A Guide to the Leading OLAP Platform

Applied Microsoft Analysis Services 2005 and Microsoft Business Intelligence Platform

Teo Lachev

Prologika Press

Applied Microsoft Analysis Services 2005 and Microsoft Business Intelligence Platform

Published by:
Prologika Press
info@prologika.com
http://www.prologika.com

Printed in the United States of America

ISBN, print edition	0-9766353-0-5
ISBN-13, print edition	978-0-9766353-0-7
First printing	2005
Second printing	2006
Third printing	2006
Fourth printing	2008

Author:	*Teo Lachev*
Technical Editor:	*Alexzander Nepomnjashiy*
Copy Editor:	*Elena Lachev*
Cover Designer:	*Shay Zamir*

contents

preface

Analysis Services and the Microsoft Business Intelligence Platform share the common goal of making business data usable and accessible to as many people as possible and delivering on the Microsoft promise – "*BI for the Masses*". Most businesses today have OLTP-based systems to capture raw data. This is usually the first IT requirement an organization has to tackle. The IT technology has matured to a point where implementing highly-transactional, highly-available applications is not an issue. The real predicament that most organizations face in the information age is analyzing the mountains of data that are piled up every day.

Think of the last time you had to look up a person's contact. How long did it take you? Did you start with a stack of scattered name cards in your drawer, then checked the Outlook Contacts folder, and finally gave up after checking the contacts stored in your cell phone? Wouldn't it be much faster and simpler if all these pieces of data were stored in one repository? Now, give this data predicament an enterprise "dimension" and you are getting closer to what a corporate business analyst has to deal with on a regular basis. Not to mention that the numbers often don't tally from one reporting medium to another and there are different versions of the "truth" depending of what reporting tool is used.

Don't get me wrong. Enterprise reporting plays an important role as a business intelligence vehicle. However, once you've successfully addressed the basic reporting requirements, you may realize that it is time to "graduate" to the next level – efficient, consistent and rich data analytics. This is where Microsoft Analysis Services and Microsoft Business Intelligence Platform come in. By allowing you to organize your data assets and build an efficient presentation layer on top of them, they allow you to get *out* what was put *in*. As a result, you spend less time in searching for information and have more time to act upon it and make decisions.

Microsoft Analysis Services has a very strategic role in the Microsoft Business Intelligence initiative. At the same time, however, Analysis Services is not a trivial technology. An Analysis Services-based solution is often the focal point of several IT processes, including OLAP, data mining, ETL, data warehousing, standard and ad hoc reporting, performance management, etc. Understanding how these technologies fit together is not an easy task. I wrote this book to help you in this endeavor.

As its name suggests, the main objective of *Applied Microsoft Analysis 2005* it so to teach you the practical skills you need to implement Analysis Services-centric business intelligence solutions. This book doesn't assume any prior experience with OLAP and Microsoft Analysis Services. It is designed as an easy-to-follow guide where each chapter builds upon the previous to implement the components of the innovative Unified Dimensional Model (UDM) in chronological order. New concepts are introduced with step-by-step instructions and hands-on demos.

Artists say that after Picasso's Cubism, the world of art never looked the same. I hope that you will find Analysis Services 2005, code-named *Picasso*, as influential for transforming your company's BI vision to the next level. Happy data analyzing!

Teo Lachev
Atlanta, GA

acknowledgements

Writing this book has been a lot of fun and a lot of work. It would not have been a reality without the help of many people to whom I am thankful.

As with my previous book, first and foremost, I would like to thank my family for their ongoing support. They had to tolerate my total dedication to the book for almost a year! My wife, Elena, contributed directly to the book by converting my incoherent writings into a readable manuscript. To my family I owe my greatest thanks.

I would like to thank Ariel Netz, Group Program Manager with Microsoft Analysis Services for letting me harass his team with naïve questions. Special thanks to Akshai Mirchandani, Alex Bocharov, Amir Netz, Andrew Garbuzov, Dave Wickert, Jamie MacLennan, Marin Bezic, Mosha Pasumansky, Paul Sanders, Raman Iyer, Richard Tkachuk, Rob Zare, Sasha Berger, Siva Harinath, T.K. Anand, Thierry D'Hers, ZhaoHui Tang, and other Microsoft engineers who not only didn't mind my constant pestering, but were always willing to help me understand the "dark side" of OLAP and data mining.

Donald Farmer from the Integration Services team helped me tremendously with the Integration Services code samples. As with my first book, Brian Welcker and the Reporting Services team have been extremely accommodating and supportive. Special thanks to Jason Carlson and Carolyn Chao for addressing tough questions about ad hoc reporting and Rajeev Karunakaran for helping me with the report viewer controls.

Kudos to my technical reviewer, Alexzander Nepomnjashiy (Alex), for meticulously reviewing the manuscript consistency and code accuracy. As with my previous book, Alexzander helped me tremendously in transitioning the book from the yearly builds of Analysis Services to its final release – a long, painstaking and sometimes frustrating process.

Many, many thanks to my peer reviewers for supporting me with valuable feedback and encouragement. Marco Russo, Dejan Sarka (MVP – SQL Server), and Deepak Puri (MVP – SQL Server) and have been phenomenal in sharing their extensive OLAP experience and suggestions for improvement. Stacy Parish, Brendon Schwartz, and Sorin Belean helped me improve the book readability and technical accuracy.

Finally, thank *you* for purchasing this book! I sincerely hope that you will find it as enjoyable to read as it has been for me to write!

about the book

Chapter 1 provides a panoramic overview of Microsoft Analysis Services 2005 and its architecture. You will understand what UDM is and how it bridges the "great divide" between the relational and dimensional reporting models. We will finish with a hands-on lab that demonstrates how you can produce an Excel-based report that sources data from an Analysis Services cube.

Part 1, *The Unified Dimensional Model*, is meant for database modelers and developers that will implement the core dimensional model of UDM. Chapter 2 teaches you how to work with data and set up data sources and data source views. Chapter 3 introduces you to the dimensional model and shows you how to use the Cube Wizard and Dimension Wizard to build quickly the raw UDM. In chapter 4, you will refine the UDM and get more insight into the UDM building blocks – dimensions and measures. In chapter 5, we will look at some innovative features that debut in Analysis Services 2005, such as dimension relationships, semi-additive measures, linked cubes and measure groups, and error configurations.

Part 2, *Data Warehousing and Mining*, discusses the two most common usage scenarios for using Analysis Services. Chapter 6 shows you how to build a cube top-down by starting with the cube schema and implementing an ETL package to load the cube with data. Chapter 7 introduces you to the powerful data mining features in UDM and shows you how to build mining models on top of relational data sources. Chapter 8 expands the data mining concepts by teaching you how to use UDM as a data source for the mining models.

Part 3, *Programming Analysis Services*, targets developers who will be using MDX to extend the cube capabilities. Chapter 9 introduces you to MDX and walks you through many examples that demonstrate how you can navigate the dimensional model horizontally and vertically. In chapter 10, you will learn how to work with sets and subcube expressions. Chapter 11 teaches you how to extend UDM with custom code in the form of VBA functions and Analysis Services stored procedures. In chapter 11, you will build a rich end-user model by using KPIs, actions, perspectives, and translations.

Part 4, *Managing Analysis Services*, is for administrators who are responsible for managing Analysis Services servers. Chapter 13 introduces you to the management features of the SQL Server Management Studio and shows you how to perform routine tasks, such as backing up, synchronizing, deploying, and scripting databases. In chapter 14, you will learn how to work with the cube storage settings and improve the cube performance with aggregations. Chapter 15 discusses the Analysis Services processing architecture by walking you through different operational scenarios. In chapter 16, you will understand how to secure Analysis Services by using role-based security policies.

Part 5, *Building Business Intelligence Solutions*, gives developers and power users the necessary background to build Analysis Services-centric solutions. Chapter 17 teaches you how to leverage MDX and DMX to build custom business intelligence applications. In chapter 18, you will build standard and ad hoc reports with Microsoft Reporting Services. Finally, in Chapter 19, you will learn how to use Microsoft Office analytics tools to implement interactive reporting solutions and the Microsoft Office Business Scorecard Manager 2005 to build dashboards for corporate performance management.

source code

Applied Microsoft Analysis 2005 introduces the new concepts with hands-on labs where each chapter builds upon the previous to implement a complete UDM solution. Table 1 lists the software requirements to run all the code samples included in the book.

Table 1 Software requirements for running the book source code.

Software	Purpose
SQL Server 2005 Developer or Enterprise Edition	These two editions provide all Analysis Services features. Use the Developer Edition on Windows XP and Developer or Enterprise Edition if you are running Windows 2003.
Microsoft Visual Studio 2005	To edit the Visual Basic code samples and SSAS stored procedures.
Microsoft Office 2003	To use the analytics tools for building reports (Excel and OWC) in Chapter 19.
Microsoft Office Business Scorecard Manager 2005 and Windows Server 2003 with SharePoint Services	To build a performance scorecard in Chapter 19.

The code samples can be downloaded from the book web page at *http://www.prologika.com.* After downloading the zip file, extract it to any folder of your hard drive. Once this is done, you will see a folder for each chapter. The UDM code samples use the AdventureWorks and AdventureWorksDW sample databases that come with SQL Server 2005. Follow the instructions in Appendix A to install these databases. For the hands-on lab in chapter 1, you will also need the sample Adventure Works DW UDM which is included in Analysis Services 2005 samples. Chapter 1 provides instructions about how to deploy the Adventure Works DW solution.

about the author

Teo Lachev has more than a decade of experience in designing and developing Microsoft-centric solutions. He is a technical architect for a leading financial institution where he designs and implements Business Intelligence applications for the banking industry. Teo is a Microsoft Most Valuable Professional (*MVP*) for SQL Server, Microsoft Certified Solution Developer (*MCSD*), and Microsoft Certified Trainer (*MCT*). He is the author of *Microsoft Reporting Services in Action* (Manning Publications, 2004). Teo lives with his family in Atlanta, GA.

Your purchase of *Applied Microsoft Analysis Services 2005* includes free access to a web forum sponsored by the author, where you can make comments about the book, ask technical questions, and receive help from the author and the community. The author is not committed to a specific amount of participation or successful resolution of the question and his participation remains voluntary. You can subscribe to the forum from the author's personal website *www.prologika.com.*

Chapter 1

Introducing Microsoft Analysis Services 2005

Albert Einstein once said that information alone is not knowledge. This adage has never been more relevant than in today's information age where organizations are looking for ways to quickly make sense of mountains of data generated every day. Only by carefully screening and analyzing that data can an organization unlock its power and fully understand its customers, its markets, and its business. I am not aware of an official slogan for Analysis Services but the one that may best serve this purpose could be "Knowledge is power".

As its name suggests, the promise of Microsoft SQL Server Analysis Services 2005 is to promote better data analytics by giving information workers powerful ways to analyze consistent, timely, and reliable data. Empowered with Analysis Services, you are well positioned to solve the perennial problem with data – that there is too much of it and finding the right information is often difficult, if not impossible.

This introductory chapter gives you a panoramic view of Microsoft SQL Server Analysis Services 2005 (SSAS) and the Microsoft Business Intelligence platform. Throughout the rest of this book, I will use the terms Analysis Services and SSAS interchangeably to refer to Microsoft SQL Server Analysis Services 2005. In this chapter, we will discuss:

- What is SSAS?
- The services SSAS provides
- The role of SSAS in the Microsoft Business Intelligence Platform
- How SSAS unifies the relational and dimensional reporting models
- SSAS architecture
- SSAS in action hands-on lab

1.1 What is Analysis Services 2005?

The processes of collecting and analyzing information assets to derive knowledge from data are typically referred to as *Business Intelligence,* or *BI,* for short. Simply put, SSAS can be viewed as a sophisticated software platform for delivering business intelligence by providing rich and efficient ways to "get out" what was "put in". To be more specific, we can describe SSAS as a server-based platform that provides two core services -- On-Line Analytical Processing (OLAP) and data mining. Let's cover these two terms in more detail.

Definition Microsoft Analysis Services is a server-based platform for on-line analytical processing (OLAP) and data mining.

1.1.1 Introducing OLAP

There are two types of database-driven systems that serve orthogonal requirements. *On-Line Transactional Processing* (OLTP) systems are designed for fast transactional input to support business systems. On the other side, OLAP systems are optimized for fast data output to support data analytics and reporting.

Definition On-Line Analytical Processing (OLAP) applications are optimized for fast data querying and reporting.

Let's consider a popular BI scenario that can be implemented using the OLAP technology and SSAS.

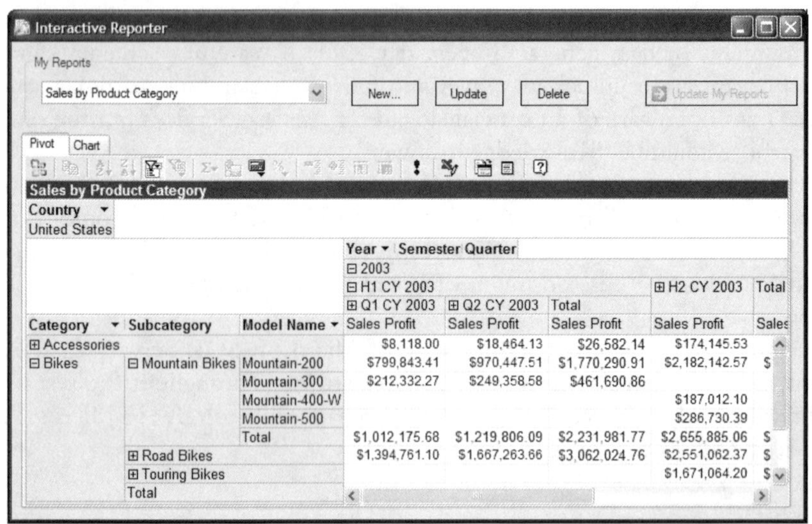

Figure 1.1 Use "smart" OLAP browsers connected to SSAS to build interactive reporting applications.

Fast and intuitive reporting

Suppose that your company's CEO is asking you for a report showing last-year sales. You run an SQL query that produces the magic number, e.g. the company made one million dollars in sales. While this figure may be great (or not so great depending on the company situation), it is unlikely to provide enough information to your CEO and marketing department.

There are a myriad of questions your business users may ask you. How do the sales of this year compare to last year? What are the top selling products? How do products sale by region, resale channels, etc? You may opt to address some of these questions by authoring standard reports but, at some point, this process may become counterproductive, especially when large datasets need to be processed.

One elegant and efficient solution is to implement an OLAP application that allows business users to produce reports interactively, as shown in Figure 1.1. It is implemented as a .NET Windows Form client application that leverages a "smart" OLAP browser connected to SSAS

2005. In this case, the browser is Microsoft Office Web Components (OWC) which is part of the Microsoft Office suite. Empowered with this application, end users could view data from different angles (called *dimensions* in the OLAP terminology) by creating dynamic views interactively. Moreover, report queries will be satisfied almost instantaneously because OLAP servers are optimized for fast retriaval.

Definition The OLAP terminology uses the term *dimension* to refer to an analytical perspective that can be used to browse the data. Common examples of dimensions include Product, Customer, and Time.

In Figure 1.1, the user has decided to see sales data broken by *Product by Category* dimension on rows and *Time* dimension on columns. The user has expanded ("drill down") the Product by Category dimension to see data broken further down by Product Category, Subcategory, and Model Name. The Time dimension is also expanded to show sales figures by Calendar Year, Semester, and Quarter levels. Data is further filtered by Country to show sales figures for United States only.

I dubbed this type of reporting "interactive" because with a few mouse clicks the user can change the report to view data from different angles. For example, assuming the SSAS model supports this, the user can opt to view the sales data by Customers on rows and Fiscal Year on columns. Optionally, this application allows the user to save the report view to a database and retrieve it on as-needed basis. I will show you how you can build this type of applications in chapter 19.

As you could see, interactive reporting is much more powerful and flexible than standard "canned" reporting. The tradeoff is that you need to spend some extra effort to design and implement your OLAP database in such a way that it conforms to the OLAP dimensional model, as we will discuss in section 1.2. Don't despair, though. SSAS definitely goes a long way in making this endeavor easier.

SSAS as OLAP server

Can you produce interactive reports from a relational database instead of going through all the trouble to implement an OLAP solution? Most likely the answer will be yes. For example, you can connect OWC directly to a relational database and achieve similar reporting results. There is really no magic that OLAP performs behind the scenes as a database engine. The same aggregation results could be achieved by just sending SQL statements. So, why should you use OLAP and SSAS for that matter?

To answer this question, consider the **F**ast **A**nalysis of **S**hared **M**ultidimensional **I**nformation (FASMI). This test was proposed by The OLAP Report, an independent organization that studies the OLAP technology and market (see the Resources section). It outlines five easy to remember criteria that each OLAP server should adhere to.

The *Fast* rule means that the OLAP server has to be optimized for fast (almost instantaneous) data retrieval. The OLAP Report suggests that most queries should be answered in five seconds. Of course, performance depends on a variety of factors, including hardware and software configuration, level of optimization, etc., but OLAP servers have to be *FAST*.

The *Analysis* rule means that the OLAP calculation engines should be superior in supporting advanced business calculations compared with RDBMS and these calculations shouldn't mandate the use of a professional programming language.

Each OLAP server should also provide *Shared* access to data. This criterion has two aspects. First, it mandates that every OLAP server should protect sensitive data preferably at the most granular (cell) level. In addition, an OLAP server should support *writeback*, i.e. allowing the users not only to read, but also to change data.

The *Multidimensional* characteristic is the most important requirement. Every OLAP system should provide a multidimensional view of data that extends beyond the two-dimensional analysis of RDBMS. OLAP users should be able to see data from different angles called *dimensions*, as we've just seen in the example shown in Figure 1.1.

Finally, the *Information* criterion measures the ability of the OLAP system to store and aggregate vast volumes of data without performance degradation. So, to sum up, the strongest motivation factors to favor the OLAP technology instead of RDBMS for reporting is its superior performance, user-friendly reporting model, and rich calculations. I hope that in this chapter and throughout this book, I will convince you to consider OLAP for implementing efficient and rich reporting solutions.

1.1.2 Introducing Data Mining

The second main service that SSAS provides is data mining. Data mining is a science in itself. Generally speaking, data mining is concerned with the process used to predict the unknown based on known statistical facts. Instead of asking us to look at a crystal ball, the SSAS team has implemented sophisticated mathematical models that can analyze large volumes of data, discover patterns and trends, and produce prediction results.

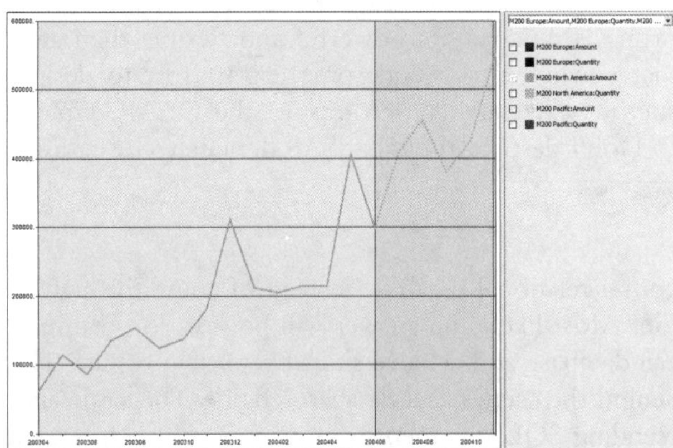

Figure 1.2 Use SSAS data mining to discover trends in data, such as forecasting future sales.

Typical examples where data mining can be used efficiently include sales forecasting and basket analysis. For example, by examining the historical sale figures, data mining can answer the following questions:

- What are the forecasted sales numbers for the next few months?
- What products may this customer buy together with the chosen product?
- What type of customers (gender, age groups, income, etc.) is likely to buy this product?

A common practical example of using data mining is shown in Figure 1.2. Imagine that your company is selling products and the marketing department is asking you to estimate the sales in North America for the next five months. Instead of dusting off your college math book, you prudently decide to use SSAS. Once you build the data mining model, with a few mouse clicks you can produce a report as the one shown in Figure 1.2. We will discuss data mining in more detail in chapters 7 and 8.

1.1.3 Overview of SSAS

Shortly after acquiring the Panorama OLAP technology in 1997, Microsoft introduced the first release of SSAS. It shipped as an add-on to the SQL Server 7.0 and was named Microsoft OLAP Services. The second version coincided with the SQL Server 2000 release. The product name was changed to Analysis Services 2000 to reflect the fact that now SSAS provided not only OLAP, but also data mining capabilities. Today, SSAS 2000 is a leading OLAP platform according to The OLAP Report (see the Resources section). After five years of gestation effort, Microsoft released SQL Server Analysis Services 2005 in November 2005.

SSAS editions and licensing

As its predecessors, SSAS 2005 ships as an add-on to SQL Server 2005. However, note that, although it is bundled with SQL Server, SSAS is not necessary dependent on the SQL Server relational engine.

Note There are some features in SSAS 2005, such as using multiple data sources in a single data source view and proactive cache notifications, that work only when SQL Server is used as a data source.

For step-by step instructions on how to install SSAS 2005, refer to Appendix A at the end of this book. Let's now briefly discuss how SSAS is packaged and its licensing requirements. To address different user needs, SQL Server 2005 is available in five editions – Express, Workgroup, Standard, Enterprise, and Developer editions. However, SSAS is available in the last three editions only (see Table 1.1). The Developer edition has the same feature set as the Enterprise edition but it is licensed for one machine only.

Table 1.1 SSAS supports three editions to address different user needs.

Edition	Choose when
Standard	You need to install SSAS on a single server. The Standard edition doesn't support advanced analytics and scalability features, such as partitioned cubes, proactive caching, and parallel processing.
Enterprise	You need all SSAS features and your OLAP solution must be highly scalable.
Developer	You design and develop SSAS databases. The Developer edition supports all SSAS features but it is not licensed for production use.

For more information about how SSAS editions and other SQL Server 2005 products compare to each other, read the document *SQL Server 2005 Features Comparison* (see Resources section). SSAS 2005 licensing model is simple. Basically, you need a SQL Server license on the machine where SSAS is installed and there are no special "middleware" exceptions. For example, suppose your operational requirements call for installing SSAS on a separate server than your SQL Server RDBMS box. In this case, you will need two SQL Server licenses – one for the SSAS server and another one for the SQL Server instance.

Why use SSAS?

Traditionally, Analysis Services and OLAP in general have been used in conjunction with data warehousing. Of course, this scenario is still applicable. Many organizations would use Analysis Services to build an OLAP layer on top of a relational data warehouse in order to take advantage of the superior query performance of SSAS. However, thanks to new enhancements in SSAS, I believe you will find new scenarios for using it, including:

- *Rich data analytics* – For many organizations, SSAS can become the logical next step for advanced data analysis and interactive reporting.
- *Data mining* – An organization could find many uses for the predictive power of data mining.
- *Corporate performance management* – With the introduction of KPIs, SSAS can be used to capture vital company performance metrics. More on this in chapter 12 and 19.
- *Centralized repository for business metrics* – SSAS supports advanced calculations and is best suited for storing business metrics and calculations.
- *Ad hoc reporting* – Besides interactive reports, end-users can create ad hoc reports from SSAS. We will see how this could be done in chapter 18.

At the same time, as there is no such a thing as a free lunch, SSAS may be overkill for small organizations because it requires an additional design and maintenance effort. As a rule of thumb, if standard reporting meets your data analytics and performance needs, it may not be time to "graduate" to OLAP yet.

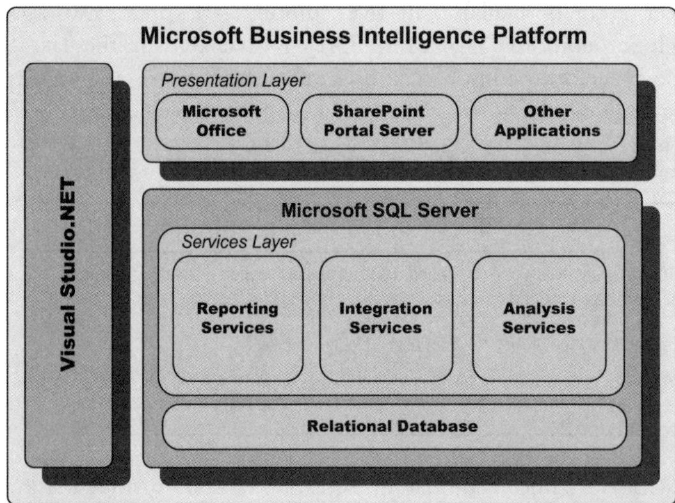

Figure 1.3 The Microsoft Business Intelligence Platform provides valuable services and tools that address various data analytics and management needs.

1.1.4 SSAS and Microsoft Business Intelligence Platform

SSAS is not the only Business Intelligence product that Microsoft provides. It is an integral part of the Microsoft Business Intelligence Platform that was initiated in early 2004 with the powerful promise to "bring BI to the masses". The Microsoft Business Intelligence Platform is a multi-product offering that addresses the most pressing data analytics and management needs that many organizations encounter every day.

To understand how SSAS fits into this initiative, it may be helpful to depict the Microsoft Business Intelligence Platform in the context of a typical three-tier architectural view that most of the readers are probably familiar with, as shown in Figure 1.3. Let's explain briefly the building blocks of the Microsoft Business Intelligence Platform.

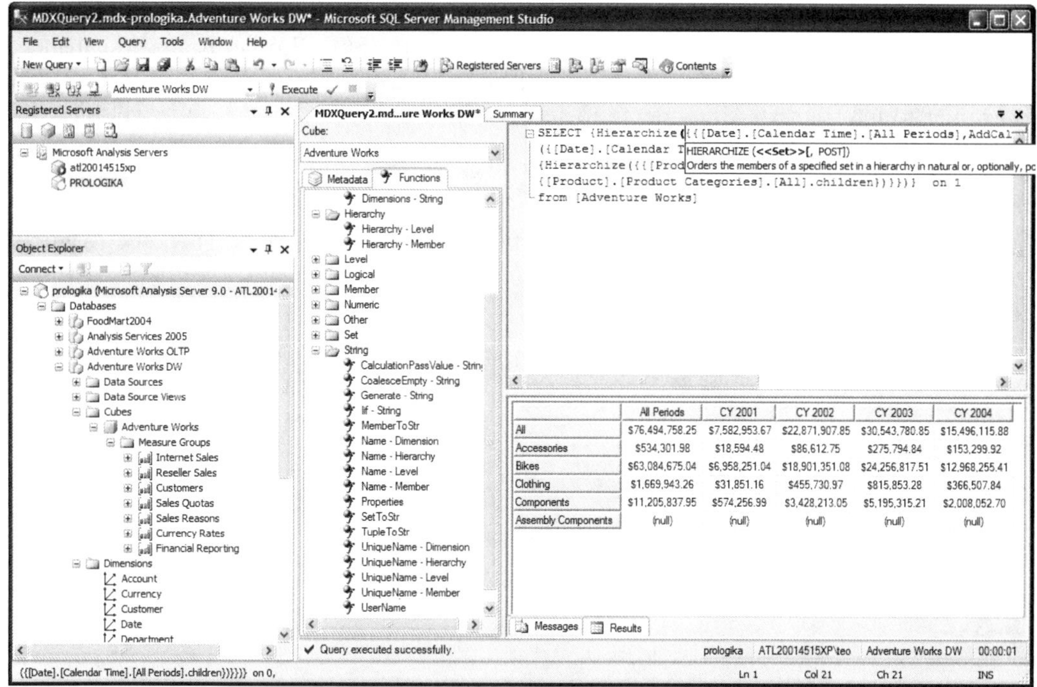

Figure 1.4 Use SQL Server Management Studio to manage all Analysis Services, Reporting Services, Integration Services, and SQL Server installations.

SQL Server

The SQL Server relational database engine forms the foundation of the BI Platform. In my opinion, SQL Server is one of the best products that Microsoft has ever invented. Its relational database has been holding the top TPC (Transaction Processing Council) benchmarks in the price/performance category, as you could see online at *www.tpc.org*. Now that SQL Server comes bundled with so many valuable add-on services, it is indeed "do more with less", as the popular Microsoft slogan goes. While discussing the SQL Server 2005 enhancements and new features may easily fill a whole book, I would like to bring your attention to a couple of SSAS-related enhancements that we will be using throughout this book

SQL Server Management Studio

SQL Server 2000 Enterprise Manager is gone and it is replaced by the new SQL Server Management Studio (see Figure 1.4). The most prominent feature of the SQL Server Management Studio is that it can be used to manage all SQL Server services. Figure 1.4 shows that I've connected to an Analysis Services server called *Prologika* and I've executed an MDX query against the Adventure Works cube.

The central pane shows the metadata of the Adventure Works cube. You can drag and drop objects from the Metadata tab, or MDX standard functions, from the Functions tab. Yes, the query editors support IntelliSense so you could check the function syntax easily! SQL Server Management Studio comes with a slew of editors, templates, designers, and other tools to meet the full spectrum of your query authoring, performance optimization and management needs.

SQL Profiler

Veteran SSAS developers know that, in the past, it was almost impossible to "peek under the hood" of the SSAS server. This has all changed now since the SQL Profiler has been enhanced to support capturing and displaying events raised by SSAS 2005. For example, you can use the SQL Profiler to intercept an MDX query to see how long it takes to execute. We will meet the SQL Profiler in chapter 13 when discussing SSAS management.

Services layer

On top of the relational database, SQL Server provides various services. The three main BI pillars are Reporting Services (SSRS), Integration Services (SSIS), and, of course, Analysis Services (SSAS) which is the subject of this book.

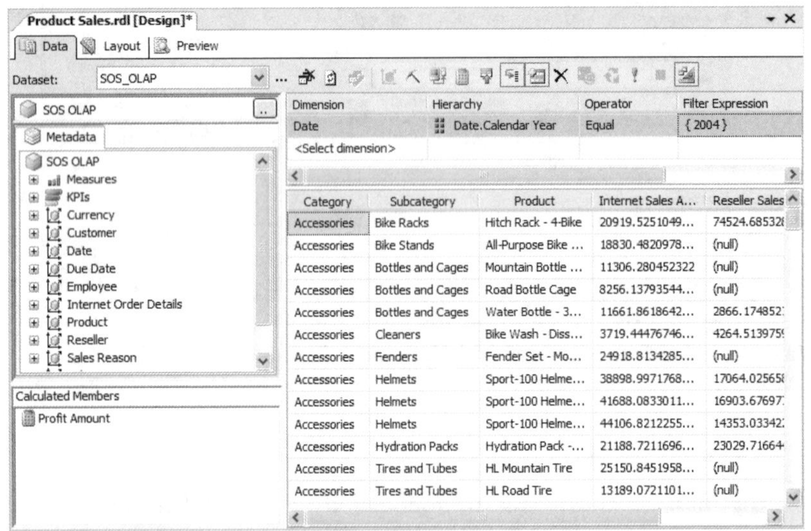

Figure 1.5 The MDX Query Builder makes authoring reports from SSAS a breeze

Reporting Services

SSRS is a server-based platform for authoring, managing, and distributing standard reports. SSRS reports can source data from virtually any data source that exposes its data in a tabular format, including SSAS. A new SSAS-related feature of SSRS 2005 is the excellent MDX Query Builder that you can use to create reports from SSAS cubes easily (see Figure 1.5). Figure 1.5 shows that I've authored a Product Sales report by dragging Product dimension and a few measures from the Metadata pane and dropping them onto the Results pane. In addition, I've parameterized this report by allowing the user to filter the report data for a given calendar year.

I've covered SSRS 2000 in details in my book *Microsoft Reporting Services in Action* (see the Resources section). In chapters 18 and 19 of this book, I will show you the most exciting new features of SSRS 2005 that relate to authoring SSAS-based reports, including the MDX and DMX query builders, the new Windows Forms and ASP.NET report viewer controls, ad-hoc reporting, and SharePoint integration.

Integration Services

Today's enterprise IT shop would typically maintain a hodge-podge of data sources and technologies. These include desktop databases, legacy mainframe systems (that no one dares to touch), RDBMS, etc.

Note One of my projects involved building a data warehouse for a call center of a major financial institution. The data integration requirements called for extracting data from six databases and consolidating it into a central data warehouse repository. Most of the project effort was spent on implementing the ETL data integration processes.

For example, the order tracking data could reside in a SQL Server database, the HR data could be stored in an Oracle database, while the manufacturing data could be located in a mainframe database. Integrating disparate and heterogeneous data sources presents a major challenge for many organizations. This is where SSIS (formerly known as DTS) could be useful. It is typically used for Extracting, Transforming, and Loading (ETL) processes for data integration.

SSIS has been completely revamped in SQL Server 2005. There are a few exciting features in SSIS that specifically target SSAS, including dealing with slowly changing dimensions, implementing low-latency OLAP, and processing partitions. One of the most common OLAP requirements that could benefit from SSIS is data warehousing. We will see how this could be done in chapter 6. There are other SQL Server add-on services that you may find more or less relevant to BI applications. These may include *Replication Services* to clone data, *SQL Server Broker* to raise event notifications, and *Notification Services* to build sophisticated notification application.

Presentation layer

The OLAP technology will be useless if users cannot browse the data. SSAS itself doesn't provide an OLAP browser. The BI platform delegates this role to the Microsoft Office suite, SharePoint, or third-party products.

Microsoft Office

In section 1.1.1 of this chapter, we had a glimpse of how Microsoft Office Web Components (part of the Microsoft Office suite) can be used to build "smart" OLAP clients. Besides OWC, in the last chapter of this book I will show you how to integrate Microsoft Excel and the Office Business Scorecard Manager 2005 with SSAS 2005 to implement interactive reporting and performance management.

SharePoint

Use SharePoint to build enterprise-level portal sites. SSAS doesn't include web parts to browse cube data. However, the Reporting Services team has built two SharePoint web parts, Report Explorer and Report Viewer, which can be used to integrate SSRS reports with a SharePoint portal. We will have a glimpse of how SharePoint Portal Services can be used to disseminate scorecards in chapter 19.

Other applications

Developers can utilize industry-standard connectivity protocols to integrate SSAS and SSRS easily with their applications. In chapter 17, I will show you how you can develop custom OLAP-based applications.

Visual Studio.NET

Finally, developers can use Visual Studio.NET to glue the components of the BI Platform together. Developers can use the excellent Visual Studio.NET IDE to custom solutions or work with BI projects. If you don't have the full-blown version Visual Studio.NET (or you are not willing to purchase a license), the SQL Server 2005 setup program gives you an option to install a scaled-down version of Visual Studio.NET, called *Business Intelligence Development Studio (BI Studio).*

BI Studio supports Analysis Services, Reporting Services, and Integration Services projects. It gives you the power of the Visual Studio.NET Integrated Development Environment at no additional cost. Using BI studio, you can centralize the design and management of your BI projects. Now that we have reviewed the components of the Microsoft BI Platform, let's find out what's so innovative about SSAS 2005.

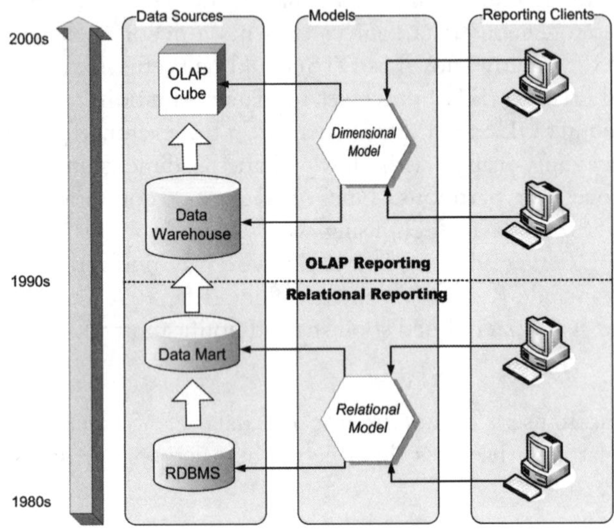

Figure 1.6 Today's BI reality is characterized by the "great divide" between relational and dimensional reporting models.

1.2 Understanding OLAP

SSAS 2005 goes beyond just being an OLAP and Data Mining server. The bold mission of SSAS is to break out of the OLAP space by *unifying* the relational and dimensional reporting models. To understand the new changes in SSAS 2005, it may be useful to take a short trip back in time and discuss the challenges that enterprise business intelligence has been facing for the past two decades. Let's use Figure 1.6 as a roadmap for our tour.

I will be quick to point out that as it currently stands, UDM shouldn't be viewed as a replacement of the relational reporting model or as a competing technology to standard reporting. Considering the unified vision of UDM however, one would expect that eventually both models will be merged in an integrated platform that provides both standard and OLAP reporting services.

Figure 1.6 depicts the evolution of both reporting models, relational and OLAP, and the "great divide" between them that is a common reality for most organizations today. On the one side of the dividing line is relational reporting where reporting processes are performed against relational models. A *relational model* could represent both a relational OLTP schema (normalized in the 3rd Normal Form) and a layer built on top of it (e.g. to serve ad-hoc reporting needs).

Note Strictly speaking, the dividing line between relational and OLAP reporting processes could be somewhat blurred. For example, standard reports can be generated from a dimensional data source (e.g. data mart) if this doesn't lead to performance issues. For this reason, Figure 1.6 shows a data mart in the relational reporting section. Chapter 2 discusses various reporting scenarios in respect to the data source type in more details.

On the other side are OLAP reporting processes that interact with dimensional models. We will use the term *dimensional model* to represent a data source that is specifically structured and optimized to address reporting and data analytics requirements, such as data marts, data warehouses, and OLAP cubes.

1.2.1 Relational Model

In the early 1980s, reporting needs were addressed by sourcing data directly from RDBMS. This model is still popular and widely used today. For example, if your preferred tool of choice for standard reporting is Microsoft Reporting Services, you can source the report data directly from RDBMS. As popular as it is, the relational reporting model has well-known deficiencies.

Not user-oriented

The relational model is designed with the system, not the end user in mind. Consequently, to create a report, the end user has to understand the database relational schema and know SQL. Isn't it strange that one of the job requirements for hiring a business analyst is to know SQL?

Performance challenges

Relational reporting could lead to performance issues. The report performance depends, to a large extent, on the data volume the report needs to process. What's more, running reports directly against RDBMS may very well slow down the performance of the OLTP system itself as a result of locking large number of rows. The reason for this is that pending transactions may be blocked while waiting for the report query to finish executing and releasing the read locks placed on the qualifying rows.

Note Once upon a time, I was called upon to troubleshoot mysterious query timeout errors that a client-server application was experiencing at random. After some troubleshooting, I pinpointed the culprit to be a popular ad-hoc reporting tool. Not only was the tool placing read locks on the SQL Server tables, but it wasn't releasing the locks even after the report was generated.

Lack of conformity

While the ad-hoc reporting models could abstract the underlying data schema to some degree, relational reporting is characterized by a lack of conformity. Business calculations and logic are not centralized in one place. For example, the database developer could define the net dollar amount calculation of a line item in the database itself, while the report designer could re-define it in the ad-hoc reporting model. This may be confusing to end users. Often, users are left to make their own interpretation of the data.

1.2.2 Dimensional Model

To solve some of the challenges of relational reporting, organizations started moving data from OLTP databases to data marts and warehouses. OLAP servers, such as Analysis Services, emerged in the late 1990s to provide the necessary CPU power to process the increased data volumes. A new *dimensional* model was born to make reporting more intuitive for less technically savvy users. SSAS embraces and extends the dimensional model, so let's spend some time explaining its terminology.

Note The terms *data warehousing* and *OLAP* are often used interchangeably but an important distinction exists. As its name suggests, a data warehouse can simply be described as a relational database that stores vast volumes of data. The term *OLAP*, on the other hand, represents the service layer introduced between the warehouse and users to make data available for fast retrieval and analysis. A data warehouse solution may not feature an OLAP server. Similarly, an OLAP server, such as SSAS 2005, may draw its data directly from the OLTP system, instead of from a data warehouse. That said, both data warehousing and OLAP use dimensional modeling as a core technique to organize data and make it more suitable for data analytics and reporting. There are some differences in their terminology though. For example, the data warehouse model refers to business metrics as *facts,* while OLAP uses the term *measures*.

Measures

Measures represent the numerical values (facts) that are used to measure business activity. Let's have a look again at our interactive report shown in Figure 1.7. This report displays the company sales performance. The only measure used in this report is *Sales Amount*. Other measures may include tax amount, discount, profit, order count, etc.

Measures are physically stored in relational tables called *fact* tables. These tables are usually narrow (don't have many columns) but can have thousands to millions rows of historical data. In addition, fact tables have foreign keys that link them to dimension tables.

Dimensions

As its name suggests, the main goal of the dimensional model is to allow users to slice and dice data using different perspectives called *dimensions*. Dimensions reflect the natural way end users would prefer to view and query data. For example, our report allows users to browse data by two common dimensions: *Product* and *Time*.

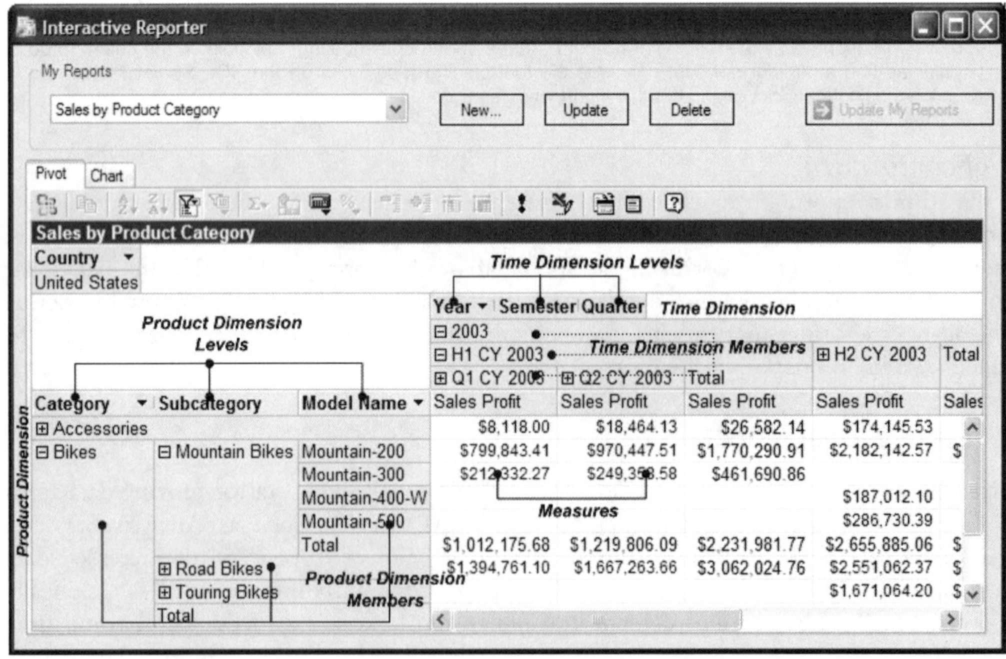

Figure 1.7 Dimensional model is designed to provide intuitive end-user reporting experience.

Dimension hierarchies

To facilitate drilling through data, dimensions may have hierarchies. For example, in our sample report, the time dimension hierarchy consists of the following dimension levels: *Year*, *Seminar*, and *Quarter*. The quarters can be further broken down into more granular levels, e.g. Month and Day. Similarly, the Product dimension hierarchy includes the *Category*, *Subcategory*, and *Model Name* levels. A dimension level summarizes *("aggregates")* data at that level. For example, since the user hasn't expanded the 2003 quarter, 2003 sales data on this report are aggregated at the Quarter level.

Dimension members

The actual dimension entities that belong to each level are called dimension *members*. Thus, the members of the Calendar Year level are *2003* and *2004*, while the members of the Category level are *Accessories*, *Bikes*, *Clothing*, and *Components*. Another way to depict the dimension hierarchy is to use an organizational chart, as the one shown in Figure 1.8.

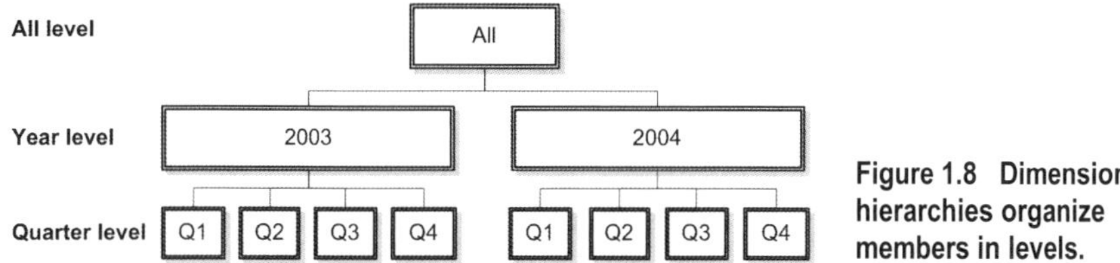

Figure 1.8 Dimension hierarchies organize members in levels.

The top level of a dimension is depicted as *All* level, which is how SSAS terminology refers to it. It is a handy way to retrieve the total aggregated value for the whole dimension. The All level usually serves as the default dimension member. For example, if I am to remove the Time dimension from the report, the report will show the product sales for all time periods. The members of the lowest level of a dimension hierarchy are called *leaf members*. For example, if the Quarter level is the lowest level in our Time dimension, the quarters are the leaf members.

Dimension tables

Dimension data are stored in relational tables called *dimension tables*. Unlike fact tables, dimension tables are usually wide (have many columns) but don't have many rows. The large number of columns is required to accommodate various dimension-related *attributes* that could be of interest to the end users. For example, a product dimension could have attributes such as product description, color, model, list price, listed date, discontinued date, etc.

The classic dimensional model defines two types of relational schemas (see Figure 1.9) that describe the relationship between the dimension and fact tables: *star* and *snowflake*. A star schema requires that a dimension hierarchy be contained within a single table. This requires the dimensional table to be denormalized. For example, going back to the sales report, if a star schema is chosen for the product dimension, the product data may look like this:

```
ProductID ProductCategory ProductSubCategory ModelName
1      Bikes     Montain    Bikes Montain-200
2      Bikes     Montain    Bikes Montain-300
```

If the dimension hierarchy is left normalized, then the schema is of a snowflake type. Over the past decade, dimensional model scholars have staged fierce battles in a quest to find out which schema type reigns supreme. The "classic" dimensional model promotes the star schema. Indeed, if the user queries the relational database (e.g. data warehouse) directly, a snowflake schema will require the user to link the dimension tables together. This assumes that the user has the necessary technical skills to do so, but wasn't this the problem that the dimensional model was trying to avoid in the first place? Moreover, in comparison with snowflake schemas, stars schemas are easier to maintain and update.

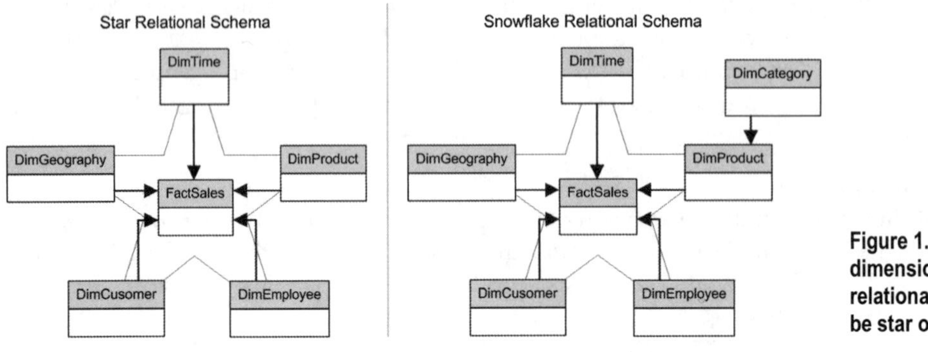

Figure 1.9 The dimension-to-fact relational schema could be star or snowflake.

On the other hand, snowflake schemas could support more flexible relationships, such as referenced and many-to-many relationships (discussed in chapter 5). In addition, they could save storage space with large dimensions. SSAS takes a nonchalant view of this schema debate and supports both schema types. A noticeable exception is the dimension writeback feature which is only supported with star dimensions. In real life you should carefully weigh out the pros and cons of both approaches and choose the schema that best meets your requirements. In general, I would recommend you gravitate toward star dimensions whenever possible and consider "upgrading" them to snowflake dimensions if needed. Dimension terminology has some additional classifications but, for time being, this is all you need to know about dimensions.

Cubes

The Sales by Product Category report (see again Figure 1.7) is an example of a two-dimensional report. SSAS is not limited to storing and displaying information in a two-dimensional format. As I've mentioned, one of the FASMI requirements is that every OLAP system must be *multidimensional*, so users can view data from as many dimensions as they want. In addition, the OLAP multidimensionality shouldn't sacrifice performance.

Definition The cube is the logical storage object in SSAS. It combines dimensions and measures to provide fast multidimensional access to the cube data.

How are cubes implemented?

To achieve these demanding requirements, SSAS employs the logical concept of a *cube* as a main storage object. The term *logical* in our definition means that, unlike relational objects (tables, views, etc.), the cube doesn't have a physical realization. Thus, if you browse the SSAS storage folder (the default is C:\Program Files\Microsoft SQL Server\MSSQL.2\OLAP\Data), you won't find any multidimensional or other exotic structures. Instead, you will find a large number of files that store data in binary format. During runtime, SSAS performs its "magic" and exposes the content of these files to clients as a multidimensional cube. Figure 1.10 shows how you can visualize a cube that has three dimensions.

Suppose that we connect OWC to this cube. We can now browse by three dimensions – Year, Product, and Territory (for the sake of simplicity, let's assume that the three dimensions don't have hierarchies). The intersection of the cube dimensions is called a cube *cell*. For example, the shaded cell in the figure is found at the intersection of the following dimension members

– *2003* (Year dimension), *Bikes* (Product Category dimension), and *North America* (Territory dimension). Each cell of the cube holds a single value.

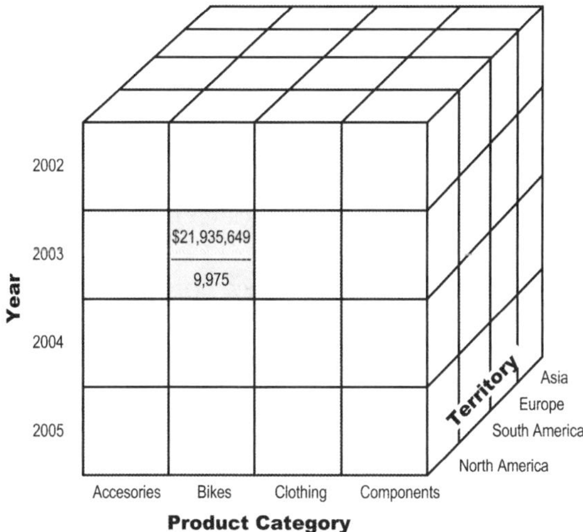

Figure 1.10 The cube is the main storage object in SSAS. The cube is a multidimensional structure that consists of dimensions and measures.

Tip When visualizing the cube, it may be helpful to think of the cube measures as separate dimensions. In our case, we have two measures (sales amount and order count). Each intersection between the cube dimensions and measures will result in a single cell. Since it is difficult to show the cube in four perspectives, I split the cell in two - the upper cell in the figure shows the sales amount; the lower shows the order count.

We live in a three-dimensional space, so it is natural for us to visualize a three-dimensional cube. However, SSAS 2005 cubes can and usually have more than three dimensions. In fact, SSAS 2005 cubes support more dimensions than you will ever need (in the range of billions). Since many of the cube limitations in the past have been removed, an SSAS 2005 cube could really be viewed as a "super-cube". In fact, you are encouraged to build your entire OLAP layer on top of an enterprise-wide data warehouse with a single SSAS 2005 cube.

Cube storage

From a user perspective, a cube appears to store all fact rows and have aggregated values for each cell. For example, if the user hasn't expanded the Calendar Year hierarchy, the cube will show the annual totals. Similarly, if the user drills down to the Quarter level, the cube will readily return the quarter aggregated values.

In reality, the cube may have neither the fact rows, nor the aggregated values stored in it. In this case, the cube will aggregate the values on the fly. As an UDM designer, you can tell SSAS where the fact data and aggregations will be kept – in the relational database (ROLAP storage), in the cube (MOLAP storage), or both (HOLAP storage). SSAS cubes usually perform best when all data (details and aggregations) are stored in the multidimensional store on the server, i.e. when MOLAP storage model is used. In this way, the cube can answer all queries *without* querying (and impacting the performance) of the underlying data source. On the downside, since the server keeps a copy of dimension and fact data (MOLAP storage option), it has to be updated (*processed*) when the dimensional structure or source data changes.

Dimensional model challenges

By now, you are probably convinced that the dimensional model has many advantages over its counterpart, the relational model. It is the cornerstone of the OLAP technology and it is very popular today. At the same time, the dimensional model is not without its shortcomings. Let's mention a couple of them.

Data fidelity lost

While dimensions reflect the natural way end-users prefer to analyze data, important dimension characteristics could be lost when transforming OLTP data to fit into the "classic" dimensional model. For example, the Product dimension we've discussed has a hierarchy that reflects the natural way end users would prefer to browse the product sales data – by category, subcategory and product name.

However, the original Product relational schema may have included columns for product color, size, model, etc. With the classic dimensional model these attributes could be simply "lost" when the Product dimension hierarchy is created or require additional dimensions to be implemented. The end result is that the user may not be able browse or filter data using these attributes.

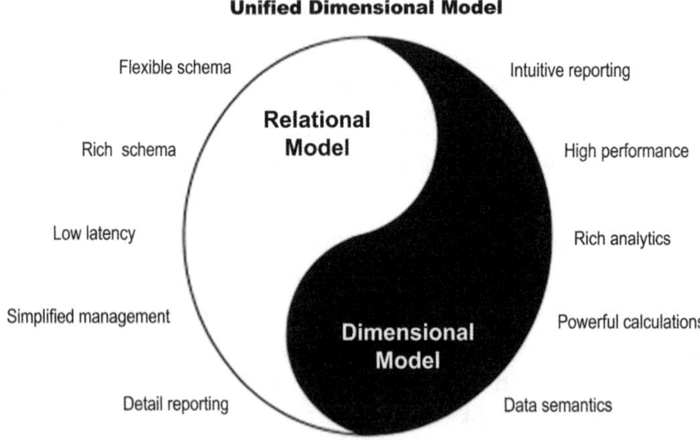

Figure 1.11 The SSAS 2005 Unified Dimensional Model solves some of today's BI challenges by uniting the relational and dimensional models.

Data latency

The second well-known issue surrounding the OLAP model is data latency, since the same data extracts would exist in all the OLAP repositories – data marts, data warehouse, and OLAP cubes. This is further aggravated by latency issues. It is not uncommon for ETL processes to take hours, if not days to complete. By the time data arrives in the OLAP cubes and it is available for reporting, it may be significantly outdated.

1.3 Understanding The Unified Dimensional Model

In summary, most of today's organizations have accumulated a mixture of two distinct storage models, relational and dimensional, and each of them has its own pros and cons. What is exciting about SSAS 2005 is that is starts a novel journey to unite both relational and dimensional models by combining the best aspects from both. This model is called *Unified Dimensional Model* or *UDM* for short, as shown in Figure 1.11. UDM is *unified* because its goal is to unite the relational and dimensional models. It is *dimensional* because it has its roots in the dimensional model.

Definition The SSAS Unified Dimensional Model (UDM) converges the relational and dimensional models. The physical manifestation of UDM is the SSAS 2005 cube.

1.3.1 Relational Model Features

At this point, some of the OLAP-savvy and perhaps skeptical readers may wonder if the notion of UDM is not too far-fetched. Let's enumerate some the most prominent characteristics of UDM that justify its bold vision to become the "next stage" for OLAP. We will start with the UDM features that bring it closer to the relational reporting model.

Rich schema

As I mentioned, one area where the classic OLAP falls behind compared to the relational model is loss of data fidelity. The end product of the classic dimensional model could be intuitive user hierarchies but at the cost of losing the ability to browse data from other perspectives. One of the most exciting new features of SSAS 2005 is *attribute-based dimensions*. With UDM, each column (attribute) from a dimensional table can be exposed as a hierarchy by itself. In fact, the UDM cube space is a product of attribute-based hierarchies, while multilevel hierarchies are optional.

For example, consider a Product dimension table that includes product attributes that are not part of or are not naturally related to the Product Category dimension, such as product name, list price, and color. UDM makes it possible to report off these attributes (see Figure 1.12).

My Sales Report

Drop Filter Fields Here

			Calendar Year			
			⊞ CY 2003		⊞ CY 2004	
Product Name	**List Price**	**Color**	Sales Amount	Order Count	Sales Amount	Order Count
⊟ All-Purpose Bike Stand	⊟ 159	NA	$16,798.21	119	$17,081.48	119
⊟ AWC Logo Cap	⊟ 8.6442	Multi	$4,362.08	197		
⊟ AWC Logo Cap	⊟ 8.99	Multi	$15,864.33	1,146	$15,690.91	1,411
⊟ Bike Wash - Dissolver	⊟ 7.95	NA	$8,898.65	621	$7,650.05	664
⊟ Cable Lock	⊟ 25	NA	$5,715.54	111		
⊟ Chain	⊟ 20.24	Silver	$5,377.26	136	$3,469.81	114
⊟ Classic Vest, L	⊟ 63.5	Blue	$4,112.30	73	$6,836.54	120
⊟ Classic Vest, M	⊟ 63.5	Blue	$50,246.23	281	$33,062.58	260
⊟ Classic Vest, S	⊟ 63.5	Blue	$80,456.95	332	$64,306.94	341

Figure 1.12 UDM is an attribute-based model and it supports both multi-level and attribute-based hierarchies.

As Figure 1.12 shows, UDM doesn't force you to use the Product Category dimension when browsing sales data by product. Instead, just like with relational reporting, you can drop the product related attributes side-by-side. To achieve the same effect in SSAS 2000, the cube designer had to create multiple dimensions which led to duplication of definitions and storage.

Flexible schema

One of the trademarks of the relational reporting model is that it enjoys a flexible database schema. Indeed, complex relationships, e.g. one-to-many, many-to-many, outer joins, etc, have been a part of the core relational schema model from its beginning. Similarly, with UDM, you are not confined to star and snowflake schemas anymore. In addition, UDM introduces new dimension roles (referenced, many-to-many, role playing, degenerate, etc) that enable new scenarios. Let's mention one scenario that UDM makes possible.

With the "classic" dimensional model it has been traditionally difficult to join two fact tables that summarize data at different levels (called grain in the OLAP terminology). For example, the grain of the time dimension in your cube may be days. At the same time, you may also have a sales quota fact table which stores the sales person quotas at a quarter level. Suppose that your requirements call for joining both tables to compare the sales person's performance and her quota side-by-side.

There were a few techniques in SSAS 2000 to address the multi-grain issue, including parent-child dimensions, inserting "fake" members, using virtual cubes, but none of them presented a clean solution. In contrast, UDM addresses this issue gracefully by simply allowing you to define the grain at which a given dimension joins both fact tables, as shown in Figure 1.13. In this case, I have specified that the time dimension will join the fact table at Calendar Quarter level. It can't be easier, really!

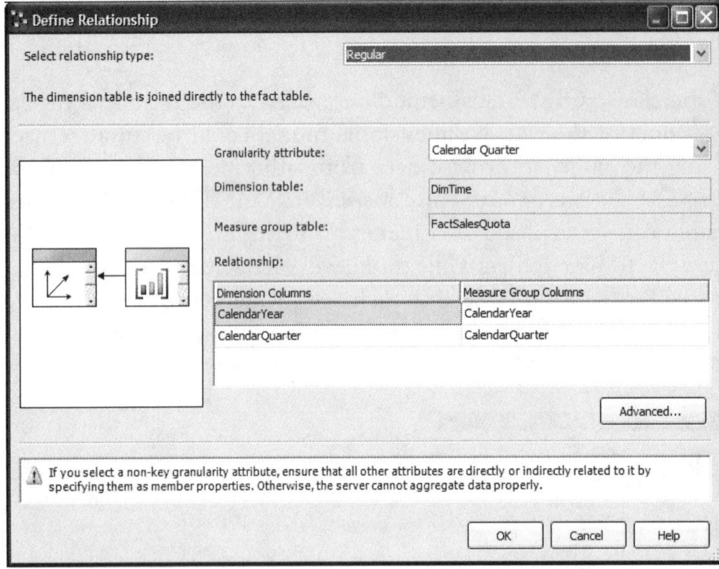

Figure 1.13 With SSAS 2005 you can easily join dimension and fact tables at different grains.

Low latency

The business requirements of today's economics mandate ever-shrinking time windows to make data available for reporting and analysis. UDM makes real-time OLAP and building low latency OLAP applications a possibility. There are two techniques to accomplish this. The first technique involves pushing the data directly into the cube (push-mode processing) without updating the underlying data source. For example, you may have a sales cube built on top of a data warehouse database. The processes of extracting, transforming, and loading the order data into the data warehouse may take significant time to execute. Yet, business requirements may dictate new order data to be available for reporting within a few hours. With SSAS 2005, you can build a light-weight data integration package that runs frequently and trickle-feeds the new orders into a cube completely bypassing the data warehouse tables. Unresolved dimensions can be defaulted to unknown values until the "full-blown" data integration package executes.

The second technique is more suitable for cubes built directly on top of OLTP databases. It allows you to put the cube in "auto-pilot" mode by leveraging the new *proactive caching* feature. When proactive caching is enabled on an SSAS 2005 cube, the cube can detect changes to the underlying data and automatically update its dimensional structures. I will show you how you can implement real-time OLAP in chapter 15.

Simplified management

There are several provisions in SSAS 2005 to simplify the management effort. SSAS 2005 removes the limitation that a cube can have only one fact table. What this means to you is that you can store the entire dimensional model into a single "super-cube". If you worry about what impact this will have on performance and scalability, rest assured that your UDM model scales well. SSAS 2005 gives you the means to scale out large deployments, e.g. by partitioning the cube across multiple servers and load-balancing these servers in a cluster.

To minimize the management and design effort, BI Studio provides a slew of wizards and designers. For example, The Cube Wizard can help you "jumpstart" the cube dimensional model by heuristically examining the relational schema and suggesting measures. As its name suggests, the New Dimension wizard walks you through the process of adding a new dimension. Finally, a brand new .NET-based object model called Analysis Management Objects (AMO) has been introduced to supersede the SSAS 2000 Decision Support Objects (DSO) model and allow developers to implement SSAS management features in their .NET applications.

Detail reporting

You shouldn't view relational and OLAP reporting as competing but, rather, complementary technologies that address different user needs. Therefore, SSAS 2005 will not be my tool of choice for generating OLTP-based relational reports, such as a common order report (order header with line items). Instead, use SQL Server Reporting Services for your standard reporting needs.

Yet, UDM provides several ways to view detail data. First, you can use a feature called *drilltrough* to see the underlying rows under a given dimension member or a cube cell. For example, the cube may aggregate sales order data on a daily basis. Yet, users may want to view the individual orders placed on a given day. You can implement this requirement by enabling drillthrough for that cube. This, of course, assumes that the OLAP browser supports this feature.

Second, you can use UDM *actions*. Considering the above example, if drilldown is not a good fit or is not supported by the OLAP browser, you can implement an action to launch a standard report (e.g. a Reporting Services tabular report) to display the invoices. Once the action is configured, the end-user could right-click on the cube cell in question to launch the report from the dropdown menu.

1.3.2 Dimensional Model Features

While SSAS 2005 comes with exciting new features, its stays close to its roots. The core dimensional concepts are the same. Now let's discuss briefly how UDM leverages and enhances the dimensional model.

Intuitive reporting

Intuitive end-user oriented reporting has been the hallmark of the dimensional model since its inception. As I mentioned, UDM makes the user experience even richer by enabling reporting scenarios that are not part of the core dimensional model, such as actions, drillthrough, and attribute-based reporting.

High Performance

OLAP user experience is directly correlated to the query performance. As noted, there are two factors that contribute most to the SSAS efficiency – the optimized query engine and the cube multidimensional model. SSAS 2005 brings additional performance enhancements. Most of them are related to the fact that SSAS 2005 cubes are not limited to having one fact table anymore. What this means to you is that you don't have to use virtual cubes anymore. Another cause of grievance in the past was that SSAS 2000 required all dimensions to be loaded in memory. To address this issue, SSAS 2005 loads dimensions in memory on as-needed basis.

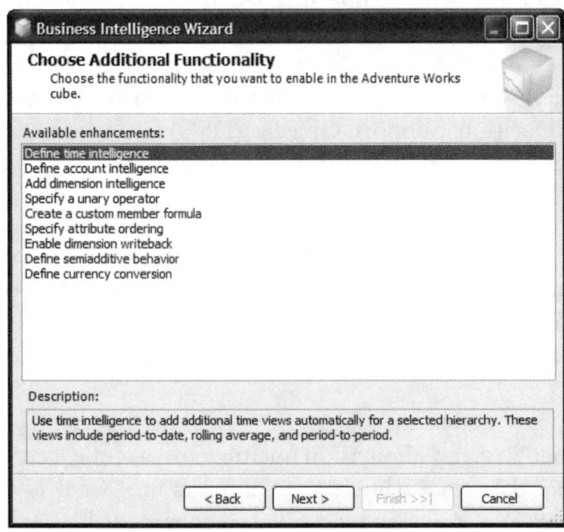

Figure 1.14 Use the Business Intelligence Wizard to add advanced business intelligence features.

Rich analytics

There are many new features in SSAS 2005 that bring rich business intelligence features to end users. Some of them were available in the previous releases as well, but they were not straightforward to implement. To facilitate defining advanced analytics features in SSAS 2005, the Analysis Services team introduces a brand new *Business Intelligence Wizard* (see Figure 1.14). For example, one of the common reporting requirements is to compare data over parallel time periods, e.g. sales figures between the first quarters of two consecutive years. As Figure 1.14 shows, the *Define time intelligence* feature of the Business Intelligence Wizard can help you save time by generating such time-related metrics for you. We will see how to add advanced business intelligence features to UDM in chapter 10.

Powerful calculations

The calculation engine has been completely redesigned in SSAS 2005. You still have to know MDX to define your calculations, but authoring and testing MDX logic is much easier now. Issues that have pestered MDX developers in the past (solve order, pass) have simply disappeared. One welcome enhancement is that all MDX constructs (calculated members, cell calculations, named sets) are centralized in one place (the Calculations tab of the Cube Designer), as shown in Figure 1.15.

In this case, I use the Calculations Script View pane to define several calculated members, named sets and MDX scripts. .NET developers will undoubtedly find many similarities between the Script View and Visual Studio.NET. Similar to working with the Visual Studio.NET IDE,

MDX developers can use breakpoints, debug MDX scripts, and see the effect of the executed script. For example, Figure 1.15 shows that I've just stepped out of a breakpoint and the Pivot Table has highlighted the effected cell. The SSAS calculation engine is also extensible. Developers can plug in additional programming logic in the form of SSAS stored procedures that can be written in any .NET-compatible language. We will cover MDX programming in part 3 of this book.

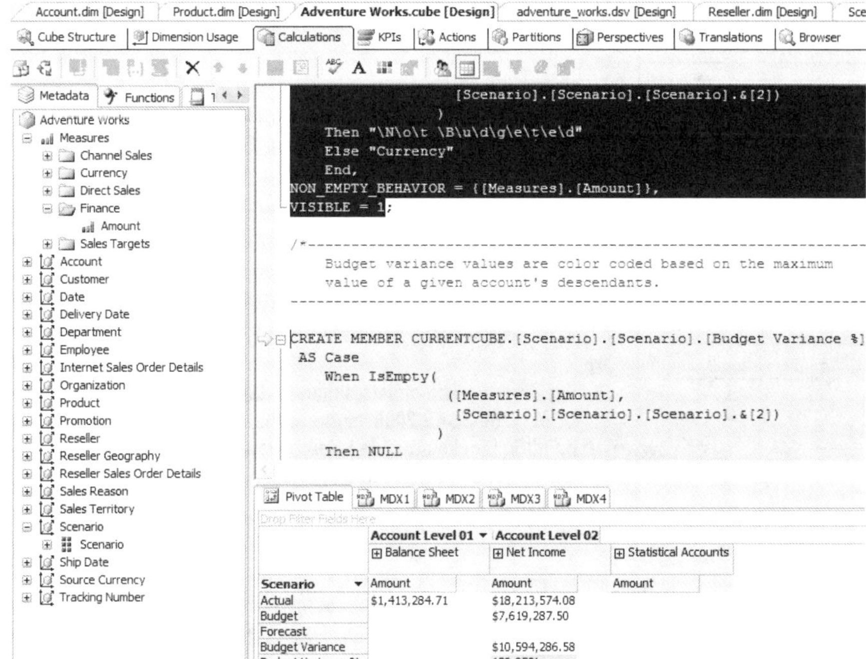

Figure 1.15 Use the MDX Script View to centralize the cube calculations in one place and debug MDX scripts.

Data semantics

Unlike the relational model, which is oblivious to the meaning of data, UDM can be "educated" to understand the data semantics. For example, UDM understands *Time* dimension and chart of accounts. In the later case, UDM knows how to map the account data to pre-defined categories, such as income, expenses, and taxes, and apply the required calculations. We will see how to implement advanced intelligence features in chapter 5.

1.3.3 UDM Components

At this point, you are probably curious about how UDM is implemented. The physical manifestation of UDM is the new Analysis Services 2005 cube. Therefore, I will use the terms *UDM* and *cube* interchangeably throughout the rest of the book. As Shrek would undoubtedly attest, just like ogres, UDM has layers. Figure 1.16 shows how you can visualize UDM. As you could notice, I've stacked the UDM components in the chronological order they will be typically implemented. To reflect this natural flow, the book is organized in the same way and the numbers shown inside the individual layers represent the chapter(s) where the corresponding layer is discussed.

Data source view (DSV)

UDM is based on a logical data schema that seeks to present the data from the relational data store in a standard and intuitive way. UDM implements the schema in the form of a data source view (DSV). Besides providing the UDM data schema, DSV isolates the cube dimensional model from changes in the underlying relational databases.

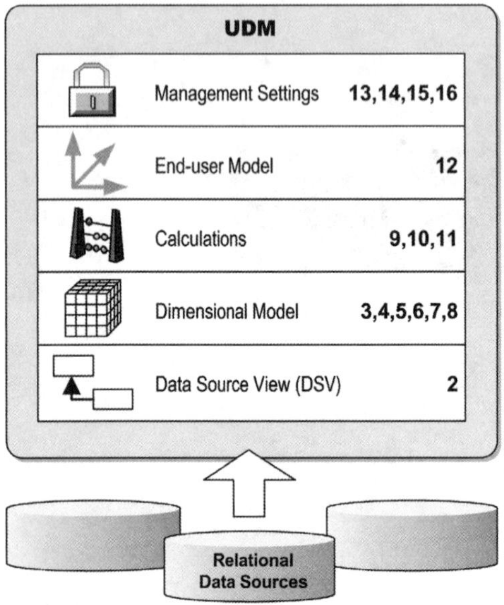

Figure 1.16 The physical manifestation of UDM is the SSAS 2005 "super-cube". Its main building blocks are data source view, dimensional model, calculations, end-user model, and management settings.

Dimensional model

Once DSV is created, the next step will be implementing the cube dimensional model. The end result of this process is the cube definition consisting of measures and dimensions with attribute and/or multilevel hierarchies.

Calculations

Only in rare cases, the dimensional model alone will fully meet your needs. As a UDM designer, you can augment your cube with specific business logic in the form of MDX expressions.

End-user model

As noted, the main design goal of the dimensional model is to provide intuitive end-user reporting and data navigation experience. By "end-user model", we will understand the additional features you can build on top of the dimensional layer to provide even richer data semantics. These features include Key Performance Indicators (KPIs), actions, perspectives, and translations. For example, if the cube will be browsed by international users, dimension levels could be localized by using translations. Or, you can use perspectives to define named subsets of large and complex cubes for easier navigation.

Management settings

At last, the cube is ready for prime time. As a last step, a savvy administrator would configure the cube to meet various operational requirements, including availability, latency, and security. For example, in this stage the cube administrator will configure which users will be able to access the cube, when and how the cube data will be updated, the cube storage model, etc.

1.3.4 To UDM and Beyond

By now, you should be able to understand the UDM goal to unite the best of both worlds (relational and dimensional) and become a bridge between the users and data. One could envision UDM to evolve in time to a point where the other relational and dimensional models are simply not needed and will disappear, as shown in Figure 1.17.

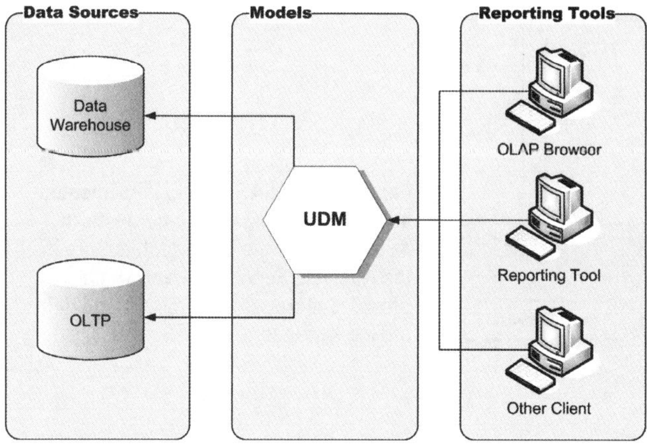

Figure 1.17 In time, UDM could replace the other reporting models to provide both relational and dimensional reporting needs.

When this happens, UDM will be able to serve both relational and dimensional reporting needs. Besides simplicity, having a single model will bring also conformity. Business logic and calculations could be defined in one place. As an added bonus, all reporting clients will be able to benefit from the performance boost they will get from SSAS.

Note To some extent, SQL Server 2005 and the Microsoft BI platform give you the tools to materialize the "unified" vision of having UDM as a focal point for data analytics. For example, as I will demonstrate in chapters 18 and 19, Reporting Services and the Microsoft Office analytics tools integrate well with UDM. However, as noted before, you shouldn't expect UDM to address all reporting requirements equally well. That's why I don't suggest you quickly throw away your reporting tools in favor of UDM. In my opinion, medium to large-size organizations will benefit most from leveraging UDM as a central repository.

1.4 Analysis Services Architecture

Readers who have prior SSAS experience have probably heard the popular saying that all roads to SSAS 2000 go through the PivotTable Service (PTS). PTS was the primary method for interacting with Analysis Services 2000 to perform tasks such as connecting to a cube and retrieving data. It was designed as a client-side component and, as such, it had to be installed on the machine where the client application was installed. PTS helped query performance by providing client-side caching. In many cases, however, PTS was simply getting in the way. For example, PTS wasn't designed to work with server-based applications. The good news is that the SSAS 2005 architecture is entirely server-based, as shown in Figure 1.18. This enables flexible client integration scenarios, e.g. implementing thin clients that require no installation footprint.

Let's discuss the SSAS building blocks starting with the Analysis Services server.

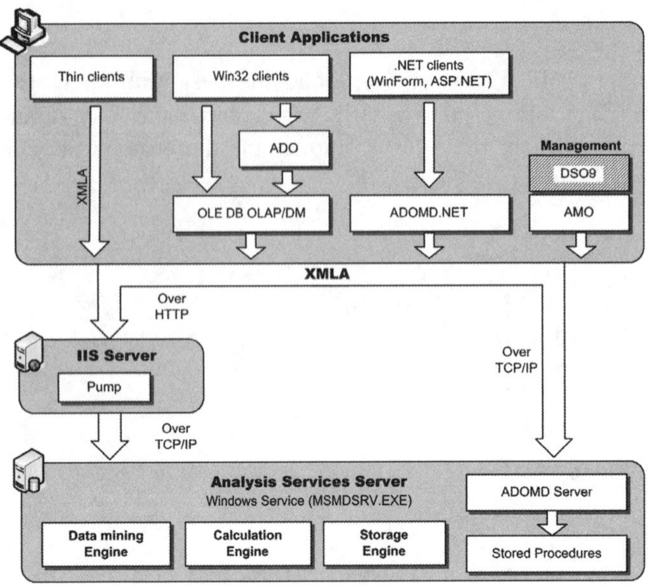

Figure 1.18 SSAS 2005 is implemented as a server-based middle-tier platform. At the heart of the SSAS architecture is the Analysis Services server which provides storage, calculations, and data mining services.

1.4.1 Analysis Services Server

At the heart of the SSAS architecture is the Analysis Services server. The SSAS server provides the following main services:

- *Storage* – The Storage Engine is responsible for storing and processing SSAS objects. It also keeps the UDM object definition (called *metadata*).
- *Calculations* – The Formula Engine handles MDX queries and expressions.
- *Data mining* – The Data Mining Engine processes mining queries and returns prediction results.

As with the previous releases, the SSAS server is implemented as a Windows service called MSMDSRV.EXE written in C++ native code. By default, the setup program installs the Analysis Services Server in C:\Program Files\Microsoft SQL Server\MSSQL.2. You can install more than one instance of SSAS 2005 on a single machine and different versions (e.g. 2000 and 2005) can co-exist side-by-side. Perhaps the most interesting SSAS architectural change is that it embraces XML for Analysis (XMLA) as a native protocol. In fact, you cannot communicate with SSAS in any other way than using XMLA. Given the strategic importance of XMLA, let's spend some time introducing this protocol.

1.4.2 XML for Analysis (XMLA) Specification

As its name suggests, the XMLA protocol conforms to XML-based grammar called XMLA specification. The purpose of this specification is to standardize the data access between OLAP clients and analytical data providers, such as SSAS. Since its debut in mid-2001, XMLA gained support with more than twenty vendors, including the three founding members -- Microsoft, Hyperion, and SAS (see the Resource section). The XMLA specification is managed by the XMLA council (*xmla.org*). As of the time of this writing, the most current version of the XMLA specification is 1.1. This is the version that is implemented in SSAS 2005.

XMLA embraces the SOAP protocol for sending and receiving XMLA messages to a XMLA-capable provider. The actual SOAP grammar is very simple (Figure 1.19). It describes just two methods, *Discover* and *Execute*, which every XMLA provider must support.

Discover

An OLAP client calls the *Discover* method to obtain the metadata that describes OLAP and data mining objects. For example, an OLAP client can ask the SSAS 2005 server to return a list of all cubes defined in an Analysis Services database by invoking the *Discover* method.

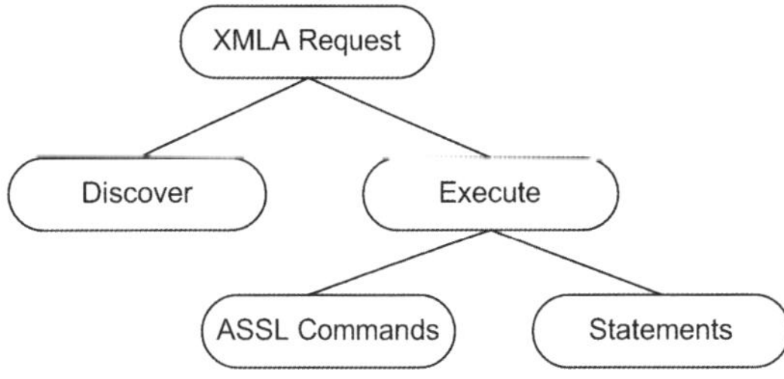

Figure 1.19 The XMLA protocol consists of Discover and Execute methods. A client can use the Execute method to send ASSL commands or statements.

Execute

Execute is an action-oriented method. A client can invoke the *Execute* method to send either ASSL commands or statements.

Analysis Services Scripting Language (ASSL)

Analysis Services Scripting Language (ASSL) is an XML-based grammar that describes the UDM metadata (DDL grammar) and commands.

- *Data Definition Language (DDL) grammar* – DDL is the internal representation of metadata in Analysis Services 2005. DDL describes the object definition, e.g. a cube definition. You can see the DDL grammar by right-clicking on the object in the BI Studio Solution Explorer and choosing *View Code.*
- *Command language grammar* – A subset of ASSL defines some action-oriented commands that could be sent to the server, e.g. for processing, altering, or creating objects. For example, each time you process a cube, BI Studio generates an ASSL script that includes a *Process* ASSL command.

The Execute method can (and most often) is used to send also statements.

Statements

With OLAP, the Execute statements describe MDX queries, while with data mining, they contain DMX queries. The query results are returned as a rowset (for SQL and data mining queries), or in the form of a more complex structure called MDDataSet in the case of OLAP (MDX) queries.

What may be confusing is that both MDX and DMX also define DDL statements. For example, MDX defines a *CREATE MEMBER* construct to create a new calculated member, while DMX supports a *CREATE MINING MODEL* to create a data mining model. It is important to understand that these DDL statements have nothing to do with the ASSL DDL grammar although they have ASSL equivalents. In addition, MDX and DMX DDL statements are less flexible than DDL.

XMLA Connectivity Options

SSAS 2005 gives you two connectivity options to send XMLA messages to an Analysis Services server. By default, the client communicates with the server via TCP/IP. However, SSAS can be configured also for HTTP connectivity to enable web-based integration scenarios.

XMLA over TCP/IP

The XMLA over TCP/IP connectivity option is more suitable for intranet deployments. With this option, the SOAP messages are serialized in binary format and sent over TCP/IP to the SSAS server. You don't need to take any extra steps to configure SSAS to use XMLA over TCP/IP. For example, if you use Office Web Components and set its connection string to use the OLE DB Provider for Analysis Services 9.0, the provider will communicate with SSAS over TCP/IP.

Compared to HTTP connectivity, the XMLA over TCP/IP connectivity option has slightly better performance since no additional layers are introduced between the client and the SSAS server. The tradeoff is that the client has to be able to connect directly to the port the SSAS server is listening to (2383, by default) which may conflict with firewall policies.

XMLA over HTTP

In this case, IIS is used as an intermediary to receive the HTTP requests. To set up SSAS 2005 for HTTP connectivity, you need to set up an IIS virtual root that will host the SSAS XMLA provider (a.k.a. *Pump*). The purpose of the Pump component is to accept the incoming HTTP requests from IIS and forward them to the SSAS server over TCP/IP. Once the HTTP connectivity is set up, change the connection string to point to the IIS virtual root, e.g. *http://<ServerName>/<VRoot>/msmdpump.dll*.

Consider the XMLA over HTTP option when you need to connect to SSAS over the Internet or when direct connectivity to SSAS is not an option. For example, security requirements may enforce access to SSAS only over port 80 (HTTP) or 443 (SSL). HTTP connectivity could be a good choice when you cannot install programming libraries, e.g. when you need to implement thin or non-Windows clients, e.g. a Java-based OLAP client running on UNIX box. The XMLA over HTTP connectivity option is described in more details in chapter 16.

1.4.3 SSAS Clients

OLAP clients have several available programming interfaces to connect to SSAS 2005. No matter which connectivity option is chosen, the interface library translates the calls to XMLA. Code samples demonstrating different integration options are provided in chapter 17.

Thin clients

Thanks to its entirely server-based architecture and support of industry-standard protocols (HTTP, XMLA, and SOAP), SSAS 2005 can be integrated with any SOAP-capable client running on any platform with no installation footprint. In this case, the client is responsible for constructing SOAP requests conforming to the XMLA specification and interpreting XMLA responses.

Win32 native clients

C++ clients would typically connect to SSAS 2005 using the OLE DB for Analysis Services. This is how OWC connects to SSAS 2005. The provider you need is OLE DB Provider for Analysis Services 9.0 (Provider=MSOLAP;3 in the connection string). You cannot use an older provider, e.g. version 8.0, because only version 9.0 knows how to translate the OLE DB for Analysis protocol to XMLA. COM-based clients, such as Visual Basic 6.0 clients, can connect to SSAS 2005 by using the ADO **M**ulti**D**imensional library (ADOMD) which is implemented as a COM wrapper on top of the OLE DB provider.

.NET clients

.NET clients can connect to SSAS 2005 using the ADO MultiDimensional for .NET library (ADOMD.NET). ADOMD.NET doesn't require the OLE DB Provider for Analysis Services 9.0 to be installed on the client machine. It is implemented as a light-weight managed wrapper on top of XMLA. Interestingly, SSAS provides also a server-side object model in the form of the ADOMD Server library (ADOMD.NET Server) residing inside the Analysis Services server. The main difference between ADOMD Server and ADOMD.NET is that the former doesn't require the developer to set up a connection with the server explicitly before sending queries or navigating the server objects. Other than that, both libraries provide almost identical set of objects.

For management tasks, .NET developers would use the brand new Analysis Management Objects (AMO) library. With the AMO library, you have access to the full Analysis Services object hierarchy, including servers, databases, data source views, cubes, dimensions, mining models, and roles. Developers would typically use the AMO library to automate routine management tasks, such as database synchronization and processing. AMO supersedes the Decision Support Objects (DSO), the object model of SSAS 2000. DSO is still available for backward compatibly in the form of the DSO9 object library. However, as the documentation states, DSO will be removed in the next version of Microsoft SQL Server and you are strongly encouraged to migrate your management applications to AMO.

1.5 Analysis Services in Action

Let's demonstrate some of the concepts that we've discussed so far in a short hands-on lab. Before we start, let's introduce an imaginary company, called Adventure Works Cycles. *Adventure Works Cycles* (or AWC, for short) manufactures and sells bicycles to resellers and individuals in North America, Europe, and Australia. In 2001, its first year of operation, AWC sales accounted for more than ten million dollars. Since then, the AWC business has been growing exponentially to reach the record high of forty million dollars in total sales in 2003. However, the AWC business took a downturn in 2004 and sales fell below the projected figures. Direct sales to customers remain constant, while resales fell almost fifty percent.

1.5.1 Introducing Adventure Works Sales OLAP System (SOS OLAP)

The AWC management has decided to implement a BI reporting solution to get more insight into the company performance and its customers. And, as you probably guessed it, AWC has hired you as an architect to lead the design and implementation of the strategic Adventure Works **S**ales **O**LAP **S**ystem, or SOS, as the AWC information workers affectionately refer to it to emphasize its much awaited arrival. It is worth mentioning that, as useful as our fictitious system could be, it is not meant to serve as a complete solution for sales analytics. Instead, you should view it as a sample whose main objective is to help you learn SSAS 2005.

The current system

After a series of acquisitions, Adventure Works Cycles operates several software systems spanning different technologies. The employee data is stored in an Oracle-based HR system, while the manufacturing data is captured in an IBM mainframe system. The sales ordering data is stored in a SQL Server database 2005 called *AdventureWorks*.

Note SQL Server 2005 comes with two sample databases. AdventureWorks simulates an OLTP sales order database, while AdventureWorksDW imitates a data warehouse database that sources its data from the AdventureWorks database. You can find the AdventureWorks OLTP Visio schema in the Database\AWC folder of the book source code. As you can see by browsing its seventy tables, the AdventureWorks database is inherently more complex than FoodMart or other SQL Server sample databases that you may have encountered in the past.

The sales representatives use a Windows Form intranet application to capture orders placed through the resale channel. Web customers purchase AWC products online through the AWC Intranet website. In both cases, the sales orders are stored in the *AdventureWorks* OLTP database. A sales order is assigned different status codes as it goes though the order management pipeline, e.g. *In Process*, *Approved*, *Shipped*, or *Cancelled*. AWC has a cutoff period of one month for the order to be considered finalized (*Shipped* or *Cancelled*).

AWC has already built a data warehouse to archive the sales history. Data from relevant systems is extracted, transformed, and loaded in the data warehouse. Shipped sales orders that are older than a month are extracted from the *AdventureWorks* OLTP system and offloaded to the warehouse. The role of the data warehouse is fulfilled by the *AdventureWorksDW* sample database, which can be installed by running the SQL Server setup program.

Reporting challenges

Currently, enterprise reporting needs are addressed by running standard reports directly against the warehouse database. This reporting model is characterized by several of the standard reporting deficiencies we enumerated in 1.2.1, including:

- *Inadequate reporting experience* – Business analysts complain that they cannot slice and dice data from different perspectives easily. Different reporting tools are used based on the user skill set, ranging from Excel spreadsheets to high-level reporting tools, such as Reporting Services.
- *Performance issues* – Reports that aggregate large volumes of data take a long time to execute.
- *Insufficient data analytics* – Complex business logic and calculations cannot be easily implemented on top of the data warehouse relational schema. Subsequently, they are often redefined from one report to another and stored as part of the report, instead of in a central repository. In addition, the current reporting model doesn't support pattern discovery and forecasting.

To address the current report deficiencies, you've decided to use SSAS 2005 as an OLAP engine that will power the new SOS system.

The solution

You envision the SOS system to provide three major functional areas – a historical layer, a real-time UDM layer, and a reporting layer.

Historical UDM

The main purpose of the SOS system is to provide fast and uniform access to the data stored in the data warehouse. This objective will be achieved by building a UDM layer in the form of an Analysis Services 2005 cube on top of the warehouse database. The historical UDM layer will serve most of the OLAP requirements and all data mining requirements.

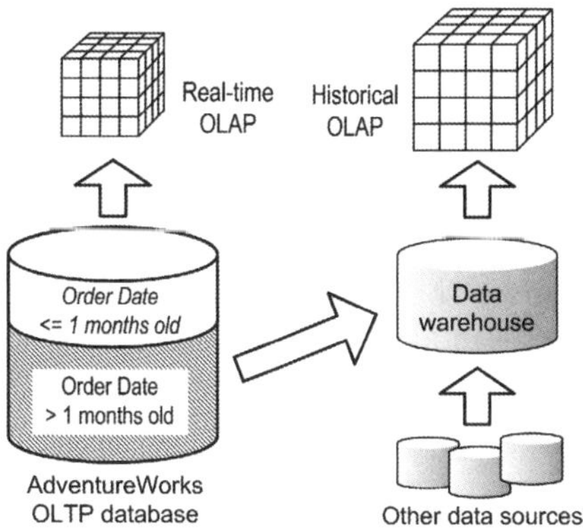

Figure 1.20 The SOS solution will feature the real-time and historical UDM layers.

Real-time UDM

To address real-time BI needs for reporting off volatile order data that hasn't been offloaded to the data warehouse, a real-time (hot) OLAP layer will be built directly on top of the Adventure-Works OLTP system. The real-time UDM layer will be implemented as a second SSAS 2005 cube that will provide a subset of the data analytics feature set of the historical UDM.

Note We will keep the real-time UDM light-weight on purpose. From a learning perspective, there is no point duplicating the same feature set in both the historical and real-time UDM models. Instead, when implementing the real-time UDM, our focus will be demonstrating UDM features that are particularly relevant to low-latency OLAP solutions, such as data source views and proactive caching. In real life, of course, you can have a more sophisticated and feature-rich real-time layer if required.

The term *real-time* here means that the cube will pick up changes in the transactional data almost instantaneously, instead of requiring explicit processing.

Reporting layer

Since the AWC business analysts have different reporting needs, you envision leveraging several BI reporting tools for presenting data to the end users, including custom applications, Reporting Services, and Microsoft Office.

1.5.2 Your First OLAP Report

Suppose the Adventure Works business analysts would like to be able to generate interactive sales reports to slice and dice data from different angles. Let's see how we can address this requirement by using two reporting technologies: standard reporting and OLAP reporting.

Standard reporting

In the absence of an OLAP reporting solution, the most common option is to author standard or ad-hoc reports that submit SELECT SQL statements directly to the OLTP database. These SELECT queries are typically multi-join statements that link several relational tables together to fetch the report data. An example of a SQL SELECT statement that will produce a standard report similar to the interactive report shown in Figure 1.1 is included in SQLQuery.sql file.

There may be several potential issues with generating reports sourced directly from an OLTP database. To start with, the report query may impact the performance of the OLTP database. The query may take long a time to execute. On my machine (HP NW8000, 1.8 GHz Pentium M single CPU, 2 GB RAM) the query in the SQLQuery.sql file takes about three seconds to execute. Not that bad, you may say. Of course, we need to factor in the amount of data processed. In our case, the SalesOrderDetail table in the sample AdventureWorks database has 121,317 order line items. Now, imagine that the same query is fired against a much bigger transactional or warehouse database. Assuming linear regression of performance, the same query will take about 30 seconds to complete if we have ten times more records. I doubt that your users will be willing to wait for that long!

If you would like to empower your end users to generate their own reports in ad-hoc fashion, they have to know quite a bit about the relational (ER) model and SQL. They have to know which tables to join and they have to know how to join them. True, ad-hoc reporting tools may abstract to a certain extent the technicalities of the relational model but they have issues of their own. Finally, standard reports are not interactive. The user cannot drill down data, e.g. double-click on a given year column to see data broken down by quarters.

Deploying the Unified Dimensional Model

Now, let's see how OLAP and UDM change the reporting experience. We will use Excel reporting capabilities to build a simple reporting solution with SSAS 2005 that will resemble the report shown in Figure 1.1. The report will source its data from an SSAS 2005 cube. To build the cube, we will use the AdventureWorks Analysis Services Project sample that comes with the SQL Server 2005 samples. It includes a sample cube called *Adventure Works*. The Adventure Works cube draws data from the Adventure Works warehouse database (*AdventureWorksDW*)

If you have installed the SQL Server 2005 samples (see Appendix A), the project will be located in C:\Program Files\Microsoft SQL Server\90\Tools\Samples\AdventureWorks Analysis Services Project folder.

Note Both Standard and Enterprise versions of the project will do fine for our demo. Choose one based on the SSAS version you are running.

Opening an Analysis Services project in BI Studio

If you haven't deployed the sample AdventureWorks Analysis Services Project sample, follow these steps:

1. Start SQL Server Business Intelligence Development Studio (found in the Microsoft SQL Server 2005 program group). Readers familiar with Visual Studio.NET will undoubtedly notice that the Business Intelligence Development Studio IDE looks similar. As I've mentioned in section 1.1.4, you will use BI Studio as a primary tool to design and maintain UDM.

2. From the File menu, choose Open, then Project/Solution… and Open the Adventure Works solution (Adventure Works.sln). This solution includes a single project (Adventure Works DW.dwproj). Don't worry if the concepts of SSAS database and projects are not immediately obvious. It will all become clear in Chapter 2. For the time being, note that the AdventureWorks DW project includes the definitions of all objects in the Adventure Works UDM.

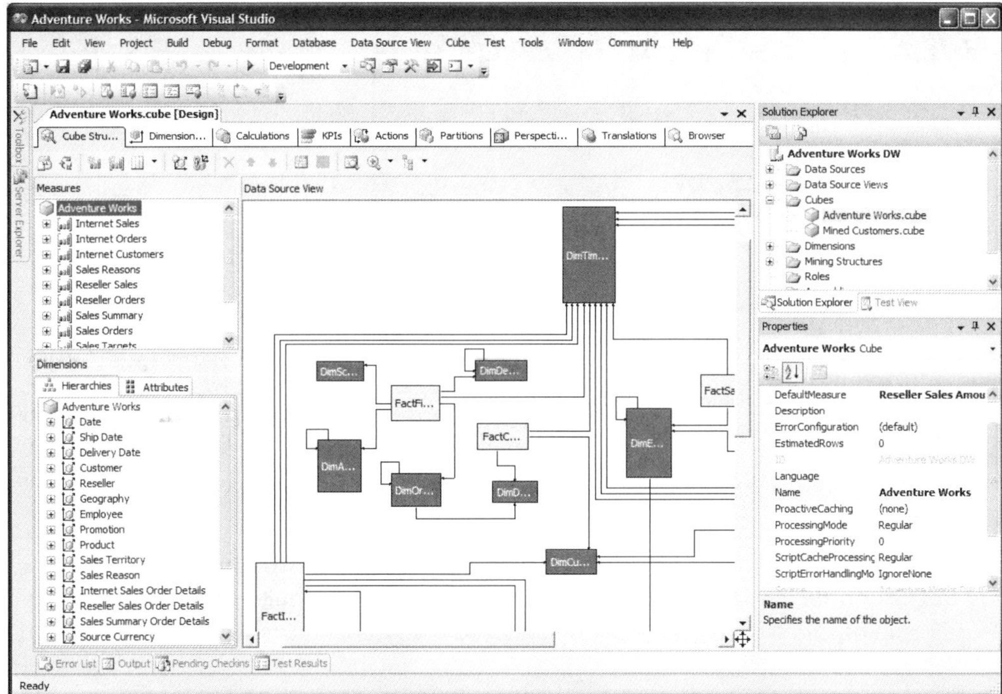

Figure 1.21 Use the Business Intelligence Studio to design SSAS objects.

3. If the Solution Explorer window is not shown, click on the Solution Explorer (View menu) or press Ctrl-Alt-L. The Solution Explorer shows the SSAS objects defined in the Adventure Works DW project in a tree view, as shown in Figure 1.21.

Double-click on the Adventure Works cube to open the Cube Designer. The Cube Designer uses the same colors (blue for dimension tables and yellow for fact tables) as Analysis Manager 2000. Note that the dimension and fact tables are linked to each other, just like relational tables are joined via referential integrity constraints. However, the big difference is that UDM enforces these relationships at a metadata level. As a result, the end user doesn't have to explicitly join UDM objects. Instead, producing an OLAP report is as easy as dragging and dropping UDM objects using your favorite OLAP client, which could be Microsoft Excel, as we will demonstrate shortly.

4. In the Solution Explorer, expand the Cube node, right-click on the Adventure Works cube and choose View Code. BI studio shows the definition of the cube described in Analysis Services Scripting Language (ASSL). When you work in project mode (default), changes are persisted locally.

Deploying projects

5. To propagate changes made in project mode, you need to deploy the project. Back to the Solution Explorer, right-click on the Adventure Works DW project node (not to be confused with the topmost solution node) and choose *Properties*. Expand the Configuration Properties and click the *Deployment* node (Figure 1.22).

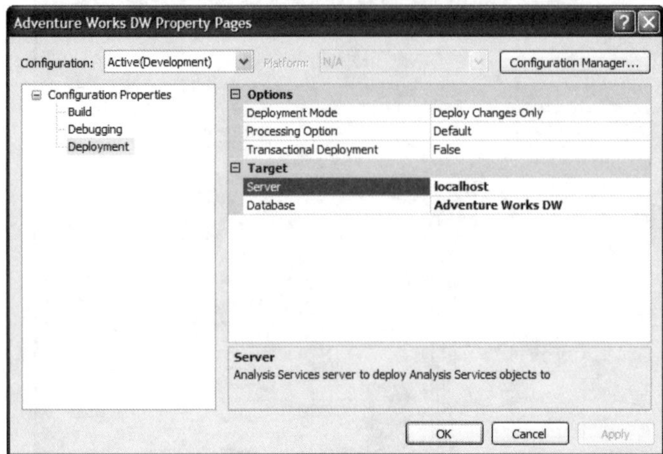

Figure 1.22 To propagate changes made in project mode, you need to deploy the project to the SSAS server specified in the Deployment Options window.

6. Verify the server name (enter **localhost** to deploy to the local server).

7. Close the Property Pages window. If you haven't deployed the Adventure Works DW project yet, right-click on the project node and choose *Deploy*. BI Studio builds and deploys the project. The end result of this process will be the creation of a new SSAS database called *Adventure Works DW*.

8. To verify that the deployment process has completed successfully, open SQL Server Management Studio (Microsoft SQL Server 2005 Program group).

9. In the Object Explorer pane, choose *Connect* ⇨ *Analysis Services* to connect to the SSAS server that you deployed the project to.

10. Expand the Databases folder and check that there is a database named *Adventure Works DW*.

11. Expand the Adventure Works DW folder and take some time to familiarize yourself with the database content. For example, expand the Adventure Works cube, then the Measure Groups measures and notice that there are eleven measure groups (with the Enterprise version).

Building OLAP Report

At this point, the SSAS database is built and its only cube has been processed. Let's now use Microsoft Excel as a reporting tool to browse the cube data. We will generate a report that shows sales data broken by product and time, as shown in Figure 1.23.

1. Start Microsoft Excel 2003

2. Create a new PivotTable report by selecting PivotTable and PivotChart Report from the Data menu.

3. In Step 1 of the PivotTable and PivotChart Report Wizard, select the "External data source" option since you will be retrieving the data from an SSAS server. Click Next.

4. In Step 2, click on the Get Data button to configure Microsoft Query. In the Choose Data Source dialog, click on the OLAP Cubes tab. Make sure the New Data Source item is selected. Click OK.

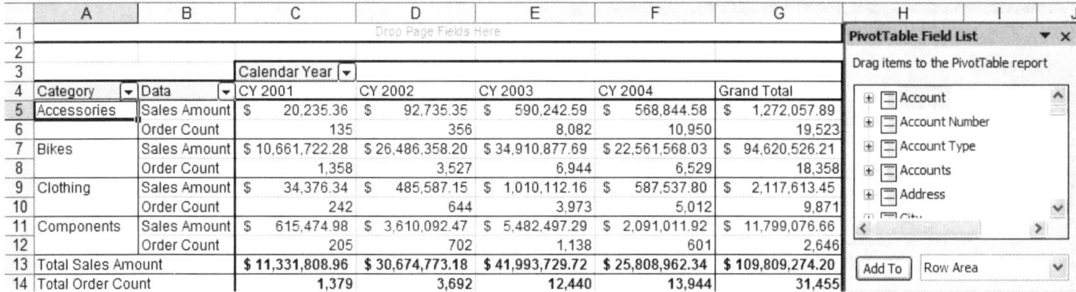

Category	Data	CY 2001	CY 2002	CY 2003	CY 2004	Grand Total
Accessories	Sales Amount	$ 20,235.36	$ 92,735.35	$ 590,242.59	$ 568,844.58	$ 1,272,057.89
	Order Count	135	356	8,082	10,950	19,523
Bikes	Sales Amount	$ 10,661,722.28	$ 26,486,358.20	$ 34,910,877.69	$ 22,561,568.03	$ 94,620,526.21
	Order Count	1,358	3,527	6,944	6,529	18,358
Clothing	Sales Amount	$ 34,376.34	$ 485,587.15	$ 1,010,112.16	$ 587,537.80	$ 2,117,613.45
	Order Count	242	644	3,973	5,012	9,871
Components	Sales Amount	$ 615,474.98	$ 3,610,092.47	$ 5,482,497.29	$ 2,091,011.92	$ 11,799,076.66
	Order Count	205	702	1,138	601	2,646
Total Sales Amount		**$ 11,331,808.96**	**$ 30,674,773.18**	**$ 41,993,729.72**	**$ 25,808,962.34**	**$ 109,809,274.20**
Total Order Count		**1,379**	**3,692**	**12,440**	**13,944**	**31,455**

Figure 1.23 Use Microsoft Excel to create SSAS 2005 interactive reports.

5. In the *Create New Data Source* dialog, name the data source Adventure Works. In the "Select an OLAP provider for the database you want to access" dropdown select Microsoft OLE DB Provider for Analysis Services 9.0 (see Figure 1.24). Recall that Win32 clients must use version 9.0 of the OLE DB Provider for Analysis Services to connect to SSAS 2005.

6. Click the Connect button. On the *MultiDimensional Connection* dialog, select the *Analysis Server* radio button, enter the machine name where SSAS 2005 is installed (Server field). Leave the credentials fields blank to use Windows Authentication. Click Next. The Database listbox appear. Select the *Adventure Works DW* database and click Finish. You are now taken back to the Create New Data Source dialog.

7. Expand the last dropdown (Figure 1.24) and select the Adventure Works cube. Click OK to close the *Create New Data Source* dialog and OK to close the *Choose Data Source* dialog. You are back to the PivotTable and PivotChart Wizard. Click Next to advance to Step 3.

8. Accept the defaults in Step 3 and click Finish.

9. A blank pivot report appears in the Excel spreadsheet. A PivotTable Field List pane contains all measures and dimensions defined in the Adventure Works cube.

Note At this point, you are probably confused by the sheer number of items shown in the PivotTable Field List pane. Most of the items are attribute-based dimensions which are derived directly from columns in the underlying dimension tables. For example, the *Color* dimension corresponds to the Color column in the DimProduct dimension table. Unfortunately, Excel 2003 was released before SSAS 2005 and it is unaware of the new features. Subsequently, the Field List is not capable of organizing the attribute hierarchies in folders, as the Cube Browser does.

10. Scroll down the PivotTable Field List pane until you locate the *Date.Calendar* hierarchy. This dimension represents a natural time hierarchy with Year, Semester, Quarter, Month and Date levels. Drag the *Date.Calendar* hierarchy to the *Drop Column Fields Here* area of the pivot report.

11. Scroll further down the PivotTable Field List pane until you locate the *Product Categories* dimension. This dimension represents a natural product hierarchy with Category, Subcategory, and Product Name levels. Drag the *Product Categories* hierarchy to the *Drop Row Fields Here* area of the pivot report.

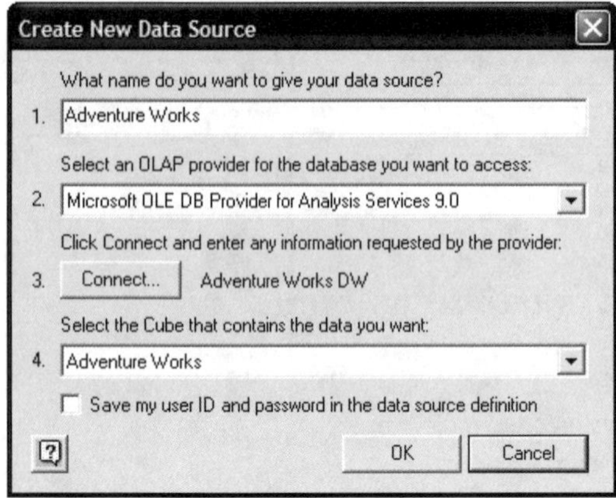

Figure 1.24 Use the Microsoft OLE DB Provider for Analysis Services 9.0 to connect to SSAS 2005.

12. Let's now add some measures to the report. Scroll the PivotTable Field List pane all the way down until you locate the *Sales Amount* measure. In the pane, measures have a different icon (0110) than dimensions. Drag the *Sales Amount* measure to the *Drop Data Items Here* report area. Do the same with the *Order Count* measure. Although the PivotTable Field lists doesn't have a special icon for MDX expressions, note that there are many calculated measures we can use in the report, such as *Reseller Ratio to All Products*, *Internet Gross Profit Margin*, etc.

13. If you wish, you can spend some time to pretty up the report by changing format, font, and color settings. At the end, your report may look like the one shown in Figure 1.23.

We are done! Feel free to experiment with the Excel PivotTable report. For example, double-click on any member of the Product Categories dimension to drill down sales data to the product subcategory and product name levels. Drag and drop other dimensions and measures. Once the cube is designed and deployed, there are many ways to build interactive reports that provide the needed level of business intelligence.

1.6 Summary

This chapter has been a whirlwind tour of the SSAS 2005 and OLAP technology. By now, you should view SSAS 2005 as a sophisticated server-based platform that provides OLAP and data mining services. Empowered with SSAS 2005, you can build intuitive and efficient BI applications. We've seen how SSAS 2005 fits into the Microsoft BI initiative. We've emphasized the ambitious goal of SSAS 2005 to converge the relational and dimensional models into a single Unified Dimensional Model.

We've also looked at the high-level of the SSAS 2005 architecture and emphasized the fact that XMLA is the native protocol of SSAS 2005. To help readers who have prior SSAS experience, I've provided a side-by-side comparison map between versions 2000 and 2005. Finally, we've put into practice what we've learned by building an interactive Microsoft Excel PivotTable report which sourced its data from SSAS 2005. Having laid the SSAS foundation, we are ready to "drill down" the UDM layers. Let's start by finding out how we can work with data.

1.7 Resources

Microsoft SSAS home page
(http://shrinkster.com/895) – First stop for the latest on SSAS.

The OLAP Report website
(http://www.olapreport.com/) – The OLAP Report is an independent research resource for organizations buying and implementing OLAP applications.

SQL Server 2005 Features Comparison
(http://shrinkster.com/62q) – Compares side by side the editions of the SQL Server 2005 products.

SSAS and the competition
(http://www.olapreport.com/market.html) – Market share analysis of the top OLAP vendors.

Microsoft Reporting Services in Action Book
(http://www.manning.com/lachev) – Following the report lifecycle, my book teaches you the necessary skills to create, manage, and deliver SSRS reports.

XML for Analysis home page
(http://www.xmla.org/) – Visit to access the latest XML/A specification, FAQ, discussion forum, and samples.

PART 1

The Unified Dimensional Model

As noted in chapter 1, UDM can be logically divided in several layers. As a first step of building up UDM, you will construct its data layer in the form of a Data Source View (DSV) that isolates UDM from the underlying relational data schema. Once the data foundation is in place, the next step is to lay out the dimensional model on top of it. The easiest way to generate the raw dimensional model is to use the Cube Wizard and Dimension Wizard provided by Business Intelligence Studio.

Readers familiar with OLAP will undoubtedly find that despite the radical changes introduced in UDM, the core concepts are still the same. The main difference is that UDM is an attribute-based model. The Cube and Dimension designers pick up where the wizards leave off. With the help of the designers, you can refine your UDM dimension model and custom-tailor it to meet your specific OLAP requirements.

Although UDM has its roots in the dimensional model, it is, in many ways, superior. Its main goal is to synthesize the best features of the relational and dimensional reporting models. Flexible dimensional relationships, advanced data analytics features, linked dimensions, and measure groups allow UDM to break out of the traditional OLAP space and meet more advanced data analytics requirements.

Chapter 2

Working with Data

In chapter 1, I introduced you to the SSAS Unified Dimensional Model. As you would recall, the main goal of UDM is to provide fast and intuitive access to large volumes of data. UDM consists of data schema, dimensional model, calculation, end-user analytics, and management settings layers. Although UDM has its roots in the dimensional model, it is, in many ways, superior. One prominent feature of UDM is its flexible data architecture which goes beyond supporting star and showflake schemas only. To demonstrate the flexible nature of UDM, in this chapter, I will show you how you can build UDM on top of arbitrary database schemas, including relational and dimensional schemas. You will learn:

- The main components of the SSAS data architecture
- How to design UDM data schemas
- How to build UDM on top of OLTP data sources
- How to work with dimensional data sources

The finished demos accompanying this chapter are available in the Ch02 solution.

2.1 UDM Data Concepts

In chapter 1, I talked briefly about the building blocks of UDM. I introduced the concepts of data source views (DSV), cubes and databases but I didn't explain the relationship among them and their purpose. Let's do this now.

2.1.1 SSAS Databases

An Analysis Services database is a logical container of UDM objects and it has no data storage of its own. How you define the database scope is totally up to you. For example, if you need to implement an OLAP solution on top of an existing enterprise-wide data warehouse, you may find that one database with a single "super-cube" is all you need. On the other hand, operational and security requirements may mandate splitting the OLAP model into several databases. For example, security requirements may dictate that the HR database will be hosted on a separate server than the Sales database. As a cube designer, you will undoubtedly find that SSAS 2005 gives you a great deal of flexibility for partitioning UDM any way you want.

UDM objects

Just like you need a SQL Server database to group a set of related objects (tables, views, stored procedures, etc), you can use an SSAS database to organize a set of related SSAS objects. Table 2.1 lists all UDM objects that can be hosted in an SSAS database.

Table 2.1 All UDM objects must be defined in an SSAS database.

Database object	Description
Data source	A data source defines a connection to a database. The term data source is used to refer to both to the connection definition and the actual database, e.g. SQL Server database.
Data Source View (DSV)	A data source view defines the data schema on top of which you build the dimensional model.
Cube	A multidimensional structure that consists of dimensions and measures. The measures are part of the cube definition while dimensions are defined as separate UDM objects.
Dimension	Represent the analytical perspectives used to organize and browse data. Dimensions can be shared among cubes within the same or external SSAS databases.
Data mining structure	Mining structures contain data mining models.
Role	Just like Windows groups, SSAS roles could be used to define security policies for end users based on their Windows identity or group membership.
Assembly	.NET assemblies that contain stored procedures for extending UDM programmatically.

Database metadata

Where does SSAS keep the database object definitions? Veteran SSAS readers would probably recall that SSAS 2000 keeps its metadata by default in a Microsoft Access database which could be optionally migrated to a SQL Server database.

Definition The term *metadata* literally means data that describes other data. In the SSAS 2005 context, metadata describes the database object definitions and relationships, e.g. which objects are part of the database, dimension hierarchies and levels, measure groups, etc.

In contrast, for performance and maintenance reasons, the Analysis Services team has decided to store the SSAS 2005 metadata as XML files. The metadata is kept on the server where SSAS is installed (by default in folder C:\Program Files\Microsoft SQL Server\MSSQL.2\OLAP\Data). You should abstain from making any manual changes to the Analysis Services metadata. Instead, you should always deploy your projects either from Business Intelligence Studio or the other supported methods that are described in chapter 13, such as backup/restore or database synchronization.

How is metadata described?

In case you would like to know more about the SSAS 2005 metadata, here are some additional details. The SSAS 2005 metadata is described in ASSL Data Definition Language (DDL). As I mentioned briefly in chapter 1, ASSL is the XML-based grammar that SSAS 2005 uses to describe its objects.

For example, assuming that you've deployed the Adventure Works DW sample database, in the metadata folder you will see a file named something like Adventure Works DW.0.db.xml. This file describes the Adventure Works DW sample database in ASSL. Navigating further the folder hierarchy, you will see additional subfolders for database objects, .dim files for dimensions, .ds files for data sources, etc.

Metadata storage overview

As you will notice, SSAS 2005 uses a special naming convention for the object names. Each object (dimension, measure, etc) has a unique identifier. In addition, every object has a version number starting with 0 (the first time the object is created). The digit inside the object name stands for the object version.

SSAS 2005 uses sophisticated technology, based on the Windows structured file storage, to update database objects in a transactional scope when they are deployed. Each time an object is updated and its transaction commits, SSAS generates a new version of the object. If, for some reason, the transaction fails, the object changes are rolled back to the previous version. Each object version has a reference to its storage entity. For example, each version of a dimension object has a reference to the dimension storage file (where dimensions levels are kept). Multiple object versions can point to the same storage.

I will stop here in my overview of the SSAS 2005 metadata storage after admitting that I've only scratched the surface. As a cube designer, you don't have control over the metadata generation and it is of no practical use for you to know more about it.

2.1.2 Data Sources

Since the focus of this chapter is working with data, I will focus here only on two UDM objects -- data sources and data source views. Figure 2.1 shows how these objects fit in the UDM data architecture. For the sake of simplicity, in this chapter, I won't discuss how data mining objects work with data sources (this is covered in chapters 7 and 8).

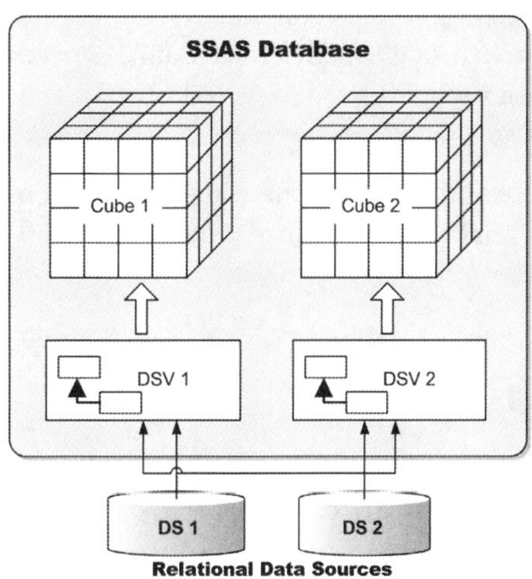

Figure 2.1 One SSAS database may contain one or more cubes. One cube has only one data source view associated with it. A data source view may draw data from more than one data source.

An SSAS 2005 database can contain more than one cube. In SSAS 2005, a cube cannot access data sources directly. Instead, you must define a data source view that isolates the cube from its underlying data source. While data source views can be shared among cubes in the same database, one cube can have a single data source view only. However, a data source view can reference one or more data sources that feed the cube(s) with data.

Data providers

A data source uses a data provider to talk to the database. Cubes and dimensions can source data from any relational data source that has an OLE DB or .NET provider. Please note that I said *relational*. SSAS cubes cannot draw data from multidimensional data sources, such as another SSAS database. That said, an SSAS cube can share UDM objects with another cube through linked dimensions and measure groups (discussed in chapter 5).

OLE DB providers

SSAS officially supports several OLE DB providers -- Microsoft SQL Server (7.0, 2000, and 2005), Oracle (8.0, 9.0, 10.0), IBM DB2 (8.1), NCR TeraData (4.1, 5.0), and Microsoft Jet (4.0). SSAS 2005 doesn't officially support ODBC data sources. ODBC connectivity was causing issues in the past and the SSAS team has decided to discontinue its support.

.NET providers

In the absence of a suitable OLE DB provider, SSAS allows you to choose a .NET managed provider. The officially supported .NET providers are the SQL Server and Oracle providers distributed with the .NET Framework. Before deciding on a .NET provider, recall the fact that the SSAS server (MSMDSRV.EXE Windows service) is implemented in native code. For this reason, if you choose a .NET provider, you will experience performance overhead associated with marshalling .NET types to native code for all data source operations. When processing fact tables with million of rows, this overhead could add up and increase processing times.

Tip Use a .NET data provider only if you don't have a native OLE DB provider available for the data source you need to connect to.

Data source integration scenarios

How can you integrate SSAS with relational data sources? To answer this question, let's consider some common OLAP reporting scenarios based on data size and complexity (see Figure 2.2). With small to medium-size data volumes (e.g. up to several gigabytes of data), reporting is typically done directly against the OLTP systems without requiring a designated OLAP server.

OLTP data sources

As the data volume increases however, OLAP activities may hinder the transactional performance. In this case, SSAS could supplement or replace relational reporting in the form of a UDM

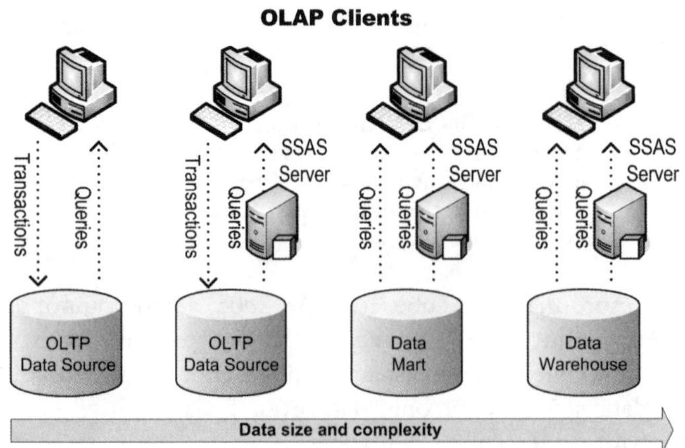

Figure 2.2 As data size and complexity increases, OLAP processes are shifted to designated databases and OLAP servers.

layer built directly on top of the OLTP database. For lack of a better term, I will dub this approach *Transactional OLAP*.

Note Now that I've coined yet another term, you may wonder how *Transactional* OLAP compares to *real-time* OLAP I introduced in chapter 1. Transactional OLAP sources its data from an OLTP data source. By real-time OLAP, we will mean synchronizing UDM with the data source changes in real time. Transactional OLAP may not require real-time synchronization. Similar to a typical data warehousing pipeline, Transactional OLAP objects may be processed on a regular basis. If you need to keep Transactional OLAP in sync with the data source changes in real time, then Transactional OLAP and real-time OLAP are basically the same with OLTP data sources.

OLAP fundamentalists may question the practical use of Transactional OLAP. Indeed, today's enterprise OLAP requirements are usually best met when data is extracted from various disparate data sources and consolidated in a dimensional data source, such as a data warehouse. In this respect, Transactional OLAP may be viewed as too unrealistic, if not an oxymoron. However, based on my experience, many BI requirements call for minimal or no data transformation and can be addressed without building a formal data warehouse. For example, a medium-size company may be using an order management system, such as Microsoft Great Plains. This system may capture a wealth of business measures (sales amount, inventory levels, etc.) and dimensions (products, vendors, customers, etc.).

Should you jump on the warehouse bandwagon if you need to implement an OLAP solution? In my opinion, this may be overkill. Instead, consider building UDM directly on top of the underlying transactional database, as we will demonstrate in section 2.3. Of course, Transaction OLAP usually precludes historical reporting since it is very likely that the OLTP database will be truncated on a regular basis to keep its performance at peak. In addition, you may need to pay attention to concurrency issues since the transactional data and your report results could be ever changing.

Data marts and warehouses

To meet more demanding performance and integration requirements, consider moving OLTP data to a designated data mart or data warehouse database. For example, OLTP systems typically don't keep a historical view of data. To keep transactional systems operating at maximum speed, administrators may need to truncate transactional data on a regular basis. The old data can be offloaded from OLTP systems to a data warehouse which can serve as an enterprise-wide reporting repository.

Definition I use the term *data mart* to refer to a data repository that is loaded with data specific to a particular subject or business activity, such as finance or customer analysis. In the classic data warehousing scenario, data from data marts is extracted and consolidated in the enterprise-wide data warehouse.

For example, the finance department may have a data mart for the purposes of financial reporting, while the sales department could have a data mart of its own to support sales reporting. At the other end of the spectrum, enterprise requirements may call for implementing a *data warehouse* to "unite" disparate and heterogeneous data into a single conformant repository.

While reporting needs can be served directly from data marts and data warehouses, consider discouraging this practice and using SSAS as a focal source for data analytics. This approach will yield better performance and analytics. For example, due to their design limitations, relational databases are not suitable for comparing data over parallel time periods, while SSAS can handle this requirement easily through business logic encapsulated in MDX calculations. Finally, the data source integration scenarios shown in Figure 2.2 are not necessarily exclusive. For example, while the data warehouse can address historical reporting needs, transactional OLAP could address real-time OLAP needs. This is the approach I will demonstrate in this book.

2.1.3 Data Source Views

One of the most prominent features of UDM is that it can be built on top of arbitrary data source schemas. In the best case scenario, UDM will source data from a formal data warehouse whose schema is already "dimensionalized". In this case, the data schema may require none or minimal changes. At the other end of the spectrum is an OLTP data source (Transactional OLAP). In this case, you may need to bend the data source schema to fit your UDM requirements. For example, you may need to define relationships between tables or create new "virtual" tables, just like you do when using SQL views in RDBMS.

To complicate things further, sometimes strict security requirements may rule out changes to the underlying relational schema. SSAS 2005 addresses these realities elegantly by introducing data source views.

Note A data source view (DSV) is a metadata logical layer which isolates the cube from the relational schema of the data source. DSV changes are not persisted to the underlying data source.

The DSV idea originated from a common requirement to provide an abstraction layer that shows only a subset of tables from a large data warehouse schema (similar to the SQL Server diagrams). But the idea took a life of its own and eventually resulted in a sophisticated logical layer that serves two main objectives. First, it defines the schema on which UDM is built. Second, it supports enhancing the schema by logical primary keys and relations, named queries, and calculations.

Interestingly, you will find the same data sources and data source views objects are shared across the three pillars of the Microsoft BI 2005 platform. The difference is in the model you build on top of DSV. In Analysis Services 2005, it is UDM; in the Integration Services, it is the task workflow; while in the RS ad hoc architecture, it is the semantic model. Besides minimizing your learning curve, this uniform model brings consistency by allowing you to share data sources and data source view across the three project types in Business Intelligence Development Studio. As noted in chapter 1, BI Studio is a light version of Visual Studio.NET.

2.2 Designing Databases

UDM modelers would probably rely on BI Studio to design SSAS databases. If you are new to BI Studio and VS.NET, read the *Overview of the Analysis Services Development and Management Environments* whitepaper by Microsoft to quickly introduce yourself to BI Studio IDE (see Resources). To meet different project scenarios, BI Studio supports two design modes for making changes to UDM objects, as shown in Figure 2.3. It is essential that you understand how these two modes differ, so let's discuss them in more details.

Figure 2.3 In project mode, changes need to be deployed to the server. In online mode, changes are reflected immediately.

2.2.1 Project Mode

This is the default and recommended design mode. BI Studio defaults to project mode when you create a new Analysis Services project (*File* ⇨ *New* ⇨ *Project* menu). In project mode, changes to the UDM objects are saved locally as XML files described in ASSL. In comparison with online mode, the project mode has two distinct advantages which are discussed next.

Project mode benefits

First, project mode facilitates team development and version control of the object definition files. For example, suppose that multiple developers are working on the same UDM. You can put the entire Analysis Services project under source control, e.g. in a Visual SourceSafe database. Once this is done, developers can make changes to objects by checking out the corresponding files without worrying that they will overwrite each other's changes.

The second advantage of project mode is not so obvious. As I mentioned in chapter 1, UDM objects needs to be reprocessed when their structure change or to refresh their data. In some cases, affected objects are inter-dependent and have to be processed in a particular order. For example, when a cube is processed, the server doesn't process its dimensions. Therefore, if you change the dimension definition, you need to process the dimension first, before processing the affected cube(s). As a novice UDM modeler, you may find these processing rules intimidating. Project mode helps you in this respect because when you deploy the project, the server automatically detects the affected objects and processes them in the correct order.

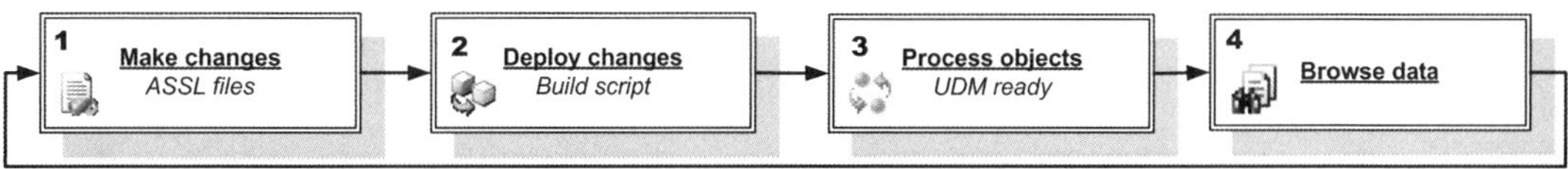

Figure 2.4 In project mode, you need to deploy the changed objects to the server and process them.

Project mode lifecycle

Since project mode changes are done in disconnected mode, to see the effect of these changes, you need to deploy the affected objects to the server. For example, after adding a new dimension to a cube, you need to deploy the project before you can browse data by the new dimension. Therefore, the project mode requires that you adopt the four-step iterative approach shown in

Figure 2.4. First, you use BI Studio to make changes to the local definition files. Next, you deploy the modified object definitions to the development server. Then, you process the affected objects. Finally, you browse the data to see the effect of the changes.

Note I hope a future SSAS release will support a preview mode which doesn't necessarily require deploying the changed objects. This could be implemented as caching data locally (similar to the way Reporting Services caches data in Preview mode), or displaying sample data (the SSAS 2000 cube browser). Currently, even a light-weight change (such as a measure formatting), requires redeployment to see its effect. One practical approach to minimize deployment and processing time is to use a very small dataset during development.

As noted, BI Studio can handle object processing for you. Moreover, BI Studio combines steps 2 and 3 into one step when the project is deployed. First, BI Studio *builds* the project to generate a deployment script of the changes. Next, BI Studio sends the script to the server to deploy the changes. Finally, BI Studio initiates the object processing by asking the server to process the affected objects in the right order.

You may find this paradigm similar to working with development projects in VS.NET. A .NET developer doesn't need to know a whole lot about the inner workings of the linker and the compiler. All that is needed to produce the project binary is building (compiling) the project. Similarly, an UDM modeler only needs to deploy the project to update and process the affected objects on the server in one step. Once the UDM has been finalized, you are ready to deploy the project to the production server. You can do so straight from BI Studio or by using the Deployment Wizard.

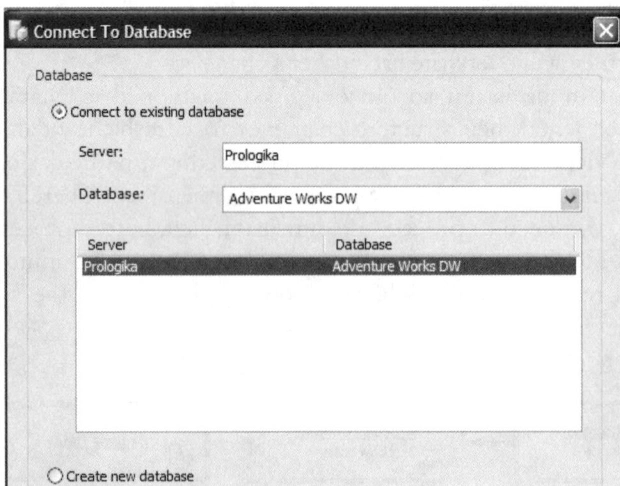

Figure 2.5 Choose an online project mode when you need to make changes directly to the SSAS database.

2.2.2 Online Mode

Readers with prior Analysis Services experience will find online mode identical to working with the SSAS 2000 Analysis Manager. As its names suggests, in this mode you are directly connected to the SSAS 2005 database and the changes are applied immediately when the object is saved. Therefore, step 2 in Figure 2.5 is eliminated. The major disadvantage of online mode is that you cannot version-control the object definitions. Even worse, multiple developers can overwrite each other's object definition changes inadvertently.

Opening an SSAS database

To work in online mode, select *File ➪ Open ➪ Analysis Services Database* menu to open the *Connect To Database* dialog. Then connect to the desired SSAS 2005 database by entering the server and database name (see Figure 2.5). In Figure 2.5, I intend to connect to the *AdventureWorksDW* database hosted on a server called Prologika. BI Studio will still create a project file but, in online mode, this file will contain only the server and database names. Once the project is created, you can start making changes to the object definitions. Again, you are making changes "live" since they are committed immediately to the SSAS database.

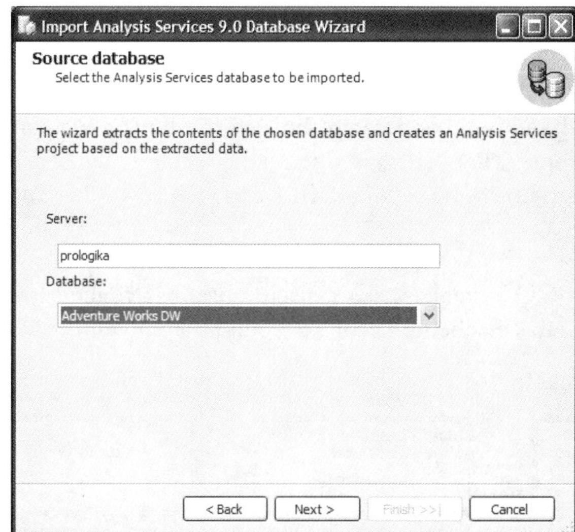

Figure 2.6 Use the Import Analysis Services 9.0 Database Wizard to reverse-engineer an SSAS database and create object definition files.

Reverse-engineering SSAS databases

But what if you don't have the ASSL files of the database objects and you want to work in project mode? For example, suppose that you've upgraded an Analysis Services 2000 database to UDM. Are you stuck in online mode forever? Luckily, the Analysis Services team has provided the means to reverse-engineer a SSAS 2005 database so you could derive the object definition files.

To reverse-engineer a database, select *File ➪ New ➪ Project.* However, instead of choosing the Analysis Services Project template, select *Import Analysis Services 9.0 Database*, specify the location of the project and click OK. BI Studio launches the *Import Analysis Services 9.0 Database Wizard* (Figure 2.6). Once you specify the location of the database, the wizard will examine the database and generate an Analysis Services project. Next, you can proceed to work with the database in a project-based mode. Reverse-engineering an SSAS database shouldn't result in any metadata loss. In other words, P (project mode) ➪ D (database) should give you identical results as D ➪ P.

2.2.3 Other Management and Design Options

SSAS gives you two more options to design UDM objects. You can use the SQL Server Management Studio to manage an SSAS database. In addition, you can design and manage UDM objects programmatically.

SQL Server Management Studio

While BI Studio will be the tool of choice for cube designers and developers, administrators will rely on the SQL Server Management Studio to perform day-to-day management activities. For example, once the BI project is deployed and the SSAS 2005 database is created, the administrator can make final changes to UDM before it goes live, e.g. defining who can access a given cube, the cube storage model, etc. Since the SQL Server Management Studio is designed to be used by administrators, its design capabilities are a subset of BI Studio feature set. For example, while you can delete and change the object properties, you cannot design new objects.

Programmatic access

As I mentioned in chapter 1, XMLA is the native (and only) protocol of SSAS 2005. Thus, client tools, including BI Studio and Management Studio, ultimately describe all actions in ASSL and send them as SOAP messages that comply to the XMLA specification. When these tools are not enough, you can take the road less traveled and build your own tools to fulfill more demanding design and management needs. For example, suppose that operational requirements call for creating the SSAS programmatically. You can do so, by writing .NET code that uses the Analysis Management Objects (AMO) object library.

Now that we know the main objects of an SSAS database, let's discuss briefly a practical methodology that could help us architect the database schema before we build the Adventure Works dimensional model on top of it.

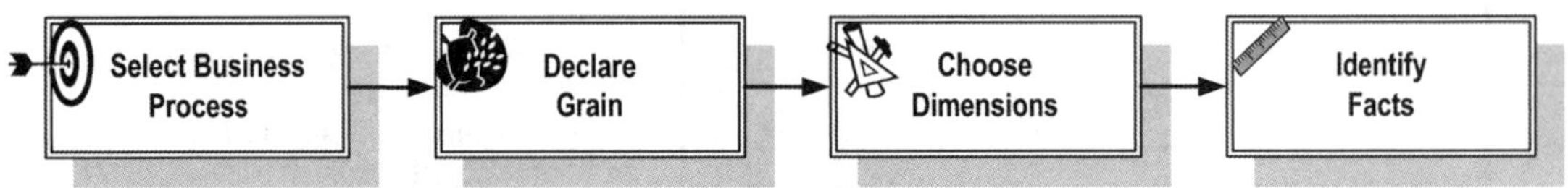

Figure 2.7 Use the four-step design process to architect the UDM data schema.

2.3 The Four-Step Design Process

As noted in chapter 1, one of the main objectives of the Adventure Works SOS solution is to provide data analytics to volatile sales data which hasn't been offloaded yet to the data warehouse (orders that are less than one month old). To address these requirements, we will build the real-time OLAP layer directly on top of the Adventure Works OLTP data source (AdventureWorks). We will do this without making any schema changes to the AdventureWorks database.

As noted, when the data source is a data warehouse, you may need only minimal schema changes. However, OLTP data sources typically require extensive schema changes to fit the relational schema into the dimensional model. To make this endeavor easier, you could benefit from a guided methodology. One such methodology is the four-step design process (Figure 2.7) which Ralph Kimball and Margy Gross outlined in their excellent book *The Data Warehouse Toolkit* (see the Resources section).

You can use this methodology both when architecting the dimensional schema of a data warehouse or "dimensionalizing" the relational schema of an OLTP database. The end result of applying the four-step process against the AdventureWorks OLTP database is the data schema shown in Figure 2.8. As simplistic as it may look, it will help us demonstrate most of the DSV features. We will crank up the complexity and build more "realistic" schema when implementing the Adventure Works historical UDM layer in section 2.4.

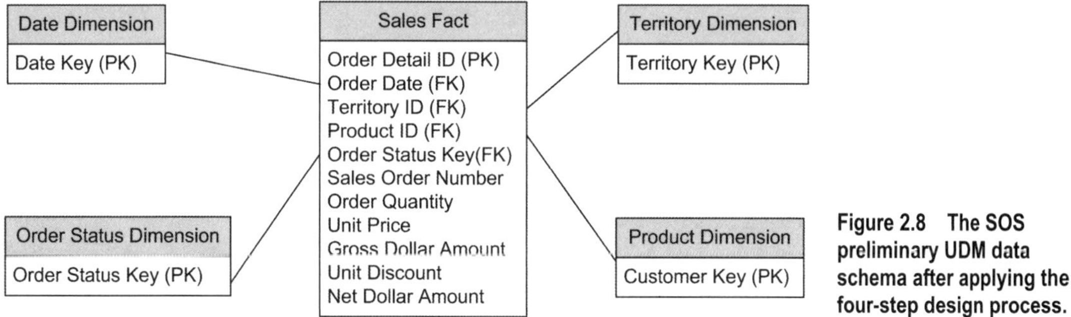

Figure 2.8 The SOS preliminary UDM data schema after applying the four-step design process.

2.3.1 Step 1: Select Business Process

As a first step of the schema design methodology, we need to select the business process to model. In our case, the user requirements call for implementing OLAP system to help business analysts analyze direct and reseller sales. Therefore, the business process that we will model is order management. Since order management processes could provide vital business metrics, such as sales volume and revenue, it is likely that your organization will tackle them first among all OLAP initiatives.

2.3.2 Step 2: Declare Grain

By "declaring the grain", we mean defining what a row in the fact table will represent. This is a critical step which determines the level of detail that UDM will support. In other words, the end result of this step is specifying the level of *data granularity*. Ralph Kimball and Margy Gross recommend that a fact table should capture data at the most atomic level. If we decide to store summarized fact data, we would be taking the risk that our UDM will not be able to answer more detailed business questions.

In the case of the Adventure Works SOS system, the most atomic level of data is the order item. In our desire to make UDM more efficient, we may be tempted to pre-aggregate data before it is imported in the cube, e.g. on a daily basis. However, if we do so, we will effectively prevent our users from browsing the individual order items. For example, they won't be able to drill through sales data and see whether there was a discount applied to a given order item.

Tip If you decide to aggregate fact data to minimize storage space or for other reasons, you may be able to use UDM actions to browse fact details, e.g. a drillthrough action to show the detail rows behind a cell. This approach assumes that the transaction details are available in the OLTP data source.

Resolving Order Header to Order Details Hierarchy

A typical order management OLTP system will capture the order data in two separate tables (an order header table and an order details table) joined with one-to-many relationship. This presents an interesting dilemma. Should we keep the order header table as a separate fact/dimension table joined to the order details fact table or should we "flatten" the order hierarchy into a single table?

Whatever approach we take shouldn't result in a loss of valuable information. For example, the *Sales.SalesOrderHeader* table in the AdventureWorks database captures the order freight. This column is a candidate for a useful measure that could indicate how much Adventure Works is spending on shipping charges. If the business users prefer to retain this measure, we could use one of the following two approaches.

First, if we decided to have a single fact table, we could split the freight amount equally between the sales fact rows. Therefore, when the rows are aggregated, the freight amounts of the individual order details rows will result in the order freight amount. A second approach is to make the order table a separate fact table.

Note If you are curious about what the **Sales** prefix in the table name stands for, it specifies the object database schema. Schemas are a new feature in SQL Server 2005 and are used to enforce more granular security than the object-level permissions. For example, you can give all sales persons rights to the *Sales* schema so they can read all objects belonging to that schema but not to the *HumanResources* schema. Consequently, the fully qualified object name in SQL Server 2005 is server.database.schema.object.

For the sake of simplicity, we will ignore the order header measures and we will merge the order header and order details tables into a single fact table Sales Fact. In real life, you need to consult with your business users to determine the best approach.

2.3.3 Step 3: Choose Dimensions

In this step, we need to determine the dimensions that will apply to each fact row. Since we've merged the order header and details facts, the Sales Fact table inherits the dimension keys from both the *Sales.SalesOrderHeader* and *Sales.SalesOrderDetail* tables. To make things simpler, we will ignore some dimensions that are undoubtedly useful in real life, such as Customer, Sales Person, etc.

The Date dimension will help us to address the most common OLAP requirement – to see sales broken down by time, e.g. year, quarter, month, and day. OLTP systems almost never have a designated date or time dimension tables. SSAS solves this issue elegantly by supporting server-based date dimensions (discussed in chapter 5). Since, during the one-month window, we can have orders in different stages of the order management pipeline, the Order Status dimension will allow us to slice data by the order status. The Territory dimension demonstrates a typical geographical dimension consisting of a continent, country, and region. It will help us see the sales figures broken by this natural hierarchy.

Finally, the Product dimension will give us the typical product natural hierarchy consisting of product category, subcategory, and model, as well as allow us to browse by other product-related attributes. It will be formed by joining the tables *Production.ProductCategory*, *Production.ProductSubcategory*, and *Production.Product*.

2.3.4 Step 4: Identify Facts

The final step is to identify the numeric facts that will be used to measure the business process. To start with, useful facts include the *Order Dollar Amount*, *Order Quantity*, and *Unit Discount* (entered as percentage of the unit price). The first two are additive, while the third is not, since percentages cannot be meaningfully summarized.

The *Gross Dollar Amount* equals *Order Quantity* times *Unit Price*, while the *Net Dollar Amount* is the adjusted *Gross Dollar Amount* after reflecting the discount. The *Gross Dollar Amount* and *Net*

Dollar Amount measures are not available in the *Sales.SalesOrderDetail* table. If changing the data source schema is not an option, you can define these facts as named calculations at a DSV level, as I will demonstrate in section 2.4.3.

Let's now see how data source views could help us build the real-time and historical data schema of the Adventure Works SOS solution. We will start with the real-time UDM.

2.4 Implementing the Real-time Schema

Now that we have designed the data schema, let's see how we can implement it. First, we will create a new Analysis Services project. Next, we will set up a data source pointing to the AdventureWorks OLTP database. Finally, we will construct a data source view to augment the schema, i.e. to transform the relational schema into a dimensional schema.

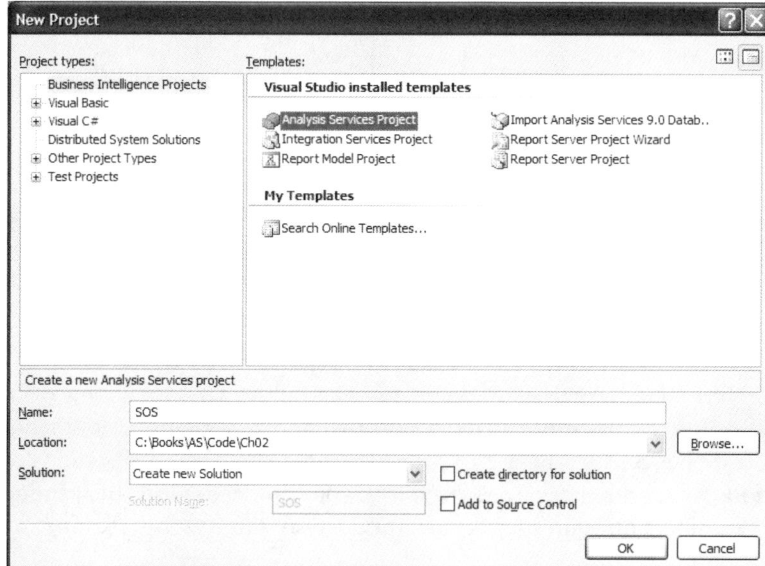

Figure 2.9 Select the Analysis Services Project template to create a new SSAS project.

2.4.1 Working with Analysis Services Projects

Follow these steps to create a new Analysis Services project that will represent our SOS Analysis Services database.

Create the Analysis Services project

1. Start BI Studio. Select *File* ⇨ *New* ⇨ *Project*. The New Project dialog appears (Figure 2.9).
2. Select Analysis Services Project as a project template.
3. Enter **SOS** as the project name. This project will include both the real-time and historical UDMs. Choose the folder where the project will be created. Click OK. BI Studio creates an empty Analysis Services project template. The Solution Explorer shows the pre-defined folders where the SSAS database objects will be placed.

Set up project settings

Before we proceed with creating the data source, let's take a moment to review quickly the project settings that BI Studio has pre-configured for us.

1. In the Solution Explorer window, right-click on the SOS project node (the second node below the Solution node) and select *Properties* to open the Property Pages dialog is shown.

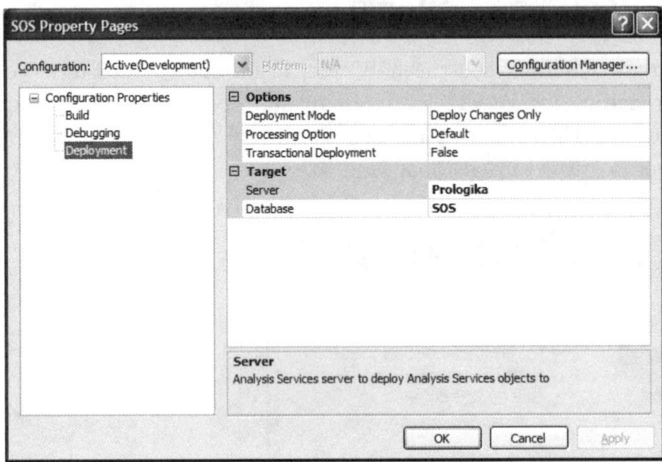

Figure 2.10 Use project configurations to define different deployment settings.

You can use the Project Properties dialog to configure the project build, debugging, and deployment settings.

Project configurations

Similar to Visual Studio.NET IDE, Analysis Services projects allow you to define different configurations to support different environment modes. For example, during development, you will probably deploy and test your SSAS database to your local server by using the settings of the Development configuration. When the database is complete, you can deploy it to the production server straight from BI Studio. You can specify the production settings by creating a new configuration, as follows:

2. In the project Property Pages (Figure 2.10), choose the *Configuration Manager* menu item.
3. From the Active Solution Configuration drop-down list choose <*New…*>.
4. In the New Solution Configuration dialog, name your new configuration **Production** and copy the settings from the Development configuration.

To switch active configurations:

5. From the "Build" menu choose the "Configuration Manager" menu item.
6. From the Active Solution Configuration drop-down list choose the preferred configuration.

Tip You can control which actions BI Studio performs when debugging and deploying a project in the Configuration Manager. By default, when a project is deployed, BI Studio builds and deploys the project. If you have a solution that includes multiple projects, it may be time consuming to re-deploy them each time. Instead, you may decide to clear these two checkboxes for the projects that you are not planning to change.

Since we are currently in the development stage, let's leave the Configuration dropdown to its default – *Development.*

Deployment settings

As noted in section 2.1.2, when working in project mode you need to explicitly deploy the changed objects. The *Server* setting specifies the NetBIOS name or TCP/IP address of the deployment server. The default setting is *localhost*, meaning that BI Studio will deploy the project to your local SSAS server. If this is not what you want, change the *Server* setting accordingly. The Database property specifies the name of the database that SSAS will create when the project is deployed.

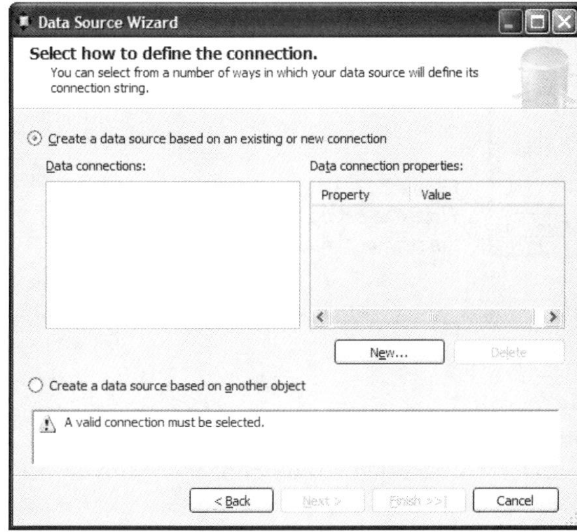

Figure 2.11 Use the Data Source Wizard to set up a connection to the relational data source.

You can specify deployment settings per project configuration. The *Default* processing option setting lets the server decide the optimum processing mode based on the changes detected. Deployment changes can be performed in a transactional scope, i.e. if an object fails to process, all changes will be rolled back. By default, BI Studio will instruct the server not to use a transactional deployment. Finally, the default setting (Deploy Changes Only) of the Deployment Mode setting is used to send only the changed objects definitions to the server. Click OK to close the Project Settings dialog.

2.4.2 Connecting to Data Sources

Let's now set up a connection (a.k.a. data source) to the *AdventureWorks* database.

1. Right-click on the Data Sources folder and select *New Data Source*. The Data Source Wizard starts. Click Next to advance to the *Select how to define the connection* step (Figure 2.11).
2. The Data Source Wizard gives you the options to reuse the connection string from an existing connection or clone the data source definition from another data source or project. Since we don't have any existing connections pre-defined, click the New button. The *Connection Manager* dialog appears.

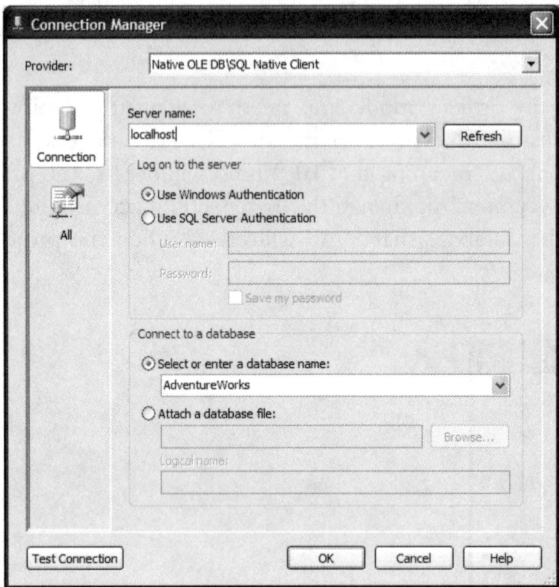

Figure 2.12 Use the Data Source Wizard to set up a connection to the relational data source.

This is where things can go wrong, so let's explain the Connection Manager options in more details.

Choosing a Native OLE DB provider

The Provider dropdown gives you the option to choose between .NET and Native OLE DB providers. As noted before, with Analysis Services you should always choose a Native OLE DB provider if available. But which OLE DB driver should you pick when connecting to a SQL Server data source? The options are the *Microsoft OLE DB Provider for SQL Server* and the *SQL Native Client* provider.

Microsoft recommends that you use the SQL Native Client provider when connecting to SQL Server databases including releases prior to SQL Server 2005 and we will follow this advice.

Note What's SQL Native Client anyway? The SQL Native Client is a provider specifically designed for SQL Server 2005. The SQL Server 2005 relational engine includes many new features which required enhancements to the Microsoft Data Access Components (MDAC) stack. The problem is that MDAC has been so pervasive that it's become a part of the core Windows operating system. Therefore, the SQL Server team can't just go ahead and update the OLE DB Provider for SQL Server each time a new feature is introduced. This is how the SQL Native Client provider was born. The SQL Native Client is implemented as a lightweight provider and it is not dependent on MDAC.

Setting the connection properties

After this detour, let's finalize the connection settings by continuing with the following steps.

1. Leave the Provider dropdown with Native OLE DB selected. Select *SQL Native Client* in the OLE DB Provider dropdown.

2. Enter the server name in the Data Source field. Use *localhost* if the data source is located on your local machine.

Tip Do *(local)*, *locahost*, and "." behave the same when connecting to a local SQL Server instance? The short answer is: it depends. When SQL Native Client or SQL Server .NET Data Provider in .NET 2.0 is used, all of the three settings are equivalent. The client will connect with different protocols depending upon the server configuration. It will first attempt shared memory, then TCP/IP, and then named pipe. For other providers, e.g. *Microsoft OLE DB Provider for SQL Server*, the last two settings are protocol dependent. To avoid confusion, I would recommend you stick to using **(local)**. The only exception would be if you want to control the TCP/IP address of the server in the Hosts configuration file. In this case, use *localhost* since it is a socket-based construct.

3. Select the *AdventureWorks* database in the Initial Catalog dropdown. Optionally, click the Test Connection button to make sure that you can connect to the database with the specified credentials. Once done, click OK to close the Connection Manager and return to the Data Source Wizard. Click Next.
4. In the *Impersonation Information* step, select the Default option and click Next, I will explain the impersonation settings in the next section. Click Next.

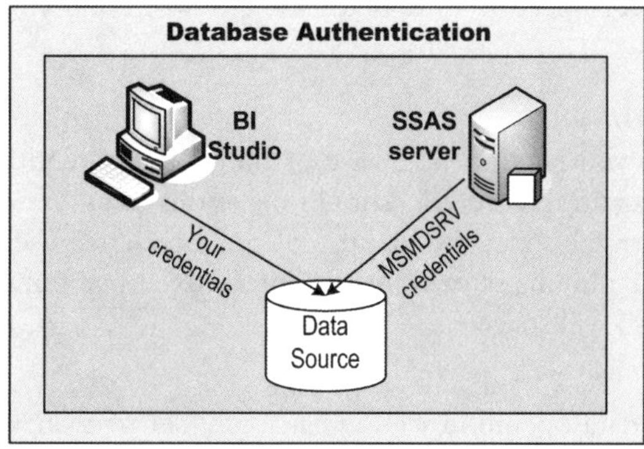

Figure 2.13 When Windows Integrated authentication is used, database operations can be performed under yours or SSAS server identity.

5. In the *Completing the Wizard* step, accept **Adventure Works** as a default name of the new data source and click Finish. You should see the Adventure Works data source under the Data Sources node in Solution Explorer. If you need to make changes to the data source definition, double-click on the data source name.

2.4.3 Choosing Data Source Authentication Mode

During the process of setting a data source, you need to decide also what authentication option to use. The options are Windows NT Integrated Security and standard SQL Server authentication (user name and password). What is not so obvious is that both BI Studio and the SSAS server use these settings to connect to the data source. BI Studio will use the connection for all interactive data source operations, e.g. browsing a relational table. On the other side, the SSAS server will use the same data source definition to connect to the data source when processing dimensions and cubes to load them with data. Therefore, always keep in mind that a data source definition has a dual life (see Figure 2.13).

Suppose that you use localhost (or ".") as a SQL Server name. When you set up a DSV and browse the relational data source tables, the connection is made from BI Studio to your local SQL Server instance. However, assuming that you deploy the project to another machine, the SSAS server on that machine will also try to resolve the connection to a local SQL Server instance, e.g. when loading the cube with data during cube processing. If there is no SQL Server installation, processing will fail. If you need to use different servers, consider using separate project configurations. The Connection Manager dialog (see Figure 2.12) gives you two authentication options to connect to data source – Windows Authentication and SQL Server Authentication (standard).

Using standard authentication

When Windows-based authentication is not an option, you can use standard database security (SQL Server Authentication radio button). Standard database authentication requires you enter a username and password. Standard authentication is straightforward because the same credentials will be used for both BI Studio and SSAS connections. However, standard authentication is less secure than Windows Integrated authentication (requires knowing and managing passwords) and you should avoid it in favor of Windows Integrated authentication.

The Connection Manager gives you an option to save the password by checking the "Save my password" checkbox. The password is saved in an encrypted format. For an added level of security, BI Studio will ask you to re-enter the password under certain circumstances. For instance, copying the data source definition between projects invalidates the password and you need to re-enter it.

Using Windows Integrated authentication

When setting Windows Integrated authentication you have to be aware of the process identity under which the data operations are carried out. Again, Figure 2.13 should make this clear. Data source operations initiated in BI Studio are performed under the identity of the interactive user (your identity). Thus, assuming that you have local administrator rights, all interactive operations (browsing data, retrieving data schema in DSV, etc.) will succeed.

Impersonation options

Determining which process identity a server-side data operation will be carried under is trickier. SSAS supports several impersonation options that are applicable only for Windows Integrated authentication. To see them, double-click on the data source to open the Data Source Designer and switch to the Impersonation Information (Figure 2.14). Since the impersonation options are applicable only with Windows Integrated data source authentication, the Credentials dropdown should get disabled when standard authentication is used, but as it stands, it is always enabled.

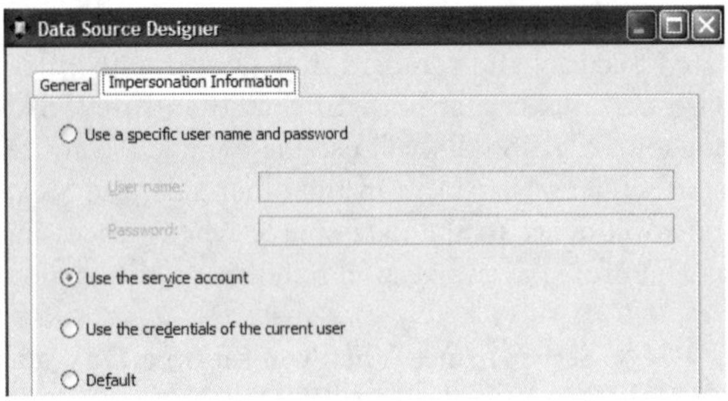

Figure 2.14 SSAS supports several impersonation options when Windows Integrated data source authentication is used.

The *Use a specific user name* option allows you to specify the credentials of a Windows account. Since this option is less secure, I would advise against its usage. The *Use the service account* (*Imper-*

sonateServiceAccount) option conducts the data source operations under the identity of the Analysis Services server (MSMDSRV Windows service). The *Use the credentials of the current user* (*ImpersonateCurrentUser*) option impersonates the identity of the interactive user. The *Default* option lets the server decide which impersonation mode is appropriate, as shown in Table 2.2.

Table 2.2 How impersonation options affect different data source tasks.

Task	Default	Impersonate ServiceAccount	Impersonate CurrentUser
Processing, ROLAP queries	Impersonate ServiceAccount	Supported	Not supported (validation error)
Out-of-line bindings	Impersonate CurrentUser	Not supported (validation error)	Recommended
Data Mining OpenQuery, SystemOpenQuery	Impersonate CurrentUser	Not Supported (validation error)	Recommended
Local Cubes and Mining Models	Same as ImpersonateCurrentUser	Same as ImpersonateCurrentUser	Recommended
Remote Partitions	Impersonate ServiceAccount	Supported	Not supported (validation error)
Linked Objects	Impersonate ServiceAccount	Supported	Not Supported (validation error)
Database synchronization (from target to source)	Impersonate ServiceAccount	Supported	Not Supported (validation error)

Don't worry if some of the tasks listed in the table are not familiar to you at this stage. As you progress through the book, you will be introduced to them gradually. For now, note that not all settings are applicable to all tasks. For example, *Impersonate Current User* is not supported with processing tasks and it will result in an error. Instead of consulting with the table each time you need to set up a data source, a good practical approach is to leave the impersonation in an "autopilot" mode by using the *Default* setting and let the server choose the most appropriate option for the task at hand.

Using a domain account

Suppose that you set up your data source to use the *ImpersonateServiceAccount* option and configure MSMDSRV to run under the Local System built-in Windows account. Since this is a highly privileged account, it would be able to log in to a local data source that supports Windows Authentication successfully.

But will the database call succeed if the SSAS server and the database server are hosted separately? The answer is that it depends. If both machines belong to the same or trusted domain, the call will go out under the SSAS server computer's domain account which must be given rights to log in to the database server. If neither server belongs to a trusted domain, the call will go out under a Windows null session and it will fail. The same will happen if MSMDSRV is running under the Network Service (available in Windows 2003) built-in account. Even worse, if the Local Service account is chosen as the MSMDSRV account, the authentication call will always fail since this account doesn't have network credentials.

To make sure the connection succeeds when connecting to both local and remote data sources, consider configuring MSMDSRV to run under a domain account when Windows

Authentication is used. Table 2.3 lists some possible authentication configurations for different phases of the project lifecycle.

Table 2.3 Example configurations for data source connectivity

Phase	Authentication	SSAS Windows service account
Development (SSAS and database installed locally)	Windows authentication	MSMDSRV running under Local System account.
Development (SSAS local, database remote)	Standard or Windows authentication	If Windows authentiction is used, MSMDSRV must run under a domain account.
Production	Windows authentication	MSMDSRV running under a domain account to connect to remote data sources.

To summarize, I would recommend the following Windows Integrated authentication best practices:

- Use Windows Integrated data source authentication for an added level of security.
- Use the Default impersonation setting.
- Configure the SSAS server (MSMDSRV) to run under a designated domain account.
- Configure your database server to grant the server account read-only permissions to the dimension and fact tables.

As noted, project configurations can be used to support various deployment needs. Suppose you need different connection strings for development and production. To meet this requirement, create two configurations. During development, use the Development configuration with Windows Integrated authentication to connect to the data source. Once it is time for deployment to production, change the project configuration to Production and modify the connection string accordingly. BI Studio will store both versions of the connection string and will use the right connection string depending on the active project configuration.

2.4.4 Constructing the Real-time Data Source View

Now that the connection to the AdventureWorks OLTP data source is set up, let's build the data schema by implementing a data source view (DSV) on top of the data source.

1. In the Solution Explorer window, right-click on the Data Source Views folder and choose *New Data Source View* item from the context menu. The Data Source View Wizard starts. Click Next to advance to the *Select a Data Source* step.
2. The only pre-selected choice in the Relational Data Sources list is the *Adventure Works* data source you created in section 2.3.2. Click Next to advance to the *Select Tables and Views* step (Figure 2.15).

Tip What tables to include in DSV? A DSV should contain only the tables that belong to the dimensional model, i.e. dimension and fact tables. Applications tables should not be added to the DSV because they can unnecessarily complicate it.

3. The Data Source Wizard displays all tables and views in the AdventureWorks database. You may want to drag the left bottom corner to enlarge the dialog. Select fact tables *Sales.SalesOrderDetail*

and *Sales.SalesOrderHeader* and dimension tables *Sales.SalesTerritory*, *Production.Product*, *Production.ProductCategory*, and *Production.ProductSubcategory* we identified in section 2.2.

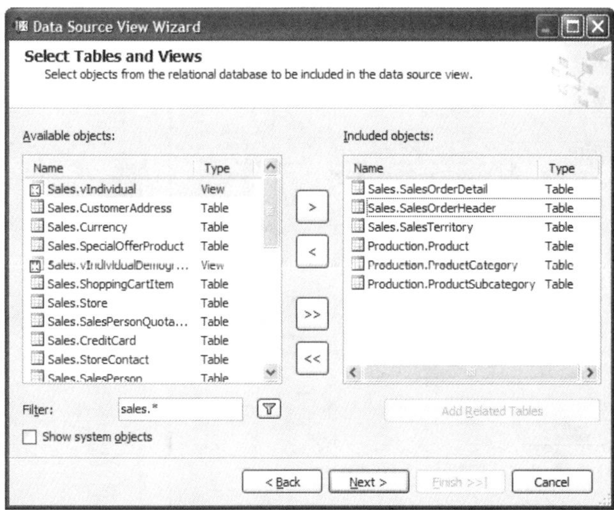

Figure 2.15 Use the Data Source View Wizard to generate a data source view quickly.

Finding the right table or view in a large database such as AdventureWorks could be difficult. To help you locate objects quickly, the Data Source Wizard has a convenient filter feature. For example, to view only the tables in the Sales schema I typed **Sales.*** in the Filter field. Wildcards are supported. You can add tables that are related to a given table through referential integrity by selecting the table and clicking the Add Related Tables button.

4. Click Next to advance to the Competing the Wizard step.

5. Change the data source view name to **SOS OLTP**. Click Finish to close the wizard to open the SOS OLTP data source view you've just created in the Data Source View designer.

DSV Designer Panes

The DSV Designer (Figure 2.16) is divided into three panes to show you different views of the data source schema.

Diagram pane

The Diagram pane shows the data source schema of the selected tables (views) and their relations. By default, the DSV Designer will analyze the table schema and join the tables based on the referential integrity relationships defined in the database schema. If you wish, you can use the *NameMatchingCriteria* property in the Property window to change this behavior, e.g. to create relationships based on a naming convention by joining two tables that have keys with the same name. You can right-click on an object to see a context menu with relevant commands. For example, if you want to see the table data, right-click on a table and select *Explore Data*.

Table pane

The Tables pane lists the tables and views that belong to the data source view. You can add additional tables and views from the underlying data source or other data sources defined in the same project (more on this in section 2.4.2). You can drag an object off this pane and drop it in the diagram pane canvas. Selecting a table in the Table pane, selects the same table in the Diagram pane and vice versa.

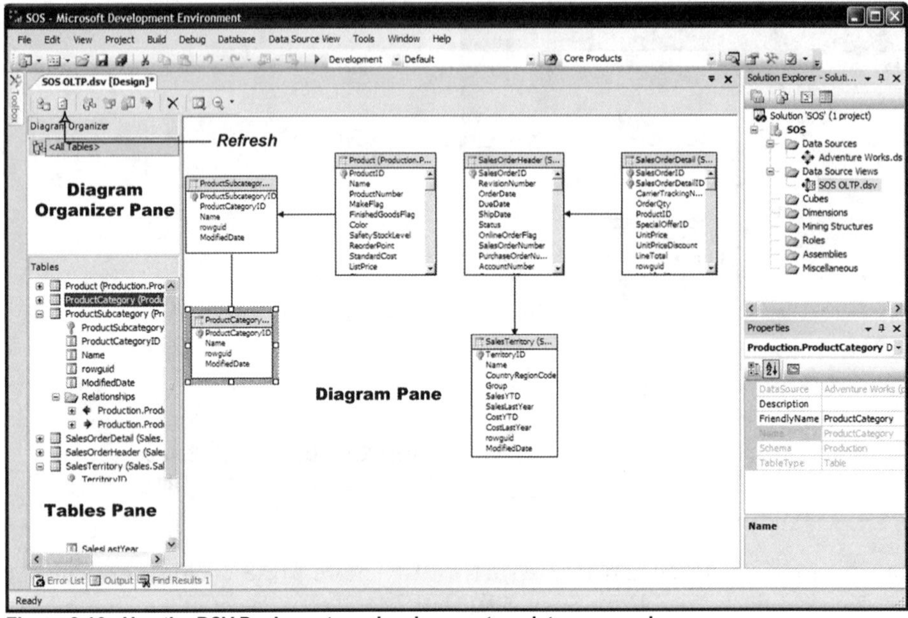

Figure 2.16 Use the DSV Designer to make changes to a data source view.

Diagram Organizer pane

A large DSV can be difficult to navigate. The Diagram Organizer pane allows you to define logical views that comprise different sections of the DSV. When the DSV view is created, there is only one diagram that contains all the objects added to the view. We will see how this feature will help us organize the more involved historical DSV in section 2.4.2

Synchronizing DSV with the data source

DSV doesn't automatically reflect changes made to the underlying data source schema. To update the view, you need to refresh it by either clicking on the Refresh button or selecting the *Refresh* command from the Data Source View menu. The refresh process compares the view schema with the underlying data source schema. If changes are detected, the view is updated and you are presented with a helpful report of the changes made. You cannot pick and update individual objects to refresh. This may look like a limitation but, in reality, you would typically want to get all changes at the same time. This way, you don't leave the view in inconsistent state that may break processing the cube.

Tip When DSV is first created, the table columns are ordered in the same way as in the underlying data source table. When you refresh your DSV, new columns that are discovered are added to the end of the table. At this point, the order of columns may get out of sync with the database. If you want to order DSV columns in a specific way, e.g. sort them alphabetically, you can do so in the DSV source file. To do so, in the Solution Explorer window, right-click on DSV and choose View Code.

Changes to the underlying data source schema are not automatically propagated up the UDM layers. For example, if a column is renamed, the new name is not reflected in the DSV schema.

This should come as no surprise to you because DSV is meant to isolate UDM from the underlying data source. Changes made to DSV schema are never propagated to the data source. In other words, DSV only reads from and never writes to the data source.

Exploring data

One handy DSV feature is the ability to explore the data in the underlying table. Realizing the common need to explore the raw data, the Analysis Services team has built in a nice data explorer which is a mini BI-application by itself. Suppose that you want to browse the Product dimension table to find out how the product list price varies.

1. Right-click on the Product dimension table in the DSV diagram and choose *Explore Data* (see Figure 2.17).

The Data Explorer allows you to see data in table, pivot table, chart, and pivot chart views. The Table mode displays data in a tabular read-only format. The pivot options use the PivotTable and ChartSpace controls from Office Web Components suite that I introduced in chapter 1. The chart mode allows you to create chart views of several columns and compare them side-by-side (see Figure 2.17). For example, I've selected the *Color* and *ListPrice* columns of the Product table. The various supported charts allow me to find quickly that the price of most products is around $350.

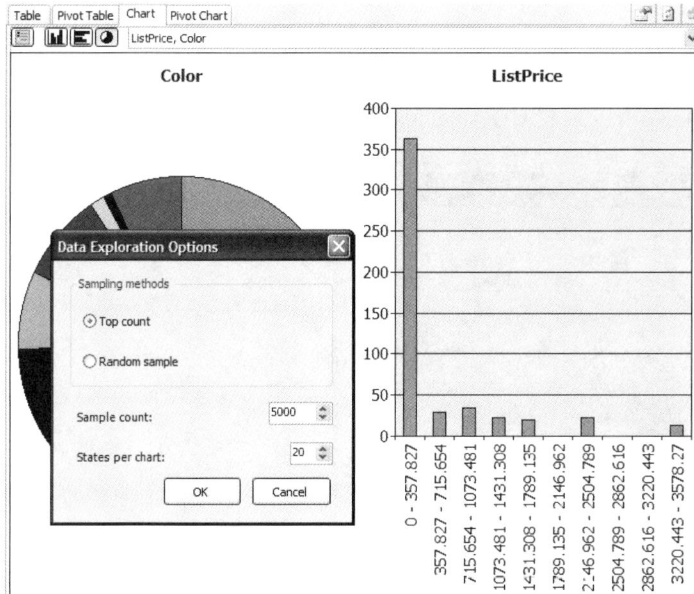

Figure 2.17 Use the DSV Data Explorer to analyze the raw data in tabular and chart views.

Retrieving all rows from a fact table that may have millions of records is definitely not desirable. Instead, use the Sampling Options button (the first toolbar button on the top right corner) to sample the underlying data in one of two ways. First, you can use the *Top count* option to cap the maximum number of rows returned sequentially (similar to the SQL TOP clause). Second, you can get more realistic data by sampling data at random.

Working with DSV schemas

The DSV great advantage is that it allows you to take the data source schema as it is and adjust it to fit your UDM needs. If you wish, you can make changes in the DSV schema even if you are not connected to the data source. Let's make the required changes to the SOS OLTP data source view so it matches the dimension model discussed in section 2.3.

Working with Named Queries

Similar to a SQL view, a named query can be used in a DSV to create a virtual view that uses a SQL SELECT statement to combine two or more tables. The statement syntax has to comply with the SQL dialect of the data source. For example, let's replace the SalesOrderHeader and SalesOrderDetails tables with a named query to "flatten" the order hierarchy into a single fact table.

Tip Should you use a DSV named query or a SQL view? In general, if you can make changes to the data source, I would recommend you use SQL views because they are more versatile. For example, since views are part of the database, they can be accessed not only from SSAS, but also from other database objects and programming logic. Also, views can be stacked on top of each other while named queries cannot. Finally, views can be indexed for better performance. However, sometimes you won't have permissions to change the data source so named queries are the only option. Another scenario where a named query could be preferable is to simplify deployment, since you have the entire database encapsulated in a single project.

1. Start by selecting both the *SalesOrderHeader* and *SalesOrderDetail* tables by holding the Ctrl key and clicking on the tables or simply lassoing both tables together. Hit the Delete key and confirm the Delete Objects dialog to remove these two tables from the DSV diagram.

2. Right-click anywhere on the empty canvas space in the Diagram pane and select *New Named Query* from the context menu. The Named Query Designer is launched in a graphical mode.

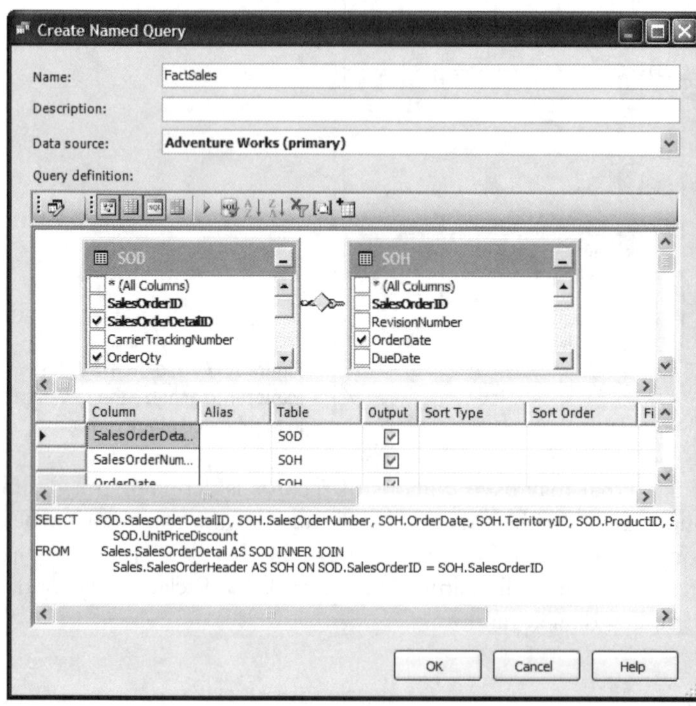

Figure 2.18 Use named queries to create virtual DSV tables that replace the physical tables.

3. Right-click on the Diagram pane and choose *Add Table* or click on the Add Table button on the toolbar. On the Add Table dialog, select both the *SalesOrderHeader (Sales)* and *SalesOrderDetail (Sales)* tables and click the Add button to add the tables to the Diagram pane (see Figure 2.18).

4. From the SalesOrderHeader table check the *SalesOrderNumber*, *OrderDate*, *TerritoryID*, *Status* columns. From the SalesOrderDetail table select the *SalesOrderDetailID*, *ProductID*, *OrderQty*, *UnitPrice* and *UnitPriceDiscount* columns.

5. Change the statement generated by the Query Designer SQL SELECT to the one below.

```
SELECT  SOD.SalesOrderDetailID, SOH.TerritoryID,
        SOD.ProductID, SOH.Status AS OrderStatusID,
        SOH.OrderDate, SOH.SalesOrderNumber,
        SOD.OrderQty, SOD.UnitPrice,
        SOD.UnitPriceDiscount,
        SOD.UnitPrice * SOD.OrderQty AS GrossDollarAmount,
        ISNULL(SOD.UnitPrice * (1.0 - SOD.UnitPriceDiscount) *
        SOD.OrderQty, 0.0) AS NetDollarAmount
FROM    Sales.SalesOrderDetail AS SOD INNER JOIN
        Sales.SalesOrderHeader AS SOH
        ON SOD.SalesOrderID = SOH.SalesOrderID
WHERE   (DATEPART(yyyy, SOH.OrderDate) = 2003)
AND     (DATEPART(mm, SOH.OrderDate) = DATEPART(mm, GETDATE()))
```

Notice that I specified a WHERE clause because the real-time UDM will pick up the sales data that is one month old (recall that the older data is offloaded to the data warehouse). I set the year to 2003 to be sure that the query will find matching rows since the AdventureWorks has sample data only for the period 2001-2004. You can verify the SQL syntax by clicking on the Verify SQL toolbar button. To execute the query and see its results click on the Run button. The Graphical Designer is not limited to supporting SQL statements only. For example, you can base your query on a stored procedure (by typing its name) or use a user-defined function as part of the SELECT statement.

6. Name the named query **FactSales** and click OK to close the Named Query designer and return to the DSV Designer. To join the *FactSales* named query to the dimension tables, you must define a primary key on *FactSales*. UDM will use this key to uniquely identify the fact rows. Since a named query is a virtual table, we cannot create a physical key. Instead, create a logic key on the *SalesOrderDetailID* column by clicking on the column and selecting the *Set Logical Primary Key* context menu. If more than one column identifies uniquely a fact row, you can select multiple columns by holding the Ctrl key.

7. The FactSales named query is ready. If you want to modify the query definition, you can right-click on FactSales and select *Edit Named Query*.

Working with the Generic Query Builder

Sometimes, you may need to base your named query on more involved SQL statement than the Graphical Query Builder can handle. If the Graphical Query Builder chokes on the named query statement, you can switch to the *Generic Query Builder* (the first toolbar button). The Generic Query Builder doesn't validate the query syntax or restructure the query. Instead, it sends the query text verbatim as a pass-through query to the data source.

Let's demonstrate how the Generic Query Builder can help us create the *OrderStatus* dimension table. Since the AdventureWorks database schema doesn't include an Order Status lookup table, we will fabricate one by introducing another named query based on a SELECT CASE statement.

8. Start the Named Query Designer again. Switch to the Generic Query Builder and type the following query.

```
SELECT DISTINCT Status, CASE Status
     WHEN 1 THEN 'In Process'
     WHEN 2 THEN 'Approved'
     WHEN 3 THEN 'Backordered'
     WHEN 4 THEN 'Canceled'
     WHEN 5 THEN 'Shipped'
     ELSE 'Status' + CAST(Status AS VARCHAR)
END AS OrderStatus
FROM Sales.SalesOrderHeader
```

Don't be alarmed that the above query results in only one order status (*Shipped*). For some reason, all orders in the AdventureWorks database have this status code. If you wish, you can correct this by changing the Status columns of some orders in the *SalesOrderHeader* table.

Note Strictly speaking, the Graphical Query Builder can handle the above statement just fine. But this won't be the case with a more involved SQL statement, e.g. an UNION query, or a query that uses the new SQL Server 2005 functions, such as *ROW_NUMBER()*.

9. Name the named query **DimOrderStatus** and click OK to return back to the DSV Designer.

10. Set the *OrderStatusID (Status)* column in the DimOrderStatus table as a logical primary key.

Changing the table names

Often, IT shops have naming conventions for object names, e.g. *Dim* prefix for dimension or Fact for fact tables. DSV gives you the flexibility to rename table and column names. Let's demonstrate this feature by changing the names of the DSV tables.

11. Click on table *Product* to select it. In the BI Studio Property pane, locate the *FriendlyName* property and change it to **DimProduct**. Following the same naming convention, prefix dimension tables ProductSubcategory, ProductCategory, and SalesTerritory with the **Dim** prefix.

12. You can assign a friendly name to a column in the DSV schema. Select the *Status* column in the DimOrderStatus table. Change its *FriendlyName* property to **OrderStatusID**. Select the *OrderStatus* column and change its friendly name to **Status Description**.

Replacing tables

When working with large fact tables, you may want to test the UDM structure and calculations on a smaller test dataset. To facilitate the above scenarios, DSV allows you to replace tables with the same structure easily by following these steps:

13. Right-click on the table in the DSV diagram and choose the *Replace Table* menu item.

14. If you already have another table with the test data, choose the *With Other Table* sub-menu item and select the appropriate table.

15. If you would like to use a query to restrict test data, choose the *With New Named Query…* sub-menu item and then edit the query definition to appropriately reduce the test data.

When you are done testing and would like to return to the original data set, simply repeat the steps above and replace the table with the original table containing your full data set.

Defining relationships

We are almost done. As a last step, we need to define the relationships between the dimension tables and the fact table so SSAS knows how to join the tables when processing the cube. Let's start with the Product dimension.

16. Select the *ProductID* column in *FactSales*.
17. Drag the *ProductID* column over and inside the *DimProduct* table. Note that DSV highlights the underlying column.
18. When you hover on top of the *ProductID* column of the *DimProduct* table and DSV highlights it, release the mouse button.

Note When creating a relationship between a fact and a dimension table, the right direction is to drag the fact column onto the dimension column. Don't worry if you do the reverse. The DSV Designer will open the dialog shown in Figure 2.19 so you could reverse the relationship direction.

To find out what the DSV Designer has done for us, select the new relationship and double-click on it. The Edit Relationship dialog comes up, as shown in Figure 2.19. As a result, the relationship links the dimension table (a primary table) and the fact table by *ProductID*. You can use the Edit Relationship dialog to create relationships manually. This could be useful when the primary key consists of more than one column.

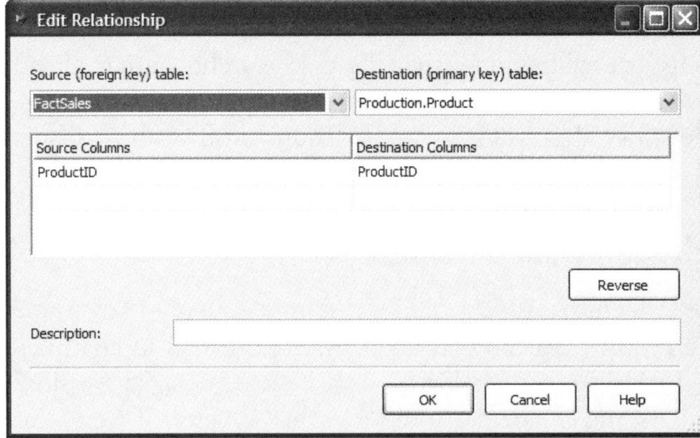

Figure 2.19 Use the Edit Relationship dialog to verify and create DSV relations.

19. Repeat the same process to create relationships between the fact table and *DimOrderStatus* dimension table on *OrderStatusID* and *DimSalesTerritory* on *TerritoryID*.
20. Optionally, right-click anywhere on an empty space in the diagram and choose *Arrange Tables* to let the DSV Designer adjust the diagram layout to look better.

At this point, your DSV should look like the one shown in Figure 2.20. Our SOS OLTP data schema consists of one fact table (*FactSales*), a snowflaked Product dimension consisting of three tables (*DimProductCategory*, *DimProductSubcategory*, and *DimProduct*), and two star-based dimensions (*DimSalesTerritory* and *DimOrderStatus*).

Let's leave the real-time UDM for now and focus our attention on the implementation of the historical data schema which we will be using exclusively throughout the rest of this book. We will revisit the real-time UDM on an as-needed basis to demonstrate applicable features.

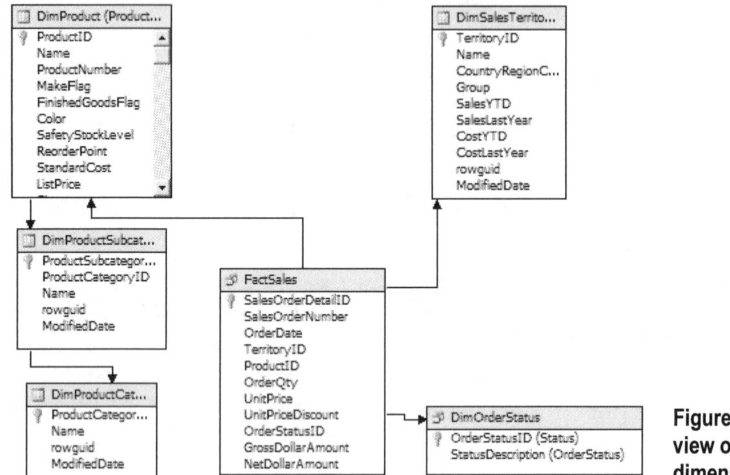

Figure 2.20 The data source view of the SOS OLTP dimensional schema.

2.5 Implementing the Historical Schema

As I mentioned in chapter 1, the historical UDM will source its data from the Adventure Works data warehouse. For the sake of simplicity, we will assume that the data warehouse has already been designed and implemented in the form of the AdventureWorksDW SQL Server database. We will proceed by implementing another DSV that will serve as the foundation of the historical UDM.

2.5.1 Designing the Data Warehouse Data Schema

Let's take a moment to explain how the Adventure Works data warehouse schema (Adventure-WorksDW) differs from its OLTP counterpart (AdventureWorks). As I explained in chapter 1, most of the changes can be attributed to the fundamental difference between the dimensional and relational models. Again, we may understand the data warehouse schema better if we discuss it in the context of the four-step design process we introduced in section 2.2.

Step 1: Select business process

The business process that the Adventure Works data warehouse represents is, again, sales order management. However, to reflect the enterprise nature of data warehousing and address a broader audience, AdventureWorksDW has additional dimensions and business metrics. For example, to allow business analysts to aggregate sales data per employee hierarchy and department, the data warehouse imports data from the HR system and captures it in tables *DimEmployee*, *DimDepartmentGroup*, and *DimOrganization*. Similarly, to serve the requirements of the finance department, the *DimAccount*, *DimScenario* dimensional tables and the *FactFinance* fact table were added. Don't worry if the meaning of these tables is not immediately clear. We will revisit them in the next chapters.

Step 2: Declare grain

Just like the real-time data schema, the fact grain in the data warehouse (fact tables *FactInternet-Sales* and *FactResellerSales*) is the individual order item. However, instead of "flattening" the schema directly through the DSV layer, we will now assume that the Adventure Works has implemented ETL processes to integrate the fact data and populate the fact tables.

Step 3: Choose dimensions

Table 2.4 lists the dimension tables and their purpose.

Table 2.4 Dimensions in the AdventureWorksDW database.

Dimensions	Purpose
DimTime	Allow data drilldown by the date natural hierarchy consisisting of year, semester, quarter, month, and day.
DimCustomer, DimReseller, DimGeography, DimSalesTerritory	Browse data by customer
DimProduct, DimSubcategory, DimCategory	Represents the product natural hiararchy
DimEmployee, DimDepartmentGroup, DimOrganzation	Browse data by HR hierarchy.
DimPromotion, DimSalesReason	View data by sale promotion as specified by the SpecialOfferID column in the SalesOrderDetail OLTP table.
DimAccount, DimScenario, DimCurrency, DimScenario	Implement financial reporting

The following dimensions deserve more explanation.

DimCustomer and DimReseller Dimensions

To support Internet and resale sales, the AdventureWorks OLTP schema defines two types of customers, *individuals* (table Sales.Individual) and *stores* (table Sales.Store), that have different characteristics. For example, a resale store has a sales person assigned to it while this is not the case for individual customers who buy products online. For this reason, the data warehouse schema preserves the same design and splits the customers into two dimension tables, DimCustomer (web customers) and DimReseller (resale stores).

DimEmployee Dimension

The DimEmployee dimension is interesting because it is a parent-child dimension that represents the employee organizational hierarchy where an employee reports to a manager who reports to a more senior manager, and so on, until the CEO level is reached. As usual, the parent-child hierarchy is defined by means of a key (ParentEmployeeKey) which links to the table primary key (EmployeeKey).

DimTime Dimension

Unlike OLTP schemas, a data warehouse schema always includes a designated date dimension table. The advantage of having a separate date dimension table is two-fold. First, it allows us to decorate the date dimension with additional attributes, such as a holiday flag. Such helpful attributes can explain why there was a drop (or a lift) in sales in certain days. In addition, a separate table may minimize the storage space of the fact tables that link to the DimTime dimension. For example, an integer primary key takes less space compared to dates stored as strings.

Reacting to dimension member changes

If you inspect the AdventureWorksDW dimension table schema you will notice that some of the tables (e.g. DimProductSubcategory) have two keys: primary (also called *surrogate* key) and alternate. Isn't this redundant? To understand why we need two keys, let's recall that the main purpose of a data warehouse is to retain a historical record of data that originated from OLTP systems. Since OLTP data is volatile, it is essential to determine to what extent the data warehouse will be resilient to dimension member changes in the OLTP data source. To clarify this concept, let's consider the example shown in Figure 2.21.

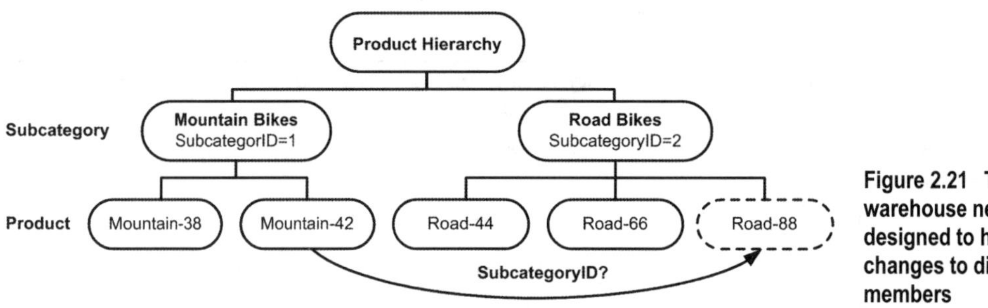

Figure 2.21 The data warehouse needs to be designed to handle changes to dimension members

As noted, the Adventure Works dimensional model supports the natural product hierarchy consisting of product category, subcategory, and product. For example, bikes Mountain-38 and Mountain-42 belong to the Mountain Bikes subcategory, while Road-44 and Road-62 belong to the Road Bikes subcategory. Suppose that the Mountain-42 has been re-classified at the beginning of 2004. Its name has been changed to Road-88 and it now belongs to the Road Bikes subcategory. An OLTP system typically handles such changes in-place. To reflect the new subcategory membership, the Adventure Works OLTP system could change the SubcategoryID column of the Product table from 1 to 2. The question is how do you want the data warehouse to react to this change? Here are the two most popular approaches.

Type 1 changes

The first choice is the "I don't care about history" approach. This type of change behaves exactly the same way as the OLTP system. When the relationship between members of a dimension level changes, the member foreign key is updated. Going back to our example, the ETL processes that load the Product dimension table would update the SubcategoryID foreign key of Mountain-42 from *1* to *2* and its name from *Mountain-42* to *Road-88* to reflect its new membership.

This type of change is easy to implement and doesn't require extending the data warehouse schema. Its downside is that it doesn't retain the historical record of the dimension member prior to the change. Once we change the CategoryID key of the Mountain-42 member and browse sales by a product subcategory, the aggregated Road Bikes total will happily pick up all of the Mountain-42 sales despite the fact that prior to 2004 Mountain-42 contributed to the Mountain Bikes subcategory. In other words, prior sales record of Mountain-42 as a subordinate of the Mountain Bikes subcategory has simply vanished.

Type 2 changes

If your business requirements call for retaining the history of dimension members, you have to extend the data warehouse schema. One way of doing so is to introduce a new column for the primary key of the Product table. The dimensional terminology refers to such a key as a *surrogate* key. The net result is that you will end up with two key columns. The alternate key column (ProductAlternateKey) will retain the value of the OLTP primary key in the Product table, while the surrogate key (ProductID) will now become the primary key and it will be maintained independently of the OLTP key. Assuming that the original primary key of Mountain-42 in the OLTP database was 10, the Type 2 change may result in the following records:

Time	ProductID	ProductAlternateKey	SubcategoryID	Name	Status
2003	1	10	1	Mountain-42	NULL
2004	2	10	2	Road-88	Current

When a given member of the Product level changes its subcategory membership, the ETL processes will insert a new row in the Product dimension table. The net effect of this is that you will end up with as many duplicate members as the number of the membership changes for this member. Now, when you browse sales data by a product subcategory, the Mountain-42 sales prior to 2004 will be correctly reflected under the Mountain Bikes subcategory. In addition, a new Status column was introduced to identify the current member, so ETL processes know which dimension member needs to be evaluated. Alternatively, a Start Date-End Date column combination can be used. Chapter 6 gives more details about how ETL processes could handle Type 2 changes.

Step 4: Identify facts

The AdventureWorkDW data warehouse schema defines several fact tables prefixed with "Fact". The most important ones are the two sales fact tables: FactInternetSales and FactResellerSales. Why was the OLTP sales data split into two fact tables? It turns out that the SalesOrderHeader table captures both Internet (orders placed online) and reseller (orders placed through resale stores) sales. Our first instinct when designing the data warehouse schema is to preserve this design pattern by having a single fact table to include both types of facts. However, upon further investigation of the AdventureWorks OLTP schema, we will discover that not all dimensions apply to both fact types.

For example, the Sales Person dimension is not applicable to sales placed on the Internet. The Customer dimension is even more troublesome because it represents both individuals (web customers) and resale stores that have different characteristics (represented by tables Sales.Individual and Sales.Store). For this reason, the data warehouse designer has decided to split the fact rows into two fact tables, Internet and Reseller Sales, respectively. The two fact tables have identical fact columns. They differ only in their dimension keys. Specifically, FactInternetSales has a CustomerKey dimension key to link the table to the DimCustomer dimension table that represents Internet customers. In comparison, FactResellerSales joins the DimReseller dimension table (sales data can be sliced by store) and DimEmployee (sales data can be browsed by sales person).

2.5.2 Constructing the Historical Data Source View

Since the data warehouse schema has been carefully architected according to the principles of dimensional modeling, the DSV schema will not require much work. Follow the same steps to set up the SOS historical data source as with its real-time counterpart. We will add the new objects to the same SOS Analysis Services project we created in section 2.4.

Creating the SOS OLAP Data Source View

Now it's time to create the data source view that the Adventure Works historical UDM will be based on.

1. Start by creating a new data source (Adventure Works DW) which points to the Adventure-WorksDW database.

Tip If you want to reuse the same data source across BI projects, you can create a *referenced* data source by selecting the *Create a data source based on another object* option in the Data Source Wizard. When I first came across the referenced data source concept, I immediately made an association with class inheritance. I thought that the derived data source can inherit some properties from the base data source while overriding others. It turns out that BI Studio is not that flexible. If you want to make changes to the derived data source, you have to break the reference to the base data source.

2. Right-click on the Data Source Views folder in Solution Explorer and choose New Data Source View. The Data Source View Wizard starts. Click Next.
3. In the Select a Data Source step, select the Adventure Works DW data source and click Next.
4. In the Select Tables and Views step, select all tables. Exclude the five views objects (names starting with "v") which are used for data mining. Click Next.
5. In the Completing the Wizard step, name the new data source view **SOS OLAP** and click Finish to create it. The Data Source View designer is launched with the SOS OLAP data source view loaded (Figure 2.22).

Working with diagrams

As you can see by quickly browsing the twenty plus tables, the new view is definitely more involved than its real-time counterpart. Finding the right table is becoming difficult.

Zooming and searching

To help us navigate through the data schema, the DSV Designer supports two zooming modes. First, there is a zoom toolbar button which allows us to zoom the diagram pane in and out. Second, we can use the interactive zoom feature (the cross in the bottom right corner of the diagram pane) to interactively select and zoom a particular area of the diagram pane. The Find Table could also help us locate and select a single table. In addition to zooming and table finding, the DSV Designer provides the ability to define logical "subviews" which can show only a subset of the DSV tables in the form of DSV diagrams.

Creating the Internet Sales diagram

Let's first create the Internet Sales diagram that will include only the tables relevant to the sales placed by web customers.

1. Right-click inside the Diagram Organizer pane and choose *New Diagram*. A new diagram is created and it is named *New Diagram* by default. Change the diagram name to **Internet Sales**.

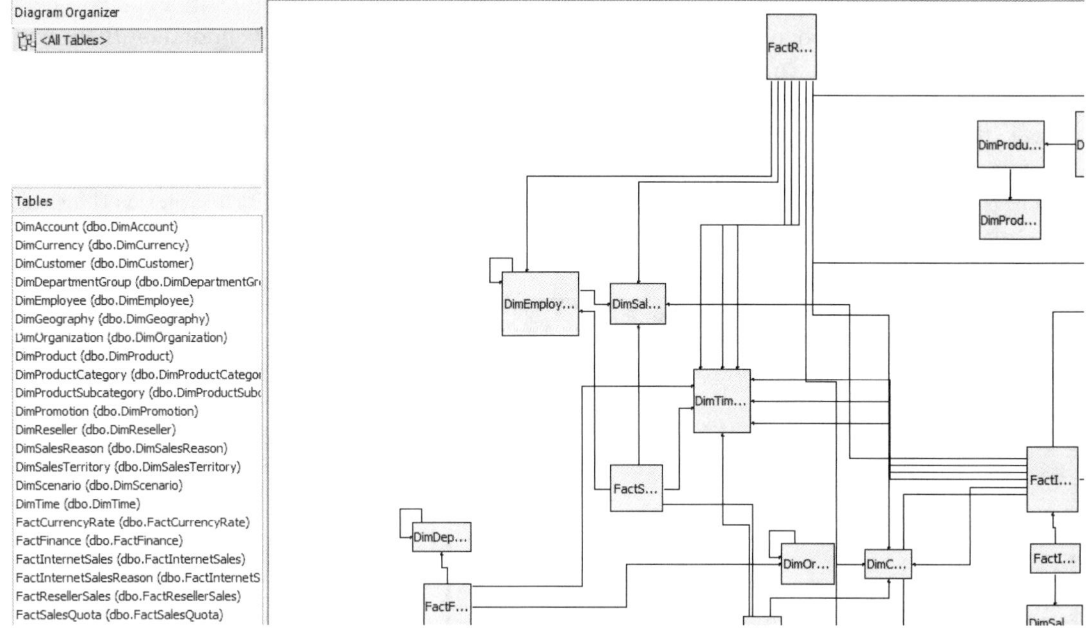

Figure 2.22 The SOS OLAP Data Source View consists of more than twenty tables.

2. Right-click inside the empty diagram pane and select *Show Tables*.

3. From the Show Tables dialog select the *DimCurrency*, *DimCustomer*, DimGeography, *DimProduct*, *DimProductCategory*, *DimProductSubcategory*, *DimPromotion*, *DimSalesTerritory*, *DimTime* dimension tables and *FactInternetSales* fact table.

Warning Remember that a DSV diagram is just a façade on top of the DSV schema. If you want to remove a table from a data diagram, don't delete the table because the table will get removed from DSV. Instead, right-click on the table and choose Hide Table from the context-menu. The Hide Table menu is available only with user-defined diagrams.

4. Save the new diagram by clicking on the *Save All* toolbar button.

5. Select the *<All Tables>* diagram and then Internet Sales. Observe that the Internet Sales diagram is easier to comprehend since it includes a subset of the DSV tables.

Creating the Reseller Sales diagram

It will be useful to create a diagram that will include the tables applicable to resale sales.

6. Create a new diagram and name it **Reseller Sales**.

7. Select *DimCurrency*, *DimEmployee*, *DimGeography*, *DimProduct*, *DimProductCategory*, *DimProductSubcategory*, *DimPromotion*, *DimReseller*, *DimSalesTerritory*, *DimTime* dimension tables, and *FactResellerSales* fact table to add them to the Reseller Sales diagram.

Defining named calculations

In section 2.4.3, I showed you how you could use expression-based columns in a named query. You can do the same when you work with relational tables (or views) by annotating them with *named calculations*. As its names suggests, a named calculation is a column that is based on an expression. The expression syntax is data source specific. If you have experience with SQL Server, think of a named calculation as a formula-based table column. Unlike a formula-based column, a named calculation is part of DSV, not the relational table definition. Let's define the ProfitDollarAmount for both the FactInternetSales and FactResellerSales fact tables as the order sales amount minus the product cost.

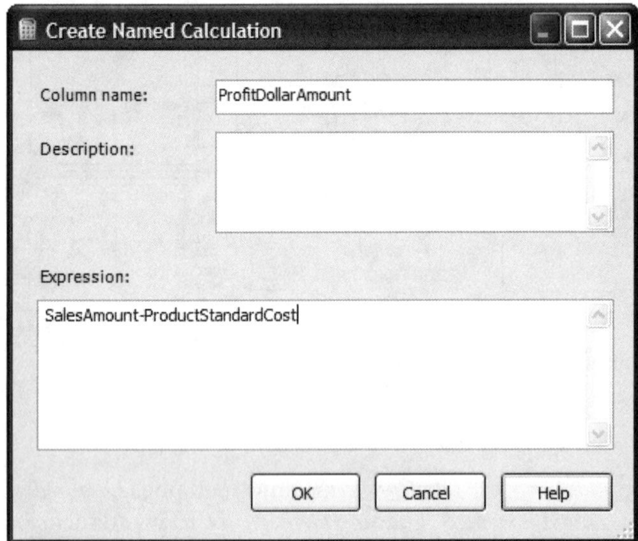

Figure 2.23 You can annotate tables with expression-based columns in the form of named calculation.

1. If the SOS OLAP data source view is closed, double-click on it in the Solution Explorer.
2. In the Diagram Organizer, click on the Internet Sales diagram to activate it.
3. Right-click on the FactInternetSales table and choose *New Named Calculation*. The Create Named Calculation dialog is shown in Figure 2.23.
4. Enter **ProfitDollarAmount** as a column name and `SalesAmount - ProductStandardCost` as the expression text. Click OK to create the ProfitDollarAmount calculation. The DSV Designer parses the expression text and validates it against the data source. You can easily tell apart the named calculations and the regular columns since they have special icons.
5. Back to the DSV Designer, right-click on FactInternetSales and chose *Explore Data*. Observe that the ProfitDollarAmount column is added to the end of the table columns as though it is part of the relational table definition.

Note that similar to SQL views, you cannot base one named calculation on another. For example, if you want to define the sales profit as a percentage of the sales amount, you cannot use the expression ProfitDollarAmount/SalesAmount. Instead, you have to use the expression that defines ProfitDollarAmount. In addition, the scope of a named calculation is restricted to the table where the named calculation is defined. Subsequently, you cannot have a named calculation whose expression spans columns from other tables. As a workaround, use a named query.

Tip If you want to derive the named calculation from a table other than the source table, you can use a subquery or a scalar user-defined function. For example, assuming that you need to retrieve the product cost from a Product dimension table to calculate the net order cost, you can set the expression of the named calculation to (SELECT ProductCost from DimProduct WHERE…). When using a subquery, you need to enclose the query text in brackets. Alternatively, you can use a scalar user-defined function, e.g. dbo.ufnGetProductStandardCost(ProductID, ProductDate). Make sure to specify the fully-qualified UDF name, including the owner.

Next, define the same ProfitDollarAmount named calculation in the FactResellerSales fact table. Finally, create additional useful named calculations, as shown in Table 2.5.

Table 2.5 Named calculations used in the SOS OLAP schema

Table	Named Calculation	Expression	Description
DimTime	DateName	DATENAME(mm, FullDateAlternateKey) + ' ' + DATENAME(dd, FullDateAlternateKey)	A descriptive name for the calendar date
	CalendarQuarterName	'Q' + CONVERT(CHAR (1), CalendarQuarter) + ' CY ' + CONVERT(CHAR (4), CalendarYear)	A descriptive name for the calendar quarter.
	CalendarSemesterName	CASE WHEN CalendarSemester = 1 THEN 'H1 '+'CY ' + CONVERT(CHAR (4), CalendarYear) ELSE 'H2 '+ 'CY '+ CONVERT(CHAR (4), CalendarYear) END	
	FiscalQuarterName	'Q' + CONVERT(CHAR (1), FiscalQuarter) +' '+ 'FY ' + CONVERT(CHAR (4), FiscalYear)	A descriptive name for the calendar semester (half year).
	FiscalSemesterName	CASE WHEN FiscalSemester = 1 THEN 'H1 '+'FY '+ CONVERT(CHAR (4), FiscalYear) ELSE 'H2 '+'FY '+ CONVERT(CHAR (4), FiscalYear) END	A descriptive name for the fiscal semester (half year)
DimCustomer	FullName	FirstName+ ' ' + ISNULL(MiddleName+ '. ', '') + LastName	Customer's full name
	Age	DATEDIFF(yy, BirthDate, GETDATE())	Customer's age
	MaritalStatusName	CASE WHEN MaritalStatus = 'S' THEN 'Single' ELSE 'Married' END	A marital status description
DimEmployee	FullName	FirstName+ ' ' + ISNULL(MiddleName+ '. ', '') + LastName	Employee's full name
DimProduct	ProductLineName	CASE ProductLine WHEN 'M' THEN 'Mountain' WHEN 'R' THEN 'Road' WHEN 'S' THEN 'Accessory'	A descriptive name for the product line

		WHEN 'T' THEN 'Touring' ELSE 'Miscellaneous' END	
DimReseller	OrderFrequencyName	CASE WHEN OrderFrequency = 'A' THEN 'Annual' WHEN OrderFrequency = 'S' THEN 'Semester' ELSE 'Quarterly' END	The reseller channel billing cycle

Sourcing data from multiple data sources

A data source view can combine tables from more than one data source. Let's say you need the SOS OLAP data source view to include the product inventory fact table which is not part of the AdventureWorks data warehouse. Instead, the product inventory data is located in an Oracle database. Suppose that you don't want to or can't change the data warehouse schema. You have at least two ways to solve this requirement and they both require SQL Server 2000 or higher as a primary database server.

First, you can use the SQL Server linked server feature and link the Oracle server to the data warehouse server. Once this is done, you can link to the product inventory tables and views as though they are part of the data warehouse database. The second approach is to define a new data source in your Analysis Services project pointing to the Oracle product inventory database and add the required tables directly to the primary data source view. For example, assuming that the Adventure Works data source points to the product inventory database, use the familiar Add/Remove dialog to add its objects to the SOS OLAP data source view (see Figure 2.24).

The caveat when combining objects from multiple data sources is that the primary data source (the one that was used to create the data source view) must be SQL Server 2000 or above because SSAS uses the SQL Server OPENROWSET feature to fetch data from other OLE-DB compliant data sources.

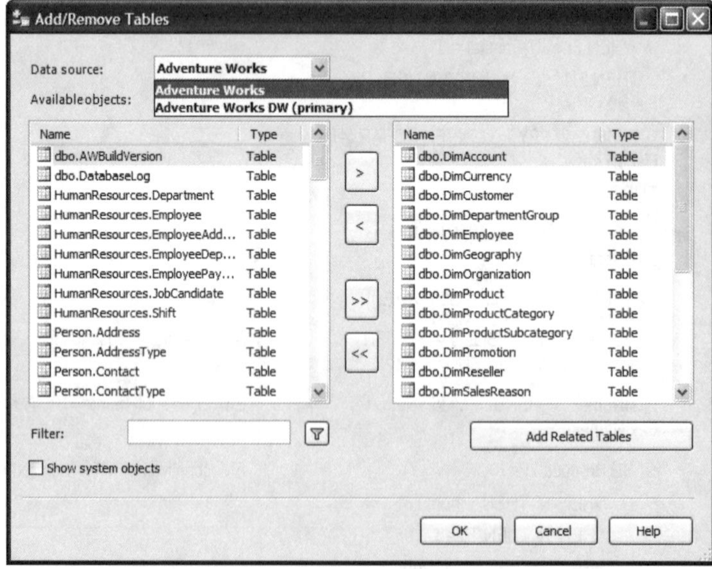

Figure 2.24 If the primary data source is SQL Server-based, you can combine objects from multiple data sources in a single data source view.

2.6 Summary

Analysis Services databases are containers of UDM objects. Follow the four-step design process to architect the UDM data schema. The UDM flexible data architecture supports both relational and dimensional data sources. The data source view defines the data schema on which UDM is built. It isolates the upper UDM layers from the underlying data source schema.

DSV gives you the flexibility to transform the data source schema to meet your UDM requirements. Use named queries to define virtual tables and named calculations to create expression-based columns. Now that we know how to work with data, let's build the most important UDM component – the dimensional model.

2.7 Resources

Overview of the Analysis Services Development and Management Environments (http://shrinkster.com/6l5) -- This paper provides an overview of the various environments for users who develop or manage OLAP or Data Mining applications.

The Data Warehouse Toolkit: The Complete Guide to Dimensional Modeling, 2nd Edition, Ralph Kimball, Margy Ross (http://shrinkster.com/6l6) – A great resource to get you up to speed with dimensional modeling and data warehouse design.

Chapter 3

Dimensional Modeling Basics

As we discussed in chapter 1, the main objective (and dilemma) of the Unified Dimensional Model and OLAP technology, in general, is to provide user-friendly data analytics without sacrificing performance. As its name suggests, UDM responds to these requirements by embracing dimensional modeling as a design technique to store and retrieve data in the most efficient way. At the same time, UDM supplements the traditional dimensional model with characteristics native to the relational model.

Again in chapter 1, we said that unlike the "classic" dimensional model, UDM is not limited to star and snowflake schemas only. Moreover, one of the main factors that help UDM break out of the OLAP core model is that it is an attribute-based model. In this chapter, we will lay out the groundwork for the UDM dimensional model on which the next few chapters will be built upon. You will learn:

- What the building blocks of UDM dimensions are.
- How measures and measure groups fit together.
- How to use BI Studio wizards to create the raw dimensional model.
- How to process and browse dimensions and cubes.

3.1 Understanding Dimensions

As its predecessor, the dimensional model, UDM facilitates intuitive data exploration by allowing end users to slice and dice data from analytical perspectives called *dimensions*. For example, provided that the underlying schema supports it, we can introduce Time, Product, Customer, etc., dimensions to allow the end user to analyze the data that way. In UDM, a dimension can be defined as a container of *attributes*, *hierarchies*, and *member properties* objects. Let's now get more insight into these objects and find how they are used in UDM.

 **SSAS 2000** UDM doesn't support private dimensions. All dimensions in UDM are shared.

3.1.1 Attributes

In UDM, attributes are the building blocks of the dimensions and the cube space. Let's explain the attribute role by considering a hypothetical Product dimension table (Figure 3.1). An attribute typically corresponds to a single column (or a named calculation) from the underlying dimension table. All columns of this star-based dimension table could potentially be useful for data analysis. Therefore, when creating the Product Dimension, we could choose to promote all table columns as dimension attributes. For the sake of brevity, Figure 3.1 shows that only four table columns have been promoted to attributes.

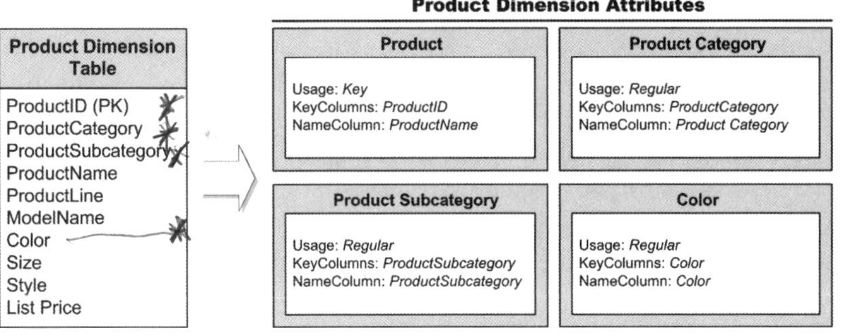

Figure 3.1 A dimension consists of attributes which may form attribute and multilevel hierarchies.

Attribute usage types

Not all attributes are created equal. In UDM, an attribute is characterized by its usage and bindings. An attribute can fulfill one of the following three usage roles in its containing dimension as specified by the attribute *Usage* property.

Key

Just like a relational table typically has a primary key, every dimension must have a *dimension key* attribute. A dimension can have only one dimension key attribute. The dimension key tells us what each row in the dimension table represents. Moreover, just as a referential integrity key joins two tables in a relational database, the dimension key is used to relate a dimension to a measure group. Typically, the role of the dimension key is fulfilled by the primary key of the dimension table. For example, in Figure 3.1, the role of the key attribute is fulfilled by the ProductID attribute.

Note Since the dimension key plays an important role, when the cube dimensions are generated, the Cube Wizard renames the dimension key attribute to match the dimension table name, e.g. *ProductID* becomes *Product*. This naming convention signifies that the dimension key represents the entities stored in the table, e.g. the ProductID dimension key is equivalent to the Product entity. The Dimension Designer assigns a special (key) icon to the dimension key for easier identification.

Parent

Sometimes you may need to design a dimension that has a parent-child (recursive) relationship among its members. For example, in section 3.3.2, we will implement a parent-child Employee dimension. This dimension will be based on the DimEmployee table which links employees to supervisors by using a designated reference key column (*ParentEmployeeKey*). To set up a parent-child dimension, you set the usage of the ParentEmployeeKey attribute to *Parent*.

You can have only one attribute with the Usage set property set to Parent. Therefore, if you want to define two views of an Employee dimension (one for the organizational view and another for the administrative reports), you need to define two separate dimensions.

Regular

An attribute whose usage is not *Key* or *Parent* is a regular attribute. A regular attribute is used to decorate the dimension with additional information. For example, end users can use the Color attribute to browse data by the product color. All attributes of the Product dimension table, besides the Parent ID attribute, are regular attributes.

Attribute bindings

Each attribute has *members*. The attribute members represent the unique values stored in the underlying attribute column. For example, the color attribute of the product dimension may have members Black, Red, and Blue, while the Product Category attribute may include Bikes, Accessories, and Clothing.

How does UDM identify attribute members? For example, the Product dimension table may have hundreds of products having the same color. Yet, UDM must determine the *unique* members so the end user doesn't see repeating colors when browsing by the Color attribute. To accomplish this, UDM evaluates three attribute properties:

- *KeyColumns (Required)* – This is the most important attribute binding. Similar to a unique index in a relational table, *KeyColumns* identifies uniquely the attribute members by one or more columns.
- *NameColumn (Optional)* – Provides the visual representation of the attribute members. If not specified, the key column will be used.
- *ValueColumn (Optional)* – Designates which column will provide the member value. If not specified, the key column will be used.

The attribute key shouldn't be confused with the dimension key attribute (Key usage role) that we've just discussed since they have different scopes. The former is used to identify the attribute members within that attribute, while the latter is used to identify the rows in the dimension table. The dimension key is an attribute itself and it has also KeyColumns property.

Attribute key

Most attributes have only a KeyColumns binding and the KeyColumns collection usually contains only one column. That's because a single column is good enough to uniquely identify the attribute members. What if you have a dimension table which has a composite primary key consisting of two columns, e.g. CompanyID and CustomerID. In this case, you can create a composite attribute key whose KeyColumns collection includes these two columns.

Member names

If you don't want the attribute members to derive their names from the attribute key column, set the attribute *NameColumn* property to the table column that will supply the member names. For example, assuming that the Product attribute doesn't have a NameColumn binding, its member names will be derived from the values of ProductID column. Since this is probably not what your users would expect when browsing the Product attribute hierarchy, you can use a NameColumn binding to derive more descriptive names from the ProductName column. One case when you definitely need to use a NameColumn binding is a composite attribute key (KeyColumns spans more than one column). That's because UDM won't know which column to use for the names of the attribute members.

SSAS 2000 If you have SSAS 2000 experience, you may be surprised to find out that none of the attribute bindings in SSAS 2005 can be expression-based. In UDM, you can use named calculations at a DSV level to create expression-based attribute members. In addition, the *MemberNamesUnique* and *AllowDuplicateNames* dimension properties have been deprecated because in UDM the attribute key is always unique. These properties still show up in the Properties window but they exist for backward compatibility only, i.e. for migrated cubes, and are not enforced during processing.

Member qualification

In UDM, the attribute key must be unique so that the Analysis Server can properly identify the attribute members. Going back to Figure 3.1, identifying the attribute key of the ProductID (Product) attribute is easy – it is the ProductID column again. When the dimension is processed, the Analysis Server will send SQL SELECT DISTINCT statements for each attribute to retrieve the unique members of the attribute. For example, assuming that the Product attribute has KeyColumns set to ProductID and NameColumn to ProductName, the Analysis Server will send a statement similar to the one below to retrieve the ProductID attribute members.

```
SELECT DISTINCT ProductID, ProductName FROM DimProduct
```

What about the rest of the attributes that don't have designated key columns in the dimension table, e.g. Color? In this case, the attribute key is set to the Color column itself and the SQL statement that retrieves the color members will be:

```
SELECT DISTINCT Color FROM DimProduct
```

If our attribute binding discussion sounds mind-boggling, don't worry, it will all become clear when we come to the step-by-step tutorial. The most important point that you need to take with you from our membership discussion is the following golden rule.

Important The attribute key must be unique in order for the attribute members to be qualified properly when the attribute is processed.

Considering the Product attribute, what do you think is going to happen if we have two products with the same ProductID? Assuming the dimension error configuration is left to its default settings, SSAS will process the product dimension successfully. However, when you browse the dimension, the second product won't show up.

Ordering

Chances are that your users would like to see the attribute members sorted in a particular way. The attribute member ordering is controlled by the *OrderBy* property. By default, OrderBy is set to *Key*. For example, in our Product Dimension, the products will be sorted by default in ascending order of the ProductID column. Suppose your users want to see products sorted by name. Assuming that the NameColumn property is set to the ProductName attribute, you can set OrderBy to *Name*. UDM also allows you to use another attribute that can define the sort order.

Member values

The attribute *ValueColumn* can be used to provide an alternative member value. For example, the Product hierarchy may contain a *Size* attribute whose key is bound to a numeric column. A smart OLAP application could inspect the attribute KeyColumns, NameColumn, and ValueColumn bindings. If a ValueColumns binding exists, the application may decide to favor the attribute value for filtering and sorting because it may have no knowledge of whether the key may be useful or not. Hence, the UDM modeler can choose if the attribute key, name, or another attribute may be used as a member value.

SSAS 2000 The ValueColumn could be compared to the Member Property, which has its own type and can be used to sort dimension level members.

In addition, the ValueColumn binding can be used to preserve the original data type of the column, while NameColumn converts it to a string. For example, if the Size attribute in the Product dimension contains pre-defined sizes, e.g. 1 ½ , 1 ¾, 2, etc., you could use NameColumn to display the name but you can preserve the real value into ValueColumn and order the attribute by that value. The ValueColumn property is exposed as a *MEMBER_VALUE* predefined property of the dimension member.

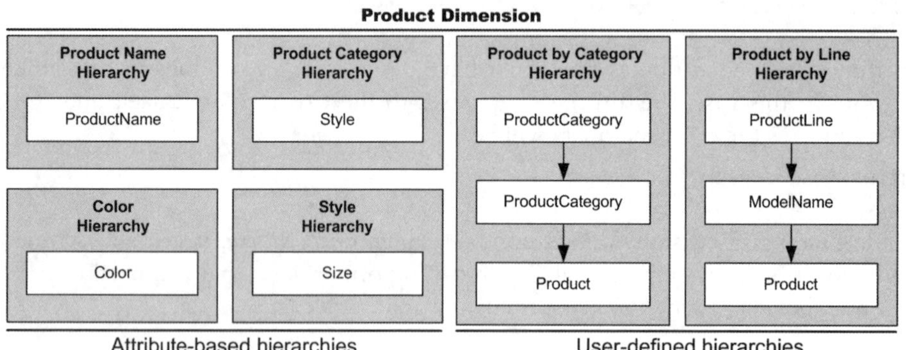

Figure 3.2 A dimension consists of attributes which may form attribute and multilevel hierarchies.

3.1.2 Hierarchies

Attributes are exposed to end users through dimension hierarchies. Dimension hierarchies define useful navigational paths for exploring data from different angles, as shown in Figure 3.2. Attributes can form *attribute* and *multilevel* hierarchies.

Attribute hierarchies

By default, in UDM, every attribute (and thus every column in a dimension table) can form its own attribute hierarchy. An attribute hierarchy contains an optional *All* level and the distinct members of the attribute. For example, the Color attribute can form an attribute-hierarchy that has two levels: the *All* level and a second level with a member for each color. End users can leverage the Color attribute hierarchy to get the aggregated totals for products of all colors (All member) or drill down data by product color.

How attributes affect the cube space

A radical departure from the traditional dimensional model is that, in UDM, it is the attribute hierarchies that define the cube space. This means that the measures stored in the cube are found at the intersecting coordinates of the attribute hierarchy members. Figure 3.3 shows how you can visualize the UDM multidimensional cube as a product of its attribute hierarchies.

For the sake of simplicity, Figure 3.3 shows a three-dimensional cube whose space is defined by the *Customer Name*, *Product Category*, and *Date Year* attribute hierarchies. The attributes forming these hierarchies belong to different dimensions, e.g. the Customer Name is in the Customer dimension, Product Category is in the Product dimension, and the Date Year attribute is in the Date dimension. The $20,000 sales amount measure exists at the intersection of members from the Customer Name attribute hierarchy (member Larry), Product Category attribute hierarchy (member Bikes), and Date Year attribute hierarchy (member 2000). Of course, in real life your cubes are likely to have many more attribute hierarchies.

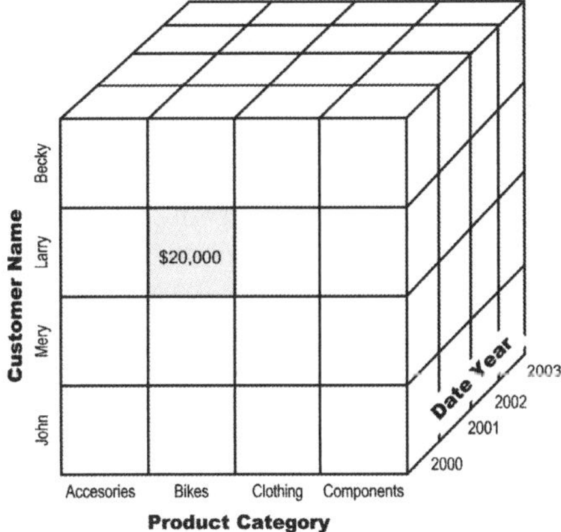

Figure 3.3 In UDM, the cube space is defined by its attribute-based hierarchies.

Autoexists behavior

If the cube space is defined by its attribute hierarchies and these hierarchies are independent of each other, how does UDM relate the attribute members when the attribute hierarchies are requested side-by-side (cross-joined) in a query? Readers familiar with database programming know that a cross join between two relational tables produces the cross (Cartesian) result set where the size of the set is the number of rows in the first table multiplied by the number of rows in the second table. Yet, in UDM, this doesn't happen with members of the attribute hierarchies contained within the same dimension (see Figure 3.4).

My Sales Report

Drop Filter Fields Here

		Calendar Year					
		⊞ CY 2003		⊞ CY 2004		Grand Total	
Product Name	Color	Sales Amount	Order Count	Sales Amount	Order Count	Sales Amount	Order Count
⊟ Mountain-500 Black, 52	Black	$28,835.47	66	$33,263.38	80	$62,098.85	146
⊟ Road-650 Red, 58	Red	$79,551.78	87			$79,551.78	87
⊟ Road-650 Red, 60	Red	$235,596.37	196			$235,596.37	196
⊟ Road-650 Red, 62	Red	$232,786.06	197			$232,786.06	197
⊟ Road-650 Red, 44	Red	$242,576.72	203			$242,576.72	203
⊟ Road-650 Red, 48	Red	$221,460.97	204			$221,460.97	204
⊟ Road-650 Red, 52	Red	$132,325.31	136			$132,325.31	136
⊟ Road-650 Black, 58	Black	$224,478.54	198			$224,478.54	198
⊟ Road-650 Black, 60	Black	$127,000.98	142			$127,000.98	142
⊟ Road-650 Black, 62	Black	$73,131.27	79			$73,131.27	79

Figure 3.4 SSAS applies a special Autoexists behavior to synchronize attribute hierarchies in the same dimension.

In this case, the user has requested to see sales data by two attribute hierarchies in the Product dimension (Product Name and Color). It turns out that, when SSAS receives a query, it examines it to determine if the query spans attribute hierarchies in the same dimension. If this is the case, SSAS applies a special behavior called *Autoexists*. Specifically, Autoexists is done at the dimension level to find the intersection between attributes of the same dimension. In our example, since the query includes the members of Product.ProductName and Product.Color attribute hierarchies, the Autoexists behavior will return the member intersection, i.e. only the product names and colors where there is at least one product matching a given ProductName and Color combination.

SSAS 2000 In SSAS 2000, the only way to create attribute hierarchies was to create separate dimensions. However, these dimensions were treated as unrelated and the server wasn't capable of applying the Autoexits behavior to correlate the dimension members.

Multilevel hierarchies

Besides attribute hierarchies, the UDM designer can optionally group attributes together to form *multilevel hierarchies* (also referred to as *user-defined hierarchies*). These hierarchies should be familiar to readers with experience in SSAS 2000. Multilevel hierarchies represent common logical paths for data navigation. The example shown in Figure 3.2 defines two multilevel hierarchies, Product by Category and Product by Line. The Product by Category hierarchy is introduced to allow the user to drill down product sales data by Product Category, Product Subcategory, and Product levels, while the Product by Line exists so that end users can explore data by Product Line and Product Model.

Again, it is the dimension attributes that are the building blocks of multilevel hierarchies. The UDM designer implements a multilevel hierarchy by identifying attributes that will form the dimension levels. For example, the Product Category level in the Product by Category dimension is represented by the ProductCategory attribute. In addition, an attribute can participate in more than one multilevel hierarchy. For example, the Product attribute (dimension key) participates in the both *Product By Category* and *Product by Line* multilevel hierarchies.

My Sales Report
Drop Filter Fields Here

Category	Subcategory	Product Name	Sales Amount	Order Count
⊟ Accessories	⊟ Bike Racks	Hitch Rack - 4-Bike Reorder Point: 3 List Price: 120 Dealer Price: 72	$133,267.84	796
	⊟ Bike Stands	All-Purpose Bike Stand Reorder Point: 3 List Price: 159 Dealer Price: 95.4	$19,080.00	249

Drop Column Fields Here

Figure 3.5 Use member properties to provide relevant member information.

3.1.3 Member properties

Besides forming hierarchies, in UDM, an attribute can be given a special role as a *member property*. Member properties fulfill two major tasks. Traditionally, dimensional modelers have used member properties to add additional information to the dimension members. More importantly, in UDM, member properties are used to define known relationships between attributes.

Data analytics

Member properties could be used to provide additional information relevant to an attribute member. Figure 3.5 shows how an OLAP browser (Office Web Components) can display member properties. In this case, the end user has configured the report to show three member properties (Reorder Point, List Price, and Dealer Price) of the Product Name attribute. Alternatively, to minimize space, OWC supports showing member properties in a tooltip activated by hovering the mouse cursor over the member.

Attribute relations

In UDM, member properties have been promoted to play a much more important role than just member decoration. All dimension attribute must be related to the dimension key attribute either directly or indirectly. For example, the Color attribute is directly related to the Product dimension key attribute because each product has one and only one color. However, attributes may also have one-to-many relationship within the containing dimension. For example, a product category is associated with many product subcategories and a product subcategory has many products. Such attribute relationships are not automatically inferred by UDM. By defining member properties, you are letting UDM know about these relationships so UDM knows how attributes forming levels in multilevel hierarchies relate to each other and to the fact table(s).

If you think of attributes as building blocks of dimension hierarchies, think of member properties as the glue that holds them together. In this respect, it may be helpful to visualize attributes as nodes of a tree, while the member properties are the connecting lines between them. Figure 3.6 should help you understand this analogy.

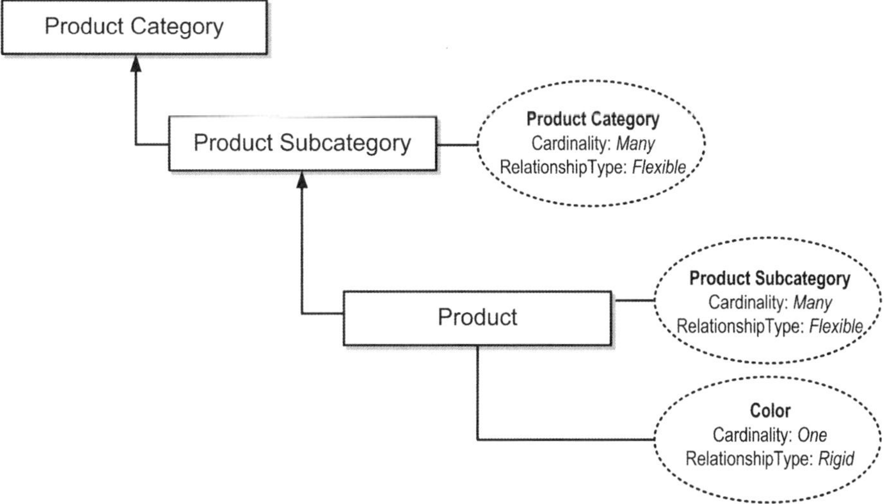

Figure 3.6 Use member properties to let UDM know about known relationship between attributes.

Here, I've added the Product Subcategory attribute as a member property of the Product attribute to inform UDM that the relationship between a product subcategory and a product is one-to-many. Similarly, I've added the Product Category attribute to the Product Subcategory attribute to tell UDM that one category can have many subcategories. In addition, I've defined the Color attribute as a member property of the Product attribute.

A member property has a couple of characteristics that help UDM optimize the attribute relationship.

- *Cardinality (One or Many)* – Similar to a SQL join, the cardinality characteristic defines the cardinality of the relationship between the two attributes. For example, the cardinality between a subcategory and a product is Many, while the cardinality between a product and its color is One.
- *RelationshipType (Flexible or Rigid)* – A rigid relationship doesn't change over time. For example, if the product color never changes, we can enforce this rule by setting the Color relationship to Rigid. If underlying data does change (e.g. a data entry error has been made and the product color is updated), Analysis Services will raise an exception and you will need to fully process the dimension. An example of flexible relationship could be the product-to-product subcategory relationship if a product may be re-classified to another subcategory.

Using member properties to define known attribute relationships is optional. However, I highly recommend you spend some time to define proper relationships and document them. Besides "gluing" attributes together, such relationships bring additional advantages, as discussed next.

Data aggregation

When member properties are defined properly, UDM can use an aggregation from one attribute to obtain the results from a related attribute in a multilevel hierarchy. For example, if the Product Category attribute is defined as a member property of the Product Subcategory attribute in the Product multilevel hierarchy, the Analysis Server can derive the aggregated sales value of the Product Category level by simply adding the aggregated values of the Product Subcategory level. In the absence of defined member property relationships between attributes, Analysis Services has no other choice but to aggregate all non-key attributes from the key attribute.

SSAS 2000 Multilevel hierarchies don't define aggregations by itself in UDM. It is the attribute relationships that tell UDM how data aggregates from one level to another. Therefore, after setting up the levels of a multilevel hierarchy, you need to define the attribute relationships among them.

Efficiency

Properly defined member properties will make UDM more efficient. For example, if the *RelationshipType* property of the Product Subcategory attribute is set to *Rigid* in respect to the Product attribute, UDM knows that a given product cannot be re-classified and assigned to a different category. In other words, the product members are fixed. When a dimension is processed incrementally, the flexible aggregations get dropped and recreated while the rigid ones are not discarded because rigid relationships guarantee that dimension members haven't changed.

While using member properties for defining known relationships makes UDM more efficient, you have to be careful not to overdo their usage. This is especially true for dimension key attributes. Member properties on the dimension key are the most expensive in terms of storage because many more values need to be processed and stored.

Validation

Just like constraints in a relational model help enforce certain rules, UDM uses member properties to validate the attribute relationship. For example, if the Product Subcategory is defined with a Mandatory optionality, at dimension processing time, UDM will raise an error if a row in the Product dimension table doesn't have a subcategory. Similarly, if the RelationshipType property of the Product Subcategory attribute is set to Rigid, UDM will complain if a product subcategory changes.

Multilevel hierarchy types

Attributes that form levels of a multilevel hierarchy may have or not have explicit relationships among each other. In this respect, we can have *natural* and *reporting* multilevel hierarchies.

Natural multilevel hierarchies

A natural multilevel hierarchy defines a strict one-to-many relationship between the attributes forming the hierarchy levels that are enforced through member properties. For example, all multilevel hierarchies in the hypothetical Product dimension shown in Figure 3.7 are natural (the screenshot is taken from the Dimension Designer which I will introduce in section 3.3.3).

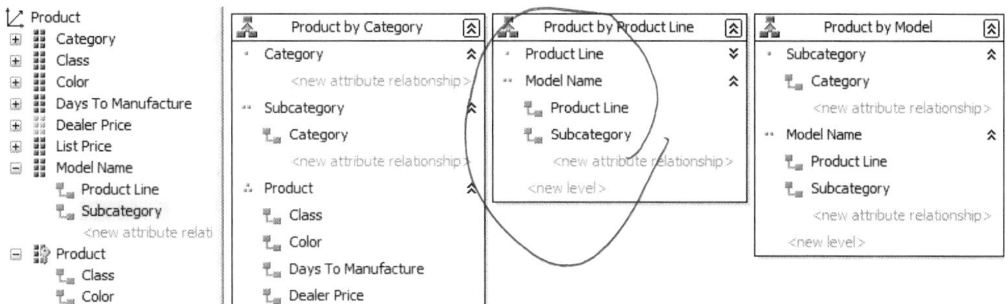

Figure 3.7 In a natural multilevel hierarchy, each member has one and only parent.

The Product by Category hierarchy has two one-to-many relationships -- a product category has many subcategories and a subcategory has many products. More importantly, each member in a natural hierarchy has only one parent. For example, a hypothetical Road-42 product member belongs to only one category (e.g. Road Bikes). To represent the one-to-many relationships between the attributes, member properties define cascading attribute relationships up the levels in the hierarchy (Cardinality is *Many*). For example, the Category attribute links the Subcategory attribute to the Category attribute.

UDM natural multilevel hierarchies are flexible. For example, not all "natural" levels must be present in a hierarchy. Back to the Product By Category hierarchy, we can remove the Subcategory level if we want the user to be able to drill down directly from Category to Product level. Although a level may be missing, cascading relationships in the form of member properties must be present. Further, attributes may exist in more than one hierarchy. For example, the Model Name attribute forms levels in both the Product by Product Line and Product by Model hierarchies. Finally, note that the dimension key doesn't have to form the bottom level of a hierarchy. For example, the bottom levels of the same two hierarchies are formed by the Model Name attribute (not Product).

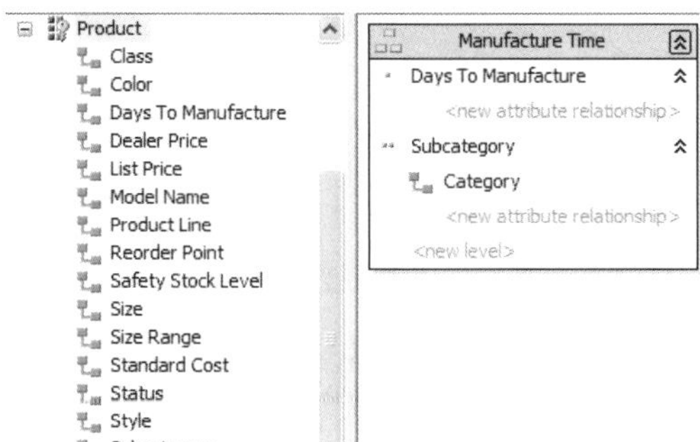

Figure 3.8 A reporting multilevel hierarchy includes attributes that don't have direct relationships.

Reporting multilevel hierarchies

Sometimes, you may need to define a multilevel hierarchy whose attributes don't have direct relationships among each other. Such attributes are only related through the dimension key (or other attribute). For example, in the Manufacture Time hierarchy (Figure 3.8), there isn't an attribute relationship between the Days to Manufacture and Subcategory levels because there isn't one-to-many cardinality between them. Yet, end users may need to browse data by this hierarchy.

Note You will end up with a reporting hierarchy if you create a multilevel hierarchy from attributes that are not related through member properties. In other words, if you don't define attribute relations, each multi-level hierarchy you create in the Dimension Designer will be a reporting hierarchy. Avoid this!

In general, you should minimize the number of reporting multilevel hierarchies. As noted, in absence of direct attribute relationships, the server has no other choice but to infer the attribute relationships which may cause performance degradation. No attribute relationships lead to poor design. You should always spend time to define useful attribute relationships and document them.

3.1.4 Dimension Classification

With the introduction of attributes, you are not restricted to star and snowflake-based dimensions only. In fact, UDM dimensions may have so many aspects that it can be difficult to categorize dimensions, e.g. to come up with a broadly accepted definition of what a dimension type is. To avoid ambiguity, I came up with the dimension taxonomy table shown in Table 3.1.

Table 3.1 Dimension classification

Characteristics	Type	Definition
Dimension type	Standard	A standard dimension is defined and contained within the current database
	Linked	A linked dimension is contained in another database
Fact table relationship	No relationship	The dimension is not related to the fact table.
	Regular	The dimension table is joined directly to the fact table, e.g. DimProduct and FactSales. A regular dimension could be interpreted as a role-playing dimension, when it is related multiple times to the same fact table
	Fact (degenerate)	The dimension members are derived from the fact table (e.g. saler oder tracking number).
	Referenced	The dimension joins the fact table through an intermediate table, e.g. DimGeorgraphy to DimCustomer to FactSales
	Many-to-Many	The dimension and fact table has a many-to-many relationship, e.g. one customer may have more than one bank account and a bank account may belong to more than one customer
	Data mining	The dimension is based on a data mining model
Semantic type	Time, Accounts, etc	Describes the data semantics.

In this chapter, we will focus only on implementing standard dimensions that have a regular relationship to the fact table.

3.1.5 Dimension Storage

Just like all other database objects, the dimension definition is described in ASSL grammar. When the dimension definition is deployed to the server, it becomes part of the metadata that describes the SSAS database.

Metadata storage

When a dimension is processed, SSAS generates various binary files to serve as containers of dimension data. While discussing the dimension store files in full is beyond the scope of this book, here are some essential concepts.

File format

Similar to SQL tables, the dimension store files contain fields (columns) and records (rows). Records are grouped into fixed size pages. SSAS employs sophisticated storage primitives to read/write data to the store files based on Windows file structured storage. Perhaps, the most important observation is that in SSAS 2005 dimension data is read on demand and it is not memory resident as it was in SSAS 2000. This allows SSAS 2005 to scale to extremely large dimensions (in the range of million key attribute members).

Dimensions stores

As I mentioned, when a dimension is processed, SSAS generates SQL SELECT statements to fetch the distinct attribute members. Next, SSAS generates a *dimension map* which contains the full path to each attribute member in attribute and multilevel hierarchies. These references are internally represented by unique numeric paths that may look like this if described in text format:

```
[Bikes] ⇨ [Mountain Bikes] ⇨ [Montain-48]
```

The above path qualifies fully the Mountain-48 member of the Product by Category hierarchy. When the cube is processed, SSAS generates map store files populated with fact data. A map file consists of attribute references and measure values and has a file extension of fact.data. You can think of a map store file as analogous to a row in a SQL table, where the measure values are the column values, while the attribute references are represented by the table keys.

Besides the map store files, SSAS generates various other files in the dimension folder. These files include attribute stores to store the member keys, bitmap index stores to index related attributes, hierarchy stores that contain the hierarchical paths for level members, and decoding stores with indexes to aggregations.

3.2 Understanding Measures

A UDM cube consists of one or more dimensions combined with one or more measures. The whole purpose of UDM and OLAP in general is to gauge the business performance across numerical facts called *measures* in the SSAS terminology. As identified in chapter 2, examples of useful facts to evaluate the Adventure Works sales performance are the order item sales amount and order count. The tables that store the measures are called fact tables. When we build the SOS OLAP dimensional layer in this chapter, we will derive measures from appropriate columns of the fact tables. If they are not enough, we can define additional measures in the form of MDX calculations.

3.2.1 Measure Bindings

A measure supports three binding modes as specified by the measure *Source* property. Typically, a measure is bound to a single column from the underlying fact table (*Column* binding). By default, a measure inherits the data type of its source column. In most cases, this is the desired behavior but sometimes you may need to override the measure data type. For example, you may need to have an Order Count measure that shows the number of the orders by counting the distinct order numbers. If the order number column is a character-based column, you need to override the Order Count measure data type to *Integer*.

Sometimes, instead of binding a measure to a particular column, you may need to bind it to the entire row (*Row* binding). For example, you may need to count the order item transactions in a sales order fact table. You can accomplish this by creating a new measure and using row binding. Finally, the measure source binding may not be known during design time (*Generate column* binding). This is useful when you create UDM top-down in the absence of a data source.

3.2.2 Measure Groups

In UDM, a cube can have more than one fact table. Just like a dimension is built on top of a dimension table, a measure group represents a fact table. For example, in chapter 2, we split the sales order items of the SOS OLAP data schema into two fact tables: FactResellerSales and FactInternetSales. Therefore, the dimensional layer we will implement in this chapter will have two measure groups, one for each fact table.

In UDM, the definition of measures and measure groups becomes part of the cube structure definition. For this reason, you won't see separate ASSL files for cube measure groups. Similar to linked dimensions, UDM supports linking to measures stored in another cube. For example, if there is an HR cube to serve the needs of the HR department, the SOS OLAP cube can link to its dimensions and measure groups.

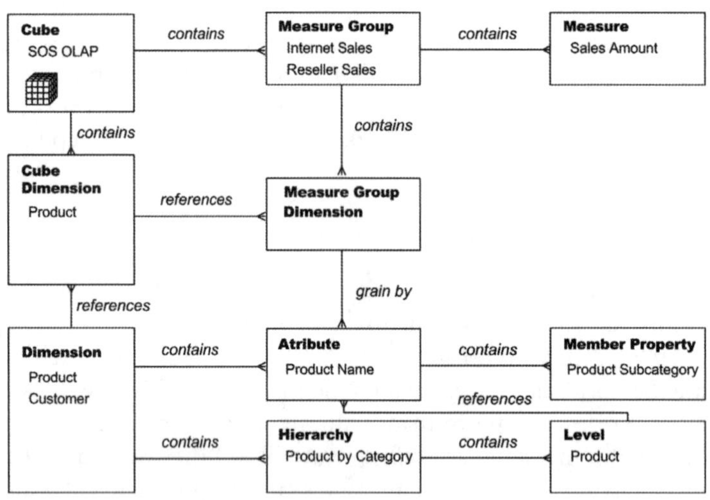

Figure 3.9 The cube object schema at a glance.

3.2.3 The Cube Object Schema

Throwing in so many UDM elements and definitions may be confusing. Figure 3.9 is meant to clarify the relationship among the UDM objects in the context of the SOS OLAP cube we will be building shortly. A cube contains one or more measure groups and references one or more dimensions. For example, the SOS OLAP cube in Figure 3.9 references the Product dimension but doesn't use the Customer dimension. A dimension may be used by more than one cube defined in the containing database or external databases. A dimension contains attributes and optionally hierarchies (attribute or multilevel). A hierarchy has levels. For example, an attribute hierarchy may have two levels (All level and the level defined by the attribute members). Each level references an attribute. For example, the Product level (the lowest level of the Product hierarchy) is represented by the Product attribute. An attribute may contain member properties that define known relationships to other attributes.

The relationship between dimensions and measure groups is many-to-many. A dimension may join more than one measure group, e.g. the Product dimension can be used by both Internet and Reseller Sales measure groups. A measure group may be, and often is, joined to more than one dimension. A measure group defines one or more measures.

3.3 Implementing the Raw Dimensional Model

Having laid out the UDM dimensional concepts, let's proceed by implementing the raw Adventure Works dimensional layer. As you would recall, in chapter 2, we implemented the real-time data schema in the form of the SOS OLTP data source view. In addition, we designed a more involved SOS OLAP data source view on top of the AdventureWorksDW database for historical data analysis. What we will be doing now is building the dimensional layer on top of the SOS OLAP data source view. The SOS OLAP dimensional model will encompass one cube and several dimensions.

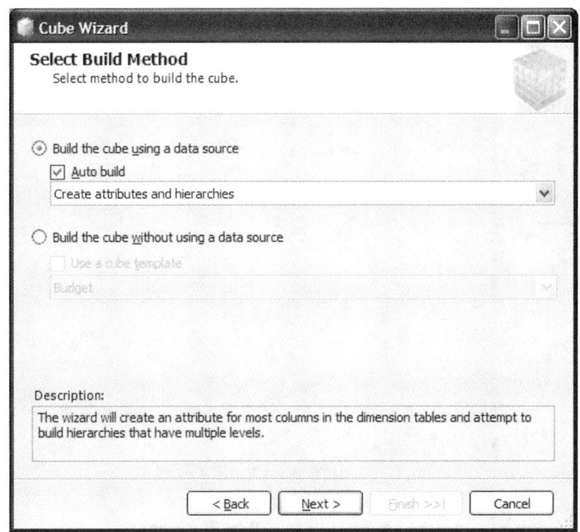

Figure 3.10 With the Cube Wizard, you can build a cube from an existing data source or from a template.

3.3.1 Building a Cube using the Cube Wizard

While you can build a cube manually, the Analysis Services team has provided a sophisticated Cube Wizard to help you build the cube quickly. You may sometimes hear people refer to the Cube Wizard affectionately as *IntelliCube*.

1. Start BI Studio and open the SOS SSAS project (SOS.dwproj) you created in chapter 2.
2. In the Solution Explorer window, right-click on the Cubes folder and choose *New Cube* to start the Cube Wizard. Click Next to advance to the *Select Build Method* step (see Figure 3.10).

The Cube Wizard supports two methods for building a cube. Use the bottom-up method (*Build the cube using a data source* option), to build the dimensional model from an existing data source. This is the approach we will be using to build the SOS OLAP cube. More formal OLAP requirements may force you to go for the top-down approach (*Build the cube without using a data source* option). I will demonstrate this approach in chapter 6.

3. Check the *Auto build* checkbox to let the Cube Wizard examine heuristically the data and suggest attribute and multilevel hierarchies. Click Next.

4. In the Select Data Source View step, choose the *SOS OLAP* data source view that we implemented in chapter 2. Click Next.

The Cube Wizard initiates the *Detecting Fact and Dimension Tables* step and probes the DSV objects to identify fact and dimension tables. The Cube Wizard follows a simple algorithm to identify dimension and fact tables. If a table doesn't reference other tables (a leaf table), the wizard assumes that it is a good candidate for a fact table. Otherwise, it is most likely a dimension table. A more complicated case is when a table is referenced by other tables, contains numeric information, and references other tables, e.g. the SalesOrderHeader table in the AdventureWorks OLTP database. In this case, the wizard takes the middle road and declares the table both a fact and dimension table.

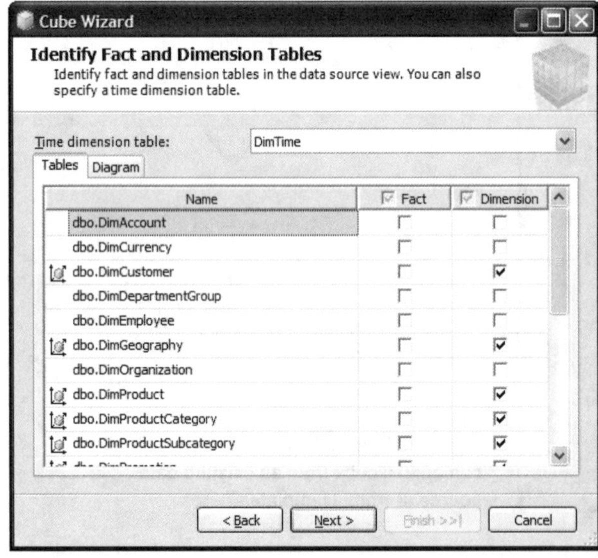

Figure 3.11 Use the Identify Fact and Dimension Tables step to select which tables will be included in the cube and their type.

Identifying dimension and fact Tables

Once the Cube Wizard is done examining the tables, click Next to advance to the *Identify Fact and Dimension Tables* step (Figure 3.11) and see how useful and informative this step really is! The *Identify Fact and Dimension Table step* is a multi-purpose step. It allows you to select which tables will be included in the cube. It also gives you the option to specify the table role – fact, dimension, or both.

SSAS 2000 For readers familiar with SSAS 2000, note that the Cube Wizard uses the same colors to depict the table types – blue for dimension tables and yellow for fact tables. The difference, of course, is that now we can have hybrid tables serving both fact and dimension roles that are colored in green.

Finally, this step allows you to designate a given dimension table as a *Time* dimension table. If you decide to do so at this time, the Cube Wizard will accomplish three things. First, it will construct date-related hierarchies based on the mappings you specify in the Select Time Periods step that will be introduced in the Cube Wizard workflow. Second, the wizard sets the dimension semantic type to *Time* which is used by date-related MDX functions, e.g. YTD (YearToDate). Finally, it enables the advanced Time intelligence page in the BI wizard (discussed in chapter 5) that can automatically construct advanced MDX calculations, e.g. year-to-date, year-to-year growth, etc.

1. Since we have a designated date dimension table (DimTime), select *DimTime* in the *Time dimension table* dropdown as a Time dimension table.
2. Scroll down the grid and observe that the Cube Wizard has identified DimReseller both as a fact and a dimension table. The reason for this is that DimReseller contains numeric information and links FactResellerSales to DimGeography. However, we won't be deriving any measures from DimReseller, so let's override the wizard's vote by clearing the Fact checkbox of DimReseller.
3. Further, the Cube Wizard has identified FactInternetSales both as a fact and a dimension table. This is because FactInternetSales is joined to FactInternetSalesReasons with one-to-many relationship. Since we will use FactInternetSales as a fact table only, clear the Dimension checkbox.
4. To keep things simple, let's select only a subset of tables that we will need to implement the raw dimensional model. We will introduce dimensions and measures based on the rest of the tables on as-needed basis. Clear the Dimension checkbox for tables *DimAccount*, *DimCurrency*, *DimEmployee*, DimDepartmentGro*up*, *DimOrganization*, *DimScenario, and DimSalesReason.* Note that when DimSalesReason is unselected, the Cube Wizard displays a warning message that the FactInternetSalesReason will be left with no dimensions. This is OK because we won't be using FactInternetSalesReason in the raw dimensional model.
5. Clear the Fact checkbox for tables FactCurrencyRate, FactFinance, FactInternetSalesReason, and FactSalesQuota.
6. Flip to the *Diagram* tab and explore the dimensional schema. If you need to see a larger view of the diagram, drag the leftmost bottom corner to enlarge the diagram. Note that you can change the table type in Diagram mode by clicking on the corresponding button.

Designing time dimensions

The Select Time Periods step (Figure 3.12) is shown only if you've mapped a dimension table as a Time dimension table in the Identify Fact and Dimension Tables step. Here, the Cube Wizard is asking you to map the columns from the time dimension table to pre-defined date entities. Many organizations support a separate fiscal calendar. For example, the AW fiscal year starts in July as you will notice by examining the DimTime table data. The Cube Wizard has a comprehensive date and time business intelligence built in. It can support five independent calendars (calendar, fiscal, reporting, manufacturing, and ISO 8601). We will discuss the calendar types in more details in chapter 4 when we will build a server-based Time dimension.

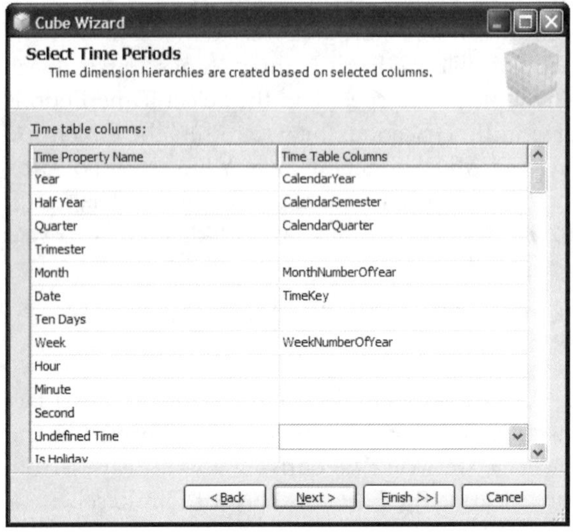

Figure 3.12 Use the Select Time Periods step to help the Cube Wizard create common Time hierarchies.

By setting the appropriate column mappings, you are helping the wizard understand the semantics of your date dimension table so it can build useful hierarchies. The Adventure Works data warehouse schema supports regular and fiscal calendars only. Also, the grain of the DimTime dimension is a calendar day. Therefore, time-related properties are not applicable to our sample UDM. Complete this step by setting the mappings listed in Table 3.2.

Table 3.2 Time table mappings

Time Property Name	Time Table Column	Purpose
Year	CalendarYear	Calendar year, e.g. 2004
Half Year	CalendarSemester	Calendar semester (1 or 2).
Quarter	CalendarQuarter	Calendar quarter, e.g. 2 (second quarter)
Month	MonthNumberOfYear	Calendar month, e.g. 10 (October)
Week	WeekNumberOfYear	Calendar week, e.g. 2 (second week)
Day of Week	DayNumberOfWeek	Day of week, e.g. 1 for Sunday.
Day of Month	DayNumberOfMonth	Day of month
Day of Year	DayNumberOfYear	Day of year
Date	TimeKey	Granularity of the AW DimTime table is a day. TimeKey represents a single day.
Fiscal Quarter	FiscalQuarter	Fiscal quarter
Fiscal Half Year	FiscalSemester	Fiscal semester
Fiscal Year	FiscalYear	Fiscal year

Since the AW fiscal year starts on July 1st, we need to offset the fiscal year hierarchy with two quarters. The AW data warehouse schema doesn't have designated columns for the lower levels of the fiscal hierarchy (months, weeks, and days) since they will be reused across both calendars. Click Next to advance to the *Select Measures* step.

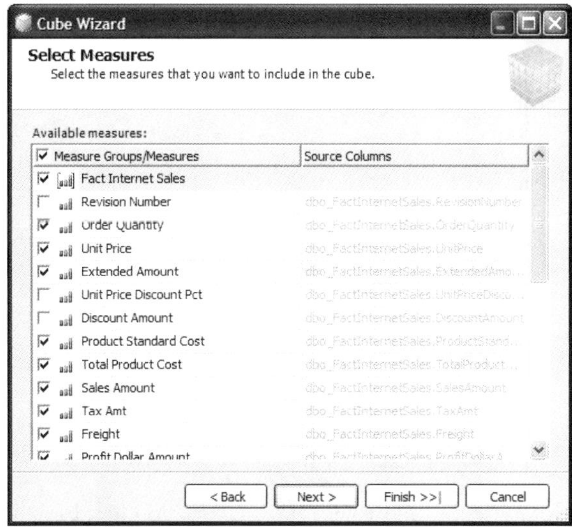

Figure 3.13 In the Select Measures step, you can review the measure groups and measures that the Cube Wizard identified.

Identifying measures

The Select Measures step (Figure 3.13) displays the measures that the Cube Wizard has identified. Each fact table is mapped to a measure group and, by default, all columns are pre-selected. Note that the measure names must be unique within a cube. To comply with this requirement, the Cube Wizard has renamed the measures of the Fact Reseller Sales by adding the table name. Upon reviewing the suggested measures, you may conclude that some of them are not that useful. For example, the Revision Number measure is not additive and it is not a very useful measure. While we can always take out or add measures in the Cube Designer later, let's use this step to remove a few measures which are not needed.

1. From the Fact Internet Sales measure group, remove *Revision Number*, *Unit Price Discount Pct*, and *Discount Amount* measures.
2. Remove the same measures from the Fact Reseller Sales measure group.
3. Click Next to advance to the *Detecting Hierarchies* step.

Identifying dimensions

During the *Detecting Hierarchies* step, the Cube Wizard examines the dimension tables searching for attribute and multilevel hierarchies. The Cube Wizard understands star and snowflake dimension schemas. Once the Cube Wizard is done discovering the dimension relationships, click Next to review them in the *Review New Dimensions* step (Figure 3.14). Take a moment to examine the dimension hierarchies suggested by the Cube Wizard. For example, notice that the Product dimension (Dim Product) has one multilevel hierarchy (*Dim Product Category – Dim Product Subcategory*) and many attribute hierarchies derived by all columns in the DimProduct table. While not all suggested hierarchies are useful, let's move on to the last step. We will later use the Dimension Designer to fine-tune our dimensions.

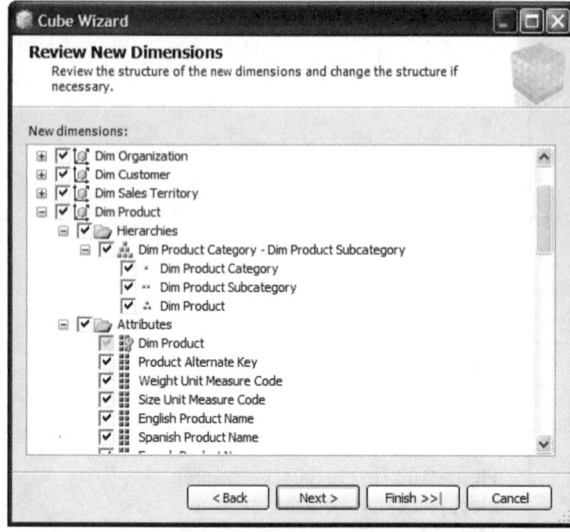

Figure 3.14 Use the Review New Dimensions step to review attribute and multilevel hierarchies.

1. In the Completing the Wizard step, accept the default cube name of *SOS OLAP* and click Finish. The Cube Wizard opens the SOS OLAP cube in the Cube Designer where you can review and edit the cube structure.

Tip How many columns should you promote to attributes? In real life, the number of the selected columns will be probably a tradeoff between convenience and disk storage space. Data explosion is a well-known issue with OLAP cubes and it is even more relevant with attribute-based models, such as UDM. Disk storage aside, my advice is to import all columns. If you don't, chances are one day someone will ask about why a given attribute is missing. Adding a new attribute requires cube re-processing which is much more expensive than hiding it if the attribute is not immediately needed.

Now that we've created the raw cube definition, the Solution Explorer lists the cube and dimension definition files in the Cubes and Dimensions folders respectively. The Cube Wizard has generated six dimension definition files, one for each dimension detected. These dimension files describe both the attribute and multilevel hierarchies.

2. Right-click on the Dimensions folder and choose the *Sort by name* context menu to sort the dimensions in alphabetical order.

3. By default, the file naming convention of a dimension file reflects the underlying table name. Having the *Dim* prefix is redundant, so rename all dimension files by removing it. Confirm when the Cube Designer prompts you to change the dimension object name in the dimension definition file.

4. Rename the Time dimension to **Date** (Date.dim) because it doesn't represent time units (calendar day is the lowest level).

5. (Optional) Select a dimension file and click on the View Code button in the Solution Explorer toolbar to view the ASSL definition. Observe that the Name attribute reflects the new name.

3.3.2 Introducing the Dimension Wizard

Before we explore the Cube Designer, let's introduce another useful wizard which you will rely on often. As your dimensional model evolves, you may need to add additional dimensions. The easiest way to create a new dimension is to use the Dimension Wizard. Let's demonstrate the Dimension Wizard by creating a parent-child dimension.

Understanding parent-child dimensions

A parent-child dimension is a dimension that has a recursive relationship among its members defined by a designated key column. For example, the DimEmployee dimension table defines such a relationship between employees and their supervisors.

1. Close the Cube Designer and open the SOS OLAP data source view.
2. In the Tables pane, click on the DimEmployee table to select in the DSV diagram.
3. Double click on its self-join and, in the Edit Relationship dialog, note that the DimEmployee table is joined to itself by linking the ParentEmployeeKey foreign key to the EmployeeKey primary key.
4. Right-click on the DimEmployee table and choose *Explore Data*. Observe that each employee has a manager and the relationship is defined by the ParentEmployeeKey column. For example, Guy Gilbert is a subordinate to Jo Brown who, in turn, has Peter Krebs as a manager.

Creating parent-child dimensions

The Dimension Wizard makes it easy to create a parent-child dimension. This is one of the dimension types that the wizard knows how to handle.

1. In the Solution Explorer, right-click on the Dimension folder and choose *New Dimension*. The welcome page of the Dimension Wizard is shown. Click Next to advance to the *Select Build Method* step. This step is identical to the Select Build Method Cube Wizard step (Figure 3.10). Click Next to continue.

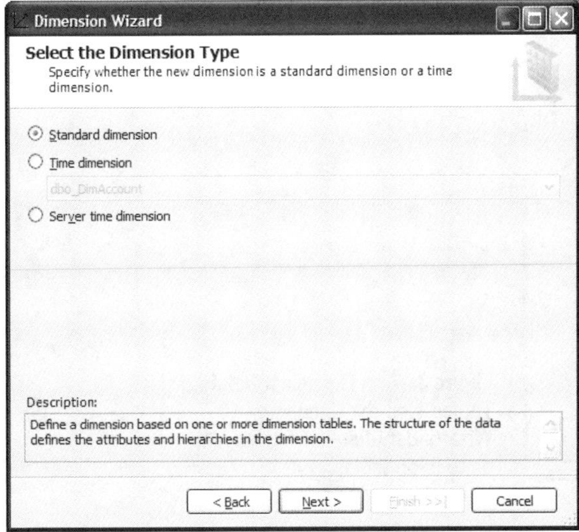

Figure 3.15 Use the Select the Dimension Type step to create a standard or time dimension.

2. In the *Select Data Source View* step, select the *SOS OLAP* data source view and click Next.
3. In the *Select the Dimension Type* step (Figure 3.15), leave the *Standard dimension* radio button selected. Click Next to advance to the Select the *Main Dimension Table* step.
4. The Select the Main Dimension Table step (Figure 3.16) is the most important step. Here, you need to tell the Dimension Wizard which table the new dimension will be based on. Select DimEmployee table.

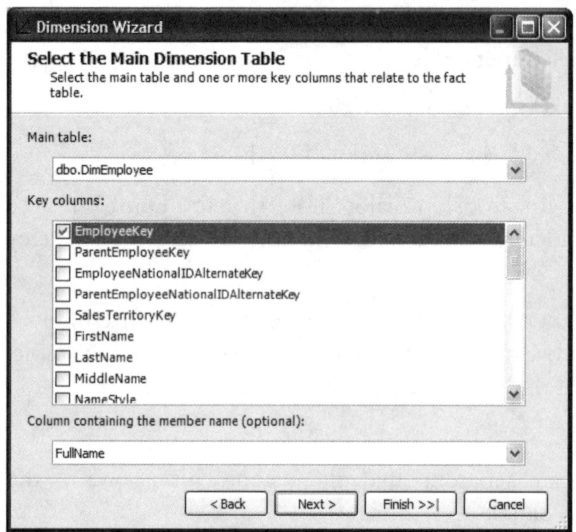

Figure 3.16 In the Select the Main Dimension Table step, you select the dimension table and the dimension key.

5. In this step, you can also specify which column(s) will form the dimension key. Select the EmployeeKey primary table key in the *Key column* list.

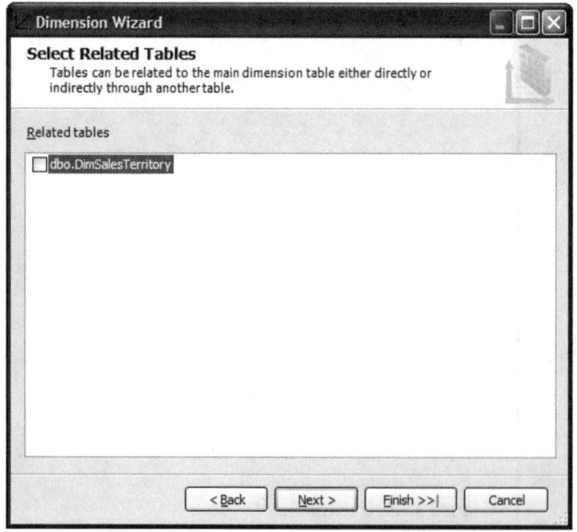

Figure 3.17 In the Select Related Tables step the Dimension Wizard identifies the related dimension tables.

6. An attribute may derive its member names from another column. Use the *Column containing the member name* dropdown if you want to specify the column that will bound to the NameColumn dimension key property. Select the *FullName* column which you added in chapter 2 as a named calculation. Click Next to proceed with the *Select Related Tables step* (Figure 3.17).

   The Dimension Wizard explores the data source to find tables that are related to the DimEmployee table. In our case, it correctly identifies that DimSalesTerritory is linked to DimEmployee. However, the Cube Wizard has already discovered that the DimSalesTerritory table is linked to other dimension tables and has created a separate Dim Sales Territory dimension. To avoid redundancy, we will not include the DimSalesTerritory table in the Employee dimension. Don't worry since nothing is lost. In chapter 5, we will configure the Sales Territory dimension with a referenced relationship to the Employee dimension, so users can still browse sales data by sales territory. Click Next to continue.

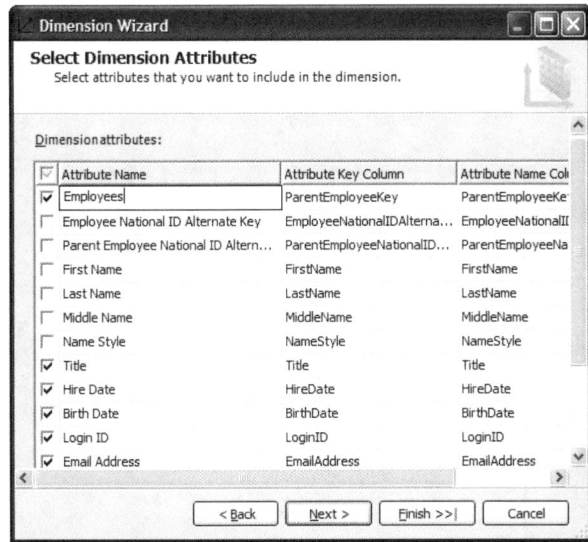

Figure 3.18 In the Select the Main Dimension Table step, you select the dimension table and the dimension key.

Configuring dimension attributes

7. In the *Select Dimension Attributes* step (Figure 3.18), the Dimension Wizard gives you an option to select the additional columns (other than the dimension keys) that will be promoted to dimension attributes.

8. You can change the attribute names and specify the attribute key and name bindings. In our case, the first row represents the recursive hierarchy, so let's give it a more meaningful name, e.g. **Employees**. In addition, unselect the attributes shown in Figure 3.18 because they are not useful for data analysis.

9. Click Next to advance to the *Specify Dimension Type* step (Figure 3.19).
   As with the Identify Facts and Dimension Tables step of the Cube Wizard (Figure 3.11), here, we are given the option to select the dimension type. There isn't a predefined type that matches the semantic meaning of the Employees dimension, so leave its dimension type to Regular and click Next to proceed to the Define the Parent-Child Relationship step (Figure 3.20).

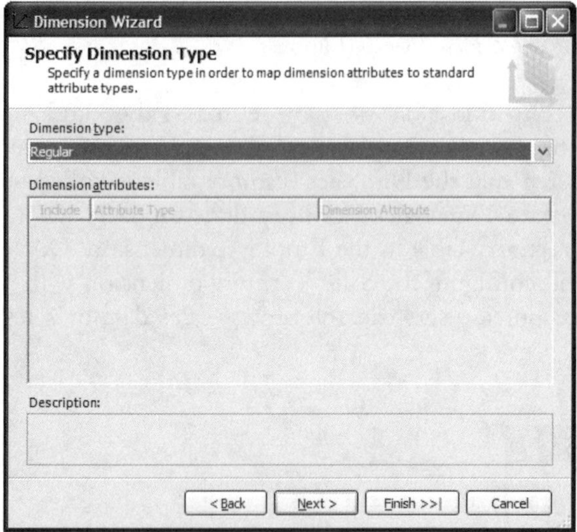

Figure 3.19 You can describe the semantic meaning of the dimension by setting its Type.

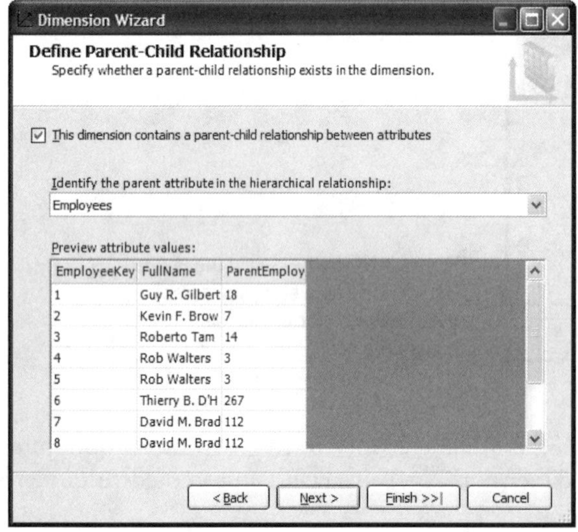

Figure 3.20 The Dimension Wizard can detect a parent-child relationship.

Configuring dimension hierarchies

10. The Dimension Wizard explores the table schema and discovers the existence of a self-join. The parent attribute is correctly set to the *Employees* attribute we've identified in the Select Dimension Attributes step.

11. Click Next to let the Dimension Wizard explore the dimension data and discover potential multilevel hierarchies in the Detecting Hierarchies step. When it is done, click Next to advance to the *Review New Hierarchies* step (Figure 3.21).

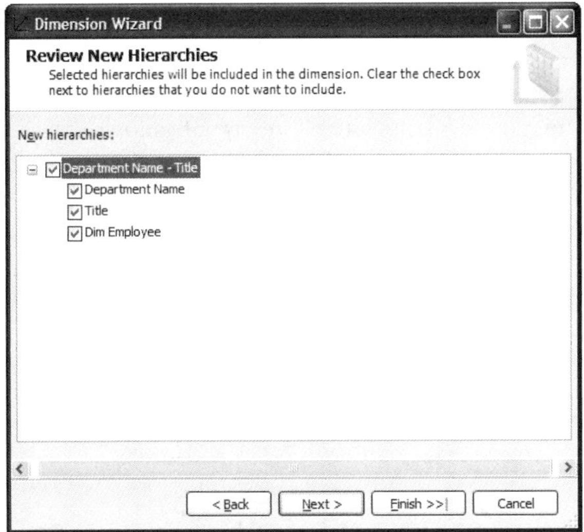

Figure 3.21 The Dimension Wizard can detect useful multilevel hierarchies.

The Dimension Wizard has discovered one-to-many relationships among the department name, employee title, and employee name. Indeed, they form a useful navigational path that allows the end-user to drill down data by Department, Title, and Employee levels. Unfortunately, you don't have an option to rename the hierarchy levels. This has to be done in the Dimension Designer.

12. Accept the wizard's recommendation and click Next to proceed to the last step.

13. In the *Completing the Wizard* (Figure 3.22) step, review the dimension structure and name the dimension **Employee**. Click Finish to complete the wizard flow. The Dimension Wizard generates the dimension definition and opens the Employee dimension in the Dimension Designer.

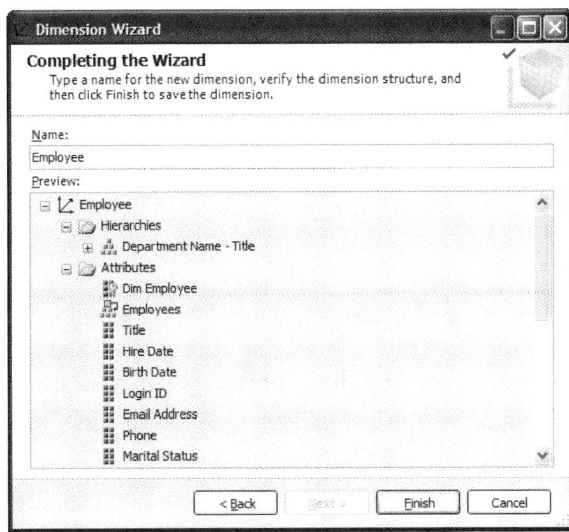

Figure 3.22 Use the Completing the Wizard step to review and name the dimension

3.3.3 Introducing the Dimension Designer

You can edit existing dimensions by using the *Dimension Designer* (see Figure 3.23). The Dimension Designer features a tabbed user interface consisting of three tabs. Use the *Dimension Structure* tab to architect your dimensions. To support international users, use the *Translations* tab to define localized versions for attribute and multilevel hierarchy names. The *Browser* tab allows you to browse the dimension hierarchies and members.

Understanding the dimension structure

Assuming that you have completed the Dimension Wizard steps, the Employee dimension definition will be loaded in the Dimension Designer.

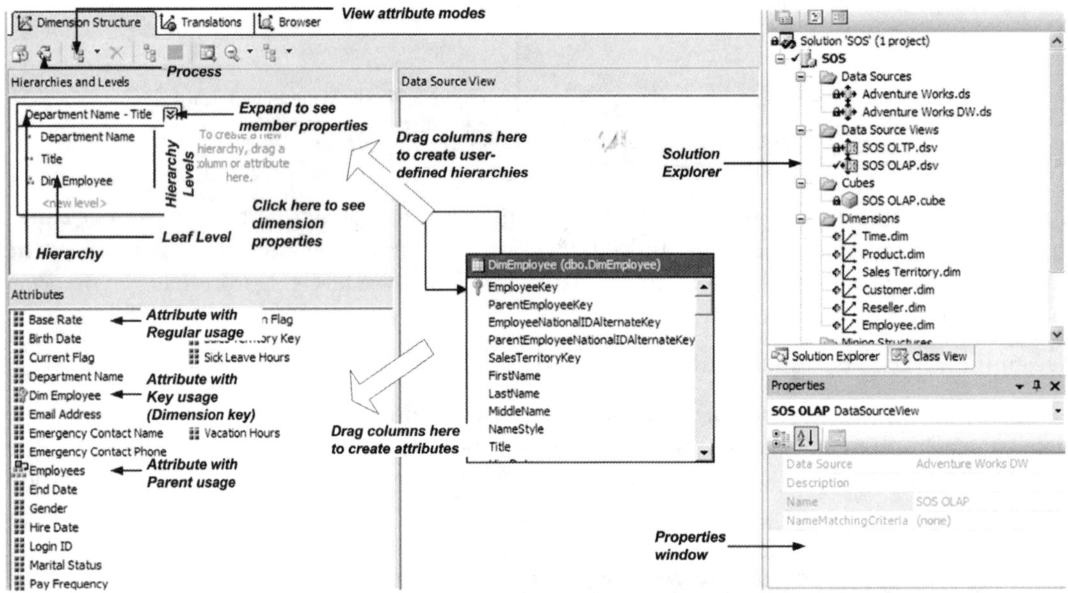

Figure 3.23 Use the Dimension Designer to edit the dimension structure, process, and browse dimensions.

Data Source View pane

This pane shows a read-only subset of the DSV tables used by the loaded dimension. If you need to add (show) a table from the underlying DSV (e.g. to create a snowflake-type dimension), right-click on empty space in the diagram and choose the *Show Tables* context menu. Next, choose the table(s) from the Show Tables dialog. Similarly, to exclude a table from the cube DSV, right-click on the table and choose *Hide Table*.

To see only the tables used by the cube dimensions and measures, right-click on an unoccupied place in the DSV diagram and choose *Show Only Used Tables*. If you need to makes changes to the DSV schema, you need to use the DSV Designer that could be launched by right-clicking anywhere on the Data Source View pane and choosing the *Edit Data Source View* context menu.

Attributes pane

The Attributes pane contains the entire list of attributes defined in the dimension. You can add, remove, and change attributes. Attributes can be created by dragging column from the dimension tables shown in the Data Source View pane to the Attributes pane. The Attribute pane supports three view modes which can be changed by clicking on the *View Attribute* toolbar button. The default mode is View Attributes As List. Use the *View Attributes as Tree* mode to view and create member properties. Use the *View Attributes as Grid* mode, to view various attribute properties in a grid format, including the attribute bindings, usage, and type.

As we've instructed the Dimension Wizard, the role of the dimension key in the Employee dimension is fulfilled by the Dim Employee attribute. The parent-child hierarchy is represented by the Employees attribute which has a Parent usage. The rest of the attributes have Regular usage. If you need to promote other columns to attributes, you can drag them from the tables shown in the Data Source View.

1. Click on the Dim Employee dimension key to select it in the Attributes pane. Note that, in the Properties window, its key (KeyColumns property) is bound to the EmployeeKey column, while its name (NameColumn) is derived from the FullName column. The attribute key column(s) is used to identify the qualifying members of the Employee attribute.

Viewing member properties

2. Click on the *View Attributes as Tree* toolbar button to view the member properties associated with a given attribute.
3. Select the *Dim Employee* dimension key attribute. By default, the Dimension Designer promotes all columns in the same table as the member properties of the dimension key (see Figure 3.24). This tells UDM that all attributes are related to each other through the key attribute.

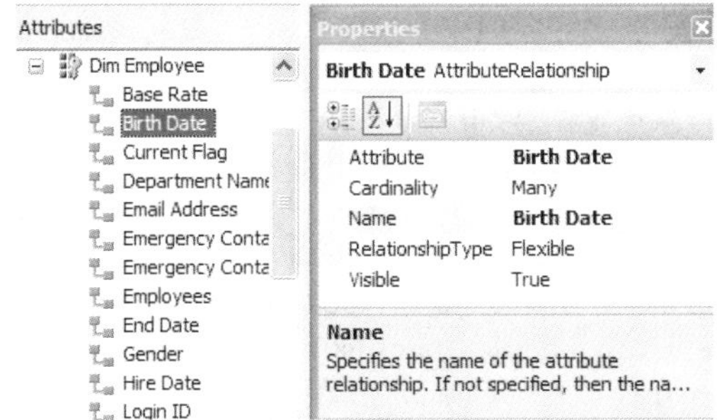

Figure 3.24 Member properties decorate attribute members and define known relationships.

4. Besides decorating the attribute members, member properties can be used to define known relationships among attributes forming levels in multilevel hierarchies. Click on the *Birth Date* member property. By default, the Dimension Designer sets the properties of a member property to the values shown in Figure 3.24.

In chapter 4, we will see how we can work with member properties to define specific types of relationships. For example, the relationship between an employee and the employee's birth date is one-to-one and it won't change over time. Knowing this, we could and should further optimize UDM by setting the Cardinality property to *One* and the RelationshipType property to *Rigid*.

Hierarchies and Levels pane

This pane enables the user to create multilevel hierarchies by dragging and dropping attributes from the Attributes pane or columns from the Data Source View pane. In the first case, you create multilevel hierarchies from existing attributes. The latter approach creates dimension attributes first and then starts a new multilevel hierarchy. In the case of the Employee dimension, the Dimension Wizard has created the *Department Name-Title* multilevel hierarchy. You can expand a multilevel hierarchy to see member properties associated to the level attributes.

Deploying and processing dimensions

Before we can browse a dimension, we must deploy its definition file to the SSAS database. In addition, you need to process the dimension to load it with data. Before initiating the dimension deployment, let's take a moment to verify the project deployment settings.

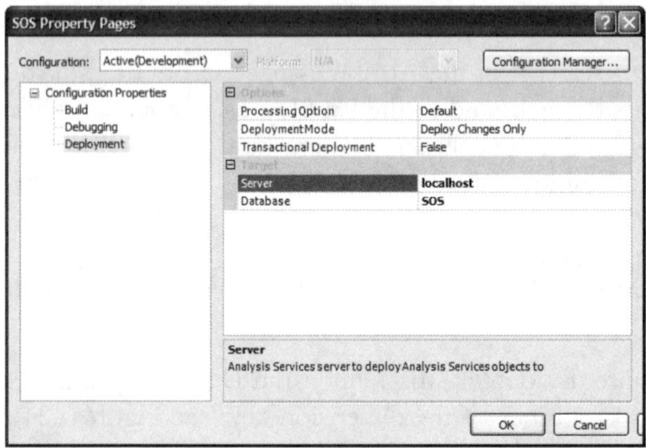

Figure 3.25 The project deployment properties specify how the cube and dimensions will be deployed and processed.

1. In Solution Explorer, right-click on the SOS project and choose Properties. Select the Deployment mode (Figure 3.25) and verify the project deployment properties.

The *Processing Option* setting should be set to *Default*. In this way, we put the dimension processing in auto-pilot mode by letting the server choose the best processing option based on the dimension structural changes. The *DeploymentMode* setting should be set to *Deploy Changes Only*. The Analysis Server can perform deployment changes within the scope of transaction. For example, we may want to roll back changes to both the Internet Sales and Reseller Sales measure groups if the deployment process results in an error. Since transactional deployment is more expensive, the default option is *False*. Finally, verify the target deployment server (*localhost* if deploying to your local SSAS instance) and database name (should be *SOS*).

You can process the affected objects by deploying the project or by clicking on the Process toolbar button. The first approach will deploy and process the objects in one step. The latter approach gives you more control by keeping these two steps separate.

2. Process the Employee dimension by clicking the Process toolbar button.
3. If the Dimension Designer detects structural changes, it will prompt you to deploy the project before proceeding with the dimension processing. Click OK to confirm. This will cause BI Studio to generate a deployment script and send it to the Analysis Server. BI Studio shows the overall deployment progress in the Output window, while the detail steps are shown in the Deployment Progress window.
4. Once the deployment process is finished, the Process Object(s) dialog is shown (Figure 3.26).

If the Dimension Designer detects structural changes to the dimension definition, it defaults the process mode (Process Options column) to *Process Full*. When a dimension is fully processed, its dimension stores are discarded and rebuilt again. As a result, not only the dimension structure is updated, but the dimension is re-loaded with data.

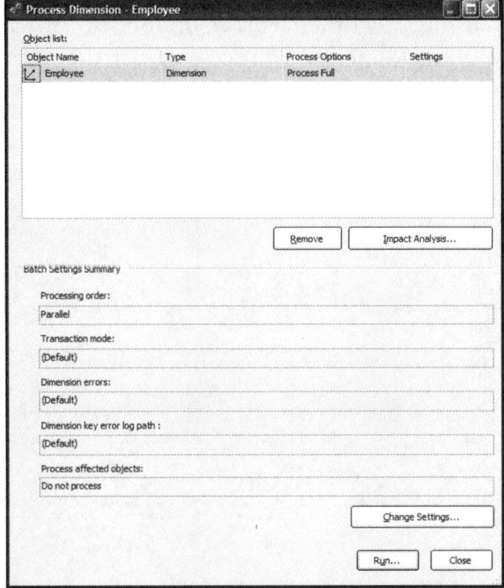

Figure 3.26 Use the Process Object(s) dialog to tell the sever how to process the object.

If there are no structural changes, the Dimension Designer sets the processing mode to *Process Update*. This processing option reads all the dimension rows and applies their changes made to the dimension members. New members are added, deleted members are removed, and existing members are updated if the underlying rows have changed.

Tip You can select multiple objects in the Solution Explorer and process them at the same time. Use the Change Settings button to instruct the server to process the selected objects sequentially or in parallel (default setting).

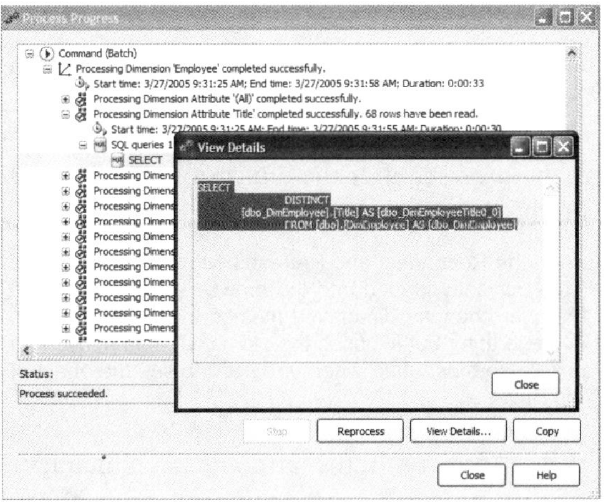

Figure 3.27 Use the Process Progress dialog to monitor and troubleshoot dimension processing.

Click on the Impact Analysis button to find out which objects will be affected and need to be re-processed after the dimension is processed. For example, if structural changes have been made to a dimension and the dimension processing option is set *Process Full*, all measure groups that this dimension is added to need to be reprocessed. However, if there are no structural changes and you just need to refresh the dimension data by using the *Process Update* option, no other objects will be affected. This is all you need to know about dimension processing for the time being. For more detailed discussion about object processing refer to chapter 15.

5. Click the Run button to start dimension processing. The Dimension Designer displays the Process Progress dialog (Figure 3.27) which is similar to the BI Studio Deployment Progress window.

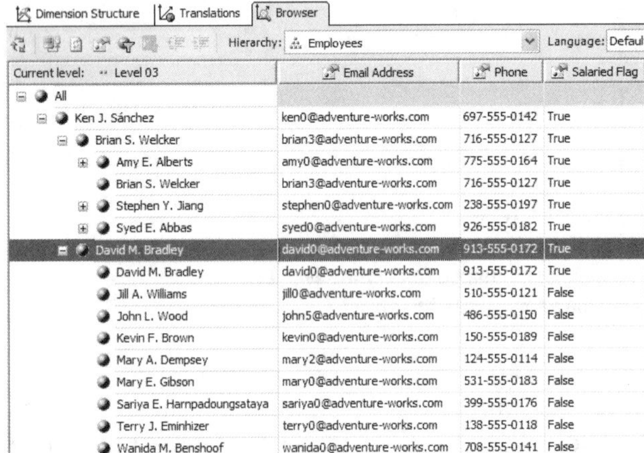

Figure 3.28 Use the Browser tab to browse attribute and multilevel hierarchies.

For each attribute, the Dimension Designer prepares and submits a SQL SELECT DISTINCT statement and sends it off to the data source to retrieve the attribute members based on the attribute key column. You can double-click on the SQL statement or choose *View Details* to see the entire statement in the View Details window. Sit and watch as the Analysis Server processes dimension attributes. In case things go wrong, error messages are reported in red.

Browsing dimensions

If all is well, the dimension will be processed successfully and can be browsed. To browse the dimension hierarchies, flip to the Browser tab (Figure 3.28) in the Dimension Designer. You can process a dimension from the Browser tab by clicking on the Process toolbar button. The Dimension Designer doesn't automatically refresh the browser after the dimension is processed. To see the results of dimension processing, click on the Reconnect button.

Note You may wonder what the difference is between the Reconnect and Refresh buttons. **Refresh** does not drop the server connection and re-reads the data currently loaded into the browser. Refreshing data could be useful for write-back dimensions when the user changes dimension members and you need to see the effect of the changes. **Reconnect** does the same thing but it closes the old server connection and opens a new one. Reconnect will be the option you will use most often when you need to see the effect of dimension processing. The same applies to the Cube Browser.

1. Expand the Hierarchy dropdown and notice that it lists both the attribute and multilevel hierarchies. As Figure 3.28 shows, I have selected the Employees parent-child hierarchy. Notice

that because the dimension members are linked to each other, you can keep on expanding the members until a leaf member is reached (an employee that doesn't have subordinates).

2. Click on the Member Properties toolbar button. Select the Email Address, Phone, and Salaried Flag member properties and click OK. The Dimension Browser refreshes and shows the selected member properties.

3. Expand the Employees hierarchy to Level 04 and select an employee associated with that level, e.g. Amy E. Alberts. Let's find all members whose names start with "B". Click on the Filter Members button to bring up the Filter Members dialog (Figure 3.29).

4. The Filter Members dialog is context-sensitive in respect to the hierarchy level selected and the Property dropdown shows only the member properties associated with that level. Expand the Property dropdown and select the *Name* property. Change the Operator to *Begins with* and enter **B** in the Value column. Click the Test button to execute the filter.

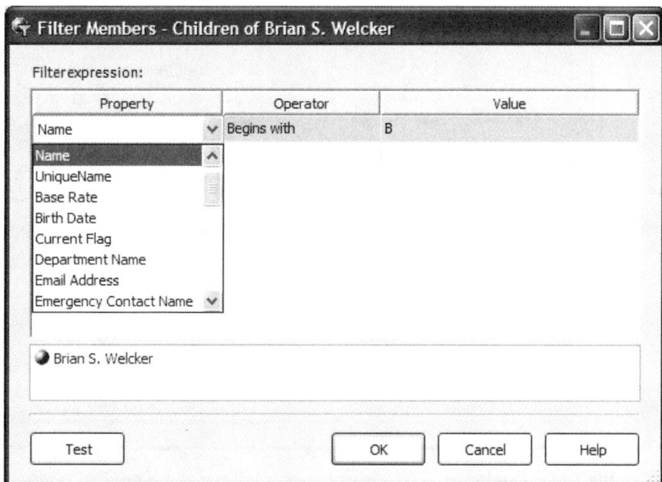

Figure 3.29 Use the Filter Members dialog to find dimension members by searching on the member properties.

3.3.4 Introducing the Cube Designer

As a UDM designer, you will spend most of your time using the Cube and Dimension designers. Once the dimensions are created, you can use the Cube Designer to define the cube structure. In the Solution Explorer, double-click on the SOS OLAP cube top open it in the Cube Designer. The Cube Designer has an intuitive user interface consisting of several tabs. The tabs are laid out in the order in which you would typically implement the UDM layers listed in chapter 1 (section 1.3.3).

When designing the dimensional model, you will probably spend most of your time using the Cube Structure and Dimension Usage tabs. As its name suggests, the Calculations tab is where you will define your MDX calculations. Next, you implement end-user analytics features using the KPIs, Actions, Perspectives, and Translations tabs. If you decide to set the cube management settings using BI Studio, you can do so by using the Cube Structure and Partitions tabs. Finally, you can browse the cube data by using the Browser tab. In this chapter, we will work only with the Cube Structure, Dimension Usage, and Browser tabs.

Understanding the cube structure

The Cube Structure tab (Figure 3.30) employs the multi-pane layout, familiar by now, to help you set up various cube, measure groups, and dimension settings.

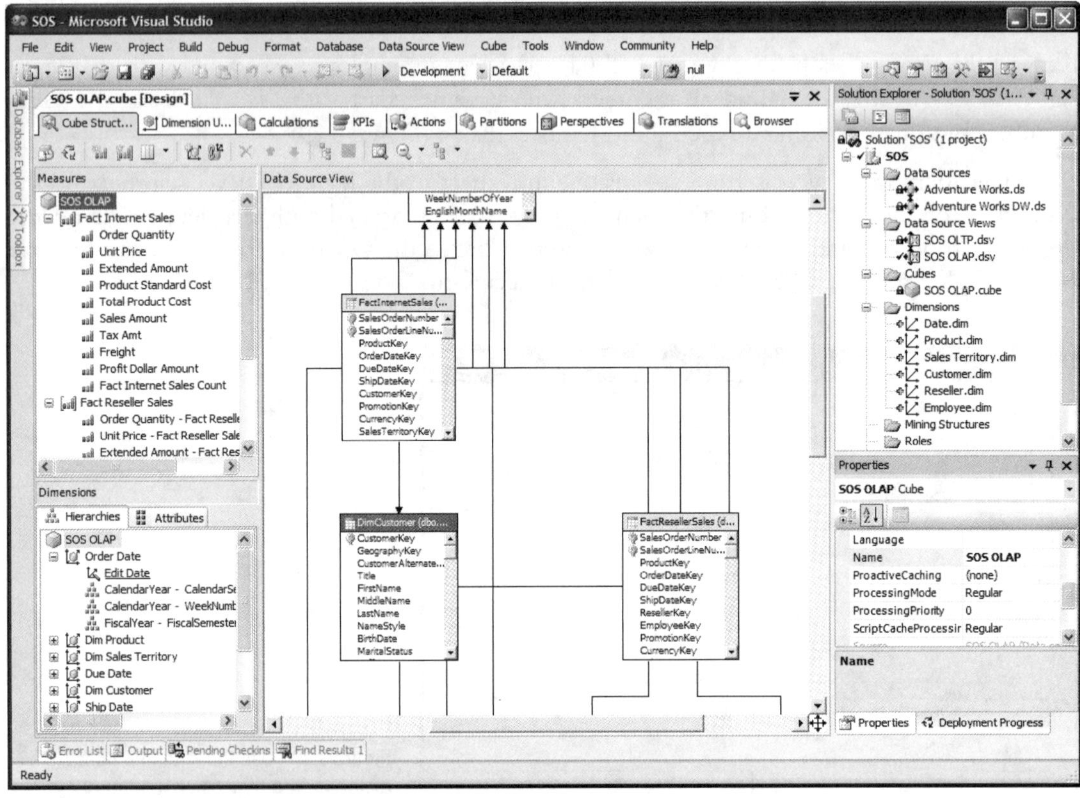

Figure 3.30 The raw SOS OLAP cube displayed in the Cube Designer.

The cube data source view

Similar to the Data Source View pane of the Dimension Wizard, the cube Data Source View pane shows the subset of the DSV tables that the cube uses. From a functionality standpoint, the cube DSV is very similar to the DSV Designer, so I will mention only some of its new features. Since a large "super-cube" may span many tables, the Cube Designer supports a tree view to show a compacted list of the cube tables. To see the DSV tables in a tree view, right-click on an empty spot of the DSV diagram and choose *Show Data Source View in* ➪ *Tree*, or click on the Show Tree View toolbar button. Finally, if you need to define a given fact column as a measure, right-click on the column and choose the "New Measure from Column" context menu.

Cube measures

Recall that measures become part of the cube definition. Therefore, there isn't a separate designer for working with measures. Instead, you create new measures or edit existing ones using the Measure pane (Cube Structure tab) of the Cube Designer. Since we've selected only two fact tables in the Select Measure step of the Cube Wizard (see again Figure 3.13), we have only two measure groups, *Fact Internet Sales* and *Fact Reseller Sales*. Each measure group contains ten measures.

Click on a few measures in the Measures pane and observe in the Properties window that the *AggregateFunction* of all measures is set to *Sum*, which is the most common aggregate function in OLAP. Note that the measure data type (*DataType* property) is inherited from the underlying columns to which the measure is bound, as specified by the Source column. The only exception is the last measure in each measure group (Sales Count), which is automatically generated by the Cube Wizard. It uses row binding to count the number of individual order items.

Cube dimensions

The Dimension pane lists the dimensions used by the cube. As you would notice, the Employee dimension that we've created using the Dimension Wizard is not listed. That's because dimensions are independent of the cube definition. A dimension could be added or removed from a cube at any time and its definition can be shared by more than one cube within the same or external SSAS database. Let's add the Employee dimension to the SOS OLAP cube since it can be used by the end users to browse sales data by sales person.

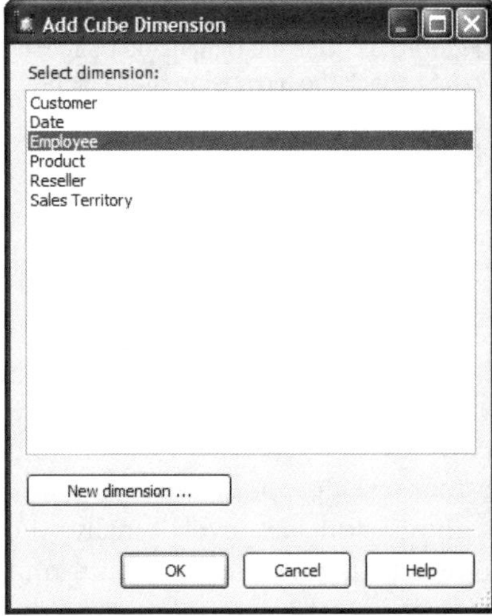

Figure 3.31 Use the Add Cube Dimension dialog to add existing or new dimensions to the cube.

1. Right-click anywhere inside the Dimension pane and choose *Add Cube Dimension*. The Add Cube Dimension dialog appears (see Figure 3.31). If you need to create a brand new dimension, you can do so by clicking on the "New dimension" button. This will launch the Dimension Wizard. Once the dimension is created, it will be added to the cube.

2. Select the Employee dimension and click OK.

You may be confused as to why the Cube Structure Dimensions pane shows different dimension names than the Solution Explorer pane, especially given the fact that we've explicitly renamed the dimensions. The reason for this is that, when the Cube Wizard created the dimensions, it stored the original dimension names in the cube definition. The Cube Designer doesn't automatically synchronize the dimension names when they are subsequently changed.

3. To "fix" this, rename the cube dimensions in the Dimensions pane (double-click slowly on the dimension name or right-click and choose *Rename*) by removing the "Dim " prefix from the dimensions that have it. Click the Save All toolbar button to persist the changes.

4. Another oddity is that the Dimension pane lists eleven dimensions while there are only six dimensions in the Solution Explorer. To understand what's going on, flip to the Dimension Usage tab of the Cube Designer (see Figure 3.32).

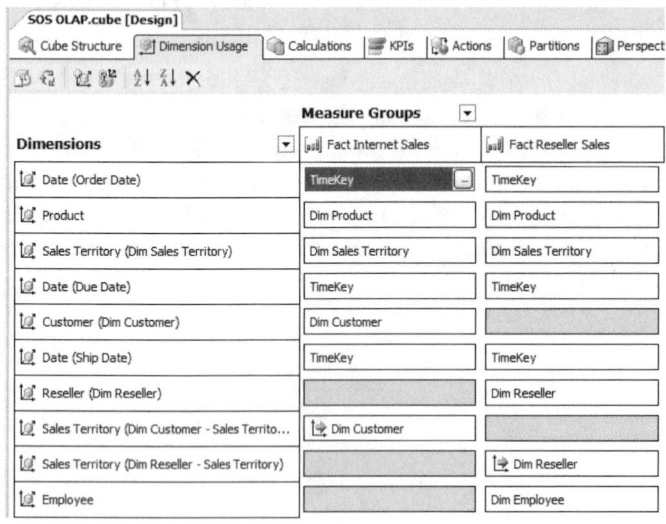

Figure 3.32 Use the Dimension Usage tab to check the dimension-to-measure group traceability, define dimension roles, and the grain at which a dimension joins a measure group.

Dimension usage

The Dimension Usage tab is one of my favorite Cube Designer features. It is a very well-designed multi-purpose screen. First, it shows the dimension-to-measure traceability matrix. By quickly glancing at the matrix, you can tell easily which measure group is related to a given dimension. For example, the Date (Order Date) dimension is joined to both measure groups, while the Customer dimension is not applicable to Fact Reseller Sales.

Second, it specifies the grain at which a dimension joins a measure group. For example, the Date (Order Date) dimension joins the measure groups at a dimension key level. Finally, the Dimension Usage tab allows you to specify the dimension role by clicking on the "…" button in the intersecting cell. Hovering the mouse over the matrix intersecting cells gives you all of the dimension information in the form of a tooltip. Follow these steps to link the Employee dimension to the Fact Reseller Sales fact table.

5. Click on the "…" button inside the cell located at the coordinates of the Employee dimension and Fact Reseller Sales measure group. The Define Relationships dialog is shown (Figure 3.33).

The Select relationship type dropdown should be set by default to *Regular*. Note that the Granularity attribute defaults to the dimension key (DimEmployee). This is correct because the Employee dimension will join the fact table at that level. In the Relationship grid, notice that the DimEmployee table and the FactResellerSales table are related by EmployeeKey.

Role-playing dimensions

Upon unraveling the dimension proliferation dilemma, we realize that the reason why the Dimensions pane lists so many dimensions is because we have two role-playing dimensions (Date and Sales Territory). Each fact table includes three dates (order date, due date, and ship date). All of the three date columns are served by only one Date dimension which plays different roles. By now seasoned dimensional modelers probably start to appreciate the UDM capabilities.

If you had to address the same requirement with SSAS 2000, you had to use separate dimensions (probably based of SQL views). This led to duplication of definition and storage. In SSAS 2005, the Analysis Server handles role-playing dimensions natively.

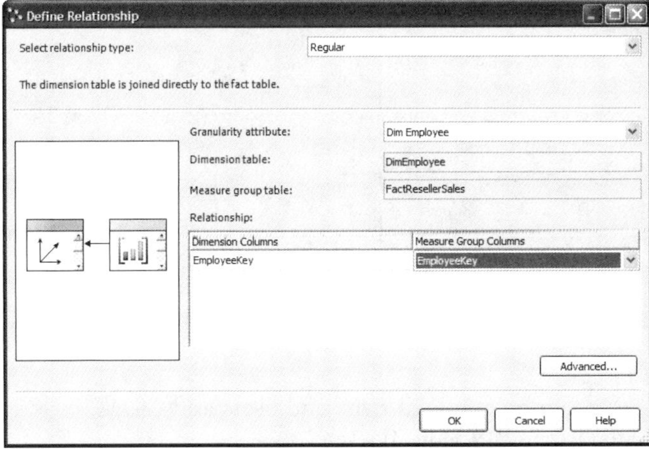

Figure 3.33 Use the Define Relationships dialog to link a dimension to a measure group.

You can use the Dimensions pane to see the dimension multilevel hierarchies (Hierarchies tab) and attributes (Attribute tabs). Expanding a dimension and clicking on the Edit tab brings the Dimension Designer where you can edit the dimension.

Deploying and processing the cube

Our SOS OLAP dimensional model is far from complete, but let's finish our introduction to the Cube Designer by finding out what the preliminary cube would look like from end user perspective. Before the user can browse the cube, we need to deploy and process the cube. BI Studio performs both actions when you deploy the project from the BI Studio environment.

1. In Solution Explorer, right-click on the SOS project mode and choose *Deploy*. This will cause BI Studio to first build the project in order to generate a deployment script.

Note When you deploy an Analysis Services project, BI Studio asks the server to process all UDM objects with *ProcessDefault* option. The server keeps track of which objects have changed and processes only the modified objects. In other words, the BI Studio deployment process is driven by the structural changes, not by data changes. As you can imagine, there is no processing option that can detect changes to the data source data. Therefore, if need to refresh the dimension or cube data, you need to process the object explicitly with ProcessFull or ProcessUpdate options because just deploying the project may not refresh the object data.

If there are any definitions errors, they will be displayed in the Errors window and build process will be interrupted. The object processing sequence is shown in the BI Studio Output window. Next, BI Studio sends send the deployment script to the Analysis Server. Note that BI Studio shows the overall deployment progress in the Output window, while the detail steps including the SQL SELECT statements are shown in the Deployment Progress window. If all is well, the cube deployment process will complete with *Deployment Completed Successfully* message displayed in the Deployment Progress window.

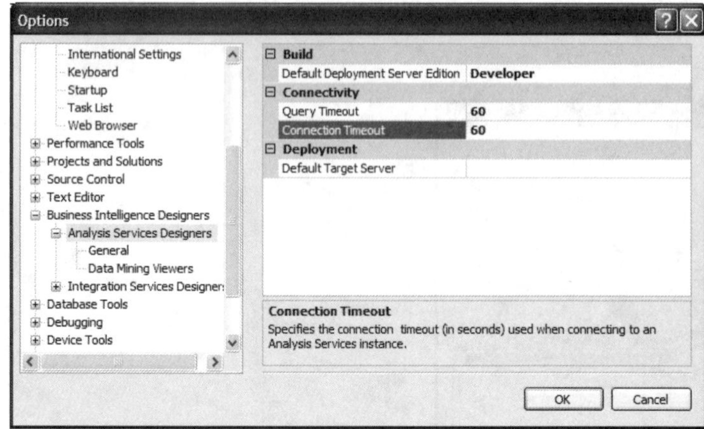

Figure 3.34 Use the Options dialog to control connection and query timeouts.

Browsing the cube

Once the cube is deployed and processed, it can be queried by the end users and OLAP browsers. Use the Browser tab to browse the cube in the BI Studio IDE.

Controlling the connection and query timeouts

When you flip to the Browser tab, the Dimension and Cube Designers establish a connection to the Analysis Server to send queries. You can control the connection and query timeouts from the BI Studio *Tools* ⇨ *Options* menu (see Figure 3.34). You can also specify the default target SSAS machine for new Analysis Services projects.

Creating PivotTable reports

The Browser tab (Figure 3.35) is powered by the pivot table OWC control, which is part of the Office Web Components (OWC) version 11 that we met in chapter 1. Unfortunately, the Office team has not upgraded OWC to support the new UDM features and enhancements. For example, OWC is unaware of the fact that UDM dimensions are now containers of attribute and dimension hierarchies. To get around the OWC limitations, the Analysis Services team has built a layer on top of on the OWC in the form of the Metadata pane. In addition, UDM perspectives (discussed in chapter 12) can be used to provide more restricted views of the cube data.

The Metadata pane organizes neatly the cube dimensions and measures in logical folders similar to the Cube Structure tab. For example, observe that the cube measures are grouped in the two folders that correspond to the cube measure groups. Let's build a simple report that shows sales broken down by the Product dimension on rows and Date dimension on columns. If you make a mistake and want to clear the pivot table report click on the Clear Result toolbar button.

1. Drag the Product dimension from the Metadata pane and drop onto the *Drop Row Fields here* area of the pivot table component. Alternatively, right-click on the Product dimension and choose *Add to Row Area*. UDM defaults to the first multilevel hierarchy in the selected dimension. In our case, we have only one multilevel hierarchy (Product Category) which gets added to the pivot table row area. Note also that the Dim Product Category level displays numeric values instead of the category names because, by default, it uses the attribute key for the member names.

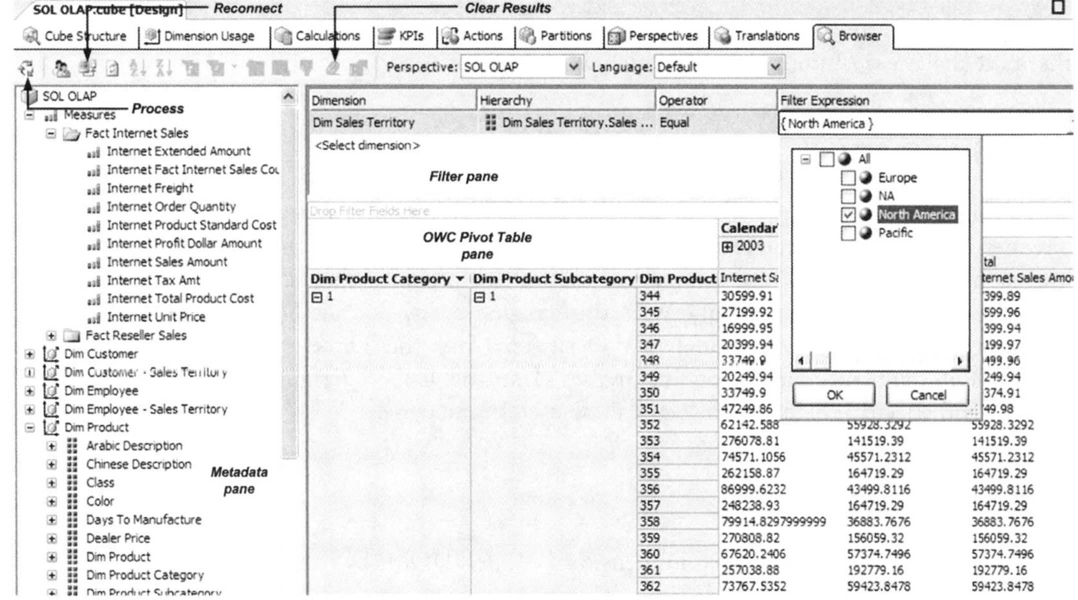

Figure 3.35 The raw SOS OLAP cube displayed in the Cube Designer.

2. Drill down the Product Category hierarchy by expanding the Dim Product Category level. Notice that the members of the lower levels of the Product multilevel hierarchy show the attribute key values too. This behavior is probably not what end users would expect from an intuitive OLAP reporting system so we need to fix it when refining our UDM in the next chapter.

3. Drag the Order Date dimension from the Metadata pane and drop onto the *Drop Column Fields here* area of the pivot table component. Alternatively, right-click on the Order Date dimension and choose *Add to Column Area.*

4. Drag some measures (e.g. Internet Sales Amount and Reseller Sales Amount) to the "Drop Totals or Detail Fields here" area of the pivot table. Observe that the measures are not formatted as currencies and this represents another potential improvement area. By default, the Cube Browser displays only dimension members that have data. If you want to see all dimension members, click on the Show Empty Cells toolbar button.

5. The Cube Browser supports filtering. Let's filter our report to show data for North America only. In the Metadata pane, expand the Sales Territory dimension and its Group level ([Sales Territory].[Sales Territory Group]).

6. Right-click on North America (Figure 3.35) and choose the *Add to Subcube area* context menu. The report is refreshed and shows data for North America Only. Experiment with various filter operators to apply different filters.

Note Why does the Cube Browser support two filtering options (pivot table filtering and filter pane)? To support more efficient filtering, SSAS 2005 introduced the CREATE SUBCUBE MDX statement. Since the OWC has not been upgraded, it is unaware of the subcube feature. OWC has its own filtering performed when a dimension is dropped on the *Drop Filter Fields here* area. When the filter pane is used, the Cube Browser creates a sub-cube and applies it to the OWC connection.

As you continue browsing the cube from different dimensions, you will undoubtedly discover other potential areas of improvement which we will address in chapter 4.

3.4 Summary

The UDM dimension model consists of measures organized across dimensions. A dimension is a container of attributes, hierarchies, and member properties. Attributes are the building blocks of dimensions and may form attribute and multilevel hierarchies. The attribute-based hierarchies define the cube space. Use the Cube Wizard to create quickly the raw UDM. Next, refine UDM by leveraging the Cube and Dimension Designers. Use the Dimension Designer to define attribute and multilevel dimension hierarchies. Use the Cube Designer to set up the UDM measures and specify which dimensions will be used in the cube.

3.5 Resources

Introduction to the Unified Dimensional Model (UDM) by Paul Senders
(http://shrinkster.com/891) – This paper provides an introduction to the Unified Dimensional Model (UDM), including the basic end-user model, and a brief overview of the architecture and security models.

UDM: The Best of Both Worlds by Paul Senders
(http://shrinkster.com/892) – Another great introductory article that discusses how UDM unifies the relational and dimensional models.

Chapter 4

Working with Dimensions and Measures

The BI Studio cube and dimension wizards go a long way to jumpstart the UDM implementation process and minimize the amount of tedious groundwork involved in creating dimensions and measures. The cube and dimension designers start where the wizards left off. With the help of the designers, you can refine your UDM dimension model and custom-tailor it to meet your specific OLAP requirements. In this chapter, we will leverage the Dimension Designer to enhance existing dimensions and create new dimensions. In addition, we will use the Cube Designer to refine measures generated by the Cube Wizard and create new measures and measure groups. You will learn:

- How to create attribute and multilevel hierarchies.
- How to implement more advanced hierarchies, such as parent-child, ragged, and discretization hierarchies.
- How to create standard and server Time dimensions.
- How to work with measures and measure groups.

By exercising the BI Studio designers through various scenarios, we will expand both the real-time and historical dimensional models we've introduced in the preceding chapter. As you would recall, we left the real-time UDM in chapter 2 with only the DSV layer implemented, while in chapter 3, we used the cube and dimension wizards to create the raw historical UDM. Up till now, for our convenience both historical OLAP (SOS OLAP cube) and real-time OLAP (SOS OLTP cube) UDMs have been hosted in a single SSAS database.

4.1 Working with Standard Dimensions

Having the historical and real-life UDMs in the same SSAS database could lead to duplication of UDM objects because each UDM needs to target a different data source. Moreover, in real life, operational and security requirements will most likely mandate that you separate the two models. Let's start this chapter by splitting the SOS database into two databases (projects) – SOS OLAP and SOS OLTP. As an added bonus, this exercise will help you practice working with projects in BI Studio.

4.1.1 Separating the Historical and Real-time UDMs

To separate the historical and real-time UDMs, we need to create a new project that will host the real-time UDM objects only by following these steps.

1. Copy the entire SOS project to another Windows folder, e.g. *SOS OLTP* folder.
2. Open the project you've just copied in BI Studio. In the Solution Explorer, click on the project node (SOS) and rename it to **SOS OLTP**.
3. Delete the Adventure Works DW data source, SOS OLAP data source view, SOS OLAP cube, and all dimension definition files. The only definition files that you need are the Adventure Works data source and the SOS OLTP data source view.
4. Open the original SOS project and rename it to **SOS OLAP**.
5. Remove the real-time objects (the Adventure Works data source and the SOS OLTP data source view) from the SOS OLAP project.
6. Optionally, add either of the two projects to the solution containing the other project, so you can have both projects in the same solution.

To save you time, I included the starting solution for this chapter (Ch04 Start.sln) in the Start Solution folder. The finished SOS OLAP and SOS OLTP projects can be loaded by opening the Ch04.sln solution. First, let's focus on extending the historical UDM. Open the SOS OLAP project that contains the raw historical UDM. With the help of the cube and dimension wizards in chapter 3, we built six standard dimensions. Specifically, we have one star-schema dimension (Sales Territory), two snowflake-schema dimensions (Customer and Product), one server-based time dimension (Date), and one parent-child dimension (Employee). Let's now refine the raw dimensions starting with the Sales Territory star-schema dimension.

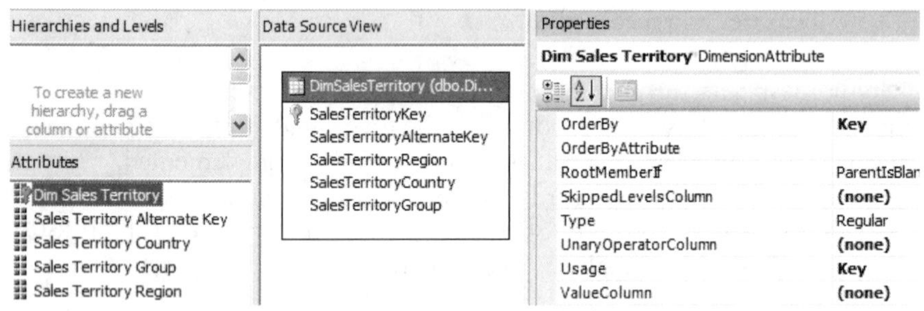

Figure 4.1 The raw Sales Territory dimension.

4.1.2 Configuring Attributes

The Sales Territory dimension is as simple as a dimension can get. It is a star dimension based on a single dimension table (DimSalesTerritory) that defines a common geographical hierarchy consisting of Group (e.g. North America), Country (e.g. United States), and Region (e.g. Southeast) levels. As simple as the Sales Territory dimension is, it will help us to demonstrate many of the dimension concepts we discussed in the preceding chapter.

Double-click on the Sales Territory.dim file in the Solution Explorer to open the Sales Territory in the Dimension Designer and note the attributes in the Attributes pane (Figure 4.1).

By default, the Cube Wizard promotes all table columns to attributes. The role of the dimension key in the Sales Territory dimension is fulfilled by the Dim Sales Territory attribute which is bound to the primary key (SalesTerritoryKey column) of the DimSalesTerritory dimension table. The rest of the attributes are regular attributes because their Usage property is set to Regular.

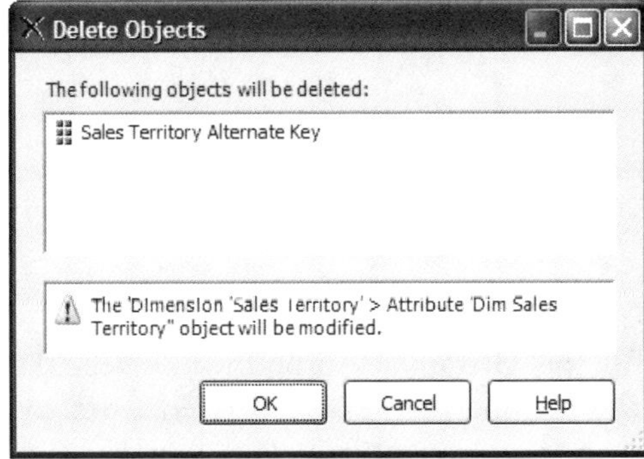

Figure 4.2 To reduce clutter and optimize UDM, review and delete the attributes you don't need.

Removing attributes

To optimize UDM storage and performance, you should remove the attributes you don't need.

1. The Sales Territory Alternate Key doesn't convey any useful information to the end users. Select it and press the Delete key to remove it. The Dimension Designer displays the Delete Objects dialog (Figure 4.2). The dialog warns you if the attribute to be deleted is related to other attributes. In our case, the Dim Sales Territory dimension key will be affected only because the Sales Territory Alternate Key is defined as its member property. Click OK to confirm.

As noted, the Cube Wizard promotes all columns in the dimension table to attributes. Sometimes, this is redundant. For example, the members of the Sales Territory Region attribute return the region names. This is definitely a useful attribute and a good candidate for an attribute hierarchy. However, as noted in chapter 3, an attribute can have distinct key and name bindings. In section 4.1.3, we will bind the Sales Territory Region to the NameColumn property of the dimension key (Dim Sales Territory).

2. To avoid redundancy, select and delete the *Sales Territory Region* attribute as well.

Renaming attributes

To make the attribute names more user-friendly, the Cube Wizard automatically delimits the words with a space. This happens if the column name follows the title case naming convention where the first letter of each word is capitalized, e.g. **S**ales**T**erritory. This is not a bad naming convention but we can do better. You can rename an attribute in-place in the Attributes pane or by changing its *Name* property in the BI Studio Properties window.

1. Select the Dim Sales Territory attribute and change its name to **Region**.
2. Rename Sales Territory Country to **Country** and Sales Territory Group to **Group**.

4.1.3 Configuring Attribute Hierarchies

By default, the Cube Wizard and Dimension Wizard set up each attribute to form an attribute hierarchy with an empty *NameColumn* property. As a result, the attribute member names will be derived from the attribute key values. You need to review these bindings against your requirements and make changes as needed.

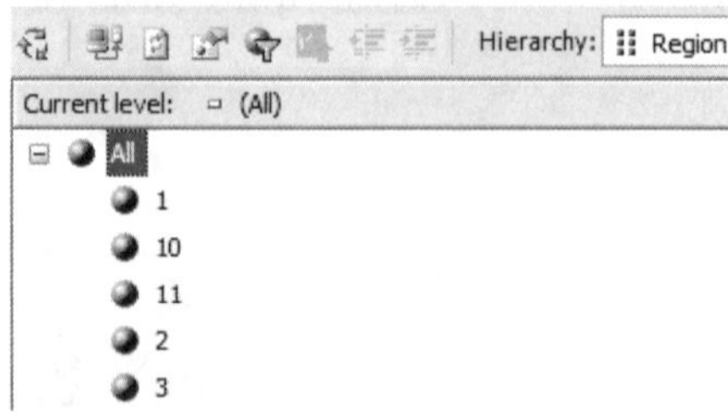

Figure 4.3 By default, the member names are derived from the attribute key binding.

Defining member names

Process and browse the Sales Territory dimension. In the Hierarchies dropdown, select the *Region* attribute hierarchy (Figure 4.3). Observe that the member names are derived from the SalesTerritoryKey column as opposed to showing the actual region names. This is unlikely to make your end users happy, so let's define a descriptive name to the dimension key by binding its NameColumn property to the *SalesTerritoryRegion* column.

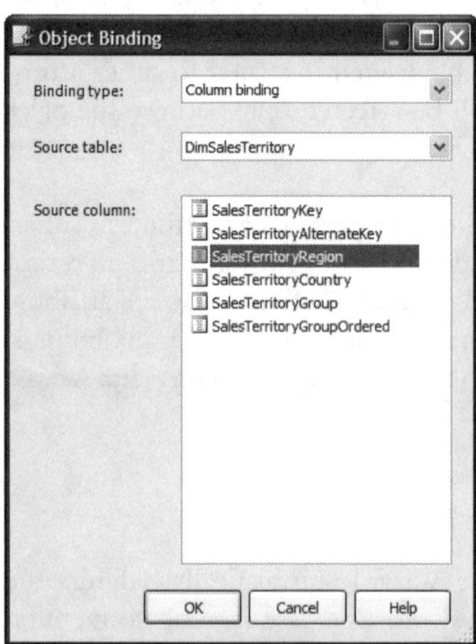

Figure 4.4 Use the Object Bindings dialog to bind to a column that supplies the member name.

1. Select the Region attribute in Attribute pane. Note that its *NameColumn* property is set to *(none)*. In the absence of an explicit name binding, the member names will be derived from the attribute key column (SalesTerritoryKey).
2. Expand the NameColumn property and select *(new)*. The Object Binding dialog appears (Figure 4.4).
3. Select the SalesTerritoryRegion column and click OK. As Figure 4.5 shows, the members of the Region hierarchy will be identified based on the attribute KeyColumns (SalesTerritoryKey), while their names will be derived from the NameColumn (SalesTerritoryRegion).

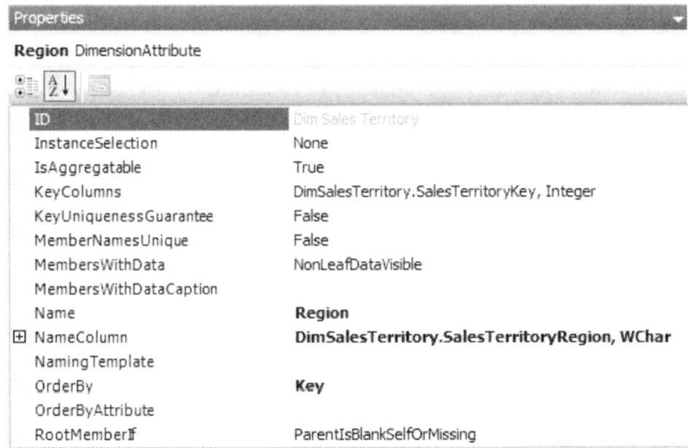

Figure 4.5 An attribute can have different key and name member bindings.

4. Process and browse the Sales Territory dimension. Click the Reconnect toolbar button to retrieve the new dimension changes. Request the Region hierarchy again and note that now the members show the region names.

Defining member properties

By default, the Cube Wizard adds all dimension attributes as member properties of the dimension key attribute. When you create a new attribute, e.g. by dragging a column from the DimSalesTerritory table and dropping it to the Attributes pane, the Dimension Designer automatically assigns the attribute as a member property to the dimension key. That's because each table column has a one-to-one relationship with the dimension key, e.g. a product has color, size, name, etc. attributes.

As I pointed out in the preceding chapter, for better performance and data analytics reasons, you need to spend some time reviewing and making changes to the member properties. For example, when member properties are properly defined, Analysis Services can use an aggregation from one attribute to obtain the results from a related attribute in a multilevel hierarchy. The easiest way to work with member properties is to change the view mode of the Attributes pane to tree.

1. Click on the *View Attributes as Tree* toolbar button. Expand the Sales Territory tree in the Attributes pane. Observe that both Country and Group attributes are defined as member properties of the dimension key. We will leave the Country member property because it correctly represents the one-to-many relationship between the region and country attributes.

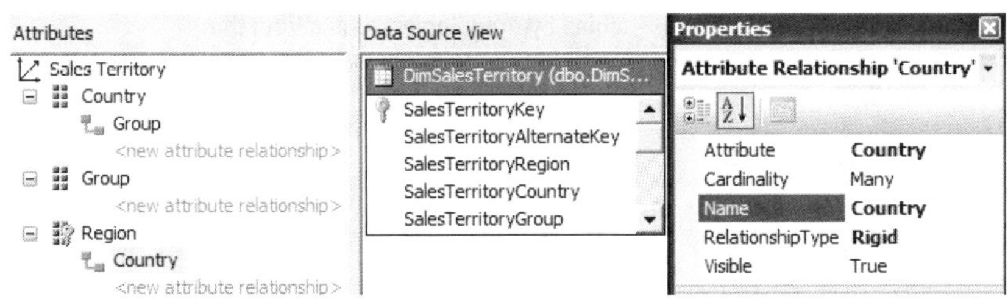

Figure 4.6 Appropriately defined member properties inform UDM about known relationships among attributes.

2. Unless the user requirements call for displaying the Group attribute as a member property of Region members, there is no good reason to keep it. Delete the *Group* member property.

3. In the next section, we will create a multilevel natural hierarchy that will represent a logical navigational path (Group ⇨ Country ⇨ Region levels). To inform UDM about the one-to-many relationship between the Group and Country levels, drag the Group attribute and drop it to the <*new attribute relations property*> placeholder of the Country attribute. The Sales Territory tree should look like the one shown in Figure 4.6.

4. Let's assume that the Country-Region relationship is fixed. In other words, the values of SalesTerritoryCountry column in the DimSalesTerritory table will not change over time (a region cannot be assigned to another country). We can optimize UDM further by defining the attribute relationship as rigid. Select the Country member property of the Region attribute and, in the Properties window, change its RelationshipType to *Rigid*.

By default, the name of the member property is identical to the source attribute it is based on. However, as shown in Figure 4.6, the *Attribute Relationship* object has a Name property which can be used to override the default name of the member property.

Note MDX has intrinsic member properties for each attribute e.g. *Name*, *UniqueName*, Key, etc. Hence, you cannot use reserved words for the name of the member property. When the Cube Wizard and Dimension Designer detect a reserved word, they automatically append _ suffix to the member property. If this is unacceptable, instead of renaming the source attribute, you can override the name of the member property in the AttributeRelationship object.

4.1.4 Creating a Multilevel Hierarchy

Each of the Country, Group, and Region attributes forms its own attribute hierarchy because their AttributeHierarchyEnabled property is set to *True* by default. These attributes also imply a useful multilevel hierarchy for drilling down the Group ⇨ Country ⇨ Region navigational path. Follow these steps to create the Sales Territory multilevel hierarchy.

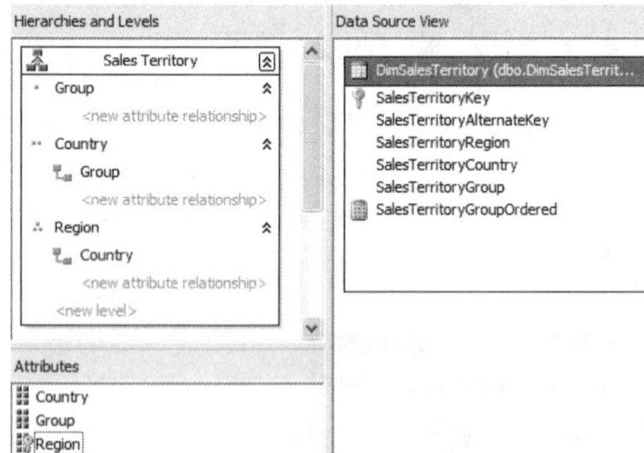

Figure 4.7 Form multilevel hierarchies by dragging attributes from the Attributes pane or columns from the Data Source View pane to the Hierarchies and Levels pane

To create a multilevel hierarchy, you can drag an attribute from the Attributes pane or a table column from the Data Source View pane to the Hierarchies and Levels pane. The latter approach will create the attribute first and then add it to the multilevel hierarchy. The highest hierarchy level in our Sales Territory hierarchy will be represented by the Group attribute.

1. Switch to View Attributes as Grid view mode.

2. Drag the *Group* attribute from the Attributes pane and drop it to the Hierarchies and Levels pane. A new multilevel hierarchy is created with a single level represented by the Group attribute.

3. By default, the Dimension Designer names the new multilevel hierarchy *Hierarchy*. Double-click slowly on the hierarchy header and change in-place the hierarchy name to **Sales Territory**.

4. Create the second hierarchy level by dragging the Country attribute and dropping it below the Group attribute. Note that the Dimension Designer prefixes the Country level with two dots to denote that it is a subordinate of the Group level.

Tip Dimension Designer is capable of detecting various error conditions when a new level in a multilevel hierarchy is created. For example, it knows that a dimension key can form only a leaf level. If the Dimension Designer determines that the level is incorrect, it marks it with a jagged red line. To view a tip that describes the problem, move the mouse pointer over the marked level.

5. Create the leaf level by dragging the Region attribute and dropping it below the Country level. The expanded Sales Territory multilevel hierarchy should look like the one shown in Figure 4.7.

6. Process and browse the Sales Territory dimension. Reconnect. Now, the Hierarchy dropdown should default to the Sales Territory multilevel hierarchy. It should look like the one shown in Figure 4.8.

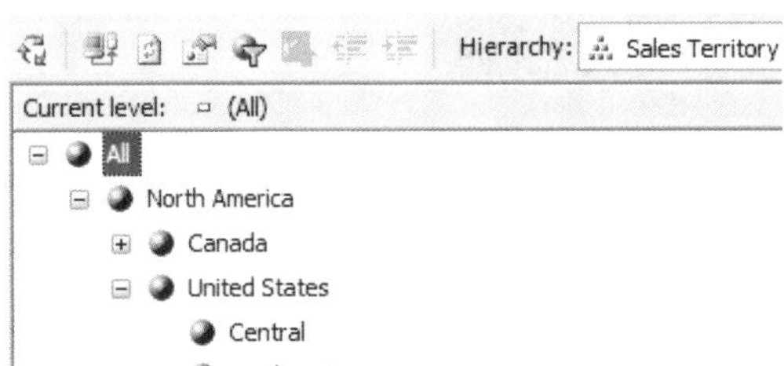

Figure 4.8 The Sales Territory multilevel hierarchy

4.1.5 Defining the Hierarchy Top Member

As you know by now, in UDM, a dimension is a container of attributes, hierarchies, and member properties. You can review and set some global dimension properties by clicking on an empty space in the Hierarchies and Levels pane and using the BI Studio Properties window. One property you may need to change is *AttributeAllMemberName*. SSAS automatically generates a top (All) level for attribute and multilevel hierarchies. As I explained in chapter 1, the (All) level has a single member named by default *All* (see Figure 4.8) that gives us the total aggregated value of the values of all members in the hierarchy.

Note To hide the (All) level for an attribute hierarchy, set the attribute *IsAggregatable* property to *False*. In this case, an attribute hierarchy will have only one level (the member level) and can be added only to the root level of a multilevel hierarchy.

For multilevel hierarchies, the *All* member name can be specified on a hierarchy basis by selecting the hierarchy and changing the AllMemberName property. Attribute-based hierarchies don't have AllMemberName property. Instead, you can set a global *All* member name that applies to all attribute hierarchies by setting the dimension-level *AttributeAllMemberName* property. Let's make the name of the *All* level member of the hierarchies in the Sales Territory dimension more descriptive by changing it to **All Sales Territories**.

1. In the Hierarchies and Levels pane, select the Sales Territory multilevel hierarchy. In the Properties window change the *AllMemberName* property to **All Sales Territories**.
2. Click on an empty space in the Hierarchies and Levels pane to see the dimension-level properties. In the Properties window, change the *AttributeAllMemberName* property to **All Sales Territories**.
3. Process and browse the dimension. Observe that both the Sales Territory multilevel hierarchy and the three attribute hierarchies have their top member displayed as All Sales Territories (see Figure 4.9).
4. Optionally, deploy the SOS OLAP cube and, in the Cube Browser, create a report to browse data by the Sales Territory dimension. Notice that OWC ignores the *All* member name we've just defined. Instead, it shows the *All* member as *Grand Total*.

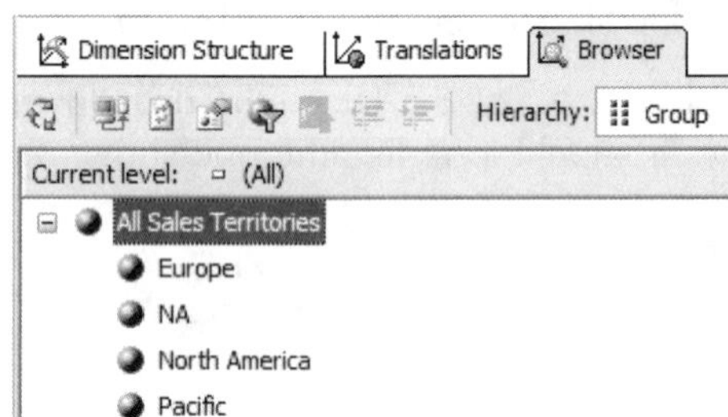

Figure 4.9 By default, UDM sorts attribute members by the attribute name in an ascending order.

4.1.6 Sorting Attribute Members

By default, UDM orders the attribute members by the attribute name. That's because the attribute OrderBy property binding is set by default to *Name*. To see the effect of the default order settings, process the Sales Territory dimension and flip to the Browser tab. In the Hierarchy dropdown, select the Group attribute hierarchy (Figure 4.9). The members of the Group attribute hierarchy are sorted in ascending order by their name because the NameColumn of the Group attribute is set to SalesTerritoryRegion. If it is the attribute key that we want to sort on (SalesTerritoryKey), we can change the OrderBy property of the Group attribute to Key.

Note When the Analysis Server processes a dimension, it orders the attribute members according to the OrderBy settings. If attribute ordering is not important, you can speed up the attribute processing by setting the *AttributeHierarchyOrdered* property to *False*.

But what if we need to sort the attribute names in a custom-defined order? For example, suppose that we would like to list the North America member first. Luckily, UDM supports sorting attribute members by using another attribute whose members define the specific order.

Creating a named calculation for sorting

1. In our case, the DimSalesTerritory table doesn't include a column that can be used for sorting. Instead of creating a new table column, we will define a DSV named calculation. Open the SOS OLAP data source view and locate the DimSalesTerritory table.
2. Create a new named calculation called SalesTerritoryGroupOrdered that is based on the following expression:

```
CASE SalesTerritoryGroup
    WHEN 'North America' THEN -1
    ELSE SalesTerritoryKey
END
```

The net effect of the above expression is to create an "artificial" key that will put the North America member on top. Save the SOS OLAP data source view.

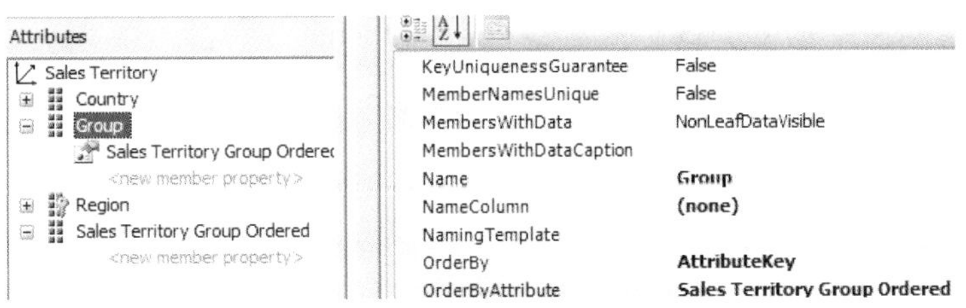

Figure 4.10 To sort attribute members by another attribute, set the OrderBy and OrderByAttribute properties.

3. To create a sorting attribute derived from the SalesTerritoryGroupOrdered column, drag the SalesTerritoryGroupOrdered column from the DSV diagram to the Attribute pane. A new attribute Sales Territory Group Ordered is created and it is automatically added as a member property of the Region attribute.

Configuring the sorting attribute

To sort by an attribute, the sorting attribute must be related to the attribute whose members you need to sort. In other words, the sorting attribute must be defined as a member property. Switch to View Attributes as Tree mode and add the Sales Territory Group Ordered attribute as a member property of the Group attribute.

1. Select the Group attribute. Change its OrderBy property to *AttributeKey*.
2. Expand the OrderByAttribute dropdown and select the Sales Territory Group Ordered attribute (see Figure 4.10).

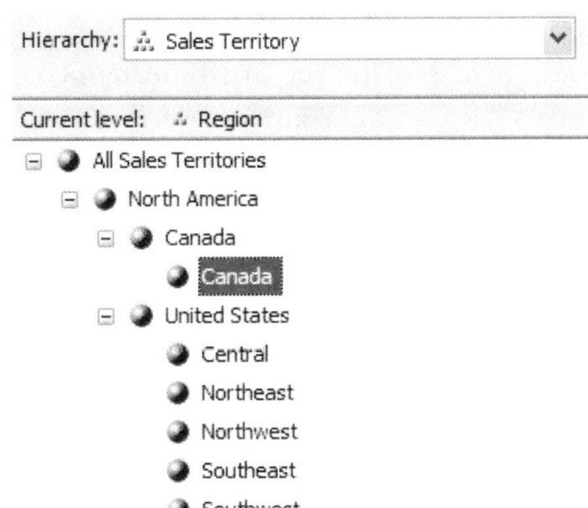

Figure 4.11 The Sales Territory hierarchy with custom sorting.

3. Process and browse the Sales Territory dimension.
4. In the Browser tab, select the Group hierarchy in the Hierarchy dropdown. Observe that North America is now the first member below the All Sales Territories top member (Figure 4.11).

Using the Business Intelligence Wizard

The Business Intelligence Wizard is designed to automate routine tasks, including attribute ordering. If you find the custom attribute ordering steps tedious, consider using the Business Intelligence Wizard to review and change the way the dimension attributes are ordered in one easy pass. To order the attributes of the Sales Territory dimension:

1. If the Sales Territory dimension is open in the Dimension Designer, click on the *Add Business Intelligence* toolbar button to launch the BI Wizard. Alternatively, right-click on the dimension in the Solution Explorer pane, and choose *Add Business Intelligence* context menu.
2. In the *Choose Additional Functionality* step, select *Specify attribute ordering* and click Next to advance to the *Specify Attribute Ordering* step (Figure 4.12).

Figure 4.12 Use the BI Wizard to set up custom attribute ordering in a single pass.

Once you know how attribute ordering works, you will probably appreciate the convenience the BI Wizard offers. The *Available attributes* grid shows all dimension attributes and their currently defined ordering options. You can change the Criteria column to sort by the attribute name or key. Or, you can choose the Ordering Attribute column to select another attribute for custom ordering.

Disabling attribute hierarchies

Not all attributes can form useful hierarchies for end-user analytics. For example, if we leave the Sales Territory Group Ordered attribute as it stands, its attribute hierarchy will be accessible to the end users, but it will show meaningless members derived from the SalesOrderGroupOrdered column. To make an attribute hierarchy not accessible to the end users, we have two choices.

First, we can choose not to create the attribute hierarchy at all by setting the attribute *AttributeHierarchyEnabled* property to *False*. A disabled hierarchy is invisible to the end users. The downside is that an attribute with a disabled hierarchy cannot be used to form a level in a multilevel hierarchy. If this is needed, you can keep the attribute hierarchy (AttributeHierarchyEnabled = True) but hide it by setting the attribute AttributeHierarchyVisible property to *False*. This hides the attribute from the end users, but the attribute hierarchy can still be used to form multilevel hierarchies or to be queried by MDX expressions. Let's disable the attribute hierarchy of the SalesOrderGroupOrdered attribute because it is used for member sorting only.

1. Select the Sales Territory Group Ordered attribute and set the *AttributeHierarchyEnabled* property to *False*. Observe that the Attributes pane grays out the attribute icon to signify that the attribute will not produce an attribute hierarchy.
2. As a further optimization step, set the *AttributeHierarchyOrdered* to *False*.
3. Set the *AttributeHiearchyOptimizedState* property to *NotOptimized* to instruct the Analysis Server not to build indexes during attribute processing.

4.2 Implementing Advanced Hierarchies

In UDM, you can group attributes in flexible ways to form different types of attribute and multilevel hierarchies. Let's discuss some of the most common analytics requirements you may face when working with hierarchies.

4.2.1 Creating Ragged Hierarchies

Under normal circumstances, members of the same level in a hierarchy have the same number of members above them. For example, every member of the Month level in our Calendar Date multilevel hierarchy always has Quarter, Semester, and Year members above it. Such hierarchies are called *balanced*. Sometimes, balanced hierarchies may get in the way. For example, as you can see by glancing at Figure 4.11, only the United States has regions. The rest of the countries have duplicated Country and Region members. Users may find this redundant and tedious. Instead, let's create a ragged hierarchy by hiding the Region members when they have the same name as the parent member (Country).

1. In the Hierarchies and Levels pane select the *Region* level of the Sales Territory hierarchy. Change its *HideMemberIf* property to *OnlyChildWithParentName*. This instructs the Analysis Server to hide a Region level member when it is the only child of a Country level member and its name is the same as its parent. In the Sales Territory multilevel hierarchy, the same effect can be achieved by choosing the *ParentName* option which hides a member if it has the same name as the parent *regardless* of the number of children.
2. The Sales Territory dimension table includes a *NA* record that ETL processes can use to link fact records whose regions cannot be successfully resolved to a known region. If you would like to suppress duplicated Group and Country members with the same *NA* name, select the Country level and set its *HideMemberIf* property to *OnlyChildWithParentName*.

> **Note** In real life, you may want to keep all dimension members visible (including members with incomplete data) to avoid confusion.

3. Process and browse the Sales Territory dimension. Observe that now the Sales Territory hierarchy is ragged and there are no parent and child members with the same name.

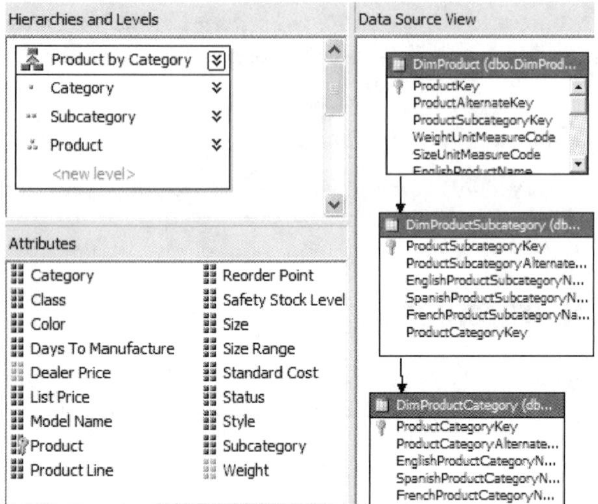

Figure 4.13 The Product dimension has a snowflake schema consisting of the three tables.

4.2.2 Implementing Multiple Hierarchies

In UDM, a dimension can have as many multilevel hierarchies as needed. Let's switch to the Product dimension to demonstrate this. The Product dimension is based on a snowflake data schema that spans three tables. When analyzing the database schema, the Cube Wizard has identified a single multilevel hierarchy called Dim Product Category – Dim Product Subcategory. Each level in this hierarchy represents a table from the snowflake dimension schema.

The role of a dimension key is fulfilled by the Product attribute which uniquely qualifies the rows of the Product Table. Table DimProductSubCategory is represented by the Subcategory attribute, while table DimProductCategory is represented by the Category attribute. The Cube Wizard has promoted all columns from the three snowflake tables to attributes. However, some columns aren't that useful for data analytics. Before creating multilevel hierarchies, let's spend some time reviewing and fine-tuning the dimension attributes.

Note If the Dimension Designer discovers the absence of member properties that define mandatory attribute relationships, it underlines the affected attributes with a jagged red line. For example, while the Dimension Designer knows how to relate attributes in a star dimension, it doesn't know how to do so in a snowflake dimension. If you hover on top of the line, you will see the message "The attribute <attribute name> is not related (directly on indirectly> to the '<attribute name' key attribute." displayed in a tooltip. If you build the Analysis Services project at this point, the build will not succeed and several build errors (as the one shown above) will appear in the Output window. To fix this issue, you need to define relationships among these attributes in the form of member properties.

Identifying attributes

For example, while the locale-specific attributes (French Product Name, Spanish Product Name, etc.) can be used for localizing the member names, it is unlikely that the end users will be interested to browse the standalone attribute hierarchies formed. After deleting the insignificant attributes and renaming the rest, the Product dimension definition looks like the one shown in Figure 4.13. I've disabled the attribute hierarchies of the Dealer Price and Weight attributes because their values are continuous and not that useful for end-user analytics.

Creating multiple hierarchies

Upon exploring data in DimProduct category, we could identify other useful hierarchies besides the Category-Subcategory-Product hierarchy that the Cube Wizard has created. For example, a multilevel hierarchy can be created with the Product Line, Model Name, and Product levels. Note that the leaf level of a multilevel hierarchy doesn't have to be formed by the dimension key attribute (Product). Follow these steps to create the Product by Product Line hierarchy with Product Line and Model Name levels only.

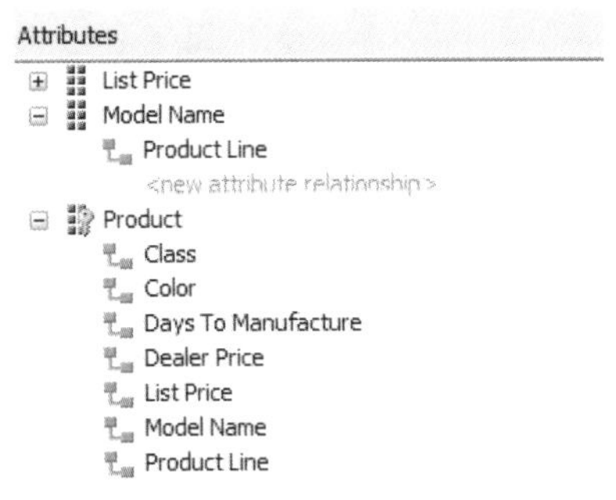

Figure 4.14 Member properties define one-to-many relationships among the attributes that form multilevel hierarchies.

1. Review the member properties of the Product attribute (Figure 4.14). If the Model Name member property is absent, drag and drop the Model Name attribute to the <new attribute relationship> placeholder of the Product attribute. We need the Model Name to be defined as a member property of the Product attribute to tell UDM that products roll up to product models. Set the Cardinality property of the Model Name member property to *Many* because one model may encompass more than one product.
2. The Product Line member property is not needed at the Product attribute level in respect to constructing the new hierarchy and can be deleted. However, it must be defined as a member property of the Model Name attribute because models are rolled up to product lines. Again, its Cardinality property should be set to *Many*.
3. Follow similar steps as in section 3.1.3 to create the *Product by Product Line* hierarchy (see Figure 4.15).

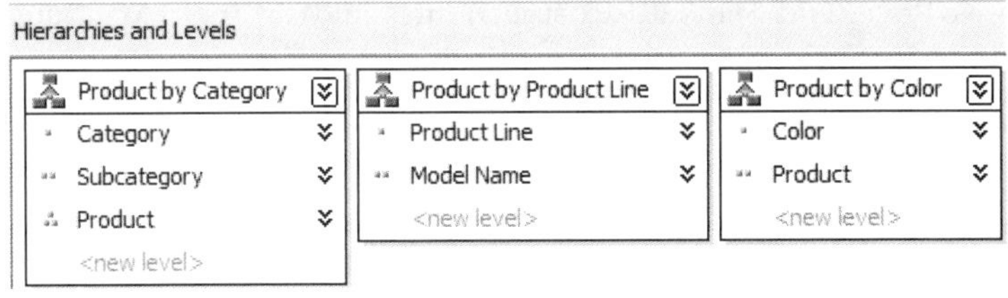

Figure 4.15 Attributes can be combined in flexible ways to create multilevel hierarchies.

4. Optionally, identify and create additional multilevel hierarchies. For example, a multilevel hierarchy can be formed by the Color and Product attributes to allow end-users to drill-down data by the product color.

Ordering hierarchies

The positional order (left to right), in which the hierarchies are placed in the Hierarchies and Levels pane, is significant. The first hierarchy in the order is the default hierarchy for queries that do not specify a hierarchy explicitly. For example, if in the Cube Browser you drag the Product dimension to the OWC PivotTable pane, it will default to the Product by Category hierarchy assuming that the product hierarchies are ordered as shown in Figure 4.15.

Note If a hierarchy is not explicitly requested, the Analysis Server picks up the first multilevel hierarchy. It doesn't default to an attribute hierarchy for performance reasons. An attribute hierarchy may have many members (e.g. the dimension key hierarchy) and may needlessly impact the query performance.

You can order the hierarchies in a particular way by dragging the title bar of the hierarchy you want to reorder and drop it to a new position on the Hierarchies and Levels pane. As you drag a hierarchy, a vertical bar appears to indicate the new position.

Organizing hierarchies in folders

To reduce clutter, you can group logically related attribute and multilevel hierarchies in folders just as you can save physical files in Windows folders. A UDM-aware OLAP browser can pick up these folder settings and organize hierarchies accordingly.

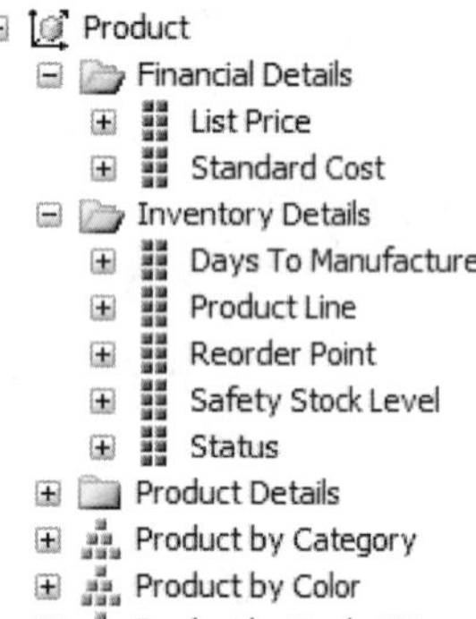

Figure 4.16 Organize logically related attributes in display folders for better user experience.

1. In the Attribute pane, select the Category, Class, Color, Model Name, Product, Size, Size Range, Style, Subcategory, and Weight attributes and set their AttributeHierarchyDisplayFolder property to **Product Details**.
2. Select the Days to Manufacture, Product Line, Reorder Point, Safety Stock Level, and Status attributes and set their AttributeHierarchyDisplayFolder property to **Inventory Details**.
3. Finally, select the Dealer Price, List Price, and Standard Cost attributes and set their Attribute-HierarchyDisplayFolder to **Financial Details**.
4. Deploy the project. Open the SOS OLAP cube in the Cube Designer and flip to the Browser tab. Observe that the Product dimension hierarchies are organized neatly in the display folders we've just created (see Figure 4.16). Note that the Dealer Price and Weight attributes don't show up because we disabled their attribute hierarchies (*AttributeHierarchyEnabled = False*).

Setting the dimension type

You can use the dimension Type property to specify the dimension semantics type. UDM understands the semantics of the Account, Currency, and Time dimension types only. The rest are for the OLAP browsers to inspect if they choose to do so. For instance, the OLAP client could change the dimension icon in accordance to its type. It so happened that there is a predefined Product dimension type so let's use it to let clients know that this is indeed a product-related dimension.

1. In the Dimension Designer, select the Product dimension.
2. Expand the Type dropdown property and select **Product**. You could also set the Type property of the Customer dimension to **Customers**.

Setting attribute default member

Each attribute has a default member. If a query doesn't request a given attribute hierarchy explicitly, the Analysis Server will use the default member of the attribute. A typical scenario where this is useful is the Time dimension. Often it makes no sense to see multiple years data aggregated together. Removing the *All* level and defining a default attribute member (for example the current Year) is a common practice.

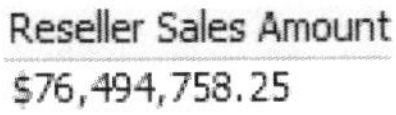

Reseller Sales Amount
$76,494,758.25

Figure 4.17 When an attribute is not explicitly requested, the default member will be used.

Suppose that you need to create a simple report that shows the grand total of the resale sales (Figure 4.17). The MDX query behind this report doesn't include any dimensions. However, the Analysis Server always retrieves cube cell values found at the intersection of all attributes (recall, that it is the attributes that define the cube space). In the absence of an explicitly defined default attribute member, the Analysis Server uses the attribute *All* member, which is the behavior you would typically need. For example, if the Product hierarchy is not explicitly requested, you would want to see the aggregated total for all products.

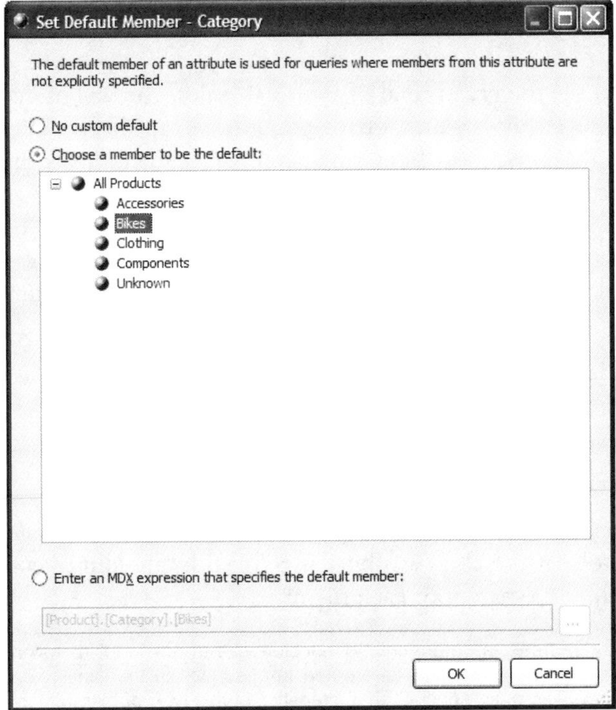

Figure 4.18 When an attribute is not explicitly requested, the default member will be used.

Sometimes, you may need to define a default attribute member explicitly. For example, suppose that, if the user doesn't request the Product dimension, you would like the query to default to the Bikes category. You can implement this requirement as follows:

1. Open the Product dimension in the Dimension Designer and select the *Category* attribute in the Attributes pane.
2. In the Properties window, click the **...** button inside the *DefaultMember* property to open the Set the Default Member dialog (Figure 4.18). You can define a default member by selecting a given member or by using an MDX expression.
3. Select the *Choose the member to be the default* option, expand the *All Products* hierarchy, and select *Bikes*. Note that the default member path in the MDX formula changes to *[Product].[Category].[Category].[Bikes]* which specifies the full path to the Bikes member of the Category attribute inside the Product dimension. Click OK to close the dialog

Note If the attribute key value is different than the attribute name, UDM will use the key. For example, if we were setting the default value for the Product attribute to the *Chain* member, the default member path will be [Product].[Product].[Product].&[559]. The ampersand here tells UDM to select the member by its key value. UDM favors the attribute key because it uniquely qualifies the attribute members.

4. Deploy the project and open the Cube Browser.

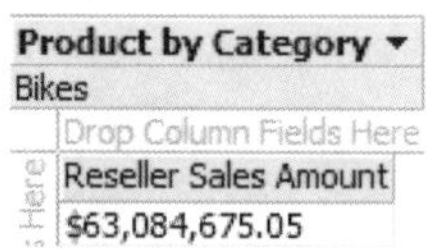

Figure 4.19 An explicitly defined default member acts as a query filter.

If you now browse the cube and request to see the grand total of the resale sales, you will notice that its value is now less than it used to be. To understand what's going on, drop the Product dimension to the report filter area. Notice that the report filter defaults to Bikes since this is the Product dimension default member (Figure 4.19).

As you could imagine, not using the *All member* as the default attribute member may be confusing to the end users. You will surely have some explaining to do as to why the sales numbers don't tally. For this reason, avoid setting explicitly the attribute default member unless you have a good reason to do so.

5. Going back to the Dimension Wizard, select the Category attribute and clear its *DefaultMember* property to revert to using the *All* member as a default member.

4.2.3 Working with Parent-child Hierarchies

A parent-child hierarchy is a hierarchy formed by two columns that define a recursive relationship among the hierarchy members. The role of the child attribute is fulfilled by the dimension key. An attribute with a Parent usage identifies the parent of each member.

SSAS 2000 In SSAS 2000, the only way to create a parent-child dimension was to run the Dimension Wizard. In SSAS 2005, the parent-child attribute hierarchy can be created from scratch in the Dimension Designer just like any other attribute hierarchy. The only "special" characteristics of this type of hierarchy is the presence of a parent attribute with a Usage type set to Parent.

Understanding parent-child hierarchies

Typical examples of parent-child hierarchies include organizational and employee hierarchies. The Employee dimension you created in chapter 3 contained a parent-child hierarchy defined between an employee and her manager. Double-click on the Employee dimension to open it in the Dimension Designer. As you would recall, what makes this dimension special is the Employees attribute which has Parent usage (Figure 4.20) that defines the recursive relationship.

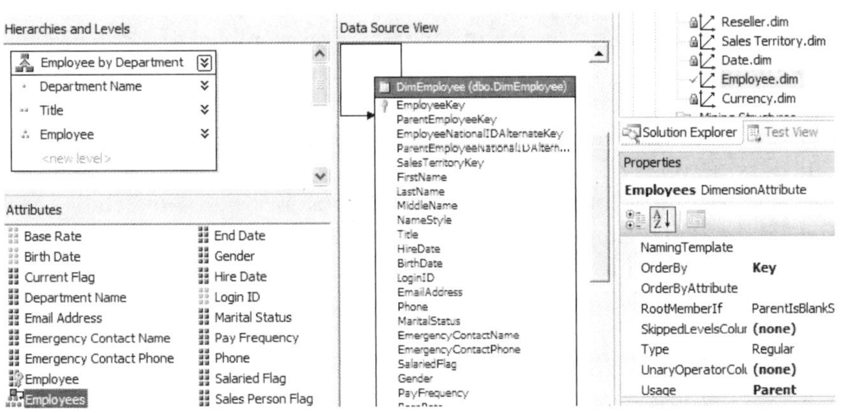

Figure 4.20 A parent-child dimension has an attribute with Parent usage.

1. Process and browse the Employee dimension. Select the Employees hierarchy in the Hierarchy dropdown (Figure 4.21).

2. Observe that the root node of the Employees hierarchy is named All Employees. That's because the dimension-level AttributeAllMemberName property is set to *All Employees*.

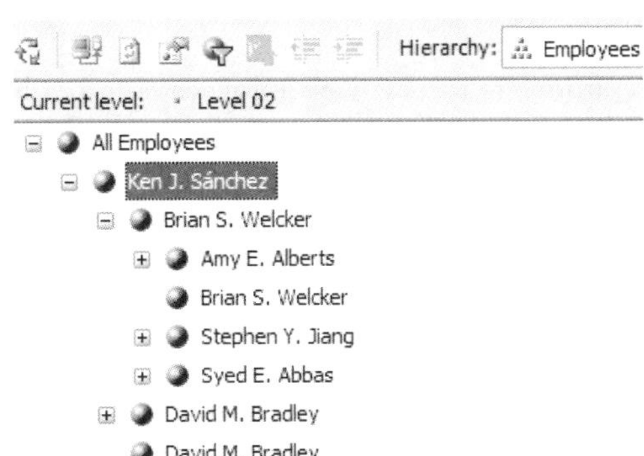

Figure 4.21 Members in a parent-child hierarchy have a recursive relationship.

3. Expand the All Employee node and note that Ken Sanchez forms the top level of the employee hierarchy because he is at the top of the organizational chart.

4. Back on the Dimension Structure tab, select the *Employees* attribute and note that its RootMemberIf property is set to *ParentIsBlankSelfOrMissing*. In the Data Source View pane, explore the data of the DimEmployee table. Locate the Ken Sanchez (EmployeeKey of 112) and note that his ParentEmployeeKey is set to NULL.

Note You may wonder why there are duplicated members in the Employees hierarchy (e.g. David Bradley appears twice). If you inspect the data in the DimEmployee table, you will see that it has duplicated records with different values in the Status column. The status of the most recent record is set to *Current*. The idea here is to demonstrate how a client application can inspect the status of a record in a changing dimension. Ideally, the UDM designer will set the Type property of the Start Date, End Date, and Status attributes to the predefined SCDStartDate, SCDEndDate, and SCDStatus types. Then, OLAP browsers could ask for the most recent members in the MDX queries. The same approach is demonstrated in the DimProduct table.

The RootMemberIf property tells UDM how to identify the top-level members of a parent-child hierarchy. If set to *ParentIsBlank*, UDM will promote all members to the top level that have NULL or zero values in their parent key column. *ParentIsSelf* will examine the values of the parent (ParentEmployeeKey) and child key (EmployeeKey) values. If they are the same, the member will be identified as a top-level member. If the RootMemberIf property is set to *ParentIsMissing*, a member will become a top-level member if no member with a matching child key is found. For example, if the ParentEmployeeKey of a member in the DimEmployee table is set to -1, that member will be promoted to a top-level member if *ParentIsMissing* is used. Finally, *ParentIsBlankSelfOrMissing* combines all these three conditions.

Removing the All level

1. Back to the Dimension Browser, click on Ken Sanchez to select it. Note that his hierarchy level is Level 02. That's because the employee hierarchy has an *All* level enabled. In our case, this is redundant because we have only one member (Ken Sanches) at the top level of the hierarchy.
2. Flip to the Structure tab, select the Employees attribute and change its IsAggregatable property to False. When doing so, make sure that you don't select the Employee dimension key attribute because it must be left aggregatable (IsAggregatable=True) since it forms the second level of the parent-child hierarchy.
3. Process and browse the Employees hierarchy again and notice that the All Employees member is gone and Ken Sanches is now at Level 01.

Level 01	Level 02	Level 03	Level 04	Reseller Sales Amount
⊟ Ken J. Sánchez	⊟ Brian S. Welcker	⊟ Amy E. Alberts	⊞ Amy E. Alberts	916051.860906834
			⊞ Jae B. Pak	5462192.57198848
			⊞ Rachel B. Valdez	1650763.59502623
			⊞ Ranjit R. Varkey Chudukatil	4466319.73830856
			Total	12495327.7662301
		⊞ Stephen Y. Jiang		63144531.0756333
		⊞ Syed E. Abbas		854899.413048955
		Total		76494758.2549124
	Total			76494758.2549124

Figure 4.22 Creating recursive reports is easy with parent-child dimensions.

A parent-child hierarchy is an odd type of hierarchy. A regular hierarchy has fact records linked to its leaf hierarchy members only. A parent-child hierarchy, however, may have fact records linked to members of any level because of the recursive relationship.

4. Deploy the project and open the SOS OLAP cube in the Cube Browser. In the Metadata pane of the Cube Browser, locate and expand the Employee dimension. Right-click on the Employees parent-child hierarchy and select the Add to Row Area context menu.

5. Expand the Measures node and then Fact Reseller Sales folder. Right-click on the *Sales Amount - Fact Reseller Sales* measure and select *Add to Data Area* context menu. Note that only employees that have associated data (sales persons) are shown in the report. To see all members in the Employees hierarchy, click on the Show Empty Sales button.

6. In the PivotTable pane expand Ken Sanchez, Brian Welcker, and Amy Alberts nodes (Figure 4.22). You can compare the sales performance by manager easily. For example, the team of Stephen Jiang is responsible for most sales. Ignore the lack of proper formatting of the Reseller Sales Amount. We will fix this shortly.

Configuring non-leaf members

Amy Alberts is repeated in both Level 04 and Level 05 columns. That's because Amy Alberts is a manager of Jae, Rachel, and Ranjit, but she also has sales associated with her. By default, UDM displays data for non-leaf members. This is probably the behavior you need anyway, since it allows you to compare managers' sale performance alongside the managers' employees.

Setting non-leaf member caption

You may need to display a special indicator to tell the manager apart. You can do so by using a caption template, e.g. (<manager name> manager), where the <manager name> will be replaced by the member name.

1. Switch back to the Dimension Structure tab in the Dimension Designer.

2. Select the Employees attribute. In the Properties window (Figure 4.23, verify that the MembersWithData property is set to *NonLeafDataVisible.*

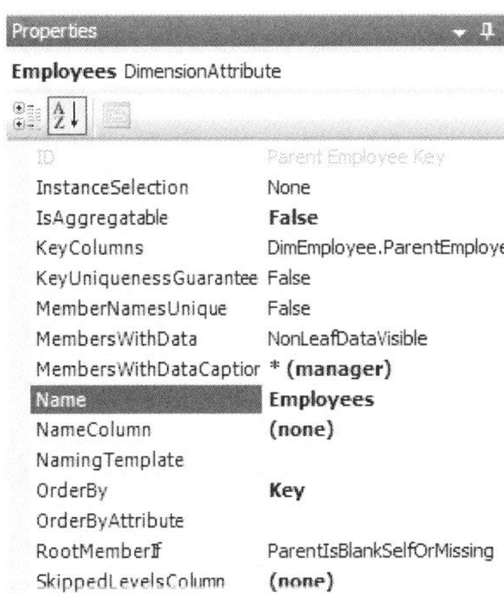

Figure 4.23 UDM gives you a lot of flexibility to custom-tailor a parent-child dimension.

3. Change the MembersWithDataCaption property to *** (manager)**. The asterisk placeholder will be replaced with the actual member name.

Level 01	Level 02	Level 03	Level 04	Reseller Sales Amount
⊟ Ken J. Sánchez	⊟ Brian S. Welcker	⊟ Amy E. Alberts	⊞ Amy E. Alberts (manager)	732078.444599999
			⊞ Jae B. Pak	8503338.64719989
			⊞ Rachel B. Valdez	1790640.2311

Figure 4.24 Use a member caption template to denote the non-leaf members that have data.

4. Switch to the Cube Browser. Process and reconnect. Note that now the Amy Alberts member at Level 04 has a (manager) suffix (Figure 4.24).

Hiding non-leaf members

In case you don't want to display the non-leaf members that have data, you can follow these steps to hide them.

5. In the Dimension Designer, select the Employees attribute and change its MembersWithData property to **NonLeafDataHidden**.

Level 01	Level 02	Level 03	Level 04	Reseller Sales Amount
⊟ Ken J. Sánchez	⊟ Brian S. Welcker	⊟ Amy E. Alberts	⊞ Jae B. Pak	8503338.64719989
			⊞ Rachel B. Valdez	1790640.2311
			⊞ Ranjit R. Varkey Chudukatil	4509888.93299997
			Total	15535946.2559003

Figure 4.25 Use a member caption template to denote the non-leaf members that have data.

6. In the Cube Browser, process the cube and reconnect. Observe that Amy Alberts is no longer shown under the Level 04 column. However, her sales are still attributed to the Total amount of that level. Hiding a member doesn't filter out its data. Now you understand why by default UDM displays the non-leaf members that have data. Otherwise, it would have been difficult to account for the gap between the visible member total and the level total.
7. Change back the MembersWithData to *NonLeafDataVisible*.

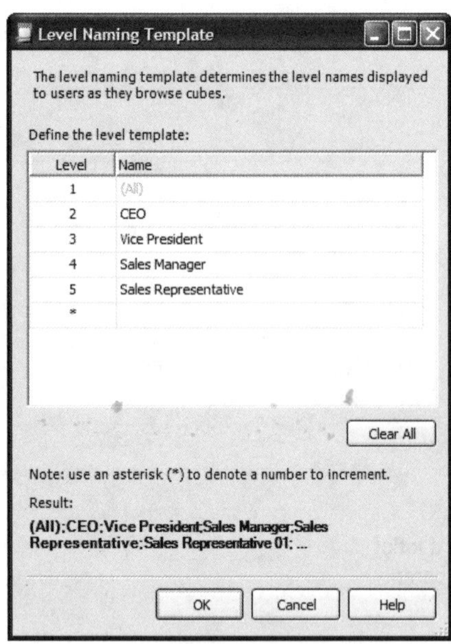

Figure 4.26 Use a naming template to provide more descriptive level names.

Changing the level caption

As you've noticed, UDM auto-generates the level names starting with Level 01. What if your users request more descriptive members? You can easily meet this requirement by creating a level-naming template for the level captions.

1. In the Dimension Designer and click the **...** button inside its NamingTemplate property. The Level Naming Template dialog is shown. The default template has only one level that will be used for the hierarchy All level.

2. Create additional level names, as shown in Figure 4.26.
3. Process the Employee dimension. Flip the Browser tab and reconnect.
4. Expand the Employees hierarchy. Select members of different levels and note that the level name changes accordingly. For example, if you select Ken Sanchez, the level name changes to CEO; when Brian Welcker is selected, it changes to Vice President, etc.
5. If you wish, re-deploy the project and browse the SOS OLAP cube. Note that the PivotTable report now shows the level names you've just defined.

4.2.4 Grouping Attribute Members

While we are still on the Employee dimension, let's demonstrate another useful UDM feature. Sometimes, you may have numeric attributes that may have many continuous values. Showing these values to the end users may not be as intuitive as grouping the member values into buckets. Take for example the Sick Leave Hours attribute. Its members are derived from the unique values in the underlying SickLeaveHours table column.

As it stands, this attribute hierarchy is not very useful. It contains many members and browsing data by so many distinct numeric values is not very intuitive. It would be much better if we could minimize the number of members by grouping the members into several buckets. This process is called *discretization*. UDM supports several pre-defined discretization algorithms that can be selected by expanding the DiscretizationMethod attribute property.

Tip Sometimes, you may need more precise discretization control than SSAS offers. For example, in the case of the person's Age attribute, you may need specific buckets, e.g. 15-18, 19-22, 23-30, 31-49, 40-55, 56 and more. To address this requirement, you may need to implement the discretization manually in the relational data warehouse.

Grouping members automatically

1. Back to the Dimension Structure tab, select the SickLeaveHours attribute.
2. Change its DiscretizationMethod to *Automatic*. This setting lets the Analysis Server determine the best grouping algorithm based on the member values. Leave the DiscretizationBucketCount property to its default value of *0*. When the bucket count is not specified, the Analysis Server will sample the data and determine the number of the groups on its own.
3. Deploy the project and open Cube Browser.
4. Expand the Employee dimension and then the HR folder. Drag the Sick Leave Hours attribute to the PivotTable rows area.
5. Drag the Reseller Sales Amount measure to the data area.
6. Drag the Order Date dimension to the column area. The report should look like the one shown in Figure 4.27.

	Year ▾			
	⊞ 2001	⊞ 2002	⊞ 2003	⊞ 2004
Sick Leave Hours ▾	Reseller Sales Amount	Reseller Sales Amount	Reseller Sales Amount	Reseller Sales Amount
20 - 27	28926.2465	356222.4968	457575.391099999	249399.7218
28 - 36	7284767.95339995	17083763.7369002	18477093.9063005	8680720.09699987
37 - 45	747691.117399999	6704443.42029998	13268000.1278001	7107942.77899989
46 - 53	4049.988			
Grand Total	8065435.30529994	24144429.6539998	32202669.4252009	16038062.5978003

Figure 4.27 Member discretization groups members in buckets.

The Analysis Server has created four discretization buckets to group the Sick Leave Hours members. Notice that, when member discretization is used, it is much easier for the end user to spot trends. Strangely enough, in our case, employees with 28-36 sick leave hours make more sales than those with 20-27 hours. Well, perhaps they are using a sick leave as an excuse for working from home! It looks like the AW management has decided to cap the sick leave hours in 2001 since the 46-53 group doesn't have members after 2001.

Grouping by equal areas

Sometimes, letting the server construct member discretization automatically may be inappropriate. Suppose that you need to group the Sick Leave Hours members into four buckets distributed equally by the number of members.

1. Back to the Dimension Structure tab change the DiscretizationMethod property of the Sick Leave Hours attribute to *EqualAreas*.
2. Change the DiscretizationBucketCount to **4**.
3. Switch to the Cube Browser tab and process the cube. Reconnect to rebuild the report. Click the Show Empty Sales button to show the Sick Leave Hours members that don't have data.

	Year ▾			
	⊞ 2001	⊞ 2002	⊞ 2003	⊞ 2004
Sick Leave Hours ▾	Reseller Sales Amount	Reseller Sales Amount	Reseller Sales Amount	Reseller Sales Amount
20 - 32	2390348.8152	6599955.7132	7055130.68079996	3072143.03129999
33 - 44	5671036.50209997	17544473.9408001	25147538.7444007	12965919.5665001
45 - 57	4049.988			
58 - 80				
Grand Total	8065435.30529994	24144429.6539998	32202669.4252009	16038062.5978003

Figure 4.28 You can select the bucket count and discretization method.

When the EqualAreas method is chosen, the Analysis Server will distribute the member population equally across the buckets. In other words, if the member values are plotted in a graph, the members will be grouped in such a way that the areas on the x-coordinate (abscissa) are equal. In our case, there are 13 distinct members that fall into the 20-32 bracket range. The reason why the last bracket group (58 – 80) doesn't have any data is that none of the employees with more than 58 sick hours made any sales since they are not sales people.

Besides Automatic and EqualAreas methods, UDM supports three additional discretization methods (Clusters, Thresholds, and UserDefined). The Clusters algorithm groups members by performing single-dimensional clustering on the input values. The Thresholds algorithm breaks the input range of continuous values into buckets based on the inflection points in their distribution curve. The last discretization method (UserDefined) implies that you can implement a custom discretization algorithm. Actually, this method exists for backward compatibility with OLAP browsers that support custom grouping. For example, the Microsoft Excel PivotTable report supports selecting members and grouping them together, e.g. selecting the USA and Canada members and grouping them together into North America. This action results in Excel creating a session cube on the server with a custom grouping on the selected members.

Naming buckets

As you've seen, UDM uses the First Bucket Member - Last Bucket Member naming conventions for the bucket labels. If this is not what you want, you can customize the bucket labels by using a naming template. Suppose that you need to provide more descriptive labels for the Sick Leave Hours buckets, as shown in Figure 4.29.

1. In the Dimension Designer, select the Sick Leave Hours attribute. If the attribute uses NameColumn binding to derive the member names, you need to implement the naming template in the column bound as NameColumn. The Sick Leave Attribute derives its member names from the key attribute.
2. In the Properties window, click on the **...** button inside the KeyColumns property.
3. In the DataItem Collection Editor, define the bucket naming template by entering the following string in the Format property.

```
Less than %{Last bucket member}; From %{First bucket member} to %{Last bucket member};
%{First bucket member} and more
```

The naming template consists of three parts separated by a semi-colon. The first part represents the naming template for the first bucket group. The third defines the naming template of the last bucket group. The middle is used to define the names of the intermediate bucket groups. When the Employee dimension is processed, the *%{<bucket name>}* placeholder will be replaced with the actual member name. Thus, the *Last bucket member* will be replaced with the last member in the current bucket. For example, the last member of the first bucket in Figure 4.29 is 32. When forming its name, UDM will use the first part of the naming template (Less than) and replace the *%{Last bucket member}* placeholder with 32.

	Year ▾	
	⊞ 2001	⊞ 2002
Sick Leave Hours ▾	Reseller Sales Amount	Reseller Sales Amount
Less than 32	2390348.8152	6599955.7132
From 33 to 44	5671036.50209997	17544473.9408001
From 45 to 57	4049.988	
58 and more		
Grand Total	8065435.30529994	24144429.6539998

Figure 4.29 Use a naming template to customize the bucket labels.

4. Once the naming template is implemented, you need to *fully* process the dimension and the cubes that reference it. Process the Employee dimension and browse the Sick Leave Hours hierarchy. Note that the bucket names change.
5. Fully process the SOS OLAP cube and reconnect to update the PivotTable report. Don't forget to click the Show Empty Cells button to show the bucket groups that don't have data. Your report should look like the one shown in Figure 4.29.

4.3 Implementing Time Dimensions

A time dimension is a standard dimension whose attributes represent time periods, such as years, semesters, quarters, months, and days. The reason why this dimension is given special attention in UDM is two-fold. First, you will probably never run into an OLAP cube that doesn't have a Time dimension because evaluating the business performance over time is an essential data analytics requirement. Second, UDM understands well the semantics of time. For example, as we saw in chapter 3, the Cube Wizard supports several date calendars which can be mapped to columns of the Date dimension table. Once this is done, the Cube Wizard can generate useful multilevel date hierarchies for you. If the Time dimension is not requested in the Cube Wizard, you can use the Dimension Wizard to create it.

4.3.1 Standard Time Dimensions

When we set up the Time dimension in the Cube Wizard, we opted to have two calendars (regular and financial) and we mapped several columns from the DimTime dimension table to common time periods. As a result, the Cube Wizard has generated three user-hierarchies and several attribute hierarchies. I renamed the hierarchies and levels to make them shorter and more intuitive. Figure 4.30 shows the final version of the Date dimension.

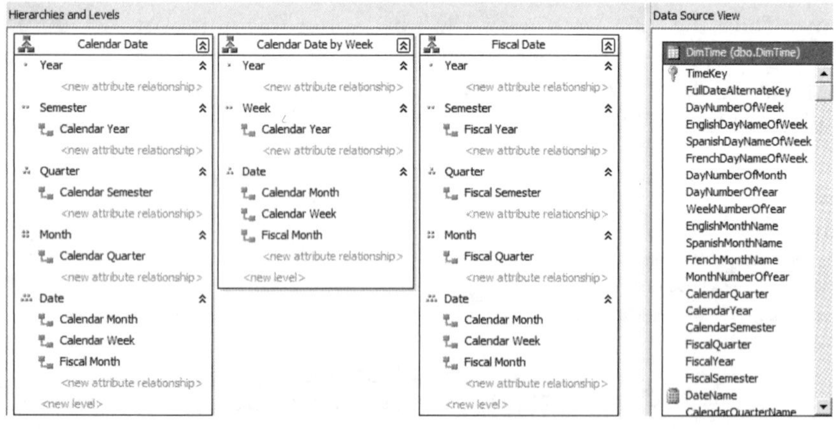

Figure 4.30 The Date dimension consists of three multilevel hierarchies and several attribute hierarchies.

Understanding the dimension structure

The Calendar Date multilevel hierarchy can be used to drill down data by the natural calendar date hierarchy (year, semester, quarter, month, and day). The Cube Wizard has created a separate Calendar Date by Week hierarchy because it knows that weeks cannot roll up to months. Finally, the Fiscal Date represents the Adventure Works financial year calendar which is offset with two quarters in respect to the standard calendar.

The role of the dimension key is fulfilled by the TimeKey attribute, which has been renamed to Date. It forms the lowest level of all hierarchies. Note that the TimeKey attribute has three member properties defined to let UDM know the hierarchical relationships. For example, the Calendar Month member property tells UDM that the Date level can be rolled up the Calendar Month level of the Calendar Date hierarchy.

Tip If your requirements call for time granularity of your fact tables (e.g. capturing individual calls in a call center), consider implementing two dimension tables – a Date dimension with a grain of a calendar day and a Time dimension with whatever grain is necessary (hour, minute, or even second). In this way, you will be able to simplify the data warehouse schema and minimize the number of members in the Date dimension. In addition, performance will be better since more coarse reporting needs can be addressed by the Date dimension only.

The unique key rule revisited

The moment you introduce a multilevel hierarchy, you need to recall the unique key rule we discussed in the preceding chapter. It stated that attribute members must have a unique key to be properly qualified. We need to be extra careful when setting the keys of the attributes that form the intermediate levels of the multilevel hierarchies in respect to the unique key rule. If you don't pay attention, you can easily fall into a nasty "gotcha" trap that we will discuss next in the context of the Calendar Date hierarchy. For the sake of simplicity, let's assume that it consists of two levels only (Quarter and Month) as shown in Figure 4.31.

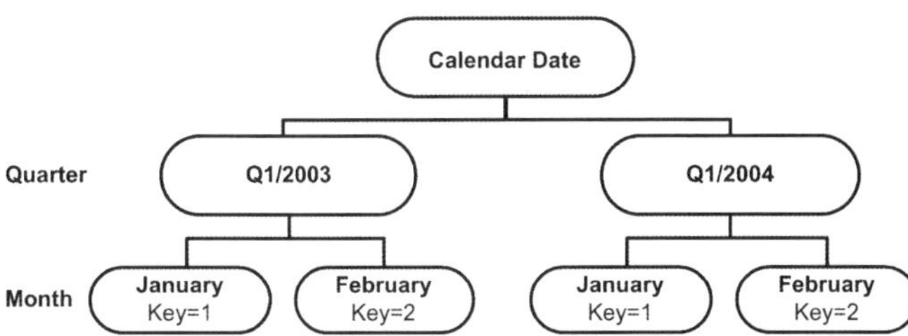

Figure 4.31 The attribute key must be unique within a hierarchy in which the attribute forms a level.

As it stands, the key of the Month attribute is formed by the MonthNumberOfYear column. You may think that we are in compliance with the unique key rule since each month member is identified uniquely, e.g. 1 for January, 2 for February, and so forth. The problem is that the Month attribute now exists in two places. First, it forms its own attribute hierarchy. Second, it exists in the Calendar Date multilevel hierarchy. Although the key of the Month attribute is unique within its attribute hierarchy scope, it is not unique within the Calendar Date hierarchy where its keys are duplicated across parallel quarters and years.

For example, the keys of the January member below the quarter 1 level of 2004 and quarter 1 level of 2005 will be identical (1). Although this dimension will process just fine, when you drill down the Calendar Date hierarchy from Quarter to Month level you may find that it doesn't give you the expected results. Measures may not roll up properly and month members may appear and vanish seemingly at random. Therefore, we could make the unique key rule more accurate by rephrasing it as follows

Important The attribute key must be unique within the containing hierarchy in which the attribute forms a level. The attribute key may need to be bound to multiple columns to be unique.

This rule may be easily compromised by any dimension, not just Time dimensions. For example, a Product dimension may have the same product member linked to different subcategories.

Using key collections

Fortunately, solving the above predicament is easy by using a key collection for the KeyColumns property to uniquely qualify attribute members. In the case of the Month attribute, this collection can be formed by the Year and Month keys. How can we identify which table columns to add to the collection? Just like creating a composite unique key of a relational table, we need to find which columns could qualify the attribute uniquely across the hierarchies in which it participates.

Table 4.1 Attribute and member properties of the Date dimension.

Attribute	Member Property	KeyColumns	NameColumn
Calendar Year		CalendarYear	CalendarYear
Calendar Semester	Calendar Year	CalendarYear, CalendarSemester	CalendarSemesterName
Calendar Quarter	Calendar Semester	CalendarYear, CalendarQuarter	CalendarQuarterName
Calendar Month	Calendar Quarter	CalendarYear, MonthNumberOfYear	EnglishMonthName
Calendar Week	Calendar Year	CalendarYear, WeekNumberOfYear	WeekNumberOfYear
Date (dim key)	Calendar Month, Calendar Week, Fiscal Month	TimeKey	DateName

On impulse, we could attempt to use the column which forms the next hierarchy level in respect to the Month attribute (CalendarQuarter). However, this will not make the Month key unique because, again, we will end up with the same key combination across two years. For example, the key collection for quarter 1 and March of 2004 will be 1-3 and it will be identical to the key collection for quarter 1 of 2003.

Note You need to explicitly bind the NameColumn property of an attribute with a composite key since UDM won't know which column to use for the member name. If the NameColumn is not set, the Dimension Designer will underline the attribute with a jagged red line. To fix this issue, bind the NameColumn property to the appropriate column.

The solution is to add the Year column to the key collection of the Month attribute. Once this is done, the January 2003 member will have a key of 2003-1, which is unique across all time periods. Fortunately, solving the above predicament is easy by using a key collection for the KeyColumns property to uniquely qualify attribute members. In the case of the Month attribute, this collection can be formed by the Year and Month keys. How can we identify which table columns to add to the collection? Just like creating a composite unique key of a relational table, we need to find which columns could qualify the attribute uniquely across the hierarchies in which it participates.

Table 4.1 shows how the unique keys are derived for attributes that form intermediate levels in multilevel hierarchies of the Calendar Date dimension. The same approach is used to identify the member properties, attribute keys and names of the Fiscal Date hierarchy. Now let's see how we can implement a unique attribute key in the form of a key collection.

Implementing a key collection

Let's go through the implementation steps to set up a key collection for the *Month* attribute.

1. Select the *Calendar Month* attribute in the Attributes pane. Click the **...** button inside the KeyColumns property. The DataItem Collection Editor is shown. The key collection has a single member based on the MonthNumberOfYear table column.

2. Click the Add button. A new binding placeholder is created with an empty Source column.
3. Click the ... button in the Source property. The Object Binding dialog is shown (see Figure 4.4).
4. In the Object Binding dialog, select *Column binding* in the *Binding type* dropdown. The selected table in the *Source table* dropdown should be DimTime.

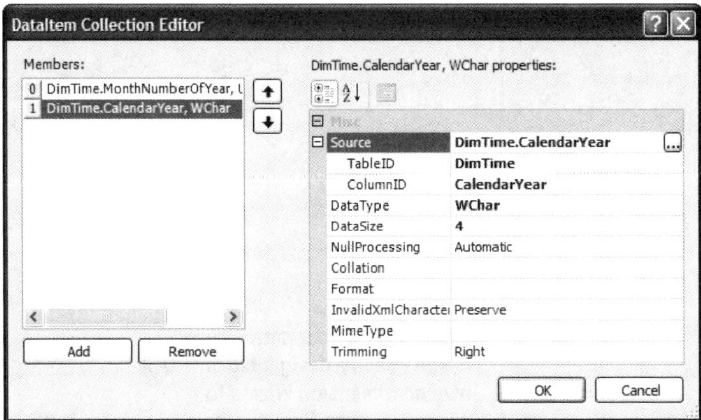

Figure 4.32 Use the DataItem Collection Editor to set up an attribute key collection.

5. Select the CalendarYear column. Click OK to close the dialog and return to the DataItem Collection Editor (Figure 4.32).

Note You may think that you can use the Format property on the DataItem Collection Editor to format attribute names, e.g. format customer's Birth Date as a short date. However, it turns out that the Format property cannot be used for member formatting. As it stands, UDM supports only trimming of the source column value by setting the Trim property to one these values – TrimLeft, TrimRight, TrimAll, TrimNone. As annoying as it could be, if you need to format the dimension members, you need to create expression-based columns either at the data source level or as named calculations.

Creating descriptive attribute names

Another interesting implementation detail of the Date dimension is that it uses several named calculations to provide descriptive names for members of the attribute hierarchies. Suppose that, instead of using the Calendar Date multilevel hierarchy, the end-user selects the Calendar Quarter attribute hierarchy. When the user expands the *All* member, the user has no way of telling apart the quarters of different years because the Year level will be missing. To address this issue, in chapter 2 we introduced several named calculations which append the year name to given members, e.g. Q1 CY 2002 for the first quarter of 2002 calendar year.

4.3.2 Server Time Dimensions

While formal OLAP stores, such as data warehouses and data marts, have a designated Time table, this is almost never the case with OLTP-based data sources. For example, the Adventure-Works database captures the order date in place. In the absence of a designated Time table, SSAS can generate a Time dimension for you. We will demonstrate a server Time dimension in the context of the Adventure Works real-time UDM (SOS OLTP). After running the Cube Wizard and fine-tuning the dimensional model, I came up with the real-time UDM that is represented by a single cube (SOS OLTP) and three dimensions (Product, Sales Territory, and Order Status). You can find the object definitions in the sample SOS OLTP project.

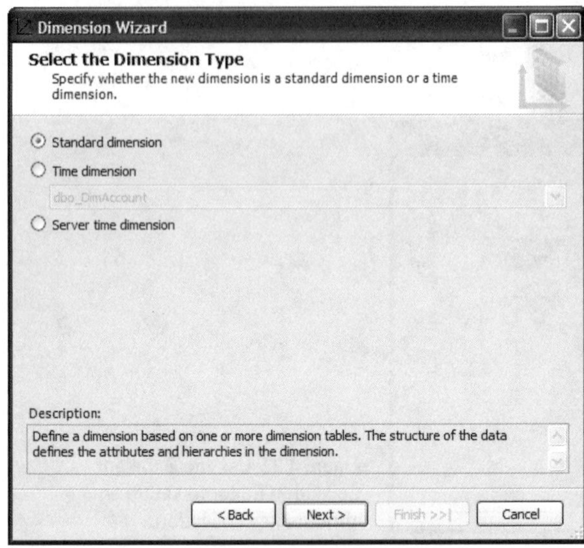

Figure 4.33 If your data source doesn't have a designated time table, use the Dimension Wizard to generate server Time dimension.

One noticeable missing piece is the ability to browse data by time. Let's complete the SOS OLTP dimensional model by introducing a server Time dimension. To build the dimension, we will use the handy Dimension wizard we met in chapter 3.

Defining time periods

1. Open the SOS OLTP project if it is not already loaded as part of your solution.
2. Right-click on the Dimensions folder and select *New Dimension* to launch the Dimension Wizard. Accept the default options in the Select Build Method step. In the Select Data Source View step, verify that SOS OLTP is the only data source view listed. Click Next to advance to the *Select the Dimension Type* step (Figure 4.33).
3. The Time dimension option allows you to generate a Time dimension from an existing table, just as we demonstrated in chapter 3 by using the Cube Wizard. To generate a server Time dimension, select the Server time dimension option and click Next to advance to the Define Time Periods step (Figure 4.34).
4. Let's instruct the wizard to generate a Time dimension spanning the period from January 1st, 2001 until December 31st, 2010. Different organizations and countries use different conventions for the first day of the week. Leave the default selection of Sunday.

SSAS 2000 If you have experience with generating server Time dimensions in SSAS 2000, you will probably appreciate the flexibility that SSAS 2005 brings. In SSAS 2000, the time range was generated by sampling the fact table data. As a result, the end time period was always restricted to last date for which there were transactions. The Dimension Wizard in SSAS 2005 removes this restriction by allowing you to specify arbitrary start and end date.

Figure 4.34 Use the Define Time Periods step to specify the time range and time periods.

5. For the purposes of our sample UDM, select all time periods to let the Dimension Wizard build all supported types of date hierarchies. Note that the Dimension Wizard allows you to localize the member names in one of the supported languages. Click Next to proceed to the Select Calendars step (Figure 4.35).

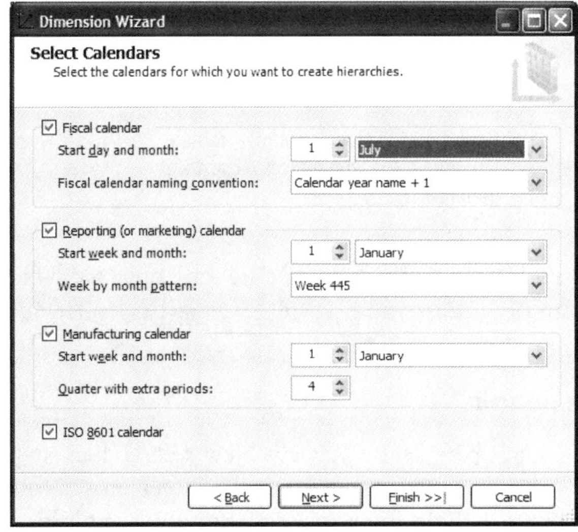

Figure 4.35 Besides the regular calendar, SSAS supports four additional calendars.

Selecting calendars

Similar to the Cube Wizard, the Dimension Wizard supports four commonly used calendars besides the regular calendar.

Fiscal calendar

Many organizations use fiscal years in addition to calendar years. As I pointed out in chapter 3, the Adventure Works financial year starts on July 1st. If the calendar year doesn't coincide with the calendar year (e.g. financial year is 2004 while the calendar year is 2003, you can specify the offset.

Reporting calendar

The marketing calendar supports dividing months into weeks by choosing a week-by-month pattern. For example, the 445 pattern defines four weeks a month, while the remaining week will be rolled into the third month. In other words, the last month of every quarter will have an extra fifth week.

Manufacturing calendar

By an industry convention the manufacturing calendar defines thirteen time periods a year, divided into three quarters of four periods and one quarter of five periods. You can choose which quarter will get the "extra" period. As with the reporting calendar, you can specify when the calendar starts. By default, its start date coincides with the start of the calendar year.

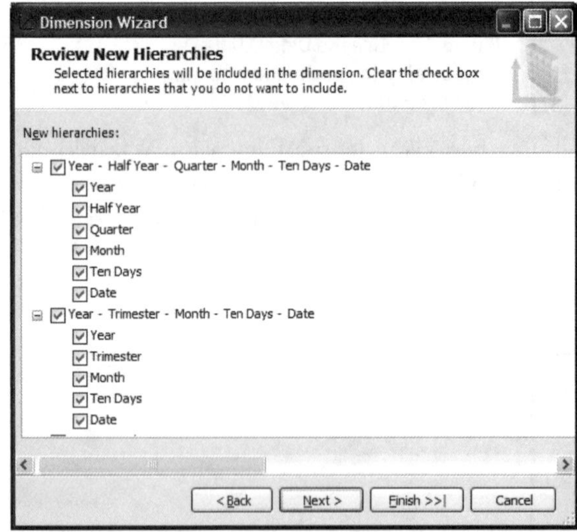

Figure 4.36 Select what hierarchies and levels the Dimension Wizard will generate.

ISO 8601 calendar

The ISO 8601 calendar employs standard numeric representations of date and time to avoid confusion in international communications. For more information on the ISO 8601 calendar, see the Resources section.

Generating the server-based Time dimension

1. Make the selections shown in Figure 4.35 and click Next. The Review New Hierarchies step (Figure 4.36) displays the hierarchies and levels that the Dimension Wizard will generate. Note that the Dimension Wizard is intelligent enough to exclude the attributes that don't apply to a given hierarchy. For example, a hierarchy cannot have both trimester and quarter levels.

2. Accept all hierarchies and click Next to proceed to the last Completing the Wizard step. Name the dimension **Date** and click Finish to let the Dimension Wizard generate the server Time dimension. This completes the wizard flow and opens the Data dimension in the Dimension Designer.

In comparison with the data-bound dimensions, one noticeable difference is that the DSV pane is missing. Its role is not fulfilled by the Time Periods pane which lists the generated time attributes. If you select an attribute in the Attributes pane and inspect its key or name bindings, you will notice that the Binding type is set to *Generate column* in respect to the fact that this is a server-generated attribute. Other than that, business is as usual. You can perform the same activities as with data-bound dimensions. For example, you can add, rename, and delete attributes, define multilevel hierarchies, etc.

Once you are satisfied with the dimension definition, process and browse the Date dimension (Figure 4.37). One thing to notice is that the Analysis Server automatically generates the member names, e.g. years in the regular calendar are prefixed with *Calendar*, quarters with *Quarter*, etc. You don't have control over this naming convention because formatting of the member names is set in the resources of the time dimension generator.

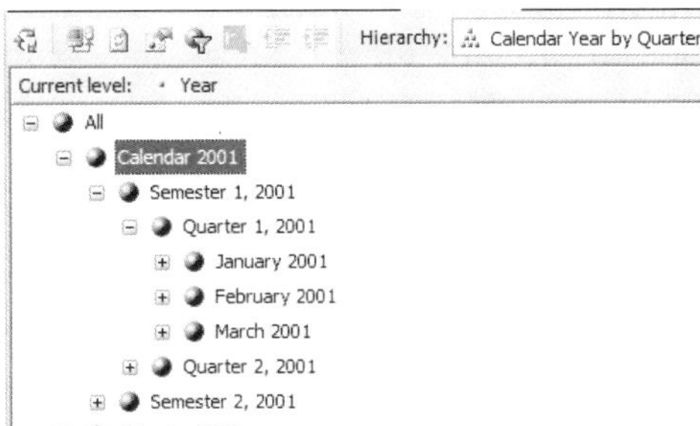

Figure 4.37 The Analysis Server automatically generates the member names of a server Time dimension.

The SSAS team has chosen this approach because custom-tailoring the member names would have been rather involved both in terms of user interface and dimension definition. That said, you can localize the members of the server-side dimension using the Translation tab of the Dimension Designer.

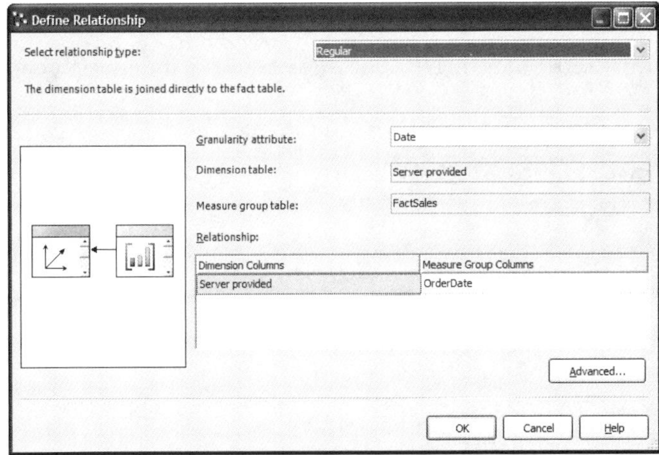

Figure 4.38 Establish a relationship between a dimension and a measure group.

Adding the Date dimension to the SOS OLTP cube

Our server Time dimension is ready. As a last step, we need to add it to the SOS OLTP cube so that end-users can browse the cube data by time.

1. In the Solution Explorer, double-click on the SOS OLTP cube definition file to open its cube definition in the Cube Designer. Make sure that the Cube Structure tab is selected.
2. Right-click anywhere inside the Dimensions pane and choose *Add Cube Dimension.* In the Add Cube Dimension dialog, select the Date dimension and click OK. At this point, the Date dimension is added to the cube structure but it is not linked to the Fact Sales measure group.
3. Flip to the Dimension Usage tab. Click the **...** button inside the intersecting cell formed by the Date dimension and Fact Sales measure group coordinates.
4. In the Define Relationship dialog, define a new relationship between the Date dimension and the FactSales measure group, as shown in Figure 4.38.
5. Process and browse the SOS OLTP cube using the Date dimension.

Back to the SOS OLAP UDM, you've completed defining the Sales Territory, Product, Employee, and Date dimensions. I've followed identical steps to fine-tune the Customer and Reseller dimensions and derive to attribute and multilevel hierarchies.

4.4 Working with Measures

Now that we are done with the dimension enhancements, let's revisit the cube measures. Open the SOS OLAP cube in the Cube Designer. Recall that we've instructed the Cube Wizard to create two measure groups from FactInternetSales and FactResellerSales fact tables. It promoted all selected columns in these fact tables to measures.

SSAS 2000 SSAS 2000 was limited to one fact table per cube. SSAS 2005 supports practically unlimited number of fact tables which can be exposed as measure groups. In this respect, you could relate an SSAS 2000 database to an SSAS 2005 cube, while the closest equivalent of an SSAS 2000 fact table is an SSAS 2005 measure group.

4.4.1 Formatting Measures

You can use descriptive names and format settings to make your measure more intuitive to end users.

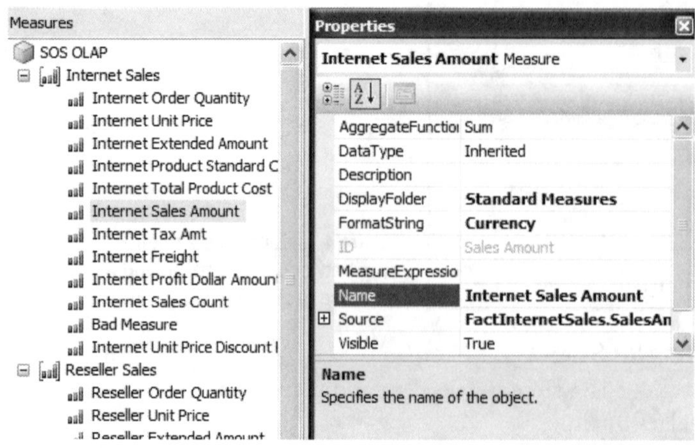

Figure 4.39 An SSAS 2005 cube can have more than one fact table. Usually, each fact table corresponds to a measure group.

1. Rename each measure in the Fact Internet Sales measure group (double-click slowly on its name or right-click and choose Rename) to start with the **Internet** prefix (e.g., Internet Order Quantity, Internet Unit Price, etc.).
2. Similarly, prefix each measure in the Fact Reseller Sales measure group with **Reseller**. Remove the table suffix from the measure name.
3. A measure can be formatted by using standard or custom format strings. OLAP browsers can pick up the UDM format settings and render the measures accordingly. Select all currency measures (price, amount, and cost facts) one by one and, in the Properties window, change their FormatString property to *Currency*. Format the rest of the measures as **#,#**.
4. Rename the Fact Internet Sales and Fact Reseller Sales measure groups to **Internet Sales** and **Reseller Sales** respectively. Note that each measure has a DisplayFolder property. Similar to dimension attributes, measures can be logically grouped in folders for easier navigation. By default, the measure display folder defaults to the name of the containing measure group. Select all measures one by one and change their DisplayFolder property to **Standard Measures**. In chapter 9, we will introduce Calculated Measures folder to group all calculated measures. At this point, your Measures pane should look like the one shown in Figure 4.39.
5. Each cube can have a default measure that will be returned by queries when no measure is explicitly requested on a given axis. In the Measures pane, select the SOS OLAP cube by clicking on the root node of the tree. Expand the DefaultMeasure dropdown and select *Reseller Sales Amount*. When an MDX query doesn't request a measure, the Reseller Sales Amount measure will be returned.

4.4.2 Understanding Measure Additivity

The most common use of OLAP is to aggregate measures across pre-defined dimensions. When the end-user browses the measure by a given dimension, the measure is aggregated according to the aggregate function specified in the *AggregateFunction* property of that measure. For example, suppose that the user requests the Internet Sales Amount measure organized by the Product by Category multilevel hierarchy that we implemented in the Product Dimension (Figure 4.40).

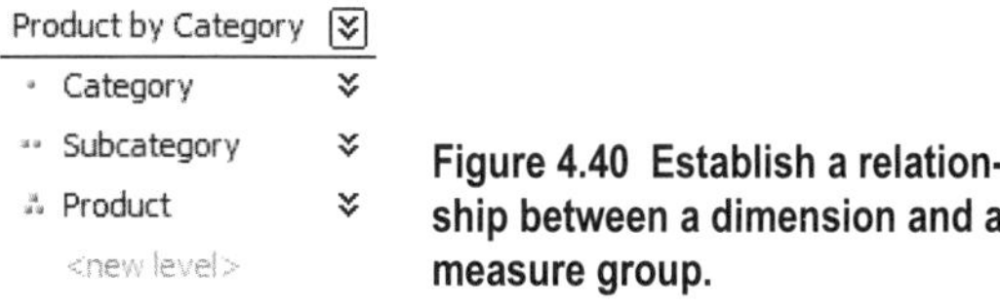

Figure 4.40 Establish a relationship between a dimension and a measure group.

The lowest level of this hierarchy is represented by the dimension key attribute (Product). It relates a set of records in the FactInternetSales fact table to a single leaf dimension member whose key matches the fact table reference key. Therefore, assuming that the aggregate function of the Internet Sales Amount measure is Sum, the aggregate measure total can be calculated by retrieving the related values from the fact table and summing them together. The aggregated values for upper non-leaf members (Subcategory and Category) in a multilevel hierarchy can be easily calculated by aggregating the members below them.

Additive measures

The most useful measures are numeric and additive (also called fully additive in the OLAP terminology), such as the Sales Amount and Order Count measures. When measures are fully additive, aggregated values can be derived from previously aggregated results. No matter how the end users slice and dice data, the aggregated measures will produce the correct total. For example, the user requests to see sales data broken by months. When the Analysis Server receives the query, it sums the sales amount and order count of the individual order items (or use pre-defined aggregations) to roll them up to months. If the user now chooses to see data aggregated by quarters, the Analysis Server will readily roll up the monthly aggregated values to quarters.

Fully-additive measures are also uniform because they are aggregatable across all dimensions. For example, you can aggregate the sales amount measure across any dimension and get the correct total. UDM supports several aggregate functions to perform common aggregation tasks with additive measures. These functions are *Sum*, *Min*, *Max*, *Count*, and *Distinct Count*.

Semi-additive measures

Some measures are semi-additive because they can be aggregated by some dimensions, but not by others. For example, an inventory closing balance measure is an example of a semi-additive measure. That's because the product inventory balances can be summed across the Product dimension, but cannot be meaningfully summed across the Date dimension. To understand this better, consider the following Inventory fact table.

Table 4.2 Semi-additive measures.

Product	March 1st	March 2nd	Total
Product A	10	15	25 (**15**)
Product B	20	25	45 (**25**)
Total by Product	30	40	70 (**40**)

This fact table stores the closing product quantity at the end of each day. Aggregating the product quantity over the Product dimension produces the correct total. However, aggregating the product quantity measure over time is meaningless and wrong. What is really needed is taking the ending balances for the requested cutoff date period (the numbers in bold). For example, if the user has requested to see the product quantities for Product A spanning two subsequent days, March 1st and March 2nd, the total product quantity should show 15.

To support semi-additive measures, UDM provides several functions, including *FirstChild*, *LastChild*, *FirstNonEmpty*, *LastNonEmpty*, *AvarageOfChildren*, and *By Account*. More complex requirements that cannot be addressed by the semi-additive functions may require MDX scripting. For example, this will be the case when a measure needs to be aggregated in different ways for different dimensions.

Non-additive measures

Finally, some measures shouldn't be aggregated at all. For example, the discount percentage of an order item cannot be meaningfully aggregated across any dimension. You can use the *None* aggregate function to instruct UDM not to aggregate a given measure. This could also be useful when you want to utilize an MDX script to aggregate the measure in a particular way, instead of letting UDM aggregate the measure.

Tip Although, discount percentage is not aggregatable by itself, you can still aggregate the discounted value and then obtain an average discount on the aggregated measures using an MDX calculated member.

4.4.3 Working with Additive Measures

All existing measures in the Internet Sales and Reseller Sales measure groups use the *Sum* aggregate function with the exception of the Internet Sales Count and Reseller Sales Count measures that use the *Count* function to calculate the number of order item transactions. Let's create a simple report that uses an additive measure.

	Year				
	⊞ 2001	⊞ 2002	⊞ 2003	⊞ 2004	Grand Total
Category	Internet Sales Amount	Internet Sales Amount	Internet Sales Amount	Internet Sales Amount	Internet Sales
⊞ Accessories			$3,252.35	$4,859.20	$8,111.55
⊞ Bikes	$28,269.60	$85,851.51	$141,020.84	$195,037.22	$450,179.17
⊞ Clothing			$2,939.77	$2,651.19	$5,590.96
Grand Total	$28,269.60	$85,851.51	$147,212.96	$202,547.61	$463,881.68

Figure 4.41 Fully additive measures can be aggregated by all dimensions.

Using the Sum function

1. In the Cube Structure tab, select the *Internet Sales Amount* measure. In the properties window, observe that its AggregateFunction property is set to *Sum*.
2. Process the SOS OLAP cube and flip to the Cube Browser tab. Reconnect if necessary.
3. Drag the *Product* dimension to Rows area of the pivot table report.
4. Drag the *Internet Sales Amount* measure from the Internet Sales measure group to the pivot table data area.
5. Drag the Order Date dimension to the Column area of the pivot table report. Your report should look like the one shown in Figure 4.41.

The Internet Sales Amount measure is fully additive because it can aggregate across any dimension. The Category Grand Total amount is equal to the total of the Category member values while the Year Grand Total represents the total across time.

Using Min and Max functions

You can easily create additional measures if needed. Suppose that you need to show the minimum and maximum unit price over time.

1. Right-click on the Reseller Sales measure group and choose *New Measure*. The New Measure dialog is shown (Figure 4.42).
2. In the Usage dropdown, select *Minimum* to use the Min aggregate function.
3. Select the *UnitPrice* source column in the *Source column* list. Click OK.
4. A new measure named Minimum Unit Price is added to the Reseller Sales measure group. Rename the measure to **Reseller Min Unit Price** and format it as currency.
5. Repeat the above steps to create a **Reseller Max Unit Price** with a Maximum usage.

Tip Suppose you realized that you've bound a measure to a wrong table column. Instead of re-creating the measure, you can just change its column binding. In the Properties window, expand the measure Source property and select a new column from the ColumnID dropdown.

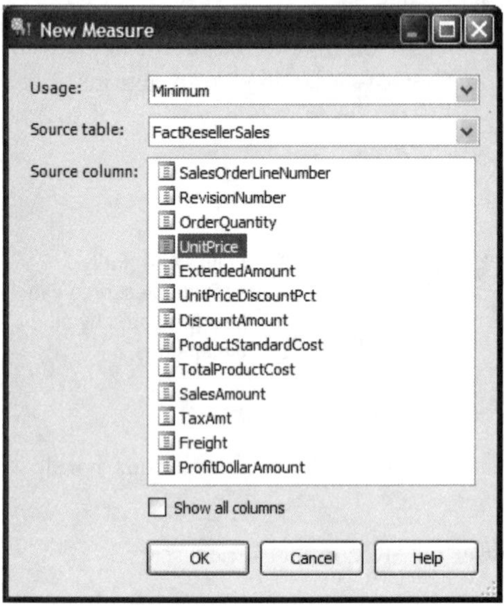

Figure 4.42 SSAS supports a variety of pre-defined aggregate functions to address common aggregation needs.

6. Process the cube or deploy the project. Switch to the Cube Browser tab and reconnect.
7. Create a new report with the Product attribute hierarchy on rows, Order Date dimension on columns, and Reseller Min Unit Price and Reseller Max Unit as measures (Figure 4.43).

	Year ▾					
	⊞ 2003		⊞ 2004		Grand Total	
Product ▾	Reseller Min Unit Price	Reseller Max Unit Price	Reseller Min Unit Price	Reseller Max Unit Price	Reseller Min Unit Price	Reseller M
AWC Logo Cap	$4.75	$5.19			$4.75	$5.19
Bike Wash - Dissolver	$3.98	$4.77	$4.37	$4.77	$3.98	$4.77
Cable Lock	$14.50	$15.00			$14.50	$15.00
Chain	$11.74	$12.14	$12.14	$12.14	$11.74	$12.14

Figure 4.43 Using the Min and Max functions.

Observe that several products have changed their unit price in 2003 and 2004. For example, the lowest price of the AWC Logo Cap in 2003 was $4.75, while the highest price was $5.19. You may be interested to find which reseller has changed the unit price of a given product for a given time period. You can do so by moving the Product dimension to the filter area and filtering the product in question. To find the reseller, add the Reseller attribute dimension to the report columns area.

Working with Distinct Count measures

Normally, you will create a new or derived measure in the containing measure group. The most noticeable exception in this approach is when creating a distinct count measure. A distinct count measure counts the unique values in the measure's source column. For example, consider the report shown in Figure 4.44 which uses a distinct count measure (Internet Order Count) to count the number of the customer orders.

Category	Internet Order Count
⊞ Accessories	18,208
⊞ Bikes	15,205
⊞ Clothing	7,461
Grand Total	27,659

Figure 4.44 Using the Distinct Count function to determine the number of orders.

Understanding distinct count measures

Notice something strange. The Internet Order Count doesn't seem to produce the correct Grand Total amount. To explain why this is happening you need to understand how the Distinct Count function works. If you query the distinct orders in the FactInternetSales table, you will find that the Grand Total figure is correct. To understand why the total of the dimension member values exceeds the grand total, consider the fact that an order may have (and usually has) more than one order item with different products. For example, an order may include one bike and one accessory product item. In this case, when we calculate the distinct orders, we need to count this order twice (for the Accessories level and second for the Bikes level). Hence, the Grand Total amount will usually be less than the distinct total amount.

When you indicate that you want a distinct count measure, the Cube Designer automatically creates a new measure group for you. While you can have a single distinct count measure defined in a measure group, there are good reasons to move it to a separate group. First, when you add a distinct count measure to a measure group, the entire measure group is treated as non-aggregatable. This reduces the effectiveness of the server-side cache by requiring more disk-based queries. Second, designing aggregations when a distinct count measure exists will result in much larger aggregations because the distinct count measure will internally be represented as a level. This level will participate in all aggregations and generally be quite large. Finally, the measure group records must be ordered by the distinct count field and ordering has to be done while SSAS queries the fact table (an ORDER BY condition is added to the SELECT statement). Since this operation could be really heavy for a large fact table, you should carefully consider the cost-benefit ratio before adding a Distinct Count measure to a cube.

Creating a distinct count measure

Let's implement a distinct count measure that represents the number of orders placed by counting the sales order numbers (SalesOrderNumber column values).

Note Aggregating distinct count measures properly may be more involved and may require MDX calculations. For more thorough discussion of the issues involved, refer to the Resources section.

1. Right-click on the Internet Sales measure group and choose *New Measure*.
2. Set the measure usage to Distinct count.
3. Select the SalesOrderNumber source column in the Source column list. Click OK.
4. A new measure group named *Internet Sales 1* is created with a single measure in it. Rename the measure group to **Internet Orders** and the measure to **Internet Order Count**. Follow the same steps to create the Reseller Order Count to count the resale orders.
5. Switch to the Cube Browser tab. Process the cube and reconnect. Create a new report with the Product dimension on rows and Internet Order Count as measures (Figure 4.44).

4.4.4 Creating New Measure Groups

As the data source schema evolves, you may need to add additional fact tables and measure groups. For example, so far we've ignored the fact that the order monetary data are actually captured in different currencies in the AdventureWorksDW database. Dealing with foreign currencies is a common data analytics requirement and different businesses deal with it in different ways. Suppose the Adventure Works management has requested that the monetary facts be converted to a common currency, which we will assume to be the US dollar.

Figure 4.45 A new measure group can be created from an existing fact table.

Creating the Currency Rates measure group

To support the currency conversion requirement, the AdventureWorksDW database schema includes a fact table (FactCurrencyRate) that tracks the currency exchange rates on a daily basis. With the help of this fact table, you can perform the currency conversion at the data source level or you can use a measure expression at the UDM level. Let's demonstrate the second approach. As a prerequisite, we need to create a new measure group, called Currency Rates, which will be based on the FactCurrencyRate fact table. Once the Currency Rates measure group is created, a monetary measure can be converted to US dollars by simply multiplying it by the Average Rate measure.

1. Right-click anywhere inside the Measures pane and choose *New Measure Group*. The New Measure Group dialog is shown (Figure 4.45). Notice that the New Measure Group dialog excludes the fact tables already bound to existing measure groups. The reason for the validation is that it's generally a bad design practice to reuse a measure group since this will lead to duplication of storage space.

2. Select the *FactCurrencyRate* fact table and click OK. A new measure group called *Fact Currency Rate* is created.

3. Rename the new measure group to *Currency Rates* and set its Type property to the pre-defined *ExchangeRate* semantic type.

4. Delete the Fact Currency Rate Count measure since it's not that useful for data analytics. At this point, the Measures pane should look like the one shown in Figure 4.46.

5. Format the Average Rate and End Of Day Rate measure as **#,#0.00**.

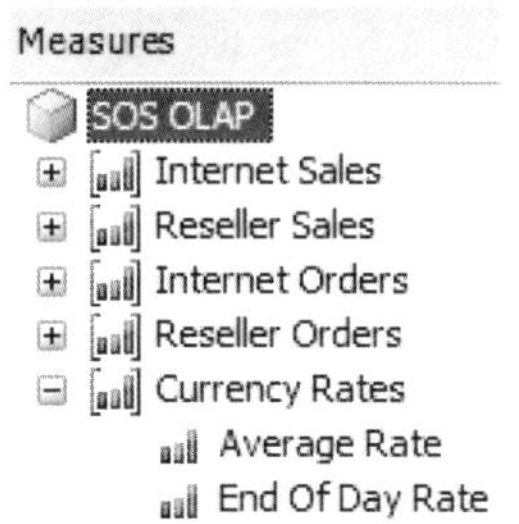

Figure 4.46 The Currency Rates measure group will be used to convert the localized sales facts.

Adding the Currency dimension

The AdventureWorks data warehouse schema includes also a DimCurrency dimension table. Assuming that the end users are willing to browse data by this dimension (e.g. to find out how many orders have been placed in a particular currency), follow these steps to create a Currency dimension and add it to the SOS OLAP cube.

1. Right-click anywhere in the Hierarchies pane of the Cube Structure tab and choose *Add Cube Dimension.*

2. In the Add Cube Dimension dialog, click on the *New dimension* button. The familiar Dimension Wizard starts.

3. Follow the wizard flow to create the Currency dimension as a standard dimension based on the DimCurrency table. In the Specify Dimension Type step, set the dimension semantic type to Currency and match the Currency Name dimension attribute to the Currency Name pre-defined attribute. Accept the defaults in the rest of the steps and name the new dimension *Currency.*

4. Back to the Add Cube Dimension dialog, make sure that the Currency dimension is selected and click OK to add it to the cube. The Currency dimension is added to the Hierarchy pane.

5. Expand the Currency dimension and click on the Edit Currency link to open the Currency dimension in the Dimension Designer.

6. Rename the Dim Currency attribute to **Currency**. Delete the *Currency Alternate Key* and *CurrencyName* attributes. Bind the NameColumn property of the Currency dimension key attribute to the CurrencyName column to use the currency name as a member name.

7. Click Save and close the Dimension Designer and return to the Cube Designer.

8. Switch to the Dimension Usage tab. The Cube Designer should have discovered the existing referential integrity relationship between the DimTime and FactCurrencyRate table and should have linked the Date dimension to the Currency Rates group automatically. In the next chapter, we will demonstrate semi-additive measures and see how the Currency Rates measure group could be useful.

4.4.5 Working with Measure Expressions

UDM allows you to create simple expression-based measures that span two measure groups. The main objective of measure expressions is to be used for implementing fast simple calculations at leaf-level dimension members, such as currency conversion. Think of a measure expression as a SQL INNER JOIN between two fact tables. To keep the calculations fast, the measure expressions are restricted to multiplication and division operators only. For more involved calculations you need to use MDX.

Understanding measure group segmentation

To understand the rationale behind supporting only multiplication and division operators in measure expressions, you need to know how the measure groups are stored. Assuming MOLAP storage model, a measure group data is split into storage objects called *segments*. When a measure group is processed, measures for a given combination of attribute members may end up in different segments. For example, the values of the Resale Sales Amount measure for a given combination of the participating attribute hierarchies (Product, Customer, Reseller, Date, etc.) can be found in multiple segments. The storage engine simply adds these values together when retrieving data.

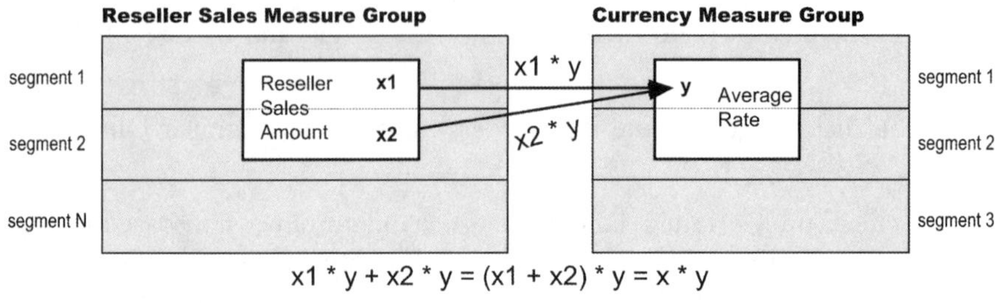

Figure 4.47 The measure group segmentation supports only multiplication and division operations.

Let's consider the example shown in Figure 4.47. Suppose that for a given combination of attribute hierarchies the values of the Reseller Sales Amount measure are split between two segments. To make things simpler, let's assume there are only two values, x1 and x2. In addition, let's assume that the Average Rate measure in the Currency Measure Group has only one value located in a single segment. If a measure expression is not used, when evaluating the value x, the storage engine simply sums the values when aggregating the Reseller Sales Amount (assuming Sum aggregation function): x = x1 + x2.

However, evaluating a measure expression is not so simple. For example, suppose that you need to calculate the Reseller Sales Amount by multiplying its value by the Average Rate (x * y). In this case, the storage engine evaluates the expression for every unique attribute members encountered in each segment. So, for the multiplication operator it does (x1 * y) + (x2 * y) which of course is the same as x * y. Now consider what would happen if other operations, such as additions, were allowed. In this case, we will have (x1 + y) + (x2 + y) which is not the same as x + y because y will be counted twice. For this reason, only multiplication (*) and division operators (/) are allowed.

Implementing a measure expression

As I've explained, consider measure expressions when you need simple and efficient calculated measures. The syntax of the measure expression is as follows:

```
Measure Z = [Measure X] operand [Measure Y]
```

Measure expressions are subject to several restrictions. As noted, the *operand* must be either * or /. The second measure must be from another measure group. The measure expression cannot reference other expression-based measures. The data type of the expression-based measure must be the same as the data type of the left operand. Deviating from the expression rules results in an error during deployment.

Let's demonstrate measure expressions by converting the monetary measures to US dollars. The Currency Rates measure group defines two measures. As their names suggests, the Average Rate measure captures the average currency exchange rate on a daily basis. The End Of Date rate gives us the currency exchange rate at the end of a given day. Depending on the user requirements, we can use either rate for currency conversion. We will use the Average Rate measure.

1. In the Measures pane, expand the Internet Sales measure group and select the Internet Sales Amount measure.

2. In the Properties window, type in the expression from the next step or click the ... button to open the Measure Expression dialog.

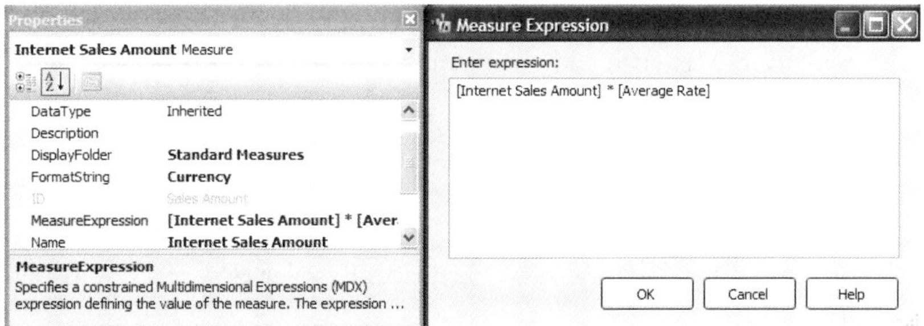

Figure 4.48 Use measure expression to implement simple and efficient calculations.

3. Type in the following expression in the Measure Expression dialog (Figure 4.48):

```
[Internet Sales Amount] * [Average Rate]
```

4. Repeat the above steps by replacing the first operand with the source measure name for measures Internet Extended Amount, Internet Profit Dollar Amount, Reseller Sales Amount, Reseller Extended Amount, and Reseller Profit Dollar Amount.

5. Process and browse the SOS OLAP cube in the Cube Browser. Drag the Reseller Sales Amount and Internet Sales Amount to report Detail Fields area. Notice that, overall, Adventure Works has made $76,494,758.25 in resale sales and $26,054,827.45 in direct (Internet) sales.

Year ▾							
⊞ 2001		⊞ 2002		⊞ 2003		⊞ 2004	
Reseller Sales Amount	Internet Sales Amount	Reseller Sales Amount	Internet Sales Amount	Reseller Sales Amount	Internet Sales Amount	Reseller Sales Amount	Internet Sales
$7,582,953.67	$2,627,031.40	$22,871,907.85	$5,681,440.58	$30,543,780.85	$8,705,066.67	$15,496,115.88	$8,992,282.96

Figure 4.49 The Adventure Works sales record broken down by years and shown in US dollars.

6. Drag and drop the Order Date dimension on columns. This makes it easy to trace Adventure Works sales performance in time (Figure 4.49). For example, notice that sales have been increas-

ing each year. The decline in 2004 is because the sample database doesn't have data for the second half of 2004.

Avoiding non-additive measure expressions

Here is one trap you may fall into when using the division operator in measure expressions. When the division operator is used, the resulting value must be additive, so that SSAS can aggregate it properly. For example, assuming the FactCurrencyRate table stores the reversed exchange rates, instead of using multiplication you can use division and the result will be additive. However, if the measure expression is used to produce a ratio, the result will not be additive and you will get the wrong results when aggregating on the measure expression. That's because the storage engine first calculates the measure expression at the leaf level of the attribute hierarchies and then rolls the measure up.

Suppose that you want to compare the product unit price for Internet and resale sales. At first, you may decide to use a measure expression to calculate the Internet Unit Price/Reseller Unit Price percentage ratio.

1. On the Cube Structure tab, right-click on the Internet Sales measure group and choose *New Measure.*
2. Select the UnitPrice column in the New Measure dialog and click OK. A new measure called *Unit Price* is created.
3. Rename the Unit Price measure to **Bad Measure** and change its format string to **#,#**.
4. Enter the following expression in the Measure Expression property of Bad Measure.

```
[Internet Unit Price]/[Reseller Unit Price]
```

5. Switch to the Cube Browser tab. Process and reconnect.
6. Drag the Product dimension on rows. Drag the Internet Unit Price, Reseller Unit Price, and Bad Measure to the data area (Figure 4.50).

Category	Internet Unit Price	Reseller Unit Price	Bad Measure
⊞ Accessories	$9,337.04	$110,522.02	267
⊞ Bikes	$505,292.11	$21,891,358.55	246
⊞ Bikes		$4,697,942.24	
⊞ Clothing	$6,156.77	$346,032.93	112
Grand Total	$520,785.92	$27,045,855.75	625

Figure 4.50 The resulting expression-based measure must be additive.

Observe that the Bad Measure values are wrong. That's because the storage engine lowers the grain of the expression-based measure to the lowest level on both measure groups, calculates the measure expression and then aggregates the results. In this example, what we really need is aggregate first and then apply the measure expression. To implement this requirement, we need to use an MDX calculation instead of a measure expression.

4.5 Summary

Dimensions and measures represent the cornerstone of dimensional modeling. Dimension attributes can be grouped in flexible ways to form attribute or multilevel hierarchies. Use attribute hierarchies to allow your end users to browse data from many aspects. Implement multilevel hierarchies to provide logical navigational paths for data exploration.

UDM allows you to implement flexible data analytics requirements. Use parent-child dimensions to deal with recursive data. Create a standard Time dimension when you have a designated table in the data source or a server-side Time dimension otherwise. Expose fact tables as measure groups containing useful measures. Use the pre-defined aggregate functions to handle additive or semi-additive measures. Leverage error configurations at dimension, measure group, and cube levels to handle data integrity issues in dimension or fact tables.

4.6 Resources

A Summary of the International Standard Date and Time Notation by Markus Kuhn (http://shrinkster.com/4ni) – Explains the International Standard ISO 8601 calendar.

DISTINCT COUNT, Basket Analysis, and Solving the Multiple Selection of Members Problem article by Amir Netz (http://shrinkster.com/4nj) – Although originally based on SSAS 2000, this is an excellent article that teaches you how to solve advanced BI requirements.

Analysis Services: Semi-additive Measures and Inventory Snapshots article by Amir Netz (http://shrinkster.com/89q) – Although originally based on SSAS 2000, read this article to understand how semi-additive measures can be used to implement inventory snapshots.

Chapter 5

Advanced Dimensional Modeling

The ambitious goal of UDM is to synthesize the best features of the relational and dimensional reporting models. In the preceding chapters, you've seen how the attribute-based nature of UDM allows it to transcend the boundaries of the classic dimensional model by not restricting it to star and snowflake dimensions only. In this chapter, we will explore other prominent characteristics that help UDM break out of the traditional OLAP space and meet more advanced data analytics requirements. You will learn how to:

- Work with dimension relationships to link dimensions and measure groups.
- Implement semi-additive measures, account intelligence, and dimension writeback.
- Link UDM to dimensions and measure groups located in an external UDM.
- Handle data integrity issues.

To demonstrate these innovative features, we will enhance the SOS OLAP cube and will build new cubes. All UDM projects can be loaded by opening the Ch05 solution file.

5.1 Working with Dimension Relationships

Back in chapter 3, I briefly mentioned that UDM supports different types of dimensions. In fact, UDM dimensions are so versatile that one may find it challenging to classify them, e.g. to come up with a common definition of what a dimension type really is. To help you in this regard, in chapter 3, I introduced a dimension taxonomy table which organizes dimensions by dimension type, semantic type, and measure group relationship. So far, the only types of dimensions that you've created and worked with were standard dimensions that have a regular relationship to the related measure groups.

Definition A regular relationship is represented by a direct foreign key relationship between the dimension table and the fact table.

Now it's time to find out how we can leverage the dimension relationships supported by UDM to their full potential.

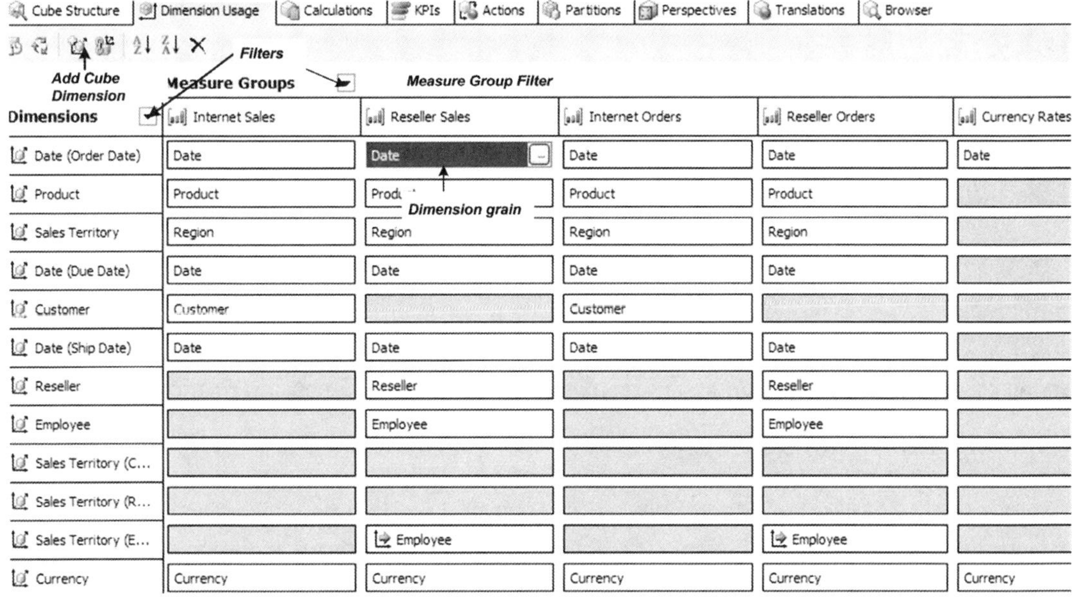

Figure 5.1 Use the Dimension Usage tab of the Cube Designer to tell UDM how dimensions relate to measure groups.

5.1.1 Understanding Dimension Usage

As you would recall from chapter 4, you use the Dimension Usage tab of the Cube Designer to define the relationships between cube dimensions and the measure groups in a cube. Let's cover the Dimension Usage tab in more details and make a few necessary changes along the way. Open the SOS OLAP cube in the Cube Designer and flip to the *Dimension Usage* tab (Figure 5.1). After the Cube Structure tab, the Dimension Usage tab is the most important tab of the Cube Designer. Just as you would use SQL joins to define known relationships among relational tables, the Dimension Usage tab allows you to set up relationships between dimensions and measures.

A large cube may include many dimensions and measure groups. Use the two filter buttons to reduce clutter and filter only the dimensions and measure groups you need. Filtering doesn't delete the selected objects, it just excludes them from the dimension tab. You can also sort dimensions and measures by name in ascending or descending order by using the corresponding toolbar buttons.

Adding dimensions

The Dimension Usage matrix shows cube dimensions in rows and measure groups in columns. You can use both the Dimensions pane of the Cube Browser or the Dimension Usage tab to add new or existing (either defined in the same project or in an external UDM) dimensions to the cube. Both tabs are synchronized, which means that dimension changes made in the Cube Browser are automatically detected in the Dimension Usage tab and vice versa.

Use the Add Cube Dimension toolbar button to add a dimension to the cube. This will bring up the Add Cube Dimension dialog that we discussed in chapter 3. You can use the Add Cube

Dimension dialog to add existing dimensions or create new dimensions. The Dimension Usage tab doesn't support adding new measure groups.

Bank Name	Internet Sales Amount	Reseller Sales Amount
⊞ Guardian Bank	$26,005,821.61	$12,820,862.09
⊞ International Bank	$26,005,821.61	$9,374,001.85
⊞ International Security	$26,005,821.61	$12,307,928.91
⊞ Primary Bank & Reserve	$26,005,821.61	$12,865,022.64
⊞ Primary International	$26,005,821.61	$9,175,522.14
⊞ Reserve Security	$26,005,821.61	$10,391,566.35
⊞ United Security	$26,005,821.61	$9,559,854.28

Figure 5.2 If IgnoreUnrelatedDimensions for a measure group is True, the unrelated dimensions will be forced to their Top level.

When a new dimension is added, the Dimension Tab examines the cube data source view for existence of data source or DSV relationships between the dimension table (primary dimension table for snowflake dimensions) and the fact tables. If a suitable relationship is detected, the Dimension Designer relates the dimension to the corresponding measure group(s). The intersecting cell between a dimension and measure groups defines the dimension relationship.

Removing dimensions

If the intersecting cell is empty (e.g. Reseller dimension and Internet Sales measure group) the dimension is not related to the measure group. The *IgnoreUnrelatedDimension* measure group property determines what will happen if a query requests an unrelated dimension to a given measure group. If IgnoreUnrelatedDimension is set to *True* (default), the dimension will be forced to its top level. In other words, the server will return the aggregated total of all unrelated measures requested in the query. For example, the report shown in Figure 5.2 repeats the grand total of the Internet Sales Amount measure because the Reseller dimension is not related to the Internet Sales measure group. If IgnoreUnrelatedDimension is *False*, empty cells will be returned for the unrelated measures.

If you want to remove the relationship between a dimension and a measure group, select the intersecting cell and press the Delete key (or click the Delete toolbar button). Once you confirm your intention on the Delete Objects dialog, the dimension relationship will be deleted and the intersecting cell will be emptied.

There is no good reason to keep a dimension that is not related to any measure group defined in the cube. To remove such a dimension from the cube, select the dimension name in the Dimensions column and press *Delete* (or click the Delete toolbar button). For example, glancing at Figure 5.1, you can see that we have four instances of the Sales Territory dimension (Sales Territory, Sales Territory (Customer), Sales Territory (Reseller), and Sales Territory (Employee). There is no need to keep the last three. The first two are not related to any measure group. Sales Territory (Employee) is a reference dimension that joins the reseller measure groups via the Employee dimension. However, the Sales Territory dimension joins these measure groups directly (at a Region dimension key level) and having the Sales Territory (Employee) is redundant.

1. Select the Customer – Sales Territory dimension in the Dimensions column and press *Delete* to remove it.
2. Click OK on the Delete Objects dialog.
3. Repeat these steps to remove the Employee – Sales Territory and Reseller – Sales Territory dimensions.

Renaming dimensions

You can use the Dimension Usage tab to change the name of a dimension or a measure group by which it is known in the containing cube. For example, we have three Time role-playing dimensions (role-playing dimensions are discussed in section 5.1.3). Among them, the Date (Order Date) is the primary date that the end users will use when drilling down data by time. As its name stands right now, this dimension will be shown to the end users as *Order Date*. For the end-user's convenience, let's rename this dimension to *Date* only.

1. In the Dimensions column, select the Date (Order Date) dimension. The Date prefix tells the UDM designer that this dimension is based on the Date dimension. The *(Order Date)* part is the name by which this dimension instance is known in the SOS OLAP cube.
2. Click twice slowly to select the dimension name and change it to **Date**.
3. Optionally, flip to the Cube Structure tab and note that the Dimensions pane reflects the name change.

5.1.2 Multi-Grain Relationships

A regular dimension relationship implies a foreign key relationship between the dimension table and the fact table it is related to. Normally, a dimension will join a measure group at the dimension key level. If this is the case, the dimension key determines the grain of the dimension relationship. Sometimes, you may need to join a dimension to two (or more) measure groups at a different grain. Since, in this case, the dimension and the measure group granularities differ, I dubbed such a relationship a *multi-grain* relationship.

Granularity revisited

To understand this better, consider the Date dimension in the SOS OLAP cube. Its dimension key (Date attribute) is bound to the primary key column (TimeKey) of the DimTime table and uniquely identifies a record in the DimTime dimension table. Since a row in the DimTime table represents a calendar day, the grain of our Date dimension is a calendar day.

EmployeeKey	TimeKey	CalendarYear	CalendarQuar	SalesAmount
272	1	2001	3	28000
272	93	2001	4	7000
272	185	2002	1	91000
272	275	2002	2	140000
272	366	2002	3	70000
272	458	2002	4	154000

Figure 5.3 Sometimes, you may need to join a dimension to a fact table at a higher grain than the dimension key.

Normally, the fact tables related to the Date dimension will have the same grain. For example, to join to the Date dimension, the FactResellerSales fact table has foreign keys (OrderDateKey, DueDateKey, ShipDateKey) that reference the TimeKey column of the DimDate table. Had FactResellerSales captured order items at a lower grain, e.g. an hour, joining the Internet Sales measure group to the Date dimension would have been impossible.

While there is nothing you can do to join a dimension to a fact table at a lower grain than the dimension key, UDM makes it very easy to do so at a higher grain. For example, the FactSalesQuota fact table in the AdventureWorksDW database captures the sales persons' quota on a quarterly basis, as you can notice by exploring its data. As Figure 5.3 shows, the sales quota for sales person 272 for the third quarter of 2001 is $28,000, while her sales quota for the next quarter is $7,000. Given this fact table, you may want to compare the sales person's actual sales against her targeted sales quota. The only issue, though, is that the FactResellerSales and FactSalesQuota tables have different grains.

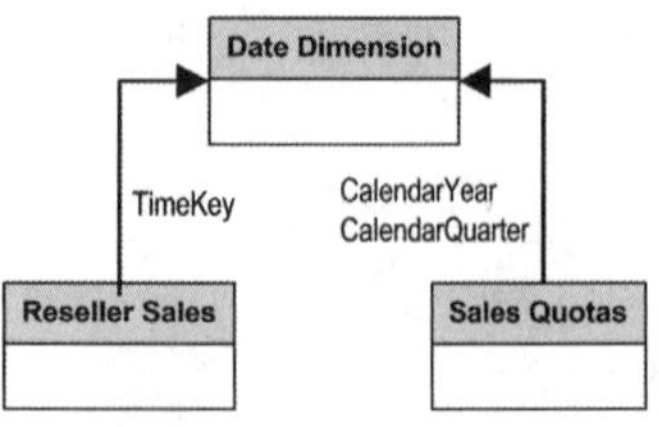

Figure 5.4 The Date dimension joins the Reseller Sales measure group at a grain of a calendar day, while it joins the Sales Quotas measure group at a grain of a calendar quarter.

To meet this requirement, we need to be able to join the Date dimension to the measure groups deriving from the two fact tables, as shown in Figure 5.4. Solving this dilemma in UDM is a matter of taking a few sample steps.

Reviewing the DSV schema

Let's start by reviewing the data schema of the DimTime and FactSalesQuota tables.

1. Open the SOS OLAP data source view (SOS OLAP.dsv) in the DSV Designer. In the Diagram Organizer, select *<All Tables>* to see all tables in the Diagram pane.
2. In the Tables pane, select the *Fact Sales Quota* table. This should select the Fact Sales Quota in the Diagram pane.
3. Double-click on the relationship (the arrow line) between the FactSalesQuota and DimTime tables to open the Edit Relationship dialog (Figure 5.5).

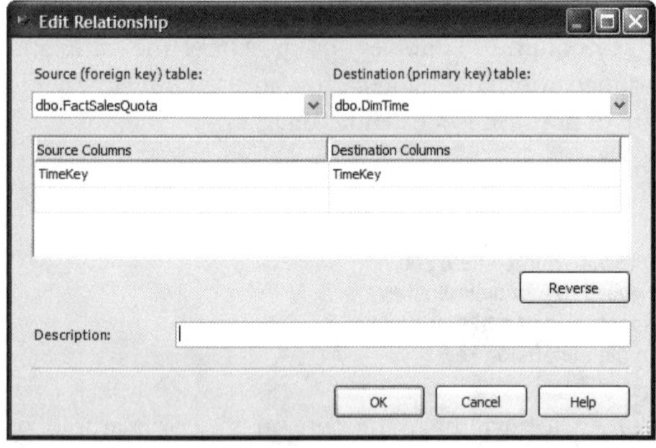

Figure 5.5 Create data schema relationship between the fact table and the dimension table that will be joined at a higher grain.

Note that the two tables are joined by the TimeKey column. Strictly speaking, a Time dimension is a special case because it can be joined at any grain of its multilevel hierarchy without requiring changes to the schema of the dimension table. That's because all members can be identified by the primary key. For example, the TimeKey values in the FactSalesQuota correspond to the first day of each quarter in the DimTime table (e.g. January 1st 2003, April 1st 2003, etc), as you can assert by comparing the key values. Therefore, we can join the DimDate dimension table to the FactSalesQuota fact table at a quarter level on the TimeKey column (as we've done with the other fact tables) regardless of the fact that the FactSalesQuota table has a higher grain.

With other dimensions, you will need to add the required key column to the dimension table. For example, suppose that the FactSalesQuota fact table stores the sales person's quota broken down by product category. Joining the DimProduct dimension table to FactSalesQuota in this case requires adding a CategoryKey column to DimProduct. To simulate this scenario, you could join the FactSalesQuota and DimTime tables by the CalendarQuarter and Calendar Year columns instead of TimeKey. The bottom line is that there must be a referential join between the dimension table and the fact table. In the absence of a referential join at the data source level, a logical relationship can be defined at the DSV level.

Creating the Fact Sales Quota measure group

Once the data schema relationship is in place, we can proceed by adding the Fact Sales Quota measure group to the SOS OLAP cube.

1. Switch to the Cube Structure tab. Create a new measure group based on the FactSalesQuota table.
2. Rename the measure group to **Sales Quotas**.

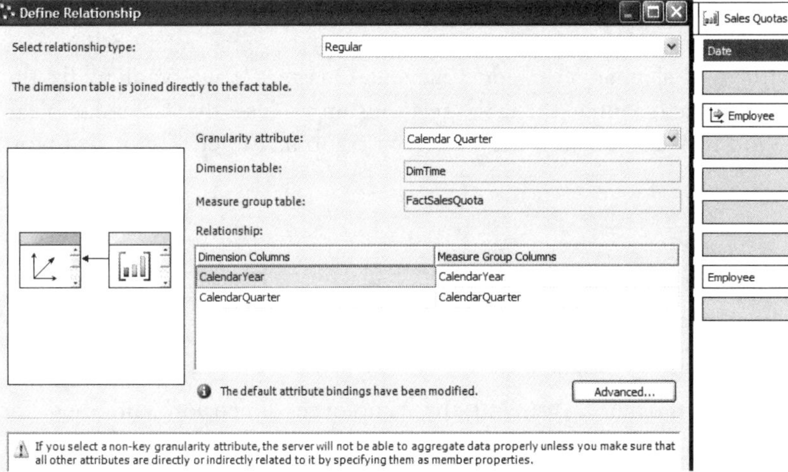

Figure 5.6 Set up an appropriate granularity attribute to define the dimension grain.

3. Remove all measures except the Sales Amount Quota measure.
4. Rename the Sales Amount Quota measure to **Sales Quota**. Change its FormatString property to *Currency*.

Defining the multi-grain relationship

Finally, let's set up a multi-grain relationship to tell UDM that Date dimension joins the Fact Sales Quotas measure group at a quarter level.

1. Switch to the Dimension Usage tab. Note that the Cube Designer has discovered and created dimension relationships to relate the Date and Employee dimensions to the Sales Quota measure group. The Date dimension joins the measure group by the Date dimension key attribute.
2. Click on the **...** button to launch the Define Relationship dialog.
3. Change the Granularity attribute dropdown to Calendar Quarter.

Note that the Define Relationships dialog displays a warning message at the bottom advising you that you need to have appropriate member properties defined. When you join a dimension table at a higher level than the dimension key, the server knows that it must aggregate measures at the level of the granularity attribute specified. However, the server has no notion of the hierarchical relationship among the dimension members and it doesn't know how to aggregate data from the leaf members up.

For example, if the granularity attribute is set to Calendar Quarter, the server needs to roll up leaf measures to the quarter level. If it is Calendar Year, it needs to roll up the leaf measures to quarters, and then to years. As we mentioned in the preceding chapter, you let UDM know about such relationships by defining appropriate member properties (e.g. Calendar Year is a member property of the Calendar Quarter). If you do not, Analysis Services will not be able to aggregate values properly.

SSAS 2000 If you had to deal with multi-grain relationships in SSAS 2000, you would probably appreciate the simplicity that UDM brings. In the past, you had to resort to all sorts of workaround techniques, ranging from using parent-child dimensions to pure hacks (e.g. introducing dummy dimension members). With UDM, this issue simply disappears.

4. Configure the relationship grid as shown in Figure 5.6. Ignore the informational message about the attribute bindings. It is displayed because we are overwriting the table relationship from TimeKey to the combination of Calendar Year and Calendar Quarter. If we want to fix this warning, we could change the data source or DSV relationship to use the Calendar Year-Calendar Quarter combination instead of using the TimeKey column. Either way, it will work just fine.

			Year			
			2001		2002	
CEO	Vice President	Sales Manager	Reseller Sales Amount	Sales Quota	Reseller Sales Amount	Sales Quota
Ken J. Sánchez	Brian S. Welcker	Amy E. Alberts			$2,605,313.93	$4,270,000.00
		Stephen Y. Jiang	$7,582,953.67	$9,513,000.00	$20,266,593.92	$24,739,000.00
		Syed E. Abbas				
		Total	$7,582,953.67	$9,513,000.00	$22,871,907.85	$29,009,000.00
	Total		$7,582,953.67	$9,513,000.00	$22,871,907.85	$29,009,000.00

Figure 5.7 Comparing employees' actual performance against sales quotas.

5. Deploy the project and browse the cube. Expand the Employee dimension and drag the Employees parent-child dimension on rows and Date dimension on columns. Drag the Reseller Sales Amount and Sales Quota measures on the report details. Your report should resemble the one shown in Figure 5.7. Multi-grain relationships make it easy to link dimensions and measure groups at different levels.

5.1.3 Role Playing Relationships

A single fact table may be related to a dimension table more than once. A classic example of this scenario is an order transaction fact table, such as the FactInternetSales table in the Adventure-WorksDW database (Figure 5.8). It has three foreign keys to the DimTime dimension table that represent the order date (OrderDateKey), ship date (ShipDateKey), and due date (DueDateKey). Since the Time dimension in this case serves multiple roles, we refer to this scenario as dimension *role-playing*. Assuming that the end users would like to browse data by all role-playing dates, with the "classic" OLAP model, you need to define separate dimensions.

Definition A role-playing relationship occurs when a single dimension is joined repeatedly to the same fact table.

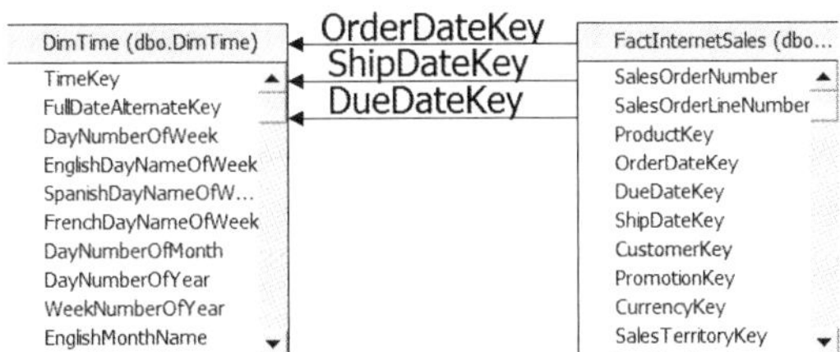

Figure 5.8 Use a role playing dimension when a fact table has more than one foreign key to a dimension table.

UDM solves dimension role-playing scenarios elegantly by introducing role playing relationships. UDM role-playing relationships reduce maintenance effort because the UDM designer has to maintain only one dimension definition. In addition, they also minimize storage space because the Analysis Server can reuse the dimension stores.

When the Cube Wizard infers a role-playing dimension, it creates automatically as many relationships as the dimension roles. Assuming that the dimension definition is already in place, implementing a role-playing relationship manually involves two steps. First, using the Cube Structure tab or the Dimension Usage tab you need to add the dimension as many times as the number of roles it will "play". In our case, we need to have three instances of the Date dimension that differ by naming convention. The end result is that the same Date dimension appears under three different names (Date, Ship Date, and Due Date) in the SOS OLAP cube (see again Figure 5.1).

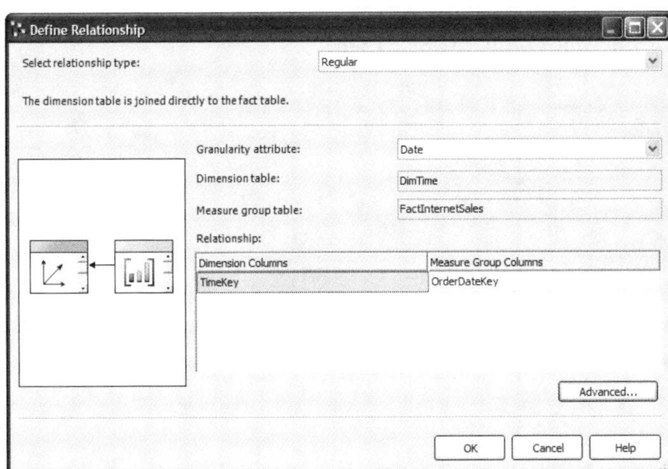

Figure 5.9 Define a role-playing relationship by matching the primary key of the dimension table to the appropriate foreign key of the fact table.

Second, we need to create a regular relationship for each role by matching the primary key column of the dimension to the appropriate reference key column in the fact table. Thus, for the Order Date (Date dimension, in our case), we need to match the TimeKey column to the OrderDateKey column of the FactInternetSales fact table (see Figure 5.9).

5.1.4 Fact Relationships

Both the FactInternetSales and FactResellerSales fact tables contain the Order Number, Line Number, and Carrier Tracking Number columns. These columns are certainly useful for end-user data analytics. For example, a data analyst may be interested to find out the total sales amount for all orders bundled under the same tracking number. Or, a customer representative may need to look up the total sales order amount for a given order number. At the same time, these columns are not suitable to form a standard dimension for two main reasons.

First, these columns don't have additional descriptive information that might form a separate dimension table. For example, all attributes associated with the order (Order Number) have already been moved out to other dimensions (e.g. Date, Customer, etc.). Since the resulting Order Number dimension is empty, the dimensional theory refers to it as a *fact* or *degenerate* dimension.

Definition A *fact (degenerate)* dimension is derived directly from the fact table and doesn't have a corresponding dimension table. The grain of a degenerate dimension is the individual item of the fact table.

Implementing fact relationship

In UDM, a fact dimension is implemented by creating a standard dimension that has a fact relationship to the respective fact table. Let's create the Internet Order Details fact dimension to encapsulate the useful attributes that cannot form standard dimensions, such as the customer PO number, order number, order line number, and carrier tracking number.

1. In the Dimension Usage tab, click on the Add Cube Dimension toolbar button. In the Add Cube Dimension dialog, click the *New dimension* button to launch the Dimension Wizard.
2. Choose the *SOS OLAP* data source in the Select Data Source View step and click Next.
3. In the Select the Dimension Type step, leave the default radio button *Standard dimension* selected and click Next to advance to the Select the Main Dimension Table.

Figure 5.10 A fact dimension is derived directly from the fact table.

4. Select the FactInternetSales fact table since we will be deriving the Internet Order Details directly from the fact table. Note that the Dimension Wizard has pre-selected the SalesOrder-Number and SalesOrderLineNumber columns for the key collection of the dimension key attribute because these columns form the composite primary key in the fact table (see Figure

5.10). In addition, notice that the name of the dimension key will be derived from the SalesOrderLineNumber column. Accept the defaults and click Next.

5. In the Select Related Tables step, clear all tables since a fact dimension is based solely on the fact table. Click Next.

6. In the Select Dimension Attributes step, clear all attributes and select only the *Carrier Tracking Number* and *Customer PO Number* attributes. Click Next.

7. Accept the defaults in the rest of the steps. In the Completing the Wizard step, name the dimension **Internet Order Details** and click Finish. The new dimension is added to the Add Cube Dimension dialog.

8. Click OK to return to the Dimension Usage tab. Note that the Internet Order Details dimension is added at the end of the Dimensions column list (Figure 5.11).

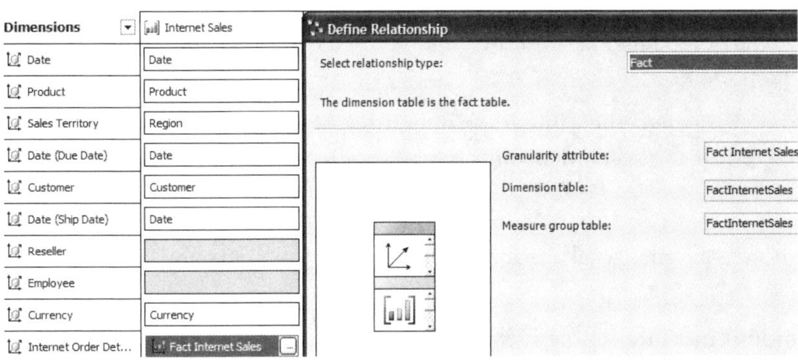

Figure 5.11 A degenerate dimension has a Fact relationship to the fact table it is derived from.

In addition, the Cube Designer has joined the Internet Order Details dimension to all measure groups that derive from the FactInternetSales fact table (Internet Sales and Internet Orders measure group). When doing so, the Cube Wizard has set the dimension relationship to Fact, as you can easily deduce by looking at the special icon (identical to the icon identifying a measure group) or by opening the Define Relationship dialog.

Working with fact relationships

Before creating a report that showcases the Internet Order Details dimension, let's briefly review its definition and add some final touches. Open the Internet Order Details dimension in the Dimension Designer. A fact dimension is no different that the standard dimensions you are familiar with. We can add or remove attribute hierarchies and create multilevel hierarchies.

1. Rename the Fact Internet Sales dimension key to **Order Line Item**. This name reflects the fact that the dimension key identifies a single item in the FactInternetSales fact table which represents an order line item.

2. Drag the SalesOrderNumber column from the Data Source View diagram to the Attribute pane. This action creates the Sales Order Number attribute. Rename it to **Order Number**.

3. A carrier tracking number may span more than one order. To inform UDM about this relationship, define the Carrier Tracking Number attribute as a member property of Order Number attribute.

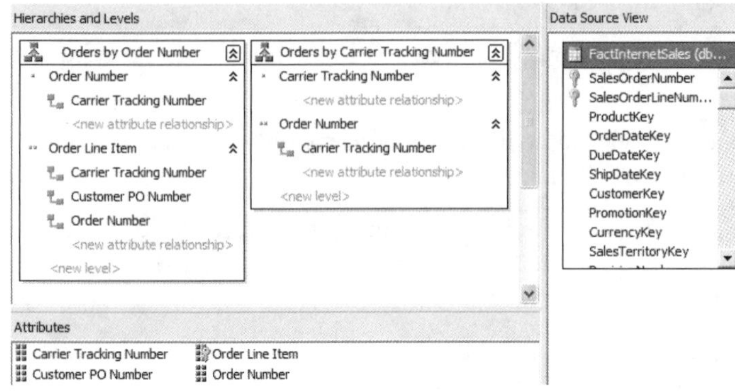

Figure 5.12 A fact dimension is a standard dimension that may have attribute and multilevel hierarchies.

4. If you wish, you can also create useful multilevel hierarchies. For example, we could create Orders by Order Number hierarchy that defines the *Order Number* ⇨ *Order Line Item* natural hierarchy. An Orders by Carrier Tracking Number hierarchy is another potentially useful multilevel hierarchy (see Figure 5.12).
5. Once you are done with the changes to the dimension definition, save the dimension and close the Dimension Designer to return to the Dimension Usage tab. Deploy the project and browse the SOS OLAP cube.

Let's create a report that shows the sales total amount broken down by orders and line items for a given customer.

6. Drag the Internet Sales Amount measure on the Detail Fields area.
7. Drag the Full Name attribute hierarchy from the Customer dimension on rows. In the OWC PivotTable report, expand the Full Name dropdown filter. Clear the *All* checkbox and select only a few customers (e.g. the first three).
8. Drag the Orders by Order Number multilevel hierarchy from the Internet Order Details fact dimension and drop it next to the Customer dimension. Your report should like the one shown in Figure 5.13.

Full Name	Order Number	Order Line Item	Internet Sales Amount
⊟ Aaron A. Allen	⊟ SO46413	1	$2,236.39
		Total	$2,236.39
	Total		$2,236.39
⊟ Aaron A. Hayes	⊞ SO49797		$782.99
	⊟ SO67240	1	$2,319.99
		2	$9.99
		Total	$2,329.98
	Total		$3,112.97
⊞ Aaron A. Zhang			$600.46
Grand Total			$5,949.82

Figure 5.13 Use the Internet Order Details fact dimension to browse sales data by order number.

As you can see, UDM automatically applies the Autoexists behavior among the requested dimensions, so that only the orders associated with a given customer are shown. For example, glancing at the report, we can see easily that Aaron Hayes has two orders. The second order with an order number of SO76240 has two line items totaling $2,319.99 and $9.99 respectively. If you wish, you could enhance UDM further to show interactively the line item details by implementing drill-through or actions, as I will demonstrate in chapter 12.

5.1.5 Reference Relationships

Typically, a dimension is directly related to a measure group by virtue of a referential or logical (DSV) relationship between the dimension table primary key and a foreign key of the measure group table. For example, the Customer dimension is directly related to the Internet Sales measure group because there is a one-to-many relationship at the data source level. However, what if you need to relate a dimension to a measure group in the absence of a direct relationship? For example, consider the data schema of the Sales Territory dimension and the Sales Quotas measure group (Figure 5.14).

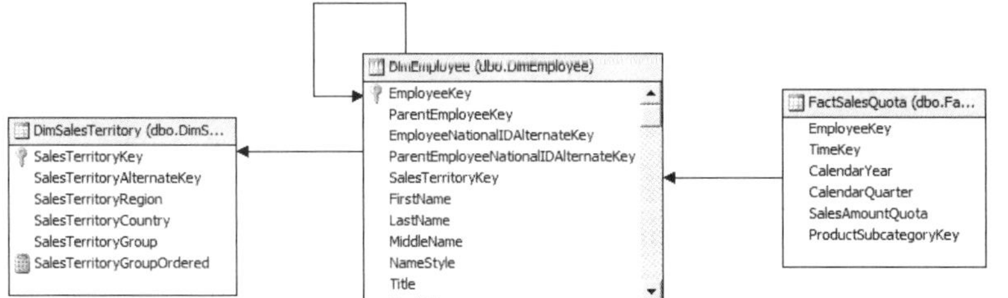

Figure 5.14 Browsing the FactSalesQuota facts by Sales Territory requires using the Employee dimension as a referenced dimension.

There is no relationship between these two tables. Yet, end users may need to browse the sales quotas facts by the Sales Territory dimension, e.g. to see the 2003 sales quota for North America. A trivial approach could be to add Sales Territory to the Employee dimension and create a multi-level hierarchy which has Sales Group, Sales Country, Sales Region, and Employee levels. If we do so, however, we will end up duplicating the Sales Territory dimension definition and storage. Ideally, we would like to leave the Sales Territory dimension intact as a standalone dimension but be able to join it to the Sales Quota dimension via another intermediate dimension. Assuming that the Employee dimension is already in place, we can use it as a "bridge". In UDM terminology, such a dimension relationship is called a *referenced* relationship and the Sales Territory dimension is called a *reference* dimension.

Implementing a referenced relationship

Implementing a referenced relationship is remarkably simple. In fact, when a new dimension or a measure group is added, the Cube Designer may have automatically detected referenced relationships after probing the cube data schema. For example, in the case of the SOS OLAP cube, the Cube Wizard has created a reference dimension between the Sales Territory dimension and the Sales Quotas measure group (Figure 5.15).

The relationship type is set to *Referenced*. The *Intermediate dimension* dropdown lists only the dimensions that can be joined to the measure group based on the existing data source or DSV relationships. In our case, there are only two dimensions, Employee and Date, with the Employee being the right choice for the task at hand. In the Relationship panel, you need to specify which attributes will be used to establish a relationship between the reference dimension and the intermediate dimension.

For the Sales Territory reference dimension, this will be the dimension key attribute (Region). For the intermediate dimension, this will be Sales Territory Key attribute. This, of course, assumes that the Sales Territory Key attribute has been added to the Employee dimension and its AttributeHierarchy property has been set to *True* (if you need to hide it, set its AttributeHierarchyVisible to *False*).

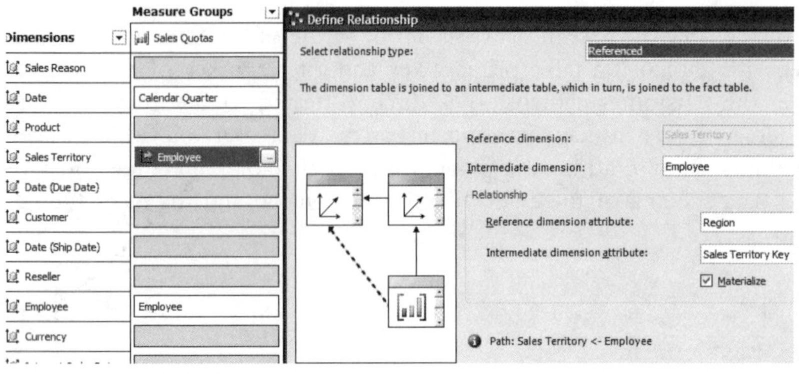

Figure 5.15 Create a referenced relationship by using an intermediate dimension.

The Materialize checkbox is used as an optimization technique. It does not affect the query results. Reference dimensions with Materialization set to *False* (as many-to-many dimensions) are resolved at query time, i.e. the server does a join between the intermediate dimension and reference dimension. The fact data stored on disk does not point to the reference dimension. When Materialization is set to *True*, the reference dimension behaves internally like a regular dimension and the fact data points to the reference dimension. No join is done at query time, so performance is better. This is the recommended approach except with linked measure groups (explained in section 5.3) where the join is not possible to materialize.

	Year ▾				
	⊞ 2001	⊞ 2002	⊞ 2003	⊞ 2004	Grand Total
Group ▾	Sales Quota	Sales Quota	Sales Quota	Sales Quota	Sales Quota
⊞ North America	$9,478,000.00	$24,284,000.00	$27,172,000.00	$12,349,000.00	$73,283,000.00
⊞ Europe		$4,162,000.00	$9,376,000.00	$4,820,000.00	$18,358,000.00
⊞ Pacific			$867,000.00	$820,000.00	$1,687,000.00
⊞ NA	$35,000.00	$563,000.00	$1,367,000.00	$421,000.00	$2,386,000.00
Grand Total	$9,513,000.00	$29,009,000.00	$38,782,000.00	$18,410,000.00	$95,714,000.00

Figure 5.16 Use a reference dimension as a bridge between a dimension and a measure group that are not directly related.

Once the referenced relationship is in place, we can author a report as the one shown in Figure 5.16. Thanks to the Employee dimension, the Sales Quota measures can be browsed by the Sales Territory dimension.

Referenced relationship pros and cons

Reference dimensions have certain advantages and disadvantages associated with them. Use reference dimensions when:

- *You need to join indirectly related dimension and measure groups* -- This is especially useful when working with linked dimensions, as we will see shortly.
- *You need to avoid duplication of dimension storage and definition* -- Just as a developer would re-factor common programming logic and move it to a function, a UDM designer could reduce maintenance effort by encapsulating the duplicated dimension definition elements into a standalone dimension.

Another example where a reference dimension could be a good choice in the SOS OLAP UDM is the Geography dimension. The Customer and Reseller dimensions both include the Dim-Geography table which is redundant. We could create a Geography dimension and join it to the

fact tables through the Customer and Reseller referenced
referenced relationships are not without tradeoffs:

- *No multilevel hierarchies* -- You cannot define multi-level hiera dimension and the intermediate dimension. For example, we c hierarchy with Sales Region and Employee Full Name attributes b tory and Employee dimensions are physically separated.
- *No Autoexist behavior* -- The Analysis Server doesn't apply Autoexists w dimension is used. For example, if we add the Employee dimension to the in Figure 5.16, it will show all combinations of the Sales Territory and Emplo bers instead of filtering the sales person based on the sales territory they are resp for. Once again, the reason for this is that the server treats the reference dimension separate dimension.
- *Performance impact* -- A reference dimension may negatively impact the query performance.

When the disadvantages of a referenced relationship get in the way, consider replacing it with a snowflake dimension (e.g. Customer dimension which absorbs the Geography dimension) or creating direct regular relationship. At the same time, the reference dimension shouldn't be viewed as a justification to create a snowflake schema when a star schema is a better option.

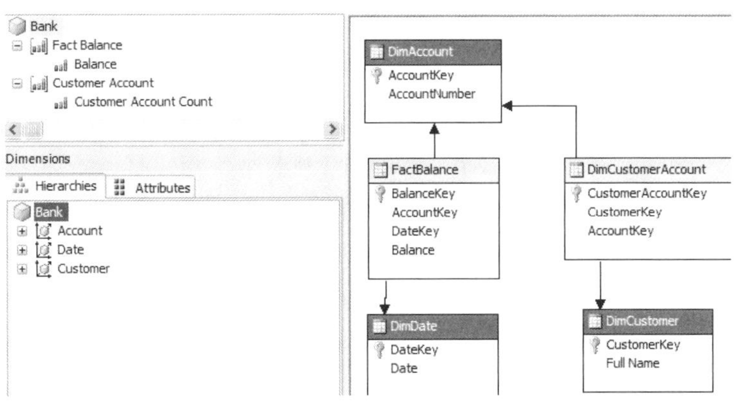

Figure 5.17 The bank account scenario is an example of a many-to-many relationship because a customer may have more than one bank account and a single account may be associated with more than one customer.

5.1.6 Many-to-Many Relationships

Typically, a single dimension member relates to one or more facts in a fact table. For example, a given customer has one or more order items. This is an example of one-to-many relationship that all of our dimensions used so far. Sometimes, you may run into the opposite situation where a single fact may actually relate to more than one dimension member. To understand this better, let's deviate for a moment from the Adventure Works UDM model and consider the "classic" bank account scenario where a customer may have more than one bank account and an account may be associated with multiple customers (a joint account), as shown in Figure 5.17.

The sample data source that will drive this scenario is a Microsoft Access database named Bank that can be found in the Ch05 folder. The Bank UDM is based on Marco Russo's weblog example (see Resource section) and is implemented in the form of the Bank cube found in the Bank Analysis Services project.

chema may look like the one shown in Figure 5.17.
the FactBalance table. What makes this scenario
be associated with more than one member of the
count. In the relational data model, a many-to-many
an additional table that breaks the many-to-many
enario, this role is fulfilled by the DimCustomerAc-

ustomer records and some of them have joint ac-
ance table has account balances for only one day and
mplistic, this bank scenario poses an issue when we
stomer. We cannot just create an additional foreign
ance table because we will end up with counting the
number of the account holders (Figure 5.18).

	Account Number				
	001	002	003	004	Grand Total
Full Name	Balance	Balance	Balance	Balance	Balance
Alice	100			100	200
Bob	100	100	100		300
Brian		100			100
John				100	100
Martin			100		100
Maya		100			100
Grand Total	200	300	200	200	900

Figure 5.18 If a many-to-many dimension relationship is not used, the facts will be counted more than once.

For example, Alice owns two accounts (001 and 004), while Bob has three accounts (001, 002, and 003). Alice and Bob share account 001. We don't want the 001 account balance to be double-counted when aggregating the balances over customers. Instead, we want to get a balance of $400 since there are four accounts, each with a balance of $100. UDM addresses this requirement by introducing many-to-many relationships.

SSAS 2000 Handling many-to-many relationships in SSAS 2000 wasn't that straightforward to implement. One approach was to use MDX calculations, which could negatively impact performance.

Implementing many-to-many relationship

Instead of joining the Customer dimension directly to the fact table, we will join it through the Customer Account measure group which will now fulfill a dual purpose: as a dimension and as a measure group in the Bank cube. In fact, when you run the Cube Wizard, it correctly identifies the DimCustomerAccount table as a fact table. The Bank UDM was implemented by following these simple steps.

1. Run the Cube Wizard and accept the default settings. The Cube Wizard should generate the UDM schema shown in Figure 5.17.
2. In the Dimension Usage tab, create a new relationship between the Customer dimension and the Fact Balance measure group of a Many-to-Many type.
3. In the Define Relationship dialog, select the *Customer Account* measure group in the *Intermediate measure group* dropdown (Figure 5.19).

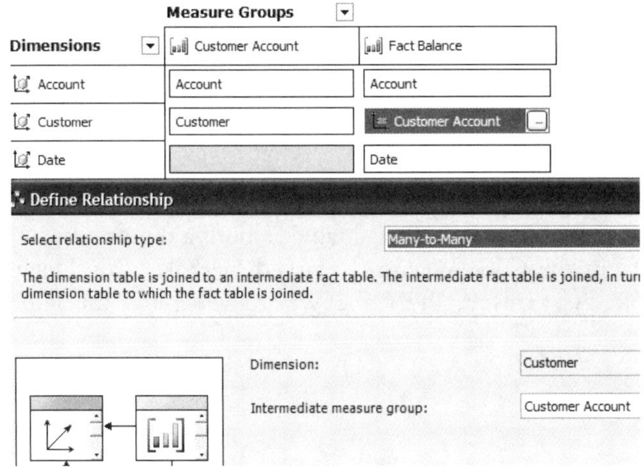

Figure 5.19 Implement a many-to-many relationship by joining the fact table to the dimension on the many side through an intermediate measure group.

4. Deploy and browse the cube. Notice that the Grand Total shows the correct total account balance of $400 and the joint account balances are not double-counted.

Going back to the Adventure Works OLAP model, the many-to-many scenario can be demonstrated by the FactInternetSalesReason table. The idea here is that a web customer may specify more than one reason when submitting an order. Naturally, the same reason can be used by more than one customer. So, if the end-user needs to browse data by the Sales Reason dimension, we need to resolve the many-to-many relationship by going through the Internet Sales Reason fact table. I won't be discussing the implementation details since they are similar to the bank account scenario. Step-by-step instructions of how the sales reason scenario could be implemented can be found in the Analysis Services tutorial that comes with the product documentation.

Sales Order Number: SO43659

Order Date	Account Number	Carrier Tracking Number	Line Item	Order Qty	Unit Price	Line Total
2001-07-01 00:00:00	10-4020-000676	4911-403C-98	1	1	2024.994	2024.994
			2	3	2024.994	6074.982
			3	1	2024.994	2024.994
			4	1	2039.994	2039.994
			5	1	2039.994	2039.994
			6	2	2039.994	4079.988
			7	1	2039.994	2039.994
			8	3	28.8404	86.5212
			9	1	28.8404	28.8404
			10	6	5.7	34.2
			11	2	5.1865	10.373
			12	4	20.1865	80.746
		Total		26	14323.7118	20565.6206

Figure 5.20 You can bend UDM to generate relational reports.

5.1.7 Treating Dimensions As Measure Groups

To wrap up our discussion about dimension relationships, I would like to mention another interesting UDM characteristic that brings it closer to the relational reporting model. Suppose that you need to create a "classic" sales order report from the AdventureWorks OLTP database consisting of two sections: a sales order header (SalesOrderHeader table) and order items

(SalesOrderDetail table). This is a requirement that relational reporting tools, such as Microsoft Reporting Services, are designed to handle with ease. Can you generate such a report with UDM? Yes, it is possible, as Figure 5.20 demonstrates. This scenario is demonstrated by the Relational UDM sample hosted in the Relational Reporting Analysis Services project. I generated the Relational UDM from scratch by running the Cube Wizard against the Adventure Works OLTP database.

Implementing the relational report

The trick to generating this report is to treat the SalesOrderDetail table as both a dimension and a fact table. To accomplish this, when I ran the Cube Wizard, I marked the SalesOrderDetail table as both a dimension and fact table. As a result, the Cube Wizard generated the cube definition shown on Figure 5.21.

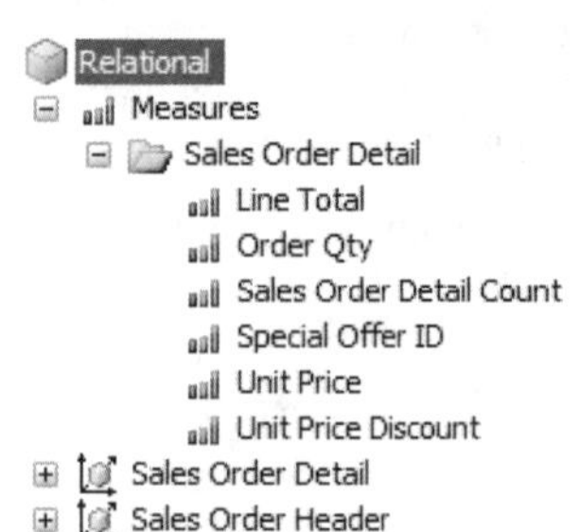

Figure 5.21 Generating the sales order report requires the SalesOrderDetail table to be treated as both a dimension and a fact table

Since the Sales Order Detail dimension is defined as both a dimension and a measure group, you can drag the line item attributes (Carrier Tracking Number and Line Item) to form the header portion of the report, while the numeric facts from the Sales Order Detail measure group can serve as measures.

Tip If you would like to morph this report into the classic header-line items template using Microsoft Reporting Services, you can use its MDX Query Designer to flatten the dataset. Next, switch to the Designer tab and use List regions to create the header and line item sections.

A word of caution

So, should you dump your favorite relational reporting tool and embrace UDM for generating relational reports? My answer is "Not yet". As I mentioned in chapter 1, you should see the relational and dimensional models as complementing, not competing with, each other. Instead, use the right tool for the job. The fact that UDM may handle relational reports doesn't mean that it is designed to be used as a relational reporting tool.

The power of OLAP is *aggregating* large volumes of data. Reports based on discrete transactional rows can be more efficiently generated by relational reporting tools, such as Microsoft Reporting Services. Doing so in UDM requires the fact table to be treated as a dimensional table, which leads to duplication of storage (unless ROLAP storage mode is used) and performance issues. Make a note of my example, but apply it with caution. Otherwise, you may feel like you are forcing square pegs into round holes. You may succeed but at what cost?

5.2 Advanced Data Analytics

In your real life, OLAP requirements may call for more sophisticated dimensional modeling techniques. UDM has been greatly enhanced to support advanced data analytics features. In this section, we will discuss and implement a few of those "special" requirements that you may face when building OLAP solutions.

	Year ▾ Semester Quarter Month							
	⊟ 2001							
	⊟ H2 CY 2001							
	⊟ Q4 CY 2001							
	⊞ October		⊞ November		⊞ December		Total	
Currency ▾	Average Rate	End Of Day Rate	Average Rate	End Of Day Rate	Average Rate	End Of Day Rate	Average Rate	End Of Day Rate
Australian Dollar	19.12	19.12	18.15	18.15	18.24	18.24	55.51	55.51
Brazilian Real	17.59	17.58	17.22	17.22	17.19	17.19	51.99	51.99
Grand Total	36.71	36.71	35.37	35.37	35.43	35.44	107.51	107.51

Figure 5.22 Sometimes, you may need to handle average or closing balances over time.

5.2.1 Handling Semi-additive Measures

Sometimes, you may need to handle semi-additive measures that don't aggregate over time, such as inventory balances, account balances, or averages. For example, in the preceding chapter, we introduced the Currency Rates measure group to help us convert the foreign currencies to the US dollar by using measure expressions. The Currency Rates measure group has two measures, Average Rate and End Of Day Rate, that represent the average exchange rate and end of day exchange rate of the currency for a given day.

Suppose that you need to find the average and end-of-date currency rates for a current time period, e.g. within the span of several days. To do so, you may create a report as the one shown in Figure 5.22. This report was created in the Cube Browser by dragging the Currency dimension on rows, Date dimension on columns, and Average Rate and End Of Date measure from the Currency Rates measure group as report data. Further, I've filtered the Date dimension to show currency rates for Q4 of 2001 only.

It doesn't take long to realize that there is something wrong in this report. While the daily measure values are correct, the totals are all wrong. The report simply sums up the measure values over time. That's because the aggregate function of both measures is set to *Sum*. What we really need is the total Average Rate figure to show the average-over-time currency rate, while the total End Of Day Rate figure to show the latest rate for the selected period. This requirement can be met easily by using the pre-defined *AverageOfChildren* and *LastNonEmpty* semi-additive aggregate functions.

SSAS 2000 If you had to work with semi-additive measures in SSAS 2000, you had no other choice but to use MDX expressions. With the introduction of the semi-additive aggregate functions in UDM, in many cases, this is no longer necessary.

1. In the Cube Designer, select the Average Rate measure and change its AggregateFunction property to *AverageOfChildren.*

2. The AverageOfChildren function sums the measure values for all dimensions except for a Time dimension. In other words, it behaves just like the Sum function except when a Time dimension is requested in the query. If a Time dimension is requested, AverageOfChildren calculates the *average* measure value, hence its name. This, of course, assumes that the dimension Type property has been set to *Time.* If you create a new measure, the AverageOfChildren is shown as the *Average over time* usage type on the New Measure dialog.

3. Select the *End Of Day Rate* measure and change its AggregateFunction property to *LastNonEmpty*. The only difference between the AverageOfChildren and LastNonEmpty functions is that the latter retrieves the ending balance for the date period requested.
4. Switch to the Cube Browser tab. Process the cube and reconnect. Observe that the report now gives you the expected output.

	Year ▾ Semester Quarter Month							
	⊟ 2001							
	⊟ H2 CY 2001							
	⊟ Q4 CY 2001							
	⊞ October		⊞ November		⊞ December		Total	
Currency ▾	Average Rate	End Of Day Rate	Average Rate	End Of Day Rate	Average Rate	End Of Day Rate	Average Rate	End Of Day Rate
Australian Dollar	.62	.61	.61	.60	.59	.57	.60	.57
Brazilian Real	.57	.57	.57	.56	.55	.54	.57	.54
Grand Total	1.18	1.18	1.18	1.16	1.14	1.12	1.17	1.12

Figure 5.23 Use the UDM semi-additive aggregate functions to handle semi-additive measures.

For example, the Average Rate Total for Australian Dollar is 60 cents which indeed equals the average currency value for the three months in Q4 2001. Similarly, the End Of Day total figure is 57 cents which is the latest exchange rate for December.

			Fiscal Year ▾			
			⊞ 2002	⊞ 2003	⊞ 2004	Grand Total
Account Level 01 ▾	**Account Level 02**	**Account Level 03**	Amount	Amount	Amount	Amount
⊟ Balance Sheet	⊞ Assets		$9,014,992.09	$14,730,369.34	$21,366,847.84	$21,366,847.84
	⊞ Liabilities and Owners Equity		$9,014,992.09	$0.00	$0.00	$0.00
	Total		$0.00	$14,730,369.34	$21,366,847.84	$21,366,847.84
⊟ Net Income	⊞ Operating Profit		$14,372,741.96	$10,312,557.51	$11,485,924.94	$36,171,224.41
	⊟ Other Income and Expense	⊞ Interest Income	$31,131.12	$45,999.81	$69,871.35	$147,002.28
		⊞ Interest Expense	$47,802.29	$70,618.29	$107,303.01	$225,723.59
		⊞ Gain/Loss on Sales of Asset	($38,167.17)	($56,280.26)	($85,561.25)	($180,008.68)
		⊞ Other Income	($23,861.00)	$89,997.79	$157,046.66	$223,183.45
		⊞ Curr Xchg Gain/(Loss)	$97,353.00	$4,643.00	($15,512.00)	$86,484.00
		Total	$18,653.66	$13,742.05	$18,541.75	$50,937.46
	⊞ Taxes		$1,622,417.70	$2,938,547.56	$2,682,825.75	$7,243,791.01
	Total		$12,768,977.92	$7,387,752.00	$8,821,640.94	$28,978,370.86

Figure 5.24 Financial reporting can be challenging since data needs to be aggregated in specific ways.

5.2.2 Implementing Accounting Intelligence

Suppose that the AW Finance department has requested the ability to generate financial reports, such as Balance Sheet, Net Income, Profit and Loss statements, etc. The final report may look like the one shown in Figure 5.24. Financial reporting can be tricky because of the way data aggregates. Account categories (referred to *account types* in UDM) can be added or subtracted from the parent category. For example, the Net Income category can be divided into Operating Profit (Gross Profit), Expenses, and Taxes subcategories, where:

```
Net Income = Operating Profit – (Expenses + Taxes)
```

UDM can help you handle financial reporting with ease and, in this section, you will learn how to implement it by creating a Finance cube. The sample Finance cube can be found in the Finance Analysis Services project (Ch05 folder). While I could have enhanced the SOS OLAP cube, I've chosen to implement the Finance cube as a standalone cube. The main reason for doing so is to show you later in this chapter how you can work with dimensions and measures located in an external UDM.

Generating the raw financial UDM

Upon a closer examination of the financial report shown in Figure 5.24, we realize that its structure resembles a recursive hierarchy. A category can be broken in subcategories, which can be further broken to an arbitrary nesting level. Does this bring any recollection? Indeed, such a structure could be handled easily by the parent-child dimension we chapter. If you explore the DimAccount table in the AdventureWork that it has a parent-child relationship set up between the ParentAc the AccountKey primary key. This data schema will help us cre dimension from which we will derive the account categories.

Creating the raw Finance cube is trivial and it is a matter of fol create an Analysis Services project called **Finance**. Next, we creat AdventureWorksDW database (or reuse its definition from the S data source view (Finance.dsv) on top of the data source which, includes only the required tables (DimAccount, DimTime, and FactFinance. Finally, Cube Wizard to create the raw UDM consisting of the Account and Date dimensions and Financial Reporting measure group. The Cube wizard should automatically detect the parent-child relationship and should set up the Account dimension as a parent-child dimension.

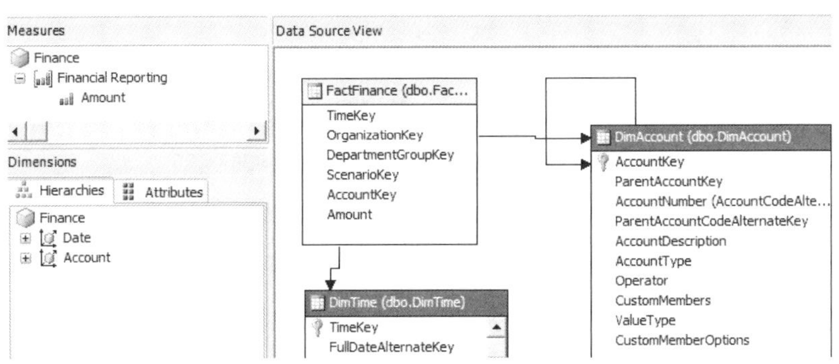

Figure 5.25 The Finance UDM consists of a Time dimension (Date), a parent-child dimension (Account), and a Financial Reporting measure group with only one measure (Amount).

After a few final touches, we derive to the Finance UDM shown in Figure 5.25. We could use the Dimension Wizard to fine-tune the Account dimension. Specifically, since we have two root members (Balance Sheet and Net Income) that don't roll up, we could disable the top member of the Accounts attribute (IsAggregatable=False) to remove the *All* member. In addition, we could make the report more intuitive by setting the NamingTemplate property of the Accounts parent-child hierarchy to **Account Level *;** in order to create the level captions shown in Figure 5.24.

If you process the Finance cube at this time and create the report shown in Figure 5.24, you will find out that it doesn't give you the expected results. There are two major issues. First, semi-additive measures are not properly aggregated over time. For example, all balance measures (assets, equity, etc.) are semi-additive in respect to the Time dimension. The report adds the balances together, instead of showing the last balance amount for the cutoff period requested. Second, account categories are not aggregated properly over the Account dimension. Since the aggregate function of the Amount measure is set to Sum, UDM just sums the measures across the Account hierarchy as opposed to adding or subtracting account categories. Let's fix these issues starting with configuring the semi-additive behavior of the Account dimensions.

Defining account intelligence

Once you match the account categories to the pre-defined account types UDM supports, you can configure the semi-additive behavior you need. The easiest way to do so is to run the Business Intelligence Wizard we've used in the preceding chapter to order attribute members.

s wizard at a cube or a dimension level. The first option is more feature-rich so ry.

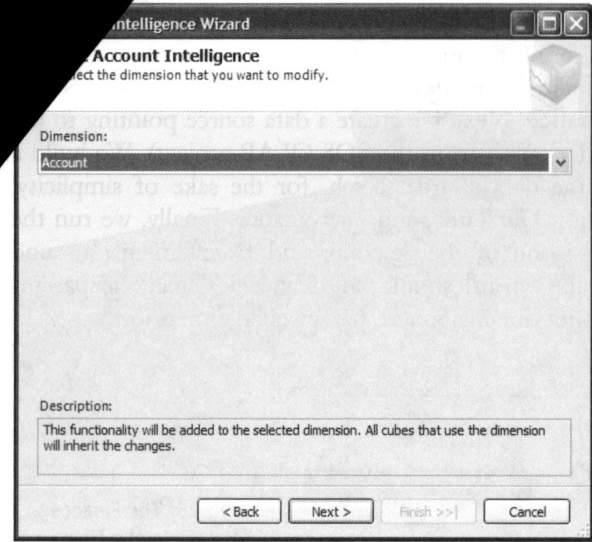

Figure 5.26 Use the Define Account Intelligence step to designate an Account dimension.

1. In the Solution Explorer, right-click on the Finance cube and choose *Add Business Intelligence* context menu to start the BI Wizard.

2. In the Choose Enhancement step, select *Define account intelligence.* Click Next.

Figure 5.27 Specify the Account attribute mappings. The most important attribute is the Account Type.

3. In the Define Account Intelligence step (Figure 5.26), the BI Wizard asks which dimension will serve as an Account dimension. Select the *Account* dimension and click Next. Behind the scenes, the BI Wizard will set the Type property of the Account dimension to *Account.*

Figure 5.28 Map the account categories to the pre-defined account types UDM supports.

4. Use the Configure Dimension Attributes step (Figure 5.27) to map the Account dimension attributes to the three pre-defined attribute types that are supported by UDM. The most important one is the Account Type attribute because its members will represent the account categories that you will need to match in the next step of the wizard. The Account Name and Account Number attributes are for client convenience only.

Note When the BI Wizard is run at the cube level, you have the option to set the aggregation function of all measures in the affected measure groups (the ones the Account dimension is related to) to *ByAccount*. The net effect of doing so is that the measures will be aggregated over time based on the respective operators you set. For example, assuming that the aggregate function of the Balance account type is set to LastNotEmpty, the closing balance amount will be shown when the account balances are requested over time.

The Define Account Intelligence step (Figure 5.28) is the most important step. The BI Wizard asks you to match your account types (the Account Type attribute members) to the seven pre-defined account types UDM supports. Additional account types could be created using the Account Mappings panel on the database properties window (see Figure 5.30). The BI Wizard makes an attempt to match the account types through a naming convention.

5. Since, in our case, not all names match, make the selections shown in Figure 5.28. You don't have to map all account types. For example, if you don't have a cash flow account type (at least in the table, I hope you will, in real life), you can ignore the Flow account type.

6. In the Completing the Wizard step (Figure 5.29), the BI Wizard gives you a summary of the changes that will be made. The BI wizard picks suitable operators based on the account type. For example, the Balance account type will be set to aggregate as *LastNotEmpty* over time. In addition, for client convenience, the BI Wizard defines additional aliases for the account types. A smart OLAP browser can use an alias as an alternative name to reference the account type. Click Finish to update the Account dimension and close the BI Wizard.

Figure 5.29 You can create one or more aliases for each account type.

You may wonder where the aggregate functions are stored and how you can change them if needed. It turns out that they become part of the database metadata.

7. Right-click on the Finance project (not cube) node in the Solution Explorer and choose *Edit Database* context menu.
8. Expand the Account Type Mapping panel and observe the Aggregation Function column (Figure 5.30).

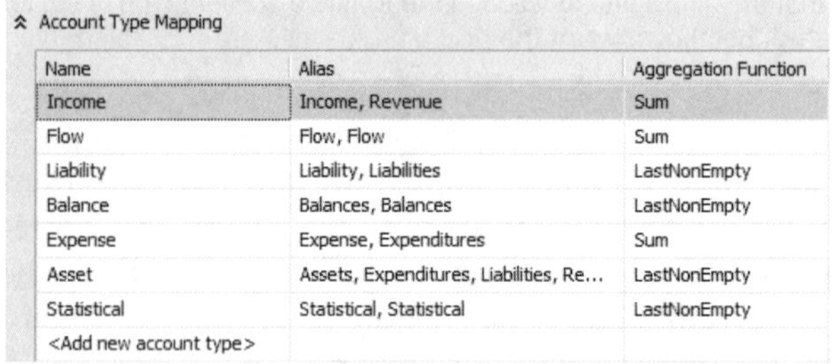

Account Type Mapping

Name	Alias	Aggregation Function
Income	Income, Revenue	Sum
Flow	Flow, Flow	Sum
Liability	Liability, Liabilities	LastNonEmpty
Balance	Balances, Balances	LastNonEmpty
Expense	Expense, Expenditures	Sum
Asset	Assets, Expenditures, Liabilities, Re...	LastNonEmpty
Statistical	Statistical, Statistical	LastNonEmpty
<Add new account type>		

Figure 5.30 Use the Account Type Mapping panel to review or change the aggregate functions.

The Account Type Mapping panel allows you to create additional account types if the pre-defined types are not enough. If you process the cube now and re-generate the report, you will see the effect of the aggregate functions. For example, back to Figure 5.24, the Grand Total column gives you the last Assets balance for the time period requested (*LastNonEmpty* function), while the Income-related account categories sum their values over time (*Sum* function).

5.2.3 Using Custom Aggregation

Parent-child dimensions can use custom aggregation rules. As we've seen, the members of the Account dimension need to be aggregated in a different way based on the account category (e.g. incomes added and expenses subtracted).

88	47	80	4	Other Income and Expense	Revenue	+
89	88	8000	80	Interest Income	Revenue	+
90	88	8010	80	Interest Expense	Expenditures	-
91	88	8020	80	Gain/Loss on Sales of Asset	Revenue	+
92	88	8030	80	Other Income	Revenue	+
93	88	8040	80	Curr Xchg Gain/(Loss)	Revenue	+
94	47	8500	4	Taxes	Expenditures	-
95	(null)	9500	(null)	Statistical Accounts	Statistical	~

Figure 5.31 A parent-child dimension can use unary operators for custom member aggregation.

Using unary operators

You can tell UDM how to aggregate the measures across a parent-child dimension by using a unary operator defined in a table column or a named calculation column. The Operator column in the DimAccount table serves this purpose (Figure 5.31). UDM supports five unary operators. Use the + operator to add the member value to its preceding sibling members. For example, the Other Income member is associated with this operator because its value needs to be added to the preceding members at the same hierarchy level when calculating the parent aggregated value. Similarly, use –, *, and / operators for subtracting, multiplying, and dividing the member value from the value of the preceding members. Finally, the ~ operator tells UDM to ignore the member value whatsoever.

Once the unary operator is set up at the data source level, you can bind the source of the UnaryOperatorColumn property of the parent-child dimension to the unary column. Alternatively, you can run the BI Wizard, as we will demonstrate next.

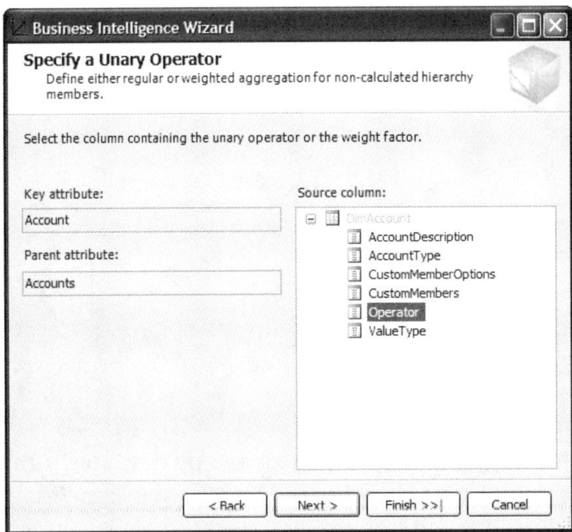

Figure 5.32 Set the UnaryOperatorColumn property of the attribute with a Parent usage to tell UDM which data source column will supply the operator value or run the BI wizard.

1. Right-click on the Account dimension in the Solution Explorer window and choose *Add Business Intelligence* to launch the BI Wizard.
2. In the Choose Enhancement step, select the *Specify a unary operator* option.
3. In the Specify a Unary Operator step, select the Operator column (Figure 5.32).
4. Deploy the project and browse the cube. Now your financial report should look like the one shown in Figure 5.24.

Using weights

The unary operator has been enhanced from SSAS 2000 to handle weights (values between 0 and 1). Weights can be used to aggregate measures based on the percentage of member contribution respective to its parent. For example, in one of my real-life projects I had to use weights for project tracking. If you are familiar with Microsoft Project, you know that it averages the parent task status when aggregating the status of its children. Hence, if the parent task has two subtasks that are completed 20% and 80% respectively, the parent task progress will be 50%.

That's all fine if the tasks are equally important, but what if one of them is more significant than the order. For example, if this is a house construction project, the first task may be Pour Foundation, while the second may be Build Fence. Although the Pour Foundation task is completed 20%, its contribution is more significant to the overall progress schedule. To reflect this, you may want to "boost" the contribution of the more significant member by multiplying its percent complete value by a given weight.

To implement this, instead of the five unary operators discussed, you can enter a value between 0 and 1 in the Operator column. In fact, you can think of the unary + operator as a weight of 1 and ~ as a weight of 0. Once the weight values are entered and the cube is processed, the Analysis Server will calculate the parent aggregated value as follows:

```
Parent value = Σ(Child N amount * Child N weight)
```

In other words, the server will multiply the member value by its associated weight before rolling it up to the parent.

Current level: · Organization Level 01	Unary Operator
[1] AdventureWorks Cycle	1
[1] European Operations	1
[1] North America Operations	1
[.75] Canadian Division	.75
[1] USA Operations	1
[1] Central Division	1
[1] Northeast Division	1
[1] Northwest Division	1
[1] Southeast Division	1
[1] Southwest Division	1
[.75] Pacific Operations	.75
[.50] Australia	.50

Figure 5.33 Use weights to change the member contribution to the parent aggregated value.

Another scenario where a unary weight operator could be useful is company ownership. In the AdventureWorksDW database, this scenario is demonstrated with the Organization dimension. Suppose that Adventure Works only partially owns foreign entities, e.g. through joint ventures (Figure 5.33).

For example, Adventure Works may own 75% of the Canadian Division, while the rest may be owned by another company. Therefore, when the Adventure Works management requests to see the company equity report, the Canadian Division figures need to be adjusted in respect to the Adventure Works ownership. You can use a unary operator to implement this requirement by allocating appropriate weights. Once you add the Organization division to the Finance cube, re-deploy, and refresh the report shown in Figure 5.24, it will notice that its values change to reflect the weights allocated.

Using a custom member formula

So far, the cell value associated with a given attribute member has always been calculated by aggregating its related measures. Sometimes, you may need to override the member aggregated value or derive it from the values of other attribute members within the same dimension. You can do so by using a custom member formula or a calculated member MDX expression.

96	95	9510	9500	Headcount	Balances	~	(null)
97	95	9520	9500	Units	Flow	~	(null)
98	95	9530	9500	Average Unit	Balances	~	[Account].[Accounts].[Account Level 04].&[50]/
99	95	9540	9500	Square Foota	Balances	~	(null)
100	27	2220	2200	Current Instal	Liabilities	+	(null)

Figure 5.34 Use a custom member formula to calculate the member value.

The first approach requires the formula expression to be stored in a table column similar to configuring a unary operator. For example, suppose that you need to calculate the value of the Average Unit Price member of the Account dimension (Statistical Accounts ⇨ Average Unit Price) by dividing the value of the Net Sales member by the value of the Units member. To do so, follow these steps:

1. Create a new column *CustomMembers* in the DimAccount table and enter the following expression for the Average Unit Price member (Figure 5.34):

```
[Account].[Accounts].[Account Level 04].&[50]/
[Account].[Accounts].[Account Level 02].&[97]
```

This expression uses the MDX syntax I explained when discussing attribute default members in the preceding chapter. It retrieves the value of Net Sales and Unit Price members by their keys. If you explore the data in the FactFinance table, you will see that there are no fact rows associated with the Average Unit Price member (*AccountKey=98*). Yet, we can set its value explicitly by using a custom member formula. If there were associated fact rows, the member value would be overridden.

2. Bind the CustomRollupColumn property of the Accounts attribute in the Account dimension to the CustomMembers table column. Alternatively, you can use the BI Wizard's *Create a custom member formula* flow. If you process now and browse the Account dimension (*Process Update* processing option is sufficient, so you don't have to reprocess the entire cube), you will see an *f* symbol added to the Average Unit Price member as an indication that its value will be derived through a formula.

Account Level 01	Account Level 02	Account Level 03	Amount
⊟ Balance Sheet	⊞ Assets		$18,140,308.53
	⊟ Liabilities and Owners Equity	⊞ Liabilities	$6,985,021.73
		⊞ Owners Equity	$10,191,603.48
		Total	$16,727,023.81
	Total		$1,413,284.71
⊟ Net Income	⊞ Operating Profit		$32,074,362.08
	⊞ Other Income and Expense		$54,086.99
	⊞ Taxes		$6,295,587.49
	Total		$25,832,861.58
⊟ Statistical Accounts	⊞ Headcount		$232.38
	⊞ Units		$7,482.63
	⊞ Average Unit Price		$37,395.65
	⊞ Square Footage		$331,000.00

Figure 5.35 Calculating the Average Unit Price by using a formula expression.

3. Deploy the project and browse the Finance cube. Click the Show Empty Cells toolbar button. Expand the Statistical Accounts level (Figure 5.35). Note that the Average Unit Price member value is now calculated according to the MDX formula.

We will postpone discussing the time intelligence and currency conversion features that BI Wizard supports until chapter 10 because they require a good grasp of MDX programming.

5.2.4 Dimension Writeback

Now that the Finance cube is ready, imagine that you've deployed it to production and you have given business users access to it. As it usually happens, the moment end users start browsing the cube, they will find data discrepancies. Perhaps, the member names are incorrect, account categories don't relate correctly to each other, members are missing, etc. As an experienced UDM designer, it is unlikely that you will be thrilled with maintaining the Account dimension. Instead, why don't allow users to make changes?

One approach could be to give users access to the underlying relational table (DimAccount). However, chances are that the DBA will vote this suggestion out at the spot. Moreover, users have to be familiar with the relational data schema of a dimension table, which is something OLAP is trying to avoid in the first place. Another approach is to allow users to make dimension changes through the Dimension Browser. As an added bonus, the nice and intuitive interface of the Dimension Browser will make it easier for users to make the right changes.

SSAS 2000 In SSAS 2000, dimension writeback was supported only for parent-child dimensions. In UDM, any star schema dimension can be write-back enabled.

Dimension vs. partition writeback

To avoid confusion, you need to differentiate between *dimension* and *partition* writeback. Dimension writeback allows you to change the dimension *members,* not the cube data. For example, given the report shown in Figure 5.35, you cannot use dimension writeback to change the dollar amount for a given account type. UDM provides a certain level of support for changing the cube data in the form of partition writeback which can be enabled on the Partition tab in the Cube Browser. We will defer discussing partition writeback to chapter 12. In this chapter, we will implement dimension writeback.

Enabling dimension writeback

By default, UDM prevents changes to the dimension members. This is controlled by the dimension-level WriteEnabled property which is set to *False* by default. Only dimensions with star schema (single dimension table) can be write-back enabled. Deviating from this rule will result in the following error when the project is built:

```
The dimension is write-enabled, but not all attribute bindings are in a single table
(dimension writeback is only possible for star schemas).
```

Follow these steps to enable writeback for the Account dimension.

1. Open the Account dimension in the Dimension Designer.
2. Click on an empty spot in the Hierarchies and Levels pane to get to the dimension properties.
3. Change the WriteEnabled property to *True*.

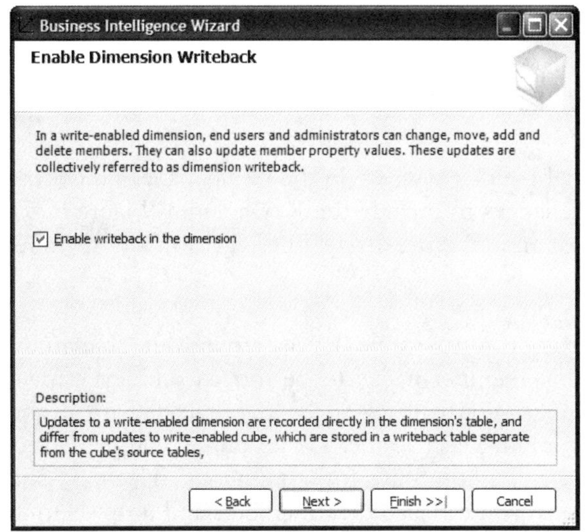

Figure 5.36 To enable writeback on a given dimension, change its WriteEnabled property manually or run the BI Wizard.

Alternatively, if you find the above steps too exhausting or not intuitive, run the Business Intelligence Wizard and select the *Enabled dimension writeback* enhancement. Use the Enable Dimension Writeback step (Figure 5.36) to turn the dimension writeback on or off. Either way, the end result will be changing the WriteEnabled property of the dimension.

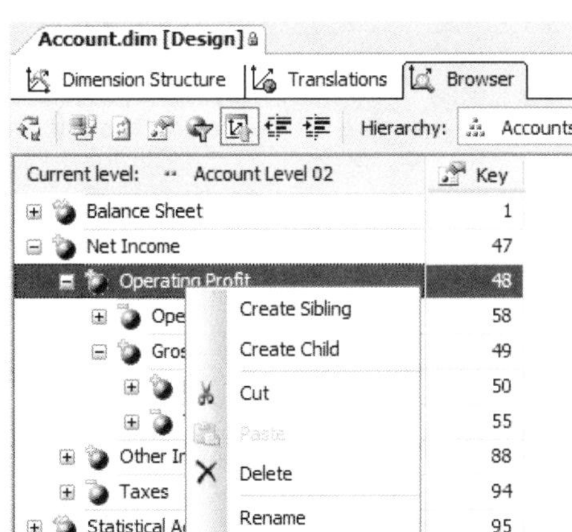

Figure 5.37 To activate writeback in the Dimension Browser, click on the Writeback toolbar button.

Activating writeback in the dimension browser

Once the dimension writeback is enabled, you need to process a dimension before you can make writeback changes to it.

1. Open the Account dimension in the Dimension Designer and process it.
2. Flip to the Browser tab. The Accounts parent-child hierarchy should be pre-selected in the Hierarchies dropdown. By default the dimension browser is not activated for writeback. That's because, in UDM, writeback is performed against the dimension attributes, while the browser is typically used to browse dimension hierarchies.

SSAS 2000 When the user makes writeback changes, the dimension browser submits writeback statements to the server. These statements indicate the dimension attributes being changed and key column values for those attributes. Therefore, there is a difference between normal dimension browsing and browsing with a writeback mode enabled. While browsing dimension members, the user most probably is not interested in viewing key column values. When browsing with write-back, those values are needed. Hence, the browser supports two modes.

3. Click the Writeback button on the toolbar or right-click anywhere in the results pane and choose the *Writeback* context menu. The results pane changes to include the Key column (Figure 5.37). You are now ready to enter a new member or modify an existing one (click on the member name).

With parent-child hierarchies, writeback allows you to move levels around the hierarchy. Suppose that the Total Cost of Sales dimension member needs to be moved one level up to become a child of the Operating Profit member. You can do so by right-clicking on it and choosing *Increase Indent*. The browser supports multi-select mode. For example, you can select several members (hold Ctrl for individual selection or Shift for continuous selection) and increase or decrease their indent at the same time. You can also drag members and drop them to a parent node to associate them with a new parent. Changes affecting multiple members are done in a transaction scope meaning that either all changes will be committed successfully, or all will fail in case of a database error.

Current level: ·· Account Level 02	Key	Account Number	Account Type	Accounts	Unary Operator	Custom Rollup
Balance Sheet	1	1			~	
Net Income	47	4	Revenue		+	
Statistical Accounts	95	9500	Statistical		~	
Headcount	96	9510	Balances	Statistical Accounts	~	
Units	97	9520	Flow	Statistical Accounts	~	
Avg Unit Price	98	9530	Balances	Statistical Accounts	~	[Account].[Account...
Square Footage	99	9540	Balances	Statistical Accounts	~	

Figure 5.38 Rename a member of a writeback-enabled dimension by clicking on the member name.

Making member changes

Suppose that the Finance department needs to change some attributes of the Average Unit Price member (a child member of the Statistical Accounts).

1. Click on the Member Properties toolbar button. Check the *(Show All)* checkbox and click OK to see all member properties.
2. Click inside the member name (Figure 5.38). The member row enters an editing mode and the member icon changes to a red pencil. Change the member name to **Avg Unit Price**.
3. Press Enter to commit the changes to the DimAccount table. If you now explore DimAccount data, you will see that the member name has been updated.
4. Suppose that the user needs to change the custom member formula of Avg Unit Price member to use the **Total Cost of Sales** instead of Net Sales. Click inside the Custom Rollup member properties of the Avg Unit Price member to enter an editing mode.
5. Instead of entering the formula by hand, you can use the MDX Builder. Click on the **...** button inside the Custom Rollup formula content to open the MDX Builder.
6. In the Expression pane, select the first operand so it will be replaced later.

7. In the Metadata pane, expand the Account Level 04 member and double-click on the **Total Cost of Sales** member. This will update the expression text to use the key of the Total Cost of Sales member. Click OK to close the dialog. You don't need to deploy or re-process the Financial cube because writeback changes are reflected immediately in UDM.

Besides changing the existing members, the UDM writeback supports adding new members. For example, to add a child member to a given member of a multilevel hierarchy, select the parent member, right-click and choose Create Child (see again Figure 5.37). Alternatively, you can create a sibling member at the same level of an existing member. The values of the table row are populated from values entered in the member property columns of the browser. If the values for a given attribute are missing, then the server will try to insert default values, which may not be what you need. Therefore, when adding new members it is important to show all member properties and populate them as needed. To delete a member, just select it and hit the Delete key.

5.3 Working with External UDM Objects

In chapter 2, I recommended that you implement your UDM as coarse as possible and I pointed out that there are certain performance and maintenance advantages for doing so. However, in real life, operational or security requirements may call for splitting UDM into two or more databases, or cubes. At the same time, you may need to reuse dimensions and measure groups across cubes. In UDM, this can be achieved by *linking* dimensions and measure groups from one cube to another.

SSAS 2000 Linking objects in UDM is essentially similar to using virtual cubes in SSAS 2000. However, UDM is more flexible because it supports linking at a more granular level. For example, you can choose to link to a specific dimension only, as opposed to the entire cube. In addition, a linked dimension can be related to a measure group in the linking cube.

You can link to both dimensions and measure groups located in an external UDM (a different Analysis Services 2005 database) and across cubes in the same database (Figure 5.39).

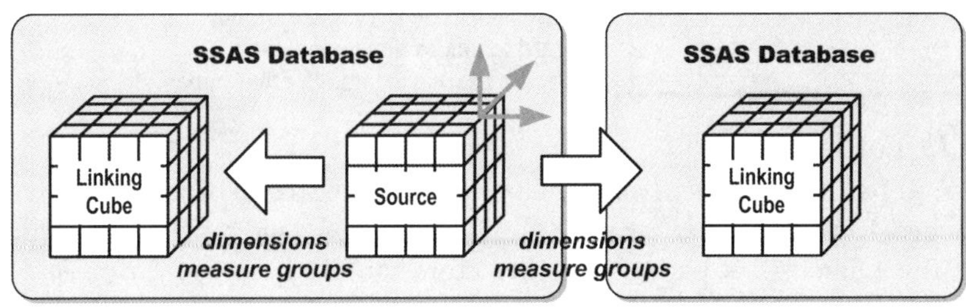

Figure 5.39 You can link objects from a cube located in the same or external database.

For example, as shown in Figure 5.39, the first SSAS database has two cubes and the first cube links to dimension and measure groups defined in the second cube. Cross-linking is also supported (although not shown), i.e. objects can be linked in both directions. Linking also works across databases. Both internal and external links are subject to security restrictions set up by the administrator.

5.3.1 Linking Dimensions and Measure Groups

Suppose that the Adventure Works management has decided that the Finance department will own the currency exchange rate database. As a result, the Currency dimension and Currency Rates measure group has been moved to the Finance UDM. However, these UDM objects are needed by the SOS OLAP database. We need the Currency Rates measure group to convert the foreign currencies to the US dollar. The Currency dimension is useful for data analytics, e.g. to find out how many orders have been placed in a given currency.

The trivial approach to address this requirement is to duplicate the object definitions and data in the SOS OLAP UDM. For example, we could replicate the currency data on a regular basis and define the Currency dimension and Currency Rates measure group as part of the SOS OLAP database. As you can imagine, from maintenance and logistics standpoints, this approach is far from ideal. A better approach could be to reuse the objects by linking them to the SOS OLAP cube. This, of course, assumes that we have connectivity to the Finance cube. You will find the completed solution implemented in the SOS OLAP Linked project. I've decided to create a separate project to avoid dependencies between the SOS OLAP project and the Finance UDM.

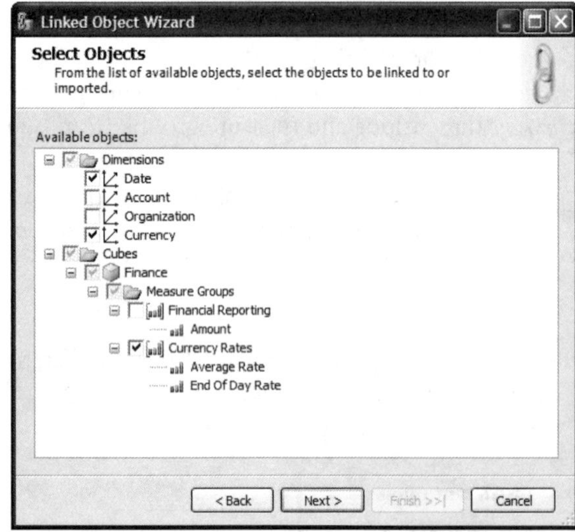

Figure 5.40 Use the Linked Object Wizard to link to dimensions and measure groups located in other cubes.

Running the Linked Object Wizard

Use the Linked Object Wizard to link an object from a cube located in the same or in an external database. It could be launched from the Cube Structure or Dimension Usage tabs in the Cube Browser or right-click on the Dimensions pane (Cube Structure tab) and choose *New Linked Object*. The same context menu is found when right-clicking on the Dimensions node in the Solution Explorer. The difference is that, when linking a dimension from the Cube Designer, once the dimension definition file is created, the dimension is automatically added to the cube. In addition, launching the wizard from the Cube Designer allows you to add both dimensions and measures at the same time. The steps are essentially the same for both scenarios, so I will only demonstrate how to link UDM object from an external database.

1. Open the SOS OLAP cube in the Cube Designer.

2. Click on the New Linked Object toolbar button found on the Cube Structure and Dimension Usage tabs or right-click on the Dimensions pane (Cube Structure tab) and choose *New Linked Object*.

3. The Cube Designer launches the Linked Object Wizard. In the Select the Data Source step, click the New Data Source button to create a new data source pointing to the Finance cube (not the Finance relational database). Name the new data source **Finance**.

Note You can only link to UDM (Analysis Services 2005) objects. For this reason, when creating a new data source for a linked object, the Connection Manager defaults to the OLE DB Provider for Analysis Services 9.0. Although the Provider dropdown may include other OLAP providers, the OLE DB Provider for Analysis Services 9.0 is the right and only option.

4. In the Select Objects step (Figure 5.40), the Linked Object Wizard asks you which dimensions and measure groups you would like to link to. Since measure groups become part of the cube definition, you need to expand the Cubes node to select the desired measure group(s). Link the Date and Currency dimensions and the Currency Rates measure group in one step.

5. Click Next. In the Completing the Wizard step, click Finish to close the wizard.

Working with linked objects

The Currency and Date dimensions are added to the Dimensions folder in the Solution Explorer. Since you've launched the Link Object Wizard from the Cube Designer, the dimensions and the Currency Rates measure group are also added to the SOS OLAP cube. The reason why we need to link to the Date dimension of the Finance UDM is that we've defined the measures of the Currency Rates measure group as semi-additive (LastNonEmpty). Semi-additive measures require a Date dimension. If you don't link the Date dimension, the Cube Designer will underline the Currency Rates measure group with a red wavy line and you will get a build error when building the project. In addition, you cannot establish a regular relationship between the local dimension and linked measure group. This limitation rules out using the local Date dimension.

To avoid naming collision, the wizard names the linked Date dimension as *Date 1*. You cannot make changes to a linked dimension since its definition is stored in the source cube. Hence, you cannot open the Date 1 dimension in the Dimension Designer. If you need to change the dimension definition, you need to do so in the Finance UDM and re-link the dimension.

1. Rename the Date 1 dimension to **Financial Date** in both the Solution Explorer and the Dimensions pane on the Cube Structure tab of the Cube Designer.

2. The Finance Date linked dimension and the local Date dimension have identical definitions. Therefore, to prevent confusion, select the Financial Date dimension in the Dimension pane of the Cube Designer and set its visible property to *False*.

Caching linked object data and metadata

A linked object (dimension or measure group) is associated with a data source that points to source UDM in which the original object is defined. After linking, linked dimensions and measure groups appear to the end user as regular objects and the end user query metadata and data for these objects. When the linked object is created and processed, a connection to the source server is established and the metadata from the source object is retrieved. Subsequently, when a client issues a query to the linked object, the linked server (the server where the linked objects are created) acts as a proxy and forwards the query to the source server. To optimize the query performance, the linked server caches the response results in memory so that subsequent identical requests do not have to be requested from the source server every time.

As with every type of caching, linked object caching is a tradeoff between performance and data latency. Both linked dimensions and measure groups expose *RefreshPolicy* and *RefreshInterval* properties which can be set at design time to specify how the linked object detects changes and refreshes its cache. The default setting of RefreshPolicy (*ByQuery*) refreshes the linked object data with every query. Alternatively, you can set RefreshPolicy to *ByInterval* and specify the refresh interval (*RefreshInterval* property) to expire the cached data and metadata of the linked object on a regular basis.

5.3.2 Working with Linked Object Relationships

You can treat a linked dimension just like a local dimension. A linked dimension can have relationships to local measure groups.

1. Switch to the Dimension Usage tab. Note that the Cube Designer has already created relationships among the linked objects. The Finance Date and Currency dimensions are related to the Currency Rates measure group. You cannot modify these relations because they are defined in the linking UDM.

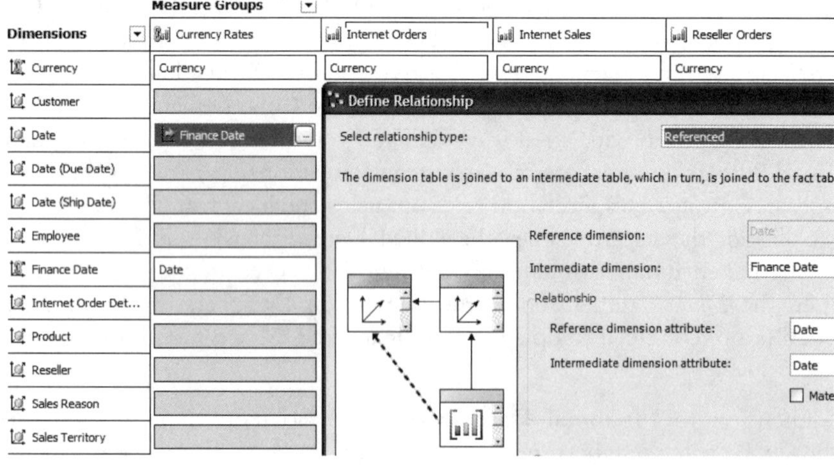

Figure 5.41 Relate a local dimension to a linked measure group by using a reference dimension.

As I mentioned, you cannot relate a local dimension to a linked measure group by using regular relationship. You can do so either programmatically through an MDX script or by creating a referenced relationship through an intermediate linked dimension. Let's use the latter approach to link the local Date dimension to the Currency Rates measure group, so the end users can browse data by the Date dimension.

2. Click on the **...** button in the intersecting cell between the Date dimension and the Currency Rates dimension to open the Define Relationships dialog (Figure 5.41).
3. Select *Referenced* relationship type and Finance Date as an intermediate dimension.
4. Relate both dimensions by the Date attribute and process the SOS OLAP cube.

Switch to the Cube Browser and create some of the reports we've authored to demonstrate the Currency dimension. The reports should display identical measure values as when the currency-related objects were locally defined. As you would recall, we converted some of the sales measures to US dollars by using measure expressions (multiplying them by the Average Currency Rate). The values of these measures should be unaffected.

5.4 Handling Data Integrity Issues

In a perfect world, you won't need to deal with data integrity issues at all. Chances are, though, that sooner or later you may face the reality of inconsistent data. For example, you may encounter referential integrity issues, such as referenced keys in the fact table that don't have matching dimension records or have NULL values. This is especially true when building your UDM directly on top of an OLTP data source, as we demonstrated with the SOS OLTP cube.

Note For more detailed discussion of handling data integrity issues, read the whitepaper *Handling Data Integrity Issues in Analysis Services 2005* (see the Resources section).

UDM gives you a great deal of flexibility in dealing with data integrity issues. Of course, the best remedy is preventing such issues from happening by handling them as soon as possible in the UDM implementation lifecycle. For example, if your UDM is built on top of a formal data warehouse, ETL processes would (and should) take care of resolving NULL values to pre-defined values, e.g. -1 for Unknown member. Even if you build UDM on top of OLTP data sources that preclude data transformations, you can still use named calculations at the DSV level to translate key values. If handling data integrity issues at the data source level is not an option, you can tackle them at the UDM level by using error configurations, unknown members, and NULL processing settings.

5.4.1 Understanding Error Configurations

You can tell UDM how to react to various data integrity issues by setting appropriate error configurations. Every cube, dimension, and measure group has an error configuration associated with it which is exposed by the *ErrorConfiguration* property.

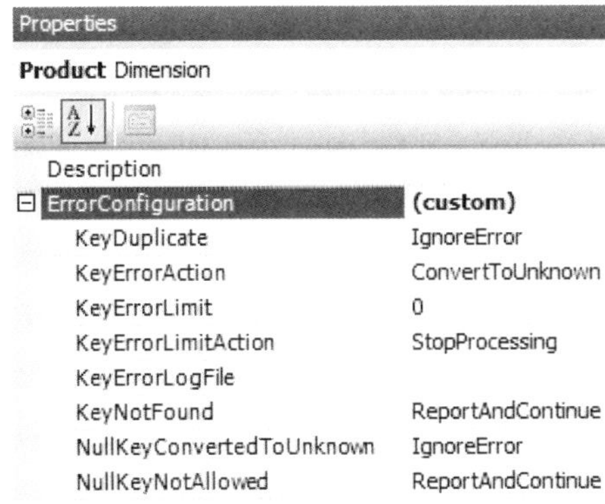

Figure 5.42 Let UDM know how to react to data integrity errors by setting the object error configuration.

Default error configuration

The default error configuration settings are stored in the SSAS configuration file (msmdsrv.ini). They can be viewed or changed permanently and applied to all SSAS objects by using the SQL Server Management Studio at the server level (General page). In addition, the default settings can be overridden in the BI Studio at a cube, dimension, and measure group levels. You can review the effective default settings of the error configuration for a given object, expand the ErrorConfiguration dropdown, and choose the *(custom)* item. For example, Figure 5.42 shows the default error configuration settings of the Product dimension. Table 5.1 summarizes the purpose of the default error configuration settings.

Table 5.1 Error configuration settings.

Setting	Default Value	Purpose
KeyDuplicate	IgnoreError	If an attribute key is encountered more than once, the duplicate member(s) are ignored.
KeyErrorAction	ConvertToUknown	If a matching dimension key is not found during processing of a snowflake dimension, the offending dimension member will be converted to unknown member.
KeyErrorLimit	0	The number of errors tolerated during processing. The default value of 0 indicates that processing willl stop when the first error is encountered
KeyErrorLogFile		The full path to the log file where the data integrity errors will be logged. No logging by default.
KeyNotFound	ReportAndContinue	The KeyNotFound error is triggered when a matching dimension member is not found during fact table processing or snowflake dimension processing. By default, processing will continue, the error will be logged, and the error will be counted toward the error limit.
NullKeyConverted ToUnknown	IgnoreError	An error will be generated when a NULL dimension key is converted to Unknown member during fact or snowflake dimension processing (NullProcesing = UnknownMember). By default, this error is ingored.
NullKeyNotAllowed	ReportAndContinue	An error will be generated when a NULL dimension key is encountered and NullProcessing is set to Error. By default, the error will be logged but processing will continue (same as KeyNotFound).

Let's go through some scenarios to demonstrate the effect of the error configuration settings when dealing with data integrity errors.

5.4.2 Enabling the Dimension Unknown Member

When the Analysis Server processes a fact table or a snowflake dimension, it tries to find a dimension member in the linked table whose dimension key matches the referenced key in the first table. If a match is not found, the offending record can be assigned to a special dimension member called Unknown member.

1. Open the Product dimension in the Dimension Designer.
2. In the DSV pane, right-click on the DimProduct table and choose *Explore Data.* Observe that the first two hundred or so products have NULL ProductSubcategoryKey values.
3. In the Attributes pane, select the Product dimension key and explore its KeyColumns settings. Note that, by default, its NullProcessing option is set to *Automatic.* This means that when a match is not found, the Analysis Server will attempt to convert the key value to zero for numeric

keys and an empty string for text-based keys. Since there is no product subcategory with ProductSubcategoryKey of zero, a KeyNotFound exception will be thrown. The default error configuration logs this error, increments the error limit counter, and continues processing the dimension. However, since the error limit will be exceeded, processing will stop with an error.

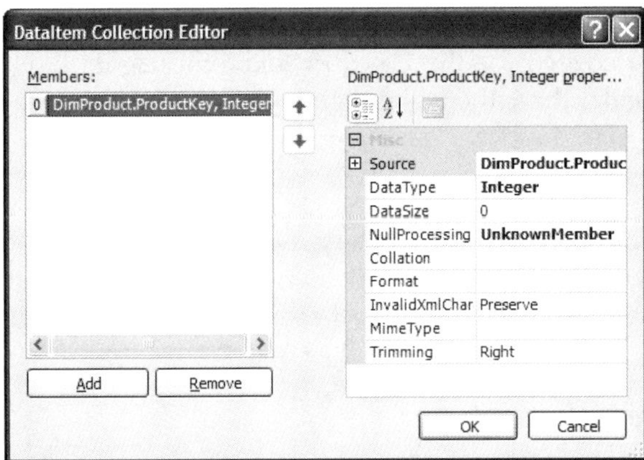

Figure 5.43 Set the NullProcessing setting of the dimension key to assign the offending member to the Unknown member.

4. Change the NullProcessing option to *UnknownMember* (Figure 5.43). As a result, when a matching dimension key is not found during dimension processing, a ConvertToUnknown error will be triggered. As Table 5.1 shows, the default error configuration will ignore this error.

   In the case of the Product dimension, the Product attribute forms several multilevel hierarchies including the Product by Category hierarchy. When a member from the Product attribute hierarchy is converted to Unknown, its key value is set to 0 for numeric columns or empty string for text-based columns. Since there is no product subcategory key with a value of 0, the ConvertToUnknown error will be triggered again when the Subcategory attribute hierarchy is processed.

5. To avoid this issue and construct the Product by Category hierarchy properly, set the NullProcessing option of the Subcategory attribute to UnknownMember as well.

6. You need to enable the Unknown member so it shows up when browsing the dimension. Click on an empty space in the Hierarchies and Levels pane to view the dimension level properties. Note that, by default, the UnknownMember property is set to *None* which disables the UknownMember member. Change UnknownMember to Visible. The third option (Hidden) will enable UnknownMember but will make it hidden to the end users.

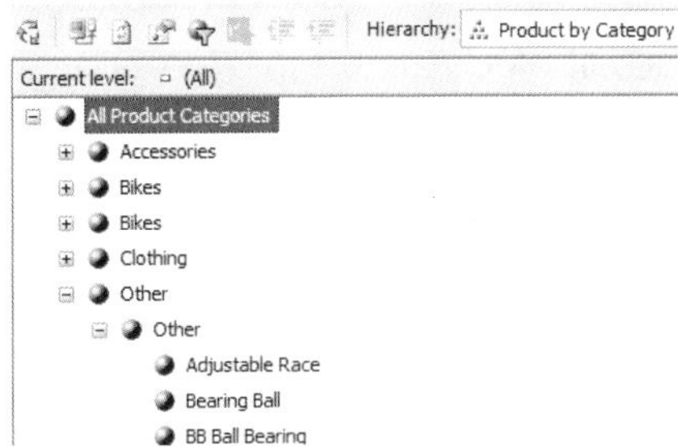

Figure 5.44 When the Unknown member of a dimension is enabled, the members with NULL keys are attributed to the unknown member.

7. By default, the UnknownMember member is named *Unknown*. You can change the UnknownMember name by using the UnknownMemberName name property. Change UnknownMemberName to *Other*.

8. Process the Product dimension. In the Dimension Browser, reconnect and browse the Product by Category hierarchy (Figure 5.44).

Observe that two new levels named *Other* are created for the Category and Subcategory levels and the products with NULL keys are found under the Other subcategory member.

5.4.3 Dealing with Fact Table Integrity Errors

When we discussed measure expressions, we converted all monetary measures to a common currency by multiplying them by the daily average exchange rate. We derived the exchange rate from the Currency Rates measure group. There are several potential issues that may come up when measures are processed.

Handling missing and NULL measure values

When the calculation engine tries to retrieve the Average Currency Rate measure for a given attribute hierarchy combination and it cannot find a match, the resulting measure value will be NULL. This issue cannot be resolved at the error configuration level. Suppose that the source column value of the Average Currency Rate is NULL. You have some degree of control to handle NULL fact values by setting the NullProcessing property of the measure. For example, click on the Internet Sales Amount measure and expand its Source property (Figure 5.45).

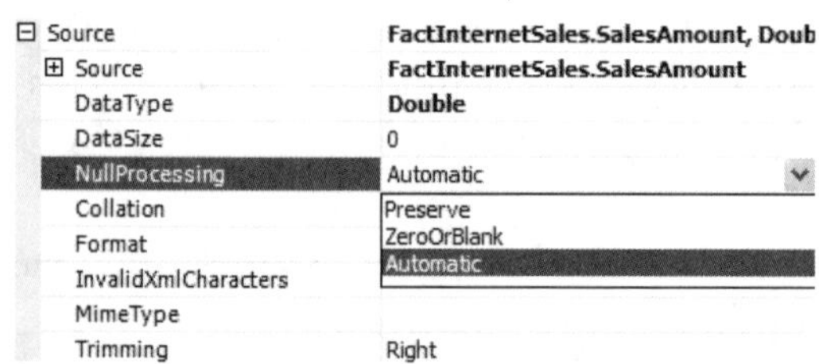

Figure 5.45 Use the NullProcessing setting to control how UDM will deal with NULL values.

Unfortunately, unlike the attribute-level NullProcessing property, you have only two NullProcessing options at a measure level. As its names suggest, the Preserve option will preserve the NULL value. The Automatic option is equivalent to the ZeroOrBlank option. It converts the null value to zero (for numeric columns) or a blank string (text-based columns). What is missing is the ability to raise an exception when NULL values are not acceptable or convert the value to a user-defined value.

Note Measure-level NullProcessing is more limited than attribute NULL processing for performance reasons. Processing facts tables that may have millions of rows should be as efficient as possible. However, I am surprised to find out that there is no None NullProcessing option that could bypass all checks. If there was such an option, then NullProcessing at a measure level could support all attribute NullProcessing options with the caveat that it would slow down the cube processing.

Handling NULL dimension keys

Suppose that a sales fact is recorded in a new currency that doesn't exist the DimCurrency table. In this case, when the Analysis Server processes the measure group, it will try to find a Currency dimension member but will not find it, which is problematic. This condition is normally prevented at the data source level by the referential constraints between the primary dimension key and the referenced fact table key. If no referential integrity exists, what will happen at the UDM level depends on the NullProcessing setting for that key.

1. Open the SOS OLAP cube definition in the Cube Designer. Flip to the Dimension Usage tab. The Currency dimension is referenced by all measure groups that we have so far.
2. Click the ... button inside the Currency cell found at the intersection of the Internet Sales measure group and Currency dimension. The Define Relationship dialog opens.
3. Click on the Advanced button to open the Measure Group Binding dialog. Note that the default Null Processing column is set to Automatic.

As we've discussed before, the default *Automatic* setting will convert the NULL key to 0 for numeric columns and an empty string for text-based columns. If a dimension record with a matching key value (0 or empty string) is not found, a KeyNotFound exception will be raised, which will be handled as indicated by the error configuration defined for that measure group. The *Error* setting will tell the server that a NULL value is illegal for this key and raise a NullKey error. The value of NullKeyNotAllowed in the error configuration determines how the server will react to the error.

The UnknownMember setting will attribute the record to the unknown member of the dimension, as I've just explained when discussing the Product dimension. UnknownMember will raise the NullKeyConvertedToUnknown error which will be dealt with according to the error configuration settings. Let's suppose that we need to prevent NULL key values at all cost by setting the NullProcessing of the CurrencyKey attribute to *Error*. You can do this at a dimension level (NullProcessing of the attribute key) or at a measure group binding level by using the Measure Group Bindings dialog. Let's try the second approach.

4. In the MeasureGroup Bindings dialog, set the Null Processing column of the CurrencyKey column to *Error*. Note that BI Studio changes the font of the Currency attribute in the Attributes grid to **bold**. That's because we are overriding the NullProcessing setting from the one specified at the attribute level in the Currency dimension.
5. Click OK to close the Measure Group Binding dialog. A little blue icon appears with an informational message "The default attribute bindings have been modified". If you want to fix this issue, open the DimCurrency dimension in the Dimension Designer and change the NullProcessing setting of the Currency dimension key to *Error* (see Figure 5.43).
6. Click OK to close the Define Relationships dialog. Repeat the same steps to set the measure group bindings of the CurrencyKey column for the Reseller Sales, Internet Orders, Reseller Orders, and Currency Rates measure groups.
7. Back on the Cube Structure tab, select the Currency Rates measure group. Expand its ErrorConfiguration property and choose *(custom)*.
8. Set the NullKeyNotAllowed setting to ReportAndStop to halt the cube processing in case of a NULL value in the CurrencyKey.

To recap, as best practice, I would recommend resolving the data integrity errors at the data source level whenever possible. You can still implement appropriate error configurations but, in my opinion, they should be used as a last line of defense to prevent errors that may have slipped through data source constraints and ETL processes.

5.5 Summary

UDM provides a plethora of advanced dimensional features to address more demanding OLAP requirements. Choose an appropriate dimension relationship when the dimension table doesn't have a direct foreign key relationship to the fact table.

Leverage the UDM aggregate functions to handle semi-additive measures that cannot be summed over time. Use the Business Intelligence Wizard to implement versatile dimension characteristics, including accounting intelligence, custom aggregation, and writeback. Consider linking dimensions and measure groups to reuse objects from an external UDM. Finally, leverage error configurations at dimension, measure group, and cube levels to handle data integrity issues in dimension or fact tables.

5.6 Resources

Marco Russo's weblog *Business Intelligence with SQL Server* (http://sqljunkies.com/WebLog/sqlbi/archive/2004/10/04/4447.aspx) – Be sure to check out this excellent blog to learn practical OLAP and Business Intelligence tips.

Analysis Services: Semi-additive Measures and Inventory Snapshots article by Amir Netz (http://shrinkster.com/4zq) – Focusing on a classic inventory problem, this article describes the implementation techniques of semi-additive measures in online analytical processing. Although originally written for SSAS 2000, many of the topics covered are still relevant.

PART 2

Data Warehousing and Mining

One traditional scenario for using OLAP and SSAS is data warehousing. A UDM layer on top of a relational warehouse database can provide fast and uniform query response times and enrich the dimensional model with calculated metrics. To help implement large data warehouse projects, Analysis Services supports architecting UDM top-down in the absence of a relational database schema. A data warehouse project is a complex undertaking. Data needs to be extracted from multiple data sources, transformed, and loaded into UDM. You will see how SQL Server Integration Services (SSIS) makes this endeavor easier.

Besides OLAP, Analysis Services provides data mining services that span data exploration, pattern discovery, and data prediction. Mining models can draw data from relational and UDM data sources. We will build a data mining model on top of a relational data source to implement a mining model for targeted campaigning. When UDM is used as a data source, data mining can be used to enrich UDM in the form of data mining dimensions and cubes. The Customer Profiling, Basket Analysis, and Sales Forecasting models demonstrate how data mining can be used to complement and extend UDM.

Chapter 6

Data Warehousing

So far, all cubes that we've implemented were built on top of an existing relational data source. BI Studio also supports reversing the UDM implementation steps by allowing you to build UDM top-down. This approach could be useful with data warehouse projects when it is essential to start with prototyping the envisioned dimensional model in the absence of a data source. Once the dimensional model is ready, you can proceed by generating the subject area database. The next step typically involves creating Integration Services packages that will handle the tasks of extracting, transforming, and loading data from the original data source (OLTP database) to its final destination (UDM). In this chapter, you will learn how to:

- Use a template to create a cube.
- Leverage the Schema Generation Wizard to generate the subject area database schema.
- Design SSIS packages to extract, transform and load data.
- Use SSIS to process UDM objects.
- Troubleshoot SSIS package execution.

We will leave the SOS OLAP and SOS OLTP UDMs for a moment to demonstrate the top-down approach by building an Inventory UDM, from which we will generate the data schema of the subject area database. We will also create the Load Inventory SSIS package to handle the data logistics. You can find both the SSAS Inventory and SSIS Load Inventory sample project inside the Ch06 solution file.

6.1 Working with UDM Templates

Just like a DBA could start implementing an ER (Entity Relationship) model by designing the data schema first, a UDM expert could architect the cube(s) in the absence of the relational data store. Once the UDM is ready, BI Studio could be used to generate the relational data schema of the staging database. If you have experience with the SQL Server 2000 Accelerator for Business Intelligence, you will undoubtedly find the UDM top-down approach similar.

6.1.1 Introducing the Inventory UDM

To demonstrate building UDM top-down, we will implement a simple Inventory cube. If you examine the AdventureWorks OLTP database, you will notice that it keeps a snapshot of the product inventory in tables Production.ProductInventory and Production.Location. As a product progresses through the manufacturing pipeline, it moves from one location to another until it is finally assembled and ready for shipment to the customer or reseller.

ProductID	LocationID	Shelf	Bin	Quantity	ModifiedDate
1	1	A	1	408	9/8/2004 12:00:00 AM
1	6	B	5	324	9/8/2004 12:00:00 AM
1	50	A	5	353	9/8/2004 12:00:00 AM
2	1	A	2	427	9/8/2004 12:00:00 AM
2	6	B	1	318	9/8/2004 12:00:00 AM

Figure 6.1 Adventure Works keeps track of the product inventory in the Production.ProductInventory table.

The Inventory pipeline

When a product changes its location, the AW inventory system adds a new record in the Production.ProductInventory table (Figure 6.1) and records the product, the new location, and the date of the change. At the same time, the system decreases the product quantity of the old location and increases the product quantity of the new location.

Imagine that, to keep the performance of the inventory OLTP system at its peek, the Inventory table is truncated on a regular basis. The AW management has requested that the SOS OLAP system be enhanced to keep a historical record of the product inventory. This could certainly be useful in analyzing the inventory flow patterns, e.g. how the inventory levels of a given product fluctuate in time, what's the longest shelf life of a given product, etc. To address this requirement, you decide to take a periodic inventory snapshot on a daily basis and import into the Inventory UDM.

The Inventory UDM

Suppose that, after analyzing the current operational requirements, you realize that a direct connectivity to the inventory system is not an option. Instead, the Adventure Works DBA will export the product (Production.Product table), location (Production.Location table), and inventory (Production.ProductInventory) data at the end of each day as flat files. ETL processes need to be implemented to extract data from these files into a staging database, perform the necessary transformations and data massaging, and load the cleansed data into a data mart (a.k.a. a subject area database). From the data mart, the data will be loaded into the Inventory cube. This typical data warehousing pipeline is shown in Figure 6.2.

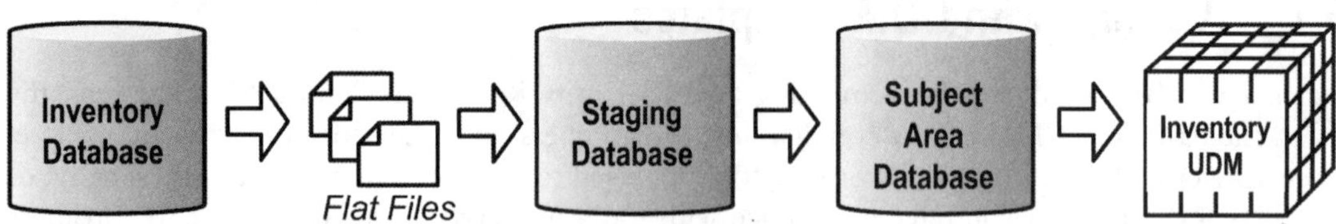

Figure 6.2 The Inventory project demonstrates typical data warehouse processes.

Implementing a data warehousing project requires expertise in several technologies, and substantial logistics and orchestration effort. Let's see how BI Studio could help us jumpstart the inventory UDM implementation by building it top-down starting from the Inventory cube.

6.1.2 Creating a Cube Template

Suppose that you are tasked to design the Inventory UDM in the absence of a relational data source. Once you are done, you will hand it over to the database developer who will generate the relational data schema and create the SSIS packages. The Cube Wizard allows you to generate UDM top-down from scratch or by using a template. The latter option promotes reuse and uniformity. Just as Microsoft Word allows you to base a new document on a pre-defined template, you can speed up and standardize the UDM implementation by using a template. Undoubtedly, third-party vendors and integrators will use this option to create standard UDM templates to be used as a foundation for building OLAP solutions.

A UDM template could have the same definition files as a regular UDM, e.g. dimensions and cube definition files. For example, the Adventure Works Inventory cube template (Adventure Works Inventory Template.dwproj) I've authored two dimensions (Location and Product). I didn't include a Time dimension because we will use a pre-defined dimension template that comes with BI Studio. The cube definition includes one measure group (Inventory) with a single measure (Quantity).

Note A dimension template is a dimension definition file stored in the C:\Program Files\Microsoft SQL Server\90\Tools\Templates\olap\1033\Dimension Templates folder.

Creating dimension definition template

You start implementing a cube template by creating the dimensions that the cube will reference.

1. Create a new Analysis Services project and name it **Adventure Works Inventory Template**.
2. Run the Dimension Wizard to create the *Product* dimension.
3. There are several pre-defined dimension templates in the BI Studio Dimension Templates folder that you can use to jumpstart your dimension definition. In addition, you can create and add your own templates by copying a dimension definition file to that folder. Select the *Product Template* as a base of the Product dimension (Figure 6.3).

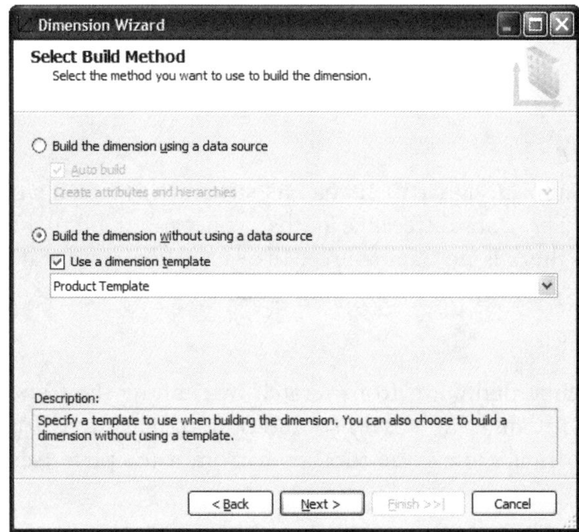

Figure 6.3 To create a dimension included in the cube template, run the Dimension Wizard and generate the dimension without a data source from scratch or by using a dimension template.

4. In the Specify Dimension Type step, select the dimension attributes you need. For the sake of simplicity, I've picked the *Product*, *Category*, *Color*, *Size*, and *Subcategory* attributes only.
5. In the Specify Dimension Key and Type step (Figure 6.4), I've selected that the Product dimension will be a slowly changing dimension, e.g. a product may change its product subcategory over time.

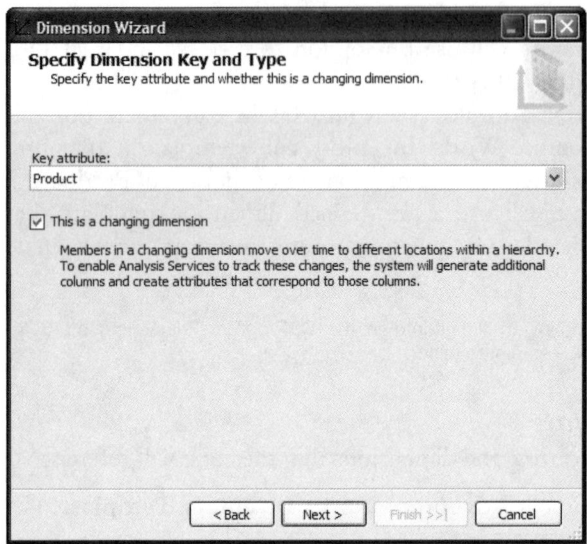

Figure 6.4 You can mark a dimension as a slowly changing dimension to tell the Dimension Wizard to create additional columns that will track the dimension changes.

When you configure a dimension as a changing dimension, the Dimension Wizard generates four additional attributes (SCD OriginalID, SCD End Date, SCD Start Date, and SCD Status) that can be used to record the member changes. When we generate the relational data schema later in this chapter, the Schema Generation Wizard will create corresponding physical columns that the SSIS packages can use when loading the dimension members.

6. In the Completing the Wizard step, don't check, name the dimension **Product**. Don't check the *Generate schema now* checkbox because we will use the Product dimension as a template only. In section 6.2.2, we will use the Schema Generation Wizard to generate the relational schema of the Inventory UDM.

Finalizing the cube definition template

Once the dimension is created, use the Dimension Designer to change its structure as usual, e.g. to create attribute and multilevel hierarchies. The only difference is that you cannot bind the dimension attributes to DSV columns because there is no data source. Instead, when you create new attributes, use the *Generate column* binding type on the Object Binding dialog.

1. Follow similar steps to create the *Location* dimension.
2. With dimensions in place, you can create the cube definition from scratch by running the Cube Wizard and choosing the Building the cube without using a data source option. The steps for creating the cube definition are very similar to building a cube top-down from a template (see section 6.2.1).

3. Create a new folder **Adventure Works Inventory** under the SSAS template folder (C:\Program Files\Microsoft SQL Server\90\Tools\Templates\olap\1033\Cube Templates).
4. Deploy the cube (*Inventory.cube file*) and dimension definition files (*Product.dim* and *Location.dim*) to the Adventure Works Inventory folder (Figure 6.5). At this point, the cube definition template is ready and you can use it as a basis for implementing the Inventory UDM.

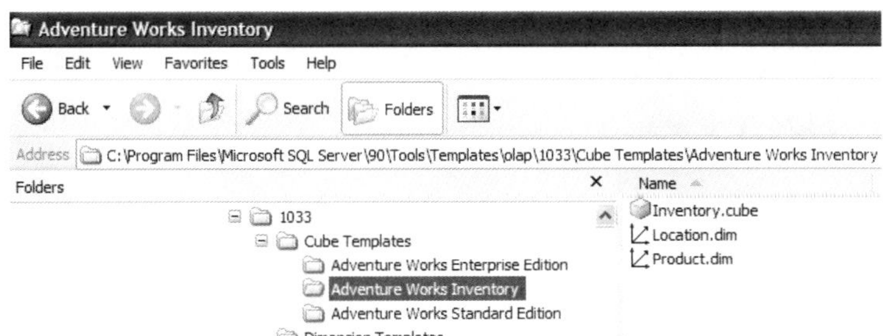

Figure 6.5 To create a cube template, copy the dimension definition files and the cube definition file to the Cube Templates folder.

6.2 Building UDM Top-down

While you can generate the Inventory UDM top-down from scratch, using a cube template makes the whole process much easier. To speed up the UDM implementation, we will use the Adventure Works Inventory template we've just created.

6.2.1 Creating a Cube without a Data Source

We will use the Cube Wizard again to create the Inventory UDM top-down. As a prerequisite, create a new Analysis Services project and name it **Inventory**. This project will host the UDM objects that the Cube Wizard will generate.

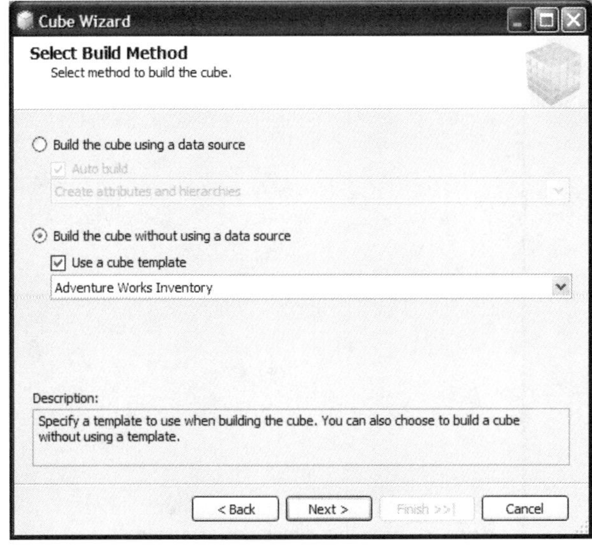

Figure 6.6 Use the Define New Measures step to make changes to the measures defined in the cube template and create new measures.

Running the Cube Wizard

1. Right-click on the Cubes folder and select *New Cube* to launch the Cube Wizard. Click Next to advance to the Select Build Method step (Figure 6.6). The Cube Wizard discovers that we don't have a data source view defined in the project and defaults to the *Build the cube using a data source* option.
2. Check the *Use a cube template* checkbox and select the *Adventure Works Inventory* template. Click Next to advance to the Define New Measures step (Figure 6.7).

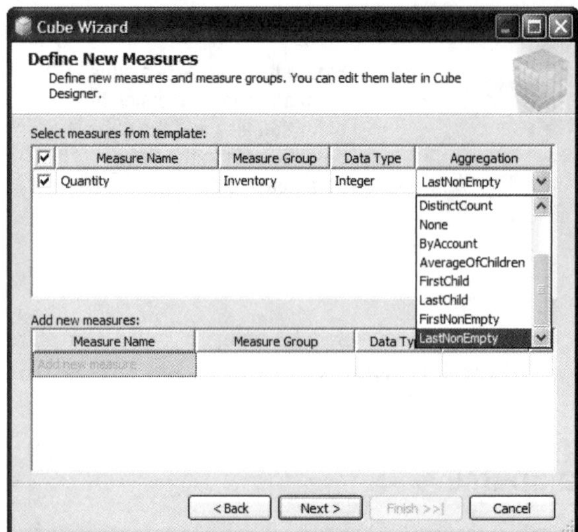

Figure 6.7 Run the Cube Wizard to build your UDM top-down. Consider using a cube template to speed up the UDM implementation.

3. The cube template defines one measure group (Inventory) that has a single measure (Quantity). When working with periodic inventory snapshots, you cannot sum product quantities over time because the Quantity measure is semi-additive. Instead, change the Aggregation function of the Quantity measure to *LastNonEmpty*.

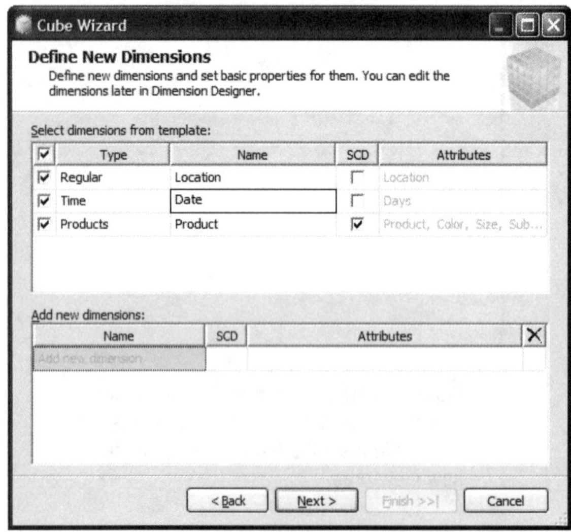

Figure 6.8 When generating UDM top-down, you can use dimension templates or create new dimensions.

4. You can create additional measures, if needed, by adding them to the *Add new measures* grid. Click Next to advance to the Define New Dimensions step (Figure 6.8).

Configuring dimensions

Now, it's time to set up the cube dimensions. The Cube Wizard examines the cube template and correctly identifies the Location and Product dimensions. In addition, the Cube Wizard discovers that the cube template doesn't have a Time dimension. As a result, the wizard suggests we consider a standard Time dimension which can be generated from a pre-defined dimension template.

We will gladly take advantage of the wizard's suggestion by leaving the Time checkbox checked. We can also use the *Add new dimensions* grid to create additional dimensions, if needed. For the purposes of our sample Inventory UDM, the three dimensions we have defined so far are sufficient.

1. Change the name of the Time dimension to **Date** and click Next to advance to the Define Time Periods step (Figure 6.8).

Since we've introduced the Time dimension, the Cube Wizard flow takes a familiar path (see section 4.3 in chapter 4). First, it brings up the Define Time Periods step where we can specify a time range. When generating the relational schema top-down in section 6.1.4, we will instruct the Schema Generation Wizard to pre-populate the Date dimension table with data within this time range.

2. In the Define Time Periods step, select a data range from January 1st 2001 to December 31st 2010. We could tell the Cube Wizard to create multilevel hierarchies based on the Time periods selected. Select the *Year*, *Month*, and *Date* time periods.
3. The Specify Additional Calendar step allows us to select additional calendars (fiscal, reporting, etc). To keep things simple, we will skip this step.

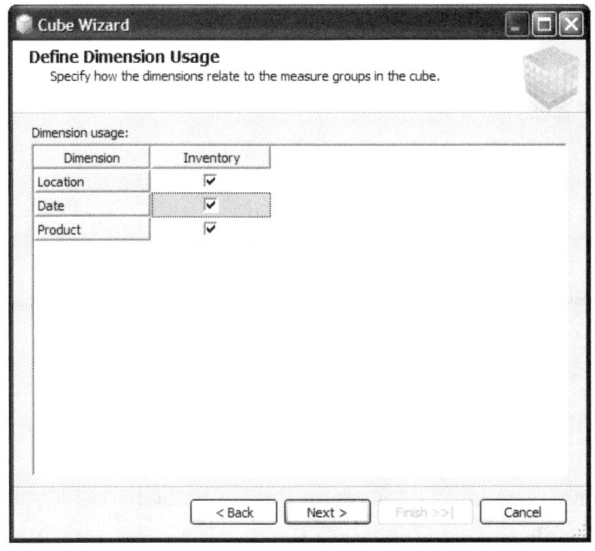

Figure 6.9 Use the Define Dimension Usage step to relate dimensions to measure groups.

4. Use the Define Dimension Usage step (Figure 6.9) to tell the Cube Wizard how the cube dimensions relate to the measure groups. This is equivalent to the Dimension Usage tab in the Cube Designer. Check the intersecting checkbox between the Date dimension and the Inventory measure group. Make a mental note that this relationship requires an ETL task to look up the dimension key of the Time dimension when loading the fact records.
5. In the Completing the Wizard step, name the new cube **Inventory**. Note that you can select the *Generate schema now* checkbox if you want to proceed with the actual database schema generation. Since, most likely, you would need to review and make changes to the cube before creating the staging and subject area databases, leave the checkbox unchecked and click Finish to let the Cube Wizard generate the cube.

Once the cube is generated, open the Inventory cube in the Cube Designer and notice that the Quantity measure is underlined with a red wavy line. Hovering on top of it pops up a tooltip with a "The Source is not specified" error message. If you try to process the cube at this time, you will get similar build errors. An unbound cube cannot be processed because it doesn't have a data source. Once we generate the subject area data schema, the Schema Generation Wizard will automatically bind the UDM objects to the underlying table columns.

6.2.2 Generating the Subject Area Database Schema

Now that the cube is ready, we can turn our attention to implementing the other pieces of the Inventory project. They include the subject area and staging databases, as well as the SSIS packages for the ETL tasks. We can generate the subject area database by running the Schema Generation Wizard. This wizard can be launched from the Cube or Dimension Designers, or from the main menu, but there is an important difference.

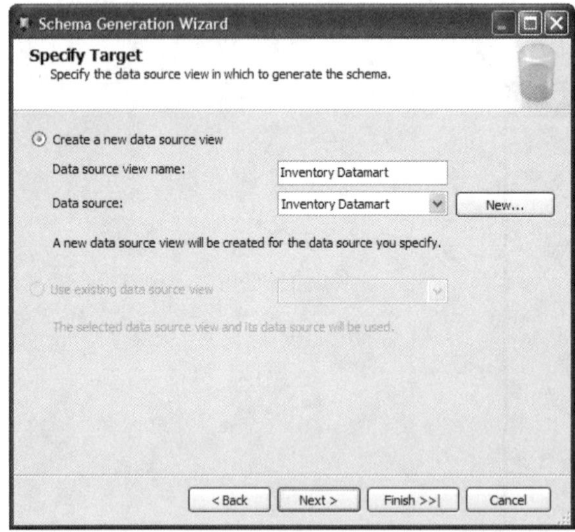

Figure 6.10 The Schema Generation Wizard generates the relational schema of the subject area database.

If the wizard is launched from the main menu (Database ⇨ Generate Relational Schema), it will not bind the UDM objects and dimensions to the subject area tables that it will create. To avoid manually binding the Inventory UDM, make sure you launch the Schema Generation Wizard from within the Inventory cube, as we will do next.

Running the Schema Generation Wizard

Before we proceed, use Management Studio to create a new SQL Server database called *InventoryDatamart* which will fulfill the role of the subject area database.

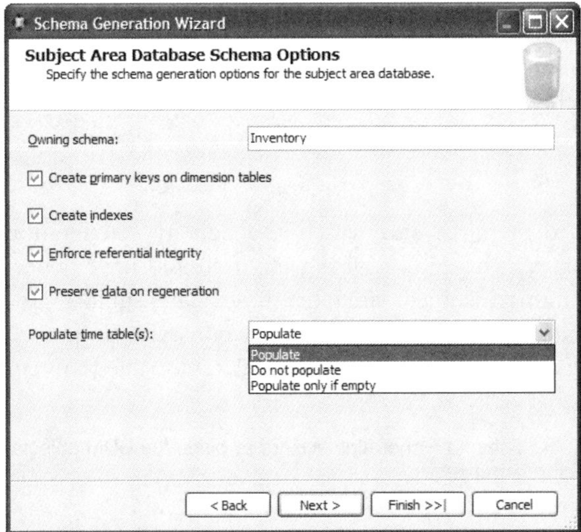

Figure 6.11 The Schema Generation Wizard can populate the Time dimension table.

1. Open the Inventory cube in the Cube Designer and click on the *Click here to generate data source view* link shown in the Data Source View pane to launch the Schema Generation Wizard. Click Next to advance to the Specify Target step (Figure 6.10).
2. Use the Specify Target step, enter **Inventory Datamart** as the name of the data source view that the Inventory UDM will be based on.

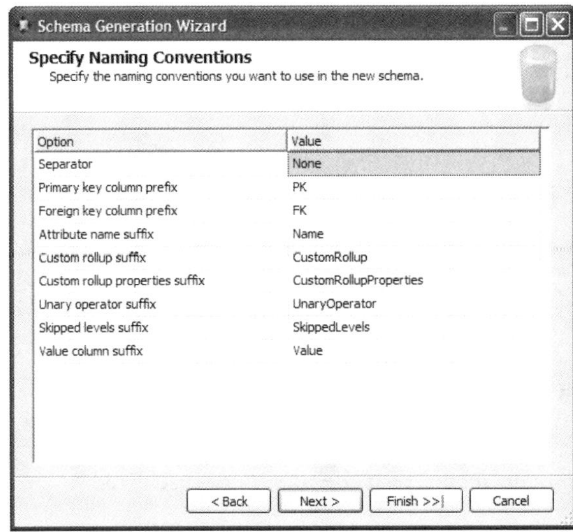

Figure 6.12 Use the Specify Naming Conventions step to tell the wizard how to name the database objects.

3. Create a new data source **Inventory Datamart** that points to the *InventoryDatamart* SQL Server database.

4. Next, use the Subject Area Database Schema Options step (Figure 6.11) to specify the owning schema of the subject area database objects. Leave the generation options to their default values. By default, the Schema Generation Wizard will create appropriate indexes and referential integrity constraints in the subject area database and populate the Time dimension table.

5. Next, in the Specify Naming Conventions step (Figure 6.12), the Schema Generation Wizard asks about the naming convention for the database object names. Most enterprise shops have database naming conventions in place for naming table objects, indexes, primary key, etc. The only change we will make in this step is to change the Separator dropdown to *None,* so the column names follow the title case naming convention, e.g. ProductName, with no separator.

Understanding the data schema

Once you confirm the Completing the Wizard step, sit and watch the Schema Generation Wizard create the subject area relational schema. At the end, if all is well, it should have generated four database tables in the InventoryDatamart subject area database. The subject area database schema is shown in Figure 6.13 and its data definition script (InventoryDatamart.sql) can be found in the Database folder. Note that I've added an additional table called Inventory.Batch for auditing SSIS package execution.

Note Once the subject area schema is created, the Schema Generation Wizard re-binds the UDM objects to the data source view you specified in the Specify Target step.

Let's review briefly the tables generated by the Schema Generation Wizard.

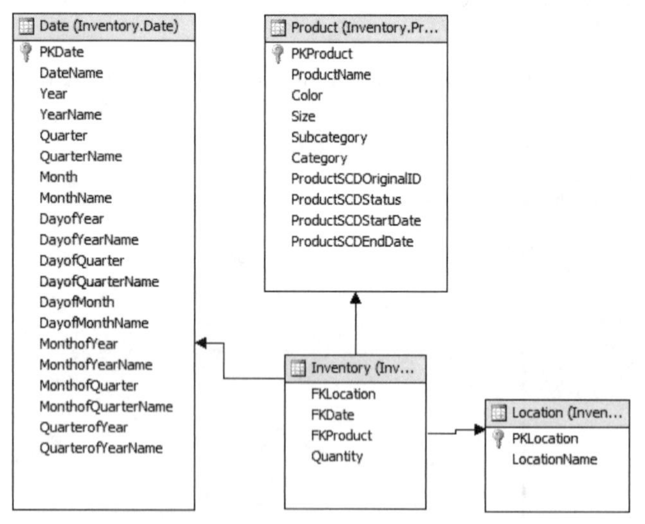

Figure 6.13 Use the Schema Generation Wizard to generate the staging and subject area databases, and the SSIS package for ETL tasks.

Date dimension table

The Date table provides the dimension members for the Date dimension. The Date table has columns for the time periods we've selected in the Cube Wizard. As we requested, the Schema Generation Wizard has populated the Date table with records for the time period selected.

Product dimension table

The Product table serves as a dimension table for the Product dimension. As we've indicated, the Product dimension is a slowly changing dimension and the wizard has generated four columns to track member changes. The original primary key from the OLTP system will be saved to the ProductSCDOriginalID column, which serves as an alternate (business) key, while the PKProduct column is the surrogate key. See chapter 2 for more information about how surrogate keys are used to handle Type 2 changes.

Should a product change its subcategory membership, a new record will be created with a new primary key (PKProduct). The ProductSCDStatus column could be used to mark the current member. For example, if a given product changes its subcategory membership twice, two records will be created in the Product table and the second one will be marked as current. Alternatively, we can use the ProductStartDate and ProductSCDEndDate columns to record the time span of the change (the end date of the old member should equal the start date of the new member).

Other tables

The Location table will be used to load the Location dimension. The Location dimension is a Type 1 dimension. As such, it doesn't keep a historic record of member changes. The Inventory table is the only fact table in the Inventory UDM. It has referential integrity relationships to all dimension tables. Finally, the Batch table is a helper table used for tracking purposes by the SSIS packages. Each package run represents a single batch. All tables have a BatchID column so you can tell which package has made the changes.

Now that the subject area database is in place, we can create the staging area database. Its schema is almost an identical copy of the subject area database. The most noticeable difference is that the staging area database doesn't have indexes for faster processing. Its data definition schema file (InventoryStaging.sql) can be found in the Database folder.

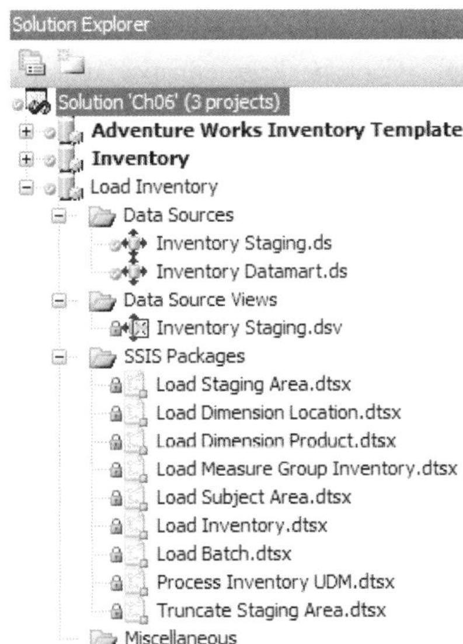

Figure 6.14 A SSIS project consists of data source, data source view, and package definitions.

6.3 Integrating Data with SSIS

A significant effort in every data warehouse project is spent on implementing ETL (**E**xtraction, **T**ransformation, and **L**oading) processes. As you can imagine, transforming and moving data from the OLTP database to the staging database, to the subject area database, to UDM is not trivial. In the past, many database developers and DBAs have relied successfully on the Data Transformation Services (DTS) which is distributed as an add-on to Microsoft SQL Server. DTS has been totally re-architected in SQL Server 2005 and the SQL Server Integration Services (SSIS) was born from its ashes. Discussing SSIS in details is, of course, outside the scope of this book. Instead, we will focus on those aspects of SSIS that are particularly relevant to data warehousing and SSAS. They are demonstrated in the Load Inventory SSIS project which is part of the Ch06 solution file.

6.3.1 Understanding SSIS projects

Just like an Analysis Services project encapsulates all UDM objects in an SSAS database, an Integration Services project serves as a logical container of SSIS objects (data sources, data source views, and packages. For example, the Load Inventory SSIS project (Figure 6.14) contains all the SSIS objects needed to perform the data logistics tasks for loading the Inventory UDM.

SSIS packages

The main object in an Integration Services project is the SSIS *package*. An SSIS package can be used to execute data integration tasks. The package definition is saved in a file with an extension *dtsx* that is described in an XML-based grammar. A package contains other objects, such as connections and tasks. For example, to move data from a flat file to a relational table, you can create a package that has two connections and one Data Flow Task.

Why are there so many packages in the Load Inventory SSIS project? Breaking down a complex data integration package into smaller packages could be useful for several major reasons. First, the project becomes more manageable and simple. Each package encapsulates the functionality and objects it needs. For example, you may need to extract data from ten flat files and upload into five different databases. Instead of having fifteen connections in one package, you can reduce complexity by logically dividing the package into smaller packages and put the objects in the package they belong. Developers may relate this approach to procedural style of programming.

Second, breaking down the flow into packages promotes an object-driven implementation approach. Different developers can work independently on different pieces of the project. You may find this approach similar to the object-oriented programming methodology where complex programming logic can be broken into objects. For example, the Load Inventory project has a package called Load Dimension Product whose sole responsibility is to load the dimension members of the Product dimension from the staging database to the subject area database. Once all packages are ready, a master package can orchestrate the entire data flow by using the Execute Package Task to start the child packages. Also, there are certain operational and performance requirements for using packages. For example, a child package could be configured to run out of the master package process.

Data sources and data source views

Just like SSAS projects, an SSIS project can contain data sources. Unlike UDM, however, in an SSIS project a data source is optional because you can define connections (called *connection managers* in SSIS) at a package level. In this respect, a pre-defined data source has a global scope and can be used across all packages. However, a package could override the data source connection, if needed. The Load Inventory project defines two data sources for connecting to the staging database (Inventory Staging) and subject area database (Inventory Datamart). Child packages may define additional package-level connections to perform their specific data integration needs. For example, the *Load staging area* package defines additional connections to perform data extraction from flat files.

Similar to SSAS, the package designer can implement a data source view to abstract the underlying data source. Again, unlike UDM, a data source view is optional in an SSIS project, but certainly encouraged as a way to isolate the packages from the underlying data sources. For example, the Load Inventory project has an Inventory Staging DSV that is laid on top of the staging database schema.

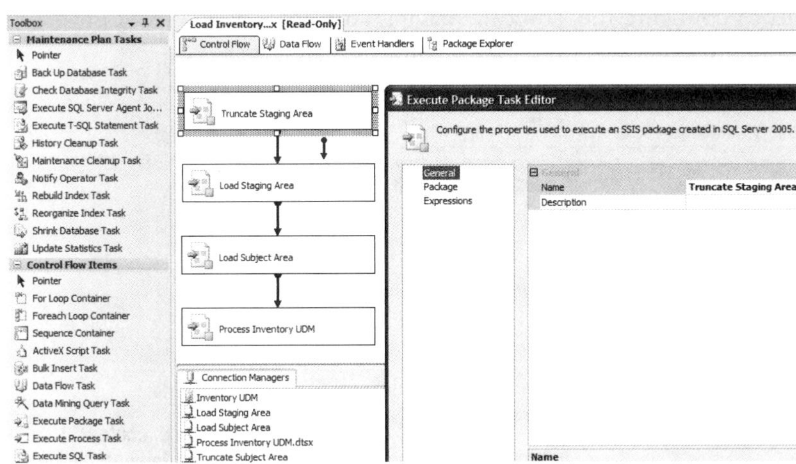

Figure 6.15 Break down a complex SSIS project into smaller, more manageable packages.

The Load Inventory master package

In our SSIS project, the role of the master package is fulfilled by the Load Inventory package. Double click its definition to open it in the SSIS Designer (Figure 6.15). Similar to the Cube Designer, the SSIS Designer features a tabbed user interface. The most important tab is the Control Flow tab. It is used to lay out the data flow by dragging tasks from the Toolbox pane and dropping them on the Control Flow canvas. To set the task execution order, you need to connect tasks by dragging a connector from one task and dropping it onto the other. You use the green connector to construct the "happy" path of the control flow, while the red connector can be used to branch the flow in case of an error condition.

The Load Inventory Package consists of four tasks that correspond to the logical steps required to load the Inventory UDM with data, arranged in their chronological order. First, the *Truncate Stage Area Execute Package* task invokes the Truncate Staging Area child package to clear the staging tables. Next, the *Load Staging Area Execute Package* task runs the Load Staging Area child package to extract data from the flat files and upload it into the staging area tables. The *Load Subject Area Execute Package* task launches the Load Subject Area child package. This is the most involved package from implementation standpoint. It retrieves the staging area data and appends it to the Inventory subject area database. For the sake of simplicity, the Load Subject Area package doesn't perform any data transformation. Finally, the Process Inventory UDM task invokes the Process Inventory UDM child package to process the objects in the Inventory UDM.

Note One thing that I find annoying is that, once you change the task name, it is difficult to tell what the task type really is. To do so, you need to resort to looking up the task in the Toolbox by its icon, double-clicking the task to open the task editor, or looking at the Description task property. For example, the task named Truncate Staging Area task is an Execute Package Task but there is no easy way to discover its type. I hope that, at some point, the SSIS team will change the Properties window to show the task type. For now, you could benefit from a good naming convention for SSIS objects that may include the task type, e.g. using the "df" prefix for the Data Flow Task.

As a prerequisite for configuring the Execute Package task, you need to create a Connection Manager of type *File system* that points to the definition file of the package to be executed. That's why the Connection Managers pane of the Load Inventory master package contains four connection managers, one for each child package. An SSIS task can be configured by double-clicking on it. For example, to configure the Truncate Staging Area task, double-click on it and set its Connection property to the Truncate Subject Area connection manager.

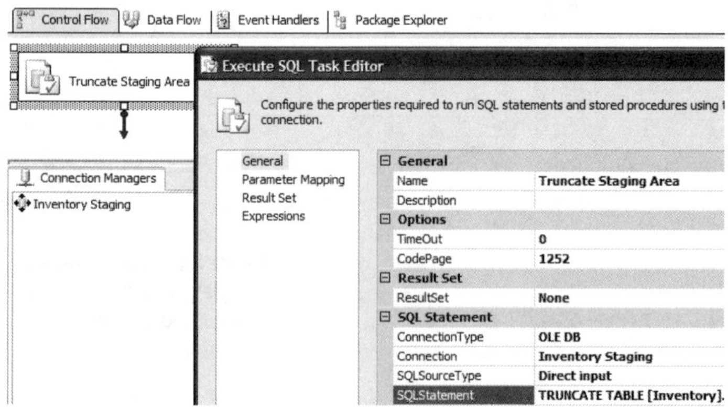

Figure 6.16 Use the Execute SQL Task to send SQL statements to the data source.

6.3.2 Loading the Staging Database

As I explained in our fictitious integration project, data excerpts of the inventory data will be exported on a daily basis in the form of comma-delimited flat files. The Load Inventory package needs to extract data from the flat files and upload it to the staging area database (InventoryStaging).

Truncating staging tables

Before the new data is loaded, the data from the previous package run needs to be truncated. The Truncate Staging Area package is as simple as a package can get. It contains a single Execute SQL Task called Truncate Staging Area (Figure 6.16). This task fires three SQL TRUNCATE statements to purge the two dimension tables (Location and Product) and the Inventory fact table. Follow these steps to execute a given SSIS task.

1. Right-click on the Truncate Staging Area task and choose the *Execute Task* context menu.

SSIS enters a debug mode and changes the task background color to yellow during the task execution. Once the task is executed, its background will change to either green (success) or red (failure).

2. Flip to the Progress tab to find a detailed log of the task execution or troubleshoot the task failure.

3. Stop the SSIS debug mode by clicking on the Stop Debugging toolbar button or pressing Shft-F6. Notice that the Progress tab changes its caption to *Execution Results*. You can use the Execution Results tab to see a detailed log history of the task or package execution.

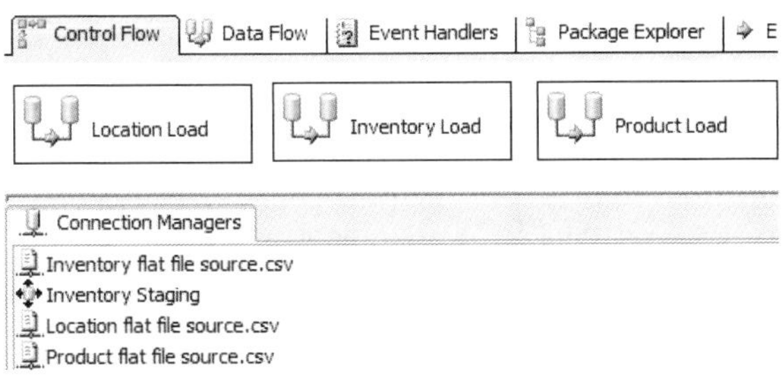

Figure 6.17 Use the Data Flow Task to transfer data between two data sources.

Loading staging tables

The Load Staging Area package loads the three staging tables by executing three instances of the Data Flow Task (Figure 6.17). The Data Flow Task is the task that you will probably use most since the most common goal of a SSIS package is to move data from one location to another. Since the staging tables don't have any referential integrity constrains, their task execution order is irrelevant. That's why the tasks are not linked to each other. As a result, the SSIS runtime will execute them in parallel in an arbitrary order.

The SSIS Designer separates nicely the package control flow from the data transformation minutia. For example, a single Data Transformation may require several steps to transform the incoming rows. You define these steps by flipping to the Data Flow tab or double-click on a Data Flow Task instance.

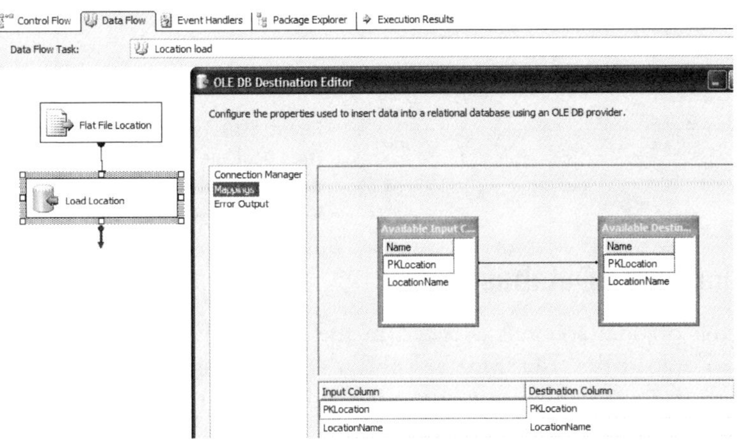

Figure 6.18 Use the OLE DB Destination task to append data to a relational table.

1. Double-click on the Load Location task in the Control Flow tab. The SSIS Designer switches to the Data Flow tab (Figure 6.18) to show its data transformation flow which, in our case, consists of two tasks. Note that you can see the data flow of another Data Flow task in the same package by selecting the task from the Data Flow Task dropdown.

   The Flat File Location task is of a Flat File Source type. It uses a Flat File Data Source Task to extract data from the Location flat file (Location flat file source.csv). The Flat File Data Source Task has a handy preview mode which allows you to see the flat file resultset as it would be parsed. The Load Location task is an OLE DB Destination Task. Its purpose is to insert the flat file resultset to the Location table.

2. Double-click on the Load Location task to open the OLE DB Connection Editor. Notice that the Connection Manager tab defines the following SQL statement:

   ```
   SELECT * FROM [Inventory].[Location]
   ```

   This statement is used to define the column mapping between the source and the destination. I personally find it strange that destination tasks use a SQL SELECT statement while they actually append data.

   Note A destination task uses the SQL SELECT statement to retrieve the column schema. The actual data contained in the table is not retrieved.

3. Flip to the Mappings tab and observe how the columns from the flat file source are mapped to the corresponding columns of the destination table.
4. Repeat the same steps to verify the data flow of the Inventory Load and Product Load tasks.
5. Let's now execute the entire Load Staging Area package. Right-click on it in the Solution Explorer and select *Execute Package*. Once the package has finished executing, you can flip to the Execution Results tab to see the execution log of the entire package. If all is well, the staging tables will be populated from the data in the flat files located in the *Flat file sources* folder.

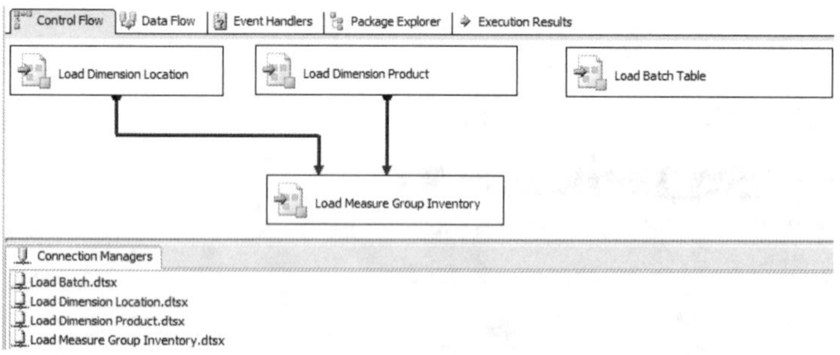

Figure 6.19 The Load Subject Area package loads the dimension tables before loading the fact tables.

6.3.3 Loading the Subject Area Database

Once data is extracted from the original source(s), loaded in the staging database, and transformed, the next step will be to upload the data into the subject area database (InventoryDatamart) that will feed the Inventory UDM. This task is performed by the Load Subject Area package (Figure 6.19).

All tasks in the Load Subject Area package are of the type Execute Package Task. Unlike the staging database load, the subject area tables need to be loaded in a well-defined order. Specifically, the dimension tables need to be loaded first followed by the fact tables. Otherwise, the referential integrity constrains will fail. The Load Batch Table task is an exception and can be executed in an arbitrary order because it doesn't load a dimension table. The purpose of this task is to insert the batch identifier in table Batch for logging purposes, as I've explained when discussing the data source schema.

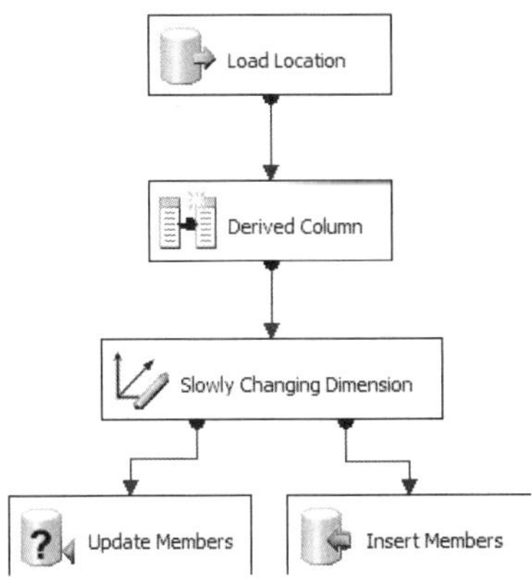

Figure 6.20 Use the Slowly Changing Dimension task to update dimension tables.

Resolving changes to dimension members is not a trivial undertaking, as every database developer can relate to. Dimension members have to be evaluated individually and dealt with according to the type of the dimension changes. As I explained, dimensions can be classified in two types according to how they react to member changes.

Type 1 dimensions are easier because changed members simply override existing members. For example, if a product changes its color, the product member could be updated in place. However, despite the fact that we are not interested in preserving the member history, we still have data logistics issues to deal with. For example, we need to find out if a given member is an existing or an entirely new member to know if we need to update it or append it to the dimension table. To help you tackle these mundane tasks, SSIS provides an extremely useful Slowly Changing Dimension Task that can handle both Type 1 and Type 2 dimensions.

Handling Type 1 dimension changes

The Load Dimension Location package demonstrates how you can handle Type 1 changing dimensions. Its data flow is shown in Figure 6.20. Its work horse is the Slowly Changing Dimension Task, which is one of the most sophisticated SSIS tasks.

Once we retrieve the rows from the Location staging table, we call the Derived Column Task to append the batch identifier column. The batch identifier itself has already been created by the Create Batch Identifier Script Task. Next, we pass the incoming resultset, which includes all columns from the Location staging table plus the batch identifier column, to the Slowly Changing Dimension task for member resolution. To configure the Slowly Changing Dimension Task, double-click on it to launch the Slowly Changing Dimension Wizard.

In the Select a Dimension Table and Keys step (Figure 6.21), we let the wizard know which dimension table it needs to handle (in this case the Location table). More importantly, you need to map the columns of the incoming row to the columns of the dimension table. Finally, you specify a Business key column (alternate key).

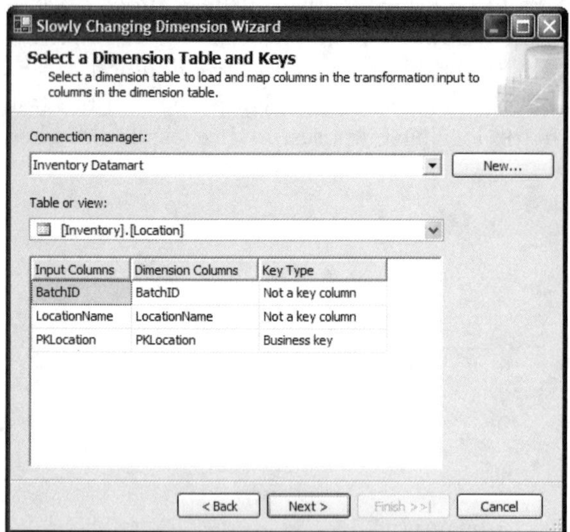

Figure 6.21 Mapping the surrogate key column.

A Type 1 dimension may not have a designated surrogate keys column although it is certainly a good practice for every dimension table to have one. If a surrogate key column is missing, as with the Location dimension table, we can map the Business key type property to the primary key column.

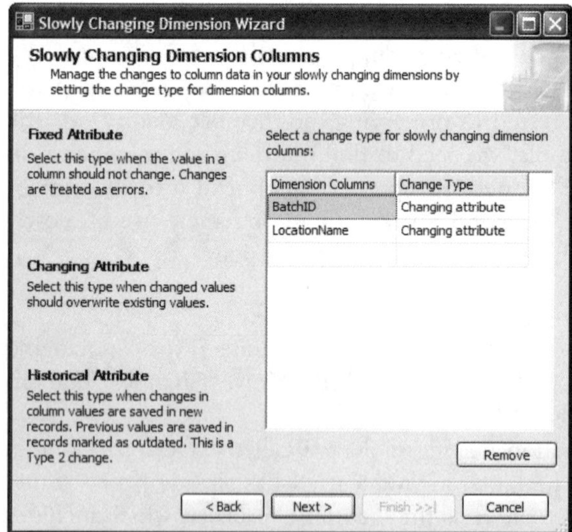

Figure 6.22 Modified values of changing attributes will overwrite the old values .

In the Slowly Changing Dimension Columns step (Figure 6.22), you need to specify which columns will be updated and how the wizard should handle the changes. The wizard supports three change types, as the step description text explains. The BatchID and Location columns are set to *Changing attribute* because we want the changes made to existing dimension members to overwrite the existing values. Accept the default settings through the rest of the wizard's flow. We will revisit them when configuring the Product dimension.

Depending on how it is configured, the Slowly Changing Dimension Task can have up to six outputs. The Load Dimension Location packages uses only two outputs – one for updates and one for inserts. At run time, the Slowly Changing Dimension Task will attempt to match each incoming row to a record in the dimension table. If no match is found, the incoming row is a new record. In this case, the Load Dimension Location package simply adds the row to the dimension table using the OLE DB Destination Task named Insert Members. Othewise, the package uses an OLE DB Command Task named Update Members to fire an UPDATE statement to change the BatchID and LocationName columns.

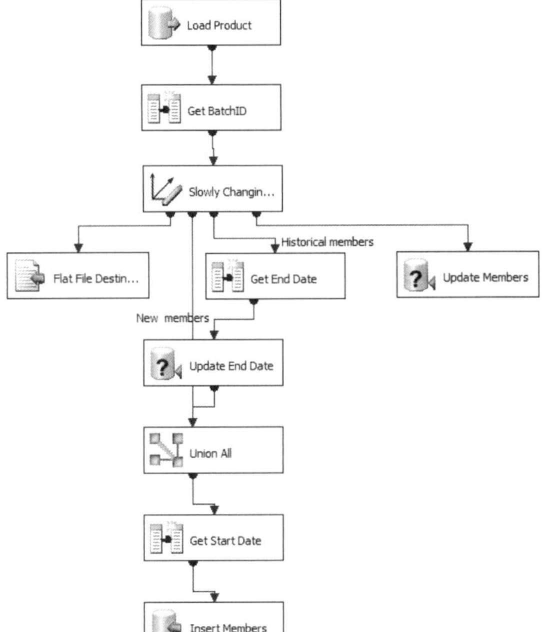

Figure 6.23 A Slowly Changing Dimension Task can have up to six inputs, including inputs for inferred, changing, and historical members.

Handling Type 2 dimension changes

Type 2 slowly changing dimensions are tricky. Not only do we need to detect if the incoming row is a new or existing member, but we also have to determine the type of change the member requires. In some cases, the column value could simply be overwritten, while in others you may need to preserve the member history. For example, if a product member is re-classified to a new subcategory, we may need to preserve its contribution to the old subcategory by creating a new record. As you can see in Figure 6.23, the Load Dimension Product package is more involved. Again, the pivot task in the control flow is the Slowly Changing Dimension task. Run the Slowly Changing Dimension Wizard to configure the Slowly Changing Dimension task.

Matching columns

The Select a Dimension Table and Keys wizard step of the Product Slow Changing Dimension Task is shown in Figure 6.24. The role of the business key in the Product table is fulfilled by the ProductSCDOriginalID column which represents the OLTP primary key. Next, you tell the wizard which columns will trigger Type 2 changes by marking these columns as historical attributes on the Slowly Changing Dimension Columns step. In our case, changes to the product category or subcategory will be treated as Type 2 changes.

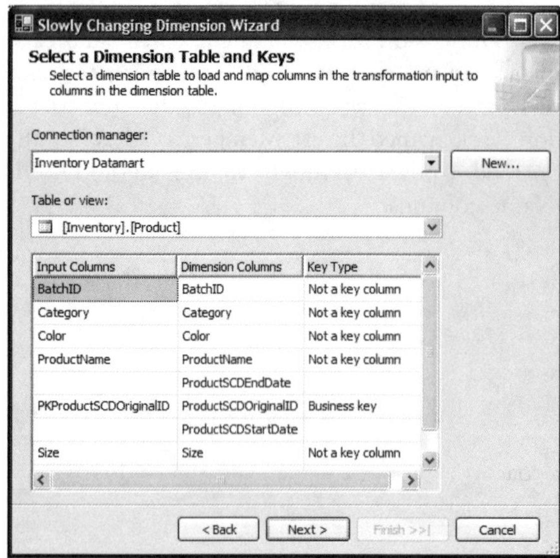

Figure 6.24 In Type 2 dimensions, the role of the business key is fulfilled by the alternate dimension key.

As you would recall from our discussion in chapter 2, a surrogate key is used to isolate UDM from Type 2 changes. In the Product table, the PKProduct column is the surrogate key. If a Type 2 change is detected and the member needs to be cloned, PKProduct changes while ProductSCDOriginalID is immutable. However, since the fact rows in the Inventory fact table need to be associated with the new member from the change forward, we need to have a way to identify the current (latest) dimension member.

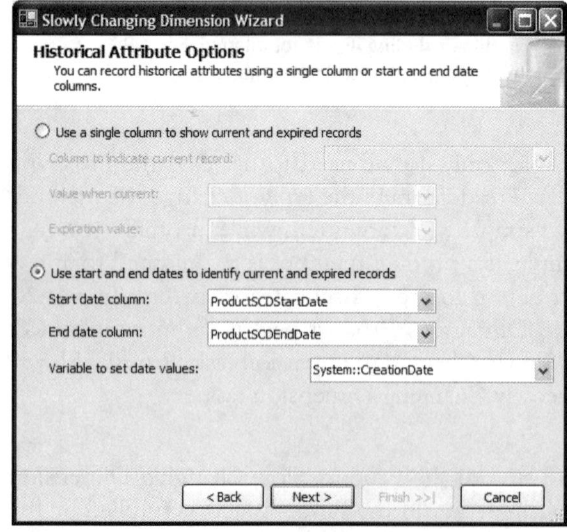

Figure 6.25 You can use either a single status column or a start-end date combination to identify the current dimension member.

Identifying the current member

The Slowly Changing Dimension Task supports two ways of identifying the current member which can be set in the Historical Attribute Options step (Figure 6.25). It can use a single column or a pair of date columns. The first approach requires a designated column that flags the current member. For example, you can use a Boolean column, as shown below.

```
ProductPK  ProductSCDOriginalKey  ProductName Category ProductSCDStatus
10     10     Chain   Bikes   0
20     10     Chain          Accessories 1
```

In this case, a product named Chain has been re-classified from the Bikes to the Accessories category. The value of ProductSCDStatus column is 1 because the second member is the current member. The second option is to use a start date/end date combination.

```
ProductPK  ProductSCDOriginalKey  ProductSCDStartDate ProductSCDEndDate
10     10     1/1/2000   6/1/2003
20     10     6/1/2003   NULL
```

In this case, the start and end date of the change validity period is recorded. The current member can be identified by looking for a NULL value in the ProductSCDEndDate column. For the purposes of our demo, we will use the latter approach to identify the current dimension member.

Identifying inferred members

Finally, you can use the Inferred Dimension Members step (Figure 6.26) to tell the wizard how to handle *inferred* members. You can think of an inferred member as an unresolved dimension member. For example, consider the product snowflake dimension we created in the SOS OLAP UDM. This dimension is based on three tables – DimProduct, DimProductSubcaegory, and DimProductCategory. Now, suppose that when loading a new product, the data transformation task attempts to look up its product subcategory in the DimProductSubcategory but fails to find a match. Instead of raising an exception, the transformation task could mark this record as unknown, similar to the way UDM handles unknown members when processing a dimension.

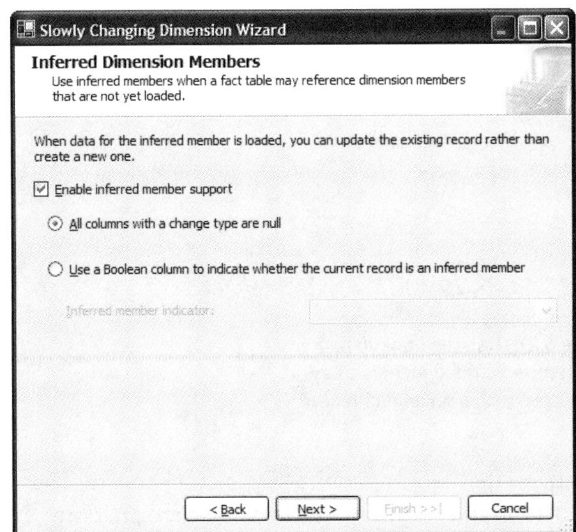

Figure 6.26 Use the Inferred Dimension Members step to tell the wizard how to handle unresolved dimension members.

The wizard can use two criteria to identify inferred rows that cannot be resolved. First, you can tell it to inspect the value of a Boolean column. For example, the data transformation process may flag inferred rows by setting a bit column. Alternatively, you can tell the wizard to treat a record that has NULL values in the changing columns (the ones that will be overwritten) as an inferred member.

Redirecting dimension members

Once you complete the Slowly Changing Dimension Wizard flow, the SSIS Designer will pre-configure the Slowly Changing Dimension task with four outputs (see again Figure 6.23). You can double-click on the connector to open the Data Flow Path Editor and find out the output type.

Handling inferred members

First, we have an output for the inferred members. This is useful if inferred members require special handling, e.g. logging them to a flat file for further inspection. This is exactly how the Load Dimension Product package handles inferred members. To replace the default OLE DB Command Destination with another destination, first remove the OLE DB Command Task. Next, add the new destination, click on the Slowly Changing Dimension Task and drag the available green connector to the new destination. In the Input Output Selection dialog, match the output of the Slowly Changing Dimension task to the input of the destination task.

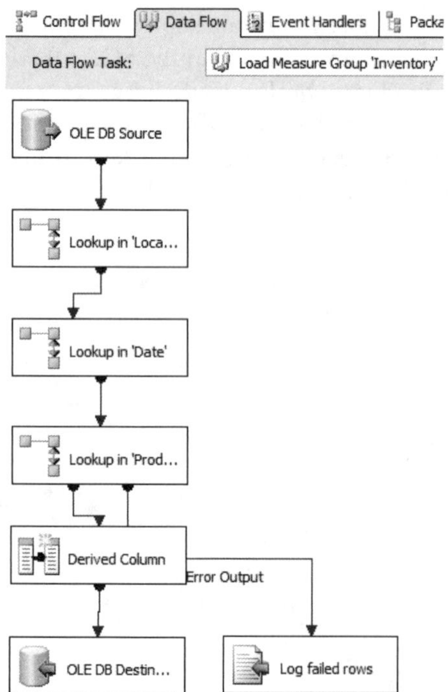

Figure 6.27 Use the Lookup task to find retrieve the dimension key associated with a given fact record.

Handling historical and new members

Next, we have an output for the new members that don't require Type 2 changes. These members need to be simply added to the dimension table with no additional transformations. In addition, there is an output for new members as a result of Type 2 changes. Before adding a new historical member, we need to update the ProductSCDEndDate column of the previous member to the current date. To do so, we use a Derived Column Task named Get End Date to get the current date. Next, we use OLE DB Command Task to update the old member. Finally, we merge both the new and historical members using Union All Transformation Task and append them to the Product table by using the SSIS Insert Members OLE DB Destination Task.

The fourth output is for members that require Type 1 changes. In this case, we just need to overwrite the changed columns. We do so by using the Update Members OLE DB Command Task. As you can see, the Slowly Changing Dimension Task is a feature-rich task that minimizes the transformation effort required to handle Type 1 or Type 2 dimension changes.

Loading the Inventory fact table

Once the dimensions are loaded, we can proceed with loading the fact table. This is a responsibility of the Load Measure Group Inventory package (Figure 6.27). The package uses three instances of the Lookup Transformation Task to look up dimension keys of the three dimension tables (PKLocation, PKProduct, and PKDate) based on the foreign key values of the incoming fact row. If a match is not found, the Lookup triggers an error which will fail the package with the default error configuration.

If this is not what you want, you can configure the error output of the Lookup Task to redirect the failed rows. For example, you may need to inspect the fact rows that failed to resolve the foreign key to the Product dimension table. You can do so by redirecting the error output of the Lookup in Product task to a flat file.

If all of the three dimension lookups succeed, the package appends the new rows to the Inventory fact table. Since the staging fact rows are loaded in memory, by using the Lookup Task you avoid multiple joins between the staging fact table and the subject dimension tables, as you had to do with DTS.

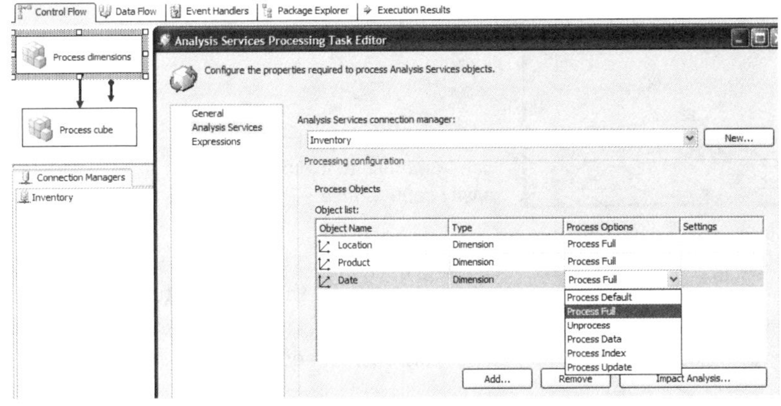

Figure 6.28 Use the SQL Server Analysis Services Task to process SSAS objects.

6.3.4 Processing Analysis Services Objects

As a final step of the Load Inventory project, you need to process the Inventory UDM to pick up the data changes made to the subject area database. The Process Inventory UDM package (Figure 6.28) is responsible for processing the Inventory UDM. Thanks to the excellent SQL Server Analysis Services Processing Task, this package is remarkably simple. The Inventory UDM processing is a matter of two steps. First, we need to process the cube dimensions followed by the cube itself.

Note Processing a cube (even full processing) doesn't process the related dimensions. That's because a dimension can be shared across cubes and, if a dimension is processed, all related cubes will be invalidated. Therefore, you need to process the related dimensions prior to processing the cube itself. If you have only one cube in the SSAS database and you don't need to process it incrementally, you can simplify the processing task by processing the entire database. The net effect will be the same; the SQL Server Analysis Services Processing Task will process the dimensions first followed by processing the cube.

In the Process dimensions task, we add the three dimensions defined in the Inventory UDM. SSAS gives you several options to process a UDM object. Picking the right option requires knowledge of what type of changes and transformations made to the dimension table. For example, if we expect only dimension member changes and know that the dimension structure won't change, we can request the Process Data option. We will discuss these options and UDM processing in more detail in chapter 15. For now, let's go for the *Process Full* option which re-creates and loads the dimensions from scratch.

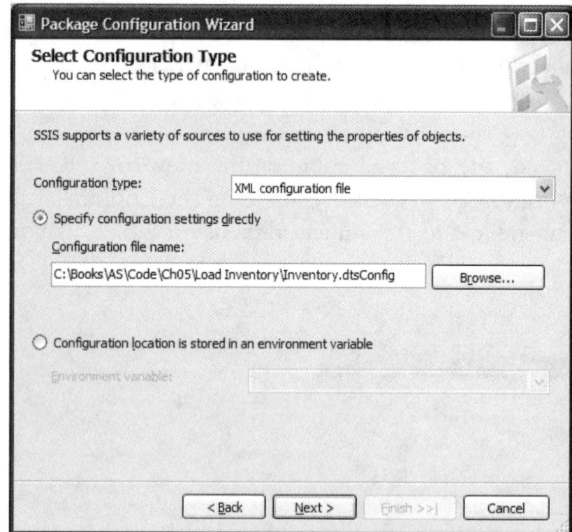

Figure 6.29 Use package configurations to make settings easily configurable.

You will find the Analysis Services tab of the SQL Server Analysis Services Processing Task very similar to the Cube Designer Process dialog. For example, it has the same Change Settings button which allows you to specify the processing options (sequential or parallel processing) and overwrite the error configuration settings for dealing with dimension key errors.

6.3.5 Working with Package Configurations

One SSIS feature that you may find especially handy in reducing the package maintenance effort is the ability to create package configurations. A package may require several connection strings to connect to source and destination databases. Instead of embedding these connection strings in the package definition file, you can store them in an external package configuration file. Once this is done, changing a connection string, e.g. when moving the package from development to production, is a matter of updating the configuration file.

When a package has a project configuration, the package will load the exported settings from the configuration file automatically at run time. A package can have more than one configuration associated with it. For example, regular settings could be kept in an XML configuration file, while more sensitive settings could be moved to a SQL Server configuration store. Let's create a project configuration for the Process Inventory UDM package so we can easily change the connection string to the Inventory cube.

1. Right-click on an empty space in the Control Flow pane and choose *Package Configurations*.
2. In the Package Configuration Organizer dialog, click the Add button to create a new project configuration. The Package Configuration Wizard is launched. Click Next to advance to the Select Configuration Type step (Figure 6.29).
3. SSIS supports different configuration stores, e.g. environmental variable, registry setting, or a SQL Server database. Select the *XLM configuration* file setting to create the configuration store as an XML file and enter the full path to the new configuration file. Click Next to proceed to the Select Properties to Export step.

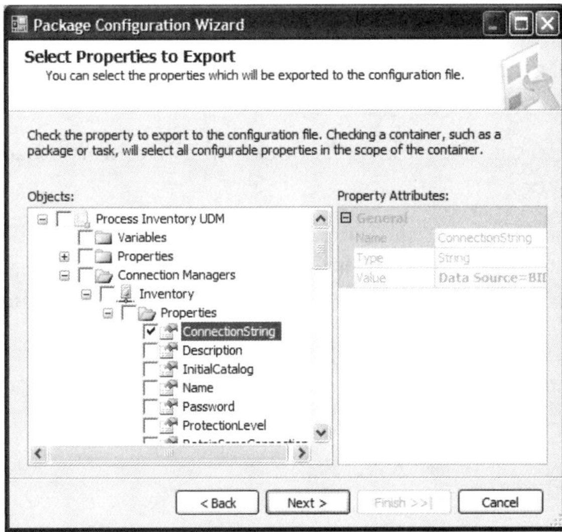

Figure 6.30 Use package configurations to maintain configuration settings easily.

4. You can make various package properties configurable. For our purposes, select the *Connection-String* property of the Inventory Connection Manager (Figure 6.30). Click Next and name the configuration section **Inventory UDM.**

The Package Configuration Wizard exports the ConnectionString setting to the specified XML configuration file. If you need to change the connection string, e.g. to change the server name, just open the configuration file and make the necessary changes. The package will pick them up the next time it is run.

6.3.6 Testing Package Execution

Now that our Load Inventory package is ready, let's give it a try. Use the files in the Flat file sources folder initial data load. Then, experiment with different inputs to test the package. For example, change the Product flat file source.csv file to simulate a Type 2 change to the Product dimension or use the sample Product Type 2.csv file. While testing the package, you may be willing to step through the package in order to verify its execution.

The SSIS Designer offers several options for troubleshooting the package execution. One useful option is debugging the package. For example, just as a developer can halt the code execution by using breakpoints, the package designer could use the breakpoint to stop the package execution at a certain task and inspect its execution results. To create a breakpoint, right-click on a given task and choose Edit Breakpoints context menu. Next, use the Set Breakpoints dialog to specify under what condition the breakpoint will be enabled. For example, to halt the project run when a task errors out, choose the OnError event. Next, run the package in debug mode (F5). Another option for troubleshooting the task execution is to use an error configuration and log the failed rows, as we did with the Load Measure Group Inventory package.

Tip When debugging a child package, set the ExecuteOutOfProcess property of its Execute Package task to *False*. If ExecuteOutOfProcess is True (default value), the child package will run in a separate process and the data viewer will not work.

Perhaps, the debugging option that will become everyone's favorite is using a data viewer to inspect the task incoming resultset. For example, suppose that you need to see the data retrieved from the Inventory flat file before it is loaded to the Inventory staging table.

1. Open the Load Staging Area package and flip to the Data Flow Tab. Select the Inventory Load Data Flow task in the Data Flow Task dropdown.
2. Double-click on the connector between the Flat File Inventory and Load Inventory tasks. In the Data Flow Path Editor, click on the Data Viewers tab and add a Grid Data Viewer. Note that when you close the Data Flow Path Editor, an icon is added next to the connection to indicate that it has an associated data viewer.
3. Right-click on the Load Staging Area package in the Solution Explorer and choose *Execute Package*.

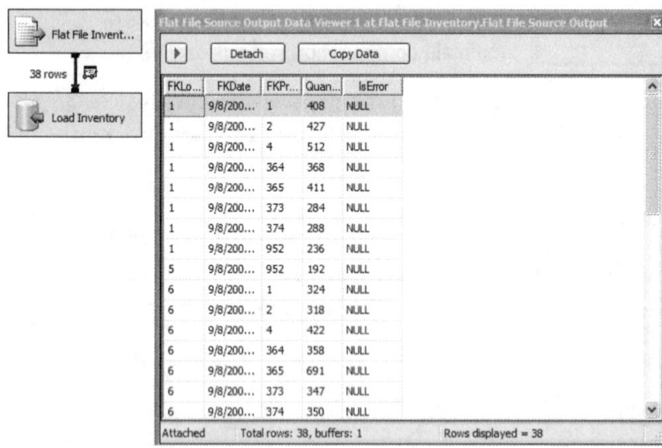

FKLo...	FKDate	FKPr...	Quan...	IsError
1	9/8/200...	1	408	NULL
1	9/8/200...	2	427	NULL
1	9/8/200...	4	512	NULL
1	9/8/200...	364	368	NULL
1	9/8/200...	365	411	NULL
1	9/8/200...	373	284	NULL
1	9/8/200...	374	288	NULL
1	9/8/200...	952	236	NULL
5	9/8/200...	952	192	NULL
6	9/8/200...	1	324	NULL
6	9/8/200...	2	318	NULL
6	9/8/200...	4	422	NULL
6	9/8/200...	364	358	NULL
6	9/8/200...	365	691	NULL
6	9/8/200...	373	347	NULL
6	9/8/200...	374	350	NULL

Figure 6.31 Data viewers help you troubleshoot the package execution.

When the flow reaches the Load Inventory task, the package execution will be halted and the Load Inventory task will change its background color to yellow. The incoming resultset will be displayed in the viewer (Figure 6.31) and the row count will be displayed at the status bar. Once you verify data, click the arrow toolbar button to resume the package execution.

6.4 Summary

A data warehouse project is a complex undertaking that may require executing tasks in parallel to shorten the project lifecycle. A modeler can blueprint UDM in the absence of a data source. Starting from a template, you can use BI Studio to define and generate the raw version of your UDM. Once the dimensional model is ready, use the Schema Generation Wizard to create the staging database schema.

Implement Integration Services packages for handling data extraction, transformation, and loading processes. Use the Slowly Changing Dimension Task to handle Type1 and Type 2 dimension changes. Leverage the SQL Server Analysis Services Processing Task to process UDM objects. Use SSIS project configurations to export package settings, such as connection strings, to reduce your maintenance effort. Add data viewers to troubleshoot the package execution.

6.5 Resources

Project REAL -- Business Intelligence in Practice
(http://shrinkster.com/6za) – Project REAL (an acronym for *R*eference implementation, *E*nd–to–end, *A*t scale, and *L*ots of users) is a cooperative effort between Microsoft and a number of technology partners in the business intelligence space. Visit the Project Real webpage for great white papers, webcasts, and other resources that showcase how the Microsoft BI components can be used to build data warehousing and OLAP solutions.

SQL Server 2005 Integration Services: Lessons from Project REAL article by Richard Waymire, Len Wyatt, John H. Miller, Donald Farmer
(http://shrinkster.com/4zr) – In this article, the Microsoft team shares their experience harvested from Project REAL where large volumes of real data were used to implement business intelligence systems with Microsoft SQL Server 2005.

Chapter 7

Data Mining Fundamentals

In chapter 1 you learned that the two core services provided by SSAS are OLAP and data mining. So far, we've been exploring UDM from the OLAP "dimension" only, completely ignoring its smaller, but no less important, cousin – data mining. Now, it's time to switch gears and give data mining its fair share of attention. In this chapter, we will see how the data mining technology complements OLAP to provide rich data analytics. You will learn:

- The fundamentals of data mining technology.
- The building blocks of SSAS data mining.
- The necessary steps to implement data mining models.
- How to construct data mining models from relational data sources.

We will put into practice what we've learned so far by implementing a data mining model for targeted campaigning. You can find the enhanced SOS OLAP UDM in the Ch07 solution file.

7.1 Understanding Data Mining

Data mining is a newcomer to the business intelligence arena. It is new because only in the past decade the computation power reached the necessary gains to support data warehousing and mining algorithms. Though a young technology, data mining has an exciting future. According to a market forecast study by IDC, data mining is the fastest growing business intelligence segment, surpassing OLAP, relational reporting, or any other business intelligence field. In 2005, the data mining market is expected to grow 32%!

Realizing that data mining is a logical next step for rich data analytics, Microsoft introduced data mining features in SQL Server 2000. Since the initial feature set was rather limited, data mining didn't enjoy broad acceptance. For example, data mining in SQL Server 2000 supported only two algorithms (Microsoft Decision Trees and Microsoft Clustering) and didn't provide adequate model building and tuning tools. In my opinion, all this is going to change with SQL Server 2005. After several years of intensive research and investment, the Microsoft data mining technology comes of age in SQL Server 2005. The data mining engine has been completely re-architected. Five new algorithms have been added to address various data mining scenarios. The data mining tools have undergone a major uplift and now support custom visualization for each algorithm. A great effort has been made to integrate data mining with other Microsoft BI technologies, including UDM, Integration Services and Reporting Services, and to enhance the programming interfaces to build intelligent applications.

7.1.1 What is Data Mining?

Data mining can be described as a business intelligence process that offers three main services -- *data exploration*, *pattern discovery*, and *prediction*. Let's find out more about these services and their practical usage scenarios.

Data mining services

Data mining could help organizations to *explore* large volumes of valuable data and derive knowledge from it. For example, you may have a huge Customer UDM dimension with thousands, if not millions, of members. Data mining can help you segment these customers to find out, for example, what is the typical profile (age, income, occupation, etc.) of customers buying a given product. Many organizations use data mining to find *patterns* in data, e.g. to recommend other items that the customer may be willing to buy together with a given product.

Finally, an organization can leverage data mining to *predict* business metrics based on existing data statistics, e.g. to find out what the next quarter sales could be given the sales statistical data for the past year. As you can imagine, market researchers and data analysts can leverage data mining as a potent and valuable tool to understand a company's business and its customers better.

Dimension	Hierarchy	Operator	Filter Expression
Customer	Customers by Geography	Equal	{ Canada }
<Select dimension>			

Drop Filter Fields Here

	Year				
	2001	2002	2003	2004	Grand Total
Customer	Internet Sales Amount	Internet Sales Amount	Internet Sales Amount	Internet Sales Amount	Internet Sales Amount
Katherine Gonzalez	$2,454.91			$1,566.33	$4,021.23
Paige Reed	$2,469.13		$1,546.93		$4,016.06
Isabella L. Bryant		$2,417.75	$1,594.24		$4,011.99
Xavier Martin	$2,467.94		$1,543.16		$4,011.10
Jordan C. Henderson		$2,431.22	$1,576.73		$4,007.95
Caitlin T. Richardson		$2,438.51		$1,569.30	$4,007.81
Paige Brooks	$2,467.09		$1,540.41		$4,007.50
Alexandra P. Barnes	$2,407.34			$1,598.80	$4,006.14
Madeline H. Parker	$2,446.18		$1,557.64		$4,003.82
Makayla Brooks	$2,397.66			$1,596.75	$3,994.41
Grand Total	$17,110.25	$7,287.48	$9,359.10	$6,331.17	$40,088.01

Figure 7.1 OLAP is a great technology for efficient data aggregation.

Data mining and OLAP

Considering the services that data mining provides, your first impression may be that it is a technology competing with OLAP. True, both technologies seek to provide rich data exploration and reporting. Also, both technologies are used typically in conjunction with data warehousing to process and analyze vast volumes of data. At the same time, however, data mining seeks to provide different services than OLAP and it should be viewed as a complementing, rather than competing technology.

To understand this better, consider the report shown in Figure 7.1. I generated this report from our sample SOS OLAP cube. It shows the top ten Canadian customers that have purchased Adventure Works products for four consecutive years. This report demonstrates one of the main strengths of the OLAP technology which is data *aggregation*. As you know by now, SSAS is designed to aggregate data across dimensions fast.

However, as useful as this report is, it doesn't tell us much about the customers themselves. For example, using just OLAP we have no easy way to find out data patterns, such as customer buying habits, perform basket analysis, or recommend products based on a customer's past purchase history. That's because once the data has been aggregated, hidden data patterns, data relationships, and data associations are often no longer discernable. Moreover, OLAP doesn't provide prediction capabilities. For example, we can't forecast product sales for the fourth quarter of 2004.

Table 7.1 OLAP is suitable for model-driven analysis, while data mining provides data-driven analysis.

Characteristic	OLAP	Data mining
Pattern discovery	Limited	Core service
Prediction	No	Core service
Object model	Cubes, dimensions, and measure groups	Structrures and mining models
Business metrics	Measures	Dimensions (usually)
Analytics process	On-going, historical analytics	Done typically on as-needed, "ad hoc" basis

The above business requirements can be addressed easily by using data mining, as the examples in this and next chapters will demonstrate. Table 7.1 outlines other major differences between data mining and OLAP. They will be explained throughout the course of this chapter.

7.1.2 Data Mining Tasks and Algorithms

Instead of looking at a crystal ball, data mining practitioners perform their "magic" by leveraging well-known mathematical models that originate from three academic fields: statistics, machine learning, and database theory. Statistical models that are particularly related to data mining are those that are designed to find data correlations, such as Naïve Bayes and Clustering. Other models come from the machine learning (or Artificial Intelligence) research field, such as decision trees and neural networks models. Finally, database algorithms are used to process large data volumes efficiently.

Data mining can be applied to a number of different tasks. The most popular data mining tasks are association, classification, segmentation (clustering), regression, and forecasting. An essential coverage of these tasks is provided in the OLE DB for Data Mining Specification (OLE DB/DM) and the excellent webcasts from the SSAS data mining team (see Resources). Discussing them in this chapter will be redundant.

Note The OLE DB for Data Mining specification was created in 2000 by Microsoft with the assistance of other data mining partners to define an industry standard for creating and modifying data mining models, train these models, and then predict against them. I highly recommend that you read the specification (see Resources section). It is a great resource for understanding not only the Microsoft data mining implementation details, but also the data mining technology and algorithms in general. Currently, data mining is part of the XMLA specification.

The mining tasks are realized by well-known mathematical algorithms. SSAS 2005 implements seven data mining algorithms. Choosing an algorithm to perform a given task can be challenging. Table 7.2 should help you choose the right algorithm for the task at hand.

Table 7.2 Data mining tasks and algorithms to implement them.

Task	Decision Trees	Clustering	Association	Naïve Bayes	Sequence Clustering	Neural Network	Time Series
Classification	✓	✓		✓	✓	✓	
Segmentation		✓			✓	✓	
Association	✓		✓				
Regression	✓	✓			✓		
Forecasting							✓

Note that in some cases a given task can be performed by several algorithms. The ones that are most suitable are highlighted in Table 7.2. For example, the classification task can be realized by the Decision Trees, Clustering, Naïve Bayes, Sequence Clustering, and Neural Network algorithms, but the Decision Trees algorithm should be your best choice.

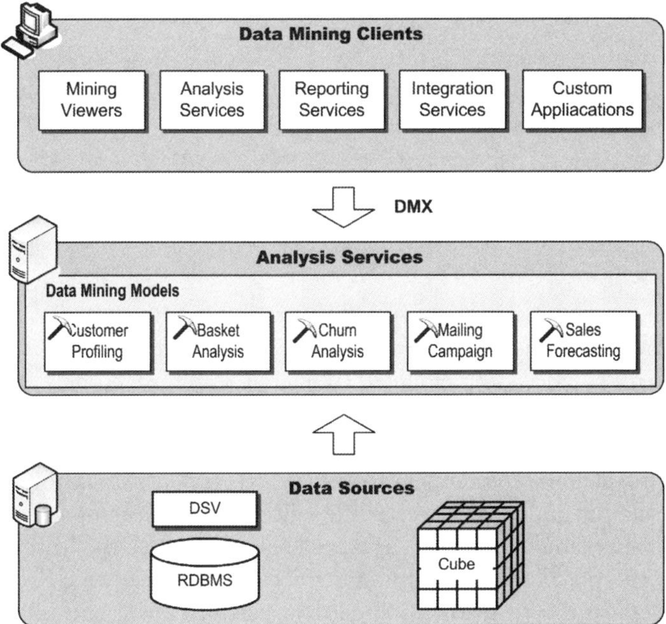

Figure 7.2 Data mining models can source data from relational databases or UDM cubes and can be integrated with different types of clients.

It is also important to note that the SSAS data mining architecture is extensible. Custom data mining algorithms can be plugged in (see Resources section for more information) and custom mining viewers can be implemented to replace the ones provided by Microsoft.

7.1.3 Data Mining Architectural View

Now, let's see how SSAS data mining works and how it fits in the Microsoft Business Intelligence Platform. Figure 7.2 shows a high level architectural view of SSAS data mining. The SSAS data mining architecture consists of data mining models (processed and executed on the server), data sources that feed the models, and mining clients that retrieve and analyze the predicted results.

Data mining models

As shown in Figure 7.2, data mining technology in SSAS is exposed to clients as one or more *data mining models* hosted in an Analysis Services database. I will explain in more detail what a data mining model is in section 7.2.1. For now, know that a data mining model is just a UDM object that takes some input data and outputs the predicted results using the selected mathematical algorithm. A data mining model can be designed and managed using BI Studio or programmatic interfaces, such as Analysis Management Objects (AMO).

Data sources

Data mining models can be fed with data from two types of data sources.

- *Relational data sources* – A data mining model can source its data from any data source that has an OLE DB driver, including SQL Server, Oracle, Teradata, etc. If data is available as text files, Integration Services can be used to extract, transform, and load the source data into a relational data source or directly in the model. Similar to SSAS cubes, a data mining model doesn't access the data source directly. Instead, it uses a data source view to isolate itself from the relational data source schema and optionally enhance it.
- *UDM* – A data mining model can be built on top of an SSAS 2005 cube. In this case, the cube and the data mining models must be hosted in the same database. A DSV is not needed when a data mining model draws data from a cube.

In this chapter, I will show you how to build a data mining model from a relational data sources. The next chapter demonstrates how you can use UDM as a data source of mining models.

Data mining clients

In the simplest scenario, the end user could use Microsoft-provided or third-party data mining viewers to browse the data mining models inside the BI Studio IDE. At the other end of the spectrum, a custom application front end could be implemented to query the mining models and display the predicted results.

Data mining is well integrated with the other products of the Microsoft Business Intelligence Platform. For example, the results of the data mining model can be used to create a dimension to enrich an SSAS cube. Integration Services include tasks specifically tailored for data mining. For example, in the next chapter, we will implement an SSIS package that uses the Data Mining Query Task to classify customers on the fly. Finally, Reporting Services can be used to deliver the data mining results to the end users in the form of a standard or ad-hoc report. An SSRS integration example is demonstrated in chapter 18.

7.1.4 Data Mining Extensions (DMX)

Clients can create and query data mining models and obtain predictions by sending DMX (**D**ata **M**ining E**X**tensions) statements. To facilitate a wide spread adoption of data mining and minimize the learning curve, the SSAS team was set to provide a query language that is familiar to database developers and easy to use. Since almost everyone knows SQL, the SSAS team decided to adopt it as a foundation for mining queries and extend with data mining-specific features (documented by the OLE DB for Data Mining Specification). Similar to SQL, DMX provides both Data Definition Language (DDL) and query constructs. For example, here is what the basic form of a DMX SELECT query looks like:

```
SELECT <expression list> FROM <mining model>
[NATURAL] PREDICTION JOIN
<source data> AS <alias> ON <column mappings>
```

Let's briefly explain the DMX-specific constructs in the SELECT statement.

Expression list

As an SQL SELECT statement specifies which columns from a relational table will be returned, the expression list in a DMX SELECT statement enumerates the predictable columns from the model that will be retrieved. For example, if I have a cluster mining model for customer profiling, the expression list can bring some customer-related columns, such as Age, Occupation, Education, etc.

In addition, DMX supports a set of functions (about thirty) that can be used in prediction queries. For example, you can use the *PredictCaseLikeliHood* function to determine the possibility for a customer to belong to a cluster. Again, similar to SQL joins, the PREDICTION JOIN...ON clause links the mining model with the source data. If the names of the mining model match the source data columns NATURAL PREDICATION JOIN can be used and the ON clause can be omitted. In this case, the columns relationships are automatically inferred through a naming convention.

Source Data

The source data specifies the input dataset that will be predicted against the mining model and it could be:

- *Database OPENQUERY or OPENROWSET query* – Use a database query to feed the mining model with data fro a relational table.
- *Singleton query* – In this case, the data values are embedded in the SELECT statement.
- *Another DMX query* – DMX queries can be nested.
- *Rowset parameter* – A client can pass an application rowset, such as an ADO.NET dataset or a data reader, as an input to the mining model.

Examples of the first two options are provided in this chapter. Chapter 17 includes more examples that demonstrate how custom applications can create and query data mining models.

7.2 Data Mining Objects

Now, let's see how the data mining technology is realized in SSAS. UDM defines two main data mining objects -- data mining *models* and data mining *structures*. Let's explain structures and models in more details. We will start with the data mining model since it is the cornerstone of the SSAS data mining technology.

7.2.1 Data Mining Models

The OLE DB for Data Mining Specification describes a data mining model as a virtual object that is similar to a relational database table. A mining model defines how data should be analyzed and predicted. For example, suppose that you need to implement a data mining model to promote the latest bicycle product as part of a mailing campaign effort. To identify which customers are most likely to respond to the campaign, you may design your model as the one shown in Figure 7.3.

Customer ID	Name	Age	Gender	Education	Commute Distance	Bike Buyer
Usage: *Key*	Usage: *Ignore*	Usage: *Input*	Usage: *Input*	Usage: *Input*	Usage: *Input*	Usage: *Predict*
1	John	25	M	Graduate Degree	1-5 Miles	Y
2	Alice	30	F	Partial College	5-10 Miles	N
3	Bob	35	M	High School	1-5 Miles	Y

Figure 7.3 A data mining model consists of set of columns with different usage types.

Model definition

Just like a relational table, the mining model definition consists of columns. Each column can have different usage inside the model. If a column identifies a row in the model (also called a *case*), the column usage type needs to be set to *Key*. For example, in our mailing campaign model, the role of the key is fulfilled by the Customer ID column because it identifies uniquely a row in the model. A column with a usage type of *Input* is used as an input parameter to the data mining algorithm. In our case, all demographics-related columns could be used as input columns. For example, we may wish to find the correlation between the Commute Distance column and the probability that a customer will purchase a bicycle. To do so, you set the Usage type of the column to Input.

A data mining model can have one or more columns with Predict or PreductOnly Usage types. A column with a *Predict* Usage type is used both for input and predictions. In comparison, as its name suggests, a *PredictOnly* column is used only for predictions. In the mailing campaign scenario, we need to predict what category of customers is likely to become bike buyers based on past purchases. Therefore, we need to set the Bike Buyer Usage type to *Predict*. Finally, we may decide to ignore a given column. For example, the Name column is not useful to find patterns. That's why we set its Usage to *Ignore*.

Does the column usage type bring any recollection? Indeed, we can loosely relate a data model to a UDM dimension. Just like a UDM dimension, a data model consists of columns (attributes) which can have different usage types within the containing model. I will be quick to point out that one noticeable difference between a UDM dimension and a data mining model is that a mining model doesn't store the input dataset. Instead, the input dataset is used only to train the model. The server stores only the results of the prediction process in the form of rules or patterns.

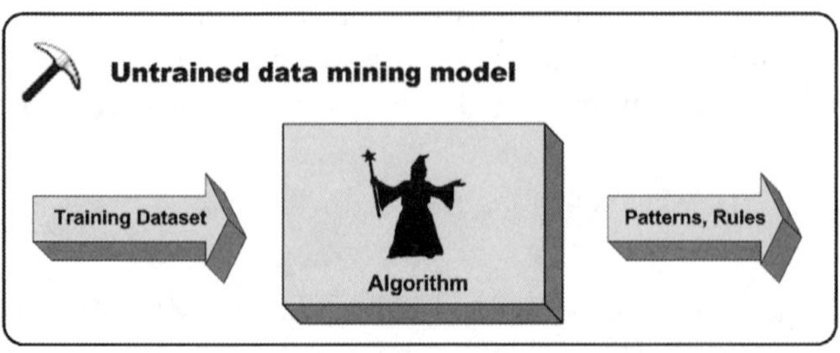

Figure 7.4 A data mining model must be trained before it can be used for predictions.

Training the model

Before a mining model can be used, it must be *trained* by loading the model with data. SSAS trains a model by executing the mathematical algorithm associated with the model to derive useful patterns or rules from input data (Figure 7.4). You can train a model by either processing it (e.g. using BI Studio or an SSIS package), or by submitting a DMX INSERT INTO statement. The latter option is typically used when creating the model programmatically, e.g. by using ADOMD.NET. For example, you can use the following statements to create and train a hypothetical CustomerProfilingMC mining model that uses the Microsoft Clustering algorithm:

```
CREATE MINING MODEL [CustomerProfilingMC]
(
    Customer LONG KEY,
    Age LONG CONTINUOUS,
    [Yearly Income] DOUBLE CONTINUOUS,
    [Occupation] TEXT DISCRETE
)
Using Microsoft_Clusterting

INSERT INTO  CustomerProfiling (Customer, Age, [Yearly Income], Occupation)
OPENQUERY(MyLinkedServer, 'SELECT CustomerID, Age, Income, Occupation FROM Customers')
```

In this case, an OPENQUERY clause is used to load the model with data from a relational table Customers. Note that we cannot query the table by using a SELECT statement because the model resides in an SSAS database (thus the OPENQUERY statement). The time needed for training a data mining model depends on the amount of input data and the complexity of the algorithm. The end result of training a data model is patterns or rules that are saved on the server.

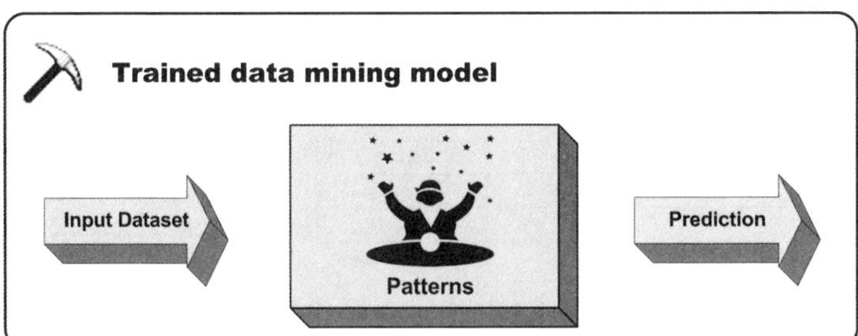

Figure 7.5 A trained mining model takes an input dataset, applies the learned patterns, and returns predications.

Performing predictions

Finding patterns in historical data is just half of the work in a typical data mining project. The next logical step is to query the mining model and obtain predictions against *new* data. For example, after training a customer profiling mining model with historical data, the model could identify (predict) a particular class of customers that are likely to purchase a product. Given the predicted results, we may need to know how likely it is that a new customer will become a potential buyer. To understand this better, it may be helpful to visualize a data mining model as a black box, which takes the data to be predicted as an input, applies the learned patterns, and outputs the predicted results (Figure 7.5).

Here, the term *prediction* is used rather loosely to describe the result of the mathematical calculation that the mining algorithm performs against the new dataset. The result may not even have a time dimension. For example, the output of the data mining model could be classifying a customer to a given cluster if the data mining task is customer profiling. Considering the CustomerProfilingMC model example, this is how an intelligent application can send a DMX SELECT query to find out how likely it is that a given customer with the supplied demographics criteria may belong to a given cluster.

```
SELECT ClusterProbability('Cluster 8')
FROM [CustomerProfilingMC]
NATURAL PREDICTION JOIN
(SELECT 35 AS [Age],
  'Professional' AS [Occupation],
  80000 AS [Yearly Income]
) AS t
```

In this case, the application uses a *singleton* query to pass the data values directly to the model. Alternatively, the second SELECT statement can retrieve the data to be predicted from a data source.

Data mining tables

When a model is trained, input data must be passed to the model as a single table which is called a *case table*. In the simplest case, each row column in this table will have only one value, as with the mailing campaign scenario shown in Figure 7.3. Sometimes, you may need to find correlations between related datasets. For example, suppose that you need to perform customer basket analysis to recommend related products to customers (customers who bought A product also bought B product). To implement the basket analysis mining model, you will need two tables, as shown in Figure 7.6.

Customer ID	Name	Age	Gender	Education	Products Bought
1	Bob	35	M	College	

Product ID	Name	Price
1	Beer	$12
2	Chips	$3
3	Milk	$2.50

Figure 7.6 A correlated dataset can be exposed as a nested table.

This model has two tables, Customer and Product, linked with a one-to-many relationship. Since a mining model can have only one input table, this schema presents an issue because we need to "flatten" the dataset to a single table. SSAS solves this dilemma by allowing us to "embed" the child table (the one on the many side of the relationship) into a column of the parent table in the form of a *nested table*. For example, in our case, the child table (Product) could be defined as a nested table embedded inside the Products Bought column of the Customer parent table. SSAS supports a single level of nesting only. In other words, a child table cannot have another nested table. The OLE DB for Data Mining Specification also defines the term *case* and *case set*.

Definition A case is a collection of data associated with a single row in the input table. A case set is the collection of all cases (all records of the parent table plus all records of the nested tables).

For example, in our fictitious basket analysis model, a case represents a single customer and its associated products. In the mailing campaign example, a case simply corresponds to an individual customer because the Customer table doesn't have nested tables.

7.2.2 Data Mining Structures

As you've seen, a data mining model could simply be described as a collection of table columns and a mining algorithm that acts upon the data contained in these columns to analyze it and perform predictions. At the same time, we've learned that a particular data mining task may be performed by using different algorithms. Naturally, you may be willing to try a few algorithms with a given mining task to select the most accurate algorithm. Since, in this case, all task algorithms will use the same data schema, it may make sense to re-factor the database schema definition in its own object, just like a data source view may be shared by several cubes. In SSAS, a data mining structure gives you this level of abstraction.

What is a data mining structure?

You can think of a data mining structure as a blueprint of the database schema which is shared by all mining models inside the structure. In this respect, developers familiar with object-oriented programming may relate a data mining structure to a class, while the actual data mining models that share the same structure can be described as concrete instances (objects) of the class. The relationship between mining structures and models is shown in Figure 7.7.

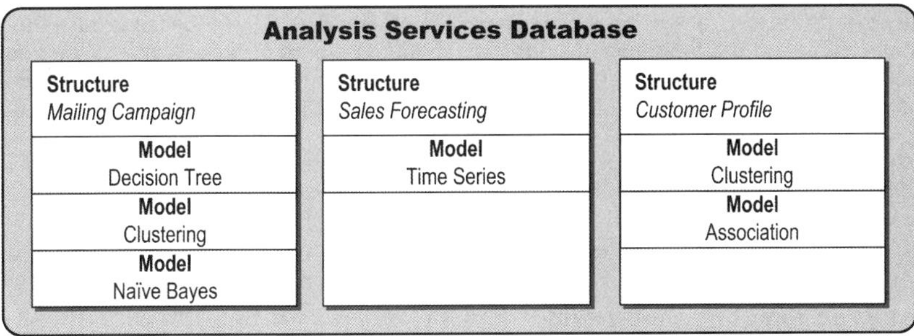

Figure 7.7 Data mining structures are containers of data mining models.

An Analysis Services Database may have many data mining structures. Each structure may contain one or more data mining models.

Why have data mining structures?

Why do we need separate data mining structures instead of uniting them into a coarser model, e.g. a cube? As I've mentioned, the main reason for this is to reduce complexity. Data mining models may be rather involved and may require experimenting with several algorithms. A structure encapsulates the logical mining domain at hand and the associated prediction algorithms. For example, a mailing campaign structure may have three data mining models associated with it that use three different algorithms, e.g. a Decision Tree, Clustering, and Naïve Bayes algorithms. Second, once the structure is processed, it is loaded with data and this data can be shared by all models within this structure. In other words, all mining algorithms contained in a structure can be trained with the same dataset.

Note With the introduction of structures in SSAS 2005, one potential source of confusion could be the naming convention that Microsoft has chosen for data mining objects. A mining model definition (a file with extension *.dmm) in fact represents a mining structure, while the mining models inside the structure actually represent one or more mathematical algorithms which perform the task. To make things even more confusing, the term *data mining model* is used to describe both a mining domain (e.g. sales forecasting), and a specific algorithm (model) inside the structure.

Finally, there are certain performance advantages of using structures as a method of data model isolation. For example, you can make changes to a data model inside a structure and even add new models, without having to re-process the structure.

The "structure" of a data mining structure

Just as a dimension definition in UDM describes the dimension attributes and their bindings, a data mining structure definition contains columns and column bindings. In this respect, a column in a mining structure can be related to a dimension attribute. As such, a structure column has a Type which denotes the column data type of the underlying table. The column type could be one of the five data types supported by the OLE DB/DM specification (Text, Long, Boolean, Double, and Date).

Column bindings

Again, similar to a dimension attribute, a structure column has KeyColumns and NameColumn properties that specify how the structure column is bound to the underlying data source column. Similar to a dimension key attribute, the KeyColumns property is used to identify the mining cases.

Warning Usually, the structure key coincides with the primary key of the relational case table (relational data source) or the dimension key of the case dimension (OLAP source). That's because all other columns (attributes) are related to the table (dimension) key. Therefore, you can choose any column as an input column. However, there is nothing stopping you from choosing another column as a structure key. For example, if you source data from the Customer dimension (SOS OLAP cube), you may choose to set the structure key to the Country attribute. In this case you will have as many input cases as the number of unique country members. When you do so, however, you may automatically disqualify other attributes, e.g. customer's age, gender, because they are not related to the key.

The NameColumn property could be used to supply alternative names of the attribute members if they need to be different than the key column values. Finally, when a SSAS 2005 cube is used as a data source, the Source property specifies which dimension attribute the structure column is bound to.

Column content

To predict data properly, a data mining algorithm needs to know in advance the content type of the column. The model designer uses the Content column property to specify the column content type. SSAS data mining supports several column content types which are explained thoroughly in the OLE DB for Data Mining specification. The most common ones are *Discrete* and *Continuous*. An example of a discrete content type is a customer gender column because it would contain only a few distinct values, e.g. *male* and *female*. An example of a continuous column is a customer income column because it may contain arbitrary values.

Some algorithms may not support all content types. For example, the Naïve Bayes algorithm supports only discrete columns as an input. If you need to use a continuous column, you can use the Data Mining Designer to discretize it into buckets by setting its *Content* property to *Discretized* and specifying the discretization bucket count and method. This is very similar to the process of discretizing attribute members of a UDM dimension, as we discussed back in chapter 4.

Processing mining structures and models

Just as a cube needs to be processed before it is first used, or when the cube structure changes, mining objects (structures and models) need to be processed occasionally.

Processing structures

Some common reasons for processing a mining structure include changes to the structure definition (e.g. a column is added or deleted), re-processing the source OLAP dimension is re-processed (OLAP data mining only), and loading the structure with new data. During the structure processing, the server retrieves the distinct values of each structure column (similar to dimension processing). To optimize the performance of the mining models contained in the structure, the structure data is compressed and stored on the server using the same storage primitives as UDM dimensions and measures.

Tip You don't need to process a structure if you've only made changes to its mining model(s). For example, the structure need not be processed if you add a new data model.

An interesting processing detail is that, behind the scenes, the server creates private cubes and dimensions to store the structure data. Specifically, the server generates a private dimension for each discrete structure column and a private measure for each continuous structure column. Each nested structure table is mapped to a measure group.

Processing mining models

As the data evolves (e.g. records are added, changed, or deleted), the mining model needs to be re-trained to keep its prediction capability on a par with the changes in the historical data. The terms *processing* and *training* are used interchangeably to refer to the process of loading data into a mining model to train the model. A model can be processed as part of processing the containing structure. For example, when you press the *Process the mining structure and its related models* toolbar button of the Data Mining Designer, the server initiates the processing task in two passes. During the first pass, the server processes the structure to load it with data. Next, the server processes the model(s) contained within the structure.

A model can also be processed (trained) independently of its containing structure (recall that a model doesn't store the trained dataset but just the predicted patterns). For example, after processing a structure, you may decide to train only one of the structure models with the new data while the rest should stay unaffected. To do so, you can use an SSIS package to process mining models selectively or you can train the model programmatically. Refer to the product documentation of the DMX INSERT INTO statement for more information about how structure and model processing affect each other.

Processing options

SSAS provides a number of processing options to process a structure and its mining models, including ProcessFull, ProcessStructure, and ProcessDefault. ProcessFull processes both the structure and its models in one pass. ProcessStructure processes only the structure. Specifically, ProcessStructure generates the structure metadata, loads the structure with data, and caches it on the server. Once the structure data is cached, you can process the containing mining models by choosing the ProcessDefault option.

7.2.3 The Data Mining Design Process

As with other IT projects, you may benefit from a guided methodology when implementing data mining models. One such methodology may encompass the steps shown in Figure 7.8. It is loosely based on the CRoss Industry Standard Process for Data Mining (CRISP-DM) process model developed in Germany (see Resources). The tools you can use to perform the step are shown below the task name.

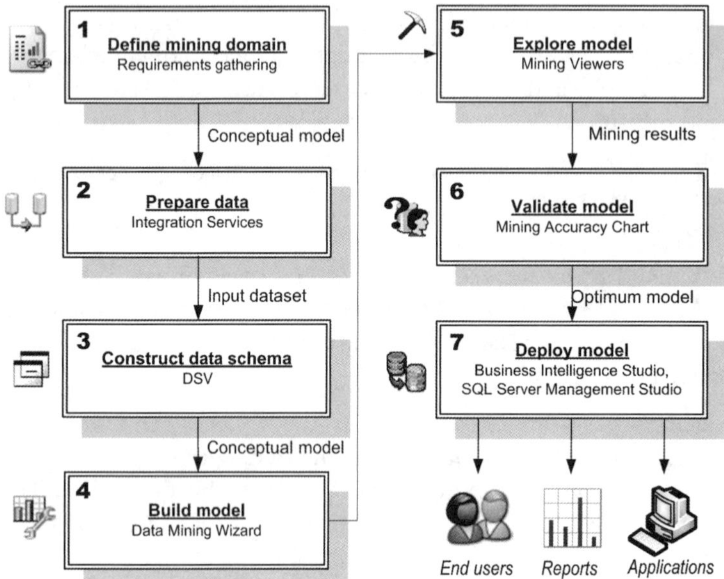

Figure 7.8 A typical data mining process consists of seven steps.

Although the flow depicted in Figure 7.8 is linear, in real life, you may find that you need several iterations to finalize the data model. Data mining models can be complex and there are really no magic rules to create an optimum mining model. For example, after validating the model, you may be surprised to find out that certain input columns have a stronger impact on the predicted results than the obvious candidates, e.g. the customer income is a stronger factor in buying a bicycle than the commute distance.

To refine the model, you may need to go back to step 2, e.g. to add more demographics-related columns, e.g. a column that indicates if the customer is a homeowner. This shouldn't discourage you (unless you need to collect a fine when going back, perhaps). Remember, data mining is more of an art than a science. Let's explain briefly the purpose of each step in the design process.

Step 1: Define mining domain

Start your data mining project from the drawing board by gathering the business requirements. What business problem are you trying to solve? Sales forecasting? Customer profiling? Basket analysis? End of the world, as we know it? As with every project, it is essential to start with a clear objective. This objective may be formulated as "Perform a data mining analysis to profile customers and identify those who are most likely to respond to a product X mailing campaign based on customer demographics". Once you've defined the mining domain, you need to conduct data availability study to identify the dataset that will support the model. This may translate into questions, such as:

- *What input columns do I need?* – For the mailing campaign scenario, these could be customer gender, income, age, etc?

- *Where is the data that will represent the input dataset stored?* – You need to identify which data source captures the data you need.
- *How can data be extracted?* – As noted, SSAS data mining can source data from a relational data source or a UDM cube. To prepare the input dataset, you may need to extract data from its original data source, which may require an ETL project of its own (now you know where data *mining* derives its name from).

Step 2: Prepare data

As noted, the source data may not be directly available and may require ETL processes to load the data into the desired input format. For example, if the data is kept in a mainframe database, data may need to be extracted to flat files, transformed, and loaded into a relational database, as we've demonstrated in the preceding chapter. Consider SQL Server Integration Services for the data preparation step.

The result of this project step is a relational data schema (in the form of a table or a view) or a UDM cube that will feed all input columns and nested tables of the data mining structure. You should have a clear understanding about the semantics of each input column and its business purpose. People new to data mining may have unreasonable (clairvoyant) expectations by believing that data mining can do everything by just running the Mining Wizard against a database. In reality, however, you will find that the more you know your data, the more effective your prediction results will be.

For example, instead of seeking correlations between all columns of the customer table and the probability that a customer will purchase a given product, it may make sense to identify a subset of the most likely candidates that may impact the customer decision, e.g. commute distance, home owner, education, etc. A less focused approach may require more time to process the data mining models and interpret the results.

Step 3: Construct data schema

As you know by now, a data source view isolates UDM from the underlying relational data schema. If you source your input dataset from a relational database, you need to construct a data source view. This means that you can take the relational schema as it is and adjust it to meet your structure requirements. For example, if security policies rule out direct changes to the data source schema, you can define named queries and calculations at a DSV level. Or, you can create logical relationships among tables in the absence of referential joins.

The end result of this step is the definition of the data mining structure that will serve as foundation of the data mining model(s).

Step 4: Build model

Once the structure is in place, you proceed to create the actual data mining models. Start by consulting with Table 7.2 to identify one or more algorithms that can be used to perform the data mining task at hand. Next, use the BI Studio Data Mining Designer to implement the model(s). For example, the data mining task that you will be performing in the mailing campaign scenario shortly is classification. This task can be performed by the Decision Trees, Clustering, Sequence Clustering, Naïve Bayes, and Neural Network algorithms.

If multiple algorithms can be used to implement the data mining task, a good approach is to start with a quick and simple algorithm, e.g. Naïve Bayes. However, as a best practice, I recommend you build additional mining models that use different algorithms to select the optimum algorithm for the task at hand. The Data Mining Designer makes it very easy to create corresponding data mining models since they share the same structure.

Step 5: Explore model

Once the model is built and trained, you are ready to explore it and analyze its predictive results. The Microsoft-provided algorithms come with excellent graphical viewers. All viewers have multiple tabs to see data from different angles.

Step 6: Validate model

In addition, you need to validate the accuracy of the data mining model(s) you've built. This is especially important if you have a structure with several models that can perform the same data mining task. One practical approach to validate a data mining model is to prepare a smaller input dataset that you can easily train and evaluate. Once the test dataset is ready, you can use the Mining Accuracy Chart tab of the Data Mining Designer to compare the model accuracy. You can create a *lift chart* or *a classification matrix* to do so.

Step 7: Deploy model

Your data mining model is ready. As a final step, you need to deploy and configure the model to the production server. As part of the configuration process, don't forget to secure the model by specifying which users and Windows groups will have access to it. You may need to process the model occasionally if the data changes. Finally, once the model is deployed, you can use a variety of technologies to query the model and deliver the prediction results to the end users, including standard reports, or custom applications. To learn more about the data mining process, read the excellent book *Preparing and Mining Data with Microsoft SQL Server 2000 and Analysis Services* (see Resources section).

Now that we've covered the essentials, let's put data mining in action. We will demonstrate the seven-point framework we've just introduced by building a targeted campaigning mining model to identify the most likely buyers of Adventure Works bicycle products.

7.3 Targeted Campaigning Example

Suppose that Adventure Works has introduced a new bicycle product. The Adventure Works marketing department is planning a campaign to promote the new bicycle. As you can imagine, promotion campaigns are not cheap. In the case of a mailing campaign, promotion materials need to be designed, printed, and mailed to customers. Radio or TV campaigns are even more expensive. It certainly makes sense to focus the marketing effort on those groups of customers who are most likely to purchase the product. In addition, a mining model could help us identify the promotion channel where these customers are likely to be found. For example, if the data mining results indicate that predominantly teenagers purchase a given product, the management could decide to run an advertisement on MTV.

7.3.1 Defining the Mining Domain

Instead of campaigning to its entire customer base (more that 14,000 customers), the Adventure Works management has asked you to identify a subset of customers who are most likely to purchase the new bicycle. The data mining domain you need to solve is a classic example of the classification mining task. Consulting with Table 7.2, you realize that there are several algorithms that you can use to perform it. As part of the process of building the data mining model, we will try a couple of them to identify the most accurate algorithm.

7.3.2 Preparing the Data

Unlike dimensional modeling, the business metrics that need to be passed as in input to a mining model typically originate from dimension-type tables (not fact tables). Since the focus of our campaigning task is customer-oriented, we need to load the data mining model with data from a customer profile table. The DimCustomer dimension table is the natural choice since it captures the profile details of the customers who purchase Adventure Products online.

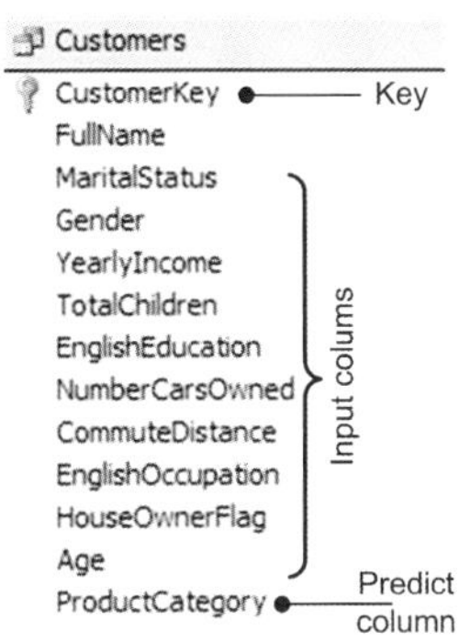

Figure 7.9 When determining the schema of the input dataset, identify which attributes could be used as input columns to influence the data mining prediction.

How do we determine the input dataset schema? Unfortunately, there are no fixed rules and you may find that knowing your data beforehand could be helpful. For example, we know that the Adventure Works OLTP sales application captures the customer demographics data. Therefore, it could certainly be useful to seek a correlation between these attributes and the customer decision to purchase a new bike. One practical approach to examine data and evaluate the usefulness of a given column is to use the data exploration feature of the DSV Designer. You can use the Pivot Table, Chart, and Pivot Char tabs to find the distribution of the column values, the content type (discrete or continuous), and possible correlation link among columns. After a few iterations, our input dataset schema may look like the one shown in Figure 7.9.

For the targeted campaign scenario, all input columns are derived from the DimCustomer table (no nested tables are needed). The most important column is the ProductCategory column which will be used both as an input and predict column. That's because we want to use the historical sales statistics to predict future behavior (the likelihood of a group of customers to purchase products from a given category). Breaking down the data mining results per product category makes our model more universal. Our data mining model will find data correlation patterns in the customer profile data based on the product category selected. When Adventure Works introduces a new bicycle, the marketing department can use the same model to find potential customers for this product by simply filtering the results.

7.3.3 Constructing the Data Schema

The only trick when constructing the input dataset is querying the customer order history to get the product category of the purchased bicycle. To accomplish this, we need to look up data in table FactInternetSales in an attempt to find an order for a bicycle product (*ProductSubcategoryKey = 1*). However, a customer may have purchased more than one bicycle. Obviously, in this case, we cannot assign a single product category to the customer since there isn't a one-to-one relationship between the customer and the product category. For the sake of simplicity, we will ignore the customers who have purchased more than one bicycle.

Since we will be using a relational data source, we need to build a data source view (Bike Buyers.dsv) on which the mining structure will be built. If you can get the database administrator to grant you permissions to create new objects, by all means, consider using a SQL view for the query statement needed to join the required tables. As noted in chapter 2, SQL views have certain performance and functional advantages over data source views. Chances are, though, that the larger the enterprise and the more people involved, the less likely it is to finish your project on time. Let's take the data source schema as it is and build a DSV named query called Customers on top of it, which is based on the following SQL statement (abbreviated):

```
SELECT  C.CustomerKey, C.MaritalStatus, … ,
     DATEDIFF(yy, C.BirthDate, GETDATE()) AS Age,
     CustomerFilter.Subcategory AS ProductCategory
FROM DimCustomer AS C INNER JOIN
        (SELECT C.CustomerKey, PS.EnglishProductSubcategoryName AS Subcategory
        FROM DimCustomer AS C
     INNER JOIN FactInternetSales AS S …
     INNER JOIN DimProduct AS P ON S.ProductKey = P.ProductKey
     INNER JOIN DimProductSubcategory AS PS
     WHERE (PS.ProductCategoryKey = 1)
GROUP BY C.CustomerKey, PS.EnglishProductSubcategoryName
HAVING(COUNT(PS.ProductSubcategoryKey)=1)) AS CustomerFilter
ON C.CustomerKey = CustomerFilter.CustomerKey
```

The subquery statement is used to filter out the customers that have purchased multiple bicycles. The first dozen rows of the dataset derived from executing this query are shown in Figure 7.10. The ProductCategory column contains the product category of the item bought by the customer. In addition, I set the CustomerKey column as a logical primary key because it uniquely identifies each customer (a mining case represents a customer).

CustomerKey	FullName	MaritalStatus	Gender	YearlyIncome	TotalChildren	EnglishEducat	NumberCarsO	CommuteDist	EnglishOccup	HouseOwne	Age	ProductCategory
11000	Jon V. Yang	M	M	90000	2	Bachelors	0	1-2 Miles	Professional	1	39	Touring Bikes
11001	Eugene L. Hu	S	M	60000	3	Bachelors	1	0-1 Miles	Professional	0	40	Road Bikes
11002	Ruben Torres	M	M	60000	3	Bachelors	1	2-5 Miles	Professional	1	40	Touring Bikes
11003	Christy Zhu	S	F	70000	0	Bachelors	1	5-10 Miles	Professional	0	37	Touring Bikes
11004	Elizabeth Joh	S	F	80000	5	Bachelors	4	1-2 Miles	Professional	1	37	Touring Bikes
11005	Julio Ruiz	S	M	70000	0	Bachelors	1	5-10 Miles	Professional	1	40	Touring Bikes
11006	Janet G. Alvar	S	F	70000	0	Bachelors	1	5-10 Miles	Professional	1	40	Touring Bikes
11007	Marco Mehta	M	M	60000	3	Bachelors	2	0-1 Miles	Professional	1	41	Touring Bikes
11008	Rob Verhoff	S	F	60000	4	Bachelors	3	10+ Miles	Professional	1	41	Touring Bikes
11009	Shannon C. C	S	M	70000	0	Bachelors	1	5-10 Miles	Professional	0	41	Touring Bikes
11010	Jacquelyn C.	S	F	70000	0	Bachelors	1	5-10 Miles	Professional	0	41	Touring Bikes
11011	Curtis Lu	M	M	60000	4	Bachelors	4	10+ Miles	Professional	1	42	Touring Bikes
11015	Chloe Young	S	F	30000	0	Partial Colleg	1	5-10 Miles	Skilled Manua	0	26	Mountain Bikes

Figure 7.10 Consider using a named query to construct the input dataset

7.3.4 Building the Model

The next step involves constructing the data mining structure and a data mining model(s). The easiest way to perform this task is to use the handy Data Mining Wizard by following these steps.

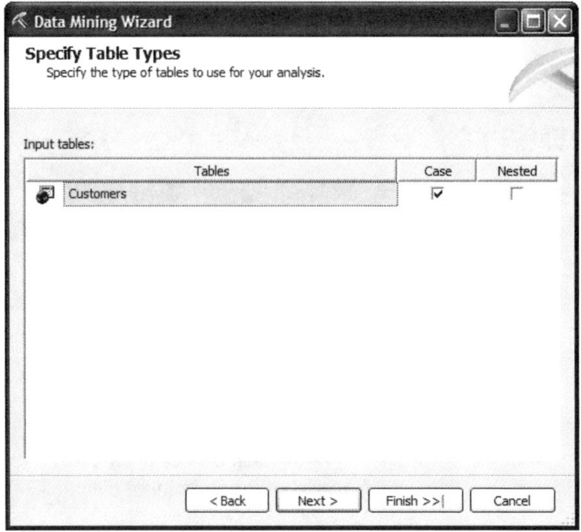

Figure 7.11 A data mining model can have only one case table.

Constructing the mining structure

1. Open the Ch07 solution file. Right-click on the Mining Structures folder and choose *New Mining Structure*. BI Studio launches the Data Mining Wizard. Click Next.
2. In the Select the Definition Method step, select the *From existing relational database or data warehouse* option since our structure will be loaded from the AdventureWorksDW relational database. Click Next.
3. In the *Select the Data Mining Technique* step, you need to pick an algorithm to perform the data mining task at hand. Glancing at Table 7.2, we determine that the Microsoft Decision Tree algorithm is especially suited for classification tasks, such as targeted campaigns. Accept the default *Microsoft Decision Tree* algorithm and click Next.

> **Note** By default, the *Algorithm name* dropdown lists only the algorithms provided by Microsoft. If you have developed and configured a custom algorithm, it will appear in the dropdown as well.

4. In the Select the Data Source View step, select the Bike Buyers data source view we discussed in the *Construct data schema* step. Click Next to advance to the Specify Table Type step (Figure 7.11).
5. In our scenario, the entire input dataset is contained in a single DSV table. The Data Mining Wizard has pre-selected the *Customer* table as a case table. Click Next.
6. In the *Specify the Training Data* step (Figure 7.12), you need to identify the input and predict columns. In our case, we need to predict the classes of customers that will buy a bike. Therefore, we only need one predict column. Select the *ProductCategory* column as both an Input and Predict column (*Predict* Usage type).
7. You can check the input columns manually (hold Shift for continuous selection), or you can ask the wizard to suggest indicative input columns by sampling the source data. Try the latter technique by clicking on the Suggest button. The Suggest Related Columns dialog appears and

starts sampling the case table in an attempt to find useful correlations between the predict column and the rest of the columns.

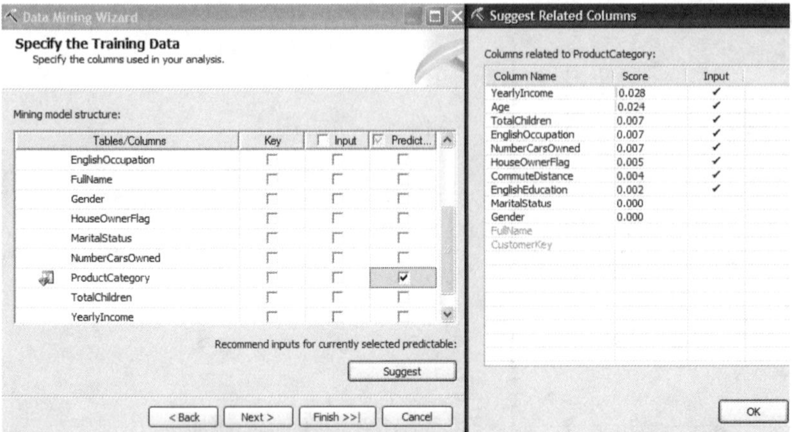

Figure 7.12 The Suggest Related Columns dialog samples case data and suggests input columns.

8. In the Suggest Related Columns dialog, select all columns with a score greater than zero and click OK to return to the Specify the Training Data step. Click Next to advance to the Specify Columns' Content and Data Type step (Figure 7.13).

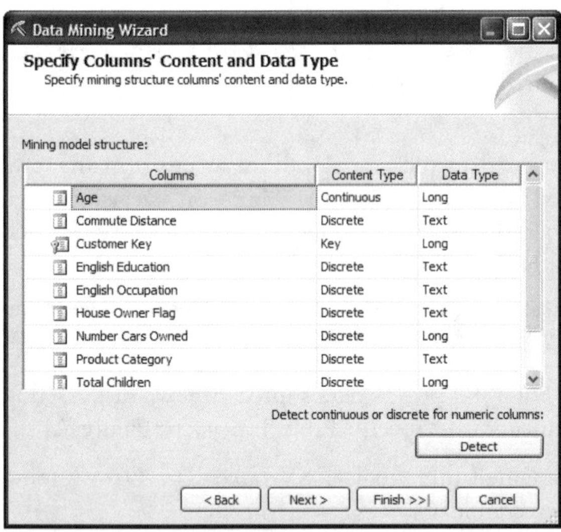

Figure 7.13 Click the Detect button to let the Data Mining Wizard probe the database schema and detect the columns' content type and data type.

9. As noted, the data mining model needs to know the content type and data type of the columns. You can specify the content type manually or ask the wizard to detect it for you by probing the database schema. We will gladly take advantage of the second approach. Click on the Detect button to let the wizard discover the column's content type and data type. Click Next.

10. In the Completing the Wizard step (Figure 7.14), name the data mining model **Targeted Campaign**. Name the Mining model **TargetedCampaignDT** to denote the fact that the model uses the Microsoft Decision Trees algorithm (recall that one structure may include several data mining models). Check the **Allow drill through** checkbox. We will find out what it does in a

moment. Click Finish to let the Data Mining Wizard create the model and open it in the Data Mining Designer.

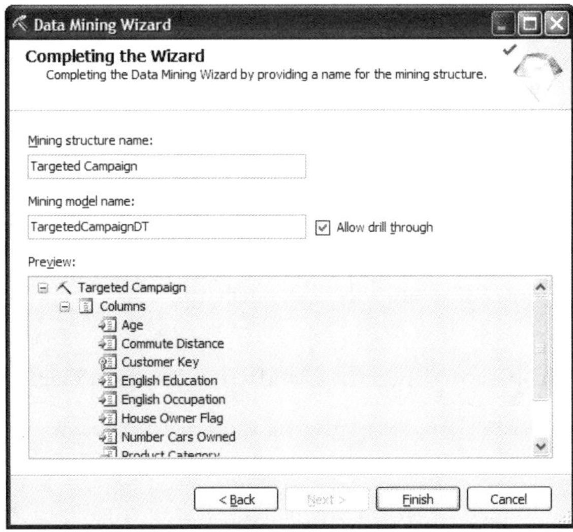

Figure 7.14 Enable drillthrough to let the end user see the source data for the model.

Introducing the Data Mining Designer

Undoubtedly, you will find the Data Mining Designer (Figure 7.15) very similar to the Dimension Designer. It has a tabbed user interface consisting of five tabs. As you would use the Dimension Structure tab to make changes to dimension attributes, use the Mining Structure tab to make changes to the mining structure. Examples of typical structure tasks you can perform are adding columns or nested tables, renaming columns, deleting columns, etc. Remember that any changes of the mining structure will require re-processing the structure.

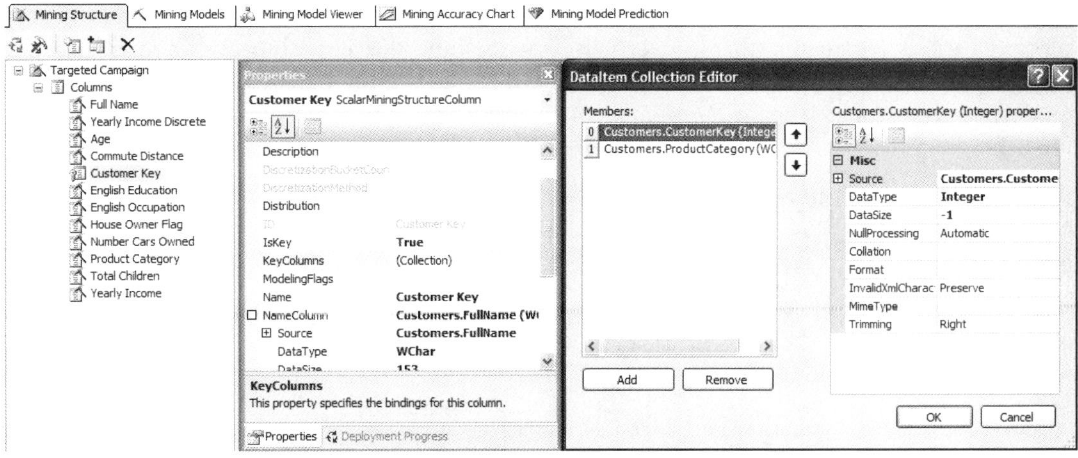

Figure 7.15 Use the Properties window to set the column properties and bindings.

One outstanding task we need to address is changing the structure key to qualify the input cases correctly. As it stands, the structure key uses the CustomerKey column only. As a result, if the case dataset has duplicated values in the CustomerKey column, these values will be ignored. This will be the case when a customer has purchased more than one bike. Indeed, if you run the Customers named query that feeds the structure, you will find that it brings 10,066 rows.

However, if you process the structure and examine the results in the Mining Model Viewer, you will find that the total number of cases contained in the structure is 7,273 only. As you know by now, the server ignores the duplicated keys when it processes the structure. We could keep this behavior and ignore the repeating customers but this will likely skew our results. Instead, let's use a key collection for the structure key. The net result of doing this is that a repeating customer will be treated as a new case and we will have 10,066 input cases.

1. In the Data Mining Designer, switch to the Mining Structure tab and select the CustomerKey column.
2. Click on the **...** button inside the KeyColumns property to open the DataItem Collection Editor.
3. Add the *ProductCategory* column to create a composite key consisting of the CustomerKey and ProductCategory columns (see again Figure 7.15).
4. Suppose you would like to see the customer name instead of the key when drilling through the customer data. Select the Customer Key column and create a new binding to bind the Name-Column property to the *FullName* column.

Adding a new mining model

The Mining Models tab (Figure 7.16) displays the mining models that are contained within the structure. Since we've just created the structure, it contains only the TargetCampaignDT model that uses the Microsoft Decision Trees algorithm. You can change the way a given column is used by the model. For example, if you decide not to use the Product Category column as an input to the Decision Trees algorithm, we can change its Usage from *Predict* to *PredictOnly*. You can also choose to ignore a column. For example, the customer's name is certainly not useful for mining purposes and we should ignore it to make our model more efficient. An algorithm may support various parameters that you can use to fine-tune the algorithm calculations. In most cases, the default settings are just fine. If you need to change the parameters, right-click on the model and choose *Set Algorithm Parameters*.

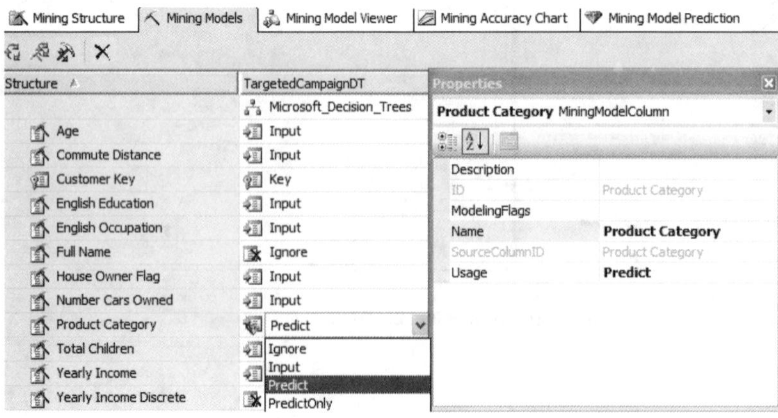

Figure 7.16 The columns of a structure may have different usage types in the containing model(s).

You may need to add additional models if you wish to compare the accuracy of different algorithms in order to choose the best fit for the task at hand. You may find the structure-model approach similar to the Controller-Viewer design pattern. You use the Mining Structure tab to define the schema definition and handle data storage and processing tasks (Controller) and then create multiple models (Viewer) on top of it to predict and show data in various ways. For example, a classification data mining task can be performed by the Microsoft Naïve Bayes algorithm as well. Follow these steps to add a new model to the Target Campaign mining structure that uses the Naïve Bayes algorithm.

1. Right-click anywhere inside the grid and choose *New Mining Model.* Alternatively, click the *Create a related mining model* toolbar button.
2. In the New Mining Model dialog, name the new model **TargetedCampaignNB** and select the *Microsoft Naïve Bayes* algorithm in the *Algorithm name* dropdown. Click OK to close the dialog.
3. The Data Mining Designer complains that the Naïve Bayes algorithm doesn't support the content type of the Age, Number Cars Owned, Total Children, and Yearly Income columns. That's because the content type of these column is continuous, while the Naïve Bayes algorithm supports only discrete columns. Accept the confirmation dialog to ignore these columns. The TargetedCampaignNB model is added as a new column in the grid. The usage type of the above four columns is set to *Ignore* and won't be used by the Naïve Bayes algorithm.

Creating a discrete column

But what if you need to use these columns? For example, there is probably a strong correlation between customer income and the type of bicycle a customer would buy. It is possible to use a continuous column with algorithms that don't support this content type provided that you discretize the column. To leave the Decision Tree model unaffected, we will add a new structure column (Yearly Income Discrete) to the Targeted Campaign mining structure and use it as an input to the TargetedCampaignNB model.

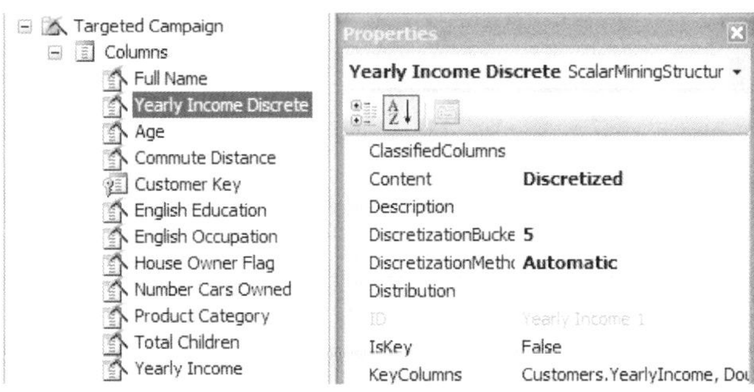

Figure 7.17 You can discretize structure columns with algorithms that don't support the continuous content type.

1. Switch to the Mining Structure tab. Right-click inside the Targeted Campaign column tree and choose *Add a Column.*
2. In the Select a Column dialog, choose the *YearlyIncome* column and click OK. A new column called *Yearly Income 1* is added to the structure.
3. Rename the new column **Yearly Income Discrete**. Click *Yes* in the confirmation dialog that follows to propagate the new name to the data mining models that use the column.

4. In the Properties window, change the column content to *Discretized*, the DiscretizationBucketCount property to 5 and leave the DiscretizationMethod to *Automatic* (see Figure 7.17). As a result of these changes, the server will group the customers into five income buckets.

5. Flip to the Mining Models tab and change the Usage type of the Yearly Income Discrete column to *Input*.

6. Deploy the project to process the mining structure and the two models. Alternatively, click on the Process button (the leftmost toolbar button) to process the structure. Processing the structure will load it with data from the Customer table and train the models.

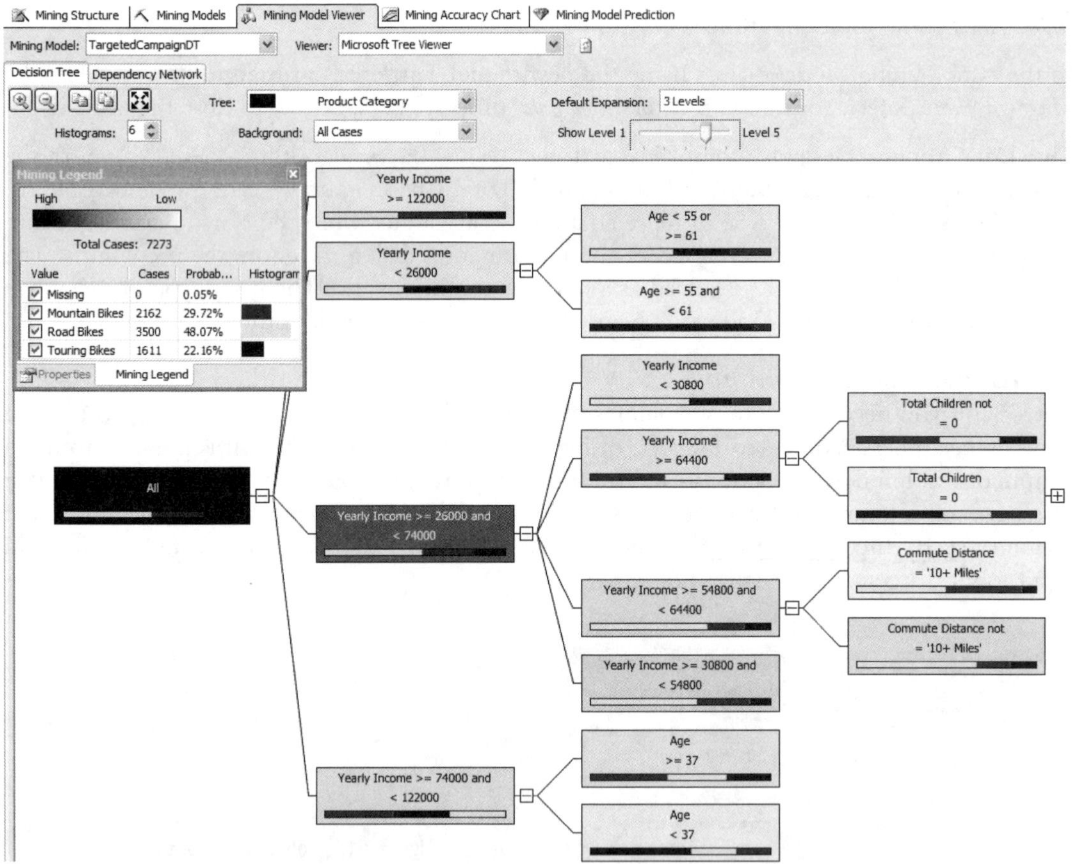

Figure 7.18 Use the Decision Tree Viewer to find the distribution of the customer population.

7.3.5 Exploring the Model

This is where the fun begins! We are ready to explore the predicted patterns found by our data mining model. Each Microsoft algorithm comes with its own viewer that is specifically designed to display the algorithm results optimally. We will start by examining the Decision Trees Viewer followed by the Naïve Bayes Viewer.

Interpreting the Decision Trees results

Switch to the Mining Model Viewer tab. The TargetedCampaignDT mining model should be selected by default in the Mining Model dropdown. The Decision Trees Viewer is displayed (Figure 7.18). Each predicted column generates a separate decision tree. Since, in our case, we have only one predicted column, there is only one entry in the Tree dropdown (Product Category). By default, the viewer displays the distribution of the customer population for all product categories (the Background dropdown is set to *All cases*).

Tip You can copy the graph as a picture by right-clicking on the graph and choosing the *Copy Graph View* or *Copy Entire Graph* context menus. If the viewer uses histogram charts, they will be copied as HTML.

Understanding the Decision Tree Graph

Let's see what educated conclusions we can make by inspecting the decision tree graph. As noted, the Microsoft Decision Trees algorithm is typically used for classification tasks. Each node of the tree corresponds to a customer class. When the background filter is set to *All Cases*, you can use the Decision Trees Viewer to find which factors may influence the customer decision to purchase a bike. For example, the model has determined that the most significant factor is customer income. That's why, the first split (after the root All node) is done on the customer age attribute.

The background color of each tree node is the most important visual indicator. The darker the color is, the larger the customer population. The root node of the tree is always the darkest. Hovering on top of the root node, or examining the mining legend, reveals that we have 10,066 cases (customers). From them, 32% have purchased mountain bikes, 47% road bikes, and 21% touring bikes. The same information can be derived approximately by glancing at the color bar inside each node. The bar has three colors because we have three distinct values in the predicted column; red for Mountain Bikes, yellow for Road Bikes, and blue for Touring Bikes).

Tracing the tree graph, we discover that the second darkest node represents 6,557customers with yearly income between $26,000 and $74,000. Therefore, this group of customers is most likely to purchase a bike. By clicking on this node and looking at the legend, we discover that more than half of these customers (56%) have purchased road bikes. Further, the Decision Trees algorithm has made another split on the customer income because it has discovered that, out of 6,557 customers, more than 5,000 customers are actually within the $26,000-$64,400 bracket.

Finally, the second most important factor after customer income is the number of cars a customer owns. The algorithm has concluded that customers with less than four cars are most likely to purchase a bicycle. Therefore, if the objective of our mining study is to identify potential bicycle buyers, this could be a good group to target.

What if the marketing department is interested in narrowing down the customers to those that are most likely to purchase a mountain bike? No problem. Change the Background dropdown to Mountain Bikes and voila! Interestingly, now we have two potential groups of customers we can target. First, we have customers with income greater than $74,000 and older than 37 years. Actually, this makes sense considering that mountain bikes tend to be more expensive. Second, we have a much smaller cluster of people with income between $64,400 and $74,000 who are 61 years old or older.

Drilling through

How can we see the individual customers that belong to a given group, so the marketing department can contact them to rekindle their interest in AW products (or spam them)? This is where the drillthrough feature comes in. As you would recall, we enabled this feature in the last step of the Data Mining Wizard. Alternatively, since drilling through is a model-level feature, you can use the *AllowDrillThrough* property of a data mining model to enable or disable drilling through the model.

Note Similar to dimension or measure group drillthrough, model drillthrough is not enabled by default for security reasons because it allows end users to browse the source data for the model. The model designer has to make a conscious decision to enable this feature.

Once AllowDrillThrough is enabled, you can simply right-click on a tree node and choose the Drill Trough context menu to browse the source data forming the corresponding group. This action will pop up the Drill Through window with the cases displayed in a grid format. The classification criterion is shown on top. You can copy all records and paste them in a text file or an Excel spreadsheet.

Understanding the Dependency Network

In real life, your decision tree may have many splits and it may be difficult to find the most significant factors by using only the Decision Tree tab. The Dependency Network tab (Figure 7.19) is designed to help you find these attributes quickly. A Decision Trees model may have more than one predicted attributes. To filter the links that are correlated to a given predicted attribute, simply select that attribute in the diagram. In our case, we have four attributes (Yearly Income, Age, Commute Distance, and Number Cars Owned) that may influence a customer's decision to purchase a bike.

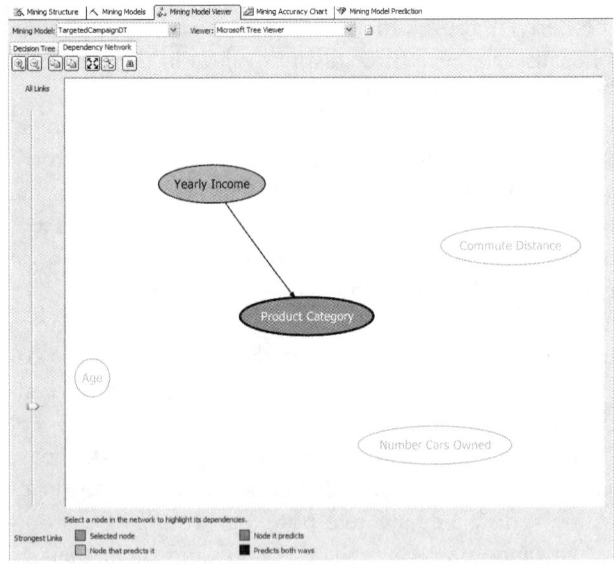

Figure 7.19 Use the Dependency Network graph to find quickly the links that have the strongest correlation factor.

To find the strongest links, slide down the slider on the left of the diagram. The slider scale will have as many nodes as the number of the distinct values of the predicted column. By sliding it down, you are in essence filtering out the less significant links. In the Targeted Campaign scenario, the Decision Trees algorithm finds that the most significant factor influencing AW customers to purchase a bike is the customer's yearly income (we don't need a mining model to figure this out, do we?). Backing up one nudge, we determine that the second important factor is customer's age.

Interpreting the Naïve Bayes results

Now, let's explore the results of the Naïve Bayes model by selecting the TargetedCampaignNB model in the *Mining model* dropdown.

Note The Naïve Bayes algorithm doesn't assume relationships among the input attributes. It is a pair-wise algorithm, meaning that it simply calculates the correlation between an input and a predict attribute, e.g. Age vs. Product Category. This is why, the algorithm is called **Naïve** Bayes. If correlating input columns is significant (e.g. Age vs. Income), you need to use more sophisticated algorithms, such as Microsoft Decision Trees. In addition, the Naïve Bayes algorithm doesn't support the drillthrough feature. As an upside, the Naïve Bayes algorithm is less computationally intensive and processes very fast.

The first tab is the Dependency Network tab algorithm:dwhich is the same as with the Decision Trees model. You can use it to get a good overall picture of the relative importance of the input columns. Since we decided to ignore the Age column when building the model, we have only three columns (attributes) with the Yearly Income Discretized being the most significant again.

Understanding the Attribute Profiles tab:attribute profiles

The Attribute Profiles tab (Figure 7.20) gives you a breakdown of the population of data in the input columns (attributes). The histogram has as many columns as the number of the discrete values of the predicted column, plus a column for *All* and missing values. For example, by just looking at the columns, we can deduce that there are 10,066 input cases (customers) from which 4,726 have bought Road Bikes, 2,125 Touring Bikes, and 3,215 Mountain Bikes.

The histogram shows the input attributes in rows and their discrete values (states) in the States column. You can roughly estimate the breakdown of the state population by inspecting the histogram columns. To find out the exact numbers, hover on top of the histogram. To determine the strongest correlation factors, examine their population distribution by comparing the Population (All) column and the predicted valued of interest.

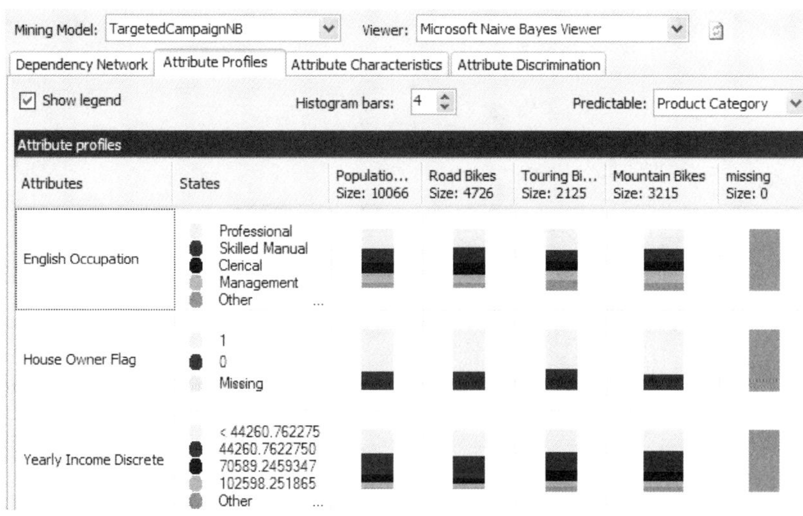

Figure 7.20 Use the Attribute Profiles chart to find the population distribution of the input attributes.

For example, if you inspect the Population column of the Yearly Income Discrete row, you can deduce that, overall, most customers have an income less than $44,000. By hovering on top of the histogram, or examining the mining legend (not shown), you can further find that this segment contributes to about 40% of the overall population. However, if you now inspect the Mountain Bikes histogram, you will find that the majority of the customers purchasing mountain bikes are within the $44,000 – $70,000 income bracket (the second stacked bar from the top) because its bar is wider. This means that this customer segment could be potentially targeted during a mountain bike promotion campaign.

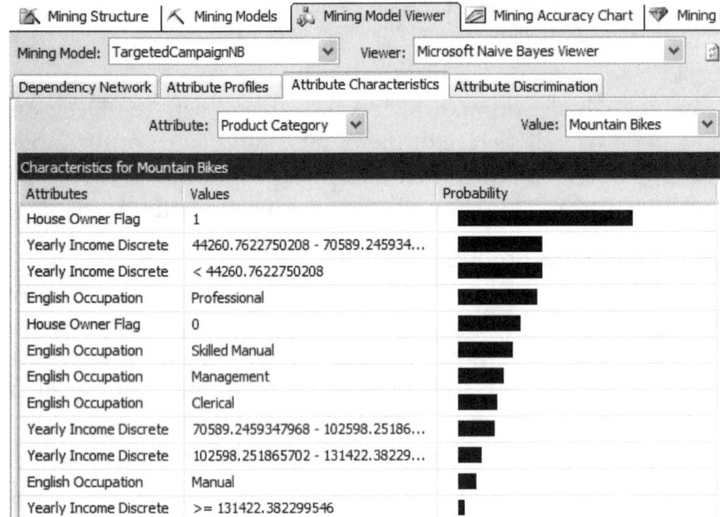

Figure 7.21 Use the Attribute Characteristics chart to determine the strongest correlation factors for a given class.

Understanding the Attribute Characteristics tabalgorithm:attribute characteristics

A more accurate picture of a particular customer class could be obtained by switching to the Attribute Characteristics tab (Figure 7.21). By examining the chart, we can deduce that most customers who purchase mountain bikes are home owners with an income between $44,000 and $70,000 and are professionals.

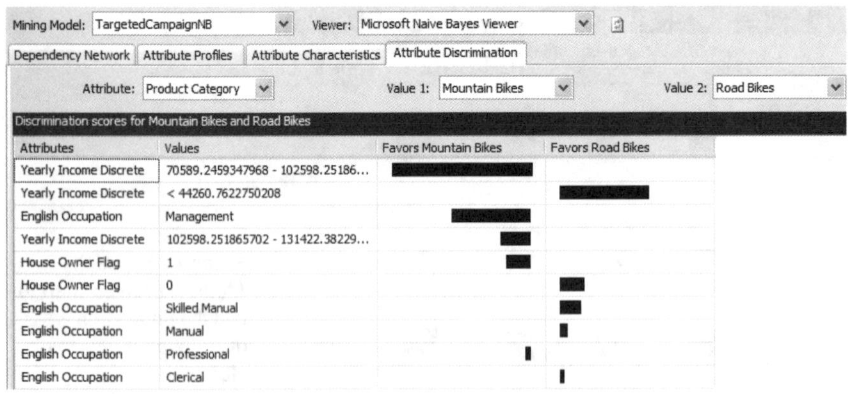

Figure 7.22 Use the Attribute Discrimination tab to compare profiles side by side.

Understanding the Attribute Discrimination tabalgorithm:d

Finally, you may be interested to compare two groups side by side. For example, you may need to find out how the Mountain Bikes customer profile compares against that of Road Bikes. You can do this by using the Attribute Discrimination tab (Figure 7.22). Now we can conclude that customers who purchase mountain bikes tend to have higher income than those buying road bikes. In addition, the mountain bike buyers tend to have managerial or professional jobs, while the second group of customers tends to have manual or skilled manual occupations.

7.3.6 Evaluating the Model

Now that we've implemented two mining models for the targeted campaign scenario, how do we know which one is better? More importantly, how do we know if our data mining model predicts efficiently? We can use the Mining Accuracy Chart tab to evaluate the accuracy of our model(s) by following these steps:

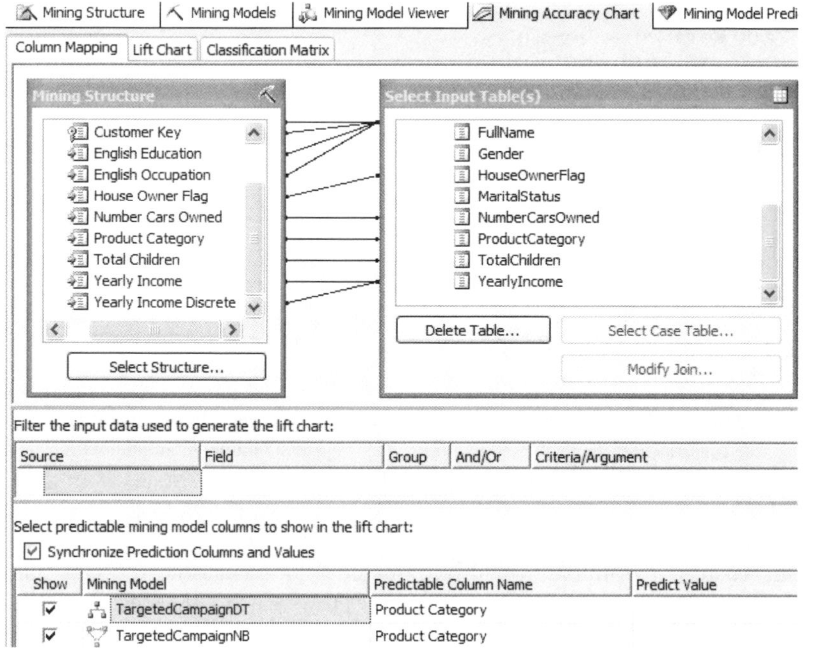

Figure 7.23 Use the Column Mapping tab to bind the columns of the mining structure to the columns of the test dataset.

Specifying column mappings

1. Click on the Mining Accuracy Chart tab. The Mining Accuracy Chart opens and its Column Mapping tab is selected (Figure 7.23). You can use the Column Mapping tab to specify an input table that holds the representative dataset that you want to test.

2. Click the Select Case Table button in the Select Input Table(s) pane and select the Customers table from the Bike Buyers DSV. For demo purposes, we will use the same input table that we used to train the model. In real life, it may make sense to prepare a smaller dataset that you can easily verify.

3. The Data Mining Designer tries to map automatically the columns of the mining structure and the input table by naming convention. If the columns have different names, you can link them manually by dragging a column from the Mining Structure pane and dropping it over the corresponding column in the Select Input Table(s) pane. Drag the Yearly Income Discrete

column which we created for the Naïve Bayes algorithm from the Mining Structure pane and drop it on the Yearly Income column in the Select Input Table(s) pane.

Optionally, you can filter the test dataset (e.g. Customers who are 25 years or older) by creating a filter criteria in the Filter grid. If you need to test the model accuracy for a particular value of the predicted column, you can specify this value in the Predict Value column of the *Select predictable columns…* grid. Leave the Predict Column empty for now to test the model accuracy irrespective of product category.

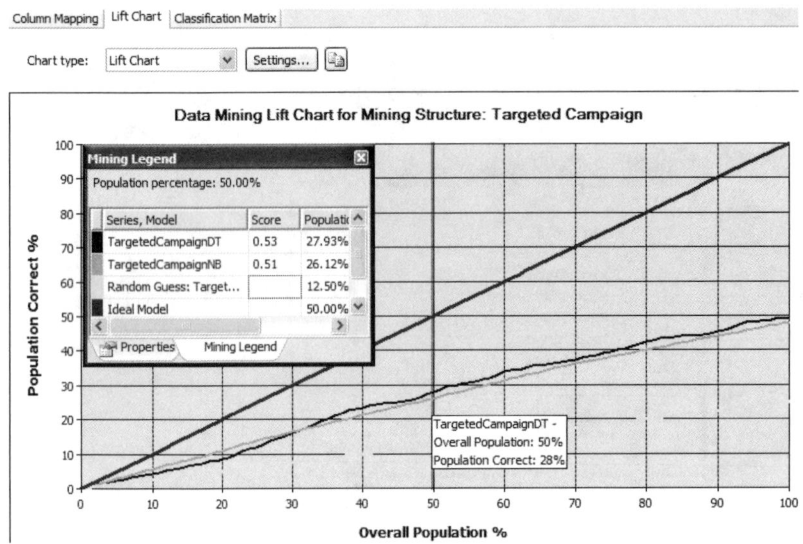

Figure 7.24 Create a lift chart to evaluate the model effectiveness.

Understanding lift charts

In our case, the customer dataset has about 10,000 customers. Suppose that, due to budget constraints, only 50% of the customer population will be targeted (5,000 customers). Naturally, not all customers will be interested in buying the new product. How can we identify the most likely buyers? Here is where a lift chart could help.

Flip the Lift Chart tab and notice that it has four lines, as shown in Figure 7.24 (the line closest to the X-axis is not easily discernable). In a perfect world, each targeted customer will respond to the campaign (100% penetration). This is what the topmost line represents. The bottom line shows the customer penetration rate if the customers are chosen at random. For example, if we are to pick 5,000 customers at random out of the entire 10,000 customer population, we will get only about 12% customer penetration.

However, if the marketing department is willing to try our model, they will get a much better response rate, as the middle two lines show. Any improvement over the random line is called a *lift*, and the more lift a model demonstrates, the more effective the model is. In our case, the darker line corresponds to the Decision Trees model, while the lighter one represents the Naïve Bayes model. As you can see, the Naïve Bayes model gives a better penetration results in a population of about 30% (3,000 customers). After that, the Decision Trees model outperforms the Naïve Bayes model.

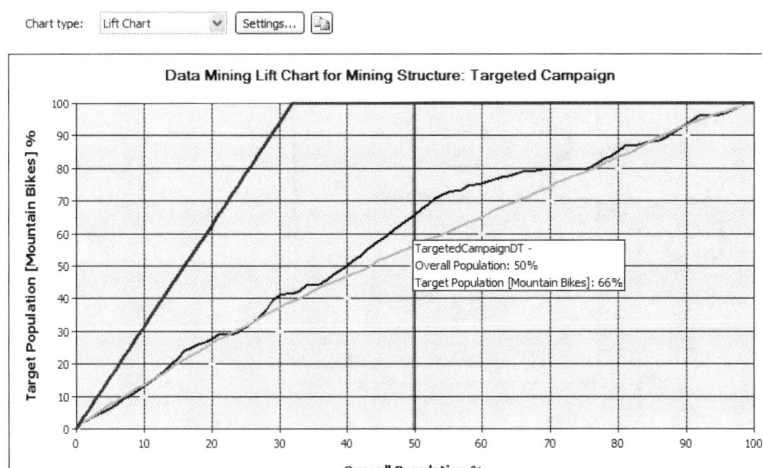

Figure 7.25 You can change the lift chart to evaluate a given predict value.

Now, hover on top of the TargetedCampaignDT line where it intersects with the 50% overall population vertical line. It turns out, that if we target 50% of the customers, the Decision Trees algorithm will give us 28% customer penetration rate, while if we select customers at random, we will get only 13% response rate.

 Tip You can re-position the population line by clicking on a vertical grid line.

Now, suppose that the marketing campaign promotes mountain bikes only. Switch to the Column Mapping tab and change Chart Type dropdown to *Lift Chart*. Select *Mountain Bikes* in the Predict Value column of the bottom grid. Flip back to the Lift Chart tab and notice that its Y-axis caption has changed to *Target Population [Mountain Bikes] %* to reflect the fact that now we evaluate the model accuracy for the Mountain Bikes product category only (Figure 7.25).

The ideal model line reveals that, in a perfect world, we need to contact about 30% of the customers to identify all mountain bike buyers. Again, the Decision Trees algorithm outperforms Naïve Bayes. At 50% overall population, the Decision Trees model will identify 66% of the potential customers interested in mountain bikes. If you are not satisfied with the accuracy results, you have several options. Start by verifying the data in the input dataset. Make sure that it is a good representative of the task you need to model. Next, re-validate the structure and mining model definitions. Finally, consider using a different algorithm.

Creating a profit chart

Now, let's add a financial dimension to our model evaluation study and find how much profit each model could generate by creating a profit chart. Change the *Chart type* dropdown to *Profit Chart*. Click on the Settings button and enter the settings shown in Figure 7.26. In our hypothetical example, we would like to target 5,000 customers. The marketing department has estimated that the fixed cost for running the campaign will be $10,000, e.g. for designing, printing, and mailing the promotion materials. In addition, there is $5 individual overhead cost per customer, e.g. for customer representatives responding to customer questions. Finally, based on past campaigns, the marketing department expects $50 as expected revenue per customer from the campaign.

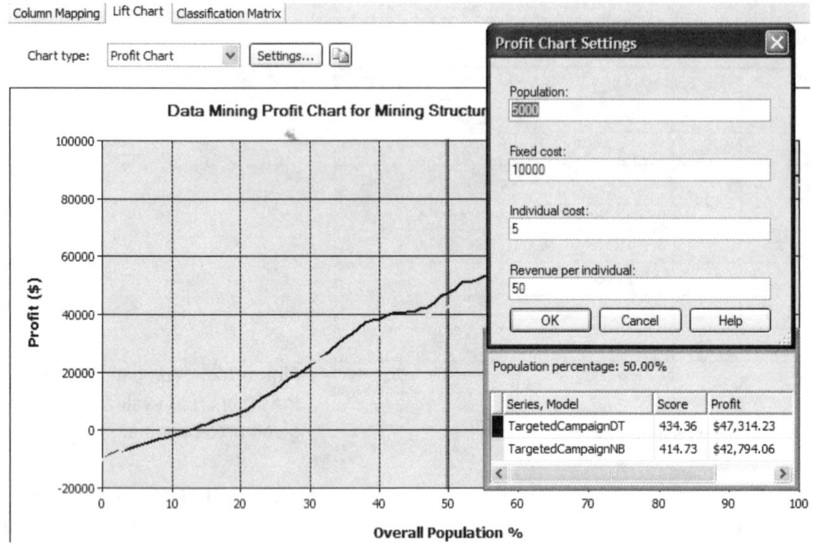

Figure 7.26 Create a profit chart to determine the profit generated by the campaign.

Based on these numbers, by examining the profit chart we could determine that we can actually lose money if we target only 10% of the customer population. Between 10% and 30%, the Naïve Bayes model will generate us more profit. After that, the Decision Trees model is the undisputed winner. If we target 50% of the customer population, we can expect our campaign to produce a profit of $47,314 with the Decision Trees algorithm. Using the profit chart, you can run what-if scenarios to find out the maximum return for your campaign investment. At this point, our models are trained and evaluated. Next, we need to deploy our model to production so it can be used for actual predictions against new customers.

Getting the predicted results

In the preceding steps, we used the Mining Accuracy Chart to compare the accuracy of the Decision Trees and Naïve Bayes models. We've identified that the Decision Trees model performs better for the classification task at hand. Specifically, the Decision Trees model could identify about 60% of the potential mountain bike buyers from a total population of 5,000 customers.

Suppose that Adventure Works Marketing department has a list of new customers. Let's run this list by the Decision Trees model to find which customers are likely to purchase a mountain bike based on the learned patterns. For the purposes of our demo, we will use the same input table (Customers) that we used to train the model. To get the model predictions, we need to query the model by submitting a DMX SELECT query. Creating the query is a child's play with the excellent DMX Query Builder provided by the Mining Model Prediction tab. Follow these steps to create a mining query to predict the mountain bike buyers.

1. Click on the Mining Model Prediction tab (Figure 7.27).

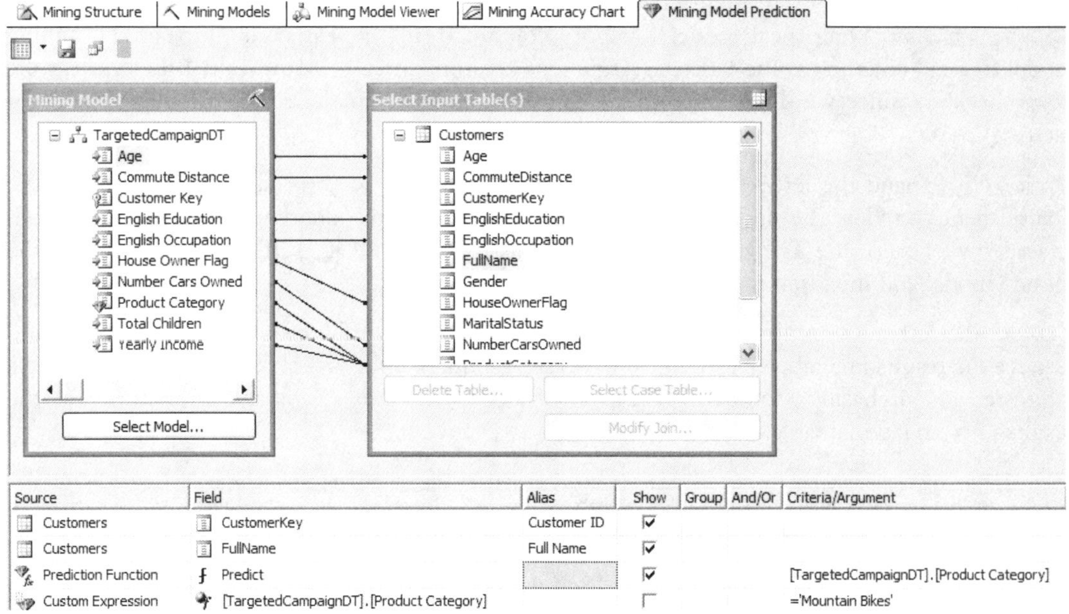

Figure 7.27 Use the Mining Model Prediction tab to build and execute a prediction query.

2. Click the Select Model button in the Mining Model pane. In the Select Mining Model dialog, expand the Targeted Campaign structure and select the *TargetedCampaignDT* model to use the Decision Tree model.

3. Next, we need to select the table that contains the input dataset. In the Select Input Table(s) pane, click the Select Case Table button and select the *Customers* table from the Bike Buyers DSV. Note that the Data Mining Designer automatically correlates the mining model and input table columns by naming convention.

   You can think of the Predict Mining Model tab as an ad hoc DMX query designer. As with the query designers included in the SQL Server Management Studio, it supports Design, Query, and Result modes. Let's use the Design mode to build our DMX query interactively.

4. First, let's select the columns we want to see in the predicted dataset. Drag the *CustomerKey* column from the input table (Select Input Table pane) and drop it onto the Source column of the grid. Alias the column as **Customer ID**.

5. Drag the FullName column and alias it as **Full Name**.

6. DMX supports various prediction functions. The function that we need is *Predict.* It allows you to predict a column from a given mining model. On the third row of the grid, expand the Source dropdown and select the *Prediction Function* item. Expand the Field column and select the first *Predict* function (there are two overloaded versions). Drag the *Product Category* column from the TargetedCampaign mining model to the Criteria/Argument column to replace the default criteria of the Predict function.

7. Since we are interested in predicting only potential mountain bike buyers, we need to filter the Product Category column. In the fourth row of the grid, expand the Source dropdown and select *Custom Expression.* Drag the Product Category column from the TargetedCampaignDT mining model to Field column. In the Criteria/Argument column, enter **= 'Mountain Bikes'**. Clear the *Show* checkbox since we don't want this column to show up in the results (it is just used for filtering).
8. Optionally, expand the left-most toolbar button and choose *Query* (or select Mining Model ⇨ Query menu) to view the underlying DMX statement. Note the query statement is actually an extended version of the T-SQL grammar and uses a PREDICTION JOIN construct to join the mining model and the input table.
9. Expand the left-most toolbar button and choose *Result* to submit the query to the server and retrieve the results in a tabular format. In my case, the query returns 3,595 customers that may be interested in purchasing mountain bikes. You can click the Save toolbar button to insert the results into a relational table.

Tip You can find my version of the DMX query saved as TargetedCampaign.dmx in the Code\Ch07\DMX folder. The DMX query builder is also available in the SQL Server Management Studio. To use it, connect to the Analysis Services database, expand the Mining Structures node, right-click on a given model, and choose Build Prediction Query. Alternatively, instead of using the query builder or the Mining Model Prediction tab, you can execute this query as a DMX query. To do so, right-click on the SOS OLAP database in the Object Explorer and choose New Query ⇨ DMX. Make sure that the TargetedCampaignDT model is selected in the *Mining model* dropdown in the Metadata pane. Next, paste the query text and execute the query by clicking the Execute button.

What if you want to specify the input values explicitly? For example, suppose you have a custom application that allows the end user to select a customer in order to find out if the customer is a likely buyer. In this case, you can use a singleton query. You can design this query by pressing the *Singleton query* button. The DMX Query Designer renames the right table to *Singleton Query Input* to denote the fact that now the values will be entered explicitly instead of retrieved from a relational table. Once the query syntax is ready, you can embed it in your application to pass the input criteria on the fly. We will see how this could be done in chapter 17.

7.4 Summary

Data mining is an exciting business intelligence technology. When properly used, data mining can help you derive valuable knowledge from mountains of data. It is a complementing, rather than competing, technology to OLAP. Use OLAP to aggregate data. Use data mining to discover patterns and trends.

Follow the seven-step data mining process to design and implement a data mining model. A data mining structure may contain more than one data mining model. Once the model is ready, train it with input data. The Mining Model Designer gives you the necessary tools to explore and evaluate a trained mining model. Once the model is in production, retrieve the predicted results by querying the model.

7.5 Resources

OLE DB for Data Mining Specification
(http://shrinkster.com/52t) – The goal of the OLE DB for Data Mining Specification is to provide an industry standard for data mining so that different mining algorithms from various data mining ISVs can be plugged easily into user applications.

Data mining models and structures and *Data mining algorithms* (part 1 and 2) webcasts
(SQL Server Resource Kit) – Your essential resource for introducing you to the SSAS data mining

CRoss Industry Standard Process for Data Mining (CRISP-DM)
(http://shrinkster.com/62h) – The CRISP-DM methodology was conceived in late 1996. It contains the corresponding phases of a project, their respective tasks, and relationships between these tasks.

SQL Server Data Mining: Plug-In Algorithms article by Raman Iyer and Bogdan Crivat
(http://shrinkster.com/53b) – Describes how SQL Server 2005 Data Mining allows aggregation directly at the algorithm level.

Preparing and Mining Data with Microsoft SQL Server 2000 and Analysis Services book
(http://shrinkster.com/8c4) – This book demonstrates how to apply data mining to a real-world situation using Microsoft SQL Server 2000, Microsoft SQL Server 2000 Analysis Services, and Microsoft Visual Basic 6.0.

Chapter 8

OLAP Data Mining

Data mining models can source data from relational data sources as well as from UDM. For lack of a better term, I will dub this approach *OLAP data mining*. Since this book is about Analysis Services and UDM, in this chapter, we will build three new mining models that draw data from the SOS OLAP cube. These mining models will perform the following mining tasks:

- Customer profiling to categorize customers into groups (segmentation task).
- Basket analysis to determine which products customers tend to purchase together (association task).
- Sales forecasting to predict future product sales based on past sales history (forecasting task).

These tasks, of course, can be implemented by using relational data sources. However, as you will see, OLAP data mining offers several distinct advantages. We will also build an SSIS package to show how data mining can be leveraged to implement "intelligent" ETL processes. You can find the enhanced SOS OLAP UDM and the Customer Profiling SSIS project in the Ch08 solution file.

8.1 OLAP vs. Relational Data Mining

Besides using a different data source type (UDM), OLAP data mining is no different than its relational counterpart. To design and implement your OLAP data mining models, you could use the same seven-step data mining methodology that I introduced in the preceding chapter. You don't need to learn new skills to set up and query your data mining models and structures.

8.1.1 Advantages of OLAP Data Mining

Why would you consider OLAP data mining? Using UDM as a data source offers several distinct advantages. To start with, the multi-dimensional data stored in UDM is well-formed and clean. It has already been transformed and organized neatly in measure groups and dimensions. As a result, you can import the data as-is in the data mining structures without having to create SQL views to link and transform the case tables.

Second, OLAP data mining fits well into the UDM mission to provide a "single version of the truth". The data from relational data sources is fed into UDM which fulfils the role of a single enterprise data repository. OLAP data mining can leverage the efficient UDM aggregations and calculations present in the cube. For example, the data mining designer can use a complex financial measure as an input column, which could otherwise be difficult to implement in a relational database.

Finally, not only can UDM data be used as an input to data mining, but also the prediction results can be applied back to UDM, in this way creating data mining cubes and dimensions. For example, the prediction results from a classification mining tasks can be used to create a new mining dimension. You can use this dimension to understand your customers better, e.g. to find out how much a particular class of customers (those most likely to purchase a given product) spent on average last year.

8.1.2 OLAP Data Mining Tradeoffs

On the downside, the obvious tradeoff with OLAP data mining is that it is more involved to set up since additional effort is required to design and build the dimensional model. In comparison, the data source for relational data mining can be faster assembled by using either SQL views or data source views. In addition, you may find the OLAP mining approach less flexible in comparison with relational data sources. For example, the Time Series algorithm requires a fairly rigid schema of the input dataset, e.g. the date column has to be numeric and no period laps are allowed. This could be problematic if a Date dimension is used as a source.

Another issue with OLAP mining is that some relational schema fidelity could be lost as part of dimensionalizing the schema. For example, the order header-order details one-to-many relationship may be lost when capturing the order facts into a fact table. This could lead to a loss of accuracy in the mining model, as I would explain in more details in the Basket Analysis scenario.

8.2 Customer Profiling

Our first OLAP data mining task will be to help Adventure Works understand its customers. We will build a Customer Profiling data mining model that will examine the Customer dimension and categorize customers into groups referred to as *clusters* by the Microsoft Clustering algorithm we will use to power the mining model. Since OLAP mining is almost identical to relational data mining, I will fast forward through the implementation steps and will focus only on the new concepts.

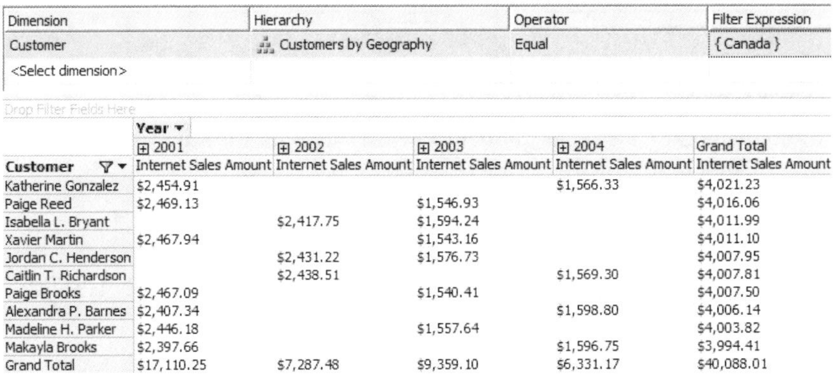

Dimension	Hierarchy	Operator	Filter Expression
Customer	Customers by Geography	Equal	{ Canada }
<Select dimension>			

Drop Filter Fields Here

	Year				
	2001	2002	2003	2004	Grand Total
Customer	Internet Sales Amount	Internet Sales Amount	Internet Sales Amount	Internet Sales Amount	Internet Sales Amount
Katherine Gonzalez	$2,454.91			$1,566.33	$4,021.23
Paige Reed	$2,469.13		$1,546.93		$4,016.06
Isabella L. Bryant		$2,417.75	$1,594.24		$4,011.99
Xavier Martin	$2,467.94		$1,543.16		$4,011.10
Jordan C. Henderson		$2,431.22	$1,576.73		$4,007.95
Caitlin T. Richardson		$2,438.51		$1,569.30	$4,007.81
Paige Brooks	$2,467.09		$1,540.41		$4,007.50
Alexandra P. Barnes	$2,407.34			$1,598.80	$4,006.14
Madeline H. Parker	$2,446.18		$1,557.64		$4,003.82
Makayla Brooks	$2,397.66			$1,596.75	$3,994.41
Grand Total	$17,110.25	$7,287.48	$9,359.10	$6,331.17	$40,088.01

Figure 8.1 Finding trends and patterns in large OLAP dimensions could be difficult without data mining.

8.2.1 Defining the Mining Domain

As noted in the beginning of this chapter, data mining can be used to complement OLAP well. Given the report shown in Figure 8.1, suppose that we have a huge customer dimension with thousands or even millions of customers. OLAP can certainly go a long way to help us slice and dice the customer-related measures across multi-level hierarchies, e.g. by customer territory.

However, we can browse data all day long and still not be able to discover interesting patterns in the customer dimension that are not easily discernable by just aggregating and slicing data. Perhaps, most sales are generated by customers with a higher income in a certain age group. Or, perhaps, demographics factors, such as commute distance and home ownership, could influence the customer decision to buy a bike.

Customer profiling is a classification mining task that could help you discover such patterns and could be the key for understanding your customers. We've already demonstrated this task in the targeted campaign scenario. The difference in this example will be that we will use the Microsoft Clustering algorithm which is specifically designed to handle classification tasks. In addition, we will derive a data mining dimension from the customer clusters. Finally, we will apply the mining dimension back to UDM to help the marketing department browse data by these clusters.

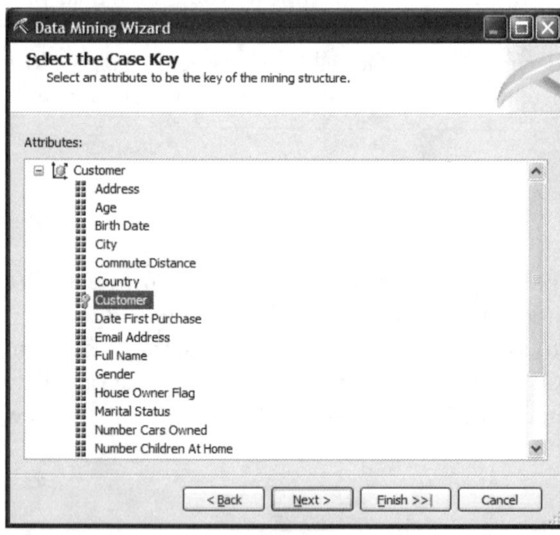

Figure 8.2 Select the dimension attribute which will qualify the mining cases.

8.2.2 Implementing an OLAP Mining Model

Again, the easiest way to build an OLAP mining model is to use the Data Mining Model Wizard. We will follow the same implementation process as with its relational counterpart.

Creating Clustering Profile Mining Model

1. Launch the Data Mining Wizard and select the *From existing cube* option on the Select the Definition Method step.
2. Select the *Microsoft Clustering* algorithm on the Select the Data Mining Technique step.

3. OLAP data mining models can draw data only from cubes in the same SSAS database. Select the *Customer* dimension in the Select the Source Cube Dimension step.

4. In the Select the Case Key step (Figure 8.2), we need to tell the wizard what our mining case will represent. In our scenario, the grain of our mining model will be the individual customer. Therefore, we will set the case key to the *Customer* dimension attribute. If we wanted to find patterns at another level, e.g. customer city, we would use that attribute instead. In this case, the input set will contain the distinct members of the City attribute.

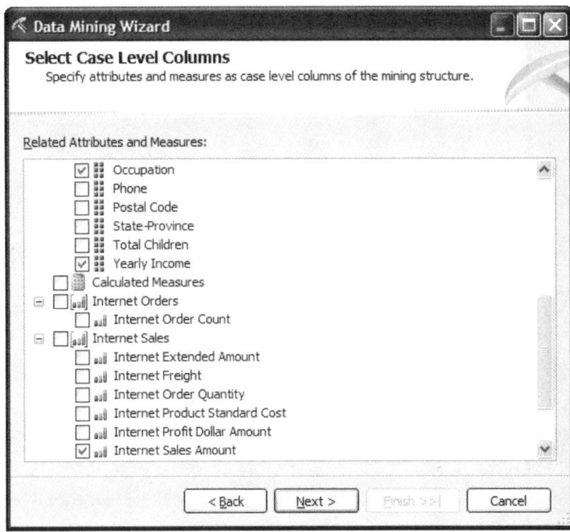

Figure 8.3 You can use dimension attributes and measures as input columns.

5. Next, in the Select Case Level Columns step (Figure 8.3), we need to specify the input columns of the mining structure. You can choose any dimension attribute which has an attribute hierarchy (AttributeHierarchyEnabled = True). In addition, you can select any regular or calculated measure (derived through an MDX expression) from measure groups related to the selected dimension. Select *Age*, *Commute Distance*, *House Owner Flag*, *Number Cars Owned*, *Number Children At Home*, *Occupation*, and *Yearly Income* attributes from the Customer dimension. Select the *Internet Sales Amount* measure from the Internet Sales measure group to find out how customer spending affects the customer profiles.

6. Accept the default settings in the Specify Mining Model Column Usage step. All the selected attributes will be used as input columns. The Microsoft Clustering algorithm doesn't require a designated predict column.

7. Accept the default settings in the Specify Columns' Content and Data Type step.

8. Just as you would use the SQL WHERE clause to limit data from a relational table, OLAP data mining allows you to apply a mining model to a subset of a cube called a *slice*. You can use any dimension to slice a cube. Suppose you are interested in profiling only customers who have purchased bikes. To do so, in the Slice Source Cube step, select the Product dimension and filer the Category attribute hierarchy members to *Bikes* (see Figure 8.4).

Tip If you want to change the cube slice criteria, or create a new slice after the wizard is done, go to the Mining Models tab, right-click on the model, and choose Define Mining Structure Cube Slice or use the Mining Model menu.

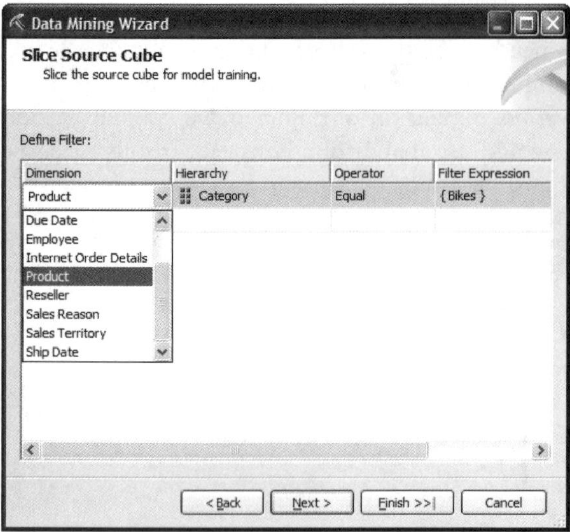

Figure 8.4 OLAP data mining allows you to slice the source cube.

9. In the Completing the Wizard step (Figure 8.5), name the structure **Customer Profiling** and the model **CustomerProfilingMC**. Enable drillthrough.

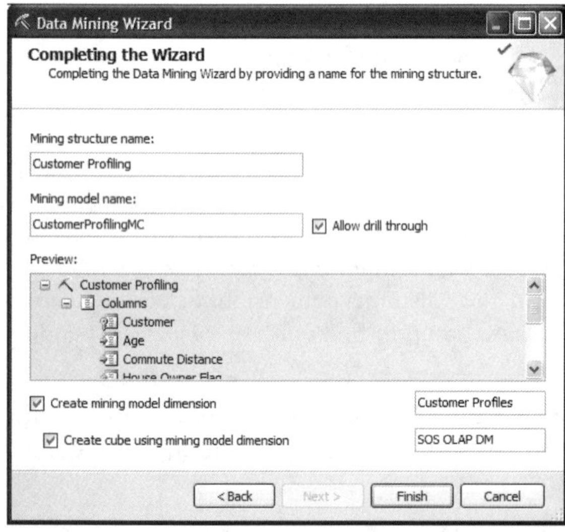

Figure 8.5 Data mining results can be applied back to UDM in the form of a data mining dimension.

Enhancing UDM

As noted, the results from the data mining model can be applied back to the UDM in the form of a data mining dimension. However, you cannot add the mining dimension back to the source cube it is derived from because it will create a circular reference. If you attempt to do so, you will get a "The objects depend on each other; they form part of a, or a whole, dependency circuit" error when building the cube.

If you need to browse the source cube data by the mining dimension, the Mining Wizard gives you an option to create a new (linked) cube. This cube will be a mirrored copy of the original cube with the exception that all of its measure groups will be linked to the original measure groups to avoid duplication of storage and definition.

1. Check the *Create mining model dimension* checkbox to instruct the wizard to create a UDM dimension and name the dimension Customer Profiles. Name the new cube **SOS OLAP DM**.

Tip If you want to generate a UDM dimension from an existing OLAP-bound model outside the wizard, right-click on the model in the Mining Models tab and choose *Create a Data Mining Dimension* or use the Mining Model menu.

Once the Data Mining wizard is done, you will see four new definition files in the Solution Explorer -- a data mining model (Customer Profiling.dmm), a data source view for the mining dimension (Customer Profiles_DMDSV.dsv), a mining dimension (Customer Profiles.dim), and a new cube (SOS OLAP DM.cube).

2. Rename the Customer Profiles_DMDSV DSV to **Customer Profiles.dsv** to make its name more compact.

3. Deploy the SOS OLAP project to reflect the changes on the server and process the Customer Profiling data mining structure.

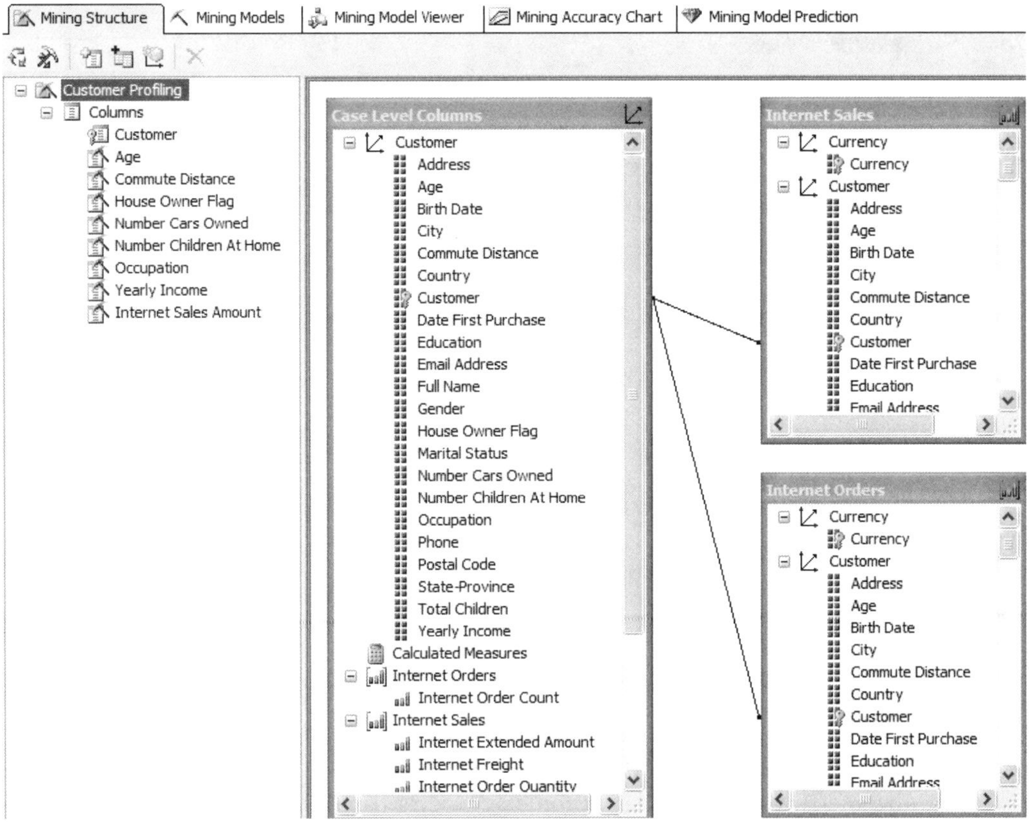

Figure 8.6 The case dimension and related measure groups are exposed as Case Level Columns.

8.2.3 Understanding OLAP Mining Structures

Before we explore the mining model results, let's take a moment to review the mining structure definition. Open the Customer Profiling mining model in the Mining Model Designer and flip to the Mining Structure tab (Figure 8.6). The diagram pane shows the UDM objects that can be used by the mining structure. Since the Customer dimension is the case dimension in our mining model, the Case Level Columns table lists the Customer dimension and its related measure groups. You can drag dimension attributes or measures from the Case Level Columns table to create additional input or predicted columns.

In addition, you can use other dimensions related to the Customer dimension as nested tables in the model. To do so, you can drag dimension attributes from the Internet Sales and Internet Orders tables. These tables correspond to the measure groups related to the Customer dimension. In this respect, you can think of a measure group as a bridge you can use to get to the dimensions that will form the nested tables. The Customer Profiling model doesn't need any nested tables. We will demonstrate how nested tables can be used with OLAP mining models in the Basket Analysis and Sales Forecasting scenarios.

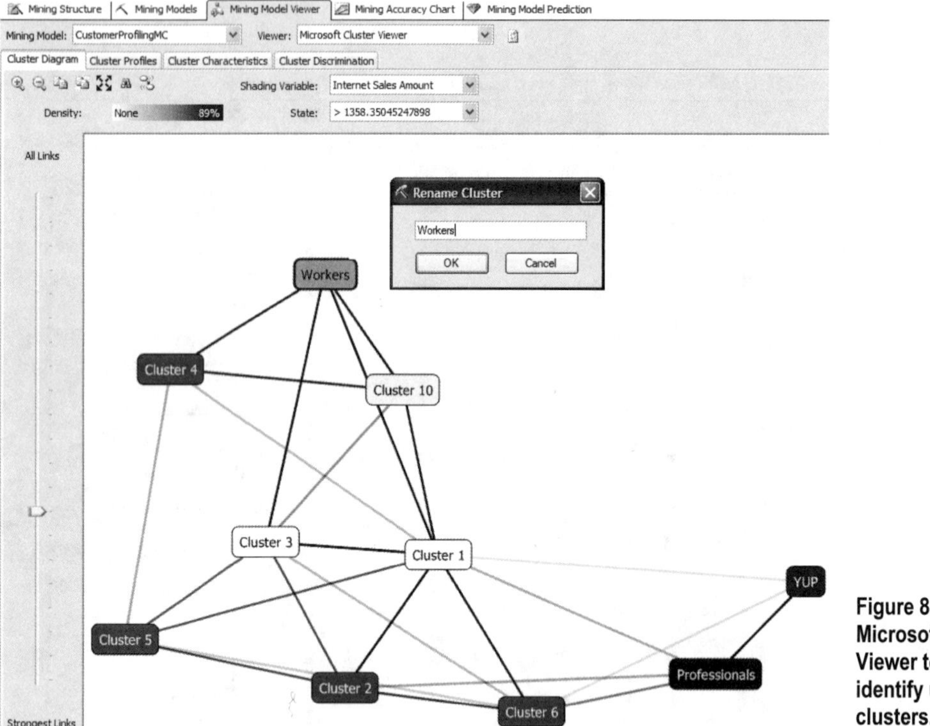

Figure 8.7 Use the Microsoft Cluster Viewer to quickly identify useful clusters.

8.2.4 Exploring the Model

Now that the Customer Profiling OLAP model is built and deployed, let's find out how it can help us categorize the Adventure Works customers. Models based on the Microsoft Clustering and Naïve Bayes algorithms have similar viewers. We can identify the most significant clusters easily by using the Cluster Diagram tab (Figure 8.7) of the Microsoft Cluster Viewer.

By using the Cluster Diagram tab, you can find out quickly which clusters have the largest population based on a given criteria. For example, to find out which groups of customers spend more than average, select the *Internet Sales Amount* attribute in the Shading Variable dropdown. As with the Decision Trees Viewer, the darker the cluster is, the larger its population is. The cluster position on the diagram is also significant. The closer two clusters are next to each other, the more characteristics they have in common. Again, similar to Decision Trees, you can identify the strongest links by sliding down the slider on the left side.

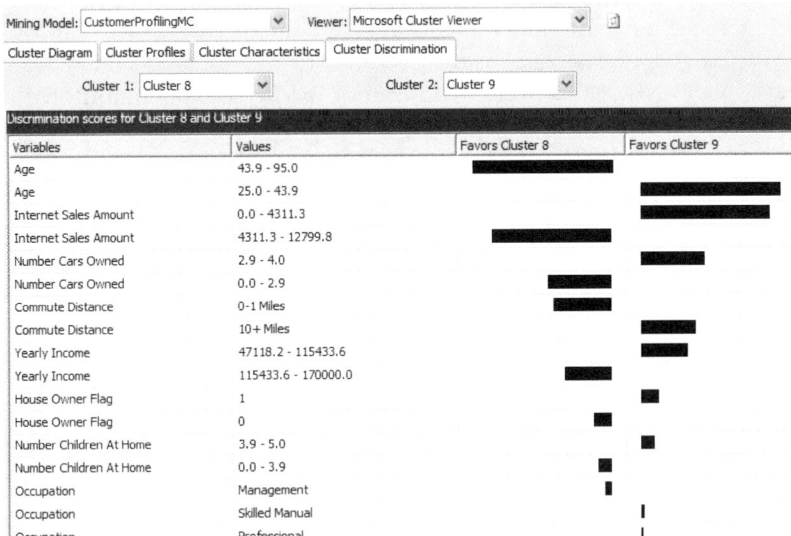

Figure 8.8 Use the Cluster Discrimination tab to find out what differentiates two clusters

In our case, clusters 7, 8, and 9 are the darkest clusters. This doesn't mean that they generate the most sales. The only conclusion we can actually make at this stage is that there are many customers in these clusters who spend more than average. For example, hovering on top of cluster 8 reveals that 89% of the customers there have spent more than the average sales amount of $1,358. Further, the Cluster Characteristics tab reveals that Cluster 7 consists predominantly of manual and skilled workers.

1. Back to the Cluster Diagram, we can rename a cluster to give it a more meaningful name by right-clicking on the cluster node and choosing *Rename Cluster.* Rename cluster 7 to ***Workers*** (see again Figure 8.7)
2. Cluster 8 and 9 include mostly customers with management or professional occupations. By comparing clusters 8 and 9 side-by-side in the Cluster Discrimination tab (Figure 8.8), we discover that the most discriminating factor that differentiates these two clusters is customer age. Specifically, most customers in cluster 8 are older than 43 years, while cluster 9 customers are between 25 and 43 years old. Rename cluster 8 to **Professionals** and cluster 9 to **YUP** (Young Urban Professionals).
3. Process the Customer Profiles data mining dimension (Process Full option) followed by processing the SOS OLAP DM cube.

8.2.5 Enhancing UDM with Data Mining

As noted, the mining results from a data mining model could be applied back to enrich UDM in the form of a mining dimension and a linked cube. Mining dimensions and cubes can be generated only from OLAP mining models.

Data mining dimensions

A mining dimension is automatically generated and synchronized with the mining model when the model is processed. If you open the Customer Profiles dimension in the Dimension Designer, you will find out that it is just a parent-child dimension where the MiningDimensionContentNodes attribute has a Parent usage. The dimension is bound to a system-generated DSV table called DIMENSION_CONTENT_ROWSET. You cannot modify the definition of this table. During runtime, the server generates a DMX query against the associated data model and populates this table with the results from the query.

The results of the DMX query are exposed as nodes grouped in levels. The node levels form the member levels of the dimension. The number of levels returned depends on the mining algorithm that the model is based on. For example, a mining model that uses Microsoft Clustering algorithm returns only one level which has as many nodes as the number of the distinct clusters found. A mining dimension derived from a Decision Trees model will have as many levels as the number of the levels formed by the tree splits.

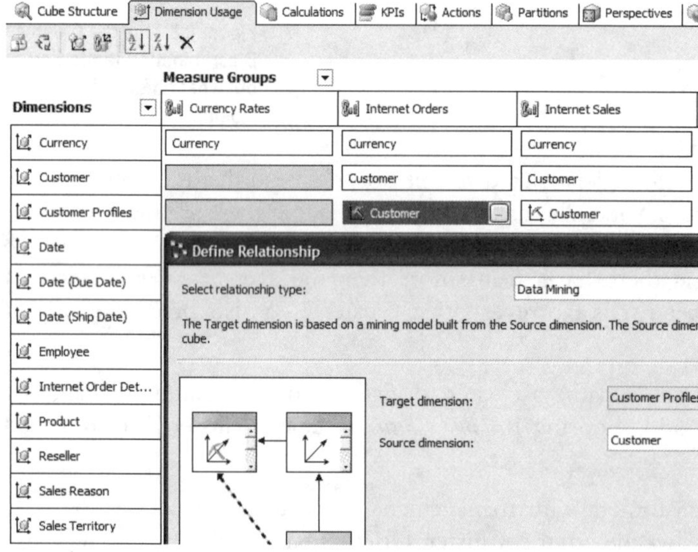

Figure 8.9 A mining dimension can be related to a measure group with a Data Mining relationship.

Adding a data mining dimension to a cube

A mining dimension can be added to any cube *other* than the cube it sources its data from. The Data Mining Dimension Wizard automatically adds the dimension to the mining cube you specified in the Completing the Wizard step. Open the SOS OLAP DM cube in the Cube Designer and switch to the Dimension Usage tab (Figure 8.9).

The Customer Profiles mining dimension is related to the two measure groups (Internet Orders and Internet Sales) the source dimension (Customer) is related to. The pickaxe icon in the intersecting cell tells us that the Customer Profiles dimension has a data mining relationship to these measure groups. Click the ... button inside to find out how the relationship is configured. The relationship type is set to *Data Mining*, the target dimension is Customer Profiles, and the Source dimension is *Customer* dimension. If you need to use the Customer Profiles dimension in another cube, you can configure it in the same way. Of course, this assumes that the cube includes the Customer dimension as well.

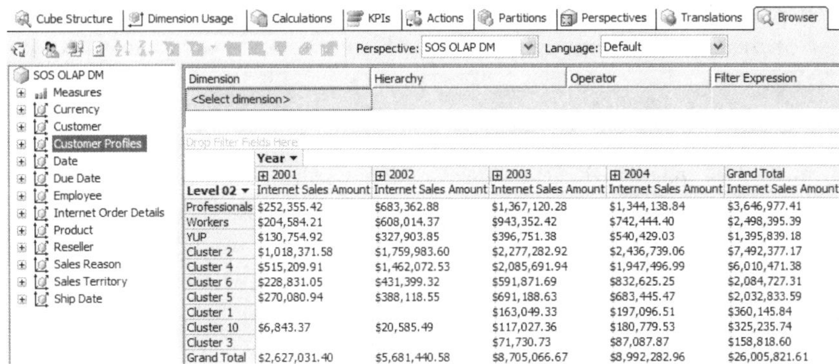

Level 02	2001 Internet Sales Amount	2002 Internet Sales Amount	2003 Internet Sales Amount	2004 Internet Sales Amount	Grand Total Internet Sales Amount
Professionals	$252,355.42	$683,362.88	$1,367,120.28	$1,344,138.84	$3,646,977.41
Workers	$204,584.21	$608,014.37	$943,352.42	$742,444.40	$2,498,395.39
YUP	$130,754.92	$327,903.85	$396,751.38	$540,429.03	$1,395,839.18
Cluster 2	$1,018,371.58	$1,759,983.60	$2,277,282.92	$2,436,739.06	$7,492,377.17
Cluster 4	$515,209.91	$1,462,072.53	$2,085,691.94	$1,947,496.99	$6,010,471.38
Cluster 6	$228,831.05	$431,399.32	$591,871.69	$832,625.25	$2,084,727.31
Cluster 5	$270,080.94	$388,118.55	$691,188.63	$683,445.47	$2,032,833.59
Cluster 1			$163,049.33	$197,096.51	$360,145.84
Cluster 10	$6,843.37	$20,585.49	$117,027.36	$180,779.53	$325,235.74
Cluster 3			$71,730.73	$87,087.87	$158,818.60
Grand Total	$2,627,031.40	$5,681,440.58	$8,705,066.67	$8,992,282.96	$26,005,821.61

Figure 8.10 A mining dimension can be used as a regular dimension when browsing data.

Now, let's generate a report to find the actual sales amount that the customer clusters have generated. Switch to the Browser tab. Drop the Customer Profiles dimension on rows and the Date dimension on columns. Drop the Internet Sales Amount measure on the report body. If you wish, drag the Professionals, Workers, and YUP members to position them on top of the report (Figure 8.10). The report shows that the customers in the Professionals cluster have generated most sales.

This report could also help us identify other potentially interesting clusters. For example, cluster 2 has generated an amount almost equal to the combined sales amount of the first three clusters. Although its customers tend to spend less on average, we can use the Cluster Characteristics tab of the Microsoft Cluster Viewer to get some insight into this category of customers and possibly target them in a future marketing campaign.

8.3 Basket Analysis

A very popular association mining task is basket analysis. It has two main objectives. First, basket analysis seeks to find the most popular products customers buy. Second, this task can be used to determine which products customers tend to buy together. The results from the basket analysis tasks are typically used for cross-selling initiatives in one form or another, e.g. customers-who-bought-this-also-bought-that model or placing products next to each other in a resale outlet. To help Adventure Works perform the basket analysis task, we will implement an OLAP mining model that uses the Microsoft Association Rules algorithm.

8.3.1 Working with Nested Tables

Implementing the basket analysis task is somewhat trickier because it requires a nested table that represents the products a customer bought, as I explained in the preceding chapter (see section 7.2.1). If we base the mining model on top of a relational database schema, the role of the case table would be fulfilled by the Order Header table. That's because we need to find out which products are purchased *together* (bundled in the same order). The Order Detail table then will be used as a nested table to give us the product correlation.

Identifying OLAP mining approaches

With OLAP data mining, however, the order header/order details hierarchy disappears when imported into the FactInternetSales fact table. We cannot derive the case table from the Order Number as a fact (degenerate) dimension too, because such a dimension will contain as many members as the number of the individual line numbers. We have two approaches to solve this dilemma.

First, we can use the Customer dimension as a case dimension joined via the Internet Sales measure group to the Product nested dimension. The issue with this approach is that the cases will not be correlated in time. In other words, if the customer buys a bike and two months later the same customer buys a helmet, the mining model will still consider these products related to each other. We can use a cube slice for a given period, e.g. day or week, to eliminate products purchased after a given time period but we may "loose" useful correlations when doing so.

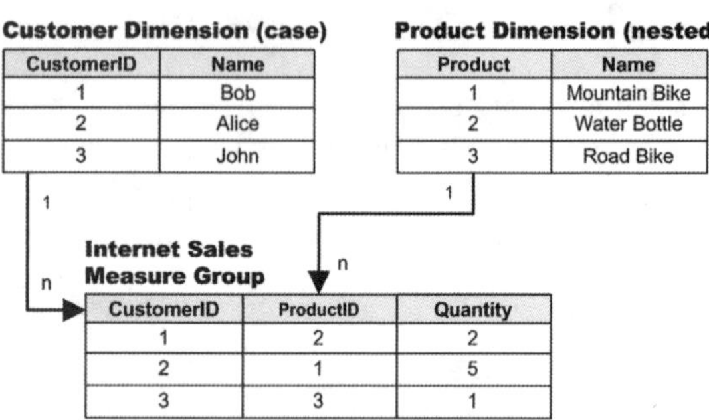

Figure 8.11 In OLAP data mining, any dimension related to the case dimension can be used as a nested table.

The second approach is trivial. We could "reverse-engineer" the FactInternetSales fact table and derive an Order Header dimension from it to get back the order header/details hierarchy. For the purposes of our demo, we will ignore the timing issue and use Customer dimension as a case dimension and Product as a nested dimension (see Figure 8.11).

To bring the OLAP data mining terminology on a par with UDM, we will call the dimension that forms the case mining table a *case dimension* (Customer) and the one used for the nested table (Product) – *a nested dimension.* Just as a relational model uses an intermediate table to translate a many-to-many relationship to one-to-many, we will use the Internet Sales measure group to join these two dimensions together.

Creating the Mining Structure

Given the considerations above, creating the Basket Analysis mining structure with the Data Mining Wizard is simple.

1. Pick the *From existing cube* option since we will create an OLAP mining model.
2. Choose the *Microsoft Association Rules* algorithm which is specifically designed to find associations.
3. In the Select the Source Cube Dimension step, select the *Customer* dimension from the SOS OLAP cube.

4. In the Select the Case Key step, select the *Customer* attribute. Once again, this is done because we want the mining case to represent the products that a given customer has purchased.
5. We won't seek any correlation between the customer-related attributes and the products they have bought. Therefore, don't select any attributes or measures in the Select Case Level Columns step.

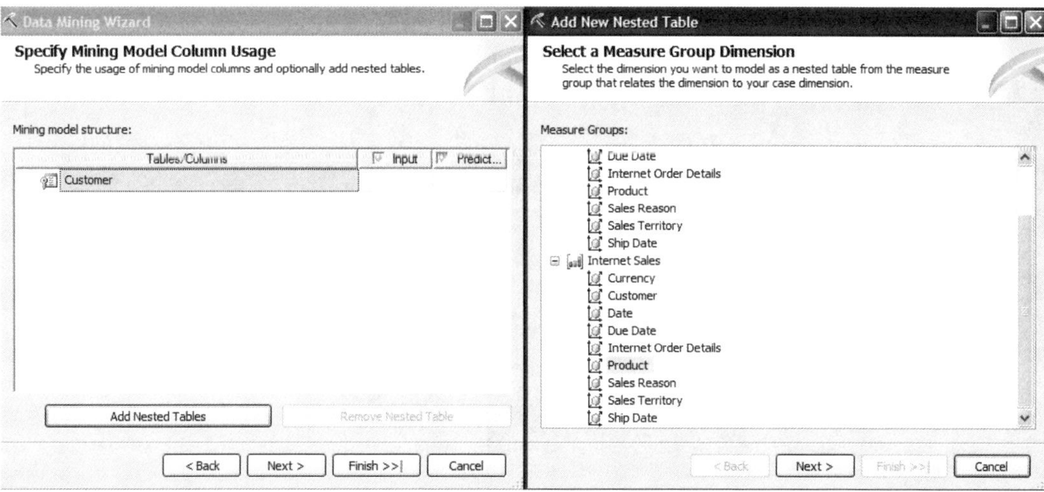

Figure 8.12 You can choose any related dimension to form a nested table.

6. In the Specify Mining Model Column Usage step, click on the Add Nested Table button to start the nested dimension wizard flow. You can choose any dimension that shares the same measure groups with the case dimension as a nested dimension. Select the *Product* dimension from the Internet Sales measure group (Figure 8.12).

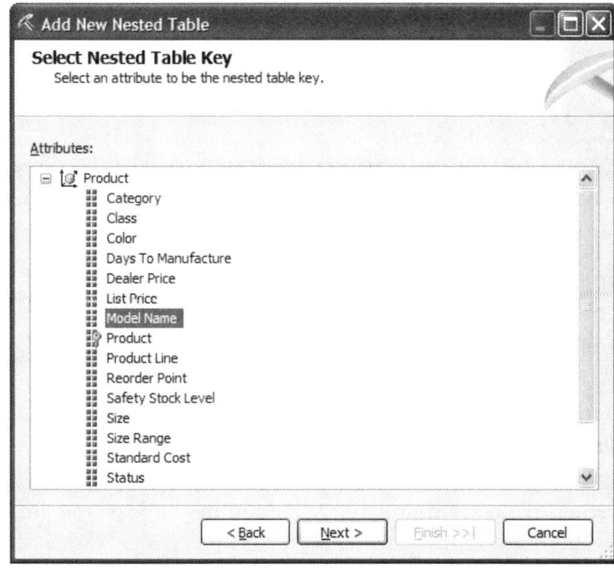

Figure 8.13 The table key doesn't have to be the dimension key.

To make things more interesting, suppose that, instead of trying to find correlations at the product level, we want our case to be scoped at the product model level (a model may span several products).

7. In the Select the Nested Table Key step (Figure 8.13), for the Product nested table, select the *Model Name* attribute.

8. Similar to the case dimension, we won't need additional attributes from the nested tables, so skip the Select Nested Table Columns step and click Finish to end the nested table flow and return to the Specify Mining Model Column Usage step. The Product dimension is added to the grid.

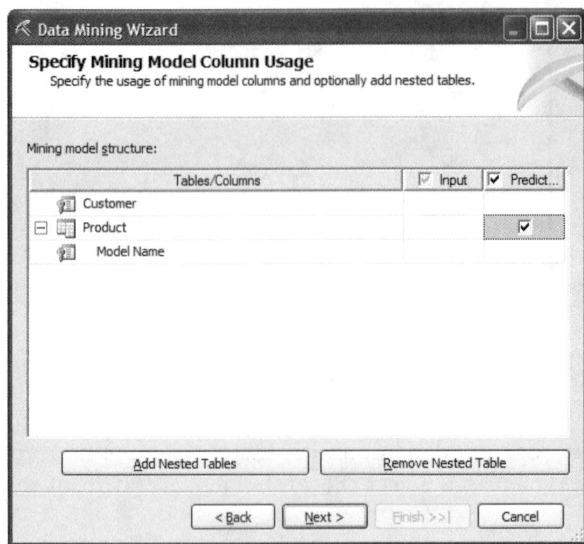

Figure 8.14 A data mining model views a nested table as a column which can be used as input for predictions.

9. Recall that the mining model treats a nested table as an input column. Check the *Predict* checkbox next to the Product column to instruct the model to predict the product associations (Figure 8.14).

10. Skip the Specify Columns' Content and Data Type step.

11. As explained in the preceding example, we could use the Slice Source cube step to slice the cube, e.g. to filter only customers who live in London. Assuming that you need to find associations among products bought by all Adventure Works customers, skip this step.

12. In the Completing the Wizard step (Figure 8.15), name the structure **Basket Analysis** and the mining model **BasketAnalysisAR**. Check the "Allow drill through" checkbox. We won't be creating OLAP mining objects in this example, so leave the bottom two checkboxes unchecked.

Once the Basket Analysis structure is created, switch to Mining Structure tab and notice that the Product column is defined as a type TableMiningStructureColumn. In addition, notice that the DSV Diagram includes the measure groups (Internet Sales and Internet Orders) related to the Customer case dimension, so we can conveniently create new structure columns by just dragging the desired measures or related dimensions.

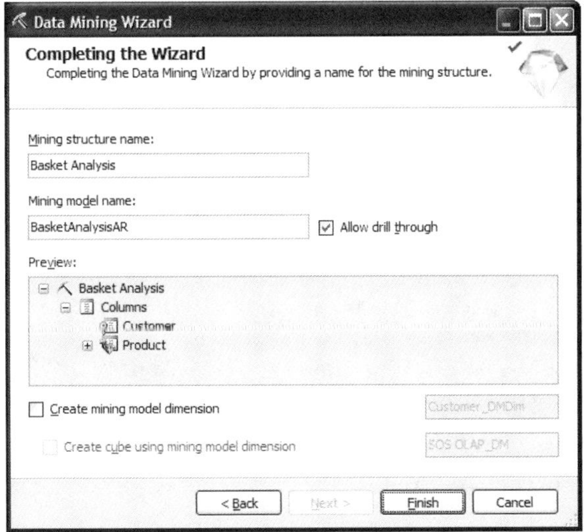

Figure 8.15 Enable drillthrough to see the underlying data in the data source.

13. Process the Basket Analysis structure either explicitly or by deploying the project.

8.3.2 Exploring the Model

Let's now analyze the predicted results using the Microsoft Associated Rules Viewer. It has three tabs that give different views of the products bought.

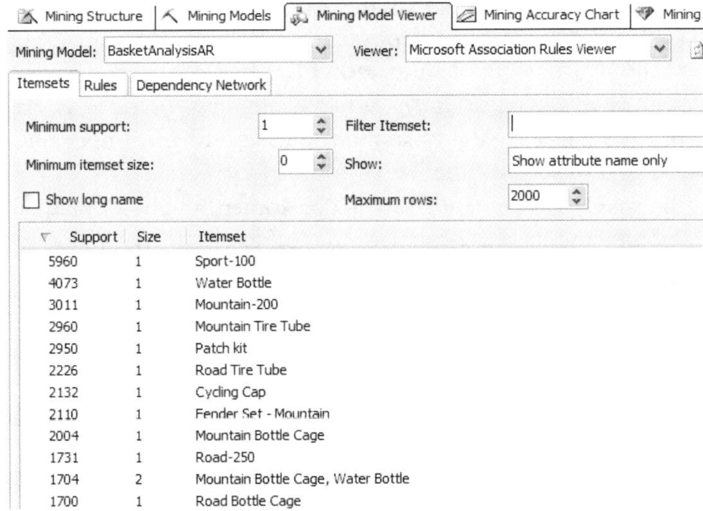

Figure 8.16 Use the Itemsets tab to determine the most popular products.

Identifying popular products

The Microsoft Association Rules algorithm uses the term *itemset* to describe a group of items contained in a case. An itemset may contain one or more items. The Itemsets tab (Figure 8.16) shows the popular itemsets that the algorithm has identified. By default, the itemsets are sorted in descending order by the Support column which indicates the frequency of the itemset.

Analyzing the table, we realize that the most popular product model is Sport-100. It was purchased by 5,960 customers.
Some itemsets have more than one item. For example, the Association Rules model has identified that 1,704 customers bought Mountain Bottle Cage and Water Bottle products together. You can use the Minimum support and Minimum itemset size parameters to filter the results, as needed.

Figure 8.17 Use the Rules tab to determine which products customers are likely to buy together.

Identifying association rules

The power of the Association Rules model is to predict recommendations (rules) based on the customer purchase history, as you can see by switching to the Rules tab (Figure 8.17). For example, the mining model predicts that 100% of the customers who will buy Mountain-500 product and Touring Tire together will also buy the Touring-1000 product (the second row). Each rule is associated with a score called an *importance factor*. When examining the rules, it may be beneficial to pay attention not only to the Probability column, but also to the Importance column. The rule importance factor takes into account the item's popularity.

For example, suppose we have the rule B⇨W, where B is 1 if a customer bought a mountain bike, otherwise 0. W is 1 if the customer purchased a water bottle, otherwise 0. Let's also say that half of the customers buy water bottles, while only 5% buy mountain bikes. Now, among those who buy mountain bikes, almost all buy water bottles, so Mountain Bike⇨Water Bottle would be a strong recommendation. On the other hand, few water bottle buyers also buy mountain bikes, so the reverse rule Water Bottle ⇨ Mountain Bike is much weaker. The Importance column gives you the reverse rule score. For you, math fans, out there, the score is calculated as follows:

```
Score(B ⇨ W) = log [ p( W | B ) / p( W | not B )],
```

where *p* stands for probability. The importance score is also known in mathematics as weight of evidence (WOE).

Finding dependent rules

Having so many rules may be confusing. For example, it is difficult to find out what other products customers will buy together with a particular product. Use the Dependency Network tab to locate an item and discover the strongest correlations to that item (Figure 8.18).

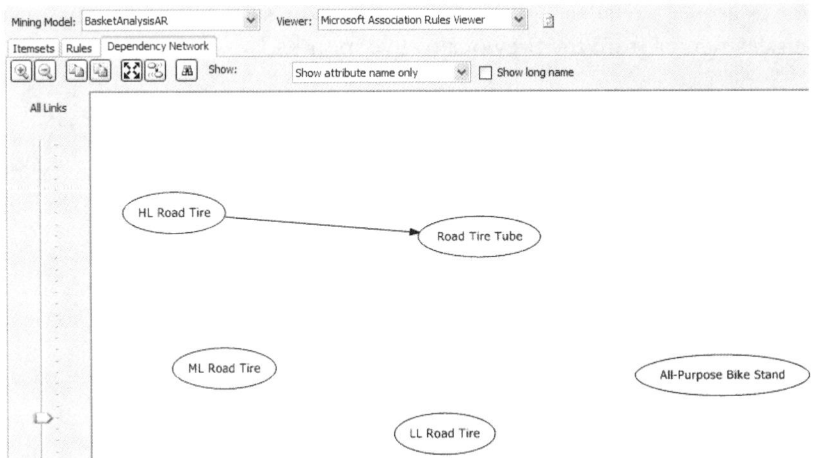

Figure 8.18 Use the Dependency Network tab to find an item quickly and determine its strongest correlations.

You can click on the Find Node button to locate a product quickly in the dependency diagram. The viewer will highlight the related products automatically. Next, slide down the links slider to find the products customers will be most likely to purchase together with this product. For example, in our case, the Association Rules algorithm predicts that, while we have other products correlated to Road Tire Tube, it is most strongly linked to HL Road Tire. In other words, customers that buy HL Road Tire are very likely to purchase Road Tire Tube as well.

8.4 Sales Forecasting

Another very popular and frequently requested data mining task is forecasting. Forecasting is the oldest and most well-known statistical task. The mathematical algorithms that are used to implement this task take a numerical dataset as an input and produce a formula that fits the data. Once you have the formula, you can plug a new dataset into it and you get the predicted results. Perhaps, the most common usage scenario for this task is sales forecasting, where future sales numbers need to be predicted given the historical sales statistics.

Readers who have read my book *Microsoft Reporting Services in Action*, would probably recall that I used the forecasting task to predict sales figures shown on a Reporting Services matrix report (see Resources for the MSDN article which is based on the book example). Behind the scenes, the report would call down to the Open Source OpenForecast package (see Resources) to obtain the forecasted monthly figures using regression analysis. The regression algorithm which Open Forecast uses doesn't care about the data semantics. It would simply take the input dataset, derive the mathematical formula, and calculate the requested number of data points.

The focus of the example was to demonstrate how an RS report could invoke custom .NET code. Of course, with the advent of SSAS 2005, this report could be easily re-designed (and simplified) to leverage the SQL Server 2005 data mining technology.

8.4.1 Designing the Model Schema

When the input data is time-dependent, the Microsoft algorithm of choice for the forecasting task is Microsoft Time Series. As its names suggests, this algorithm expects an input dataset called *time series* which is loaded with values that change over time and are recorded at regular intervals (e.g. monthly sales figures). The output of the Time Series is a forecasted value for the time period requested. For example, a retailer may need to forecast the sales figures for the next two months based on the sales figures from the previous twelve months.

Relational schema

Suppose that the Adventure Works management has requested a data mining model that shows the forecasted monthly reseller figures for 2004 broken down by product category. If we are to build the mining model from a relational data source, the input dataset would have the following simple relational schema (assuming two product categories only):

```
Product       Category Month    Sales Amount
Accessories   200307            $10,000
Bikes         200307            $20,000
Accessories   200308            $34,000
Bikes         200308            $45,000
```

The historical dataset contains the aggregated sales data broken down by product category and month. The Time Series algorithm requires the Month column to be numeric. In addition, by default, the algorithm doesn't allow gaps in the data series. For example, if there is no value for the Accessories category in August 2003, you will get an error during processing. You can get around this error by changing the algorithm MISSING_VALUE_SUBSTITUTION parameter to either use the previous value in the series (July 2003 in our case), or calculate a mean value. However, this may skew the prediction results, so make sure you have values for each time period.

OLAP schema

Implementing an OLAP-based data mining model that uses the Time Series algorithm is a somewhat more involved. I would like to thank ZhaoHui Tang, a Lead Program Manager of SQL Server Analysis Services, for helping me with a sample model. To implement our forecasting model on top of the SOS OLAP UDM, we will need the schema shown in Figure 8.19.

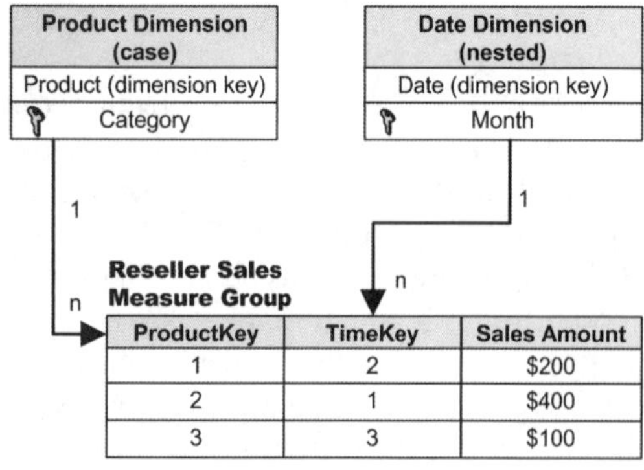

Figure 8.19 The Time Series algorithm requires a time dimension.

The role of the case dimension is fulfilled by the Product dimension. Note that, although the Product attribute is the dimension key of the Product dimension, the case key of the Product case dimension is Category. That's because sales data needs to be consolidated by product category. The net result is that we will end up with four cases only because we have four product categories (Bikes, Accessories, Clothing, and Components). If the requirements call for forecasting at a lower level, then the case key would be represented by the Product or Subcategory dimension attributes.

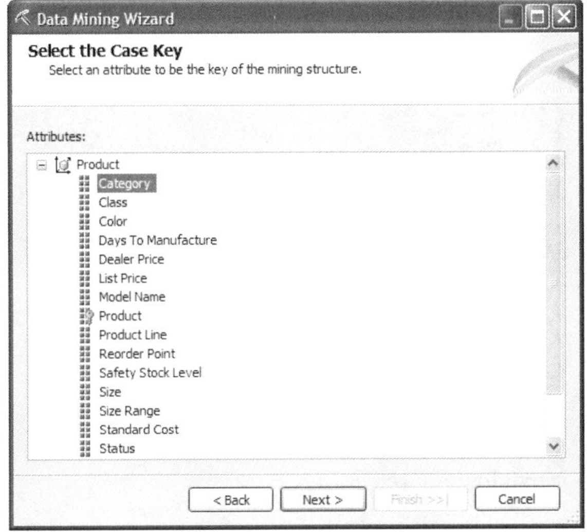

Figure 8.20 Since the sales data needs to be grouped by product category, the Category attribute forms the case key.

To get the time periods, we need to use the Date dimension as a nested table. Since the cardinality of the time series is month, we will use the Month attribute as a nested key. On first impulse, we may opt to select the MonthNumberOfYear dimension attribute. However, the attribute values of MonthNumberOfYear are not unique across years.
For this reason, we need to add a new numeric named calculation to the DimTime dimension table which uses the year-month combination for unique key values.

1. Open the SOS OLAP DSV in the Data Source View Designer. Add a named calculation called **TimeIndex** to table DimTime that is based on the following expression:

```
CONVERT(Integer, CalendarYear) * 100 + CONVERT(Integer, MonthNumberOfYear)
```

In addition, make a mental note that since we are forecasting the reseller sales, we need to join the Product case dimension to the Date nested dimension through the Reseller Sales measure group.

8.4.2 Constructing the Mining Model

Let's use the Data Mining Wizard again to quickly create the sales forecasting model.

1. Choose the *From existing cube* option and *Microsoft Time Series* as an algorithm in the first two steps of the wizard.

2. In the Select the Source Cube Dimension step, select the *Product* dimension from the SOS OLAP cube.
3. In the Select the Case Key step, select the *Category* attribute (Figure 8.20).

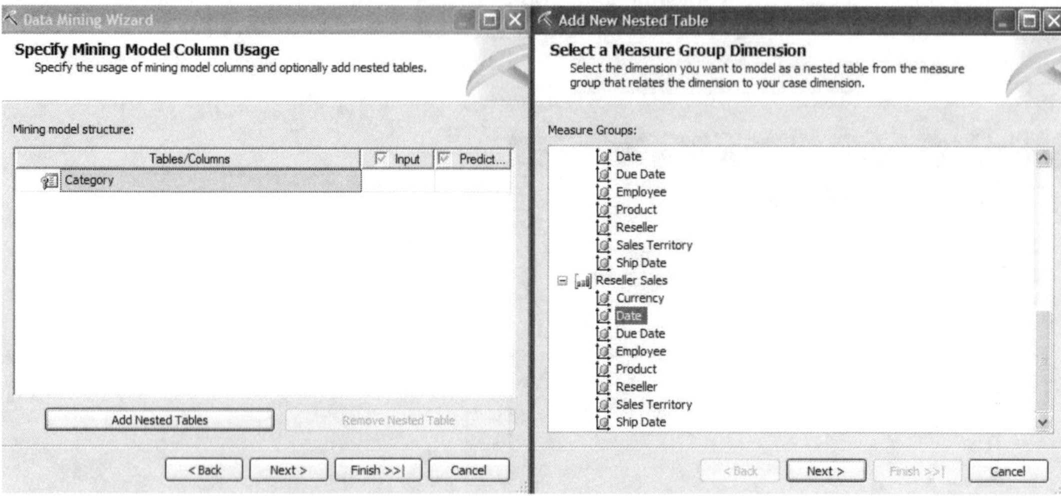

Figure 8.21 The time information is derived from the Date nested dimension.

4. Skip the Select Case Level Columns step without making any selections.
5. In the Specify Mining Model Column Usage step, click the *Add Nested Table* button to add the *Date* dimension as a nested table.
6. In the Select a Measure Group Dimension step, select the *Date* dimension (Figure 8.21) from the **Reseller Sales** measure group.

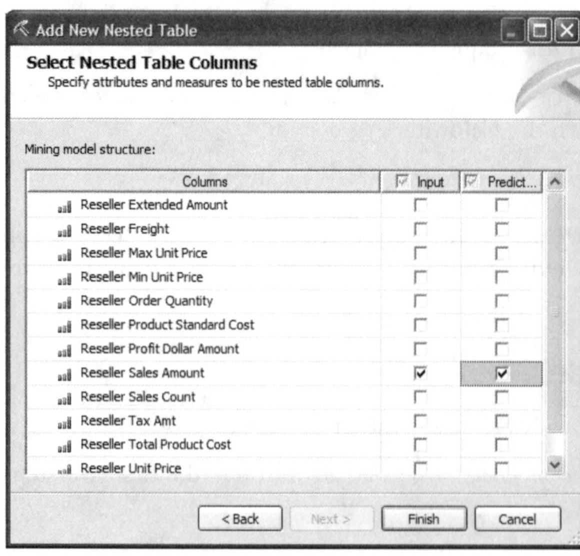

Figure 8.22 Select the predicted measure as both Input and Predict column to correlate the data series.

7. In the Select Nested Table Key step, select the *Time Index* attribute.

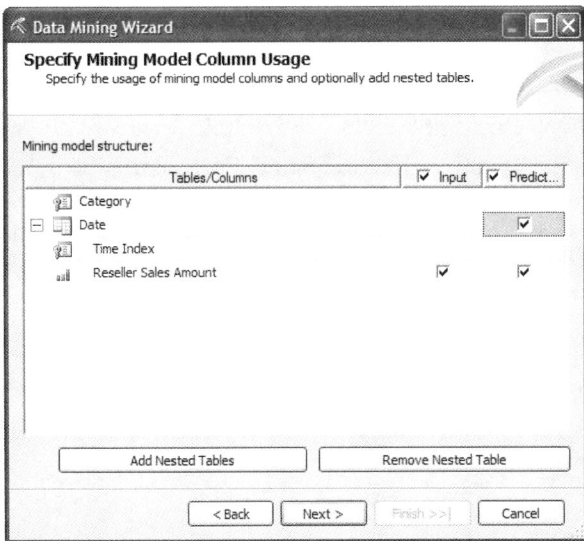

Figure 8.23 Set the nested table as a Predict column.

An interesting feature of the Microsoft Time Series algorithm is cross prediction. It can detect correlations among data series and use these correlations for predictions. For example, if the sales of Accessories and Clothing product categories follow the same historical sales pattern, the algorithm may decide to use a formula to forecast the Accessories sales from the Clothing historical sales.

8. In the Select Nested Table Columns Step (Figure 8.22), select the Reseller Sales Amount as both an Input and Predict column to enable cross prediction. Click Finish to return to the Specify Mining Model Column Usage step (Figure 8.23).

9. Check the *Predict* checkbox next to the Date nested table and click Next.

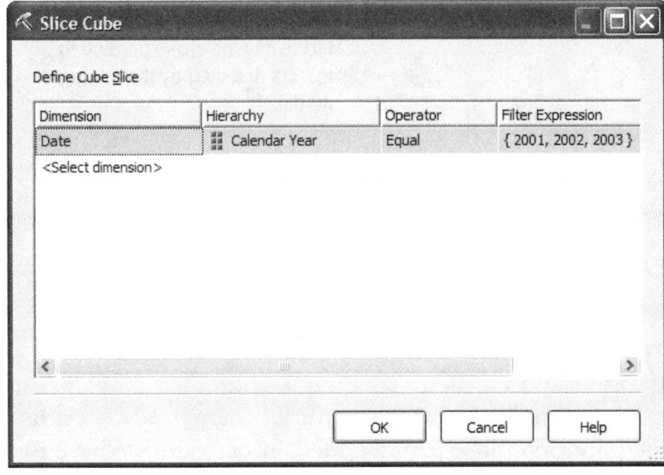

Figure 8.24 Create a cube slice to predict the 2004 sales based on the historical sales from 2001 to 2003.

10. In the Specify Columns' Content and Data Type step, change the Data Type of the Category attribute to *Text* so it matches the underlying data type of the Category attribute. The Content Type of the Time Index attribute should be set to *Key Time*. If it isn't, expand the Content Type dropdown of the Time Index attribute and select *Key Time*. Click Next.

11. Since we need to predict the 2004 sales, use the Slice Cube step to create a cube slice that filters both the case and nested table data for years 2001, 2002, and 2003 (Figure 8.24).

12. In the Completing the Wizard step, name the mining structure **Sales Forecasting** and the mining model **SalesForecastingTS**. Check the *Allow drill through* checkbox because the Time Series algorithm viewer needs to fetch the training cases to display the visualization. Leave the *Create mining model dimension* and *Create cube using mining model dimension* options unchecked. Click Finish to generate the mining structure.

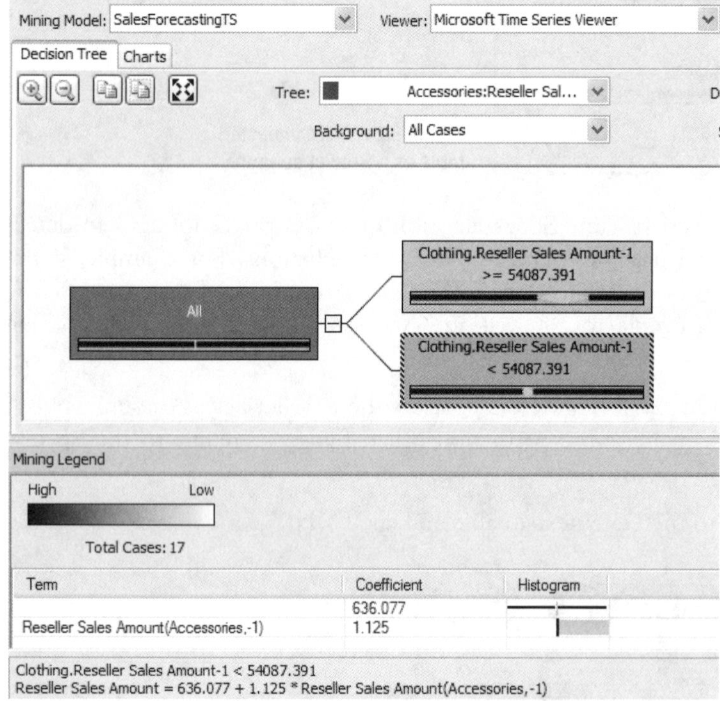

Figure 8.25 Use the Decision Tree tab to see the cross prediction results detected by the mining model.

8.4.3 Exploring the Mining Model

The Time Series Mining Model Viewer has two tabs. As noted, a unique feature of the Time Series algorithm is its cross-prediction capabilities. You can use the Decision Tree tab (Figure 8.25) to see the cross prediction results.

Understanding the Decision Trees tab

The mining model has detected a strong correlation between the historical data series of the Accessories and Clothing product categories. Similar to the Microsoft Decision Trees algorithm, the Time Series algorithm may split the population in separate nodes. In our case, we have two input variables.

Understanding the tree graph

First, we have the Accessories.Reseller Sales Amount for which the auto-regression tree is built (also called *prediction target*). Second, we have Clothing.Reseller Sales Amount which happens to be an input variable for this tree. As with the Decision Trees algorithm, the shading of the tree node signifies the number of the cases in that node. The darker the shading is, the larger the population of that node is. For example, select the Clothing.Reseller Sales Amount-1 node (see again Figure 8.25) and observe that it has 17 Accessories members out of the total 29 Accessories members.

Besides the first *All* node, each node has a prediction formula (called *auto-regression* formula) that the model will use to predict future values. In our case, the algorithm has split the tree on the Clothing.Reseller Sales Amount measure. This means that different prediction formulas will be used for the sales of Accessories depending on how well the sales of Clothing went the month before, i.e. depending on Clothing.Reseller Sales Amount-1.

Note Clothing.Reseller Sales Amount - 1 (t-1) refers to the previous period. In our case, t-1 is the previous month since the periodicity of our model is month. t-1 is **not** the last historical month (the last month before the cutoff date of December 31, 2003). It is a relative future period that comes before a given forecast period. For example, if the model is calculating the forecasted sales for March 2004, then t-1 refers to February 2004.

Selecting the Clothing Reseller Sales Amount < 54,087 node reveals that if we sold less than $54,087 of Clothing the month before, the expected Accessories sales amount would be calculated as $636.077+ 1.125*A(-1), where A(-1) is the Accessories sales amount the month before. For example, if we sold $1,000 worth of Accessories in February 2004, then the mean expectation for March Accessories sales amount will be $636+$1,125 = $1,751. Of course, the regression formula for the other node (Clothing sales > 54,087) will be rather different.

Understanding the diamond chart

Each node also has a diamond chart that represents the mean value of the node and the certainty of the prediction. The node selected in Figure 8.25 consists of Accessories data points where the Clothing sales the month before accounted for less than $54,087. The diamond is positioned almost in the center of the chart. This means that the mean value in this group almost coincides with the overall mean value of all Accessories points. In comparison, the diamond in the other group (Clothing sales > 54087) is somewhat shifted to the right, meaning that its mean value is bigger than the overall mean value.

The thinner the diamond is, the more accurate prediction this node will produce. For example, judging from the small diamond shape in the selected node, the uncertainty in predicting future Accessories sales is going to be relatively small. As our sales keep growing, the Clothing sales amount will likely cross the $54,087 threshold and the prediction formula of the node with Clothing sales > $54,087 will be considered. Regardless of what the exact formula is, its prediction uncertainty will be much higher.

Understanding the Charts tab

The Charts tab (Figure 8.26) gives you the anticipated view of the sales forecast data in a chart format that less technically savvy users can digest easily. The Y-axis represents the data series values, while the X-axis represents time. The vertical line divides the historical values and the forecasted values. By using the *Prediction steps* field, you can adjust the number of the forecasted periods. The default value is five, which, in our example, means that the chart shows the forecasted values for the first five mounts of 2004.

You can use the chart legend to select which data series you want to observe. In our case, I chose to have the Clothing (the top line in the chart), Accessories (the middle line), and Bikes (the bottom line) data series displayed on the chart. As you can see, the Clothing and Accessories lines have a strong correlation towards the end of the historical period chosen, which explains the Decision Trees results. Interestingly, there were two peaks in the Clothing and Accessories sales during the summer months in 2002 and 2003 which may be worth investigating. Perhaps, the Adventure Works customers use the summer vacation to hit the road?

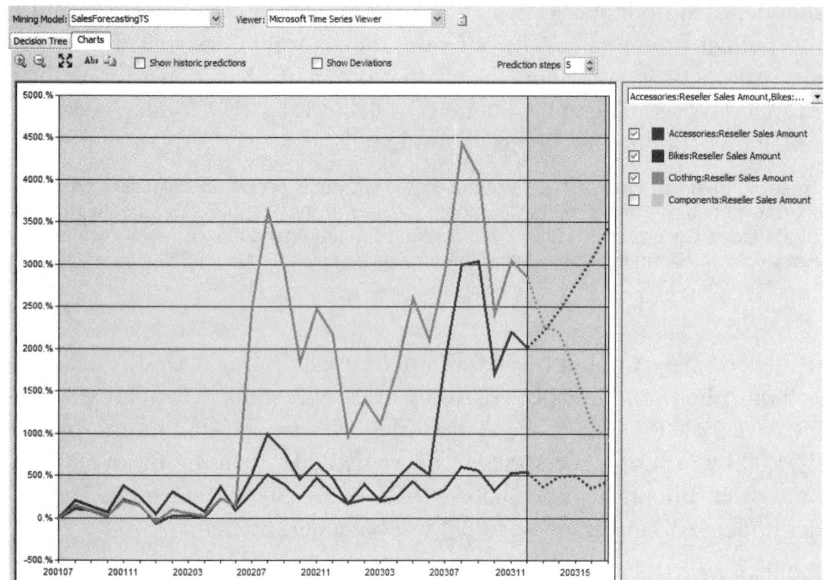

Figure 8.26 Use the Chart tab to see the historical and forecasted values over time.

Overall, the Adventure Works management is unlikely to rejoice over the forecasted results. The bike sales will remain relatively flat, while the Clothing sales will plummet. The only sunny forecast is that the Accessories sales will grow. Or will they?

8.4.4 Fine-tuning the Mining Model

At this point, the most attentive readers will probably notice something odd. The model forecasts that Accessories sales will grow almost linearly. But the Decision Trees results indicated a split at the $54,087 threshold. As the chart indicates, the Clothing sales are expected to decline and fall below $54,000 in February 2004 (select only Clothing in the chart legend to see the actual sales figures on the Y-axis). Why then are the Accessories sales unaffected?

Understanding deviation results

To solve this puzzle, check the Show Deviations checkbox. When you do this, the chart plot is updated to show deviation vertical lines for each forecasted period (Figure 8.27). Hover the mouse cursor over the Accessories line where its X-coordinate is somewhere near February 2004. The tooltip shows that the standard deviation for this prediction result is +/-- 1251%. This is a really high deviation which is likely to skew the predication results.

How can we make our forecasted results more accurate? In short, there is really no exact science to do so. The key is to try different models and compare them using our best judgment and data knowledge. For example, looking at the graph again, there is a low volume Clothing sales plateau back in 2001-2002. Is this by accident? As it stands, the model does not seem to answer this question with a high degree of certainty. Therefore, when the forward-predicted mean for Clothing sales declines below $54,087, this uncertainty propagates into the predicted results for the Accessories sales.

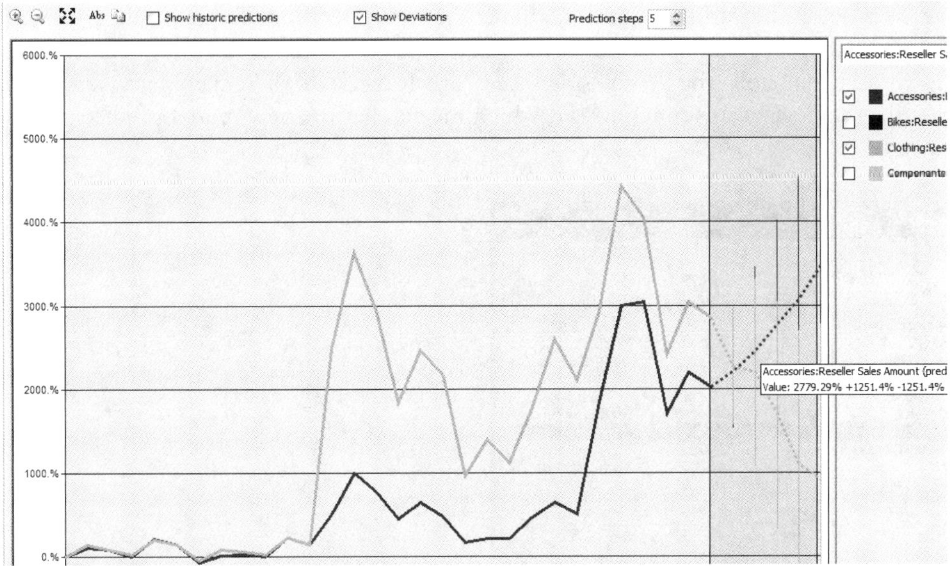

Figure 8.27 Enable Show Deviation to evaluate the accuracy of the Time Series algorithm.

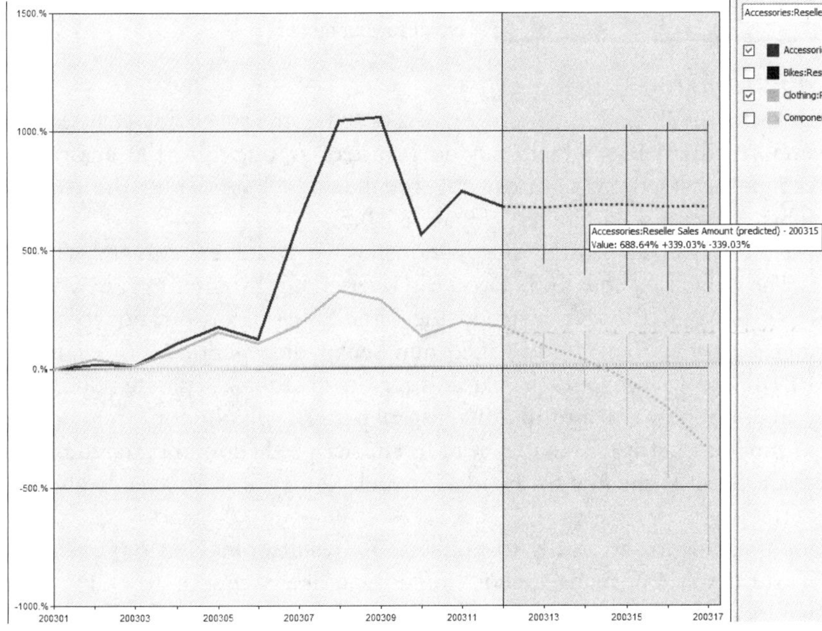

Figure 8.28 Exercise different "what-if" scenarios with the input dataset to improve the accuracy of the predicted results.

Filtering the input dataset

A more accurate forecasting model should reflect our understanding about the input data. Suppose we determine that the low values of Clothing sales are abnormal and shouldn't affect the prediction. The next step will be to filter them out by changing the cube slice to exclude years 2001 and 2002. You can access the Slice Cube dialog by flipping to the Mining Models tab, right-clicking on the SalesForecastingTS model, and choosing *Define Mining Structure Cube Slice.*

Once we re-process the structure and examine the new Decision Trees results, you will notice that there are no correlations among the data series. Examining the new chart graph (Figure 8.28) reveals that now the Accessories sales are forecasted to remain fairly constant. More importantly, the deviation is much lower, which means that the new model predicts with a higher certainty.

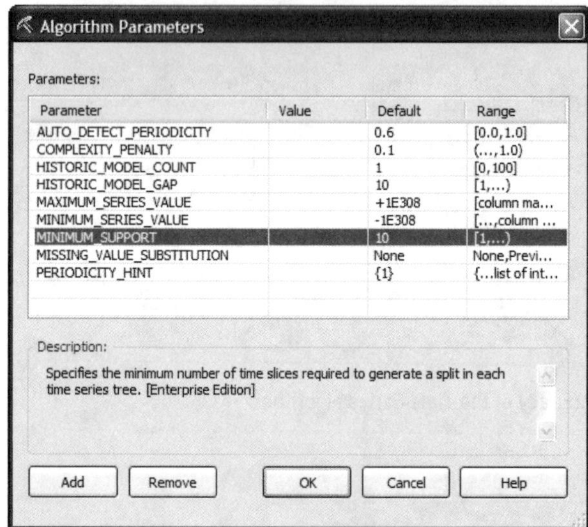

Figure 8.29 Experiment with different algorithm parameters to optimize your model.

Adjusting the model parameters

Alternatively, we could try different algorithm parameters. As noted in the preceding chapter, the Microsoft algorithms support parameters which can be adjusted to fine-tune the algorithm. Algorithm parameters can be accessed by right-clicking on the model header in the Mining Models tab and choosing Set Algorithm Parameters (Figure 8.29).

In the case of the Time Series algorithm, one parameter we could experiment with is MINIMUM_SUPPORT. The default value is 10 but you can overwrite it by entering a new value in the Value column. MINIMUM_SUPPORT instructs the Time Series algorithm not to create prediction nodes for patterns shorter than the specified number of time periods. For example, setting MINIMUM_SUPPORT to 15, prevents the algorithm from creating a separate node for a history pattern shorter than 15 months. As a result, this history pattern will not contribute to the prediction results quite as much as before. This may lead to smaller prediction uncertainties, but it does not necessarily mean that it is the key to the ideal model. Rather, it is a valuable alternative for you to explore.

Once the model is optimized, you are ready to publicize its results. Since, in our scenario, you will be the bearer of bad news, AW management would most likely request to see the time series results broken down further, e.g. to find out the forecasted trends by product subcategory.

You can address this requirement by changing the mining model (or creating a new model) to use the Subcategory attribute from the Product dimension (the Case Level Columns table in the Mining Structure tab) as a case key.

8.5 SSIS Integration

Besides its natural usage scenario to build intelligent application, data mining can be used in interesting ways to implement flexible data integration scenarios. SSIS includes a variety of data mining transformation tasks that allows you to perform predictions and react to the predicted results in the data integration flow. For example, imagine that Adventure Works has contacted a marketing agency and obtained a mailing list of potential customers as a comma-delimited flat file. Adventure Works would like to pass the customer dataset by the Customer Profiling mining model we've built to find out which customers will be willing to purchase an expensive bike model.

As you would recall, in section 8.2, we identified three customer clusters that tend to spend more on average – YUPs, Professionals, and Workers. Suppose that Adventure Works management is interested only in targeting the first two clusters. We will create an SSIS package that filters the customer list and splits it into two files (one for YUPs and one for Professionals).

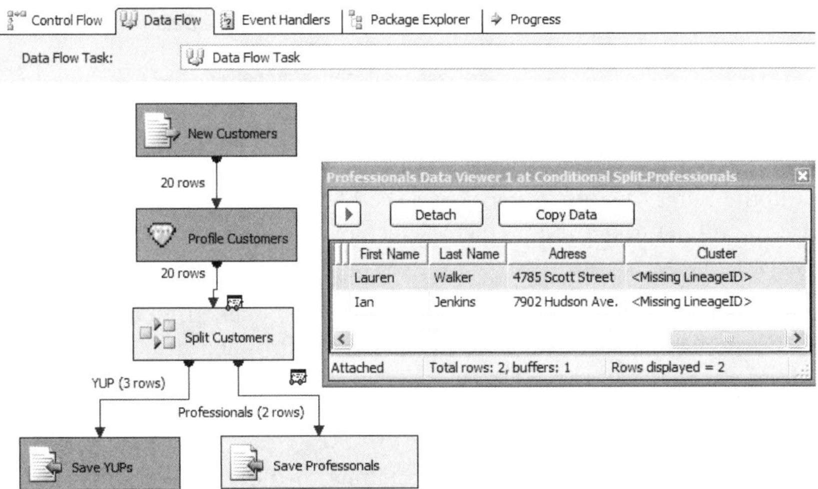

Figure 8.30 The Data Mining Query task can be used to obtain prediction results from a model.

8.5.1 Building a Data Mining-aware Integration Package

The SSIS project (Customer Profiling) and a sample input flat file can be found in the Ch07 folder. Thanks to the handy Data Mining Query Task, implementing the SSIS integration package (Filter Customers.dtsx) is trivial. The package control flow consists of a single data transformation task. The data flow of this task in action is shown in Figure 8.30.

First, a Flat File Source Task (New Customers) is used to parse the comma-delimited file and expose its content as an input to the Data Mining Query Task. The Data Mining Query Task (Profile Customers) passes the dataset as an input to the CustomerProfilingMC mining model. The mining model profiles the customers and assigns them to clusters. Next, a Conditional Split

Task (Split Customers) is used to redirect the YUP cluster customers and Professionals cluster customers to different flows. For example, in Figure 8.30, the mining model has classified two customers as professionals (belonging to the Professional cluster). These customers are shown in the Data Viewer. Finally, the results of the Data Mining Query task are saved in two flat files using two Flat File Destination tasks.

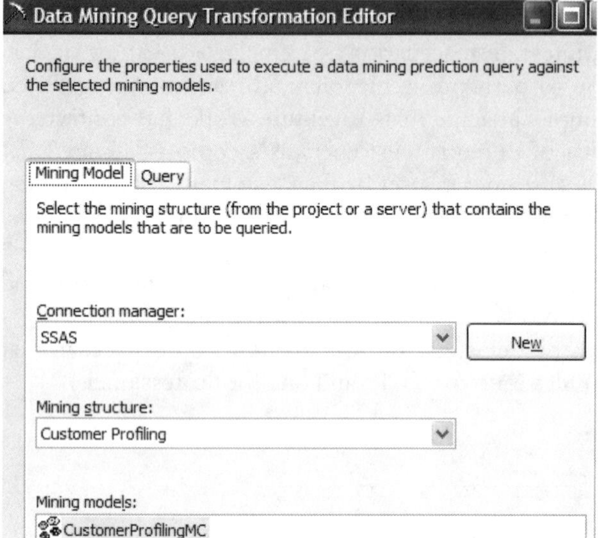

Figure 8.31 Configure the Data Mining Query Task to use the required mining model.

8.5.2 Working with the Data Mining Query Task

The most important task in the Filter Customers package is the Data Mining Query Task (Profile Customers) which queries the model to get the predicted clusters. Follow these steps to configure the Profile Customers task.

1. Use the Mining Model tab (Figure 8.31) to specify which model will be queried. In our case, this is the CustomerProfilingMC model that is contained in the Customer Profiling structure.
2. Switch to the Query tab and click on the Build New Query button to open the Data Mining Query Builder (Figure 8.32).
3. Drag the FirstName, LastName, and AdressLine1 input columns to the grid so the marketing department can contact the identified customers.
4. Use the *Cluster* prediction function to retrieve the predicted cluster.

Note that when launched from the Data Mining Query Task, the Data Mining Query Builder doesn't give you an option to execute the query. That's because the input dataset will be supplied during runtime. If all is well, when you execute the package, you will see two files in the root folder of the C drive. In my case, the yup.txt file contains three customers, while the professionals.txt has two.

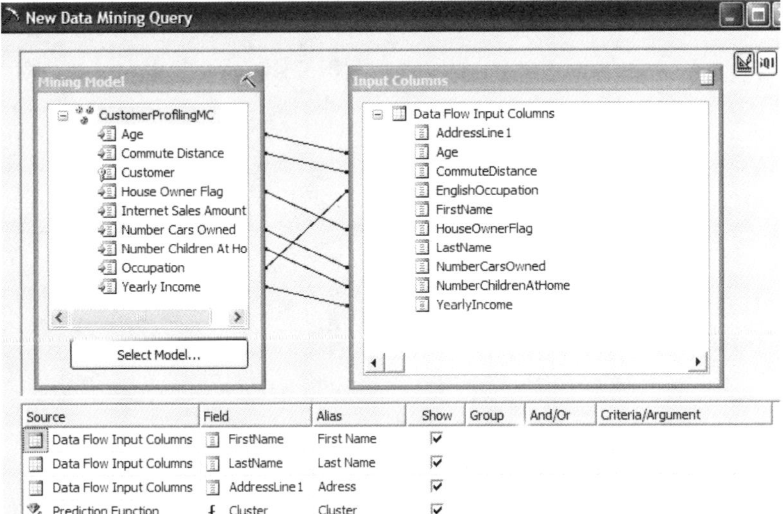

Figure 8.32 Use the Cluster function to predict the customer cluster.

8.6 Summary

If you already have UDM in place, OLAP data mining models can extend and complement the dimensional model to provide richer data analytics. Any UDM dimension can be used as an input table to the mining model. When nested tables are needed, they can be derived from related dimensions. The results from the OLAP mining model can be applied back to enhance UDM in the form of data mining dimensions and cubes.

The Microsoft Business Intelligence Platform is an integrated framework whose components can be combined together to form synergetic solutions. Leverage mining predictions to build intelligent business applications. Use the SSIS mining tasks to implement intelligent integration flows.

8.7 Resources

Extending Microsoft SQL Server 2000 Reporting Services with Custom Code
(http://shrinkster.com/5k7) – Excerpted from my book, *Microsoft Reporting Services in Action*, this article demonstrates how you can use mathematical regression algorithms to forecast data series using the OpenForecast Open Source package.

The OpenForecast website
(http://openforecast.sourceforge.net) -- OpenForecast contains forecasting models written in Java that can be applied to any data series.

Autoregressive Tree Models for Time-Series Analysis
(http://shrinkster.com/8cu) – This paper from Microsoft Research covers the Autoregressive Tree mathematical model that powers the Microsoft Time Series algorithm.

PART 3

Programming Analysis Services

By now, we've implemented the Data Schema and Dimensional Model layers of the fictitious Adventure Works OLAP UDM. Now it's time to build the Calculations UDM layer. MDX is the query language we can use to extend UDM and help you address more involved business requirements.

MDX supports a variety of functions that allow you to navigate the dimensional model both horizontally and vertically. There are three main types of MDX expressions that you can author – calculated members, named sets, and subcube expressions. Calculated members can be used for creating expression-based measures and dimension members. Use named sets to alias commonly used MDX sets. Subcube expressions allow you to retrieve and change the cube data down to the individual cells.

No programming language is perfect. MDX can be extended by using pre-defined and custom functions. Analysis Services comes with many canned functions encapsulated in the Excel and VBA libraries. Consider moving more complicated programming logic in the form of Analysis Services stored procedures.

The end-user model helps you implement a rich semantic layer in the form of KPIs, actions, perspectives, and translations. Its main focus is extending UDM to make the user experience more intuitive and feature-rich.

Chapter 9

MDX Fundamentals

As you would probably agree, Microsoft Analysis Services 2005 allows you to build quickly dimensional models that provide essential OLAP and data mining features. Chances are, however, that in real life you may need to go beyond building basic cubes only. Business needs may require transcending the dimensional model boundaries and enhancing UDM with business logic. MDX gives you the programmatic power needed to travel the "last mile" needed to unlock the full potential of UDM.

In this chapter, I will introduce you to MDX programming. You will learn:

- What MDX is and how it is used in UDM.
- How the cube space is defined and how you can reference it.
- How the cube aggregates.
- How to write MDX expressions.
- How to use MDX to navigate dimensions both horizontally and vertically.

We will put our MDX knowledge in practice by extending the SOS OLAP UDM with useful MDX expressions that solve real business needs. You can find the finished solution by opening the Ch09 solution file.

9.1 Understanding MDX

Back in chapter 1, we said that one of the FASMI rules for evaluating an OLAP server is *Analysis*. The Analysis rule implies that every OLAP server should support complex calculations that are otherwise difficult or impossible to implement in a relational database. At the same time, implementing such calculations shouldn't mandate learning a professional programming language and advanced programming skills. Instead, business calculations and logic should be implemented in the form of expressions that are simple to understand and maintain. With Analysis Services, database developers can use MDX to fulfill the Analysis rule.

9.1.1 What is MDX?

MDX stands for **M**ulti**D**imensional E**X**pressions. Just like a relational database understands SQL, MDX is the programming language that UDM "speaks". MDX is not exclusive to SSAS though. Over the years, MDX has become the lingua franca of OLAP. Most OLAP vendors (see the full list at *www.xmla.org*) have embraced or are currently adopting the XMLA specification. As a result, there are many OLAP servers and browsers on the market that leverage MDX as a programming language in one form or another.

Note Originally introduced in 1997 as a part of the OLE DB for OLAP specification (see Resources), MDX grammar is now part of the XMLA specification. As of the time of this writing, the XMLA council is working on a new MDX-based specification for querying OLAP servers called mdXML. The mdXML grammar will be XML-based and programming language independent.

MDX is specifically designed for multi-dimensional reporting and analysis. Once you step beyond the basic dimensional model, you need MDX to implement more involved business logic. For example, in the preceding chapters, we built a dimensional model (SOS OLAP) to address the main data analytics requirements posed by the Adventure Works information workers. Undoubtedly, our model provides a solid foundation for efficient data aggregation and data mining. However, as useful as it is, our model cannot answer some important questions that your business users may be interested in. For example, they may want to see the percentage profit of each product. Or, they may want to compare the percentage change in revenue between two parallel time periods. How about implementing key performance indicators (KPIs) to track vital business metrics?

Such requirements can only be addressed programmatically by using MDX. As noted, the *Analysis* rule emphasizes that the expression language should be simple to use. To this extent, MDX is designed as an expression-based language, not a full-blown programming language, such as Visual Basic or C#. For example, MDX doesn't support variables, loop statements, object-oriented constructs, etc. However, although MDX is light-weight, it is very powerful.

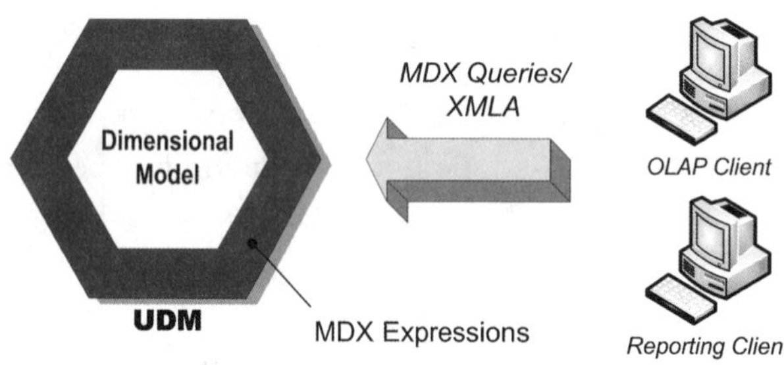

Figure 9.1 Use MDX to query UDM or enhance it with business logic in the form of MDX expressions.

9.1.2 How is MDX Used in UDM?

In UDM, MDX is used in two main ways, as Figure 9.1 demonstrates. First, custom applications and OLAP browsers use MDX to query UDM. In addition, MDX expressions can be used to implement the Calculations layer of UDM and enhance its analytic power.

MDX queries

Just like you can use SQL to extract data from a relational database, you can send MDX query statements to an SSAS server to retrieve multidimensional data. A smart OLAP browser, of course, could (and should) shield end users from the MDX technicalities, so the user can be totally oblivious to the MDX existence. For example, the Microsoft OWC PivotTable component, which powers the Cube Browser tab of the Cube Designer, constructs and sends MDX queries behind the scenes every time you change the pivot report.

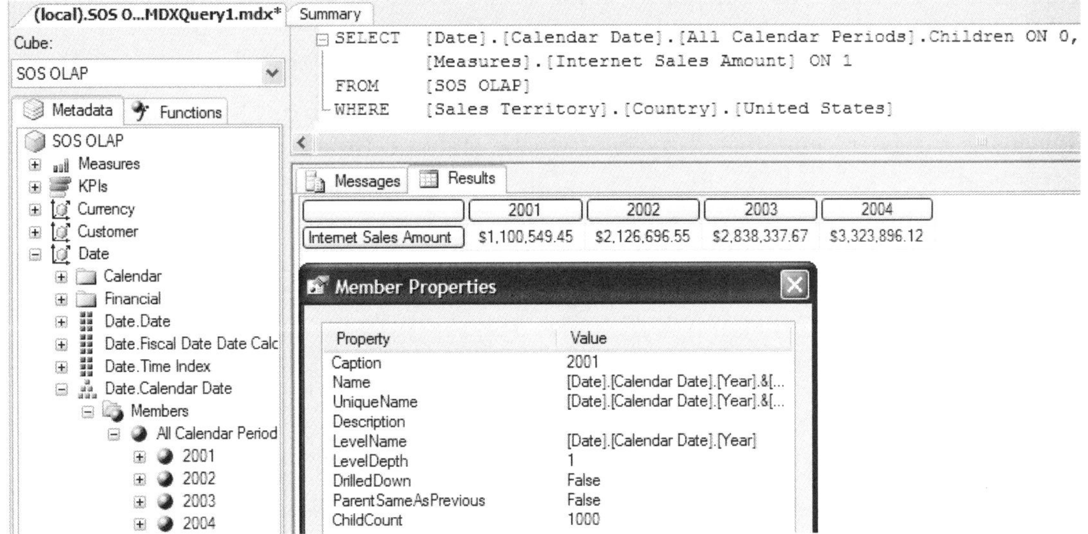

Figure 9.2 Although MDX resembles SQL, it is very different since it's designed for multi-dimensional data source.

Basic MDX query

I will cover MDX queries in more details in chapter 17. In case you need the basics fast, Figure 9.2 shows a simple MDX statement which I've authored using the SQL Server Management Studio. The MDX statement queries the SOS OLAP UDM and retrieves the Adventure Works Internet sales for the United States broken down by years.

The MDX Designer included in the SQL Server Management Studio makes it easy to create MDX queries. Once you connect to the SSAS Server you want to query, you can just drag dimensions and measures from the Metadata tab. In this case, I wanted to see the sales numbers in a tabular format with Years on columns. To show the members of the Year attribute hierarchy, I used the *Children* function. This MDX function returns the members below a given dimension member (in this case, the *All* member). The actual report values are derived from the Internet Sales Amount measure.

Tip In the MDX Designer Results grid, you can double-click on the member name to open the Member Properties dialog (Figure 9.2) and see the member standard properties, such as UniqueName and Caption.

Sometimes, you may hear MDX experts referring to the ROWS and COLUMNS axes of the query as *dicers* since they are used to dice the cube by the requested dimensions and measures. MDX supports *Axis* function, so COLUMNS is Axis(0) and ROWS is Axis(1). You can omit the Axis function and use only the index as follows:

```
SELECT  [Date].[Calendar Date].[All Calendar Periods].Children ON 0,
        [Measures].[Internet Sales Amount] ON 1
FROM    [SOS OLAP]
WHERE   [Sales Territory].[Country].[United States]
```

Another term you may hear is *slicer*, which refers to the WHERE clause that is used to filter the cube data. For example, the query slicer in the sample MDX query shown in Figure 9.2 filters sales in the United States only.

MDX vs. SQL

At a glance, the MDX syntax looks deceptively similar to SQL. But, as Shrek would conclude, sometimes things are not what they appear to be. Table 2.3 outlines the major differences between MDX and SQL.

Table 9.1 Comparing SQL and MDX.

Characteristic	SQL	MDX
Database schema	Relational (two-dimensional)	Multi-dimensional
Object relationships (joins)	Must be specified	Pre-defined in the metadata
Data relationship	Position (agnostic)	Position-aware
Data Definition Language	Full support	Limited support

To start with, the fundamental difference between the two languages is the type of data sources they are designed to query. SQL is designed to retrieve data from relational (two-dimensional) schemas. In comparison, MDX targets multi-dimensional data sources. For example, MDX has commands that you can use to navigate the dimensional hierarchies, such as *Children*, *Parent*, *Descendants*, etc. In addition, with SQL, you need to specify how two tables are related by using JOIN constructs. With MDX, joins are not needed because the object relationships are defined at the metadata level.

SQL is position-agnostic and it doesn't care about where a given row is located in a relational table. With MDX, however, the position of a given member in a dimension hierarchy is of utmost importance. The location-aware nature of MDX allows you to correlate data across dimension members, e.g. to find out how sales figures compare between two parallel quarters. Finally, besides data retrieval commands, SQL provides full support for DDL commands, such as CREATE, INSERT, ALTER, etc. In comparison, MDX provides limited support for manipulating the cube structure, e.g. the CREATE MEMBER statement that we will use in this chapter to create a calculated member.

MDX expressions

MDX can also be used for writing *expressions*. MDX expressions are small chunks of MDX programming logic which you can use to enhance your cubes with business calculations. The advantage of implementing these calculations in MDX is that they will be centralized in one place, the UDM, instead of being defined and re-defined in Excel spreadsheets, reporting tools, etc. UDM supports three main types of MDX expressions:

- *Calculated members* – As its name suggests, a calculated member is a dimension member whose value is derived during runtime by using an MDX expression. For example, you can create a calculated member Total Sales Amount as a sum of Internet Sales Amount and Reseller Sales Amount.
- *Named sets* – Just like a SQL view can be used to encapsulate a complex SQL statement, an MDX named set can be used to assign an alias to a given subset of the cube data. For

example, you can create a set named Bestselling Products that will return the ten top selling products. Once this is done, the end user can use the named set to slice the cube, if the user wants to see the sales figures for these products only. In the absence of a named dataset, the user has to use the capabilities of the OLAP browser to sort the product sales in descending order to be able to identify the bestselling products.

- *Subcube expressions* – Sometimes, you may need to overwrite the value of a given cube cell or a range of cells. Subcube expressions allows you to implement such targeted calculations. You can specify the scope of the expression. Once you assign the value of the scope, the values of all cube cells inside that scope will be changed.

Besides the abovementioned expression types, MDX expressions can be used for other things. For example, as I demonstrated in chapter 5, you can use MDX expressions to derive default dimension members, custom member formulas, and unary operators.

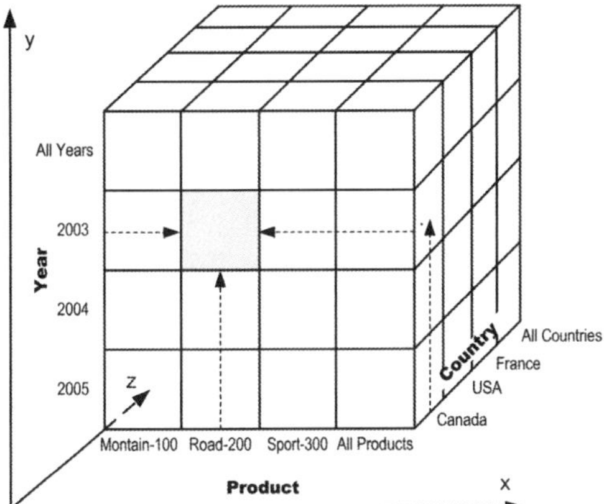

Figure 9.3 The cube space is defined by its attribute hierarchies; multi-level hierarchies are optional.

9.1.3 Tuples and Sets

MDX expressions give you the ultimate power to programmatically query and change the cube space all the way down to the individual cells. To use MDX effectively, you need to understand how to navigate the cube space. As noted in chapter 3, UDM is an attribute-based model. What this means is that the cube space is defined by its attribute hierarchies. Take for example the cube shown in Figure 9.3, which represents a simplified version of the SOS OLAP cube. It has only three attribute hierarchies (Product, Country, and Year) and each attribute hierarchy has only four members. In addition, for the sake of simplicity, let's assume that the cube has a single measure (let's call it Sales Amount).

Tuples

Each cell in this cube is found at the intersection of members taken from *all* attribute hierarchies defined in the cube. For example, the shaded cell in Figure 9.3 is located at coordinates Product ⇨ Product ⇨ Mountain-100, Date ⇨ Year ⇨ 2004, Sales Territory ⇨ Country ⇨ All Countries. To visualize this better, you may find it easier to map the cube space to the familiar three-dimensional coordinate system with its origin (0, 0, 0) found at the intersection of the All members taken from all hierarchies in the cube (assuming that all attribute hierarchies have All members defined).

Then, the x axis coordinate is defined by the Mountain-100 member of the Product attribute hierarchy in Product dimension. The y axis coordinate is represented by the 2004 member of the Year attribute hierarchy, which is part of the Date dimension. Finally, the z axis coordinate is defined by the All Countries member of the Country attribute hierarchy in the Sales Territory dimension.

Since our fictitious cube has three attribute hierarchies only, each cell is identified by a triple geometrical coordinate. If we add a fourth hierarchy, each cell will be identified by a quadruple coordinate. Five hierarchies will produce a quin*tuple*; six – sex*tuple*; seven – sep*tuple*, and so on. For the sake of simplicity (and preserving your sanity!), the MDX terminology introduces a generic coordinate called *tuple*.

Definition A tuple is a multi-dimensional coordinate produced by *one* member taken from one or more attribute hierarchies. A tuple identifies a single cell in the cube space.

By the way, there is no consensus about how tuple should be pronounced. The SSAS team tends to pronounce it as *too-ple* (as in pupil), but you may hear it being pronounced as *tup-ple* (as in couple). Lexical ambiguities aside, note that our definition stresses that a tuple can include only one member from a given attribute hierarchy. That's because if we have more than one, e.g. Year.2003 and Year.2004, then the tuple will reference more than one cell, which contradicts its definition.

Tuple syntax

From a syntactical standpoint, the attribute members included in the tuple must be enclosed in parenthesis and separated by comma. Dot separators are used to delimit the hierarchy levels. Thus, `Product.Product.[Road-200]` specifies the Road-200 member of the Product attribute hierarchy which is defined in the Product dimension. Ordering of the attribute hierarchies inside a tuple is irrelevant (with a forthcoming caveat which I will explain when discussing MDX sets). In addition, if the attribute hierarchy or the member name is an MDX reserved word, contains an empty space, or is a number, it must be enclosed in parentheses (square brackets), e.g.:

```
(Product.Product.Road-200, Date.Year.[2003], [Sales Territory].Country.Canada)
```

It is a good practice to use parentheses anyway, so from now on, I will use them to enclose all hierarchies and members names. Finally, note also that MDX is not case-sensitive, so [Product], [product], and [PRODUCT] can all be used interchangeably.

Complete and partial tuples

If a tuple includes a member from each attribute hierarchy defined in the cube, the tuple is a complete tuple. As you can imagine, having to specify all attribute hierarchies could be a recipe for an ultimate nightmare. Even a relatively moderate cube, as our SOS OLAP cube, could have tens and hundreds of attribute hierarchies. Instead of using complete tuples, MDX allows us to use partial tuples that include only the attribute hierarchies we are interested in. However, if we omit the rest of the hierarchies, how would UDM identify cell uniquely? It's like trying to identify a point in a three-dimensional space with only X and Y coordinates.

If turns out that if a member of a given attribute hierarchy is not explicitly specified, MDX will use the concept of the *current member* to resolve the members of the omitted attribute hierarchies. Figure 9.4 should make this clear. Here, I created a pivot report that shows the resale sales broken down by the *Country* attribute hierarchy (Sales Territory dimension) on rows and

Year attribute hierarchy (Date dimension) on columns. In addition, a cube slicer is used to filter only sales for the member *Mountain-100 Black, 38* from the Product.Product attribute hierarchy.

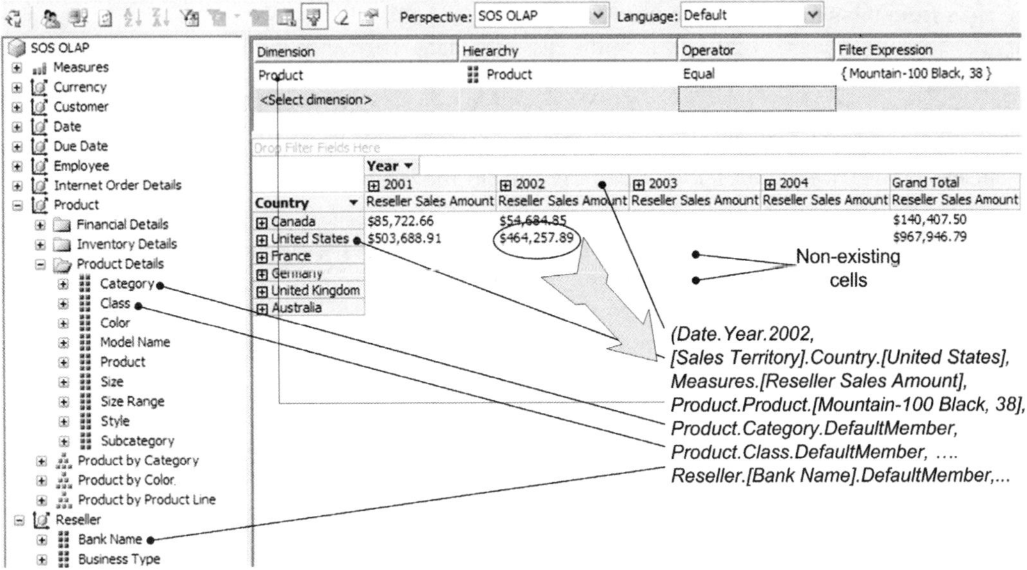

Figure 9.4 Partial tuples are resolved by using the current member of all attribute hierarchies defined in the cube.

Although not so obvious, the tuple of the highlighted cell with a value of $464, 257.89 is produced by the current members of *all* attribute hierarchies defined in the cube. Behind the scenes, the calculation engine will inspect the CurrentMember property of each attribute hierarchy. Next, the calculation engine will resolve CurrentMember according to how the hierarchy is used by the query. In this case, members of three attribute hierarchies ([Date].[Year].[2002], [Sales Territory].[Country].[United States], and [Measures].[Reseller Sales Amount]) are specified explicitly in the resulting query. Therefore, the CurrentMember property of these hierarchies returns exactly these members.

Definition The dimensions explicitly indicated in the tuple describe the tuple *dimensionality*. For example, the dimensionality of the tuple ([Date].[Year].[2002], [Sales Territory].[Country].[United States], [Measures].[Reseller Sales Amount]) consists of the Date, Sales Territory, and Measures dimensions.

From the example shown in Figure 9.4, it should be clear that MDX treats all measures as members of a dimension called *Measures* irrespective of the measure group they belong to. The Measures dimension has only one level. For example, to MDX the Reseller Sales Amount measure is a member of the Measures dimension.

The fourth member of the tuple (Mountain-100 Black, 38) comes from the cube slicer. The rest of the attribute hierarchy members are implicitly inferred. Specifically, the calculation engine will map CurrentMember to the default member of each hierarchy. As noted in chapter 4, for attribute hierarchies (attributes with IsAggregatable=True), the default member is usually the *All* member. For instance, going back to Figure 9.3, if we want to reference the cell above the highlighted cell, the All member (All Years) from the Date.Year hierarchy will be used. The net result returned from the query will be the Canada sales for Road-200 aggregated over *all* years (all members of the Year attribute hierarchy). What if the *All* member for a given attribute hierarchy is suppressed (IsAggregatable=False)? In this case, the server will select the first member.

Empty cells from missing or NULL fact data

So far, we assumed that all tuples will find cells with data. In reality, however, most cubes are rather sparse. For example, glancing back at Figure 9.4, we could see that there are no sales for the Mountain-100 Black in any country for years 2003 and 2004. Empty cells don't take any storage space in the cube. To visualize this, you may think of the cube space as a rather porous Swiss cheese, whose holes correspond to empty cells in the cube.

Tip By default, the Cube Browser suppresses empty cells. To produce the exact report shown in Figure 9.4, make sure you click on the Show Empty Cells toolbar button.

The MDX *IsEmpty* function can be used to check for empty cells. MDX, however, doesn't support a function to determine if a given cell is empty because there were no rows in the fact table or because the fact values were simply NULL. If you need to differentiate between these two conditions, you can convert NULL fact values to zeros (or empty strings) when transforming data, by using named calculations at a DSV level, or by using the NullProcessing option of the measure Source property.

The take-home note about the cube empty cells is that they can still be referenced by tuples. In other words, they are part of the cube addressable space even though they don't take any storage space. For example, the tuple ([Sales Territory].[Country].[France], [Date].[Year].[2002], [Product].[Product].[Mountain-100 Black, 38]) is valid and can be used in an MDX expression to overwrite the value in the empty cell.

Sets

Many MDX expressions take as input (or return) a collection of tuples called a *set* in the MDX terminology. A *set* is a collection of tuples with the same dimensionality.

Definition A *set* is a collection of tuples with the same dimensionality. While the order of the dimensions inside a tuple is irrelevant, all tuples in a set must have the same dimension order.

When requested in MDX queries, a set must be enclosed in braces {}.

SSAS 2000 Moving to UDM, you will find that the syntax rules for using tuples and sets have been relaxed and UDM does automatic type conversion for you. Specifically, UDM converts automatically *Member ⇨ Tuple ⇨ Set*. For example, in SSAS 2000, you needed to enclose a tuple with braces inside a WHERE clause of an MDX query, because the WHERE clause expects a set. In UDM, you don't have to do this, since the calculation engine casts a tuple to a set automatically for you.

Given our definition of a set, Figure 9.5 shows a valid set which consists of two tuples:

```
{([Sales Territory].[Country].[All Countries], [Date].[Year].[2004],
[Product].[Product].[Mountain-100]),
([Sales Territory].[Country].[All Countries], [Date].[Year].[2004],
[Product].[Product].[Road-200])}
```

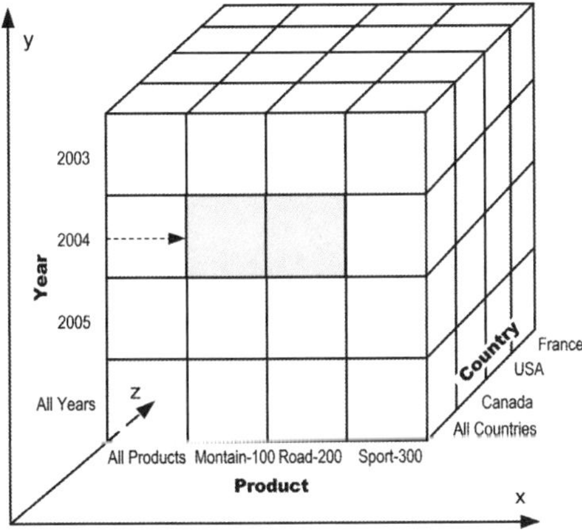

Figure 9.5 A set is a collection of tuples with the same dimensionality.

As our definition of a set stands, a valid set must consists of tuples with the same dimensionality. In this respect, the following set is invalid because its tuples have different dimensionality (the first tuple uses the Customer dimension, while the second uses the Territory dimension):

```
{([Customer].[John Doe], [Date].[Year].[2003], [Product].[Product].[Mountain-100]),
([Sales Territory].[Country].[Canada],
[Date].[Year].[2003], [Product].[Product].[Road-200])}
```

The following set is also invalid because its tuples have different dimension ordering on the Date and Sales Territory dimensions:

```
{([Date].[Year].[2003],[Sales Territory].[Country].[Canada],
[Product].[Product].[Mountain-100]),
([Sales Territory].[Country].[Canada], [Date].[Year].[2003],
[Product].[Product].[Road-200])}
```

		Year				
		2001	2002	2003	2004	Grand Total
Group	Country	Reseller Sales Amount	Reseller Sales Amount	Reseller Sales Amount	Reseller Sales Amount	Reseller Sales Amount
North America	Canada	$1,030,877.82	$3,176,620.29	$3,602,887.84	$1,528,956.15	$9,339,342.10
	United States	$6,552,075.85	$17,622,549.51	$20,071,116.48	$9,362,059.37	$53,607,801.21
Europe	France		$847,630.05	$2,344,926.22	$1,370,433.57	$4,562,989.84
	Germany			$973,543.72	$855,759.82	$1,829,303.54
	United Kingdom		$1,225,107.99	$3,108,609.04	$1,966,705.12	$6,300,422.15
Pacific	Australia			$442,697.55	$412,201.86	$854,899.41

Figure 9.6 Attribute members that do not exist with one another, do not exist in the cube.

9.1.4 How Autoexists Affects The Cube Space

It turns out that the Autoexists behavior, which I introduced in chapter 3, has implications on the cube space. As you would probably recall, the server automatically applies the Autoexists behavior when a query requests attribute hierarchies within the same dimension. For example, the report shown in Figure 9.6 is produced by a query that requests (cross-joins) both the Group and Country attribute hierarchies from the Sales Territory dimension.

When the server receives this query, it determines that both attribute hierarchies belong to the same dimension and returns only the intersection of the attribute members. In our sample report, after applying the Autoexists behavior, the server returns only the countries that are part of the same geographical group, e.g. countries Canada and United States in the North America region.

Non-existing cells

Since Autoexists never returns attribute members from the same dimension that don't exists with one another, it is meaningless to have the corresponding cells in the cube space at all. Indeed, such cells simply do not exist in the cube space. For example, the tuple *([Group].[North America], [Country].[France])* doesn't reference an existing cell in the cube space. Although such tuples can be used in MDX queries and expressions, they will always return empty cells. You cannot place expressions into these cells, nor can you write data.

Autoexists and empty cells

It is important to understand that Autoexists has nothing to do with the fact data. It is applied at a dimension metadata level. What may be confusing is that tuples that reference cells that have missing or NULL fact data and tuples that reference non-existing cells (as a result of the Autoexists), both return empty cells. However, the difference is that, in the first case, the cells *are* part of the cube space and their data can be changed with MDX expressions.

In comparison, non-existing cells simply do not exist in the cube space and cannot be written to. Although MDX expressions trying to write to non-existing cells won't trigger an exception, they won't produce anything because they will be writing to void. It is a bit like this naval game that you used to play with your friend on a piece of paper, whose objective was to sink the opponent's ships by giving two-dimensional coordinates. If the cell coordinates don't find a ship, there is no penalty, but you simply don't score.

Navigational invariance

If the cube space is defined by attribute hierarchies, you may be curious as to what effect the multilevel hierarchies have on the cube space. It is simple – none. The cube space is independent of multilevel hierarchies. Specifically, navigational paths in multilevel hierarchies are translated behind the scenes to attribute coordinates. For example, suppose that a query requests the following tuple:

```
(Product.[Product Category].Bikes.[Mountain Bikes].Mountain-100,
[Measures].]Sales Amount])
```

This path is equivalent to the following tuple:

```
([Product].[Product Category].[Bikes],
[Product].[Product Subcategory].[Mountain Bikes],
[Product].[Product Name].[Mountain-100],
[Measures].]Sales Amount])
```

Now, consider the following tuple:

```
([Product].[Product Name].[Mountain-100], [Measures].]Sales Amount])
```

In this case, a member from the Product Name attribute hierarchy is used in the tuple. What cell will this tuple reference? To answer this question, it is important to note that a member of one attribute hierarchy does not imply members of other attribute hierarchies. Although the [Mountain-100] product is found under the [Mountain Bikes] product subcategory in the Product by Subcategory natural hierarchy, this tuple is *not* identical to the previous one. That's because, UDM will not imply any of the multilevel hierarchies. Instead, the tuple references the cell found at the intersection of the Mountain-100 product member and the current members of the rest of the attribute hierarchies:

```
([Product].[Product Name].[Mountain-100],
[Product].[Product Subcategory].[All],
[Product].[Product Category].[All],
<current members from the rest of the attribute heirarchies>
[Measures].]Sales Amount])
```

Note Again, the current member may not be the *All* member. For example, if you have a pivot report in the Cube Browser and you drill down the Product by Subcategory hierarchy, the current members of the Product Category and Product Subcategory levels will be the members referenced by the current cell. Moreover, in some MDX expression functions, such as *Order* or *Filter*, a tuple is evaluated for each member of a given set and the current member for some dimensions changes for each iteration. In other words, the current member depends on the context of the expression evaluation.

Understanding how navigational invariance affects referencing the cube space is especially important when you are writing to the cube space. If it is not immediately obvious at present, don't worry, it will all become clear when practicing subcube expressions in the next chapter. For now, I would like to conclude our cube space discussion with an advice. Use attribute hierarchies in your MDX expressions whenever it makes sense. The cube space is best described by attribute hierarchies. If you use user-defined hierarchies, you may over-restrict your calculations. For example, *[Product].[Product].[Product].Members* returns all members of the Product attribute hierarchy (all products), while *[Product].[Product by Category].[Subcategory].[Road Bikes].Members* returns the products that belong to the *Road Bikes* subcategory only. In some cases, this may be exactly what you need, while in others, you may need access to the all members in your expression.

9.2 Understanding MDX Scripting

As noted in section 9.1.2, the main types of MDX expressions are calculated members, named sets, and subcube expressions. You author these expressions by adding MDX-compliant code to the MDX *script* for that cube. An MDX script is simply a collection of MDX *commands* separated by commas. Calculated members and named sets consist of only one command. A subcube expression may have several nested commands.

Note Currently, SSAS 2005 supports only one MDX script inside a given cube. A future release may allow multiple scripts to be associated with a cube, just like a development project may have several source files.

You can add expressions to the MDX script of a cube by using the MDX Designer hosted inside the Calculations tab of the Cube Designer (Figure 9.7). From now on, I will use the terms *MDX Designer* and *Calculations tab* interchangeably since there is one-to-one relationship between them.

9.2.1 Introducing the MDX Designer

A welcome improvement from SSAS 2000, which many MDX developers will undoubtedly appreciate, is that, in UDM, all cube-level expressions are centralized in one place – the Calculations tab. Thanks to its integration with the Visual Studio.NET IDE, the Calculations tab gives you an MDX editor that supports everyone's favorite features, including Intellisense, color-coding, on-the-fly syntax checking, and debugging (the world's first MDX debugger!).

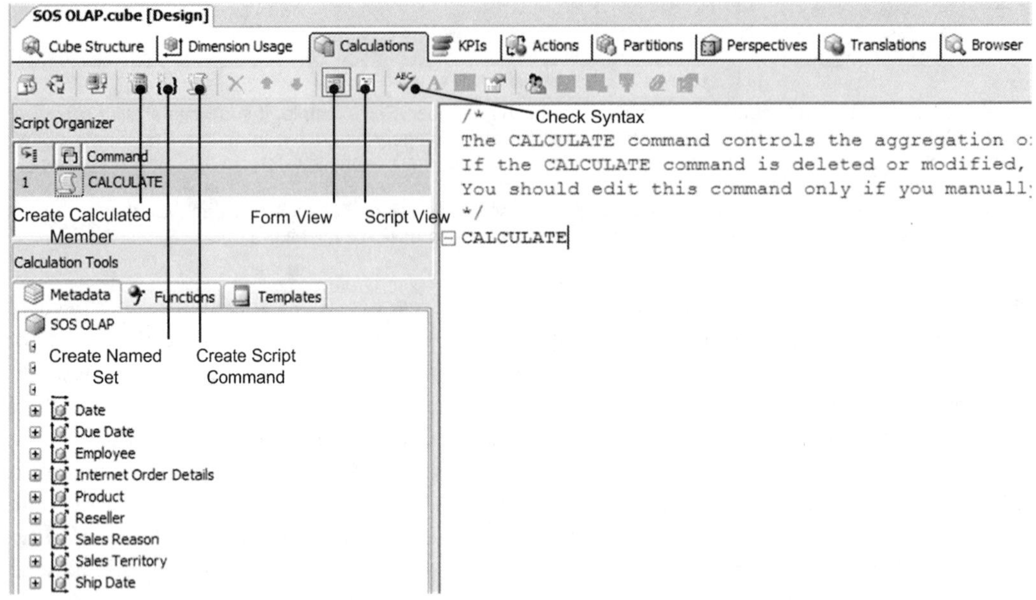


```
/*
The CALCULATE command controls the aggregation o:
If the CALCULATE command is deleted or modified,
You should edit this command only if you manuall:
*/
CALCULATE
```

Figure 9.7 In UDM, cube-level MDX expressions are centralized in one place – the Calculations tab

While there is nothing to prevent you from writing MDX expressions directly in the cube definition file (under the <MdxScript> element), you can use the Calculations tab of the Cube Designer to do so in a civilized manner. The net effect is the same – all MDX expressions become part of the cube definition and metadata (once the cube is deployed). Therefore, MDX expressions don't take storage space. Instead, they are evaluated during runtime. The calculation engine processes MDX expressions very efficiently, but complex calculations may impact the cube performance. Dimension-level calculations, (unary operators, custom member formulas, and default members), remain in the dimension metadata.

Form and Script modes

The Calculations tab supports two view modes. The Form View mode (Form View) toolbar button is targeted to novice MDX developers. As its name suggests, it provides a form user interface that has separate sections for different parts of the MDX expression, including sections for the MDX expression itself, formatting, color expressions, font expressions, etc. The Form View abstracts you from the syntax technicalities, e.g. separating different sections of an MDX expression with commas and using semi-colon as a command delimiter.

Note The Form View mode is not that useful when writing subcube expressions. Since subcube expressions could include several commands, it doesn't make sense to break them down in separate UI sections. Form View is still available with cube expressions, but it just shows the selected command of the subcube expression.

Once you become more experienced in MDX, you can "graduate" from the Form View mode to the Script View mode. In the Script View mode, the MDX Designer shows all cube expressions, just like the VS.NET Code Editor shows all code inside a source file with development projects.

The Script View allows you to have quick access to all expressions defined in the cube, so you can make changes quickly.

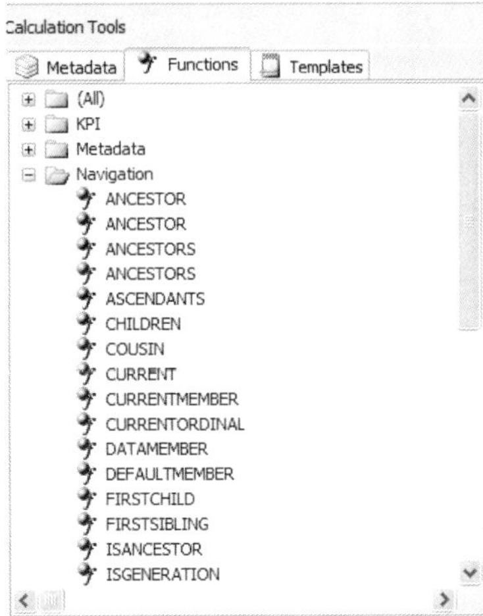

Figure 9.8 The Functions tab organizes the MDX functions in logical categories.

Script Organizer pane

The Script Organizer pane lists the currently defined commands in the cube. It is shown only in a Form View mode. You can easily tell the expression types apart by their icons. A calculated member has an icon that resembles a calculator. A named set is prefixed with **{...}**. Commands inside a subcube expression can be identified by the script icon (recall that a subcube expression may have more than one command).

The command ordering in the Script Organizer pane reflects the position of the command in respect to the other commands in the MDX script. In other words, commands are sorted in the way they are laid out in the MDX script. For subcube expressions that change cell values, the position of the expression in the script is very important because the last expression that writes to a given cell wins. I will explain the script execution model in more details in chapter 10. For now, note that you can re-order a script either by using the Script View mode by just moving the script block, or by right-clicking on the script in the Script Organizer pane and choosing Move Up or Move Down. Alternatively, you can use the Move Up and Move Down toolbar buttons.

You have at least three ways to create a new MDX expression. You can right-click anywhere on the Script Organizer pane and indicate the expression type. You can use the New Calculated Member, New Named Set, and New Script Command toolbar buttons to create a calculated member, a named set, or a command for a subcube expression. Finally, you can switch to the Script View mode and enter the expression manually.

You can also delete expressions, either by right-clicking on the script in the Script Organizer pane and choosing Delete, or by selecting the entire script block and deleting it in the Script View mode.

Calculation Tools pane

The Calculation Tools has three tabs. The Metadata tab is the same as the one in the Cube Browser. Since a cube may have many attribute and multilevel hierarchies, remembering navigational paths could be difficult. Use the Metadata pane to drag hierarchy levels or members to construct quickly your expressions.

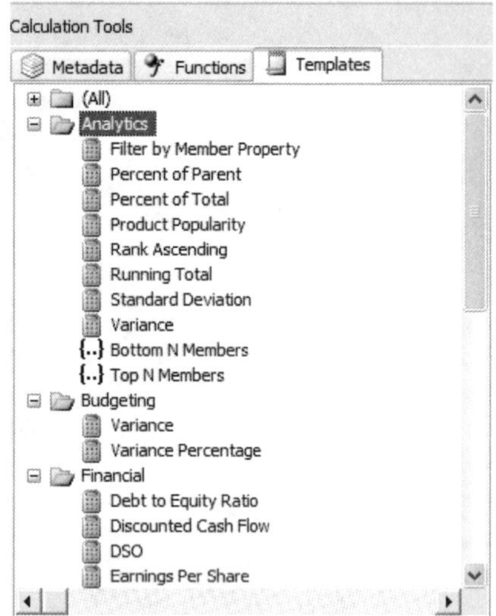

Figure 9.9 The Templates tab lists pre-defined or custom MDX expression templates to help you write MDX expressions.

MDX supports many functions (the exact count depends on how you count them but 200 is probably right) and finding the right function for the task at hand can be difficult. Use the Functions tab (Figure 9.8) to locate a function quickly and check its syntax. The Functions tab organizes the MDX functions in logical groups. For example, all functions for navigating the cube space are found under the Navigation node. Hovering on top of a given function reveals the function syntax in a tooltip. Finally, the Templates tab (Figure 9.9) lists commonly used MDX expression templates, which you can leverage to jump-start your expressions. For example, use the Top N Members template as a starting point for creating a named set that contains the top attribute members based on a given criteria. You can add custom templates to the list, if needed.

9.2.2 How the Cube Aggregates

As noted, the default MDX script of a cube contains a single command called *Calculate*. The comment above it warns you about the consequences of deleting this command. Specifically, if you remove this command, the cube will not aggregate. To understand why you need the Calculate command, you need to know how the cube aggregates. Figure 9.10 should help you visualize the cube aggregation process. The cube data is aggregated in passes. The value of each cell in the cube space is either fact data (leaf cells), or derived via an expression. Initially, the cube is not populated and its cells are empty.

Pass 0

Pass 0 occurs when the cube is processed. When this happens, the cube leaf cells are populated with fact data. If the grain of your dimensions is higher than the grain of the fact table, the only way to see the fact rows is to define a drillthrough action on the corresponding measure group. That's why, in Figure 9.10, Pass 0 data is shown below the pivot report, as coming from the fact table. During the cube processing, the fact data is copied into the cube leaf cells.

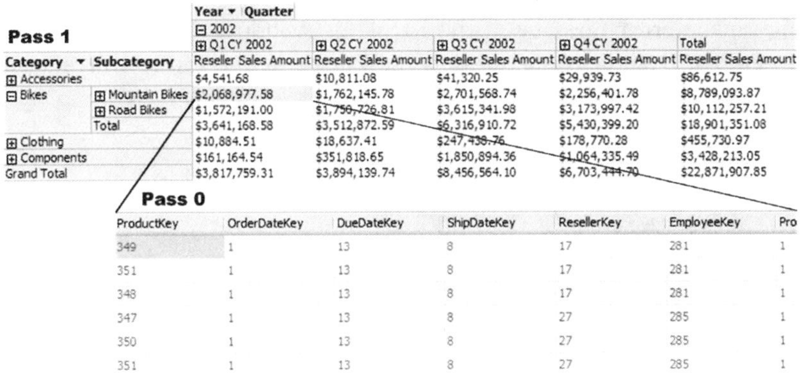

Pass 1

Category	Subcategory	Q1 CY 2002 Reseller Sales Amount	Q2 CY 2002 Reseller Sales Amount	Q3 CY 2002 Reseller Sales Amount	Q4 CY 2002 Reseller Sales Amount	Total Reseller Sales Amount
Accessories		$4,541.68	$10,811.08	$41,320.25	$29,939.73	$86,612.75
Bikes	Mountain Bikes	$2,068,977.58	$1,762,145.78	$2,701,568.74	$2,256,401.78	$8,789,093.87
	Road Bikes	$1,572,191.00	$1,750,726.81	$3,615,341.98	$3,173,997.42	$10,112,257.21
	Total	$3,641,168.58	$3,512,872.59	$6,316,910.72	$5,430,399.20	$18,901,351.08
Clothing		$10,884.51	$18,637.41	$247,438.76	$178,770.28	$455,730.97
Components		$161,164.54	$351,818.65	$1,850,894.36	$1,064,335.49	$3,428,213.05
Grand Total		$3,817,759.31	$3,894,139.74	$8,456,564.10	$6,703,444.70	$22,871,907.85

Pass 0

ProductKey	OrderDateKey	DueDateKey	ShipDateKey	ResellerKey	EmployeeKey	Pro
349	1	13	8	17	281	1
351	1	13	8	17	281	1
348	1	13	8	17	281	1
347	1	13	8	27	285	1
350	1	13	8	27	285	1
351	1	13	8	27	285	1

Figure 9.10 The cube aggregation is done in passes.

Pass 1

Pass 1 happens when the Calculate command in the default script is executed. When this happens, the calculation engine aggregates the cube measures in accordance with their aggregate functions. For the report shown in Figure 9.10, this means summing the fact data since the aggregate function of the Reseller Sales Amount measure is *Sum*. Other measures are aggregated using the aggregation function specified in the *AggregateFunction* property of the measure.

Expression passes

MDX expressions are resolved in subsequent passes according to their positional order. For example, if you create a subcube expression that changes the value of a given cell, it will create a new pass that's guaranteed to happen after pass 1. Results of expressions are cached in memory but not persisted to the disk. Since MDX expressions are resolved during runtime, complex expressions may impact the server performance.

We will continue expanding on the calculation pass concept in the next few sections of this chapter and in the next chapter.

9.2.3 Troubleshooting MDX Errors

As with every programming language, MDX provides comprehensive error handling. There are three types of errors that you will encounter when writing MDX expressions. First, there are syntax errors, e.g. when making a typo in the MDX script. Second, you may run into runtime errors, such as when the calculation engine fails to resolve a hierarchy, level, or a member, or when an expression results in a division by zero error. Finally, you may introduce logical errors as a result of incorrect MDX logic which executes just fine but produces wrong results. Logical errors are, of course, the most difficult to fix. In this section, I will focus on syntax and runtime errors only.

Handling syntax errors

The MDX Designer detect syntax errors as you type by underlying the syntax errors with red wavy lines in both Form and Script View modes. You can also click on the Check Syntax to let BI Studio verify if the script is syntactically correct. In addition, if you switch from the Script View mode to the Form View mode and there is a syntax error, you will see a descriptive message, as the one shown in Figure 9.11. I personally found the syntax-related error messages to be very descriptive. You can use the line and column information to pinpoint the offending expression. Double-clicking on the error message in the Error List window throws you in the Script View mode and the MDX Designer will position the cursor at the error. Unresolved syntax errors are reported during cube deployment.

The Form View cannot be displayed because the MDX script has the following syntax error: 'Query (71, 109) Parser: The syntax for ')' is incorrect. [Line:70; Column:108]' To correct this error, click Script View on the toolbar, and then edit the MDX script to correct the syntax.

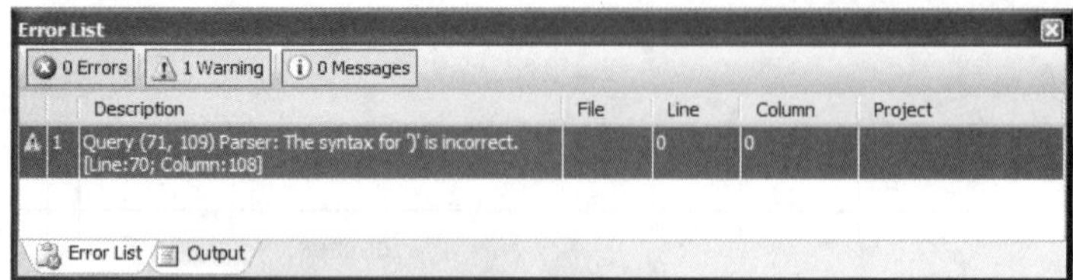

Figure 9.11 The MDX Designer shows descriptive error messages in case of syntax errors.

You will find out UDM is very lenient about misspelled object names, e.g. instead of Product you type *Produc* as the dimension name. Such errors are reported during runtime when the expression is requested.

Handling runtime errors

When the calculation engine encounters an MDX expression error, it sends the error code to the client. If you use OWC or the Cube Browser, these codes will be displayed in the affected cells. For example, the error code that you will encounter most often is *#VALUE!*. To troubleshoot runtime expression errors, just hover on top of the cell. Say, you request the Sales Profit calculated member in an MDX query and you get the dreaded #VALUE! displayed in a cube cell (Figure 9.12).

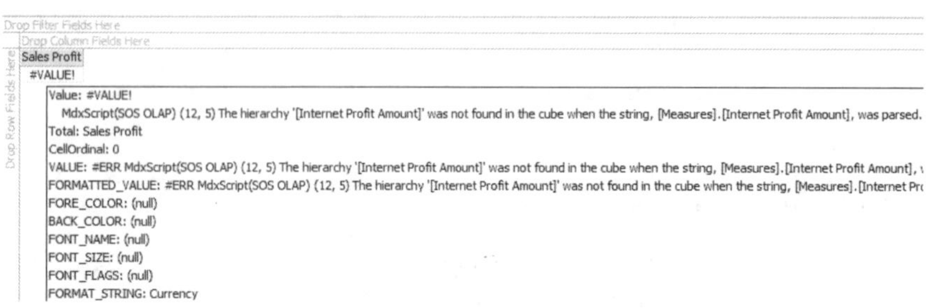

Figure 9.12 To troubleshoot a runtime MDX expression error, hover over the affected cell.

Don't panic! Just hover on top of the affected cell (the one with the error code). A tooltip will pop up and display troubleshooting information. In this case, I've misspelled the name of the Internet Profit Dollar Amount measure to Internet Profit Amount in the Sales Profit calculated member. Use the line and column numbers to locate the error in the MDX script of the cube, and fix it quickly (hopefully). Next, you need to re-deploy the cube.

Tip MDX syntax is verified during cube deployment processing after the cube is processed. As a result, even a small typo would fail the cube processing. Although you can correct the MDX error and re-deploy the cube without having to re-process the cube again, sometimes it is better to ignore the MDX errors, e.g. if you don't want to fail an SSIS package. You can tell the server to ignore MDX errors by setting the *ScriptErrorHandlingMode* cube-level property to *IgnoreAll* either programmatically, or at design time, using the Cube Structure tab of the Cube Designer.

There are a few more concepts that you need to know about MDX scripting which are best illustrated with examples. Therefore, let's get our feet wet by creating our first MDX expression. When we were architecting the SOS OLAP model back in chapter 3, we introduced two measure groups, Internet Sales and Reseller Sales, whose measures were loaded from the corresponding fact tables (FactInternetSales and FactResellerSales).

9.2.4 Your First MDX Expression

One of the first requirements that we would most likely have to tackle programmatically is the calculating the Adventure Works sales profit amount. We can do this by adding the Internet Dollar Profit Amount measure (from the Internet Sales measure group) to the Reseller Dollar Profit Amount measure (from the Reseller Sales measure group) by using the following formula:

```
Sales Profit = Internet Dollar Profit Amount + Reseller Dollar Profit Amount
```

Instead of using an MDX expression, we could have derived the Sales Profit measure by using a measure expression inside either the Internet Sales or Reseller Sales measure groups. The problem with this approach is that the Sales Amount measure doesn't belong logically to either of these two measure groups and shouldn't reside in either of them. Instead, we will implement the Sales Amount measure by creating a new MDX expression and we will place the new measure in a separate *Sales Summary* display folder.

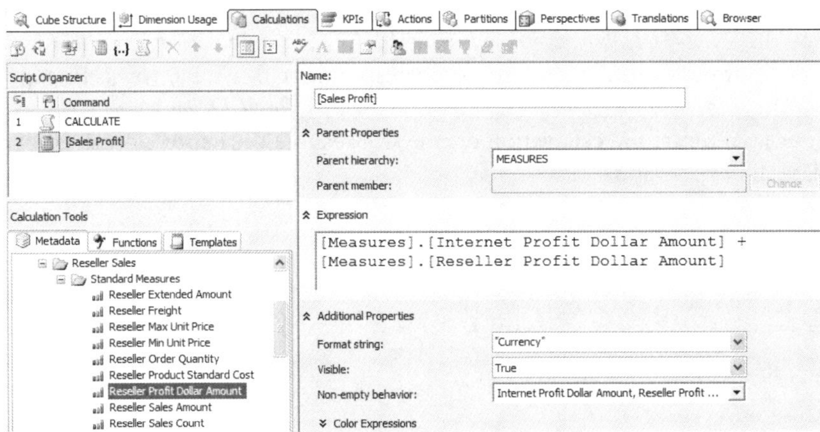

Figure 9.13 Creating a new calculated member using the Form View mode.

Creating a calculated member

Since we will be adding a new member to the Measures dimension (recall that MDX treats measures as members of a pre-defined MEASURES dimension), we need to create a new calculated member.

1. Open the SOS OLAP cube in the Cube Designer. Switch to the Calculations tab and make sure that Form View button is selected.
2. Click the New Calculated Member toolbar button to create an empty calculated member.
3. Replace the [Calculated Member] default name with **[Sales Profit]**.

A calculated member can be added to any dimension hierarchy in the cube (recall that all measures belong to a special dimension called *Measures*). Most calculated members that you will probably create will be calculated measures. Leave MEASURES as a pre-selected value of the Parent Hierarchy dropdown.

4. In the Metadata tab of the Calculation Tools pane, expand the Internet Sales measure group below the Measures folder. Drag and drop the Internet Profit Dollar Amount measure to the Expression textbox. The MDX Designer automatically resolves the measure to *[Measures].[Internet Profit Dollar Amount]*. If you want, you can omit the Measures dimension since it is automatically assumed in UDM.
5. Remove the dot separator. Observe how the MDX Designer underlines [Internet Sales Amount] with a red wavy line to give you a hint that there is a syntax error. Enter back the dot separator.
6. Type + (a plus sign) after the *[Measures].[Internet Profit Dollar Amount]* measure. Drag the Reseller Profit Dollar Amount measure and drop it after the plus sign to create the required expression. Click the Check Syntax toolbar button to test the expression syntax.
7. A calculated member can be formatted with pre-defined or custom format strings. In the *Format string* dropdown, select *Currency* to format the Sales Profit measure as a currency (see Figure 9.13).

Tip You can hide a calculated member from the end users by setting its Visible property to False. This could be useful if the measure is created as an interim measure that will be used in other expressions.

8. As a performance enhancement technique, you can tell the calculation engine how to evaluate the measure as empty. If the *Non-empty behavior dropdown* is blank, the calculation engine must evaluate the expression every time, even if there are no correspondent fact table rows. Expand the dropdown and select the *Internet Profit Dollar Amount* and *Reseller Profit Dollar Amount* measures. If these two measures are empty, the calculation engine will resolve the expression as empty without having to calculate the expression.

```
/*
The CALCULATE command controls the aggregation of leaf cells in the cube.
If the CALCULATE command is deleted or modified, the data within the cube is affected.
You should edit this command only if you manually specify how the cube is aggregated.
*/
CALCULATE;

/* Calculates the sales profit amount. */
CREATE MEMBER CURRENTCUBE.[MEASURES].[Sales Profit]
 AS [Measures].[Internet Profit Dollar Amount] + [Measures].[Reseller Profit Dollar Amount]
FORMAT_STRING = "Currency",
NON_EMPTY_BEHAVIOR = { [Internet Profit Dollar Amount], [Reseller Profit Dollar Amount] },
VISIBLE = 1  ;
```

Figure 9.14 Use the Script View mode to see all scripts defined in the cube.

9. Flip to the Script View mode (Figure 9.14). Note that Sales Profit is defined as a calculated member using the MDX **CREATE MEMBER** statement. In addition, note that the calculated member elements are separated by commas, while the script ends with a semi-colon.

Tip To make your code more readable, you may want to spread long MDX expression on several lines. MDX scripts don't require a special line continuation character when the expression wraps to the next line. That said, each MDX command must end with semicolon.

10. You can add descriptive comments to MDX expressions to improve their readability and help others understand their purpose. You can enclose your block comments with /* */, or use (--)

for inline comments. Enter the comment text that immediately precedes the CREATE MEMBER statement in Figure 9.14.

Browsing a calculated member

Let's now test the Sales Profit calculated member.

1. Deploy the project to apply the new calculated member. Since MDX expressions are calculated during runtime, the cube should process very fast.

Tip When experimenting with MDX, you may need to process and deploy your project quite often. For this reason, it makes sense to keep your UDM as light as possible. For example, in the case of the SOS OLAP UDM, you could speed up the project deployment by excluding all data mining objects that we've created in chapters 7 and 8. They include the SOS OLAP DM cube, Customer Profiles dimension, and all mining models. To exclude these objects, select them, right-click, and choose Exclude From Project. This action will remove the object definition files from the project only (it won't delete them). You can always add the definitions later by right-clicking on the project node and choosing the Add ⇨ Existing Item menu.

2. Switch to the Cube Browser tab and create the report shown in Figure 9.15. Observe that no matter how you slice and dice the cube, the Sales Profit measure always equals the sum of the Reseller Sales Amount and Internet Sales Amount. As noted in section 9.1.3, that's because the calculation engine aggregates measures using the current member of all attribute dimensions.

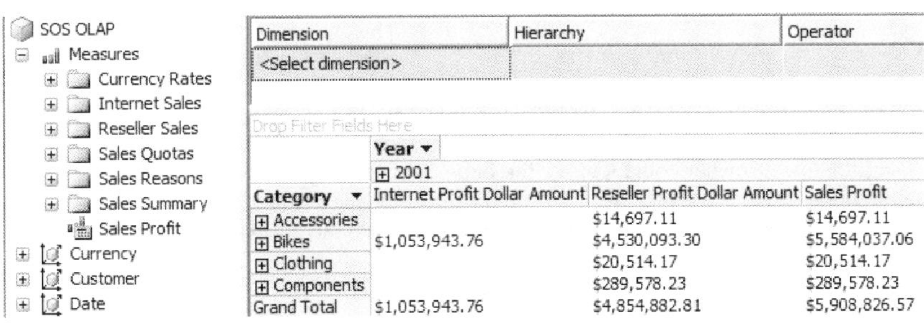

Figure 9.15 A calculated member is exposed to the end users as a regular measure.

Using display folders

Note that you can tell calculated measures apart from the regular measures in the Metadata pane of the Cube Browser by their special icon. As it stands, the Sales Profit measure is outside the measure group folders. To reduce clutter, you may want to organize calculated members in display folders, in the same way you can organize regular measures. Follow these steps to place the Sales Profit measure in a new folder called Sales Summary.

1. Switch to the Calculations tab.
2. Click on the Calculation Properties toolbar button to launch the Calculation Properties dialog (Figure 9.16). The Calculation Properties dialog applies to all measures, so there is no need to select the Sales Profit measure before displaying the dialog.
3. Expand the Calculation Name dropdown and select the *[Measures].[Sales Profit]* calculated member.

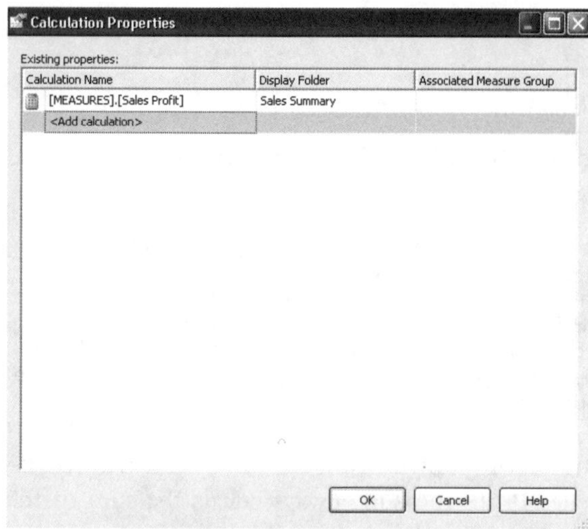

Figure 9.16 Use display folders to organize calculated members that are logically related.

4. Enter **Sales Summary** in the Display Folder column. Note that there is also an Associated Measure Group column. Since, in our case, the Sales Profit measure spans two measure groups, leave the Associated Measure Group column empty.

Tip Both Display Folder and Associated Measure Group are UI-related features. Use Display Folder to place a given calculated member into a given folder. Use the Associated Measure Group column to associate a calculated member that uses measures from a single measure group to that measure group. Once this is done, a smart OLAP browser could inspect the cube schema (e.g. by using ADOMD.NET) and determine which measure group is associated with the calculated member. Next, the browser could also find out which dimensions are related to that measure group and exclude the dimensions that are not relevant when the calculated member is selected.

5. Re-deploy the project. Switch to the Cube Browser tab and re-connect to refresh the report. Notice that the Sales Profit measure is now in the Sales Summary folder.

You can use similar steps to create other simple calculated members that span the Internet Sales and Reseller Sales measure groups, such as Sales Amount, Tax amount, etc.

9.2.5 Calculating Averages

Another common programming task is calculating average values. In chapter 5, we saw that UDM offers the AverageOfChildren semi-additive aggregate function. This function calculates the average value for all non-empty child members of a given member over time. How can you calculate averages over any dimension? For example, you may want to find the average profit amount generated by different products. There is no standard aggregate function to do so. Instead, you need to create a calculated member which uses an MDX expression to divide the measure value by the item count.

Implementing a simple average measure

We can calculate the average profit amount across any dimension by dividing the Sales Profit calculated member that we've just created, by the total number of sales orders.

```
[Average Profit] = [Sales Profit] / ([Internet Order Count + Reseller Order Count])
```

1. Create a new calculated member called **Average Profit** based on the above expression.
2. Format it as currency.
3. Use the [Internet Order Count] and [Reseller Order Count] measures to evaluate the member non-empty behavior.
4. Open the Calculation Properties dialog and place the Average Profit measure into the Sales Summary display folder.

Note If you create a new calculated member in the Script View mode, you need to switch to the Form View mode to refresh the Calculated Name dropdown and get the new member to show up the Calculated Properties dialog.

5. Deploy the project and create the report shown in Figure 9.17.

		Year				
		2001	2002	2003	2004	Grand Total
Category	Subcategory	Average Profit	Average Profit	Average Profit	Average Profit	Average Profit
Accessories		$108.87	$204.82	$50.77	$32.01	$43.46
Bikes	Mountain Bikes	$10,391.71	$6,903.56	$3,024.94	$1,855.03	$3,578.04
	Road Bikes	$2,215.39	$3,255.36	$2,593.13	$1,417.42	$2,404.42
	Touring Bikes			$3,378.89	$2,424.92	$2,809.75
	Total	$4,111.96	$4,274.21	$2,873.06	$1,816.76	$2,858.22
Clothing		$84.77	$589.15	$185.46	$74.13	$152.80
Components		$1,412.58	$3,185.28	$2,982.59	$2,037.51	$2,700.07
Grand Total		$4,284.86	$4,811.36	$1,968.80	$990.26	$1,970.19

Figure 9.17 Simple averages can be created by dividing the measure value by the item count.

Observe that the Average Profit measure is non-additive. For example, Adventure Works has made $43.46 profit on average from selling accessories. The overall profit is not the sum of the average annual profit amounts.

Calculating an average value over a set

Sometimes, you may need to calculate an average from a set of values. For example, the Average Profit From Top Five Resellers calculated measure calculates the average profit amount that the top five resellers have generated. You can use the MDX *Avg* function for this purpose. First, you need a set to get the top five resellers that have generated the most profit. To do so, you can use the *TopCount* MDX function.

```
TopCount([Reseller].[Reseller].[Reseller].Members, 5, [Reseller Profit Dollar Amount])
```

Note In real life, it may make more sense to implement this expression as a calculated dimension member (explained in section 9.4.3) on the Reseller dimension since it logically belongs to that dimension. In this case, you wouldn't probably specify the last argument, so it works on the current measure (current member of Measures).

The TopCount function gets all resellers and sorts them in descending order based on the expression you supply as a third argument. Then, TopCount returns as many members as you specify in the second argument. Remember that dimensions are containers of attribute hierarchies. Attribute hierarchies may have up to two levels; an optional (All) level and the level at which the attribute members are found. When writing expressions, it is very important you reference the right object for the task at hand. For example, [Reseller].[Reseller].Members will give you all resellers *plus* the All member. One way to exclude the All member is to go down to the Reseller level (prefixed with dot), hence the triple notation ([Reseller].[Reseller].[Reseller] ↵ .Members).

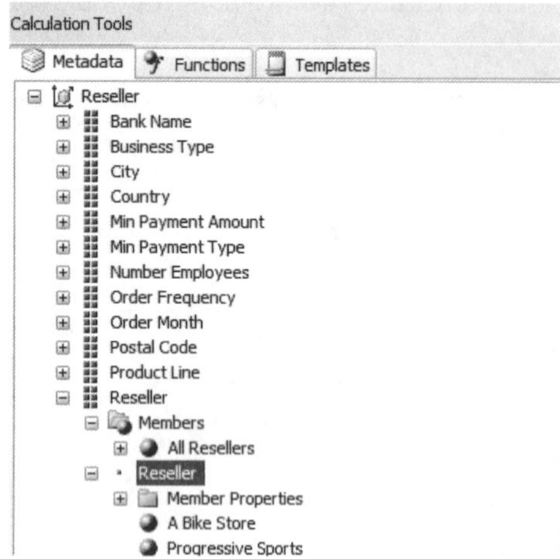

Figure 9.18 Use the Metadata pane to resolve the object hierarchy.

The Metadata goes a long way to help you get the object hierarchy right. As Figure 9.18 shows, I've selected the Reseller level to exclude the All member. If I had selected the Reseller attribute hierarchy (the node one level above, whose icon has 6 dots), I would have gotten 703 sales persons, instead of the correct count of 702. The *TopCount* function returns a set which is exactly what the Avg function takes. Similar to the TopCount function, *Avg* accepts a second argument -- the set that will be averaged. The complete expression of the Average Profit For Top Resellers calculated measure is:

```
Avg(TopCount(
    [Reseller].[Reseller].[Reseller].Members, 5,
    [Reseller Profit Dollar Amount]),[Reseller Profit Dollar Amount])
```

9.3 Navigating Hierarchies Horizontally

Multilevel hierarchies could be extremely useful for creating MDX expressions that address common business needs. The measures that we will demonstrate next leverage a range of extremely useful MDX functions for navigating multilevel hierarchies both horizontally and vertically.

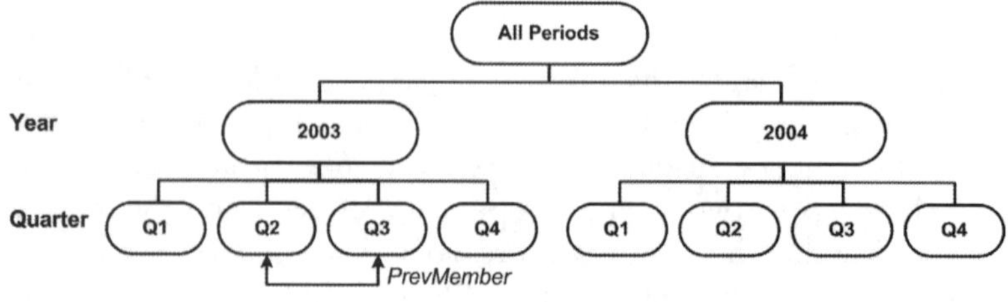

Figure 9.19 A common requirement is to analyze measures from one time period to another.

9.3.1 Working With Time Dimensions

The Time dimension is an omni-present dimension that exists in almost all dimensional models that you will build. A common analytical requirement is to compare values between different time periods, e.g. comparing the current month value with the previous month value, comparing values between parallel periods, etc. We can implement these requirements by navigating the Time hierarchy horizontally.

Note Before using time-related MDX functions, you need to set up the semantic type of the Time dimension and its attributes correctly. As noted in chapter 4, you can do so by setting the Type property at a dimension and attribute level.

The reason why I call time navigation *horizontal* can be understood by projecting the Time dimension as shown in Figure 9.19. As noted in chapter 4, Time dimensions usually have balanced hierarchies, e.g. months roll up to quarters which, in turn, roll up to years. If you imagine that time progresses linearly, then you can implement time-related calculations by simply navigating the hierarchy levels horizontally. For example, to compare sales figures between quarters 3 and 4 of year 2003, you simply need to find the value of the previous member at the Quarter level.

9.3.2 Comparing Values Between Adjacent Time Periods

One of the most common programming techniques that you need to master is the ability to compare a value for the current time period to a value for the previous time period. Let's implement a calculated member that returns the sales growth of the reseller sales between the current and previous time period. Our pseudo expression for the Reseller Profit Growth calculated member looks like this:

```
Reseller Profit Growth = Current Month Reseller Profit - Previous Month Reseller
Profit
```

Determining the current time period

As a first step for authoring the Reseller Profit Growth calculated member, we need to find the reseller profit for the current time period. To identify the corresponding cell, we need a tuple with the following pseudo coordinates:

```
(Current Time Period, Reseller Profit)
```

The CurrentMember function

How do we get the current time period? As noted in section 9.1.3, MDX provides a handy function called CurrentMember which is specifically designed for this purpose. To understand how this function works, create the following calculated member:

```
CREATE MEMBER CURRENTCUBE.[MEASURES].[Show Current Time Member]
AS ([Date].[Calendar Date].CurrentMember.Name), VISIBLE = 1 ;
```

Note When referencing a hierarchy, make sure you use the [DimensionName].[HiearachyName] syntax. Recall that a dimension is just a named container of attribute and multilevel hierarchies. Therefore, just using the dimension name will give you a #VALUE! error displayed in the affected cube cells.

You can find the CurrentMember function by expanding the Navigation node of the Functions tree. Hovering on top of CURRENTMEMBER reveals that the function syntax is *<<Hierarchy>.CURRENTMEMBER*. Therefore, CurrentMember takes a hierarchy and returns the current member in respect to a given cell coordinate. The member object has a number of properties. The one that we need is the *Name* property because it returns the member name as specified by the NameColumn property of the corresponding attribute. For a full list of the properties, see the Member Class topic in the ADOMD.NET Managed Programming Reference section in the product documentation.

Deploy the project and create the report shown in Figure 9.20. Observe that the CurrentName function resolves the member of the Calendar Date multilevel hierarchy based on the cell coordinates. Think of the CurrentMember function as a Global Positioning System (GPS). No matter where we are, CurrentMember gives you the cell coordinate from the specified hierarchy.

Year	Semester	Quarter	Month	Date	Show Current Time Member
⊞ 2001					2001
⊟ 2002	⊟ H1 CY 2002	⊞ Q1 CY 2002			Q1 CY 2002
		⊟ Q2 CY 2002	⊞ April		April
			⊞ May		May
			⊞ June		June
			Total		Q2 CY 2002
		Total			H1 CY 2002
	⊞ H2 CY 2002				H2 CY 2002
	Total				2002
⊞ 2003					2003
⊞ 2004					2004
Grand Total					All Calendar Periods

Figure 9.20 The CurrentMember MDX function returns the current member of an attribute hierarchy.

Referencing dimension members

While we are still on the member properties subject, let's explain how you can reference a dimension member. When you reference a dimension member in a tuple, you can use the member name, e.g. [Product].[Product].[Mountain-100] to reference a member named Montain-100 from the Product attribute hierarchy of the Product dimension. However, this syntax will only work if there is only one product with that name.

Instead of using the member name, you can resolve the member uniquely by using its key. As explained in chapter 3, UDM identifies members uniquely by using the attribute key. To reference a member by key, you prefix the key with ampersand. Assuming that you have a product with a key of 10, [Product].[Product].&[10] will resolve that member uniquely even if there are other products with the same name. One way to retrieve the member key is to hover on top of that member in the Metadata tab of the Calculation Tools pane. Another way to retrieve the member key is to use the *UniqueName* property of the member. For example, if you replace the Name property of the [Show Current Time Member] expression with UniqueName, the report will change as shown in Figure 9.21.

Year	Semester	Quarter	Month	Date	Show Current Time Member
⊞ 2001					[Date].[Calendar Date].[Year].&[2001]
⊟ 2002	⊟ H1 CY 2002	⊞ Q1 CY 2002			[Date].[Calendar Date].[Quarter].&[2002]&[1]
		⊟ Q2 CY 2002	⊞ April		[Date].[Calendar Date].[Month].&[4]&[2002]
			⊞ May		[Date].[Calendar Date].[Month].&[5]&[2002]
			⊞ June		[Date].[Calendar Date].[Month].&[6]&[2002]
			Total		[Date].[Calendar Date].[Quarter].&[2002]&[2]
		Total			[Date].[Calendar Date].[Semester].&[2002]&[1]
	⊞ H2 CY 2002				[Date].[Calendar Date].[Semester].&[2002]&[2]
	Total				[Date].[Calendar Date].[Year].&[2002]
⊞ 2003					[Date].[Calendar Date].[Year].&[2003]
⊞ 2004					[Date].[Calendar Date].[Year].&[2004]
Grand Total					[Date].[Calendar Date].[All Calendar Periods]

Figure 9.21 Use the member UniqueName property to find out the fully-qualified name of the member.

As you would notice, UDM uses the attribute key to resolve the current member. What may seem strange is that sometimes the key contains more than one value, e.g. [Date].[Calendar Date].[Month].&[4]&[2002] to reference the member April of year 2002. This could be explained easily by recalling that an attribute could have a composite key when a single column is not enough to identify the attribute members. We discussed composite attribute keys in chapter 3. Going back to our programming task at hand, the tuple that references the resale profit for the current time period is:

```
([Date].[Calendar Date].CurrentMember, [Measures].[Reseller Profit Dollar Amount])
```

Note Since our Time dimension contains multiple multilevel hierarchies, the above expression specifies explicitly the Calendar Date multilevel hierarchy. If you need the same expression for another multilevel hierarchy, e.g. Fiscal Date, you need to clone the expression and target that hierarchy. Alternatively, you can use the BI Wizard to do it for you, as I will demonstrate in the next chapter.

Determining the previous time period

As you probably guessed, MDX provides a handy function to reference a previous member in a hierarchy. The function is *PrevMember* and has the same syntax as CurrentMember. So, the tuple that will give us the resale profit for the previous time period is:

```
([Date].[Calendar Date].CurrentMember.PrevMember,
[Measures].[Reseller Profit Dollar Amount])
```

Since the CurrentMember happens to be the default member property, we could make the tuple more concise.

```
([Date].[Calendar Date].PrevMember,
[Measures].[Reseller Profit Dollar Amount])
```

Besides making the tuple syntax more compact, it turns out that there are some runtime performance advantages of omitting CurrentMember. Taking this road, we can also omit CurrentMember from the tuple that references the current period resale profit. So, the final expression is:

```
([Date].[Calendar Date], [Measures].[Reseller Profit Dollar Amount]) -
([Date].[Calendar Date].PrevMember, [Measures].[Reseller Profit Dollar Amount])
```

Tip If you are really ambitious, you can omit [Date].[Calendar Date] from the first tuple whatsoever. As you know, the calculation engine will resolve a missing dimension to its current member.

Note that you need to specify the CurrentMember property if you want to display the *name* of the current member, as we did in the report shown in Figure 9.20. If you just type [Date].[Calendar Date].Name, the calculation engine will resolve this to the Name property of the Calendar Date multilevel hierarchy. In other words, the calculation engine will cast to CurrentMember only if you don't request an existing property. For example, since there is no PrevMember property off the dimension class, the engine will cast [Date].[Calendar Date].PrevMember to [Date].[Calendar Date].CurrentMember.PrevMember.

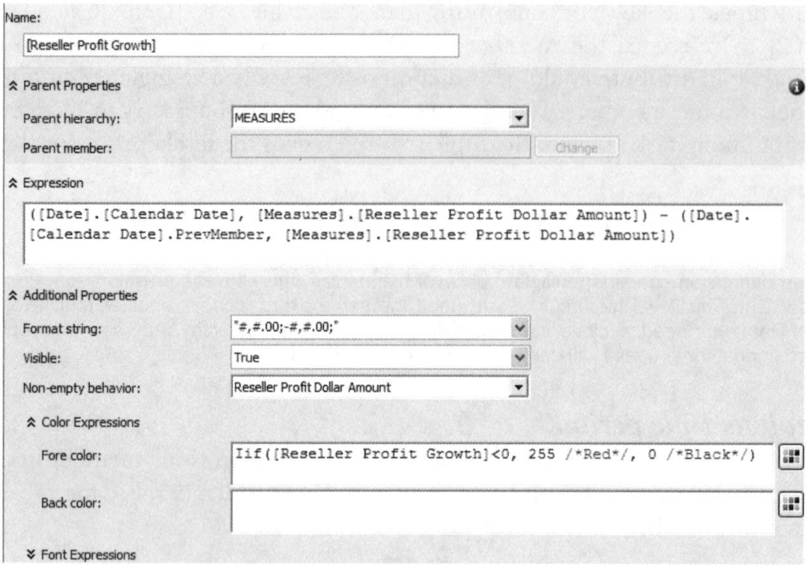

Figure 9.22 You can use conditional formatting in the form of MDX expressions.

Creating the Reseller Profit Growth calculated member

Now that we have the expression, constructing the calculated member is easy. Figure 9.22 shows Reseller Profit Growth in a Form View. You can use conditional formatting in your expressions. For example, suppose that you need to show negative growth in red to alert the end user. You can do so by using the *Iif* operator. This operator consists of three parts. The first part is the expression that needs to be evaluated. If the expression evaluates to *True*, the result of the expression entered in the second part will be returned; otherwise *Iif* will return the result of the third expression. In our case, we are evaluating the value of the calculated member itself. If it is negative, we set the fore color to Red. Of course, this will work only if the OLAP browser knows how to handle server-side formatting (not all do).

In addition, you can use custom format specifiers when the standard format settings are not enough. If we format Reseller Profit Growth as Currency, the negative numbers will show enclosed in parenthesis, e.g. ($10,000). If this is not what you want, you can use custom format specifiers. For numbers, the custom format specifier consists of up to four parts, separated by semi-colons. The first part specifies formatting for positive numbers. The second part is for negative numbers. The third part applies to zeros, and the fourth part is for NULL values.

Assuming that you want to display the negative values of Reseller Profit Growth prefixed with a minus sign, e.g. -10,000, the custom format specifier you need is *#,#.00;-#,#.00;*. For more information about how to use custom formatting, refer to the FORMAT_STRING Contents topic in the product documentation. For final touches, use the Calculation Properties dialog to place the Reseller Profit Growth member in the Reseller Sales folder and associate it with the Reseller Sales measure group. A sample report that uses the Reseller Profit Growth measure is shown in Figure 9.23. We can see that we have negative sales growth for September 2001. Colors could be really useful to illustrate the negative numbers in red, but unfortunately we are restricted to monochrome in this book.

their position in the hierarchy. In other for this to work, each level must have the same number of children (no holes at any levels).

Note IsEmpty or IS NULL? You may be curious about why I am using IS NULL to check for a missing member instead of IsEmpty. The IsEmpty function checks if a given expression results in an empty value (a.k.a. NULL). The IS operator checks if two object expressions are the same. In the expression above, IS NULL checks if the ParallelPeriod member is outside the cube space. Since NULL.Value is always Empty, IsEmpty(NULL) is always true. However, the reverse is not always true. If IsEmpty(<Expression>) is true, then Expression IS NULL may or may not be true. To make this story short, use IsEmpty to check for empty cells, and IS NULL to check for members that may fall out of the cube space (e.g. PrevMember, FirstChild, ParallelPeriod, etc).

As you could imagine, ParallelPeriod has no way to determine which members are missing and re-adjust the existing members properly. To fix the issue with our report, you need to populate the DimTime dimension table with dates for the first half of 2001. I will leave this exercise to the reader.

9.3.4 Period-to-Date Aggregations

Another common data analytics requirement is to provide period-to-date aggregations, such as year-to-date calculations from the beginning of the current year, or a running total for all periods. Let's find out how you can implement these requirements by leveraging a few more time-related functions.

Year-to-Date aggregations

Suppose that you need to calculate the sales amount generated by Internet sales from the beginning of the year. Needless to say, the year doesn't have to coincide necessarily with the current calendar year. Instead, we will use the current member of the Year attribute hierarchy. First, we have to filter the Time members for the YTD period. For example, if the current cell is found at the coordinate March 2003, we need to retrieve members January 2003, February 2003, and March 2003. It so happens that the SSAS team has already provided such a function for us. This function is YTD and the following expression will give us exactly what we need.

```
YTD([Date].[Calendar Date])
```

The YTD function takes a given member from a hierarchy in the Time dimension and returns a set of members since the beginning of the parent Year member. Summing the values of these members can be done by using the *Sum* aggregate function, which can be found under the Statistical node in the Functions tab. This function takes a set as a first argument and a measure expression that will be aggregated over the set. So, the final calculated member expression will be:

```
CREATE MEMBER CURRENTCUBE.[MEASURES].[YTD Internet Sales] AS
SUM(YTD([Date].[Calendar Date]), [Measures].[Internet Sales Amount])
```

Year	Semester	Quarter	Month	Internet Sales Amount	YTD Internet Sales
⊟ 2001	⊟ H2 CY 2001	⊟ Q3 CY 2001	⊞ July	$362,056.83	$362,056.83
			⊞ August	$418,532.34	$780,589.17
			⊞ September	$403,888.49	$1,184,477.66
		⊟ Q4 CY 2001	⊞ October	$429,188.62	$1,613,666.28
			⊞ November	$414,130.49	$2,027,796.77
			⊞ December	$599,234.63	$2,627,031.40
	Total			$2,627,031.40	$2,627,031.40

Figure 9.26 Use the YTD function to calculate year-to-date values.

Figure 9.26 shows a report using the YTD Internet Sales measure. As you can see, the YTD Internet Sales column produces a running total of the sales figures for a given month.

Period-to-Date aggregations

What if we need to produce a running total for all periods to date? It turns out that YTD function is just a shortcut version of another time-related function called *PeriodsToDate.* The PeriodsToDate function allows you to specify a time period from a starting level of a given Time hierarchy to a given member. For example, consider the following expression:

```
PeriodsToDate([Date].[Calendar Date].[(All)], [Date].[Calendar Date])
```

This expression will return all members of the Calendar Date dimension starting from the (All) member all the way across to the current member. Given this, producing a running period-to-date total can be implemented by using the following calculated member:

```
CREATE MEMBER CURRENTCUBE.[MEASURES].[PTD Internet Sales] AS
Aggregate(PeriodsToDate([Date].[Calendar Date].[(All)],
[Date].[Calendar Date]), Measures].[Internet Sales Amount])
```

Tip Should you use the Aggregate function or the Sum function? The Sum function sums a given measure irrespective of the aggregate function associated with the measure, while the Aggregate function will honor the aggregate function of the measure. For example, the Currency Rates measure group has an Average Rate measure whose AggregateFunction property is set to AverageOfChildren. If you use the Sum function in a measure expression, it will ignore the semi-additive behavior of this measure. Generally, a calculated member placed on a dimension other than Measures should use Aggregate function, so it behaves correctly when it's crossed against any measure. When you define a calculated member on Measures dimension, you know what other measure(s) you are aggregating. In this case, use the appropriate aggregation function, which may be different than the one of the underlying measure(s).

Figure 9.27 shows a report that uses the PTD Internet Sales measure. As you would notice, the PTD Internet Sales measure produces a running total for all time periods, while the scope of YTD Internet Sales is always a year.

Year	Semester	Quarter	Month	Internet Sales Amount	YTD Internet Sales	PTD Internet Sales
⊟ 2001	⊟ H2 CY 2001	⊟ Q3 CY 2001	⊞ July	$362,056.83	$362,056.83	$362,056.83
			⊞ August	$418,532.34	$780,589.17	$780,589.17
			⊞ September	$403,888.49	$1,184,477.66	$1,184,477.66
		⊟ Q4 CY 2001	⊞ October	$429,188.62	$1,613,666.28	$1,613,666.28
			⊞ November	$414,130.49	$2,027,796.77	$2,027,796.77
			⊞ December	$599,234.63	$2,627,031.40	$2,627,031.40
	Total			$2,627,031.40	$2,627,031.40	$2,627,031.40
⊟ 2002	⊞ H1 CY 2002			$3,280,162.68	$3,280,162.68	$5,907,194.08
	⊞ H2 CY 2002			$2,401,277.91	$5,681,440.58	$8,308,471.99
	Total			$5,681,440.58	$5,681,440.58	$8,308,471.99
⊞ 2003				$8,705,066.67	$8,705,066.67	$17,013,538.66
⊞ 2004				$8,992,282.96	$8,992,282.96	$26,005,821.61

Figure 9.27 Use the PeriodsToDate function to calculate a running total for an arbitrary time period.

9.4 Navigating Hierarchies Vertically

Horizontal hierarchy navigation is unique to Time dimensions. You probably can't think of other dimensions where comparing values to a previous or a parallel member actually makes sense. For example, it is meaningless to compare members horizontally across the Product dimension. What would a previous or a parallel product member mean? At the same time, a common requirement for almost any hierarchy (attribute or multi-level) is the ability to compare values of members vertically (up and down the hierarchy), i.e. to find the ratio of a given member to an aggregate produced by a member up the hierarchy.

9.4.1 Calculating Ratios

There are many kinds of ratios that you may need to implement, including percentages, allocations, and averages. Some of them are simple to implement, others may require some MDX wizardry. In this section, I will show you how you can implement common expressions that use ratios.

Relative percentage to (All)

Suppose that you need to find out the percentage contribution of a member to grand total aggregate value (*All* member) for a given dimension, e.g. the profit contribution of any member of the Product dimension to the profit amount of all products. In addition, to make things more interesting, suppose that you want your expression to work with any hierarchy (attribute or multi-level) of the Product dimension.

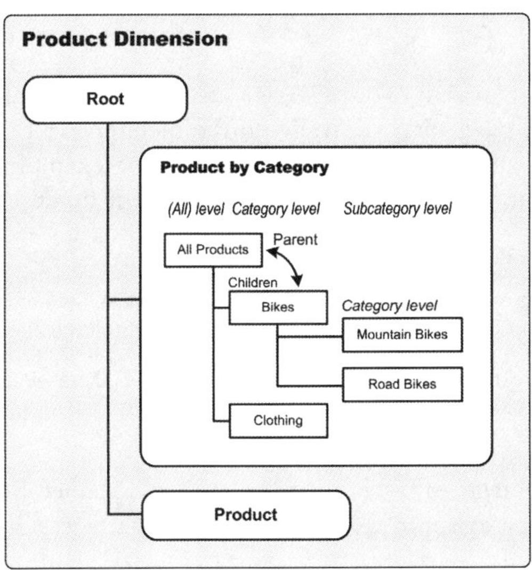

Figure 9.28 MDX supports useful functions to navigate hierarchies vertically.

To fulfill the latter requirement, MDX provides a useful function called *Root*. As shown in Figure 9.28, the Product dimension contains many hierarchies, including multi-level hierarchies (e.g. Product by Category), and attribute hierarchies (e.g. Product or Color). Use the Root function as a shortcut to get to the value of the *All* members from *all* attribute hierarchies. Given this, our MDX expression is simple:

```
CREATE MEMBER CURRENTCUBE.[MEASURES].[Profit Ratio To All]
AS
  Iif (IsEmpty( [Measures].[Sales Profit]), 0,
  ([Measures].[Sales Profit]) /( Root([Product]), [Measures].[Sales Profit]))
```

First, we use the *Iif* operator to check if the grand total value of the Sales Profit measure is NULL. It is a good idea to implement such safety "valves" to prevent division by zero errors. Next, we just divide the sales profit for the current member by the Sales Profit grand total amount. We also need to format the calculated member as Percentage. The result is shown in Figure 9.29.

Category	Subcategory	Profit Ratio To All
⊞ Accessories		1.37%
⊟ Bikes	⊞ Mountain Bikes	35.71%
	⊞ Road Bikes	36.97%
	⊞ Touring Bikes	11.99%
	Total	84.67%
⊞ Clothing		2.43%
⊞ Components		11.53%
Grand Total		100.00%

Figure 9.29 Use the Root function to get to the top level of any hierarchy in a given dimension.

Thanks to the new calculated member, we can easily find out the relative contribution of each member. For example, the Bikes product category has contributed almost 85% to the overall profit. Drilling further into its subcategories, we can tell that the Road Bikes product subcategory is the bestselling product subcategory because it contributes 36.97% to the overall profit amount. If you replace the Product by Subcategory hierarchy with another attribute or multi-level hierarchy, you will find that the Profit Ratio To All calculated member still works thanks to the Root function.

Relative percentage to parent

You can also calculate the member contribution to its parent. To do so, we just need to replace the Root function with another helpful function for navigating vertically up the hierarchy called *Parent*. The Parent function returns the parent member of a given member. For example, glancing at Figure 9.28, the parent of the Bikes member is the *All* member. The Parent function requires that you specify a hierarchy.

Tip As a result of Type 1 dimension changes, members can move within a hierarchy. For example, members can be deleted or moved from one parent to another. In SSAS 2000, an MDX expression that references a missing member always produced an error. SSAS 2005 introduces a new dimension-level property, called *MdxMissingMemberMode*. By default, UDM will ignore missing members. If you want MDX expressions referencing missing members to generate an error, you can set MdxMissingMemberMode to Error.

Suppose that you need to find the relative percentage of each member of the Product by Category multilevel hierarchy to its parent. In our first attempt, we can code the new expression as:

```
CREATE MEMBER CURRENTCUBE.[MEASURES].[Profit Ratio To Parent]
 AS Iif ( IsEmpty( [Measures].[Sales Profit]), 0,
    ([Measures].[Sales Profit]) /([Product].[Product by Category].Parent,
    [Measures].[Sales Profit]))
```

Category	Subcategory	Profit Profit Ratio To Pare
⊞ Accessories		1.37%
⊟ Bikes	⊞ Mountain Bikes	42.18%
	⊞ Road Bikes	43.66%
	⊞ Touring Bikes	14.16%
	Total	84.67%
⊞ Clothing		2.43%
⊞ Components		11.53%
Grand Total		1.#INF

Figure 9.30 Expressions going outside of the cube space result in errors.

This expression will work for all members except the *All* member, as shown in Figure 9.30. The reason for this is that the *All* member doesn't have a parent. Therefore, when querying the Parent member of the All member, we are thrown outside the cube space. As a result, the tuple ([Product].[Product by Category].Parent, [Measures].[Sales Profit])) evaluates to NULL, which triggers the 1.#INF error. We can avoid this error by checking if the current member is the All member, and if this is the case, return 1 (so it could be formatted as 100%). Nesting Iif expressions could result in difficult to read, spaghetti-like code. To avoid this, let's use the MDX Case statement (new to SSAS 2005).

```
CREATE MEMBER CURRENTCUBE.[MEASURES].[Profit Ratio To Parent]
 AS
    Case
        When
            IsEmpty( [Measures].[Sales Profit])
        Then 0
        When
           [Product].[Product by Category].CurrentMember.Level Is
           [Product].[Product by Category].[(All)]
        Then 1
        Else
           ([Measures].[Sales Profit]) /
          ([Product].[Product by Category].Parent, [Measures].[Sales Profit])
        End
```

You can use different When clauses inside the Case statement to check for various conditions. If they all evaluate to False, the Else clause will be used. Figure 9.31 shows a report that uses the Profit Ratio to All and Profit Ratio to Parent measures side by side. The difference between the Profit Ratio to All and Profit Ratio to Parent measures is that in the first case contributions of *all* members add up to 100%, while in the latter, contributions of *all children* of a given member add up to 100%.

Category	Subcategory	Profit Ratio To All	Profit Ratio To Parent
⊞ Accessories		1.37%	1.37%
⊟ Bikes	⊞ Mountain Bikes	35.71%	42.18%
	⊞ Road Bikes	36.97%	43.66%
	⊞ Touring Bikes	11.99%	14.16%
	Total	84.67%	84.67%
⊞ Clothing		2.43%	2.43%
⊞ Components		11.53%	11.53%
Grand Total		100.00%	100.00%

Figure 9.31 Use the Parent MDX function to calculate the member contribution to its parent.

Relative percentage to ancestor

You can explicitly indicate a given member up the hierarchy by using the *Ancestor* function. This is another flexible function which can either take a specific level, or a numeric offset relative to the current member. For example, the following expression calculates the contribution of a given member to the Product Category level.

```
CREATE MEMBER CURRENTCUBE.[MEASURES].[Profit Ratio To Product Category]
 AS Case
        When IsEmpty( [Measures].[Sales Profit])
        Then 0
        When [Product].[Product by Category].CurrentMember.Level.Ordinal <= 1
        Then "N/A"
        Else
          [Measures].[Sales Profit])/(Ancestor([Product].[Product by Category],
         [Product].[Product by Category].[Category]),[Measures].[Sales Profit])
       End
```

We use the Ordinal property to obtain the numeric value of the level where the current member is located. That's because we want to apply the contributions only to those members whose level is below the Category level. Otherwise, we return *N/A*.

Category	Subcategory	Product	Profit Ratio To All	Profit Ratio To Parent	Profit Ratio To Product Category
⊞ Accessories			1.37%	1.37%	100.00%
⊟ Bikes	⊞ Mountain Bikes		35.71%	42.18%	42.18%
	⊞ Road Bikes		36.97%	43.66%	43.66%
	⊟ Touring Bikes	Touring-1000 Blue, 46	1.42%	11.82%	1.67%
		Touring-1000 Blue, 50	0.90%	7.50%	1.06%
		Touring-1000 Blue, 54	0.51%	4.26%	0.60%
		Touring-1000 Blue, 60	1.64%	13.64%	1.93%
		Touring-1000 Yellow, 46	1.17%	9.77%	1.38%

Figure 9.32 Use the Ancestor function to calculate contributions to a specific member up the hierarchy.

As the report shown in Figure 9.32 demonstrates, the Profit Ratio to the Product Category expression shows the contribution that each descendant has to a member at the Category level.

9.4.2 Allocating Values

Sometimes, you may need to distribute values proportionally down the hierarchy. For example, you may need to assign each department a budget based on the expenses that the department incurred during a previous period. You can solve such requirements by using allocation expressions.

Basic allocations

Suppose that you need to distribute each sales territory a sales quota for the current year based on the profit generated by that territory last year. We will assume that the annual sales quota is a measure of the Sales Quotas measure group. As I pointed out in chapter 5, the FactSalesQuota measure group captures the sales quota at a quarter level. Strictly speaking, for the purposes of our allocation expression, it is sufficient to have only annual sales quotas because our expression will distribute them down the time hierarchy. To accomplish this, we will break our expression in two parts. First, we need to get the annual sales quota for the current year. This part could be accomplished with the following tuple:

```
([Measures].[Sales Quota], Root([Sales Territory]))
```

Next, we need to allocate this value down the Sales Territory hierarchy based on the sales profit amount from the previous year. To allocate the sales quotas proportionally, we need to find out the sales profit ratio between a given member and the *All* level for the last year. The following expression will do the trick:

```
([Measures].[Sales Profit], ParallelPeriod([Date].[Calendar Date].[Year], 1,
[Date].[Calendar Date])) /
([Measures].[Sales Profit], Root([Sales Territory]), ParallelPeriod([Date].[Calendar
Date].[Year], 1, [Date].[Calendar Date])),
```

The first tuple (before the division operator) returns the sales profit for each member for the same time period in the previous year. The second tuple returns the total profit amount for the previous year. Finally, we just need to multiply the annual sales quota amount by the calculated ratio.

```
CREATE MEMBER CURRENTCUBE.[MEASURES].[Allocated Quota]
 AS ([Measures].[Sales Quota], Root([Sales Territory])) *
    ([Measures].[Sales Profit],
```

```
   ParallelPeriod([Date].[Calendar Date].[Year], 1, [Date].[Calendar Date])) /
     ([Measures].[Sales Profit], Root([Sales Territory]),
ParallelPeriod([Date].[Calendar Date].[Year], 1, [Date].[Calendar Date])),
```

Very elegant code given the complex task at hand, don't you think? Figure 9.33 shows the results for years 2003 and 2004.

	Year					
	2003			2004		
Group	Sales Quota	Sales Profit	Allocated Quota	Sales Quota	Sales Profit	Allocated Quota
North America	$27,172,000.00	$17,544,804.10	$31,617,870.63	$12,349,000.00	$8,652,945.10	$12,886,430.68
Europe	$9,376,000.00	$6,076,966.44	$4,777,605.07	$4,820,000.00	$4,387,781.80	$4,463,452.90
Pacific	$867,000.00	$870,153.48	$1,019,524.30	$820,000.00	$767,422.18	$639,116.42
Grand Total	$37,415,000.00	$24,491,924.01	$37,415,000.00	$17,989,000.00	$13,808,149.08	$17,989,000.00

Figure 9.33 MDX makes it easy to allocate values down the hierarchy.

Note that the allocated quota for 2004 is distributed accordingly to the sales profit distribution for 2003. At the same time, the totals for the original Sales Quota measure and the Allocated Quota measure are the same (only the distribution is different).

Allocations based on the number of children

Another allocation example is distributing a member value based on the number of its children. To understand this type of allocation, think of elderly parents who are willing to distribute their assets equally among their children, so each child gets an equal share. Applying this example to the SOS OLAP UDM, suppose that we need to change the previous allocation scenario. Now, we need to distribute the sales quota of the parent sales territory equally among its children. Breaking down this requirement in pieces, let's start with finding out how we can get the parent sales quota amount. The tuple that we need is:

```
([Measures].[Sales Quota],[Sales Territory].[Sales Territory].CurrentMember.Parent)
```

Next, we need to count the number of children a given parent member has. We could use CurrentMember.Parent.Children to do so, but it turns out that MDX has another trick up its sleeve. The *Siblings* property of a given member returns a set of all members at the same level of that member (including the current member) that have the same parent. For example, going back to Figure 9.28, if the current member is Bikes, Siblings will return both Bikes and Clothing. This is exactly what we need in our scenario. To count the sibling members, we will use the *Count* MDX function.

```
Count([Sales Territory].[Sales Territory].Siblings)
```

Finally, we need to calculate the ratio of the distribution by simply dividing 1 by the expression above. The complete expression for the Allocated Quota by Children calculated member follows.

```
CREATE MEMBER CURRENTCUBE.[MEASURES].[Allocated Quota by Children]
 AS
    Case
        When [Sales Territory].[Sales Territory].Parent Is Null Then
          ([Measures].[Sales Quota], [Sales Territory].[Sales Territory])
        Else
            ([Measures].[Sales Quota], [Sales Territory].[Sales Territory].Parent) *
            (1/Count([Sales Territory].[Sales Territory].Siblings))
    End
```

Figure 9.34 shows the report. The overall sales quota is $95,714,000. It is split equally between the children of each member.

Group	Country	Region	Allocated Quota by Children
⊞ North America			$23,928,500.00
⊟ Europe	⊟ France	Total	$6,119,333.33
	⊞ Germany		$6,119,333.33
	⊞ United Kingdom		$6,119,333.33
	Total		$23,928,500.00
⊞ Pacific			$23,928,500.00
⊞ NA			$23,928,500.00
Grand Total			$95,714,000.00

Figure 9.34 Allocations performed based on the number of the children.

9.4.3 Creating Dimension Calculated Members

All calculated members that we've authored so far were created in the *Measures* dimension. As such, these "virtual" measures can be browsed by any dimension that intersects them. Sometimes, you may need to author a dimension calculated member.

Understanding dimension calculated members

A common scenario for doing so is comparing the performance of one member to another. For example, you may need a dimension calculated member to:

- Calculate the variance between two members of the Time dimension, e.g. Sales for 2004 – Sales for 2003.
- Calculate the average performance of all sales representatives in the Employee dimension.
- Calculate the average product category performance.

It is important to understand that a dimension calculated member becomes a "virtual" member of the hierarchy it is created in. In addition, it doesn't roll up to the parent hierarchy. Therefore, calculated dimension members do not affect the cube aggregations. How do you decide between a dimension and measure calculated member? If you want to the calculated member to intersect with *all* measures, it is a good candidate for a dimension member. On the other side, if it doesn't make sense for the member to intersect with all measures, it may be better to add the member to the Measures dimension.

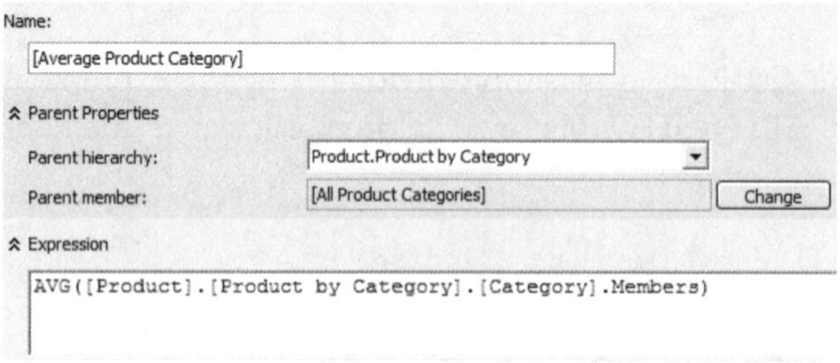

Figure 9.35 Create a dimension calculated member using the Form View.

Creating a calculated dimension member

Suppose the Adventure Works users have requested to see the average of the product categories when they browse the Product by Category multi-level hierarchy. The average amount will be calculated for *all* measures that intersect with the Product dimension (as defined in the Dimension Usage tab). Follow these steps to create the Average Product Category calculated dimension member. We will use the Form View mode since it makes it easier to place the calculated member to the correct hierarchy level.

1. Switch to the Form View mode. Select the last command in the Script Organizer pane (it should be [Allocated Quota by Children]) and click the New Calculated Member button.
2. Enter **[Average Product Category]** as the name of the dimension calculated member.
3. In the *Parent hierarchy* dropdown, select the Product by Category multi-level hierarchy from the Product dimension.
4. Click the Change button next to the Parent member label and select the [All Product Categories] member. That's because we want to place the [Average Product Category] member below the All member (at the Category level).
5. Flip to the Functions tab of the Calculation Tools pane. Expand the Statistical node and drag the AVG function to the Expression textbox. It should get resolved to `AVG( «Set»[, «Numeric Expression»])`. Remove the `[«Numeric Expression»]` argument since we want the dimension calculated member to work across all measures.
6. Switch to the Metadata tab of the Calculation Tools pane. Expand the Product dimension and the Product by Category hierarchy. Drag the Category level to replace the `«Set»` placeholder in the AVG function. Your expression should look as the one shown in Figure 9.35.
7. Deploy the project and switch to the Cube Browser tab. Create the report shown in Figure 9.36.

	Year				
	⊞ 2001	⊞ 2002	⊞ 2003	⊞ 2004	Grand Total
Category	Sales Profit	Sales Profit	Sales Profit	Sales Profit	Sales Profit
⊞ Accessories	$14,697.11	$72,916.07	$410,362.66	$350,484.52	$848,460.36
⊞ Bikes	$5,584,037.06	$15,075,127.52	$19,950,531.77	$11,861,594.89	$52,471,291.24
⊞ Clothing	$20,514.17	$379,415.53	$736,846.06	$371,527.29	$1,508,303.06
⊞ Components	$289,578.23	$2,236,070.06	$3,394,183.51	$1,224,542.38	$7,144,374.18
⊞ Average Product Category	$1,477,206.64	$4,440,882.29	$6,122,981.00	$3,452,037.27	$15,493,107.21
Grand Total	$5,908,826.57	$17,763,529.18	$24,491,924.01	$13,808,149.08	$61,972,428.84

Figure 9.36 A dimension calculated member is a virtual member which doesn't affect the cube aggregations.

Observe that the Category level now includes the Average Product Category member which is used to calculate the average value of the measures added to the report. In addition, note that the Average Product Category member doesn't affect the Grand Total values.

Note MDX functions that operate on dimension members, such as Children and Members, exclude dimension calculated members. MDX provides an *AllMembers* function that returns all members (including the calculated members) from in the specified dimension, hierarchy, or level. For example, [Measures].AllMembers return both standard and calculated members of the MEASURES dimension.

9.5 Summary

MDX expressions take off where the dimensional model leaves. The benefits of using MDX expressions are two-fold. First, you can leverage MDX expressions to derive business calculations that are difficult to implement in relational database or reporting tools. Second, you can publish such calculations in a single repository – the Unified Dimensional Model, and make them available across the entire enterprise.

There are three main types of expressions that you will author using MDX – calculated members, named sets, and subcube expressions. You write these expressions by adding commands to the MDX script of the cube. Calculated members, named sets, and subcube expressions become part of the cube definition file and are accessible from the cube Calculation tab of the Cube Designer.

Calculated members can be used for creating expression-based measures and dimension members. You author calculated members by using MDX functions that allow you to navigate both horizontally and vertically across dimension hierarchies. The cube space is defined by its attribute hierarchies. Each cube cell can be referenced by a multi-dimensional coordinate called a tuple. A collection of tuples with identical dimensionality forms a set.

9.6 Resources

The OLE DB for OLAP specification
(http://shrinkster.com/5pz) – Describes the MDX grammar for expressions and formulas and the syntax for the MDX statements.

Fast Track to MDX
(http://shrinkster.com/5v9) – Written by the creators of MDX, this book is your essential resource to get up to speed with MDX. As of time of the time of this writing, the authors are working on an updated revision for SSAS 2005.

MDX Solutions: With Microsoft SQL Server Analysis Services
(http://shrinkster.com/5vb) – An excellent and more advanced book to complement your MDX knowledge. As of the time of this writing, the author is working on a revised edition for SSAS 2005.

Chapter 10

Advanced MDX Expressions

MDX is a versatile and powerful programming language. Besides calculated members, MDX has a few other tricks up its sleeve which you can leverage to address more demanding programming tasks. Mastering the techniques presented in this chapter will help you implement versatile expressions that unleash the full potential of UDM. In addition, they give you the ultimate control over the cube space, all the way down to the individual cube cells.

In this chapter, you will discover how advanced MDX expressions can solve common analytical requirements. You will learn how to:

- Construct and filter MDX sets and create named sets.
- Leverage subcube expressions to read and write anywhere in the cube space.
- Apply time intelligence.
- Implement currency conversions.

You can explore the finished code samples by opening the Ch10 solution.

10.1 Working with MDX Sets

MDX sets are very useful constructs that can be used in variety of programming scenarios. I introduced MDX sets in the preceding chapter. MDX sets are frequently used in expressions, so knowing them well is essential. In this chapter, we will drill down further into the MDX sets to find out how we can take the most out of them in UDM.

10.1.1 Constructing Sets

As you would recall, an MDX set is just an ordered collection of tuples that have the same dimensionality. Tuples have the same dimensionality when they share identical dimensions and these dimensions are ordered in the same way. From a syntactical standpoint, the tuples in the set need to be separated by a comma, and the set needs to be enclosed in braces {}. In the preceding chapter, we said that there are many MDX functions that accept or return an MDX set. For example, the Average function returns the average value calculated over an MDX set. We also came across the *Children* and *Siblings* functions which return MDX sets too. Let's introduce two additional MDX functions that you may find useful when working with MDX sets.

Descendants and members

The *Descendants* function is a more flexible (and powerful) version of the Children function because it has several overloads. Usually, you will use the Descendants function to get the members below a given member at a specified level of the hierarchy. For example, suppose you need to find the average monthly sales for 2001. The following expression does just this.

```
CREATE MEMBER CURRENTCUBE.[MEASURES].[Average Monthly Sales for 2001]
 AS Avg(
       Descendants ([Date].[Calendar Date].[Year].&[2001],
       [Date].[Calendar Date].[Month]),[Internet Sales Amount]))
```

To achieve the desired goal, we need a set that contains all months of the year 2001. Assuming the Calendar Date multilevel hierarchy, starting from the year level, we need to skip two levels (semester and quarter levels) to get to the Month level. The Descendants function is designed for exactly this kind of tasks. As a first argument, we need to specify the year. As a second argument, we specify the level at which the member will be found (Month). Note also that I leave it to the calculation engine to automatically cast the set when passing the results to the *Avg* function and I don't enclose the set in braces.

Date.Calendar Year ▾		
2001		
	Drop Column Fields Here	
Group ▾	Internet Sales Amount	Average Monthly Sales for 2001
⊞ North America	$1,200,784.22	$200,130.70
⊞ Europe	$612,365.51	$102,060.92
⊞ Pacific	$813,881.67	$135,646.94
Grand Total	$2,627,031.40	$437,838.57

Figure 10.1 Use the Descendants function to return a set of descendants of a given member at any level of the hierarchy below that member.

In our case, the output of the Descendants function is a set consisting of six months because there is data only for the last half of 2001 in the Adventure Works database. Next, we use the familiar *Avg* function to calculate the average monthly sales. To validate the expression, create the report shown in Figure 10.1. The values of the Average Monthly Sales for 2001 can be verified by just dividing the Internet Sales Amount measure by six.

Another versatile set-producing function is the *Members* function. This function returns all members of a specified dimension, attribute hierarchy, or level. For example, the Employee Count calculated member uses the Members function to count the employees in Adventure Works.

```
CREATE MEMBER CURRENTCUBE.[MEASURES].[Employee Count]
AS Count([Employee].[Employee].[Employee].Members)
```

First, the expression [Employee].[Employee].[Employee].Members returns an MDX set of all employees. Specifically, it returns all members at the Employee level of the Employee attribute hierarchy, which is defined in the Employee dimension. Next, we pass the resulting set to the *Count* function. The Count function is a polymorphic function which, among other things, can count the number of cells in a set. That's exactly what we need for the task at hand.

Requesting tuples explicitly

Suppose that you need to calculate the aggregated total of Internet Sales Amount measure for years 2001, 2002, and 2003 (the first three years of Adventure Works sales). The Sales for 2001-2003 calculated member gets the job done.

```
CREATE MEMBER CURRENTCUBE.[MEASURES].[Sales for 2001-2003]
AS Aggregate ({[Date].[Calendar Year].&[2001], [Date].[Calendar Year].&[2002],
         [Date].[Calendar Year].&[2003]}, [Internet Sales Amount])
```

To filter the Internet sales for the first three years of Adventure Works operations, we request the corresponding members of the Calendar Year explicitly. We can request a member by either referencing it by its key (<<member>>.&[Key] syntax), or by its name, assuming that all members of the attribute hierarchy have unique names.

Note Although I will use the terms **members** and **tuples** somewhat interchangeably to refer to the elements of a set, it is important to note that each member of a set is a tuple. For example, [Date].[Calendar Year].&[2001] represents a tuple whose first coordinate is the explicit member and the rest are derived from the current members of the other attribute hierarchies in the cube. A set is always composed of tuples.

Figure 10.2 shows a report that compares the Internet sales for all years (including 2004) against the sales for the first three years.

Category	Internet Sales Amount	Internet Sales for 2001-2003
⊞ Accessories	$608,191.39	$264,609.69
⊞ Bikes	$25,107,749.76	$16,625,916.38
⊞ Clothing	$289,880.46	$123,012.58
Grand Total	$26,005,821.61	$17,013,538.66

Figure 10.2 You can construct an MDX set by requesting members of attribute hierarchies explicitly.

Requesting a range of members

As you can imagine, having to explicitly enumerate each tuple in a set could quickly become tedious. Moreover, this approach may lead to brittle expressions. For example, if the key (or name, if members are referenced by name) of an explicitly requested member changes, that member will be either ignored or the expression will fail (depending on how the *MdxMissingMemberMode* property for that dimension is set). When the set consists of tuples formed by consecutive members, consider using the range operator (:) as a shortcut. This approach resembles requesting a range of cells in Excel (Figure 10.3).

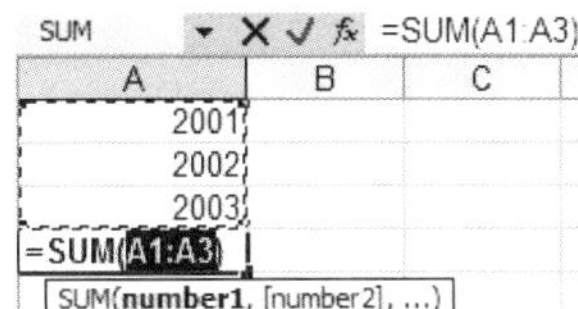

Figure 10.3 Request a range of consecutive members by using the range operator.

For example, given the Excel spreadsheet shown in Figure 10.3, the formula *SUM(A1:A3)* sums all cells within that range. The new version of the Internet Sales for 2001-2003 calculated member that uses the range operator follows.

```
CREATE MEMBER CURRENTCUBE.[MEASURES].[Internet Sales for 2001-2003 Simplified]
 AS Aggregate ({[Date].[Calendar Year].&[2001]:
[Date].[Calendar Year].&[2003]}, [Internet Sales Amount])
```

Note that the calculation engine selects the qualifying tuples in a set based on the way the members are ordered within the attribute hierarchy. Assuming that the product members are ordered by the Name attribute, the set

```
([Product].[Product].&[348]:[Product].[Product].&[595]
```

will select all products with keys from 348 to 595, exactly as they appear when you browse the product hierarchy using the Dimension Browser or the Metadata tab. Suppose that the name of the [Product].[Product].&[348] member is Mountain-100, while the name of the [Product].[Product].&[595] member is Mountain-300. Even if Mountain-200 has a key of 340, it will be included in the set because, when designing the Product dimension, we decided to order products by name (not by key).

Tip You can use NULL as a range boundary to define an "infinite" limit on one side of the range. For example, *[Date].[Year].Members(1) : NULL* will return all years starting with the first member and including new members as they come along. The Time Intelligence script (see section 10.3 demonstrates this approach).

10.1.2 Using Sets in MDX Queries

Since a calculated member cannot return an MDX set, you may wonder how you can test the set before passing it as an input parameter to an aggregate function. Let's take a moment to demonstrate a useful technique for visualizing and troubleshooting MDX sets. Suppose that you would like to see the set produced by the Descendants function in the Average Monthly Sales for 2001 calculated member. You can use the MDX set expression in an MDX query to display the set. You don't have to know a whole lot about MDX queries to use them for testing purposes.

1. Open the SQL Server Management Studio.
2. Expand the Connect dropdown in the Object Explorer and choose Analysis Services. Provide the login information to log in to your Analysis Server, e.g. *localhost*.

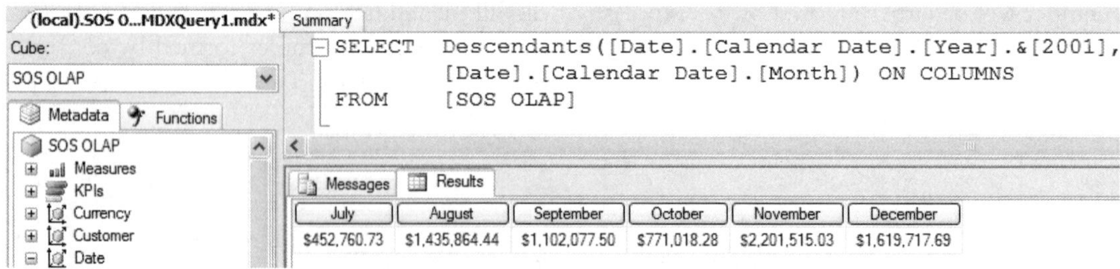

Figure 10.4 Use MDX queries to display and troubleshoot MDX sets.

3. In the Object Explorer pane, right-click on the SOS OLAP database and choose *New Query ⇨ MDX*.
4. In the MDX query pane, create a basic MDX query that projects the set expression on Columns (see Figure 10.4).
5. Run the query by clicking on the Execute toolbar button or pressing Ctrl+E. The query should return the members of the set on columns.

Tip You can have more than one MDX statement in the same MDX Query window. To avoid the red wavy line for syntax errors, separate the queries with a semicolon. To execute a query, select the query text and press Ctrl+E. The MDX Designer doesn't support executing multiple queries in one batch.

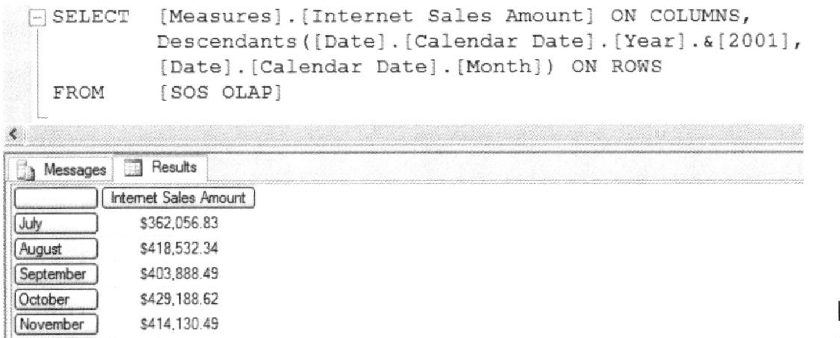
SELECT [Measures].[Internet Sales Amount] ON COLUMNS,
Descendants([Date].[Calendar Date].[Year].&[2001],
[Date].[Calendar Date].[Month]) ON ROWS
FROM [SOS OLAP]
Messages
Results
Internet Sales Amount
July $362,056.83
August $418,532.34
September $403,888.49
October $429,188.62
November $414,130.49
December $599,234.63

Figure 10.5 Requesting an MDX set on rows.

If you would like to see a given measure (calculated or regular) broken down by the set members, change the query to request the set on rows and the measure on columns, as shown in Figure 10.5. The Messages tab reveals a trace of the query execution. Among other things, it shows you the number of columns or rows returned, e.g.:

```
Executing the query ...
Obtained object of type: Microsoft.AnalysisServices.AdomdClient.CellSet
Formatting.
Cell set consists of 7 rows and 2 columns.
```

10.1.3 Crossjoining Sets

You can construct an MDX set by combining two or more other sets. This is especially useful when you need to request more than one attribute or multilevel hierarchy on the same axis of an MDX query, e.g. to show the sales profit broken down by both product and sales territory on rows. The OLE DB for OLAP specification defines a *Crossjoin* function that can be used to take the cross-product of two sets, e.g. Crossjoin (set1, set2). Analysis Services supports an alternative syntax in the form of the asterisk operator (e.g. set1 * set 2), which is functionally equivalent to the Crossjoin function. Finally, UDM introduces an implicit crossjoin behavior when you request sets side-by-side, e.g. (set1, set2, … setN), which I will discuss in more details shortly. What resulting set you will get back from the crossjoin functions depends on whether the hierarchies requested belong to the same or different dimensions.

		Year				
		2001	2002	2003	2004	Grand Total
Group	Category	Sales Profit	Sales Profit	Sales Profit	Sales Profit	Sales Profit
North America	Accessories	$14,697.11	$63,845.40	$250,577.06	$191,229.38	$520,348.96
	Bikes	$5,009,212.67	$12,667,788.18	$14,216,865.90	$7,393,145.62	$39,287,012.37
	Clothing	$20,514.17	$327,017.29	$541,442.63	$246,059.28	$1,135,033.36
	Components	$289,578.23	$1,952,573.71	$2,535,918.50	$822,510.82	$5,600,581.26
	Total	$5,334,002.19	$15,011,224.58	$17,544,804.10	$8,652,945.10	$46,542,975.95
Europe	Accessories		$9,070.67	$133,721.26	$129,067.57	$271,859.49
	Bikes	$246,198.95	$1,923,299.53	$4,942,362.04	$3,769,339.42	$10,881,199.94
	Clothing		$52,398.24	$178,617.31	$109,929.72	$340,945.27
	Components		$283,496.35	$822,265.83	$379,445.09	$1,485,207.27
	Total	$246,198.95	$2,268,264.79	$6,076,966.44	$4,387,781.80	$12,979,211.98
Pacific	Accessories			$26,064.34	$30,187.57	$56,251.91
	Bikes	$328,625.44	$484,039.81	$791,303.83	$699,109.85	$2,303,078.93
	Clothing			$16,786.13	$15,538.30	$32,324.42
	Components			$35,999.18	$22,586.47	$58,585.64
	Total	$328,625.44	$484,039.81	$870,153.48	$767,422.18	$2,450,240.91
Grand Total		$5,908,826.57	$17,763,529.18	$24,491,924.01	$13,808,149.08	$61,972,428.84

Figure 10.6 Crossjoining two sets from different dimensions results in a set that contains all possible combinations of their members.

Crossjoining sets from different dimensions

When sets from different dimensions are crossjoined, the resulting set contains all possible combinations of the members from the requested attribute hierarchies. For example, consider the report shown in Figure 10.6. This report requests the Group attribute hierarchy from the Sales Territory dimension and Category attribute hierarchy from the Product dimension on the same axis of the query. Behind the scenes, OWC uses the Crossjoin function that may look like this.

```
Crossjoin(
     [Sales Territory].[Sales Territory].[Group].Members,
     [Product].[Product by Category].[Category].Members)
```

Since the two sets come from different dimensions, their cross product contains all combinations of their members. Specifically, the resulting set has 3 x 4 = 12 members (each sales territory group has four products). If you add additional attribute hierarchies from different dimensions (e.g. from the Customer dimension), you will see that OWC starts nesting the Crossjoin functions. That's because the Crossjoin function can take only two sets. Alternatively, in UDM, you can use the * (Crossjoin) syntax, to combine conveniently more than two sets, e.g.:

```
[Sales Territory].[Sales Territory].[Group].Members *
[Product].[Product by Category].[Category].Members  *
[Customer].[Customers by Geography].[Country].Members
```

Crossjoining sets within the same dimension

Crossjoining two sets from different dimensions results in a superset consisting of all combinations of the members from the input sets. However, when you crossjoin attribute hierarchies from the *same* dimension, the calculation engine applies the Autoexists behavior (introduced in chapter 3). In this case, the resulting set is made of the intersecting members of the joined sets, as Figure 10.7 illustrates.

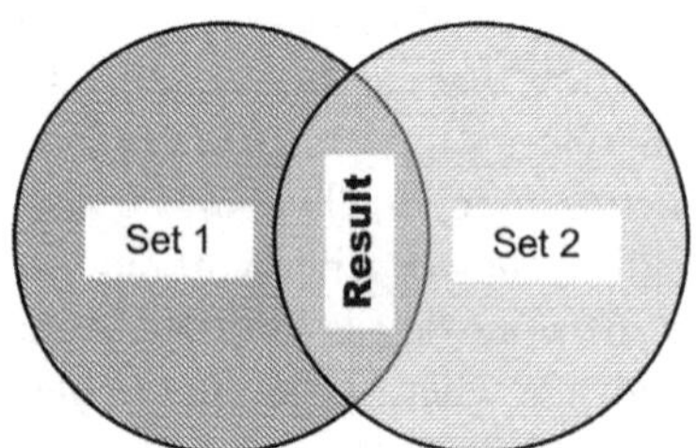

Figure 10.7 Crossjoining two sets from the same dimension results in a set that contains the intersecting members, as a result of the Autoexists behavior.

Figure 10.8 shows a report that demonstrates the effect of crossjoining two attribute hierarchies from the same dimension. In this report, I requested the Category and Subcategory attribute hierarchies on rows.

As a result of the Autoexists behavior, the subcategory members are not repeated for every product category. Instead, only the matching members that exist with one another are returned. An interesting side effect of Autoexists is that you can use attribute hierarchies to simulate multilevel hierarchies. For example, as the report in Figure 10.8 shows, requesting the Category and Subcategory attribute hierarchies on the same axis has the same effect as using the Product by Category multilevel hierarchy. Of course, in real life, end users would prefer a multilevel hierarchy instead of having to combine attribute hierarchies. However, Autoexists could be really useful in an absence of suitable multilevel hierarchies, e.g. browsing products by color when there is no Product by Color multilevel hierarchy.

		Year				
		2001	2002	2003	2004	Grand Total
Category	Subcategory	Sales Profit	Sales Profit	Sales Profit	Sales Profit	Sales Profit
Accessories	Bike Racks			$108,961.37	$77,335.55	$186,296.92
	Bike Stands			$10,515.68	$10,693.01	$21,208.69
	Bottles and Cages			$16,921.22	$21,010.79	$37,932.01
	Cleaners			$7,257.20	$5,869.18	$13,126.38
	Fenders			$10,676.63	$14,181.97	$24,858.60
	Helmets	$14,697.11	$58,394.96	$145,224.95	$114,975.89	$333,292.91
	Hydration Packs			$43,356.78	$32,851.06	$76,207.84
	Locks		$7,908.20	$4,640.49		$12,548.69
	Pumps		$6,612.91	$4,005.11		$10,618.02
	Tires and Tubes			$58,803.24	$73,567.06	$132,370.31
	Total	$14,697.11	$72,916.07	$410,362.66	$350,484.52	$848,460.36
Bikes	Mountain Bikes	$3,273,387.83	$6,800,008.28	$7,743,841.97	$4,312,937.67	$22,130,175.75
	Road Bikes	$2,310,649.23	$8,275,119.24	$8,601,413.22	$3,722,136.08	$22,909,317.76
	Touring Bikes			$3,605,276.59	$3,826,521.14	$7,431,797.73
	Total	$5,584,037.06	$15,075,127.52	$19,950,531.77	$11,861,594.89	$52,471,291.24
Clothing		$20,514.17	$379,415.53	$736,846.06	$371,527.29	$1,508,303.06
Components		$289,578.23	$2,236,070.06	$3,394,183.51	$1,224,542.38	$7,144,374.18
Grand Total		$5,908,826.57	$17,763,529.18	$24,491,924.01	$13,808,149.08	$61,972,428.84

Figure 10.8 With Autoexists, only members that exist with one another are retained in the result set.

Implicit crossjoins

A new UDM feature in comparison with SSAS 2000 is the ability to implicitly crossjoin sets when they are enclosed in parenthesis and separated by comma. Implicit crossjoins were introduced for developer's convenience. For example, suppose that you need a calculated member that filters the Adventure Works employees and returns the sales people only. You can implement this by using a filter (see next section) or by crossjoining two sets. To implement the later approach, first we need to construct a set that contains all employees. Next, we could apply an implicit crossjoin to retain only those employees that are also sales people.

```
([Employee].[Employee].[Employee].Members, [Employee].[Sales Person Flag].&[True])
```

This expression is syntactically equivalent to:

```
[Employee].[Employee].[Employee].Members * {[Employee].[Sales Person Flag].&[True]}
```

Strictly speaking, the second part of the expression is a tuple. The calculation engine automatically casts it to a set that has one member only.

Employee Count	Salesperson Count
296	17

Figure 10.9 Demonstrating an implicit crossjoin.

The Salesperson Count calculated member passes the result set to the Count function to compare the Employee Count and Salesperson Count measures side-by-side (see Figure 10.9).

10.1.4 Filtering Sets

You've just seen how crossjoins can be used to produce a superset or a subset of two or more MDX sets. Sometimes, you may need to exclude certain members from an MDX set, just like you may want to exclude relational rows from a SQL SELECT statement by using a WHERE clause. MDX provides two constructs for excluding members.

The Except function

If you just need to remove a member (or set of members) from a set, use the *Except* function. The Except function has two syntax versions.

- (Except)

The first version of the Except function has syntax: *Set_Expression - Set_Expression*

For example, the following expression returns the aggregated sales total for all categories except the Unknown and Components categories.

```
Aggregate(
      [Product].[Category].[Category].Members -
      {[Product].[Category].[Category].[Unknown], [Product].[Category].[Components]},
      [Internet Sales Amount] )
```

Except (Set1, Set2)

The same result can be obtained by using the second syntax version of the Except function:

```
Except( Set_Expression [ , Set_Expression... ] )
```

In this case the expression will be:

```
Aggregate(
         Except([Product].[Category].[Category].Members,
              {[Product].[Category].[Category].[Unknown],
              [Product].[Category].[Components]}), [Internet Sales Amount])
```

In both cases, the Except function takes as a first argument the input set to be filtered and, as a second argument, the subset to be excluded.

Filters

What if you need to exclude members from a set based on more involved criteria? The MDX *Filter* function comes to the rescue. The Filter function takes a set as an input, passes it by a given expression, and returns only the members that satisfy that expression.

Basic filter expression

For example, suppose you need to count the most profitable Adventure Works products. For demo purposes, we will assume that a product is considered highly profitable if it has generated more than half a million dollars for all time periods. The following calculated member satisfies this requirement.

```
CREATE MEMBER CURRENTCUBE.[MEASURES].[Highly Profitable Products]
  AS Count(
    Filter([Product].[Product].[Product].Members, [Sales Profit] > 500000))
```

The first argument of the Filter function passes a set consisting of all products (excluding the *All* member). The second argument specifies the expression to be evaluated. Any Boolean expression can be used as a criterion. Counting the members of the filtered set results in 40 products.

Filtering on member properties

You can also filter on member properties. Say, you need a set that contains the most expensive Adventure Works products with a list price exceeding $2,000. Glancing at the Metadata tab (Figure 10.10), we can see that the List Price attribute is defined as a member property. By default, member properties are returned as strings, so you need some help to cast the property value to a number if the expression needs it that way. One way do so, is to use the *Val* function which MDX borrows from the Visual Basic for Applications (VBA) library. I will discuss the MDX extensibility and the VBA library in more details in chapter 11. Here is a calculated member that uses the Filter function to filter products based on the List Price member property.

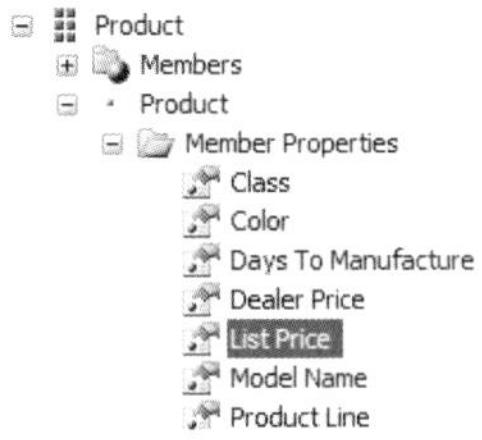

Product
Members
Product
Member Properties
Class
Color
Days To Manufacture
Dealer Price
List Price
Model Name
Product Line

Figure 10.10 Member properties can be used in expressions.

```
CREATE MEMBER CURRENTCUBE.[MEASURES].[Expensive Products]
AS Count(Filter(
    [Product].[Product].[Product].Members,
    Val([Product].[Product].Properties("List Price")) > 2000))
```

You will find that there are 46 products whose price exceeds the $2,000 threshold. Another way to return to cast the property value to the underlying data type is to use the TYPED argument, e.g. [Product].[Product].Properties("List Price", *TYPED*), as demonstrated by the Expensive Products 1 calculated member. Considering the fact that member properties are actually attributes, we can accomplish the same result by the following expression.

```
CREATE MEMBER CURRENTCUBE.[MEASURES].[Expensive Products 2]
AS Count(Filter([Product].[Product].[Product].Members *
    [Product].[List Price].[List Price].Members,
    [Product].[List Price].MemberValue > 2000))
```

Here, we are crossjoining a set of all products with a set of all members of the List Price attribute (All member excluded) to obtain a set that consists of all products that have a list price. Next, we filter on the value of the List Price attribute by using the *MemberValue* property. As you would recall, if the attribute *ValueColumn* property is not explicitly set, the attribute value is derived from the attribute key column, which corresponds to the ListPrice column from the DimProduct table.

Finally, a fourth variant of the above expression is:

```
Count([Product].[Product].[Product].Members *
  Filter ([Product].[List Price].[List Price].Members,
    [Product].[List Price].MemberValue > 2000))
```

Here, first we filter the List Price attribute to get its members that exceed $2,000. Then, we crossjoin these members with the product set. As you can see, the attribute-based nature of UDM gives you a lot of flexibility for constructing your expressions.

Using a filter to find declining sales

Here is a more involved filter example. Suppose, you need to find how many products have experienced a decline in sales from the previous time period. By "previous time period", we mean the period that immediately precedes the current member at the same level of the Time hierarchy. Our first MDX filter expression may look like this:

```
Filter (
    [Product].[Product].[Product].Members,
    ([Date].[Calendar Date], [Measures].[Sales Profit]) <
    ([Date].[Calendar Date].PrevMember, [Measures].[Sales Profit]))
```

The first part of the Filter expression returns all products except the *All* member (since we've requested the Product level). The purpose of the second part of the expression is to select only the products which have sold less than the period before. This filter expression will get the job done. The only problem with it is that it is somewhat inefficient. That's because no matter what level of the hierarchy we are at, the expression will use all products as a starting point and recursively filter the expression result.

When writing MDX expressions, you should try to minimize recursion for better performance. Instead of evaluating the *entire* product set each time the user drills down, let's use only the members below the currently selected product. To do so, we will leverage again the handy Descendants function, so our filter expression will be:

```
Filter (
    Descendants([Product].[Product by Category].CurrentMember,
    [Product].[Product by Category].[Product]),
    ([Date].[Calendar Date], [Measures].[Sales Profit]) <
    ([Date].[Calendar Date].PrevMember, [Measures].[Sales Profit]))
```

Since our requirements call for counting the products, we need to pass the filtered set as an input to the Count function. Of course, the only thing left is to create a calculated member which we will name Products with Declining Sales (Figure 10.11).

		⊟ Q2 CY 2004		
		⊞ April	⊞ May	⊞ June
Category	**Subcategory**	Products with Declining Sales	Products with Declining Sales	Products with Declining Sales
⊞ Accessories		6	7	15
⊟ Bikes	⊞ Mountain Bikes	11	8	8
	⊞ Road Bikes	10	3	13
	⊞ Touring Bikes	17	5	9
	Total	38	16	30
⊞ Clothing		3	10	14
⊞ Components		20	5	31

Figure 10.11 Using a filter to find out how many products have declining sales.

Just to give you an idea of the effect of our optimized expression, on my machine, the first version of the report takes about 15 seconds to render, while the second version takes about 5 seconds. This is a three-fold increase in performance, so it does make sense to understand how a given expression works and find ways to make it more efficient.

10.1.5 Named Sets

A named set is an MDX expression that returns a set of dimension members. For example, you can create a named set to return the top 10 customers. Named sets have the following advantages:

- *More readable and concise code* – You can reference named sets in expressions by name, just as you can do so with calculated members. In addition, you can pass a named set to an MDX function that takes a set as an input.
- *Business logic encapsulation* – You can define a named set once and use it as is, without having to redefine the same business logic in multiple places.
- *Improved end-user experience* – End users can use named sets on query axes to slice the cube.

We've already created several set-producing expressions that are good candidates for named sets. Let's "promote" some of them to named sets.

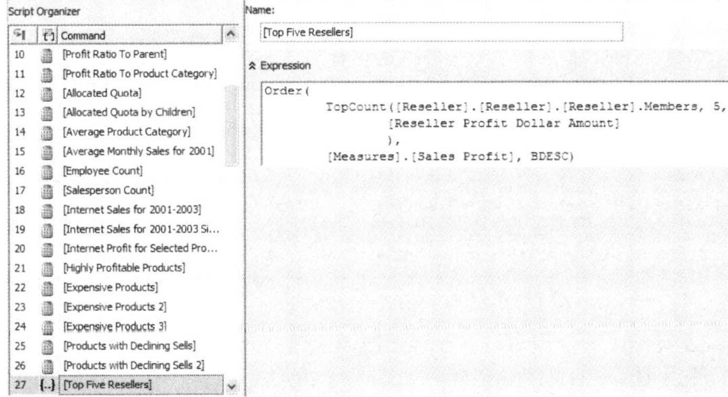

Figure 10.12 Creating a named set in a Form View mode.

Creating a new named set

In the preceding chapter, we authored a calculated member called Average Profit From Top Five Resellers that uses the *TopCount* function to return the most profitable resellers.

Let's turn the TopCount expression into a useful named set by following these steps:

1. In the Script View mode, locate the Average Profit From Top Five Resellers calculated member and copy the following expression:

```
TopCount([Reseller].[Reseller].[Reseller].Members, 5,
[Reseller Profit Dollar Amount])
```

2. Although you are probably used to Script View mode by now, let's create our first named set in the Form View mode. Switch to the Form View mode and select the last calculated member in the Script Organizer pane. As noted, the ordering of the script commands is important because expressions are resolved according to their positional order in the MDX script.

3. Click on the New Named Set {..} toolbar button. The Form View interface changes (see Figure 10.12). Specifically, the Additional Properties section gets hidden since a named set cannot have format settings.

4. Enter **[Top Five Resellers]** as the name of the set. Paste the TopCount expression that you just copied.

5. Similar to calculated members, named sets can be organized in display folders to reduce clutter. Open the Calculation Properties dialog. Scroll all the way down the grid, expand the Calculation Name dropdown and select the Top Five Resellers named set. Enter **Sets** in the Display Folder column to place the set in the Sets folder.

6. Switch to the Script View mode. The entire expression to create the Top Five Resellers named set is:

```
CREATE SET CURRENTCUBE.[Top Five Resellers]
  AS TopCount([Reseller].[Reseller].[Reseller].Members, 5,
            [Reseller Profit Dollar Amount]);
```

The MDX CREATE SET statement is used to produce a named set.

7. Deploy the SOS OLAP project.

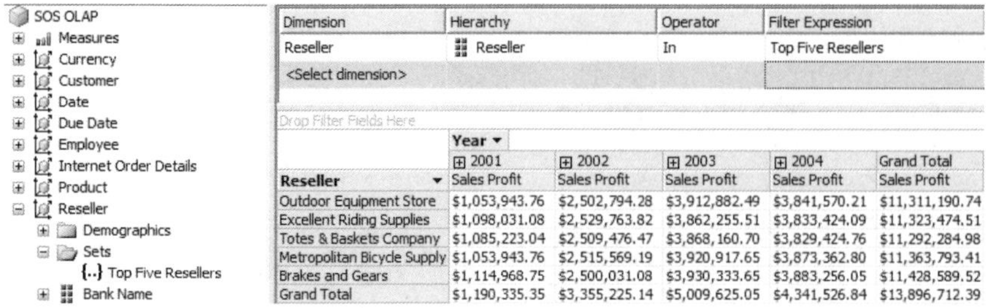

SOS OLAP
Measures
Currency
Customer
Date
Due Date
Employee
Internet Order Details
Product
Reseller
Demographics
Sets
{..} Top Five Resellers
Bank Name
Dimension
Hierarchy
Operator
Filter Expression
Reseller
Reseller
In
Top Five Resellers
<Select dimension>
Drop Filter Fields Here
Year
2001
2002
2003
2004
Grand Total
Reseller
Sales Profit
Outdoor Equipment Store $1,053,943.76 $2,502,794.28 $3,912,882.49 $3,841,570.21 $11,311,190.74
Excellent Riding Supplies $1,098,031.08 $2,529,763.82 $3,862,255.51 $3,833,424.09 $11,323,474.51
Totes & Baskets Company $1,085,223.04 $2,509,476.47 $3,868,160.70 $3,829,424.76 $11,292,284.98
Metropolitan Bicycle Supply $1,053,943.76 $2,515,569.19 $3,920,917.65 $3,873,362.80 $11,363,793.41
Brakes and Gears $1,114,968.75 $2,500,031.08 $3,930,333.65 $3,883,256.05 $11,428,589.52
Grand Total $1,190,335.35 $3,355,225.14 $5,009,625.05 $4,341,526.84 $13,896,712.39

Figure 10.13 You can use a named set to slice the cube.

Testing the named set

Let's put the Top Five Resellers named set to practical use by authoring a new report in the Cube Browser and using the named set to filter the report data.

1. Flip to the Cube Browser tab and reconnect.
2. Expand the Reseller dimension and the Sets folder below it. Note that the Cube Browser has automatically placed the Top Five Reseller set in the Reseller dimension. That's because a named set is always associated with a single dimension.
3. Drag the Reseller attribute hierarchy from the Reseller dimension on rows, Date dimension on columns, and Sales Profit measure on the report data section. As a result, a long report is generated that has more than 700 resellers on rows.
4. To use the Top Five Resellers as a cube slicer, drag it from the Reseller dimension and drop it onto the cube slicer section of the report (not the pivot table Drop Filter Fields Here section). The report refreshes to show the top five resellers only.

Note The Cube Browser tab doesn't allow you to use a named set on the report rows or columns. This is a limitation of the OWC PivotTable component. MDX queries can place named sets on any axis of the query.

From a performance standpoint, the set expression is evaluated the first time it is requested by a query. The calculation engine caches the set until the session expires or the set is explicitly removed by sending the DROP SET statement.

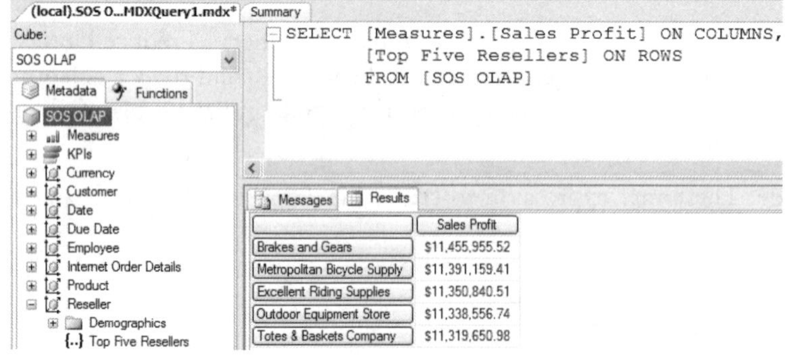

Figure 10.14 MDX queries can request a named set on any axis.

Using the named set in MDX queries

A smart browser could allow the end users to filter report data by placing the named set on the report rows or columns. To do so, the browser could send an MDX, such as the one shown in

Figure 10.14. This screenshot is taken from the SQL Server Management Studio. I've authored an MDX statement that requests the Top Five Resellers on rows. The net result is the same but the underlying process is different. In the case of the report created in the Cube Browser, a subcube is created first and then the MDX query is evaluated against the cube. In the second case, there is only one MDX query.

Ordering members of a set

If you'd like, you can sort a set by a given criteria by using the MDX *Order* function. The Order function takes the set to be sorted and optionally an expression for the sort criterion. For example, suppose you need to sort the [Top Five Reseller] named set by the Reseller Sales Amount measure in a descending order.

```
SELECT [Measures].[Reseller Sales Amount] ON COLUMNS,
    Order([Top Five Resellers],[Measures].[Reseller Sales Amount], BDESC) ON ROWS
    FROM [SOS OLAP]
```

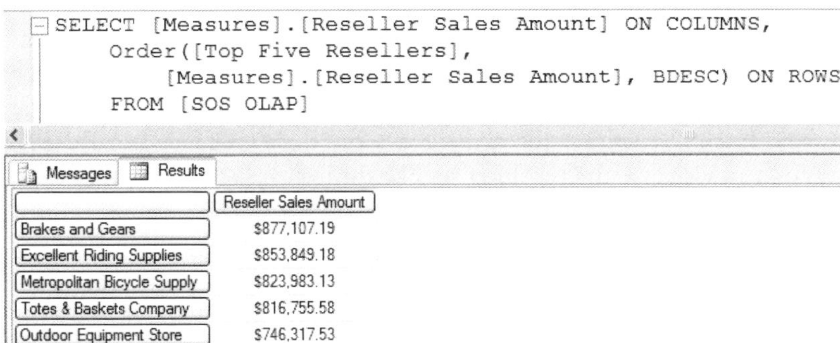

Figure 10.15 Using the Order function to sort members of a set in descending order.

By default, if a multi-level hierarchy is requested in the set, the calculation engine first sorts the set members according to their position in the hierarchy and then by the member level. The *B* prefix (stands for "break hierarchy") can be used to ignore the hierarchy membership. Due to the limitations of the PivotTable component, to see the ordered set, you need to use SQL Server Management Studio (Figure 10.15).

Aliasing a set inline

Sometimes, you may need to author complex MDX expressions where a given MDX set is referenced multiple times. You can make your code more readable by aliasing the set inline. For example, suppose that you need to find programmatically the last time period with data. This is useful for inventory analysis where you may need to determine the closing quantity at the end of the time period for a given product or a set of products.

Tip The expression example that I will demonstrate for finding the last non empty child is essentially the programmatic equivalent of the *LastNonEmpty* standard aggregate function that SSAS supports.

Translating this requirement to the Adventure Works OLAP model, let's assume that we need the last day in the SOS OLAP cube with data. The measure that we will evaluate will be the Reseller Order Quantity measure.

Getting Last Non Empty Child

Although it sounds simple, finding the last period with data may take a few iterations to get the expression right, so let's bite this elephant one step at a time. First, we need to exclude from the Time dimension those days that don't have values of Reseller Order Quantity. That's exactly what the filter expressions are for, so our first step produces the following expression:

```
Filter ([Date].[Date].[Date].Members * [Measures].[Reseller Order Quantity] AS s,
      Not IsEmpty(s.Current))
```

The day period is represented by the Date attribute hierarchy (the dimension key) in the Date level of the Date dimension (hence the triple notatation). The result of the crossjoin expression is a set that consists of all days that have associated Reseller Order Quantity values. However, the intersecting cells found at the Date and Reseller Order Quantity attribute hierarchies may be empty (NULL fact values). To exclude the empty cells, we use the *Not IsEmpty* criteria. The *Current* property of an MDX set returns the current member (tuple) of the set. In other words, when the calculation engine qualifies the members of the set, it processes them in a forward-only fashion. The Current property points to the member that is currently evaluated. Instead of referencing the same set again, we could make our code more readable by aliasing the set inline using the *AS* operator.

You can think of the resulting set as a one-dimensional array which has as many elements as the number of days with data. Each element of the array is a tuple that has Date and Reseller Order Quantity members. You can visualize the resulting set like this:

```
{('01/01/2001', 200,000), ('01/02/2001', 100), …, ('8/31/2004', 214,378)}
```

This example assumes that the first day with data is January 1st 2001 and we have 200,000 orders placed that day. The last day is August 31st 2004 where we have 214,378 orders.

Getting a subset using the Tail function

The next step will be to get the last day. It so happens that MDX supports a handy function to retrieve the last N members of a set. This function is called *Tail* and it returns a subset that has the specified number of members found at the end of the input set. Therefore, the expression:

```
Tail (
     Filter ([Date].[Date].[Date].Members *
       [Measures].[Reseller Order Quantity] AS s,
        Not IsEmpty(s.Current))
    , 1)
```

returns a set that has only one member -- the ('8/31/2004', 214,378) tuple in our sample set. By the way, the opposite of the Tail function is the *Head* function, which returns a subset with the specified number of members taken from the *beginning* of the set. If you want to display the actual date, you need to know how to reference the appropriate tuple. The Item indexer of an MDX set allows you to reference any tuple of the set. So, <<*set*>>*.Item(0)* will give the first and, in our case, the only tuple of the set. Then, <<*set*>>*.Item(0).Item(0)* will return the first member of the tuple (the day member), which was our ultimate goal in the first place. Use the SQL Server Management studio to fire the MDX query shown in Figure 10.16.

The results of this query reveal that the last day with data is August 31. We can't tell which year that is because the member names of the Date attribute are not prefixed with the name of the year. That's because the Date attribute is shared by the multilevel hierarchies in the Date

Dimension. We can use Item(0).Item(1) to get the actual value of the Reseller Order Quantity measure which turns out to be $214,378.

```
SELECT Tail (
        Filter ([Date].[Date].Members *
            [Measures].[Reseller Order Quantity] AS s,
            Not IsEmpty(s.Current))
    , 1).Item(0).Item(0) ON COLUMNS
FROM [SOS OLAP]
```

Messages | Results

August 31
(null)

Figure 10.16 Use the Tail function to return a subset consisting of the last N members of a given set.

10.2 Using Subcube Expressions

Calculated members and named sets allow you to extend the cube programmatically in the form of expressions that are calculated during runtime. The values of these expressions are produced by *reading* and aggregating cube data. Sometimes, you may also need to change the values of individual cells or a range of cells by *writing* to the cube space. For example, you may need to distribute (allocate) the parent values down a multi-level hierarchy by using different ratio formulas for different levels. Or, as a last resort, when you can't get the expression for a calculated member or a named set right, you may want to "fix" it by overwriting the affected cells directly. The last example was a poor attempt at a joke, of course.

SSAS 2000 Subcube expressions essentially replace cell calculations in UDM. The cell calculation syntax is still supported, but it has been deprecated in favor of the more intuitive and flexible subcube expressions that use the SCOPE statement.

In UDM, subcube expressions gives you the flexibility to create targeted calculations that assign formulas to cells located anywhere in the cube space.

10.2.1 Understanding Subcube Expressions

You implement subcube expressions by using the SCOPE statement, which has the following basic syntax:

```
SCOPE(<subcube definition>);
 <assignment statement>;
END SCOPE;
```

Subcube definition

First, you need to decide what subset of the cube (called *subcube* in the MDX terminology) your expression will target. For example, you may want to apply a formula to the children of a given member in an attribute hierarchy. The subcube definition may consist of one or more cross-joined MDX sets. There are certain restrictions that govern what constitutes a valid subcube definition. Specifically, a subcube definition could be:

- One or more members of an attribute hierarchy, excluding the All member.
- One or more members at a given level of a multi-level hierarchy.
- Descendants of a member in a multi-level hierarchy.

If you don't specify a subcube expression to limit the scope, the default scope is the entire cube.

Assignment statements

Once the scope is defined, you can have one or more assignment statements that place values or formulas in the cells located in that scope. You can use any expression that returns intersecting cells and comply with the above rules on the left side of the assignment statement. Typically, the assignment statement will be in the form:

```
THIS = <MDX expression>;
```

Think of the THIS statement as a pointer to the enclosing subcube. Typically, the MDX expression on the right side of the assignment assigns formulas to the cells in the enclosing subcube.

Note Strictly speaking, subcube expressions don't have to necessarily change the cell values inside the subcube. For example, you can have an MDX expression that applies conditional formatting, e.g. to change the background color of the subcube cells.

The active scope remains in effect until the END SCOPE statement is reached or until the scope is changed as a result of another SCOPE statement.

10.2.2 Your First Subcube Expression

Suppose that, due to worsening economic conditions, the Adventure Works management has decided to lower the 2004 sales quota for all sales regions by 50%. You have two approaches to address this requirement – database-driven and programmatic. The trivial solution is to update the FactSalesQuota table.

The first tradeoff of the database-driven approach is that it may not work that well with more complicated calculations, e.g. formulas that apply different calculations based on the hierarchical level or use different ratios (weights) based on the position of the given member in the hierarchy. Second, it entails re-processing the measure group to re-load the updated data. In addition, updating the original source data is something you would advise against. What if the management cancels the decision and asks you to revert back to the old data? In such cases, handling this issue programmatically may be a better option.

Creating the expression

To follow the tradition, let's create our first subcube expression using the Form View of the Calculation tab.

1. In the Script Organizer, select the last MDX expression, which should be the [Last Day with Data] calculated member.
2. Our business requirements state that we need to change the 2004 sales quota for all sales regions. Therefore, we need to scope our cube expression to a set defined by the intersection of the Region, Calendar Year, and Sales Quota hierarchies. Click the New Script Command button to create a new MDX command and enter the following expression as the expression text (you can drag the appropriate hierarchies from the Metadata tab).

```
SCOPE ([Sales Territory].[Region].[Region].Members,
[Date].[Calendar Year].&[2004], [Sales Quota])
```

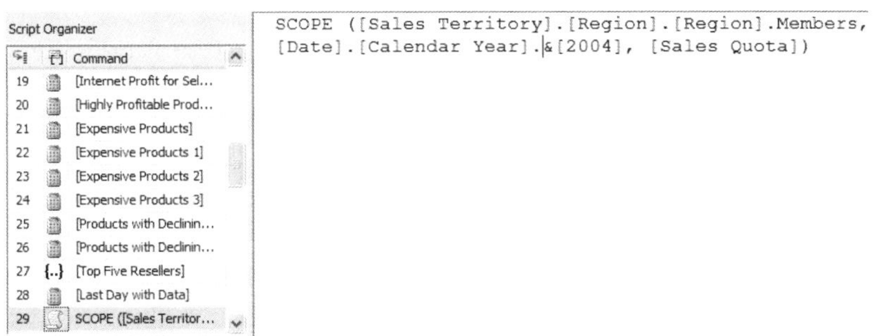

Figure 10.17 In the Form View mode, you create subcube expressions by adding script commands.

Here, we are resetting the expression scope and creating a subcube which includes all members of the Region attribute hierarchy (Sales Territory dimension), 2004 member of the Calendar Year multi-level hierarchy, and the Sales Quota measure. That's because we need to target our expression to this specific slice of the cube only. Note the scope is defined entirely by attribute hierarchies.

Tip As a best practice, use attribute hierarchies whenever possible in scope definitions and when writing to the cube space (on the left side of the expression assignment). In comparison, do use multi-level hierarchies when reading data (on the right side of the assignment) to make the expression more compact and easier to read.

3. At this point, you are probably convinced that the Form View mode is more trouble than it's worth when authoring subcube expressions, but we are almost done. Create a new command and enter the following expression:

```
This = [Sales Quota] * 0.5
```

This expression places the above formula in all cells of the subcube defined by the SCOPE operator. Once the expression is executed, the cell values in the subcube (the Sales Quota figures) inside our subcube will be decreased in half.

4. Finally, add two more commands to close the two scopes with matching END SCOPE statements. Figure 10.17 shows the final result in the Form View mode. The entire subcube expression spans five commands (lines 28-32)

5. To verify the expression text, flip to the Script View mode and compare it with the following subcube expression.

```
SCOPE ([Region].[Region].Members, [Date].[Calendar Year].&[2004], [Sales Quota]);
    This = [Sales Quota] * 0.5;
END SCOPE;
```

If all is well, we are ready to test our subcube expression.

Debugging the expression

While we can test our expression by using the Cube Browser or MDX queries, the Calculation Tab sponsors a handy MDX debugger which is specifically designed to help you with subcube expressions that write to the cube space. That's because the MDX debugger highlights automatically the affected cells.

1. In the Solution Explorer, right-click on the SOS OLAP project and select *Set as Startup Project*. Verify that the Start Object setting on the Debugging section of the SOS OLAP project properties is set to *<Currently Active Object>*.
2. Switch to Script View mode and scroll to the end of the editor window.
3. Locate the subcube expression and place a breakpoint on the SCOPE statement. You can do this either by clicking on the gray margin on the left of the SCOPE statement or placing the mouse cursor on the line and hitting F9. When you do this, a red dot appears in the margin and the SCOPE statement is highlighted in red to indicate that there is a breakpoint on that line.
4. Hit F5 to initiate the debug session. If BI Studio detects any changes, it will deploy the project and process the Sales Quota measure group. Next, the debugger will stop at the breakpoint.

   Notice the multi-tab data pane that appears at the bottom of the Calculations tab to assist you with debugging. The Pivot Table tab hosts the familiar Pivot Table OWC. If you have .NET development experience, think of the Pivot Table tab as the Auto window in VS.NET. It shows you the changes made to the cube space as you step through the subcube expression. Besides, the Pivot Table tab, the MDX debugger has four additional tabs you can use to fire free-form MDX queries. If you have .NET development experience, think of each MDX tab as the VS.NET Immediate window which you can use to send MDX ad hoc queries.
5. Drag and drop the Region attribute hierarchy (Sales Territory dimension) on rows, the Calendar Year attribute hierarchy (Date dimension) on columns, and the Sales Quota measure on details. If you wish, filter Calendar Year to show year 2004 only since our expression scope targets this year only. The report shows the original sales quota figures broken down by region and year. The Pivot Table tab highlights all cells that have data in yellow.

Tip If you need to skip expressions (and their results) in the current debug session, right-click on the expression you want to jump to and choose *Set Next Statement*. This action will advance the execution pointer to the desired expression. Of course, if you are not debugging, all expressions will be executed in the order they appear in the script.

6. Press F10 (or Debug menu ⇨ Step Over) to advance to assignment expression. The Pivot Table remains unchanged because we haven't executed the THIS statement yet.
7. Hit F10 again to execute the assignment expression. Observe that the Pivot Table highlights the Year 2004 and Grand Total columns because their values have changed (Figure 10.18). Specifically, the Sales Quota values for 2004 are now half of the original values.

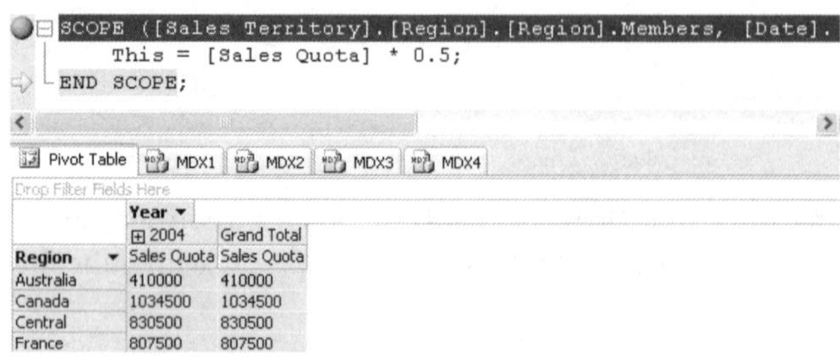

Figure 10.18 Use the MDX debugger to test and troubleshoot subcube expressions.

You may be curious as to why the Grand Total figures (the All member of the Year attribute hierarchy) change, given that we didn't target the All member in our subcube expression. That's because the corresponding cells still contain the aggregation formulas to sum the years. If our subcube expression has placed values in the All member cells *(SCOPE ([Region].[Region].Members, [Sales Quota])*, the All member will not aggregate, since its cells will have values instead of formulas.

Note As noted in chapter 5, DistinctCount measures aggregate differently, because the scope calculation doesn't propagate to "upper" levels.

8. Stop the debugging session by clicking on the Stop Debugging button located on the Debug toolbar (only visible in debug mode) or choose the Debug ➪ Stop Debugging menu. If you'd like, use the Cube Browser to create a similar report and confirm that you get the same results.

Other testing techniques

Besides the debugger, you may find other techniques useful for testing your subcube expressions, such as changing the cell values to constant values and coloring cells. For example, replace the previous expression as follows:

```
SCOPE ([Region].[Region].Members, [Date].[Calendar Year].&[2004], [Sales Quota]);
    This = 0;        -- zero out the subcube cells
    Back_Color (this) = 12632256;  -- change the background color to silver
    Format_String (this) = "Currency"   -- format cells as currency
END SCOPE;
```

Changing the subcube cell values to constants allows us to observe easily the effect of the expression from MDX queries. Another visual technique for troubleshooting expressions is to change the cell background or the font color. You can use the Color toolbar button to pick up a color. The color statements (FORE_COLOR and BACK_COLOR) can use the integer code of the color (e.g. 12632256 for silver), or the VBA RGB function, e.g. RGB (192,192,192) to achieve the same effect. Finally, format the expression value as currency using the Format_String function.

			Year				
			2001	2002	2003	2004	Grand Total
Group	Country	Region	Sales Quota	Sales Quota	Sales Quota	Sales Quota	Sales Quota
North America	Canada		$1,892,000.00	$3,592,000.00	$3,910,000.00	$0.00	$9,394,000.00
	United States	Central	$1,437,000.00	$4,750,000.00	$4,350,000.00	0	$10,537,000.00
		Northeast	$923,000.00	$3,805,000.00	$4,716,000.00	0	$9,444,000.00
		Northwest	$1,213,000.00	$2,693,000.00	$4,102,000.00	0	$8,008,000.00
		Southeast	$1,586,000.00	$2,963,000.00	$2,768,000.00	0	$7,317,000.00
		Southwest	$2,427,000.00	$6,481,000.00	$7,326,000.00	0	$16,234,000.00
		Total	$7,586,000.00	$20,692,000.00	$23,262,000.00	$0.00	$51,540,000.00
	Total		$9,478,000.00	$24,284,000.00	$27,172,000.00	$0.00	$60,934,000.00
Europe	France	Total		$1,002,000.00	$2,940,000.00	$0.00	$3,942,000.00
	Germany	Total			$1,294,000.00	$0.00	$1,294,000.00
	United Kingdom	Total		$3,160,000.00	$5,142,000.00	$0.00	$8,302,000.00
	Total			$4,162,000.00	$9,376,000.00	$0.00	$13,538,000.00
Pacific					$867,000.00	$0.00	$867,000.00
NA			$35,000.00	$563,000.00	$1,367,000.00	$0.00	$1,965,000.00
Grand Total			$9,513,000.00	$29,009,000.00	$38,782,000.00	$0.00	$77,304,000.00

Figure 10.19 Use MDX queries to test the subcube expressions.

1. Flip to the Cube Browser tab. Create a similar report as the one shown in Figure 10.18 but use the Sales Territory multilevel hierarchy on rows.

2. Drill down North America ➪ United States to expand the US regions, as shown in Figure 10.19.

Observe that the Sales Quota cells for the US regions are zeroed out and their background color has changed to silver. By using such visual techniques, you can quickly determine which scope the subcube expression targets.

10.2.3 Script Execution Revisited

As basic as our subcube expression is, it demonstrates some important script concepts which I would like to take a moment and point out. They will help you understand better how the MDX script and expressions work.

Procedural or declarative execution

An interesting characteristic of an MDX script is that it combines certain aspects from both the procedural and declarative execution models. The script itself doesn't actually "run". The MDX debugger gives you the illusion that the script executes linearly from top to bottom, as a C# or VB.NET code would. In reality, however, the calculation engine doesn't execute the script that way. Instead, the expressions contained within a script are always consistent with the cube data and are always in effect. In this respect, the MDX script is still a declarative model similar to the SSAS 2000 calculation model.

What makes the MDX script execution closer to the procedural model is the script is aware of where the expression is located in the script. For example, if you have two expressions and they both are writing to the same cell, the expression that appears further down the script will win. In other words, the last writer to a given cell always wins. This is a simple but very important concept which makes MDX programming much easier in comparison with the previous releases of Analysis Services.

Calculation Pass and solve order

To understand the simplification that the procedural execution model brings, consider the concepts of the expression pass and solve order which you had to master when writing MDX expressions with SSAS 2000. SSAS 2000 didn't have a notion of an MDX script. Instead, the MDX expressions were located in different places. For example, if you wanted to create a calculated member, you would use the Cube Editor.

The Solve Order Issue

Just like with SSAS 2005, when the cube was calculated, the calculation engine would determine the expression pass number and solve order to resolve the expression. However, the big difference in comparison with UDM is that you didn't know what solve order would be associated with a given expression. This presented an issue when two or more calculations from different dimensions were intersecting with each other. Let's consider the example shown in Figure 10.20.

Category	Sales $	Units	Sales / Units
Accessories	100	10	10
Bikes	200	2	100
Clothing	300	3	100
Category Average	***200***	***5***	***40???***

200/5 = 40

100+100+10 = 210

Figure 10.20 Use MDX queries to verify the correctness of subcube expressions.

In the preceding chapter, we authored a dimension calculated member [Average Product Category] to calculate the average sales amount by using the *Avg* MDX function. Suppose you have a report that requests the Product Category dimension on rows. On columns we have three measures: two regular measures (Sales and Units), and a calculated measure member which divides the Sales measure by the Units measure to produce the average sales amount per unit.

In SSAS 2000, what Sales/Units value you will get for the Category Average member was not predictable. If the Sales/Units formula (the horizontal pass in Figure 10.20) would reach the cell first, you would get $40, which is the correct value. However, if the Sum formula (the vertical pass) is the winner, then the cell value will be $210. Since ambiguity is something you want to avoid in your reports, SSAS 2000 had the concept of the expression solve order. To set the solve order of the two expressions in our example in SSAS 2000, you could use the Advanced tab of the calculated member properties and set the Solve Order property accordingly. The higher the solve order was, the later the expression will be calculated.

Positional pass resolution

In UDM, the expression pass and solve order concepts still exist but they are pushed to the background. Expressions are resolved according to their position in the script, which is the behavior you would expect naturally. If you need to evaluate one expression before another, you could just re-arrange it to appear before the second expression. You can still overwrite the expression solve order explicitly (by using the SOLVE_ORDER property) but, in most cases, this is not needed and you can just leave it up to the calculation engine to resolve it for you.

An added benefit of the automatic pass resolution in UDM is preventing the dreaded infinite recursion error that was plaguing SSAS 2000 MDX developers. For example, our first subcube expression had the following assignment:

```
This = [Sales Quota] * 0.5;
```

This expression is essentially equivalent to:

```
[Sales Quota] = [Sales Quota] * 0.5
```

In SSAS 2000, the above expression would result in an infinite recursion error because the cell essentially relies on its own value. In UDM, the calculation engine will use the previous pass value to prevent an infinite recursion loop.

Nesting scopes

One important aspect of working with scopes is that you can nest them within each other. For example, consider the subcube expression shown in Listing 10.1.

Listing 10.1 Nested scopes can be used for targeted calculations.

```
SCOPE ([Sales Territory].[Sales Territory].[Region].Members, -- All regions
     [Date].[Calendar Year].&[2004], [Sales Quota]);

    SCOPE ([Sales Territory].[Sales Territory]. -- North America regions only
     [Group].&[North America].Children);

         SCOPE ([Sales Territory].[Sales Territory]. -- US regions only
       [Country].&[United States].Children);

              This = [Sales Quota] * 0.5;
         END SCOPE; -- Scope reverted to North America
   END SCOPE;    -- Scope reverted to All regions
END SCOPE; -- Scope reverted to entire cube
```

This expression changes the sales quota for the US regions only. The first scope returns a set consisting of all sales regions and their sales quotas for 2004. The second scope uses the Sales Territory multilevel hierarchy to filter the sales regions in North America only. The third and final scope narrows down the targeted calculation to the regions in the US.

Tip If you want to prevent nested subcube expressions from overwriting the parent scope, you can use the FREEZE statement at the parent scope level. It pins the cell values of a given subcube, preventing subsequent expressions from changing its values.

Going back to Listing 10.1, what do think will happen when an END SCOPE statement is executed? Just like a procedure call stack, the scope statement will unwind. Thus, after the innermost END SCOPE statement, the scope is reverted to the North America regions. Here, if this is what we want, we could apply a different aggregation formula instead of summing the sales quota taken from the children of the North America member. Of course, if the whole purpose of the entire subcube expression shown in Listing 10.1 is to change the sales quota of the US regions, we could use only one SCOPE statement to create the required subcube, as follows:

```
SCOPE([Sales Territory].[Sales Territory].[Country].&[United States].Children);
```

10.2.4 Implementing Targeted Allocations

Having covered the basics, let's see a more realistic business scenario for using subcube expressions that builds upon the previous example. Suppose the Adventure Works management would like to allocate a sales quota to each sales person for the first semester of next year. Since we are in the Adventure Works time warp where the last year of data is 2003, we will assume that next year is 2004.

In the preceding chapter, I demonstrated how you can distribute allocations proportionally by creating a new calculated member. This time, let's demonstrate a different approach. Specifically, we will use different distribution formulas at the Month level of the Date dimension. The complete MDX script that drives the custom allocations can be found in the Calculations tab of the SOS OLAP cube (starting with the */* Sales person quota allocation using custom ratios */* comment). Let me walk you through the script, as you would step through it in the MDX debugger.

Semester allocations

As with most challenges in life, when writing subcube expressions, the key to success is to have a clear objective about what you need to accomplish right off the bat. In our case, we want to perform *sales quota* allocations for *all sales* persons for the *first semester* of *2004*. The words in italic immediately define our initial scope as:

```
Scope (
     [Measures].[Sales Quota],
     [Employee].[Employees].Members,
     [Employee].[Sales Person Flag].&[True],
     [Sales Territory].[Region].[Region].Members,
     [Date].[Calendar Semester].&[2004]&[1] ) ;
```

Note that we also bring the sales regions in scope. The reason for this is that in Adventure Works one sales person may be responsible for more than one sales region. If we don't slice by region, we will get the sales quota for the current member (All member) of the Region attribute hierarchy. The net result will be that our allocations won't work correctly when sales quota is broken down by region. In addition, note that I use only attribute hierarchies in the scope statement. Suppose that our business requirements state that the overall quota for the first semester of 2004 will be the same as the quota for the first semester of 2003. The following assignment accomplishes this requirement:

```
This = ( ParallelPeriod([Date].[Calendar Date].[Year],
    1, [Date].[Calendar Date].[Semester].&[2004]&[1]));
```

Here, we need to bring in the Calendar Date multilevel hierarchy because we need to retrieve the previous year data. We use the familiar *ParallelPeriod* function to get the value of the corresponding semester one year ago (H1 2003) and bring its value into the first semester of 2004. The net effect of the above assignment is that we are overwriting the default aggregation formula for first semester level of 2004 by placing a fixed value in its cell. As a result, the children (quarter cells) will not roll up automatically anymore, which is the behavior we need anyway, since we are allocating values top-down. If you are stepping through the code with the debugger, your screen should look like the one shown in Figure 10.21.

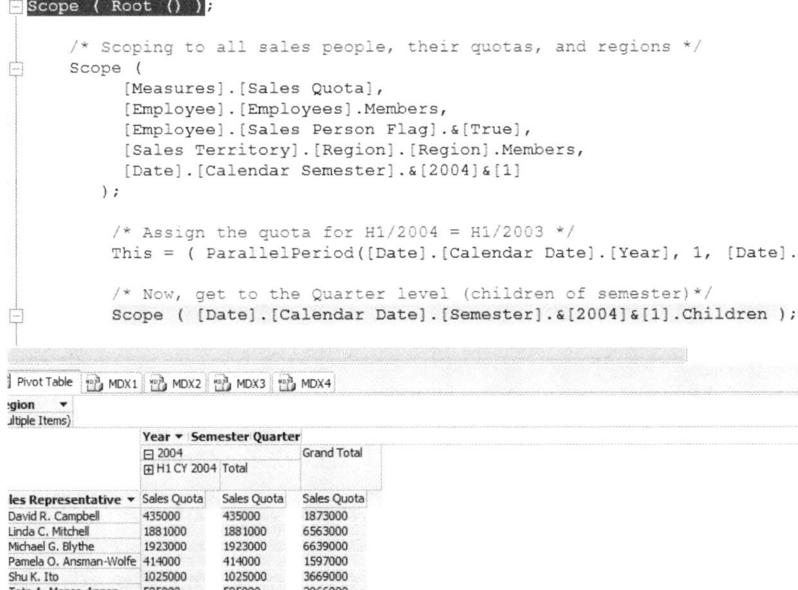

Figure 10.21 The sales quota example after the semester allocation.

To minimize the amount of data shown, I've filtered the data on the report by the regions in the USA only (Northeast, Northwest, Southeast, Southwest). What we've accomplished at this point in our expression is allocating the quota at the top (semester level). The cells below the semester level (quarter, month, day levels) retain their original values. However, because the expression pass happens after the data aggregation pass, we have effectively overwritten the aggregations at the semester level. In other words, the semester values will not roll up automatically anymore, since we've removed the Sum formula (or whatever aggregation formula is associated with the Sales Quota measure).

Quarter allocations

Our quarter allocation is simple. We will assume that the quota for the first semester of 2004 will be equally distributed to its two quarters.

```
Scope ([Date].[Calendar Date].[Semester].&[2004]&[1].Children ) ;
    This = [Date].[Calendar Date].CurrentMember.Parent / 2 ;
End Scope ;
```

First, we narrow the scope down to the quarters of the H1 2004. Since we know that each semester has two quarters, we can just divide the semester quota by two. If we don't know the number of the children below a given member, we could use the Count function to count them. At this point, your debugger window should resemble Figure 10.22.

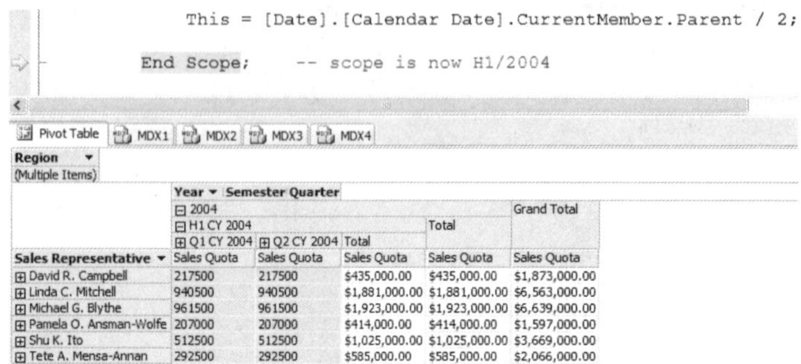

	Year / Semester Quarter				
	2004				Grand Total
	H1 CY 2004			Total	
	Q1 CY 2004	Q2 CY 2004	Total		
Sales Representative	Sales Quota	Sales Quota	Sales Quota	Sales Quota	Sales Quota
David R. Campbell	217500	217500	$435,000.00	$435,000.00	$1,873,000.00
Linda C. Mitchell	940500	940500	$1,881,000.00	$1,881,000.00	$6,563,000.00
Michael G. Blythe	961500	961500	$1,923,000.00	$1,923,000.00	$6,639,000.00
Pamela O. Ansman-Wolfe	207000	207000	$414,000.00	$414,000.00	$1,597,000.00
Shu K. Ito	512500	512500	$1,025,000.00	$1,025,000.00	$3,669,000.00
Tete A. Mensa-Annan	292500	292500	$585,000.00	$585,000.00	$2,066,000.00
Tsvi Michael. Reiter	571500	571500	$1,143,000.00	$1,143,000.00	$3,911,000.00

Figure 10.22 The sales quota example after the quarter allocation.

Month allocations

Suppose that we need to use different ratios to distribute quotas at month level. In addition, to make things more interesting, suppose that we don't want the month percentage allocations to roll up to 100%. The first challenge is getting to the children of a given quarter. As a first attempt, we may try the *CurrentMember* function believing that it would give us the current quarter. However, you will find that this approach will not work. That's because scope definitions are *static* and are not re-evaluated at each cell. Developers can associate this concept with static methods which cannot reference instance methods or variables and cannot use the *Me* (VB.NET) or *this* (C#) operators. So, the only way to get the members of the Month level of the Calendar Date dimension is to have a static scope declaration, e.g. by using the *Descendants* function.

Listing 10.2 Performing month allocations.

```
Scope (Descendants ([Date].[Calendar Date].[Year].&[2004],
     [Date].[Calendar Date].[Month])) ;

   This = Case
     When [Date].[Calendar Date].CurrentMember Is
             [Date].[Calendar Date].[Month].&[1]&[2004]
        Then .15 * [Date].[Calendar Date].Parent
        When [Date].[Calendar Date].CurrentMember Is
             [Date].[Calendar Date].[Month].&[2]&[2004]
        Then .25 * [Date].[Calendar Date].Parent
          <more monthly allocations follow>
   End ;
End Scope;
```

Once we get all months of 2004, for each month we apply a custom allocation formula to assign its quota value as a certain percentage of the quarter quota. As Figure 10.23 shows, the monthly quota values don't add up to the quarter value. Again the reason for this behavior is that the quarter level cell has been overridden and now contains the formula *[Date].[Calendar Date].CurrentMember.Parent / 2*. If this wasn't the case, changing the new month values would automatically roll up to the quarter level.

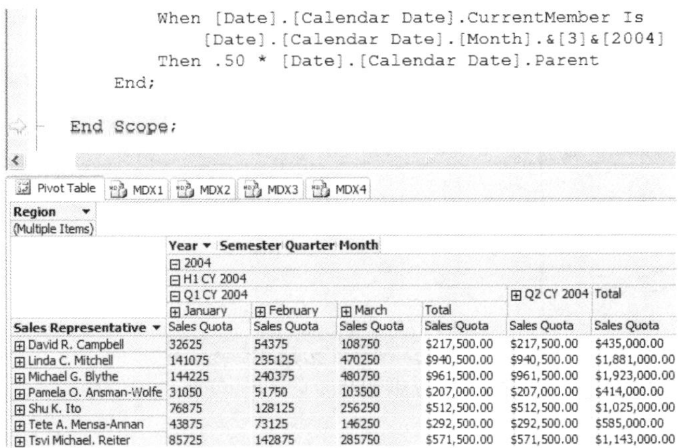

	Q1 CY 2004				Q2 CY 2004	Total
	January	February	March	Total		
Sales Representative	Sales Quota	Sales Quota	Sales Quota	Sales Quota	Sales Quota	Sales Quota
David R. Campbell	32625	54375	108750	$217,500.00	$217,500.00	$435,000.00
Linda C. Mitchell	141075	235125	470250	$940,500.00	$940,500.00	$1,881,000.00
Michael G. Blythe	144225	240375	480750	$961,500.00	$961,500.00	$1,923,000.00
Pamela O. Ansman-Wolfe	31050	51750	103500	$207,000.00	$207,000.00	$414,000.00
Shu K. Ito	76875	128125	256250	$512,500.00	$512,500.00	$1,025,000.00
Tete A. Mensa-Annan	43875	73125	146250	$292,500.00	$292,500.00	$585,000.00
Tsvi Michael. Reiter	85725	142875	285750	$571,500.00	$571,500.00	$1,143,000.00

Figure 10.23 The sales quota example after the month allocation.

10.3 Implementing Business Intelligence

Although UDM brings many programming simplifications, you would probably agree that MDX expressions can get rather involved. This is especially true in the case of the subcube expressions which may take hours of troubleshooting and debugging. Yet, it is likely that your business requirements will call for common analytics tasks that can only be addressed programmatically.

Realizing this, Microsoft has incorporated two frequently requested business intelligence enhancements into the Business Intelligence Wizard. They are the time intelligence and currency conversion enhancements. The end result is boiler-plate code which you can leverage to minimize the programming effort required to implement similar features. Even if you don't need these enhancements in your UDM, I will strongly suggest you explore the code generated by Business Intelligence Wizard to hone your MDX skills and harvest best practices for using MDX expressions.

10.3.1 Applying Time Intelligence

In the preceding chapter, we implemented a few expressions that used the Time dimension to compare values across adjacent and parallel time periods. Many OLAP requirements call for calculations that aggregate data over time, such as Year to Date, Twelve Month Average, Year to Year Growth %, etc. Let's find out how the Business Intelligence Wizard can help us enhance UDM with time intelligence.

Note The Time Intelligence enhancement of the BI Wizard will only work if you have set up the Type attribute of the Time dimension and its attributes to the pre-defined semantic types, as our sample Time dimension demonstrates.

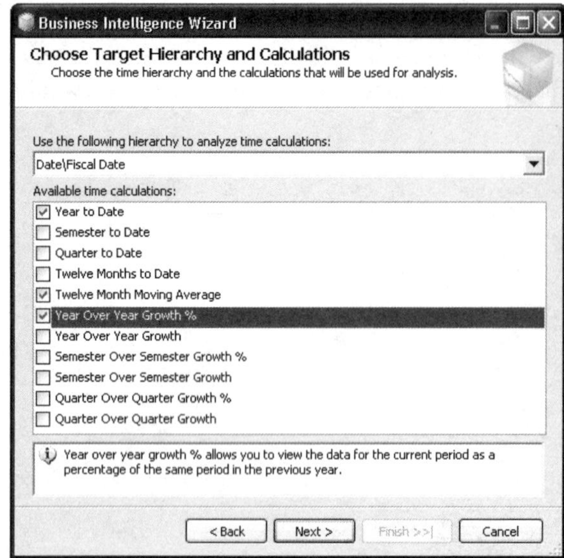

Figure 10.24 The Business Intelligence Wizard supports several commonly used time calculations.

Running the Business Intelligence Wizard

You've already used the Business Intelligence Wizard to implement account and dimension intelligence features. Follow these steps to add time intelligence to the SOS OLAP cube.

1. Right-click on the SOS OLAP cube and choose *Add Business Intelligence* to launch the Business Intelligence Wizard.

2. Click Next to advance to the Choose Enhancement step and select the *Define time Intelligence* option (the first item on the list). Click Next to move to the Choose Target Hierarchy and Calculations step (Figure 10.24).

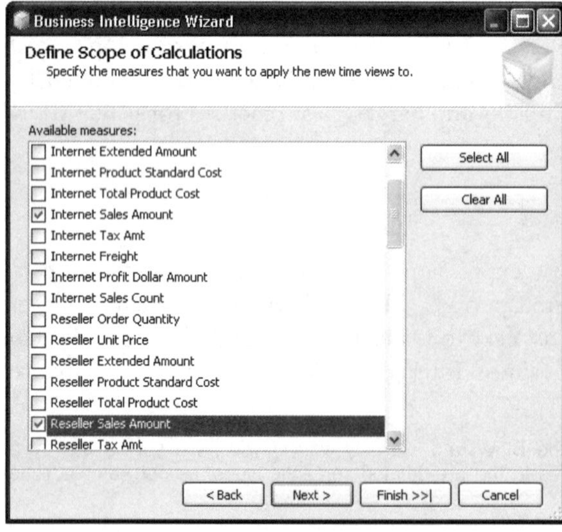

Figure 10.25 Select one or more measures that the time calculations will use.

The wizard automatically queries UDM to find if there is a Time dimension defined (its semantic Type property is set to Time). If so, the wizard loads the dimension and its role-based derivatives in the dropdown. You can select any attribute or multi-level hierarchy for the base of the time-related calculations. You can select only one hierarchy for a given wizard run. If you need to create calculations based on different hierarchies (e.g. Calendar Date and Financial Date), you need to run the Business Intelligence Wizard for each hierarchy.

3. Select the *Fiscal Date* multi-level hierarchy of the Date dimension.

4. You can choose one or more pre-defined time calculations. Select Year to Date, Twelve Month Moving Average, and Year Over Year Growth % calculations. When you select a calculation, a brief description of its purpose is shown in the bottom pane.

5. In the Define Scope of Calculations step, you need to select which measures these calculations will use to produce the aggregated values. Select the *Internet Sales Amount* and *Reseller Sales Amount* measures (Figure 10.25).

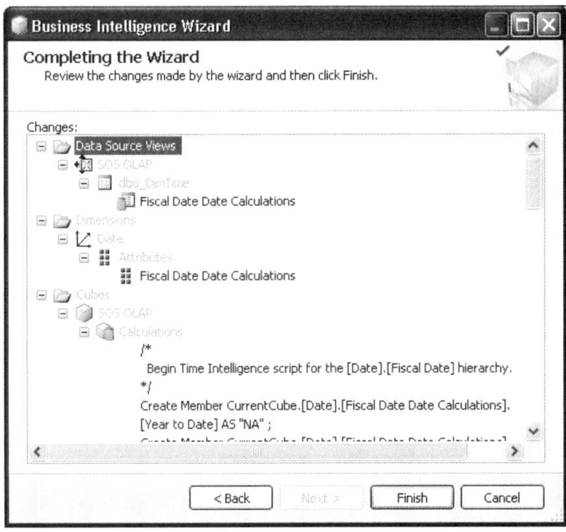

Figure 10.26 Review the changes that the Business Intelligence Wizard will make.

6. Completing the Wizard step lists the changes that the Business Intelligence Wizard will make to the underlying data source view, Time dimension, and the MDX script of the cube (Figure 10.26).

Understanding the schema changes

Each time you run the wizard, it will add a new named calculation to the DimTime dimension table, a new attribute to the Date dimension, and a new script block to the cube script. The named calculation and the attribute follow the *<HierarchyName N> Date Calculations* convention, where N is the number of times you run the wizard for the same hierarchy. Obviously, ending up with many named calculations and attribute hierarchies for the same source attribute hierarchy could become counter-productive. Unfortunately, you cannot copy the code from the last step of the wizard. Therefore, the only option to minimize the number of the time intelligence "byproducts" is to let the wizard run, manually remove the named calculation plus the hierarchy, and change the script.

Reseller by Geography ▾
United States

	Fiscal Date Date Calculations ▾			
	Current Date	Year to Date	Twelve Month Moving Average	Year Over Year Growth %
Year ▾ Semester	Reseller Sales Amount	Reseller Sales Amount	Reseller Sales Amount	Reseller Sales Amount
⊞ 2002	$13,208,634.95	$13,208,634.95	$13,208,634.95	
⊞ 2003	$19,471,989.04	$19,471,989.04	$16,340,312.00	47.42%
⊞ 2004	$20,927,177.22	$20,927,177.22	$17,869,267.07	7.47%
Grand Total	$53,607,801.21	NA	NA	NA

Figure 10.27 Use MDX queries to verify the correctness of subcube expressions.

The generated named calculation serves as a dummy source column for the new attribute hierarchy that the wizard adds to the Date dimension. For example, the report in Figure 10.27 uses the Fiscal Date Date Calculations hierarchy on columns and the Fiscal Date multi-level hierarchy on rows to show the time-based measures for resellers in the USA. As you can see, the Fiscal Date Date Calculations hierarchy has four members. The Current Date member gives the actual measure values. The other three correspond to the time calculations we selected in the Choose Target Hierarchy and Calculations step.

Understanding the time intelligence script

The BI Wizard adds the Time Intelligence expressions to the end of the MDX script of the cube. The time intelligence MDX script that the Wizard generates is template-based. The default location of the template is C:\Program Files\Microsoft SQL Server\90\Tools \Templates\ ↵ olap\1033\TimeIntelligence.xml. You can change the template to fit your needs and custom-tailor the script. The script starts by creating dimension calculated members for the Date Calculations hierarchy.

```
Create Member CurrentCube.[Date].[Fiscal Date Date Calculations].
[Year to Date] AS "NA";
```

The default value of the member is *NA* which is displayed when the calculation doesn't apply to the current cell. For example, in the report shown in Figure 10.27, the three calculations show *NA* for the Grand Total value. The same will happen if the source Date hierarchy is not requested in the report. Next, the script creates a subcube for the selected measures by the user.

```
Scope ({
          [Measures].[Internet Sales Amount],
          [Measures].[Reseller Sales Amount]});
```

This is the scope the calculations will operate upon. All other measures will return *NA*. Next, the script performs the actual calculations. For example, if you selected the Year to Date calculation, the subcube expression may look like:

```
([Date].[Fiscal Date Date Calculations].[Year to Date],
    [Date].[Fiscal Year].[Fiscal Year].Members ) =

  Aggregate(
          { [Date].[Fiscal Date Date Calculations].DefaultMember } *
          PeriodsToDate(
                        [Date].[Fiscal Date].[Year],
                        [Date].[Fiscal Date].CurrentMember
          ) ) ;
```

As you can see, here the assignment is made without using the THIS statement. Instead, the left side of the operand selects the subcube which, in this case, consists of all cells that intersect with the members of the Fiscal Year attribute hierarchy and Year to Date member of the Fiscal Date

Date Calculations. The values of these cells are overwritten with the result of the *Aggregate* function. For more information about time intelligence, read the excellent article *Analysis Services 2005 Brings You Automated Time Intelligence* by Mosha Pasumansky and Robert Zare (see the Resources section).

10.3.2 Handling Currency Conversions

Another frequently requested analytics task in today's global economy is currency conversion. Of course, as a prerequisite of implementing currency conversion, you need to have a fact table that stores the currency exchange rates. Once this table is in place, you can run the Business Intelligence Wizard to create currency conversion calculations.

Currency conversion scenarios

The Business Intelligence Wizard can handle currency conversions of foreign currencies stored both in the facts (facts are entered in foreign currencies), or in an attribute hierarchy, e.g. an Organization dimension which indicates in what currency each subsidiary reports its numbers. For example, both the FactResellerSales and FactInternetSales fact tables in the AdventureWorksDW database have a CurrencyKey foreign key that references the DimCurrency table.

Tip To avoid ambiguity, I would recommend you perform the currency conversion as a part of the ETL processes before the facts enter UDM or when the facts are captured in the OLTP system. Otherwise, it may be confusing for the end user which measures represent the converted and original currency amount. Sometimes, however, business requirement may rule out pre-UDM currency conversion, so you are left with no other choice but to solve currency conversion programmatically.

When we designed the SOS OLAP UDM, we converted the sales-related measures to US dollars, by multiplying them with the average currency rate for that day. We used measure expressions to do so very efficiently (e.g. [Internet Sales Amount] * [Average Rate]). Suppose that the end users would like to run reports that show the sales number in the original currency. You can use the Business Intelligence Wizard to create currency conversion calculations to convert the dollar amount to the foreign currency amount for reporting purposes.

OrganizationK	ParentOrganiz	PercentageOf	OrganizationN	CurrencyKey
1	(null)	1	AdventureWo	100
2	1	1	North Americ	100
3	14	1	Northeast Div	100
4	14	1	Northwest Di	100
5	14	1	Central Divisi	100
6	14	1	Southeast Div	100
7	14	1	Southwest Di	100
8	2	.75	Canadian Divi	19
9	1	1	European Op	36
10	1	.75	Pacific Operat	6
11	9	.50	France	36
12	9	.25	Germany	36
13	10	.50	Australia	6
14	2	1	USA Operatio	100

Figure 10.28 Consider automated currency conversions when the company subsidiaries report their figures in local currencies.

Another suitable scenario for automated currency conversion is when an organization spans multiple subsidiaries and each subsidiary reports its quarterly or annual performance numbers in local currencies. For example, take a moment to examine the DimOrganization table which the Organization dimension is based on (Figure 10.28).

In the case of the Adventure Works, US-based subsidiaries report their numbers in US dollars (CurrencyKey of 100), the European subsidiaries in euros (CurrencyKey of 36), the Canadian Division in Canadian dollars, and the Pacific subsidiaries in Australian dollars. Our challenge is to allow the Adventure Works headquarters to report in a single corporate currency (the US dollar), while each foreign subsidiary could see the report numbers in the original foreign currency. This is an example of a many-to-many currency conversion and it is the most involved scenario out of the three conversion scenarios supported by the Business Intelligence Wizard. An example that demonstrates the many-to-many conversion follows.

Running the Business Intelligence Wizard

We will use the Finance UDM located in the Finance Analysis Services project to demonstrate the many-to-many automated currency conversion. The reason for this is that the Finance UDM contains the Adventure Works chart of accounts which we will use for reporting purposes. As a prerequisite for automated currency conversion, remember to set the semantic types of the Currency conversion and its attributes to the pre-defined currency types (already done in the SOS OLAP Currency dimension).

1. Right-click on the Finance cube and choose *Add Business Intelligence* to launch the Business Intelligence Wizard.
2. In the Choose Enhancement Step, select *Define currency conversion* and click Next.
3. In the Set Currency Conversion Options step (Figure 10.29), you need to make several important selections. First, you need to select the measure group that contains the currency exchange rates. The BI Wizard lists the two measure groups in the Finance UDM that reference the Currency dimension (as specified in the Dimension Usage tab). Select the *Currency Rates* measure group.

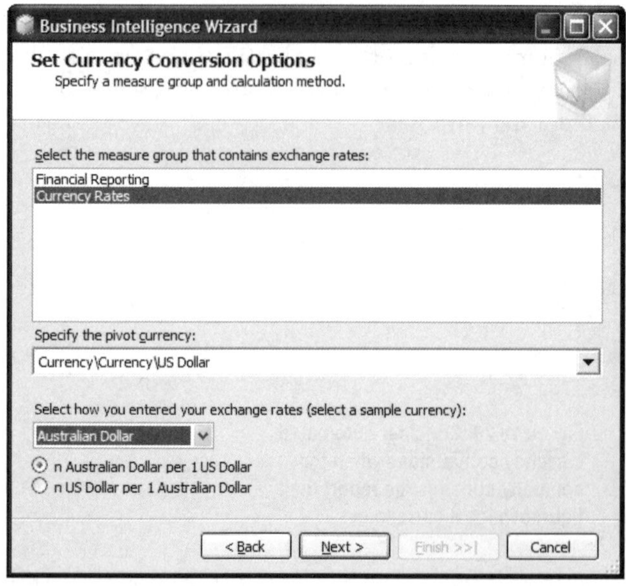

Figure 10.29 Select the pivot currency that Analysis Services will use to manage currency conversions and how the currency rate is entered.

4. Next, you need to specify the pivot currency. The pivot currency is the currency which will be used as the basis for the currency conversion. This is usually the standard corporate currency. Expand the second dropdown and notice that it lists all attribute members of the Currency

attribute hierarchy because the semantic type of the Currency attribute is set to the CurrencyName pre-defined type. Select *US Dollar*.

5. Next, you need to tell the wizard how the currency exchange rates are captured. Typically, this will be in the form of many foreign currencies to a single US dollar (the first option). If you select this option, the conversion calculations will multiply the currency amount by the exchange rate to produce the converted amount. Select Australian Dollar as a sample currency and leave the *n Australian Dollars per 1 US Dollar* radio button selected.

Specifying the currency conversion options

Use the Select Members step (Figure 10.30) to tell the wizard how to apply the currency conversion and which currency measures will be used. As noted, the wizard is capable of converting the individual facts or of using a chart of accounts. If you decide to use the latter option, you have two choices. First, you can specify how each member of the Account parent-child hierarchy will be converted (the Account hierarchy option.) Specifying conversion options for a large chart of accounts could be labor-intensive. Instead, consider using account types, if available (the third option). As you would recall, the account types are derived from an attribute which is mapped to the AccountType semantic type.

Note The BI Wizard shows the account type aliases under the Account Type column as specified in the Account Type Mapping grid of the SSAS database properties (right-click on the database node in the Solution Explorer and choose Edit Database). If you see duplicated account types, make sure to remove the duplicated account type aliases.

1. Select the *Account hierarchy based on type* option. Suppose that we want to convert the Liabilities and Assets account types using the average currency rate, while we use the end of date currency rate for converting the Balances and Expenditures account types. To do so, make the selections shown in Figure 10.30.

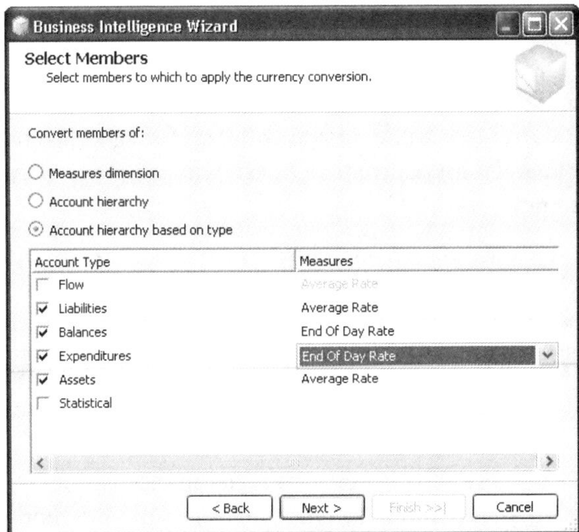

Figure 10.30 Currency conversion can be applied at the fact table level or across a chart of accounts.

2. In the Select Conversion Type step, you can choose a conversion type. Use the Many-to-many option, when the facts are captured in foreign (local) currencies and you need to report in multiple currencies. Use the One-to-many option when the facts are captured in a single cur-

rency but you need to report in multiple foreign currencies. Finally, use Many-to-one when the facts are captured in foreign currencies but you need to report on the pivot currency only. In our fictitious example, we will assume the first conversion scenario. Select the *Many-to-many* option.

3. In the Define the Currency Reference step (Figure 10.31), you need to tell the wizard how to look up the currency rate. If the currency code is captured in the fact row (as with the FactInternetSales and FactResellerSales fact tables), use the *Identifiers in the fact table* option. If the wizard needs to use an intermediary dimension table to resolve the currency code, use the second option. In the Finance UDM, the currency codes that the Adventure Works subsidiaries report in are stored in the DimOrganization dimension table. Therefore, select the second option.

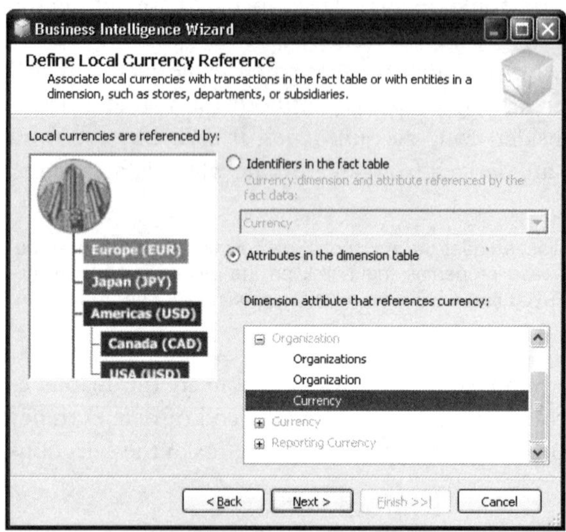

Figure 10.31 You can associate foreign currencies with transactions in the fact table or with entities in a dimension.

4. To tell the wizard which attribute captures the currency code, scroll down the list, expand the Organization dimension, and select the *Currency* attribute.

5. Finally, in the Specify Reporting Currencies step, you need to select the reporting currencies you would like to report in. Naturally, the reporting currencies will coincide with the foreign currencies, so select *Australian Dollar*, *Canadian Dollar*, and *EURO* currency codes. The pivot currency will be automatically included as a reporting currency.

6. Review the wizard's changes in the Completing the Wizard step and click Finish to let the wizard generate the calculations.

Note If you run the currency conversion BI enhancement consequently, the BI Wizard will introduce a new step (Define Currency Conversion) before the last step. This step will ask you whether you want to overwrite the existing script or append the new script at the end.

Once the BI Wizard has generated the script, we can use the currency conversion calculations in a report. The only alteration we need to make to the script is changing the StrToMember function to use the member key (&) as opposed to the member name. That's because the Currency attribute hierarchy in the Organization dimension uses the currency key.

```
StrToMember("[Currency].[Currency].&[" +
[Organization].[Currency].CurrentMember.Name+"]")
```

The BI Wizard adds a new dimension called Reporting Currency to the Finance UDM. The Reporting Currency dimension is based on a named query with an identical name, which the wizard has added to the Finance data source view. The purpose of the Reporting Currency named query is to return the selected reporting currencies as members of the Reporting Currency attribute hierarchy. Figure 10.32 shows a report that uses the Reporting Currency dimension.

Fiscal Year ▾						
2003						
			Currency ▾			
			Australian Dollar	Canadian Dollar	EURO	US Dollar
Account Level 01 ▾	Account Level 02	Account Level 03	Amount	Amount	Amount	Amount
⊟ Balance Sheet	⊟ Assets	⊞ Current Assets	$6,985,100.39	$8,811,244.15	$12,544,046.97	$13,774,617.97
		⊞ Property, Plant, Equipment	$533,135.62	$672,515.47	$957,420.49	$1,051,343.43
		⊞ Other Assets	$80,625.75	$101,704.07	$144,790.07	$158,993.98
		Total	$7,598,861.76	$9,585,463.69	$13,646,257.52	$14,984,955.38
	⊟ Liabilities and Owne	⊞ Liabilities	$2,522,376.10	$3,181,811.34	$4,529,756.55	$4,974,125.66
		⊞ Owners Equity	$4,988,832.73	$6,293,083.95	$8,959,091.29	$9,837,978.14
		Total	$7,400,304.00	$9,334,996.15	$13,289,681.71	$14,593,399.48
	Total		$198,557.76	$250,467.54	$356,575.82	$391,555.90
⊟ Net Income	⊞ Operating Profit		$19,398,943.81	$15,924,542.16	$9,236,680.25	$6,360,575.44
	⊞ Other Income and Expense		$43,207.70	$34,757.18	$18,554.07	$11,570.21
	⊞ Taxes		$1,615,935.72	$2,009,110.34	$2,772,856.37	$3,094,233.67
	Total		$17,826,215.79	$13,950,188.99	$6,482,377.95	$3,277,911.99

Figure 10.32 This report shows the chart of account numbers converted to the original foreign currencies.

The report has the Account parent-child hierarchy on rows, the Reporting Currency calculated dimension on columns, and Amount measure on the report details. The Amount numbers are calculated using the currency conversion script generated by the BI Wizard. Let's take a moment to examine the script. In the case of Many-to-many scenario, the currency conversion is done in two passes.

Understanding the Many-to-one currency conversion

During the first pass, the measures reported in foreign currencies are converted to the pivot currency. This would allow the Adventure Works management to see the report in a single corporate currency, which in our case is the US dollar.

```
Scope ({Measures.[Amount]});
    Scope( Leaves([Date]), [Reporting Currency].[Currency Code].&[US Dollar],
    Leaves([Organization]));
```

The first scope eliminates all cube measures except the measures in the measures groups that reference the Account dimension. Next, the scope is narrowed down to the leaf members of the Date and Organization dimensions. The leaf members are defined by the dimension grain. In most cases, the leaf members will be qualified by the dimension key attribute. However, as I explained in chapter 5, a dimension may join a measure group at a higher grain. The *Leaves* function returns the leaf member of the specified dimension. Next, we perform the actual conversion to the pivot currency by using the specified currency rate.

```
Scope({([Account].[Account Type].[Liabilities]),([Account].[Account Type].[Assets])});
    This = [Reporting Currency].[Currency].[Local] / (Measures.[Average Rate],
    StrToMember("[Currency].[Currency].&["+
    [Organization].[Currency].CurrentMember.Name+"]"));
End Scope;
```

As you recall, we told the BI Wizard that the Liabilities and Assets account types will be converted using the average currency rate. First, we re-scope to narrow the cube scope to include these two members only. Next, we need to look up the currency code associated with each subsidiary. The *StrToMember* allows us to construct a dynamic member of the [Currency].[Currency Code] attribute hierarchy. The script retrieves the currency code associated with the current subsidiary from the Organization dimension and looking up the corresponding average rate for that currency code. Finally, we divide the foreign currency amount by the rate to get the US dollar amount.

Understanding the One-to-many currency conversion

During the second pass, the script converts the reported measures to their foreign currency equivalents. This allows the Adventure Works subsidiaries to see the reports in their native currency.

```
Scope(Leaves([Date]), Except([Reporting Currency].[Currency].[Currency].Members,
    {[Reporting Currency].[Currency].[Currency].[US Dollar],
    [Reporting Currency].[Currency].[Currency].[Local]}));
```

Again, we get to the leaves of the Date dimension but this time we exclude the USD and local members. Next, we perform the actual currency conversion.

```
Scope({([Account].[Account Type].[Liabilities]),([Account].[Account Type].[Assets])});
    This=[Reporting Currency].[Currency].[US Dollar]*(Measures.[Average Rate],
    LinkMember([Reporting Currency].[Currency].CurrentMember, [Currency].[Currency]));
End Scope;
```

To do so, we need to find again the corresponding average rate of the current foreign currency. Since the dollar amount is already calculated, we could look up the exchange rate from the Currency dimension without having to use the Organization dimension as a "bridge". The *LinkMember* MDX function returns the corresponding member from a specified hierarchy given a member from another hierarchy. This of course assumes that the lookup hierarchy intersects the same measure group.

10.4 Summary

In this chapter, we discussed how you can leverage advanced MDX expressions to solve more demanding programming scenarios. Besides calculated members, MDX supports named sets and subcube expressions. Named sets promote code encapsulation and can be used to facilitate end-user reporting experience. You've seen how you can manipulate sets in various ways, including filtering, ordering, and crossjoining.

Subcube expressions allow you to write anywhere in the cube space. Use the SCOPE statement to narrow down the scope of the targeted calculations. Use the THIS statement to assign values or formulas to the subcube cells. Finally, consider the time intelligence and currency conversion enhancements of the Business Intelligence Wizard to learn best programming practices and minimize programming effort.

10.5 Resources

Analysis Services 2005 Brings You Automated Time Intelligence (http://shrinkster.com/8fi) – This article looks at how the new Business Intelligence Wizard makes implementing time intelligence easy.

Chapter 11

Extending UDM with Custom Code

An important requirement of every enterprise framework, such as Analysis Services, is that it has to be extensible. As flexible and powerful as MDX is, it alone may not address all of your programming needs. One of the main characteristics of UDM is that it can be extended with custom code that you or somebody else has already written. This chapter shows you how you can extend UDM programmatically through external libraries and stored procedures. You will learn how to:

- Call external VBA functions.
- Create and deploy stored procedures.
- Use the server ADOMD.NET object model.
- Troubleshoot and debug SSAS stored procedures.

I will be quick to point out that, although the focus of this chapter will be MDX extensibility, SSAS stored procedures can be used to perform data mining tasks, as our last example will demonstrate. You can find the finished code samples by opening the Ch11 solution.

11.1 Understanding MDX Extensibility

You can extend MDX in two ways. First, you can "borrow" functions from the two external function libraries that are pre-installed with SSAS. They are the Excel library and the Visual Basic for Applications (VBA) library. Second, you can supercharge the MDX capabilities by writing custom code in the form of SSAS stored procedures.

11.1.1 Extensibility Scenarios

Why would you extend SSAS programmatically? Some of the most common extensibility scenarios are in order. First, you may need to extend MDX when you've reached the limit of its capabilities. For example, you may need to perform a custom aggregation over an MDX set, or to filter a set using some sophisticated programming logic. Second, you may find yourself using the same MDX expressions over and over. For example, you may need to author several calculated members that use the same expression. In such cases, you may be better off centralizing your code in stored procedures.

Finally, another scenario that requires extensibility is complex validation rules. Since SSAS stored procedures can tap into the power of the .NET framework, your custom code can extend UDM in versatile and innovative ways. For example, your security requirement may call for restricting access to UDM by authorizing the users against security policies stored in a database. I will demonstrate a similar example in chapter 16.

11.1.2 What's New in MDX Extensibility

Programmatic extensibility has been supported in the previous releases of SSAS. In my opinion, the two most important extensibility enhancements that UDM brings are server-side code execution and .NET-based stored procedures.

Server side code execution

In UDM, all external functions are executed on the server side. One of the deficiencies of the previous release of Analysis Services was that external functions (called user-defined functions or UDF) were executed on the client side. Subsequently, you were forced to distribute and install your function libraries on every end-user machine, which presented a maintenance issue. This limitation has been removed in UDM. Custom .NET function libraries need to be deployed and registered on the server only.

.NET-based stored procedures

.NET-based stored procedures replace the user-defined functions in SSAS 2000. As you can imagine, this brings a lot of flexibility to the MDX extensibility model. Moreover, you have the entire ADOMD.NET object model available in your stored procedures. Among other things, it allows you to create tuples and sets in an object-oriented way.

Let's go through some examples to demonstrate the MDX extensibility model.

11.2 Using Standard External Libraries

As with its previous releases, SSAS provides two pre-registered external function libraries that encapsulate many popular Excel and VBA functions. In fact, we used one of them in the preceding chapter. This was the VBA *Val* function, which helped us convert a string representation of a number to its numeric equivalent. Let's find what other gems await us in the external libraries.

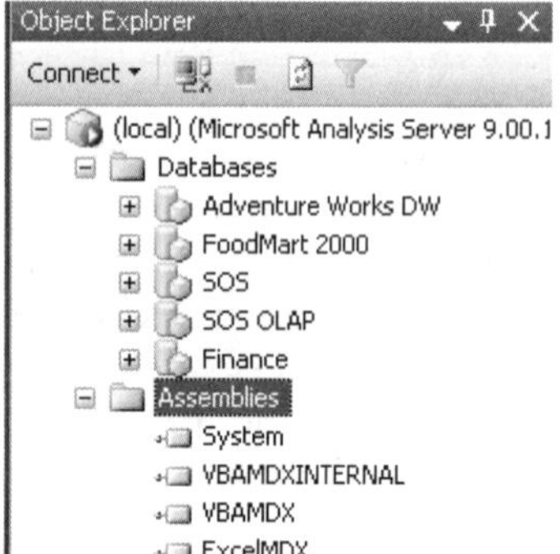

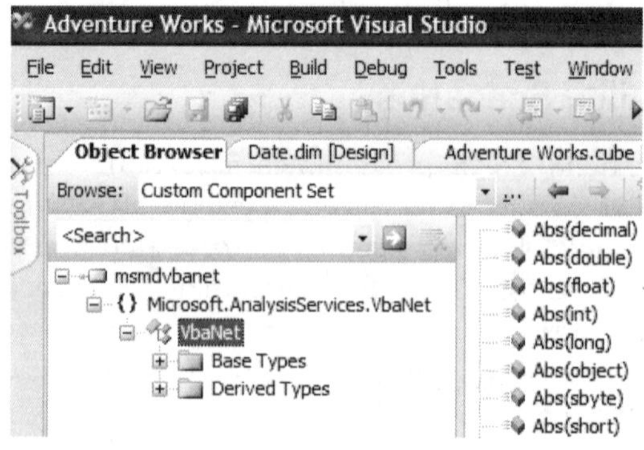

Figure 11.1 You can use functions from the Excel and VBA function libraries in your MDX expressions.

11.2.1 Exploring the External Libraries

The Excel and VBA function libraries are pre-registered on the SSAS server. You can verify their existence by using the SQL Server Management Studio and expand the Assemblies folder of the SSAS server (Figure 11.1). As you can see, the VBA and Excel libraries are deployed as server assemblies and thus can be called from MDX expressions in any database.

Tip You can make a stored procedure available across all SSAS databases by registering its hosting library globally in the server Assemblies folder.

The VBAMDX library exposes a subset of the VBA functions that can be used in MDX. If you inspect the properties of the VBAMDX function library, you will notice that it points to a .NET managed assembly called msmdvbanet.dll. To see the list of the exported VBA functions and their call syntax, open this file in the BI Studio Object Explorer. To do so, start BI Studio, press Ctrl+Alt+J, and click the **...** button next to the Browse dropdown to load the msmdvbanet assembly (it is located in the C:\Program Files\Microsoft SQL Server\MSSQL.2\OLAP\bin folder).

There is no corresponding assembly for the ExcelMDX function library because it is a COM wrapper on top of the native Excel library. The System assembly contains data mining-related functions. VBAMDXINTERNAL library is a COM-based library and, as it name suggest, it is for internal use only.

Date.Date ▾			
June 29			
			Drop Colum
Category ▾	**Subcategory**	**Product**	Sales Profit
⊟ Bikes	⊟ Mountain Bikes	Mountain-200 Black, 38	$1,886.58
		Mountain-200 Black, 42	$943.29
		Total	$2,829.86
	⊞ Road Bikes		$296.28
	Total		$3,126.15
Grand Total			$3,126.15

Figure 11.2 For the convenience of the end user, you can set the default member of a Time dimension to the current calendar day.

11.2.2 Setting the Default Member Programmatically

Let's practice a few VBA functions in MDX expressions. Suppose that your business requirements call for setting the default member of the Date attribute hierarchy to the current calendar day. This could be useful to quickly generate a report that shows some business measures for the current day, without having to filter the date dimension. For example, once the default member is programmatically set, an end user could just drag the Date attribute hierarchy on the report filter and it will automatically default to the current day (see Figure 11.2).

Understanding the expression

The MDX expression that does this may seem a bit scary at first but it is really not that complicated. This is how it looks, delimited by the date parts (Year, Semester, Quarter, Month, and Day):

```
StrToMember ("[Date].[Calendar Date].[2003].[H" +
CStr(IIf(Month(Now()) <= 6, 1, 2)) + " CY 2003].[Q" +
CStr(DatePart("q", Now())) + " CY 2003].[" + Format(Now(), "MMMM") + "].[" +
Format(Now(), "MMMM") + " " + CStr(Day(Now())) + "]")
```

To understand what's going on, note that our MDX expression needs to return the current day in the following format (assuming that the current day is June 29th 2003).

```
[Date].[Calendar Date].[2003].[H1 CY 2003].[Q2 CY 2003].[June].[June 29]
```

Why can't we use the Date attribute hierarchy directly? To do that, we need to know the dimension key, e.g. [Date].&[729], to identify uniquely the calendar day. We cannot use the day name because it is not unique across years. As you can imagine, there is no easy way to find out the attribute key for the current day. Instead, we will use the Calendar Date multi-level hierarchy and concatenate the day member using a handful of VBA functions. By the way, I am explicitly setting the year to 2003 so the expression doesn't leave the Adventure Works cube space (we have sample data up to year 2004 only). In real life, you can use the *Year* VBA function to retrieve the current calendar year.

Constructing the navigational path

The *Now* function returns the current date. Getting the current semester is the only tricky part of the expression since there is no VBA function to do so. I use the *Iif* operator to find out the current semester based on the month number. The *Month* function returns the ordinal number of the month which we need to cast to string using the *CStr* VBA function. Similarly, the *Day* function returns the day number. The *DatePart* function returns the ordinal number of the quarter. I use the VBA *Format* function to get the full name of the month. That's because the VBAMDX library doesn't include the VBA *MonthName* function. Finally, I use the MDX *StrToMember* function to resolve the string representation of the member to the actual member.

In my first attempt to set up the default member, I tried using the *DefaultMember* property of the Date attribute of the Date dimension. Much to my surprise though, I got the following error during deployment:

```
The specified default member '[Date].[Calendar Date].[Date].&[729]' must be from the
'[Ship Date].[Date]' hierarchy.
```

It turned out this happens because the Date dimension is a role playing dimension. You cannot set the DefaultMember property of a role playing dimension in the Dimension Designer because it is not clear which specific role version it is intended for. Instead, the only way to set up the default member is to do it programmatically by using the ALTER CUBE statement.

```
ALTER CUBE CURRENTCUBE
UPDATE DIMENSION [Date].[Calendar Date],
DEFAULT_MEMBER = StrToMember ("[Date].[Calendar Date].[2003].[H" +
    CStr(IIf(Month(Now()) <= 6, 1, 2)) + " CY 2003].[Q" + CStr(DatePart("q", Now())) +
    " CY 2003].[" + Format(Now(), "MMMM") + "].[" + Format(Now(), "MMMM") + " " +
    CStr(Day(Now())) + "]") ;
```

You can find this statement at the end of the MDX script for the SOS OLAP cube. If you want to test the default member expression quickly, you can use the following MDX query:

```
SELECT {[Internet Sales Amount], [Sales Profit], [Average Profit]} ON ROWS,
     StrToMember ("[Date].[Calendar Date].[2003].[H" +
     CStr(IIf(Month(Now()) <= 6, 1, 2)) + " CY 2003].[Q" + CStr(DatePart("q", Now()))
     + " CY 2003].[" + Format(Now(), "MMMM") + "].[" + Format(Now(), "MMMM")
     + " " + CStr(Day(Now())) + "]") ON COLUMNS
FROM [SOS OLAP]
```

If you don't feel like typing, I will show you in a moment how you can invoke a stored procedure that returns the default member. Figure 11.3 shows the results of executing the above MDX query in Management Studio. Your results will vary depending on the calendar day when the query is executed.

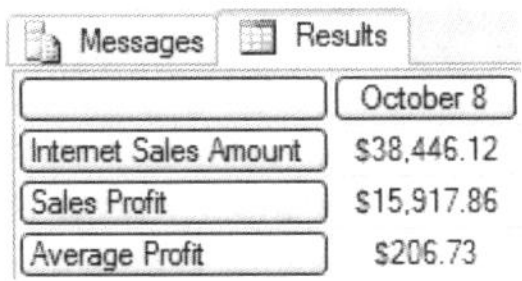

	October 8
Internet Sales Amount	$38,446.12
Sales Profit	$15,917.86
Average Profit	$206.73

Figure 11.3 Testing an MDX query that retrieves data for the current day.

11.3 Implementing Stored Procedures

Sometimes, you need to take the road less traveled and whip out custom code to address more demanding extensibility needs. In UDM, custom libraries give you this level of flexibility. Custom library can contain .NET managed or native COM code. Since COM-based user-defined functions would most likely be used only for backward compatibility, I will focus only on .NET-based stored procedures. To implement the sample stored procedures, you will need Visual Studio.NET since BI Studio doesn't support code projects.

11.3.1 Understanding SSAS Stored Procedures

SSAS stored procedures offer two major benefits. First, you can encapsulate common programming logic and reuse it in your MDX expressions or queries. Second, your stored procedures can transcend the capabilities of MDX, VBA and Excel functions. You can extend MDX by writing custom code in .NET using your favorite .NET language, e.g. VB.NET, C#, or C++ with managed extensions.

I have to admit that, at first, the term *stored procedure* got me profoundly confused until I realized that it represents a method in a plain vanilla .NET library assembly. The SSAS team decided to call .NET extensibility methods *stored procedures* to bring the terminology inline with SQL Server CLR stored procedures. This makes sense considering the fact that both types share the same code access security model and configuration approach.

Definition An SSAS stored procedure is an instance or static method in a .NET library assembly. If needed, the stored procedure can reference the server-side ADOMD.NET model. Before MDX expressions can call custom stored procedures in a given assembly, the assembly needs to be registered on the server.

One noticeable difference is that the assembly that hosts SSAS stored procedures is installed in the SSAS database (or server for global scope), while the SQL Server stored procedure assembly is registered in the relational database. In addition, the individual stored procedures contained in the SSAS library assembly are not exposed in the SQL Server Management Studio and are not securable items.

Calling stored procedures

A .NET library assembly may have more than one stored procedure in it. All public instance or static (shared in VB.NET) methods in the .NET assembly automatically get exposed as SSAS stored procedures. Once the .NET assembly is registered, you can call its stored procedures from

MDX expressions or queries just as they are standard MDX functions. You can use any of the following syntax conventions to call a stored procedure.

```
Assembly.Namespace.Class.StoredProcedure(parameter1, parameter 2, … parameterN)
Assembly.StoredProcedure(parameter1, parameter 2, … parameterN)
Assembly!StoredProcedure(parameter1, parameter 2, … parameterN)
```

For example, suppose that you have a public method (static or instance) with a fully qualified name of `AdventureWorks.Extensibility.StoredProcedures.PctDiff`. Here, the *AdventureWorks* is the assembly name, *Extensibility* is the namespace, *StoredProcedure* is the class name, and *PctDiff* is the method (stored procedure) name. You can call PctDiff from MDX expressions using either of the following conventions:

```
AdventureWorks.Extensibility.StoredProcedures.PctDiff(…)
AdventureWorks.PctDiff(…)
AdventureWorks!PctDiff(…)
```

Note Although you can call instance methods, you cannot maintain state in class-level variables. If you try to do this, you will find out that the instance state is lost between method invocations. In other words, you can only maintain state within a single stored procedure call, e.g. when a stored procedure executes other helper methods or stored procedures.

Interestingly, SSAS doesn't require that you specify the fully-qualified method name (including the namespace). Another interesting implementation detail is that you don't have to use different calling conventions to execute instance vs. static (shared) methods. For developer's convenience, the calculation engine maps both method types to a single calling convention.

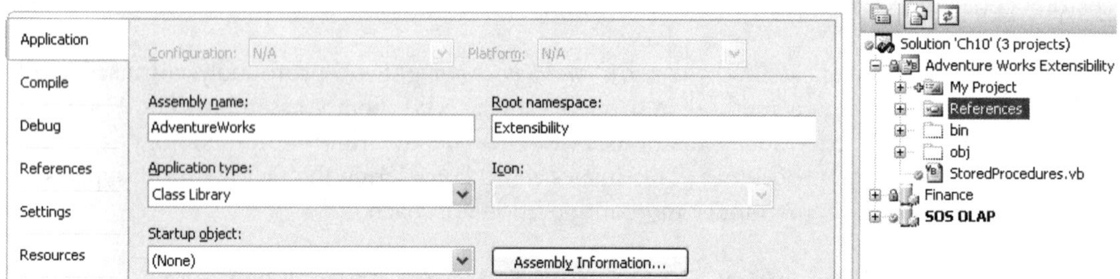

Figure 11.4 Stored procedures are hosted in .NET assemblies.

Your first stored procedure

Suppose that you need to calculate the percentage difference between two measures (x and y) as:

```
PctDiff = (x - y) / x
```

As you know by now, you can create a calculated member that is based on the above MDX expression. However, a calculated member must specify the names of the measures explicitly. What if you want to reuse the same formula for another set of measures? You have to create a new calculated member. At some point, this can get counterproductive. A better approach could be to encapsulate the formula in a stored procedure. Follow these steps to create an SSAS stored procedure called *PctDiff* written in VB.NET.

1. Start by creating a new VB.NET library project. In the VS.NET Solution Explorer, right-click on the SOS OLAP solution and choose *Add ➪ New Project*. In the Add New Project dialog that follows, click on the *Visual Basic* project type and select the *Class Library* template. Name the new project **Adventure Works Extensibility** and click OK to create the project.

2. In the Adventure Works Extensibility project properties, click on the Application tab. Change the assembly name to **AdventureWorks** and the root namespace to **Extensibility** (Figure 11.4).

3. Delete the Class1.vb file and add a new source file (right click on the project node and choose *Add ➪ Class*) named *StoredProcedures*. Double-click to open the source code in the VS.NET code editor.

4. Add the PctDiff stored procedure code to the StoredProcedure class (Listing 11.1).

Listing 11.1 The PctDiff stored procedure

```
Public Class StoredProcedures
    Public Shared Function PctDiff(ByVal x As Decimal, ByVal y As Decimal) As Object

        If y = 0 Then
            Return "NA"
        Else
            Return (x - y) / y
        End If
End Class
```

To call this function from MDX, you need to pass two tuples as input arguments. When MDX invokes the PctDiff function, it will cast automatically the cell values referenced by the tuples to decimals (or whatever the argument type is). If a cell value is empty, MDX will coerce it to zero. The PctDiff function checks for this condition and returns *NA* if the second value is zero to prevent division by zero error.

5. Build the project (Ctrl+B). If it compiles fine, you are ready to deploy the stored procedure assembly to the server.

Encapsulating complex expressions

Before we see the PctDiff stored procedure in action, here is another example that emphasizes the encapsulation advantage of using store procedures. In section 11.2.2, I showed you a rather nasty and long MDX expression to set the default member of the Date attribute hierarchy to the current calendar date. Such expressions are difficult to troubleshoot and manage. When expression complexity increases, consider moving expressions to stored procedures. Besides centralizing the expressions in one place, the added bonus is that you can debug .NET assemblies much easier.

The *GetCurrentDay* stored procedure encapsulates the original expression to set the default member of the Date attribute hierarchy.

```
Public Shared Function GetCurrentDay() As String
        Return "[Date].[Calendar Date].[2003].[H" +
    CStr(IIf(Month(Now()) <= 6, 1, 2)) + _
        " CY 2003].[Q" + CStr(DatePart("q", Now())) + " CY 2003].[" + _
    Format(Now(), "MMMM") + "].[" + Format(Now(), "MMMM") + " " _
    + CStr(Day(Now())) + "]"
End Function
```

The ALTER CUBE statement can call this expression just like the original one by using the MDX *StrToMember* function to convert the result to a member.

11.3.2 Deploying Stored Procedures

A stored procedure assembly can be deployed from VS.NET or by using the SQL Server Management Studio. The first is more convenient during design time, so let's start with it.

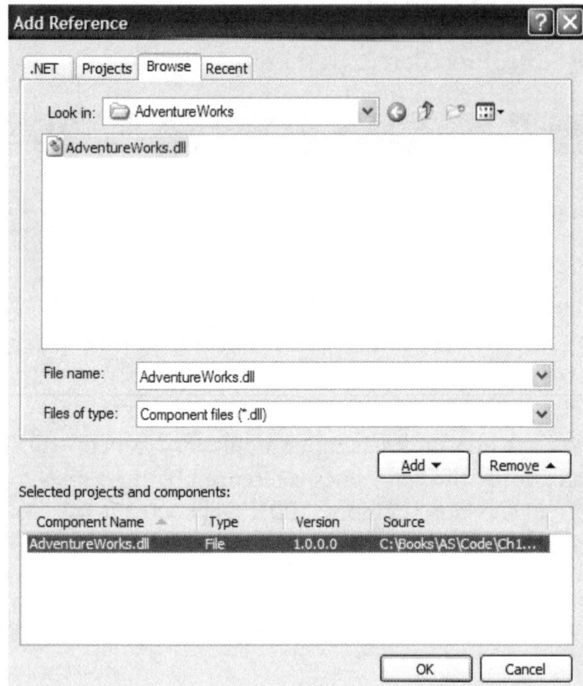

Figure 11.5 If you need to deploy the library assembly as part of deploying your project, you need to add a reference to it in the Assemblies folder.

Deploying from VS.NET

1. Back to the SOS OLAP project, right-click on the Assemblies folder and chose *New Assembly Reference.*
2. In the Add Reference dialog that follows, click on the Browse tab.
3. Navigate to the folder where the AdventureWorks.dll library is located (typically in the bin\debug subfolder).
4. Click the Add button to add the AdventureWorks.dll to the selected assemblies list and the OK button to create a reference to it. At this point, your Assemblies folder should list the library assembly, as shown in Figure 11.6.

Note Unlike .NET development projects, you don't need to reference the library assembly in the SSAS project which will use the assembly. Adding a reference to the assembly is convenient because you can deploy the assembly to the server together with the project.

When you deploy a library assembly, SSAS physically copies the assembly to a special folder in the SSAS metadata folder structure. The name of this folder follows the <Assembly-Name>.<Version>.asm naming convention, e.g. AdventureWorks.23.asm. This folder typically contains two files per each library assembly (a DLL and a PDB file). The PDB file contains the library debug symbols and it is required if you need to debug stored procedures. If the PDB file is missing, you can copy it to that folder. However, you cannot deploy the assembly by just copying it to the physical folder (XCOPY deployment) because the assembly needs to be registered in the SSAS metadata.

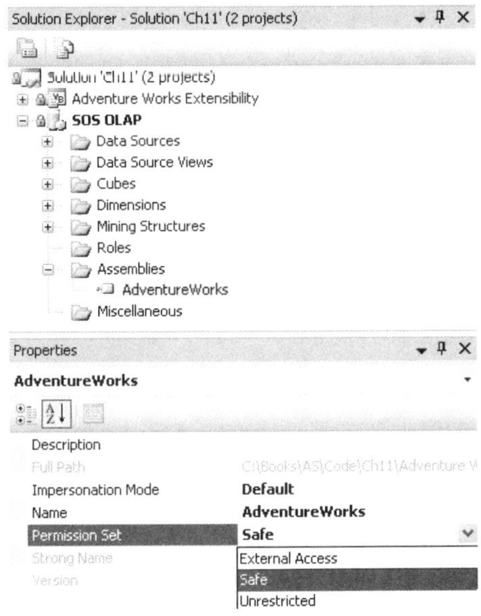

Figure 11.6 A library assembly can be deployed as part of deploying the Analysis Services project from VS.NET.

5. Optionally, if you would like, you can reference the library by a different name in your expressions. To do so, click on the assembly reference and change the assembly *Name* property.

6. Deploy the SOS OLAP project. If all is well, the StoredProcedures.dll assembly will be deployed to the SOS OLAP database. You can verify this by using the SQL Server Management Studio and expanding the Assemblies folder of the SOS OLAP database.

Once the library assembly is referenced in an SSAS project, making code changes to its stored procedures requires a two-step deployment process. First, you build the library assembly to compile the new code changes. Second, you deploy the assembly by simply deploying the hosting SSAS project.

Deploying with the SQL Server Management Studio

You don't have to deploy the Analysis Services project if you have made stored procedure changes only. If there are no changes made to the dimensional or calculation layers of UDM, you can refresh the library assembly by using the SQL Server Management Studio:

1. Connect to the SSAS server. Expand the database Assemblies folder and delete the assembly.

2. Expand the SSAS database that will host the assembly. Expand the Assemblies folder. Select the assembly you want to refresh and press the Delete key to delete it.

3. Right-click on the Assemblies folder and choose *New Assembly* to launch the Register Database Assembly dialog (Figure 11.7).
4. As you would expect, the assembly type defaults to .NET. Specify the assembly path and name.
5. If you want to debug the stored procedures contained in the assembly, check the *Include debug information* checkbox. This will copy the PDB file to the server.

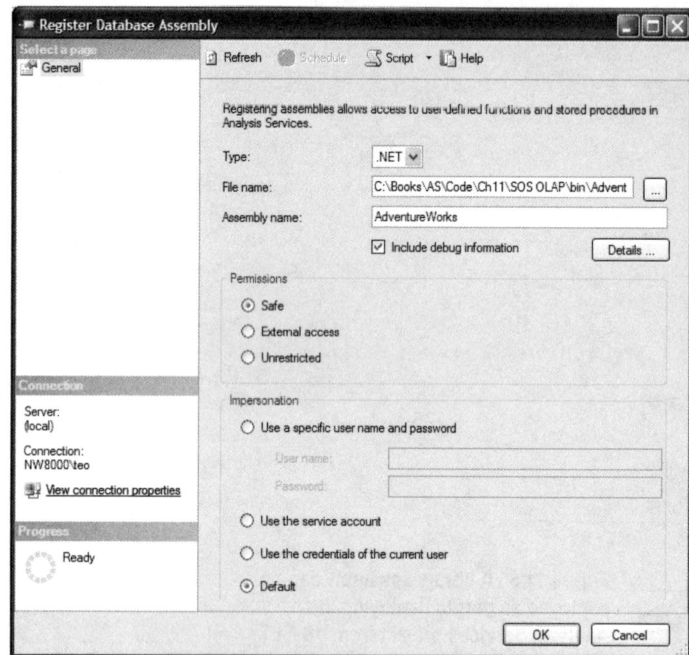

Figure 11.7 You can deploy the library assembly using the SQL Server Management Studio.

Next, I will cover the library permission settings and impersonation mode next.

11.3.3 Securing Stored Procedures

Similar to the SQL Server stored procedures, the allowed actions that an SSAS stored procedure can execute are "sandboxed" by the CLR code access security model. When the server loads an assembly, the CLR goes through some decision making to determine what the assembly can do. As part of this process, the CLR gathers some information about the assembly, such as the assembly origin, strong name and publisher (for strong-named assemblies). The assembly evidence is then passed to the CLR code-access security policy for evaluation which has a final say about what the assembly code can do. To simplify the code access security setup, SSAS provides three permission sets to configure a library assembly (see Figure 11.7):

- *Safe* – This is the most restrictive and default permission set. Only internal code execution is allowed.
- *External Access* – The assembly code can access external resources, such as files, opening database connections, etc.
- *Unrestricted* – All bets are off. The assembly can do whatever it likes, including calling unmanaged code.

As a security best practice, you should start with the Safe permission set and switch to less restrictive level only as needed. For example, all stored procedures that we will implement in this chapter can execute just fine with the Safe permission set. External operations, such as opening database connections, accessing network files, are done by default under the server identity. A library assembly (External Access or Unrestricted permission sets only) can be configured to impersonate the interactive user by setting the Impersonation Mode property of the assembly.

	Year ▾		
	⊞ 2004		
Category ▾	Reseller Sales Amount	Internet Sales Amount	PctDiff
⊞ Accessories	$153,299.92	$343,581.70	-55.38%
⊞ Bikes	$12,968,255.41	$8,481,833.38	52.89%
⊞ Clothing	$366,507.84	$166,867.88	119.64%
⊞ Components	$2,000,052.70		NA
⊞ Other			NA
Grand Total	$15,496,115.88	$8,992,282.96	72.33%

Figure 11.8 MDX expressions can call a stored procedure form calculated members.

11.3.4 Invoking Stored Procedures

We can invoke a stored procedure just like we can invoke any MDX function. I provide an example of how the stored procedure could be called in the comment header preceding each sample stored procedure. For example, to invoke the PctDiff stored procedure, you can create a calculated member as follows:

```
CREATE MEMBER CURRENTCUBE.[MEASURES].[PctDiff]
AS AdventureWorks!PctDiff([Measures].[Reseller Sales Amount],
     [Measures].[Internet Sales Amount]),
FORMAT_STRING = "Percent",
VISIBLE = 1;
```

Once you deploy the project, you can create a report that uses the new calculated member, as the one shown in Figure 11.8. Note that the PctDiff measure for the Components and Other categories is *NA* because the Internet Sales Amount measure (the second argument to our function) is empty.

11.3.5 Debugging Stored Procedures

One of the advantages of using stored procedures is that you can easily troubleshoot their execution by debugging them using the powerful VS.NET debugger. Follow these steps to attach to the Analysis Services server process and debug an SSAS stored procedure.

1. Set one or more breakpoints inside your stored procedure.
2. Select Debug ⇨ Attach to Process main menu.
3. Check the *Show processes from all users* checkbox at the bottom of the Attach to Process dialog.
4. Select the msmdsrv.exe process (Figure 11.9) and click the Attach button. VS.NET will display progress messages in the Output window as the DLL symbols get loaded.

Tip Before you invoke the stored procedure to debug it, wait until your breakpoint is activated (its circle becomes solid red). If it doesn't, most likely the server code is outdated. You can find out if this is the case, by hovering over the breakpoint and inspecting the error message. If the server debug symbols are different, you won't be able to debug. You need to re-deploy the library to the server.

5. Invoke the stored procedure by sending an MDX query that uses it. If the stored procedure is used in an MDX expression, use the Cube Browser to create a report that uses that expression.

At this point, your breakpoint should be hit and you should be able to step through the code.

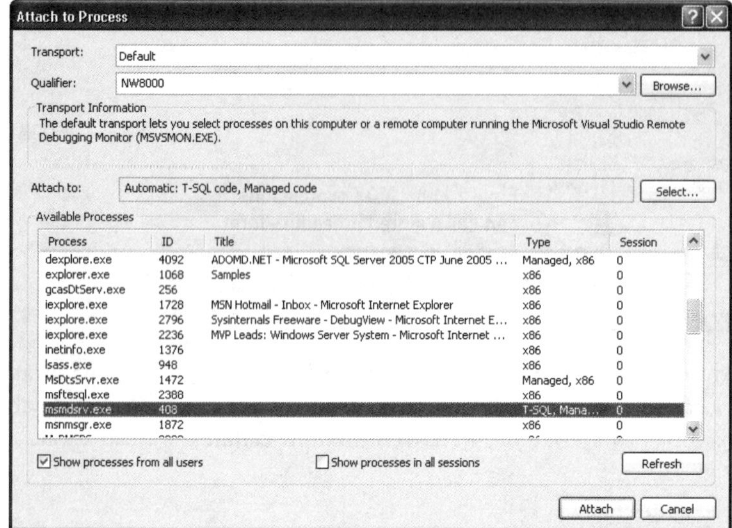

Figure 11.9 Debug a stored procedure by attaching to the SSAS server process.

11.4 Using the ADOMD.NET Server library

As noted in chapter 1, Analysis Services introduces ADOMD.NET, a .NET-based object model that can be used in stored procedures and by client applications to access and work with Analysis Services objects and data. ADOMD.NET comes in two flavors – client and server object libraries. Client applications will use the ADOMD.NET client library to connect to the server, send queries, and retrieve results.

Custom code in SSAS stored procedures could leverage the server version of ADOMD.NET, which has been optimized for fast in-process access to the server objects. For example, the server version doesn't require you to connect to the Analysis Services server. That's because all operations are performed in the current database context. In addition, an additional level of efficiency is achieved by eliminating the network overhead.

Note One limitation of the server-based ADOMD.NET version is that you can't use it to send MDX queries. DMX queries can be executed though, as I will demonstrate in section 11.4.4.

11.4.1 Exploring the ADOMD.NET Object Model

To access the ADOMD.NET object model in your library assembly, you need to reference the Microsoft. AnalysisServices.AdomdServer library, as shown in Figure 11.10. The AdomdServer reference appears as **msmgdsrv** under the References folder (Figure 11.11). To get yourself introduced to the ADOMD.NET model, you may find it helpful to explore it in the Object Browser (right-click on the msmgdsrv reference and choose *View in Object Browser*). As you would notice, the entire server model (databases, cubes, dimensions, measure groups, mining models, etc.) are available to you.

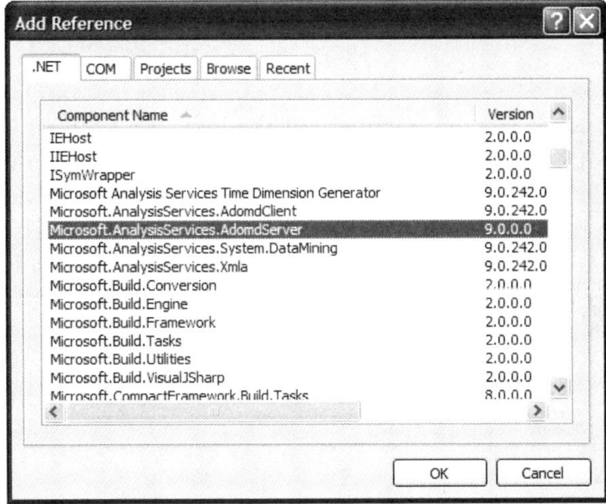

Figure 11.10 To use ADOMD.NET, reference its library in the .NET assembly.

As Figure 11.11 shows, I have selected the Context object which is one of the ADOMD.NET objects. You can use it to reference the current context in which the stored procedure executes. The next example demonstrates how the Context object can be used.

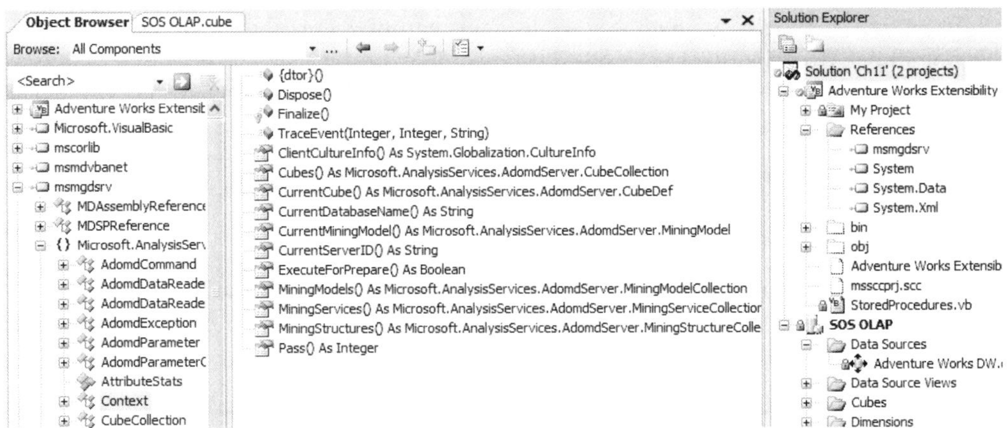

Figure 11.11 MDX expressions can call a stored procedure to form calculated members.

11.4.2 Working with Current Context

When I was experimenting with MDX expressions, I wanted to find an easy way to output the unique names of the members that are explicitly requested in an MDX set. In addition, I wanted to see the calculation pass number to understand when the calculation engine processes the expression. So, I wrote a small stored procedure called *ShowSet* for this purpose.

```
Public Shared Function ShowSet(ByVal inputSet As String) As [Set]
        Trace.WriteLine(String.Format("Input set: {0}, Pass: {1}",
      inputSet, Context.Pass.ToString()))
```

```
        Return AdomdServer.MDX.StrToSet(inputSet)
End Function
```

This function takes a given MDX set as an input, outputs its members and the calculation pass to the active trace listener, and returns the same set to the client.

Passing the string representation of a set

The first challenge that I have to address is how to get the members of the input set. Unfortunately, time constraints have prevented the SSAS team to implement all MDX functions. As you will notice by selecting on the MDX node in the object browser, ADOMD.NET supports only a handful of MDX functions, including the *Aggregate*, *CrossJoin*, *Filter*, and *StrToSet* functions. The function that I needed to convert an MDX set to its string representation is *SetToStr*. Since this function is not implemented, I had to do the conversion on the client. This is how a client could invoke the ShowSet stored procedure.

```
SELECT AdventureWorks.ShowSet(
SetToStr(
     {TopCount([Reseller].[Reseller].[Reseller].Members, 5,
     [Reseller Profit Dollar Amount])}
     )) ON COLUMNS
FROM [SOS OLAP]
```

In this case, the set consists of the top five most profitable resellers. Of course, instead of using an MDX query, you can invoke ShowSet from an MDX expression.

Watching the trace output

To watch its output, you need to attach a trace listener that intercepts the messages sent by the OutputDebugString API. The one I have relied on most in my projects is the excellent DbgView tool from SysInternals (see Resources). Once the stored procedure is executed, its output will show up in DbgView (Figure 11.12).

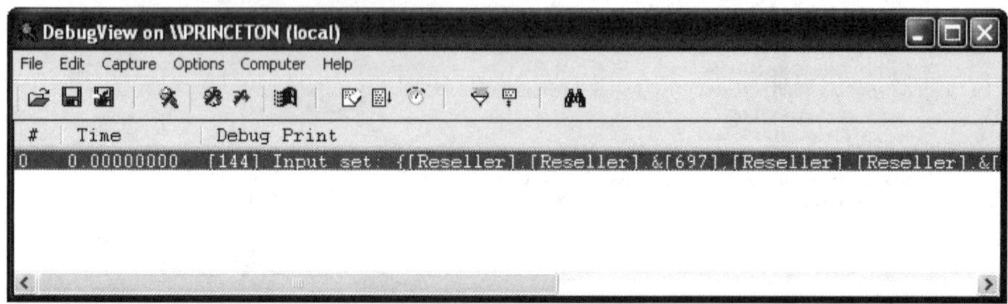

Figure 11.12 Using DbgView to watch trace messages from ShowSet.

Given the above query, the ShowSet output may look like this:

```
Input set: {[Reseller].[Reseller].&[697],[Reseller].[Reseller].&[502],
[Reseller].[Reseller].&[170],[Reseller].[Reseller].&[72],
[Reseller].[Reseller].&[328]}, Pass: 4
```

The output tells us the unique names of the set members, as well as the calculation pass during which the expression is resolved.

11.4.3 Constructing a Set Dynamically

Sometimes, you may need to construct an MDX set inside your stored procedure. For example, you may need to evaluate the cell values of an input MDX set and filter out those that don't meet a given condition. Or, you may need to construct an MDX set from scratch. The *FilterSetByCeiling* stored procedure demonstrates how this could be done. It builds upon the *FilterSet* sample stored procedure which is included in the AmoAdventureWorks code sample project that comes with the Analysis Services samples. For this reason, let me first walk you through the FilterSet stored procedure.

Building a set using ADOMD.NET

The FilterSet stored procedure demonstrates how you can filter an input set using the SetBuilder ADOMD.NET object.

Listing 11.2 Filtering an MDX set using the SetBuilder object

```
Public Shared Function FilterSet(ByVal inputSet As Set,
      ByVal filterExpression As String) As [Set]
        Dim tuple As Tuple
        Dim expr As Expression = New Expression(filterExpression)
        Dim resultSetBuilder As SetBuilder = New SetBuilder()

        For Each tuple In inputSet.Tuples
            If CType(expr.Calculate(tuple), Boolean) Then
                resultSetBuilder.Add(tuple)
            End If
        Next

        Return resultSetBuilder.ToSet()
End Function
```

This stored procedure takes an MDX set as an input and an expression that will be used to filter the set. Suppose that you have an MDX set with all Adventure Works customers that needs to be filtered in different ways, e.g.:

```
Filter({[Customer].Customer.Members}, NOT IsEmpty([Measures].[Internet Sales Amount]))
```

This expression uses the MDX Filter function to return a set of the Adventure Works customers who have purchased a product. You can pass the filter expression under the second argument to the FilterSet stored procedure. To evaluate the expression dynamically, FilterSet uses the Expression ADOMD.NET object. Next, it instantiates the SetBuilder object which is designed to construct MDX sets.

The code proceeds by enumerating the tuples in the set. For each tuple, FilterSet determines if the tuple meets the expression criteria. If so, the tuple is added to the result set. Finally, FilterSet calls SetBuilder.ToSet() to return the resulting subset of the original set. You can test the FilterSet stored procedure from an MDX query as follows:

```
SELECT [Measures].[Internet Sales Amount] ON 0,
AdventureWorks.FilterSet( [Customer].Customer.Members,
"NOT IsEmpty([Measures].[Internet Sales Amount])")  on 1
FROM [SOS OLAP]
```

Building a set using ADOMD.NET

What if you need to evaluate the cell value of a tuple before you add it to the set? This is where the *FilterSetByCeiling* function comes handy.

Listing 11.3 Evaluating the tuple values of a set

```
Public Shared Function FilterSetByCeiling(ByVal inputSet As [Set], _
                        ByVal measure As String, ByVal ceiling As Integer) As [Set]
   Dim tuple As Tuple
   Dim expr As Expression = New Expression()
   Dim resultSetBuilder As SetBuilder = New SetBuilder()
   Dim context As String
   Dim mdxValue As MDXValue

   For Each tuple In inputSet.Tuples
       context = GetCurrentContextFromTuple(tuple)
       expr.ExpressionText = String.Format("({0} {1})", context, measure)
       expr.ExpressionText = expText
       mdxValue = expr.Calculate(tuple)
       If mdxValue.ToInt32() <= ceiling Then   ' ! assume the cell value will be int
            resultSetBuilder.Add(tuple)
       End If
   Next
   Return resultSetBuilder.ToSet()
End Function

Private Shared Function GetCurrentContextFromTuple(ByVal tuple As Tuple) As String
     Dim context As String = String.Empty
     Dim member As Member
     For Each member In tuple.Members
         context += member.UniqueName + ", "
     Next
     Return context
End Function
```

The function takes a set, a name of a measure (e.g. Measures.[Sales Profit], and a maximum value of that measure as an integer. The resulting set will include only the tuples whose cell values don't exceed the maximum value. We start by looping through the tuples in the set. A tuple itself doesn't have a value. Instead, as you know, it is simply a multi-dimensional coordinate that points to a single cell in the cube space.

How do we get the cell value? Again, we can use the Expression object for this purpose. If we pass the tuple definition to it, the Expression object will give us back the cell value, which we can cast to whatever type that measure is defined in. To get the dimension members of the tuple, we call the *GetCurrentContextFromTuple* helper function. It simply enumerates through the tuple members to reverse-engineer the tuple, e.g.

```
"([Customer].[Customers by Geography].[City].London,
[Product].[Product by Category].[Subcategory].&[1])"
```

Once we have the tuple definition, we are ready to construct the expression text, which simply consists of the tuple definition and the measure we need to evaluate. The Calculate method of the Expression object returns the cell value found at these coordinates as an MDXValue object. MDXValue.ToInt32 gives us the integer equivalent of the value which we compare against the maximum value. If its cell value doesn't exceed the threshold, the tuple is added to the set. You can call the FilterSetByCeiling as follows:

```
Select {[Internet Sales Amount], [Reseller Sales Amount],
[Sales Profit], [Average Profit]} on 0,
AdventureWorks.FilterSetByCeiling(([Customer].[Customers by Geography].[City].Members,
[Product].[Product by Category].[Subcategory].&[1]),
"Measures.[Internet Sales Amount]", 20000) on 1
From [SOS OLAP]
```

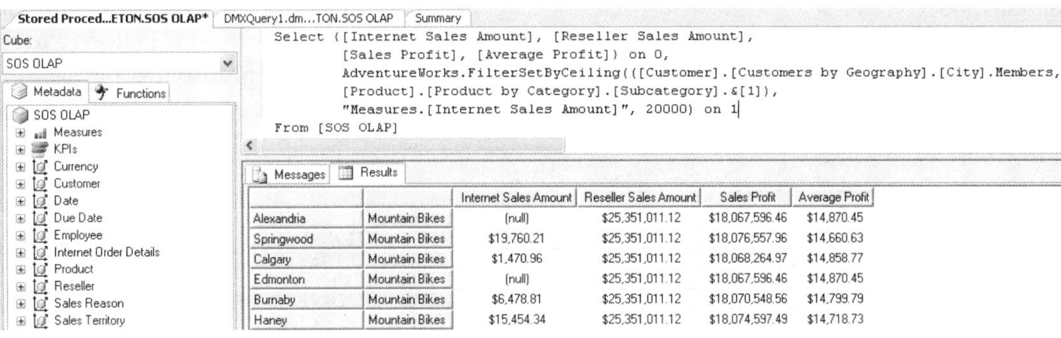

Figure 11.13 Calling the FilterSetByCeiling stored procedure to filter tuples in a set.

In this case, we pass an MDX set that contains all cities where bikes have been sold. The measure that we need to evaluate is [Internet Sales Amount], and the maximum value is $20,000. Figure 11.13 shows the results.

11.4.4 Getting Data Mining Prediction Results

As I mentioned, as it stands, ADOMD.NET supports only DMX (not MDX) queries inside a stored procedure. My last example demonstrates how an SSAS stored procedure can be used as a regular SQL Server stored procedure. This allows the end-user or a client application to pass parameters to the stored procedure, which in turn queries a mining model and returns the predicted results.

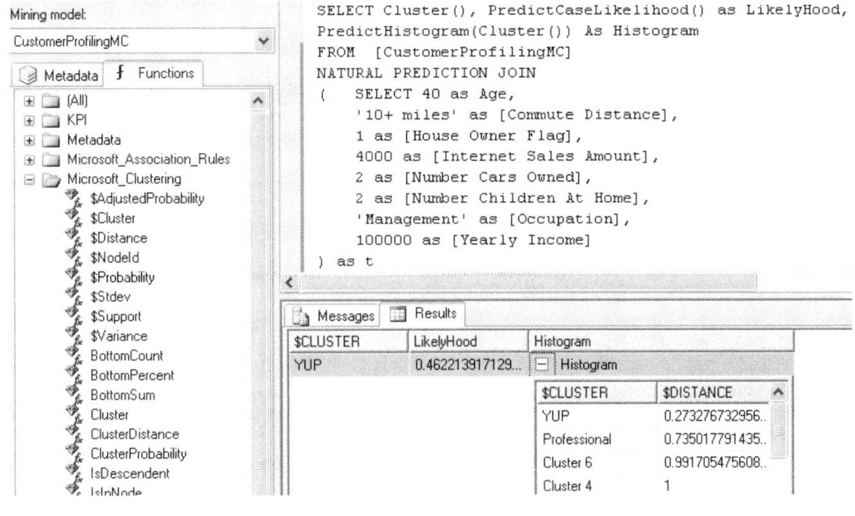

Figure 11.14 Predicting the cluster a given customer may belong to.

Using a singleton query

As you would recall, in chapter 8, we created the Customer Profiling mining model to classify the Adventure Works customers. Given this model, finding out which cluster a given customer most likely belongs to, is a matter of firing the singleton statement shown in Figure 11.14. I use SQL Server Management Studio to create and send this DMX query to the CustomerProfilingMC mining model. Given the specified customer details, the model has predicated that there is about 46% probability that this customer may belong to the YUP cluster. The *Cluster* function returns the cluster name. The *PredictCaseLikelyhood* function returns the predicted probability. Finally, the *PredictHistogram* function returns a histogram that shows the distance of the prediction to the clusters.

Using a stored procedure

Using ad hoc DMX queries like the example above are useful to test the mining model quickly. In real life, however, it may be more practical to encapsulate the DMX query in a stored procedure, just as you would encapsulate SQL statements inside an SQL Server stored procedure. That's what the *GetClusterProbability* stored procedure does (Listing 11.4).

Listing 11.4 Determining the customer probability

```
Public Shared Function GetClusterProbability(ByVal age As Integer, _
                 ByVal commuteDistance As String, ByVal houseOwner As Integer, _
                 ByVal salesAmount As Double, ByVal carsOwned As Integer, _
                 ByVal childrenHome As Integer, ByVal occupation As String, _
                 ByVal yearlyIncome As Double, yRef clusterName As String) As Double

        Dim command As New AdomdCommand()
        command.CommandText = "SELECT ClusterProbability('" & clusterName & "') " & _
                "FROM [" & Context.CurrentMiningModel.Name & "]" & _
                "NATURAL PREDICTION JOIN " & _
                "(SELECT @Age as Age, @CommuteDistance as [Commute Distance], " & _
                "@HouseOwner as [House Owner Flag]," & _
                "@SalesAmount as [Internet Sales Amount], " & _
                "@CarsOwned as [Number Cars Owned], " & _
                "@ChildrenHome as [Number Children At Home]," & _
                "@Occupation as [Occupation], " & _
                "@YearlyIncome as [Yearly Income] ) as t"
        command.Parameters.Add("Age", age)
        command.Parameters.Add("CommuteDistance", commuteDistance)
        command.Parameters.Add("HouseOwner", houseOwner)
        command.Parameters.Add("SalesAmount", salesAmount)
        command.Parameters.Add("CarsOwned", carsOwned)
        command.Parameters.Add("ChildrenHome", childrenHome)
        command.Parameters.Add("Occupation", occupation)
        command.Parameters.Add("YearlyIncome", yearlyIncome)
        Dim result As Double = command.ExecuteScalar()
        Return result
End Function
```

This time the customer details are passed as parameters to the GetClusterProbability stored procedure. I've changed slightly the purpose of the stored procedure to return the probability of the given customer to belong to a *specific* cluster, which can be passed as the last argument. You can use the AdomdCommand object to send DMX queries, just as you would use the .NET SqlCommand object to send SQL queries. Developers familiar with the ADO.NET data model will undoubtedly appreciate the similarity of the programming interfaces and language dialects.

One thing to notice is that the code doesn't create a connection. Again, that's because we use the ADOMD.NET server model. The code runs within the context of the hosting database, so a connection is not necessary.

The *ClusterProbability* function is used to determine what the probability is for a customer to belong to the requested cluster. The rest of the input parameters are passed as parameter values to the command. Finally, the ExecuteScallar method is used to retrieve the results because the DMX query returns a single row with a single column. If the DMX query returns a rowset, we can use the ExecuteReader method to obtain a DataReader object, which we can use to iterate over the rows. You can test the GetClusterProbability stored procedure from SQL Server Management Studio by sending the following DMX query to the ClusterProfilingMC data mining model located in the SOS OLAP database:

```
SELECT AdventureWorks.GetClusterProbability (40, '10+ miles',
    4000, 2, 2, 'Management', 100000, 'YUP')
FROM [CustomerProfilingMC]
```

In this case, we retrieve the probability of the customer to belong to the YUP cluster.

11.5 Summary

In this chapter, we saw how to extend the UDM capabilities with custom code. When MDX doesn't provide the functions you need, try the Excel and VBA function libraries. As a last resort, create your own functions in the form of SSAS stored procedures.

Before it is available to MDX expressions or queries, the library needs to be registered on the server. You can use VS.NET or the SQL Server Management Studio to deploy and register the assembly. As part of the deployment process, set the library permission set to the most restrictive level which allows the code to execute successfully. When you need to debug stored procedures, you can do so by attaching to the Analysis Services server process. Inside your stored procedures, you can use the ADOMD.NET server object model to work with dimensional objects, such as tuples and sets. You can also query data mining models to obtain prediction results.

11.6 Resources

The SysInternals DgbView trace listener
(http://shrinkster.com/6d9) – DbgView is an application that lets you monitor debug output on your local system, or any computer on the network that you can reach via TCP/IP.

Chapter 12

End-user Model

The main objective of OLAP is to provide an intuitive reporting framework for translating large data volumes quickly into business decisions. UDM is an end-user oriented model that facilitates interactive reporting and data navigation. By the term *end-user model*, we will mean the additional layer that can be built on top of the dimensional model to augment it with even richer reporting and data analytics features. These features are Key Performance Indicators (KPIs), actions, perspectives and translations. Implementing the first two requires MDX programming knowledge, which is why this chapter appears in the programming section of the book.

We will discuss the features of the end-user model in the order they appear in the Cube Designer tabbed interface. You will learn how to:

- Implement vital business metrics in the form of KPIs and retrieve them from a client application.
- Construct UDM actions for requesting URL resources, drilling down data, launching SSRS reports, and writing back data to the cube cells.
- Define perspective to provide subviews of large and complex cubes.
- Localize the UDM metadata and data in different cultures.

You can find the finished code samples by opening the Ch12 solution.

12.1 Measuring Business Performance

In today's fast-paced competitive economy, many organizations use KPIs to gauge business performance. Business managers would track KPIs on a regular basis, compare them against agreed upon goals, and plan improvement initiatives if needed. KPIs could help these managers confront the adage "If you can't measure it, you can't manage it". UDM provides a framework for implementing KPIs in the form of MDX calculations. Once defined, these KPIs can be used to aid decision making. Since providing KPIs is a common business analytics requirement, let's get a better understanding of what a KPI is and how you can implement it in UDM. I will also show you how a client application can use ADOMD.NET to retrieve and display KPIs.

12.1.1 Understanding KPIs

There doesn't seem to be a common, widely accepted definition of what a KPI is. To set our terminology straight right from the start, by the term *KPI* we will mean a *quantifiable* measure that represents a critical success factor in an organization. In our definition, the emphasis is on the word *quantifiable* because a KPI must be measurable in order to be successfully monitored and compared against a given objective.

Naturally, in UDM, you would create KPIs from existing regular or calculated measures. However, not all measures are good KPI candidates. As the second part of our definition states, a measure should be promoted to a KPI only if the company management agrees that it represents a *critical* success factor to gauge the company performance. Consequently, the list of KPI measures should be kept relatively small. For example, the following measures can be good KPI candidates: Sales Profit, Revenue Growth, Customer Satisfaction Rate, etc.

KPI characteristics

Besides being measurable and performance-oriented, KPIs should be used to track the organizational progress against strategic, typically long-term, goals. These goals should have a clear correlation to business objectives, such as *Attain sales profit of X dollars in the next quarter* or *Achieve 90% customer satisfaction at the end of the next financial year*. Because the goals will change infrequently, the KPI definitions should remain fairly static. There are additional criteria that can be used to evaluate a good KPI, as explained in the article *Ten Characteristics of a Good KPI* by Wayne Eckerson (see Resources).

The results from monitoring the KPIs are typically used to get the big picture of how the company is performing and where it is going. To aid decision making, the KPIs could be published in various Business Performance Management (BPM) channels, such as standard reports, portals, and digital dashboard applications. One way to categorize KPIs reflects their relationship to time and classifies them as leading, lagging, and coincident indicators. *Leading indicators* signal future events. For example, good customer satisfaction could be a good indicator of a higher sales profit. Or, an increasing employee turnover may impact the company's ability to provide services on time.

Lagging indicators occur after a given event. For example, as a result of a good company performance, the net profit margin indicator could be high. On the negative side, if the economy is doing poorly, the unemployment rate could be rising. Finally, *coincidental indicators* happen at the same time as the event. For example, personal income is a coincidental factor of the economy because a strong economy coincides with higher personal income.

While we are getting our terminology straight, let's clarify another popular term, *scorecard*, which you may have encountered together with KPIs.

About scorecards

As noted before, KPIs may not be useful if they are not part of a strategic performance measurement framework, commonly known as a *scorecard*. A scorecard can be described as a comprehensive set of performance measures that provides the framework for strategic measurement and management. The most popular methodology for implementing scorecards is the balanced scorecard methodology developed by David P. Norton and Robert S. Kaplan (see Resources). A balanced scorecard consists of:

- *Objectives* – Objectives state the strategies that the organization is trying to achieve, e.g. Increase revenue, Maintain overall margins, Control spend.
- *KPIs* – KPIs are used to track the objectives. For example, the Increase revenue objective can be monitored by the Year over Year (YoY) Revenue Growth (the ratio of this year's sales to the preceding year) indicator and the New Product Revenue indicator,

while the Control spend objective can be tracked by the Expense Variance % and Expenses as % of Revenue KPIs.

- *Targets* – Targets represent the performance level required as measures. For example, the Increase revenue objective can have a target of 20%.
- *Initiatives* – Initiatives represent the actions or programs required to achieve the target. For example, one of the initiatives to achieve the planned target of the Control spending objective could be introducing an expense tracking system.

Realizing the importance of performance management, Microsoft has released several scorecard offerings for different verticals in the form of Solution Accelerators. Perhaps, the most popular of them is the Microsoft Office Business Scorecards Accelerator. It allows organizations to build web-based scorecard solutions using Microsoft Office, SharePoint Services, and Analysis Services 2000. Microsoft Office Business Scorecards Accelerator supports both balanced and general scorecards. The Microsoft implementation of the balanced scorecard methodology focuses on the four key perspectives to make the company performance management successful. These perspectives are collectively known under the *FOSH* acronym, which stands for **F**inancial, **O**perational, **S**ales, and **H**uman Resources metrics (Figure 12.1).

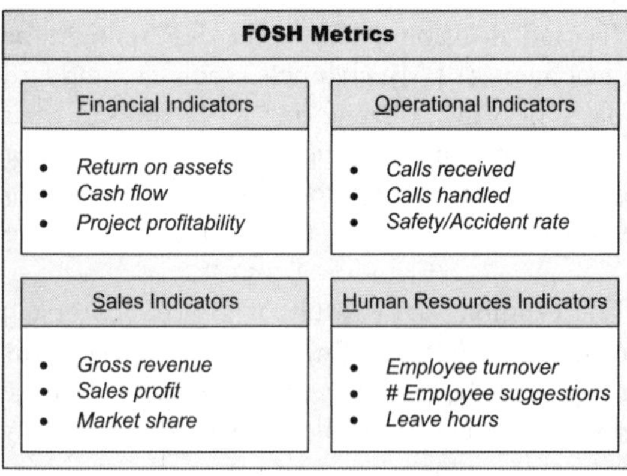

Figure 12.1 The Microsoft FOSH methodology defines four metrics areas of an organization-wide balanced scorecard.

By the time you read this book, Microsoft would have released an upgraded commercial version of the Office Business Scorecards Accelerator under the name *Microsoft Office Business Scorecard Manager 2005* (code named Maestro) offering that provides both scorecard and dashboard features. Naturally, the Office Business Scorecard Manager 2005 can leverage UDM as a KPI provider, as I will demonstrate in chapter 19.

How KPIs are implemented in UDM

KPIs in UDM are implemented as metadata wrappers on top of regular or calculated measures. Think of a UDM KPI as an extended measure that has the following expression-based properties:

- *Value* – Represents the current value of the KPI.
- *Goal* – Defines the targeted goal value.
- *Status* – Resolves the KPI value within the range of -1 (bad) to 1 (good) for displaying purposes.
- *Trend* – Indicates how the KPI value is doing over time.

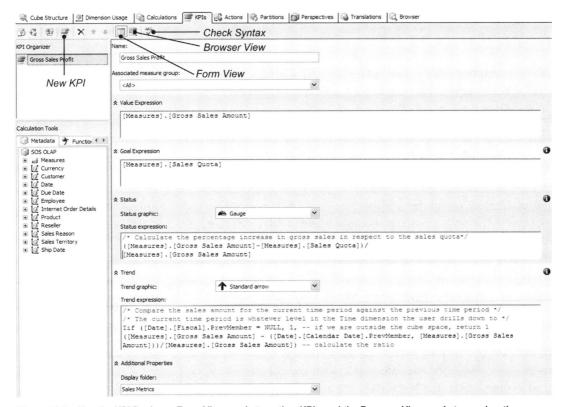

Note Although measure-like, UDM KPIs are not measures and you won't be able to find them under the Measures node in the Cube Browser. Instead, the client has to query UDM explicitly to retrieve the KPI metadata and values.

Just like cube measures, KPIs are *centralized* because they are an integral component of UDM. For example, KPIs can be used in MDX expressions or localized in different languages. They are also *multidimensional* because they can be sliced across dimensions, just as you can do with measures. Finally, since MDX can be extended through stored procedures, KPIs can also be *personalized*. For example, the status or trend values can be retrieved via a call to the stored procedure which takes the user identity as a parameter and evaluates them per user.

12.1.2 Your First KPI

Suppose that Adventure Works has embraced the balanced scorecard methodology to measure its performance. You are asked to implement a Gross Sales Profit KPI to help the AW sales management track the company gross profit from sales for a given time period against the forecasted quota for the same period. This is an example of a lagging sales-related KPI in respect to the FOSH methodology I just introduced.

Figure 12.2 Use the KPI Designer Form View mode to author KPIs and the Browser View mode to preview them.

Defining the value measure

To simplify the KPI expressions, as a prerequisite of implementing Gross Sales Profit, we will first create a calculated member *Gross Sales Amount* as a sum of Internet and reseller sales.

```
Gross Sales Amount = [Internet Sales Amount] + [Reseller Sales Amount]
```

You can find the Gross Sales Amount definition toward the end of the MDX script for the SOS OLAP cube. You need to deploy the cube to update the SOS OLAP metadata with the new measure.

Introducing the KPI Designer

You implement KPIs using the KPIs tab of the Cube Designer (Figure 12.2). The KPI Designer supports two modes. Similar to the Script Designer, use the Form View mode to set up the KPI details. Use the Browser View mode to preview the KPI.

Note The KPI Browser is not available as a standalone component. Client applications are responsible for requesting the KPI metadata and render the KPI(s).

The KPI Organizer pane lists the currently defined KPIs. The Calculation Tools pane is identical to the one in the Script Designer with the only exception that the Templates tab now provides KPI templates. You can right-click on the template and choose *Add Template* to base your KPI implementation on an existing template. Finally, you can use the Check Syntax button to verify if the KPI expressions are syntactically correct. All expression-based fields except the Value Expression field are optional.

Implementing the Gross Sales Profit KPI

Follow these steps to implement the Gross Sales Profit KPI:

1. Click on the New KPI button. The KPI Designer displays the Form View and defaults the KPI name to KPI.

2. Enter **Gross Sales Profit** in the Name textbox.

   Similar to implementing calculated members, you can associate a KPI with a given measure group. This is useful for display purposes. For example, a client application can query the associated measure groups and organize the KPIs accordingly. Leave the associated measure group to *<All>* since the value of the Gross Sales Profit KPI will be produced by adding measures from different measure groups.

3. Expand the Measures metadata node. Drag the Gross Sales Amount measure and drop it inside the Value Expression field. The Gross Sales Amount will be used as a value of the Gross Sales Profit KPI.

4. The Goal expression field defines the KPI target. This is where we want our KPI to be in the perfect world. The KPI goal could be expression-based or a constant value. In our case, we want to compare the gross sales amount against the forecasted quota. Enter [Sales Quota] as a KPI goal or drag it from the Metadata tree (under the Sales Quotas measure group).

5. Use the Status graphic dropdown to select an image indicator to represent visually the KPI value that you will define in the next step. The Gauge indicator should be selected by default. The

sample images in the Status dropdown are available in the KPI Browser only and are not streamed to the client. Instead, the client tool is responsible for rendering the KPI visually. That said, the client can query the KPI metadata to find what image was chosen at design time.

6. You can use the Status Expression field to enter an MDX expression for evaluating the KPI status. Type the following expression:

```
([Gross Sales Amount]-[Sales Quota])/[Gross Sales Amount]
```

The MDX status expression should return a normalized value between *-1* (we are doing bad) and *1* (we are doing very well). If the value exceeds the range, the status graphics will assume the end of the spectrum (*-1* if the value is less than *-1* or *1* otherwise). In any case, the calculated value will be returned to the client even if it exceeds the range. In our case, the expression simply calculates the percentage increase between the Gross Sales Amount and Sales Quota measures.

7. Use the Trend graphic dropdown to select an image that indicates the KPI trend over time, as specified in the Trend expression field. Leave the Standard arrow selected.

8. Similar to the Status Expression, the Trend Expression should return a value between -1 and 1. You can use any expression that makes sense to calculate the KPI trend. Typically, you would evaluate the current value of the monitored measure against a past value. Enter the following expression:

```
Iif (IsEmpty([Date].[ Calendar Date].PrevMember), 1,
([Gross Sales Amount] - ([Date].[Calendar Date].PrevMember,
[Gross Sales Amount]))/[Gross Sales Amount])
```

The first part of the *Iif* operator checks if a previous time period exists. If it doesn't, we return 1 since we don't have anything to compare the current time period with. Otherwise, we compute the percentage difference between the Gross Sales Amount for the current time period against the previous time period. For example, if the user has selected year 2004, the expression calculates the percentage difference between years 2004 and 2003.

The metadata settings under the Additional Properties section are used to hint the client browser how the KPI should be displayed and interpreted. Similar to measures, KPIs can be organized in display folders. For example, if you adopt the FOSH methodology, you could have Financial Metrics, Operational Metrics, Sales Metrics, and Human Resources Metrics folders. Folders can be nested. For example, if you want to place the Gross Sales Profit indicator in the Sales Summary subfolder below the Sales Metrics folder, you can enter \Sales Metrics\Sales Summary as a display folder.

9. Enter *Sales Metrics* as a display folder.

Let's discuss briefly the rest of the additional KPI properties that are not shown in Figure 12.2. Instead of using a display folder, you can chain the KPIs hierarchically by setting the Parent KPI dropdown. In this case, you can associate a weight to the child KPI using the Weight field. The display folder and Parent KPI settings are mutually exclusive (the latter overwrites the former). Sometimes, a given KPI may not be known by the current member of the Time dimension. For example, the Value Expression of the Gross Sales Profit may be calculated for the previous quarter. The UDM modeler can indicate the Time member to which a given KPI applies by entering the appropriate MDX expression in the *Current time member* fields. Again, this expression is just for client convenience only and has no effect on the way the KPI value, status, and trend expressions are calculated.

10. Enter "Compares the actual sales revenue against the forecasted quota." in the Description field and deploy the SOS OLAP cube

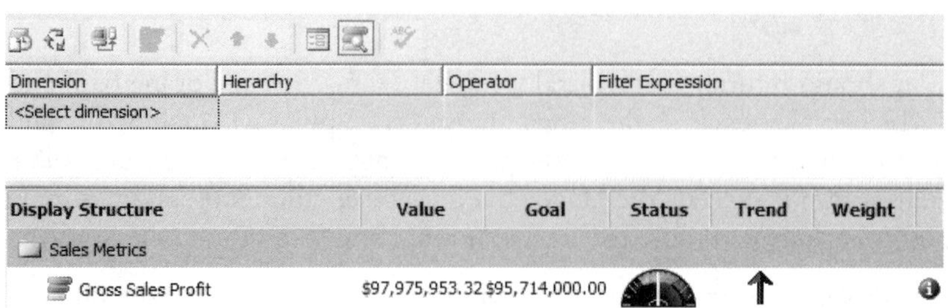

Figure 12.3 Use the KPI Browser View mode to test the KPIs.

Browsing KPIs

Flip to the Browser View mode (Figure 12.3) to test the Gross Sales Profit KPI. Note the Gross Sales Profit KPI appears under the Sales Metrics folder. Since no Time hierarchy is selected, the current Time member defaults to all periods. Overall, the Adventure Works is marginally exceeding its goal (if you can call two million dollars a marginal difference). It would be nice to show the Status indicator in its entire colorful splendor but unfortunately we are restricted to monochrome.

Tip If all MDX expressions are syntactically correct, hovering over the rightmost information glyph will display the KPI description (if any) in a tooltip. In case of an error, its icon will change and the tooltip will reveal the error message. In addition, hovering on top of the Status graphic shows the actual status value.

Unfortunately, the KPI browser doesn't support interactive KPI reports where you can drag and drop hierarchies on rows or columns and drill down data. That's because OWC doesn't support KPIs at present. Your only filtering option is using the cube slicer. For example, you can drag the Calendar Date multilevel hierarchy of the Date dimension and filter the KPI expressions for year 2004 only.

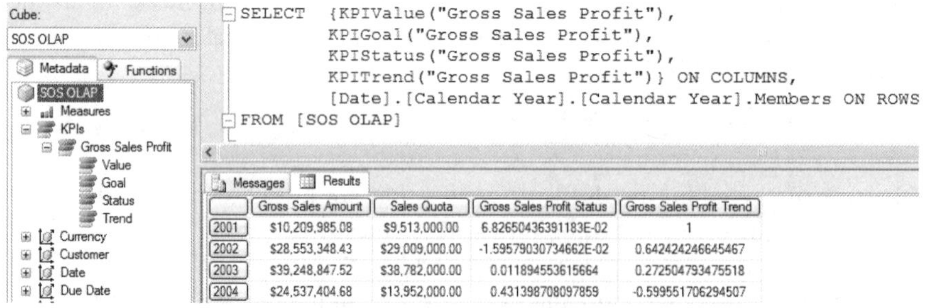

	Gross Sales Amount	Sales Quota	Gross Sales Profit Status	Gross Sales Profit Trend
2001	$10,209,985.08	$9,513,000.00	6.82650436391183E-02	1
2002	$28,553,348.43	$29,009,000.00	-1.59579030734662E-02	0.642424246645467
2003	$39,248,847.52	$38,782,000.00	0.011894553615664	0.272504793475518
2004	$24,537,404.68	$13,952,000.00	0.431398708097859	-0.599551706294507

Figure 12.4 MDX exposes several functions to work with KPIs.

KPI Functions

If you want to see quickly the KPI details across a given hierarchy, e.g. Time hierarchy, you may find it more convenient to send an MDX query from the SQL Server Management Studio. MDX supports several KPI-related functions, which you can find under the KPI node on the Functions tab. For your convenience, the most popular functions are exposed as child nodes of the KPI itself, as shown in Figure 12.4. I authored the MDX query by dragging the Value, Goal, Status, and Trend nodes below the Gross Sales Profit KPI and dropping them in the MDX Query Designer. The Query Designer automatically translated them to the appropriate MDX functions. Alternatively, you can flip to the Functions tab and drag KPI functions from there.

12.1.3 Implementing FOSH Metrics

Let's go through a few more KPI examples. We will implement a sample financial, operational, and HR KPIs to track the business performance of Adventure Works.

Implementing a financial indicator

Suppose that the Adventure Works finance department has requested the ability to track vital financial metrics. One of them is the Gross Profit Margin KPI, which represents the ratio between the company sales revenue and the cost of sales. Since we implemented the Adventure Works Finance UDM in a separate database, we will implement Gross Profit Margin KPI in the Finance cube.

Creating the source expression

As a first step of implementing this KPI, we need to determine which measures or calculated members can be used to define the KPI. In the absence of appropriate measures, we need to create them or use MDX expressions instead.

Tip Strictly speaking, we don't have to create standalone calculated members necessarily since we can embed MDX expressions in the KPI expression fields. However, this approach may lead to very verbose and hard to read KPI expressions. Besides, since KPIs track important metrics, it may make sense to expose the underlying MDX expressions as calculated members anyway.

Open the Finance cube (Finance project) and add the following calculated member at the end of the MDX script for the cube.

```
CREATE MEMBER CURRENTCUBE.[MEASURES].[Gross Profit Margin %]
 AS
    IIF (([Measures].[Amount], [Account].[Accounts].[Net Sales])=0, NULL,
        (([Measures].[Amount], [Account].[Accounts].[Total Cost of Sales])/
        ([Measures].[Amount], [Account].[Accounts].[Net Sales]))),
   FORMAT_STRING = "Percent", NON_EMPTY_BEHAVIOR = { [Amount] }, VISIBLE = 1;
```

Implementing the Gross Profit Margin KPI

Follow these steps to implement the Gross Profit Margin KPI.

1. Create a new KPI and name it **Gross Profit Margin**.
2. Associate it with the Financial Reporting Group.
3. Enter the following expression as the Gross Profit Margin value:

```
[Gross Profit Margin %]
```

4. As noted, the Goal Expression could be a constant numeric or string value. Enter "35%" in the Goal Expression field. This assumes that the finance department wants to target the company gross profit margin at 35%. The higher the margin, the better the company operates.
5. Choose the Traffic Light image as a status graphic.

6. Enter the following expression as a Status Expression:

```
Case
    When [Gross Profit Margin %] <=.18
    Then -1
    When [Gross Profit Margin %] >=.19 And
         [Gross Profit Margin %] <=.24
    Then -.5
    When [Gross Profit Margin %] >=.25 And
         [Gross Profit Margin %] <=.28
    Then 0
    When [Gross Profit Margin %] >=.29 And
         [Gross Profit Margin %] <=.32
    Then .5
    Else 1
End
```

Here, we simply compare the margin against a fixed range of values to return a normalized value between -1 and 1.

7. Choose *Faces* as a trend graphics.

8. Enter the following expression in the Trend Expression field:

```
Case
    When IsEmpty([Date].[Calendar Date].PrevMember)
    Then 1
    When [Gross Profit Margin] >
         (ParallelPeriod([Date].[Calendar Date].[Year], 1,
       [Date].[Calendar Date]), [Gross Profit Margin %])
    Then 1
    When [Gross Profit Margin] =
         (ParallelPeriod([Date].[Calendar Date].[Year], 1,
       [Date].[Calendar Date]), [Gross Profit Margin %])
    Then 0
    Else -1
End
```

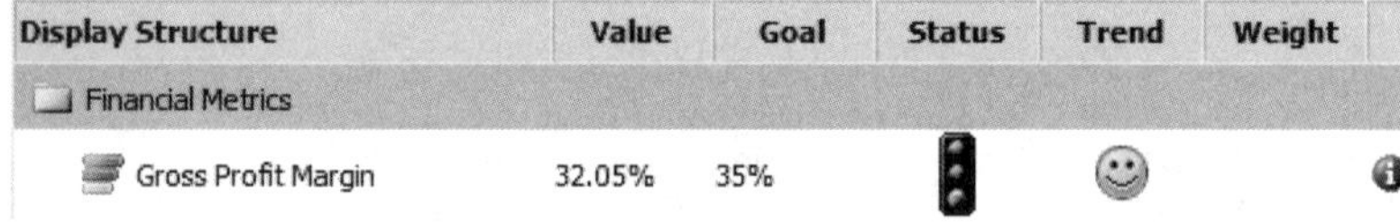

Display Structure	Value	Goal	Status	Trend	Weight
Financial Metrics					
Gross Profit Margin	32.05%	35%			

Figure 12.5 Browsing the Gross Profit Margin financial KPI.

This expression compares the KPI value in respect to the parallel period from the previous year. For example, if the user has drilled down the Calendar Date hierarchy to Q1 of 2004, the gross profit margin will be compared against Q1 of 2003.

9. Enter *Financial Metrics* as a display folder. Deploy the project.

10. Flip to the Browser View to test the Gross Profit Margin KPI. If all is well, the KPI browser should look as the one shown in Figure 12.5.

Overall, the Adventure Works Gross Profit Margin KPI is below the targeted margin of 35%. The good news is that the KPI is on an upward trend. The traffic graphic is a tree-state image. In this case, its light is green because the status value is above zero. If it is zero, we will get amber light. If the status value is negative, it will be red.

Implementing an operational indicator

Our third KPI example will track the Revenue Per Salesperson operational KPI which we will implement in the SOS OLAP cube. For our purposes, the average salesperson's revenue will be calculated as follows:

```
[Reseller Sales Amount]/[Salesperson Count]
```

We set the goal of the Revenue Per Salesperson KPI to be 10% more compared to the previous period:

```
1.1 * ([Revenue Per Salesperson], [Date].[Calendar Date].PrevMember)
```

The status expression of the Revenue Per Salesperson KPI is computed as a percentage difference between its value and its target, similar to the Gross Sales Profit KPI. The trend expression is simple. If the revenue variance between the current and previous time period is less or equal 5%, we are in trouble (trend is -1). If it exceeds 10%, we doing great (trend is 1). Otherwise, the trend is so-so. Since the goal and the status expressions are time-dependent, using the KPI Browser to render the Revenue Per Sales Person KPI won't be that useful. That's because the current member of the Time dimension will default to the *All* member. Instead, you can use an MDX query similar to the one shown in Figure 12.26 to track the KPI details over time (years in this case).

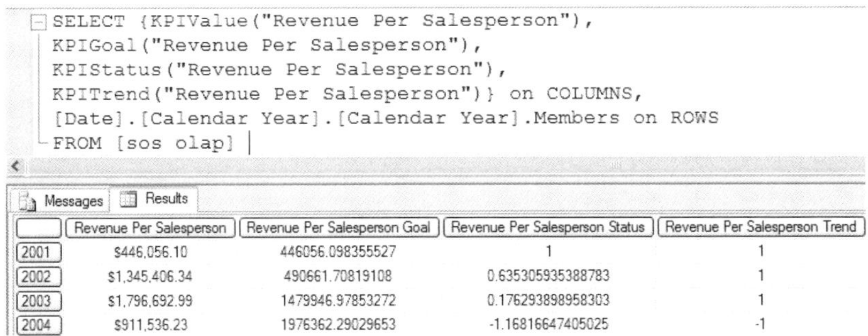

```
SELECT {KPIValue("Revenue Per Salesperson"),
KPIGoal("Revenue Per Salesperson"),
KPIStatus("Revenue Per Salesperson"),
KPITrend("Revenue Per Salesperson")} on COLUMNS,
[Date].[Calendar Year].[Calendar Year].Members on ROWS
FROM [sos olap]
```


	Revenue Per Salesperson	Revenue Per Salesperson Goal	Revenue Per Salesperson Status	Revenue Per Salesperson Trend
2001	$446,056.10	446056.098355527	1	1
2002	$1,345,406.34	490661.70819108	0.635305935388783	1
2003	$1,796,692.99	1479946.97853272	0.176293898958303	1
2004	$911,536.23	1976362.29029653	-1.16816647405025	-1

Figure 12.6 Browsing the Revenue Per Sales Person operational KPI.

As Figure 12.6 shows, each year except 2001, the Revenue Per Salesperson Goal column is set to be 10% more than the previous year. In years 2002 and 2003, Adventure Works exceeds the goal. In 2004, the trend is negative but that's because we have incomplete data for this year.

Tip Unlike calculated members, the KPI Designer doesn't support formatting the values of the KPI expressions. For example, the Goal expression of the Revenue Per Sales Person KPI "loses" the format settings of the underlying measure because it uses a formula to derive the goal value. As a workaround, the client application can handle the formatting of the KPI details. Alternatively, if formatting needs to be handled in UDM, you can move the KPI expression whose value needs to be formatted to a calculated member.

Implementing an HR indicator

Finally, let's implement a KPI which will measure the employee turnover rate. Since we don't have an HR-related fact table, we need to improvise a bit and calculate the annual employee turnover rate, as shown in Listing 12.1.

```
Listing 12.1 Implementing a calculated member to measue the employee turnover rate.
```

```
CREATE MEMBER CURRENTCUBE.[MEASURES].[Employee Turnover Rate]
 AS Case
        When [Date].[Calendar Year].CurrentMember.Level.Ordinal = 0
        Then "NA"
    When IsEmpty (
             [Date].[Calendar Year].CurrentMember.PrevMember,
             [Measures].[Employee Count] )
    Then Null
    Else
        Count(
            Filter([Employee].[Employee].[Employee].Members,
               CDate([Employee].[Employee].Properties( "End Date" )) >
      CDate('1/1/' + [Date].[Calendar Year].CurrentMember.PrevMember.Name)
               And CDate([Employee].[Employee].Properties( "End Date" )) <
      CDate('1/1/' + [Date].[Calendar Year].CurrentMember.Name)
                )
        ) / Count(
            Filter([Employee].[Employee].[Employee].Members,
               CDate([Employee].[Employee].Properties( "End Date" )) <
      CDate('1/1/1900'))
               ) * 10
    End
```

First, we display *NA* if we are at the *All* member of the Calendar Year hierarchy. Next, we check if we have a previous year and return *Null* if this is not the case. If all is well, we filter the employees that have left the company last year based on their termination date. Then, we count them. Finally, we calculated the turnover rate by dividing the count by the number of the employees that are still with the company. To make the results more "realistic" we multiply the result by 10. The rest of the implementation details are nothing that you haven't seen so far, so I will skip to the final result (Figure 12.7).

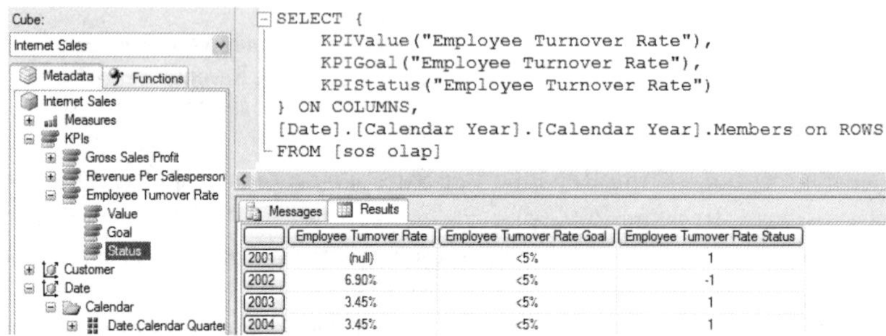

Figure 12.7 Browsing the Employee Turnover HR KPI.

The goal is to have a turnover rate below 5%. The status expression compares the current rate against three ranges (0%-4%, 4%-5%, and above 5%). The Employee Turnover Rate KPI doesn't have a trend expression.

12.1.4 Retrieving the KPI Metadata

Clients can connect to UDM and retrieve the list of KPIs and their associated metadata and values. UDM provides a dedicated schema rowset (MDSCHEMA_KPI) for KPI discovery by client applications. Even easier, for convenience of .NET clients, the ADOMD.NET or AMO object libraries expose the UDM KPIs under the KPIs property of the cube object. The KPI Explorer VB.NET application (included in the Ch12 solution) demonstrates how a .NET client can query the UDM metadata to discover its KPIs (Figure 12.8).

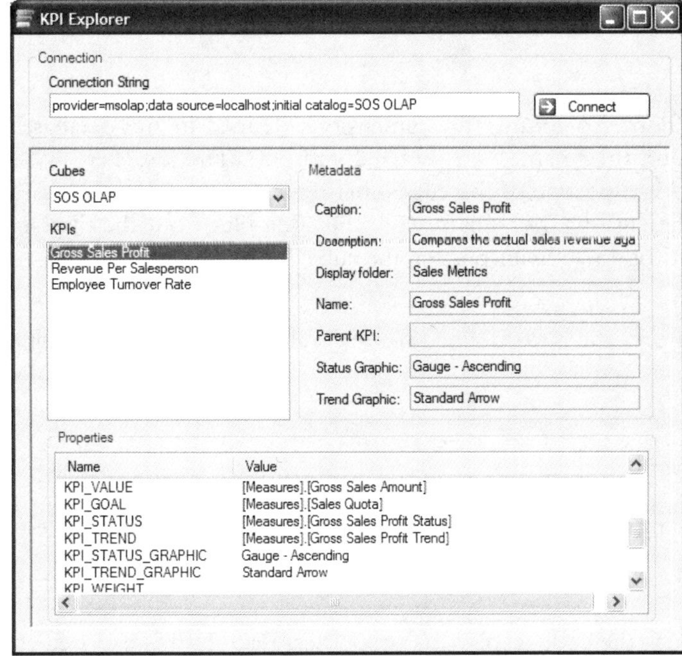

Figure 12.8 The KPI Explorer VB.NET application demonstrates how a .NET client can retrieve the KPI metadata.

The KPI Explorer Application

After specifying the connection string, click Connect to establish a connection to the SSAS database of your choice. Once connected, the KPI Explorer proceeds with retrieving and displaying the cubes in the Cubes dropdown. Next, select the cube from which you would like to retrieve the KPI metadata. The KPIs defined for the cube will be displayed in the KPIs listbox. Once a KPI is selected, its metadata details will be shown in the Metadata panel, while its properties will be enumerated in the Properties list.

Behind the scenes of the KPI Explorer

Implementing the KPI Explorer is remarkably simple. The KPI explorer uses the ADOMD.NET client library to connect to the server. As I pointed out in the preceding chapter, there are two versions (server and client) of the ADOMD.NET library. The one you need to connect from .NET applications is Microsoft.AnalysisServices.Adomd.Client.

Connecting to the SSAS database

Connecting to an SSAS database takes two lines of code:

```
m_connection = New AdomdConnection(Me.txtConnectionString.Text)
m_connection.Open()
```

Tip You may have more than one Analysis Services OLEDB providers installed on your machine. The one you need is **msolap.3**. If you don't specify the version, ADOMD.NET will use the provider that is registered the latest.

Retrieving the cubes

The database cubes are exposed under the Cubes collection. Each cube is represented by a *CubeDef* object.

```
For Each cube In m_connection.Cubes
    If cube.Type = CubeType.Cube Then
     cmbCubes.Items.Add(cube)
    End If
Next
```

Besides the cubes, the Cubes collection also returns the dimensions defined in the database. They are exposed as implicit cubes and their names are prefixed with "$". The idea here is to allow developers to query dimensions irrespective of the cubes that reference them. In our case, we are not interested in the UDM dimensions. For this reason, the code filters out the dimensions and loads only the cubes in the dropdown by inspecting the cube Type property.

Retrieving the KPIs

Once a cube is selected, the code retrieves the KPIs defined for that cube. This takes three more lines of code.

```
For Each kpi In cube.Kpis
    lstKPI.Items.Add(kpi)
Next
```

As noted, the ADOMD.NET object model exposes the KPIs under the CubeDef.Kpis collection.

Retrieving the KPI metadata

When the user selects a KPI to preview, the code displays its properties. Each KPI is exposed as a *KPI* object.

```
txtCaption.Text = kpi.Caption
txtDescription.Text = kpi.Description
' Loading more properties ...

For Each p In kpi.Properties
    lsvItem = lsvProperties.Items.Add(p.Name)
    lsvItem.SubItems.Add(p.value)
Next
```

Besides common properties, e.g. Caption, Description, etc., the KPI metadata exposes many additional properties in the Properties collection. Among other things, the KPI schema returns the names of the graphics specified at design time to hint the client how the KPI should be rendered. As it stands, the KPI Explorer doesn't retrieve and display the KPI details but enhancing it to support this feature is trivial. As noted, a client application can retrieve the KPI details (value, goal, status, trend, etc.) by submitting an MDX query, as the one shown in Figure 12.4.

12.2 Extending UDM With Actions

Actions allow you to integrate UDM with external applications and extend UDM in versatile ways. For example, suppose that a customer disputes a given order transaction and asks a representative to provide further breakdown e.g. per order or even line item. To do so, the representative has to drill down the aggregated order total to retrieve the individual transactions. In this respect, the OLAP application could behave as an OLTP-based application.

Assuming that there is a fact (degenerate) Order Details dimension defined, a drilldown action can be used to retrieve the fact rows behind the aggregated order amount. These are the fact rows whose measures roll up to produce the aggregated cell value. In the absence of a fact dimensions, the order details (if available) could be retrieved from the OLTP system by initiating a reporting action to request a Microsoft Reporting Services report.

12.2.1 Understanding Actions

Let's "drill down" a bit further into how the actions are realized in UDM. A UDM action is a pre-defined MDX expression that targets a specific part of the cube. With the exception of a drilldown action, which is carried out by the server, UDM actions are interpreted and executed by the client application. UDM actions are user-initiated. What this means is that the user has to select a part of the cube to which the action applies and invoke the action. This, of course, assumes that the client application, whether a third-party OLAP browser or a custom application, supports actions.

How actions are implemented in UDM

The action details are stored in the cube metadata. You implement the main part of the action in the form of an MDX expression. For example, if the customer scenario above requires a reporting action, an MDX expression could be used to pass parameter values to the report, e.g. the order number or the customer name. You can think of a UDM action as analogous to Windows shell actions. If you right click on a Microsoft Word (*.doc) file, you will see several actions (verbs) at the top of the menu, e.g. Open, Edit, New, and Print. These actions are registered with the Windows shell processor, as you can see by starting Windows Explorer and observing the File Types tab of the Folder Options dialog (Tools ⇨ Folder Options menu). In this example, the Windows shell processor resembles UDM, while Microsoft Word is the OLAP browser that will interpret and execute actions.

As part of setting up the action, you need to specify its target. The target of the action is the cube scope to which the action applies, such as the entire cube, dimension, level, attribute, set, or a cell. For example, an E-mail Customer action could target the members of the Customer attribute only because it is irrelevant in other scopes.

Types of actions

UDM supports different types of actions. The action type informs the client application how it should interpret the action. To keep the action terminology consistent with the UI of the Actions tab, we could introduce three main types of actions:

- *Regular actions* – These are multi-purpose actions that can target different client applications. In this case, the action expression returns a command that represents one of the action types listed Table 1
- *Drillthrough actions* – Allow the client to access the details behind a cube cell. This is the only action that is executed by Analysis Services.
- *Reporting actions* – This type of actions can be used to request a Microsoft Reporting Services report. The action command is the report path with optional report parameters.

When a regular action is used, you can let the client know how the action should be interpreted by specifying one of the action semantic types shown in Table 12.1.

Table 12.1 Regular action types.

Type	Purpose
Dataset	The resulting string is an MDX statement. For example, if you use ADOMD.NET, you can create an AdomdCommand object, set its CommandText to the action string, and send the query to SSAS to retrieve the results in the form of a Cellset object.
Proprietary	The resulting string is client-specific. The client is responsible for interpreting the semantic meaning of the action.
Rowset	Like the Dataset action type, a rowset actions specifies commands to retrieve data. However, a rowset action can be run againts any OLE DB-compliant data source, including relational databases. For example, you can have a Rowset action that queries external relational databases with standard SQL.
Statement	The resulting string represents an OLE DB command. Unlike the Dataset and Rowset actions, the statement should not bring any results (only a success or failure result). For example, a statement action can be used to perform data modifications.
URL	The resulting string is a URL and should indicate one of the standard protocols, e.g. http, https, ftp, file, mail, etc. For security reasons, the client applications may ignore protocols other than http and https.

Each of the three action types supports additional properties to provide further information to the client about how the action should be carried out. For example, one of these properties is the Invocation property, which could be *Batch*, *Interactive*, or *On Open*. UDM itself doesn't process these options in any way. They are just for the convenience of the client application.

Action discovery

Not all end-user model features are exposed as properties of the CubeDef object. A client application can request a list of actions defined for the cube by querying the cube metadata and retrieving the MDSCHEMA_ACTIONS schema. As part of the action discovery stage, the client needs to provide the cube scope in the form of coordinates to retrieve the actions defined for that scope. Upon receiving the request, the server evaluates the action condition (if any) to determine if the action is applicable. If so, UDM resolves the action command and returns it to the client. The client has a final say if the action will be presented to and executed by the user. Having covered the basics, let's put UDM actions into "action".

12.2.2 Requesting URL Resources With Regular Actions

Suppose that the Adventure Works technical support needs to perform warranty service requests onsite. Faulty bikes could be expensive to ship back! It could certainly be useful if the SOS OLAP UDM provides a map of the customer's location to help a technician plan her route. Unfortunately, as it stands, UDM doesn't provide mapping capabilities. However, Yahoo and a few other popular websites offer such services. The only thing left on our part is to implement a regular action to integrate the SOS OLAP UDM with the Yahoo website.

Implementation approach

From end-user perspective, our envisioned implementation approach follows. First, the end-user uses an action-aware OLAP browser to find the customer of interest. Next, the end user right-clicks on the customer's name. Behind the scenes, the OLAP browser sends an action discovery request to the server. The server returns the *Display Customer Map* action. The OLAP displays the action in the context menu. The end user initiates the action to display the customer map. The OLAP browser sends a URL request to the Yahoo Maps website and displays the map in the web browser. To implement the above scenario, we need a regular URL action which produces the following action command:

```
http://maps.yahoo.com/maps_result?addr=<customer address>
&csz=<customer zip>&country=<customer country>
```

The Display Customer Map URL action has a couple of limitations. First, maps can be generated only for US customers. That's because the Yahoo Maps website supports only US maps. Second, the action targets the Customer attribute hierarchy only. In other words, the action is available only if the end user selects a member of the Customer attribute hierarchy.

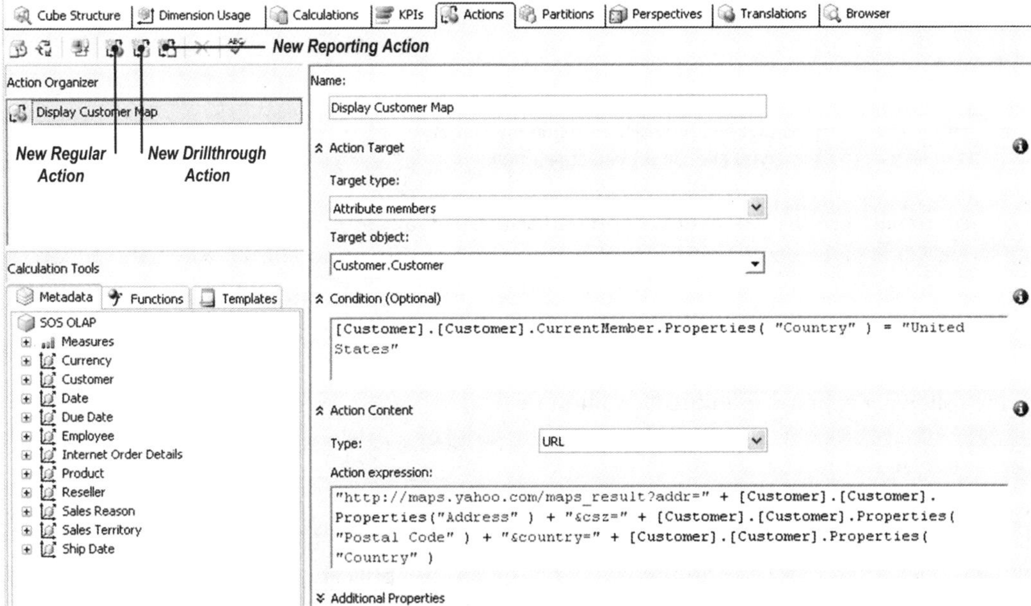

Figure 12.9 The Action Designer supports regular, drillthrough, and reporting actions.

Implementing the Display Customer Map action

You create new actions or update existing ones by using the Action Designer hosted in the Actions tab of the Cube Browser (Figure 12.9). The Action Designer has several panes (Did you spot the trend yet?). The Action Organizer pane lists the currently defined actions. The Calculations tool pane should be familiar to you by now. Finally, the Form View pane is where you enter the action details. The implementation steps of the View Map action follows:

1. Open the SOS OLAP cube in the Cube Designer and switch to the Actions tab.
2. Click on the New Action toolbar button to create a regular action.
3. Enter **Display Customer Map** as the action name.
4. As noted, an action can target different parts of a cube. You should narrow the action scope down to where the action is applicable. In our case, we want to apply our action to the Customer

attribute hierarchy only. Select **Attribute members** in the *Target type* dropdown (Figure 12.10). This effectively enables the action for the Customer attribute hierarchy and all multilevel hierarchies where it is used.

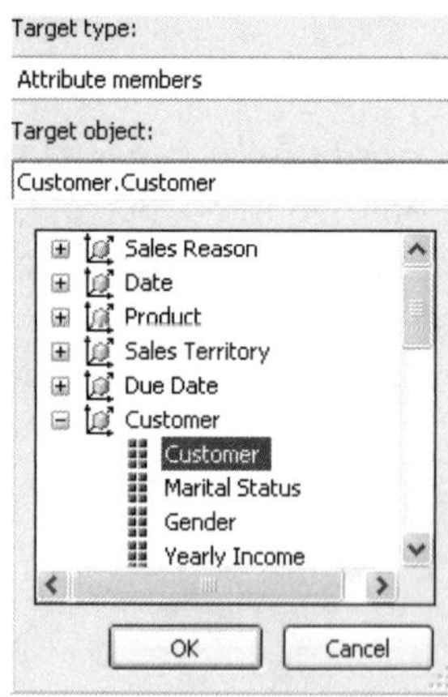

Figure 12.10 Target your action to a given cube scope by using the Target type and Target object settings.

You can optionally specify an MDX expression in the Condition field to further restrict the action scope. This gives you a lot of flexibility to control programmatically when the action is activated. For example, the conditional expression can call an SSAS stored procedure to validate a business rule that determines if the action is applicable. The server doesn't return the action to the client if the conditional expression evaluates to False.

5. Enter the following expression in the Condition field:

```
[Customer].[Customer].CurrentMember.Properties("Country") = "United States"
```

Since the maps can be generated for the customers in the USA only, our conditional expression validates that the Country property of the current member contains *United States*. Leave the *URL* action type selected in the Type dropdown to tell the client application that this is a URL-based action. Typically, the client application will just shell out the URL string to the web browser.

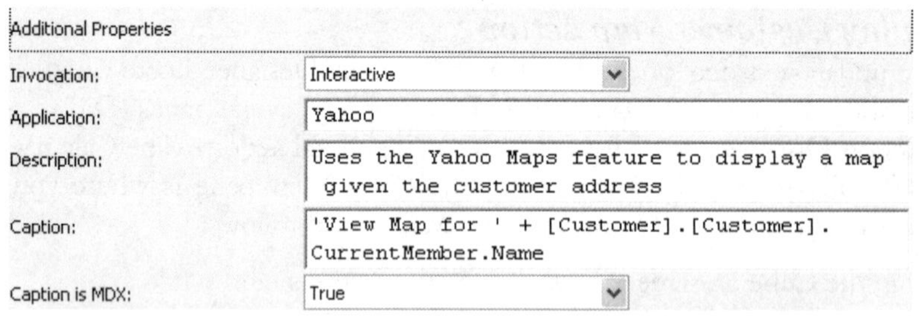

Figure 12.11 You can pass additional properties to the client application to indicate the action semantics.

6. The trickiest part of setting the Display Customer Map action is setting the actual URL string. Enter the following expression in the Action expression field.

```
"http://maps.yahoo.com/maps_result?addr=" +
[Customer].[Customer].Properties("Address") + "&csz=" +
[Customer].[Customer].Properties("Postal Code") + "&country=" +
[Customer].[Customer].Properties("Country")
```

This MDX expression simply extracts the values of the Address, Postal Code, and Country properties of the selected customer. It concatenates the values together to form a valid URL string as per the Yahoo Maps URL specification.

7. You can pass additional properties to the client application to describe further the purpose of the action. Expand the Additional Properties panel and enter the properties shown in Figure 12.11.

   You can programmatically set the action caption by using an MDX expression and setting the Caption is MDX dropdown to *True*. When the action is requested, the server will evaluate the Caption expression and set the action caption accordingly. In our case, the caption will be *View Map for <Customer Name>*, where the <Customer Name> will be set to the name of the current member of the Customer attribute hierarchy.

8. Deploy the SOS OLAP project.

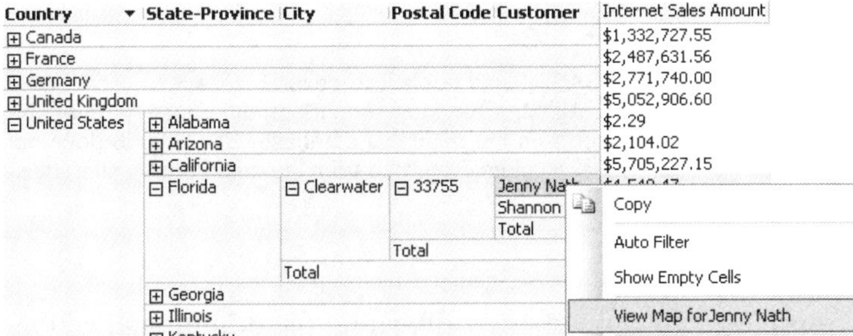

Country
State-Province
City
Postal Code
Customer
Internet Sales Amount
Canada
$1,332,727.55
France
$2,487,631.56
Germany
$2,771,740.00
United Kingdom
$5,052,906.60
United States
Alabama
$2.29
Arizona
$2,104.02
California
$5,705,227.15
Florida
Clearwater
33755
Shannon
Total
Total
Total
Georgia
Illinois
Copy
Auto Filter
Show Empty Cells
View Map forJenny Nath

Figure 12.12 You can pass additional properties to the client application to indicate the action semantics.

Testing the action

It's show time! Let's create a report in the Cube Browser to test the action.

1. Create a report with the Customer by Geography (or just the Customer attribute hierarchy) on rows and the Internet Sales Amount measure on details (Figure 12.12).

2. Expand the hierarchy to find a customer in the US, e.g. Jenny Nath from Clearwater, FL.

3. Right-click on the customer. The context menu should include the *View Map* action.

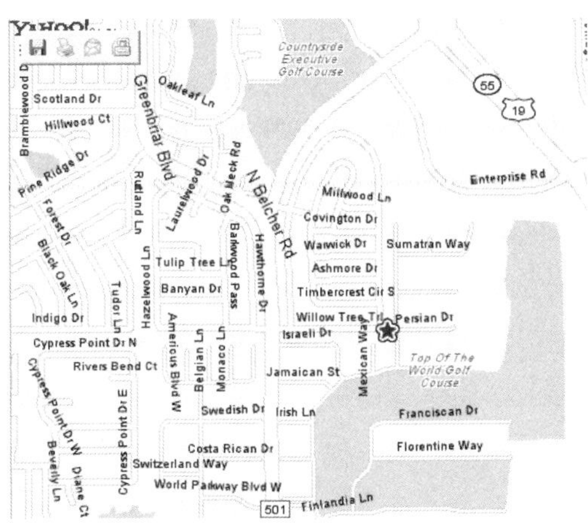

Figure 12.13 Integrating UDM with URL-addressable resources is just one way of extending it with actions.

4. Click on the View Map menu to trigger the action. Since this is an URL action, OWC hands out the URL request to the web browser, which in turn, sends the request to the Yahoo Maps website.

   If all is well, you should see the customer's map displayed in a new window of the web browser (Figure 12.13).

12.2.3 Displaying Detail Cell Data With Drillthrough Actions

Often end users may need to access detailed data behind the grain of a measure group. For example, the grain of the FactInternetSales and FactResellerSales fact tables and their associated measure groups is a day. Normally, end users cannot drill down behind the daily aggregated values although the individual transactional details are stored in the cube. Suppose that an Adventure Works business analyst reviews the sales order data and drills down the Calendar Date multilevel hierarchy to its lowest level – a calendar day. What if the analyst questions the aggregated daily total and would like to inspect the individual fact rows? Drillthrough actions can be used to provide a level of detail behind a cube cell.

SSAS 2000 Although drillthrough was available in SSAS, it was subject to several limitations. The SSAS team has redesigned the drillthrough architecture in UDM. The most important difference is that the drillthrough results are returned from within the cube, not from the relational database. SSAS 2005 does not send any SQL queries to the database. Consequently, each column returned from the drillthrough action must have a corresponding UDM attribute.

Understanding drillthrough actions

Drillthrough actions can target measure groups only. As part of setting the drillthrough action, you need to specify which measures will be returned. In addition, the drillthrough action can optionally return dimension attributes from the dimension related to the targeted measure group. Since the value of a single cube cell could be produced by aggregating many fact rows, you can restrict the number of rows returned to prevent performance degradation.

The drillthrough action expression results in an MDX DRILLTHROUGH statement that the client application can execute against the server to display the results to the end user. For more information about the drillthrough internals can be found in the excellent *Enabling Drillthrough in Analysis Services 2005* whitepaper by T.K. Anand, a Program Manager of the Analysis Services team (see Resources).

Implementing a drillthrough action

Let's implement a drillthrough action that displays the Adventure Works resale order transactions behind a given cube cell. Since the process is similar to creating a regular action, I will focus only on the new concepts.

1. Click on the New Drillthrough Action toolbar menu.
2. Name the action *Drillthrough To Reseller Facts* (Figure 12.14).
3. Expand the Action Target dropdown and observe that it lists only the measure groups in the SOS OLAP cube. Select the *Reseller Sales* measure group.

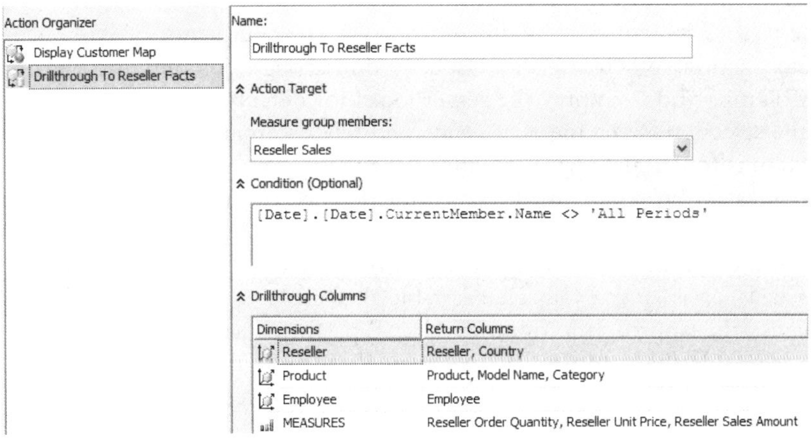

Figure 12.14 Drillthrough actions can target only measure groups but can return attributes from related dimensions.

4. To prevent information overflow and performance degradation, it's a good idea to limit the scope of the drillthrough action as much as possible. For example, our Drillthrough To Reseller Facts action is enabled only if the user drills down to the leaf cells of the Date attribute hierarchy. To enforce this rule, we use the following condition expression:

```
[Date].[Date].CurrentMember.Name <> 'All Periods'
```

The Date attribute represents the dimension key of the Date dimension. If this hierarchy is not present in the query or the user hasn't drilled down to its level (in the case where the Date attribute is a part of a multilevel hierarchy, e.g. Calendar Date), then the current member is the *All* member and the server won't return the action.

5. In the Drillthrough grid, specify the drillthrough columns that the action will return as per your business requirements. As noted, the drillthrough columns can be derived from measures of the targeted measure group or/and attributes from related measures. Measures from other measure groups cannot be used unless you use the default drillthrough actions, as I will explain in the next section.

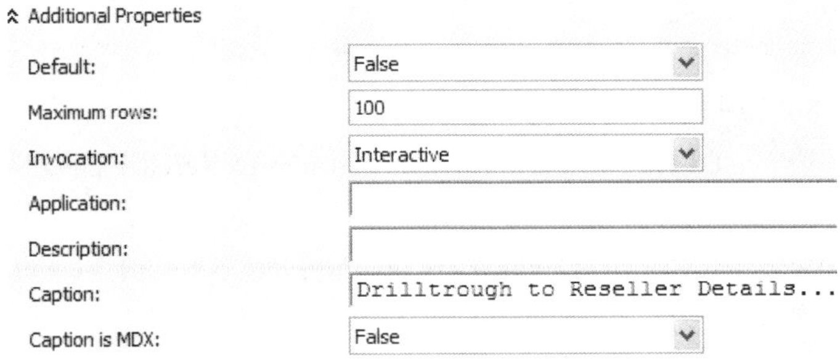

Figure 12.15 When implementing a drillthrough action, it is important to limit the number of returned rows by using the Maximum rows field.

Drillthrough actions have two properties that regular actions don't support (Figure 12.15). The *Maximum rows* property sets the maximum number of rows returned (100 in our case). The *Default* property deserves more attention.

Using default actions

Setting the Default property to *True* marks a drilldown action as a default action. A cube can have more than one default action. When you don't specify drillthrough columns for a given action (the Drillthrough Columns grid is empty), the server looks for default drillthrough actions that apply to the same cube selection (same measure group and related dimensions). If a matching default drillthrough action is found, the server executes the action.

Although this may sound very boring, it enables some interesting scenarios. For example, it allows the drillthrough results to be returned from a fact table other than the fact table that the action targets. Suppose that a call center cube has two fact tables – e.g. a Daily Calls fact table that aggregates calls on a daily basis, and a Call Details table that captures the individual calls. Many warehouse schemas use this approach to optimize OLAP performance of queries that are answered by a "master" fact table that captures the aggregated data. At the same time, detail queries are answered from the transactional fact table.

Default actions allow end users to drill through the aggregated fact table (the Daily Calls cube in our example) to the transaction-level fact table (Call Details). Implementing this scenario requires creating two drillthrough actions – a drillthrough action on the master measure group that doesn't return any columns and a default drillthrough action on the transaction-level measure group. The server will automatically enable the default action when the user initiates drillthrough.

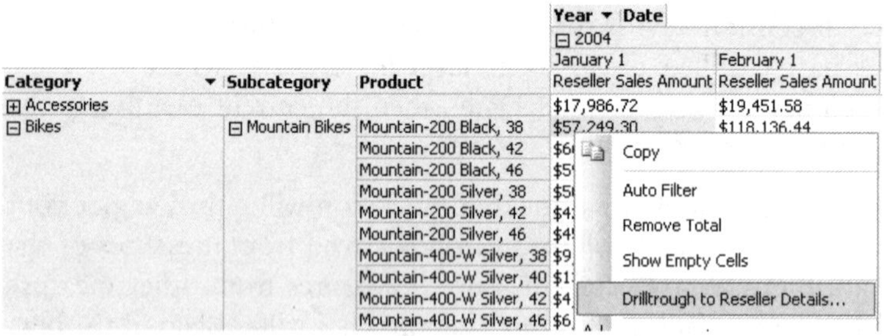

Figure 12.16 Using a drillthrough action to retrieve the detail rows behind a cell.

Testing the drillthrough action

Follow these steps to test the Drillthrough To Reseller Facts action:

1. Deploy the SOS OLAP project and create the report shown in Figure 12.16.
2. Drill down the Calendar Date dimension to a given day.
3. Right-click on any Reseller Sales Amount cell. OWC displays the Drillthrough to Reseller Details action in the context menu.
4. Click on the action to drill through the selected cell. OWC pops up the Date Sampler Viewer window to display the detail rows (Figure 12.17).

Even if you don't cap the maximum rows returned, the Data Sampler Viewer will display the first 1,000 rows only. In my case, the drilldown action that targets the $57,249.30 cell results in 16 rows. If you would like to verify the results, you can do so by executing the following SQL query against the AdventureWorksDW database:

```
SELECT      FRS.ProductKey, T.FullDateAlternateKey,
            P.EnglishProductName, FRS.SalesOrderNumber
```

Topham, Kendra - CIF 00000 000511997

617 653-

506-676-0952

Henry

Cammercial Bids

Home Equity

Cammercial lending

VAT 3829862

cammercial non Accrual Report

```
FROM        FactResellerSales AS FRS INNER JOIN
            DimTime AS T ON FRS.OrderDateKey = T.TimeKey
INNER JOIN  DimProduct AS P ON FRS.ProductKey = P.ProductKey
WHERE       T.FullDateAlternateKey = '01/01/2004'
            AND P.EnglishProductName = 'Mountain-200 Black, 38'
```

The query should return the same rows that are displayed in the Data Sample Viewer.

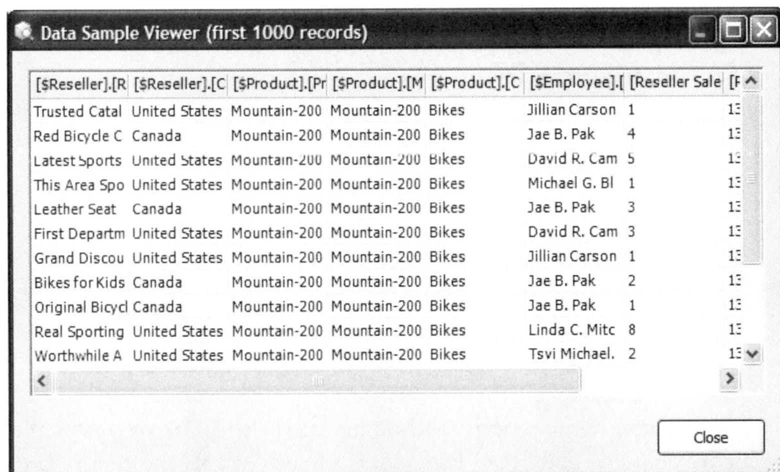

Figure 12.17 When testing the drillthrough action in the Cube Browser, OWC displays the detail rows in the Data Sample Viewer.

12.2.4 Generating Reports With Reporting Actions

SSAS 2005 introduces a reporting action. End users can use reporting actions to generate Reporting Services reports. For example, suppose that a customer representative queries the SOS OLAP UDM to retrieve the orders placed by a customer. At some point, the customer representative may need to generate a standard sales order report with sales header and order details sections.

Once the reporting action is in place, the customer representative could right-click on the sales order and pass the order number as a parameter to the report. The report data doesn't have to originate from the UDM data source necessarily. An SSRS report can be fed with data from any OLE DB-compliant data source, e.g. the AdventureWorks OLTP database. After the report is generated, the customer representative can print the report or export it in any of the supported export formats, e.g. PDF, Excel, etc.

Understanding reporting actions

A reporting action provides a level of integration between UDM and Microsoft SQL Server Reporting Services (SSRS). If you are new to Microsoft Reporting Services, you may find useful the chapter *Introducing Reporting Services* from my book *Microsoft Reporting Services in Action* (see Resources). SSRS provides two addressability options for client applications to request RS reports – URL and Web service. UDM reporting actions use the URL addressability option. The URL addressability option uses a typical HTTP-GET syntax where additional arguments can be passed to the Report Server as query parameters:

```
http://<ReportServer>/<ReportServerVroot>?[/<ReportPath>]&prefix:param=value1...n
```

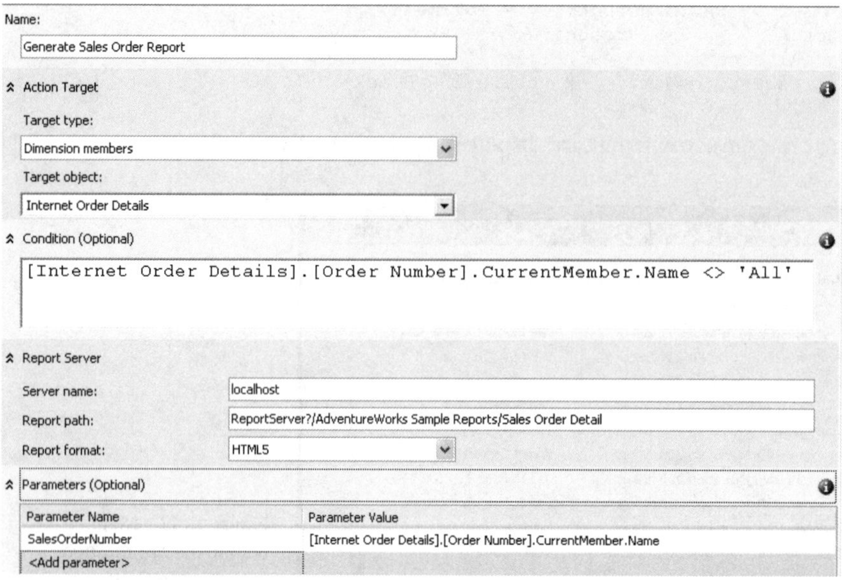

Figure 12.18 Use a reporting action to integrate UDM with Reporting Services.

The *ReportServer* parameter is the machine name where SSRS is installed, *ReportServerVroot* is the SSRS virtual root (ReportServer by default), and *ReportPath* is the folder path to the report (e.g. /AdventureWorks Sample Reports/Sales Order Detail). The Report Server supports a set of report commands. In the URL string, these commands are prefixed with the *rs* prefix. For example, to request a report in Adobe PDF format, you can use the *rs:Format=PDF* command. If the report takes report parameters, you can pass them as *param=value* pairs and delimit each pair with &.

Assuming that you have deployed the SSRS sample reports to the default AdventureWorks Sample Reports folder, this is how you can request the Sales Order Detail report in a PDF format by URL.

```
http://localhost/ReportServer?/AdventureWorks Sample Reports/
Sales Order Detail&SalesOrderNumber=SO50750&rs:Format=PDF
```

It's simple -- you open the web browser, enter the above link, and the SSRS renders the report in the requested export format. In fact, instead of implementing a reporting action, you can use a regular URL action to request an SSRS report with the same effect. At the end, both actions send the same URL request to the Report Server. The reporting action just provides a friendlier interface so you can enter the report details more conveniently. Of course, a potential benefit of using a reporting action is that the client can query for this action type and adjust the user interface accordingly.

Implementing the reporting action

Back in chapter 5, we implemented the Internet Order Details fact (degenerate) dimension by deriving it directly from the FactInternetSales fact table. In a sense, this dimension preserves the original order-order details hierarchy by allowing the end user to browse data by the sales order number. Let's implement a Generate Sales Order Report reporting action that requests the Sales Order Detail report passing the selected order number (Figure 12.18). The target object to the reporting action is the Internet Order Details dimension. As with the Drillthrough To Reseller Details example, the Condition expression enables the reporting action only if the Order Number hierarchy is requested. That's because we need the sales order number.

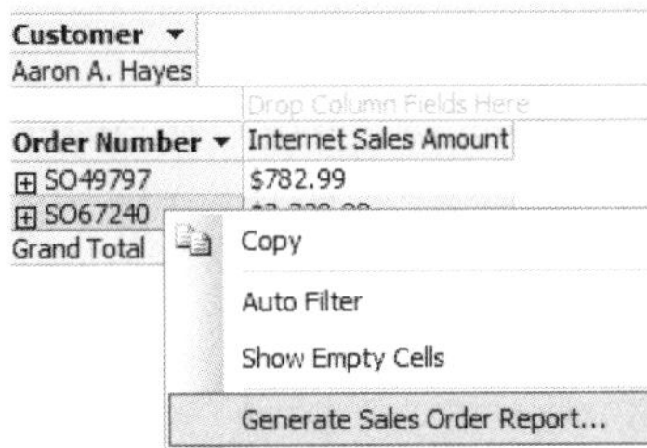

Figure 12.19 Initiating the report action to request a Reporting Services report.

You enter the Report Server details in the Report Server pane. In this case, the report server is installed locally. The server path spells out the full catalog path to the report. Use the *Report format* dropdown to specify the desired export format (by default, the report will be exported in HTML). The Sales Order Detail sample report accepts the order number as an input parameter. This is just what we need because the Generate Sales Order Report action needs to generate the report for the currently selected order number. The name of the report parameter is SalesOrderNumber. The Parameter Value expression ([Internet Order Details].[Order Number].CurrentMember.Name) extracts the order number from the selected order and passes it as a parameter value.

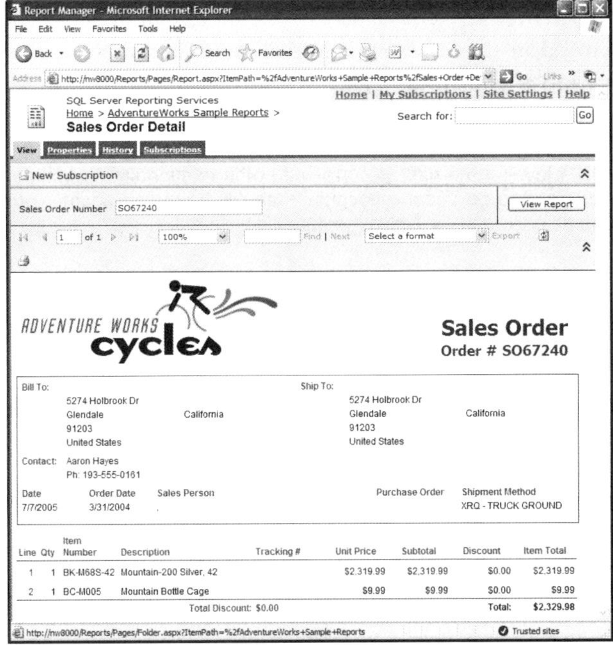

Figure 12.20 SSRS generates the Sales Order Detail report requested by the reporting action.

Testing the reporting action

To test the Generate Sales Order Report action, in the Cube Browser, create the report shown in Figure 12.19.

Tip To avoid performance degradation when requesting all orders, drop the Customer dimension on the Pivot Table filter area and select a customer. Next, drop the Internet Sales Amount on the report details. Finally, drop the Order Number attribute hierarchy or the Orders by Order Number multilevel hierarchy of the Internet Order Details dimension.

Right-click on a given order number and select the *Generate Sales Order Report* action from the context menu that follows. OWC will make a URL request to the Report Server. If all is well, the Report Server will respond by generating the Sales Order Detail for the sales order requested (Figure 12.20).

12.2.5 Changing Cell Data With Cube Writeback

UDM supports the ability to change the cube data by *writing back* to the cube. No, you won't find a Writeback action type on the Actions tab. Instead, this feature must be enabled on the Partitions tab. The reason I am discussing it here is two fold. First, in my opinion, the ability to write back to the cube is part of the end-user model. Second, I will show you how you can support writeback in your client applications with UDM actions.

SSAS 2000 The UDM writeback architecture is essentially the same as in SSAS 2000. Writeback is only available with the Enterprise Edition of SSAS.

Understanding cube writeback

In chapter 5, I demonstrated how you can use dimension writeback to change the dimension members. *Cube writeback* allows end users to change the cell data. For example, suppose that a financial analyst browses the finance data stored in the cube and she realizes that certain data is entered wrong. If the cube is write-enabled and the client application supports cube writeback, she can update, or write back to, the cube cell.

Note Since writeback is performed at the UDM level, if the data is corrected in the relational data source and the cube is reloaded, writeback changes need to be undone because data will be wrong again. You should always attempt to eliminate data errors as early as possible in the data lifecycle.

Although cube writeback gives the user an illusion that the cube cell is updated in-place, writeback changes are not written to the cube cell. Instead, when you enable cube writeback, SSAS creates a relational table to store the changes. This table is referred to as a *writeback* table. The writeback table stores the delta changes made to the cube. For example, if the initial value of a given cell is 1,000 and the user changes is to 800, the writeback table row will record a change of -200. Therefore, rows are only added to the writeback table and never updated or deleted.

Tip Since the writeback table is a relational table, a client application or the administrator can add, update, or delete rows outside UDM. The changes made directly to the writeback table may not show immediately when browsing the cube because SSAS may have cached the data.

Writeback-enabled cubes don't need to be re-processed to view the updated cells. Instead, the server applies the writeback changes to the query results during runtime. When a query asks for the value of an updated cell, the server queries the writeback table to calculate the aggregated value for that cell. Therefore, cube writeback may impact the query performance.

Storing the writeback changes in a separate writeback table, allows the administrator to review the changes. At some point, the administrator could decide to convert the writeback table to a partition, e.g. for performance reasons. When this happens, the writeback data is written to the partition, the writeback table is automatically deleted, and the writeback feature for that cube gets disabled. If the administrator wants to continue supporting the writeback feature, she must re-enable cube writeback.

Enabling cube writeback

So, the cube writeback feature sounds like a cool feature, doesn't it? Unfortunately, as it stands, cube writeback supports only the Sum aggregation function. You cannot enable the cube writeback if one or more measures in a given measure group use aggregate functions other than Sum, which may automatically disqualify your real-life measure groups. However, when there is a need, there is a solution. Even if you cannot use the native writeback functionality, you may be able to implement custom writeback by using the technique I will demonstrate shortly.

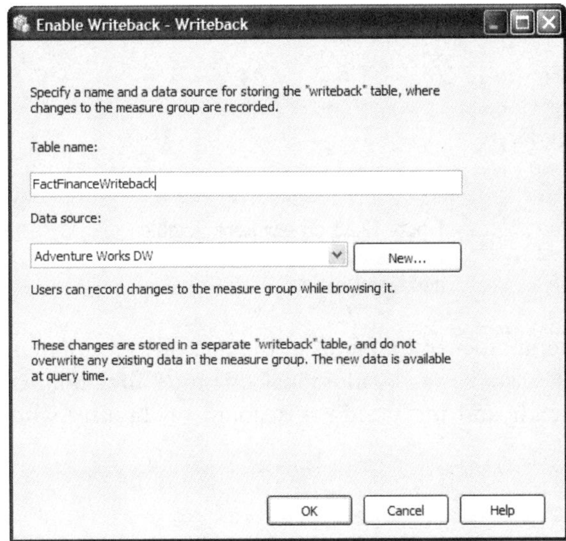

Figure 12.21 Before users can change the cube cells, you need to enable cube writeback.

All of the measure groups in the SOS OLAP cube include measures with aggregate functions other than *Sum*. To demonstrate the cube writeback feature, I had no other choice but to create a new measure group based on the Fact Finance table. I named the new measure group *Writeback*. It has a single measure (Finance Amount) that aggregates using the Sum function. Once the writeback Sum aggregation requirement is met, enabling cube writeback is easy.

1. Open the SOS OLAP cube in the Cube Designer and switch to the Partitions tab.
2. Expand the panel of the measure group you need to enable writeback for and click on the *Writeback Settings* link. At this point, UDM will check the Sum aggregate requirement and if the measure group doesn't meet it, it will display an error message.
3. In the Enable Writeback dialog that follows (Figure 12.21), enter **FactFinanceWriteback** as the name of the writeback relational table and choose the data source where it will be created. The

writeback table data source doesn't have to necessarily be the same as the UDM data source. Click OK.

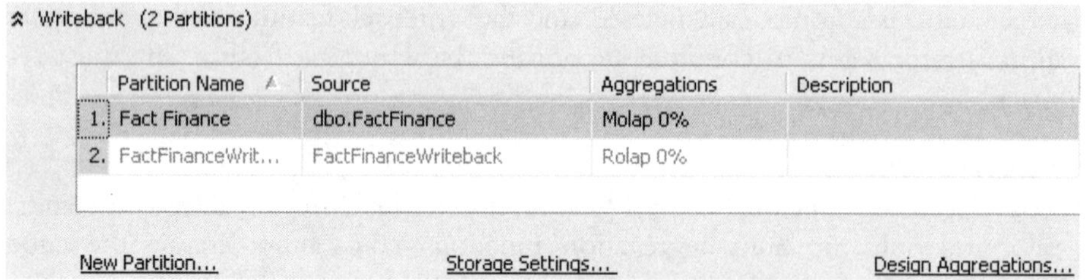

Figure 12.22 Once cube writeback is enabled, the writeback partition represents the writeback table.

At this point, your Partition tab should look like the one shown in Figure 12.22. A new partition is added to the partitions of the Fact Finance measure group. The cube is enabled for writeback but the writeback table is not created yet. If in the future you need to disable writeback, click on the Writeback Setting link again.

4. Deploy the cube to create the writeback table (Figure 12.23).

	Amount_0	TimeKey_1	MS_AUDIT_TIME_2	MS_AUDIT_USER_3
	-11374884.51	1	7/10/2005 2:17:59 AM	NW8000\teo
	10000	1	7/10/2005 2:33:49 AM	NW8000\teo
	-5000	1	7/10/2005 2:38:07 AM	NW8000\teo
	2000	1	7/10/2005 2:40:07 AM	NW8000\teo
▸	NULL	NULL	NULL	NULL

Figure 12.23 The writeback table records the delta changes and audit information.

The writeback table has as many columns as the number of measures in the measure group, plus the number of the intersecting dimensions. It also has two additional columns for auditing purposes that store the time the change was made and the Windows account of the user who made the change.

Performing cube writeback

As with the rest of the features of the end-user model, you need to have a writeback-aware client application to perform the actual write back changes. As of the time of this writing, none of the Microsoft OLAP browsers (OWC, Excel PivotTable, Excel Add-in for Analysis Services, etc.) supports writeback. This forces you to take the road less traveled and implement writeback programmatically, which brings us to the Writeback Demo VB.NET application. This application demonstrates the following features:

- Integrating cube writeback with UDM actions
- Displaying actions in OWC
- Performing writeback changes with ADOMD.NET

You can find the Writeback Demo application included in the Ch12 solution.

Creating the Writeback action

When implementing the Writeback Demo application, I wanted to provide the end user with an easy way to initiate the cube writeback. While writeback could be initiated directly from the OWC PivotTable component, in my opinion, a better approach is to use a UDM action. That's mainly because you can easily set the action target at design time. For example, suppose that you need to support writeback only at the leaf cell level, e.g. when the user has expanded the Date hierarchy to its lowest level. The easiest way to implement this is to use a Condition expression at design time as part of defining your writeback action.

The Writeback action (Figure 12.24) in the SOS OLAP cube demonstrates this approach. It targets the cube cells. If we don't restrict the action further, the action will apply to any cell of the cube. The Condition expression limits the action scope to the Finance Amount measure and the leaf members (Day level) of the Date dimension.

Tip The MDX UPDATE CUBE statement, which is used for writeback, is capable of updating non-leaf cells. You can use one of the four allocation functions that UPDATE CUBE supports to specify how the value will be distributed down the dependent leaf cells. For example, the USE_EQUAL_ALLOCATION option distributes the value equally among the leaf cells that contribute to the updated cell.

We also set the Action Content type to *Proprietary* and the action expression to *Writeback* to indicate that this action is only understood by OWC.

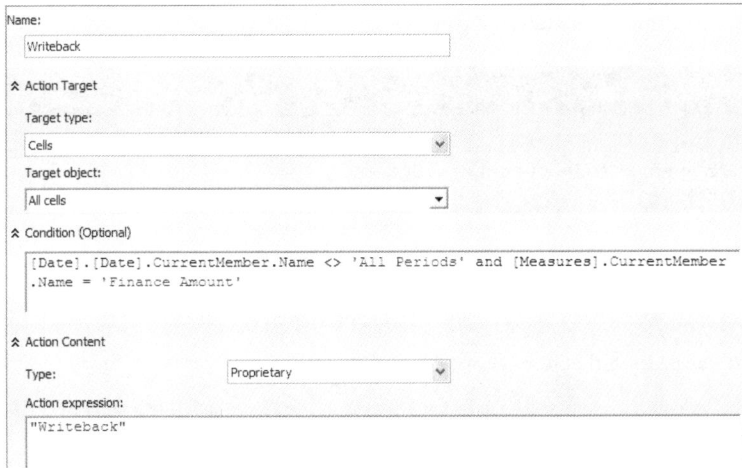

Figure 12.24 Use a UDM action to initiate cube writeback.

Retrieving actions in ADOMD.NET

Retrieving the list of actions that are applicable to a given portion of the cube is easy with ADOMD.NET. Conceptually, the mechanism is similar to retrieving KPIs (see Listing 12.2).

Listing 12.2 Retrieving actions in ADOMD.NET

```
Private Function GetActions(ByVal coordinate As String, ByVal coordinateType As
CoordinateType) As DataTable
    Dim connection As New AdomdConnection(m_connectionString)
    Dim actions As DataSet
    Dim action As DataRow
    Dim i As Integer
    Dim restrictions As New AdomdRestrictionCollection()

    restrictions.Add(New AdomdRestriction("CATALOG_NAME", "SOS OLAP"))
    restrictions.Add(New AdomdRestriction("CUBE_NAME", "SOS OLAP"))
    restrictions.Add(New AdomdRestriction("COORDINATE", coordinate))
    restrictions.Add(New AdomdRestriction("COORDINATE_TYPE", _
```

```
        Int32.Parse(coordinateType)))
    connection.Open()
    actions = connection.GetSchemaDataSet("MDSCHEMA_ACTIONS", restrictions)
    Return actions.Tables(0)
End Function
```

The *GetActions* function queries the MDSCHEMA_ACTIONS schema by passing a list of restrictions in the form of an AdomdRestrictionCollection collection. These restrictions need to specify the catalog name, cube name, coordinate of interest, and the coordinate type. The coordinate type corresponds to the action target type property you specify when setting up the action (6, if the action target is the cube cells). The *GetSchemaDataSet* ADOMD.NET method returns the actions found at the specified coordinate as an ADO.NET DataSet object.

Displaying actions in OWC

As it stands, OWC doesn't support actions by default. Instead, the developer is responsible for implementing actions programmatically. Examples of how this could be done in Java script are available in the Office XP Web Component Toolpack (see Resources). To display the Writeback action, the Writeback Demo intercepts the *BeforeContextMenu* event that the PivotTable component fires each time the user invokes the context menu (right click on a given cell). The abbreviated version of the BeforeContextMenu event handler follows.

Listing 12.3 Intercepting the BeforeContextMenu OWC event

```
Private Sub pivotTable_BeforeContextMenu(ByVal sender As System.Object, _
     ByVal e As IPivotControlEvents_BeforeContextMenuEvent) _
     Handles pivotTable.BeforeContextMenu

    If pivotTable.SelectionType = "PivotAggregates" Then
        coorType = CoordinateType.Cell
             coorCaption = pivotTable.Selection(0).Total.Caption
             aggregates = CType(pivotTable.Selection, PivotAggregates)
             aggregate = aggregates(0)
               coorValue = GetCoordinateFromCell(aggregate.Cell)
    Else
     Return
    End If

    actions = GetActions(coorValue, coorType)
    actionCount = actions.Select("ACTION_NAME='Writeback'").Length

   If actionCount > 0 Then
       Dim menu As Object() = CType(e.menu.Value, Object())
     newMenu = New Object(menu.Length + actionCount) {}
       menu.CopyTo(newMenu, 0)
       newMenu(menu.Length) = Nothing   ' placeholder
     For i = 0 To actionCount - 1
       newMenu(menu.Length + 1 + i) = New Object() _
         {actions.Rows(i)("ACTION_NAME"), coorValue}
       Next
       e.menu.Value = newMenu
    End If
End Sub
```

At different points in time, different PivotTable areas may be selected by the user. We are only interested in cube cell selections. If a cell is selected, the Selection property will return PivotAggregates. Next, the code calls the *GetCoordinateFromCell* to translate the selected cell to its tuple coordinates, e.g. ([Measures].[Finance Amount], [Date].[Date].&[1]).

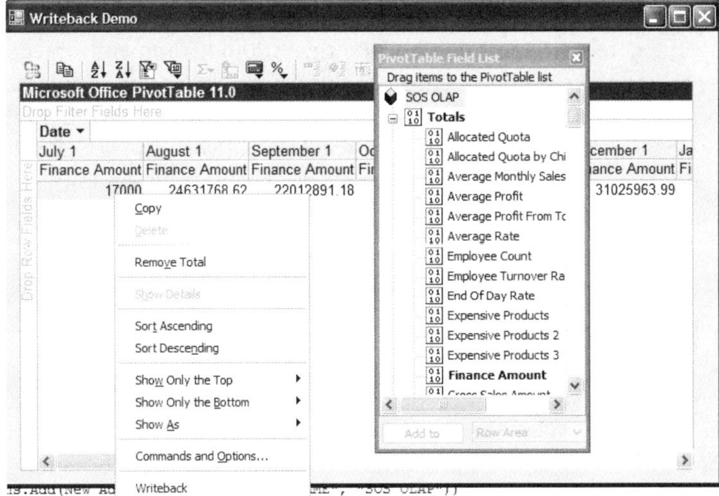

Figure 12.25 Use a UDM action to initiate cube writeback.

Next, the code calls the *GetActions* function to retrieve a list of actions that target that tuple and filters the list to find if the Writeback action is returned. If this is the case, the code overwrites the PivotTable context menu to show the Writeback action at the end of the menu list (see Figure 12.25).

Performing the cube writeback

Once the user selects the Writeback action from the context menu, the PivotTable *CommandExecute* event fires (code not shown). The Writeback Demo application intercepts the event and pops up a VB.NET InputBox to ask the user to specify the new cell value. Next, the event code calls the *DoWriteback* function (Listing 12.4) to write the value to the selected cell.

Listing 12.4 Updating the cube data with the UPDATE CUBE statement

```
Private Sub DoWriteback(ByVal tuple As String, ByVal value As Double)

    Dim command As New AdomdCommand()
    Dim connection As New AdomdConnection(...)
    Dim transaction As AdomdTransaction = Nothing

    connection.Open()
    command.Connection = connection
    transaction = connection.BeginTransaction()
    command.CommandText = String.Format("UPDATE CUBE [SOS OLAP] SET {0}={1}", _
        tuple, value)
    command.ExecuteNonQuery()
    transaction.Commit()
End Sub
```

We use the UPDATE CUBE statement to write the value back to the cube. The UPDATE CUBE changes are not immediately written to the writeback table. The idea here is to minimize the writeback performance overhead by performing the writeback changes in a batch fashion. In order for this to work in ADOMD.NET, the actual changes to the writeback table must be enclosed in a scope of a transaction.

Once we establish a connection to the SOS OLAP cube, we start call the *BeginTransaction* method off the AdomdConnection object. BeginTransaction returns an AdomdTransaction object that represents the pending transaction. Then, we fire the UPDATE CUBE statement to write the changed value using the ExecuteNonQuery method of the AdomdCommand object. Finally, we commit the changes by calling the Commit method of the AdomdTransaction object.

At this point, the changes should be written to the writeback table. To see their effect, refresh the PivotTable report by clicking on the Exclamation toolbar button. The writeback mechanism is transparent to the end user. As noted, it appears that the change is done in-place, while in reality, the delta change actually gets stored in the writeback table and the cell value is calculated during runtime.

12.3 Putting UDM Into Perspective

UDM enhancements, such as multiple measures groups per cube and attribute-based dimensions, encourage you to centralize and encapsulate the dimensional model into a large cube. In real life, your cubes may have tens of measures and dimensions, with each dimension containing tens or hundreds of attributes. While having such super-cubes may be desirable and recommended, the sheer size of the model may be overwhelming to end users.

For example, the SOS OLAP UDM has an enterprise level scope. It contains sales, financial, and even HR data. However, different groups of users are usually interested in their domain of expertise only. It may not make sense for the financial department to see sales-related data, and vice versa. Perspectives provide the means to define subsets of the cube that simplify the end-user navigation and reporting.

12.3.1 Understanding Perspectives

We've seen how display folders can be used to group logically-related measures, attributes, and KPIs to reduce clutter. However, as useful as display folders are, they don't allow you to *filter* UDM objects. This is where perspectives come into play. Think of perspectives as virtual views on top of a cube. The main purpose of a perspective is to reduce the perceived complexity of a large cube by exposing only a subset of UDM objects. By default, a cube has a single perspective that exposes the entire cube content. You cannot remove the default perspective. Additional perspectives can be added to the cube to serve the analytics needs of different groups of users.

A perspective defines which cube objects will be visible to the end user. These objects include measure groups, measures, dimensions, hierarchies, attributes, KPIs, and calculations. From end-user point of view, there is no difference between the cube and its perspectives. When connecting to UDM, perspectives appear as cubes. How do you determine the number of the perspectives you need and the objects a given perspective will expose? There are really no fixed rules here. Typically, perspectives will reflect some logical criteria, such as the company departmental structure or product line division. In this respect, the Adventure Works could have Reseller Sales, Internet Sales, Finance, and HR perspectives.

Note It is important to note that perspectives are *not* a security mechanism. You cannot use perspectives to enforce restricted access to portions of the cube. Perspectives cannot be secured because only UDM objects are securable. Object security polices pass through the containing perspectives. For example, if the user doesn't have access to a given dimension, that dimension will not show in the perspectives that contain it.

Let's define a few perspectives in the SOS OLAP UDM to demonstrate how this end-user analytics feature can be used to tailor UDM to different user needs.

12.3.2 Defining Perspectives

Suppose that the Adventure Works business analysts find the SOS OLAP UDM too complex to navigate. They have requested you implement several simplified views on top of the SOS OLAP cube that align with their subject matter expertise. After evaluating the business requirements, you decide to define the Reseller Sales, Internet Sales, and Sales Summary perspectives. Follow the steps below to create the Reseller Sales perspective that will filter the reseller-related UDM objects.

1. Open the SOS OLAP cube in the Cube Designer and switch to the Perspectives tab. The Perspectives pane lists all UDM objects and their object type.
2. Click on the New Perspective toolbar button. A new column called *Perspective Name* is added to the right. By default, a new perspective is named Perspective and it exposes all objects (the checkboxes of all objects are checked).
3. Rename the perspective in-place to **Reseller Sales**.
4. Each perspective can have a default measure that is different than the default measure of the cube. Select *Reseller Sales Amount* as a default measure for the Reseller Sales measure group.
5. Clear the checkboxes of all UDM objects that are not logically related to resale sales (Figure 12.26). Unselect the *Sales Quota* measure group. Unselecting a measure group removes all of its measures from a perspective. Remove also the *Internet Sales*, *Internet Orders*, *Currency Rates*, and *Sales Reasons* measure groups.

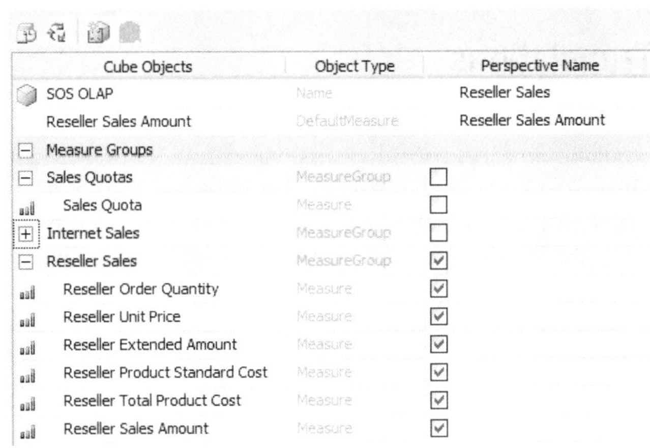

Figure 12.26 Use perspectives to provide subviews of a large cube.

6. You can remove entire dimensions from a perspective or specific hierarchies. Remove the *Sales Reason*, *Customer*, and *Currency* dimensions from the Reseller Sales perspective.
7. A perspective can expose a given subset of the cube calculated measures. Remove the *Employee Turnover Rate* KPI. Remove the *Display Customer Map* action. Finally, remove the *YTD Internet Sales*, *PTD Internet Sales*, *Internet Sales for 2001-2003*, *Average Monthly Sales for 2001*, *Internet Profit for Selected Product Categories*, and *Employee Turnover Rate* measures. That's because these objects are not applicable to the reseller channel.
8. Follow similar steps to create the Internet Sales and Summary Sales perspectives.
9. Deploy the cube and flip to the Cube Browser tab. Reconnect if necessary.
10. Expand the Perspective dropdown (Figure 12.27). Observe that besides the SOS OLAP default perspective, the Perspectives dropdown lists the Reseller Sales, Internet Sales, and Summary Sales perspectives we've just defined.

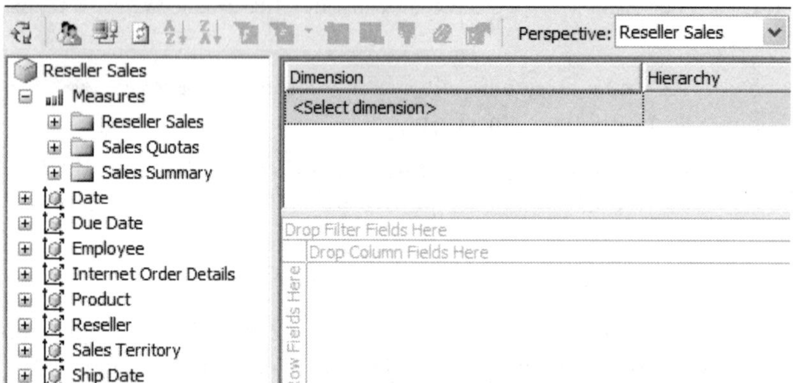

Figure 12.27 A perspective filters out the objects that are not included in the perspective.

11. Select the Reseller Sales perspective. Observe that the Metadata pane on the left filters out the objects that are not contained in the perspective. For example, the entire Internet Sales display folder and its measures are excluded from the Metadata pane. So is the Customer dimension. However, calculated measures that reference these objects will still continue to work. That's because UDM just hides objects that are not contained in a perspective.

12.4 Localizing UDM With Translations

So far, our SOS OLAP UDM has been blissfully ignorant about supporting different cultures. Both the model metadata and data are available in English only. This will definitely present an issue if we need to support international users. SSAS certainly makes it very easy to localize your UDM in different languages. For example, in chapter 10, we implemented programmatic currency conversion to provide the Adventure Works foreign subsidiaries with reports where measures are converted to local currencies. However, we didn't translate the attribute and measure captions, nor did we translate the attribute members to the official language of the foreign subsidiary. This is where translations come handy.

12.4.1 Understanding Translations

In UDM, a translation is a localized representation of an object name in a given language. UDM supports translations of:

- *Metadata* – For example, you can localize captions of measures, dimensions, and perspectives.
- *Data* – UDM also supports localizing members of an attribute hierarchy. This requires as many additional table columns as the number of the languages supported. Each column stores the translated name of the member in a given language.

Translations for different types of UDM objects are done using different designers. Consult with the *Working with Translations* topic in the product documentation to determine which designer to use for the translation task at hand. The best way to explain how UDM translations work is in the context of a few examples. We will translate a limited set of objects in the SOS OLAP database. Unfortunately, Spanish and French (the languages used to localize the attribute members in the AdventureWorksDW database) are not among the languages I speak. So, I will "borrow" the translation text from the Adventure Works sample UDM which is fully localized.

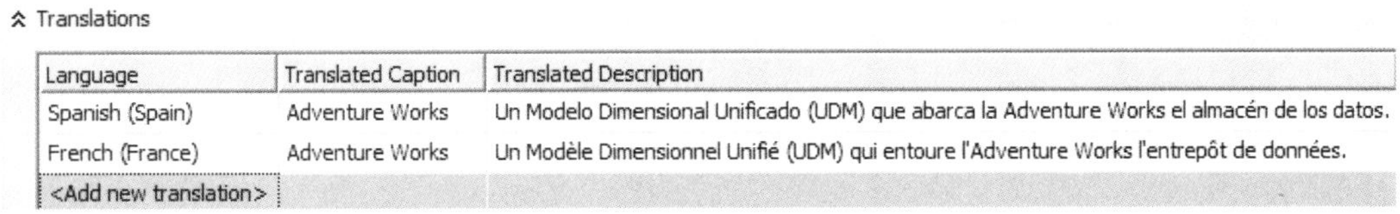

Translations

Language	Translated Caption	Translated Description
Spanish (Spain)	Adventure Works	Un Modelo Dimensional Unificado (UDM) que abarca la Adventure Works el almacén de los datos.
French (France)	Adventure Works	Un Modèle Dimensionnel Unifié (UDM) qui entoure l'Adventure Works l'entrepôt de données.
<Add new translation>		

Figure 12.28 You can localize the database caption and description.

12.4.2 Translating Metadata

UDM supports localizing captions and descriptions of many UDM objects. These translations become part of the cube metadata. UDM doesn't localize date and time format settings. For example, if you have a measure with a Currency format specifier, UDM won't format it automatically as euros, e.g. if a user with French regional settings browses the cube. Format settings translation is a responsibility of the client application.

Translating the database metadata

One metadata translation task is localizing the caption and description of the Analysis Services database.

1. Right-click on the SOS OLAP database node in the Solution Explorer and choose *Edit Database.*
2. In the database properties window, expand the Translations pane and enter the localized database caption and description in Spanish and French, as shown in Figure 12.28.

Translating the cube metadata

You can translate the captions of many cube objects using the Translations tab of the Cube Designer.

1. Open the SOS OLAP cube in the Cube Designer and flip to the Translations tab (Figure 12.29). You will see a similar grid as the one on the Perspectives tab (Figure 12.29).

Default Language	Object Type	French (France)	Spanish (Spain)
SOS OLAP	Caption		
Measure Groups			
Dimensions			
Sales Reason	Caption		
Date	Caption	Fecha	Date
Product	Caption	Producto	Produit
Sales Territory	Caption		
Due Date	Caption		
Customer	Caption		
Ship Date	Caption		
Reseller	Caption		
Employee	Caption		
Currency	Caption		
Internet Order Details	Caption		
Perspectives			

Figure 12.29 Use the Translations tab of the Cube Designer to localize the captions of measures, measure groups, display folders, dimensions, perspectives, KPIs, actions, named sets, and calculated members.

2. Click the New Translation toolbar button to create the French metadata translations. In the Select Language dialog that follows, select *French (France)* to translate the cube metadata in French as spoken in France.
3. Create another translation that will contain the Spanish metadata translations.
4. Enter the localized captions of the Date and Product dimensions, as shown in Figure 12.29.

As you can see, the process of translating the UDM metadata is repetitive and simple. In real life, once the UDM is finalized, you would probably hand out the cube definition file to professional translators to localize the UDM metadata in the languages that you need to support.

Dimension Structure | Translations | Browser

Default Language	Object Type	French (France)	Spanish (Spain)
Product	Caption	Produit	Producto
All Products	AttributeAllMemberName	Tous les Produits	Todos los Productos
Other	UnknownMemberName	Produits Inconnu	Productos Desconocidos
Attributes			
Product	Caption	Produit	Producto

Figure 12.30 Use the Dimension Designer to translate both the dimension metadata and attribute member data.

12.4.3 Translating Data

UDM goes beyond just supporting translations of the object metadata. It allows you to localize the actual attribute data based on the translations stored in another attribute. Use the Dimension Designer to localize the attribute data. Let's demonstrate how this could be done with the Product dimension.

1. Open the Product dimension in the Dimension Designer and select the Translations tab.

2. Click the New Translation button to create a column for the French translation. Repeat to create a Spanish translation.

3. You can use the Dimension Designer to translate the dimension metadata (dimension, hierarchy, attribute names, etc.). Localize the name of the Product dimension to French and Spanish, as shown in Figure 12.30.

   Note that you can overwrite the translation of the dimension name in the cube that contains it by using the Translation tab of the Cube Designer, as I demonstrated in section 12.4.2. Moreover, the Dimension Designer allows you to translate the attribute members. For example, the DimProduct table contains columns that provide the French and Spanish equivalents of the attribute members, such as FrenchProductName and SpanishProductName to localize the members of the ProductName attribute.

Note Attribute member translations are data-driven. As a prerequisite of translating the member names, you need to have a column in the dimension table that stores the translated member captions for each supported language.

4. Click on the translation cell found at the intersection of the Product attribute and French translation column. A command button with a triple-dot caption (...) appears in the cell. Click on the button to open the Attribute Data Translation dialog (Figure 12.31).

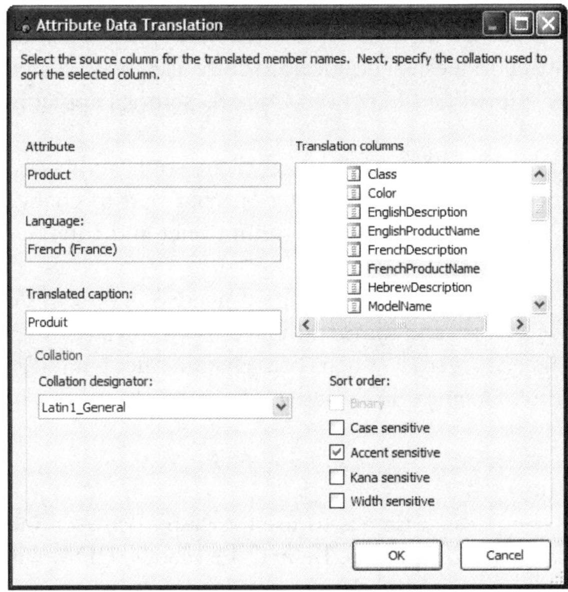

Figure 12.31 Attribute member translations are data-driven.

5. Scroll down the *Translation columns* list until you locate the FrenchProductName column. Select the *FrenchProductName* column. Click OK to close the dialog.

Tip As you can see in Figure 12.31, UDM translates the member Caption property. When requesting the localized member names from ADOMD.NET remember to request the *Caption* property. It is the Caption property which is localized, not the member Name property.

The Collation pane specifies how the translation data is stored and sorted. These settings are identical to collation settings of the SQL Server relational database. For example, the default collation designator Latin1_General uses the U.S. English character set (code page 1252). The default sort order *Accent sensitive* distinguishes between accented and unaccented characters. For example, "a" is not equal to "à".

6. Click OK to close the Attribute Data Translation dialog and repeat the last two steps to localize the Product attribute to Spanish. Deploy the project.

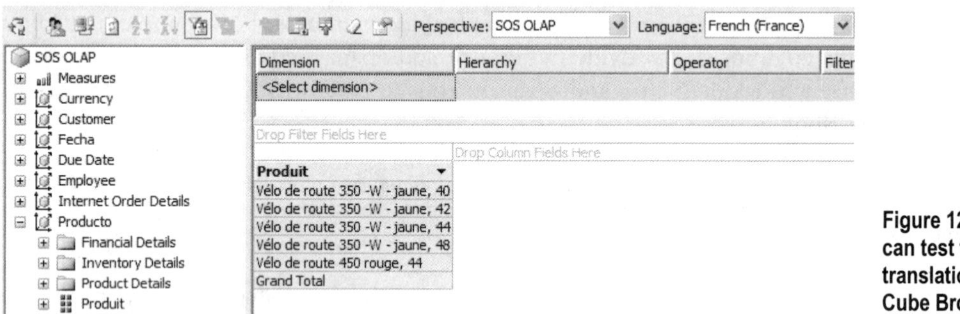

Figure 12.32 You can test the UDM translations in the Cube Browser.

12.4.4 Testing Translations

By default, UDM resolves translations based on the locale culture of the current thread. For Windows applications, the current thread is the main UI thread. For web-based applications, the current thread is the thread that services the user request. The locale culture can be changed when installing Windows or later by using the Regional and Language Options settings applet in the Control Panel (requires reboot).

Once set, the locale culture gets picked up by both Windows-based client applications and the Internet Explorer browser. Normally, you don't have to do anything on your part to change the thread culture programmatically. Translations will just work with both intranet and Internet-based OLAP applications.

You can overwrite the default locale detection to a specific language if needed. You can do so by changing the Language property at database, cube, and dimension levels (mining structures and mining models also support the Language property). When you change the Language property of an object, UDM will use the specified language irrespective of the locale culture of the thread.

Testing translations during design time

The most convenient way to test translations during design time is to use the Cube Browser and select the language you want to test from the Language dropdown. Behind the scenes, UDM will change the thread culture and apply it to the Metadata pane and the pivot report. For example, as shown in Figure 12.32, I selected the French language in the Language dropdown to test the French translations. As a result, the French language equivalents are applied to both the Product dimension metadata (Metadata pane) and the members of the Product attribute hierarchy. In other words, UDM simulates what a user with French locale settings will see when browsing UDM.

Testing translations during runtime

I will mention two options to test translations during runtime. The first one is more involved. It requires you to change the regional settings in the Windows Control Panel, reboot the machine, and run your client application to see the translations for the selected locale. The second option involves just changing the connection string. The OLE DB Provider for Analysis Services supports the *Locale Identifier* setting in the connection string, which you can set to the locale code (LCID) for the language you need to test. A full list of the language code is provided in the List of Locale ID (LCID) Values as Assigned by Microsoft document (see Resources).

For example, if you would like to test the French translations from an OLAP browser, you can use the following connection string:

```
Provider=MSOLAP.3;Initial Catalog=Adventure Works DW;
Data Source=localhost;Initial Catalog=Adventure Works DW;
Locale Identifier=1036;
```

The Locale Identifier setting will overwrite the default language detection and UDM will apply the French translations.

12.5 Summary

The UDM end-user model helps you implement a rich semantic layer on the top the dimensional model. Its main focus is extending UDM to make the user experience more intuitive and feature-rich. Use KPIs to define business measures that gauge your company business performance. Retrieve KPIs metadata and values by leveraging the ADOMD.NET object library and the MDX KPI functions.

Integrate UDM with external applications in the form of actions. Use regular URL actions to request URL resources. Allow users to see the detail rows behind a cube cell with drillthrough actions. Integrate UDM with Reporting Services by implementing reporting actions. Write-enabled cubes coupled with UDM actions allow end users to make changes to the cube cells. With large cubes, consider perspectives to expose selected portions of the cube. Finally, if you need to support international users, define UDM translations to localize both the cube metadata and attribute members.

12.6 Resources

The Balanced Scorecard Collaborative Website
(https://www.bscol.com/) – The home website of the balanced scorecard methodology developed by David P. Norton and Robert S. Kaplan. Balanced scorecards link together perspectives, objectives, KPIs, themes, and initiatives, and use them collectively to evaluate how an organization is supporting its strategic goals.

Ten Characteristics of a Good KPI
(http://shrinkster.com/6fb) – When developing KPIs for scorecards or dashboards, you should keep in mind that KPIs possess 10 distinct characteristics, as explained by the Wayne Eckerson, Director of Research, TDWI.

Office XP Web Component Toolpack Download Page
(http://shrinkster.com/6gg) – Includes code samples that demonstrate how various features can be implemented with OWC, including actions, drillthrough, conditional formatting, and printing.

Enabling Drillthrough in Analysis Services 2005 Whitepaper
(http://shrinkster.com/8j1) – This whitepaper describes the UDM drillthrough architecture in detail. It uses some typical examples to illustrate how drillthrough can be set up effectively in Analysis Services 2005. It also provides guidance on migrating drillthrough settings from Analysis Services 2000 databases.

Introducing Microsoft Reporting Services
(http://shrinkster.com/6ip) – The first chapter of my book *Reporting Services in Action* provides a panoramic view of Reporting Services and introduces you to Microsoft Reporting Services and its architecture.

List of Locale ID (LCID) Values as Assigned by Microsoft
(http://shrinkster.com/6jp) – This document lists the locales/languages with an assigned LCID.

PART 4

Managing Analysis Services

An enterprise-level platform, such as Analysis Services, must be trustworthy. A trustworthy system is easy to manage and support. It is also highly-available and scalable. Finally, it must provide the means to protect the data assets it captures by enforcing restricted access to authorized users only.

The tool that SSAS administrators rely on most to carry out various management tasks is SQL Server Management Studio. Its management console can be used to administer all SQL Server services and perform routine tasks, such as backing up, restoring, synchronizing, and deploying databases. It provides scripting capabilities to automate SSAS tasks and objects. More advanced management tasks can be carried out programmatically using the Analysis Management Objects (AMO) object library.

An optimal storage architecture produces fast queries while maintaining reasonable cube processing times. As an administrator, you have several options to optimize the UDM performance and scalability. Cube storage designs (MOLAP, HOLAP, and ROLAP) allow you to achieve the optimum tradeoff between speed and storage space. Use partitioning and aggregations abundantly to minimize the cube processing and query times.

SSAS supports flexible processing options to address various deployment and operational needs. Classic OLAP solutions rely on pull-mode processing to load cubes with data. Real-time OLAP solutions could leverage push-mode processing and proactive caching to avoid explicit cube processing and reduce data latency.

Maintaining robust security policies is an essential task that every administrator has to master. SSAS offers a robust role-based security model which administrators can leverage to enforce restricted access to the UDM objects and data.

Chapter 13

Management Fundamentals

In a typical enterprise environment there are usually three different groups of people that get involved in the different phases of the UDM's lifecycle. Database *developers* focus on designing and programming the UDM. *Administrators* are concerned with managing the server and UDM. *End users* query the server and run reports. In this chapter, we will wear administrator's hats and discuss how we can manage Analysis Services. As we will find, Analysis Services provides not one but several options to address various management tasks. You will learn how to:

- Use SQL Server Management Studio to manage servers and databases.
- Deploy, synchronize, back up, and restore SSAS databases.
- Monitor the server performance and troubleshoot errors.
- Use Analysis Management Objects (AMO) to program management tasks.

You can find the finished code samples for this chapter by opening the Ch13 solution.

13.1 Understanding Analysis Services Management

As an SSAS administrator you will be performing various day-to-day tasks, such as managing the SSAS server instance(s), deploying, backing up, restoring, and synchronizing databases, automating repetitive tasks, managing storage, processing UDM objects, securing UDM, and monitoring the server performance. SSAS provides a comprehensive management framework to help you perform all of the above activities. Typically, you will use different management tools in different phases of the UDM management lifecycle.

13.1.1 The UDM Management Lifecycle

At a high level, the UDM management lifecycle consists of three phases - development, testing, and production (see Figure 13.1). Under the name of each phase, I listed the tools that you will use to perform management activities related to that phase.

Development phase

This phase should be familiar to you by now. The main deliverable of the Development phase is the UDM definition. The tool of choice for database developers will be BI Studio or its big brother – VS.NET. If multiple developers are involved in the UDM design, the object definition files can (and should be) put under version control, e.g. by using Visual SourceSafe.

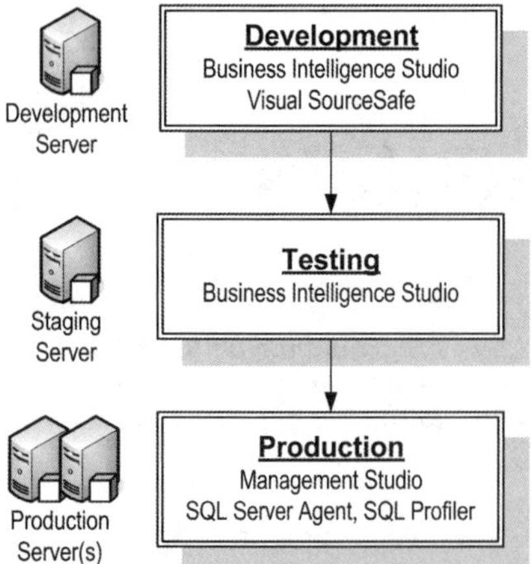

Figure 13.1 The UDM management lifecycle consists of development, testing, and production phases.

During the Development phase you will frequently deploy the project to your local SSAS server to test the latest changes. Deploying to a shared server may be impractical with team development. That's because developers may overwrite each other's changes if they are deploying to the same database. Sometimes parallel work on the same object definition file may be unavoidable (e.g. changes made to the cube definition file). In this case, the source control system can be configured for multiple checkouts. This scenario may require resolving the conflict changes manually.

Testing phase

Once the UDM definition is ready, you would deploy the SSAS database to a staging server for rigorous functional and QA testing. As a developer, you can deploy the project straight from the BI Studio IDE. To facilitate this deployment scenario, you should consider using different project configurations (e.g. Development and Production), as I explained in chapter 2. Alternatively, you can use the Deployment Wizard utility (see section 13.2.1) to deploy the database..

Production phase

The third and final stage of the management lifecycle involves deploying the UDM to the production server (or multiple load-balanced servers). During the initial deployment, you would copy the full metadata and data of the SSAS database. As an ongoing management task, you would need to make incremental updates to the definitions and data on the production server. This process requires that you differentiate between management and development changes, as I would discuss next.

Management and development changes

A production database may potentially incur changes from two sources (Figure 13.2). First, database developers could make enhancements and bug fixes in project mode using BI Studio, e.g. adding new calculations, changing definition files, etc. Second, as an administrator, you may need to apply "pure" management changes. Examples of such changes include changing storage and security settings. Such changes are done in online mode and are applied directly to the SSAS database.

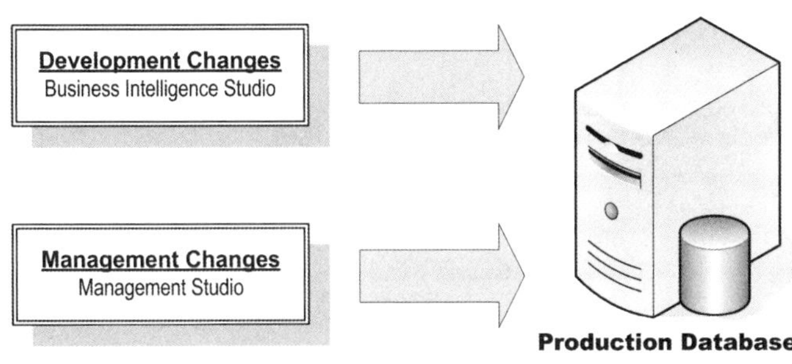

Figure 13.2 As an administrator, you may need to consolidate development and management changes.

The tool of choice for making configuration and management changes would be the SQL Server Management Studio (referred to as Management Studio for short throughout the rest of this book). If you are new to Management Studio, I suggest you read the *Overview of the Analysis Services Development and Management Environments* document (see Resources) for a comprehensive introduction to its environment and features. After reading this document, I felt that a tour of the SQL Server Management Studio will be redundant.

Tip Should you use BI Studio or Management Studio for applying management changes to a production database? I would recommend you use Management Studio for non-structural changes only, which are mainly partition and security settings. All definition changes should be done in project mode first to avoid leaving the project out of synch with the production database.

It is unlikely that you may need to propagate management changes, such as partition and security settings, to the Analysis Services project. Moreover, SSAS doesn't support synchronizing a database with its project counterpart. However, it is very likely that you may need to consolidate the development changes to the production database. For example, while applying the latest enhancements and bug fixes, you may need to preserve the storage settings defined in the production database. SSAS supports several deployment options to facilitate production deployment needs and routine management tasks, as I will demonstrate in section 13.2.

13.1.2 Managing the Analysis Server

Besides the brief overview of the Analysis Server Windows service in chapter 1, we didn't discuss how it integrates with the rest of the SQL Server add-on services and, more importantly, how you can manage its settings. Let's fill this gap now and discuss how you can configure and manage the Analysis Server.

Understanding the Analysis Services server

As noted in chapter 1, the Analysis Services Server is implemented as a Windows service named msmdsrv.exe, as you can see by opening the Services applet (Figure 13.3). In my case, I have two instances of Analysis Services running side-by-side on my computer – a *default* instance (highlighted) and a *Production* instance.

By default, the setup program installs the server binaries in the C:\Program Files\Microsoft SQL Server\MSSQL.2\OLAP\bin folder. The server supports various configuration properties that are stored in the msmdsrv.ini configuration file. The default location of this file is the C:\Program Files\Microsoft SQL Server\MSSQL.2\ OLAP\Config folder. You should abstain from making changes directly to the file to avoid accidentally changing the structure and damaging the file. Instead, use the SQL Server Management Studio to manage the server settings.

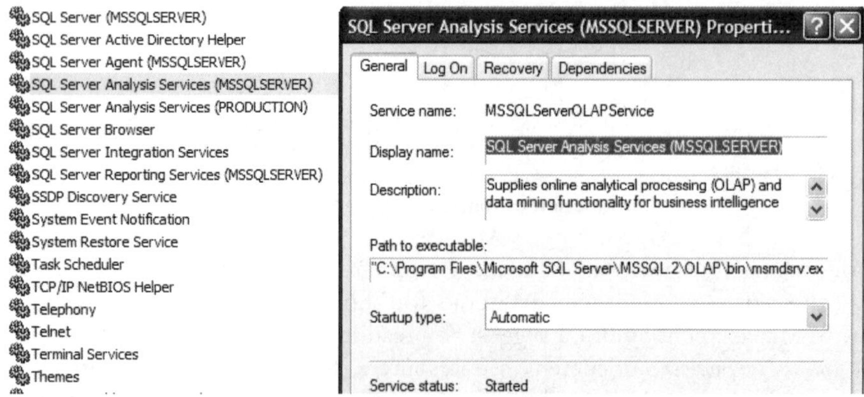

Figure 13.3 The Analysis Server is implemented as a Windows service named msmdsrv.exe.

Managing the server settings

Follow these steps to view and manage the server properties in SQL Server Management Studio.

1. Use the Object Explorer to connect to the Analysis Services server you want to manage.

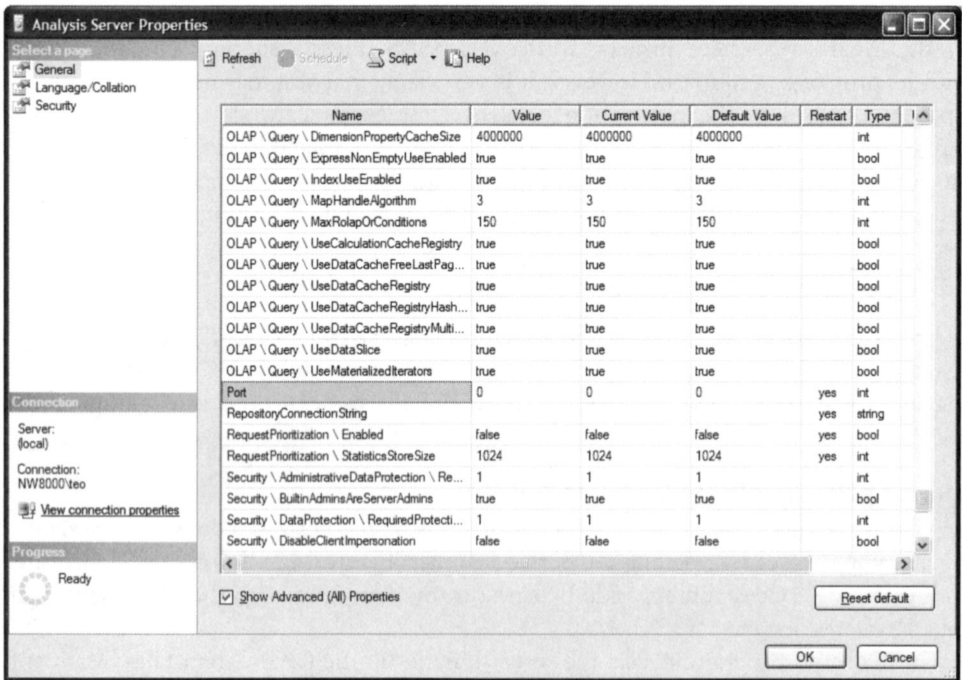

Figure 13.4 Use the Analysis Services Properties dialog to manage the server properties.

2. In the Object Explorer, right-click on the server and choose *Properties* to bring up the Analysis Services Properties dialog (Figure 13.4).

3. The Analysis Server Properties dialog reads the configuration settings from the msmdsrv.ini configuration file and displays them in the grid. To change a property, update the corresponding Value column of that property. By default, the dialog doesn't show all settings. Click on the *Shows Advanced (All) Properties* checkbox to see all properties.

For example, one of the advanced properties is the *Port* number. The value of 0 specifies the default port on which the server listens (2383). If this is not acceptable, you can change the port number. Changing certain properties requires restarting the server. The Restart column indicates if a server restart is required.

Managing dependent services

Your Analysis Services instance may rely on other SQL Server services to function properly. For example, if you install two or more instances of the Analysis Services Server on the same computer, you also need to enable the SQL Browser service. This service listens for incoming requests and redirects them to the port on which a given server instance listens. For example, if I need to connect to the localhost\Production instance (Data Source=localhost\production in the connection string), the connection request will first reach the SQL Browser which will redirect it to the Production instance.

Tip Use the *netstat* command line utility to find which ports a given service listens on. This could be useful if you need to know which firewall ports to enable, e.g. if you are trying to connect to Analysis Services installed on a Virtual PC guest OS with enabled Windows XP firewall. The command *netstat -a -b -n* will give you all connections and listening ports in numeric format.

If you would like to automate management tasks, you also need the SQL Server Agent service. This service allows you to schedule jobs and run them in an unattended mode. Finally, if your UDM sources data from a local SQL Server relational database, the SQL Server service must be running as well. You can manage all of the above mentioned services from the SQL Server Configuration Manager tool (Start ⇨ Programs ⇨ Microsoft SQL Server 2005 ⇨ Configuration Tools program group). Some features of these services may be disabled by default for security reasons, so take a moment to review the service configuration in the SQL Server 2005 Surface Area tool, which can also be found in the Configuration Tools program group.

13.1.3 Scripting Objects and Tasks

As an administrator, you may need to perform certain management tasks repeatedly or run them in an unattended mode. For example, you may need to clone the database definition from one machine to another. One of my favorite SQL Server Management Studio features is its context-aware scripting support. With the exception of editors (e.g. MDX Query Editor or XMLA Query Editor), most objects and tasks can be scripted in the scripting language the server supports. For example, the SSAS script language is ASSL, while for Reporting Services is VB.NET. Scripts can be executed immediately or saved as files for later execution.

Scripting objects

Suppose that you need to replicate the definition (not data) of the SOS OLAP database from one machine to another, e.g. from the staging to the production server. With SQL Server Management Studio, this is a three-step process.

1. Right-click on the SOS OLAP database and choose *Script Database as* ⇨ *CREATE TO* ⇨ *New Query Editor Window* to generate a CREATE DDL script of the SOS OLAP database (Figure 13.5).

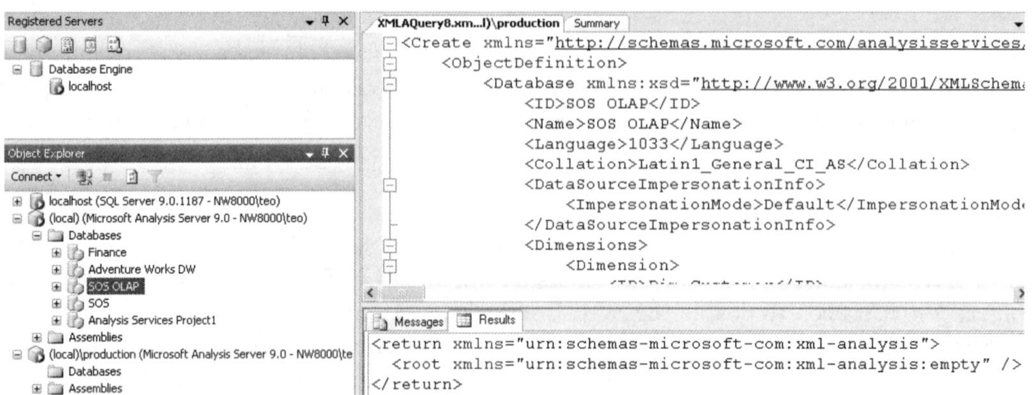

Figure 13.5 Script a database to deploy its metadata to another server.

2. Right-click inside the generated script and choose *Connection* ⇨ *Change Connection* to connect to the target SSAS server.
3. Click on the exclamation toolbar button or hit F5 to run the script.

Behind the scenes, the SQL Server Management Studio uses the AMO object library to send the script packaged in the XMLA envelope to the target server. The target server executes the script and returns a status code. If the database is created successfully, the status code will be empty. Note that you won't be able to browse the SOS OLAP cube in the new database because it doesn't have data (it hasn't been processed yet).

ALTER scripts may not work as you expect with some type of changes. That's because all impacted objects need to be altered in the same script. For example, if you script the Sales Territory dimension for ALTER (Script dimension as ⇨ ALTER TO ⇨ New Query Editor Window), remove an attribute form the dimension definition, and then try to execute the script, the server will abort the script because it discovers that this metadata change invalidates the SOS OLAP cube.

That's because altering a dimension could cause a cube to unexpectedly become unavailable – for example, if you delete an attribute that a cube depends on, then the cube would be left in an inconsistent state. In case you are wondering how BI Studio deploys the changes, it sends a request to the server to perform impact analysis and the server returns a result that indicates which dependent objects need to be altered. Consequently, the recommended approach is to use BI Studio or the Deployment Wizard to deploy object definition changes.

Scripting tasks

You can script not only objects but also management tasks. For example, suppose that the AdventureWorks CLR assembly that we created in chapter 11 is being updated every day. You would like to automate the task of deleting the old assembly and registering the new one.

1. In the Object Explorer, expand the SOS OLAP database and its Assemblies subfolder.

Tip Management Studio comes with several pre-defined XMLA, MDX, and DMX templates you can use as a starting point for creating scripts. To explore see them, open the Template Explorer in Management Studio (Ctrl+Alt+T) and the Analysis Services toolbar button. The management scripts are listed under the XMLA ⇨ Management node.

2. Right-click on the AdventureWorks assembly and choose *Delete.*

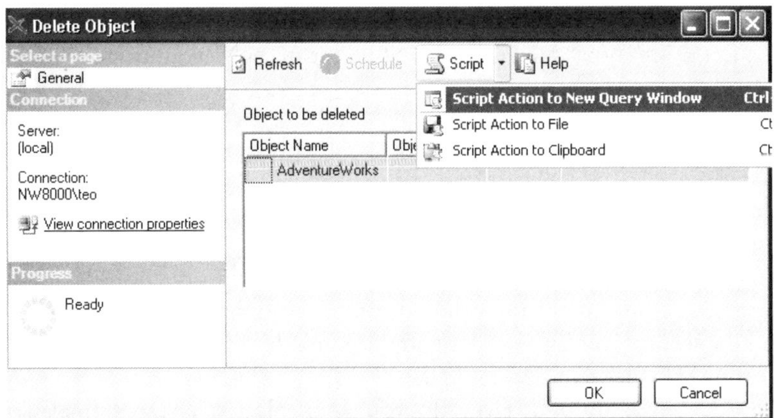

Figure 13.6 Use the Script dropdown to generate a script for the current object.

3. On the Delete Object dialog (Figure 13.6), expand the Script dropdown and select *Script Action to New Query Window* to generate the delete action. Alternatively, you can just click the Script button since *Script Action to New Query Window* happens to be the default menu. Your script should look like this:

```
<Delete xmlns="http://schemas.microsoft.com/analysisservices/2003/engine">
  <Object>
    <DatabaseID>SOS OLAP</DatabaseID>
    <AssemblyID>AdventureWorks</AssemblyID>
  </Object>
</Delete>
```

4. Run the script and observe that the AdventureWorks assembly has been removed from the Assemblies folder.
5. Right-click on the Assemblies folder and choose *New Assembly*. Specify the assembly location, permissions, and impersonation options.
6. Use the Script dropdown again to script the assembly registration task.
7. Execute the script to register the AdventureWorks assembly programmatically.

Tip In most cases, scripting an object or a task can be done by clicking on the Script dropdown in the corresponding dialog. In some cases, when a dialog is missing, the scripting action is exposed in the context menu for the selected object.

What can you do with a script? You can use it to automate the task execution. For example, you may want to back up a database at 10 PM every night. Once you generate the database backup script, you can schedule it with the SQL Server Agent. I will show how this could be done in section 13.2.4. In addition, you can put your scripts under version control just like you can with

UDM definition files. For example, you can script a database on a daily basis so you could compare what changes have been made between daily builds.

13.2 Managing Databases

One ongoing activity that every administrator has to master is database management. The database management tasks I will focus on in this section are deploying, synchronizing, backing up, and restoring databases. Let's see how Management Studio can help you perform and automate these routine tasks.

13.2.1 Deploying Databases

Once the database is in production, you need to keep it up to date by deploying changes made in project mode. As I pointed out in section 0, you should implement most of your database design changes in project mode using BI Studio. This approach ensures that your production database and its project counterpart are synchronized. In my opinion, there are only two types of management changes -- partition and security settings -- that should be made directly in the production database (online mode) using Management Studio.

This brings an interesting dilemma, though. How do you apply design changes made in project mode to your production database? One approach is to deploy the changes straight from the BI Studio environment. This will work with a caveat. BI Studio will not preserve any existing settings in the production database. It will overwrite the entire database definition. The same will happen if you script the database and deploy from Management Studio. This is where the Deployment Wizard comes in. It is specifically designed to support incremental deployment to production servers.

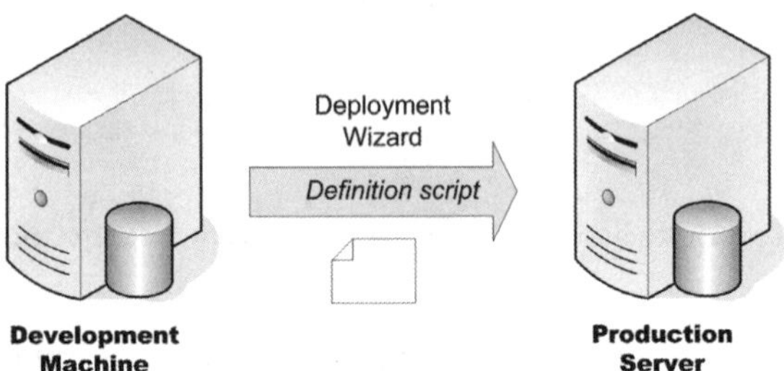

Figure 13.7 The Deployment Wizard prepares and sends a deployment script to the production database.

Figure 13.7 shows how the production deployment model works with the Deployment Wizard. The wizard takes the database project definition and applies it to the production database. However, unlike the BI Studio deployment model, the Deployment Wizard gives you an option to preserve the partition, security, and configuration settings on the production database.

Using the Deployment Wizard

Back in chapter 2, I mentioned that when you build an Analysis Services project, BI Studio creates a set of files in the build folder of the project (the project bin folder). The Deployment Wizard uses these files as a basis to deploy changes to the production database. The Deployment Wizard supports three deployment modes -- interactive deployment, scripting, and command line modes. In scripting mode, the wizard produces a script which could be run at a later time.

The wizard also supports command line mode that can be used to automate the wizard, e.g. to run it as a scheduled job.

In command line mode, the wizard execution can be controlled by various switches. To see them, open the command prompt, navigate to C:\Program Files\Microsoft SQL Server \90\Tools\Binn\VSShell\Common7\IDE and type:

```
microsoft.analysisservices.deployment.exe /?
```

For example, use the /a switch to make changes to configuration files which the wizard will use as a starting point the next time it is run. Or, use the /s switch to run the Deployment Wizard in silent mode. Let's demonstrate production deployment with the Deployment Wizard executed in interactive mode.

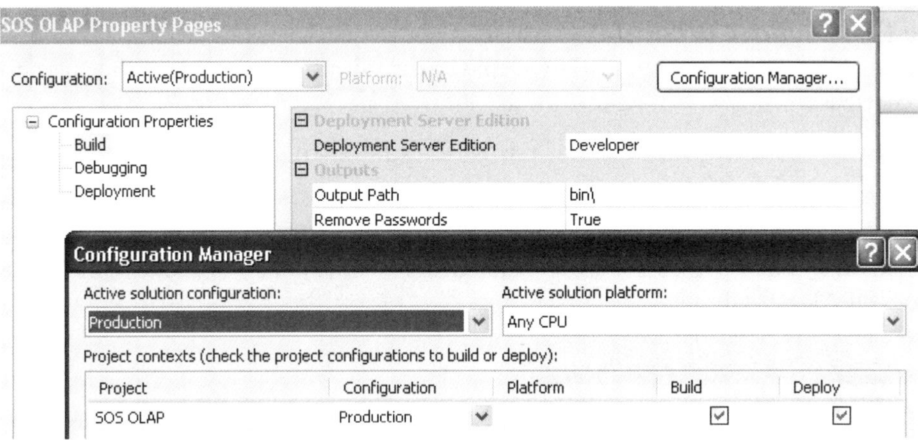

Figure 13.8 Before running the Deployment Wizard, create a Production project configuration that will store the name of the deployment server and connection string settings.

Preparing the project for deployment

Follow these steps to prepare the SOS OLAP project for deployment with the Deployment Wizard:

1. Open the SOS OLAP project in BI Studio.
2. If you haven't done this already, create a Production project configuration. To do so, go to the project properties and click on the Configuration Manager button (Figure 13.8). In the Configuration Manager dialog, expand the *Active solution configuration* dropdown and choose New to create a new project configuration named **Production**. Select the Production project configuration and click Close to return to the SOS OLAP Property Pages dialog.
3. Make sure to update the deployment server name in the Deployment settings. In addition, don't forget to update the connection strings of your data sources to point to the production database servers. As noted in chapter 2, BI Studio is capable of maintaining a separate set of connection strings for different project configurations. Build the project.
4. Open Windows Explorer and navigate to the project build folder, e.g. C:\Books\AS\Code\Ch13\SOS OLAP\bin (see Figure 13.9).

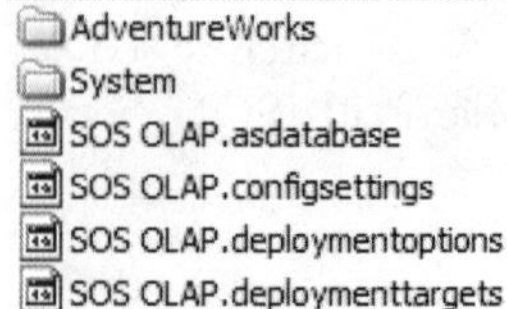

Figure 13.9 The Deployment Wizard uses the build output for deployment.

When you build an Analysis Services project, BI Studio generates a set of files in the project build folder. The file with *.asdatabase* extension contains the definition of the entire database described in ASSL. The rest of the files contain additional project configuration settings and deployment options, as specified in the project properties. The deployment utility uses these files as input.

Running the Deployment Wizard

Once the project build is ready, you can run the Deployment Wizard to reconcile the changes to the production database.

1. Launch the Deployment Wizard from the Analysis Services program group (Start ⇨ Programs ⇨ Microsoft SQL Server 2005 ⇨ Analysis Services).
2. In the Specify Source Analysis Services Database step, enter the full path to the database file (.asdatabase) that the build process has generated (e.g. C:\Books\AS\Code\Ch13\SOS OLAP\bin\SOS OLAP.asdatabase).

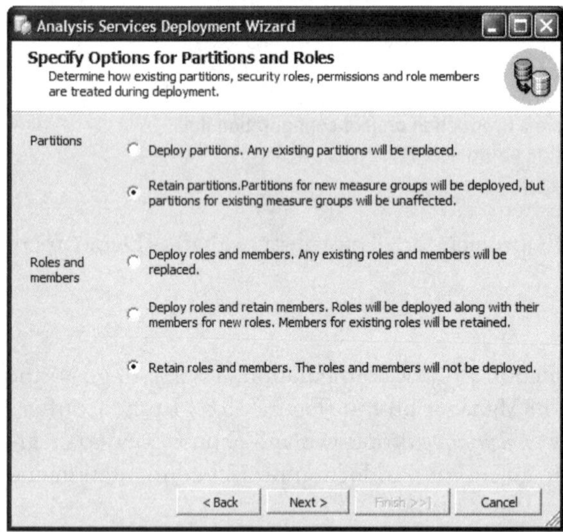

Figure 13.10 The Deployment Wizard can preserve storage and security settings of the production database.

3. In the Installation Target step, specify the target server name and database. If the database doesn't exist, the Deployment Wizard will create it.
4. In the Specify Options for Partitions and Roles step (Figure 13.10), tell the wizard which target settings to preserve. In my case, I decided to preserve the partition and security settings on the target database.

By default, the Deployment Wizard will apply the configuration settings from the current project configuration (*.configsettings* file) to the target database. In the Specify Configuration Properties step (Figure 13.11), you have the option to overwrite these settings. Alternatively, you can decide to preserve the current configuration and optimization settings on the target database. The settings you can overwrite include data source connection strings, impersonation account (if Integrated Windows Authentication is used to connect to the data sources), error log files, storage location folders, and the report paths to SSRS reports (if you have report actions).

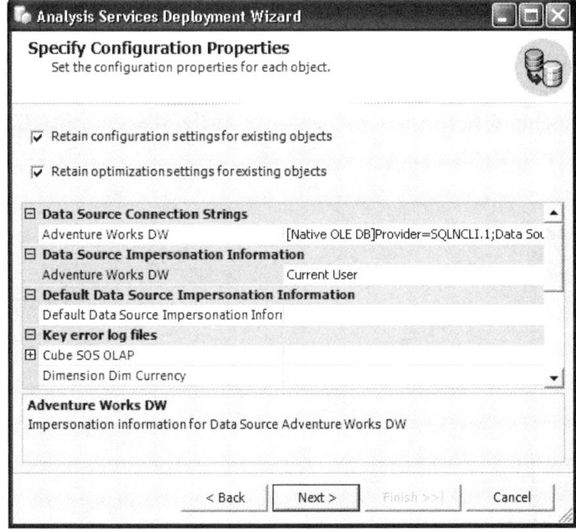

Figure 13.11 You can overwrite configuration and optimization settings of the production database.

5. In the Specify Configuration Properties step, check the *Retain configuration settings for existing objects* and *Retain optimization setting for existing objects* to preserve the existing production settings.

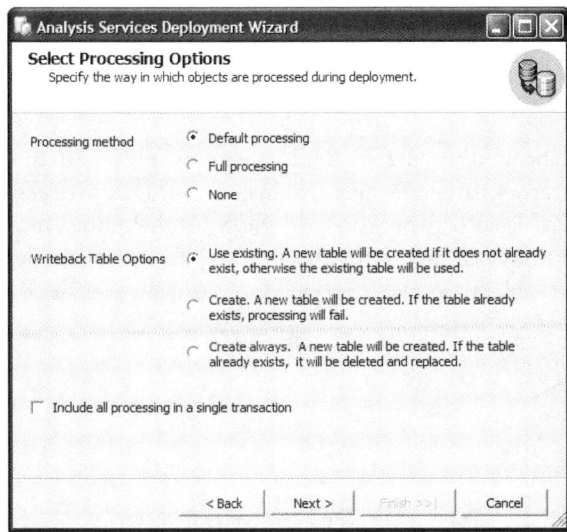

Figure 13.12 Specify how the server will process the changed objects and handle partition writeback.

In the Select Processing Options step (Figure 13.12), you can tell the wizard how to process the target database after the changes are applied. If the Deployment Wizard detects discrepancies between the object definition files of the target and source databases, it will overwrite the target definitions. Different definition changes require different processing options, as I will discus in more details in chapter 15. You can let the server figure out the most appropriate processing option based on the changes performed, fully process the affected objects, or skip the processing step altogether.

In addition, if you have partition writeback enabled, you can tell the wizard how to handle the writeback table options. Usually, you would want to preserve the existing writeback table to avoid erasing the writeback changes made by the users. Finally, you can instruct the target server to perform transactional deployment where all objects are processed within a transactional scope.

6. Accept the default and click Next to the Confirm Deployment step which gives you two options. First, you can execute the deployment immediately. Alternatively, you could choose to save the settings as a script which can be run at a later time. Click Next to deploy the database immediately to the server.

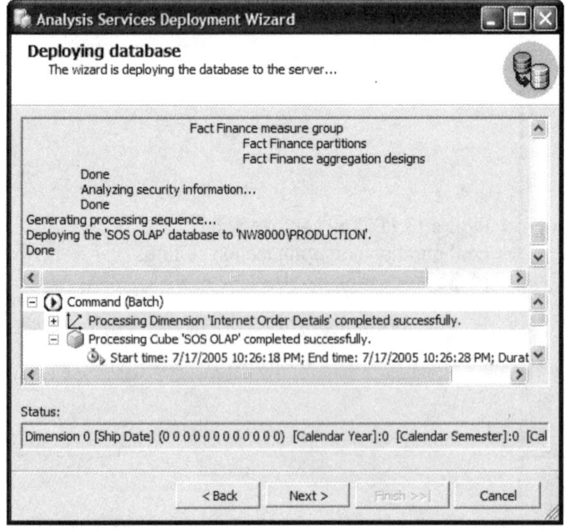

Figure 13.13 The Deployment Wizard is deploying the database definition to the target server.

The Deploying Database step (Figure 13.13) shows the current deployment progress. In this case, the wizard had detected changes to the Internet Order Details dimension. Because processing a dimension invalidates the cube, the wizard is also processing the SOS OLAP cube. It is important to note that the Deployment Wizard does not merge definition changes. For example, if you have changed the definition of a given object on the production database outside BI Studio, your changes will be lost.

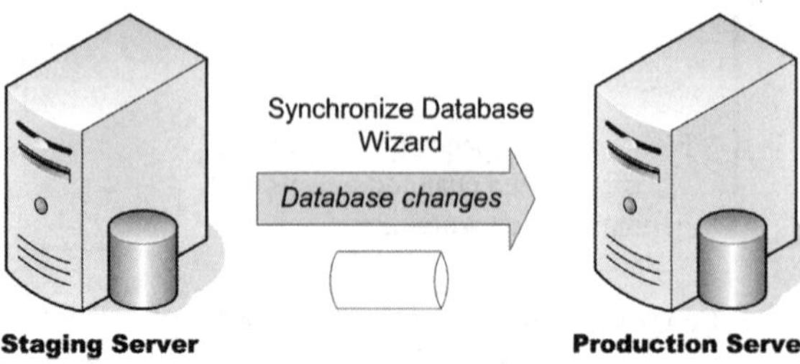

Figure 13.14 The Synchronize Database Wizard copies the data and metadata incrementally from a source (staging) server to a target (production) server.

13.2.2 Synchronizing Databases

Synchronizing two SSAS databases is a common management task. For example, one company I worked for had a terabyte-size warehouse database with an SSAS 2000 OLAP layer on top of it consisting of four presentation SSAS servers. As you can imagine, building the cubes four times on each server is not a very efficient approach. Instead, the team decided to build the cubes on a dedicated staging server. Once the cubes were built and tested, they were distributed to the load-balanced presentation servers. This is exactly the task the Synchronization Wizard is designed to handle.

SSAS 2000 In SSAS 2000, it was possible to copy the data files (XCOPY deployment) from one server to another. This was a semi-supported mechanism (some people may call it a "hack") which many organizations used to replicate SSAS databases from staging to production environments. In SSAS 2005, file-based replication is absolutely not supported. You must use the Synchronize Database Wizard to copy the data and metadata from one database to another.

If the database doesn't exist on the target server, the Synchronize Database Wizard copies the entire database. Otherwise, the wizard copies incremental (delta) changes only.

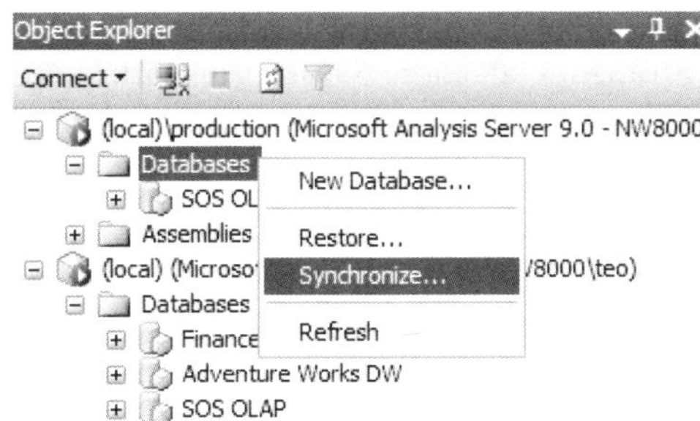

Figure 13.15 Using the Synchronize Database Wizard to synchronize a production database from a staging database.

Using the Synchronize Database Wizard

Let's use the Synchronize Database Wizard to synchronize a production database from a staging database. I will use the *(local)\production* SSAS instance to simulate a production server. Suppose you've built the SOS OLAP cube on the staging server (the default local instance in my case). Now, you need to synchronize it with the (local)\production instance using the Synchronize Database Wizard.

1. You need to run Synchronize Database Wizard on the target server. Right-click on the Databases folder (Figure 13.15) on the (local)\production server and choose *Synchronize* to launch the Synchronize Database Wizard.

2. In the Select Database To Synchronize step, select the *SOS OLAP* database as a source database and click Next. In the Specify Locations for Local Partitions step, you can optionally overwrite the default location of the cube partitions. For example, if the data folder of the staging server is on C: drive but the production server stores data on D: drive, you can change the partition locations accordingly.

3. Also, the wizard supports a limited customization. For example, you can use the Specify Query Criteria step (Figure 13.16) to preserve the security settings on the production server. Assuming that we want to preserve all security settings, select the *Ignore all* option.

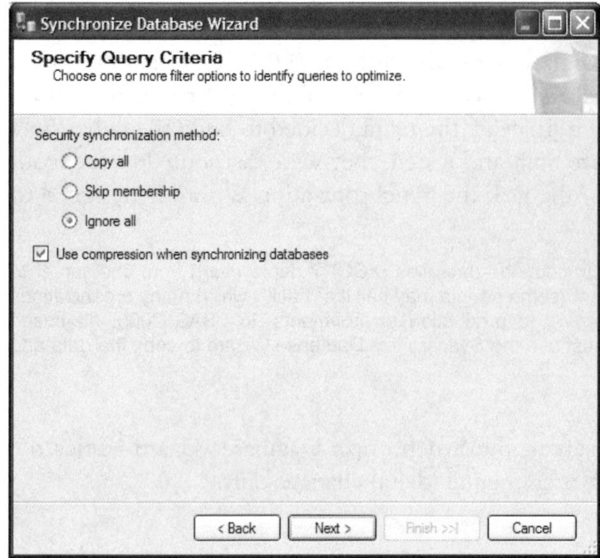

Figure 13.16 The Synchronize Database Wizard allows you to preserve the security settings on the target serer.

4. Real-life cubes can be very large in size. The Synchronize Database Wizard supports very efficient compression to send the data changes across the wire. Leave the *Use compression when synchronizing databases checkbox* selected and click Next.

5. Use the Select Synchronization Method step to specify the deployment method. You can start the synchronization process immediately or generate a script and run it later. Let's go for the second option. Choose the *Save the script to a file* option and specify the file location, e.g. C:\Books\AS\Code\Ch13\synch_sos_olap.xmla.

This is what the synchronization script may look like:

```
<Synchronize xmlns:xsi="http://www.w3.org/2001/XMLSchema-instance"
    xmlns:xsd="http://www.w3.org/2001/XMLSchema"
    xmlns="http://schemas.microsoft.com/analysisservices/2003/engine">
  <Source>
    <ConnectionString>Provider=MSOLAP.3;Data Source=(local);ConnectTo=9.0;
     Integrated Security=SSPI;Initial Catalog=SOS OLAP</ConnectionString>
    <Object>
      <DatabaseID>SOS OLAP</DatabaseID>
    </Object>
  </Source>
  <Locations />
  <SynchronizeSecurity>IgnoreSecurity</SynchronizeSecurity>
  <ApplyCompression>true</ApplyCompression>
</Synchronize>
```

As you can see, behind the scenes, the wizard uses the *Synchronize* XMLA command for its work. You can run this script manually using the SQL Server Management Studio. Alternatively, you can automate the synchronization job to run on a regular basis with the SQL Server Agent.

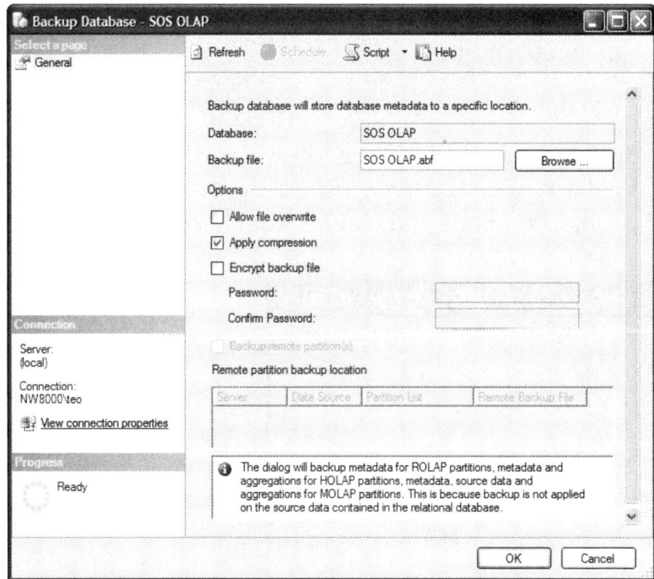

Figure 13.17 Make databases backups part of your regular maintenance schedule.

13.2.3 Backing up and Restoring Databases

A routing maintenance task is backing an SSAS database on a regular basis. A database backup copies the entire database (both metadata and data). I hope you will never need it, but a common scenario for backing up a database is restoring it as part of your disaster recovery plan. Another scenario where backing up a database can be useful is if you are working on a prototype database and you want to send the entire database to someone else. Of course, in the latter case, you can send only the object definition files but the database must be processed to load it with data.

SSAS 2000 With SSAS 2000, there was a 3GB limit per a partition when backing up a database. With SSAS 2005, this restriction has been lifted and you can now back up partitions of any size.

Follow these steps to back up the SOS OLAP database.

1. In the SQL Server Management Studio, right-click on the SOS OLAP database and choose *Back Up*. The Backup Database dialog pops up (Figure 13.17).
2. Specify the location of the backup file.
3. Optionally, you can encrypt sensitive data by leaving the *Encrypt backup file* checkbox selected.

Hopefully, you will never need your backup database but if you do, you can restore a database from its backup by right-clicking on the database (or the Databases folder) and choosing *Restore*.

13.2.4 Automating Management Tasks

As a savvy SSAS administrator, you may want to automate recurring management tasks. The SQL Server Agent service (a component of SQL Server) is capable of executing SSAS scripts.

Here is what it takes to automate the database backup task to back the SOS OLAP database on a regular basis.

1. Right-click on the SOS OLAP database and choose *Back Up*.
2. In the Backup Database dialog, expand the Script dropdown and choose *Script Action to Clipboard.*
3. Connect to the SQL Server Database Engine instance where the job will run. Make sure that SQL Server Agent service is running. In the Object Explorer, right-click on the SQL Server Agent node (should be the last one in the Object Explorer and choose *New* ⇨ *Job*.

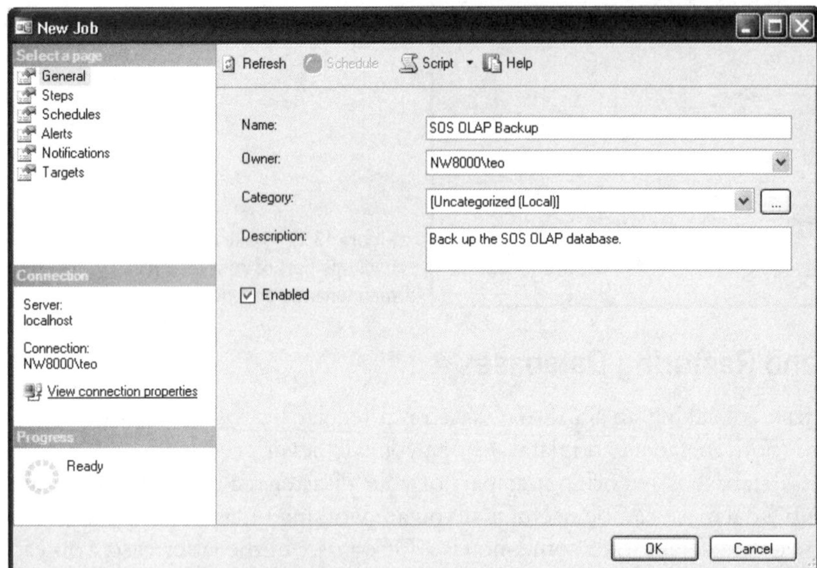

Figure 13.18 Use the SQL Server Agent to automate repetitive maintenance tasks.

4. In the New Job dialog that follows (Figure 13.18), name the new job **SOS OLAP Backup**.
5. A job can contain one or more steps. In the New Job dialog, click on the *Steps* page in the *Select a page* pane. The SOS OLAP Backup job needs only one step to back up the SOS OLAP database.
6. Click the *New* button to create a new step. Enter **Back up database** as a name of the step.
7. Expand the Type dropdown and select *SQL Server Analysis Services Command* as a step type.
8. Enter **(local)** in the Server field.
9. Paste the backup script you copied to the clipboard in the Command field (Figure 13.19).
10. Click OK to return to the New Job dialog.
11. Click on the Schedules page to schedule the job execution as desired. Alternatively, if you want to run the job immediately, click OK to create the job. Next, expand the Jobs folder under SQL Server Agent, right-click on the SOS OLAP Backup job and choose *Start Job*. The SQL Server Agent will start the job and display its progress in the Start Jobs dialog.
12. To view the job history log, right-click on the job and choose *View History*.

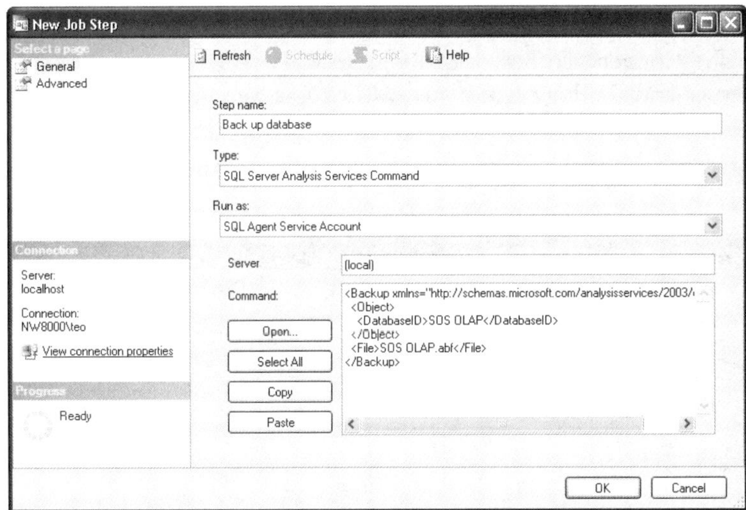

Figure 13.19 Use the SQL Server Analysis Services Command step type to automate script execution.

13.3 Monitoring Analysis Services

It is unrealistic to expect that your management duties will come to an end once the database is deployed to the production server. In real life, end users may occasionally report errors or degradation of the server performance. By monitoring the server, you can ensure that it functions correctly and it is performing optimally. SSAS provides a variety of tools to help you track the health and performance of the server.

13.3.1 Tracing With SQL Server Profiler

Veteran SSAS administrators would probably agree that one of the most significant SSAS 2000 limitations was that it was virtually impossible to monitor the server activity and understand what was going on under its "hood". The SQL Server 2005 Profiler changes all of this. The SQL Server Profiler has been enhanced to support monitoring of both the SQL Server and SSAS events side-by-side.

Understanding the SQL Server Profiler

The SQL Server Profiler allows you to create traces to monitor the server activity and performance of MDX queries. In addition, it supports filtering trace events and saving the trace events to a file to replay them later. A trace is an Analysis Services object that lives on the server. As part of creating the trace, you specify which events you want to monitor. Once configured, the trace object would output the selected events. Behind the scenes, the events are raised using the WMI (Windows Management Instrumentation) infrastructure baked into the Windows operating system. A WMI-aware application, such as the SQL Server Profiler, can intercept the events and display them for monitoring purposes.

Starting an Analysis Services Trace

Let's see how we can leverage the SQL Server Profiler to monitor an SSAS server.

1. Start the SQL Server Profiler (Start ➪ Programs ➪ Microsoft SQL Server 2005 ➪ Performance Tools ➪ SQL Server Profiler)

2. Choose File ➪ New Trace. In the Connect To Server dialog, select *Analysis Services* as a server type. Enter the name of the server and the login credentials. Click Connect to connect to the server.

3. The Trace Properties is displayed (Figure 13.20).

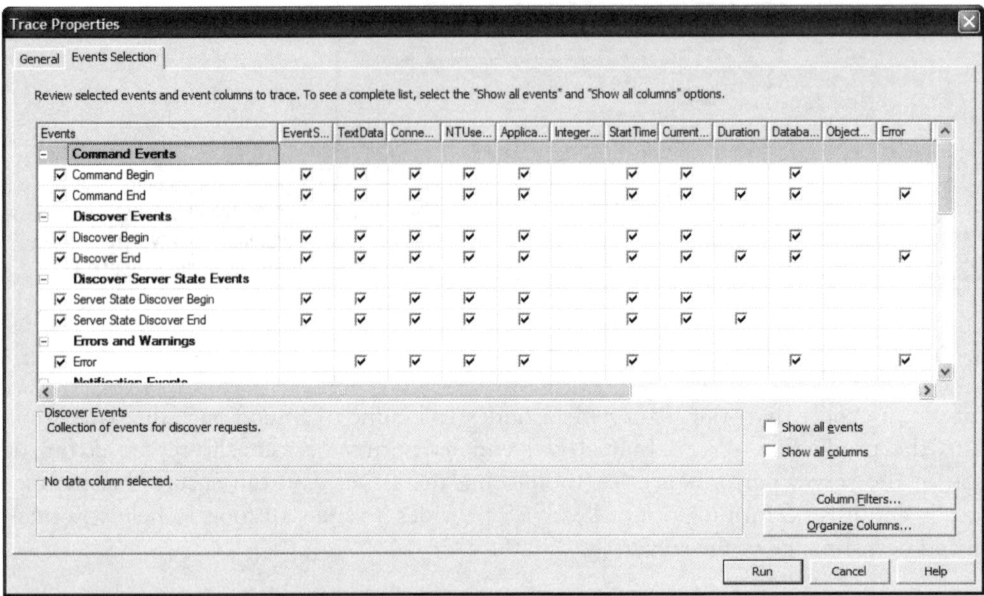

Figure 13.20 Use the Event Selection tab to filter the events you would like to monitor.

4. In the General Tab, name the trace **SOS OLAP**. Note that you can save the trace to a file with an extension .trc or a SQL Server table. Capturing the trace output to a file is useful if you want to replay the trace later.

5. Switch to the Events tab. SSAS provides many events that are grouped in event categories. A brief description of the event categories is in order.

Understanding event categories

Command events are raised when action-oriented statements are sent to the server. Examples of such statements are the scripting tasks we performed in this chapter, including deploying, synchronizing, backing up, and restoring databases. *Discover* events are generated when you query the SSAS metadata, e.g. when you retrieve the KPI schema to find what KPIs are implemented in a given cube. *Discover Server State* events are a subset of the Discover events raised as a result of querying the server state, e.g. to find the number of the currently open connections, sessions, transactions, and locks.

As their name suggest, the *Errors and Warnings* category contains events that the server raises when it encounters an error condition. For example, if you send a syntactically incorrect MDX query to the server, you will see an error event generated. This is the most important category that you would want to monitor to troubleshot failed queries. Every now and then the server raises *Notification* events when it performs tasks triggered by internal events (events that are not initiated explicitly). For example, if proactive caching is enabled, the server will raise this event when it detects that the underlying data has changed. You are already familiar with the *Progress* events which the server raises to inform the client about the progress of a given task, e.g. backing up or processing a database.

The *Query* events output the MDX statements sent to the server. As a first stop for troubleshooting query performance issues, I would recommend you track the query sent to the server and find how long it takes to execute (Duration column). You can monitor *Security Audit* events to find out who has logged in/out of the server. The *Session Events* category lets you know when a session starts or ends. Undoubtedly, you have already experienced session timeout events if you had the MDX Query Designer inactive for a long time in Management Studio.

Note Most requests to the server work in the context of a session – a session encapsulates the server "state", just like an ASP.NET session can be used to hold user state. An SSAS session holds things such as the current catalog, and other stateful properties, as well as the state of calculations in each cube that the session has accessed (session calculated members, sets, uncommitted writebacks, etc.). Since sessions can be expensive, the server has a mechanism for expiring old sessions – the typical timeout is 1 hour with no activity. This timeout can be changed by the administrator using the server properties (*MaxIdleSession-Timeout*).

The default trace output can be overwhelming. You can use the Column Filter button to filter the trace output if needed, e.g. to filter only the queries send to a specific SSAS database. Once you've made your selections, click Run to start the trace.

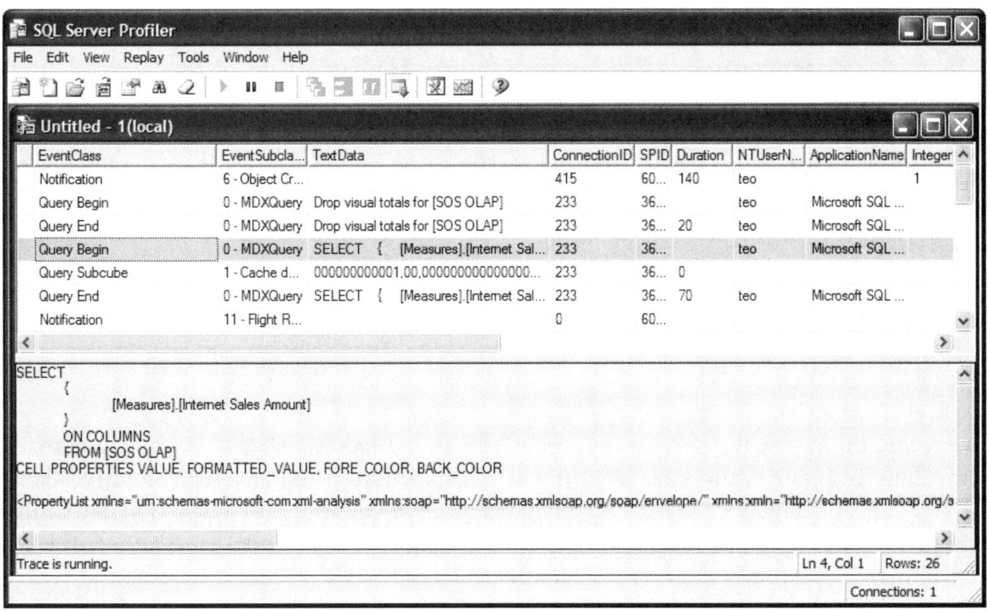

Figure 13.21 Use the Event Selection tab to filter the events you would like to monitor.

Monitoring the server activity

Let's see how the SQL Server Profiler can help us monitor the server activity and the query performance. Go back to the SQL Server Management Studio. Browse the SOS OLAP cube and create a pivot report. Switch to the SQL Server Profiler and examine the trace output (Figure 13.21).

Assuming that you've accepted the default trace events, you should get quite a verbose trace output. For example, you will see discover events which OWC sends to the server to retrieve the cube metadata for the Metadata pane. You should also find Query Begin/Query End event pairs. When you select a *Query Begin* or *Query End* event, the profiler reveals the underlying MDX query that OWC sends to the server. The Duration column shows the query duration in milliseconds.

An interesting event is the *Query Subcube* event. The server uses this event data to populate the Query Log which is used as a basis for the Usage Based Optimization. Usage Based Optimization could help you design a smarter set of cube aggregations and it is discussed in chapter 14. You may wonder what the meaning of the 0's and 1's is in the TextData column. If you recall that UDM is an attribute-based model, these binary sections tell you which attributes were used or required to solve the MDX query request. Thus, in the example shown in Figure 13.21, only the last attribute from the first dimension was used to satisfy the query.

Tip Since the Query Subcube event was designed to be as compact as possible, there is no easy way to derive the name of the attributes and dimensions. However, the Query Subcube Verbose event can give you this answer. The Query Subcube Event is not enabled by default. To enable it, click the Pause button to temporarily suspend the trace. Next, open the trace properties, flip to the Events tab, and check the *Show all events* checkbox. Scroll the Events grid until you locate the Query Events category and select the Query Verbose Event. Once you refresh the pivot report, this event will fire immediately after the Query Subcube event and it will give you a human-readable list of the attributes and dimensions that the server used to satisfy the query.

Canceling commands

Sometimes, you may need to cancel a long-running query or a session that drains the server resources. SQL Server administrators can perform the relation equivalent of this task by using the Activity Monitor and "killing" the connection. Unfortunately, the SQL Server Profiler UI doesn't support a similar feature. However, the server supports a *Cancel* command which you can use to kill a session, connection, or a process.

Suppose that you spot a long-running MDX query in the Performance Monitor and you want to cancel the user connection. You can get the connection identifier from the ConnectionID column. Next, in Management Studio, create an XMLA query with the following statement:

```
<Cancel xmlns="http://schemas.microsoft.com/analysisservices/2003/engine">
  <ConnectionID>22</ConnectionID>
</Cancel>
```

Once you execute the query, the server will destroy the requested connection or return an error if no connection is found with that identifier. A connection could contain multiple client sessions. The Cancel command supports passing a session identifier to destroy a particular session within a connection but keep the connection alive. However, the Profiler UI doesn't provide a column that exposes the session identifier. Therefore, you need to query the server (DISCOVER_SESSIONS schema) to obtain the current sessions by sending the following XMLA query:

```
<Discover xmlns="urn:schemas-microsoft-com:xml-analysis">
  <RequestType>DISCOVER_SESSIONS</RequestType>
  <Restrictions/>
  <Properties/>
</Discover>
```

You will get back a list of all open sessions and their identifiers. If this sounds like too much of a hassle, the SSAS team has provided a useful .NET application called *Activity Viewer*. If you have installed the SSAS samples, you will find the Activity Viewer in the C:\Program Files\Microsoft SQL Server\90\Samples\Analysis Services\Administrator\ActivityViewer folder.

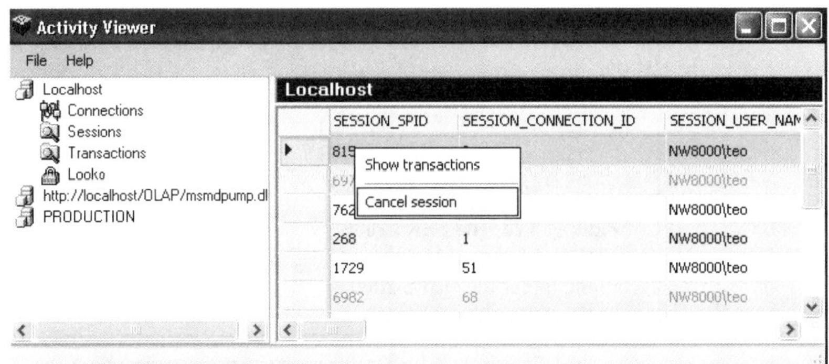

Figure 13.22 Use the Activity Viewer sample to explore the current server activity and cancel connections and sessions.

Figure 13.22 shows the Activity Viewer in action. It simulates the SQL Server Activity Monitor. The Activity Viewer allows you to connect to local and remote SSAS servers, including those configured for HTTP access (as discussed in chapter 17). You can click on the Sessions node to find the open sessions and you can cancel a given session by right-clicking on it and choosing *Cancel session*. Behind the scenes, the Activity Viewer uses AMO and ADOMD.NET to query the server. I highly recommend you explore the source code of the application if you are interested in programming management tasks.

13.3.2 Monitoring the Server Performance with Performance Counters

Another way to track the server utilization and activity is to monitor SSAS performance counters. As a part of the setup process, SSAS installs various performance counters that cover essential server statistics, including caching, connection management, memory utilization, MDX query coverage, processing, and more. You can use the Windows Performance console to monitor this statistics for local or remote servers. For example, follow these steps to track how fast the server processes relational rows when you process an UDM object.

Selecting performance counters

1. Start the Performance console (Start ⇨ Programs ⇨ Administrative Tools ⇨ Performance). Alternatively, you can launch the console from the SQL Server Profiler (Tools ⇨ Performance Monitor). Click on the + toolbar button to add a performance counter.
2. Enter the server name in the *Select counters from computer* dropdown (Figure 13.23).
3. Expand the Performance object dropdown and scroll down until you see the MSAS 2005 performance objects. SSAS 2005 supports several performance objects and counters. For the purposes of our demo, select the *MSAS 2005:Processing* performance object. This performance object exposes several processing-related metrics which you can use to monitor the server processing activity.

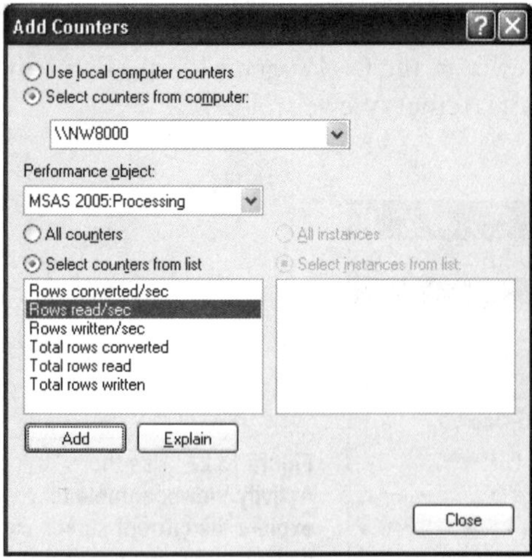

Figure 13.23 The SSAS 2005 performance counters are found under the MSAS 2005 performance object category.

4. In *Select counters from list*, select the Rows read/sec (Figure 13.23). This counter shows how fast the server processes rows from the relational database expressed in rows/sec.
5. Click on the Explain button to see a brief description of the selected counter. Click on the Add button to add the counter to the performance graph.

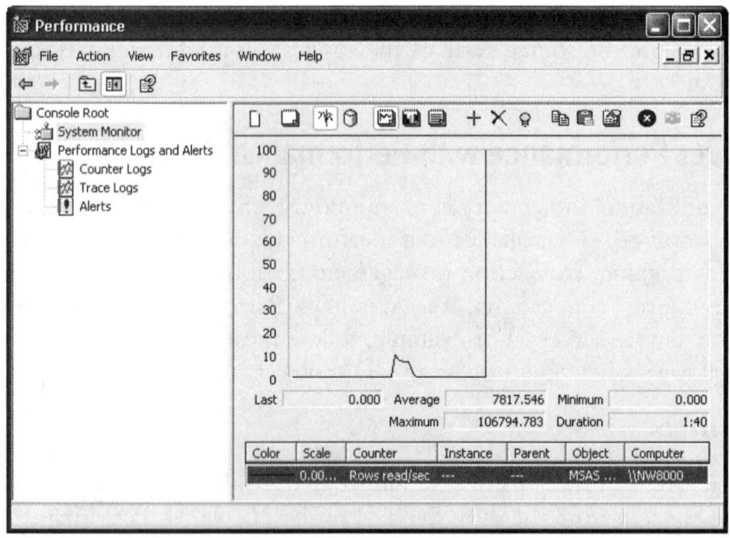

Figure 13.24 Use the Rows read/sec to monitor how fast the server processes rows from the data source.

Monitoring performance counters

To monitor the Rows read/sec performance counter:

1. Go back to Management Studio and process an SSAS object, e.g. the entire SOS OLAP cube.
2. While the server is processing the cube, switch to the Performance console and watch the Rows/sec counter (Figure 13.24). You should see a spike as the server starts extracting and

processing rows from the AdventureWorksDW data source. In my case, the server maximum throughput was 106,794 rows per second. On average, the server has read 7,817 rows/sec.

Note An optimized production server should yield even better processing performance results. For example, I know of an SSAS 2000 production server which was capable of processing 90,000 rows/sec! I will outline several performance optimization techniques harvested from this project in the next two chapters.

The SSAS performance counters are well explained in the product documentation and the *Microsoft SQL Server 2000 Analysis Services Performance Guide* whitepaper (see Resources).

13.3.3 Capture and Replay With Flight Recorder

The SQL Server Profiler and Performance console are great tools to monitor the server activity in real time. However, sometimes you may need to investigate the server state *after* it has taken place. For example, an MDX query may have crashed the server, or a customer may have reported performance degradation. Every administrator knows one of the most frustrating aspects of troubleshooting issues is not being able to reproduce them. The SSAS Flight Recorder could help you diagnose server issues by allowing administrators to replay failure conditions. Similar to an airplane "black box", the Flight Recorder captures the server activity during runtime.

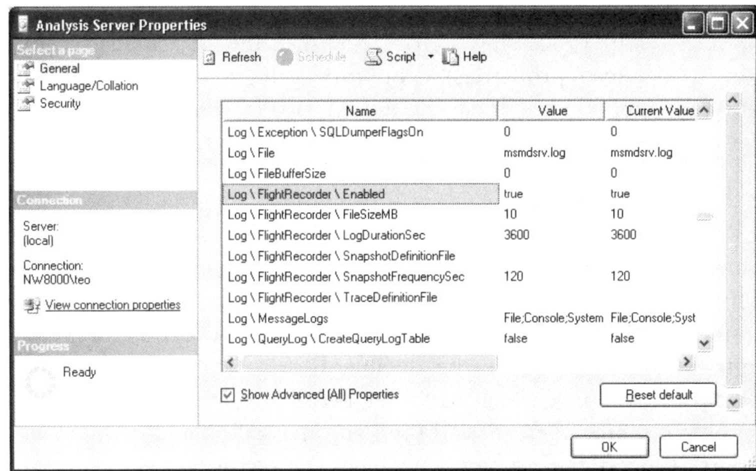

Figure 13.25 Configure the Flight Recorder using the Analysis Server Properties.

The Flight Recorder is enabled by default. You can configure its settings using the Analysis Server Advanced Properties window (Figure 13.25). By default the Flight Recorder saves its trace file (FileRecroderCurrent.trc) in the C:\Program Files\Microsoft SQL Server\MSSQL.2\↵ OLAP\Log. Each time the server is restarted, a new trace file is generated. You can tell the Flight Recorder when to roll over the file, e.g. by setting the maximum file size (FileSizeMB property). Once you have the Flight Recorder trace file, replaying it is easy.

1. Open the trace file in the SQL Server profiler (File ⇨ Open ⇨ Trace File).
2. Click the Start Reply toolbar button or hit F5.
3. You will be asked to connect the target server. Enter the server name and login credentials in the Connect To Server dialog.

4. Use the Replay Configuration dialog that follows to configure the server replay, e.g. to replay only the statements within a given timeframe.

Once you confirm the Replay Configuration dialog, the SQL Server Profiler will start executing the captured statements against the server. Moreover, the SQL Server Profiler will simulate the server state and load as close as possible. For example, the server will create the same number of open connections and sessions as existed during the capture.

13.3.4 Error Logging and Reporting

Besides the Flight Recorder capture and replay features, SSAS supports other options for troubleshooting error conditions. They range from comprehensive error logging to preparing and sending crash dumps of the server state.

Error logging

As a first stop for troubleshooting SSAS server error conditions, I would suggest you inspect the Windows Event log using the Event Viewer console (found under Administrators program group). When things go sour, the SSAS server outputs various informational and error messages to the Application log.

SSAS supports also a system-wide error log file whose default path is C:\Program Files\Microsoft SQL Server\MSSQL.2\OLAP\Log (can be changed in the server properties). In addition, SSAS can optionally log processing errors to the file specified in the Log\ErrorLog\FileName setting (Advanced properties). You can configure what processing errors are logged by turning on properties matching the UDM object error configuration settings. For example, to log key duplicate errors, turn on the KeyDuplicate setting from 0 to 1.

Dr. Watson crash dumps

You can help the Microsoft Product Support investigate server issues by using Dr. Watson minidumps. A minidump captures stack traces of the server process (msmdsrv.exe) and could assist the Microsoft Product Support investigate the internal state of the server. One example of when a minidump would be desired is a problem report of a server hang or a server crash.

The Dr. Watson minidump feature is turned on by default. It can be controlled by the *Log\Exception\CreateAndSendCrashReports* setting, which has three possible values – 0 (minidump is not generated), 1 (create a minidump) and 2 (create and send automatically the minidump file to the Microsoft Product Support). Once this property is enabled, the server will automatically generate minidumps when a critical (STOP) server error is encountered. The minidump files (*mdmp) are sequentially numbered and are generated by default in the C:\Program Files\Microsoft SQL Server\MSSQL.2\OLAP\Log folder. This location is configurable by changing the *CrashReportsFolder* server property.

13.4 Programming with AMO

Sometimes (very rarely, indeed!) the SSAS tools and scripting functionality may not be enough to meet your management needs. For example, you may need to generate a cube definition programmatically or evaluate some conditions before processing an SSAS database. SSAS provides two programmatic interfaces to meet more demanding management requirements, as I will discuss next.

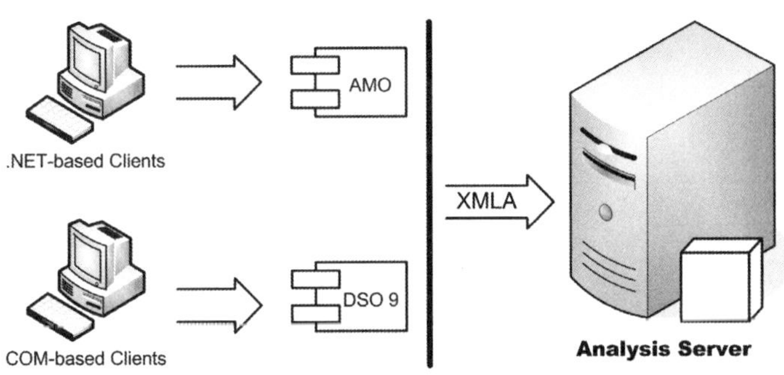

Figure 13.26 .NET-based management clients use AMO, while COM-based clients use DSO for programmatic management.

13.4.1 Understanding Management API

To support different clients, SSAS provides two object libraries to manage the server programmatically – *Decision Support Objects* (DSO) and *Analysis Management Objects* (AMO). Figure 13.26 shows a high-level architectural overview of the SSAS management API. As you would probably recall from our discussion in chapter 1, the XMLA is the native (and only) protocol that SSAS 2005 supports. Therefore, both management object libraries are essentially object-oriented wrappers on to top of the XMLA protocol. They take incoming management API calls, convert them to XMLA requests, and send the requests to the server.

Decision Support Objects (DSO)

The Decision Support Object library is COM-based. Thus, it would be the library of choice for Windows native clients, such as Visual Basic 6 or C++ clients. DSO is provided for backward compatibility only. You can take an existing DSO management application as it-is and integrate it with SSAS 2005. The only configuration change you need to make to these applications to upgrade them to UDM is referencing the DSO 9.0 library. That's because prior versions don't support XMLA.

SSAS 2000 The DSO 9.0 library still persists metadata changes to the repository. Changes made outside DSO, e.g. with Management Studio or AMO, can get the repository out of synch.

No model changes have been made to DSO and the new UDM features are not supported. DSO is a deprecated object library and it is highly recommended you embrace .NET and AMO.

Analysis Management Objects (AMO)

SSAS introduces a brand new management API in the form of the Analysis Management Objects (AMO) object library. AMO is a .NET wrapper on top of XMLA and it is intended to be used by .NET managed clients, such as VB.NET or C# applications. In fact, Management Studio and Business Intelligence Studio, which are .NET-based application, use AMO behind the scenes for all SSAS 2005 management tasks. AMO supports SSAS 2005 servers only.

AMO provides a .NET class for every UDM object, e.g. server, database, measure group, dimensions, etc. As Figure 13.27 shows, AMO organizes these objects in neat hierarchies for easier navigation. For example, backing up a database using AMO takes four lines of code:

```
Dim server as new Server()
server.Connect("Data Source=(local);")
Dim databases as DatabaseCollection = objServer.Databases
databases("SOS OLAP").Backup("C:\SOS OLAP.abf", true)
```

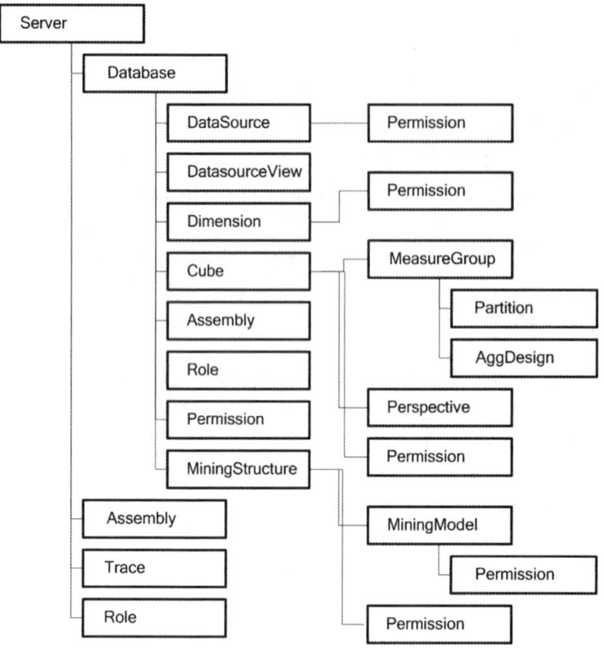

Figure 13.27 AMO organizes UDM objects in a hierarchy of .NET classes.

The AMO Server object represents an instance of an Analysis Server. Once connected to the server, you can retrieve all databases as a *DatabaseCollection* object. Each object exposes properties you can use to set the object state and methods to perform management tasks. For example, use the *Backup* method of the Database object to back up programmatically a database. Or, once you are done changing the object properties, call the object *Update* method to propagate the changes to the server. Another interesting AMO characteristic is that it supports offline metadata changes (used by BI Studio), serializing the object definition in XML, capturing the XMLA requests without sending them to the server (*Server.ExecuteCaptureLog*), and session tracing (raising events for all session activities).

13.4.2 AMO vs. ADOMD.NET

You will undoubtedly find many similarities between the ADOMD.NET and AMO object models and may wonder how they differ. The ADOMD.NET object is optimized for querying the server metadata and data in a read-only mode. For example, you cannot use ADOMD.NET to make changes to the server metadata, e.g. to change a dimension name. AMO requires only view security permissions to the database when querying the server metadata.

On the other side, AMO is optimized for making metadata changes. The AMO Server object supports an *Execute* method for sending DDL statements to the server, e.g. to create a cube. AMO doesn't support result-based MDX or DMX queries. AMO requires at least read permissions to the SSAS metadata.

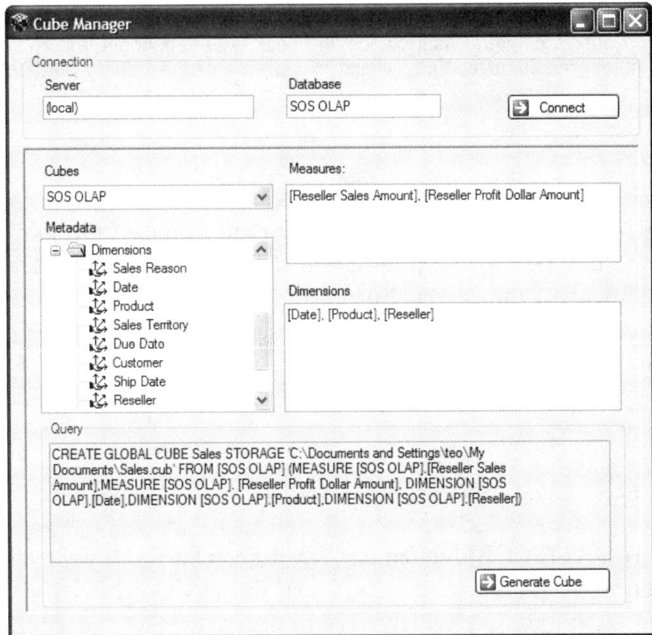

Figure 13.28 The Cube Manager demonstrates how you can leverage AMO and ADOMD.NET to create local cubes.

13.4.3 Creating Local Cubes with AMO

Let's put AMO to practical use. A common business scenario is supporting OLAP reporting in disconnected mode. For example, suppose that the Adventure Works sales people spend most of their time away from the corporate office. While on the road, they may need to download the SOS OLAP cube (or a subcube from it) to their laptops, so they can browse the company data offline.

Tip Besides the Activity Viewer sample, the SSAS team has provided other AMO code samples (see the code samples in the C:\Program Files\Microsoft SQL Server\90\Samples\Analysis Services\Programmability\AMO folder). I definitely recommend you explore this buried treasure.

The Cube Manager demonstrates how you can use AMO and ADOMD.NET to support offline OLAP reporting scenarios.

Introducing the Cube Manager

The Cube Manager (Figure 13.28) is a VB.NET Windows Forms application. When the user connects to the SSAS database of choice, the Cube Manager populates the Cubes dropdown with the names of the cubes found in the database. Once a cube is selected, the Cube Manager loads the Metadata tree with the measures and dimensions defined in that cube.

The end user designs a subcube by dragging measures to the Measures textbox and dimensions to the Dimensions textbox. The Query pane shows the resulting CREATE GLOBAL CUBE statement that will be used to create the local cube. When the user clicks the Generate button, the Cube Manager generates the local cube it the user's My Documents folder. At this point, the user can disconnect from the network. Offline cube browsing can be done with any OLAP browser that supports local cubes, e.g. Microsoft Excel.

Note Since the Cube Manager doesn't carry out any management tasks, it could be implemented entirely in ADO MD.NET. AMO is used to demonstrate how you can navigate the object hierarchy which can be done with ADO MD.NET as well, though the syntax is different. As it stands, the only AMO-dependent feature in the Cube Manager is serializing the object metadata in XML, which is implemented for demonstration purposes only.

Creating local cubes

As with its previous release, SSAS supports two options for creating a local cube. First, you can create the cube definition from scratch, followed by INSERT statements to populate the local cube with data. Second, you can delegate this task to the programming library by submitting a single CREATE GLOBAL CUBE statement to the server. For example, the statement below creates a local cube from the server-based SOS OLAP cube. Its space is defined by two dimensions (Product and Date) and one measure (Reseller Sales Amount) only.

```
CREATE GLOBAL CUBE Sales STORAGE 'C:\Documents and Settings\teo\My
Documents\Sales.cub'
FROM [SOS OLAP]
(MEASURE [SOS OLAP].[Reseller Sales Amount],
DIMENSION [SOS OLAP].[Product],DIMENSION [SOS OLAP].[Date])
```

When the server receives a CREATE GLOBAL CUBE statement, it verifies that the connected user has at least *ReadDefinition* permission to the SOS OLAP cube. Next, the server streams back the local cube definition. The programming library (ADOMD.NET in my case) takes the DDL statement, generates the local cube, and populates it with data. Let me walk you through the most important implementation details of the Cube Manager.

Enumerating cube objects

Once the Cube Manager connects to the server, it calls the *LoadCubes* function which populates the Cubes dropdown with the cubes found in the requested database.

```
Dim cubes As CubeCollection = m_server.Databases.GetByName(txtDatabase.Text).Cubes

For Each cube In cubes
    Dim listItem As New ListItem(cube.Name, cube)
    cmbCubes.Items.Add(listItem)
Next
```

Note that when using AMO, you don't connect to a database but to a server. In this respect, you can think of an AMO connection as having a larger scope than an ADO MD.NET connection. As noted, the code references the requested database by using the *GetByName* method of the *Databases* object. The *Cubes* property of the *Database* object returns a collection of the cubes in that database. The only thing left for us to do is to loop through the Cubes collection to load the cmbCubes dropdown. I am using a helper class (ListItem) to bind both the cube name (item text) and the cube object reference (item value) to the cmbCubes dropdown. We will use the cached object reference to manipulate the cube object later.

Serializing objects to ASSL

AMO supports serializing the object definition to ASSL. BI Studio uses this feature to create the object definition files when you reverse-engineer an SSAS database. The Cube Manager demonstrates how you can carry out the same task programmatically.

```
Dim myStream As New MemoryStream()
Dim writer As New XmlTextWriter(myStream, New System.Text.UTF8Encoding())
```

```
Utils.Serialize(writer, cube, False)
Debug.WriteLine(System.Text.Encoding.UTF8.GetString(myStream.GetBuffer()))
```

Only AMO *major* objects that inherit from the *MajorObject* class can be serialized to XML. Major objects are container objects, such as databases, cubes, dimensions, and measure groups. The AMO *Utils.Serialize* method takes an *XmlWriter* object to write the ASSL definition to. To get the definition in a string variable, the code writes the XML output to the memory. Alternatively, you can use a *FileStream* stream to write the definition to a physical file. Finally, the code outputs the cube definition to the active trace listener. In debug mode, the XML definition will be outputted to BI Studio Output Window. During runtime, you can attach trace utilities, such as the Sysinternals DbgView, to watch the trace output.

Loading the cube metadata

Upon selecting a cube in the Cubes dropdown, the code loads the cube measures and dimensions in the Metadata tree. Listing 13.1 shows the abbreviated code of the LoadMetadata function.

Listing 13.1 Loading the cube metadata with AMO

```
Private Sub LoadMetadata(ByVal cube As Cube)

    Dim measureGroup As MeasureGroup
    Dim measure As Measure

    For Each measureGroup In cube.MeasureGroups
     parentNode = New TreeNode(measureGroup.Name,Icons.DisplayFolder,
        Icons.DisplayFolder)
     treeMeta.Nodes.Add(parentNode)

     For Each measure In measureGroup.Measures
        tempNode = New TreeNode(measure.Name,
        Icons.AttributeHierarchy, Icons.AttributeHierarchy)
               tempNode.Tag = measure
               parentNode.Nodes.Add(tempNode)
           Next
     Next

    parentNode = New TreeNode("Dimensions", Icons.DisplayFolder, Icons.DisplayFolder)
    treeMeta.Nodes.Add(parentNode)

    Dim dimension As CubeDimension
     For Each dimension In cube.Dimensions
        tempNode = New TreeNode(dimension.Name, Icons.Dimension, Icons.Dimension)
      tempNode.Tag = dimension
      parentNode.Nodes.Add(tempNode)
        Next dimension
End Sub
```

We start by looping through the cube measure groups to load them in the Metadata tree. For each measure group, we loop through its measures and add them to the tree. Next, the code creates a placeholder node (Dimensions) which will serve as a parent node for the cube dimensions. Finally, we loop through the Dimensions collection to load all dimensions referenced in the cube in the Metadata tree.

Generating the local cube

As noted, the users can define the local cube definition by simply dragging measures and dimensions and dropping them to the Measures and Dimensions textboxes respectively. When this happens, the code generates the CREATE GLOBAL CUBE syntax and displays it in the Query textbox. The *CreateLocalCube* function uses ADOMD.NET to send the statement to the server. Its abbreviated code is shown in Listing 13.2.

Listing 13.2 Generating a local cube with CREATE GLOBAL CUBE

```
Private Sub CreateLocalCube()
    Dim connection As New AdomdConnection(String.Format("Data Source={0};
     Initial Catalog={1};", txtServer.Text, txtDatabase.Text))
    Dim command As New ADOMD.AdomdCommand(txtQuery.Text)
    connection.Open()
    command.Connection = connection
    command.ExecuteNonQuery()
End Sub
```

The code configures an AdomdCommand with the generated CREATE GLOBAL CUBE statement. Next, it calls the *ExecuteNonQuery* method to send the statement to the server to get the subcube definition. Next, the ADOMD.NET library builds the cube definition and processes the cube. Once the cube is generated, you should be able to use Management Studio (or an OLAP client) to connect to it and query it just like a server cube. The only difference is that when connecting you need to specify the full path to the local cube file.

Areas for future enhancements

The CREATE GLOBAL CUBE statement supports more granular cube slicing by dimension levels and members. For example, the following statement slices the server cube by year 2004 only.

```
CREATE GLOBAL CUBE Sales STORAGE 'C:\Sales.cub'
FROM [SOS OLAP]
(MEASURE [SOS OLAP].[Reseller Sales Amount],
DIMENSION [SOS OLAP].[Product],
DIMENSION [SOS OLAP].[Date](LEVEL Year, MEMBER [Calendar Year].&[2004]))
```

If you need to support member slicing, you can enhance the Cube Manager to display the full dimension metadata (hierarchies, levels, and members). In addition, you need to change the Cube Manager to generate the appropriate syntax according to the type of the object dropped in the Dimensions textbox.

13.5 Summary

As an SSAS administrator, you need to ensure that the server functions correctly and performs optimally. In this chapter, we covered essential management techniques that will help you meet this goal. The tool that you rely on most to carry out various management tasks is the SQL Server Management Studio. Use the server properties dialog to configure the server settings. Use the scripting functionality of Management Studio to script and automate SSAS tasks and objects.

SSAS provides different options for database deployment. Use the BI Studio deployment capabilities or scripting when you don't need to preserve the management settings of the target database. The Deployment Wizard allows you to deploy the database definition while preserving the storage and security settings. Use the Synchronize Database Wizard to synchronize data between two databases. Incorporate a back up and restore database plan in your management plan.

SSAS provides various options for monitoring the server. Use the SQL Server Profiler to watch the server activity in real time, or to replay a captured activity. Inspect the SSAS server logs to troubleshoot error conditions. Activate the Dr. Watson feature to send minidumps to the Microsoft Product Support when troubleshooting server crashes.

Finally, when scripting and management tools are not enough, you can create your own management applications. .NET-based management clients can leverage AMO object library to read and change the database metadata, as well as carry out server or database management tasks.

13.6 Resources

Overview of the Analysis Services Development and Management Environments (http://shrinkster.com/6l5) -- This paper provides an overview of BI Studio and SQL Server Management Studio environments.

Optimizing Cube Performance Using Microsoft SQL Server 2000 Analysis Services (http://shrinkster.com/6op) -- This paper by Unisys discusses the design and implementation of a series of test scenarios that include building and querying cubes using Microsoft SQL Server 2000 and Analysis Services.

Microsoft SQL Server 2000 Analysis Services Performance Guide (http://shrinkster.com/6pe) -- This paper describes techniques you can use to optimize query responsiveness and processing performance in SSAS. Although originally written for SSAS 2000, many of its findings are still applicable for SSAS 2005.

Chapter 14

Managing Storage

As you know by now, the first criteria of the FASMI test evaluates the ability of OLAP servers to provide **F**ast query performance. So far, we've been designing our UDM without knowing or caring about how SSAS stores multidimensional data. As long as your cubes are relatively small, you will be fine by using the default storage settings. However, chances are that in real life, your cubes will be many times larger than our sample cubes and you may need to optimize their storage design and performance. A good storage design goes a long way to decrease the cube query and processing times.

This chapter provides a comprehensive understanding of the SSAS storage options and optimization techniques. You will learn how to:

- Manage partition and dimension storage modes.
- Design and optimize cube aggregations.
- Partition measure groups to improve processing and query performance.

You can find the code samples for this chapter by opening the Ch14 solution.

14.1 Designing Storage

The dilemma that SSAS and the OLAP technology face is how to maximize the query performance by requiring minimum storage space. An optimal storage produces fast queries while maintaining reasonable cube processing times. SSAS goes a long way to meet your performance and scalability requirements. You can help it by choosing an optimum storage mode and creating useful cube aggregations.

The SSAS storage architecture is based on sound and flexible design goals. First, it allows the administrators to select a storage mode that provides an optimum balance between the cube performance and storage space. Second, the storage design is transparent to the client applications. The cube represents the logical view of UDM that hides the physical implementation details. Finally, while the cube storage design can be implemented during design time, the administrator can change it once the model is deployed to production. Changes to the UDM storage design require reprocessing the cube.

14.1.1 Understanding Storage Modes

UDM data containing objects (dimensions and measure group partitions) can be configured with one of the following three standard storage modes:

- Multidimensional OLAP (*MOLAP*) – Data and aggregations are stored in the multi-dimensional store.
- Hybrid OLAP (*HOLAP*) – Data is left in the relational database; aggregations are stored in the multi-dimensional store. Only applicable to measure groups.
- Relational OLAP (*ROLAP*) – Data and aggregations are stored in the relational database.

SSAS 2000 The SSAS 2005 standard storage modes remain the same as those in the previous release. While it is true that proactive caching (discussed in section 15) adds an additional "dimension" to the storage architecture, the main storage options correspond to the standard OLAP storage modes -- MOLAP, ROLAP, and HOLAP.

To understand how these storage modes differ, you need to know some details about the cube storage architecture. Once you understand the storage modes in the context of a cube, it is easy to apply them to dimensions.

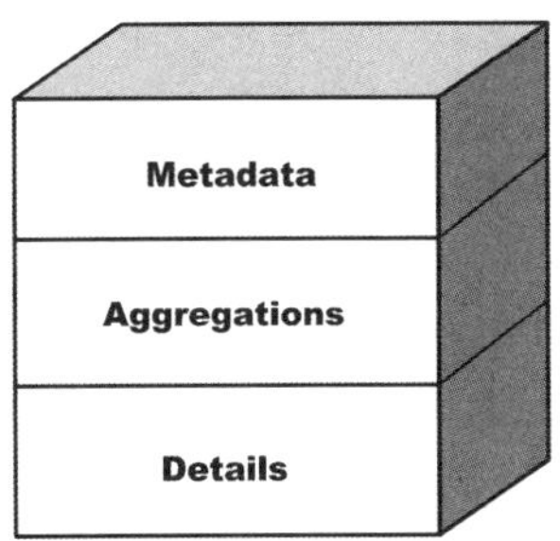

Figure 14.1 The cube storage consists of metadata, aggregations, and details.

Cube storage architecture

Figure 14.1 provides a simplified view of the cube storage architecture. At a high level, the cube storage is defined by the cube *details*, *aggregations*, and *metadata* layers. A cube may contain *detailed data* that is pulled from the data source when the cube is processed. A cube may optionally have *aggregations*. Aggregations are pre-calculated summaries of data that the server can use to answer queries faster. Finally, the metadata is what makes the cube appear as a logical storage medium (cube) to the client application. For example, when you open the SOS OLAP cube in the Cube Designer, the Metadata pane shows you the dimensions and measures defined in the cube.

Table 14.1 The cube storage modes define the location of the details and aggregations.

Storage layer	MOLAP	HOLAP	ROLAP
Metadata	✓	✓	✓
Aggregations	✓	✓	
Details	✓		

When you are setting up the cube storage mode, you are basically specifying the location of the cube aggregations and details (Table 14.1). The cube metadata is not affected by the choice of a cube storage mode because it is always stored on the server. The three storage modes only differ in the location of the cube aggregations and details.

MOLAP Storage Mode

MOLAP stores both cube data and aggregations in the server multidimensional store. When a MOLAP cube is processed, the server brings the cube data from the data source into the cube. Therefore, with MOLAP, data is duplicated because it exists in both the data source and in the cube itself. In fact, once a MOLAP cube is processed, the relational data source is not accessed at all when the server is queried.

Note Normally, you can't see the fact data when browsing a cube. That's because you can drill down as far as the grain of the measure group. For example, since the grain of the Reseller Sales measure group is a calendar day, you cannot drill further down to see the individual fact rows. The only way to browse the detail-level data is to implement a drillthrough action, as we demonstrated in chapter 12.

MOLAP pros and cons

MOLAP is the default cube storage mode and for a reason. MOLAP cubes have the fastest query performance. There are several reasons for the MOLAP efficiency. First, the MOLAP mode eliminates the network overhead of moving data across the wire from the data source to the Analysis Services server. Second, data is kept in a highly efficient multidimensional file store on the server side. This allows the server to index the data and aggregations that will give queries best performance.

Note MOLAP is the fastest in querying but uses the most disk space.

Since there is no such thing as a free lunch, there are some tradeoffs when choosing the MOLAP storage mode. Obviously, additional disk storage space is needed on the server to duplicate the detail-level data. This additional data load impacts the cube processing time. Finally, since MOLAP is essentially a disk-based cache, the cube has to be refreshed as the source data changes.

MOLAP disk storage

To minimize the storage space, MOLAP stores data very efficiently. For example, empty cell values are not persisted. In addition, the server uses very efficient algorithms to compress data. As a result, MOLAP cubes can actually take less space than the relational database. For example, the AdventureWorksDW database takes about 85 Mb of storage space, while the SOS OLAP database (no aggregations) occupies about 40 Mb. In SSAS 2000, you could use the following formula to estimate the MOLAP data storage:

```
cube storage (bytes) = (((2 * total number of dimension levels) +
       (4 * number of measures)) * number of fact records) / 3
```

Of course, with the introduction of attributes, the above formula is not applicable to UDM. As of the time of this writing, I am not aware of an official formula to estimate UDM storage needs. However, based on my experiments, the following formula seems to get the job done:

```
measure group storage (bytes) = (((2 * total number of attributes) +
       (4 * number of measures)) * number of fact records) / 3
```

When applying this formula, recall that a UDM cube may have more than one measure group. Use the formula to estimate the storage space for each measure group in the cube and then sum the results. The *total number of attributes* argument reflects the number of attributes in dimensions that intersect the measure group.

HOLAP Storage Mode

As its name suggests, HOLAP is a hybrid between MOLAP and ROLAP. With this mode, the cube data remains in the relational store, while the aggregations are stored on the SSAS server. You can think of HOLAP as an attempt to give you the best of the relational and multidimensional worlds. HOLAP is most efficient in terms of disk space since detail-level data is not duplicated as with MOLAP and it requires less space to store aggregations than ROLAP. For example, a study conducted by Unisys (see Resources) found that ROLAP storage space surpasses HOLAP when the aggregation level exceeds 30%. The study measured the cube performance of SSAS 2000 but similar results should be expected with HOLAP in SSAS 2005 as well.

In terms of query performance, HOLAP scores in the middle. It is not as fast as MOLAP, but it outperforms ROLAP (with aggregations). With HOLAP, queries are sent to the relational store to retrieve data. As far as processing times, HOLAP cubes may process faster because data is read only once to create aggregations (no need to populate the multi-dimensional store). However, due to the efficient storage architecture of SSAS, in real life, MOLAP and HOLAP should give you comparable processing times.

 **Note** HOLAP is best in storage and second best in querying.

In my opinion, the practical usage scenarios for HOLAP are limited. HOLAP may look like a good bet for large data warehouses because it allows you to minimize the storage space. In theory, most queries will be answered from the pre-calculated aggregations and rarely reach the relational database. However, in real life, an SSAS 2005 cube may (and often will) have many dimensions with significant number of attribute hierarchies. Even with a good aggregation design, it is likely that a large number of queries may not find appropriate aggregations and have to be satisfied by the relational database. The net result of this HOLAP-but-actually-ROLAP scenario is performance degradation. It is unreasonable to expect that end users will tolerate well a sudden drop in performance when HOLAP reverts to ROLAP.

A good fit for HOLAP may be a historical partition that is infrequently accessed, as I will demonstrate in section 14.3.2. Assuming that most of the queries target recent data, you may decide to leave the historical data (e.g. more than several years old) in the relational database to save space. Next, you can create a separate HOLAP partition for the historical data and implement a good aggregation design to satisfy most of the historical queries from pre-calculated aggregations.

ROLAP Storage Mode

With ROLAP, both the cube data and aggregations remain in the relational database. Consequently, the server must create additional relational tables to hold the cube aggregations. With no aggregations defined, ROLAP is most efficient in terms of storage. However, queries incur a performance penalty because they must be satisfied from the relational database.

 **Note** ROLAP is worst in querying and second best (after HOLAP) in storage.

So, why do we have ROLAP at all? In my opinion, there are only a few practical usage scenarios for ROLAP. First, as you saw in chapter 12, a writeback partition requires ROLAP storage. Another scenario that may benefit from ROLAP is a constantly changing dimension that takes very long to process. In this case, it makes sense to leave the dimension data in the relational database. Finally, consider ROLAP with large fact (degenerate) dimensions which are used only for drillthrough queries.

One popular scenario with SSAS 2000 for using ROLAP was large dimensions, e.g. dimension with millions of members. Now that the dimensions are not memory-bound anymore (no more 2GB memory limit), a large MOLAP dimension could give you better performance than its ROLAP counterpart. As for the maximum number of members, a UDM dimension can have up to two billion members. The exact number depends on the hardware platform (32-bit versa 64-bit, memory, etc).

14.1.2 Configuring Partition Storage

You can design the cube storage mode both during design time (using BI Studio), or after the cube is deployed (using Management Studio). In my opinion, the latter option will be a more popular choice with larger cubes. During design time database developers would typically work on a smaller datasets that are not partitioned. Only when the cube is deployed to the staging or production database, it makes sense to finalize its partition and storage design. That said, I will use BI Studio for education purposes. In this way, the settings are stored in the Analysis Services project and you don't have to reproduce the implementation steps to review them.

By default, a measure group is configured with a single partition that spans the entire fact table. With SSAS 2005 Enterprise Edition, additional partitions can be created to optimize the UDM performance. You define the partition storage mode by setting the StorageMode property for that partition. Also, cubes and measure groups have a StorageMode property but it's used to define the default storage mode for new partitions. For example, if the cube storage mode is set to MOLAP, but one of its measure groups is HOLAP, new partitions in that measure group will default to HOLAP storage mode. Remember that the storage mode only affects data-containing objects (partitions and dimensions). Assuming that you have Administrator rights to the relational data source, you may find a SQL Server Profiler trace useful when experimenting with different partition storage settings.

1. Launch the SQL Server Profiler (Start ⇨ Programs ⇨ Microsoft SQL Server 2005 ⇨ Performance Tools program group).
2. Select File ⇨ New Trace. In the *Server type* dropdown, select *Database Engine* and click the Connect button. Click Run on the Trace Properties dialog to start a trace.
3. Open the SOS OLAP cube in the Cube Designer and click on the *Partitions* tab.
4. Expand the Internet Sales measure group panel and observe that, as it stands, the Internet Sales measure group has only one partition called Fact Internet Sales. That's because, by default, BI Studio creates a new measure group with one partition.
5. Select the Fact Internet Sales partition. Note that its *StorageMode* property is set to *Molap* (the default storage mode).

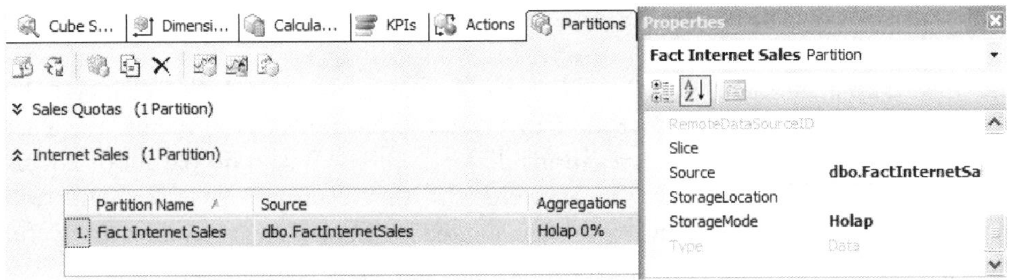

Figure 14.2 Use the Partitions tab to change the storage mode for a partition.

6. Switch to the Cube Browser tab and create a report that uses measures from the Internet Sales measure group, e.g. just drag the Internet Sales Amount measure. In the SQL Server Profiler, you shouldn't see any SELECT statements sent to the AdventureWorksDW database. That's because MOLAP queries are always satisfied from the multi-dimensional server store.

7. Let's change the storage mode of Fact Internet Sales partition to *HOLAP*. In the Properties window, expand the StorageMode property dropdown and select *Holap* (Figure 14.2).

> **Note** You may wonder why I don't use the Storage Settings link below the partition. My advice is to avoid using Storage Settings link if you don't have a good understanding of how proactive caching works. The Storage Settings link exposes a few pre-defined storage modes. Besides MOLAP (the right-most setting), all other options enable proactive caching which may not be what you are after.

8. Process the SOS OLAP cube. If you inspect the disk storage space occupied by the SOS OLAP database (C:\Program Files\Microsoft SQL Server\MSSQL.2\OLAP\Data\SOS OLAP.0.db), you will notice that it has been reduced substantially.

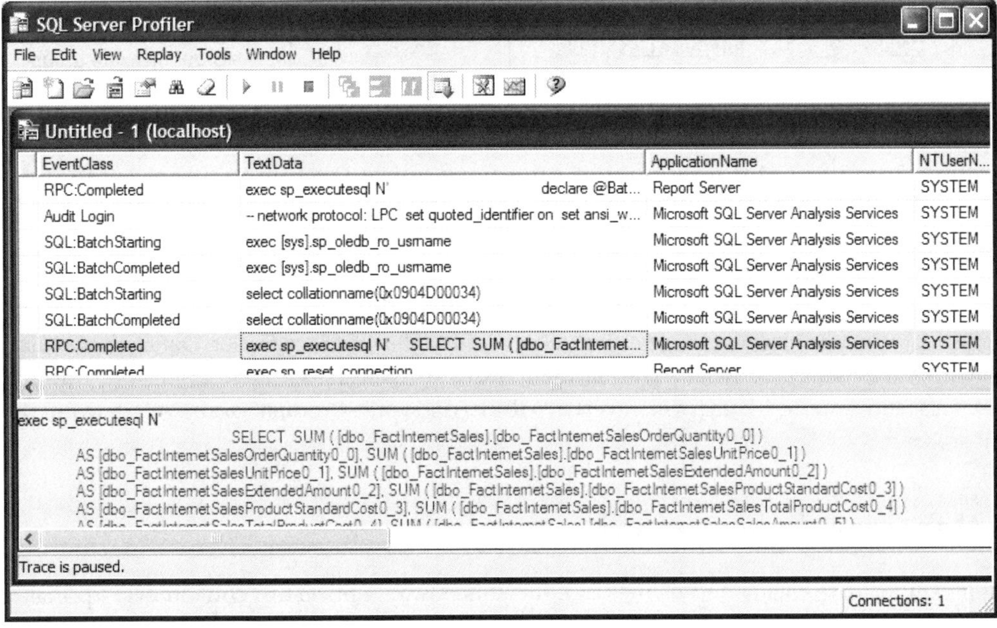

Figure 14.3 In the absence of cube aggregations, all HOLAP queries are satisfied from the relational store.

9. Refresh the report in the Cube Browser. Going back to the SQL Server Profiler, you should see a SQL SELECT statement that the server sends to retrieve the aggregated values for the report.

   To understand this, take a moment to reflect on what we've accomplished. We changed the storage mode of the Fact Internet Sales partition to HOLAP. However, as it stands, the Fact Internet Sales partition doesn't have any aggregations defined. HOLAP with no partitions equals ROLAP. In other words, all queries will be answered by the relational database. This will definitely slow down the query performance with large databases. However, pre-computed useful aggregations could help the server satisfy queries from the multidimensional store. I will show you how to define aggregations in section 0.

14.1.3 Configuring Dimension Storage

As you would probably recall, the SOS OLAP UDM includes a fact (degenerate) dimension (Internet Order Details) to support browsing the individual order transactions. Fact dimensions are good candidates for ROLAP storage because they contain as many members as the fact table they are derived from and may take a substantial storage space. Moreover, usually a relatively small number of queries request fact dimensions. Let's change the storage mode of the Internet Order Details dimension from MOLAP (default) to ROLAP.

1. Open the Internet Order Details dimension in the Dimension Designer.
2. In the dimension properties, note that the *StorageMode* property is set to *MOLAP*. Expand the StorageMode dropdown. Note that it lists only MOLAP and ROLAP storage modes. As I mentioned, a dimension cannot have HOLAP storage.
3. Change the StorageMode property to *ROLAP* and process the cube.

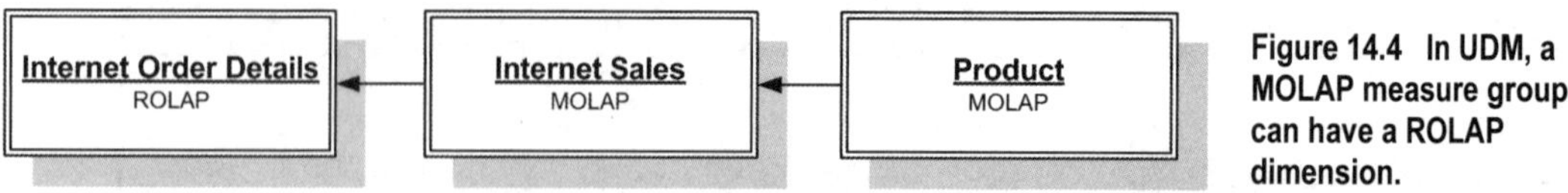

Figure 14.4 In UDM, a MOLAP measure group can have a ROLAP dimension.

An interesting feature in UDM is that a MOLAP measure group can have an associated ROLAP dimension (Figure 14.4). For example, the Internet Sales measure group and its related dimensions can have MOLAP storage mode, while the Internet Order Details can be configured as ROLAP. In this scenario, the Internet Sales measure group cannot store references to the ROLAP dimension members. It has to behave like a ROLAP measure group when a ROLAP dimension is part of the query. Queries that don't request the Internet Order Details dimension are satisfied entirely from MOLAP. The moment a query requests the fact dimension, Internet Order Details and Internet Sales will revert to ROLAP, while Product is answered from the MOLAP store.

14.2 Managing Aggregations

No matter how you are slicing and dicing data, the cube always appears to contain every possible aggregated value. For example, consider the Product Sales by Date report shown in Figure 14.5. Regardless of the level the user has drilled down to, the cube returns the correct aggregated cell value for the requested Reseller Sales Amount measure. The server can derive the aggregated cell value for a given cell in one of two ways. In the absence of pre-defined aggregations, the server has no other choice but to query the lowest level of data (facts) for the requested cube slice and sum up their values. In comparison, if appropriate intermediate aggregations exist, the server could use them to satisfy the query.

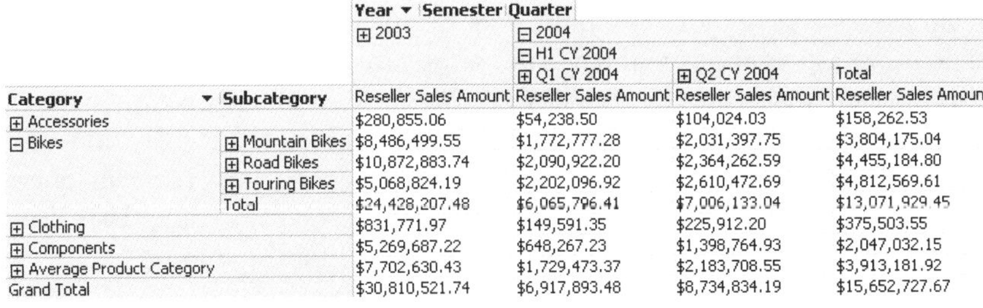

	Year ▾ Semester Quarter			
	⊞ 2003	⊟ 2004		
		⊟ H1 CY 2004		
		⊞ Q1 CY 2004	⊞ Q2 CY 2004	Total
Category ▾ Subcategory	Reseller Sales Amount	Reseller Sales Amount	Reseller Sales Amount	Reseller Sales Amount
⊞ Accessories	$280,855.06	$54,238.50	$104,024.03	$158,262.53
⊟ Bikes ⊞ Mountain Bikes	$8,486,499.55	$1,772,777.28	$2,031,397.75	$3,804,175.04
⊞ Road Bikes	$10,872,883.74	$2,090,922.20	$2,364,262.59	$4,455,184.80
⊞ Touring Bikes	$5,068,824.19	$2,202,096.92	$2,610,472.69	$4,812,569.61
Total	$24,428,207.48	$6,065,796.41	$7,006,133.04	$13,071,929.45
⊞ Clothing	$831,771.97	$149,591.35	$225,912.20	$375,503.55
⊞ Components	$5,269,687.22	$648,267.23	$1,398,764.93	$2,047,032.15
⊞ Average Product Category	$7,702,630.43	$1,729,473.37	$2,183,708.55	$3,913,181.92
Grand Total	$30,810,521.74	$6,917,893.48	$8,734,834.19	$15,652,727.67

Figure 14.5 A cube appears to have every possible aggregated value.

For example, the first column of the Product Sales by Date report in Figure 14.5 shows the 2003 sales figures. As it stands, the SOS OLAP cube doesn't have any aggregations. Therefore, to produce the 2003 sales figures, the server has to retrieve the leaf cells for 2003 and the current product member. Next, the server has to sum the cell values to produce the aggregated total. If there were aggregations for the members of the Quarter attribute hierarchy, the server could produce the year aggregate value by just summing the four quarter values.

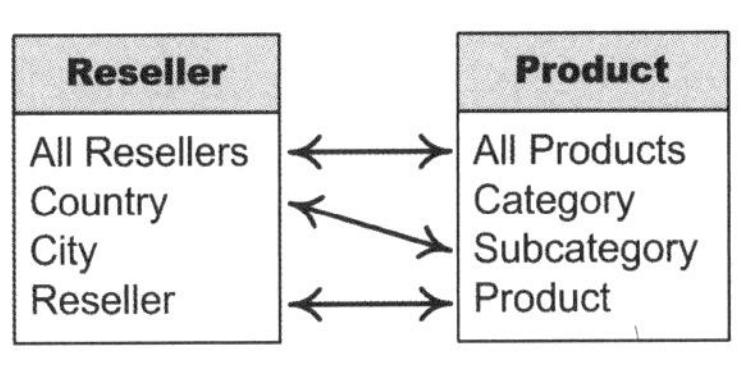

All level aggregation

Reseller	Product	Sales Amount
All	All	$120,546

Intermediate aggregation

Country	Subcategory	Sales Amount
US	Road Bikes	$10,456

Fact-level aggregation

Reseller	Product	Sales Amount
A Bike Store	Road-42	$1,234

Figure 14.6 Aggregations are pre-calculated subtotals of attributes from every dimension referenced in a cube.

14.2.1 Understanding Aggregations

An aggregation is a subtotal of attributes from every dimension. A cube may have aggregations at different levels. For example, consider the basic cube shown in Figure 14.6 which has only two dimensions – Reseller and Product. If the cube has an All-level aggregation, a query that asks for the grand sales totals will be satisfied by that aggregation. Similarly, more detail queries can be answered by intermediate and fact-level aggregations.

SSAS 2000 Strictly speaking, in UDM, subtotaling is done on an attribute level instead of on a dimension level. I chose to show dimension levels in Figure 14.6 because there are easier to understand and illustrate.

Goal for using aggregations

So, if aggregations are so useful, why not create all possible aggregations in the cube to achieve the best performance? The short answer is that this will cause data explosion because the total number of aggregations will equal the number of the dimension attributes raised to the power of the number of the dimensions. For example, suppose you want to create all possible aggregations between the Reseller and Product dimension (see again Figure 14.6). Just for the four attributes forming the dimension levels, we will end up with $4^2 = 16$ aggregations. However, a more realistic cube with ten dimensions that have four levels each will result in $4^{10} = 1{,}048{,}576$ aggregations. Now, throw in the other attribute hierarchies to the mix...

As with storage modes, choosing the optimal number of aggregations is a tradeoff between performance and storage space. The size of an aggregation is a factor of the number of cells it aggregates (lower level aggregations have more cells), the data that is aggregated, and the number of the cube measures. The more aggregations you have, the more storage space they will take. In addition, cube processing time increases proportionally with the number of aggregations. That's because aggregations are computed when the cube is processed. Therefore, your goal should be finding the optimal subset of the aggregations that gives you the necessary increase in query performance without taking too much space and impacting the cube processing time. Usually, a good aggregation design contains aggregations in the tens or hundreds (not thousands).

Working with aggregations

Aggregations are defined at partition level. A single aggregation always includes all measures in the measure group excluding the calculated members. You cannot specify different aggregation levels for different attribute members. For example, it is not possible to set the aggregation level for the Accessories product category to 20% and Bikes to 40%. As with the rest of the storage settings, managing aggregations is totally transparent to the client; you can add or remove aggregations as you wish.

Aggregations can be designed, processed, and used in queries. When you design aggregations, you select which combinations of attributes to use. The aggregation design is stored in the cube partition definition file (<cube>.partitions). When the server processes the aggregations, it calculates the aggregations and materializes them (saves them to disk). When the server receives a query, it decides which aggregations (if any) will be used. The server may decide to use intermediate aggregations to satisfy a query that asks for aggregated data at a higher level. If no suitable aggregations are found and the query results are not cached, the server scans the multidimensional store to retrieve the qualifying cells and aggregates them.

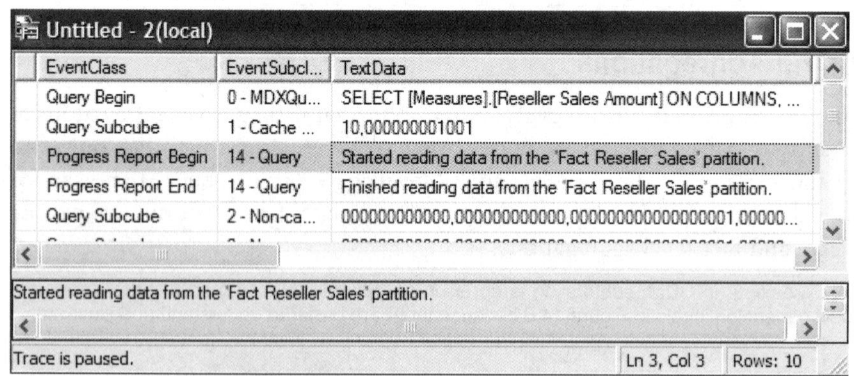

Figure 14.7 Use the SQL Server Profiler to monitor aggregation hits and misses.

Monitoring aggregation usage

You can use the SQL Server Profiler to determine if a given query is satisfied from the cube aggregations or not. However, the SQL Server Profiler won't tell you why the server has decided to use a particular aggregation. If the server didn't use aggregations, the Progress Report event

(Figure 14.7) will show "*Start reading data from the 'Partition Name' partition.*' Otherwise, the report will say '*Start reading from the 'Aggregation Name' aggregation.*' As Figure 14.7 shows, in my case, the server didn't find any useful aggregations when processing the MDX query.

14.2.2 Designing Aggregations

There are two ways to create aggregations. First, you can use the Aggregation Design Wizard to select useful aggregations for you. Second, after the cube is deployed to production, you can use the query usage statistics and refine the aggregation design with the Usage-Based Optimization Wizard. Therefore, a good approach is to use the Aggregation Design Wizard *before* the cube is deployed in production. Once representative query set is available, you could fine-tune the aggregation design with Usage-based Optimization Wizard. Examples that demonstrate how to use both wizards are in order.

How the Aggregation Design Wizard works

The Aggregation Design Wizard doesn't take into account what queries will be submitted to the server or what dimensions will be used most. This information is not available at design time. Instead, the Aggregation Design Wizard assumes that all queries will cover dimension levels with an equal probability. For example, the Aggregation Design Wizard assumes that the number of queries that request the Product attribute will equal the number of queries that ask for the Color attribute. This, of course, is an optimistic assumption that may not reflect the real-life query patterns.

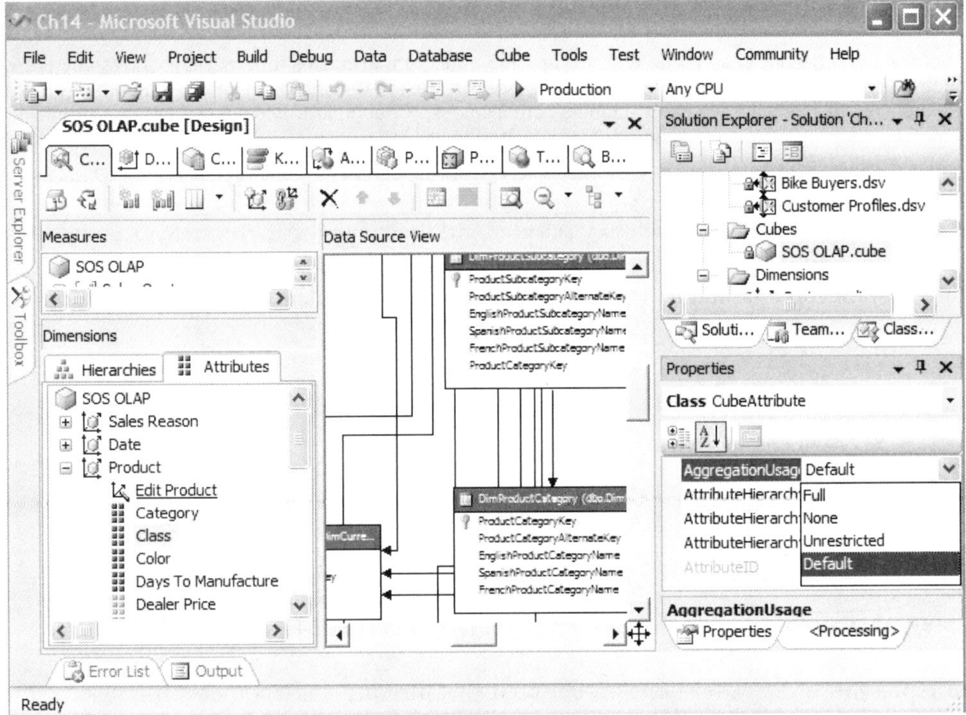

Figure 14.8 You can control which attribute will be considered for aggregation design by changing the AggregationDesign property of the attribute.

The Aggregation Designer Wizard performs three steps to select aggregations. First, it identifies dimension attributes based on their AggregationUsage property. Second, the wizard builds an attribute chain. Finally, it runs a statistical algorithm that assigns weights to different paths in the attribute chain. Let's discuss each step in more details.

Step 1: Evaluating aggregation usage

By default, only attributes that participate in multi-level hierarchies can be considered for the aggregation design. However, you can control this behavior by setting the *AggregationUsage* property at an attribute level to tell the Aggregation Wizard whether it should consider a given attribute for aggregations. You will find the AggregationUsage property in the Attributes tab of the Cube Structure tab (Figure 14.8) in the Cube Designer (not the Dimension Designer). That's because aggregations are a function of the cube measures and attributes.

Full aggregation usage means that every aggregation in this cube must include this attribute. If you set the AggregationUsage property to *None*, no aggregations will use this attribute. If an attribute is configured for *Unrestricted*, it is up to the Aggregation Design Wizard to consider the attribute when designing aggregations. Finally, the *Default* setting will escalate *All* and dimension key attributes to *Unrestricted*. The aggregation usage of attributes participating in many-to-many, referenced, and data mining dimensions will be to *None*.

For multilevel hierarchies, the wizard will scan the hierarchy from the top level and evaluate each level. If the attribute relationships exist for the attribute (natural hierarchy), the attribute will be promoted to *Unrestricted* level. Otherwise, the Aggregation Design Wizard will move to the next level in the multi-level hierarchy. Again, note that setting proper attribute relationships at design time is very important. If the attribute doesn't participate in a multi-level hierarchy, its AggregationUsage property will be set to *None*.

Tip Set the AggregationUsage property to *None* if the attribute participates in a multilevel hierarchy but is used infrequently or when you want to tell the Aggregation Design Wizard to ignore the attribute (e.g. with rich natural hierarchies that have many attribute combinations). Change to *Unrestricted* if this is a commonly used attribute and you want to improve the query performance.

Step 2: Building the attribute chain

Once the Aggregation Design Wizard has selected the qualifying attributes, it examines the attribute relationships and creates a chain of dependencies (Figure 14.9). Each arrow in the graph is an attribute relationship. Natural multilevel hierarchies form complete chains from the bottom level of the hierarchy to the top level.

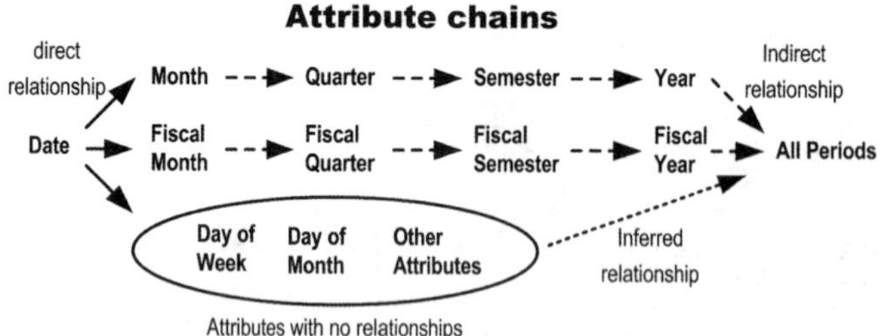

Figure 14.9 Aggregations could be defined only for attributes that form multi-level hierarchies.

A solid line represents a direct relationship between the attribute and another attribute. Attributes that don't form multilevel hierarchies but have an *All* level are assigned inferred relationships. When identifying useful aggregations, the Aggregation Design Wizard prefers long and complete paths. In the absence of attribute relationships, the wizard cannot distinguish one attribute from another and will most likely ignore such attributes. Once the attribute chains are defined, the wizard applies a coverage algorithm to filter the most useful aggregations.

Step 3: Algorithm coverage

In this step, the wizard builds a tree structure of aggregations recursively to identify how each attribute relates to other aggregations. Then, it assigns a cost-benefit weight to each aggregation. The more space an aggregation takes, the more costly it is. The closer a given aggregation is to another aggregation, the more useful it is. The wizard takes in consideration the number of partition rows and attribute members. Partition row counts are used to estimate the data density of the aggregation. Attribute member counts are used to estimate the size of the aggregations.

Starting the Aggregation Design Wizard

Now, that you know how the Aggregation Design Wizard works, let's see it in action. The Aggregation Design Wizard is available both in BI Studio and Management Studio. I will use BI Studio to demonstrate how you can design aggregations. Suppose that you would like to improve the performance of queries that target the Reseller Sales measure group in the SOS OLAP cube.

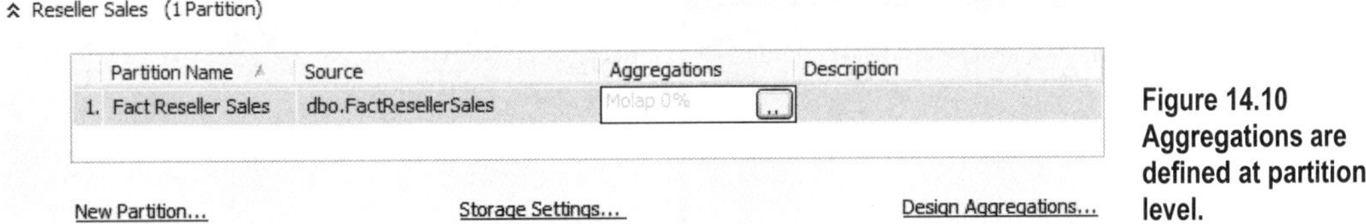

Figure 14.10 Aggregations are defined at partition level.

1. Open the SOS OLAP cube in the Cube Designer and switch to the Partitions tab.
2. Expand the Reseller Sales measure group (Figure 14.10) and note that the Aggregations column of the Fact Reseller Sales partition has no aggregations defined (0%).
3. You can launch the Aggregation Design Wizard by clicking on the **...** button inside the Aggregations cell or click the Design Aggregations link. Alternatively, you can right-click on the Fact Reseller Sales partition and choose *Design Aggregations.*

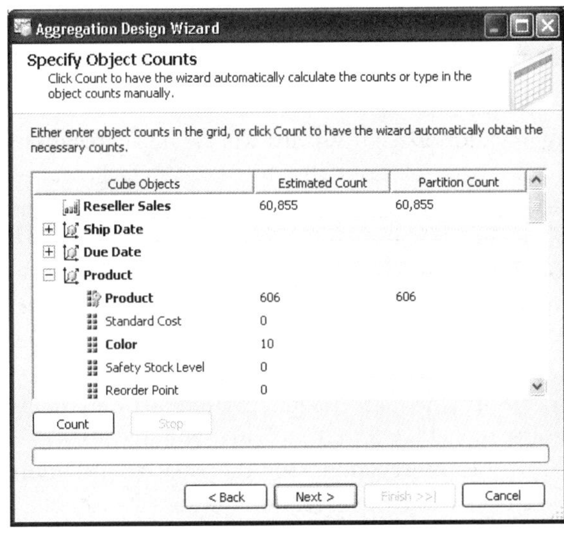

Figure 14.11 Aggregations could be defined only for attributes that form multi-level hierarchies.

4. Click Next on the Specify Storage and Caching Options step to advance to the Specify Object Counts step (Figure 14.11). Bolded attributes shown in the Cube Objects column are those that participate in attribute chains.

5. Click the Count button to let the Aggregation Design Wizard count the members of attributes that participate in attribute chains. Blank partition counts will use the estimated fact table values. You can validate and overwrite the count numbers if needed.

SSAS 2000 In SSAS 2000, you had to set the Member Count property of a dimension *prior* to running the Storage Design Wizard. A Count Dimension Members menu was provided in the Cube Editor to count the dimension members. In SSAS 2005, the Count Dimension Members feature is implemented in the Aggregation Design Wizard. Once the wizard obtains the member count, it updates the *EstimatedCount* property for the affected attributes.

Setting the aggregation options

The Set Aggregation Options step (Figure 14.12) gives you several options to design the number of aggregations.

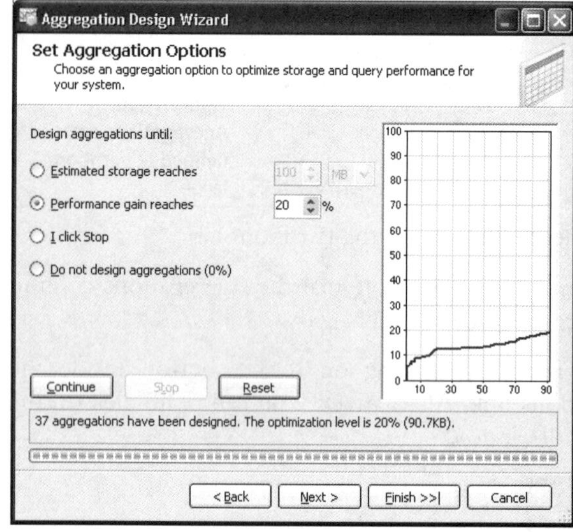

Figure 14.12 The Performance Gain Reaches option is the most useful method for designing aggregations.

The *Estimated storage reaches* option allows you to limit the number of the aggregations by the storage space they take. With this option, the Aggregation Design Wizard will create aggregations until they consume the specified amount of disk space or until the 100 percent aggregation threshold is reached. The estimated storage space is calculated based on the aggregation size and member counts set in the Specify Object Counts step. If the member counts are not accurate, the estimated storage space will be inaccurate too. It's a common error to define a member count limit which will be overtaken by dimension member growth. My recommendation is to enter estimated member counts in the Specify Object Counts step that project the cube growth after one to two years of use.

Use the *Performance gain reaches* option to specify the percentage improvement in query performance that you expect the aggregation design to yield. Contrary to what you may expect, a performance gain of 100% doesn't create all possible aggregations for the selected partition. Instead, it simply means that the wizard will keep on adding aggregations until a hypothetical

100% improvement in query performance is reached. As you can guess, there are no fixed rules to give you the "ultimate" truth. As with other performance-related process optimizations, optimizing the aggregation design is an empirical activity rather than an exact science.

In general, I would recommend you keep the performance gain below 50%. Twenty percent to thirty percent will be adequate for most cubes. Setting it any higher may be counterproductive since it may result in too much of a waste in storage space without substantial performance gain. "The more, the better" principle doesn't play very well here. A good approach is to start with a lower percentage and work up from there if the query performance is not adequate. For example, start with 20% (5-10% with large partitions). If the queries are slow, increase with 5%. If you are still not satisfied with the query performance, repeat the process.

Tip The key to successful aggregation design is to keep increasing the performance gain percentage until you reach the point of diminishing returns. You need to stop when increasing the performance gain percentage doesn't yield additional improvement in the query performance. If the wizard runs for more than 30 minutes or produces many aggregations (more than 100-200), then cube may be too complex for statistical algorithms. If this case, you should collect query logs and use the Usage Based Optimization Wizard.

The *I click Stop* option allows you to start the aggregation and stop it when you are satisfied with the results or when the performance gain reaches 100%. Finally, the *Do not design aggregations* options sets the number of aggregations to zero (no aggregations).

1. Select the *Performance gain reaches* option and enter **20**%.
2. Click the Start button to kick off the aggregation design process. The graph on the right will keep on changing to reflect the current percentage improvement on the y-axis and the estimated storage space taken by the aggregations on the x-axis.

In my example, the wizard has designed 37 aggregations to reach the targeted query optimization level of 20% and has estimated that these aggregations will take about 90KB of storage space.

Completing the wizard

As noted, the Aggregation Design Wizard doesn't actually create the aggregations. To do so, you need to process the affected partition. In the Completing the Wizard step, you have the options to save the aggregation design only or process the cube to create the aggregations.

1. To create the aggregations, choose *Deploy and process now* and click Next.
2. BI Studio brings up the Process Partition dialog and defaults the processing option to *Process Full.* Click Run to process the Reseller Sales partition and create the aggregations. The server builds the MOLAP multidimensional fact table and aggregations in parallel, and indexes them for fast member access.

Tip Creating aggregations for a multi-partition measure group could quickly become tedious. Management Studio allows you to duplicate the aggregation design among partitions in the same measure group. To use this feature, right-click on the target partition and choose *Copy Aggregation Design.* In the Copy Aggregation Design dialog that follows, check all destination partitions that will have the same aggregations as the selected partition.

14.2.3 Usage-Based Optimization

While the Aggregation Design Wizard may suffice for small to medium-size cubes, large cubes can benefit from usage optimization by running the Usage-Based Optimization Wizard. As its name suggests, this wizard will select aggregations based on the server usage, i.e. the actual queries that have been submitted to the server. Once you obtain a representative query statistics, you should run the Usage-Based Optimization Wizard to fine-tune your aggregation design.

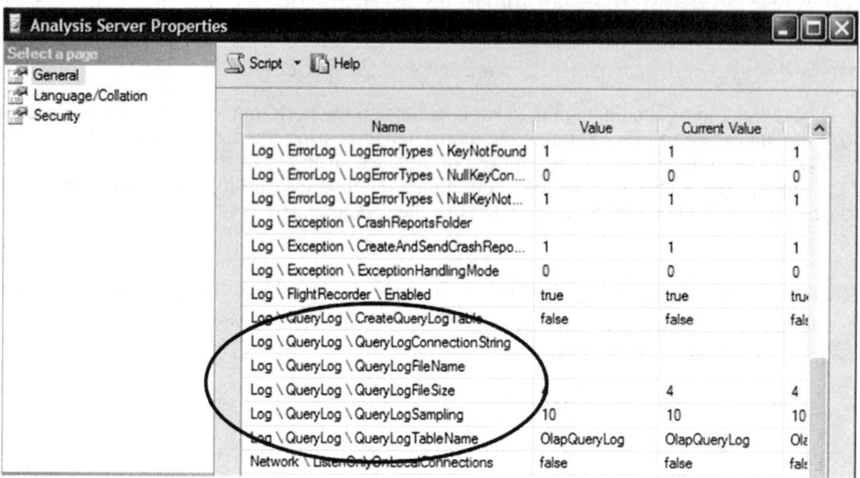

Figure 14.13 You need to enable the Query Log before using the Optimization-Based Wizard.

Enabling the Query Log

How do you get the query statistics? To do so, first you need to enable the server Query Log feature. The Query Log captures the query activity as client applications interact with the server. It can be hosted in any data source that comes with OLE DB or .NET provider. Alternatively, if operational requirements prevent logging to the relational database, the Query Log can be saved to a flat file. Follow these steps to enable the SSAS Query Log:

1. In Management Studio, open the SSAS Server Properties dialog (Figure 14.13).
2. For the purposes of our demo, we will create the Query Log table in the AdventureWorksDW relational database. Locate the *CreateQueryLogTable* setting and change its value to *true*.
3. Click the "..." button inside the Value cell for the *QueryLogConnectionString* and use the Connection Manager dialog to set up a connection to the AdventureWorksDW relational database.
4. By default, the server captures every tenth query that is sent to the server (the *QueryLogSampling* setting is 10). To get enough query statistics fast, change the *QueryLogSampling* to **1** to capture all of the queries sent to the server.
5. You can use the *QueryLogTableName* setting to specify the name of the QueryLog table. By default, the server will name the table *OlapQueryLog*. Click OK to create the Query table. Connect to the SQL Server that you specified in the connection string and verify that the OlapQueryLog is created in the AdventureWorksDW database. The Query Log changes take effect immediately without having to restart the server.

	MSOLAP_Datab...	MSOLAP_ObjectPath	MSOLAP_User	Dataset	StartTime	Duration
▶	SOS OLAP	NW8000.SOS OLAP.SOS OLAP.Fact Currency Rate	NULL	10,000000001001	7/26/2005 10:22...	100
	SOS OLAP	NW8000.SOS OLAP.SOS OLAP.Fact Sales Quota	NW8000\teo	0000000000000000000000,1000000000...	7/26/2005 10:23...	0
	SOS OLAP	NW8000.SOS OLAP.SOS OLAP.Fact Sales Quota	NW8000\teo	0000000000000000100000,1100000000...	7/26/2005 10:23...	0
	SOS OLAP	NW8000.SOS OLAP.SOS OLAP.Fact Sales Quota	NW8000\teo	0000000000000000100000,1110000000...	7/26/2005 10:23...	0
	SOS OLAP	NW8000.SOS OLAP.SOS OLAP.Fact Sales Quota	NW8000\teo	0000000000000000000000,0000000000...	7/26/2005 10:23...	0
	SOS OLAP	NW8000.SOS OLAP.SOS OLAP.Fact Sales Quota	NW8000\teo	0000000000000000000000,1000000000...	7/26/2005 10:23...	0
	SOS OLAP	NW8000.SOS OLAP.SOS OLAP.Fact Internet Sales	NW8000\teo	00000000001,00,0000000000000000,0...	7/26/2005 10:23...	0
	SOS OLAP	NW8000.SOS OLAP.SOS OLAP.Fact Currency Rate	NW8000\teo	10,100000001001	7/26/2005 10:23...	20
	SOS OLAP	NW8000.SOS OLAP.SOS OLAP.Fact Internet Sales	NW8000\teo	10000000001,00,0000000000000000,0...	7/26/2005 10:23...	330

Figure 14.14 The Query Log table captures the query statistics, including the targeted measure group and attributes.

Populating the Query Log

In real-life you should give the Query Log enough time to capture a representative query set, e.g. capture queries for a week or a month. For test purposes, spend some time browsing the SOS OLAP cube to populate the Query Log table. Once you are done with the logging, you can disable the Query Log by changing the QueryLogSampling setting to 0.

Let's take a moment to see what gets captured in the Query Log table. In the Adventure-WorksDW database, right-click on the OlapQueryLog table and choose *Open Table* to browse the table data (Figure 14.14). Despite its name, the Query Log table doesn't capture the actual query statements. If this is needed, you can use the SQL Server Profiler to save the SSAS trace to a file. The most important column in the Query Log table is the *Dataset* column. It captures the attributes that were used to satisfy the query. As noted in the preceding chapter, the server uses the results from the Query Subcube event to populate this column.

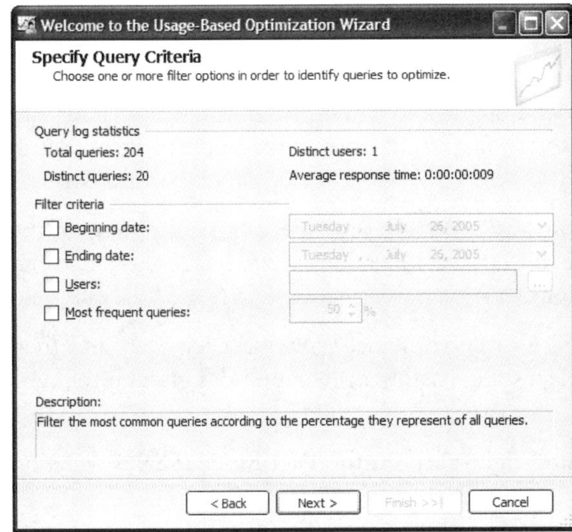

Figure 14.15 Use the Specify Query Criteria step of the Usage-Based Optimization Wizard to filter the captured queries.

Running the Usage-Based Optimization Wizard

Once you have the Query Log populated, you are ready to create usage-based aggregations. You can do so using BI Studio or Management Studio. Both options will start the Usage-Based Optimization Wizard.

1. In BI Studio, open the SOS OLAP cube in the Cube Designer and flip to the Partitions tab.

2. Expand the Reseller Sales measure group pane. Right-click on the Fact Reseller Sales partition and choose *Usage Based Optimization.*

   The Specify Query Criteria step (Figure 14.15) shows a summary of the query statistics. For example, in my case, the Query Log table has captured 204 queries. You can use the *Filter criteria* to select a subset of the captured queries.

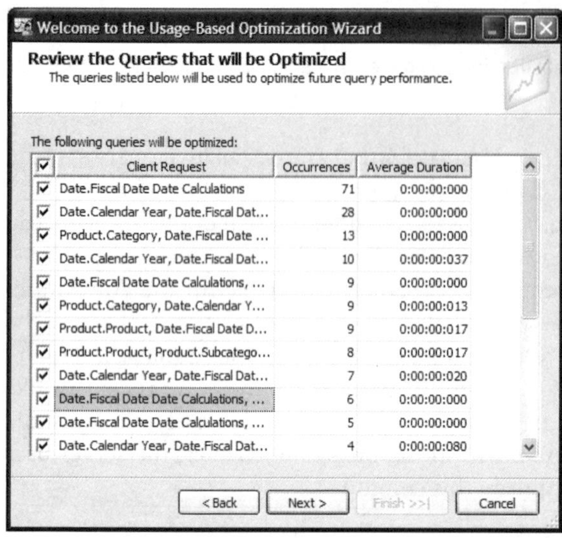

Figure 14.16 You can exclude queries from usage-based optimization.

3. Click Next to advance to the *Review the Queries that will be optimized* step (Figure 14.16). The wizard groups the identical queries and shows the names of the attributes that were used to satisfy the query. By default, all queries will be used for the aggregation design but you could filter out queries. For example, if a given query executes very fast, it may not make sense to include it in the usage-based optimization process.
4. The wizard steps that follow *Review the Queries that will be optimized* are identical to the steps of the Aggregation Design Wizard. Since the Usage Based Optimization Wizard takes as an input known query patterns, I would recommend you use a large performance gain (e.g. 70-80%).
5. In the Set Aggregation Options step, enter **80**% as a performance gain and click Start and then Continue. The Usage Optimization Wizard replaces the existing aggregation design with the new design.
6. After completing the Optimization Based Wizard, right-click on the Fact Reseller Sales partition and choose *Process* to create the aggregations.

Let's sum up our discussion about aggregation design and provide some recommendations. At design time, use the Aggregation Design Wizard to create aggregations needed to reach 20% performance gain. Once the cube is in production for a while, collect query logs and run the Usage-Based Optimization Wizard to prepare a more accurate design. Another practical approach, especially with large cubes, is to deploy the cube to production with no aggregations to save storage space and processing time. Next, once you've collected enough query statistics, add usage-based aggregations incrementally until the desired query performance goal is reached.

14.2.4 Examining the Aggregation Design

It may be interesting to examine the aggregation designs produced by the wizards. This will help you understand better what a UDM aggregation is. The easiest way to examine the aggregation designs is to use the AMO Browser application that is included with the SSAS samples. By default, the AMO browser is installed in the C:\Program Files\Microsoft SQL Server\90\Samples\Analysis Services\Programmability\AMO\AmoBrowser folder. As its name suggests, the AMO Browser is used to browse the SSAS metadata. Follow these steps to examine the aggregations in the SOS OLAP database.

1. Open the AMO Browser project in VS.NET and hit Ctrl+F5 to run the application.
2. Enter the name of the SSAS server you want to connect to and click Connect.
3. In the metadata tree, expand the server and Databases node. Next, expand the SOS OLAP database and the SOS OLAP cube.
4. Expand the MeasureGroups node and the Reseller Sales measure group under it.
5. One of the child nodes of the Reseller Sales measure group is AggregationDesigns (see Figure 14.17). In my case, there are six aggregation designs. Your results may vary.
6. Expand one of the aggregation designs.

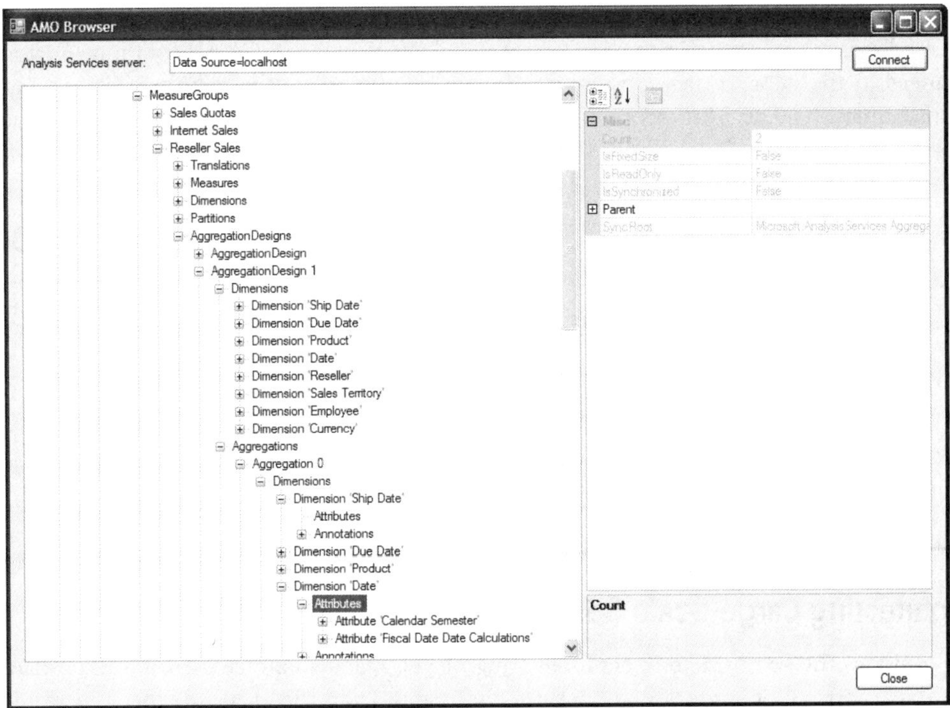

Figure 14.17 Use the AMO Browser application to examine the aggregation design.

The Dimensions node lists the dimensions that join the measure group. If you drill down the Aggregations node, you will see a list of aggregations. If you expand further the Dimensions node below a given aggregation, you will notice that there is Attributes node. That's because a UDM aggregation is an aggregated subtotal based on combination of *attributes* (not hierarchies as with SSAS 2000). Some dimension aggregations have empty Attributes node. For example, the Ship Date dimension has no attributes (no pre-calculated aggregations). In the absence of attributes, the dimension will be subtotaled at the All level of its attributes.

For other dimensions, the wizards may have decided to create pre-calculated attribute totals that could be used to subtotal the dimensions. For example, when subtotaling the Date dimension, the server will use the Calendar Semester and Fiscal Date Date Calculations (produced by the Time Intelligence Wizard) attribute aggregations. Again, this ties with the notion that the attributes are the building blocks of the dimension.

The Aggregation Design Wizard (during design time) and Usage-Based Optimization Wizard (during runtime) discover which attributes could be useful to subtotal the dimension. When the cube is processed, the server uses the aggregation design produced by the wizard to pre-calculate the attribute totals per dimension. When a query requests a dimension with aggregations, the calculation engine uses the pre-calculated attribute totals. The second way to examine the aggregations is to generate a CREATE script for the database in Management Studio. Once the XML script is generated, search for the *<AggregationDesigns>* element. You will find the aggregations below that element.

14.3 Optimizing Storage

I would like to discuss this section in the context of a real-life large-scale OLAP solution. As you will see, changes to the cube storage design can dramatically improve the cube processing and query response times. The real-life project I am referring to utilized SSAS 2000 but the same concepts apply moving forward to SSAS 2005.

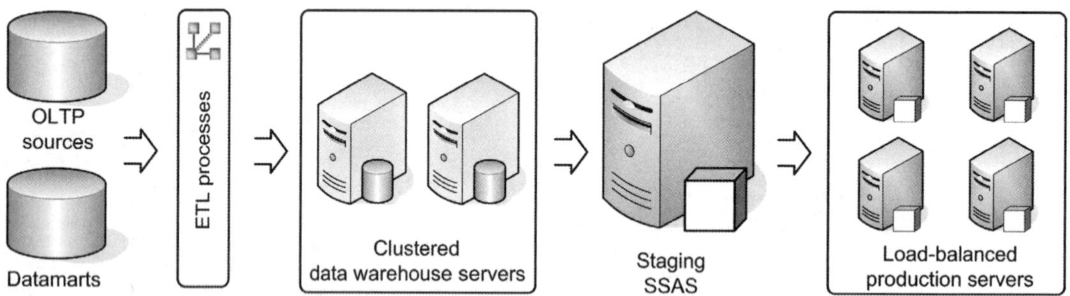

Figure 14.18 With Microsoft Windows OS and SSAS, you can build large-scale, highly-available SSAS solutions.

14.3.1 Architecting Large-Scale SSAS Sites

Figure 14.18 outlines the solution architecture at a high level. Data is extracted from OLTP data sources and data marts. ETL processes transform the raw data and load it into the data warehouse. A designated staging server was used to build and validate the SSAS cubes. Finally, the cubes from the staging server were replicated to four production servers. Since SSAS 2000 doesn't provide database synchronization capabilities, the cubes were replicated by copying the physical data folder containing the cube data. This approach is not supported with SSAS 2005. Instead, use the database synchronization feature.

Designing for high availability

One of the key project challenges was to implement a highly available OLAP solution. A highly-available site continues to perform even if individual servers within that site crash as a result of software or hardware outages. To achieve high availability, the team followed the reference architecture outlined in the paper *Creating Large-Scale, Highly Available OLAP Sites* by David Wickert (see Resources). I hope Microsoft will provide an updated version of this excellent resource in the near future.

Windows Clustering

Windows Clustering was used to cluster the database and SSAS servers. Windows Clustering (available in Windows 2000 and 2003 Advanced Server editions) supports two clustering technologies. Microsoft Cluster Server (MSCS) provides failover support for database servers. MSCS requires both servers to have identical hardware. The two data warehouse servers were configured in a database (back-end) MSCS cluster in active-to-passive mode. In this mode, only one server is active at a time. In case the primary server crashes, the backup server is activated and takes over the cluster.

Network Load Balancing

Windows Advanced Server also provides Network Load Balancing (NLB) technology that balances the incoming traffic among servers (nodes) configured in a web farm. Unlike MSCS, with NLB servers participating in the web farm can have different hardware configurations. The four production (presentation) SSAS servers were configured in a web farm using Network Load Balancing.

NLB was set up in *multiple host* configuration mode in which all nodes handle incoming requests. An SSAS client sends query requests to the virtual IP address of the cluster. NLB maintains utilization statistics of all clustered servers and sends the request to the least utilized server. In this way, the SSAS site can scale out almost linearly by adding new servers to the NLB cluster.

Designing for scalability

Another key challenge in this project was scaling out to both large data volumes and high utilization. Here, by the term *large*, I mean a solution that needs to accommodate hundreds of gigabytes of data. To bring some dose of reality, the solution had to meet the following scalability requirements:

- Support three fact tables with 200 million rows.
- Scale to potentially 20,000 end-users generating reports against the presentation cubes.
- Maintain average query response time below 10 seconds (as recommended by the FASMI guidelines).

As you would probably imagine, an OLAP site of such magnitude brings a completely new "dimension". It was estimated that fully processing the non-optimized SSAS database could take 8-16 hours! There were several techniques that the team used to optimize processing and performance but the one that yielded a quantum leap in performance was *partitioning*.

14.3.2 Optimizing Partition Storage

A partition represents the physical storage medium for measure groups. A measure group can have one or more partitions. Small to medium-sized cubes may provide adequate performance with a single partition per measure group. With large data volumes, partitions provide the means to scale out your UDM. For that reason, partitioning is only available with the SSAS Enterprise Edition.

Partition, partition, partition

The main reason for creating partitions is to minimize the cube processing times. That's because when a measure group is partitioned, partitions can be processed independently of each other. For example, it makes sense to process new data more frequently because it is more volatile. At the same time, historical data (e.g. data that is a few years old) may seldom be changed and may require only occasional processing.

In addition, SSAS 2005 supports processing partitions in parallel without requiring any additional configuration steps. In comparison, SSAS 2000 provided no direct support for parallelizing partition processing. Instead, you had to use a special utility. You should always try to perform tasks in parallel to utilize the server resources better. For example, the team noticed that only one to two processors in the staging server (out of eight available) were utilized when SSAS objects were processed sequentially. Not only did parallel partition processing distribute the server utilization more efficiently, but it also led to processing 90 K rows/sec. In other words, instead of the initial enormous processing times, it was possible to process a fact table with 100 million rows in 20 minutes!

Partitioning could also improve query performance. That's because queries can be satisfied by a single partition and return results faster due to the smaller dataset being accessed. Having stressed the importance of partitioning, let's find out what an SSAS partition is and how to optimize the UDM storage with partitions.

Understanding partitions

As with the other components of the SSAS storage architecture, partitions are totally transparent to client applications. The administrator can add or remove partitions to/from measure groups at will. A measure group returns the combined data from all partitions. New partitions must be processed before their data can be accessed. Each partition in a measure group can have (a) different:

- *Fact table* – As long as fact tables share the same schema, different partitions may be based on different fact tables.
- *Storage settings* – MOLAP, HOLAP, or ROLAP. For example, recent data which is heavily queried could be configured for MOLAP, while historical data could remain in the relational database (HOLAP or ROLAP).
- *Proactive caching settings* – For example, a partition with volatile changes can be configured for proactive caching to minimize data latency.
- *Aggregation design* – To optimize the query performance, you may choose to design more aggregations with heavily-utilized partitions, e.g. 30%. In comparison, a historical partition may have minimum or no aggregations whatsoever.
- *Storage location* – An interesting feature that SSAS storage architecture supports is *remote partitions*. A remote partition is processed by another Analysis Services server. In this de-

ployment scenario, the local server receives queries and dispatches them to the remote server. Remote partitions give you additional options to scale a very large UDM.

As you can imagine, partitioning can be a potent and flexible tool to optimize the UDM performance. Let's see how we can split a measure group into partitions.

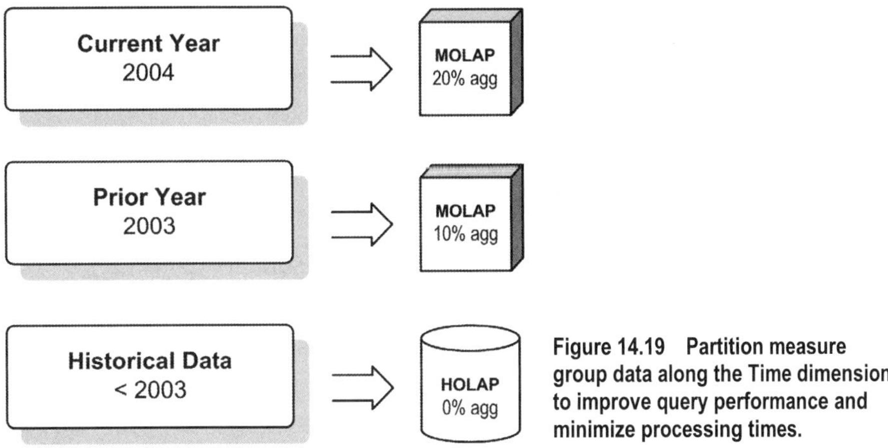

Figure 14.19 Partition measure group data along the Time dimension to improve query performance and minimize processing times.

Designing partitions

As it stands, the Internet Sales measure group in the SOS OLAP cube has some 60,000 rows. This is a trivial job for the SSAS processing engine even if the measure group has a single partition. On my machine, it takes the server six seconds to process the entire measure group. Now, let's think big and imagine that this measure group has one thousand times that number of rows (sixty million rows). Undoubtedly, having so many orders is great news for Adventure Works management, but what does it mean for our SOS OLAP UDM? Assuming linear increase in processing times, now we are talking about 6,000 seconds (around 1.5 hours).

As noted, it is not uncommon for a large data warehouse to store millions and millions of rows, so time spent in processing could become a significant latency factor. Let's see how partitioning can help. Figure 14.19 demonstrates one possible partitioning strategy. You would typically partition measure groups along the Time dimension. For example, we could define three discrete units based on how old the data is. The assumption here is that the more recent the data is, the more frequently it will be changed and the more often it needs to be processed.

First, we have a partition with data for the current year. This is a "hot" partition that will undergo frequent changes, e.g. new orders will be appended at the end of each day. In addition, this storage area will probably take the most queries. Therefore, it makes sense for this partition to have MOLAP storage with a high number of aggregations (e.g. 20%). In terms of processing frequency, this partition is a good candidate for daily processing.

Second, we have a partition that captures data for the previous year. Often, end-users need to compare data between the current period and a parallel period of the prior year. Therefore, we may decide to configure this partition for OLAP too. To minimize the aggregation storage space, we may decide to introduce fewer aggregations, e.g. 10%. This partition has a relatively stable data, so it makes sense to process it less frequently, e.g. once a month.

Finally, we have a partition that holds the company historical data. This partition will be the largest in size and it will be infrequently queried. To minimize processing times and storage space, we could configure the historical partition with HOLAP storage mode and no aggregations. We assume that changes to this partition will happen once in a blue moon, so we may decide to process this partition only on as-needed basis, e.g. when the UDM metadata changes.

Using a partition filter

Now that we've designed the partition storage, let's implement it. For demonstration purposes, I will use the Internet Sales measure group in the SOS OLAP cube. We will start by creating the partition for the historical data that captures orders for years prior than 2003.

SSAS 2000 In SSAS 2000, it was possible to use two criteria in order to specify the partition scope – data slice and partition filter. The data slice option allowed the modeler to slice the cube by a dimension, while the partition filter option used a SQL query. Since UDM is an attribute-based model and, for the most part, attributes map to table columns, having two options is redundant. Therefore, SSAS 2005 supports only the filter option.

1. In Management Studio, connect to the AdventureWorksDW relational database and query the DimTime dimensions table to locate the last member for year 2002 (FullDateAlternateKey = '12/31/2002'). The TimeKey primary key value should be 549. We need the TimeKey value because the DimTime dimension table joins the FactInternetSales fact table by the primary key.
2. Open the SOS OLAP cube in the Cube Designer and switch to the Partitions tab. Expand the Internet Sales measure group. As it stands, the Internet Sales measure group has only one partition (Fact Internet Sales) which is configured for HOLAP storage.
3. If the HOLAP partition has any aggregations (percentage aggregations is greater than 0%), run the Aggregation Design Wizard and in the Set Aggregations Options step, select the *Do not design aggregations (0%)* option to remove all existing aggregations.
4. Click inside the Source column and press the "..." button to open the Partition Source dialog (Figure 14.20). By default, a measure group has a single partition which is bound to the entire fact table (the partition Binding type is *Table Binding*).

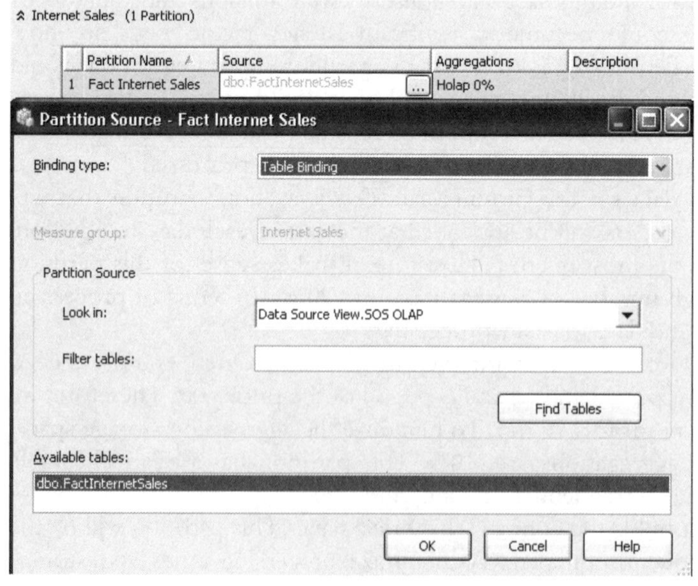

Figure 14.20 By default, a measure group has a single partition which is bound to entire fact table with Table Binding option.

5. Expand the Binding type dropdown and select *Query Binding*. When you do this, BI Studio replaces the partition table binding with a SELECT query (Figure 14.21).

Warning The SELECT query with the Query Binding option represents the partition filter. The partition filter specifies which rows from the fact table will be loaded into the partition. As the warning message at the bottom says, when defining multiple partitions within a measure group, it is very important to specify the WHERE clause correctly so no rows are lost or duplicated. You can use any WHERE clause to filter the returned rows (stored procedures cannot be used).

6. By default the query retrieves all fact table columns and it contains an empty WHERE clause. To scope the partition for all data prior to year 2003, change the WHERE clause to:

```
WHERE OrderDateKey <= 549
```

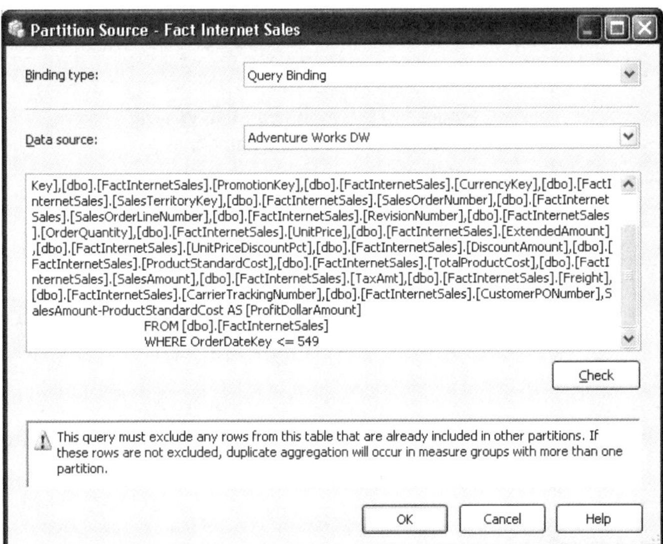

Figure 14.21 Create a partition filter by specifying a WHERE clause for the source query.

7. Click the Check button to verify the SQL syntax. Click OK to create the partition.

8. Back to the Partitions tab, right click on the Fact Internet Sales partition and choose *Rename Partition*. Change the partition name in-place to **Historical Sales**.

Creating a new partition

Let's now create a partition for the prior year. Querying the DimTime table again, we determine that the TimeKey value for December 31st 2003 is 914. Therefore the 2003 partition will include all fact rows where TimeKey is between 550 and 914 inclusive.

1. In the Partitions tab of the Cube Designer, select the Historical Sales partition and click the New Partition toolbar button or click on the New Partition link below the partition. BI Studio launches the Partition Wizard. Click Next to advance to the Specify Source Information step.

The Internet Sales measure group is pre-selected in the *Measure group* dropdown. The partition data doesn't necessarily have to reside in the same fact table or relational database. For example, you may have separate fact tables for years 2002 and 2003. You use any table as a partition source provided that it has the same structure as the original partition.

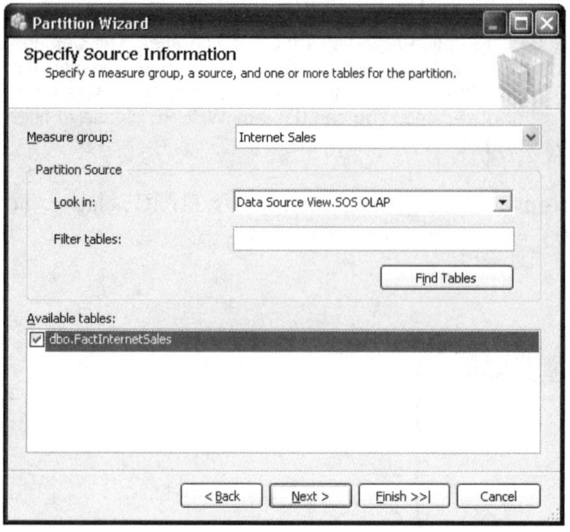

Figure 14.22 Use the Partition Wizard at design time to create additional partitions.

2. Check the FactInternetSales fact table and click Next.
3. In the Restrict Rows step, specify the following WHERE clause for the partition filter query:

```
WHERE OrderDateKey >= 550 AND OrderDateKey <= 914
```

4. Click Next to advance to the Processing and Storage Locations step (Figure 14.23).
5. As noted, a partition can be defined on the local server (the server where the rest of the UDM resides) or on a remote server. Accept the default settings and click Next to define the new partition as local.

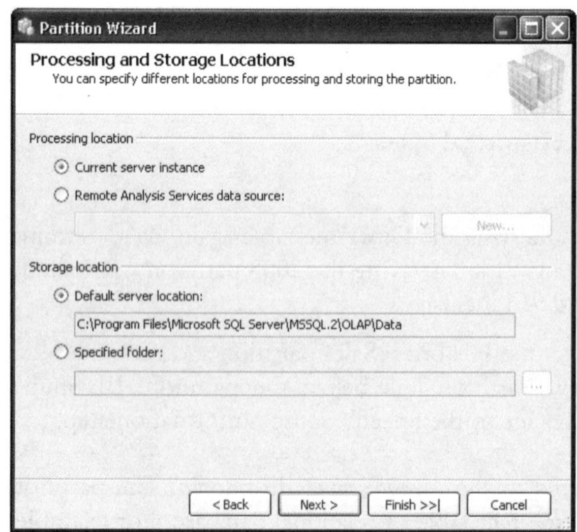

Figure 14.23 Use the Processing and Storage Locations step to configure the partition as local or remote.

6. In the Completing the Wizard step, name the new partition **2003 Internet Sales**. You also have a choice to proceed with designing aggregations for the partition (default option), create the partition with no aggregations, or copy the aggregation design from another partition in the same measure group. Accept the default aggregation option and click Finish to launch the Aggregation Design Wizard.
7. Configure the 2003 Internet Sales for MOLAP storage mode with 10% aggregation design.
8. Finally, create a **2004 Internet Sales** partition with the following filter:

```
WHERE OrderDateKey >= 915 and OrderDateKey <= 1280
```

9. Configure the 2004 Internet Sales partition for MOLAP storage mode with 20% aggregations.
10. Back to the Partitions tab, select all the three partitions. To do so, hold Ctrl key and click on each one of them or use the Shift key for continuous selection. Right-click on the selected partitions and choose *Process*. Confirm the BI dialog to deploy the changes.
11. The Process Objects dialog should list the three partitions. Click on the Change Settings button to verify that by default the server will process the partitions in parallel. Click OK to close the Change Setting dialog and click Run to process the partitions.

As noted, you can process partitions individually. For example, if data changes are restricted to the 2004 Internet Sales partition, you can minimize processing time by processing that partition only.

Merging partitions

Management Studio allows you to merge two partitions into a single partition. Why merge partitions? In some cases consolidating partitions may improve the query performance. For example, you may scope your partitions at a month level to minimize the cube processing time. However, after the monthly data is processed, you can merge the partitions so that annual reports could access a single partition instead of accessing twelve partitions.

Two partitions can be merged if they have the same storage and aggregations design. If the partitions have different aggregation design, before you merge them you can copy the aggregation design from one partition to the other. To do so, in Management Studio, right-click on the partition you want to change and choose *Copy Aggregation Design*. Follow these steps to merge the 2004 Internet Sales partition into the 2003 Internet Sales partition.

1. Right-click on the 2004 Internet Sales partition and choose Copy Aggregation Design. In the Copy Aggregation Design dialog, select the 2003 Internet Sales partition and choose OK. Process the Internet Sales partition.
2. Right-click on the 2003 Internet Sales partition and choose *Merge Partitions*.
3. In the Merge Partitions dialog (Figure 14.24), select the 2004 Internet Sales partition and choose OK. Process the Internet Sales Partition.

Management Studio will merge the data from the 2004 Internet Sales partition into the 2003 Internet Sales partition and will delete the 2004 Internet Sales partition. I would also recommend you review the partition filter after the partition merge to make sure that it is set correctly.

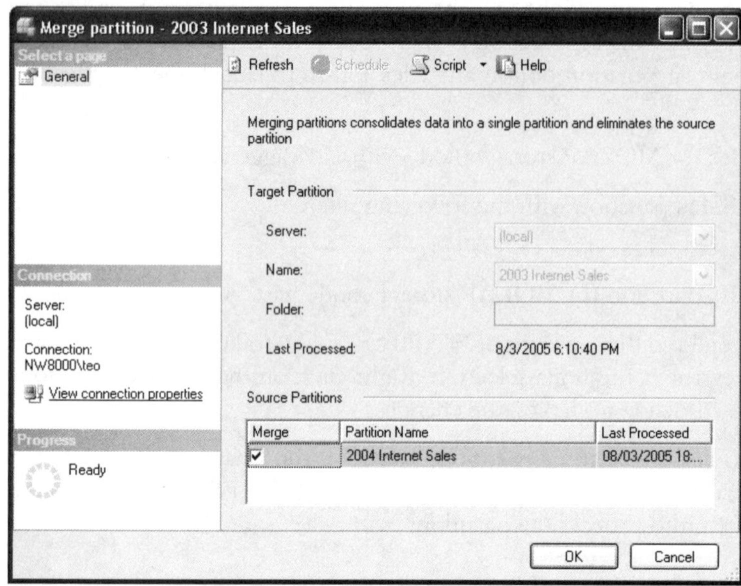

Figure 14.24 You can merge two partitions into one with Management Studio.

You would probably agree that partitions introduce an ample opportunity for automating management tasks. For example, you may want to automate creating new partitions and deleting old ones. Provided that you are willing to put in some AMO programming effort, you can easily automate partition management tasks. Next, I will walk you through two scenarios that demonstrate how this could be done. The first one uses an SSAS stored procedure, while the second leverages the SSIS Create Partition task.

14.3.3 Creating Partitions Programmatically with AMO

Suppose that you need to create a new partition every *N* months. Instead of defining a recurring monthly appointment in your Outlook calendar and manually creating partitions, you could write some AMO code to perform this task for you. One way of implementing this scenario is to create an SSAS stored procedure and schedule its execution with the SQL Server Agent service.

To make this scenario more flexible, the stored procedure could take as input parameters the target cube, the containing measure group (where the partition needs to be created), and the time span for the partition (e.g. in months). For easier testing and troubleshooting of the AMO code, you may find it more convenient to implement the programming logic as a .NET application first. Once the application is tested, you can easily migrate it to an SSAS stored procedure. Enclosed in the Ch14 solution, you will find a Partition Manager application that we will later migrate to an SSAS stored procedure.

Introducing the Partition Manager

The Partition Manager is implemented as a Visual Basic.NET console application. A console application doesn't have UI. Instead, it reads from the standard input device (usually the keyboard) and writes to the standard output device (usually the monitor). Console applications are great for quickly testing programming code. The core partition logic is encapsulated in the Create Partition procedure (Listing 14.1).

Listing 14.1 Creating partitions programmatically is easy with AMO

```
Public Sub CreatePartition(ByVal cubeName As String, _
      ByVal measureGroupName As String, ByVal months As Integer)

   Dim part As Partition
   Dim mg As MeasureGroup
   Dim maxOrderDateKey As Integer = 0
   Dim svr As New Server()

   svr.Connect("Data Source=(local)")

   Dim db As Database = svr.Databases.GetByName("SOS OLAP")
   Dim cube As Cube = db.Cubes.GetByName(cubeName)

   mg = cube.MeasureGroups.GetByName(measureGroupName)
   ' Get the last partition
   part = mg.Partitions(mg.Partitions.Count - 1)

   If TypeOf part.Source Is QueryBinding = False Then
       Throw New ApplicationException("The partition must have Query Binding")
   End If

   ' Get the last date index from the partition query
   Dim lastDateIndex = GetLastDateIndex(part)

   ' Get the new date index.
   Dim newDateIndex As Integer = GetNewDateIndex(lastDateIndex, months)

   ' If there are no enough data in the partition, exit
   If newDateIndex = 0 Then
       Return
   End If

   ' Get the fact table name from the old partition
   Dim factTableName As String = GetFactTableName(CType(part.Source,_
     QueryBinding).QueryDefinition.ToLower())
   ' Create a new partition
   part = mg.Partitions.Add(measureGroupName & " _" & newDateIndex)
   part.StorageMode = StorageMode.Molap

    ' Create the query text
   Dim queryText As String = String.Format("SELECT * FROM {0} WHERE " _
     & "OrderDateKey >= {1} and OrderDateKey <= {2}", factTableName,_
     lastDateIndex + 1, newDateIndex)
   part.Source = New QueryBinding(db.DataSources(0).ID, queryText)
   ' Save the changes
   part.Update()
   ' Process the partition
   part.Process()
   svr.Disconnect()
End Sub
```

This procedure is loosely based on the *CreatePartitions* SSAS stored procedure that is included in the AmoAdventureWorks project (part of the SSAS samples). The major difference is that AmoAdventureWorks saves the last date index (the upper boundary of the new partition) in the partition metadata in the form of an *annotation*.

Note An *annotation* is an open-ended property collection that most UDM objects support. It allows the programmer to save some data (in a name-value format) as part of the object metadata. For example, if you want the partition to "remember" the last date it was processed, you could programmatically create a new partition annotation to preserve the date. The next time the procedure is run, it could read the date from the partition annotation.

My version takes a more flexible approach by retrieving the last date index from the filter query. The easiest way to explain how *CreatePartition* works is to walk you through its code. The first several lines of code are nothing that you haven't seen so far. The code connects to the server, references the SOS OLAP database, then the cube name, and finally the requested measure group. Next, the code references the most recent partition from the *Partitions* collection of the measure group.

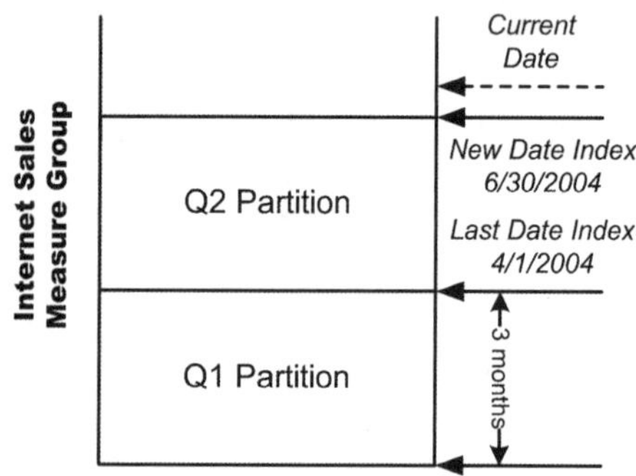

Figure 14.25 Calculating the partition scope is done by retrieving the last date index (the upper boundary of the most recent partition) and adding the requested number of months.

Determining the partition scope

The code checks if the partition is bound to a query. For example, if there is only one partition in the Partition collection, most likely it is bound to the entire table (DsvTableBinding). In this case, it is meaningless to create a new partition and the code throws an exception. Figure 14.25 depicts how CreatePartition determines the new partition scope assuming that a new partition is created every 3 months. In this case, there is an existing partition for the first quarter of 2004. The code calls the *GetLastDateIndex* helper function (not shown in the listing), which parses the partition query of the most recent partition to return the last date index. For example, if the query WHERE clause for the Q1 partition is *WHERE OrderDateKey >= 550 AND OrderDateKey <= 914*, GetLastDateIndex will return 914. Incrementing the result with one (915) gives us the starting index of the new partition.

At this point, we have the lower boundary of the new partition. The only missing piece is the new boundary which we have to compute by adding three months. The tricky part here is that we need to translate the last date index to the actual date from the DimTime dimension in order to perform the date arithmetic. This is what the *GetNewDateIndex* function does (not shown in the listing). It uses ADO.NET to query the DimTime dimension table in order to retrieve the actual date (FullDateAlternateKey column) related to the last date index. Next, *GetNewDateIndex* adds the requested number of months to compute the end date of the partition (6/30/2004). If the current date is exceeding the end date, it's time to create a new partition. *GetNewDateIndex* derives the new date index by retrieving the TimeKey value from DimTime corresponding to the end date. If the current date is less than the end date, *GetNewDateIndex* returns zero.

Setting the partition filter

Once *CreatePartition* receives the new date index, it proceeds by creating the new partition. It calls the *GetFactTableName* helper function to retrieve the name of the fact table from the filter query of the old partition. Next, it creates the new partition and configures it for MOLAP storage. Then, it constructs the filter query with a WHERE clause that specifies the scope of the partition and binds it to the partition *Source* property. The *partition.Update* method persists the changes to the server. Finally, we process the partition. At this point, the partition is available for querying from client applications.

Converting Partition Manager to SSAS stored procedure

To make the most use out of the Partition Manager, you will probably want to schedule it so it executes on a regular basis in an unattended mode, e.g. every day. One way to accomplish this is to convert the Partition Manager to an SSAS stored procedure that is scheduled to run with the SQL Server Agent service. As an added benefit, the stored procedure runs under the context of the database it is deployed to, so you don't have to worry about the server and database connection details. Converting the Partition Manager is simple. You can find the *CreatePartition* stored procedure in the Adventure Works Extensibility project.

1. In the Adventure Works Extensibility project, create a reference to the Analysis Management Object library.
2. Copy the CreatePartition function from the PartitionManager and paste it into the StoredProcedures.vb source file.
3. Instead of specifying the server name when connecting with AMO, connect to SSAS as:

```
svr.Connect("*")
```

4. To take advantage of the current execution context, reference the SOS OLAP database as:

```
Dim db As Database = svr.Databases.GetByName(Context.CurrentDatabaseName)
```

5. Build the Adventure Works Extensibility project.
6. Assuming that the SOS OLAP project already has a reference to AdventureWorks, deploy the SOS OLAP project to deploy the updated AdventureWorks assembly to the server.

Automating the stored procedure execution

At this point, the stored procedure is deployed and ready for execution. Unlike the rest of the stored procedures we've authored, you probably don't want to call CreatePartition from an MDX expression or a query. That's because this stored procedure is not designed to extend MDX. Instead, it may be preferable to execute CreatePartition in a standalone mode, similar to the way you can execute a SQL Server stored procedure with the *EXECUTE* statement. The SSAS equivalent of the EXECUTE statement is the *CALL* statement.

1. Connect to the SQL Server on which you want to schedule the CreatePartition execution.
2. Create a new SQL Server Agent Job called *Create Partition.*
3. Create a single step for the Create Partition job and configure it as shown in Figure 14.26.

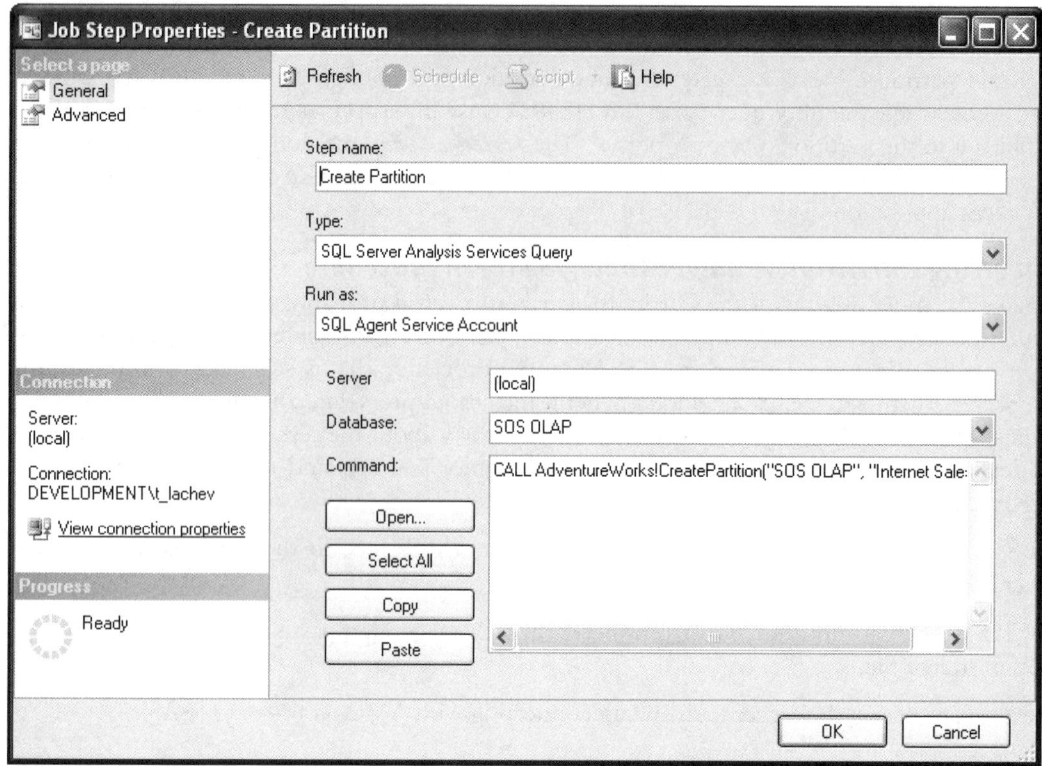

Figure 14.26 Use the CALL statement to execute SSAS maintenance stored procedures.

The step type is *SQL Server Analysis Services Query*. The command text is

```
CALL AdventureWorks!CreatePartition("SOS OLAP", "Internet Sales", 3)
```

In this case, the *CreatePartition* stored procedure will add a new partition to the Internet Sales measure group in the SOS OLAP cube every three months. As a final step, configure the job to run on a regular schedule, e.g. every day.

14.3.4 Generating Partitions with SSIS

Another way to automate partition maintenance tasks is with an SSIS package. This approach is demonstrated by the SyncAdvWorksPartitions project which is included with the SSIS samples. The default location of the SyncAdvWorksPartitions project is C:\Program Files\Microsoft SQL Server\90\Samples\Integration Services\Package Samples\SyncAdvworksPartitions Sample. The SyncAdvWorksPartitions sample was harvested from project REAL. I highly recommend you review the project REAL resources for additional business intelligence best practices and tips (see Resources). The SyncAdvWorksPartitions project includes a single package called *Sync Partitions* (Figure 14.27).

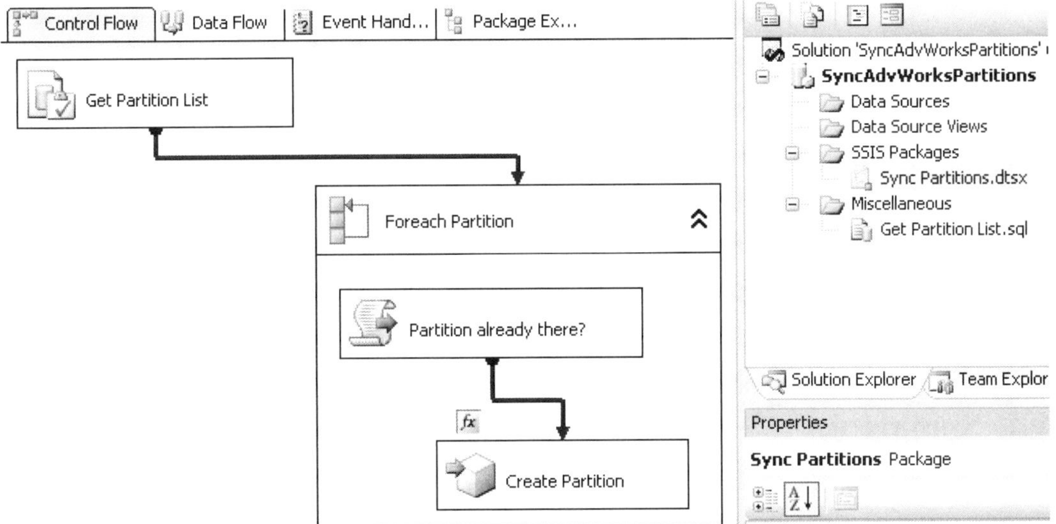

Figure 14.27 Use the CALL statement to execute SSAS maintenance stored procedures.

Let me walk you briefly through the package implementation. First, the Get Partition List task executes a complex SQL statement against the AdventureWorksDW database. The statement includes several SELECT statements that segment the fact tables in several date ranges (Figure 14.28).

Internet_Sales_2001	SELECT [dbo].[FactInternetSales].[ProductKey],[dbo].[FactInternetSales].[OrderDateKey],[dbo].[FactInterne...	1	184
Internet_Sales_2002	SELECT [dbo].[FactInternetSales].[ProductKey],[dbo].[FactInternetSales].[OrderDateKey],[dbo].[FactInterne...	185	549
Internet_Sales_2003	SELECT [dbo].[FactInternetSales].[ProductKey],[dbo].[FactInternetSales].[OrderDateKey],[dbo].[FactInterne...	550	914
Internet_Sales_2004	SELECT [dbo].[FactInternetSales].[ProductKey],[dbo].[FactInternetSales].[OrderDateKey],[dbo].[FactInterne...	915	1158

Figure 14.28 The Sync Partitions package uses a SQL SELECT statement to retrieve the partitions to be created.

Each row in the resulting rowset represents a single partition. This rowset is then sent to the *Foreach Partition* loop container. The Foreach Partition task enumerates the rowset one row at a time and passes each row to the *Partition already there* Script Task. The VB.NET logic in the script tasks uses AMO to find out if the partition with that name already exists. If no matching partition is found, the *Partition already there* task prepares a DDL script to create the partition. Assuming that the package creates the Internet Sales measure group, the abbreviated script may look like:

```
<Create xmlns="http://schemas.microsoft.com/analysisservices/2003/engine">
    <ParentObject>
     <DatabaseID>SOS OLAP</DatabaseID
     <CubeID>SOS OLAP</CubeID
     <MeasureGroupID>Internet Sales</MeasureGroupID>
    </ParentObject>
   <ObjectDefinition>
        <Partition xmlns:xsd=http://www.w3.org/2001/XMLSchema
       xmlns:xsi="http://www.w3.org/2001/XMLSchema-instance>
         <ID>Internet_Orders_2004</ID>
      <Name>Internet_Orders_2004</Name>
      <Source xsi:type="QueryBinding">
```

```
        <DataSourceID>Adventure Works DW</DataSourceID>
          <QueryDefinition>
      SELECT ... WHERE OrderDateKey >=185 AND OrderDateKey <= 549
        </QueryDefinition>
      </Source
         </Partition>
   </ObjectDefinition>
</Create>
```

Finally, the script is sent to a SQL Server Analysis Services Execute DDL Task (*Create Partition*). You can use this task to send any DDL statement (CREATE, ALTER, DROP) to an SSAS server. In this case, the CREATE PARTITION statement instructs the server to create a new partition. As you can see, AMO and SSIS provide flexible ways to automate partition management tasks.

14.4 Summary

Partition and dimension storage designs have important ramifications on the query performance and processing time. In general, UDM performs best with MOLAP. Consider using HOLAP with very large databases. ROLAP is almost never a good choice. The easiest way to increase the query performance is to design useful aggregations. At design time, you can do so by running the Aggregation Design Wizard. Once the cube is deployed and you have query statistics available, consider refining the aggregation design with the Usage-Based Optimization Wizard to reflect the actual query patterns. With large-scale cubes, consider partitioning the cube measure groups. Partitions can be processed independently and could have different storage and aggregations settings. For easier maintenance, automate partition management tasks with AMO and SSIS.

14.5 Resources

Optimizing Cube Performance Using Microsoft SQL Server 2000 Analysis Services
(http://shrinkster.com/6op) -- This paper by Unisys discusses the design and implementation of a series of test scenarios that include building and querying cubes using Microsoft SQL Server 2000 and Analysis Services.

Microsoft SQL Server 2000 Analysis Services Performance Guide
(http://shrinkster.com/6pe) -- This paper describes techniques you can use to optimize query responsiveness and processing performance in SSAS. Although originally written for SSAS 2000, many of its findings are still applicable for SSAS 2005.

Project REAL website
(http://shrinkster.com/8kj -- Project REAL demonstrates best practices for creating BI systems with SQL Server 2005.

Chapter 15

Managing Processing

During design time BI Studio shields you from the processing technicalities. It really doesn't matter what processing option you use because, usually, you will be working against relatively small datasets. You can live a happy and oblivious life by letting BI Studio handle object processing for you. However, things change once the cube is deployed to production. Fully processing cubes with terabytes of data may take hours to complete. This may force you to abandon the nonchalant attitude and seek more conservative processing options.

The processing architecture in SSAS 2005 has been expanded significantly to provide flexible options for addressing various processing needs. In fact, the sheer number of processing options may be overwhelming even for veteran SSAS administrators. In this chapter, you will learn how to:

- Differentiate between data and metadata changes.
- Analyze impact of processing UDM objects.
- Fully and incrementally process dimensions and cubes.
- Automate processing tasks.
- Leverage various techniques to implement low-latency OLAP solutions.

You can find the finished code samples for this chapter by opening the Ch15 solution.

15.1 Understanding UDM Processing

In SSAS, by the term *processing* we will mean loading UDM data containing objects with data. Traditionally, OLAP servers including SSAS have relied on pull-mode (explicit) processing. In this mode, the cube is explicitly processed by the administrator or an application (e.g. ETL package). To respond to the demand for building low-latency OLAP solutions, SSAS 2005 offers two new approaches for implicit cube processing, *push-mode processing* and *proactive caching*, which we will look at in section 15.5.

Note Structural changes (dimension or cube definition changes, storage setting changes, etc) always require you explicitly process the UDM. Implicit cube processing and proactive caching options are only applicable when refreshing UDM data. However, adding or removing new measure groups and partitions doesn't affect existing measure groups and partitions and doesn't require re-processing them.

I will start by discussing the pull-mode processing approach which you will probably rely on most often with both classic and transactional OLAP solutions. Different objects require different types of processing but the underlying concept is the same. When data changes in the underlying data source, the processing task (or series of tasks) turns the data changes into multidimensional structures that are ready for querying.

Before continuing any further, I strongly suggest you stop and read the excellent whitepaper *Analysis Services 2005 Processing Architecture* (see Resources) in which T.K. Anand explains the internals of the SSAS 2005 processing architecture. After reading the document, I realized that I don't have much more to say on this subject. Instead, I decided to focus on the practical aspects and implications of processing UDM objects with hands-on examples.

15.1.1 Types of Data Changes

Pull-mode processing supports several options to give you a fine-grained control over the amount of data that is loaded (e.g. all data vs. new data only). To understand how different processing options play together, it may be beneficial to differentiate between metadata and data changes. As noted in the preceding chapter, the cube storage architecture consists of metadata, aggregations, and details.

Metadata changes

The metadata layer is what "ties" the UDM objects together and exposes them as logically related entities (collectively known as a *cube*) to client applications. Dimension and cube metadata changes require fully reprocessing (*Process Full* option) the affected object and its dependent objects. For example, adding a new attribute to a given dimension necessitates fully re-processing the dimension to apply the changes. Consecutively, all cubes that reference that dimension are invalidated and must be fully processed.

It is important to note that dimension data (attribute members) is also part of the cube metadata. For example, adding a new attribute member (e.g. a member *Singapore* to the *Country* attribute hierarchy in the Sales Territory dimension) affects the cube metadata because the end-users could browse the cube data by that member. SSAS provides different options to mitigate the effect of the dimension data changes to cubes that reference it.

Fact data changes

By fact data changes we will mean modifications to data stored in the fact tables. Examples of data changes include adding, changing, or deleting fact rows. These changes are scoped at measure group (partition) level. It is important to differentiate data from metadata changes because data changes don't require re-processing the cube dimensions and invalidating the cube. Instead, you can incrementally process the affected partitions without affecting the rest of the UDM objects. For example, if you know that only data in the FactResellerSales fact table has been changed, you can process the Reseller Sales measure group (all partitions or a specific partition) to apply the changes to the cube.

15.1.2 Analyzing Processing Impact

When estimating the impact analysis of processing a given UDM object, you need to account for its dependencies to other objects in an SSAS database. UDM objects could be intra and/or inter-dependent with one another.

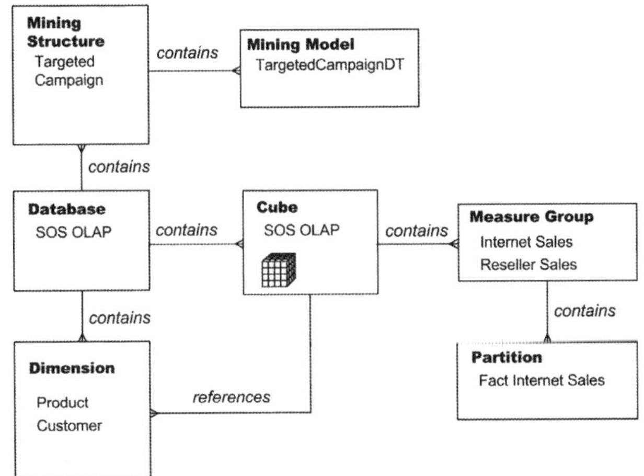

Figure 15.1 When designing your processing steps, you need to account for inter and intra-dependencies among UDM objects.

Intra dependencies

Intra dependencies reflect the relationships among objects in the context of the database object schema. The SSAS database schema shown in Figure 15.1 is meant to help you visualize the intra dependencies among UDM objects. As Figure 15.1 shows, a UDM object may contain other objects. For example, an SSAS database contains mining structures, cubes, and dimensions. Further, a cube contains dimensions and measure groups. Processing a given object always causes recursive processing of its child objects. For example, if you process the entire SSAS database, the server will process all mining structures, cubes, and dimensions in the database.

Tip Fully processing the entire database is the simplest way to process all UDM objects in the database. If processing the database is not very expensive and bringing it offline while processing lasts is not an issue (e.g. overnight scheduled processing), this may very well be everything you need to know about UDM processing.

When processing a given cube, the server will also process the measure groups defined in the cube. Similarly, when processing a measure group, the server will process all of its partitions.

Inter dependencies

Some objects are inter-dependent. In other words, processing object A may affect object B although B is not contained within A. If B is inter-dependent object, when the server processes A, it will invalidate B. The most common example is dimension processing. A dimension may be referenced by one or more cubes. The side effect of fully processing a dimension is invalidating the cubes that reference it. This necessitates fully processing the affected cubes. The *Analysis Services 2005 Processing Architecture* document provides a full list of the inter-object dependencies.

15.2 Processing Dimensions

A cube has one or more dimensions for browsing the cube measures from different angles. As a prerequisite for processing a new cube, you need to process all dimensions that are referenced by the cube. Once the cube is in production, you have to process its dimensions on a regular basis to reflect dimension member changes.

15.2.1 Understanding Dimension Processing

You may be curious what happens when a dimension is processed. As you know, UDM is an attribute-based model. When the server processes a dimension, it constructs an attribute map for each attribute that forms a hierarchy (AttributeHierarchyEnabled = True). When doing so, the server sends a SQL query to the data source to extract the attribute key, name, and value (assuming that the attribute NameColumn and ValueColumn columns are different than KeyColumns). Table 15.1 shows what the query results may look like for the first three members of the Region attribute.

Table 15.1 During dimension processing, the server creates an attribute map for each attribute.

Key	Name	Member ID
3	Central	1
2	Northeast	2
1	Nortwest	3

Next, the server orders the attribute members according to the OrderBy attribute column (or by the key if the OrderBy column is not set). Finally, the server assigns a unique Member ID number to each attribute that reflects the attribute positional order and stores the attribute map as a physical map file. You can find these attribute files with extension *.map* in the dimension metadata folders. The attribute map is stored in a binary format and it is not human readable. During cube processing, the server combines the attribute maps to create paths to all non-empty cells of the cube.

Let me walk you through a few examples that demonstrate the effect of different dimension processing options. Since we will be making data changes to the dimension tables, I recommend you back up the AdventureWorksDW database.

15.2.2 Rebuilding Dimensions

By rebuilding a dimension, we will mean fully processing a dimension. This entails discarding all dimension stores (data, index, map, etc.), rebuilding them from scratch, and populating them with data. As noted, all dimension metadata changes require rebuilding a dimension (Process Full option). For example, some common scenarios that require rebuilding a dimension are adding and deleting attributes.

SSAS 2000 With the introduction of new dimension processing options in UDM (e.g. Process Update), you may find that the scenarios for fully processing a dimension have been reduced. For example, moving a member from one parent to another (re-parenting) doesn't require Full Process in UDM. The Process Update option can handle this without invalidating the cubes.

Rebuilding a dimension has major implications to UDM. Specifically, the server invalidates all cubes that reference that dimension. Let's demonstrate the side effects of fully processing a dimension. Suppose that you need to reload the Sales Territory dimension with data, e.g. after the ETL processes have completed. One way of doing so is by rebuilding the dimension from scratch using the *Process Full* option.

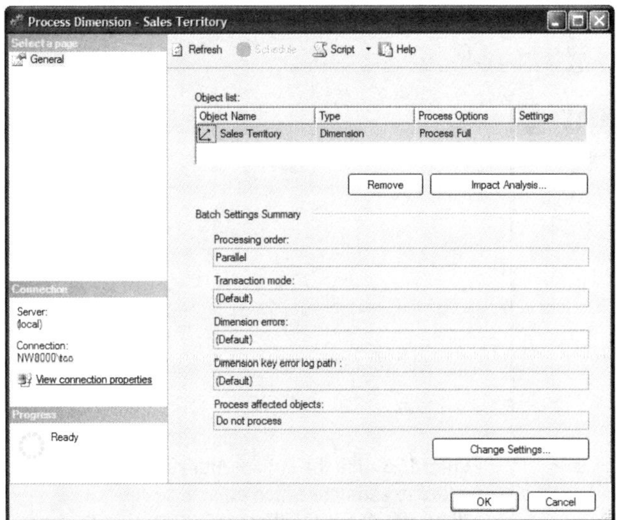

Figure 15.2 Fully processing a dimension discards the storage contents of the object and rebuilds them from scratch.

Scripting the processing action

1. In Management Studio, right-click on the Sales Territory dimension and choose *Process*.
2. Management Studio brings the familiar Process Dimension dialog. The most noticeable difference when this dialog is launched from Management Studio is that it includes the Script button to script the processing task. Management Studio defaults the Process Options column to *Process Update* because it has inspected the state of the Sales Territory dimension and has discovered that no metadata changes have been made.
3. Change the Processing Options to *Process Full* (Figure 15.2).
4. Click on the Script button to script the dimension processing action as it stands. Management Studio should generate the following script (XML namespaces excluded for brevity):

```
<Batch xmlns="...">
  <Parallel>
    <Process xmlns:xsd="...">
      <Object>
        <DatabaseID>SOS OLAP</DatabaseID>
        <DimensionID>Dim Sales Territory</DimensionID>
      </Object>
      <Type>ProcessFull</Type>
      <WriteBackTableCreation>UseExisting</WriteBackTableCreation>
    </Process>
  </Parallel>
</Batch>
```

The Batch command allows you to send multiple processing commands to the server in one shot. In our case, we have only one command (Process). Management Studio will send this command to the server to process the Sales Territory dimension.

Estimating the impact of processing a dimension

As noted, the Process Full dimension processing option could potentially be an expensive proposition with large databases because it invalidates the cubes that reference that dimension.

The cubes will remain offline and cannot be queried until they are re-processed. To find which UDM objects will be impacted by fully processing a dimension, click on the Impact Analysis button. This brings the Impact Analysis dialog (Figure 15.3).

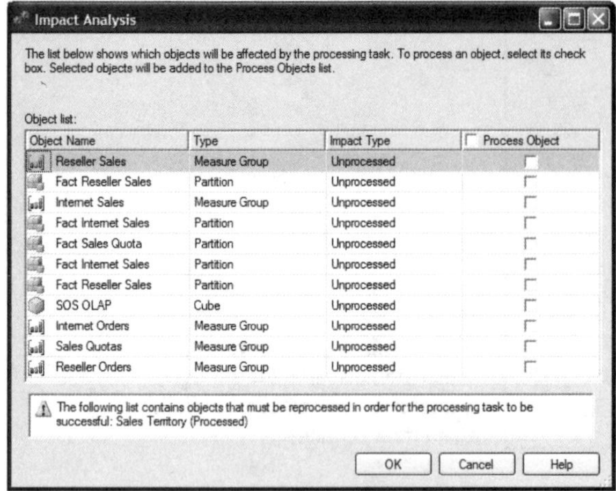

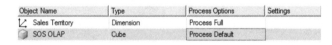

Figure 15.3 Use the Impact Analysis feature to estimate which objects will be affected with different processing options.

As you can see, fully processing the Sales Territory dimension would invalidate all measure groups and cubes that reference the dimension.

Note One potential area of improvement with the Impact Analysis dialog is consolidating the affected objects. Given that fully processing a dimension invalidates the entire cube, it is sufficient to process only the cube. Since cube measure groups and partitions are intra-dependent object, the server will process them as well.

Once you select the SOS OLAP cube and confirm the Impact Analysis dialog, the cube is added to the objects to be processed with the *Process Default* option. The Process Default option lets the server figure out the most appropriate processing method based on the state of the object. Fully processing a dimension clears the cube storage. As a result, the server will escalate Process Default to Process Full for the affected cubes.

Object Name	Type	Process Options	Settings
Sales Territory	Dimension	Process Full	
SOS OLAP	Cube	Process Default	

Figure 15.4 Use the Process Default option to let the server determine the appropriate processing method.

If you now script the Process Dimension dialog, you will get the following script:

```
<Batch xmlns="http://schemas.microsoft.com/analysisservices/2003/engine">
  <Parallel>
    <Process xmlns:xsd="..." xmlns:xsi="...">
      <Object>
        <DatabaseID>SOS OLAP</DatabaseID>
        <DimensionID>Dim Sales Territory</DimensionID>
      </Object>
      <Type>ProcessFull</Type>
      <WriteBackTableCreation>UseExisting</WriteBackTableCreation>
    </Process>
    <Process xmlns:xsd="..." xmlns:xsi="...">
```

```
      <Object>
        <DatabaseID>SOS OLAP</DatabaseID>
        <CubeID>SOS OLAP</CubeID>
      </Object>
      <Type>ProcessDefault</Type>
      <WriteBackTableCreation>UseExisting</WriteBackTableCreation>
    </Process>
  </Parallel>
</Batch>
```

The Parallel element indicates that the server will process the objects in parallel on multiple threads. If you want to process the objects sequentially, you can overwrite the default behavior by clicking on the Change Settings button and choosing the *Sequential* option.

Processing affected objects

Instead of processing the affected objects explicitly, you can let the server process them automatically. To enable this behavior, all it takes is selecting the *Process affected objects* checkbox on the Change Settings dialog (Figure 15.5).

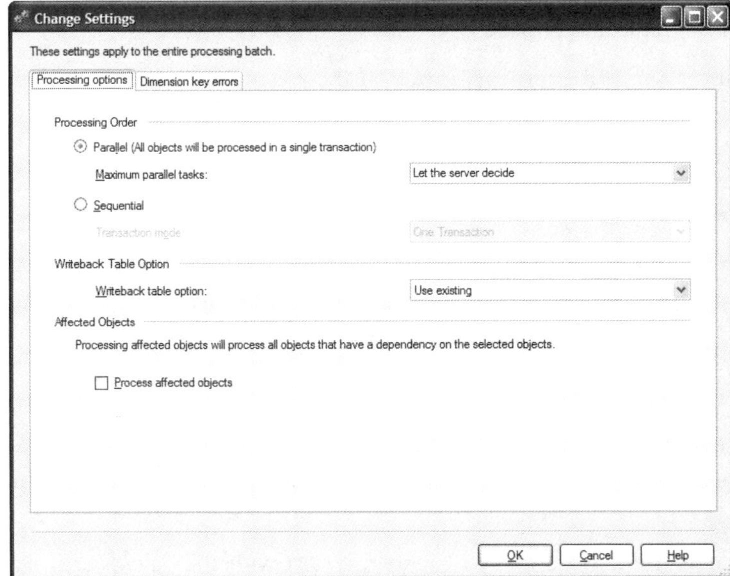

Figure 15.5 Use the Change Settings dialog to control the object processing behavior.

If needed, before you initiate the processing task, you can overwrite the dimension error configuration that you specified at design time. I demonstrated in chapter 5 how you can leverage error configurations to deal with data integrity and processing errors. By default, processing exceptions are logged in the msmdsrv.log file (C:\Program Files\Microsoft SQL Server\MSSQL.2-\OLAP\Log folder).

15.2.3 Incrementally Processing Dimensions

If the dimension metadata hasn't changed, consider a more light-weight dimension processing option, such as *Process Update* or *Process Add*. For example, suppose that the SOS OLAP cube is in production and you know that its dimension metadata hasn't changed from the last time the cube was processed. Further, let's assume that minimizing the cube offline time is more significant than minimizing the cube processing time.

Note The Process Add option is an even lighter processing option than Process Update because it targets the new dimension members only. Unfortunately, this option is not exposed in the Process Dimension dialog and scripting it is not that easy. Please refer to the *Analysis Services 2005 Processing Architecture* document to find out how to script the Process Add dimension processing option.

Process Update

The *Process Update* option sends SQL queries to scan the dimension table, determine what data changes have been made to the dimension members and apply the changes. It detects member updates, additions, and deletions. The difference between Process Update and Process Full is that Process Update on a dimension doesn't invalidate the cubes that reference that dimension. Its downside is that it is slower compared to Process Full. Let's demonstrate the effect of the Process Update option for processing a dimension incrementally.

1. In Management Studio, connect to SQL Server and expand the AdventureWorksDW database.
2. Right-click on the DimSalesTerritory table and choose *Open Table.*
3. To simulate a re-parenting scenario, change the territory group of the France dimension member to **Pacific**, as shown in Figure 15.6.

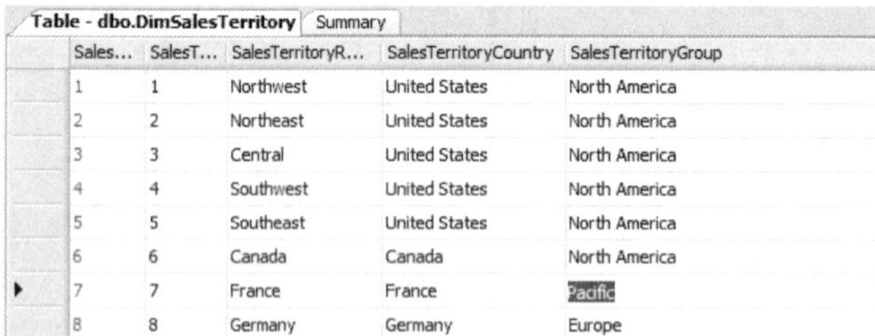

Table - dbo.DimSalesTerritory | Summary

Sales...	SalesT...	SalesTerritoryR...	SalesTerritoryCountry	SalesTerritoryGroup
1	1	Northwest	United States	North America
2	2	Northeast	United States	North America
3	3	Central	United States	North America
4	4	Southwest	United States	North America
5	5	Southeast	United States	North America
6	6	Canada	Canada	North America
7	7	France	France	Pacific
8	8	Germany	Germany	Europe

Figure 15.6 Simulating re-parenting change by changing a star schema dimensional table in place.

I agree that this change doesn't make much sense from a business standpoint but it will help us understand how the Process Update processing option can be used to apply member changes in a smart manner.

4. Right-click on the SOS OLAP cube and choose *Browse.* Create a report with the Sales Territory multi-level hierarchy on rows and Reseller Sales Amount measure on details. Note that the France Country member is still a child of the Europe Group member.
5. Process the Sales Territory dimension using the **Process Update** option (should be set by default).
6. Go back to the report and reconnect.

Group	Country	Reseller Sales Amount
⊞ North America		$62,947,143.31
⊟ Pacific	⊞ Australia	$854,899.41
	⊞ France	$4,562,989.84
	Total	$5,417,889.25
⊞ Europe		$8,129,725.69
Grand Total		$76,494,758.25

Figure 15.7 Use the Process Update option to apply dimension changes.

The France Country member is now found under the Pacific Group member (Figure 15.7). More importantly, the cube is not invalidated.

Note Process Update reflects dimension changes only. You still need to reprocess the cube to reflect fact data changes. However, since processing a cube doesn't bring the cube offline, Processing Update will not result in any downtime and the cube will be available to clients.

7. To restore the database to its original state, change the SalesTerritoryGroup column of France back to **Europe** and re-process the Sales Territory dimension with Process Update again.

How aggregations are effected

Process Update has an interesting effect on the existing partition aggregations. If there is an aggregation on an attribute that is changed during Process Update, the aggregation is temporarily removed from the cube, although it still exists in the aggregation design. At this point, queries give correct results and aggregations not affected by the dimension processing are still in use. If you want to bring back the deactivated aggregation, you don't have to re-process the whole cube/measure group/partition. Instead, you can use the Process Index option. When Process Index is used, the server rebuilds the missing indexes. If you are not sure what processing option you need, you can always use Process Default. Process Default morphs to the least expensive process type that gets the job done at minimum cost.

15.3 Cube Processing

Cube processing is an ongoing task that the administrator needs to perform to update the cube metadata, data, and aggregation layers. Cubes with MOLAP, HOLAP, and ROLAP storage mode require different processing. At a high level, one can differentiate among three common cube processing scenarios (full process, data refresh, and incremental process modes) that are described in this section.

15.3.1 Understanding Cube Processing

As noted, the cube storage architecture consists of metadata, aggregations, and data layers. Here is a simplified picture of what happens behind the scenes when you fully process a cube. First, the server sends SQL SELECT statement to load each measure group with data from the underlying fact table. Next, the server processes the returned resultset one row at a time. When doing so, the server calculates the path to every leaf cell by combining the attribute coordinates that reference that cell.

Table 15.2 During cube processing, the server creates a master cube map.

Region	Year	Month	Reseller Sales Amount
Central	2002	January	$1,000
Northeast	2003	February	$2.000
Nortwest	2004	March	$3,000

Given the hypothetical fact table shown in Table 15.2, the path to the $1,000 Reseller Sales Amount is *Central* ⇨ *2002* ⇨ *January*. The server translates the member names to their numerical equivalents taken from the attribute map files, so the actual path may look like *0* ⇨ *1* ⇨ *0*. Next, the server creates the cell and stores the aggregated value from the fact details in the cell. The cell paths are subsequently combined into a master cube map and stored in the cube metadata layer. Finally, the server creates the cube aggregations based on the aggregation design produced by the Aggregation Design Wizard or Usage-Based Optimization Wizard.

How dimension processing affects cube processing

You may wonder how the different dimension processing options impact the cube processing. While discussing all possible processing permutations is beyond the scope of this book, Table 15.3 lists the most common scenarios to bring the cube to the fully processed state.

Table 15.3 How dimension processing impacts cube processing.

Processing Option	MOLAP	HOLAP
Process Full	Process Full	Process Full
Process Update	Process Data (data refresh) + Process Default (indexes and aggregatons)	Process Default
Process Add	Process Add (data additions) + Process Default (indexes and aggregatons)	Process Default

Table 15.3 excludes the ROLAP cube storage mode because it has limited usage scenarios. Let's discuss these three processing scenarios in more details.

15.3.2 Rebuilding Cubes

Fully processing a dimension always requires rebuilding the affected cubes. Other common reasons to fully process a cube include metadata changes, including adding or removing dimensions, measure groups, and measures, as well as changing the partition storage mode. When the server does a full process on a MOLAP cube, it discards and rebuilds its data stores. Aggregations and indexes are erased and rebuilt irrespective of the cube storage mode (MOLAP, HOLAP, or ROLAP).

An interesting implementation detail of the SSAS processing architecture is that dimension and cube processing jobs are done in a transactional scope. If there is an error during processing an object, all processing changes are rolled back and the object is reverted to its previous state. Consecutively, you need to account for the extra space that is required to process a cube. As a rule of thumb, you need to have at least the same amount of free disk space as the space currently occupied by the cube to fully process it, plus the storage space required for the new data.

15.3.3 Refreshing the Cube Data

Assuming that only the cube data has changed, you can use a more light-weight processing option than Process Full, such as *Process Data*. It is important to note that Process Update on a dimension doesn't refresh the cube data in any way. If you watch the Process Progress dialog when you process the dimension, you will notice that the server does some processing on the measure groups that reference the Sales Territory dimension. However, if you expand the measure group nodes in the tree, you will find that no SQL statements are sent to the server. So, what's going on?

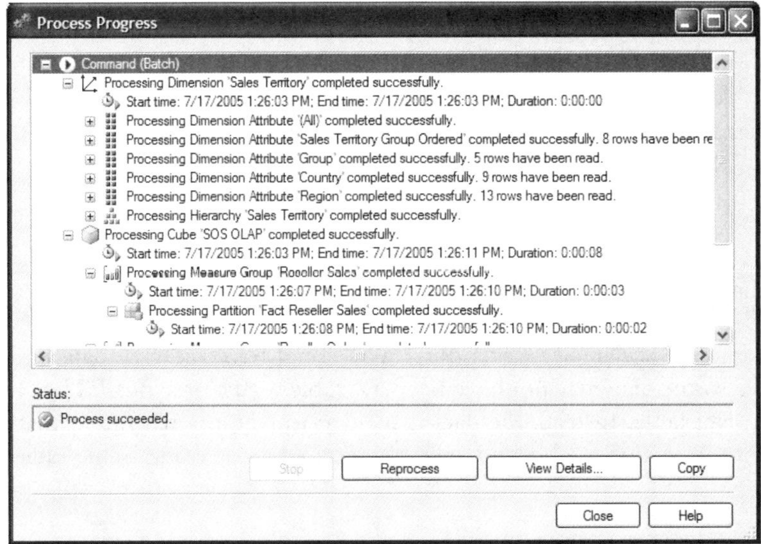

Figure 15.8 Process Update on a dimension clears indexes and aggregations on the affected partitions.

If you consult with the Side Effects table in the *Analysis Services 2005 Processing Architecture* document, you will see that Process Update on dimension clears indexes and aggregations in the affected partitions. So, after the Sales Territory dimension is processed with Process Update, the server proceeds with removing the indexes and aggregations from the affected partitions. Therefore, there are two important considerations when using Process Update. First, queries against the affected partitions will run slower.

Second, Process Update on a dimension must be followed with processing the cube itself. With MOLAP, you need to refresh the cube data (Process Data or Process Full options). Unfortunately, Process Data refreshes the cube data only. It doesn't build the partition indexes and aggregations. Therefore, with MOLAP, Process Data must be followed with *Process Default* to bring the affected objects to fully processed state. With HOLAP, it is sufficient to process the cube with the *Process Default* option after Process Update on the cube dimensions. That's because HOLAP cube data is kept in the relational data source. Instead, you need to build the partition indexes and aggregations only.

15.3.4 Processing Cubes Incrementally

Many ETL processes only add new fact rows to the fact tables. In this case you can consider using the *Process Incremental* option to bring only the new fact data to a partition. For example, suppose that Reseller Sales measure group only takes new rows. To minimize the cube processing time, you decide to process its partitions incrementally.

 **Note** Incremental updates are supported with MOLAP partitions only.

1. Right-click on the Reseller Sales measure group and choose *Process*.

2. Expand the Process Options dropdown and select *Process Incremental*. Notice that a *Configure* link appears in the Settings column (Figure 15.9).

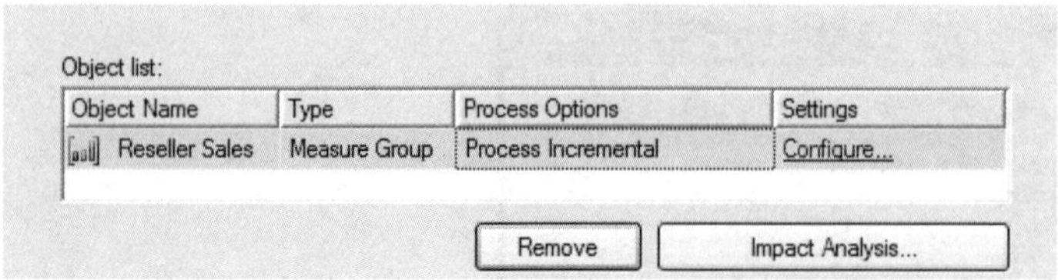

Figure 15.9 Consider Process Incremental option to add only new data to the cube.

3. Click on the Configure link to bring up the Incremental Update dialog.
4. If the measure group spans more than one partition, expand the Partition dropdown to select the partition that will be incrementally updated.

The dialog supports two incremental update scenarios. First, you could have the new data in a separate fact table. For example, some data may not have been available with a previous ETL run and may not be present in the fact table. Instead, the data is handed to you in a flat file format. You can import the flat file into a relational table and specify the table name using Table radio button.

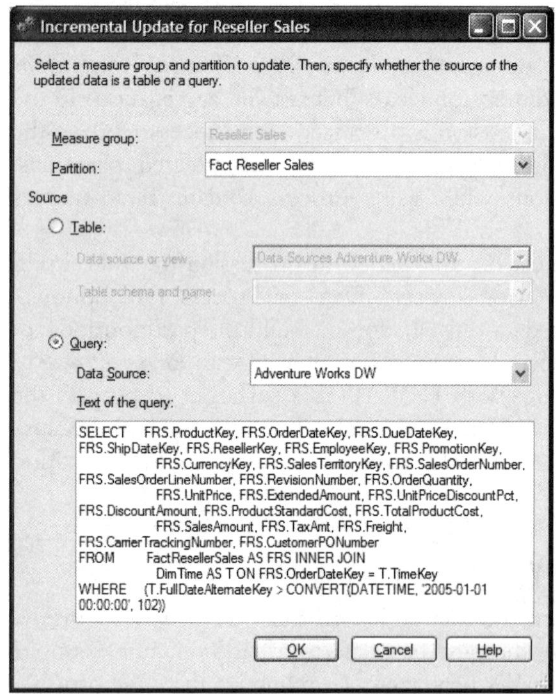

Figure 15.10 You can incrementally update a partition from a separate fact table or from a query.

Alternatively, use the Query option if the data has already been imported in the fact table. In this case, you need to specify a SQL SELECT statement to retrieve the new data only.

Warning It is very important that the query doesn't overlap the existing data in the fact table. If this happens, you may duplicate fact table rows, which is something you don't want to do for sure.

5. Choose the Query option. In the *Text of the query* textbox, enter the SQL SELECT statement that fetches the new rows *only*.

   No, I didn't type in this statement manually and nor should you. Instead, in BI Studio, open the SOS OLAP cube in the Cube Designer and switch to the Partitions tab. Change the source of the Reseller Sales partition to Query Binding to let BI Studio generate the query statement for you. Select the entire statement, copy it (Ctrl+C), and cancel the Partition Source dialog. Paste the statement text into the *Text of the query* textbox (Figure 15.10). Change the WHERE clause of the statement as indicated in the screenshot. For demonstration purposes, I use a fixed date in the query WHERE clause to bring only the rows from the Fact Reseller Sales fact table that are newer than 1/1/2005. In reality, this query will return an empty set since there is no data for 2005 in the FactResellerSales table.

6. Click OK to close the dialog. Click OK on the Process Measure Group dialog to process the selected partition incrementally.

15.4 Automating Processing Tasks

In real-life you would probably want to automate the processing of UDM objects in an unattended mode. For example, you may need to process UDM objects at the end of the ETL pipeline, or you may need to schedule processing tasks to be executed on a regular basis. The most popular options for automating UDM processing are executing an SSIS package and scripting.

15.4.1 Automating Processing With SSIS Packages

Back in chapter 6, we designed the Load Inventory SSIS project to extract, transform, and load data into the Inventory UDM. As a last step of the ETL pipeline, the Load Inventory master package executes the Process Inventory UDM child package to process the dimensions followed by processing the Inventory cube. ETL processes are typically automated to execute on a regular schedule. Here is what it takes to automate the Load Inventory SSIS package.

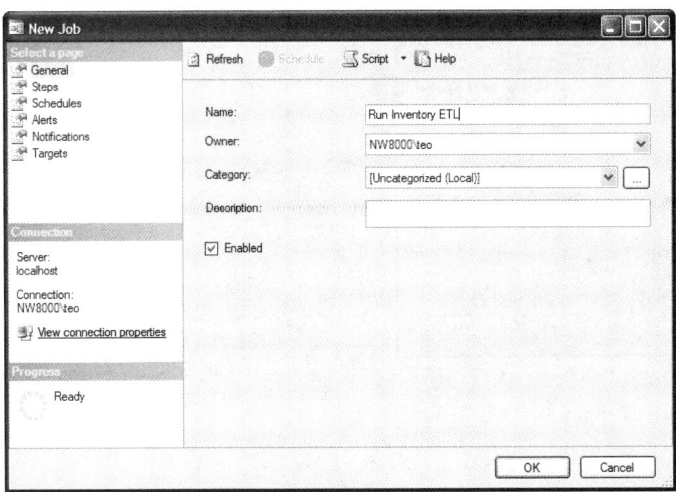

Figure 15.11 Use the SQL Server Agent to schedule and execute tasks in an unattended mode.

1. Deploy the Load Inventory project from the Ch06 solution to the SQL Server. There are different ways of doing this and the product documentation provides step-by-step instructions. Once the SSIS package is deployed, you can use the SQL Server Agent to schedule its execution. As a prerequisite, make sure that the SQL Server Agent service is running on the server where the package is deployed.
2. Connect to the SQL Server where the package is deployed. In the Object Explorer, right-click on the SQL Server Agent node and choose *New ⇨ Job.*
3. Name the new job **Run Inventory ETL** (Figure 15.11).
4. Click on the Steps page in the *Select a page* pane. The Load Inventory ETL job will have only one step which will launch the *Load Inventory* master SSIS package.
5. Enter **Load Inventory** as a name of the step.
6. Expand the Type dropdown and select SQL Server Integration Services Package.
7. Expand the Sever dropdown and select the server where the package is located, e.g. *(local)* if the SSIS package is deployed locally.
8. Click on the ... button next to the Package textbox and in the Select an SSIS Package dialog that follows select the Load Inventory master package (Figure 15.12).

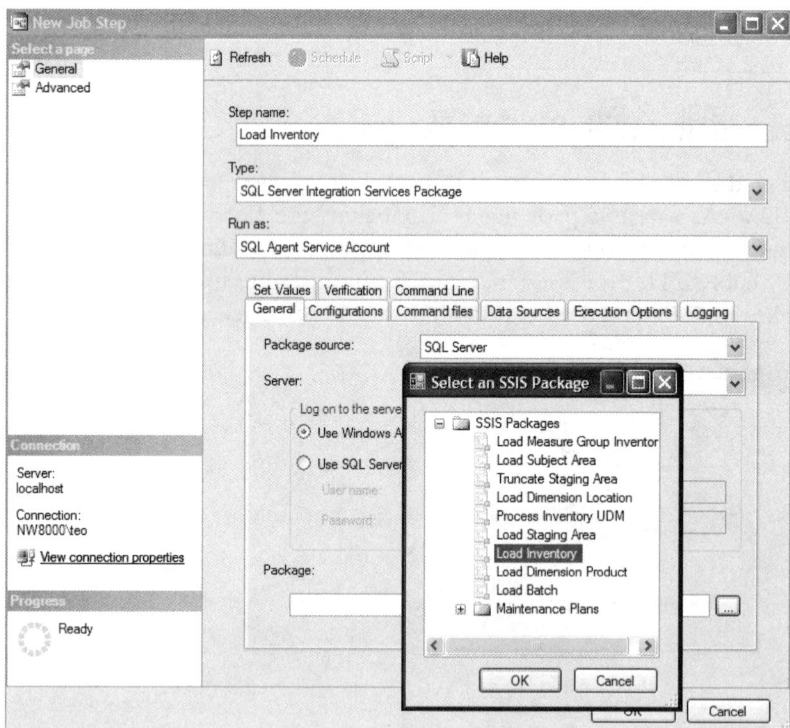

Figure 15.12 Create an SQL Server Integration Services Package step to run an SSIS package.

9. Click OK twice to return to the New Job dialog.
10. Click on the Schedule page to schedule the job execution as desired.

11. Alternatively, if you want to run the job immediately, click OK to create the job. Next, expand the Jobs folder under SQL Server Agent, right-click on the Run Inventory ETL job and choose *Start Job*. The SQL Server Agent will start the job and display its progress in the Start Jobs dialog.

12. To view the job history log, right-click on the job and choose *View History*.

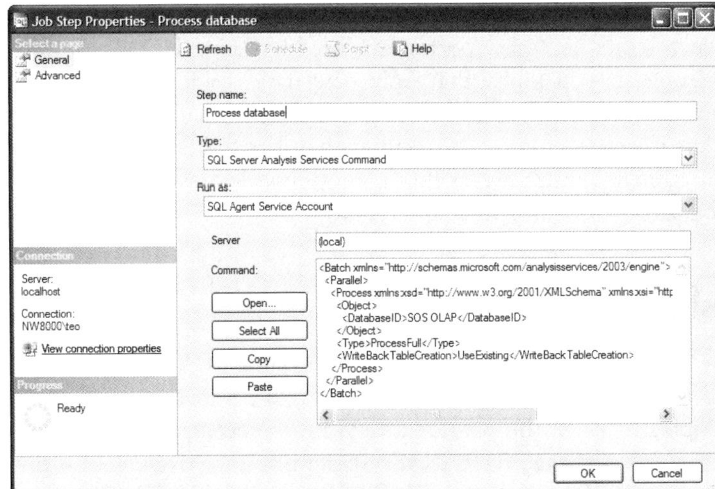

Figure 15.13 Use the SQL Server Analysis Services Command step type to automate script execution.

15.4.2 Automating Processing With Scripting

As noted in chapter 13, the SQL Server Agent is capable of executing SSAS scripts. Suppose that you have a UDM built directly on top of the OLTP data source. Instead of processing the UDM explicitly, you've decided to leverage proactive caching (discussed in section 15.5) which propagates the data changes automatically to the UDM. No matter how well proactive caching is doing its job, it may make sense to give the SSAS database a "healthy" reprocess once in a while just to make sure that no data is lost between notification events. Here is how you can automate processing with scripting.

1. Right-click on the SOS OLAP database and choose *Process*.
2. In the Process Database dialog, expand the Script dropdown and choose *Script Action to Clipboard*.
3. Create a new job with the SQL Server Agent and name it **Process SOS OLAP Database.**
4. Create a new step and name it **Process database**.
5. Expand the Type dropdown and choose SQL Server Analysis Services Command.
6. Paste the script you created in step 2 into the Command textbox (Figure 15.13). Click OK twice to create the job.

If you need a more granular workflow, the processing job may contain more than one task, e.g. Process Dimensions followed by Process Cubes, as we did with the Process Inventory UDM SSIS package. Moreover, you can use the Advanced page to specify "on success" and "on failure step" conditions for a given step. In this way, you can create multi-step sequential, albeit relatively basic, processing workflows.

15.4.3 Processing Best Practices

If you find our processing discussion mind-boggling, here are some best practices you may want to consider when trying to simplify your processing framework. If fully processing your UDM gives you adequate performance, by all means go for it. Fully processing UDM objects is the cleanest and easiest way to apply data changes and the only way to reflect structural changes. However, it is also the most expensive.

If fully processing doesn't give you the necessary performance with a large UDM, consider other processing options. For example, if you know that only new data is added, choose the Process Add option. However, choosing the "right" processing could be a challenge especially when automating processing tasks. Imagine an ETL workflow that has different processing branches for new and updated data! Finally, don't forget that a good storage design goes a long way in optimizing UDM processing, as we discussed in chapter 14.

15.5 Low-Latency OLAP Solutions

OLAP solutions are typically built on top of large relational databases, such as data warehouses. As the data volumes increase, OLAP has definite performance advantages compared to relational reporting. That's because SSAS copies (caches) the relational data into specialized multidimensional stores that are optimized for fast retrieval. The SSAS efficient storage architecture improves the query performance dramatically. However, as with any form of caching, caching data into the multidimensional stores brings additional challenges and one of them is *data latency*. Once you take a data "snapshot" by processing a cube, the data becomes stale until you reprocess again. How much OLAP data latency is acceptable will depend on your business requirements. In some cases, your end-users may mandate up-to-date (even *real-time*) information. For example, they may want to compare the sales data of today with the same day of last month.

In this section, we will discuss different techniques for implementing real-time OLAP solutions. These techniques bring UDM closer to relational reporting by allowing you to shorten the time window from the moment data is captured in the OLTP system until the moment it is available for OLAP reporting. We will spend most of our time exploring the innovative proactive caching feature which debuts with UDM.

15.5.1 The Reality of Real Time OLAP

The trivial solution for minimizing the data latency issue is to process the cubes more often. However, data logistics and operational factors may make this approach unrealistic. To understand this better, consider the common OLAP lifecycle (Figure 15.14).

Understanding data latencies

Once an end user (or a system) enters the transactional data into the OLTP database(s), each stage of the OLAP lifecycle introduces a latency delay. For example, data extracts from OLTP systems may be available once a day. Next, data would typically undergo some processing before it enters UDM. Complex data extraction, transformation, and loading (ETL) processes may be required to cleanse and validate the data. Data is then moved to a staging and warehouse (subject area) databases. Next, the cubes are built on the staging server and pushed to the production server. Finally, data is available for end-user reporting.

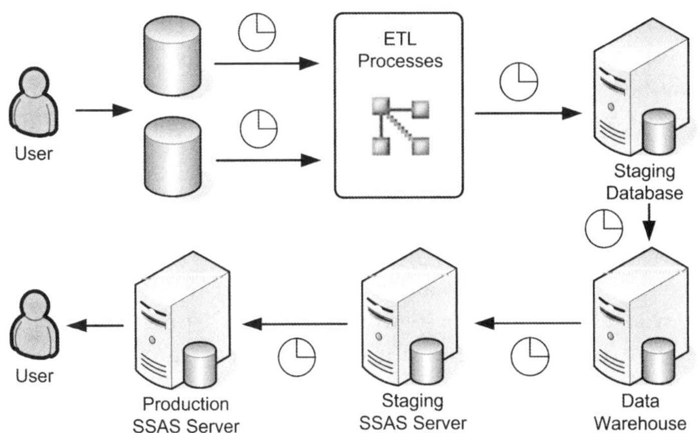

Figure 15.14 The OLAP pipeline introduces numerous data latency delays.

As a result of these data logistics processes, the user is drifted further away from data she should be acting upon. Of course, Figure 15.14 shows the full-blown classic OLAP pipeline which may or may not be applicable to your particular situation. But even when the OLAP layer is built directly on top of a clean OLTP data source, data will get stale with MOLAP cubes. That's because each time you process a cube, you essentially take a snapshot of the source data. The snapshot latency represents the time period between two cube processing cycles.

OLAP scenarios and low latency techniques

Not all latency delays can be eliminated by SSAS. Therefore, before we delve into the technical details, it may make sense to point out when and how Analysis Services can help you implement low-latency OLAP solutions. Table 1 is meant to be used as a starting point.

Table 15.4 Low latency scenarios that SSAS can address.

OLAP Scenario	SSAS Solution
Classic OLAP (OLTP, ETL, data warehouse, OLAP)	Actions Push-mode processing
Transactional OLAP (OLAP built on top of an OLTP data source)	Multiple data sources, Snapshot isolation Proactive caching

As noted in chapter 2, we can divide OLAP implementations in two categories. *Classic OLAP* refers to the scenario depicted in Figure 15.14. This is a common architecture for most data warehouse projects. In this case, data is extracted from one or more data sources, transformed, and loaded into UDM. In comparison, with *transactional OLAP*, UDM is built directly on top of the OLTP data source. Undoubtedly, real-life solutions may not exactly fit into these two categories but, for the sake of simplicity, we will ignore variations. The most important factor that differentiates classic OLAP from transactional OLAP is that in the first case data cannot be used as it is. Instead, data must be pre-processed before it reaches its final destination – UDM.

Classic OLAP

In my opinion, SSAS may not be of much help in reducing data latency with the classic OLAP scenario. This shouldn't be viewed as a limitation of the product though. If you have experience with data warehousing, you would probably agree that the factors that introduce latencies are for the most part outside of the SSAS realm. Here, we are talking about essential data logistics processes, such as how often data will be extracted from the source systems, time spent in ETL processes, data validation and testing, etc. Yet, the features that you can consider for providing up-to-date data with classic OLAP are *actions* and *push-mode (aka pipeline) processing*. You've already seen how actions can be leveraged to integrate UDM with external applications. For example, in chapter 12, I demonstrated how a reporting action can be used to generate an SSRS report from the relational database.

An interesting UDM feature is allowing an external application to push data into a cube. Normally, a cube pulls the data from a relational database when the cube is processed. With push-mode processing, the data source is bypassed and data is blasted directly into the cube. I will demonstrate this feature in section 15.5.2.

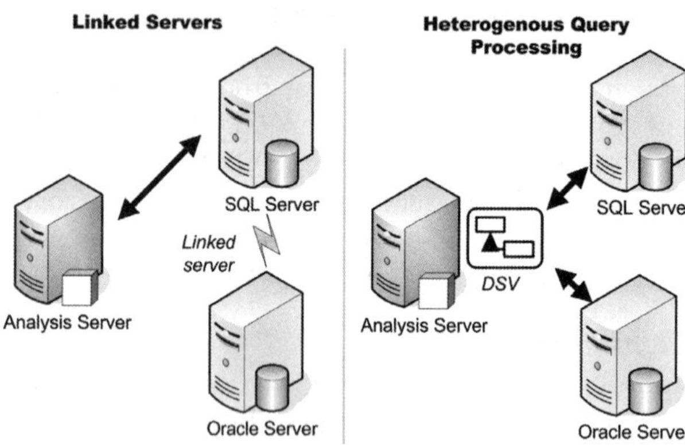

Figure 15.15 Consider using linked servers and heterogeneous processing when data comes from multiple data sources.

Transactional OLAP

For the most part, transactional OLAP doesn't incur ETL latencies. In the ideal case, no data transformations are necessary. If this is not the case, DSV named queries and named calculations can be used to enrich the relational schema, as the SOS OLTP UDM demonstrated. SQL Server and SSAS could help you implement transactional OLAP solutions in several ways. Most noticeably, SSAS allows you to put the cube into an "auto-pilot" mode by enabling the proactive caching storage setting. Proactive caching is discussed in details in section 15.5.3. Two other features that you may find useful with transactional OLAP are multiple data sources and snapshot isolation.

Note Transactional OLAP and proactive caching should not be viewed as a substitute for classical OLAP. Both approaches have strengths and weaknesses. Transactional OLAP may shortcut the implementation of an OLAP solution but it may offer limited reporting capabilities. Take this as a cautionary note before you get too excited about transactional OLAP and proclaim the demise of classical OLAP.

Multiple data sources

When data originates from multiple data sources, consider using the SQL Server linked server feature (see Figure 15.15). For example, suppose that the sales data resides in the SQL Server database, while the HR data is in an Oracle database. One option to bridge data is to register the Oracle server as a linked server. Registering a linked server is easy with Management Studio.

1. Set up a linked server login as explained in the Security for Linked Servers topic in the product documentation.
2. Connect to the SQL Server that will link with the Oracle server.
3. Expand the Server Objects folder. Right-click on the Linked Servers node and chose *New Linked Server.*
4. In the New Linked Server dialog, select the *Microsoft OLE DB Provider for Oracle* provider and specify the connection details.

The second option for data sourcing from multiple sources is to do so at DSV level by leveraging the Heterogeneous Query Processing (HQP) feature of SSAS. Use this option when security policies prevent you from registering linked servers. I discussed the pros and cons of HQP in chapter 2.

Snapshot isolation

Although much simpler than classic OLAP, transactional OLAP may bring additional challenges. One of them is rapidly changing data in the data source. For example, suppose that you start processing a cube built directly on top of the OLTP data source. The SSAS server has processed the dimensions and is currently processing the fact rows. Meanwhile, the OLTP system adds a new dimension member and updates a fact row to reference the new member. When the server processes that row, it may fail to find the new dimension member. The exact outcome of this scenario depends on the error configuration for that measure group which may not be what you want.

One way to prevent such issues is to "freeze" the source data by taking a snapshot at the moment the server starts processing the cube. Fortunately, the SQL Server 2005 introduces a new SNAPSHOT transaction isolation option to address exactly this problem. Of course, the SQL Server doesn't make a copy of the entire database (that will be suicidal with large data warehouse databases). Instead, it uses a technique called *row versioning* to keep track of changes made after the SNAPSHOT transaction has been initiated. For more information about how SNAPSHOT transactions work, read the *T-SQL Enhancements in SQL Server 2005* chapter from the *First Look at SQL Server 2005 for Developers* book (see Resources). You can tell the SSAS server to use a SNAPSHOT transaction during processing at a data source level. To do so, double-click on the data source and change the Isolation setting to *Snapshot* in the Data Source Designer dialog.

Next, I will demonstrate how the data push and proactive caching options can be used to implement low-latency OLAP solutions.

15.5.2 Push-Mode Processing

Suppose that the Adventure Works warehouse pipeline introduces data latency of several days spent in ETL processes, testing, and deploying the SOS OLAP UDM. Further, let's assume that the Adventure Works Sales department finds this latency unacceptable. Instead, you are tasked to reduce the latency so new sales data is available for reporting within a few hours after it is captured in the source OLTP database. After analyzing the SOS OLAP solution, you realize that delays are introduced in each stage of the OLAP pipeline (Figure 15.16).

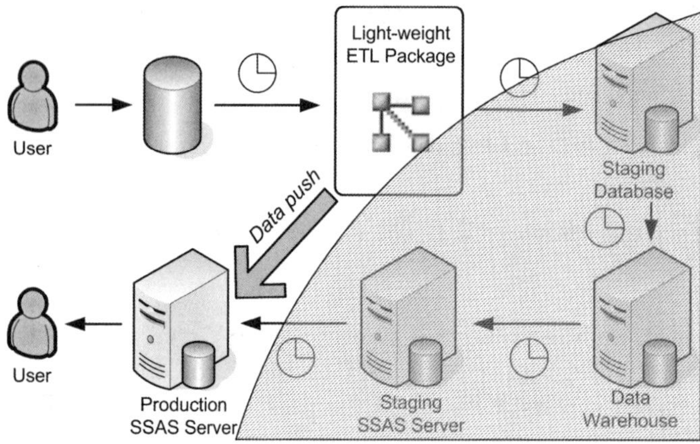

Figure 15.16 Consider push-mode processing to trickle-feed UDM.

Most of these delays are out of your control and are unavoidable. For example, you discover that significant latency is introduced to consolidate and validate data from multiple data sources, e.g. data from HR, Sales, and Manufacturing databases.

Push mode pros and cons

After talking with business users, you've come up with a reasonable compromise. You will build a light-weight SSIS package that will run frequently to extract the new data from the Sales database and trickle-feed the SOS OLAP UDM. Here, "frequently" means running the package as often as required to meet the latency requirements, e.g. every few minutes to an hour or so. The package could extract the new data by querying the Sales database directly, apply the bare minimum data transformation required, and push the new data to the SOS OLAP database. The benefit of this approach is that it bypasses several stages of the data warehouse pipeline (Figure 15.16) and thus eliminates their latencies.

Obviously, our "trick" is not without tradeoffs, which is why I used the phrase *reasonable compromise*. For example, a valid question could be "What will happen with the other dimensions that don't originate from the Sales database?" The answer is that the users won't be able to browse the new data by these dimensions. Now, you know why I called the package *light-weight*. In real life, the package could resolve the missing dimensions to their unknown values. As long as the users can tolerate a reasonable data inconsistency, the push-mode approach may be a solution for low-latency OLAP. The new data fed into the UDM may leave the data warehouse temporarily in a "limbo" state until the "master" OLAP pipeline is executed at a later stage to erase the trickle feeds and restore the warehouse to a consistent state again.

How push-mode processing works

As noted, you would process SSAS objects typically in pull mode, where the server pulls the data from the data store. Push-mode processing is the opposite. With a push-data mode, the data source is bypassed. Instead, the data is blasted straight into the multidimensional store. Both dimensions and partitions can be processed in push mode. A client application initiates this mode by preparing a rowset containing the new data and passing it as a parameter to the *Process* command. In addition, the Process command must overwrite the bindings of the object by using an advanced processing feature called *out-of-line bindings*. For more information about push-mode processing, read the excellent *Analysis Services 2005 Processing Architecture* whitepaper (see Resources).

In SSIS, Dimension Processing and Cube Processing tasks can be used to push data to UDM dimensions and partitions respectively. As a prerequisite for using push-mode processing, the target UDM object (dimension or partition) must be in a processed state. The client application must supply values for each attribute of the target dimension (in case of dimension push-mode processing) and for each measure of the target measure group (partition push-mode processing).

Only attribute keys can be fed with data (attribute NameColumn and ValueColumn properties cannot be bound). Since push-mode bypasses the attribute and measure NullProcessing settings, the client application must resolve NULL values before pushing data to numeric attributes and measure groups. Finally, the out-of-line bindings processing feature supports single-table dimensions only. If the dimension is built on top of multiple tables from the underlying DSV (snowflake schema), you will get the following SSIS error when trying to process the dimension:

```
Pipeline processing can only reference a single table in the data source view.
```

Group	Country	Reseller Sales Amount
⊞ North America		$62,947,143.31
⊟ Pacific	⊞ Australia	$854,899.41
	Total	$854,899.41
⊞ Europe		$12,692,715.53
⊞ NA		
Grand Total		$76,494,758.25

Figure 15.17 The SSIS package will add a new member to the Sales Territory dimension and a new row to the Reseller Sales measure group.

The Push to SOS OLAP SSIS package

Our push-mode example is kept simple on purpose. We will create an SSIS package (Push to SOS OLAP) that adds new data to the SOS OLAP UDM. You can find the Push to SOS OLAP package inside the Data Push SSIS project. Open the SOS OLAP cube in the Cube Browser (BI Studio or Management Studio) and create the report shown in Figure 15.17. The package will add a member *Singapore* as a child of the *Pacific* member in the Sales Territory multi-level hierarchy. In addition, the package will add a new row to the Reseller Sales measure group that references the new dimension member.

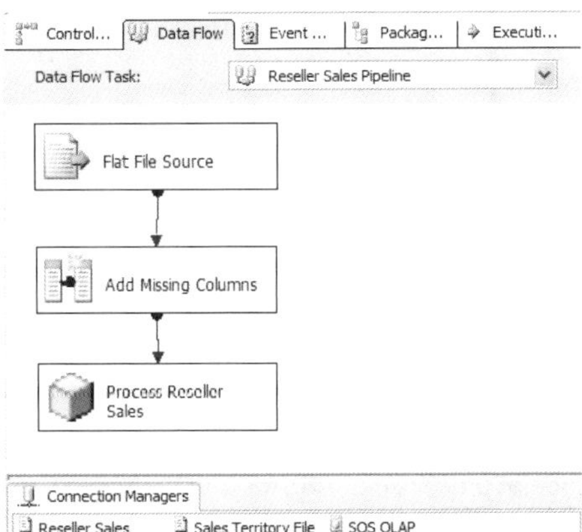

Figure 15.18 The Reseller Sales Pipeline data flow retrieves the new rows from a flat file, adds missing columns, and processes the Reseller Sales partition in push-mode.

Ideally, to minimize data latency even further, you would read the new data directly from the OLTP database. However, it is unlikely that in real life you will be given direct access to the relational database. Instead, our package will import the new data from a couple of flat files located in the Input Files folder. At a high-level, the Push to SOS OLAP control flow consists of two Data Flow tasks (Sales Territory Pipeline and Reseller Sales Pipeline) that add new data to the Sales Territory dimension and Reseller Sales measure group respectively. For the sake of brevity, I will walk you only through the data flow of Reseller Sales Pipeline (Figure 15.18).

Implementing push-mode processing

The Reseller Sales Pipeline starts by reading the new sales facts from the Reseller Sales flat file. Next, it adds four new columns for the missing measures that are not provided in the flat file. Specifically, it adds a *Reseller Profit Dollar Amount* (calculated as SalesAmount -- ProductStandardCost), *Reseller Sales Count* (set to 1), and *Reseller Minimum Unit Price* and *Reseller Maximum Unit Price* (set to 0). Despite the fact that all of these measures are formula-based and calculated automatically during pull-mode processing, we need to explicitly set their values because push mode bypasses the SSAS internal processing architecture. The actual data push is accomplished with the Partition Processing Task (Process Reseller Sales). In the process of configuring this task, you need to specify which UDM partition will be processed in push mode (Figure 15.19).

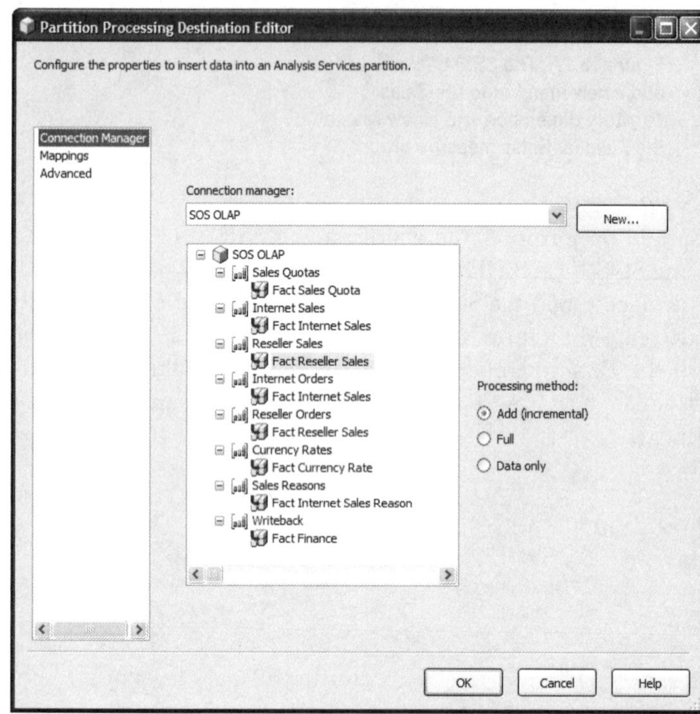

Figure 15.19 Use the Partition Processing task to push data to a partition.

In our case, the Reseller Sales group has only one partition (Fact Reseller Sales). SSAS supports incrementally processing a dimension or a measure group with the *ProcessAdd* option.

SSAS 2000 Although its name suggests otherwise, incremental processing in SSAS 2000 refreshes the entire dimension (inserts, deletes, and updates). The SSAS 2005 equivalent option of SSAS 2000 incremental dimension processing is Process Update. Process Add (a new processing option with SSAS 2005) processes new members only.

Since we will be adding new data only, *Add Incremental* will be the most efficient processing option. Next, we switch to the Mappings page where we need to map the columns from the input rowset to the measures and dimension keys in the Reseller Sales measure group. The Reseller Sales measures and dimension keys are listed in the Available Destination Columns list. The naming convention for dimension attributes is *Dimension.DimensionKey*. You map input columns to measures by dragging the input column and dropping it onto the corresponding dimension key or measure. Finally, you can use the Advanced page if you need to overwrite the default error configuration settings for the measure group.

Testing push-mode processing

Before running the package, take a moment to review the settings of the three connection managers. I attached two Data Viewers to the incoming connectors flowing into the two processing tasks so you can see the rows retrieved from the flat files. If all is well, the package should execute successfully and the Singapore dimension member should get added to the Sales Territory dimension followed by a fact row appended to the Reseller Sales measure group. Refresh the report to verify the package execution (Figure 15.20).

Group	Country	Reseller Sales Amount
⊞ North America		$62,947,143.31
⊟ Pacific	⊞ Australia	$854,899.41
	⊞ Singapore	$727.70
	Total	$855,627.11
⊞ Europe		$12,692,715.53
⊞ NA		
Grand Total		$76,495,485.96

Figure 15.20 After executing the package, a Singapore member is added to the Pacific member and Reseller Sales Count is updated to 1.

As noted, push-mode processing completely bypasses the data source. Therefore, the new data that the package writes to the cube is not added to the relational database. This is the behavior you would probably need anyway. You should regard the push-mode changes as temporary. Typically, once the master package processes the SOS OLAP cube in pull mode, the push-mode changes are discarded and replaced with data from the relational database.

15.5.3 Proactive Caching

Before we delve into the proactive caching internals, I would like to take something off my chest. In my opinion, after CLR stored procedures, proactive caching could very well win the runner-up place as another most oversold SQL Server 2005 feature. Don't get me wrong. I do believe that proactive caching is well architected and has its practical uses. I just think the "no explicit cube processing" slogan is over-emphasized and in many cases unrealistic.

Think for yourself. The most common use for OLAP (and SSAS) is data warehousing. In general, data warehousing implies well-defined processes to transform, validate, and load data in the warehouse or the data mart. This means that you can process UDM objects in a deterministic fashion (usually at the end of the ETL processes). So, what value does proactive caching bring to the table except a coolness factor that you are not processing cube explicitly?

Moreover, besides performed in a well-defined manner, changes made to a data warehouse are typically done in batches. As an example, an ETL package may blast all daily transactions to the fact tables in a batch mode. Such bulk changes may upset proactive caching. Finally, as we will discuss shortly, there could be performance implications when proactive caching is used with large data volumes, e.g. when the MOLAP cache is invalidated and proactive caching decides to answer queries from the relational database (ROLAP mode). Given what I just pointed out, I believe that with classic OLAP, pull-mode cube processing is the easiest, cleanest, and most efficient way to refresh UDM. Low-latency needs can be addressed by leveraging push-mode processing.

When to use proactive caching

Having thrown the "proactive" classic OLAP scenario out of the window, the logical question is when can proactive caching help? In my opinion, proactive caching could be useful for implementing low-latency (almost real-time if needed) *transactional* OLAP solutions. As noted, with transactional OLAP, you build UDM directly on top of the OLTP data source. One approach to bring your UDM up-to-date is to process the UDM objects on a regular basis (pull-mode processing). However, some scenarios may require reducing the data latency even further. For example, the Adventure Works business users may need to analyze the sales order activity in *real time*, as the orders are captured in the OLTP database, e.g. to determine the number of canceled, shipped, and unprocessed orders. This is potentially an excellent scenario for proactive caching.

Of course, you may seek alternative ways to address low-latency reporting needs instead of going for transaction OLAP. For example, you may decide to author standard SSRS reports that the end users can generate on as-needed basis. Each reporting solution has its strengths and benefits. In the case when you decide to build a transactional UDM layer, consider proactive caching to reduce the data latency.

Understanding proactive caching

Now that you know when to consider proactive caching, let's find how this technology works. Figure 15.21 is meant to help you visualize the proactive caching activity diagram at a high level.

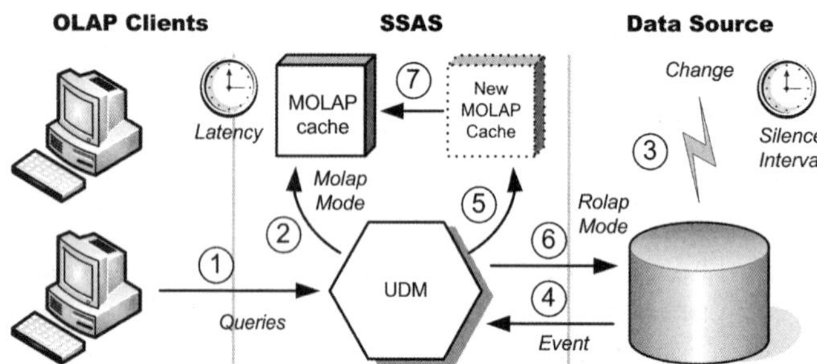

Figure 15.21 Proactive caching defines policies for the MOLAP cache.

For the sake of simplicity, we will assume that we have a MOLAP cube. As you know by now, a MOLAP cube is basically a disk-based cache of relational data. Traditionally, the only way to update the cube data was to process the cube. The time period between two processing cycles represents the latency of the cached data. Proactive caching allows you to define policies for refreshing the cube automatically without requiring explicit cube processing.

Definition Proactive caching describes management policies for the MOLAP cache. These policies define when and how to rebuild the MOLAP cache. Proactive caching is disk-based (not memory-based) caching. Once you configure proactive caching, you can leave the cube in "auto-pilot" data refresh mode without having to process the cube explicitly.

Here is how proactive caching works in a nutshell.

Steady state

In steady mode, life is as usual and no changes are being made to the relational data. Client applications submit (1) MDX queries to UDM. UDM satisfies (2) the queries from the MOLAP cache. UDM listens for data change events by using one of the three notification schemes discussed later in this section.

Unsteady state

At some point, a data change (insert, update, or delete) occurs (3) in the data source. This triggers (4) a notification event to UDM. UDM starts two stopwatches immediately. The Silence Interval stopwatch measures the time elapsed between two consecutive data change events. The idea here is to minimize the amount of "false" starts for building the new cache until the database is quiet again. For example, the data changes may be coming in batches. It is meaningless to start rebuilding the cache with each data change event. Instead, the administrator can optimize proactive caching by defining a silence interval to give some time for the batch changes to finish.

Once data in the relational database is changed, UDM knows that the MOLAP cache is stale and starts building (5) a new version. The Latency stopwatch specifies the maximum latency period (also configurable by the administrator) of the MOLAP cache. While we are within the latency period, the queries are still answered by the old MOLAP cache. Once the latency period is exceeded, the old cache is discarded. While the new version of the MOLAP cache is being built, UDM satisfies (6) client queries from the relational database (ROLAP).

Reverting to ROLAP could be a dangerous proposition. As you could imagine, querying a large warehouse database may be expensive. For example, suppose that the end user has requested to see the overall aggregated values for all periods. If proactive caching has been reverted to ROLAP meanwhile, the end user could be in for a long wait! To avoid such scenarios, the administrator could fine-tune the Latency stopwatch to give the server enough time to rebuild the new cache. A special setting of -1 can be used to prevent a ROLAP mode whatsoever. In this case, the server won't drop the old cache until the new cache is ready. Finally, once the new MOLAP cache is ready, the server activates it (7) and redirects client queries to it. Proactive caching enters a steady state again until the next data change event takes place. Sounds complicated? Well, it very well may be, but synchronizing two data stores is not a trivial problem to solve.

Enabling proactive caching

Proactive caching can be enabled for the two UDM data containing objects – dimensions and partitions. Proactive caching is not applicable for data mining objects.

Note You would find the ProactiveCaching property for cubes and measure groups as well. However, at these levels, ProactiveCaching properties specify the default settings for the nested objects. For example, proactive caching settings specified at a measure group level don't affect existing partitions. Instead, the settings will be applied to new partitions only.

To demonstrate proactive caching, it's time to dust off the SOS OLTP UDM. As I noted in chapter 1, the SOS OLTP model represents the transactional OLAP layer that is built directly on top of the AdventureWorks OLTP database. We built the SOS OLTP UDM to satisfy the low-latency needs of the Adventure Works analysts. Specifically, the SOS OLTP UDM supports browsing data for the current month. With the help of proactive caching, we will now turn the transactional OLAP layer into a *real-time* transactional OLAP layer. As data changes are committed into the AdventureWorks relational database, they will be reflected instantaneously in the SOS OLAP UDM without requiring explicit cube processing.

1. Open SOS OLTP cube in the Cube Designer and switch to the Partitions tab.

2. *Select* the Fact Sales partition (Figure 15.22). Make sure the partition is selected because if you don't select the partition, the storage settings will be applied at the measure group level. This is probably not what you want since measure group storage settings define default policies for new partitions.

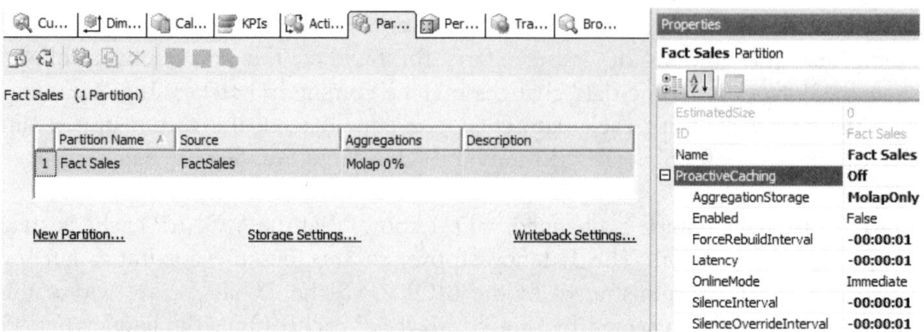

Figure 15.22 Proactive caching can be applied to partitions and dimensions only.

3. Observe the Properties window. The ProactiveCaching setting should be *Off* and StorageMode should be set to *Molap*. As it stands, the Fact Sales partition is not enabled for proactive caching and you must explicitly process the partition to refresh its data.

4. Click the Storage Settings link below the partition to open the Partition Storage Settings dialog (Figure 15.23).

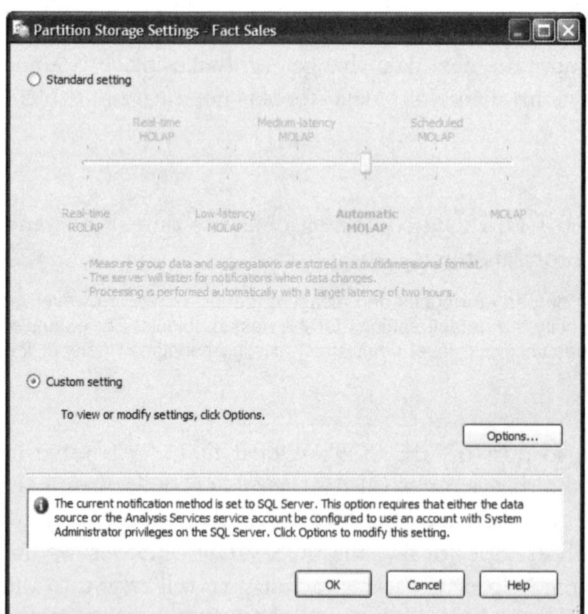

Figure 15.23 UDM defines a few standard proactive caching settings which can be fine-tuned by choosing the Custom settings option.

5. The *Standard setting* option is pre-selected. UDM defines a few standard settings which you can use to quickly set up proactive caching. Select the *Automatic MOLAP* setting.

6. You can refine the standard settings if needed. Let's find what the default Automatic Molap settings are and make adjustments as necessary. Select the *Custom settings* option and click the *Options* button to open the Storage Options dialog (Figure 15.24).

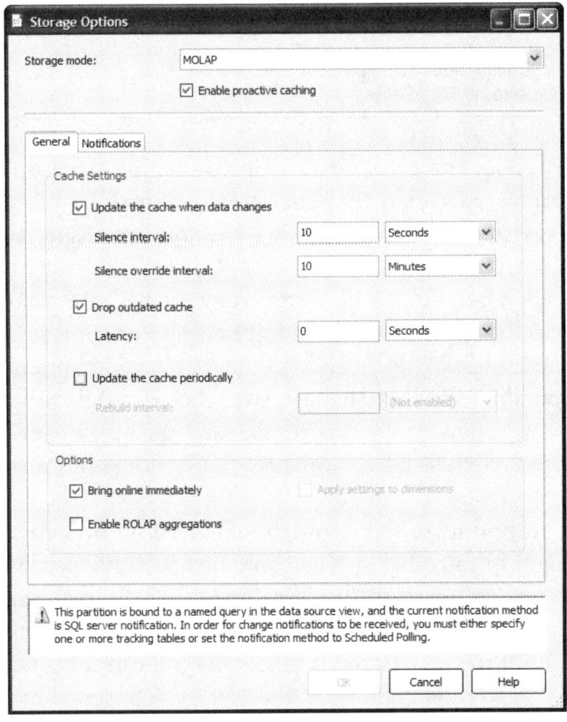

Figure 15.24 Use the Storage Options dialog to fine-tune the proactive caching settings.

Notice that the *Enable proactive caching* checkbox is selected and the *Silence interval* setting (Silence Interval stopwatch) is set to 10 seconds. This means that UDM will wait for 10 seconds before it starts to build the new version of the MOLAP cache in anticipation of a quiet period in the Adventure Works database. Again, this is useful to avoid repeated false starts for building the cache with data changes performed in batches.

Configuring caching policies

Table 15.5 summarizes the proactive caching settings and their purpose. The settings are listed by their names in the Properties window (see again Figure 15.22).

Table 15.5 Use the proactive caching settings to balance between latency and performance.

Setting	Description	Special Setting
SilenceInterval	Defines the minimum period to wait for a quiet time in the relational database.	-1 (infinite) Ingore database notifications.
SilenceOverrideInterval	If no quiet period occurs (perpetual data changes), defines the treshhold period after which the server will start rebuilding the cache.	-1 (infinite) No override period.
Latency	Defines the lifetime of the old MOLAP cache within which queries are still answered by it, albeit retrieving stale data.	-1 (infinite) Never revert to ROLAP.

ForceRebuildInterval	Schedules the new cache to be built automatically irrespective of the data activity.	-1 (infinite) No periodic update.
OnlineMode	When set to Immediate (On), the server satisfies queries from ROLAP while the cache is being rebuilt. When set to OnCacheComplete (Off), the server will never revert to ROLAP (infinite latency).	
AggregationStorage (Partitions only)	When On, the server attempts to create materialized SQL views for aggregations while queries are answered in ROLAP mode.	

In general, the purpose of the policy settings listed in Table 15.5 is to help you define a reasonable compromise between latency and performance (always orthogonal requirements). The key questions that you have to ask yourself are "How important is it to provide uniform response query times?" and "How much cache latency is acceptable?"

Suppose that you have a large relational database. In this case, reverting to ROLAP may impact the query performance. Imagine the user browsing the cube and getting superior performance while queries are answered in MOLAP mode. All of a sudden a data change happens and proactive caching reverts to ROLAP. Depending on the database size, the ROLAP query performance may be much worse than its MOLAP equivalent. As a result, the user may believe that the system has hanged and may attempt to restart the client application. Or, someone may get a phone call!

If the query performance is of an utmost importance, then you shouldn't allow proactive caching to revert to ROLAP at all. In the Storage Options dialog, this could be accomplished by disabling the Latency setting (selecting the *Not enabled* item in the dropdown) and clearing the *Bring online immediately* checkbox. The net result of this combination will be that the server will satisfy the queries from the old MOLAP cache until the new cache is ready. As you can imagine, the actual proactive caching behavior will vary greatly depending on the settings chosen. Let's overwrite the default Automatic MOLAP settings to demonstrate the typical proactive caching behavior, which is MOLAP (steady mode) ⇨ ROLAP (data change) ⇨ MOLAP (steady mode again).

1. Select the *Drop outdated cache* checkbox and specify a latency of *0* seconds. This corresponds to latency value of -1 which sets proactive caching never to revert to ROLAP mode.
2. Select the Bring online immediately checkbox.

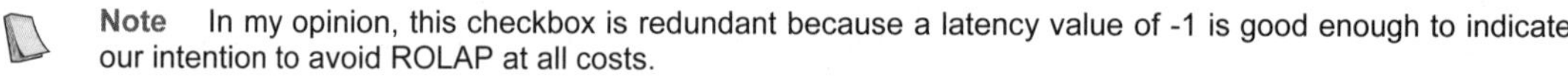

Note In my opinion, this checkbox is redundant because a latency value of -1 is good enough to indicate our intention to avoid ROLAP at all costs.

At this point, the OK button should be disabled because we still have some outstanding work to do, as indicated by the message displayed at the bottom of the Storage Options dialog. The specific issue here is that the Fact Sales measure group is built on top of a named query and the server has no idea which relational tables to track for data changes. If that wasn't the case (if the dimension or measure group was built directly on top of the relational table), we should be good to go assuming that we would like to use the default SQL Server notifications.

Speaking of notifications, let's get some insight into the notification options that proactive caching supports for discovering data changes.

Notification options

Proactive caching supports three notification options to address different deployment and security needs. You can set these options in the Notifications tab.

SQL Server notifications

This option is only available with SQL Server 2000 and above. It leverages the SQL Server trace events which are raised when data is changed. The option is the easiest to set up but it has a few caveats. First, it requires that SSAS connects to the data source with administrator rights and there is no workaround for this limitation. When setting up the data source connection, you have to specify credentials of an account with administrator rights to the data source. Alternatively, if Windows integrated security is used, the account which the Analysis Server service runs under must be a privileged account.

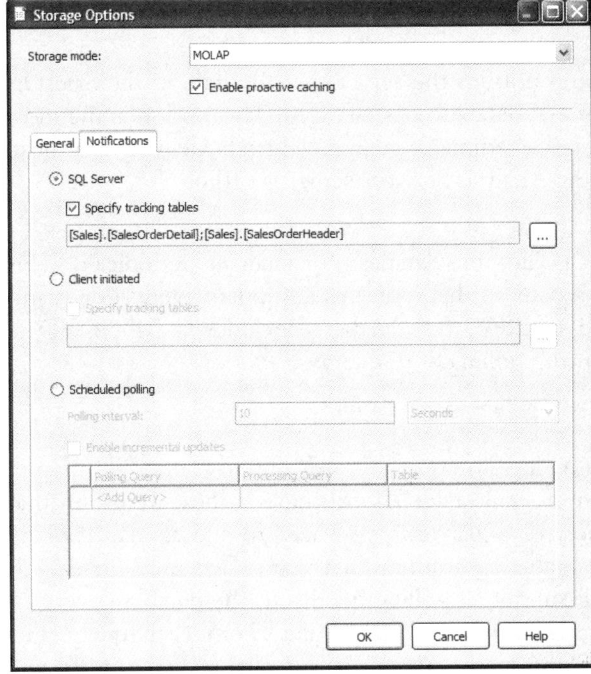

Figure 15.25 Use the Notifications tab to select one of the three supported notification options.

Second, the SQL Server notifications don't guarantee event delivery (no event queuing is supported). This may lead to losing data changes in the proactive cache. For example, if the Analysis Services service is restarted while the data is changed in the relational database, proactive caching will not pick up the data change events.

Tip Regardless of the notification option chosen, I would recommend you give your UDM a full "healthy" reprocess once in a while to make sure you haven't missed any data changes with proactive caching.

Finally, SQL Server notifications always result in Full Process for partitions and Process Update for dimensions. One scenario where this may get in the way is when you know that only new data will be added to a partition or dimension. In this case, Process Add will be a more efficient option but, as it stands, the SQL Server notification option doesn't support Process Add.

Client initiated

This option could be useful when you want an external application to notify the server when data is changed. For example, suppose that only the Adventure Works online sales application makes changes to the Internet Sales partition. In this case, the application can notify SSAS when it changes data. To do so, the application must send a *NotifyTableChange* XMLA command, as follows:

```
<NotifyTableChange>
    <Provider>SQLOLEDB</Provider>
    <DataSource>localhost</DataSource>
    <InitialCatalog>AdventureWorks</InitialCatalog>
    <TableNotifications>
     <TableNotification>
       <DBTableName>SalesOrderDetail</DBTableName>
       <DBSchemaName>Sales</DBSchemaName>
     <TableNotification>
    </TableNotifications>
</NotifyTableChange>
```

In this case, the NotifyTableChange command notifies the server that the data in the SalesOrderDetail table of the AdventureWorks relational database has changed. This option is the most involved to set up but it excels in flexibility. For example, if guaranteed event delivery is a must, the application can queue the events in case the Analysis Services server is offline.

Scheduled polling

Finally, a third and more common option is polling the database for changes periodically. This option assumes that the relational table has a column that indicates an update event. For example, the SalesOrderDetail table in the AdventureWorks database includes a ModifiedDate column. Given this, you can specify the following polling SQL query:

```
SELECT MAX(ModifiedDate) FROM Sales.SalesOrderDetail
```

The polling query must be a singleton query. A singleton query returns one row and one column. Each polling query tracks data changes from a single table. If you have a measure group that spans multiple tables (based on a named query or SQL view), you need to add as many polling queries to the grid, as the number of tracked tables. Assuming that you've accepted the default polling interval of 10 seconds, the server will submit all polling queries to the database every 10 seconds. Internally, the server will keep track of the returned value from each query. For example, in our case, we have only one polling query. When data is changed, the query will return a new value for the ModifiedDate column and the server will know that it is time to update the cache.

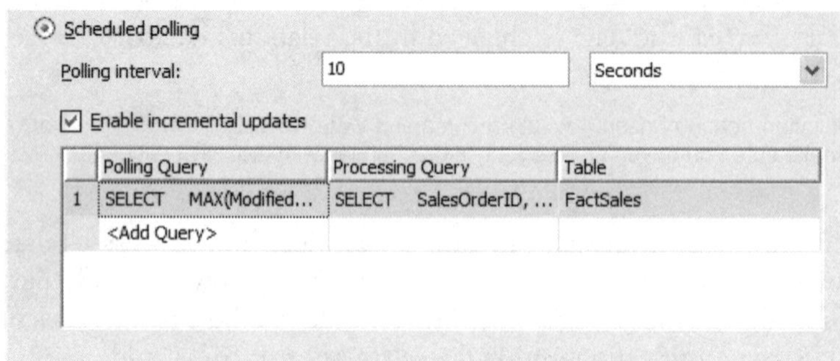

Figure 15.26 Consider incremental cache update when data is only added to a partition or dimension.

Often, data is only added (never changed or deleted) to a table. In this case, you can improve the proactive caching performance by incrementally updating the cache. To do so, you have to specify an additional processing query next to the polling query (Figure 15.26). For example, assuming the polling query above, we can define the following parameterized query to pick up new data only:

```
SELECT * FROM   Sales.SalesOrderDetail
WHERE (ModifiedDate > COALESCE (?, -1)) AND (ModifiedDate <= ?)
```

Note that the query syntax is database-specific. It is very important to get the query WHERE clause right to avoid data duplication or loss. Here is how the server performs incremental updates to the cache. First, the server will execute the polling query to retrieve the latest modified date. Next, the server will execute the processing query passing the returned ModifiedData value from the polling query as a second parameter to the processing query. When the query is executed for the first time, the actual processing query will be translated as follows:

```
SELECT * FROM   Sales.SalesOrderDetail
WHERE (ModifiedDate > -1) AND (ModifiedDate <= #last modified date#)
```

The net result will be that all table rows will be loaded in the cache. During the next polling interval, the server will run the polling query again. If new data has been added, the server will pick up the new ModifiedDate value. Now the server has two date values – the expired last modified date and the current last modified date. Next, the server will pass the two dates to the two parameter placeholders.

```
SELECT * FROM   Sales.SalesOrderDetail
WHERE  (ModifiedDate > #previous modified date#) AND
(ModifiedDate <= #last modified date#)
```

As a result, only the new rows will be retrieved and added to the cache. As you can imagine, incrementally processing a cache can greatly improve the scalability of the server.

Using tracking tables

As noted, the server has no means of detecting which relational tables it needs to monitor when the target object is based on a named query or a SQL view. In this case, you can help the server by explicitly specifying the tracking tables. Both SQL Server and client initiated notification options support tracking tables. Since the Fact Sales measure group is based on a DSV named query, follow these steps to specify the tracking tables:

1. Select the Specify tracking table option below the SQL Server notification option.
2. Click on the ... button and select the *Sales.SalesOrderDetail* and *Sales.SalesOrderHeader* relational tables.
3. At this point, proactive caching is all set up. Deploy the project and give proactive caching a spin.

Testing proactive caching

Since we will be making data changes to the AdventureWorks database, you may want to back up the database. To minimize the scope of the changes, in our test, we will be inserting only two database rows – one sales order in the Sales.SalesOrderHeader table and a related sales order item in the Sales.SalesOrderDetail table. You can find the INSERT statements in the INSERT

CHANGES.sql script file located in the Proactive Caching subfolder of Ch15 folder. In addition, for your convenience, I provided a corresponding DELETE CHANGES script to "undo" the changes when you are done testing. Finally, the MDX query that we will use to test proactive caching can be found in the Test Proactive Caching.mdx script. When you experiment with different policies or just research proactive caching, you may find it useful to monitor the relational database and SSAS activity using the SQL Profiler.

1. Open the SQL Profiler and create two new traces – a Database Engine trace and Analysis Services trace.

2. Open SQL Server Management Studio.

3. Double-click on the INSERT CHANGES.sql file and connect to the SQL server that hosts the AdventureWorks database. Make sure that the AdventureWorks database is selected.

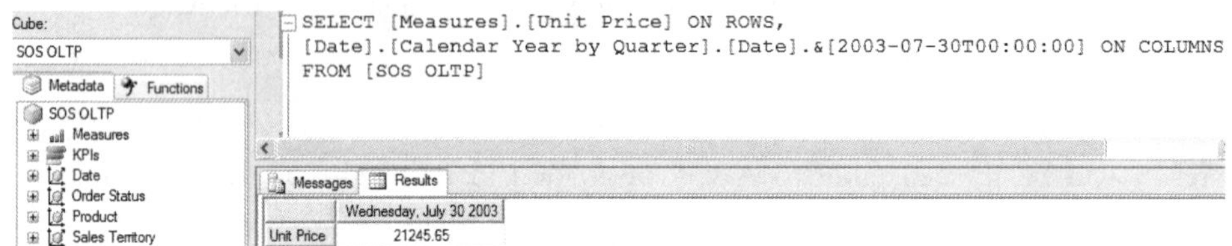

Figure 15.27 Testing proactive caching with SQL Server Management Studio.

4. Double-click on the Test Proactive Caching.mdx script file and connect to the SSAS instance where you've deployed the SOS OLTP UDM. Make sure that the SOS OLTP cube is selected in the MDX designer Cube dropdown (Figure 15.27).

5. Change the month and date of the [Date].[Calendar Year by Quarter].[Date] attribute hierarchy to match the current date but don't change the year (recall that we are in the 2000-2004 Adventure Works time warp).

6. Run the MDX query in the script. In my case (July 30th, 2003), the query returns Unit Sales of $21,245.65 for that day.

7. Switch to the SQL Profiler and observe that the database engine trace doesn't show any activity. That's because the MDX query is satisfied entirely by the MOLAP cache.

Tip You may find it helpful to disable the Reporting Services and SQL Server Agent Windows services to avoid extra "noise" for the duration of the test. Aternatively, you can use SQL Profiler event filtering to filter out the events you don't need (e.g. by filtering by database name or user name)

8. Now, let's disturb the steady mode by making a data change. Run the INSERT statements from the INSERT CHANGES file.

If you now look at the SQL Profiler traces, you will notice database activity and SSAS activity. The database activity reflects the INSERT statements, while the SSAS activity reveals the proactive caching activity. Since we specified a latency of 0, once the server receives a data change notification, it invalidates the existing MOLAP cache immediately.

9. Switch back quickly to Management Studio (in less than 10 seconds after firing the INSERT statement) and run the MDX statement again. You should see the Unit Prices measure incremented to $24,645.64.

More interestingly, SQL Profiler should show a SQL query submitted to the AdventureWorks database. That's because the server has reverted the query processing to ROLAP while the new cache has been built. In addition, once the latency interval has elapsed, you should see additional database activity as a result of the SSAS server rebuilding the new MOLAP cache.

10. Wait for a few seconds for the new cache to become available. Run the MDX query again and observe that no queries are made to the AdventureWorks database. Proactive caching is now in steady mode again.

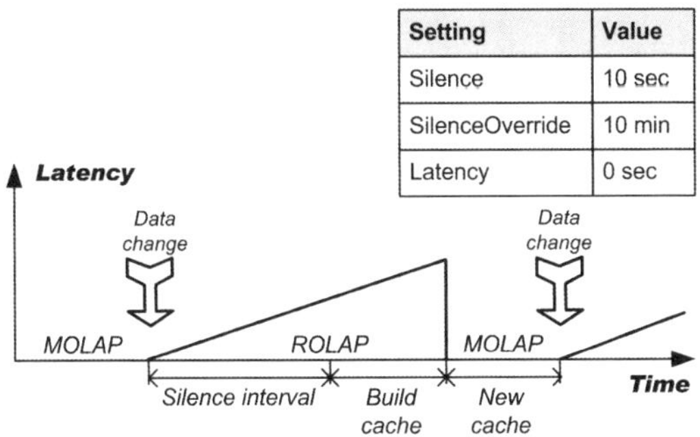

Figure 15.28 The Latency vs. Time graph for the test scenario.

Latency vs. Time graph

Figure 15.28 shows the Latency vs. Time graph and the sequence of events for our testing scenario. First, the system is in a steady state. When the INSERT statement is fired, the server detects the data change almost instantaneously and drops the old cache. However, we have a silence interval window of 10 seconds to wait for a quiet time. While we are within the silence interval, queries are answered in ROLAP mode. Once the silence interval is passed, the server starts processing the new cache by loading it with data from the relational database. An interesting implementation detail is how the server commits the new cache. The server waits for the current MDX queries to complete. During the process of committing the new cache, the server queues new MDX queries. Once the cache is built and committed, the queries are answered in MOLAP mode again.

A more complicated scenario is when database changes are perpetually arriving and the database doesn't enter a quiet mode within the silence interval. After 20 minutes, the SilenceOverride interval will be exhausted. When this happens, the server will start building the cache anyway. It is important to note that, while the cache is being built as a result of exceeding the SilenceOverride interval, the server will ignore new data change events. Of course, once the cache is built and committed, a new data change event will invalidate it again. Therefore, a more efficient cache policy with highly transactional databases will be to schedule the cache to be built on a regular basis to avoid dropping and rebuilding the cache constantly.

ROLAP and HOLAP proactive caching

As Figure 15.23 shows, there are also ROLAP and HOLAP standard storage settings. Interestingly, these settings enable proactive caching too. You may wonder what benefit proactive caching may bring to the table if the cube detail-level data remains in the database and it is updated directly anyway. It so happens that the server maintains various other caches behind the scenes. One of them is the query cache.

Tip You can use the Performance console to track the query cache utilization using the performance counters in the Cache performance category.

When you enable proactive caching on a partition or dimension with ROLAP or HOLAP storage settings, you are actually achieving real-time ROLAP (or HOLAP). If proactive caching is not enabled, the server may potentially answer MDX queries from the old query cache. With proactive caching enabled, the server will listen for data change events (as with MOLAP) and invalidate the query cache to ensure that MDX queries don't retrieve stale data. You can use the same notification options for ROLAP and HOLAP storage settings as with MOLAP. The settings on the General tab don't apply to real-time ROLAP and HOLAP.

15.6 Summary

SSAS supports flexible processing options to address various deployment and operational needs. Traditionally, classic OLAP solutions have used the pull-mode processing to load cubes with data. The Process Full option is the easiest and cleanest way to process UDM cubes and dimensions. When Process Full doesn't give the performance you need, consider incremental processing.

Automating processing tasks is a common management requirement. I showed you how you can script processing tasks and execute them on a regular schedule with the SQL Server Agent service. Alternatively, to perform processing tasks inside SSIS packages, use the Analysis Services Processing Task.

Sometimes, your business requirements may call for low-latency OLAP solutions. With classic OLAP (data warehousing), consider using report actions and push-mode processing to reduce data latency. With transactional OLAP (OLAP build on top of an OLTP data source), consider using proactive caching.

15.7 Resources

Analysis Services 2005 Processing Architecture
(http://shrinkster.com/6pn) – A must-read whitepaper which describes the Analysis Services 2005 processing architecture in detail and provides guidance on how and when to use the various processing options.

Creating Large-Scale, Highly Available OLAP Sites: A Step-by-Step Guide
(http://shrinkster.com/73f) – This paper introduces various techniques needed to create large-scale, highly available online analytical processing (OLAP) sites using Microsoft SQL Server 2000 Analysis Services and Network Load Balancing.

T-SQL Enhancements in SQL Server 2005 chapter
(http://shrinkster.com/8kq) – Understand how snapshot transaction isolation works.

Chapter 16

Securing Analysis Services

Security cannot be downplayed anymore. The explosion of viruses and hacker attacks in recent years has pushed security concerns to the forefront of development and application design. Microsoft has responded by declaring trustworthy computing as a top priority. In an open letter to Microsoft employees, Bill Gates wrote "Our products should emphasize security right out of the box". You won't get very far with Analysis Services if you don't have a good grasp of how its security model works. SSAS offers a robust role-based security model which administrators can leverage to enforce restricted access to the UDM objects and data.

In this chapter, you will learn how to:

- Control which users can administer the SSAS server and databases.
- Enforce restricted access to cubes, dimensions, and cells.
- Choose a security strategy for different application deployment models.

Because the SSAS security model is layered on top of Windows, understanding security is not easy and explaining this topic in details is beyond the scope of this book. Therefore, I will assume that you have a basic knowledge of how Windows authentication and authorization work. The Microsoft MSDN Security Center (see Resources) is a great place to start if you want to get up to speed with Windows security.

16.1 Understanding SSAS Role-based Security

You will probably find the SSAS role-based security similar to the security models of other Microsoft or home-grown solutions you have come across. The implementation details are SSAS-specific but the underlying concepts are the same. In a nutshell, the user is authenticated based on her Windows account and authorized according to the security policies the administrator has set up.

Note As it stands, SSAS doesn't support custom security to replace the Windows-based security model. SSAS will authenticate and authorize incoming requests based on the Windows account the request is made under.

Figure 16.1 is meant to clarify the SSAS security model at a high level. The server enforces restricted access to UDM objects through *roles*. A role specifies the UDM *permissions* that are granted to a given Windows *user* or a *group*. Let's drill down into the SSAS role-based security model starting with roles.

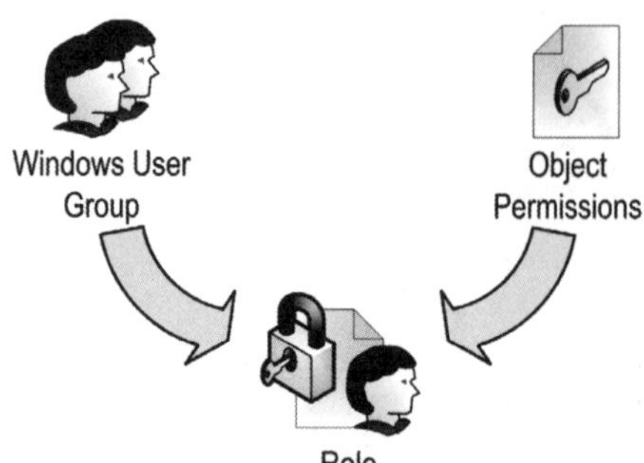

Figure 16.1 Restricted access to UDM is enforced with roles. A role is assigned set of permissions to a Windows user or a group.

16.1.1 Understanding Roles

In SSAS, by the term *role* we will mean a declarative security policy that enforces restricted access to UDM metadata and data. Out of the box, there is only one pre-defined *Server* role that controls access to the entire server. The Server role cannot be removed. Members of the server role can create database roles to define more granular security policies at the database, cube, dimension, and even cell levels.

Server role

The SQL Server setup program creates an implicit *Server* role and assigns the members of the local Administrators Windows group to that role. The Windows users and groups assigned to the Server role become the server administrators and have unrestricted access to the server and all UDM objects. For example, they can create, modify, delete, process objects, and read data from all objects. In addition, they can manage security and assign permissions to other users. You can think of the SSAS Server role as the equivalent of the SQL Server system administrator (*sa)* account. Now you understand why you were able to accomplish all the hands-on exercises in this book on your local SSAS server without configuring or knowing anything about security. Since you have Administrator rights on your machine, your account was added to the Server role.

SSAS 2000 The SSAS 2000 equivalent of the Server role was OLAP Administrators Windows user group. Since SSAS 2005 supports multiple server instances running side-by-side, the Server role is defined on an instance level. For example, you can have several development teams working on the same server and each team can have administrator rights to their server instance.

Assigning other members to the Server role

Besides the members of the local Administrators, you may want to assign additional Windows users or groups to the Server role.

1. In Management Studio, connect to the SSAS server and open the server properties (right-click on the server node in the Object Explorer and choose *Properties*).
2. Click on the Security page and note that the Server role doesn't have any members. As noted, the members of the local Windows Administrators group are implicitly assigned to the Server role.
3. Click on the Add button to bring up the standard Windows Select Users and Groups dialog (Figure 16.2). Enter the Windows user name or group in the Domain\MemberName naming

convention (or click Advanced and then Find Now to search). Click the Check Names button to verify the member.

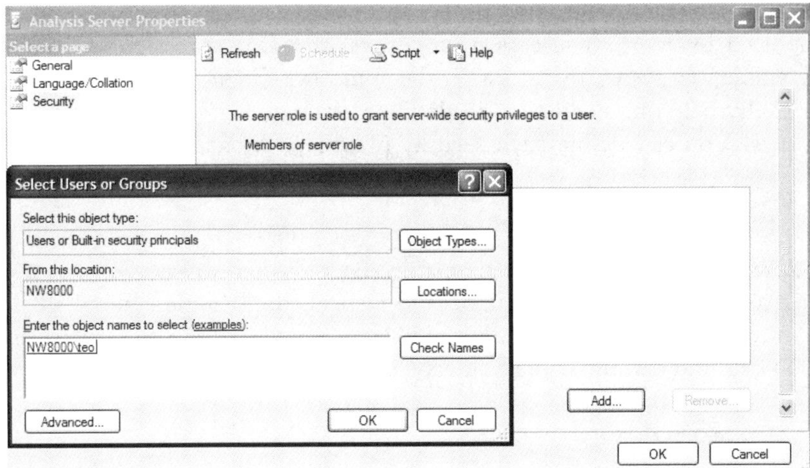

Figure 16.2 Use the server properties to grant Administrator rights to Windows users and groups.

4. Click OK to add the selected member to the Server role.

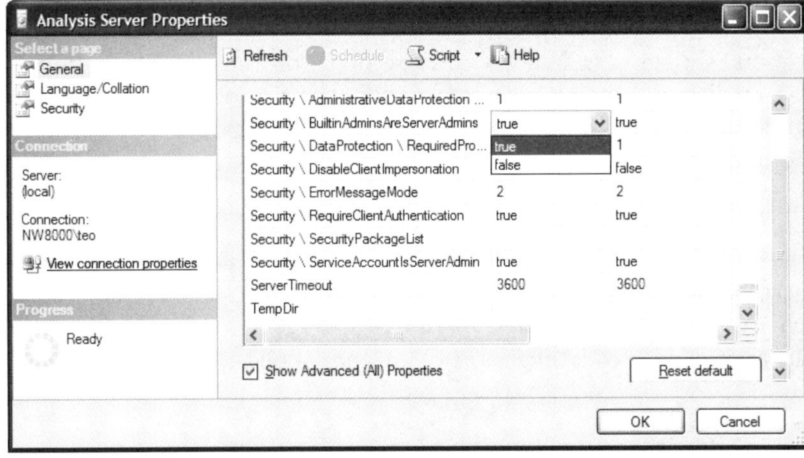

Figure 16.3 Use the server properties to remove local Aministrators from the Server role.

Removing the local Administrators from the Server role

Sometimes, you may need to remove the members of the local Windows Administrators group from the Server role after you have assigned new members explicitly.

Warning To prevent accidental server lockout, make sure that you have explicitly assigned members to the Server role before removing the local Administrators from the Server role.

5. Open the server properties and select the General page. Check the Show Advanced (All) Properties to see the advanced properties.
6. Change the Security\BuiltinAdminsAreServerAdmins property to *false* (Figure 16.3). You don't need to restart the server for this change to become effective.

One cautionary note is that the above steps prevent local administrators from accessing SSAS objects only. However, there is nothing stopping a local administrator from making system-wide changes, e.g. uninstalling the server or deleting the SSAS metadata. The Server role is the only server-wide role supported by SSAS. The easiest way to grant UDM access to all users (and achieve a completely vulnerable system) is to assign the Windows *Everyone* group to the Server role. In real-life, it is likely that you would need to define more granular security policies to the UDM metadata and data. You can define such security policies at a database level by creating database roles.

Role definitions

Before I show you how you can create a database role, I would like to clarify one potential source of confusion. If you open the Ch16 solution and inspect the definition file of the Database Administrators role I created (*Database Administrators.role* under the Roles folder in the Solution Explorer), you will find that it has the following structure:

```
<Role>
    <ID>DatabaseAdministrators</ID>
    <Name>Database Administrators</Name>
    <More role properties.../>
     <Members>
       <Member>sosdan1</Member>
     </Members>
</Role>
```

As you could see, the actual role definition doesn't contain the object permissions. Instead, it stores only Windows users (sosdan1 is a Windows user account you will create in section 16.1.3) and/or groups the role applies to, which is what you would expect a role to contain anyway. In other words, the role definition contains only the membership settings that you specify in the Membership tab when configuring the role.

So, where are the actual security policies stored then? Well, they become part of the object definition itself. For example, if you grant a given user rights to read the cube data, the security policy gets saved in the cube definition file. I wish the SSAS team had named the Roles folder in BI Studio and Management Studio *Security Polices* to avoid confusion because that's precisely what you are defining when setting up database roles. Anyway, I will stick to the official SSAS terminology and will use the term *role* as a collective name of a security policy.

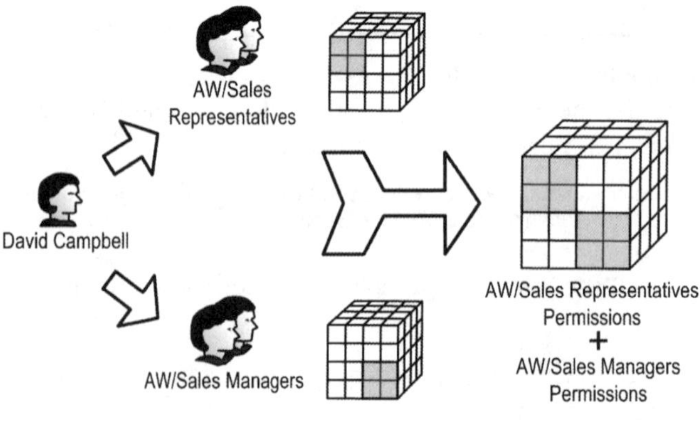

Figure 16.4 SSAS roles are additive and the user is granted the union of the permitted role permissions.

Combing roles

In SSAS, roles are additive. That is, if the user is a member of multiple role definitions, the effective permission set is the union of the allowed role permissions. As Figure 16.4 shows, the user David Campbell is a member of both Sales Representatives and Sales Manager groups in the AW domain. Assuming that both groups are given rights to read different slices of the cube, David will be able to read data contained in both slices.

While explicitly denied rights take precedence over implicit or explicit allowed rights **within** a role, SSAS doesn't support the concept of a strong deny **across** multiple roles. For example, if the Sales Representatives role explicitly denies access to the Bikes member of the Product Category hierarchy but the Sales Manager role doesn't explicitly deny it, David *will* be able to browse data by that member. For this reason, I recommend you avoid explicit denied rights whenever possible.

Interestingly, if a user belongs to multiple roles and so wishes, the user could elect to connect to the server with a given role(s). Suppose that David doesn't want to apply the permissions assigned to him by the Sales Managers role. The SSAS connection string property supports a *Roles* setting, which the end-user or the application can use to specify a comma-delimited list of Roles the user wants the server to evaluate. We will revisit the Roles connection string setting in section 16.4.1 to find how it can be useful with Internet-based solutions.

Note The user can select only roles that the user is a member of. For example, if David is not a member of the SOS OLAP Administrator role, he cannot elect this role.

16.1.2 Permissions and Access Rights

During the process of configuring a role, you specify which objects will be affected by the security policies defined in that role. These security policies get saved as a collection of *permissions* inside the object metadata (Figure 16.5).

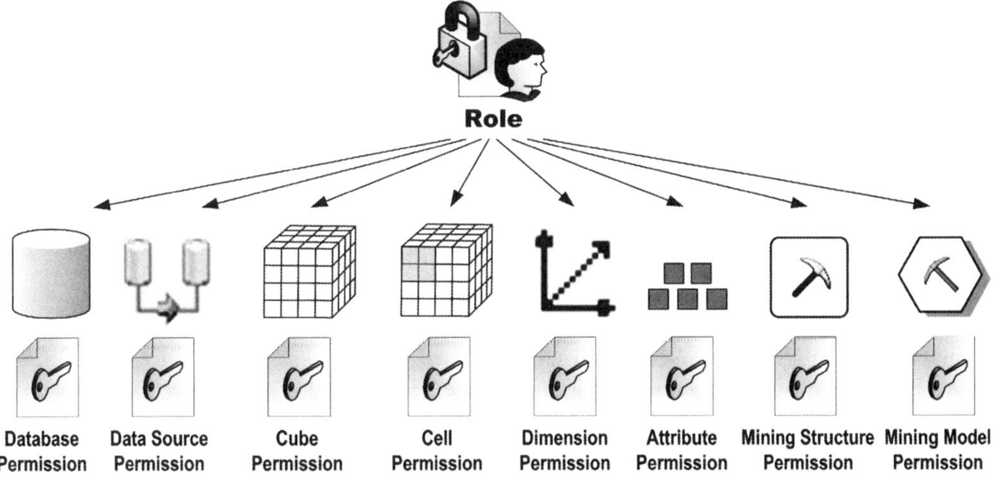

Figure 16.5 The security polices defined in a role are saved as permissions inside the object metadata.

For example, suppose you grant members of the SOS OLAP Administrators role rights to process the SOS OLAP cube. In addition, you grant the members of the Sales Managers role rights to read the cube data. Once the role is defined, BI Studio will create a collection of two *CubePermission* objects and save it inside the definition file of the SOS OLAP cube. The abbreviated definition of the CubePermission collection may look like the one below.

```
<CubePermissions>
  <CubePermission>
    <ID>CubePermission</ID>
    <Name>CubePermission</Name>
    <RoleID>SOS OLAP Administrators</RoleID>
    <Process>true</Process>
  </CubePermission>
  <CubePermission>
    <ID>CubePermission 2</ID>
    <Name>CubePermission 2</Name>
    <RoleID>Sales Managers</RoleID>
    <Read>Allowed</Read>
  </CubePermission>
</CubePermissions>
```

Each permission inside the permission collection references the role that the permission applies to. In the example above, we have two roles that define security policies for the SOS OLAP cube. UDM has corresponding permissions for all objects shown in Figure 16.5. For example, if you define a dimension security policy, a *DimensionPermission* collection will be created in the definition file of the affected dimension.

Access rights

The actual actions permitted by the role are defined as *access rights*. One of the main reasons for the new security enhancements in the SSAS 2005 was to make the security model more granular. An access right represents the most granular level in the SSAS role-based security model. Different UDM objects support different access rights. For example, in the CubePermissions XML definition above, members of the SOS OLAP Administrator role are given the Process access right to process the database. Consult with the product documentation (*Permissions and Access Rights* topic) for a full list of the access rights supported by different object permissions.

To minimize the number of explicit security policies, access rights have default values. For example, the Read cube access right has a default setting of *None*. Therefore, in the definition above, the SOS OLAP Administrator role is not allowed to read the cube data. In comparison, the administrator has granted explicitly a Read access right to the members of the Sales Managers role. Access rights could also be inheritable. For example, by default, the Process access right on a database propagates to the child objects contained in the database unless is specifically overwritten by the object permission policy.

The role-based security model schema

To summarize role-based security, you can think of a database role as a logical container of database-wide security policies that define permissions and access rights to UDM objects within a database. Object security policies become part of the object metadata and are realized as a collection of permissions (Figure 16.6). Each permission references a single role and one or more access rights that apply to that role within the containing object.

Now that you have a good understanding of the SSAS role-based security, let's find out how you can create new database roles.

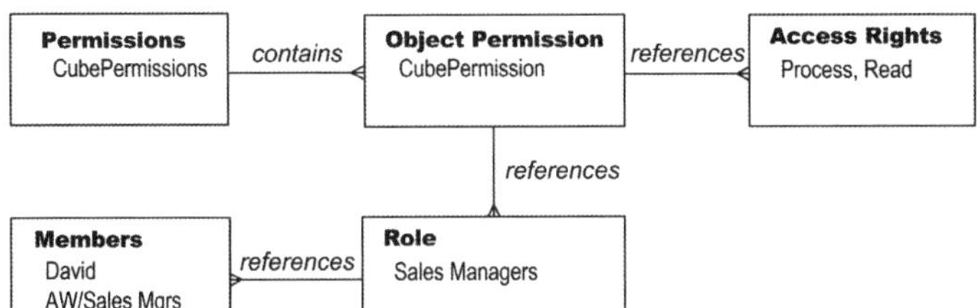

Figure 16.6 The object security policy (role) consists of a collection of permissions.

16.1.3 Creating Database Administrator Role

Suppose that as a server administrator you want to offload managing the SOS OLAP database task to another person. You can do this by creating a new database role and granting the Administer access right for the SOS OLAP database to that person. To bring a touch of reality, we will grant the Process rights to Dan Wilson, a Database Administrator for Adventure Works according to the DimEmployee table in the AdventureWorksDW database.

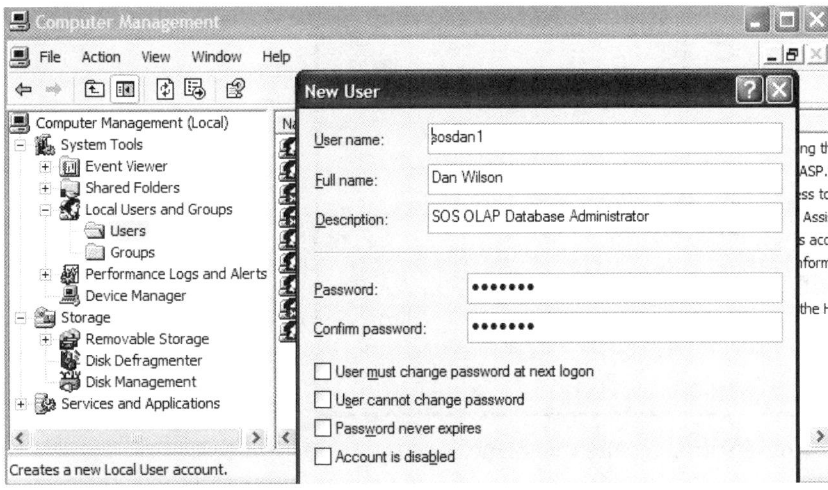

Figure 16.7 The SSAS security model is built on top of Windows security.

Creating a Windows test account

In real life, it is likely that Dan will already have a Windows account in the Adventure Works Active Directory (e.g. *adventure-works\dan1* as DimEmployee table suggests). This means you will be able to assign Dan as a member of an SSAS database role using his existing Windows account (or a Windows group he belongs to). However, for testing purposes only, we will create local Windows accounts for a few Adventure Works users.

1. Click Start ⇨ Run and type **compmgmt.msc** in the Windows Run dialog. Click OK to start the Computer Management Console.
2. Create a new Windows user named *sosdan1* and full name of *Dan Wilson* (Figure 16.7). The *sos* prefix will help you locate easily the new accounts you will create in this chapter and remove them without a problem when you are done testing.

3. Unselect the *User must change password at next logon* checkbox and click OK to create the account.

Creating a database role

Both BI Studio Role Designer and Management Studio Create Role dialog allow you to set up database roles, although a slightly different user interface. In real life, the server administrator would most likely set up security polices *after* the cube is deployed in Management Studio. For these reasons, I will use Management Studio to demonstrate creating a new database role. As an added benefit, you don't need to deploy the SOS OLAP database each time you modify a role, since changes made in Management Studio are made in online mode. Also, I duplicated some of the role settings in the SOS OLAP project (Ch 16 solution).

1. In Management Studio Object Explorer, connect to the SSAS server that hosts the SOS OLAP database.
2. Expand the SOS OLAP database folder. Right-click on the Roles folder and choose *New Role* to bring the Create Role dialog (Figure 16.8).

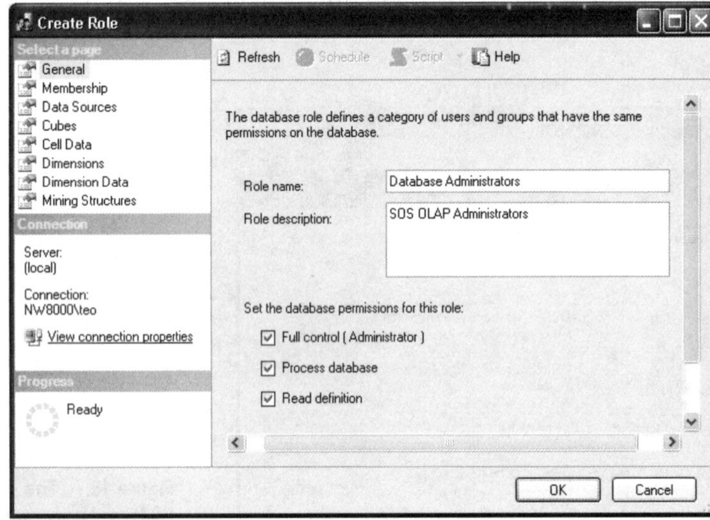

Figure 16.8 The DatabasePermission object includes Administer, Process, ReadDefinition, and Access Read (implicit) access rights.

3. Enter **Database Administrators** as the role name.
4. Check the *Full control* (Administrator) right.
5. Switch to the Membership page and add the *sosdan1* Windows account.
6. Click OK to create the Database Administrators role.
7. In the Object Explorer, right-click on the SOS OLAP database and choose *Script the database as* ⇨ *CREATE TO* ⇨ *New Query Editor Window*. Once the database CREATE DDL script is ready, search for DatabasePermissions to locate the permission definition you've just created.

```
<Roles>
    <Role>
     <ID>Role 1</ID>
       <Name>SOS OLAP Administrators</Name>
     <Description>Manage SOS OLAP Database</Description>
    </Role>
</Roles>
```

```
<DatabasePermission>
    <ID>DatabasePermission</ID>
    <Name>DatabasePermission</Name>
    <RoleID>Role 1</RoleID>
    <Process>true</Process>
    <ReadDefinition>Allowed</ReadDefinition>
    <Read>Allowed</Read>
</DatabasePermission>
```

As you can see, the DatabasePermission defining includes the Process, ReadDefinition, and Read access rights. The Administer right is not stored in the definition file.

Tip As you would notice, permission objects reference roles by the identifiers which are numbered sequentially. The UI doesn't provide a way to assign more meaningful identifiers. If this bothers you, change the object identifiers directly in the object definition file inside BI Studio. Change the role identifier immediately after an empty role is created. Otherwise, you will loose the references and you will need to reconfigure the role.

Understanding database permissions

The Create Role dialog is subdivided in as many pages as the number of the permissions supported by SSAS, plus the Membership page to set up the members of the role. Use the General page to grant access rights to the entire database (DatabasePermission object). The DatabasePermission is the highest permission object in the UDM permission hierarchy. Table 16.1 summarizes the access rights that can be assigned to the DatabasePermission object and how they map to the Create Role dialog.

Table 16.1 Access rights supported by the DatabasePermission object.

Access right	Create Role dialog	Description
Administer	Full control (Administrator)	Unrestricted rights to the affected database only. Cannot load stored procedures.
Process	Process database	Process the database and its child objects. Inheritable. No implied rights to read data.
ReadDefinition	Read definition	Read the database definition (DDL). Inheritable. No implied rights to read data.
Read	N/A	Allowed to connect to the database or read data. Not inheritable to containing objects.

To give Dan unrestricted access to the SOS OLAP database, we need to grant him the *Administer* access right. The closest SQL Server equivalent to the Administer access right is the database owner (DBO) role. However, in UDM, there are some actions that are disallowed even if you are the database administrator. For example, you cannot load assemblies and stored procedures because they may impact the server. Sometimes, you may need to grant more restricted rights. At a database level, you can restrict role members to process the database (*Process* right) only. By default, the Process right doesn't apply rights to read data. You can verify this by switching to the Cubes page and observing that the Access column is set to *None* for the SOS OLAP cube.

The *Read* access right is an interesting one because it is not exposed in the UI. Instead, the server implicitly enables it when any of the first three rights are granted. In essence, the Read access right in the database allows role members to connect to the database. For data containing objects, it permits reading the object data. It is not inheritable, meaning that a right to read a database doesn't imply rights to read data contained in the child objects. You can perform various role management tasks by right-clicking on the role inside Management Studio, including deleting, renaming, and scripting roles. Also, you can duplicate role definitions by using the Duplicate context menu.

Testing database roles

Once the database management role is in place, you may wonder how you can test it. Testing cube data permissions is easy with the handy Change User button on the Cube Browser toolbar. Unfortunately, neither BI Studio, nor Management Studio, provides an easy way to change the security context and impersonate a user or a role for testing database management tasks. You may find the following testing methodology useful if you know the password of the Windows user you are impersonating.

1. Assuming your Windows account is a member of the Server role, open a Management Studio instance to set up the required role policies.
2. Open a new Management Studio instance under the identity of the user you need to test. To do so, right-click on Management Studio shortcut and choose *Run As* (for Windows 2000 use Shift+right mouse click).
3. In the Run As dialog, select *The following user* option and type in the user name and the password. Once you click OK, Windows will run Management Studio under the impersonated user.

With this approach, role changes made in the first instance of Management Studio require only refresh of the Object Explorer in the second instance to apply the changes. Alternatively, instead of using *Run As* when connecting to Management Studio, you can enter the user credentials in the Connect to Server dialog. I wish a future release exposed all connectivity settings supported by SSAS. This will allow using the Roles connection string setting to simulate the user role membership.

16.1.4 Managing Cube-level Security

By default, only members of the Server role (server administrators) have the right to see the cube data. Suppose you need to grant rights to the Adventure Works Sales department to browse the SOS OLAP cube.

Creating a Windows testing account and group

Let's start by creating a new Windows group to represent the Adventure Works sales department and assign a Windows account to it.

1. In the Computer Management console, create a new local Windows group named *SOS Sales*.
2. Create a new Windows user account with a user name of **sosbrian3**. Enter **Brian Welcker** (Vice President of Sales in Adventure Works) as a full name of the user.
3. Assign Brian as a member of the SOS Sales Windows group. Optionally, create other Windows user accounts and assign them to the SOS Sales group.

Creating Sales database role

As you know by now, an end-user must be assigned to an SSAS database role before being able to perform any action against an SSAS database. Follow these steps to create a new database role in the SSAS database to serve the needs of the Adventure Works sales department.

1. In Management Studio, create a new database role. In the General page, enter **Sales** as the role name.
2. Select the Membership page and click the Add button to open the Select Users and Group Windows dialog. Click the Object Types button, select the *Groups* object type, and click OK.
3. Back to the Select Users and Groups dialog, enter **SOS Sales** and click Check Names to test the group name. Click OK to add the SOS Sales windows group as a member of the Sales database role in the SSAS database.
4. In the Create Role dialog, click the Cubes page. Note that, by default, the members of the SOS Sales role don't have access to read the cube data (Access is None), to create local cubes or perform drillthrough (Local cube/Drillthrough is None), and to process the cube (Process checkbox is cleared).

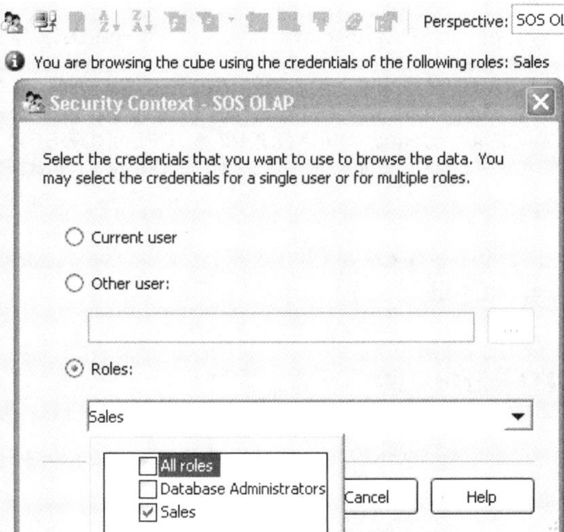

Figure 16.9 Use the Change User feature to impersonate a Windows user or a database role.

Impersonating users and roles

The Cube Browser allows you to test how security polices affect the user experience by using the Security context dialog (Figure 16.9). The *Current user* option (default) sends the query requests to server using the identity of the interactive user (that's you). The *Other* user option allows you to impersonate another user provided that Windows Server 2003 domain controller is used for authentication. The reason for this limitation is that this option uses the S4U (Service-for-User) extensions available only on Windows Server 2003.

In a nutshell, S4U allows a privileged Windows account (e.g. administrator or Local System) to impersonate another user without having the user password. For more information about the S4U extensions, read Keith Brown's article *Exploring S4U Kerberos Extensions in Windows Server 2003* (see Resources). The Roles option supports simulating a database role. Follow these steps to test the security policies assigned to the Sales role.

1. To verify the access rights granted to the Sales role (or lack thereof), right-click on the SOS OLAP cube and choose *Browse.*
2. In the Cube Browser, click the Change User toolbar button (the leftmost toolbar button) to launch the Security Context dialog.

3. Select the *Roles* option. Expand the dropdown and check the *Sales* role.
4. Click OK to close the Security Context dialog and attempt to browse the cube. The cube browser shows an error message "The cube cannot be browsed. Verify that the cube has been deployed and processed." While the message text may mislead you, the real reason why you are not able to browse the cube is that the Sales role doesn't have rights to the SOS OLAP cube.

Granting cube-level access

Let's grant the Sales role permissions rights to read the cube data.

1. In Management Studio, double-click on the Sales role to open its properties.
2. In the Edit Role dialog (Figure 16.10), select the Cubes tab and change the Access column from None to *Read*. In case you are curious, the Read/Write setting allows to you perform partition writeback if it is enabled.

Note You may wonder why you can browse HOLAP and ROLAP cubes provided that the Data Source access right is set to None (Data Sources page). As noted in chapter 2, when Windows Integrated authentication is used, the server always connects to the data source under the identity of the service account. Data sources used for DMX queries, however, can be configured to use the interactive user credentials. Therefore, the Data Sources access rights affects only DMX queries (OPENQUERY or OPENROWSET) that perform predictions against user-provided data. In this case, the interactive user must have at least Read access.

3. Browse the SOS OLAP cube again under the security context of the Sales role (or reconnect). Now, you should be able to browse the cube successfully.

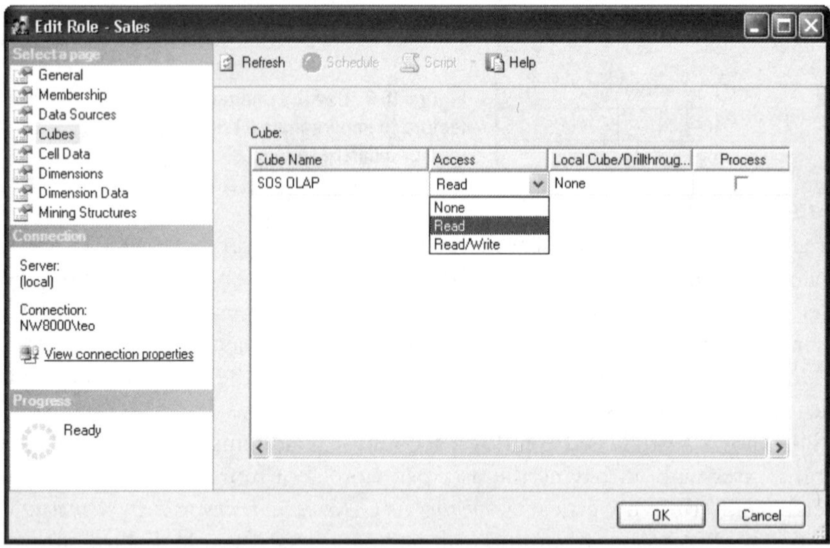

Figure 16.10 Use the Cubes page to grant a role rights to read the cube data.

So, this is easy. You assign all users that should be able to browse the cube data to a database role and grant Read rights to that role. Once the role is set, the role members can read the cube data across all dimensions.

16.2 Managing Dimension Security

Chances are that your real-life requirements may call for more granular security polices than controlling cube-level security only. For example, you may need to disallow certain roles from browsing data by given dimension members. Or, in the more involved scenario, you may need to customize the security policies based on the identity of the interactive user, e.g. allow the sales managers to view data for their regions only. You can address more involved security requirements by defining dimension and cube cell security policies.

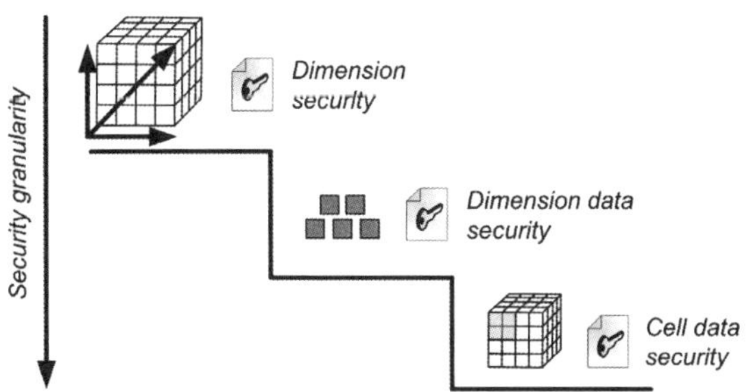

Figure 16.11 You can secure UDM data at dimension, dimension data, and cell data level.

16.2.1 Understanding UDM Data Security

UDM allows you to implement three defense lines for data security with different levels of granularity, as Figure 16.11 shows. At a *dimension* level, you could grant access rights to entire dimensions. At a *dimension data* level, you can enforce restricted access to individual members of the attribute hierarchies. Finally, the most granular security level is *cell data* security where you can define security policies for individual cells.

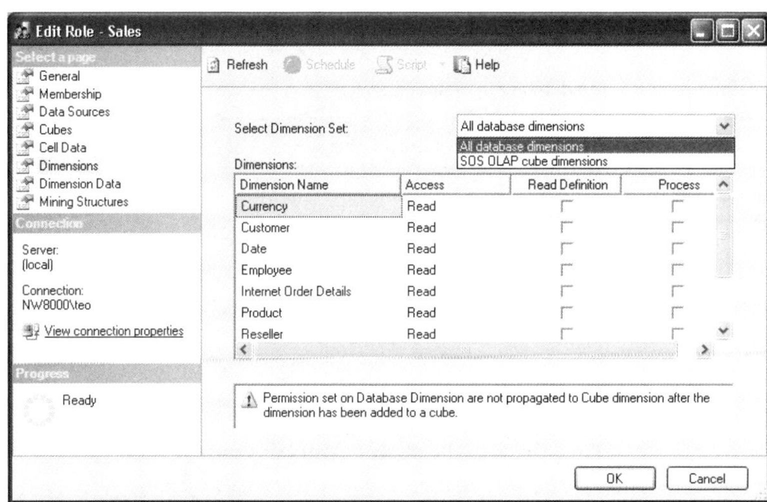

Figure 16.12 Use the Dimensions page to grant Read or Read/Write access right to dimensions.

Dimension security

You manage dimension security using the Dimensions page in the Edit Role dialog (Figure 16.12 shows). This dialog allows you to control dimension security at a database level or a cube level.

To understand this, recall that dimensions are database-level objects. A dimension may or may not be referenced in a cube.

If you haven't granted the selected role Read access to cubes in the SSAS database, the only option available in the dropdown is *All database dimensions*. This option allows you to set dimension security policies at a database level. If the role has access to a cube in the SSAS database (controlled by the Cubes page), you can select a specific cube dimension set (e.g. SOS OLAP cube dimensions). This allows you to overwrite the security polices of the *All database dimensions* set. The available access rights are Read (default) and Read/Write. The latter option allows you to control dimension writeback.

Dimension data vs. cell data security

Dimension data (attribute members) and cell data (cube cells) security policies can be defined in the Dimension Data and Cell Data pages respectively. Use dimension data security to secure members of a dimension and any data associated with those members. Use cell data security to protect cell values only. For example, consider the report shown in Table 16.2. If you don't take any extra measures to secure the cube data, members of the Sales role will have access to all data in the SOS OLAP cube.

Table 16.2 In the absence of dimension or cell data security, users can see all cube data.

Sales Territory	Reseller Sales Amount	Reseller Order Count
North America	✓ **$62,947,143.31**	✓ 3,166
Europe	✓ **$14,012,997.74**	✓ 505

Dimension data security

Suppose that you need to prevent the Sales role from seeing any data associated with the Europe member of the Sales Territory attribute hierarchy. Once dimension data security is configured for the Europe member, the report will not show the second row at all (Table 16.3).

Table 16.3 Dimension data security removes the dimension member.

Sales Territory	Reseller Sales Amount	Reseller Order Count
North America	✓ **$62,947,143.31**	✓ 3,166

Note that the end-user won't be able to browse any measures by the Europe member, not only the ones shown in the report. The Europe dimension member simply won't exist for the Sales role.

Cell data security

Cell data security is more granular. For example, if you apply a cell data security policy to prevent the members of the Sales role from seeing the Reseller Sales Amount and Reseller Order Count measures for the Europe member, the report will change as shown in Table 16.4.

Table 16.4 Cell data security controls access to the individual cube cells.

Sales Territory	Reseller Sales Amount	Reseller Order Count
North America	✓ **$62,947,143.31**	✓ 3,166
Europe	✗ **#N/A**	✗ #N/A

In this case, the user will see the Europe member but not the cell values of the measures.

16.2.2 Configuring Basic Dimension Security

Dimension data security is enforced with DimensionPermission permission objects. The DimensionPermission object is the most complex permission object supported by UDM. As you know by now, a UDM dimension is nothing more than a container of attributes. Attributes may and usually form attribute hierarchies; multi-level hierarchies are optional and are for user convenience only.

Note When you are defining dimension data security, you are essentially securing the dimension attribute hierarchies. Attribute security (AttributePermission) transcends all multi-level hierarchies which use that attribute.

Since a large UDM may contain dimensions with many attributes, the challenge of the dimension data security architecture is to give you simple ways to configure the allowed and denied attribute members. To minimize the maintenance effort, UDM supports allowed and denied sets.

Allowed and denied sets

If you inspect the DimensionPermission object once the dimension data security policy is set, you will find that it contains a collection of AttributePermission objects.

```
<DimensionPermissions>
   <DimensionPermission>
    <ID>DimensionPermission</ID>
    <Name>DimensionPermission</Name>
    <RoleID>Sales</RoleID>
    <Read>Allowed</Read>
    <AttributePermissions>
       <AttributePermission>
     <AttributeID>Product</AttributeID>
     <DeniedSet>{[Product].[Product].[Montain-100 Black, 38],
         [Product].[Product].[Montain-100 Black, 42]}
     </DeniedSet>
       </AttributePermission>
    </AttributePermissions>
   </DimensionPermission>
</DimensionPermissions>
```

The AttributePermissions collection contains as many elements as the number of the secured attributes. The actual secured attribute members will be enumerated in the AllowedSet or DeniedSet elements. An AllowedSet element enumerates the attribute members that a role is allowed to see. On the other side, a DeniedSet element specifies a list of attribute members that a role cannot see. In this case, we allow access to all attribute members in the Product dimension except for the two mountain bikes that are explicitly denied. Given this security policy, the members of the Sales role won't be able to see these members at all when browsing the Product attribute hierarchy and the multi-level hierarchies it participates.

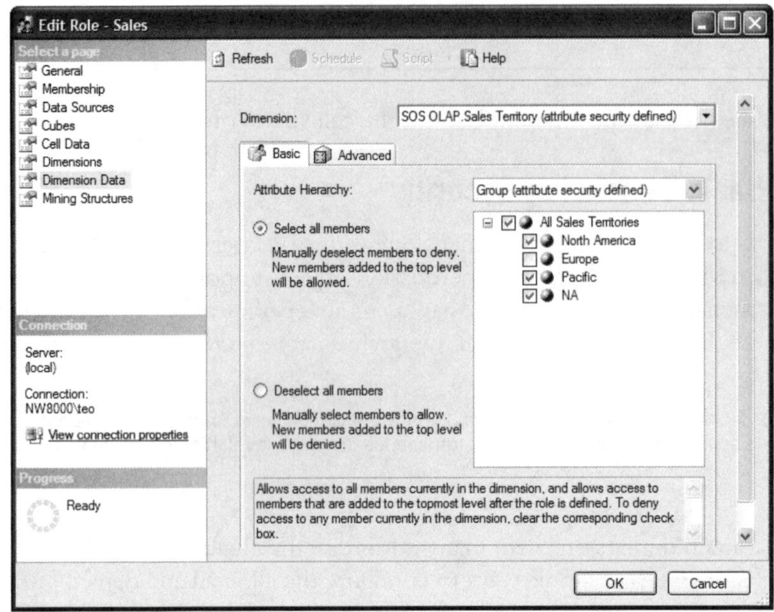

Figure 16.13 Implement basic dimension data security by selecting allowed and denied attribute members.

Disallowing attribute members

You implement basic dimension data security by using the Basic tab of the Dimension Data page in the Edit Role dialog (Figure 16.13). The Dimension dropdown allows you to select a database or cube dimension. If you select a database dimension, the security policies are inherited by cubes that reference that dimension and are stored in the database metadata. This may reduce maintenance effort when an SSAS database contains more than one cube. In the case of a cube dimension, the security policies are scoped at that cube only and are stored in the cube metadata.

Tip When you define security polices for a cube dimension, you break the inheritance chain of database-level dimension security policies. You can restore the inheritance chain by completely removing all cube-level dimension polices.

Suppose that you need to deny the members of the Sales role access to the Europe member of the Group attribute hierarchy (Sales territory dimension). Further, let's assume that we would like to scope the security policy for the SOS OLAP cube (cube-level dimension security).

1. Expand the Dimension dropdown and select the *Sales Territory* dimension below the SOS OLAP cube.
2. Expand the attribute hierarchy and select the *Group* attribute hierarchy. The right-side pane shows the members of the Group attribute hierarchy. The Select all members option is pre-selected.
3. Clear the checkbox of the *Europe* member. Click OK to apply the security policy.
4. In the Cube Browser, author the report shown in Figure 16.14.

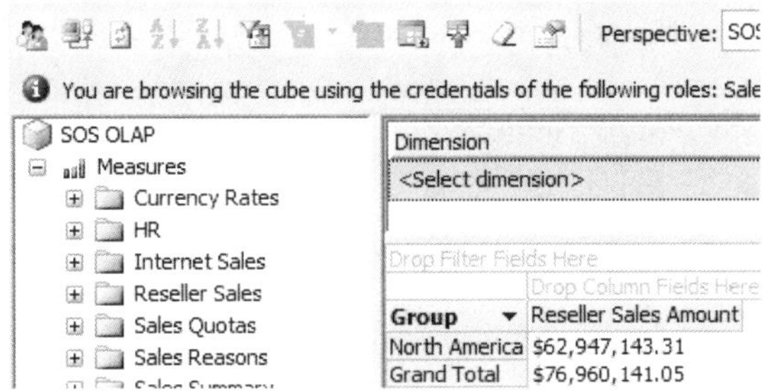

Figure 16.14 By applying dimension data security, we deny access to the Europe member.

5. Change the user context to the *Sales* role. Notice that the Europe member is not shown in the report.

Note You can easily tell the secured attribute hierarchies and dimensions in the Attribute Hierarchy and Dimension dropdowns by the *(attribute security defined)* suffix.

The Select and Deselect options on the Basic tab work in reverse. By default, UDM allows access to all members in all attribute hierarchies. You can deny access to specific members by clearing their checkboxes. This will produce a denied set (*DeniedSet* element). Alternatively, you can enable the *Deselect all members* option. In this case, all members will be disallowed by default (disallowed members are the norm, allowed members are the exception). When this option is enabled, clearing a member checkbox allows that member (*AllowedSet* is produced).

16.2.3 Configuring Advanced Dimension Security

The Advanced tab in the Dimension Data page gives you more control to specify the allowed and denied sets. For example, you can use any set-producing MDX expression or call stored procedures to implement dynamic security, as I will demonstrate in section 16.2.4. For now, let's get a better understanding of how allowed and denied sets work.

Country: Canada

City	Reseller	Reseller Sales Amount
Aurora	Online Bike Warehouse	$439.68
	Total	$439.68
Barrie	Standard Bikes	$31,928.73
	Total	$31,928.73

Figure 16.15 The Autoexists behavior returns only members that exist with one another in the same dimension.

How Autoexists affects dimension security

An interesting characteristic of dimension security is that it is affected by the Autoexists behavior. Recall that Autoexists returns attribute members that exist with each other in the same dimension. For example, the Reseller dimension includes City and Reseller attribute hierarchies. Even if there isn't a multi-level hierarchy that spans these attribute hierarchies, thanks to Autoexists, we can request the City and Reseller attribute hierarchies side-by-side to return the cross product of the City and Reseller attribute hierarchies (see Figure 16.15). In this case, only resellers that are found in a given city are returned.

The security policies defined for allowed or denied sets propagate to the other attribute hierarchies in a dimension. For allowed sets, the dimension data security is straightforward.

Members of other attribute hierarchies are accessible only if they exist with members of the allowed set. This is similar to the way Autoexists affects query results.

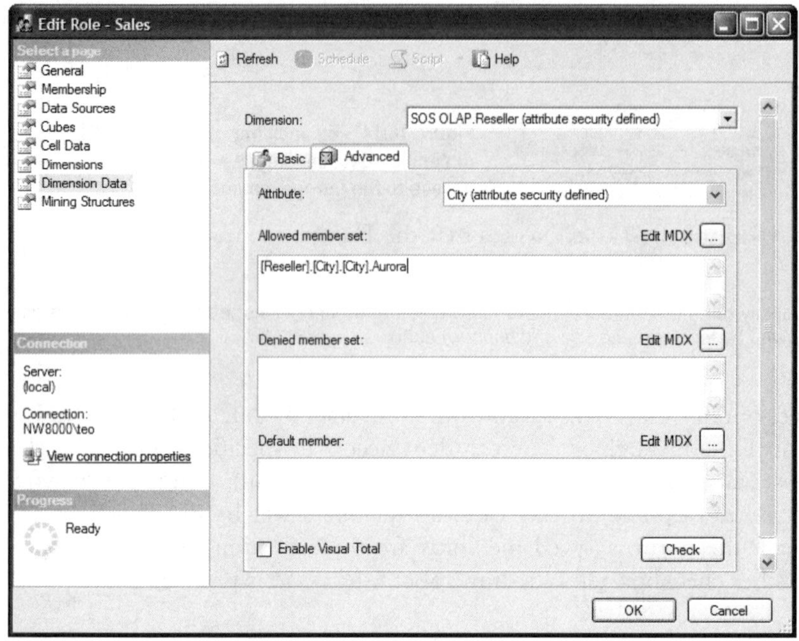

Figure 16.16 Use the Adavanced tab to specify the allowed and denied sets with MDX set-producting expressions.

Autoexists and allowed sets

Suppose, you want to grant the Sales role rights to see only the *Aurora* member of the City attribute hierarchy.

1. In the Advanced members set field, enter the following MDX expression (Figure 16.16).

```
[Reseller].[City].[City].Aurora
```

2. Open the SOS OLAP cube in the cube browser.
3. Click on the *Change user* toolbar button and impersonate the Sales role.
4. Create the report shown in Figure 16.17 by dragging the *City* attribute hierarchy (Reseller dimension) on rows and the Reseller Sales Amount measure on rows.

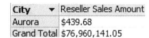

City	Reseller Sales Amount
Aurora	$439.68
Grand Total	$76,960,141.05

Figure 16.17 The Sales Role can see only the Aurora member.

As expected, the Sales role can see only the Aurora member.

5. Replace the City attribute hierarchy with the *Reseller* attribute hierarchy (Figure 16.18).

Reseller	Reseller Sales Amount
Online Bike Warehouse	$439.68
Grand Total	$76,960,141.05

Figure 16.18 The Sales Role can see only the resellers in Aurora.

As a result of Autoexists on dimension data security, the Sales role can only see the resellers in Aurora city despite the fact that we haven't explicitly defined security polices for the Reseller attribute hierarchy.

Autoexists and denied sets

End users cannot see members defined in a denied set. If included in a denied and allowed set, the member is denied (a denied set takes precedence). Autoexists on denied set takes some mental effort to comprehend. Let's lay out the rule first.

Note Members of other attribute hierarchies (within the same dimension) are disallowed if they are found at lower levels in the attribute relationship chain than the attribute containing the denied member.

An example may be better than a thousand words.

6. Cut the *[Reseller].[City].[City].Aurora* expression from the Allowed member set field.
7. Paste the expression in the *Denied member set* field and click OK to set up the new security policy.
8. Open the SOS OLAP cube in the cube browser.
9. Click on the *Change user* toolbar button and impersonate the Sales role.
10. Create the report shown in Figure 16.19 by dragging the *Reseller by Geography* multi-level hierarchy.

Country	State-Province	City
⊟ Canada	⊟ Ontario	⊞ Barrie
		⊞ Brampton
		⊞ Chalk Riber
		⊞ Etobicoke
		⊞ Kanata

Figure 16.19 Autoexist on denied set removes the attribute members that are descendants of the denied attribute member.

11. Expand the *Country* level of the Reseller by Geography hierarchy all the way down to the *City* level.

As expected, Aurora city is excluded from the cities in Ontario. More interestingly, the Sales role will not see any postal codes in Aurora, nor will it see any resellers in Aurora. That's because, when we set up the Reseller dimension in chapter 4, we set up the *Reseller* ⇨ *Postal Code* ⇨ *City* ⇨ *State-Province* ⇨ *Country* attribute relationship chain. The Reseller and Postal Code attribute hierarchies are found below the City attribute hierarchy. Therefore, the members that are descendants of the Aurora member will be excluded.

Of course, this will not work with missing attribute relationships among the Reseller, Postal Code, City, and State-Province attributes. The Autoexists behavior on denied sets emphasizes once again the importance of setting appropriate attribute relationships when designing your dimensions. More allowed and denied set scenarios and examples can be found in the article *Introduction to Dimension Security in Analysis Services 2005* (see Resources) and the product documentation.

Setting the default member

The Advanced tab of the Dimension Data security page also allows you to configure the default member of the attribute hierarchy for the selected role. As you would recall, the default member of an attribute hierarchy determines the result set returned to a client when the attribute is not explicitly included in a query. Normally, the default member is defined at an attribute hierarchy level and applies to all roles.

Overwriting the default member on a role basis could be useful when you need to "personalize" the default member for different roles. For example, the members of the Sales USA role may prefer the default member to be set to USA when browsing sales data by region. In comparison, you could set the default member to Europe to accommodate the preferences of the Sales Europe role members. You can use any MDX expression that returns a single member to set the default member for the role. I demonstrated how the attribute default member can be set programmatically in chapter 11.

Understanding Visual Totals

By default, the server aggregates data irrespective of the denied attribute members (Enable Visual Total is off). For example, when we configured a denied set for the Region attribute hierarchy, we disallowed the members of the Sales role to see Aurora city in Canada. However, if you author the report shown in Figure 16.20 and add up the country totals, you will notice that they don't add up to the Reseller Sales Amount Grand Total. What's going on?

Country	Reseller Sales Amount
⊞ Canada	$9,339,342.10
⊞ Germany	$2,889,040.58
⊞ France	$4,823,535.02
⊞ United Kingdom	$6,300,422.15
⊞ United States	$53,607,801.21
Grand Total	$76,960,141.05

Figure 16.20 By default, the server includes the denied members when aggregating data.

It turns out that for better performance the server ignores the denied attribute members when calculating the parent aggregated values. Although beneficial for performance, this behavior may present a security issue. For example, an end user could drill down to the City level, add up the individual city numbers and deduce the Aurora number. If this is a security concern, you can turn the *Enable Visual Total* property on.

Country	Reseller Sales Amount
⊞ Canada	$9,338,902.42
⊞ Germany	$2,889,040.58
⊞ France	$4,823,535.02
⊞ United Kingdom	$6,300,422.15
⊞ United States	$53,607,801.21
Grand Total	$76,959,701.37

Figure 16.21 When Visual Total is on, denied members are not included in aggregations.

Once Visual Totals is on and your refresh the report, the server excludes the Aurora contribution ($439.68) when calculating the Grand Total (Figure 16.21). Visual Totals prevents users from inferring secured data, albeit with some degradation of performance because the server needs to spend additional time filtering the cells that qualify for the calculation.

Dimension security scalability

Readers who have prior experience with SSAS probably know that there were certain scalability issues with dimension security in SSAS 2000. In SSAS 2000, the server handled dimension security by creating a special *replica* dimension. Replica dimensions contained only the unsecured members. With large secured dimensions (millions of members) and many database roles, it was possible for replica dimensions to grow and cause scalability issues. The reason for this was that in SSAS 2000 all dimensions (including the replicas) were always loaded into memory.

In SSAS 2005, dimension scalability has been improved significantly. To start with, dimensions are not memory-bound anymore. Instead, dimensions are disk-based (just like measure groups) and are loaded and swapped on demand. In addition, dimension replicas are now implemented as virtual bitmaps on the secured attributes where each bit represents a secured attribute member. In reality, the number of the secured attribute members compared to the total number of attributes would probably be relatively small. Even if this is not the case, and dimensions replicas become large, these bitmaps could be swapped out to disk and loaded on demand.

16.2.4 Implementing Dynamic Dimension Security

The Basic and Advanced tabs of the Dimension Data page allow you define a *static* list of attribute members that are explicitly denied or allowed. Static security polices are simple but not very flexible. More involved security requirements will mandate resolving the allowed and denied sets dynamically.

Why use dynamic security?

There are many real-life scenarios that may call for dynamic security. For example, you may need to allow each sales manager to see only her data. Or, each user is allowed to see a restricted list of members of the account chart. One approach for addressing such requirements is to create a role for each user. However, this approach may quickly become counterproductive and may impact the server performance. Even with the scalability improvements in dimension security, loading tens or hundreds of roles in the memory could stress out the server. In addition, enterprise deployments may require externalizing the dimension security. For example, you may need to set up your authorization security policies in Windows Authorization Manager or a data store and resolve these policies during runtime.

Note Authorization Manager (AzMan) is a component of Windows 2003 OS that can be used for role-based authorization based on the Windows identify of the user. It can be installed on Windows 2000 and Windows XP as well.

SSAS supports dynamic dimension security to minimize the maintenance effort required to administer security roles and avoid creating a role per user. SSAS exposes the identity of the interactive user (or client application) through the *Username* MDX function. For example, if Alice logs in the *adventure-works* domain as *alice*, the Username function will return *adventure-works\alice*.

Simple dynamic security policies can be implemented via MDX expressions in the Advanced tab. For example, suppose you need to allow sales managers to see data for the regions they are responsible for. Let's assume that the Region attribute of the Sales Territory dimension has a Sales Representative member property that returns the login id of the sales person responsible for the that region. In this case, returning the allowed set of the sales regions for the interactive user could be accomplished with the following MDX filter expression.

```
Filter(
    [Sales Territory].[Region].Members,
    StrComp([Sales Territory].[Region].CurrentMember.Properties
    ("Sales Representative"),
    username)=0)
```

Here, the *StrComp* VBA function is used to compare the Windows identity of the interactive user with the value returned by the Sales Representative property of the Region attribute. If they are identical, the region is added to the allowed set.

Using SSAS stored procedures to externalize security

More complicated programming logic and dynamic security rules could be encapsulated in SSAS stored procedures. Let's build upon the previous scenario and see how we can implement it with an SSAS stored procedure. Here are the high-level design requirements which will drive our implementation.

- *Externalize the Adventure Works dynamic security implementation* – We will author an SSAS stored procedure (GetRegionsByEmployee) that takes the user name as an input and returns the associated sales region for that user.
- *Implement data-driven security policies* – GetRegionsByEmployee will query the AdventureWorksDW to retrieve the sales region assigned to the interactive user.
- *Return the results as an MDX set* – GetRegionsByEmployee will create an MDX set to hold the sales region. The MDX set could be plugged in as an allowed set for the Sales role.

Listing 16.1 shows the *GetRegionsByEmployee* stored procedure.

Listing 16.1 Implementing data-driven dynamic security with SSAS stored procedures

```
Public Shared Function GetRegionsByEmployee(ByVal userName As String) As [Set]

    Dim conn As New SqlConnection("...")
    conn.Open()

    Dim cmd As New SqlCommand()
    cmd.Connection = conn

    cmd.CommandText = "SELECT DISTINCT '[Sales Territory].[Region].&[' " _
    & "CAST(ST.SalesTerritoryKey AS VARCHAR(5)) + ']' AS Region " _
    & "FROM DimEmployee AS E INNER JOIN " _
    & "DimSalesTerritory AS ST ON E.SalesTerritoryKey=ST.SalesTerritoryKey " _
    & "WHERE E.LoginID = " & userName

    cmd.CommandType = CommandType.Text

    Dim reader As SqlDataReader=cmd.ExecuteReader()

    Dim expr As AdomdServer.Expression = New Expression()
    Dim resultSetBuilder As SetBuilder = New SetBuilder()
    Dim tupleBuilder As New TupleBuilder()

    While reader.Read()
     expr.ExpressionText = reader(0).ToString()
     Dim member As Member = expr.CalculateMdxObject(Nothing).ToMember()
        tupleBuilder.Add(member)
      resultSetBuilder.Add(tupleBuilder.ToTuple())
    End While

    reader.Close()
    Return resultSetBuilder.ToSet()

End Function
```

The code starts by creating a SQL SELECT query to retrieve the sales regions assigned to the employee from the DimSalesTerritory dimension table in the AdventureWorksDW database. In Adventure Works, a sales person is responsible for only one region which is referenced by the SalesTerritoryKey foreign key. Assuming that the interactive user is a sales person (has a region assigned), the query result set will contain a single row with a single column (e.g. *[Sales Territory].[Region].&[9]*), which holds the unique name of the sales region member.

Tip Instead of hard coding the connection string in the stored procedure, you can use a Universal Data Link (UDL) file and pass the full file path as an argument to the stored procedure. In addition, if you decide to use Windows Integrated security for authentication, make sure to configure correctly the Impersonation Info setting of the stored procedure assembly on deployment (see chapter 11).

Of course, if the schema supports it, the stored procedure can handle multiple regions per sales person with no modifications. Also, the authorization store that returns the allowed members is irrelevant. In our case, the role of the authorization store is fulfilled by the AdventureWorksDW database. In real life, it could be the Authorization Manager, custom security service, or a third-party security framework that returns the allowed set.

Building an MDX set

Next, the code loops through the resultset and builds an MDX set from scratch. The stored procedure demonstrates two approaches for building MDX sets. The first (not shown in Listing 16.1) uses the MDX *StrToSet* function to construct the set from a concatenated string containing the unique names of the sales regions.

SSAS 2000 Since UDF functions in SSAS 2000 were limited to returning a scalar value, the only option to build a set was to use *StrToSet* on the client to convert the returned string to a set. This approach had performance and functionality implications imposed by the maximum length of the string data type. In comparison, an SSAS stored procedure can construct an MDX set and return it as a set.

The second approach is to build the set from scratch by using the *Expression* object we met in chapter 11. Since each row in the resultset contains the unique member name, first we use the *Expression* object to cast the member name to an ADOMD.NET *Member* object. As you know, an MDX set consists of tuples. Next, we build a tuple for each Member object by using the *TupleBuilder* object (also provided by ADOMD.NET). Then, we add the tuple to a *SetBuilder* object. Finally, we call the *SetBuilder.ToSet()* method to get the actual MDX set and return the set to the client.

Testing GetRegionsByEmployee

Before using the Adventure Works Extensibility assembly, make sure you elevate its permission set to *External Access*. The reason for this is that *GetRegionsByEmployee* opens ADO.NET connections. You can change the assembly permission set before deployment (add the assembly to the SOS OLAP Project and use the assembly properties) or after the assembly is deployed by using Management Studio. You can use the following MDX query to test *GetRegionsByEmployee* for an arbitrary user name.

```
SELECT [Measures].[Reseller Sales Amount] ON COLUMNS,
AdventureWorks.GetRegionsByEmployee("adventure-works\michael9") ON ROWS
FROM [SOS OLAP]
```

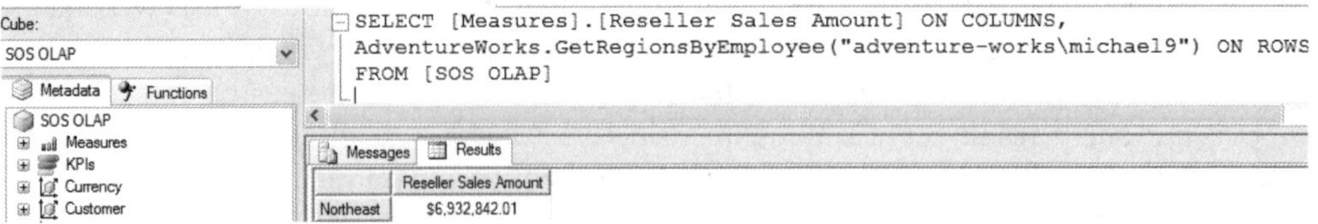

Figure 16.22 Testing dynamic dimensions security with an MDX query.

You should get the results shown in Figure 16.22. The next step is to plug in the stored procedure call as an allowed set for the Sales role (Figure 16.23).

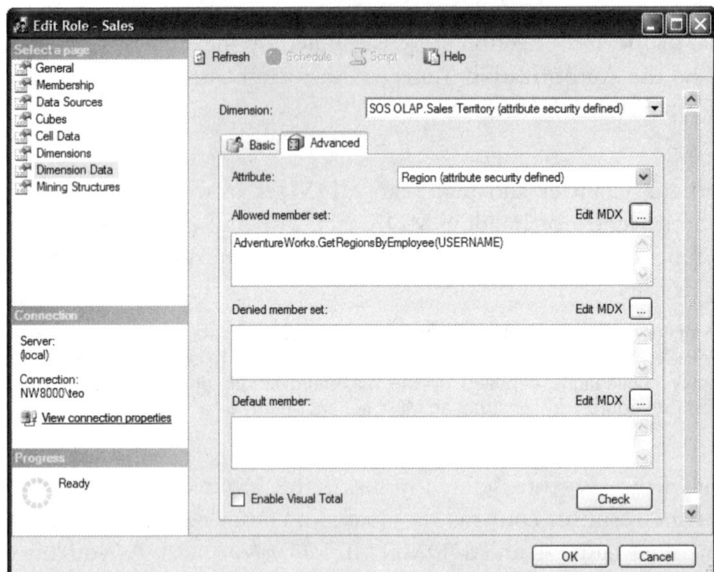

Figure 16.23 Generating an allowed set by calling an SSAS stored procedure.

When the end user browses the Region attribute (either standalone or part of a multi-level hierarchy), the Username function will pass the Window login name of the user as an argument to *GetRegionsByEmployee*, which will return the region assigned to that employee.

If the AllowedSet is empty (no regions are found for the interactive user), no attribute members will be returned to the user. An empty allowed set is not the same as a missing allowed set. In addition, if you profile the database activity with the SQL Profiler, don't be surprised if there is no activity when testing dynamic security. That's because the server executes the stored procedure upon startup and caches the dimension replica instead of executing the stored procedure each time the security policy is enforced. You won't be able to debug the stored procedure either because it is executed once for the lifetime of the cached replica. Instead, use a standalone MDX query to debug stored procedures that control dynamic security.

Note Another approach for implementing custom dynamic security is saving the security policies in a separate cube instead of a relational database. The advantage of this approach is that the security infrastructure is located in one place (UDM) and an SSAS stored procedure is not needed. The tradeoff is that a cube-based security model may be less flexible. Using a cube for implementing dynamic security is described in the Russ Whitney's Customizing Dimension Security article (see Resources).

16.3 Managing Cell Security

We said that, by default, members of a database role don't have rights to read cube data. The administrator must grant a role at least Read access rights (using the Cube page of the Role properties dialog) to make cube data accessible to end users. The administrator can tighten security further by defining dimension security policies that disallow browsing the cube data by given attribute members. Cell security is the most detailed level of security. As an administrator, you use cell security to restrict access to cell values. Cell security polices can be defined on the Cell Data page of the Role properties dialog.

SSAS 2000 In SSAS 2000, cell security was resolved on the client, i.e. the server would send the results of the query to the client and the cell security policies were enforced on the client. This made the cell security model vulnerable to attacks and exploits. With SSAS 2005, cell security is applied on the server. As a result, only data that the user can see is transmitted to the client.

16.3.1 Understanding Cell Security

If you imagine the cube as a spreadsheet, you can think of dimension security as *horizontal* security that restricts access to rows, while cell security is *vertical* security because it applies to columns (Figure 16.24).

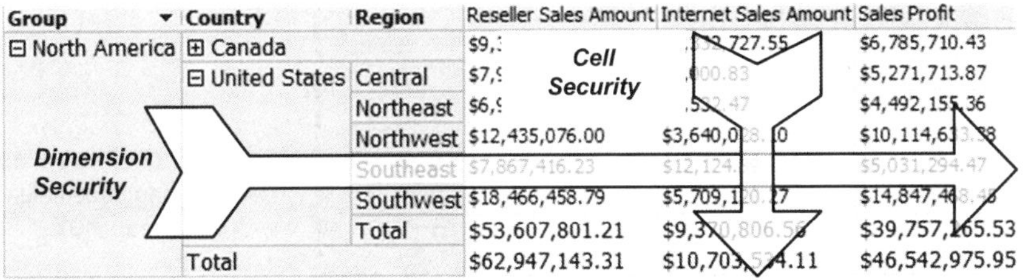

Figure 16.24 Dimension security restricts access to rows, while cell security applies to colulmns.

For example, by setting dimension security policies, the administrator can prevent the Sales role from seeing the Southeast member of the Region attribute hierarchy. However, in the absence of cell security policies, the members of the Sales roles will be able to see *all* measures for the allowed attribute members. But what if you need to prevent the Sales role from seeing the Internet Sales Amount measure?

One approach to enforce simple security cell security policies is to use dimension security. Recall that all cube measures are exposes as members of a system-defined *Measures* dimension. Therefore, preventing a given role from seeing the Internet Sales Amount measure could be as simple as setting the *[Internet Sales Amount]* measure as a denied member (*<Denied-Set>{[Measures].[Internet Profit Dollar Amount]}</DeniedSet>*). However, more involved security rules may require cell-level security.

SSAS 2000 Setting security policies on the Measures dimension will only work if there are no calculated members that derive from the denied measures. If this is not the case, you need to go for cell-based security.

MDX expressions

You define cell security policies by using MDX expressions. The server will deny cell access if the expression evaluates to *False* and grant access if the cell returns *True.* As with dynamic dimension security, consider using stored procedures to simplify the maintenance of the cell security policies. For example, you may want to allow or disallow access to all measures of a given measure group. I will demonstrate a similar scenario in section 16.3.3.

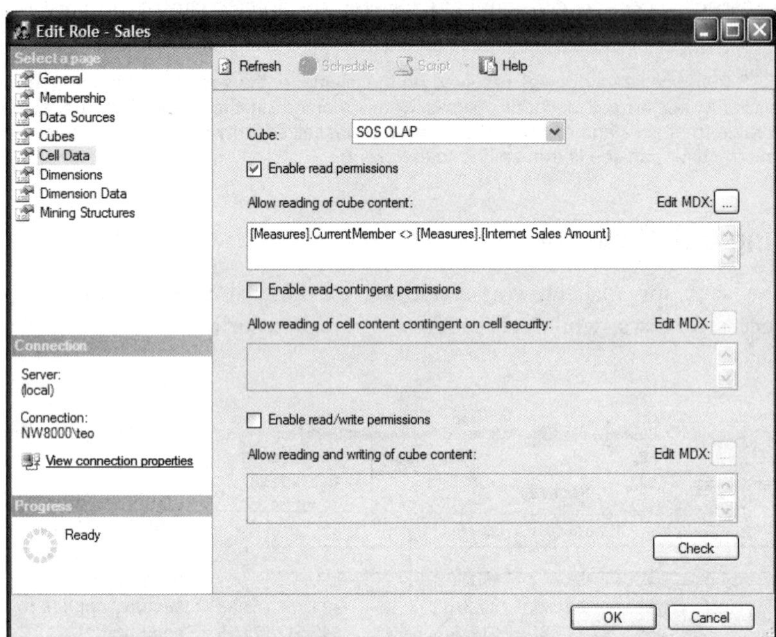

Figure 16.25 Prevent a role from reading cube cells with a Boolean MDX expression.

Types of cell permissions

There are three types of cell permissions that you can use to define cell security policies.

- *Read* – Read permission determines the cells that are viewable to members of the role. If the MDX expression evaluates to True, access to affected cells is granted regardless of whether they are derived from other cells that are restricted.
- *Read Contingent* – Determines if cells derived from restricted cells are permitted. Cells are allowed if derived from permitted cells. Cells are disallowed if derived from restricted cells. In other words, even if the MDX expression returns true, to read the affected cells, the role must have access to the cells used to derive these cells.
- *Read/Write* – Determines the cells the users can update when writing back to the cube (partition writeback). The measure group partition must be write-enabled for this permission to take effect.

Let's go through some examples that demonstrate the difference between *Read* and *Read Contingent* permissions.

16.3.2 Restricting Cell Data Access

Suppose that the members of the Sales roles are not permitted to see the *Internet Profit Dollar Amount* measure. We cannot using dimension security to deny access to *[Measures].[Internet Profit Dollar Amount]* because we have calculated members deriving from it, e.g. [Sales Profit]. Instead, we will use cell security.

1. In the Edit Role dialog (Figure 16.25), click on the Cell Data page.
2. Check the *Enable read permissions* checkbox and enter the following expression in the Allow reading of cube context field.

```
[Measures].CurrentMember <> [Measures].[Internet Profit Dollar Amount]
```

3. Browse the SOS OLAP cube under the context of the Sales role and produce the report shown in Figure 16.26.

Category	Reseller Profit Dollar Amount	Internet Profit Dollar Amount	Sales Profit
⊞ Accessories	$477,485.86	#N/A	$813,225.90
⊞ Bikes	$42,594,154.94	#N/A	$50,834,740.53
⊞ Clothing	$1,417,839.00	#N/A	$1,519,173.29
⊞ Components	$7,228,818.12	#N/A	$7,228,818.12

Figure 16.26 By default, a role can read derived cells even if some of the cells used for the derivation are denied.

As expected, the Sales role is denied access to the *Internet Profit Dollar Amount* measure. What is more interesting is that the role is allowed access to the *Sales Profit* calculated member, which is produced by adding the *Reseller Profit Dollar Amount* and *Internet Profit Dollar Amount* measures. That's because by default, the read contingent permissions on the *Sales Profit* cell are disabled (evaluate to False).

4. Back to the Cell Data page of the Edit Role dialog, check the *Enable read contingent* permissions checkbox.
5. In the *Allow reading of cell content contingent on cell security* field, enter the following expression:

```
[Measures].CurrentMember IS [Measures].[Sales Profit]
```

6. Refresh the report. Notice that the Sales Profit measure now shows *#N/A*.

Tip SSAS supports a *Secured Cell Value* connection string setting which a client application can use to specify what text will be displayed in secured cells. By default, Secured Cell Value is 0 which translates to showing #N/A in the secured cells.

Enabling *Read Contingent* access right on the Sales Profit calculated member requires at least read permissions on the cells that are used to derive the Sales Profit value. In this case, the Sales Role doesn't have rights to read the Internet Profit Dollar Amount measure. Therefore, the server refuses access to the Sales Profit measure as well.

16.3.3 Externalizing Cell Data Security

As you can imagine, using MDX expressions to specify the cell security policies could quickly become counterproductive. For example, suppose that you need to deny access to all measures of a given measure group or display folder. You will end up with a log of AND (or OR) operators! Again, consider stored procedures to externalize more involved programming logic. The *IsMeasureAllowed* stored procedure demonstrates how this could be done (Listing 16.2).

Listing 16.2 Implementing cell data security with SSAS stored procedures

```
Public Function IsMeasureAllowed(ByVal cubeName As String, _
    ByVal measureGroupName As String, ByVal measureName As String) As Boolean

   Dim mg As MeasureGroup
   Dim measure As Microsoft.AnalysisServices.Measure
   Dim svr As New Server()
   Dim measureFound As Boolean = False

   svr.Connect("data source=local")
   Dim db As Database = svr.Databases.GetByName(Context.CurrentDatabaseName)
   Dim cube As Cube = db.Cubes.GetByName(cubeName)

   mg = cube.MeasureGroups.GetByName(measureGroupName)

   For Each measure In mg.Measures
       If measure.Name = measureName Then
      measureFound = True
         Exit For
       End If
   Next

   svr.Disconnect()
   Return measureFound
End Function
```

The *IsMeasureAllowed* stored procedure uses AMO to deny (or allow) access to all measures of a given measure group.

Tip If you need to secure measures in a given display folder, you can code *IsMeasureAllowed* entirely in ADOMD.NET (no need to use AMO). That's because each Measure object in ADOMD.NET exposes a DisplayFolder property. You can get to the current cube (CubeDef object) from the Context object (Context.CurrentCube). The CubeDef object exposes a Measures collection that contains all measures in the cube.

It takes the cube name, the measure group name, and the current measure (*[Measures].CurrentMember.Name*). The code connects to the current database and the requested cube. Next, the code references the requested measure group. Then, the code loops through the measures contained in the measure group in an attempt to find if the current measure is one of them. If that's the case, *IsMeasureAllowed* returns *True* to deny the measure. For example, to deny all measures in the Reseller Sales measure group, enter the following expression in the *Allowed reading of cube content* field:

```
AdventureWorks.IsMeasureAllowed("SOS OLAP", "Reseller Sales",
    [Measures].CurrentMember.Name)
```

One cautionary note about cell security performance is that the server calls the MDX expressions repeatedly when calculating the returned set. This is very different from dimension security where the secured attribute members are identified on startup time and cached on the server. Therefore, complex cell data security expressions may impact the query performance. As a best practice, I would recommend you consider dimension security whenever possible and use cell-based security as a last resort.

16.4 Deployment Scenarios And Security

You may wonder how SSAS security affects the deployment model of your OLAP solution. As noted, SSAS supports Windows-based security only and will attempt to authenticate the requests using Windows authentication. At a high level, we can identify two major deployment scenarios, intranet and Intranet, which I discuss next.

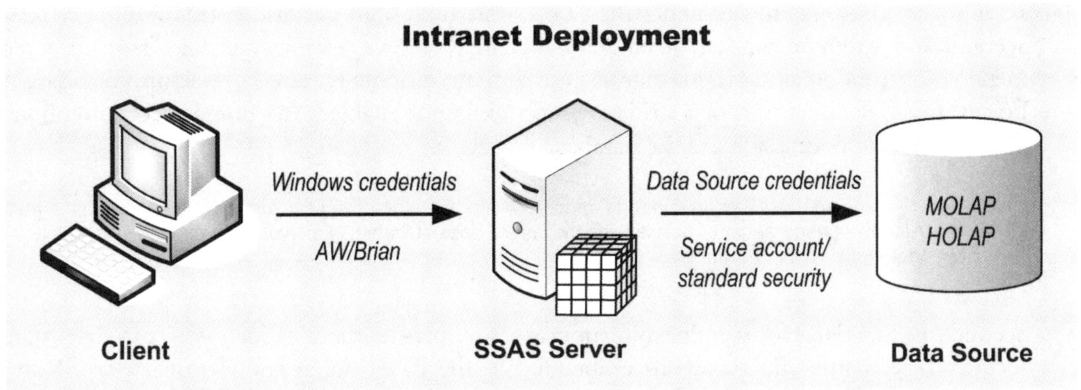

Figure 16.27 In the intranet deployment scenario, SSAS sees incoming requests under the indentity of the interactive user.

16.4.1 How Security Impacts Intranet Applications

Traditionally, Analysis Services-based solutions have been intranet-based. Figure 16.27 depicts a typical intranet deployment model. In this scenario, the entire solution (OLAP clients and the SSAS server) are deployed in a well-defined intranet environment.

Server authentication

Ideally, all end users will log in to the same domain. If this is not the case (e.g. no Active Directory is present), one workaround is to clone the local user accounts on the server. For example, if the user logs in to his machine as *MyComputer/Brian*, the administrator can create an identical Windows account (same name and password) on the server where SSAS is installed to avoid prompting the user for login credentials. When the client application generates an MDX query, the request goes under the Windows identity of the interactive user. For example, if Brian logs in to his machine with his domain account (AW/Brian), the server will see the request coming as AW/Brian. This means that the MDX *Username* function will return AW/Brian and dynamic security (if needed) will work as intended.

A slight variation of the intranet deployment model is when the client is web-based. For example, you may have an ASP.NET application that presents the query results. In this case, you can choose to impersonate the user. In ASP.NET, this could be done by changing the web.config file for the application (`<identity impersonate="true"/>`).

Data source authentication

With MOLAP storage, all query requests will be satisfied from the multidimensional store on the server and the data source is not accessed at all. With HOLAP and MOLAP, the server may need to connect to the relational data store to retrieve data. With HOLAP, this may happen when the query is not satisfied from existing aggregations, while ROLAP will always require a trip to the data source. As noted in chapter 2, you have two data source authentication options for OLAP solutions. The first and recommended option is to connect using Windows authentication with the identity of the Windows account the server runs under. This could be accomplished by specifying *Integrated Security=SSPI* in the connection string of the data source definition.

If the database server is on another machine, you cannot configure the Analysis Services service (msmdsrv.exe) to run under the Local System account because Local System is a machine account and a remote call will go under a NULL Windows session (and fail). Instead, I recommend you use a domain account that has the minimum rights required to perform database tasks. For example, if dimension or partition writeback is not enabled, the domain account should be given only Read permissions to the database server.

Note As noted, Data Mining supports impersonating the interactive user for predication queries. If maintaining Windows-based security policies for the users doesn't bother you, you can explore this authentication option with data mining solutions.

Second, if the data source doesn't support Windows authentication, you can use standard security (user name and password embedded in the data source connection string). With this approach, the obvious challenges are that it is more vulnerable for exploits and more difficult to maintain. To minimize the security risk with standard database security, the server encrypts the password and never stores it in a clear text.

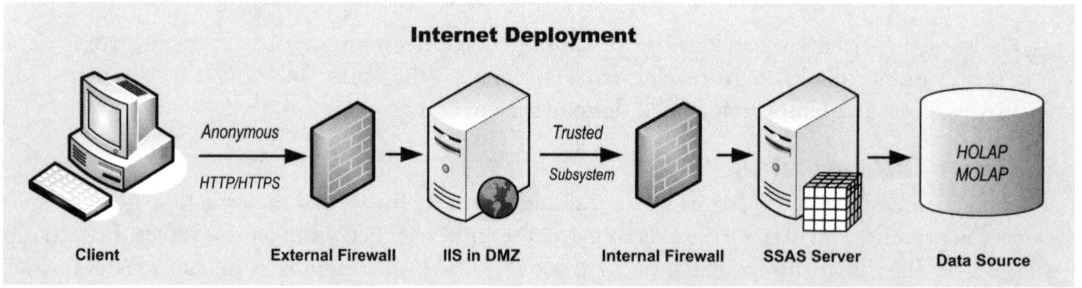

Figure 16.28 Consider configuring SSAS for HTTP access when implementing Internet-oriented OLAP solutions.

16.4.2 Internet Security Approaches

Sometimes, you may need to expose UDM outside the boundaries of your company's intranet environment. With the advent of XMLA as a standard server protocol and the elimination of client dependencies (PTS), SSAS 2005 is well-suited for building global OLAP solutions. Figure 16.28 shows one possible Internet-oriented deployment scenario.

HTTP connectivity

In this case, Internet clients send requests to SSAS via HTTP or HTTPS. As noted in chapter 1, SSAS can be configured for HTTP connectivity.

SSAS 2000 The HTTP connectivity architecture of SSAS 2005 is very similar to SSAS 2000. The major differences are that the Pump component is implemented as an XMLA provider that is hosted as an ISAPI filter in IIS (not ASP page as in SSAS 2000).

The configuration steps are well-documented in the product documentation (see the How to: Configure Analysis Services for the Web topic) and the *Configuring HTTP Access to SQL Server 2005 Analysis Server* document (see the Resources section). Once you configure SSAS for HTTP connectivity, clients can connect to it specifying the URL endpoint of the server. For example, a Windows client with installed Microsoft OLE DB Provider for Analysis Services 9.0, can connect to SSAS as follows:

```
Provider=MSOLAP;Data Source=http://<server>/<vroot>/msmdpump.dll;
Initial Catalog=SOS OLAP;
```

Here, *server* is the Internet-facing server name (e.g. ssas.abc.com) and *vroot* is the virtual folder that hosts the Pump component. Non-Windows clients can integrate with SSAS by sending XMLA-based requests.

With HTTP connectivity, IIS receives the incoming HTTP requests and forward them to the SSAS server. If you decide to expose SSAS to Internet clients, I strongly recommend you implement a comprehensive firewall infrastructure, as you would do with typical Internet-facing web applications. In Figure 16.28, the external firewall permits only HTTP traffic (or HTTPS). The IIS server is deployed in the DMZ zone. The internal firewall filters the incoming requests to go through the port the server listens on (port 2383 by default).

SSAS 2000 With SSAS 2000, you had to enable a range of NETBIOS ports for the internal firewall. SSAS 2005 doesn't require NETBIOS connectivity anymore.

For an added level of protection, the server requires client requests to be encrypted and sends encrypted data back to the client. If the HTTPS protocol is used to encrypt the communication channel, the SSAS encryption may be redundant and can be disabled through configuration settings (*RequiredProtectionLevel* and *RequiredWebProtectionLevel*) that are well-documented in the product documentation.

Authentication options

Although expanding the client base to clients running on any platform, the Internet deployment model may bring some challenges for authenticating the user.

Note Although it is not recommended, you can configure the server to accept requests from unauthenticated clients (Anonymous access). The administrator can configure Anonymous access by changing the Security\RequireClientAuthentication server configuration property from its default value of 1 to 0. Since this is a huge security vulnerability, I suggest you avoid Anonymous access and instead consider more secure approaches for user authentication.

Impersonating the user

If Windows authentication is an option (e.g. large organization where satellite offices are connecting to an HTTP-enabled server at the company headquarters via a wide area network), you can configure IIS to impersonate the user. You can do this by enabling the *Integrated Windows authentication* setting on the virtual root that hosts the Pump component in IIS (Figure 16.29).

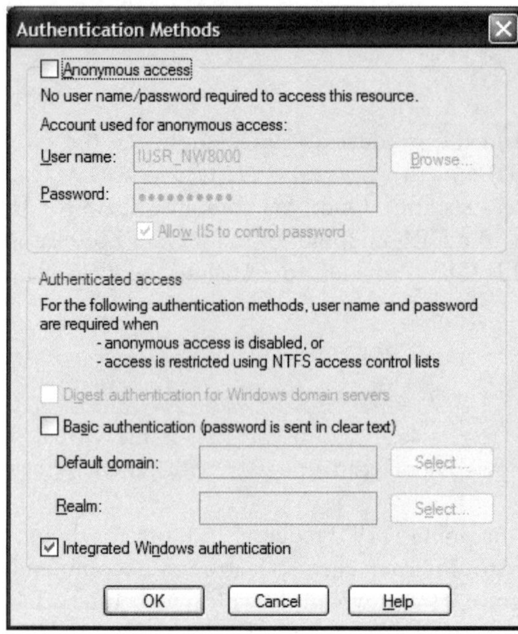

Figure 16.29 Impersonate users by enabling Integrated Windows authentication.

In this scenario, the Windows identity of the end user will flow into the server, as with the Intranet scenario. However, there is a catch with user impersonation. By default, IIS will pass the user identity successfully only if the SSAS server is on the same box as IIS. If it isn't, you need to enable Kerberos delegation because it is the only supported SSPI provider which implements delegation. Since this approach requires Active Directory and essential negotiation skills to solicit cooperation from the infrastructure group, Kerberos may be ruled out right off the bat (who wants to mess up with Active Directory, anyway?). If enabling Kerberos sounds like an exciting adventure you would like to pursue, please read the document *Enabling Kerberos and Delegation in Analysis Services 2005* to learn how to enable SSAS 2005 for Kerberos (see Resources).

Using trusted subsystem

Windows authentication may be impractical with many Internet deployment scenarios. That's because it requires maintaining Windows accounts for all web users and prompting users to enter login their Windows credentials. Instead, with Internet-based OLAP solutions, consider the *trusted subsystem* approach for authenticating requests to SSAS. With this approach, the IIS virtual root is configured for anonymous access (the Anonymous access checkbox is enabled in Figure 16.30). This means that all users will be able to send requests to IIS. Once IIS intercepts the request, it will forward it to SSAS under a single Windows account that is trusted by SSAS (hence, the name *trusted subsystem*). In Windows 2003, you can implement trusted subsystem by following these steps.

1. Create a new application pool in IIS that will host the Pump component.
2. Open the application pool properties and flip to the Identity tab.

3. Select the *Configurable* option and enter the credentials of the domain account that SSAS will trust. Click OK.

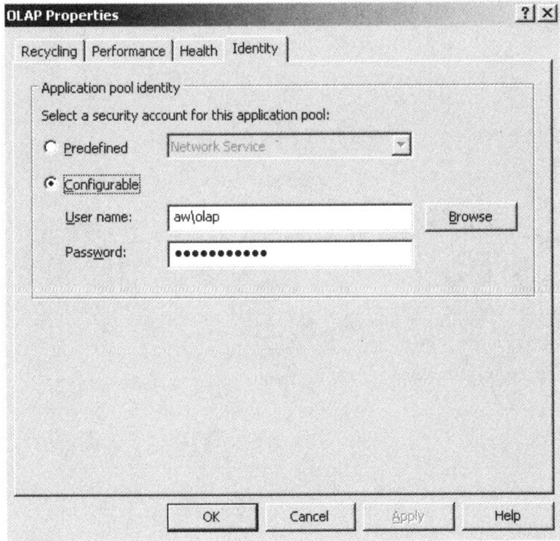

Figure 16.30 In Windows 2003, implement a trusted subsystem by changing the identity of the application pool that hosts the Pump component.

4. Use the Computer Management Console to assign the domain account to the *IIS_WPG* local Windows group.
5. Create an SSAS database role and assign the trusted account as a member of the role. Grant the necessary permissions and access rights to the new role.

If your goal is to give all web users the ability to query the server, the above steps are all you need. In some cases, however, they won't be enough. There are two tradeoffs associated with the trusted subsystem approach. First, SSAS will see all requests coming under a single identity. In other words, SSAS won't be able to tell the users apart. Therefore, SSAS won't be able to authorize the users. Second, dynamic security and MDX expressions that rely on the user identity (*Username* function) won't work. Here are a couple of variations of the trusted subsystem approach that you can consider in order to address these tradeoffs.

Custom authorization

In many cases, organizations won't permit web users to access directly the SSAS server. Instead, a web portal will probably be created to present selected subviews of the OLAP data. For example, you may have an ASP.NET business intelligence application that among other things may allow the user to generate OLAP reports. In this case, it is likely that the application will be responsible for user authentication and authorization.

For example, the same ASP.NET application may be configured for ASP.NET Forms Authentication that forces the user to authenticate before accessing the reporting features (see Figure 16.31). Upon successful authentication, the application can generate an authentication ticket (e.g. a cookie) which the user must send with each subsequent request. Here is how custom authorization may work in this scenario from an SSAS point of view.

1. The web user submits a report request.
2. The web application authorizes the request, e.g. by querying a custom authorization repository to find if the user is authorized to run a report. The role of the authorization repository could be

fulfilled by any store (e.g. XML file, database, Active Directory, etc) that captures the authorization polices.

3. If the user is authorized, the application connects to the SSAS server using the trusted subsystem approach described above.

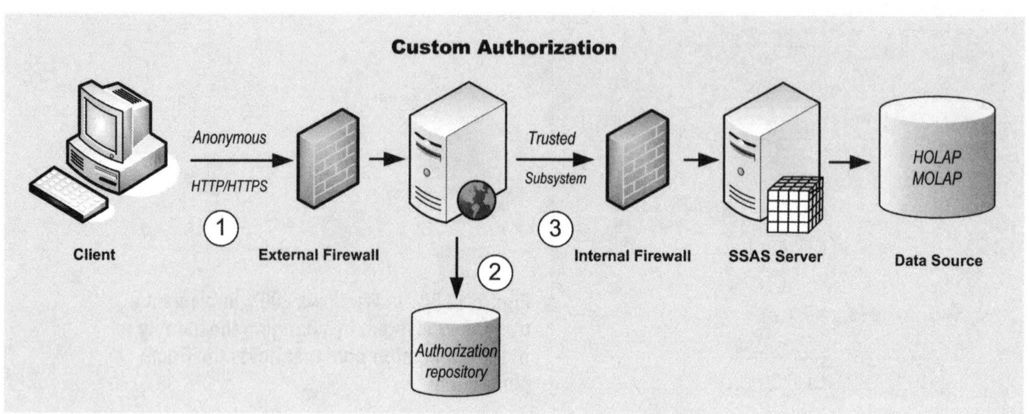

Figure 16.31 Consider custom authorization with Internet-based OLAP solutions.

As you can see, with custom authorization, the responsibility for authorizing the users is shifted to the application.

Passing the user identity and role

In some cases, you may be willing to harden the custom authorization approach even further by telling SSAS who the user is, so SSAS can apply different role security polices based on the user identity. You can do this by using the *Roles* and *EffectiveUserName* connection string settings.

Passing the database role

Instead of relying on the application front end to enforce restricted access to SSAS, the application could just look up the user role(s) in the authorization repository. Then, the application can pass the role(s) in the connection string and leave it up to SSAS to authorize the request, as I explained in section 16.1.1. For example, if the user belongs to the SOS Reports role, the application can retrieve it and construct the following connection string:

```
Provider=msolap; Roles=SOS Reports; <other connection string settings>
```

As I explained, the application can advertise which role(s) SSAS should authorize. This assumes that the trusted subsystem account is added as a member to all database roles that can be potentially passed under the *Roles* setting. As a security measure, the server will reject the request if the account is not a member of the advertised role.

Using EffectiveUserName

Most SSAS dynamic security implementation will rely on the user identity returned by the *UserName* MDX function. This presents an issue with the trusted subsystem approach because all requests will share the same identity. As a workaround, SSAS 2005 supports a new connection string setting called *EffectiveUserName*.

```
Provider=msolap; Roles=SOS Reports; EffectiveUserName=Brian;
```

When *EffectiveUserName* is passed in the connection string, the server will impersonate the specified user account and the *UserName* MDX function will return that user name, e.g. Brian in the above example. Behind the scenes, EffectiveUserName uses the same S4U services that the Change User dialog uses to impersonate the EffectiveUserName Windows account and it shares the same limitations. First, it requires Windows 2003 domain controller. Second, it requires the application to log in as an SSAS administrator (a member of the SSAS Server role). For this reason, EffectiveUserName may present security vulnerability and should be used with caution.

16.5 Summary

Setting and maintaining robust security policies is an essential task that every administrator has to master. Members of the Server role have unrestricted rights to administer the server and all UDM objects. More granular management and data access security policies can be enforced with database roles.

A database role can control data security at different levels. End users can access cube data only if they have at least Read rights to the cube. Implement dimension security policies to restrict roles from seeing data by given attribute members (horizontal security). To simplify the dimension security maintenance, consider dynamic security and SSAS stored procedures. Cube permissions represent the most granular security policies. Use Boolean MDX expressions to control access to cube cells. SSAS security can have major implications on your application topology. With intranet-based applications, consider Windows authentication for user authentication and authorization. With Internet-oriented applications, consider the trusted subsystem approach.

16.6 Resources

The Microsoft MSDN Security Center
(http://msdn.microsoft.com/security) -- Tons of excellent information including entire books to help you secure your applications.

Introduction to Dimension Security in Analysis Services 2005
(http://shrinkster.com/7co) – An essential introduction to the SSAS security model.

Customizing Dimension Security article by Russ Whitney
(http://shrinkster.com/8mi) – Demonstrates how a separate cube can be used for dynamic security.

Enabling Kerberos and Delegation in Analysis Services 2005 by Marius Dumitru
(http://shrinkster.com/7de) – Lists the steps involved in configuring Analysis Services 2005 to use Kerberos as an authentication protocol and enabling delegation.

Exploring S4U Kerberos Extensions in Windows Server 2003 by Keith Brown
(http://shrinkster.com/7ef) – Covers the S4U service in Windows 2003.

Configuring HTTP Access to SQL Server 2005 Analysis Server paper by Edward Melomed
(http://shrinkster.com/7dd) -- The paper explains the steps required to set up HTTP access. It also discusses different performance and security settings.

PART 5

Building Business Intelligence Solutions

By itself, UDM is useless if there is no one to deliver the message. Analysis Services provides a plethora of programming interfaces for integrating different types of clients. You will see how OLAP clients can query UDM and retrieve the results in different ways. We will implement data miming clients that leverage DMX to send prediction queries.

Microsoft Reporting Services is an excellent platform for disseminating UDM data in the form of standard and ad hoc reports. Report authors can use the Query Builder to create quickly complex MDX and DMX queries and embed the results in "smart" reports. End-users can leverage the Report Builder to generate reports ad hoc straight from UDM.

Microsoft Office provides several tools for analyzing UDM data. The Excel PivotTable component can be used to generate structured reports from server-based and local cubes. The Excel Add-in for Analysis Services supports more analytics features and it is better integrated with UDM. Developers can use Office Web Components (OWC) to add business intelligence features to custom applications without having to know much about MDX and UDM.

Corporate management dashboards can be implemented with the Microsoft Office Business Scorecard Manager 2005. It can extract KPI metrics defined in UDM by using the KPI-related MDX functions. Scorecards can be published to the SharePoint web portal or disseminated in the form of standard reports.

Chapter 17

Integrating Applications with UDM

Typically, end users won't query UDM directly. Instead, smart OLAP clients and browsers shield the users from the MDX and OLAP technicalities. Such clients present the query results in ways users can easily understand and analyze. Ideally, Microsoft-provided or third-party browsers would satisfy the reporting needs of your users. However, sometimes you may need to take the road less traveled and create custom OLAP solutions to meet more involved integration and end-user requirements.

In this chapter, I will show you how you can integrate custom applications with UDM. You will learn how to:

- Choose the right programming interface to meet the integration requirements.
- Build thin clients that use the XMLA protocol to integrate with UDM.
- Build classic clients that use the ADOMD object library.
- Use ADOMD.NET to implement .NET-based OLAP clients.
- Leverage ADOMD.NET and DMX to create custom data mining clients.

This will be a code intensive chapter targeted to developers. Throughout the course of the chapter we will implement several client applications to demonstrate a variety of integration tasks. In the process, we will gain more experience in authoring MDX and DMX queries. You will find the programming samples enclosed in the Ch17 solution. You will need VS.NET to open and run them.

17.1 Understanding Integration Options

When we discussed the SSAS architecture in chapter 1, we saw that SSAS provides various programming interfaces to support different types of clients. As a developer, you need to choose the optimum integration option based on the programming language the client application is written in and the platform it will be running on. Figure 17.1 is meant to assist in making the correct choice.

Custom clients can integrate with UDM via XMLA, OLE DB, ADO MD, and ADOMD.NET programming interfaces. As you know by now, SSAS provides also management API in the form of the DSO COM-based API (deprecated) and AMO .NET-based object libraries. The management interfaces were covered in chapters 13-16. In this chapter, I will focus only on the programming interfaces.

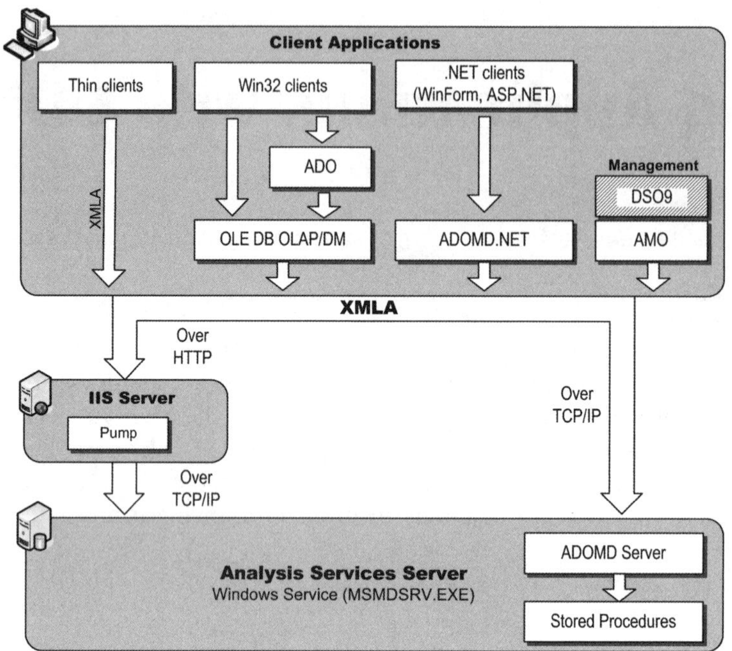

Figure 17.1 SSAS supports serveral programming interfaces to integrate with different types of clients.

17.1.1 Thin Clients

By the term *thin client*, we will mean a client that does not depend on any programming libraries to interact with UDM. Instead, thin clients will favor the XMLA integration option and send XMLA statements directly to the server. You would choose the thin client integration approach when operational or implementation requirements prevent you from installing the OLE DB, ADO MD, and ADOMD.NET object libraries on the client machines. Typical examples of thin clients include a Java client running on non-Windows OS or a handheld device.

Thin client in SSAS 2000

SSAS 2000 was originally released without XMLA support. Shortly after the first XML specification was unveiled (April 2001), Microsoft came up with its first implementation of XMLA in the form of the XML for Analysis SDK (see Resources). After the SDK was installed on the SSAS 2000 server, thin clients could query the server using XMLA. Figure 17.2 shows the SSAS 2000 XMLA deployment model.

One performance implication of the XMLA deployment model with SSAS 2000 was its dependence on the Pivot Table Service (PTS). Once IIS receives the request, it would forward it to pump component. Since all integration roads to SSAS 2000 would go through PTS, the pump sends the request to PTS which, in turn, translates the request to OLE DB and sends it to the server. The problem with PTS is that it is designed to be used by client applications and it is resource-intensive. For example, PTS caches query results, dimension members, etc. In the middle tier, PTS may impact the server scalability under heavy loads.

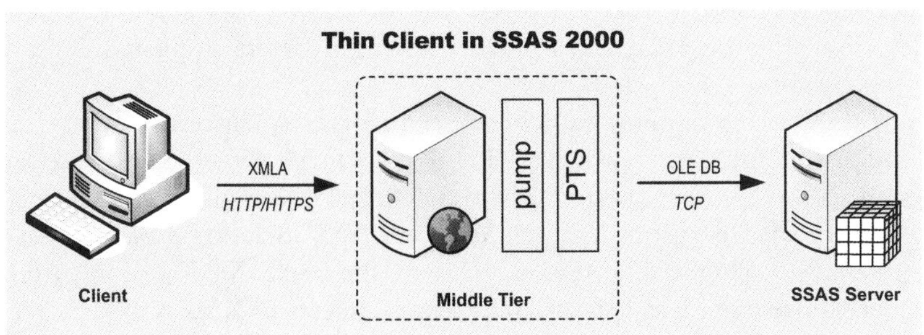

Figure 17.2. The XMLA deployment model in SSAS 2000 requires PTS on the middle tier.

Thin client in SSAS 2005

In SSAS 2005, PTS is not needed because SSAS 2005 handles XMLA natively. XMLA requests can be sent through TCP and HTTP. By default, programming libraries send XMLA requests via TCP for better performance. However, a thin client on the web would most likely favor HTTP or HTTPS transport protocols because they are firewall-friendly. By default, SSAS is not configured for HTTP access. I included a link in the previous chapter that points to detailed instructions for configuring HTTP connectivity.

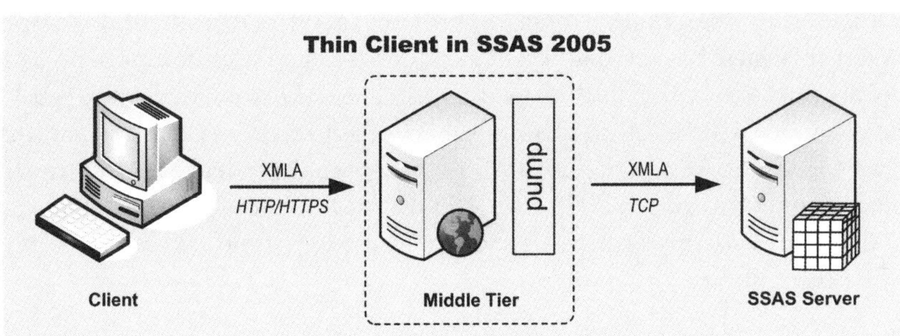

Figure 17.3. XMLA is the native protocol of SSAS 2005.

Figure 17.3 shows the thin client deployment model with HTTP connectivity in SSAS 2005. The pump component fulfils the role of a web-enabled XMLA provider. It is implemented as an ISAPI filter running under IIS. Thin clients send XMLA requests over HTTP/HTTPS to the pump endpoint (e.g. http://localhost/olap/msmdpump.dll). Once the pump receives the request, it forwards it to the SSAS server over TCP.

17.1.2 Native Clients

Windows native clients, such as C++ and COM-based clients (e.g. Visual Basic 6.0) can use the OLE DB for OLAP (or Data Mining) or ADO Multidimensional (ADO MD) object libraries. Deciding which native library is a better choice depends on the type of the client. Let's discuss these two integration options in more details.

OLE DB for OLAP

The OLE DB for OLAP provider is a set of COM-based APIs which target primarily applications written in C/C++. The OLE DB for OLAP provider is the manifestation of the OLE DB for OLAP specification that extends the Microsoft OLE DB universal access platform. You don't have to distribute the OLE DB for OLAP provider because it is included in the Windows OS. See the Resources section for a link to the OLE DB for OLAP specification, which also includes code samples. Similarly, the OLE DB for Data Mining provider implements the OLE DB for Data Mining specification.

The OLE DB for OLAP programming model has been supported since the first release of SSAS. Each version of SSAS comes with its own OLE DB for OLAP provider and you need to specify the right version in the connection string. The first release (Microsoft OLAP Services) came with *msolap.1*, the second (Microsoft Analysis Services 2000) included *msolap.2*, while the SSAS 2005 comes with *msolap.3*. Unlike the previous releases, the SSAS 2005 version (msolap.3) is a light-weight provider whose main task is translating client requests to XMLA.

The OLE DB for OLAP library gives you the most flexibility but it is also the most difficult to use compared to the rest of the object libraries. For example, as one of the code samples included in the library documentation demonstrates, sending an MDX query and obtaining the results requires more than a hundred lines of C++ code. Choose the OLE DB for OLAP library when you need unrestricted access to the OLE DB for OLAP interfaces and maximum efficiency at the expense of more programming effort. This will be the integration option of choice when you create lower-level OLAP clients and controls, e.g. ActiveX control. For example, the PivotTable OWC component calls directly to the OLE DB for OLAP object library.

ADO Multidimensional Object Library (ADO MD)

SSAS 2000 introduced the ADO MD object library to provide an OLE Automation wrapper for COM-based clients, such as Visual Basic 6.0 and ASP. ADO MD is a sister component of ADO and its purpose is to abstract the OLE DB provider just like ADO abstracts the OLE DB programming interfaces. Similar to the OLE DB for OLAP, ADO MD is a part of and distributed with the Windows OS. In SSAS 2005, ADO MD is supported for backward compatibility only. Legacy clients can connect to SSAS 2005 using ADO MD. However, ADO MD doesn't support the new UDM features. If this is an issue, you need to upgrade the client to .NET and use the ADOMD.NET object library.

17.1.3 .NET Clients

.NET clients will favor the ADOMD.NET object library to integrate with SSAS 2005. ADOMD.NET doesn't require the OLE DB Provider for Analysis Services 9.0 (msolap.3) to be installed on the client machine. That's because ADOMD.NET is implemented as a light-weight managed wrapper directly on top of XMLA.

Distributing ADOMD.NET

Unfortunately, ADOMD.NET is not included in the .NET framework and it has to be distributed to each client machine. ADOMD.NET was first released under version 8.0 in early 2005 after the XML for Analysis SDK was released. You can use ADOMD.NET version 8.0 (see Resources for download link) to integrate with both SSAS 2000 and 2005 servers. The setup program will install ADOMD.NET in the C:\Program Files\Microsoft.NET\ADOMD.NET ↵ \90 folder on the client machine.

Note SSAS 2005 comes with an updated version of ADOMD.NET object library which you should use instead of ADOMD.NET 8.0. By the time your read this book, the new version will be available for download from the Microsoft downloads website.

ADOMD.NET vs. ADO MD

When working with the ADOMD.NET object library, you will undoubtedly find it similar to ADO.NET. For example, you will find ADO.NET equivalents, such as AdomdConnection, AdomdCommand, AdomdDataAdapter, and AdomdDataReader. In addition, you will find ADO MD objects that abstracts the UDM metadata and query results in neat object hierarchies. For example, ADOMD.NET exposes metadata objects, such as CubeDef, Dimension, Hierarchy, Level, and Member. The query results are represented as CellSet, Axis, Position, and Cell objects. ADOMD.NET extends ADO MD with new objects, such as KPI, Tuple, and data mining objects.

As I demonstrated in chapter 11 and 14, SSAS also provides a light-weight version of ADOMD.NET that executes on the server (ADOMD Server). Use ADOMD Server in stored procedures. Because a stored procedure executes in the context of a database, ADO MD server provides the current database in the Context object, so you don't have to establish an explicit connection.

Now that I introduced you to the programming interfaces, let's go over some code samples that demonstrate how custom applications can use them to integrate with UDM.

17.2 Implementing Thin Clients

As noted, the natural integration choice for thin clients will be XMLA since most programming platforms support SOAP and XML. Thin clients are the most difficult to implement. That's because you need to learn the XMLA specifications and code against it without a higher-level object oriented wrapper that abstracts the raw XML requests and responses. There are different integration options you can consider with thin clients depending on the level of protocol abstraction and deployment constraints. The Web service integration isolates you the most from the SOAP plumbing details but it requires the programming platform to support Web services. Sending network requests and scripting options remove this dependency but are more difficult to implement.

17.2.1 Web Service Integration

XMLA is built on top of the Simple Object Access Protocol (SOAP), consider the Web service integration approach. Considering the fact that Web services are the industry standard for cross-platform communication, all modern programming tools provide an adequate support for handing Web services and SOAP. For this reason, the Web service approach will be the preferred XMLA integration option for most applications.

Note Perhaps, you may not agree, but it is hard for me to accept the pump component as a Web service. By definition, a Web service has to be self-describing, while the pump component doesn't advertise its contract to the outside world. Specifying an end point to a DLL binary seems strange to me too. Perhaps, one day I would add SOAP-enabled ISAPI filters to the Web service family, but until then I hope that a future SSAS release would provide a true .NET Web service for HTTP connectivity. As an added bonus, an SSAS Web service would be easier to extend (e.g. through HTTP modules) and bring conformity to the BI stack by complementing the SSRS Web service.

The XMLA for Analysis Services Sample Application

The XML for Analysis 1.1 SDK (see the Resources section for the download location) includes a sample application called *XMLA for Analysis Services Sample Application* that demonstrates how COM-based and .NET clients can integrate with Analysis Services via XMLA. The application code is provided in both Visual Basic 6.0 and .NET. The VB 6.0 sample uses the XmlHTTP component (distributed with Internet Explorer) to send and receive XMLA messages. The VB.NET sample uses the .NET Web service infrastructure that hides the SOAP plumbing details.

Although the purpose of the SDK is to XMLA-enable Analysis Services 2000, the sample application can connect to an HTTP-enabled instance of SSAS 2005 as well. That's because both the SDK and SSAS 2005 conform to version 1.1 of the XMLA specification. Once again, you don't need the SDK for XMLA to integrate with SSAS 2005. You can install only the samples.

Tip If not for anything else, you need the XML for Analysis 1.1 SDK to get the WSDL contract for Web service integration because the pump component doesn't provide it. As of the time of this writing, the only place that I was able to find the WSDL contract was in the .NET sample application included in the XML for Analysis 1.1 SDK. The default location is *C:\Program Files\Microsoft XML For Analysis SDK\Samples\↵ Sample.NET\Web References\MsXmlAnalysis\vs.wsdl*.

To run .NET version of the *XMLA for Analysis Services Sample Application*:

1. Load the Visual Basic.NET project (Sample.vbproj) in Visual Studo.NET 2005. The default location of the project file is C:\Program Files\Microsoft XML For Analysis SDK\-Samples\Sample.NET.
2. Confirm the prompt to upgrade the project to Visual Studio 2005. Once the upgrade process is complete, build the application and run it.
3. In the Connect application dialog, enter **http://<server name>/<XMLA vroot>/ msmdpump.dll** as URL and **SOS OLAP** as a data source name, where the *<server name>* is the SSAS server machine name and *<vroot>* is the name of the IIS virtual root folder that hosts the Pump component. Click OK to connect to the SOS OLAP database.

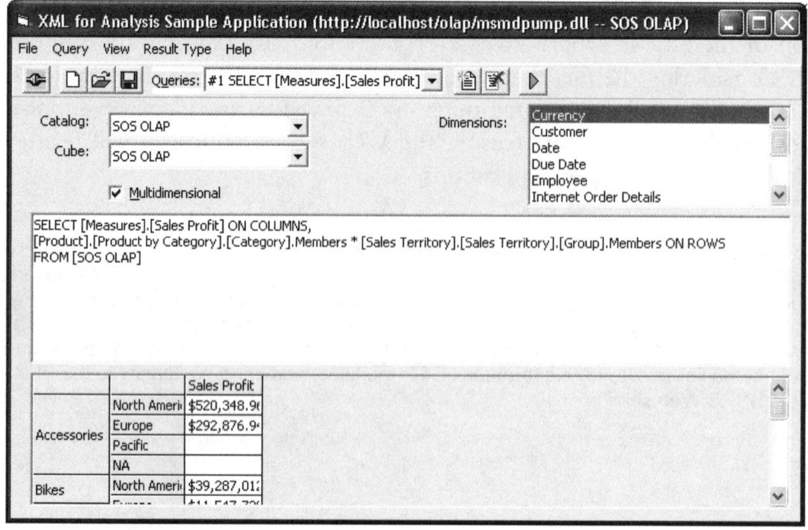

Figure 17.4 The XML for Analysis Services Sample Application demonstrates how COM-based and .NET clients can integrate with SSAS 2000 and 2005 via XMLA.

The main user interface of the XMLA for Analysis Services Sample Application is shown in Figure 17.4. Readers who have prior experience with SSAS 2000 will undoubtedly notice that this demo mimics the MDX Sample Application that ships with SSAS 2000. You can select a catalog from the Catalog dropdown and a cube that you want to query from the Cube dropdown. Once this is done, the application populates the Dimensions dropdown with the list of dimensions found in the cube. Since the application was originally written for SSAS 2000, it has no notion about the attribute-based nature of UDM and it doesn't allow you to drill down further the dimension level.

You enter a free-form MDX or DMX query statement in the query pane. In the case of an MDX statement, you should select the Multidimensional checkbox because the server will return a multidimensional (MDDataSet) structure. In the example shown in Figure 17.4, I am sending a crossjoin MDX query to show the Sales Profit measure broken down first by Product Category and then by Sales Territory Group. The results of the query execution are shown in the grid. Alternatively, you can tell the application to show the XMLA payload by selecting *View ⇨ As XML* main menu.

Behind the scenes of XMLA for Analysis Services Sample Application

If you examine the References folder in the VS.NET Solution Explorer, you will see that the application doesn't have any dependencies on the SSAS object libraries. Instead, the application sends the query requests as Web service calls.

Generating the Web service proxy

To shield developers from the SOAP technicalities, the .NET Web service infrastructure can generate a web service proxy. Think of a Web service proxy as a local copy of the Web service that is distributed with the client application. When the client wants to invoke a web method, it interacts with the proxy which acts as a gateway to the actual Web service. Once the proxy receives the call from the client, it generates a SOAP request and sends it across the wire. Upon receiving a SOAP response from the Web service, the proxy unpacks it and exposes its content to the client as an object.

By definition, a Web service must advertise its contract to the outside world and the contract must be described in a Web Service Definition Language (WSDL) format. VS.NET abstracts you from the WSDL technicalities by generating the Web service proxy automatically once you create a web reference to a Web service endpoint. As noted, the pump component doesn't expose the contract and you cannot generate it by establishing a web reference. Instead, if your application is written in VB.NET, you can "borrow" the proxy (Reference.vb file) from XMLA for Analysis Services Sample Application. If your language of choice is not VB.NET, you can generate the proxy by creating a web reference in you project that points to *vs.wsdl* as a file.

Besides solving the proxy hurdle, you will undoubtedly find other potential areas for code reuse with the sample applications, such as handling sessions and useful classes for abstracting the arguments to the Discover and Execute methods.

Invoking XMLA methods

The XMLA specification defines only two methods – Discover and Execute. A client application invokes the *Discover* method to retrieve the UDM metadata. For example, Listing 17.1 shows a Discover statement that the sample application sends to retrieve the cubes within the SOS OLAP database.

Listing 17.1 A sample Discover call to retrieve a list of cubes.

```
<SOAP-ENV:Envelope>
    <SOAP-ENV:Body>
     <Discover xmlns="urn:schemas-microsoft-com:xml-analysis">
       <RequestType>MDSCHEMA_CUBES</RequestType>
       <Restrictions>
         <RestrictionList>
           <CATALOG_NAME>SOS OLAP</CATALOG_NAME>
         </RestrictionList>
       </Restrictions>
       <Properties>
         <PropertyList/>
       </Properties>
     </Discover>
    </SOAP-ENV:Body>
</SOAP-ENV:Envelope>
```

An XMLA request is packaged in an SOAP envelope. The Discover statement has a complex definition which conforms to the XMLA specification. For example, the Restrictions element represents a collection of restrictions to be applied during the execution of a Discover method. The Restriction name specifies the rowset column name that is being restricted (CATALOG_NAME in the example). The Restriction value defines the data for the column (SOS OLAP database). The Properties element may contain additional information to describe the call.

Tip To execute the above statement in Management Studio, connect to the Analysis Services server and create a new XMLA query (in Object Explorer, right-click on the server and choose New Query ⇨ XMLA). Then, type in the text of the Discover element only (omit the SOAP-ENV elements) and execute the query. The Management Studio Template Explorer lists sample XMLA queries you can use to perform management tasks, execute Discover statements, and check the status of the server.

The Web service proxy equivalent of the Discover statement is the *Discover* method (see References.vb class) which has the following signature (namespaces and attributes excluded):

```
Public Function Discover (ByVal Discover1 As Discover,
    ByRef Session As Session, _
    ByVal BeginSession As BeginSession,
    ByVal EndSession As EndSession) As DiscoverResponse
```

The first argument represents the Discover element structure as an object of type Discover which contains RequestType, Restrictions, and Properties collections. The sample application provides additional classes to facilitate loading the Discover object with the XML representation of the property collections.

17.2.2 Other XMLA Integration Options

Of course, you don't have to choose the Web service approach when using the XMLA integration option. For example, a legacy client that doesn't support web services may prefer to interact with the SSAS pump component via HTTP POST requests. Or, a SSAS administrator may prefer to create script-based utilities for carrying out management tasks programmatically.

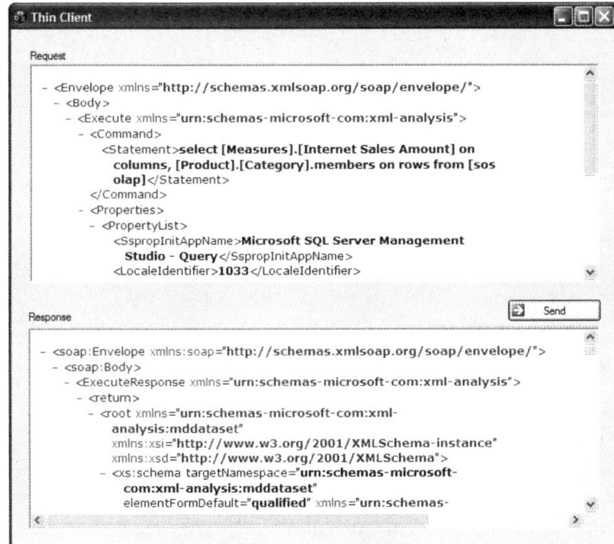

Figure 17.5 When Web service integration is not an option, applications can use the HTTP POST protocol to communicate with an SSAS instance that is configured for HTTP addressability.

Sending HTTP POST requests

I wrote the ThinClient application (Figure 17.5) to demonstrate a non-Web service integration scenario. Implemented as a VB.NET Windows Forms application, ThinClient uses the .NET HttpWebRequest and HttpWebResponse objects to send XMLA Execute requests via HTTP POST. I kept the ThinClient design simple. The application loads the Execute query from a physical file and dumps its content to the Request pane. When the user clicks the Send button, ThinClient sends the request through the wire and receives the response from the server. The whole interaction is encapsulated in the SendXMLAQuery function whose abbreviated code is shown in Listing 17.2.

Listing 17.2 The ThinClient sample sends XMLA Execute requests via HTTP POST.

```
Private Sub SendXMLAQuery()
    Dim xmlDoc As New XmlDocument()
    xmlDoc.Load(Application.StartupPath & "\" & FILE_IN)
    Dim data As Byte() = ASCIIEncoding.Default.GetBytes(xmlDoc.OuterXml)
    Dim request As HttpWebRequest =
     CType(WebRequest.Create("http://localhost/olap/msmdpump.dll"), HttpWebRequest)

  request.Credentials = CredentialCache.DefaultCredentials
  request.Accept = "*/*"
  request.UserAgent = Application.ProductName

  request.Headers.Add("Accept-Encoding", "gzip,deflate")
  request.Headers.Add("SOAPAction", "urn:schemas-microsoft-com:xml-analysis:Execute")
  request.Method = "POST"
  request.ContentType = "text/xml"
  request.ContentLength = data.Length
  Dim stream As Stream = request.GetRequestStream()

  stream.Write(data, 0, data.Length)
  stream.Close()

  Dim response As HttpWebResponse = CType(request.GetResponse(), HttpWebResponse)
```

```
  Dim receiveStream As Stream = response.GetResponseStream()
  Dim readStream As New StreamReader(receiveStream, Encoding.UTF8)
  Dim result As String = readStream.ReadToEnd()
  response.Close()
  readStream.Close()

  xmlDoc.LoadXml(result)
  xmlDoc.Save(Application.StartupPath & "\" & FILE_OUT)
  responseBrowser.Navigate(New Uri(Application.StartupPath & "\" & FILE_OUT))
End Sub
```

The code starts by loading the XMLA Execute statement from a physical file. Since the HttpWebRequest object expects the input data as a byte array, the code uses the .NET ASCIIEncoding object to convert the Execute request payload to a byte array. Then, the code instantiates an HttpWebRequest object that will send the request to the pump endpoint. Next, the code set the Credentials property to the DefaultCredentials so the request goes out under the identity of the interactive user. This is helpful when the pump virtual root is configured for Windows integrated authentication and SSAS security polices are setup to authorize the user.

With the Web service integration option, the proxy and the .NET CLR take care of the wire technicalities and provide object wrappers for developer's convenience. In this case, we are on our own. The code configures the request by setting the appropriate headers, content type, and length, etc., and sends the query through the wire as a byte array. Once the code gets the response from the server, it converts it to a string. Finally, ThinClient saves the results as an XML file and displays the file content in the Response pane.

Using Windows Scripting Host

Is my ThinClient sample not thin enough? You may say it isn't since it requires the .NET framework where the HttpWebRequest and HttpWebResponse classes are defined. If this is an issue, you can implement the client entirely in VBScript or JavaScript. For various code samples demonstrating how this could be done, check Chris Harrington's web site (see Resources).

In one of his samples, Chris demonstrates how a thin client can be implemented in JavaScript. Once this is done, the administrator can use Windows Scripting Host (WSH) to launch the script file and send Discover or Execute queries saved as files. Behind the scenes, the script sample uses the same XmlHttp ActiveX component that the Visual Basic 6.0 version of the XMLA for Analysis Services Sample Application uses to interact with the pump.

17.2.3 Tracing XMLA Traffic

When implementing thin clients, most of your development effort will be spent getting the XMLA requests right. Even if you take the Web service approach, which provides the highest level of abstraction from the XMLA plumbing details, you still need to make sure that the outgoing XMLA requests conform to the XMLA specification. Tracing can help you a long way in intercepting what is sent across the wire and troubleshooting XMLA errors.

Preparing to tracing

Suppose that you encounter an SOAP exception when the XMLA Sample Application sends an MDX query and you need to verify the request the application sends out to the server. You can use tracing utilities, such as TcpTrace and Microsoft Soap Trace to intercept the outgoing and incoming XMLA traffic by following these steps.

1. Install TcpTrace or Soap Trace. I provide links to the download locations in the Resources section. For demo purposes, I will use Microsoft Soap Trace which, as its name suggests, is specifically targeted to tracing and displaying SOAP requests and responses.

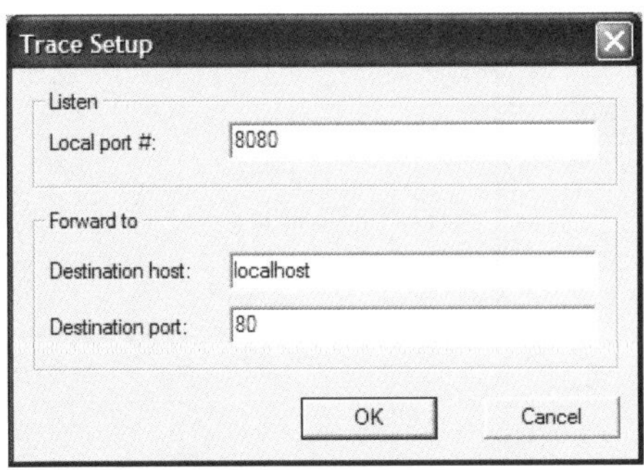

Figure 17.6 Use *localhost* when connecting to the local server or the server name when connecting to a remote server.

2. Start Microsoft Soap Trace Utility. Click *File* ⇨ *New* ⇨ *Formatted Trace*, or press Ctrl+F to connect to the server. Soap Trace allows you to monitor SOAP traffic to a local (localhost) and remote server. Assuming that you want to monitor XMLA traffic to the local server, accept the defaults in the Trace Setup dialog (Figure 17.6). If you need to interact with a remote server, replace the destination host with the name of the remote server, e.g. *ssas.abc.com*.

3. Click OK to initiate the trace.

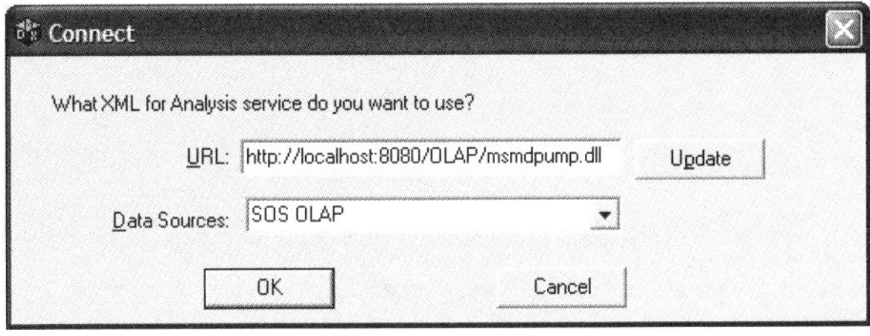

Figure 17.7 When tracing a local or a remote server, redirect the requests to Soap Trace by changing the connection string to *localhost:8080*.

Performing tracing

Now, let's configure the client.

1. Start the XMLA Sample Application or whatever client you are using to send XMLA requests. Change the connection string (Figure 17.7) to redirect traffic to *localhost:8080* irrespective of whether you use a local or a remote SSAS server. Essentially, a trace utility tricks the client application into believing that it sends requests to a real server while, in practice, the trace utility intercepts the request and forwards it to the remote server.

2. Let the client send XMLA requests to the server. If you use the XMLA Sample Application, you will see several XMLA requests (Figure 17.8) for retrieving UDM metadata immediately after closing the Connect dialog.

   If the Pump virtual root is configured for Windows authentication, the first requests represent the handshake between the client and the server to establish the authentication channel. Essentially, you will see the client repeating the XMLA request a couple of times before the server sends the response. In our case, the first request (shown in the upper right pane) retrieves the list of the SSAS databases (DBSCEMA_CATALOGS). Since the SSAS response wraps the actual

SOAP envelope with some prefix and suffix numbers, the Soap Trace chokes up when trying to render the response in the lower pane. To see the actual response, right click on the lower pane and choose *View Source*.

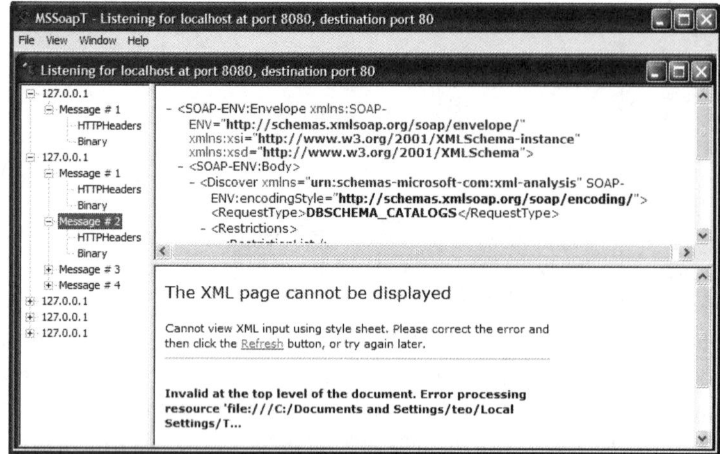

Figure 17.8 The upper right pane of the SOAP Trace utility shows the outgoing request, while the lower pane shows the response from the server.

Tracing with non-thin clients

Since all object libraries are essentially XMLA interpreters, you can use the tracing approach described above with clients that use higher-level programming interfaces, e.g. ADOMD.NET or AMO. For example, you could watch the traffic exchanged between Management Studio and the SSAS 2005 server by taking these steps.

1. Configure Soap Trace as described in the previous section.
2. In the Object Explorer pane of Management Studio, connect to the server HTTP address as you did with the sample application, e.g. *http://localhost:8080/OLAP/msmdpump.dll.*
3. Perform whatever action you need trace and watch the XMLA traffic with the Soap Trace utility.

The XMLA protocol certainly enables interesting scenarios that were not possible with Analysis Services before. Chances are, however, that most of the OLAP client applications will be deployed in an intranet environment. If this is the case, consider using the SSAS programming libraries to gain more productivity.

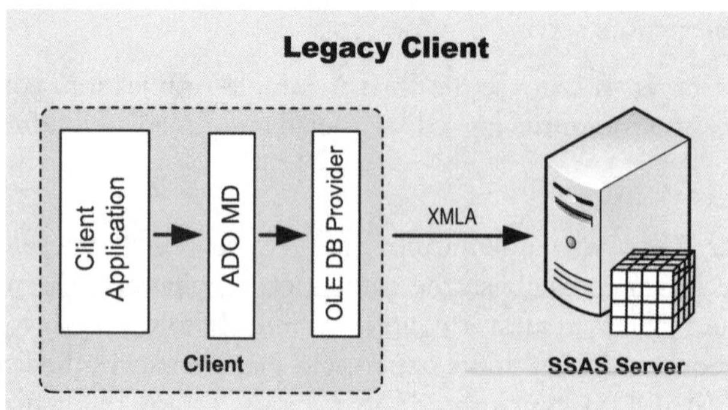

Figure 17.9 The ADO MD object library abstracts the OLE DB Provider.

17.3 Implementing Legacy Clients

Granted, .NET is omni-present nowadays but every now and then you may bump into legacy applications, such as clients written in Visual Basic 6.0 and ASP. If upgrading these applications is nowhere near the top of your to-do list, consider using the ADO MD object library to bring business intelligence to legacy clients. Figure 17.9 shows a common integration approach with legacy clients. The client interacts with ADO MD which provides an object-oriented access to the OLE DB Provider for Analysis Services 9.0. Typically, the client-to-server communication will happen over TCP. The client chooses TCP connectivity on connect by specifying the server name in the connection string only, e.g.

```
Data Source=localhost;Provider=MSOLAP;Initial Catalog=SOS OLAP
```

Alternatively, if the server is configured for HTTP addressability, the client can request to connect via HTTP, e.g.

```
Data Source=http://localhost/OLAP/msmdpump.dll;Provider=MSOLAP;
Initial Catalog=SOS OLAP
```

When the OLE DB Provider for Analysis Services 9.0 sees http (or https) in the connection string, it attempts to connect to the specified endpoint by HTTP.

17.3.1 Introducing the Legacy Client Sample Application

To demonstrate integrating legacy applications with UDM, I wrote a simple Visual Basic 6.0 application which has been a great experience considering the fact that I haven't touched VB 6.0 for five years. Along the implementation I process I had to pay homage to .NET for making our lives as developers so much easier. You can find the application in the LegacyClient subfolder under the Ch17 code folder. Figure 17.10 shows the Legacy Client UI.

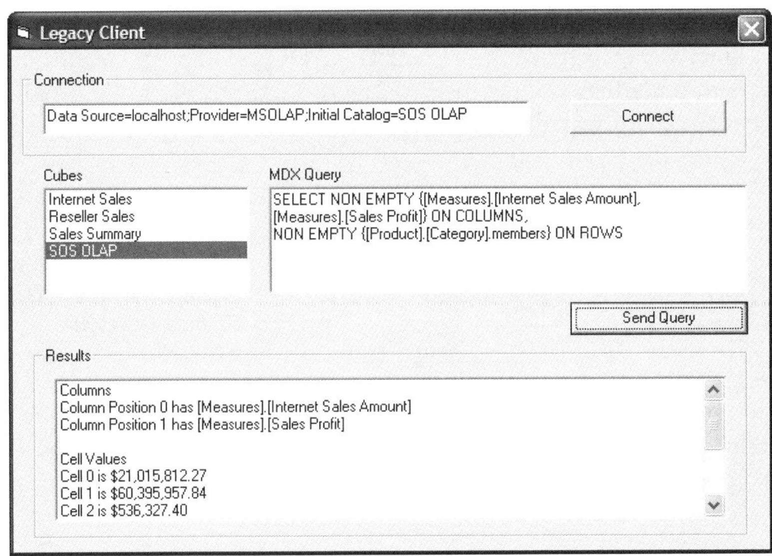

Figure 17.10 The ADO MD object library abstracts the OLE DB Provider.

Once the end user enters the connection string and clicks Connect, the application populates the Cubes list with the list of cubes found in the requested database. Then, the end user can enter an MDX query and click the Send Query button to send it to the server. Once the query results are received, the client shows the results in the Results list box.

17.3.2 Retrieving the UDM Metadata

To integrate a legacy client with UDM, you need to first reference the correct libraries.

1. In the Visual Basic 6.0 IDE, select the *Project* ⇨ *References* menu (Figure 17.11).
2. Select the Microsoft ActiveX Data Objects (Multidimensional) and the latest version of the Microsoft ActiveX Data Objects that is installed on your computer.

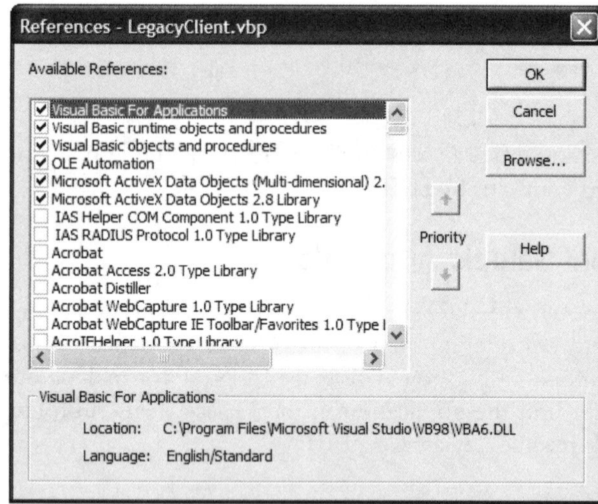

Figure 17.11 Use the ActiveX Data Objects (ADO MD) object library to connect to SSAS from Visual Basic 6.0 clients.

We will use the ADO object library to connect to the server. The ADO MD library extends the ADO library to provide access to multi-dimensional objects. Figure 17.12 shows the ADO MD object hierarchy that represents the UDM metadata.

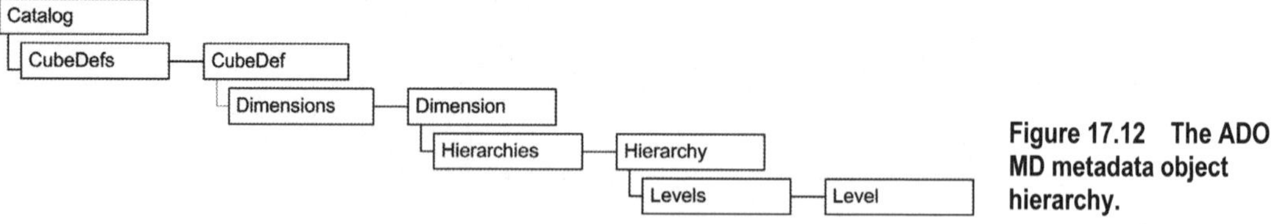

Figure 17.12 The ADO MD metadata object hierarchy.

As noted, ADO MD doesn't support the new UDM features. For example, it exposes only multi-level dimension hierarchies. The Legacy Client application opens an ADO connection to the server. Then, it retrieves the list of cubes (see Listing 17.3).

Listing 17.3 Retrieving metadata with ADO MD.

```
Private Sub LoadCubes()
    Dim cat As New ADOMD.Catalog
    Dim cube As CubeDef
    cat.ActiveConnection = gConnection

    lstCubes.Clear
    For Each cube In cat.CubeDefs
       lstCubes.AddItem (cube.Name)
    Next

End Sub
```

The Catalog object represents the SSAS database specified under Initial Catalog connection string setting. The CubeDefs collection exposes the cubes in the database as objects of type CubeDef. The code simply enumerates the cubes and adds them to the list.

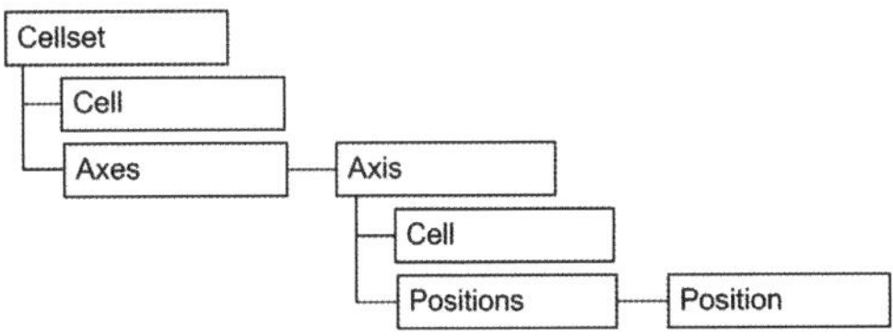

Figure 17.13 The ADO MD Cellset object hierarchy exposes the query results in an object-oriented way.

17.3.3 Working with MDX Queries

The ADO MD object model provides a Cellset object for sending MDX queries and traversing the query results. The Cellset object is similar to the ADO Recordset object, but it supports more than two axes. A Recordset has rows and columns; a cellset can have many axes. Figure 17.13 shows the Cellset object hierarchy.

Most MDX queries contain only two axes that are formed by the *ON COLUMNS* and *ON ROWS* clauses. That's because client applications would typically display the query results in a tabular format, e.g. in a grid. If the client application can handle results from multiple axes, MDX supports up to 128 axes. Three additional axes have aliases – PAGES, SECTIONS, and CHAPTERS. ADO MD returns the query axes in the Axes collection. For example, once the sample query shown in Figure 17.10 is executed, the Axes collection will contain two Axis objects.

Tip The sample query demonstrates also how you can exclude empty cells from the query results (similar to default Cube Browser behavior) by using the NON EMPTY clause.

Listing 17.4 shows how the Legacy Client application sends MDX queries and manipulates the query results.

Listing 17.4 Retrieving metadata with ADO MD.

```
Private Sub SendQuery()

    Dim oCellSet As Cellset
    Set oCellSet = New Cellset
    oCellSet.Open txtQuery.Text & " from [" & lstCubes.Text & "]", gConnection
```

```
    Dim oAxis As Axis
    Dim nDim As Integer
    Dim oMember As Member

    lstResults.Clear
    lstResults.AddItem ("Columns")
    Set oAxis = oCellSet.Axes(0)
    Dim oPosition As Position
    For Each oPosition In oAxis.Positions
       lstResults.AddItem ("Column Position " & oPosition.Ordinal & " has " _
      & oPosition.Members(0).UniqueName)
    Next

    lstResults.AddItem ("")
    lstResults.AddItem ("Cell Values")
    Dim nCell As Integer
    For nCell=0 To oCellSet.Axes(1).Positions.Count*oAxis.Positions.Count - 1
       lstResults.AddItem ("Cell " & nCell & " is "  & oCellSet(nCell).FormattedValue)
    Next nCell

    Set oCellSet = Nothing
End Sub
```

The code starts by calling the Cellset.Open method to send the MDX query to the server. Once the query is executed successfully, ADO MD populates the Cellset object. Axes(0) corresponds to the first query axis (ON COLUMNS in our case). Each axis exposes a Positions collection that defines the points of the axis. In this case, the Positions collection will give us the columns of the query if we map the query results to a two-dimensional recordset. The code enumerates the Positions collection to show the column details.

The actual cell values are laid out sequentially and are returned as a Cell collection of the Cellset object. To show all values we need to multiply the number of columns (*oCellSet.Axes(0).Positions.Count*) by the number of rows (*oCellSet.Axes(1).Positions.Count*). Finally, we loop through the cells of the Cellset object to show the formatted cell values.

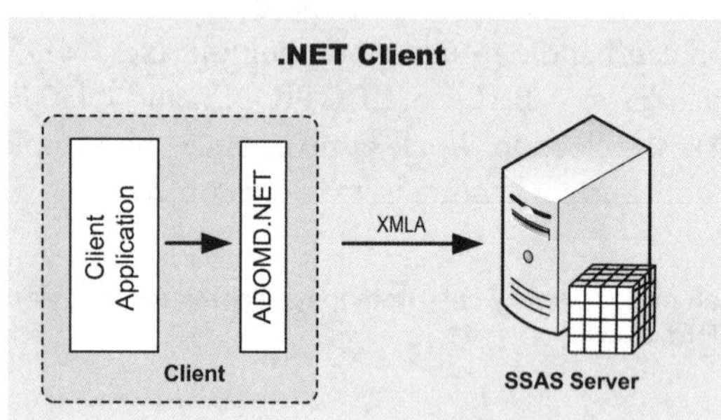

Figure 17.14 The ADOMD.NET object library wraps the XMLA protocol and eliminates the OLE DB provider.

17.4 Implementing .NET Clients

Going back to the present times and the .NET era. The natural choice for .NET client applications would be the ADOMD.NET object library. This library extends ADO MD with new objects to bring it on a par with the UDM object model. On the downside, you need to distribute the ADOMD.NET library to all machines on which the client application will be installed. Figure 17.14 depicts the .NET client deployment view.

The client application interacts with the ADOMD.NET object library which provides an object-oriented access to the XMLA protocol. Specifically, it translates the client requests to XMLA queries and maps the results to objects. The ADOMD.NET library doesn't require the OLE DB Provider for Analysis Services.

17.4.1 Understanding ADOMD.NET Object Hierarchy

The ADOMD.NET object model exposes a rich object model that maps both the UDM metadata and query results. Refer to the product documentation for a diagram of the full ADOMD.NET object model (ADOMD.NET Object Architecture topic).

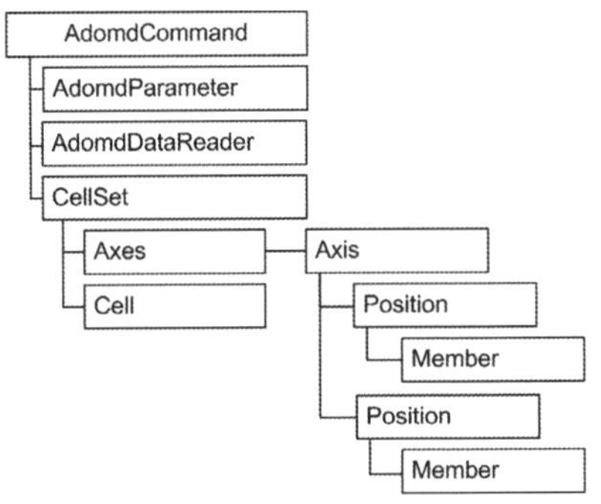

Figure 17.15 ADOMD.NET supports several options to expose the query results.

Metadata hierarchy

In chapter 12, I demonstrated how you can use ADOMD.NET to retrieve the UDM metadata. For example, the KPI Explorer sample used the CubeDef.Kpis collection to display the KPIs defined in a cube. Not all of the UDM metadata is exposed as objects though. For example, the cube actions don't have an object equivalent. In this case, use the AdoMdConnection.GetSchemaDataSet method to retrieve the metadata schema of interest, as we did in the Writeback Demo sample (chapter 12) to obtain the list of actions defined in a cube.

Data hierarchy

The ADOMD.NET data hierarchy is shown in Figure 17.15. You execute MDX queries by using the AdomdCommand object. This object exposes several methods to expose the query results in different ways, including returning a data reader, XMLA, or a CellSet object. The DotNet client demo demonstrates them all. Another welcome addition is parameterized queries which weren't supported in SSAS 2000. In UDM, MDX queries can be parameterized just like ADO.NET queries. For example, suppose that you need to restrict the query to return results for a given year that the application collects during runtime.

```
AdomdCommand command = new AdomdCommand()
commmand.Text = "SELECT ...FROM [SOS OLAP] WHERE @Year"
command.Parameters.Clear()
command.Parameters.Add(new AdomdParameter("Year", 2005))
Dim cellset as CellSet = command.ExecuteCellSet()
```

The query statement defines a named parameter *@Year*. The actual parameter value is appended to the Parameters collection of the AdomdCommand object.

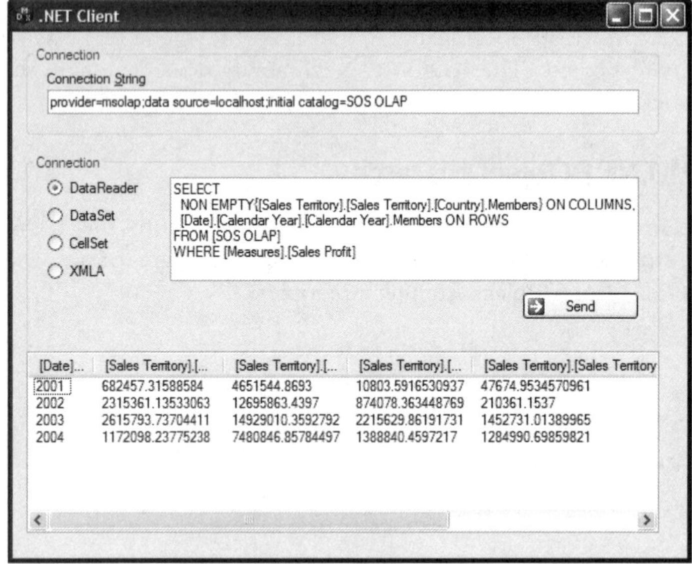

Figure 17.16 The .NET Client application leverages ADOMD.NET to query UDM.

17.4.2 Introducing the DotNetClient Application

The *DotNetClient* sample applications demonstrate common ADOMD.NET tasks for sending MDX queries and manipulating the results. Figure 17.16 shows the application user interface. The application supports four different ways of returning the query results. The DataReader option exposes the results as a forward-only cursor. The DataSet option returns the query results as an ADO.NET dataset. Use the CellSet object to manipulate the results as a multidimensional CellSet object. Finally, the XMLA option returns the raw XML payload which maps directly to the server XMLA response.

17.4.3 Managing Connections and Sessions

You can make your client application more efficient by following correct connection and session management practices. As noted in chapter 13, for performance reasons, the server maintains sessions to store some state for each connected client, such as the current catalog, calculations, etc. If there is no session activity, the server destroys the session after a configurable interval (MaxIdleSessionTimeout setting). You can think of the SSAS sessions as similar to user sessions in ASP.NET.

Session management

By default, opening a new connection creates a new session and closing the connection destroys the session. However, as a performance enhancing technique, a new connection can use an existing session. At the same time, closing a connection can leave the session open, so the session can be potentially reused by another connection. A session that is not associated with a connection is called an *orphan* session. The server automatically disposes of orphan sessions that have been idle for a configurable period of time (IdleOrphanSessionTimeout server setting). Listing 17.5 demonstrates how a client application can manage sessions.

Listing 17.5 Consider reusing sessions as a performance enhancement technique.

```
Private ReadOnly Property Connect() As AdomdConnection

    Get
     Dim connection As AdomdConnection
     Try
     Connect:
     connection = New AdomdConnection(Me.txtConnectionString.Text)
     connection.SessionID = m_sessionID
     connection.Open()
     m_sessionID = connection.SessionID
     Return connection

     Catch ex As AdomdConnectionException
      If (ex.InnerException Is Nothing) = False Then
       If ex.InnerException.Message.Contains(m_sessionID) Then
        m_sessionID = Nothing
        GoTo Connect
        grpQuery.Enabled = True
       Else
        Throw ex
       End If
      End If
     Catch ex As Exception
      Throw ex
    End Get
End Property
```

The DotNetClient application caches the session identifier in a form-level variable. When the application is first launched, the session identifier is not set (*Nothing*). Once the connection is successfully established, the application gets the session identifier (Guid data type) from the AdomdConnection.SessionID property and caches it. When a new connection is needed, DotNetClient attempts to reuse the session. If the server hasn't timed out the session, the connection will succeed. Otherwise, the server will raise an exception that the session with the requested identifier is not found. DotNetClient catches this exception and attempts to re-connect.

Connection pooling

A server connection is an expansive resource. You should try to minimize the number of open connections to scale better. For this reason, DotNetClient opens a connection to the server on demand and closes it once the results are retrieved. Closing an AdomdConnection returns the connection to the pool of available connections that other clients can potentially reuse. For more information about additional connection pooling considerations with SSAS, read the *Connection Pooling with SQL Server 2000 Analysis Services* whitepaper (see Resources).

When you are done processing the query results, you should close the connection to return it to the connection pool. The AdomdConnectiond.Close method has an overload that takes an endSession Boolean parameter. If endSession is set to True, server will dispose the session when closing the connection. DotNetClient passes *False* to this argument to preserve the session open.

Connection Settings

ADOMD.NET exposes some interesting features that can be controlled with connection settings. By default, the connection will perform metadata caching (controlled via Cache Mode, Cache Policy, Cache Ratio, and Client Cache Size settings). In addition, the connection will compress data exchanged on the wire (Compression Level setting). Moreover, by default, the connection object will also encrypt the data traffic (Protection Level setting).

Tip You will probably be surprised by the sheer number of the connection settings supported by the OLE DB Provider for Analysis Services. One way to see all settings is to use the Connection Manager dialog and select the Microsoft OLE DB Provider for Analysis Services 9.0 in the Provider dropdown (see Figure 17.17).

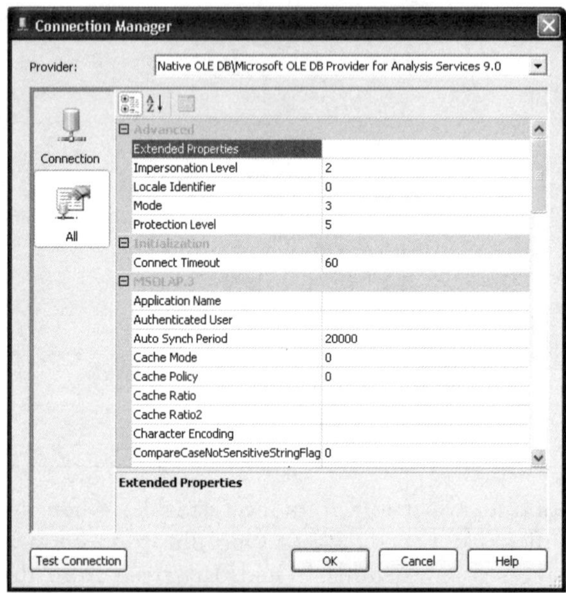

Figure 17.17 Use the All data source properties with an Analysis Services provider to view all connection settings.

17.4.4 Retrieving the Query Results

Different .NET applications may need to manipulate the query results in different ways. For example, a sophisticated OLAP browser may prefer to work with a multi-dimensional Cellset object that preserves the full fidelity of the MDX query. At the same time, a Windows Forms application may prefer ADO.NET datasets that could be bound easily to smart controls, such as the DataGridView control which debuts in .NET Framework 2.0.

Listing 17.6 Consider using DataReader for best performance.

```
Private Sub DoDataReader()
    Dim connection As AdomdConnection = Me.Connect
    Dim command As New AdomdCommand(txtQuery.Text, connection)
    Dim reader As AdomdDataReader

    Try
     connection = Connect()
     reader = command.ExecuteReader(CommandBehavior.CloseConnection)

     Dim schema As DataTable = reader.GetSchemaTable()

     ' display column captions
     For Each row As DataRow In schema.Rows
        lsvResults.Columns.Add(row("ColumnName"),200,HorizontalAlignment.Left)
     Next
```

```
    Do While reader.Read()
      value = IIf(reader.IsDBNull(i),String.Empty, reader(i).ToString())
      ' ... display data
    Loop
   Finally
    If Not (reader Is Nothing) Then
         reader.Close()
    End If
   End Try
End Sub
```

Using DataReader

Using the DataReader ADO.NET object is the most efficient way to retrieve the query results. That's because DataReader simply exposes the results as a read-only forward-only stream which is blasted to the client as fast as the client can process data. Although processing data in a forward-only pass may not seem that useful, consider the fact that you can bind the DataReader object to the data-bound ASP.NET controls (repeater, grid, list, etc.) to render its data. Listing 17.6 shows the abbreviated version (display logic excluded) of the DoDataReader function.

The AdomdCommand object exposes an ExecuteReader method which returns an AdomdDataReader object. AdomdDataReader implements the IDataReader interface (a common interface implemented by most .NET data reader objects, including SqlServerDataReader). The code calls IDataReader.GetSchemaTable to retrieve the underlying schema that describes the resultset in order to configure the columns of the ListView controls. The schema is exposed as an ADO.NET data table object that describes the column metadata, e.g. the column name, data type, etc.

Next, the code loops through the reader rows by calling repeatedly the IDataReader.Read method to add the rows to the ListView controls. After all rows are processed, the code closes the reader which, in turn, closes the associated connection. Use the CommandBehavior.CloseConnection argument when opening a data reader to close the connection when closing the reader.

Using DataSet

While data readers could be an excellent data carrier for ASP.NET applications, they may be impractical for distributed applications with Windows Forms clients. That's because, a reader requires the connection to be open until all rows are read. With distributed applications, every row will require a round trip to the database server. This is definitely something you should avoid.

Instead, consider using ADO.NET datasets. An ADO.NET dataset represents a cached copy of the query results. While behind the scenes, an ADO.NET uses a data reader to fetch the data, it closes the reader and its associated connection once all data is fetched. Moreover, the .NET framework automatically serializes the ADO.NET dataset when it is transported from one application domain to another. Exposing the MDX query results as an ADO.NET dataset is remarkably simple, as Listing 17.7 shows.

Listing 17.7 Consider using DataSet when you need a cached copy of the data.

```
Private Sub DoDataSet()
     Dim connection As AdomdConnection = Me.Connect
     Dim command As New AdomdCommand(txtQuery.Text, connection)
     Dim adapter As New AdomdDataAdapter(command)
```

```
    Dim dataset As New DataSet

    adapter.Fill(dataset)
    dgvResults.DataSource = dataset.Tables(0)
    connection.Close(False)
End Sub
```

The code obtains an ADO.NET DataSet object by calling the Fill method of the AdomdDataAdapter object. Next, the code binds the DataSet object to the DataGridView control to render the results.

Using CellSet

DataReader and DataSet objects are great options for displaying tabular (two-dimensional rowsets. They can also be used for queries that request data on more than two axes but the results will be "flattened" where each axis/tuple adds new rows. Another option for working with the query results is using a CellSet object. A CellSet object preserves the full object hierarchy of the MDX query. For example, the query axes will be exposed as the Axes collection of the CellSet object. Consider using a CellSet object when your application needs a multi-dimensional view of the data. On the downside, you cannot bind the CellSet object to the data-bound controls provided by .NET.

Listing 17.8 A CellSet object preserves the multi-dimensional view of the MDX results.

```
Private Sub DoCellSet()

    Dim connection As AdomdConnection = Me.Connect
    Dim command As New AdomdCommand(txtQuery.Text, connection)
    Dim cellset As CellSet
    Dim lvItem As ListViewItem

    cellset = command.ExecuteCellSet()

    For i As Integer = 0 To cellset.Axes(0).Positions.Count - 1
        For j As Integer = 0 To cellset.Axes(1).Set.Tuples.Count - 1
           lvItem = New ListViewItem(cellset.Axes(0).Set. ↵
              Tuples(i).Members(0).Caption & ", " & cellset.Axes(1).Set. ↵
                  Tuples(j).Members(0).Caption & ": " &
                 cellset.Cells(i, j).FormattedValue)
           lsvResults.Items.Add(lvItem)
        Next
    Next
    connection.Close(False)
End Sub
```

The DoCellSet function (Listing 17.8) demonstrates how a .NET client can work with cellsets. The AdomdCommand object supports an ExecuteCellSet method that returns a CellSet object. DotNetClient supports only two-axis cellsets. The code walks down the CellSet object hierarchy (see again Figure 17.15) to retrieve the query results. Each axis has a set property which returns the MDX set that the axis represents. As you know by now, an MDX set is a collection of tuples, and a tuple is a collection of members. The code uses the Member.Caption to display the member name. The actual cell values are found in the Cells array which has as many dimensions as the number of axes.

Getting the results in XMLA

Finally, the client can retrieve the results in the raw XMLA format as streamed back from the server. This could be useful for cross-platform integration scenarios, e.g. when a .NET Web service is consumed by clients running on different platforms. Listing 17.9 demonstrates how the query results could be obtained in XMLA.

Listing 17.9 Use the AdomdCommand.ExecuteXmlReader to get the results in XML.

```
Private Sub DoXMLA()
    Dim connection As AdomdConnection = Me.Connect
    Dim command As New AdomdCommand(txtQuery.Text, connection)
    Dim xmlReader As System.Xml.XmlReader
    Dim doc As New XmlDocument()
    Dim filePath As String
    Dim xdcResults As New Xml.XmlDocument
    filePath = Application.StartupPath + "\out.xml"

    Try
        ' Execute XML query
        xmlReader = command.ExecuteXmlReader()
        doc.Load(xmlReader)
        doc.Save(filePath)
        ' Display the results in the web browser
        wbrResults.Navigate(filePath)
    Finally
        xmlReader.Close()
        connection.Close(False)
    End Try

End Sub
```

Call the AdomdCommand.ExecuteXmlReader method to get the XMLA payload. For displaying purposes, the code saves the results to a physical file and renders the file in the Web browser control, as I demonstrated with the ThinClient application. Interestingly, the CellSet object supports loading itself from an XmlReader object. This could enable some interesting disconnected scenarios. For example, while at the company office, a sales representative could retrieve the query results and save them as an XML file. When the sales representative disconnects from the network, she could still generate reports from the saved-to-disk cellsets. Of course, another implementation option is when the client supports offloading data to a local cube, as I demonstrated in chapter 13.

.NET supports various objects that inherit from XmlReader. One such a class is XmlNodeReader that can be obtained easily from an XmlDocument object.

```
Dim doc as New XmlDocument()
' ... fill the document
Dim nodeReader As New XmlNodeReader(doc)
Dim disconnectedCellSet as CellSet = CellSet.LoadXml(xmlReader)
```

In this case, the persisted cellset payload is loaded in XmlDocument. Then, an XmlNodeReader is obtained from a document and is fed into the CellSet.LoadXml method to deserialize the CellSet object.

Before we move on to the data mining part of this chapter, I would like to mention one sample application that I recommend you check out, especially if you are planning to implement web-based client applications. Richard Tkatchuk, a Lead Program Manager with the Analysis

Services team, has a full-featured web control called CellSetGrid which simulates the Cube Browser. The CellSetGrid control (see Resources) can be used for browsing both SSAS 2000 and 2005 cubes. I hope that in the near future Richard will enhance this great application to support the new UDM features.

17.5 Implementing Data Mining Clients

Intelligent applications can leverage data mining to perform predictions against server or ad hoc mining models and display the predicted results. Such applications can design, manage, and query data mining models programmatically via the same programmatic interfaces as OLAP clients (XMLA, OLE DB, ADO, and ADOMD.NET). However, instead of using MDX, data mining clients send DMX queries to the server.

Win32 native clients (e.g. a C++ application) can send DMX statements by using the Microsoft OLE DB Provider for Data Mining Services. COM clients (e.g. Visual Basic 6.0 application) would use ADO. The natural choice for .NET clients will be the ADO MD.NET library. A thin client can choose to bypass the programming interface libraries altogether and send XMLA commands directly to the server.

In addition to the information presented in this section, I highly recommend you read the article *SQL Server Data Mining Programmability* by Bogdan Crivat (see Resources) to learn more about incorporating data mining features in your applications. In addition, take a moment to review the resources available on the website sponsored by the SSAS data mining team *www.sqlserverdatamining.com*. Many goodies await you there, including using AMO to administer cubes, complete sample applications, whitepapers, and more.

17.5.1 Querying Mining Models

As explained in chapter 7, you need to train a mining model first before you can query it. Typically, you would train a mining model with a large historical dataset. For example, in chapter 8, we trained the CustomerProfilingMC model with all Adventure Works customers. SSAS stores the mining structure data (training cases) that was used to train the model and the patterns derived from the training process on the server.

Once the model is trained, you can query the model to obtain predictions. Often, a data mining client won't be interested in original (historical) dataset used to train the model. Instead, the client may want to pass a new dataset to obtain predicted results based on the discovered patterns. For example, a customer evaluation application may pass the details of the new customer to find the probability that the customer belongs to a given cluster.

Note Time Series is the only algorithm in SSAS 2005 that doesn't support input data and prediction joins. That's because forecasted values are closely dependent on the historical values and using the discovered patterns may be meaningless for a new set. In other words, the time series algorithm doesn't support "what if" scenarios, only forecasting based on "what was". Therefore, the only way to plug in a new dataset (other than the one stored in the mining structure) is to build a new Time Series mining model from scratch and train it with the new data.

Introducing the WinDataMiner Application

The WinDataMiner application demonstrates three different ways of passing an input dataset to a mining model – OpenQuery, Singleton, and Rowset. It is designed as a Windows Forms application (Figure 17.18). For the sake of simplicity, all prediction queries target the Customer-

ProfilingMC mining model. As you would probably recall, we created this mining model in chapter 8 to implement the customer segmentation mining task using the Microsoft Clustering algorithm. Based on the original Adventure Works customer training set, the model has predicted ten clusters. As new customers enroll, the Adventure Works sales department would certainly be interested to know which ones are potential buyers. To do so, the end user can open the WinDataMiner application to pass the new customer cases to the CustomerProfilingMC mining model.

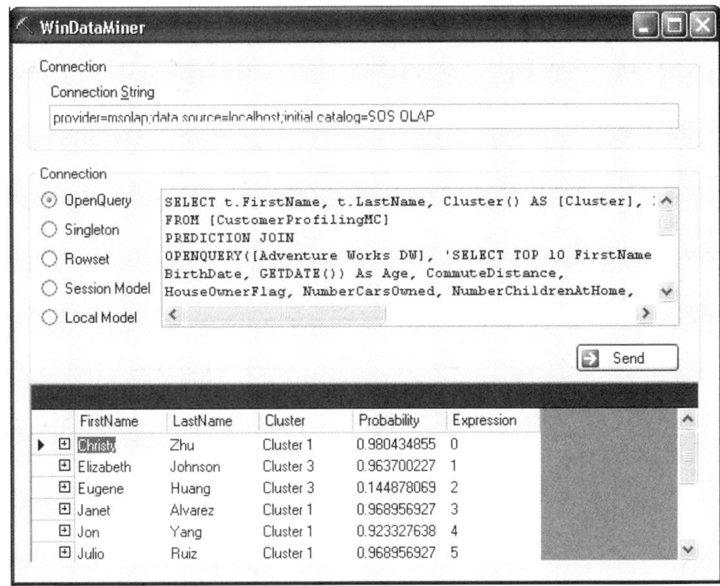

Figure 17.18 The WinDataMiner application demonstrates three different ways to pass input dataset to mining models – OpenQuery, Singleton, and Rowset.

The OpenQuery option assumes that the customer list is stored in a relational database. The Singleton option allows the end user to pass the details of a single customer to the mining model. In real life, you can use the Singleton approach to predict which cluster a customer may belong to as the customer enrolls, e.g. when the customer subscribes to the Adventure Works mailing list.

Finally, the Rowset option passes the input data as a data structure to the mining model object. You can use any data structure that implements the IRowset interface defined in the OLE DB specification. For example, the application can pass a System.Data.DataTable or data reader. As you could imagine, this option enabled some interesting scenarios. For example, a client application may support "what-if" analysis where the user can change the input data in a data-bound grid control. Once the user enters the changes, the application can pass the dataset to the mining algorithm to obtain the predictions.

The last two options demonstrate how users can create mining models if they don't have Administrator rights (Session Model option) or work in a disconnected mode (Local Model option). All options use ADOMD.NET to return the predicted results as ADO.NET datasets. The query statements used by all options are stored in the WinDataMiner.resx resource file.

Input data stored in a relational table

The OpenQuery option assumes that the new cases to be predicted are accessible through an existing data source in the SSAS database hosting the mining model. For example, the SOS

OLAP database has a data source (Adventure Works DW) which can be used to get to the data stored in the AdventureWorksDW database. The DMX SELECT statement that powers the OpenQuery option is shown in Listing 17.10.

Listing 17.10 Use the OpenQuery option when the new data is stored in a relational table.

```
SELECT t.FirstName, t.LastName, Cluster() AS [Cluster],
PredictCaseLikelihood() AS [Probability], PredictHistogram(Cluster())
FROM [CustomerProfilingMC]
PREDICTION JOIN
OPENQUERY([Adventure Works DW], 'SELECT TOP 10 FirstName, LastName, DATEDIFF(yy,
BirthDate, GETDATE()) As Age, CommuteDistance,
HouseOwnerFlag, NumberCarsOwned, NumberChildrenAtHome,
EnglishOccupation, YearlyIncome
FROM DimCustomer') AS t
ON
   t.Age=[CustomerProfilingMC].Age AND
   t.CommuteDistance=[CustomerProfilingMC].[Commute Distance] AND
   t.HouseOwnerFlag=[CustomerProfilingMC].[House Owner Flag] AND
   t.NumberCarsOwned=[CustomerProfilingMC].[Number Cars Owned] AND
   t.NumberChildrenAtHome=[CustomerProfilingMC].[Number Children At Home] AND
   t.EnglishOccupation=[CustomerProfilingMC].[Occupation] AND
   t.YearlyIncome=[CustomerProfilingMC].[Yearly Income]
 ORDER BY t.FirstName
```

I authored this long SELECT statement using the DMX Query Designer in the SQL Server Management Studio. At a high level, the prediction query joins the new cases stored in DimCustomer to the mining model in order to obtain the predicted results from these cases.

Constructing the DMX query

The inner SELECT statement specifies the input columns of the input table and relates them to the columns of the mining model. For demonstration purposes, I will use the same table (DimCustomer) that was used to supply the historical data. In real life, the new cases will probably be found in another table or repository (e.g. an Excel spreadsheet).

Similar to joining two relational tables, DMX supports a PREDICTION JOIN construct. Since input data resides in a different database than the SSAS database hosting the mining model, we can use the OPENQUERY statement or OPENROWSET statement to fetch the input data. The OPENQUERY statement uses an existing data source defined in the SSAS database (Adventure Works DW) and requires the end user to have a Read access right to the data source. This is the preferred method to fetch data because it has performance and security advantages. If you don't have an exiting data source, you can use the OPENROWSET statement. In this case, the data mining engine will attempt to establish a connection to the data source. In both cases, the inner SELECT statement specifies the input columns of the input table and relates them to the columns of the mining model.

Finally, the outer SELECT statement describes which columns from the nested table will be returned. In addition, you can use DMX functions to expose the predicted results. In my case, I use the *Cluster* function to display the predicted cluster, to which the customer is most likely to belong, the *PredictCaseLikelihood* function to return the estimated probability, and the *PredictHistogram* function to predict the distance between the new case and each cluster. The results from the PredictHistogram function are returned as a nested table which can be seen by expanding the row.

Retrieving the input data

Once the DMX query is ready, sending it using ADOMD.NET takes a few lines of code, as the *DoOpenQuery* function demonstrates.

```
Private Sub DoOpenQuery()
    Dim connection As AdomdConnection = Me.Connect
    Dim command As New AdomdCommand(txtQuery.Text, connection)
    Dim adapter As New AdomdDataAdapter(command)
    Dim dataset As New DataSet

    adapter.Fill(dataset)
    dgvResults.DataSource = dataset.Tables(0)
    connection.Close(False)
End Sub
```

I chose to return the results as an ADO.NET dataset so I can bind it conveniently to the grid control. Interpreting the results is easy. As Figure 17.18 shows, the mining algorithm predicts that the first customer (Christy Zhu) is classified to Cluster 1 with 98% probability.

Input data as a singleton query

The Singleton option predicts a single customer. While you can hardcode the customer data inside the query, most real-life applications will probably use a parameterized singleton query. In this way, the same query can be reused by changing the parameters, as shown in Listing 17.11.

Listing 17.11 Use the singleton option to perform a single case prediction.

```
SELECT [First Name], Cluster() AS [Cluster],
PredictCaseLikelihood() AS [Probability]
FROM [CustomerProfilingMC]
NATURAL PREDICTION JOIN
(SELECT
   @FirstName as [First Name],
   @Age AS Age,
   @CommuteDistance AS [Commute Distance],
   @HouseOwnerFlag AS [House Owner Flag],
   @NumberCarsOwned AS [Number Cars Owned],
   @NumberChildren AS [Number Children At Home],
   @Occupation AS [Occupation],
   @YearlyIncome AS [Yearly Income]
) AS t
```

This DMX query uses the NATURAL PREDICTION JOIN construct because the columns of the input table match exactly the columns of the mining model (there is no need to relate the columns by using ON clause). Given the above DMX query, Listing 17.12 shows the ADOMD.NET code to configure and send the query.

Listing 17.12 Creating a parameterized singleton query.

```
Private Sub DoSingleton()
    Dim connection As AdomdConnection = Me.Connect
    Dim command As New AdomdCommand(txtQuery.Text, connection)
    Dim adapter As New AdomdDataAdapter(command)
    Dim dataset As New DataSet

    command.Parameters.Add("FirstName", "John")
    command.Parameters.Add("Age", 40)
```

```
    command.Parameters.Add("CommuteDistance", "5-10 Miles")
    command.Parameters.Add("HouseOwnerFlag", 1)
    command.Parameters.Add("NumberCarsOwned", 2)
    command.Parameters.Add("NumberChildren", 3)
    command.Parameters.Add("Occupation", "Management")
    command.Parameters.Add("YearlyIncome", 90000)

    adapter.Fill(dataset)
    dgvResults.DataSource = dataset.Tables(0)
    connection.Close(False)
End Sub
```

The DoSingleton function needs to set the query parameters before executing the query. For the sake of simplicity, the parameter values are explicitly specified. In real life, the application will most likely pass the values dynamically to the singleton query.

Input data as a dataset

The Rowset option is my favorite because it's the most flexible option. In this case, the new data can be obtained from virtually anywhere. For example, your application can call a web service to get an ADO.NET dataset.

```
SELECT t.FirstName, t.LastName, Cluster() AS [Cluster],
PredictCaseLikelihood() AS [Probability], PredictHistogram(Cluster())
FROM [CustomerProfilingMC]
NATURAL PREDICTION JOIN
@InputTable as t
```

With this option, the DMX query takes a single parameter called @InputTable. During runtime, the application could pass any object that implements IRowset interface to it. For example, the DoRowset function (Listing 17.13) shows how the application can pass an ADO.NET DataSet object as a parameter value.

Listing 17.13 Use the Rowset option to pass the input data as a DataTable.

```
Private Sub DoRowset()
    Dim connection As AdomdConnection = Me.Connect
    Dim command As New AdomdCommand(txtQuery.Text, connection)
    Dim adapter As New AdomdDataAdapter(command)
    Dim dataset As New DataSet
    Dim input As DataSet = GetData()

    command.Parameters.Add("InputTable", input.Tables(0))
    adapter.Fill(dataset)
    dgvResults.DataSource = dataset.Tables(0)
    connection.Close(False)
End Sub

Private Function GetData() As DataSet
    Dim connection As New SqlConnection("<connection string")
    Dim selectQuery = ResourceManager.GetString("qrySQL")
    Dim command As New SqlCommand(selectQuery, connection)
    Dim adapter As New SqlDataAdapter(command)
    Dim dataset As New DataSet

    adapter.Fill(dataset)
    Return dataset
End Function
```

In our scenario, the *GetData* function retrieves the input dataset from the relational database. Next, DoRowset passes the first table in the dataset (an ADO.NET dataset may contain more than one table) as a parameter value to the DMX query.

17.5.2 Generating Session Mining Models

All of the three application scenarios presented above have used already trained mining models that exist on the server. This approach gives you the best performance and centralized control. Sometimes, your applications may need to generate mining models in an ad hoc fashion and perform predictions against those models. SSAS provides two options for ad hoc model generation – session and local mining models. A *session* mining model exists for the duration of the user session, while the *local* mining model is hosted in a cube file located on the user's hard drive.

Understanding session mining models

Creating a server mining model requires *Administrator* rights to the SSAS database, which end users may not have. At the same time, your application may need to generate a mining model, train it, predict against it, and dispose of the model when it disconnects. For example, suppose that the application needs to support different customer datasets that require different mining model definitions. Creating many mining models on the server could be counter-productive. Instead, consider using temporary session models.

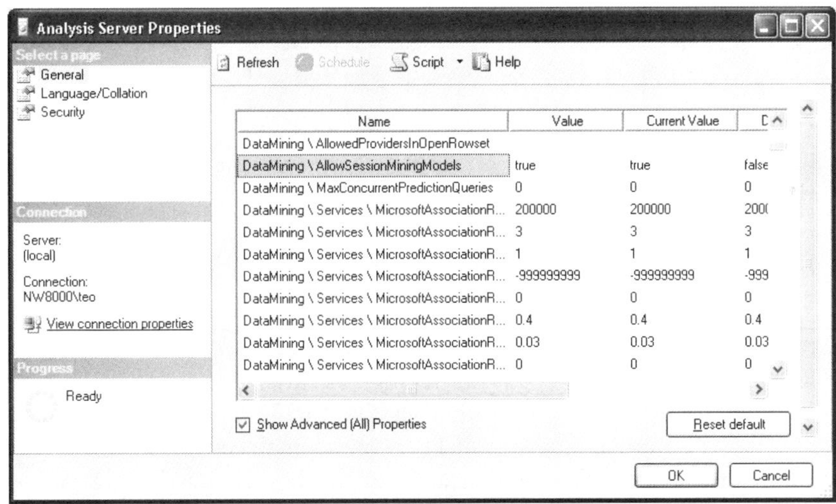

Figure 17.19 Enable session mining models by turning the AllowSessionMining-Models setting on.

You can think of a session mining model as the equivalent of a local temporary table in SQL Server. The session mining model is available only to the user who has created the model. The user needs to have only *Read Definition* access right to the database she connects to. The mining model lifetime coincides with the duration of the user session (not connection, since a session can survive a connection). When the session times out or it is explicitly closed by the application, the server automatically drops the mining model. By default, the session mining model feature is disabled on the server. To enable it, go the server advanced properties and turn the DataMining\AllowSessionMiningModels setting on (see Figure 17.19).

Creating a session mining model

Listing 17.14 shows the abbreviated code of the DoSessionModel function that generates, trains, and predicts against a session model.

Listing 17.14 Create a session mining model programmatically.

```
Private Sub DoSessionModel()

    Dim query As String
    Dim connection As AdomdConnection = New AdomdConnection(...)
    Dim command As New AdomdCommand()
    Dim adapter As New AdomdDataAdapter()
    Dim dataset As New DataSet

    Try
        connection.Open()
        Try
            command.CommandText="DROP MINING STRUCTURE SessionModel_Structure"
            command.Connection = connection
            command.ExecuteNonQuery()
        Catch ex As Exception
        End Try

        query = ResourceManager.GetString("qryCreateSession")
        command.CommandText = query ' Create model
        command.ExecuteNonQuery()

        query = ResourceManager.GetString("qryInsertSession")
        command.CommandText = query ' Train model
        command.ExecuteNonQuery()

        query = txtQuery.Text
        command.CommandText = query ' Predict
        adapter.SelectCommand = command
        adapter.Fill(dataset)

        dgvResults.DataSource = dataset.Tables(0)
    Finally
        connection.Close(True)    ' Destroy the model
    End Try
End Sub
```

First, DoSessionModel attempts to drop the old session mining structure. The server generates a session mining structure automatically when you create a session mining model with the CREATE MODEL statement. That's because a mining model is always contained by a structure. The name of the session mining structure consists of the name of the model and the *"_Structure"* suffix. Normally, the DROP MINING STRUCTURE statement will fail because when the connection is closed in the Finally block of the Try statement, we tell ADOMD.NET to end the session. As a result, the server drops the session mining model and its containing structure. Next, DoSessionModel creates the session model. To do so, it submits the following DMX DDL statement to the server.

```
CREATE SESSION MINING MODEL SessionModel
(
  CustomerID                  LONG KEY,
  Age                         LONG CONTINUOUS,
  [Commute Distance]          TEXT DISCRETE,
  [House Owner Flag]          TEXT DISCRETE,
```

```
  [Number Cars Owned]         LONG CONTINUOUS,
  [Number Children At Home]   LONG CONTINUOUS,
  [Occupation]                TEXT DISCRETE,
  [Yearly Income]             DOUBLE CONTINUOUS
) USING Microsoft_Clustering
```

DMX supports a limited set of DDL statements including the ability to create mining models with the CREATE MINING MODEL statement. To indicate that the model must be scoped at a session level, we use the SESSION clause. When this statement is executed, the server creates the model for the user session and an associated mining structure to host the model.

Training and querying the session mining model

Once the model is created, *DoSessionModel* populates the model with data using the following insert statement.

```
INSERT INTO SessionModel
(   CustomerID, Age, [Commute Distance],
    [House Owner Flag], [Number Cars Owned],
    [Number Children At Home], [Occupation], [Yearly Income])
OPENQUERY([Adventure Works DW], 'SELECT TOP 10 CustomerKey,
    DATEDIFF(yy, BirthDate, GETDATE()) As Age, CommuteDistance,
    HouseOwnerFlag, NumberCarsOwned, NumberChildrenAtHome,
    EnglishOccupation, YearlyIncome
FROM DimCustomer')
```

You can use any of the three options we discussed (OpenQuery, Singleton, or RowSet) to load the model with data. In this case, we use first option to populate the model with the first ten customers from the DimCustomer table. Besides loading the model, the INSERT INTO statement also causes the server to process and train the model. The end result is a trained model that is ready for prediction queries (SELECT statements).

Next, DoSessionModel predicts against the session model using the OpenQuery option, as you've seen. DoSessionModel stuffs the results into a dataset and binds the dataset to the grid. Finally, DoSessionModel destroys the model by closing the connection and the session. If the application tries to query the model after the session is destroyed, it will receive an exception "Either the user, <user name>, does not have permission to access the referenced mining model, SessionModel, or the object does not exist."

As you can imagine, the ability to generate ad hoc session mining models could be extremely useful. In the next chapter, I will demonstrate how a session mining model can be used to generate a sales forecasting report with SSRS.

17.5.3 Generating Local Mining Models

Sometimes, your application may need to provide data mining features in the absence of a SSAS server. For example, suppose that you have a commercial off-the-shelf application which doesn't require the customer to have SSAS installed. Or, the application needs to support a disconnected mode which allows the user to take the mining model with her on the road. To address similar scenarios, consider generating a local mining model.

Understanding local mining models

In chapter 13, I demonstrated how a client application can create a local cube which is stored on the user's hard drive. A local mining model is hosted inside a local cube. A local mining model has the same capabilities as its server counterpart except that it supports only one connection at a time.

In the disconnected scenario that I mentioned, the application would create the local mining model using AMO or ADOMD.NET. Next, the application will train the model with data. Once the model is trained, the application can disconnect and answer mining queries from the local mining model. Similar to a server model, a local mining model must be hosted inside an SSAS database. Consider using a pre-defined local cube to minimize the programming effort to create the cube and the database.

This is the approach the WinDataMiner application takes. It uses an existing LocalCube.cub local cube file as a "template" database. This local cube already has an empty SSAS database which will host the local mining model. Before executing the Local Mining option, make sure you copy the LocalCube.cub file to the root C: folder where WinDataMiner expects to find it.

Creating and querying local mining models

The code to generate a local mining model is almost identical to the one used to create a session model except for a couple of noticeable differences. First, the connection string of the AdomdConnection points to the local cube.

```
provider=msolap;data source=c:\LocalCube.cub;Initial Catalog=SOS OLAP
```

Second, we cannot use OPENQUERY anymore to train and predict against the model because it assumes a named data source inside an SSAS database. Instead, we have to use to OPENROWSET option to retrieve data.

```
INSERT INTO CustomerClusters
(   CustomerID, Age, [Commute Distance], [House Owner Flag],
    [Number Cars Owned], [Number Children At Home],
    [Occupation], [Yearly Income]
)
OPENROWSET('SQLNCLI',
     'Data Source=localhost;Initial Catalog=AdventureWorksDW;
      Integrated Security=SSPI',
'SELECT TOP 10 CustomerKey, DATEDIFF(yy, BirthDate, GETDATE()) As Age,
    CommuteDistance, HouseOwnerFlag, NumberCarsOwned,
    NumberChildrenAtHome, EnglishOccupation, YearlyIncome
    FROM DimCustomer')
```

The OPENROWSET option takes a provider as a first argument. Since we are retrieving data from a SQL Server relational database, we use the SQL Server Native Client provider. The second argument takes a connection string to the data source. WinDataMiner drops the mining structure if it exists, creates a local mining model, trains the model, and sends a prediction query.

17.5.4 Displaying Data Mining Results

Results from data mining prediction queries are best analyzed when they are presented graphically. As they say, a picture is worth a thousand words. The SSAS data mining team has provided two sample applications that demonstrate how you can provide rich user experience with Windows Forms and web-based clients.

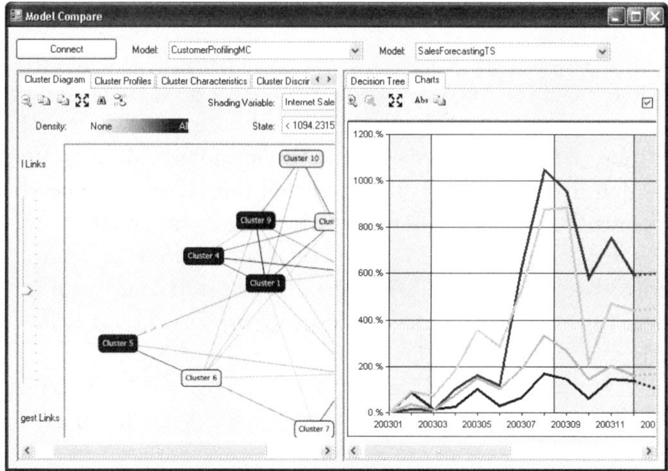

Figure 17.20 The DataMiningViewerClient application demonstrates how a Windows Forms client can integrate with the mining viewers that ship with SSAS.

Using the Data Mining Viewers with Windows Forms clients

As you saw in chapter 7, SSAS ships with excellent viewers for each of the supported mining algorithms. Moreover, the SSAS team was kind enough to package the same viewers in a standalone .NET assembly (Microsoft.AnalysisServices.Viewers.DLL) which you can use in your Windows Forms applications. As an added bonus, you can freely distribute the viewers to your end users. The source code of the viewers is not provided, though.

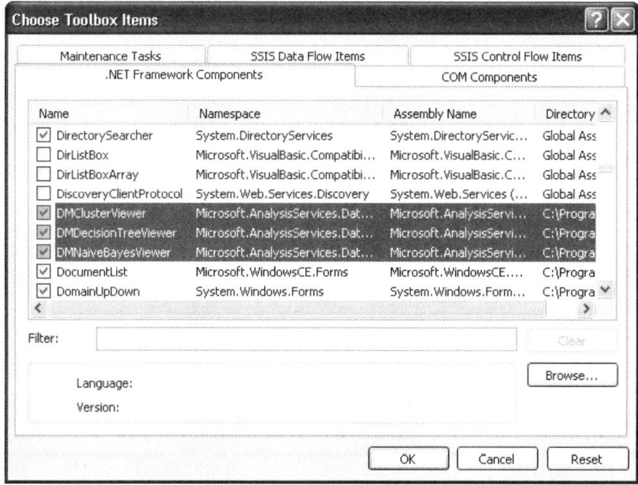

Figure 17.21 The WebControls application comes with three web viewers.

The DataMiningViewerSample (see Resources for a download link) demonstrates how a client application can leverage the viewers. Once the end user connects to an SSAS database, DataMiningViewerSample populates the two Model dropdowns with the available mining models in that database. Then, the user can select up to two mining models to see them side-by-side. For example, as Figure 17.20 shows, I have selected to see the CustomProfilingMC and SalesForecastingTS mining models. Once the user selects a model, DataMiningViewerSample instantiates the associated viewer control, passes the connection string to it, and configures the control. Next, it calls the viewer's LoadViewerData method which takes care of rendering the viewer.

Creating your own viewers

Another sample (WebControls) demonstrates how you can create a custom web-based viewer for visualizing the mining results. The default location of the WebControls sample is C:\Program Files\Microsoft SQL Server\90\Samples\Analysis Services\DataMining\Data Mining Web Controls. Follow the instructions provided in the ReadMe files to install the viewers. Once you run the setup program, it copies the control assembly (Microsoft.AnalysisServices.DataMining-HtmlViewers.dll) to the C:\Program Files\Microsoft.AnalysisServices.DataMiningHtmlViewers folder. Next, you need to add the controls to the VS.NET Toolbox by right-clicking on it and choosing the *Choose Toolbox Items* menu. Once you reference the control assembly, you will see that it hosts three viewers (Figure 17.21).

Included in the Ch17 solution is a sample ASP.NET application (WebDataMiner) which showcases the DMClusterViewer web viewer. It simulates the Cluster Discrimination tab of the Microsoft Cluster Viewer that ships with SSAS. Once the Default.aspx page is rendered, the user can select two clusters to determine how they differ (Figure 17.22). Interestingly, the WebControls sample uses OLE DB object library to query the mining models which returns the results as an OleDbDataReader object. In real life, ADOMD.NET will probably be a better choice for .NET clients since it is much easier to use.

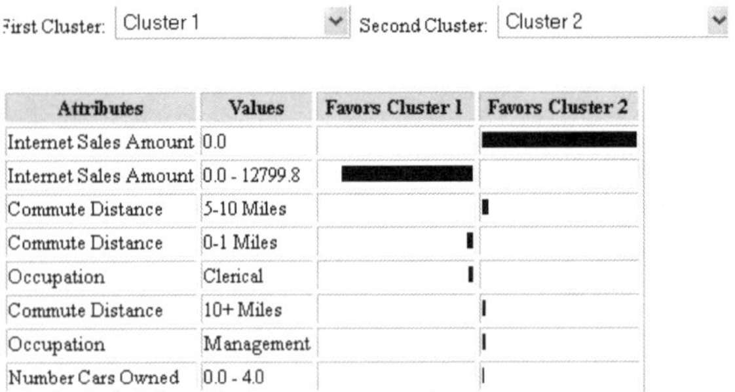

First Cluster: Cluster 1 Second Cluster: Cluster 2

Attributes	Values	Favors Cluster 1	Favors Cluster 2
Internet Sales Amount	0.0		
Internet Sales Amount	0.0 - 12799.8		
Commute Distance	5-10 Miles		
Commute Distance	0-1 Miles		
Occupation	Clerical		
Commute Distance	10+ Miles		
Occupation	Management		
Number Cars Owned	0.0 - 4.0		

Figure 17.22 The WebControls application demonstrates how you can create custom viewer controls.

17.6 Summary

SSAS provides various programming interfaces to support different integration scenarios. Thin clients that seek to eliminate platform and deployment dependencies can send raw XMLA requests. Native clients can target the OLE DB object library, while legacy clients could use the ADO MD library. SSAS provides an ADOMD.NET library for .NET managed clients.

OLAP clients have several options to retrieve the results of MDX queries. Use the DataReader option to process the results one row at a time. Use the DataSet option to get the results as an ADO.NET dataset. Retrieve data as a CellSet when you need to preserve the full fidelity of the multidimensional MDX set. Finally, use the XMLA option to retrieve the results in the raw XMLA format.

Data mining clients also have several options to send DMX prediction queries. Use the OPENQUERY or OPENROWSET when the new data resides in a relational database. Consider the singleton query option when you need to predict a single case. Finally, the Rowset option gives the ultimate flexibility to pass a structure that implements the IRowset interface on the fly. Consider session mining models to generate ad hoc mining models. Applications that need to support a disconnected mode could create a local mining model. Windows Forms client can display the data mining results using the viewers bundled with SSAS. When the standard viewers are inadequate, custom viewers can be implemented.

17.7 Resources

XML for Analysis 1.1 SDK
(http://shrinkster.com/7dd) -- The Microsoft XML for Analysis 1.1 SDK contains the Microsoft XML for Analysis provider and sample client applications.

A command-line thin XMLA client
(http://shrinkster.com/7ip) -- Chris Harrington demonstrates how you can implement a thin XML client with Windows Scripting Host.

TcpTrace Utility
(http://shrinkster.com/7is) – Use TcpTrace to trace HTTP traffic between a client and the server.

SOAP Toolkit 3.0
(http://shrinkster.com/7it) – Includes the Microsoft SOAP Trace utility which you can get by installing the Debugging Utilities only. The rest of the toolkit is deprecated because the .NET framework provides Web services infrastructure.

OLE DB for OLAP Specification
(http://shrinkster.com/7iu) – Describes the OLE DB for OLAP specification and provides code samples.

ADOMD.NET Version 8.0 Redistributable
(http://shrinkster.com/7iv) – Download ADOMD.NET 8.0.

Connection Pooling with SQL Server 2000 Analysis Services
(http://shrinkster.com/7j7) – Learn how the SSAS connection pooling works.

The CellSetGrid web control
(http://shrinkster.com/7ke) – CellSetGrid is a simple asp.net control for browsing Analysis Services 2000 and 2005 cubes. The control and source code are available.

SQL Server Data Mining Programmability article by Bogdan Crivat
(http://shrinkster.com/53j) – In this fifty-page document, Bogdan Crivat describes the data mining API and explains how they can be used in business intelligence applications.

Data Mining Samples
(http://shrinkster.com/7mz) – The SSAS data mining team has made several samples available on the website www.sqlserverdatamining.com, including the DataMiningViewerClient application.

Chapter 18

Standard and Ad hoc Reporting with Reporting Services

Reporting is an essential feature of every business intelligence application. One way to extract and disseminate the wealth of information captured in UDM is to author standard "canned" reports that end users can review and print. Once a standard report is created and published by the report author, it cannot be changed by the end users. In comparison, ad hoc reporting empowers the business users to create their own reports by abstracting them from the technicalities of the underlying database schema and query syntax.

You can use Microsoft SQL Server Reporting Services (SSRS) to author, manage, and deliver standard and ad hoc reports across the enterprise. Moreover, you can use SSRS and SSAS together to build synergetic reporting solutions. In chapter 12, you saw how you can implement UDM actions to render SSRS reports. In this chapter, you will see how you can build SSRS reports that consume data from UDM. You will learn how to:

- Author standard OLAP reports that use MDX to report from multidimensional data.
- Author standard data mining reports that use DMX to display prediction results.
- Deliver standard reports to the end users with the SSRS Report Viewer controls.
- Generate ad hoc reports from UDM.

This chapter starts with a panoramic overview of the SSRS architecture. Besides the basic UDM reports we will build, this chapter shows you how to implement advanced reports that leverage CLR stored procedures. You will find the sample reports and code in the Ch18 solution.

18.1 Understanding Reporting Services

Microsoft introduced the first release of SSRS (SQL Server Reporting Services 2000) in January 2004. Despite its short history, SSRS has been enjoying increasing popularity and has established itself as the reporting tool of choice for building small to enterprise-level cost-effective reporting solutions. One reason for this success is its open and extensible architecture which I will discuss next.

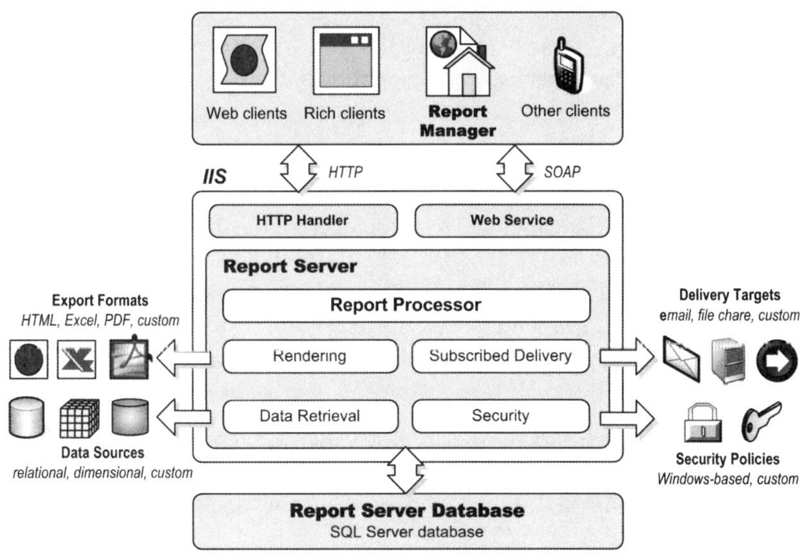

Figure 18.1 SSRS is a server platform for authoring, managing, and delivering standard and ad hoc reports.

18.1.1 Reporting Services Architecture

Similar to SSAS, SSRS is implemented as a server-based platform that ships as an add-on component to Microsoft SQL Server. To meet different reporting needs, SSRS is available in four editions – Express, Workgroup, Standard, and Enterprise. This flexible licensing model permits organizations to find the right compromise between cost and reporting features. For more information about how the SSRS editions compare refer to the document *Resources SQL Server 2005 Reporting Services Feature Matrix* in the Resources section. Figure 18.1 outlines the high-level SSRS architectural view. The major components are the Report Server, Report Server Database, and the Report Manager. Excluded from the diagram are the SSRS ad hoc components which are discussed in section 18.5.

Report Server

At the heart of the RS architecture is the Report Server, a web-based middle-tier layer that receives incoming report requests and generates reports. The Report Server encompasses several components installed by default in the C:\Program Files\Microsoft SQL Server\MSSQL.3\ ↵ Reporting Services\ReportServer\bin folder. For example, the Report Processor orchestrates all activities required to generate a report. One of the features that I like best about SSRS is its modularized and extensible architecture. Each of the services listed under the Report Processor box in Figure 18.1 is performed by specialized .NET modules called *extensions*. When the standard extensions don't provide the features you need, you can implement and plug in your own extensions.

Data retrieval

Similar to UDM, an SSRS report can draw data from a variety of data sources. Out of the box, SSRS supports standard data extensions for SQL Server, Oracle, SAP, and Microsoft SQL Server Analysis Services. The last one is particularly interesting because it allows us to report off UDM. If you need to integrate with another OLE DB or ODBC - compatible data source, you can do so by using the generic OLE DB or ODBC data extensions. Reports can be integrated with non-standard data sources through custom data extensions. For example, you can create a custom data extension to produce live reports (reports running under the Report Server) from ADO.NET datasets (see Resources for a sample custom data extension).

Rendering

SSRS comes with several rendering extensions for popular output formats, including HTML (default), Adobe PDF, Excel, CSV, Image (TIFF, JPG, GIF, etc.) and XML. The HTML rendering extension dynamically discovers the capabilities of the client and streams the appropriate HTML output. Specifically, the extension renders HTML 4.0 (default format) for uplevel browsers, e.g. Internet Explorer 6.0, or HTML 3.2 otherwise. When the standard rendering extensions are not enough, developers can implement custom rendering extensions. For example, a good scenario for a custom renderer is targeting a handheld device that expects cHTML.

Subscribed delivery

Besides on-demand (live) report delivery, SSRS supports also *subscribed* report delivery where users can subscribe to reports. With this option, SSRS schedules and renders the report asynchronously in an unattended mode. Out of the box, SSRS provides email and file share delivery extensions to deliver subscribed reports via e-mail or save them as files. When they are not enough (you guessed it), developers can implement custom delivery extension. For example, my book *Microsoft Reporting Services in Action* demonstrates a custom delivery extension that delivers reports in XML format to a web service (see Resources).

Security

Similar to SSAS, by default, SSRS is configured for Windows-based security, where the Report Server authenticates and authorizes the user based on her Windows account or group membership. When this is not adequate, developers can replace the Windows-based security model with a custom security extension (see Resources for a sample extension).

Report Server Database

Just like the Analysis Server stores the metadata that describes the UDM objects, SSRS keeps the report metadata in the Report Server Database (a.k.a. report catalog). The report metadata includes all items associated with the report, including the report definition, security policies, associated folder which hosts the reports, schedules, subscriptions, etc. By default, the SQL Server setup program creates the Report Server Database (ReportServer) on the same server where SSRS 2005 is installed. You can use the Reporting Services Configuration tool (*Microsoft SQL Server 2005* ⇨ *Configuration Tools* ⇨ *Reporting Services Configuration* program group) to change the location of the Report Server database after install, e.g. to host it in an SQL Server 2000 server.

Report Manager

To facilitate the report and model management, SSRS provides a web-based application called *Report Manager* (Figure 18.2). The Report Manager is implemented as an ASP.NET application (*http://<ReportServer>/Reports*) that fulfills two main tasks. First, it allows the report administrator to manage the report catalog, e.g. to organize reports in folders or set up security polices. Second, organizations can use the Report Manager portal to generate reports quickly. Behind the scenes, the Report Manager leverages the Report Viewer ASP.NET control (discussed in section 18.4.2) to render the reports.

SSRS 2005 introduced a second (recommended) management option. The administrator can use SQL Server Management Studio to manage report servers from a single location. SQL Server Management Studio supports all Report Manager features and adds new features not available in the Report Manager. For example, the SSRS administrator can use Management Studio to script report objects and management tasks.

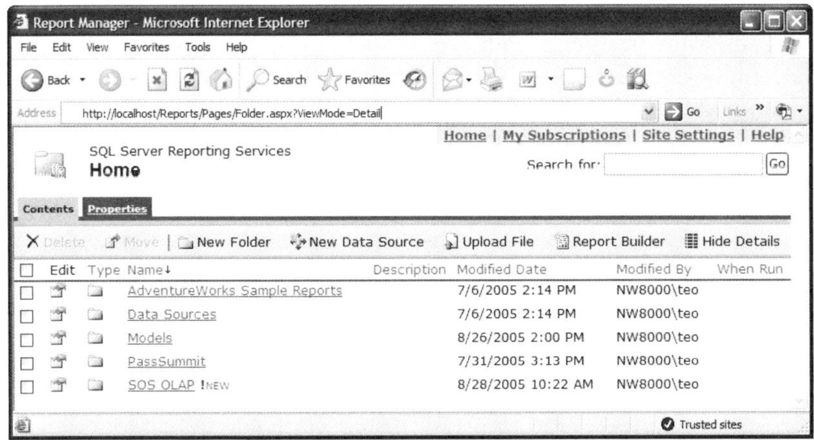

Figure 18.2 Use the Report Manager to manage the report catalog and generate reports.

18.1.2 Integrating Reporting Clients

To facilitate integration with external client applications, the Report Server provides two communication facades -- *HTTP Handler* and *Web service*. Both facades are hosted under the Internet Information Server (IIS). Let's describe the two communication facades in more details.

HTTP Handler

The SSRS HTTP handler allows external clients to request a report by submitting an HTTP GET or HTTP POST request that specify the report URL (URL addressability). For example, here is how you can render the Sales Forecast report that we will author in this chapter.

```
http://localhost/ReportServer?/SOS OLAP/Sales Forecast&Year=2003&NumberMonths=3 ↵
&rs:Command=Render&rs:Format=PDF
```

This assumes that the Sales Forecast report is deployed to the local SSRS server and it is uploaded to the SOS OLAP folder. The report takes two parameters, *Year* and *NumberMonths*, whose values are passed as query parameters. In addition, as an optimization technique, we use the *Render* command to inform the server about our intention to render the report, so the server doesn't have to figure out what type of a resource we are requesting. Finally, we instruct the server to render the report in PDF format.

URL addressability is the easiest way to request reports. In its simplest implementation, you can embed the report URL link in your application. For example, in chapter 12, you saw how you could implement a reporting action by specifying the report URL. On the downside, URL addressability may present a security risk because it exposes the report parameters. Another limitation with URL addressability is that it supports requesting reports only. You cannot use this integration option to perform management tasks. Because of these limitations, URL addressability may be deprecated in the long run in favor of the SSRS Web service.

Web service

The Web service option exposes the entire SSRS feature set to external clients. One significant limitation of the SSRS 2000 Web service was that it didn't support report interactive features (drilldown, toggled visibility, document maps, etc.). As a result, developers were forced to use URL addressability when business requirements called for rich report experience. This limitation has been lifted in SSRS 2005 and the SSRS Web service has been enhanced to support interactive features.

On the downside, integrating report clients with the SSRS Web service is inherently more difficult than URL addressability. That's because developers need to learn how to access the SSRS Web service programmatically and take extra steps to handle report images, report sessions, and other features that come for free with URL addressability. To shield developers from the Web service technicalities, Visual Studio.NET 2005 provides the freely redistributable ASP.NET and Windows Form report viewer controls, which I will demonstrate in section 18.4.

18.2 Authoring OLAP Reports

A typical report lifecycle consists of report authoring, management, and delivery. During the authoring phase, the report author creates the report definition. Once the report is ready, the administrator (or the report author) publishes the report to the report catalog to make it available to the end user and client applications. A published report can be distributed to report clients on-demand or through subscribed delivery, e.g. via e-mail.

18.2.1 Report Authoring Basics

The end result of the report authoring phase is the report definition that contains the report data retrieval and layout information. The report definition is described in Report Definition Language (*RDL*).

About Report Definition Language

Similar to ASSL, Reporting Services reports are described in an open XML-based grammar called *Report Definition Language* (RDL). RDL conforms to the Report Definition Language Specification (see Resources for a download link). Having SSRS reports stored in an open format is great for developers and third-party vendors. For example, in one of my projects, we were faced with complex ad hoc requirements that went beyond the SSRS 2005 ad hoc capabilities. Instead, we built an object model to abstract the Report Definition Language Specification which we used to manipulate ad hoc reports as objects. Alternatively, you can use the XML APIs of your programming platform (e.g. the XmlDocument object in .NET) to manipulate the report definition directly in XML.

The Report Designer

While RDL can be generated programmatically to meet more involved reporting scenarios, the preferred tool of choice for authoring standard reports is the Report Designer. The Report Designer is tightly-integrated with the BI Studio IDE and is available when you create a Report Server project. Figure 18.3 introduces you to the Report Designer components. The Report Designer features a tabbed user interfaces consisting of Data, Layout, and Preview tabs. The tab order reflects the natural steps to author a report.

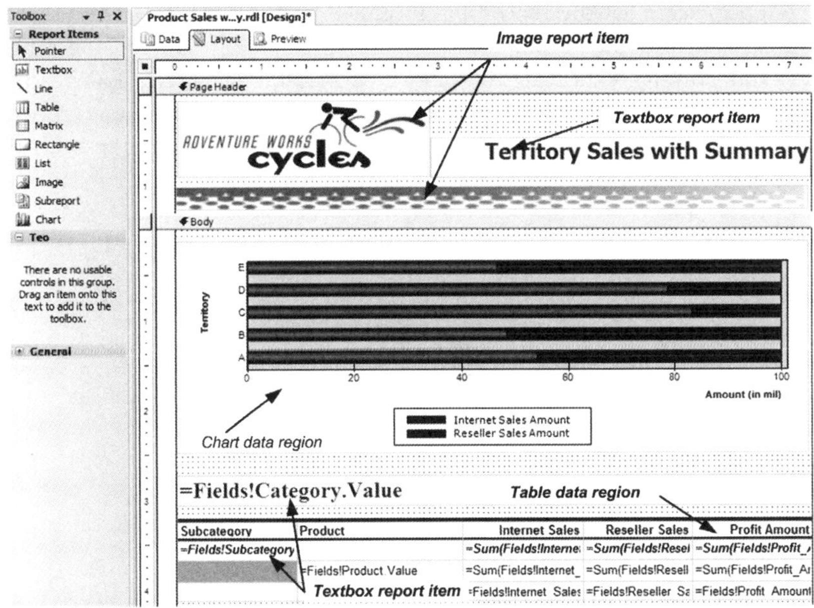

Figure 18.3 The Report Designer included in BI Studio is the preferred choice for authoring standard reports.

Data tab

You use the data tab to configure the report data by creating one or more datasets. A *dataset* is a data structure that holds the results of the query sent to the report data source. A report can have more than one dataset. For example, one dataset can feed the main portion of the report, while another may be used to derive the available values for a report parameter. When using a relational database as a data source, you can construct a dataset by using a free-form SQL SELECT statement or a stored procedure. When you target UDM, you use MDX to create OLAP reports and DMX for data mining reports. Finally, a report can combine data from different data sources. For example, you can have a report when one dataset is fed with data from a relational database, while another with data from UDM.

Layout tab

The Layout tab represents the report canvas that is the What-You-See-Is-What-You-Get (WYSIWYG) representation of the report. The report author constructs the report by dragging items from the Report Items toolbar and dropping them onto the report. The report items supported by SSRS can be classified in two groups: regular *report items* and *data regions*. The regular report items are *textbox* (used to display a fixed string, expression-based string, or a data field), *line* (for decorative purposes), *rectangle* (encloses other items, e.g. to keep them together when rendering to HTML), and image (can display external, embedded, and data-bound images).

A data region can be bound to a dataset just like an ASP.NET or Windows Form data-bound controls can be bound to ADO.NET datasets. The *table* region displays the dataset data in a tabular (grid) format. The *matrix* region is for generating crosstab reports. You can use the list region to place the report data in a freeform format. Finally, the chart region displays the dataset in a graphical format. All out-of-the-box data regions except the chart region use textboxes to display the dataset fields.

Preview tab

You can use the Preview tab to see what the report will look like in its final form. The Preview tab features a handy toolbar that provides a plethora of features including handing the report parameters, print preview and printing, exporting the report, zooming, paging, etc. To speed up the report generation, the Report Preview tab caches the report data the first time the report is run in a local file (<report name>.data). Click the Refresh button to render the report with the most recent data.

18.2.2 Creating Tabular Reports

Now that you have a good grasp of the SSRS architecture and Report Designer, let's create a few sample reports that source data from the SOS OLAP UDM. We will start with a step-by-step exercise in which we will use the Report Wizard to create a tabular OLAP report. Later, we will enhance the report to include a chart region and interactive features.

Creating Report Server project

Start by creating a Report Server project to host the Reporting Services reports.

1. Open BI Studio and choose *File ⇨ New ⇨ Project.*
2. Select the Business Intelligence Projects in the Project types pane and Report Server Project as a template.
3. Name the project **Reports**. Choose a location for the project and click OK to let BI studio create the project template.

Creating a data source

Similar to UDM, an SSRS report retrieves report data via a data source object that represents a connection to a database. Unlike UDM though, a Report Server project doesn't support data source views. SSRS supports shared and private data sources. As its name suggests, a *shared data source* can be shared among several reports. A shared data source minimizes the maintenance effort to configure database access. For example, if the administrator changes the security settings on a shared data source, all reports that reference that data source will pick up the new settings.

A private data source is scoped at a report level and gets embedded inside the report. A private data source may simplify the report deployment when you need to distribute everything that the report needs in the report definition file. Let's create a shared data source that points to the SOS OLAP UDM.

1. In the Solution Explorer window, right-click on the Shared Data Sources folder and select *Add New Data Source.*
2. Enter **SOS OLAP** as a data source name.

Note SSRS connects to UDM using ADOMD.NET client which doesn't use the OLE DB Provider for Analysis Services. The correct data extension to use when connecting to UDM is *Microsoft SQL Server Analysis Services*. To verify, you can check the *Data provider* list in the Change Data Source window. The only item in the list should be *.NET Framework Data Provider for Analysis Services*. To connect to previous SSAS releases, use the OLE DB extension with the appropriate provider, e.g. OLE DB Provider for Analysis Services 8.0 to connect to SSAS 2000.

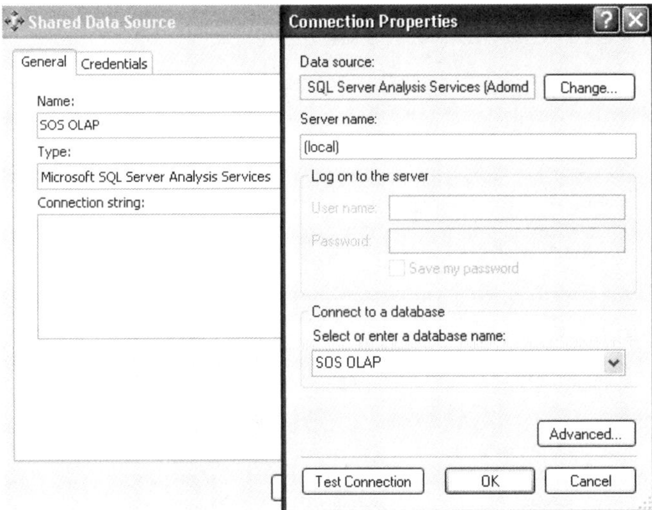

Figure 18.4 Use the Microsoft SQL Server Analysis Services extension to connect to UDM.

3. Expand the Type dropdown and select the *Microsoft SQL Server Analysis Services* data extension. Click the Edit button to configure the data source.

4. Set up the Connection Properties dialog as shown in Figure 18.4 and click OK to close the dialog. Back to the Shared Data Source dialog, click OK to create the SOS OLAP data source.

Launching the Report Wizard

BI Studio provides a handy Report Wizard for creating basic tabular and matrix reports. Let's create a tabular report that shows Adventure Works sales broken down by product category, subcategory, and product levels (Figure 18.5). The Product Sales report also demonstrates the drilldown (toggled visibility) interactive feature. By default, the subcategory level is collapsed to save space. The end user can click on the + image to see the product details. At this point, an additional request is made to the Report Server to render the hidden section.

Product Sales

Accessories

Subcategory	Product	Internet Amount	Reseller Amount	Profit Amount
⊞ Bike Racks		$30,406.81	$188,175.24	$218,582.05
⊞ Bike Stands		$28,751.95		$28,751.95
⊟ Bottles and Cages		$44,684.86	$7,275.23	$51,960.09
	Mountain Bottle Cage	$16,586.98		$16,586.98
	Road Bottle Cage	$11,402.81		$11,402.81
	Water Bottle - 30 oz.	$16,695.08	$7,275.23	$23,970.31

Figure 18.5 The Product Sales report demonstrates a tabular OLAP report.

1. In the Solution Explorer, right-click on the Reports folder and choose *Add New Report* to launch the Report Wizard. The SOS OLAP data source you've just created should be selected by default in the Select the Data Source step.

2. The Design Query step gives you an option to type (or paste) the query statement or use a query builder to assist you in constructing the query. Click on the Query Builder button. The Report Wizard launches the excellent Query Builder (Figure 18.6).

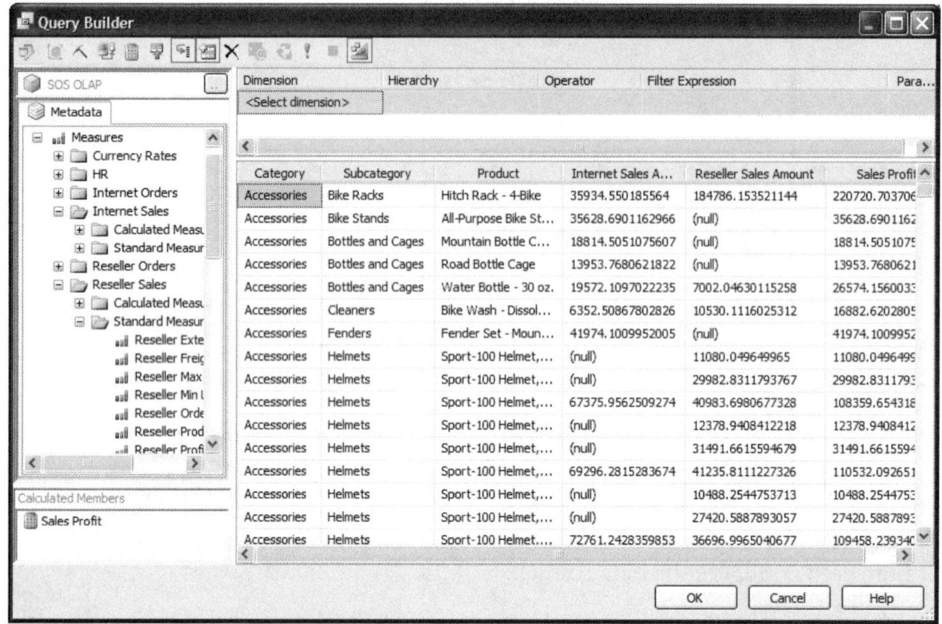

Figure 18.6 The Query Builder supports authoring MDX and DMX queries.

The Query Builder is available in both the Report Wizard and the Data tab of the Report Designer. The Query Builder supports two command modes when it targets UDM data sources. By default, the Query Builder is launched in MDX command type mode (Figure 18.6), which allows you to author MDX queries to create OLAP reports. If you need to author data mining reports, you can click on the pickaxe toolbar button to switch to DMX command type.

Creating MDX queries

In MDX command mode, the Query Builder mimics the familiar Cube Browser with a few important differences. The Query Builder doesn't use the PivotTable OWC for displaying the query results. That's because SSRS expects data in a tabular format. As noted in chapter 17, ADOMD.NET can return the query results in one of two formats -- a multidimensional cellset (CellSet object) or as a tabular rowset (DataReader and DataSet options). SSRS uses the second format. As a result, the query results are essentially flattened into a two-dimensional grid.

Note One implication of the flattened query results is that the *All* members are discarded from the attribute hierarchy. From a report layout perspective, a trivial solution to fix the problem is to create group totals to aggregate data at the desired level.

Unlike the Cube Browser, the Query Builder exposes the KPIs defined in the cube. Each KPI exposes the KPI-related functions (Value, Goal, Status, and Trend) as properties, so the report author can just drag them to the query results pane to include them as columns. Finally, the Query Builder supports creating calculated members ad hoc (as a part of the MDX query). For example, assuming that the SOS OLAP UDM doesn't have a Sales Profit member, you can define in the Query Builder. In my opinion, this approach should be used sparingly. Instead, business calculations and metrics should be centralized in the UDM itself to prevent redefining them from one report to another.

That said, ad hoc calculated members could be very useful to address more involved query requirements, e.g. to include member properties in the dataset. By default, the Query Builder allows you to return only measures and dimension hierarchies (attribute or multi-level). If a member property doesn't have an attribute equivalent, you can create a calculated member to include it in the dataset.

1. Click on the **...** Cube Selection button and select the SOS OLAP cube.
2. Expand the Product dimension. Drag the Product by Category multi-level hierarchy from the Metadata pane and drop it in the query results pane.
3. Repeat the same with the Reseller Sales Amount and Internet Sales Amount measures.
4. If the Auto Execute toolbar button is not pressed, click the *No Rows Found. Click to execute the query* link to send the MDX query and display the results.
5. Let's create a Profit Amount calculated member. Click the Add Calculated Member toolbar button to open the Calculated Member Builder dialog. Name the calculated member **Profit Amount**.
6. Expand the Metadata tree and drag the Internet Sales Amount and Reseller Sales Amount measures to form the following expression:

```
[Measures].[Internet Sales Amount] + [Measures].[Reseller Sales Amount]
```

7. Click OK to close the dialog. The Profit Amount member is added to the Calculated Members pane.
8. Drag the Profit Amount member to the end of the of the query results grid to create a new column.

Analyzing the MDX query

Behind the scenes, the Query Builder generates an MDX SELECT statement when you drag and drop dimensions and measures. You can switch to the Generic Query Designer (deselect the rightmost toolbar button) to inspect the raw query statement and make changes to the MDX query.

Note Changes done in Generic mode are lost when switching back to Designer mode. In other words, the Query Builder cannot reverse-engineer the Generic mode changes.

Let's take a moment to see what the Query Builder has done for us.

```
WITH MEMBER [Measures].[Profit Amount] AS
 '[Measures].[Internet Sales Amount] + [Measures].[Reseller Sales Amount]'
SELECT NON EMPTY { [Measures].[Internet Sales Amount],
 [Measures].[Reseller Sales Amount], [Measures].[Profit Amount] } ON COLUMNS,
NON EMPTY{([Product].[Product by Category].[Product].ALLMEMBERS)}
 DIMENSION PROPERTIES MEMBER_CAPTION, MEMBER_UNIQUE_NAME ON ROWS
FROM [SOS OLAP]
 CELL PROPERTIES VALUE, BACK_COLOR, FORE_COLOR, FORMATTED_VALUE,
 FORMAT_STRING, FONT_NAME, FONT_SIZE, FONT_FLAGS
```

The WITH MEMBER statement defines the Profit Amount calculated member. Next, the MDX query asks for the requested measures on columns, and dimension hierarchies on rows. The *AllMembers* MDX function returns all members at the Product level, including calculated dimension members (if any). The MDX sets on both axes are enclosed in the NON EMPTY clause because by default the empty cells are suppressed (Show Empty Cells toolbar button is not selected).

By default, the MDX query results return some basic member properties that describe each member in a tuple, including the member name, parent level, the number of children, and so on. DIMENSION PROPERTIES and CELL PROPERTIES clauses fetch some of these properties. The member properties extend the query axes although the Query Builder doesn't display them. A client can use these properties to configure the user interface, e.g. to set the font color, cell format, etc. The member properties are ignored by the Report Designer.

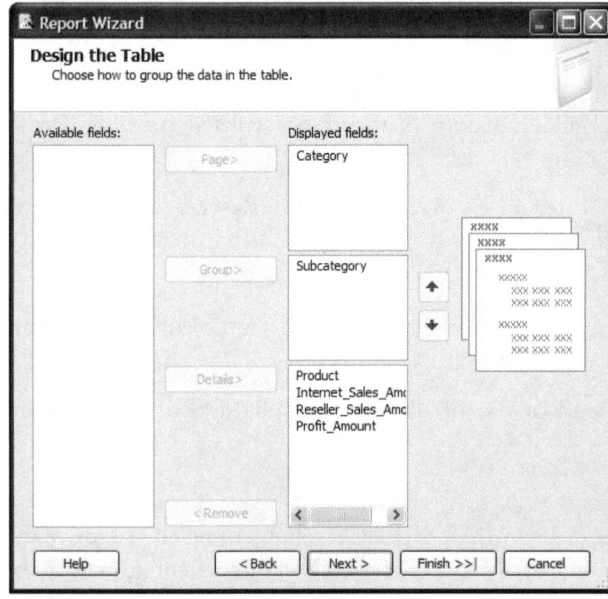

Figure 18.7 Use the Design the Table step to specify how the report data will be grouped.

Defining the report layout

Let's finish the Report Wizard and generate the report definition.

1. Click OK to close the Query Builder and go back to the Design Query step. Click Next.
2. In the Select the Report Type step, leave the default option (Tabular) selected to create a tabular report. Click Next.
3. In the Design the Table step (Figure 18.7), we need to specify how the report data will be grouped. Select the Category field and click the Page button to move it to the *Displayed fields* list. As a result, the Report Server will group data on the product category first. In addition, the Report Server will generate a page break after each product group.
4. Select the Subcategory fields and click the Group button to group the report further by product subcategory.
5. Select the remaining fields and move them to the Details list.

6. In the Choose the Table Layout step, accept the default layout (Stepped). Enable the *Include Subtotals* checkbox to generate subtotals for each product subcategory group. Check also the *Enable Drilldown* checkbox to implement the drilldown interactive feature on the subcategory level.
7. In the Choose the Table Style step, select *Bold* as a report style.
8. In the Completing the Wizard step, name the new report **Product Sales** and click Finish. Once the Report Wizard generates the report, it opens the report in the Layout tab of the Report Designer (Figure 18.8).

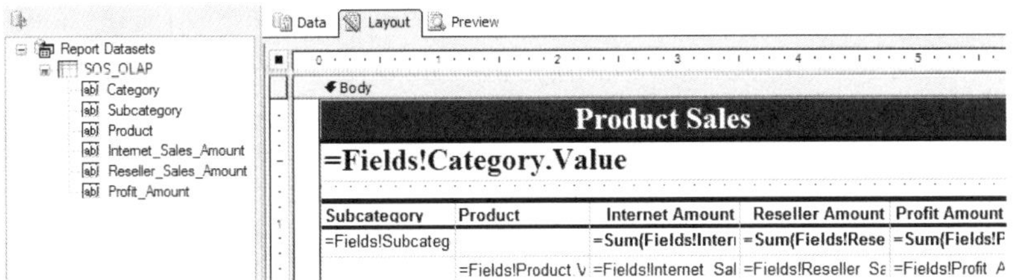

Figure 18.8 The Product Sales report contains one list region that groups data by product category and a nested table region that groups by product subcategory.

Reviewing the report

Let's review quickly what the Report Wizard has done for us. The report wizard has placed all report items (including the title) in the Body band of the report. As it stands, SSRS doesn't support designated report header/footer bands. Therefore, if the report has a title that needs to appear only on the first page, you need to place the title in the report body. The Report Datasets pane on the left side shows the datasets defined in the report. As it stands, the Product Sales report has only one dataset. The dataset fields correspond to the columns returned by the MDX query. Data-driven textbox report items in the report are mapped to the fields of the dataset, while the data regions are bound to the dataset itself.

Tip To select the parent container of an item quickly, select the item and press the Esc key. Alternatively, use the BI Studio Properties window to pick an item from the dropdown to select that item in the report canvas.

The Report Wizard has generated two data regions. The list region encloses all report elements except the report title. The reason why the Report Wizard included the list region in the first place is because the Category field is placed as a standalone page-level field and is used to group the report data. If you inspect the list region properties (select the region, right-click, and choose Properties) and click on the *Edit details group* button, you will see the list data is grouped at a Category level and a hard page break is specified at the end of each group. As a result, the list region will be repeated as many times as the number of the product categories and each category (except the first) will start on a new page.

The table region is nested inside the list region and it will be rendered for each product category. Besides details grouping, the table region supports table-level groups. In our case, a table-level group is created at a product subcategory level. The group totals are specified as expressions. Specifically, the expressions use the *Sum* aggregate function, which is one of the several aggregate functions supported by SSRS. In addition, I've done numerous formatting changes to pretty up the report, including decreasing the page margins, reducing the font size, formatting all numeric textboxes as currencies (select the textboxes and change the Format property to *C*), etc. During the design process, I used the Review tab on a regular basis to verify how the report is rendered and make sure that it doesn't exceed the page margins.

18.2.3 Implementing Parameterized Reports

As it stands, the Product Sales report reads from the entire multidimensional space and users cannot restrict the data shown on the report. Chances are that in real life your users may call for more flexible reports. A common reporting requirement is allowing the user to filter the information shown on the report by using parameters. For example, the end user may want to filter the report for a given time period. Let's enhance the Product Sales report to support filtering the report data for one or more years that will be passed as report parameters. You can find the new version saved under *Product Sales by Year.*

SSAS 2000 The only way to implement a parameter-driven OLAP report with SSAS 2000 was to use an expression-based MDX query by concatenating the query text and the parameter values. With SSAS 2005, there is a better way. You can create parameterized MDX queries by adding parameter placeholders, just like you can do with SQL queries.

Creating a parameter

The Query Builder can generate parameterized MDX queries automatically for you.

1. Switch to the Data tab of the Report Designer.
2. Filter the MDX query by defining a cube slice (see Figure 18.9), the same way you can do in the Cube Browser. In this case, I have filtered the cube space for the 2004 calendar year.

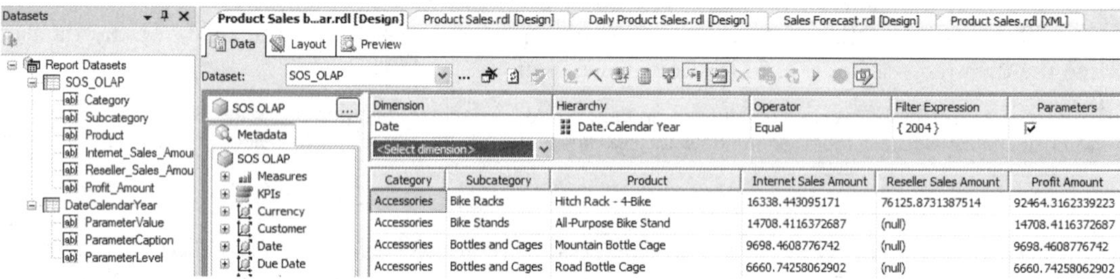

Figure 18.9 Creating a parameterized MDX query by defining a cube slice.

3. Check the Parameters checkbox and save the report. The moment you save the parameterized MDX query, the Query Builder performs its "magic" and generates a data-driven multi-value parameter for each filter row.

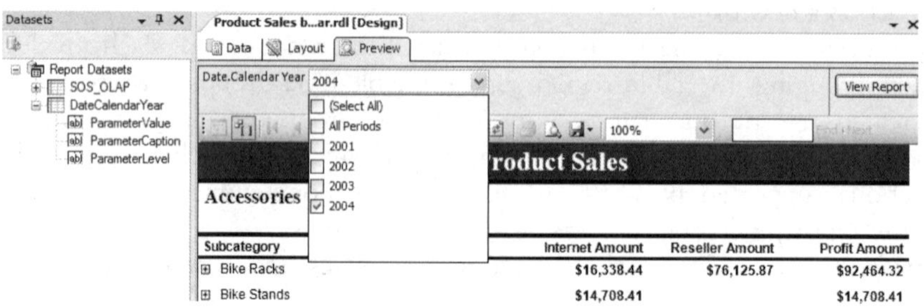

Figure 18.10 The DateCalendarYear dataset defines the available values for the CalendarYear parameter.

4. Switch to the Preview tab (Figure 18.10). Observe that a new *DateCalendarYear* dataset is added to the Dataset pane and the report now has a *Date.Calendar Year* parameter that matches the filtered hierarchy by naming convention.

5. Expand the *Date.Calendar Year* parameter and notice that year 2004 is pre-selected. In addition, notice that you can select multiple years because the Query Builder has created *Date.Calendar Year* as a multi-value parameter.

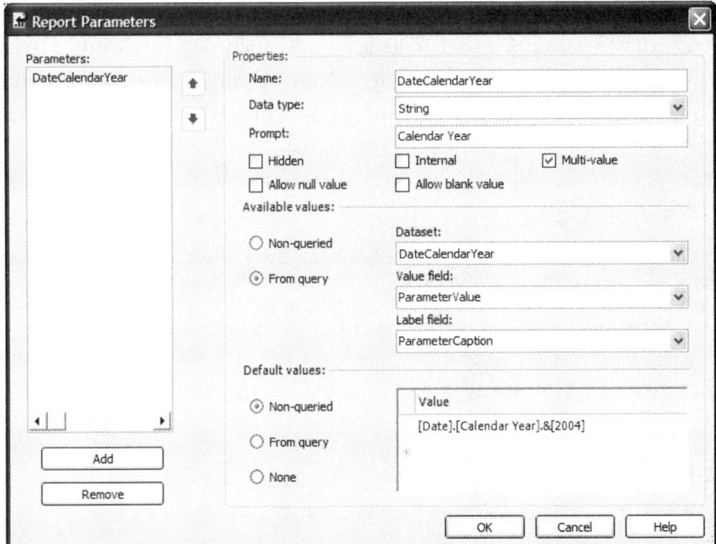

Figure 18.11 By default, the Query Builder creates a multi-value data-driven parameter when the Equal operator is used.

Understanding Report Parameters

The only way an end-user (or a client application) can change the report data and layout of a Reporting Services report is by using report parameters. Let's take a moment to understand the changes the Query Builder made when setting up the report parameter.

1. With the Layout tab active, select the *Reports* ➪ *Report Parameters* main menu. BI Studio opens the Report Parameters dialog (Figure 18.11)

The Query Builder has created a report parameter called *DateCalendarYear*. The Query Builder has configured the parameter available values to be derived from the *DateCalendarYear* dataset, which uses on the following MDX query.

```
WITH MEMBER [Measures].[ParameterCaption] AS
    '[Date].[Calendar Year].CURRENTMEMBER.MEMBER_CAPTION'
MEMBER [Measures].[ParameterValue] AS
    '[Date].[Calendar Year].CURRENTMEMBER.UNIQUENAME'
MEMBER [Measur es].[ParameterLevel] AS
    '[Date].[Calendar Year].CURRENTMEMBER.LEVEL.ORDINAL'
SELECT {[Measures].[ParameterCaption], [Measures].[ParameterValue],
    [Measures].[ParameterLevel]} ON COLUMNS,
    [Date].[Calendar Year].ALLMEMBERS ON ROWS
FROM [SOS OLAP]
```

Figure 18.12 shows the parameter dataset.

Calendar Year	ParameterCaption	ParameterValue	ParameterLevel
(null)	All Periods	[Date].[Calendar Year].[All Periods]	0
2001	2001	[Date].[Calendar Year].&[2001]	1
2002	2002	[Date].[Calendar Year].&[2002]	1
2003	2003	[Date].[Calendar Year].&[2003]	1
2004	2004	[Date].[Calendar Year].&[2004]	1

Figure 18.12 The parameter dataset defines the parameter available values.

The flattened parameter dataset returns parameter label (caption) and value as columns. However, MDX expects a set expression on the column axes. The Query Builder gets around this limitation by creating "pseudo" measures as calculated members (another good use for ad hoc calculated members). SSRS supports binding two columns for each parameter to derive the parameter value and label properties which are exposed as the *Parameters!<ParameterName>.Value* and *Parameters!<ParameterName>.Label* respectively.

Tip When you use multi-value parameters, bear in mind that the Value property of a parameter returns an array, not a scalar. For example, if you reference a multi-valued parameter via *=Parameters! <Parameter-Name>.Value* in a textbox, you will see *#Error* when you preview. To get around this, you can use the *Join* function. This function creates a single string from an array of strings with an optional delimiter.

2. Change the parameter Prompt property to **Calendar Year** and click OK to close the Report Parameters dialog.

Defining a parameter placeholder

Flip to the Data tab and select the SOS_OLAP dataset in the Dataset dropdown to open it in the MDX Query Builder. To see the raw MDX query, switch to the Generic Query Designer by deselecting the Design Mode button. Notice that the Query Builder has automatically defined a parameter placeholder in the FROM clause of the query.

```
FROM (SELECT(STRTOSET(@DateCalendarYear, CONSTRAINED)) ON COLUMNS FROM [SOS OLAP])
```

When used in the FROM clause, the SELECT statement defines a subcube on which the outer SELECT statement operates. In this case, this will be a subcube of the SOS OLAP cube that is sliced for the selected years. Subcube filters are a new feature of SSAS 2005. When the query is executed, the *@DateCalendarYear* placeholder will be replaced with a comma-delimited string with all selected parameter values. SSRS matches the placeholder and the actual parameter by name. Therefore, don't change the name of the parameter. If you do, you will find that the Report Designer will ignore the changed parameter and create a new one. The *StrToSet* MDX function converts the value list to an MDX set.

Deploying the report

Now that the Product Sales Report is ready, let's deploy it to the report catalog.

1. Open the project properties. Enter SOS OLAP as TargetReportFolder and http://localhost/ReportServer as TargetServerURL. As a result of these settings, all reports in the Report Server project will be deployed to the Home/SOS OLAP folder on the local Report Server.
2. In Solution Explorer, right-click on the project node (Reports) and choose *Deploy*. BI Studio deploys the SOS OLAP data source and the Product Sales report to the Report Server.

3. Start Internet Explorer and navigate to the Report Manager URL address (*http://localhost/reports*). Navigate to the SOS OLAP folder.
4. Click on the SOS OLAP data source link and verify that SOS OLAP data source used the correct credentials to connect to the SOS OLAP UDM.

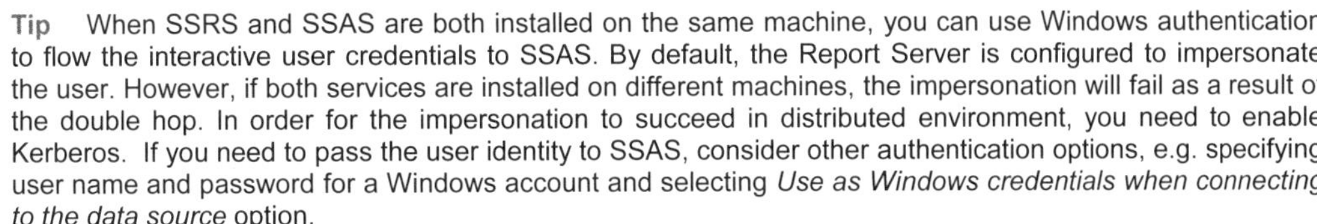

Tip When SSRS and SSAS are both installed on the same machine, you can use Windows authentication to flow the interactive user credentials to SSAS. By default, the Report Server is configured to impersonate the user. However, if both services are installed on different machines, the impersonation will fail as a result of the double hop. In order for the impersonation to succeed in distributed environment, you need to enable Kerberos. If you need to pass the user identity to SSAS, consider other authentication options, e.g. specifying user name and password for a Windows account and selecting *Use as Windows credentials when connecting to the data source* option.

5. Click on the *Product Sales* report link to launch the Product Sales report. Once the report is rendered, you can use the Export dropdown in the standard report toolbar to export the report in the desired format.
6. If your security requirements call for securing the report, use the report Properties page and Security link to enforce restricted access to the report for specific Windows users or groups.

These simple steps completed the report lifecycle of the Product Sales report. You saw how SSRS makes it easy to author, manage, and deliver reports. Another report you may find interesting is the Product Sales by Dates report. It demonstrates a date range filter. To implement it, I had to manually change the parameter datasets. In addition, the report demonstrates how you can retrieve the member value (MEMBER_VALUE property) to preserve the underlying data type (DateTime in this case).

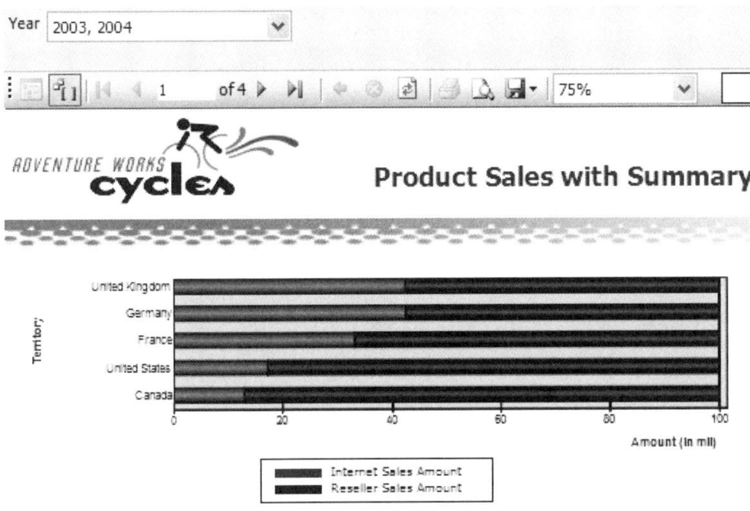

Figure 18.13 Author multi-section reports by placing data regions side-by-side.

18.2.4 Designing Chart Reports

SSRS supports more advanced reports. For example, a common reporting requirement is authoring a multi-section report (e.g. a board report), where different sections present information in a different way. SSRS supports placing regions side-by-side to the meet similar needs. The *Product Sales with Summary* report (Figure 18.13) builds upon the Product Sales by Year report to demonstrate how you can implement a multi-section SSRS report.

This report features a summary section that is implemented by using the SSRS chart region. Behind the scenes, the chart region is bound to a new dataset (*dsTerritory*), as you can notice by inspecting the *DataSetName* property of the chart region. The MDX query that feeds the dataset is defined as a parameterized query that is bound to the same *DateCalendarYear* parameter. This is done to keep the restrict chart data for the same time period as the one used to select the tabular data.

The Product Sales with Summary report demonstrates also the new SSRS 2005 user sort feature. The end user can click the Profit Amount header to sort the subcategory totals as the arrow glyph hints. The user sort feature works in a toggle mode. Each time you click the header, the report is refreshed and the subcategory sort order changes direction.

18.3 Authoring Data Mining Reports

Business intelligence should help users analyze patterns from the past to plan for the future. Data mining presents ample opportunities to implement a new generation of reports with predictive analytics features. Such reports could process historical patterns to present views of opportunities and trends. The two sample reports (Targeted Campaign and Sales Forecast) included in this chapter demonstrate how you can leverage data mining features of SSAS to author "smart" reports. The first report presents a list of the top ten customers that are most likely to purchase a given product. The second report uses the past sales history to forecast future sales.

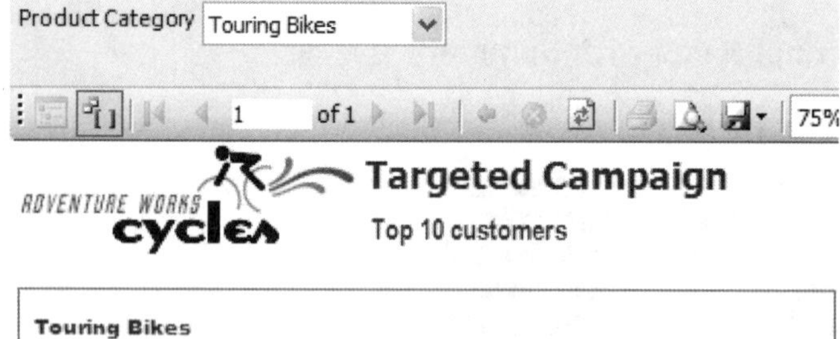

Touring Bikes

Customer ID	Customer Name	Probability
11451	Ruben Muñoz	92.58 %
12340	Stacy Diaz	92.58 %
11446	Bethany Chander	92.58 %
11447	Jennifer Roberts	92.58 %
12338	Monica Vance	92.58 %
12339	Clayton Jai	92.58 %
11444	Tina Mehta	92.58 %
11445	Kari Kim	92.58 %
12667	Maria Wood	92.58 %
12342	Morgan Young	92.58 %

Figure 18.14 The Targeted Campaigning report uses a data mining model to display a list of potential buyers.

18.3.1 Targeted Campaigning

In chapter 7, we implemented the Targeted Campaign mining model to identify potential customers that may be interested in buying a new bicycle product. Suppose that you need to prepare a standard report that lists the most likely buyers. Figure 18.14 shows the Targeted Campaign report that meets this requirement. The end user can filter the report by product category. The report shows the top ten customers that may purchase a product from the selected category and the estimated probability.

Constructing the DMX query

As you know by now, you need DMX to query a mining model. Constructing a DMX query statement is easy with the Query Builder.

1. Create a new dataset *dsCampaign* that uses SOS OLAP as a data source.
2. In the Dataset dropdown (Data tab), select the dsCampaign dataset to open it in the Query Builder.
3. Select the pickaxe toolbar button to switch to the DMX command mode (Figure 18.15).

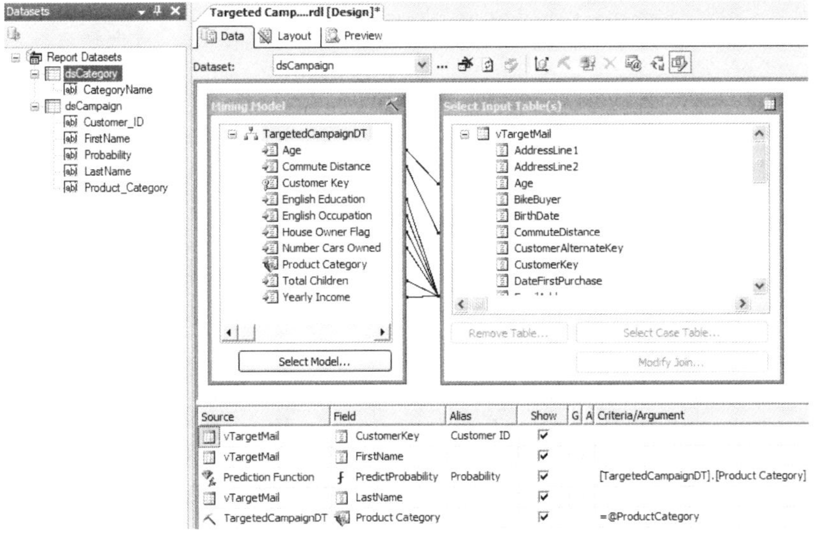

Figure 18.15 Switch to the DMX command mode to create a DMX query.

The DMX query builder is very similar to the DMX Designer available on the Mining Model Prediction tab of the Data Mining Designer. For this reason, I won't discuss it in details. To produce the query needed for the Targeted Campaign report, I used the Design mode of the Query Builder. The vTargetMail view fulfils the role of the case table that contains the new customers. As with MDX, DMX queries can have parameters. The *@ProductCategory* parameter placeholder will be replaced during runtime with the value of the selected product category. If you want to test the parameter during design time, you can click on the Query Parameters toolbar button. In the Query Parameters dialog that follows, enter @ProductCategory as a parameter name and the category name as the parameter value.

Since the report needs the top ten customers who are most likely to buy a product from the selected category, I had to finalize the query in SQL mode (right-click outside the two tables and choose *SQL*). I needed to introduce an ORDER clause in the query to sort by the predicted probability column and use *SELECT TOP 10* to cap the query.

Constructing the report parameter

As with the MDX command mode, the moment you introduce a parameter placeholder in the DMX query, the Report Designer creates a report-level parameter. To make the parameter data-driven, I used a second dataset (*dsCategory*) that fetches the product categories from the AdventureWorks database. I used this dataset to derive the parameter available values.

Note DMX doesn't support an IN clause in the WHERE portion of the query since the DMX parser is not a complete SQL implementation. As a result, you cannot easily implement multi-value report parameters with data mining reports. As a workaround, you can create a linked query from SQL Server and execute the where clause on the result of the OPENQUERY statement.

Once the report query and parameters have been taken care of, authoring the report layout is nothing you haven't seen so far. I used a table region that is bound to the dsCampaign dataset. Next, I dragged the dsCampaign fields from the Datasets pane and dropped them on the table region to create the three columns. The report also demonstrates how expression-based conditional formatting can be used to alternate the background color of the table rows.

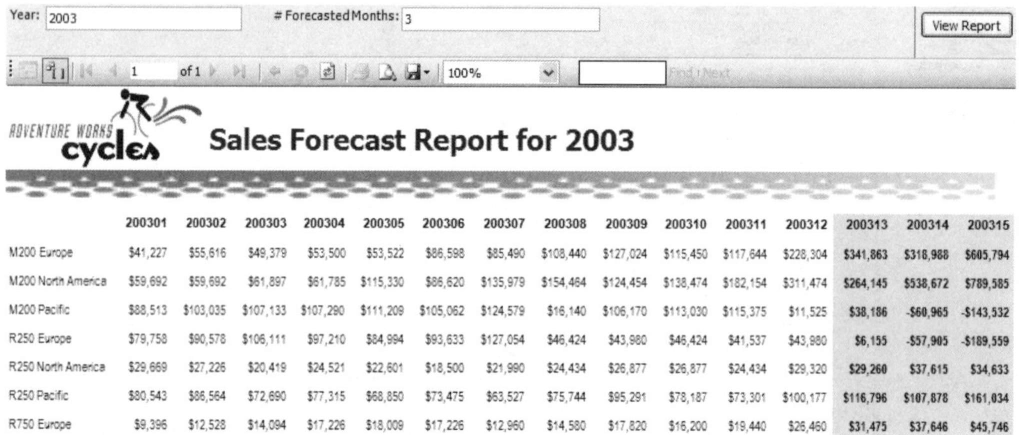

	200301	200302	200303	200304	200305	200306	200307	200308	200309	200310	200311	200312	200313	200314	200315
M200 Europe	$41,227	$55,616	$49,379	$53,500	$53,522	$86,598	$85,490	$108,440	$127,024	$115,450	$117,644	$228,304	$341,863	$318,988	$605,794
M200 North America	$59,692	$59,692	$61,897	$61,785	$115,330	$86,620	$135,979	$154,464	$124,454	$138,474	$182,154	$311,474	$264,145	$538,672	$789,585
M200 Pacific	$88,513	$103,035	$107,133	$107,290	$111,209	$105,062	$124,579	$16,140	$106,170	$113,030	$115,375	$11,525	$38,186	-$60,965	-$143,532
R250 Europe	$79,758	$90,578	$106,111	$97,210	$84,994	$93,633	$127,054	$46,424	$43,980	$46,424	$41,537	$43,980	$6,155	-$57,905	-$189,559
R250 North America	$29,669	$27,226	$20,419	$24,521	$22,601	$18,500	$21,990	$24,434	$26,877	$26,877	$24,434	$29,320	$29,260	$37,615	$34,633
R250 Pacific	$80,543	$86,564	$72,690	$77,315	$68,850	$73,475	$63,527	$75,744	$95,291	$78,187	$73,301	$100,177	$116,796	$107,878	$161,034
R750 Europe	$9,396	$12,528	$14,094	$17,226	$18,009	$17,226	$12,960	$14,580	$17,820	$16,200	$19,440	$26,460	$31,475	$37,646	$45,746

Figure 18.16 The Sales Forecast report uses a session data mining model to forecast future sales.

18.3.2 Sales Forecasting

Sales forecasting is a critical reporting requirement for most businesses. At the same time, sales forecasting has been traditionally difficult to implement and forecasts have been often wrong as a result of the incorrect output from the mathematical models used. In this section, I would like to show you how SSAS data mining can be used to create compelling and consistent sales forecast reports.

From a user's standpoint, the Sales Forecast report (Figure 18.16) is simple. The end user would enter the year for the historical period and the number of the forecasted months. The report displays the sales figures for the selected year followed by the forecasted figures (shaded in gray). The data is broken down by the product model and territory on rows and time (in months) on columns.

Choosing implementation approach

As noted in the previous chapter, the Time Series algorithm doesn't support passing an input dataset by using a *Prediction Join* statement. As a result, the only way to predict from an arbitrary dataset is to build a new Time Series data model that is bound to that dataset. One way to do this is to create a session mining model which the server automatically disposes of at the end of the user session. From an SSRS standpoint, you have at least three options to author a report that uses a session mining model. First, you can implement a custom data extension to generate the model, retrieve the results as an ADO.NET dataset (or reader), and translate the results to a format that SSRS understands.

Second, you can call custom code in an external .NET assembly that generates the session mining model and retrieves the results via expressions in your report. I demonstrated a similar approach in my book *Microsoft Reporting Services in Action* (see Resources). Both approaches mentioned above share the same tradeoffs. They are difficult to implement and debug. You have to distribute and register the custom dataset extension (or external assembly) with the Report Server. Finally, custom extensions are supported only by the Standards and Enterprise editions of SSRS.

With the advent of the CLR stored procedures in SQL Server 2005, a third approach is to move the programming logic into a CLR stored procedure. A *CLR stored procedure* is .NET code packaged as a stored procedure. In my opinion, CLR stored procedures will open a new world of implementation and integration scenarios that were difficult, if not impossible, with prior releases of SQL Server. Once the CLR stored procedure is implemented and deployed, it can be called from your report just like a regular stored procedure. The downside of this approach is that it requires SQL Server 2005. Let's use a CLR stored procedure to implement the Sales Forecast report.

Implementing the SalesForecast mining model

When implementing a CLR stored procedure, you may find it easier to adopt a two-step approach. First, for faster development and testing, you write and debug the .NET code in a standard .NET project, e.g. a console application. Once the code is ready, you move it to a CLR stored procedure and register the procedure with the SQL Server 2005. In the Ch18 solution, you will find a TimeSeries console application that demonstrates the first step of the process, and the AdventureWorks assembly that includes the final version of the *CreateSessionModel* stored procedure.

You can use AMO or DMX DDL statements to create the mining model. Listing 18.1 shows the abbreviated code of the TimeSeries console application that generates and queries the session model using DMX only. In the TimeSeries folder, you will find a SalesForecast.dmx file which you can use to test the DMX statements in Management Studio.

Listing 18.1 Creating a session mining model that returns the historical and forecasted data.

```
Private Sub CreateSessionModel(ByVal Year As Integer, _
     ByVal numberMonths As Integer)

    command.CommandText = "DROP MINING STRUCTURE SessionForecast_Structure"
    command.Connection = connection
    command.ExecuteNonQuery()

' Create a session model
    query = "CREATE SESSION MINING MODEL SessionForecast ( " _
```

```
    & "TimeIndex LONG KEY TIME, ModelRegion TEXT KEY," _
    & "Amount LONG CONTINUOUS PREDICT" _
    & ") Using Microsoft_Time_Series WITH DRILLTHROUGH"

    command.CommandText = query
    command.ExecuteNonQuery()

    Dim startMonth As Integer = Int32.Parse(Year.ToString() & "01")
    Dim endMonth As Integer = Int32.Parse(Year.ToString() & "12")

    ' Train the model
    query="INSERT INTO SessionForecast,TimeIndex,ModelRegion,Amount,Quantity) " _
    & "OPENQUERY([Adventure Works DW], " _
    & "'Select TimeIndex, ModelRegion, Amount " _
    & "FROM [vTimeSeries] WHERE (TimeIndex >= " & startMonth & _
    &  "And TimeIndex <= " & endMonth & ") ORDER BY TimeIndex')"

    command.CommandText = query
    command.ExecuteNonQuery()

    Dim predictions As New DataSet
    ' Get predicted results
    query = "SELECT ModelRegion, " _
    & "(SELECT $TIME, [Amount], PredictVariance([Amount]) " _
    & "FROM PredictTimeSeries([Amount], @NumberMonths)) " _
    & "FROM [SessionForecast]"

    command.CommandText = query
    command.Parameters.Add("NumberMonths", numberMonths)
    adapter.SelectCommand = command
    ' Fill the dataset
    adapter.Fill(predictions)

    ' Get the cases
    query = "SELECT ModelRegion, TimeIndex, Amount  FROM [SessionForecast].CASES"
    command.CommandText = query
    adapter.SelectCommand = command
    Dim cases As New DataTable
    adapter.Fill(cases)

    ' Merge cases and predictions
    Dim results As DataTable = PopulatePredictedColumns(predictions.Tables(0))
    results.Merge(cases)
End Sub
```

First, the code attempts to drop the session mining structure. Normally, the code will fail to find it and will error out. That's because a session mining model is automatically disposed of when the user session terminates. However, you may find the DROP MINING STRUCTURE statement useful during debugging, e.g. if you need to change a query and recreate the structure without restarting the application.

Creating the mining model

Next, the code creates the SalesForecast session mining model. For the purposes of the Sales Forecast report, we need only three columns – TimeIndex (the month), the Model Region (we are forecasting by the model-region combination on rows), and Amount (the column we are predicting against). The mining model has the same columns as the vTimeSeries SQL view which serves as a data source for the model. When the server executes *CREATE SESSION MINING*

MODEL statement, the server creates the SalesForecast model and the SalesForecast_Structure to host the model.

Training the model

Once the session model is generated, we are ready to train the model with the historical dataset. We do this by sending an INSERT INTO DMX statement which feeds the model with data from the vTimeSeries SQL view for the time period selected in the report. This statement is the workhorse of the *CreateSessionModel* function and it takes the most time to execute. During the statement execution, the server populates the model with data and processes (trains) the model to produce the predicted results.

ModelRegion	Expression		
R250 Pacific	⊟ Expression		
	$TIME	Amount	Expression
	200313	121415	52182277.25281...
	200314	115050	76133738.53521...
	200315	161004	78695437.5942782
M200 North America	⊞ Expression		

Figure 18.17 The forecasted results are returned as a nested table.

Querying the model

The code proceeds by sending a prediction query to get the predicted results. A Time Series model exposes the predicted results as a nested table that contains as many rows as the number of the prediction steps. Therefore, to retrieve the forecasted numbers, the SELECT statement uses a subquery that returns the forecasted month (*$TIME* function), amount, and the estimated variance of the prediction (*PredictVariance* function). Given the results shown in Figure 18.17, the SalesForecast model has forecasted that the sales amount for the first predicted month (January 2004) will be $121,415.

Tip In real life, you should spend some time optimizing the mining model to reduce the variance and obtain more accurate predictions. Chapter 8 gives some optimization tips to fine-tune a Time Series mining model.

Note that the number of the predicted months is passed as a parameter to the prediction query. The forecasted results are loaded into the *predictions* ADO.NET dataset.

ModelRegion	TimeIndex	Amount
R250 Pacific	200301	80543
M200 North Ameri...	200301	59692
M200 Europe	200301	41227
M200 Pacific	200301	88513

Figure 18.18 The historical data is obtained from the cases table.

Besides the forecasted values, the Sales Forecast report displays the historical data. The second SELECT statement queries the mining model to retrieve the cases used to train the model. Each mining model exposes a CASES property which returns the case table. Needless to say, we can obtain the cases directly from the vTimeSeries view for the time period requested.

Combining the historical and forecasted results

We need to combine the historical and forecasted results in a single dataset that contains all data needed to generate the report. However, as they stand, both datasets have different schemas. Only datasets with identical schemas can be merged together. The *PopulatePredictedColumns* helper function (not shown in Listing 14.1) converts the *predictions* dataset to the schema of the *cases* dataset by creating a new DataTable object.

Since the *predictions* dataset has two tables that are joined with a relation (see Figure 18.17), *PopulatePredictedColumns* loops through each parent row (ModelRegion), retrieves the child records (forecasted monthly values), and flattens both rows into a single row. Finally, the code merges the predicted results and the case results into one table. The Sales Forecast report uses a matrix region to rotate the TimeIndex field on columns.

18.3.3 Working with CLR Stored Procedures

The last implementation task is to convert the .NET code into a CLR stored procedure which will be invoked by the Sales Forecast report. This involves creating an SQL Server database project and changing the code to serialize the ADO.NET DataTable object. You will need VS.NET to create a SQL Server project. If you don't have VS.NET, you can deploy the AdventureWorks assembly found in the C:\Books\AS\Code\Ch18\AdventureWorks\bin\folder.

> **Tip** If you need to execute just a DMX prediction query, consider using an SSAS stored procedure that returns *IDataReader* as a data source for your report. For example, an SSAS stored procedure can query a mining model and return the results using the *AdomdDataReader.ExecuteReader* method. The Sales Forecast report uses a CLR stored procedure for two main reasons. First, it needs the mining results as an ADO.NET dataset so it can combine the forecasted dataset with the historical dataset. As it stands, the ADOMD Server object library doesn't expose the AdomdDataAdapter object and I wanted to avoid populating an ADO.NET table programmatically. Second, CLR stored procedures are more flexible because they are not restricted to using ADOMD Server only.

Creating an SQL Server project

The easiest way to work with a CLR stored procedure is to create an SQL Server project. An SQL Server project can include stored procedures, user-defined functions, user-defined types, and triggers written in .NET code. In addition, an SQL Server project automatically deploys the CLR objects to the database server and supports debugging.

1. Select the *File ⇨ New ⇨ Project* menu. Expand the *Visual Basic* project type and select *Database*.
2. In the Templates pane, choose *SQL Server Project*. Enter **AdventureWorks** as the project name. Choose the location where the project will be created and click OK.
3. Rename the Class1.vb file to *Predictions*. Rename the *Class1* class in it to **StoredProcedures**.
4. Copy the *CreateSessionModel* function and paste it inside the StoredProcedures class and add the Shared modifier. That's because, all CLR stored procedures must be shared (static in C#).
5. To tell BI Studio that the *CreateSessionModel* function is a CLR stored procedure, decorate it with the following attribute *<Microsoft.SqlServer.Server.SqlProcedure()>*.

The *CreateSessionModel* requires a reference to the AdomdClient object library. Much to my surprise, when I opened the Add References dialog in an SQL Server project, I found that the SQL Server tab lists only a few trusted assemblies and AdomdClient is not among them. To get AdomdClient to show up in Add References, you need to first register this assembly in the AdventureWorksDW database.

6. In Management Studio, connect to the SQL Server hosting the *AdventureWorksDW* database. Right-click on the *AdventureWorksDW*, select *New Query* to open a new query window and execute the following T-SQL command:

```
ALTER DATABASE [AdventureWorksDW] SET TRUSTWORTHY ON
```

This command tells the SQL Server to trust the AdventureWorksDW database and it is required because we need to elevate the permissions of the AdomdClient assembly to *Unsafe*.

7. Expand *AdventureWorksDW database* ⇨ *Programmability* ⇨ *Assemblies*.

8. Right-click on the Assemblies folder and choose *New Assembly*.

9. Browse to the location of Microsoft.AnalysisServices.AdomdClient.dll (default install location is C:\Program Files\Microsoft.NET\ADOMD.NET\90).

10. Change the permission set to *Unsafe* (Figure 18.19). Click OK to register AdomdClient.

11. Back to the AdventureWorks SQL Server project, choose *Project* ⇨ *Add Reference*. In the Add References dialog, flip to the SQL Server tab, select the AdomdClient assembly and click OK to create a reference to it.

12. Build the project. If all is well, the project should compile successfully.

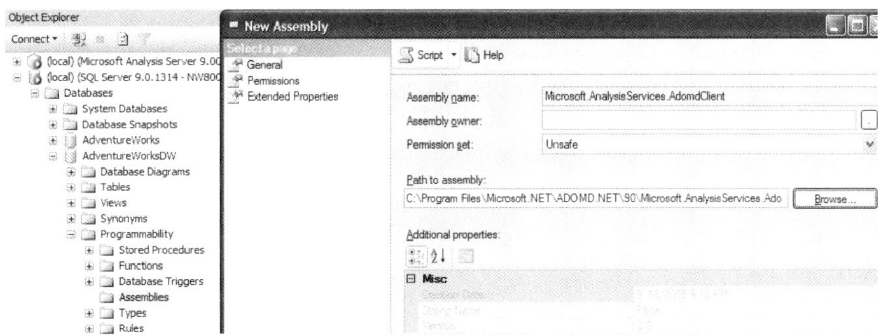

Figure 18.19 You need to register a non-trusted assembly explicitly before you can reference it from an SQL Server project.

Returning the results

The only conversion task left is to serialize the results of the stored procedure. A CLR stored procedure cannot return tabular results as a DataTable object. Instead, the results must be streamed in a well-defined format using a connected pipe (SqlPipe object). Listing 18.2 demonstrates how this could be done.

Listing 18.2 A CLR stored procedure must pipe tabular results.

```
Dim results As DataTable = PopulatePredictedColumns(predictions.Tables(0))
results.Merge(cases)
Dim record As SqlDataRecord = TableRowToSqlDataRecord(results)
SqlContext.Pipe.SendResultsStart(record)

For Each row As DataRow In results.Rows
    record.SetValues(row.ItemArray)
    SqlContext.Pipe.SendResultsRow(record)
Next
SqlContext.Pipe.SendResultsEnd()
```

First, the CLR stored procedure must inform the caller about the format of the returned results by sending back a metadata header (*Pipe.SendResultsStart*). The *TableRowToSqlDataRecord* (not shown in Listing 18.2) function is used to generate the header. Its task is to map the .NET data types to SQL Server data types. Next, *CreateSessionModel* loops through the table rows and calls *Pipe.SendResultsRow* to pipe each row. Finally, *CreateSessionModel* calls *Pipe.SendResultsEnd* to let the caller know that the end of the resultset is reached.

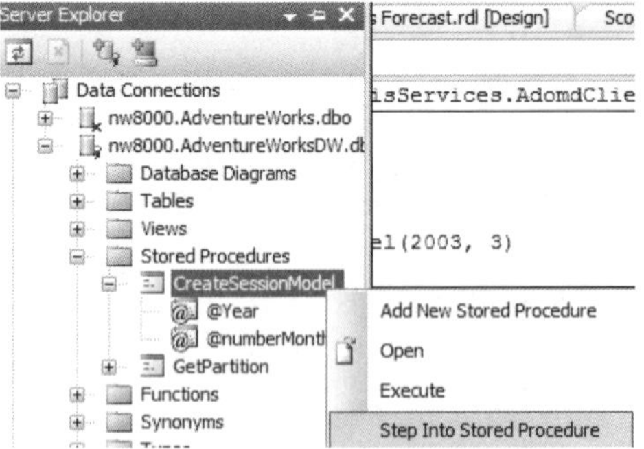

Figure 18.20 You can debug a CLR stored procedure from BI Studio.

Testing CLR stored procedures

Testing CLR stored procedure is easy with BI Studio. Follow these steps to debug the *CreateSessionModel* stored procedure.

1. Open the AdventureWorks project properties and select the Database tab. Click the Browse button and choose the AdventureWorksDW database reference to deploy the project to the AdventureWorksDW database. If the AdventureWorksDW doesn't exist, create a new database reference that points to the AdventureWorksDW database.

2. Back to the Solution Explorer, right-click on the AdventureWorks SQL Server project and choose *Deploy*. BI Studio registers the AdventureWorks assembly and all of its CLR objects in the AdventureWorksDW database.

3. Place a breakpoint inside the CLR stored procedure.

4. Press Ctrl+Alt+S to open the Server Explorer. Expand the *AdventureWorksDW connection* ⇨ *Stored Procedures*. Right-click on the CreateSessionModel stored procedure and choose *Step Into Stored Procedure* (Figure 18.20).

5. In Run Stored Procedure dialog that follows, enter the parameter values, e.g. **2003** for the @Year parameter and **3** for the @NumberMonths parameter.

Once you've tested the *CreateSessionModel* procedure, you can use it to feed a report dataset.

18.3.4 Implementing Drillthrough Navigation

The Sales Forecast report demonstrates also the drillthrough navigation interactive feature that SSRS supports. Similar to a drillthrough UDM action, a drillthrough SSRS action can be used to generate a report that shows the details behind a report item. Once the Sales Forecast report is rendered, the user can click on any historical sales figure. This generates the Daily Product Sales report that displays the daily product history for the corresponding month and sales territory.

For example, if the user clicks on the first cell ($41,227), the Daily Product Sales report will show the aggregated product sales in Europe broken down by day.

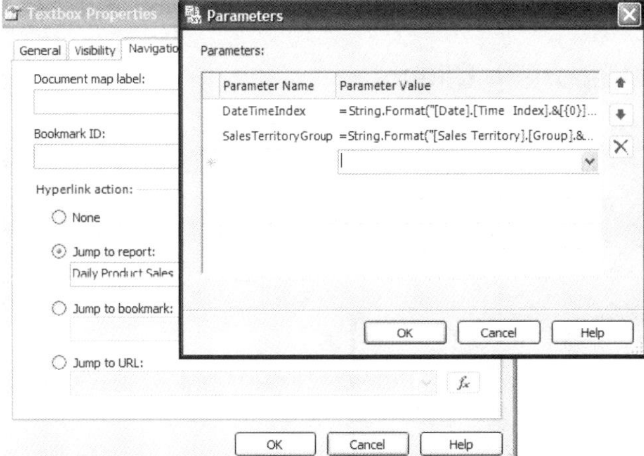

Figure 18.21 Implement report drillthrough by attaching a hyperlink action to a report item.

To implement a drillthrough action on the Amount textbox in the matrix region:

1. Right-click on the Amount textbox, choose *Properties* and flip to the Navigation tab.
2. In the Hyperlink panel, select the Jump to report option and select the Daily Product Sales report.
3. Click the Parameters button and match the parameters of the master report and the drillthrough report (Figure 18.21).

Initially, I was planning to demonstrate the Jump to URL option which gives more flexibility to construct the URL link. For example, assuming that you have an embedded function that sets the reportLink variable to contain the URL address of the Daily Product Sales report, the following URL navigation action would open the report in a new window and resize the window.

```
"javascript:void(window.open('" & reportLink & "','_blank',
 'location=no,toolbar=no,left=100,top=100,height=600,width=800'))"
```

The problem with URL navigation and OLAP reports is that the parameter values would typically contain ampersand (&), e.g. [Date].[Time Index].&[200312]. This presents an issue with the URL addressability option because the Report Server interprets & as a query parameter placeholder. Even escaping the parameter value (JavaScript *escape* function or using %26 for &) doesn't help because Internet Explorer automatically unescapes the value. If someone discovers a workaround for using special characters and URL addressability, please let me know.

18.4 Delivering Reports

Once the report is implemented and deployed to the report catalog, it is ready to be distributed to the report clients either on-demand or via subscriptions. As we saw, end users can leverage Report Manager to generate reports. However, chances are that, in real life, you may need to integrate custom applications with SSRS. To facilitate report-enabling .NET applications with SSRS 2005, Visual Studio.NET 2005 includes two report viewer controls (Windows Form and ASP.NET). While discussing the report viewers in detail is beyond the scope of this book, I would like to introduce them to you briefly.

18.4.1 Report-enabling Windows Reporting Clients

The WinReporter application (Figure 18.22) generates reports using the WinForm version of the Report Viewer control. The Report Viewer control can be found under the Data section on the standard VS.NET Toolbox. Both the WinForm and ASP.NET report viewers can generate remote and local reports.

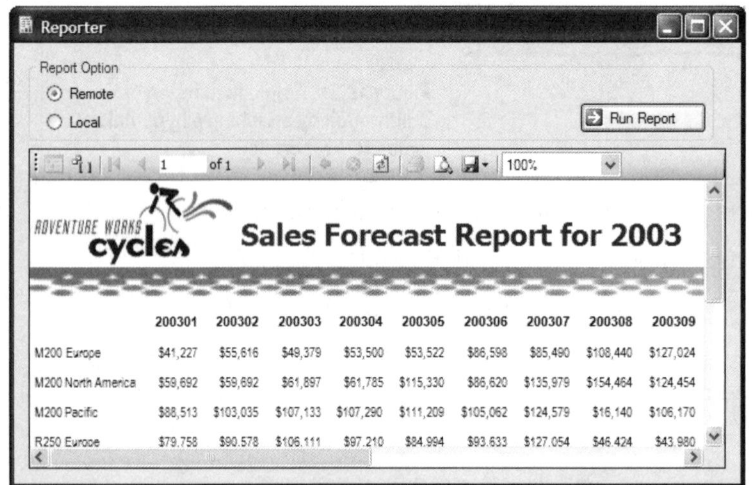

Figure 18.22 The WinReporter uses the Report Viewer control to demonstrate generating remote and local reports.

Generating remote reports

In remote mode, the Report Viewer can render *managed* reports, i.e. reports that are deployed to the report catalog and are processed by the Report Server. Generating a remote report is a matter of a few lines of code as Listing 18.3 shows. Any developer who has used the Web service addressability with SSRS 2000 will undoubtedly appreciate the simplicity that report viewers bring to the table.

Listing 18.3 Rendering a remote report with the Report Viewer control.

```
Private Sub RunRemote()
    reportViewer.ProcessingMode = ProcessingMode.Remote
    reportViewer.ServerReport.ReportServerUrl = "http://localhost/ReportServer"
    reportViewer.ServerReport.ReportPath = "/SOS OLAP/Sales Forecast"

    Dim parameters(1) As ReportParameter
    parameters(0) = New ReportParameter("Year", 2003)
    parameters(1) = New ReportParameter("NumberMonths", 3)
    reportViewer.ServerReport.SetParameters(parameters)
    reportViewer.RefreshReport()
End Sub
```

It is important to note that WinForm version of the Report Viewer always renders the report asynchronously. If the application needs to be notified when the report is ready, the application can subscribe to the *RenderingComplete* event. The Report Viewer control exposes a few properties that developers can use to customize the control appearance. For example, WinReporter sets the *PromptAreaColapsed* to *True* to collapse the parameter area.

Finally, both the WinForm and ASP.NET report viewers support different security modes (DefaultCredentials, Basic Authentication, and custom security). The first two security modes can be enabled by simply setting the *ReportViewer.ServerReport.ReportCredentials* property to a .NET NetworkCredentials object. Custom security requires setting ReportCredentials to a class that implements *IReportServerCredentials* and maintaining the authentication ticket (cookie) returned from the *LogonUser* API. For a code sample of how this could be done, refer to AdventureWorks sample on my website (see Resources).

Generating local reports

When configured for local mode, the Report Viewer control processes the report locally instead of calling down to the Report Server. Generating local reports is a great option for software vendors who need to bundle reports with their application and distribute them without requiring the client to have SSRS installed. The obvious tradeoff is that the rest of the Report Server features are not available, e.g. the report catalog, security, subscribed delivery, etc. In addition, the Report Viewer export formats are restricted to HTML, Excel, and PDF only.

To differentiate remote reports from local reports, the local report has a file extension of *rdlc* as opposed to *rdl*. Just like a regular report, a local report is described in RDL. The only difference is that the report definition cannot include datasets that are bound to external data sources. That's because it is the application that is responsible for collecting the report data, e.g. as an ADO.NET dataset, and binding it to the report. Creating a local report consists of three steps:

- Create one or more data sources.
- Design a report based on the data source schema.
- Configure the Report Viewer control to render the local report.

Configuring the report data source

A data source describes the dataset definition that will feed a local report. There are two ways to create a data source in Visual Studio.NET. First, once you create a new local report (or open an existing one), you can click on the *Add New Data Source* link inside the Data Source window. This starts the Data Source Configuration Wizard which allows you to create a data source from a database (table, view, or stored procedure), Web service, or an application object. However, as it stands, the Data Source Configuration Wizard does not support free-form SQL queries.

A second (and recommended) way is to add a new dataset to the project (*Add ⇨ New Item ⇨ Dataset*). Then, right-click on the Dataset Designer canvas and choose *Add ⇨ TableAdapter*). This launches the TableAdapter Configuration Wizard which supports SELECT queries and it is available in ASP.NET projects as well. Point the wizard to the *CreateSessionModel* stored procedure and name the dataset SalesForecast. The end result of running the TableAdapter Configuration Wizard is a typed dataset (SalesForecast.xsd), which contains the three fields returned by the CreateSessionModel CLR stored procedure (see Figure 18.23).

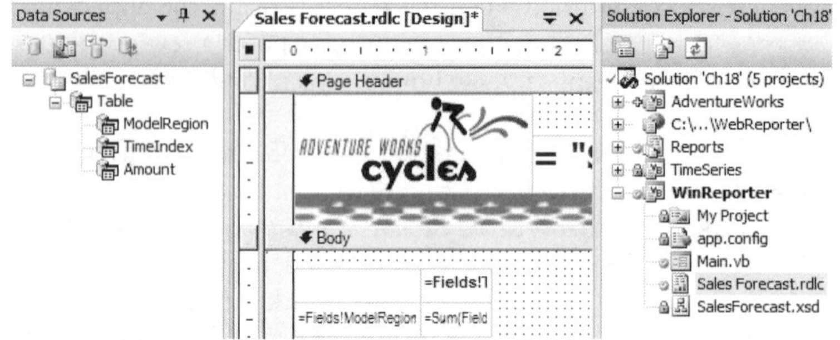

Figure 18.23 As part of setting up a local report, you need to create a data source which represents the dataset definition.

Designing a local report

Visual Studio.NET includes a scaled-down version of Report Designer which doesn't support report preview. For this reason, you may find it more convenient to adopt the following procedure for authoring local reports.

1. Create the report(s) in a Report Server project using the full-featured Report Designer.
2. Change the extension of the report definition file to *rdlc* and add the file to your application project. When you are done authoring the report, you can exclude the report definition file from the project. Upon deployment, the application setup program could copy the report definition to a known location where the Report Viewer can find it.
3. Removing the existing datasets from the report.
4. Rebind the report to the local data source(s). For example, in the Sales Forecast report, rebind the matrix region to the SalesForecast_Table dataset.

Note An ADO.NETdataset can have more than one table. When you are binding a local report, you are essentially binding to a table inside the ADO.NET dataset. Each table can be referenced by the *<DatasetName>_<TableName>* convention. For example, the matrix region in the Sales Forecast report is bound to the SalesForecast_Table dataset.

Setting up the Report Viewer

Generating a local report requires a couple of extra steps in comparison to generating a remote report – setting the report path and adding the data sources (Listing 18.4).

Listing 18.4 Rendering a local report with the Report Viewer control.

```
Private Sub RunLocal()

    Dim dataset As New SalesForecast
    ' ... Code to load the dataset
    reportViewer.ProcessingMode = ProcessingMode.Local
    reportViewer.LocalReport.ReportPath = "Sales Forecast.rdlc"
    reportViewer.LocalReport.DataSources.Add(New ReportDataSource _
     ("SalesForecast_Table", dataset.Tables(0)))
    Dim parameters(1) As ReportParameter
    parameters(0) = New ReportParameter("Year", 2003)
    parameters(1) = New ReportParameter("NumberMonths", 3)
    reportViewer.LocalReport.SetParameters(parameters)
    reportViewer.RefreshReport()
End Sub
```

The code starts by loading the SalesForecast dataset that we will feed the report. Next, the code sets the *ReportPath* property of the Report Viewer to the location of the report definition file. In this case, the code expects to find the report file in the application executable path. Next, the code binds the report to the first table in the SalesForecast dataset by adding the table to the Report Viewer *DataSources* collection.

Working with events

The Report Viewer control exposes various events which are raised as the user interacts with the report. The WinReporter sample demonstrates how a developer can programmatically respond to the *Drillthrough* and *Hyperlink* events. For example, the Daily Product Sales report is available only as a remote report. The trivial solution to prevent the end-user from drilling through the Sales Territory local report is to remove the Jump To Report hyperlink action from the local version (Sales Forcast.rdlc). Alternatively, WinReporter intercepts the *Drillthrough* event, determines if this is a local report, and if this the case, ignores the event.

You can use the *Hyperlink* (or Drillthrough) event to pass context from the report to your application. Suppose that you need to allow the end user to click on a given region in the Sales Forecast local report and open a form that can be used to update the region details. Implementing this requirement is simple.

5. Implement a Jump to URL hyperlink action attached to the ModelRegion textbox in the Sales Forecast local report and set the hyperlink expression to *="region:" & Fields!ModelRegion.Value.*

6. Implement the Report Viewer *Hyperlink* event.

Listing 18.5 Implementing the Report Viewer drillthrough event with local reports.

```
Private Sub reportViewer_Hyperlink(ByVal sender As System.Object,_
            ByVal e As Microsoft.Reporting.WinForms.HyperlinkEventArgs)

    Dim uri As New Uri(e.Hyperlink)

    If uri.Scheme = "region" Then
        e.Cancel = True
        Dim regionEditor As New RegionEditor()
        regionEditor.SelectedRegion =
            System.Web.HttpUtility.UrlDecode(uri.AbsolutePath)

        If regionEditor.ShowDialog(Me) = Windows.Forms.DialogResult.OK Then
            RunLocal()
        End If
    End If

End Sub
```

First, the code checks if the heperlink URL targets the region. If so, the code cancels the Drillthrough event because we will handle it manually. Next, the code opens the maintainance form that the end user will use to update the region details. When the event is raised, the Report Viewer will retrieve the region identifier from the ModelRegion field and pass it as an event argument. Once, the user is done making changes and closes the RegionEditor form, the code re-generates the report.

18.4.2 Integrating Web Reporting Clients

The WebReporter application (Figure 18.24) demonstrates how an ASP.NET application can use the web version of the Report Viewer to render a remote report. Since both versions support identical feature set and object model, I won't discuss how we set up the web Report Viewer. Readers familiar with the Report Viewer sample that ships with SSRS 2000 may assume that this is the same control. In reality, only the UI presentation of the control is the same. The SSRS 2000 Report Viewer used URL addressability to submit the report request on the client side of the application. In comparison, the SSRS 2005 Report Viewer calls down to the SSRS Web service to generate the report entirely on the server side of the application.

This is a very important advantage that may simplify your reporting architecture and security model. For example, suppose you have an Internet-facing ASP.NET application which is configured for Forms Authentication. In SSRS 2000, most Internet reporting scenarios required custom security. That's because interactive features were available only with URL addressability, which required direct access to the Report Server.

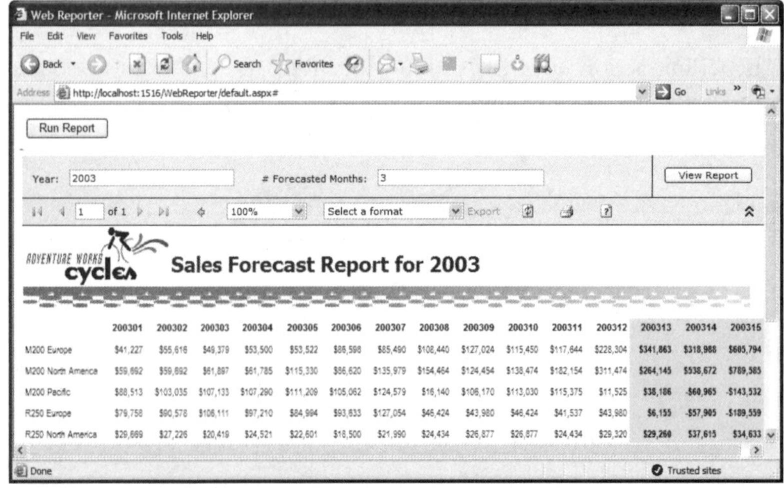

Figure 18.24 Use the web version of the Report Viewer to generate local or remote reports.

With the advent of the new ASP.NET Report Viewer and the ReportExecution2005 Web service, web reports can be rendered entirely on the server side of the application and they *can* have interactive features. Moreover, if passing the user identity to the Report Server is not needed (e.g. the *My Reports* feature is not required), the application (not the Report Server) can authenticate and authorize the users. The report requests to the Report Server can go under the application identity (trusted subsystem approach) which can significantly simplify your security architecture. For more information about how this scenario can be implemented, you may find my PowerPoint presentation and AdventureWorks custom security sample useful (see Resources).

18.5 Generating UDM Ad hoc Reports

While developers may rejoice over Visual Studio.NET Report Designer's ease-of-use, less technically-savvy users may find it too complex and intimidating. Still, one of the most common data analytics feature that business users request is the ability to generate reports in an ad hoc fashion. Ad hoc reporting lets end users run queries and create reports without having to know the technicalities of the underlying database schema and SQL query syntax.

18.5.1 Understanding Ad hoc Reporting Architecture

To support ad hoc reporting, the RS 2005 architecture enhancements include several new components, as shown in Figure 18.25. They are the Model Designer (for creating the ad hoc model), Report Builder (end-user tool to create ad hoc reports), and the Query Translator (to translate ad hoc queries to native queries).

Model Designer

Business users need not be familiar with the technical aspects of the database schema to generate an ad hoc report. When targeting relational data sources, you design and implement one or more ad hoc models that abstract the underlying schema. To do so, you need to create a Report Model Project BI project. Next, you use the Model Designer to create the model. When the model is ready, you publish it to the report catalog so it becomes available to the end users.

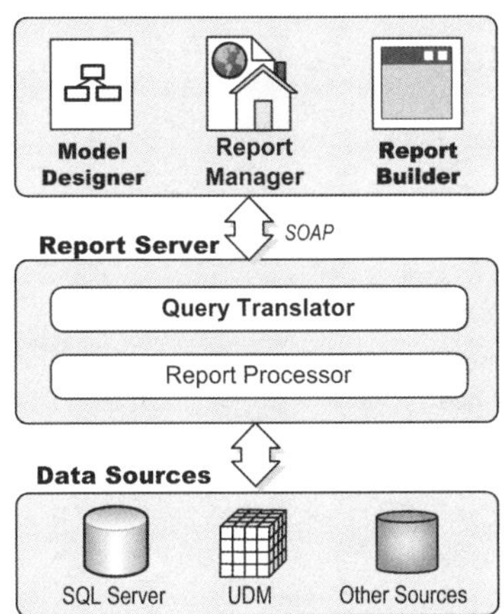

Figure 18.25 The RS Ad hoc architecture adds the Model Designer, Report Builder, and the Query Translator.

When the ad hoc reports target UDM, you don't need to create an explicit ad hoc model. After all, one of the main reasons for having UDM in the first place is to provide intuitive end-user model, so building another layer on top of it is redundant. Instead, SSRS automatically maps UDM to the format the Report Builder expects.

Report Builder

End users interact with the Report Builder to create reports against the ad hoc model. The Report Builder is implemented as a .NET Windows Form application. The Report Server machine hosts the Report Builder assembly, distributing it to end users via the "click-once" technology provided by .NET 2.0. As part of the deployment process, the Report Builder detects and optionally installs the .NET 2.0 framework if it is not already present on the target machine.

When users launch Report Builder, it prompts them to select an ad hoc model, then it downloads the model definition from the report catalog. Next, users build reports by choosing entities from the ad hoc model. The Report Builder user interface is intuitive—similar to

PowerPoint 2003. To author a report, you simply select one of the pre-defined report templates and drag–and-drop model entities to the report canvas.

Query Translator

While designing reports, users can preview them in the Report Builder. Behind the scenes, the Report Builder generates the report definition on the fly. This differs from generating standard RS reports because the ad hoc report definition includes a semantic query that describes the model entities selected by the user, rather than being pre-defined by a developer. The Report Builder sends the report definition to the Report Server by invoking the Render method of the new *ReportExecution2005* Web service.

Upon receiving the request, the Report Server extracts the semantic query and forwards it to the Query Translator. The Query Translator translates the semantic query to a native query (SQL, MDX, or DMX), using the syntax of the underlying data source. Then, it executes the query against the data source, retrieves the data, and passes the report definition and data to the Report Processor, which is responsible for rendering the report in its final format.

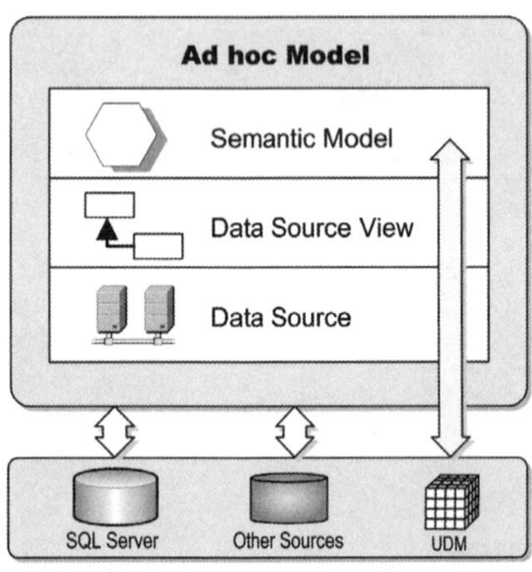

Figure 18.26 When the ad hoc model targets relational data sources, it has semantic model, DSV, and data source layers. With UDM data sources, the semantic model is mapped directly to UDM.

18.5.2 The Ad Hoc Model

The main characteristic of the SSRS ad hoc model is that it is designed with the user (not system) in mind. The ad hoc model consists of data source, data source view, and semantic model layers (see Figure 18.26).

Understanding the SSRS ad hoc model

Does the SSRS ad hoc model bring any recollection? Indeed, it resembles UDM because it has data source and DSV layers. The difference is the top layer. In SSAS, the top layer is the dimensional model, while with ad hoc reporting it is the semantic model.

Note Out of the box, SSRS can target SQL Server data sources only because the Query Translator is limited to supporting TSQL. However, developers can plug custom query processors that can retrieve data from other data sources.

As noted, with UDM data sources, the data source and DSV layers are redundant and the semantic model layer is mapped transparently to UDM. For this reason, if you report off UDM only, you don't need to know a whole lot about the SSRS ad hoc layer. In case you need the basics, you may find my article *Ad hoc Reports with Microsoft Reporting Services 2005* useful (see Resources).

Generating ad hoc model

You can use both the Report Manager and Management Studio to generate a UDM-based ad hoc model. Let's use Management Studio to create the model from the same SOS OLAP data source that we used to create OLAP and data mining reports.

1. In the Object Explorer pane of Management Studio, connect to the Reporting Services instance.
2. Navigate through the folder namespace to the folder which contains the SOS OLAP data source, e.g. *Home* ⇨ *SOS OLAP*.
3. Right-click on the SOS OLAP data source and choose *Generate model*. This menu is available only if the data source points to an SSAS database.
4. In the Generate Model dialog that follows, enter **SOS OLAP Model** as the model name. Accept the default folder location to generate the ad hoc model in the Home/SOS OLAP folder (see Figure 18.27). Click OK.

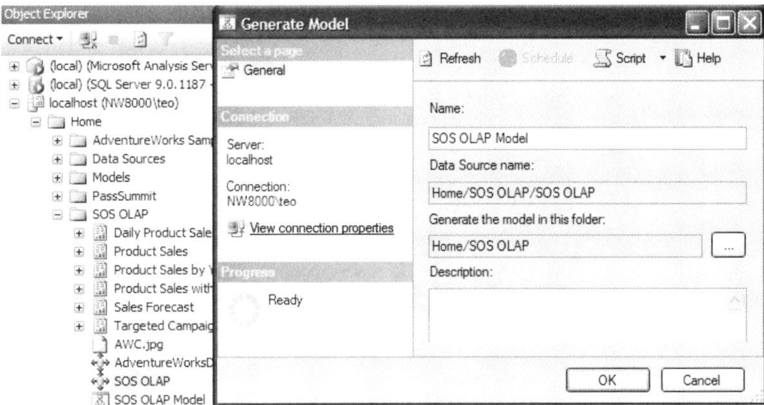

Figure 18.27 Generate the UDM ad hoc model directly from the data source.

If you are curious to find what the model looks like, use the Report Manager to navigate to the model and click on it. Then, click on the Edit link (General tab) to download and open model definition. You will see that the ad hoc model is described in an XML-based grammar called *Semantic Model Definition Language* (SMDL). In the case of using UDM as a data source, the model entities are mapped directly to the UDM hierarchies and measures. In real life, once the model is generated, you may need to secure access to the model, as you would do with standard reports.

18.5.3 Authoring Ad hoc Reports

After deploying and configuring the model, end-users can author ad hoc reports using the Report Builder. The Report Builder can be launched from the Report Manager or by requesting its click-once URL link. Let's use the Report Builder to create the *Internet Sales* chart report.

Note The Report Builder goes a long way to make authoring ad hoc reports a breeze. Unfortunately, as it stands, the Report Builder is not extensible. There isn't a single extensibility hook (not even command line parameters) that a developer can use to customize the Report Builder or integrate it with a custom application. This is surprising to me considering the fact that extensibility has been an SSRS hallmark since its first release. I hope that a future release will make the Report Builder more modular and extensible, e.g. decouple it from the ad hoc model and support pluggable formula libraries.

1. Open Internet Explorer and navigate to http://localhost/ReportServer/ReportBuilder/ReportBuilder.application. If the Report Builder is launched for the first time, the .NET framework downloads its assemblies to the client.
2. Once the Report Builder UI appears, select the *SOS OLAP Model* in the New Report dialog. Note that instead of reporting off the entire UDM, the end user can choose a specific cube perspective.

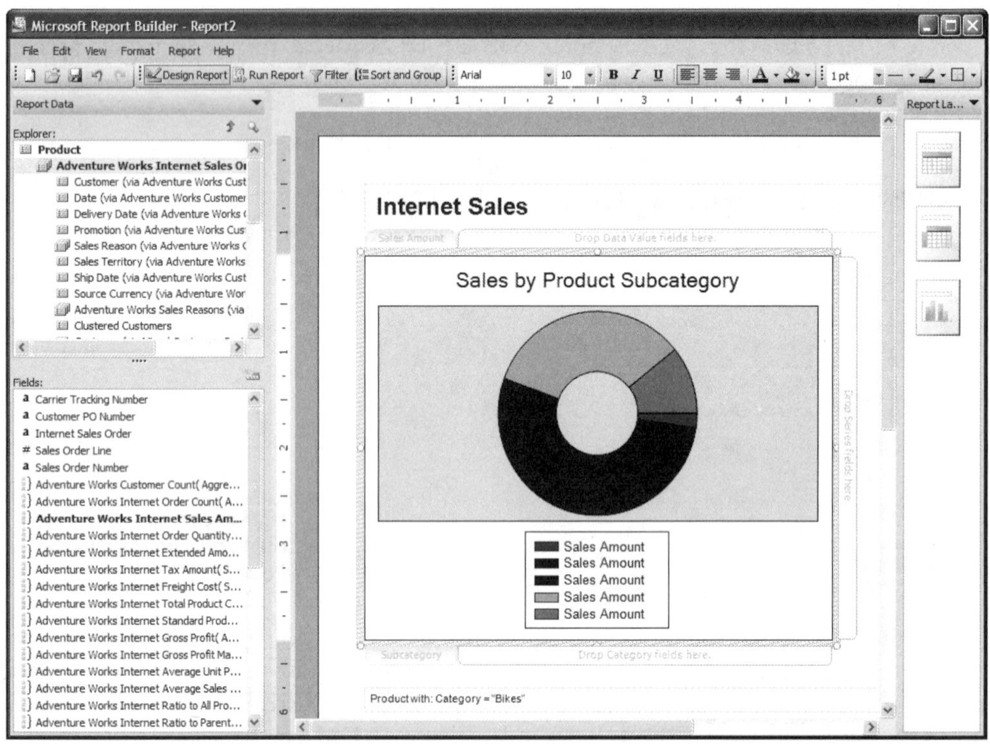

Figure 18.28 End users would use the Report Builder to generate ad hoc reports from the ad hoc model.

The Report Builder loads and parses the SOS OLAP Model. The Explorer pane shows the dimensions and measure groups mapped as entities. Once an entity is selected, the Fields pane lists the attribute (if a dimension entity is selected) or measures (if a measure group entity is selected). Text attributes are prefixed with **a** icon, while numeric attributes are prefixed with **#**. You can tell measures from attributes easily by their special three-dot icon. The Report Layout pane lists several pre-defined report layouts to jumpstart the report design process.

3. In the Report Layout pane, select the *Chart report* template.

4. In the report canvas, right-click on the chart region and change the chart type to *Simple Doughnut*. Click on the Chart report to activate it in design mode.
5. In the Explorer pane, click on the *Product* entity. Drag the *Subcategory* attribute from the Fields pane to the chart *Drop Category Fields here* area (Figure 18.28).

   Notice that once an entity attribute is added to the report, the Explorer pane changes to a tree that lists only the dimensions and measure groups that are referenced by the dimension containing the attribute. This prevents the user from using attributes and measure groups that are not applicable to the selected attribute. Behind the scenes, the semantic model enforces valid links by using *roles* that define known entity relationships.
6. In the Explorer pane, select the Adventure Works Internet Sales Orders (via Product) role. Drag the Internet Sales Amount from the Fields pane and drop it to the *Drop Data Fields here area of the chart* region.
7. Experiment with the chart control settings until you are satisfied with its appearance.
8. Click the Run Report toolbar button to preview the report. Notice that the report doesn't look that great because the Subcategory attribute has many members.
9. Click on the Filter button. In the Fields pane, double-click the Category attribute to add it to the Filter pane. Expand the *Category equals* dropdown and select *Bikes* to filter the report to show only the bike subcategories.
10. Click the Run Report to verify the report. When you are satisfied with the report, click the Save button to upload the report definition to the report catalog. e.g. to My Reports folder (not enabled by default).

Once saved, the ad hoc report can be managed and modified as it is a regular report. For example, it can be loaded and modified in the Report Designer.

Note Not all Report Designer changes are supported by the Report Builder. The Report Builder will ignore RDL elements it doesn't recognize.

18.6 Summary

SSAS and SSRS are completing technologies that can be used together to implement end-to-end business intelligence solutions. The Report Server is web-enabled middle-tier component that can generate standard and ad hoc reports. You author Reporting Services reports by using report regions that are bound to datasets. OLAP reports display data by sending MDX queries to UDM. Use the Query Builder graphical interface to create easily MDX queries that support multi-value parameters. Data mining reports fetch data by sending DMX queries. Use the DMX mode of the Query Builder to create DMX queries. Consider SSAS and CLR stored procedures to encapsulate more involved programming logic.

On-demand standard reports can be requested via URL and Web service addressability options. I highly recommend you consider the Visual Studio.NET 2005 report viewer controls to report-enable .NET Windows Form and ASP.NET applications. Ad hoc reporting requires implementing an ad hoc model. With UDM as a data source, the ad hoc model can be generated easily from a data source. End users interact with the Report Builder to author the ad hoc report and upload it to the report catalog.

18.7 Resources

SQL Server 2005 Reporting Services Feature Matrix
(http://shrinkster.com/7nc) – Provides feature comparison for SQL Server 2005 Reporting Services. New for SQL Server 2005 will be the inclusion of Reporting Services into editions beyond Standard and Enterprise.

Custom Dataset Data Extension for Microsoft Reporting Services
(http://shrinkster.com/7nu) – This custom dataset extension allows the application to pass a serialized dataset to the Report Server as a report parameter.

Harden MS Reporting Services Using Custom Extensions article by Teo Lachev
(http://shrinkster.com/7nw) – This two-part article demonstrates how developers can replace the default SSRS Windows-based security model with a custom security extension.

Report Definition Language Specification
(http://shrinkster.com/7nx) – Report Definition Language (RDL) is an XML-based schema for defining reports. It conforms to the Report Definition Language Specification.

Extending Microsoft SQL Server 2000 Reporting Services with Custom Code
(http://shrinkster.com/7t7) – Demonstrates how you can leverage custom code to author an advanced report with sales forecasting features by integrating with the OpenForecast Open Source package.

AdventureWorks Custom Security sample
(http://shrinkster.com/7tu) – Demonstrates how an ASP.NET application can use the Report Viewer web control configured for custom security. The PowerPoint presentation can be found at same location.

Generate Ad hoc Reports with Microsoft Reporting Services 2005 article by Teo Lachev
(http://shrinkster.com/7tv) – Provides step-by-step instructions to design an ad hoc model from a relational data source and create an ad hoc report from it.

Microsoft Reporting Services In Action book by Teo Lachev
(http://shrinkster.com/8tq) – A detailed and practical guide to Reporting Services 2000.

Chapter 19

Business Intelligence with Microsoft Office

Microsoft Office Suite is the leading platform for document management, document sharing, and workgroup collaboration. With every new release, it takes further steps to make business intelligence available to every person at every level of an organization and fulfill Microsoft slogan "BI for the Masses". Microsoft Office includes several analytics tools which you can leverage to build business intelligence solutions that source data from UDM.

Unfortunately, as of the time of this writing, Microsoft doesn't have a UDM browser that supports the new UDM features. Third-party tools will most likely attempt to fill this gap. Meanwhile, Microsoft is hard at work on the next version of Office (Office 12). Details remain scarce at this point, but expect UDM to play a major role in the next-generation BI "wave". In this chapter, you will learn how to:

- Author Excel reports using Microsoft Excel PivotTable Report component and Microsoft Office Excel Add-in for SQL Server Analysis Services.
- Implement interactive reporting in custom applications with Microsoft Office Web Components (OWC).
- Build corporate performance management dashboards with the Microsoft Office Business Scorecard Manager 2005.

The analytics tools we will cover in this chapter target business users and don't require MDX or OLAP knowledge. Business users can leverage the PivotTable Report, Excel add-in, and OWC to create interactive ad hoc reports. Microsoft Office Business Scorecard Manager 2005 helps organizations measure, monitor, and manage business performance metrics that originate from a variety of data sources. I also suggest you evaluate the Microsoft Data Analyzer, which is a commercially available add-on to Microsoft Office (see Resources). You will find the sample reports and applications in the Ch19 folder.

19.1 Using Excel Analytics Tools

Excel is omnipresent in today's enterprise. It's the main tool of choice for business analysts, accountants, financiers, sales persons, and the list goes on and on. Perhaps, the most common reporting requirement is "make it work like Excel". Therefore, Excel is a natural environment for building business intelligence solutions that target UDM. Using Excel, business users can author interactive free-form or structured reports using the PivotTable component or/and the Excel add-in for Analysis Services.

19.1.1 Authoring PivotTable Reports

The PivotTable and PivotChart components built in Excel have been using Analysis Services cubes as data sources since Office 2000. Consider PivotTable and PivotChart when:

- Your business users have Excel 2000 and above installed on their machines.
- Users need to author basic ad hoc interactive reports from UDM.
- Operational requirements call for minimum client installation footprint.

Understanding PivotTable reports

Among all Microsoft-provided OLAP browsers, the PivotTable component requires a minimum installation footprint because it is bundled with Excel. When sourcing data from UDM, you need to distribute and install the Pivot Table Service (see Resources for a download link to PTS). On the downside, the Excel PivotTable Report component is not as feature-rich as other Office analytics tools that target Analysis Services only. For example, it doesn't differentiate between attribute and multi-level hierarchies, doesn't support actions, drillthrough, and free-form reports. In addition, PivotTable cannot be integrated with custom applications because it is not available as a standalone component. Let's create a simple Excel PivotTable report to demonstrate how Excel can be used as a UDM browser.

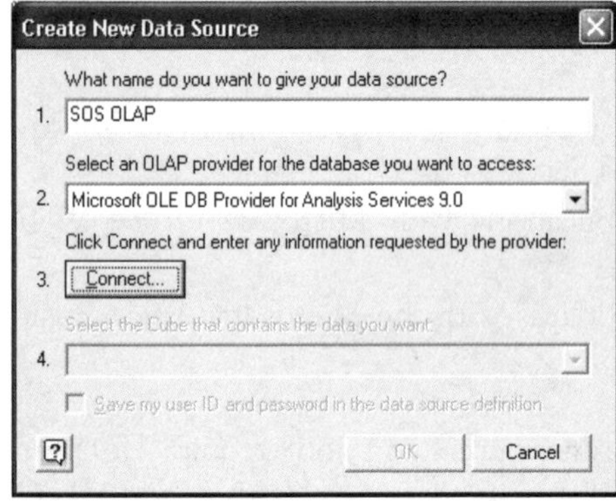

Figure 19.1 Start building a PivotTable report by setting up the report data source.

Setting up the report data source

Use the PivotTable and PivotChart Report Wizard to author a PivotTable report in three easy steps. The first time you create the report, there are extra steps required to set up the report data source.

1. Start Microsoft Excel 2003. Choose *Data* ➪ *PivotTable and PivotChart Report* main menu to launch the PivotTable and PivotChart Report Wizard.
2. In *Step 1*, select the *External data source* option and click Next.
3. In *Step 2*, click the Get Data button to start Microsoft Query. As its name suggests, Microsoft Query is a component of Microsoft Office which allows you to create queries that retrieve data from external data sources. It is installed the first time it is used (requires the Office Setup CD).

4. In the Choose Data Source dialog, click the *OLAP Cubes* tab. Select the *<New Data Source>* item in the list and click OK.

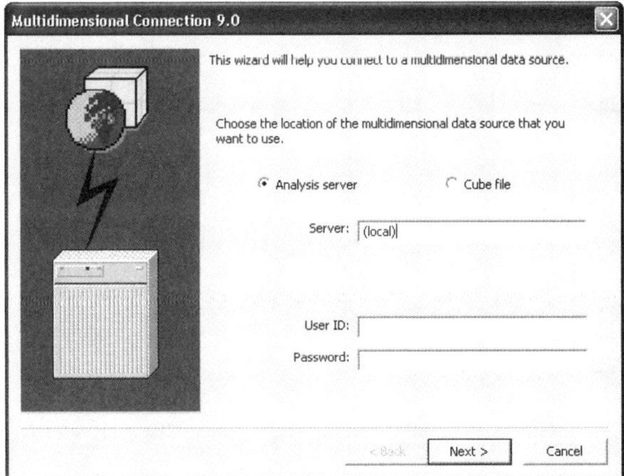

Figure 19.2 A PivotTable report can source data from server-based and local cubes.

5. In the Create New Data Source dialog (Figure 19.1), enter **SOS OLAP** as a data source name.

6. Select the *Microsoft OLE DB Provider for Analysis Services 9.0* as an OLAP provider and click the Connect button.

7. In the *Multidimensional Connection 9.0* dialog (Figure 19.2), select the *Analysis Services* option. Note that you can use a local cube file as a data source. Assuming that you need to connect to your local Analysis Services server, enter **(local)** as a server name and click Next.

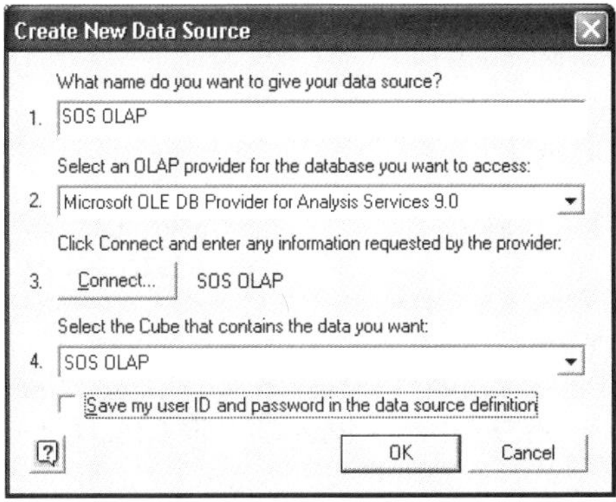

Figure 19.3 When using UDM as a data source, use the Microsoft OLE DB Provider for Analysis Services 9.0 and specify the cube (or perspective) you need to connect to.

8. In the next step, select *SOS OLAP* as an SSAS database and click Finish.

9. Back to the *Create New Data Source* dialog, expand the *Select the Cube* dropdown. Notice that that it lists all cubes and perspectives defined in the SOS OLAP database. Select the *SOS OLAP* cube (Figure 19.3) and click OK to let Microsoft Query create the data source.

Note Microsoft Query creates a data source file in the C:\Documents and Settings\<User>\Application Data\Microsoft\Queries folder. The data source file follows the *<DataSourceName>.oqy* naming convention (e.g. SOS OLAP.oqy) and contains the connection string. Double-clicking the file, launches Excel and creates a new PivotTable report that uses that data source.

10. The PivotTable and PivotChart Report Wizard's flow continues with the next (and last) step (Figure 19.4). Notice that you can define the report layout optionally in this step. However, we will perform these tasks outside the wizard flow. Accept the defaults and click Finish to create the report.

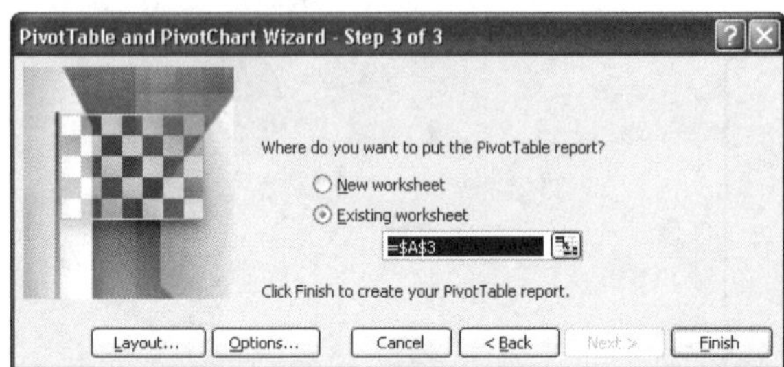

Figure 19.4 Select the location of the report and optionally define the report layout and format.

Once the report data source is created, the wizard prepares a report template as a starting point for building the report interactively.

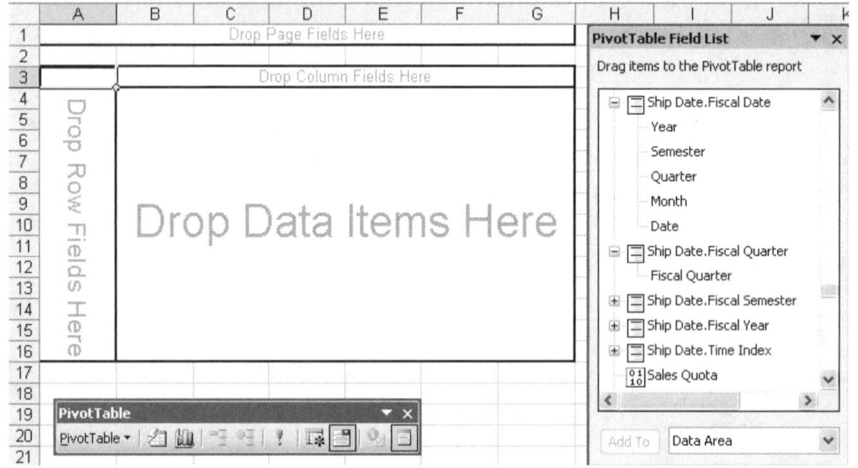

Figure 19.5 A PivotTable report can have up to three axes.

Building an interactive report

The PivotTable report template (Figure 19.5) resembles the Cube Browser report pane. The PivotTable Field List is the equivalent of the Cube Browser metadata pane. It lists the cube hierarchies (attribute and multi-level) and measures. You can easily tell the measures apart by their "digital" icon. As noted, PivotTable doesn't differentiate between attribute and multi-level hierarchies (we are still in the 2003 time warp).

For example, the Field List doesn't differentiate between attribute and multi-level hierarchy. As Figure 19.5 shows, the multi-level hierarchies (e.g. *Ship Date.Fiscal Date*) and attribute hierarchies (e.g. *Ship Date.Fiscal Quarter*) have the same icon. Named sets are exposed as measures. The Field List doesn't organize the attribute hierarchies in dimension folders, nor does it support display folders. It would have been nice if, at least, the Field List allowed you to sort the fields so you can locate them faster. Tell those end users who have a hard time finding a particular dimension that you are currently working on a solution and you will make it all better in a few months (when Office 12 comes out).

Tip It appears that the Field List sorts the hierarchy names in an ascending order with the containing dimension. Similarly, measure names appear to be sorted by a measure group. Of course, since the dimension folders are missing, this sort order doesn't help much. If you decide to target PivotTable as a reporting tool, I would suggest you define more limited cube views in the form of perspectives and encourage your users to select a perspective when defining the data source to limit the number of fields shown in the Field List.

The report template itself can have up to three query axes – pages (Drop Page Fields Here area), columns (Drop Column Fields Here area), and rows) (Drop Row Fields Here area). Only measures can be dropped in the *Drop Data Items Here* area, while dimensions can be dropped on any of the three axes but not on the *Drop Data Items Here* area.

Note A PivotTable report "owns" its section of the Excel worksheet. You cannot insert rows and columns in the report space.

1. Drag the *Sales Territory* multi-level hierarchy to the *Drop Page Fields Here* area.
2. Expand the *All Sales Territories* dropdown and enable the *Select multiple items* checkbox. Unselect the *All Sales Territories* checkbox and select the *United States* member (Figure 19.6). This will filter the report to show data for the United States and its subordinates only.

Figure 19.6 End users can filter the report data by selecting dimension members.

3. Drag the *Product by Category* multi-user hierarchy on rows and *Date.Calendar Date* on columns.
4. Drag the Sales Profit measure on the report data. Your report should look like the one shown in Figure 19.7.

Tip Excel does not use NON EMPTY keywords or NONEMPTYCROSSJOIN() function in the MDX query. This fact can negatively impact the report performance. You can get around this behavior with advanced technique described at http://blogs.msdn.com/bi_systems/articles/162852.aspx.

5. With multi-user hierarchies, you can double-click on a dimension member (or click the Show Detail button on the PivotTable toolbar) to drill-down to its children. Double-click on the *Bikes* member to see the report broken down by bike subcategories. Double-click on *2002* Year

A	B	C	D	E	F
Sales Territory	United States				
Sales Profit	Year				
Category	2001	2002	2003	2004	Grand Total
Accessories	11756.1065	51272.8946	200727.6739	151692.2482	415448.9232
Bikes	4378952.06	10754714.96	12172018.16	6456203.824	33761889
Clothing	16968.5332	263564.219	439965.976	195828.813	916327.5412
Components	243868.1693	1626311.367	2116298.552	677121.9729	4663600.061
Average Product Category	1162886.217	3173965.86	3732252.59	1870211.714	9939316.382
Grand Total	4651544.869	12695863.44	14929010.36	7480846.858	39757265.53

Figure 19.7 The raw report that shows the sales profit by product group for products sold in the United States.

member to see the annual amount broken down by semesters. Double-click works in reverse. Double-click on an expanded member to collapse it.

Tip Double-clicking could become tedious with deep multi-level hierarchies. Instead, expand the top-level dropdown (e.g. Year) and select the levels you want to see. The PivotTable report will automatically expand to show the selected levels. The PivotTable Field List highlights the expanded levels.

6. You can place more than one hierarchy on the same axis. Drag the *Region* hierarchy and drop it next to the *Category* hierarchy on rows. The report shows data broken down by product category and region.

7. Users can remove field by dragging the field away from the report. Select the *Region* field on the report and drag it away from the report to remove it. Alternatively, your most beloved Undo feature (Ctrl+Z) is always standing by to help you cancel the last action(s).

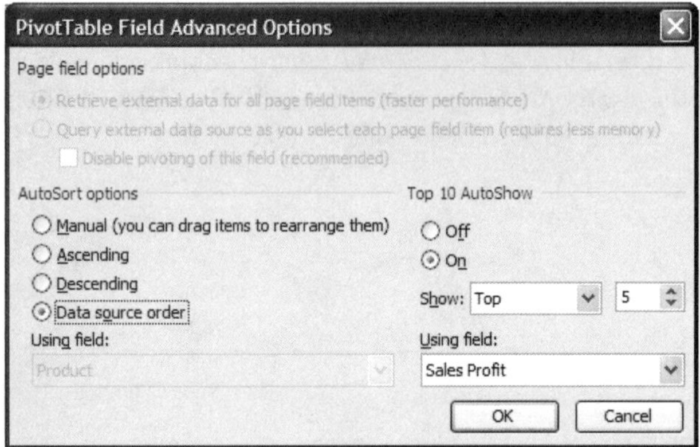

Figure 19.8 Filter the top N members for a given measure.

8. Suppose you need to see the top five selling bikes in each product subcategory. Double-click on the *Bikes* product category member to expand it. Double-click on the *Mountain Bikes* member to expand it to the product level.

9. Right-click on any product member and choose *Field Settings*. In the PivotTable Field dialog that follows, click the Advanced button. Enable the *Top Autoshow* feature, as shown in Figure 19.8. If the report includes multiple measures, expand the *Using field* dropdown to select the measure to filter on.

10. You can get the latest report data (re-execute the MDX query) by clicking on the exclamation button in the PivotTable toolbar. If the PivotTable toolbar is not shown, select *View ⇨ Toolbars ⇨ PivotTable.*

Tip You can create a report, save it, and open it a few days later but forget to refresh the report. To avoid this, you can automate the report refresh. Right-click on any report cell and choose *Table Options*. In the Data Source Options pane, enable *Refresh on open* or *Refresh every N minutes*.

Formatting the report

PivotTable supports various options to format a report.

1. Click a cell inside the report to activate the toolbar. Click the Format Report button on the PivotTable toolbar.

2. PivotTable comes with several pre-defined report styles that are categorized in two groups. Use the report styles to make the PivotTable report look as a standard report. The table styles preserve the tabular structure of the report. Scroll down the AutoFormat list and pick *Table 3* style to pretty up the report.

3. The PivotTable report doesn't pick up the UDM format settings. Let's format the Sales Amount as currency. Double-click on the Sales Profit header. In the PivotTable Field dialog that follows, click the Number button and choose the *Currency* format specifier. Your report should look like the one shown in Figure 19.9.

A	B	C	D	E	F
Sales Territory	United States				
Sales Profit	Year				
Category	2001	2002	2003	2004	Grand Total
Accessories	$11,756.11	$51,272.89	$200,727.67	$151,692.25	$415,448.92
Bikes	$4,378,952.06	$10,754,714.96	$12,172,018.16	$6,456,203.82	$33,761,889.00
Clothing	$16,968.53	$263,564.22	$439,965.98	$195,828.81	$916,327.54
Components	$243,868.17	$1,626,311.37	$2,116,298.55	$677,121.97	$4,663,600.06
Average Product Category	$1,162,886.22	$3,173,965.86	$3,732,252.59	$1,870,211.71	$9,939,316.38
Grand Total	**$4,651,544.87**	**$12,695,863.44**	**$14,929,010.36**	**$7,480,846.86**	**$39,757,265.53**

Figure 19.9 Use the pre-defined report styles to format the report.

If you want to format individual report cells, you can use Excel cell formatting features. For example, right-click on the cell to be formatted and use the *Format Cells* context menu.

Creating a PivotChart report

You can create a PivotChart report from the PivotTable report easily and the chart report is always linked to the source pivot report. As a result, changing the pivot report changes the chart report and vice versa – manipulating the chart data updates the pivot report. This automatic linkage may get in the way. For example, it is not possible to show the Date dimension on the X axis if the PivotTable report shows the Date dimension on columns. Another annoying issue is that PivotChart loses the custom settings you set when you refresh the PivotTable it is linked to.

Tip If you want to make the PivotTable report independent of the PivotChart report, copy the pivot report to a new sheet.

1. Right-click on any cell in the PivotTable report and choose *PivotChart*. Excel creates a new sheet and generates a bar chart in it.

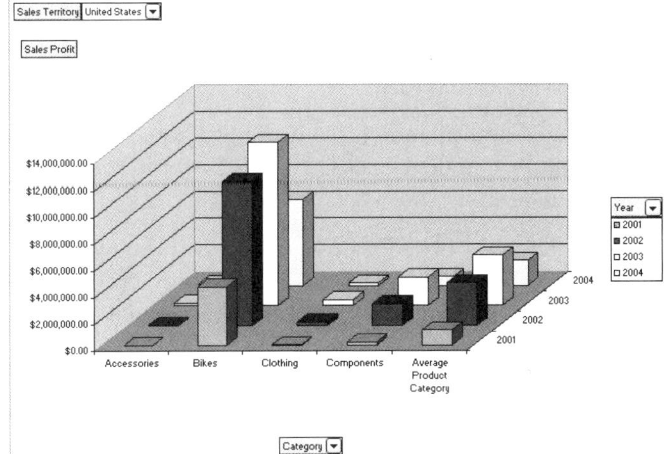

Figure 19.10 A PivotChart report is always synchronized with the PivotTable source report.

2. In the Chart toolbar, expand the Chart Type dropdown and select the 3-D surface chart button (Figure 19.10).

3. Optionally, right-click on the chart and use the chart options to adjust the chart. Different options are available based on the chart area selected.

19.1.2 Building Local Cubes

In chapter 13, you saw how you can create local cubes programmatically using AMO and ADOMD.NET. The PivotTable component also supports creating a local cube from a server-based cube. A local cube typically contains much less data so the user can save it on her local hard drive or on portable storage device. Once the local cube is created, the user can disconnect from the server cube and the network and connect to the local cube to perform offline data analytics.

1. Switch to the Excel sheet containing the PivotTable report. Click on any cell in the PivotTable report.

2. Expand the PivotTable dropdown located on the PivotTable toolbar and choose *Offline OLAP*. In the Offline OLAP Settings dialog that follows, click the *Create offline data file* button to launch the Create Cube File wizard.

3. In Step 2 (Figure 19.11), select the dimensions and levels that need to be exported to the local cube. By default, the wizard has pre-selected the dimensions used in the PivotTable report and the expanded levels. Accept the defaults and click Next.

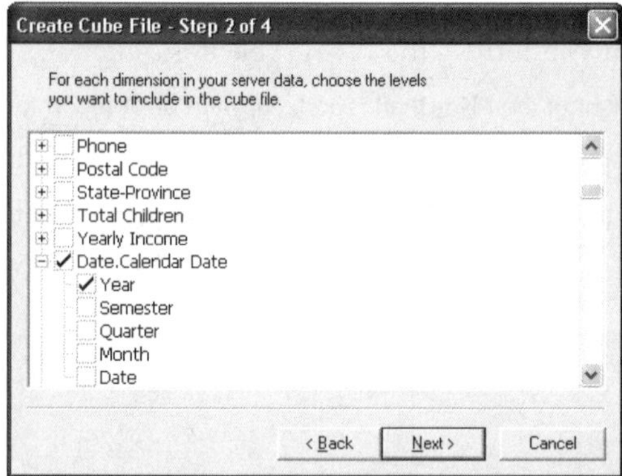

Figure 19.11 Select the dimensions and levels to be included in the cube.

4. In Step 3 (Figure 19.12), you can select measures and members from the attribute hierarchies that will be exported to the cube. Expand the *Measures* node. Unselect the *Measures* root node and select only the *Internet Sales Amount* and *Reseller Sales Amount* measures.

5. In Step 4, specify the full path to the cube file and click Finish to create it. Next, you can configure the PivotTable component to connect to the local cube file when setting up the data source connection (see Figure 19.2) or at a later time by using the Offline OLAP Settings dialog.

Tip Microsoft Query can create a local cube file from a relational database. To use this feature, select *Data ⇨ Import External Data ⇨ New Database Query* and create a connection to the relational database. Then, use the Query Wizard to define the query. Once the query is ready, use *File ⇨ Create OLAP Cube* to export a subset of the relational data to a local cube file.

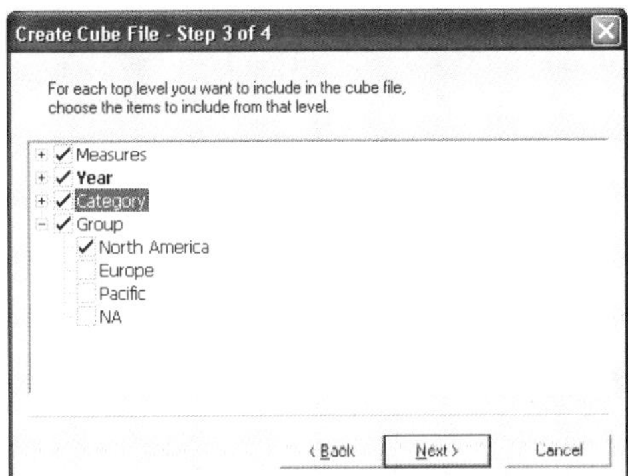

Figure 19.12 Choose the dimension members and measures to be included in the cube.

19.1.3 Creating Structured Reports

Realizing the growing trend to use Microsoft Excel as an OLAP browser with SSAS, in 2004 Microsoft released the Microsoft Office Excel Add-in for SQL Server Analysis Services (referred to as *Excel add-in* for short throughout the rest of this chapter). The Excel add-in is freely available to licensed users of Microsoft Excel XP and above (see Resources section for a download link). I highly recommend you review the Microsoft whitepaper *Designing Reports with the Microsoft Excel Add-in for SQL Server Analysis Services* for an excellent coverage of how to author reports with the Excel add-in. You can find the sample reports we will create in this chapter included in the Excel Analytics workbook file (Excel Analytics.xls).

Understanding the Excel add-in

The Excel add-in is designed to complement rather than replace the PivotTable component, and as such, there is some feature overlap between both analytical tools. My favorite features not present in PivotTable are separation between multilevel and attribute hierarchies, the ability to create free-form reports, displaying the underlying report MDX query, and support of actions. There are also PivotTable features that are not supported by the Excel add-in, such as automatic charting and advanced formatting.

With the Excel add-in you can create both structured and free-form reports. A structured report resembles a PivotTable report because the user can drag and drop items to pre-defined sections (page, row, column, and data). A structured report can source its data from a single connection only. Structured reports are subject to other limitations. For example, you cannot display member properties on the report, sort on dimension members, or insert rows and columns within the report.

As its name suggests, a free-form report doesn't have pre-defined sections. Instead, you can connect any Excel cell to UDM and connected cells can be moved anywhere in the report. This allows you to intersperse OLAP and Excel data. Moreover, a free-form report can draw its data from more than one data source. You can display member properties in rows and columns and you can insert new rows and columns.

Note Unfortunately, due to an incompatibility issue with the free-form *CubeCellValue* function and SSAS 2005, I am not able to demonstrate free-form reports.

Connecting to UDM

Once the Excel add-in is installed, it adds a new Cube Analysis main menu. As a first step in using the Excel add-in, you need to define a connection to a server or local cube.

1. Expand the Cube Analysis menu and choose *Manage Connection* (Figure 19.13).
2. Click the New button and create a connection to the SOS OLAP UDM.

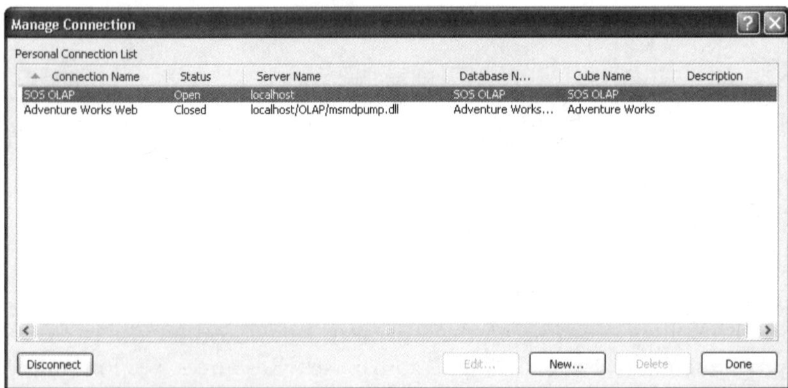

Figure 19.13 The Excel add-in supports multiple open connections.

The connection settings are saved as a standard Office Data Connection (*.odc) file in the C:\Documents and Settings\<UserName>\Application Data\ORSLN folder. You can define more than one connection and you can have multiple connections open at the same time. For demonstration purposes, as Figure 19.13 shows, I have defined two connections (via TCP and HTTP) to my local Analysis Services Server.

Before you start authoring the report, you need to specify which connection the report will use to source its data. At this point, the Excel add-in opens the selected connection. The Manage Connections dialog shows you which connections are currently open. If you close the Excel worksheet, the Excel Add-In doesn't automatically establish the connection when you reopen the worksheet. As a result, the report interactive features will be disabled. You need to open the connection manually by selecting *Cube Analysis* ⇨ *Refresh Report* or automatically by enabling the *Refresh data on open* option (*Cube Analysis* ⇨ *Options* ⇨ *Global tab).*

Authoring a structured report

Similar to a PivotTable report, to create a structured report you need to define the report layout first. The Excel add-in supports several pre-defined templates which are listed in the Layout pane of the Report Builder window.

Setting up the report layout

1. Make sure the Layout pane of the Report Builder window is selected. Select the *Row, Column, and Page Filters* template (the most complex template) found in the *Insert New Report* section. The Excel add-in creates a four-section report that consists of row axis, column axis, page filter axis, and data grid (Figure 19.14).

Tip The default Excel security settings disallow the Undo command for reports. To enable Undo, go to *Tools* ⇨ *Macro* ⇨ *Security*, activate the Trusted Publishers tab, and select the *Trust access to Visual Basic Project* checkbox.

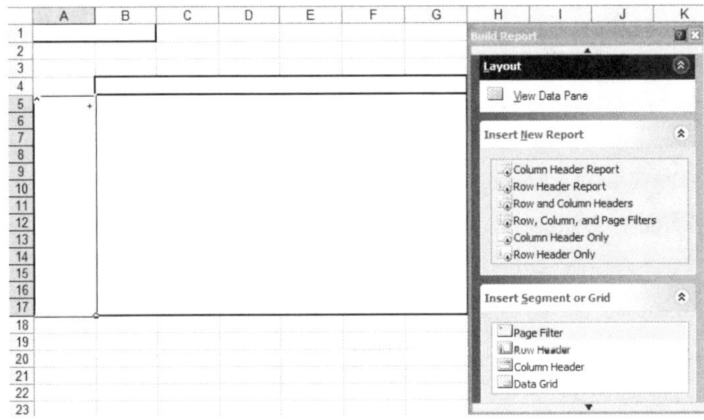

Figure 19.14 Start creating a structured report by defining its layout first.

Unlike PivotTable, the Excel add-in supports partitioning an axis in segments. For example, you may need two page filters to slice the cube by two dimensions. To add a segment, select the axis, and then select the corresponding segment type in the *Insert Segment or Grid* section. To delete a segment, axis, or the entire report, use the *Cube Analysis* ⇨ *Delete* menu.

You can re-position the entire report section by clicking on the ^ glyph in any axis and dragging the report. You can also change the location of the particular axis by dragging the + glyph to the new location. This could be useful if you want to move a dimension from one axis to another. Let's compare the process of creating structured report to the PivotTable report by creating a similar report as the one we authored in section 19.1.1. The report will show the product sales broken down by product category and date.

2. To configure the Excel add-in to carry over the server format settings, go to *Cube Analysis* ⇨ *Options* ⇨ *Format tab* and select *Color*, *Font Style*, and *Formatted Value* checkboxes. While we are in the Options window, switch to the *Global* tab and select the *Auto resize cells* checkbox.

Note For some reason, the server cell format settings didn't work for me even with the Formatted Value checkbox enabled. This may be a compatibility issue with UDM.

Define the report data

3. In the Report Builder window, click the *View Data Pane* link to switch to *Data* mode.
4. Select the *SOS OLAP* connection in the Connection Name dropdown. The Excel add-in opens the connection and loads the cube metadata. The Dimension dropdown contains the cube dimensions. The Hierarchy dropdown contains the attribute and multi-level hierarchies defined in the selected dimension (Figure 19.15).
5. In the Dimension tree, select the *Product* dimension. Expand the Hierarchy dropdown and notice that the Excel add-in understands multi-level and attribute hierarchies and uses different icons to designate each type. Let's congratulate the Excel add-in developers for the forward thinking! Select the *Product by Category* multi-level hierarchy.

The Display options allow you to select dimension members (Members Tree option) or levels (Dimension Level option). The Browse/Search pane provides several ways to select dimension members. The most versatile option is the *Custom Expression* option which supports filtering by custom expressions. For example, you can use this option to filter products that have generated more than $1,000,000 in sales profit.

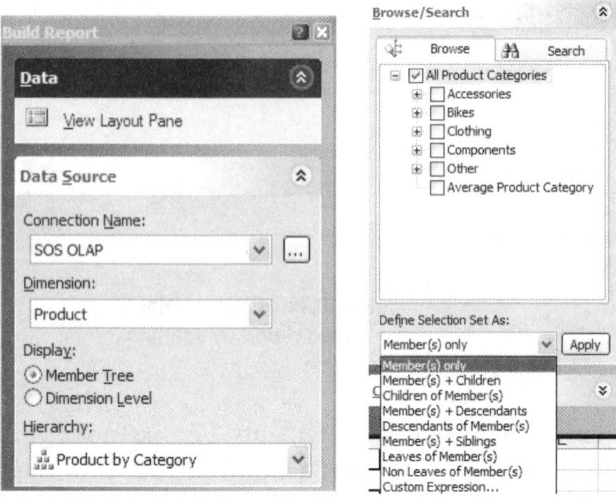

Figure 19.15 Define the report data by selecting dimension members and dropping them to the desired axis.

6. Check the *All Product Categories* member and drag it on rows.
7. Select the *Date* dimension in the Dimension dropdown and *Calendar Date* hierarchy in the Hierarchy dropdown. Check the *All Calendar Periods* member and drag in on columns.
8. Select the *Measures* dimension in the Dimension dropdown. Notice that it contains only one hierarchy (Measures). Also, observe that Browse tab organizes the cube measures in measure groups (kudos again to the Excel team!). Check the *Sales Profit* measure and drag it to the data grid.

	A	B
1	Sales Territory.Sales Territory.	All Sales Territories
2		
3		All Calendar Periods
4	All Product Categories	60395957.84
5	Accessories	813225.9045
6	Bikes	50834740.53
7	Clothing	1519173.288
8	Components	7228818.121
9	Other	
10	Average Product Category	15098989.46

Figure 19.16 A structured report contains pre-defined sections for the row, column, page, and data axes.

9. Finally, check and drag the *All Sales Territories* member of the Sales Territory hierarchy (Sales Territory dimension) on pages. Your report should look like the one shown in Figure 19.16.

Interacting with a structured report

As with PivotTable, the end user can interact with the report to filter data or drill down data.

10. Expand the *All Sales Territories* page dropdown to the *United States* member and double-click on the *United States* member to filter the report data.
11. The easiest way to drill down the report data is to double-click on a member. Double-click on the *Bikes* member to drill down to the product subcategory level.

Often, you may need to place multiple measures on the same report. Suppose that you need to have the *Internet Sales Amount* and *Reseller Sales Amount* measures side-by-side. To accomplish this, you need to first insert a new row segment.

12. Select the *All Product Categories* cell. Flip to the Layout tab in the Data window and click the *Row Header* item in the *Insert Segment or Grid* section to add a new rows segment.

13. Back to the Data mode, check the Internet Sales Amount measure and drag it to the new row segment. Repeat the same with *Reseller Sales Amount* measure. Your report should look like the one shown in Figure 19.7.

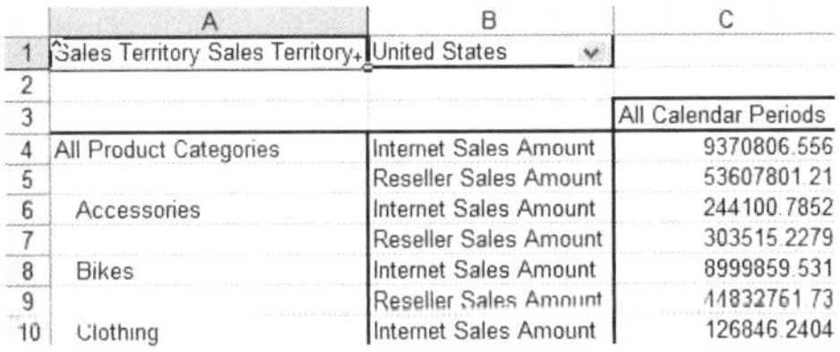

	A	B	C
1	Sales Territory Sales Territory	United States	
2			
3			All Calendar Periods
4	All Product Categories	Internet Sales Amount	9370806.556
5		Reseller Sales Amount	53607801.21
6	Accessories	Internet Sales Amount	244100.7852
7		Reseller Sales Amount	303515.2279
8	Bikes	Internet Sales Amount	8999859.531
9		Reseller Sales Amount	44832761.73
10	Clothing	Internet Sales Amount	126846.2404

Figure 19.17 Create a new row segment to display multiple measures.

14. Optionally, use the Excel formatting features to change the report style and apply format settings.

15. Select *Cube Analysis* ➪ *Show MDX* main menu to view the MDX query behind the report. The MDX query text cannot be changed.

16. Structure reports support various member navigation features (Drill Up, Drill Down, Expand, Collapse Only, Isolate and Eliminate) which can be invoked from the context mouse menu when the member is selected. For example, you can remove the Accessories member by right-clicking on it and selecting *Eliminate.*

17. Suppose that you need to have only the *Bikes* member shown in the report. Right-click on the Bikes member and choose *Isolate.* To show the entire hierarchy again, right-click on the Bikes member and choose *Drill Up.* This will display the *All Product Categories* member collapsed.

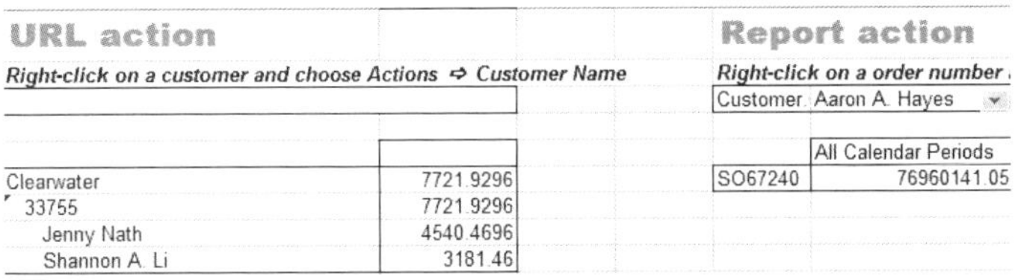

URL action

Right-click on a customer and choose Actions ➪ Customer Name

Clearwater	7721.9296
33755	7721.9296
Jenny Nath	4540.4696
Shannon A. Li	3181.46

Report action

Right-click on a order number

Customer: Aaron A. Hayes

	All Calendar Periods
SO67240	76960141.05

Figure 19.18 The Excel add-in automatically discovers URL-based actions and adds them to the context menu.

Advanced analytics

Both structured and free-form reports support advanced analytics features, including actions, drillthrough, and writeback. Unfortunately, based on my experiments, the last two features are not supported with SSAS 2005 cubes due to the radical architectural changes that these drillthrough and writeback have undergone in UDM. The drillthrough action fails to execute. When initiating the what-if analysis feature (*Cube Analysis* ➪ *What-if Analysis* ➪ *Begin*), the Excel add-in correctly determines that the cube is write-enabled but refuses to write-enable the measures of the writeback measure group.

Use the Actions worksheet (Figure 19.18) to test some of the actions we implemented in chapter 12. The Excel add-in supports URL-based actions only. To try the URL action report, right-click on a customer (e.g. *Jenny Nath*) and choose the *Actions* ➪ *View Map* context menu. This will display a Yahoo map of the customer location. The report action can be initiated by right-clicking on a customer order (e.g. SO67240) and choosing *Actions* ➪ *Generate Sales Order*

Report. This launches the Sales Order Detail Reporting Services report and passes the selected order number as a parameter.

19.2 Interactive Reporting with OWC

OWC were first introduced with Microsoft Office 2000 as a collection of COM (ActiveX) controls, covering spreadsheet, charting, and pivot (crosstab) functions. Similar to the Excel PivotTable Report, OWC comes with pivot (PivotTable) and chart (ChartSpace) components. Unlike the PivotTable Report though, OWC are implemented as ActiveX controls. This allows you to integrate OWC in your applications, as the SSAS team has done with the Cube Browser. Therefore, OWC may be a good fit when you need to report-enable custom applications, e.g. to allow the end users to build interactive reports from UDM.

Unfortunately, as with the Excel PivotTable Report, the Office team didn't bother to upgrade OWC in time to support the new UDM features. As of the time of this writing, it is unclear if Microsoft would keep and enhance OWC in the next release of Office. I personally hope that OWC will stay on and evolve with SSAS. Better yet, I would like to see OWC ported to .NET at some point for easier integration with managed clients.

19.2.1 Understanding Office Web Components

The latest version of OWC included with the Microsoft Office 2003 suite is version 11. It is also available as a separate download from the Microsoft website (see Resources). If the end users don't have Office 2003 installed, the components will work in read-only mode and the interactive features will be disabled.

Integrating OWC with SSAS

The integration between OWC and the data source follows the client-server model, as shown in Figure 19.19. The OWC components communicate with the Analysis Services server via an OLE DB provider. For example, in the case of Analysis Services, OWC uses Microsoft OLE DB Provider for Analysis Services 9.0.

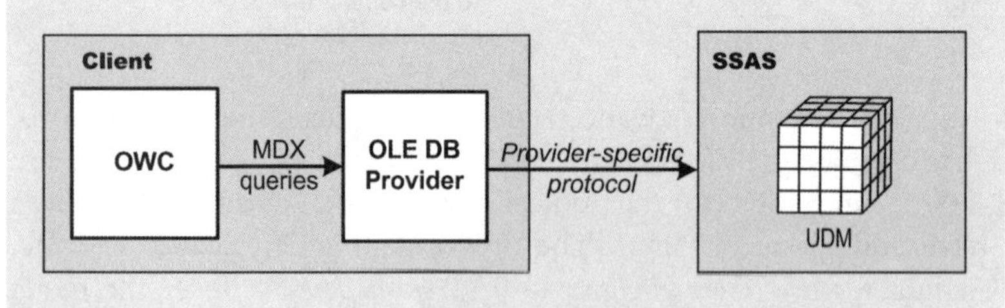

Figure 19.19 When the user interacts with an OWC component, it creates and sends MDX queries through the OLE DB provider to the SSAS server.

As the user interacts with an OWC component, e.g. drags and drops dimensions and measures, behind the scenes OWC creates and sends MDX queries to the OLE DB provider, which in turn communicates with the server to fetch the data. Therefore, as a developer, you don't need to know much about MDX and UDM to build successful BI solutions.

Setting up OWC

To use OWC with .NET-based applications, you will also need the OWC Primary Interop Assemblies (*PIAs*). PIAs are included in the Microsoft Office 2003 setup CD but they are not installed by default. To install them, you have to run the Office setup and select the .NET Programmability Support component from the Office Shared Features section, as shown in Figure 19.20. You need to install PIAs on your development machine, as well as on all clients that will run your application.

Figure 19.20 Install the OWC PIAs to integrate OWC with .NET applications.

There are extra steps required to integrate OWC with Visual Studio.NET. The Office setup program will install PIAs in the .NET Global Assembly Cache. Once you have installed OWC PIAs, you can add the components to your toolbox in Visual Studio.NET. The PivotTable control is listed as Microsoft Office PivotTable 11.0 control under the Choose Toolbox Items (*COM Components* tab), while the ChartSpace control name is Microsoft Office Chart 11.0. Once you reference the controls, check the Visual Studio.NET references. There should be a reference to the OWC11 library which should point to the .NET Global Assembly Cache (GAC) folder. If it doesn't, either PIAs are not installed or you have to refresh the reference.

You will also notice that after you establish the reference, Visual Studio.NET creates an interop assembly called *AxOWC11* to integrate OWC with managed code. Unfortunately, this assembly won't allow you to sink many of the OWC events, as documented in Knowledge Base Article 328275. The article outlines the steps to regenerate the wrapper assembly for OWC version 10 which are also applicable for version 11. For you convenience, I included the correct version of AxOWC11.dll in the bin folder of the Interactive Reporter demo application. When creating a new application, you need to remove the auto-generated reference to the AxOWC11 inside Visual Studio.NET and replace it with a reference to my version so you could handle events successfully. You don't have to do this for the Interactive Reporter sample since its project file already has the correct references.

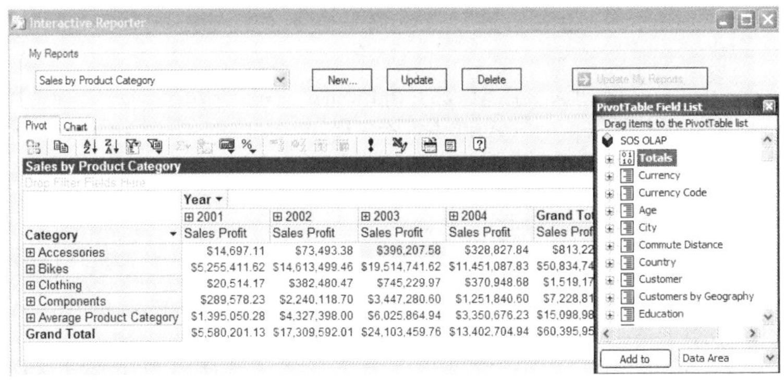

Figure 19.21 The Interactive Reporter application leverages Office Web Components to provide interactive reporting.

Now that we have a good understanding of how OWC work, let's see how we can leverage them for the purposes of the Interactive Reporter demo.

19.2.2 Programming OWC

Let's start by a quick walk-through of the Interactive Reporter application (Figure 19.21). The OWC PivotTable component is the workhorse of the application. The end-user can drag measures and dimensions from the PivotTable Field List and drop them on rows or columns to see data from different angles.

Interactive Reporter also supports the concept of standard and user-defined reports. By default, the administrator can name and save standard report views. These reports are viewable by all users but cannot be modified. Instead, a standard report can serve as a starting point for defining a new interactive report. For example, as Figure 19.21 shows, I've selected the Sales by Product Category standard report in the My Reports dropdown. I could change the report any way I want (e.g. by dragging new dimensions or measures) and save the new report as a user-defined report.

A user-defined report is accessible only by the user who created the report. This resembles the *My Reports* feature of Reporting Services. Of course, since this is a custom application, you can tweak it any way you want, e.g. you can let end-users change standard reports as well. End users can generate a chart report from the current pivot report by simply clicking on the Chart tab.

Implementing My Reports

Interactive Reporter follows a similar design pattern as the one demonstrated by Dave Stearns in his book *Programming Microsoft Office 2000 Web Components.* This approach has proven very successful in some of my real-life BI applications. In its simplest implementation, you may find that one screen, as the one shown in Figure 19.21, may be able to satisfy most of your users' interactive reporting requirements.

Most of the implementation effort went into implementing the *My Reports* feature. Interactive Reporter obtains the current report definition from the *XMLData* property of the PivotTable component. *XMLData* returns only the report layout (excluding the data), e.g. the dimension members and measure used in the report including the format settings. *XMLData* is a read/write property and can be used to save and restore the report layout. All of the three UI Office Web Components, PivotTable, ChartSpace, and Spreadsheet, expose this property. Although Interactive Reporter persists only the PivotTable report definition, with a minimum amount of programming effort, you should be able to enhance it to support saving and restoring chart report layouts as well.

The report definitions are kept in a Microsoft Access database (AdventureWorks.mdb), which you can find in the Ch19\OWC\AWReportService folder. Table Reports has a Category field which classifies the report as standard or user-defined. The table also captures the identity of the user who has created the report in the format *DomainName/UserName.* End users can only see the standard reports defined in this table plus the user-defined reports they have authored. To facilitate the access to the database, I built a web service façade *(MyReports)* which is included in the Ch19 solution. The façade exposes two web methods, *GetReports* and *SaveReports*, to retrieve or change the report definitions respectively.

When Interactive Reporter starts, it calls down to the façade to retrieve a list of standard and user-defined reports. It caches the reports in an ADO.NET dataset. The presentation layer prevents the user from making modifications to standard reports. All changes to the user-defined reports are cached locally in the dataset. When the *Update My Reports* button is clicked, the changed user-defined reports are sent to the façade, which, in turn, propagates the changes to the database.

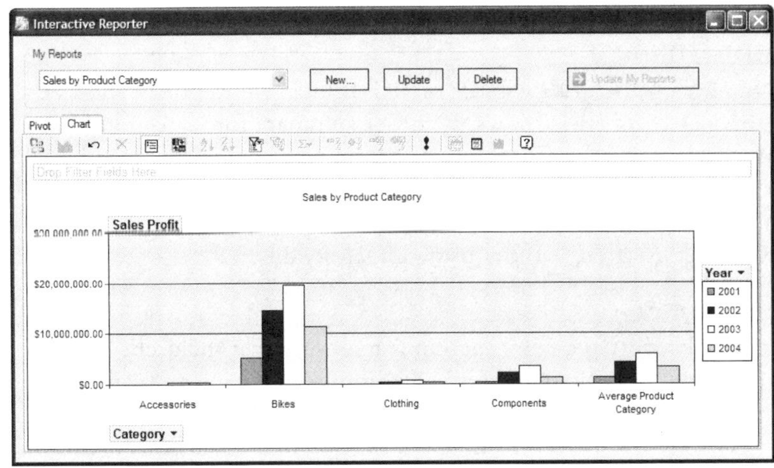

Figure 19.22 The Interactive Reporter application leverages Office Web Components to provide interactive reporting.

Implementing dynamic chart reports

As noted, the end user can generate a chart view of the current pivot report by clicking on the Chart tab (Figure 19.22). To generate the chart report when the Chart tab is clicked, the code binds the ChartSpace component to the PivotTable component, as shown in Listing 19.1.

Listing 19.1 Creating chart reports bound to the PivotTable component

```
Private Sub LoadChart()
    Dim chart As ChChart
    Dim pview As PivotView = pivotTable.ActiveView

    chartSpace.DataSource = CType(pivotTable.GetOcx(), msdatasrc.DataSource)
    chartSpace.DisplayFieldList = True
    chartSpace.AllowUISelection = True

    If chartSpace.Charts.Count = 0 Then
        chart = chartSpace.Charts.Add(0)
    Else
        chart = chartSpace.Charts(0)
    End If
    chart.HasTitle = True
    chart.Title.Caption = pview.TitleBar.Caption
End Sub
```

The code loads the ChartSpace component by setting the chart data source to the PivotTable control. Once this is done, the chart series will be automatically generated from the pivot columns. The chart categories are derived from pivot rows. Next, the code sets some chart properties to allow users to drag dimensions and measures from the Field List and select chart elements. The ChartSpace control can have more that one charts associated with it. In our case, we need only one chart. Once the chart is created, we set its title to match the title of the pivot report.

19.2.3 Integrating OWC with Reporting Services

In chapter 12, I showed you how you can program OWC to retrieve and handle UDM actions. You can use the same approach to implement report actions. Alternatively, if UDM actions don't give you the control you need, you can implement them by coding against the OWC object model. Because OWC retrieves the query results as a CellSet, it exposes a rich object model that preserves the multidimensional data structure.

To demonstrate programming with the OWC object model, Interactive Reporter allows the user to generate a Reporting Services report that shows the order summary for a given month. If the user has requested the Month level of the Date dimension on rows or columns (either by using a multi-level hierarchy or the Month attribute hierarchy), the user can generate the *Monthly Order Summary* report by right-clicking on a data cell and initiating the report from the context menu. This is handled entirely in custom code, without using UDM actions.

Determining the user selection

The most challenging aspect of implementing a report action is to ensure that the user's selection gives us enough information to set the report parameter. For example, in the above scenario, the user must have the Date dimension expanded all the way down to the Month level so we can determine the selected month.The PivotTable control exposes the user selection under its *Selection* property. Each time the user selects an item (data cell or a dimension member), the *SelectionChanged* event fires. When the user double-clicks on a cell or right-clicks to access the mouse context menu, we validate the user selection in function *IsSelectionValid* which is shown in Listing 19.2.

Listing 19.2 Determining if the user selection is valid.

```
Private Function IsSelectionValid() As Boolean
    Dim selection As String = pivotTable.SelectionType
    Dim aggregates As PivotAggregates = Nothing
    Dim aggregate As PivotAggregate = Nothing
    Dim valid As Boolean = False
    Dim uniqueName As String = Nothing

    If selection <> "PivotAggregates" Then
        Return False 'data cell is not selected
    End If
    aggregates = CType(pivotTable.Selection, PivotAggregates)
    aggregate = aggregates(0)

    If TypeOf aggregate.Value Is System.DBNull Then
        Return False 'no data
    End If

    ' seek the time dimension in columns and rows
    valid = Not (GetMonthMember(aggregate.Cell) Is Nothing)
    Return valid
End Function
```

At different points of time, different PivotTable areas may be selected by the user. We are only interested in the case when a data cell is selected. If this is true, the *Selection* property will return *PivotAggregates*. Next the code checks whether the cell is empty. After that, the code calls the *GetMonthMember* function which parses the PivotTable axes to determine if the Month attribute hierarchy is present. If this is the case, we consider the selection to be valid because we can retrieve the corresponding year and month to construct the report parameter.

Implementing custom actions

OWC allows you to change the mouse context menu and add your own items easily. Before the context menu is expanded, the PivotTable component fires the *BeforeContextMenu* event. If the user selection is valid, we can use this event to add the Show Monthly Orders Summary Report command, as shown in (Figure 19.23).

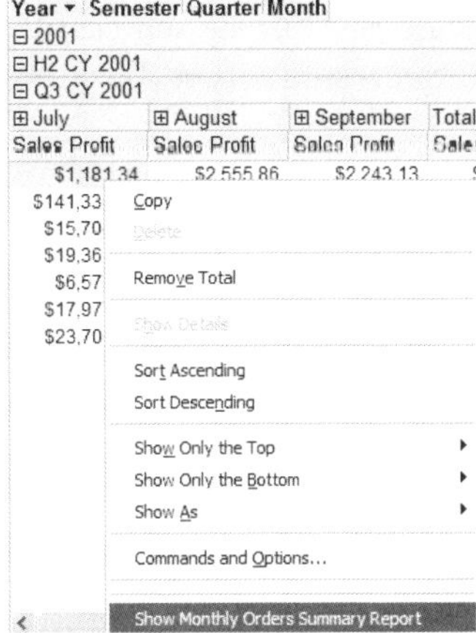

Figure 19.23 Expand the Date dimension to the Month level and right-click on a data cell to see the Show Monthly Orders Summary menu.

When the user clicks on a context menu item, PivotTable fires the *CommandExecute* event. The *CommandExecute* event handler requests the Reporting Services *Monthly Order Summary* report which you can find in the Reports project (Ch18 solution). Figure 19.24 shows the report.

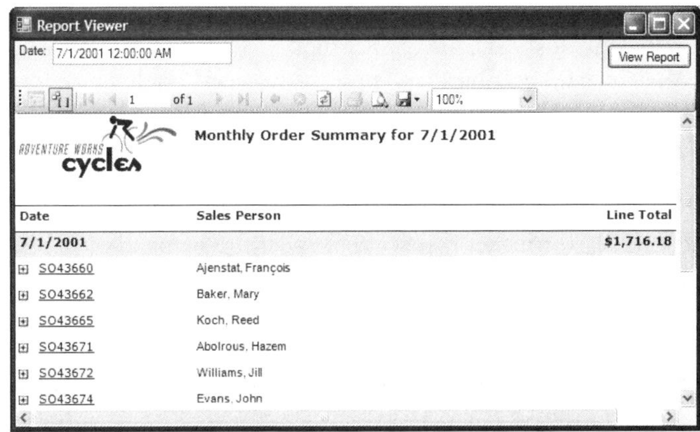

Figure 19.24 The Monthly Order Summary report shows the orders generated for the selected month in the pivot report.

Interactive Reporter generates this report by using the WinForm Report Viewer, which was introduced in the previous chapter. The report takes a single parameter *Date* which we set to the selected date in the Date dimension of the PivotTable control. As you can see, OWC components give you a lot of flexibility to perform various custom actions. In fact, Microsoft has put together an interesting sample application, Business Intelligence Portal Sample Application for Microsoft Office 2003, that demonstrates how SharePoint Portal Server, SQL Server Reporting

Services, and Office Web components can be used together to create custom business intelligence solutions. The download link can be found in the Resources section.

19.3 Corporate Performance Management

In chapter 12, we saw that UDM supports key performance indicators (*KPIs*) in the form of MDX expressions and each KPI can have value, status, goal, and trend values. A client application can call the MDX KPI-related functions (*KPIValue*, *KPIStatus*, *KPIGoal*, and *KPITrend*) to retrieve the KPI details. What's missing in UDM is the ability to define and display scorecards. This is where another component of the Microsoft Office family, Microsoft Office Business Scorecard Manager 2005 (*Scorecard Manager* for short), comes in.

19.3.1 Understanding Business Scorecard Manager

To help enterprises streamline their processes, in late 2003, Microsoft unveiled a set of seven Office Solution Accelerators -- an integrated set of components, templates and best practices designed to solve specific problems common to various organizations. One of them was the Microsoft Office Solution Accelerator for Business Scorecards. Microsoft has recently revamped this accelerator as an enterprise-level commercial offering and released the new version under the name of *Microsoft Office Business Scorecard Manager 2005*. For more information about licensing and pricing details, visit the Scorecard Manager home page (see Resources).

The Scorecard Manager offers two major functional areas. First, it provides advanced KPI and scorecard authoring and management. For example, the Scorecard Manager can source KPI metrics from multiple data sources and store them into a centrally managed repository. Similar to UDM, the Scorecard Manager allows end users to compare and contrast multiple performance targets, e.g. actual vs. targeted KPI values. Second, with the Scorecard Manager you can publish scorecard to SharePoint dashboards or disseminate them in the form of standard SSRS reports. In addition, you can define charts, graphs, spreadsheets, and SSRS reports with a scorecard and publish these views to convey the scorecard data graphically. These views stay synchronized as the user drills down for detailed analysis.

Architecture

Figure 19.25 shows the main components of the Scorecard Manager architecture. The Scorecard Manager is designed as a server-based web platform that can scale to meet the demands of large organizations. Since the Scorecard Manager is tightly-integrated with Microsoft SharePoint for publishing scorecards as SharePoint web parts, it can be installed only on Windows 2003 OS with SharePoint Portal Services (see Resources for a download link) or SharePoint Portal Server installed.

Data sources

The Scorecard Manager can source KPI metrics from multi-dimensional (via ADOMD.NET) and ODBC-enabled data sources. In the best case scenario (you guessed it!), you will have only one data store – the UDM. Even better, the KPIs will be defined in the UDM. The advantage of this approach is that you can centralize your MDX expressions in one place. In addition, you can use advanced MDX expressions (e.g. SSAS stored procedures) to build the KPIs. The only task left for you is to use the Scorecard Manager to construct and publish scorecards from these KPIs.

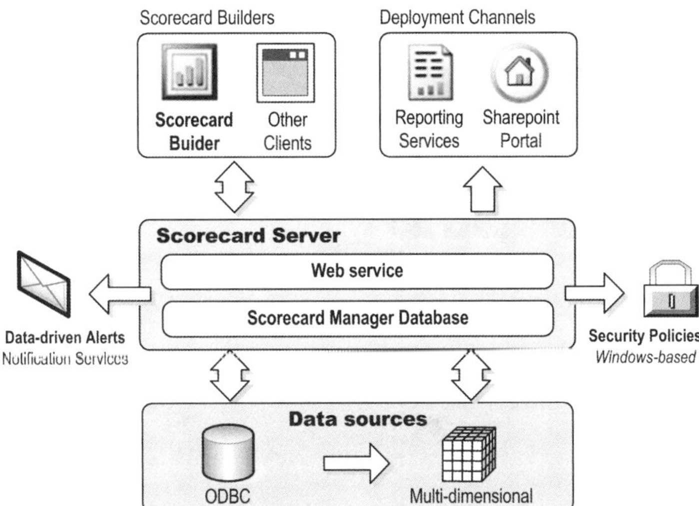

Figure 19.25 The Scorecard Manager is a server-based platform whose main components are the Scorecard Database, Scorecard Web Service, and Scorecard Builder.

With all other data sources, you need to define the KPIs (and scorecards) in the Scorecard Manager. When integrating with ODBC data sources, you have two choices. First, you can directly query the data source. Alternatively, you can extract data from the ODBC data sources and build a multi-dimensional cube(s) which can be used as a data source. As noted, you can implement a scorecard from multiple data sources if the KPI metrics are spread out in more than one database and you need a summary view of metrics.

Scorecard Server

At the heart of the Scorecard Manager's architecture is the Scorecard Server. The Scorecard Server is implemented as a middle-tier layer that orchestrates all activities for building, managing, and publishing a scorecard. Similar to the SSRS Server Database, the actual metadata describing a scorecard (scorecard elements) are stored in a SQL Server-based database -- the *Scorecard Manager Database*. The Scorecard Manager Database can be hosted in SQL Server 2000 or 2005 and can be located on a different server than the Scorecard Server.

To integrate with external clients, the Scorecard Server provides a web façade in the form of the *PmService* ASP.NET Web service. The installation program hosts the Web service in a separate IIS website called *Business Scorecard Manager Web Service*. The Scorecard Server exposes a slew of methods for managing the entire scorecard lifecycle, e.g. for getting and saving the KPIs and scorecards from the Scorecard Manager Database, defining security policies, etc. All APIs (called by SharePoint web parts and Scorecard Builder) are open and documented.

An interesting Scorecard Manager feature is data-driven alerting, which allows end users to subscribe to scorecard change events. Behind the scenes, the Scorecard Manager delegates the notification events to the Microsoft SQL Server 2000/2005 Notification Services. The Scorecard Server architecture is also extensible. For example, the scorecard XML-based metadata supports extension through object-level custom attributes. All metadata change events are written to MSMQ to support custom eventing.

Scorecard Builder

Business analysts build scorecards using the *Scorecard Builder*. The Scorecard Builder (Figure 19.26) is implemented as Windows Forms .NET-based desktop application. The Scorecard

Builder employs the concept of a *workspace* to group logically-related scorecards. Think of a workspace as similar to a Business Intelligence project. A workspace contains KPIs, data sources, scorecards, indicators, and objectives. Workspaces allow you to centralize all the scorecard elements required to create, access, and edit these elements.

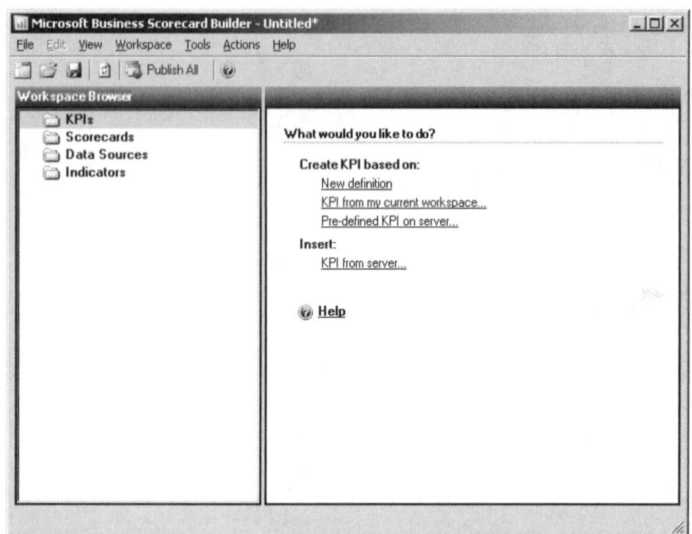

Figure 19.26 A workspace contains scorecards and scorecard elements.

The workspace definition is described in XML and saved as a local file. This allows you to define the workspace while you are disconnected from the Scorecard Server. Once the workspace is ready, you publish the workspace to the Scorecard Manager Database to make its scorecards available for viewing.

Scorecard delivery

Out of the box, the Scorecard Manager supports two channels for delivering scorecards. First, you can deploy scorecards to a SharePoint web portal. Use this approach to implement the nowadays popular *dashboards*, e.g. CFO dashboard that shows the company performance at a glance. The end users navigate to the SharePoint portal to view the scorecard and its associated views. Second, you can use the Scorecard Builder to publish a scorecard as a Reporting Services report. Use this option if you want to deliver the scorecard as a standard report managed by SSRS. As a prerequisite, you need to install and register the Scorecard custom data processing extension with the Report Server. The published report will use this extension to extract the information from the scorecard.

Now that I've introduced you to the Scorecard Manager, let me walk you through a hands-on lab in which we will build and publish a scorecard.

19.3.2 Implementing Scorecards

The scorecard lifecycle consists of several steps. First, you use the Scorecard Builder to create a workspace that will contain the scorecard elements and management polices. Next, you define the data source(s) that will supply the performance metrics. Then, you build useful KPIs to measure the business performance. Once the KPIs are in place, you implement a scorecard(s) that groups related KPIs. Next, you define one or more scorecard views to display the scorecard data. Optionally, you can associate report views with a scorecard. After the scorecard is ready, you deploy the scorecard as a SharePoint web page or SSRS report.

Let's implement a simple scorecard called *Sales Performance* that measures the sales performance of Adventure Works. Our scorecard will contain a single KPI (Gross Sales Profit) and include one scorecard view and two report views – a chart and a Reporting Services report. The scorecard view is shown in Figure 19.27.

Business Scorecard

	January		February		March	
	Actual	Target	Actual	Target	Actual	Target
Sales Performance						
Gross Sales Profit						
All Sales Territories	$2,591,343	$1,380,750	$3,804,083	$2,301,250	$3,796,566	$4,602,500
Australia		$399,000		$399,000		$399,000
Canada	$224,131	$849,000	$266,484	$849,000	$357,037	$849,000
France	$151,741	$707,000	$656,851	$707,000	$216,365	$707,000
Germany	$319,001	$366,000	$360,652	$366,000	$381,573	$366,000
Singapore						
United Kingdom	$349,043	$883,000	$507,236	$883,000	$805,270	$883,000

Figure 19.27 The Sales Performance scorecard shows the Adventure Works performance at a glance.

Having the scorecard view displayed in colors could have been useful but, unfortunately, we are restricted to monochrome view. The circle icon tells us that we are doing great. For example, the overall sales (All Sales Territories) are exceeding the target KPI values by far. This is good news. Exploring the card further, we quickly realize that several territories haven't met the expectations, including Canada and France, while the sales in the United Kingdom are so-so. Of course, we have just scratched the tip of the iceberg. Scorecard implemented with the Scorecard Manager allow you to analyze information in different ways. For example, you can filter and drill through data, subscribe to change events, associate supporting views to see data from different angles, and so on.

Creating a workspace

Start the scorecard implementation process by creating a workspace.

1. Run the Scorecard Builder application (*Microsoft Office* program group ⇨ *Microsoft Office Business Scorecard Builder 2005*).

2. Select the *File* ⇨ *New Workspace* menu (Ctrl+N) or click the *Create a new workspace* link in the Workspace browser pane. The Scorecard Builder creates a blank workspace template. The Workspace Browser pane contains pre-defined folders where you will add the scorecard elements.

3. Select *File* ⇨ *Save* (Ctrl+S) to save the workspace file. Choose a location and name the workspace file *Adventure Works.bsw*. Once the file is saved, use the Notepad to open its definition. Notice that the workspace file is described in XML.

4. To verify the connectivity to the Scorecard Server, select *Tools* ⇨ *Server Administration.*

5. The Server tab in the Server Administration dialog should be selected. The default URL of the Scorecard server is *http://localhost:46786*. If you are running the Scorecard Builder on another machine, replace *localhost* with the machine name. Click Connect to connect to the server. If all is

well, the dialog title will change to *Server Administration http://localhost:46786* and the tabs will become enabled.

6. Click on the Permissions tab and notice that you can add Windows users and groups to predefined Scorecard Server roles to enforce restricted access to the scorecard and its elements.

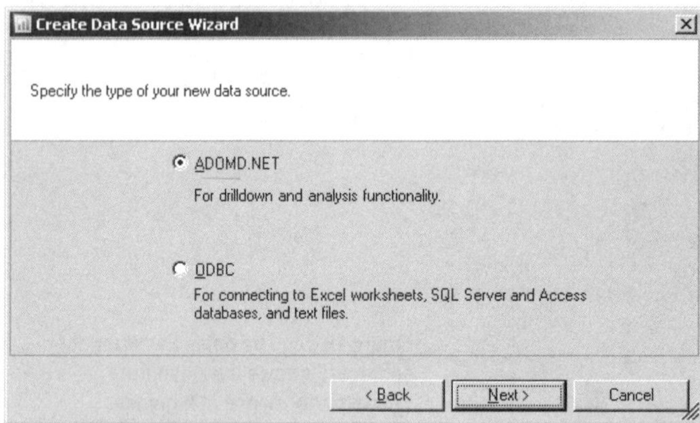

Figure 19.28 Choose the ADOMD.NET option when using UDM as a data source.

Setting up a data source

Similar to SSAS projects, a data source defines a connection string to a database that provides the KPI metrics. Follow these steps to create a data source to the SOS OLAP UDM.

1. Right-click on the Data Sources folder and choose *Create* to launch the Create Data Source Wizard.

2. You can create a data source from scratch or use an existing (workspace or server) data source definition as a starting point. In the *Create data source* step, accept the default *New definition* option and click Next.

3. As noted, the Scorecard Manager supports multi-dimensional and ODBC data sources. Since we will be using a KPI that already exists in the SOS OLAP UDM, accept the default ADOMD.NET option in the *Specify the type of your data source* step (Figure 19.28).

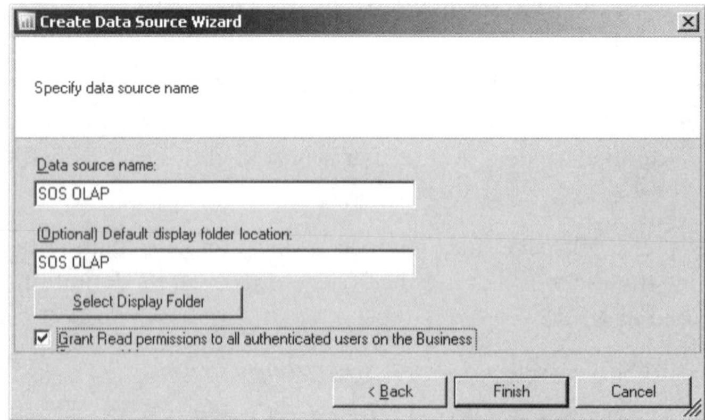

Figure 19.29 Data sources can be organized in folders and are secured items.

4. In the *Specify data source name* step (Figure 19.29), enter **SOS OLAP** as a data source name. Data sources can be grouped in folders. Enter **SOS OLAP** as a folder name.

5. Check the *Grant Read permissions...* to allow the authenticated users to read data. Click Finish to close the Create Data Source Wizard and launch the Data Source Editor (Figure 19.30).

6. Create a standard connection to the SOS OLAP UDM and click OK to create the data source.

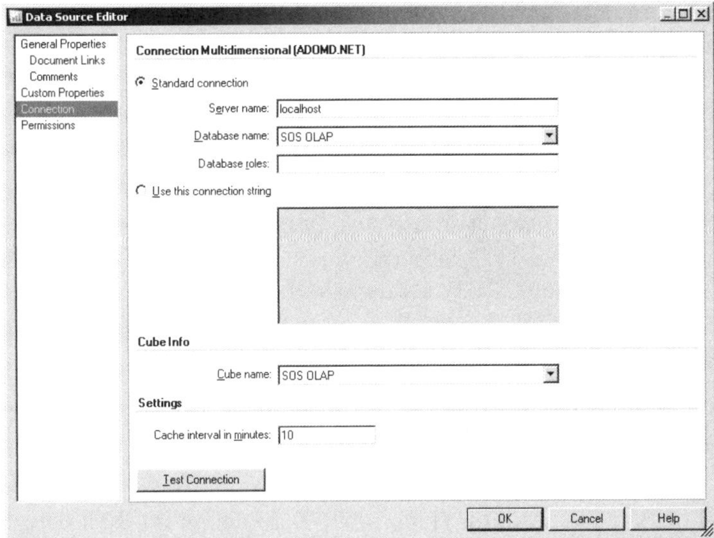

Figure 19.30 Specify the connection options to the data source.

Defining indicators

Similar to a UDM KPI, a Scorecard Manager KPI can have a graphical indicator to represent the gap between the KPI's actual and targeted value. The Scorecard Manager comes with a predefined Stop Light indicator which we will reuse in our workspace.

1. In the Workspace Browser, right-click on the Indicators folder and choose *Insert.*

2. In the Select Indicator dialog, select the Stop Light indicator and click OK.

Figure 19.31 By default, a new KPI has Actual and Target elements.

Defining KPIs

With the data source definition in place, we are ready to create KPIs from business metrics stored in the data source. In the Scorecard Manager terminology, a KPI is a set of data source mappings, business logic and application metadata representing a business metric. A KPI has one and only one actual value and one or more target values. Let's create a *Gross Sales Profit* KPI that will track the actual vs. targeted sales performance.

Creating the KPI

1. In the Workspace Browser, right-click on the KPIs folder and select *Create*. This launches the Create KPI Wizard which is very similar to the Create Data Source Wizard.
2. Name the new KPI **Gross Sales Profit** and place it in a **Sales Performance** display folder. Grant Read permissions to the authenticated users. Once the wizard creates the Gross Sales Profit KPI, it throws us in the KPI Editor (Figure 19.31). By default, the Create KPI Wizard has generated two KPI elements – Actual and Default Target. We can use them to define the KPI actual and target values respectively.
3. Select the *Actual* KPI element and double-click on it to open it in the Actual Editor. Alternatively, you can click on the *Edit the selected scorecard element* toolbar button above the Actual element.
4. Switch to the Data Mappings tab of the Actual Editor (Figure 19.32) to define the KPI actual value.

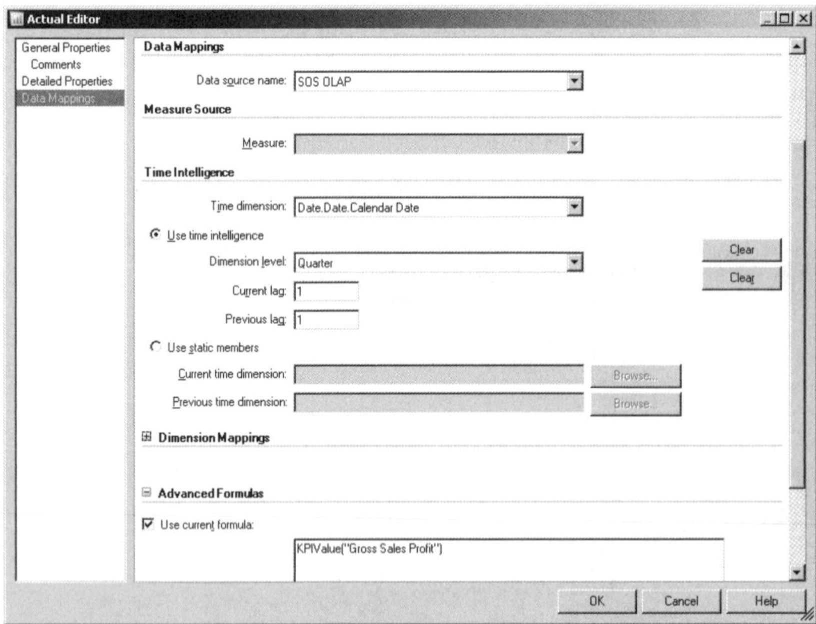

Figure 19.32 When the KPIs are defined in UDM, use the KPI-related MDX functions to derive the KPI actual and target values.

The Scorecard Manager supports two options for deriving the KPI values with multi-dimensional data sources. You can bind the KPI to an existing measure or you can use an MDX expression. If you use the first option, we will end up redefining the KPI. Since the Gross Sales Profit KPI already exists in the SOS OLAP UDM, we will use the second option.

5. Select *SOS OLAP* as a data source.

Setting time intelligence

KPI values are compared across time periods. For example, an organization may need to know how the Gross Sales Profit KPI has changed between two quarters. We have to options to evaluate the KPI. First, we can use time intelligence to define relative time periods. Alternatively, we can choose static members from the Time dimension, e.g. the current period is Quarter 4, while the last period is Quarter 3. Needless to say, with the latter option we need to "remember" to update the static members with each new period. To reduce maintenance effort, we will go for the time intelligence option, which is probably named this way because it requires some investigation to figure out the meaning of the *Current lag* and *Previous lag* fields.

Contrary to what you may believe, these fields don't specify the offset from the current time period. Instead, they are used to set the current Time member based on the number of lag periods from the last non-empty Time member. For example, let's assume you select Quarter from the Dimension Level drop-down list and type 0 in the Current Lag and Previous Lag fields. The first non-empty member found is retrieved, which gives you the quarter-to-date value. If you enter 1 in the Current Lag and Previous Lag fields, the last quarter member that exists in the cube would be returned (the current quarter).

6. Select *Date.Date.Calendar Date* (Calendar Date multi-level hierarchy in the Date dimension) as a Time dimension.
7. Select Use time intelligence option and *Quarter* level in the *Dimension level* dropdown.
8. Enter **1** as current and previous lag.
9. Expand the Advanced Formulas section and enter *KPIValue("Gross Sales Profit")*. This MDX expression will return the value of the Gross Sales Profit KPI from the SOS OLAP UDM. Click OK.
10. Now that we've set up the KPI value, let's set up its target. Back to the KPI Editor, double-click on the *Default Target* element. In the General Properties tab, change its name from *Default Target* to just **Target**.
11. Select the Data Mappings tab and enter the same settings as you entered when defining the KPI Actual value. The only difference is that instead of using the KPIValue function you need to use KPIGoal function, so the Advanced Formulas expression is *KPIGoal("Gross Sales Profit")*.
12. Target values have an additional *Thresholds* tab which you can use to associate an indicator. As with UDM-based KPIs, you can set up band settings for best, medium, and worst ranges. Expand the *Indicator name* dropdown and select the Stop Light indicator and accept the default band settings.

Implementing scorecards

Once the KPI(s) are defined, we are ready to create a scorecard. In the Scorecard Manager terminology, a scorecard is a hierarchy of KPIs. The scorecard hierarchy is defined by creating nested *objectives*. For example, if the Adventure Works wants to create different KPIs for its sales territories, we could create North America, Europe, and Pacific objectives that correspond to the sales regions. Each objective can in turn contain other objectives. For example, we can break the North America objective into the United States and Canada objectives and assign the different KPIs to these objectives. To keep the things simple, our scorecard will not have objectives.

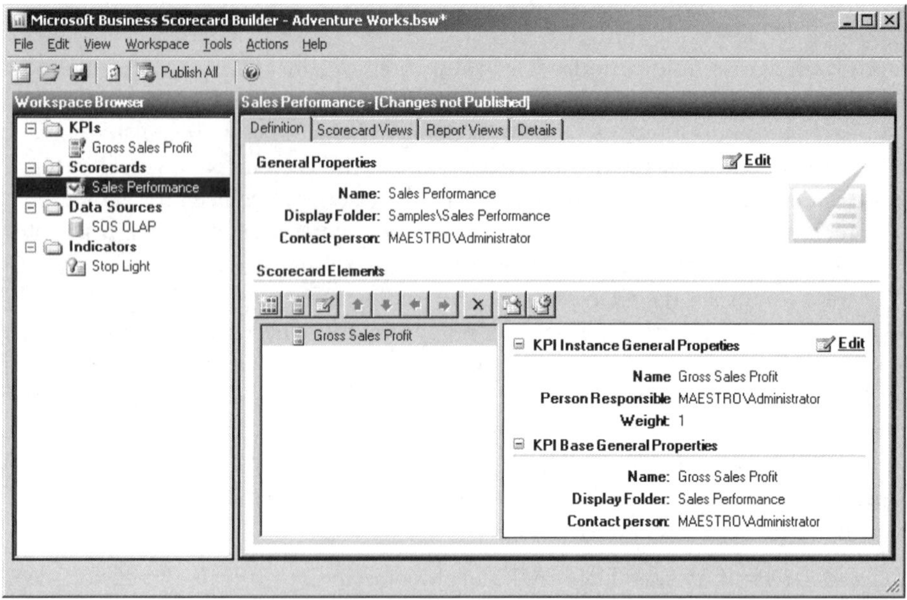

Figure 19.33 A scorecard is a hierarchy of KPIs.

1. In the Workspace Browser, right-click on the Scorecards folder and select *Create*.
2. Use the Create Scorecard Wizard to create a new **Sales Performance** scorecard and place the scorecard in a **Sales Performance** folder. Grant the authenticated users rights to read the scorecard.
3. In the Scorecard Editor, click on the *Add a KPI* toolbar button. In the Add KPI to Scorecard dialog that follows, expand the Sales Performance folder and select the Gross Sales Profit KPI. Click OK to add it to the scorecard (Figure 19.33).

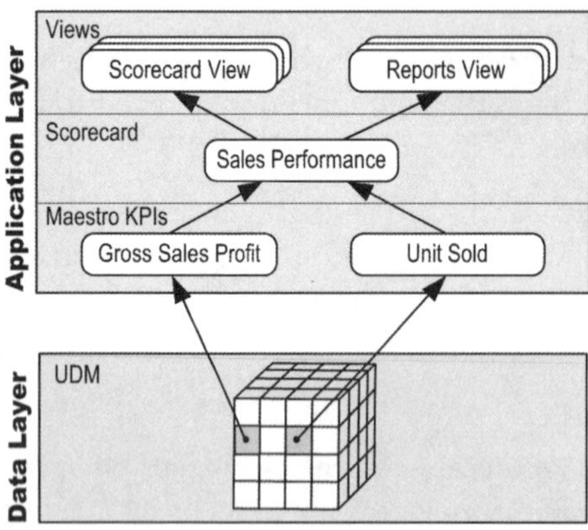

Figure 19.34 In the Scorecard Manager, a scorecard is a collection of KPIs organized in objectives. A scorecard can have one or more scorecard and report views.

A scorecard can have one or more *scorecard views* and one or more *report views* (Figure 19.34). A scorecard view is a server-generated view that shows the scorecard hierarchy with rendering specifications (e.g. headers, new labels, font sizes, etc.). A report view is a supporting report associated with the scorecard and it could be one of the following – an OWC PivotTable, an

OWC PivotChart, an Excel spreadsheet, a web page (e.g. ASP.NET page), another scorecard, or a Reporting Services report.

Creating a scorecard view

A scorecard must have at least one scorecard view before it is published.

4. Select the *Scorecard Views* tab of the Scorecard Editor. Notice that the Scorecard Editor has already created a default scorecard view called *Default View*. The process of configuring a scorecard view is very similar to creating a PivotTable report. A scorecard view can have a page filter, row and column axes. The view data is derived from the KPI actual and target values.

5. Select the Default View in the grid and click *Edit*. In the *General Properties* tab of the Scorecard View Editor, change the scorecard view name to **Sales Performance View**.

6. Switch to the *Dimensionality* tab and select the *SOS OLAP* data source in the Data source name dropdown.

7. Select the Column Members tab to define the column axis of the scorecard view (Figure 19.35).

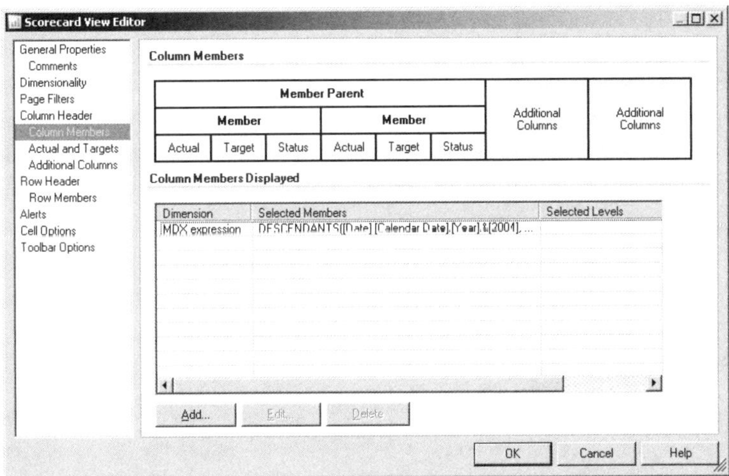

Figure 19.35 You can use static dimension members, a named set, or a custom MDX expression to define column and members of the scorecard view.

8. Click the Add button. In the Specify Dimension Members dialog that follows, select the Custom MDX Formula option and enter the following set-producing MDX expression:

```
DESCENDANTS([Date].[Calendar Date].[Year].&[2004],
[Date].[Calendar Date].[Month])
```

As a result of this expression, the column axis of the view will contain all months of 2004 for which there is data.

9. Select the *Row Members* tab. Notice that the Row Members Displayed grid already included a *Scorecard Hierarchy* row which defines the hierarchical structure of the scorecard consisting of objectives and KPIs. Enter the following MDX expression to define the rows shown in the scorecard view:

```
Except([Sales Territory].[Country].Members,
{[Sales Territory].[Country].&[NA]})
```

This expression returns an MDX set that contains all countries except the *NA* member.

Tip As it stands, the Scorecard Builder doesn't support previewing the scorecard view. For this reason, you may find it more convenient to use Management Studio to create and test the MDX expressions before using them to configure the view.

Notice that the Scorecard View Editor contains additional tabs that allow you to control various formatting and action settings. For example, you can use the Alerts tab to subscribe users for notifications when the scorecard data changes.

Creating a chart report view

Besides a scorecard view, you can attach additional reporting views to a scorecard. Follow these steps to create a PivotChart view that shows how the company sales profit is doing over time.

10. In the Scorecard Editor, click on the *Report Views* tab. The Report Views tab is empty because there are no report views defined yet.

11. Click the Add button to launch the Create Report View wizard.

12. In the *Specify report view and type* step (Figure 19.36), enter **Sales Profit Over Time** as the report view name and select *Chart* as a report type.

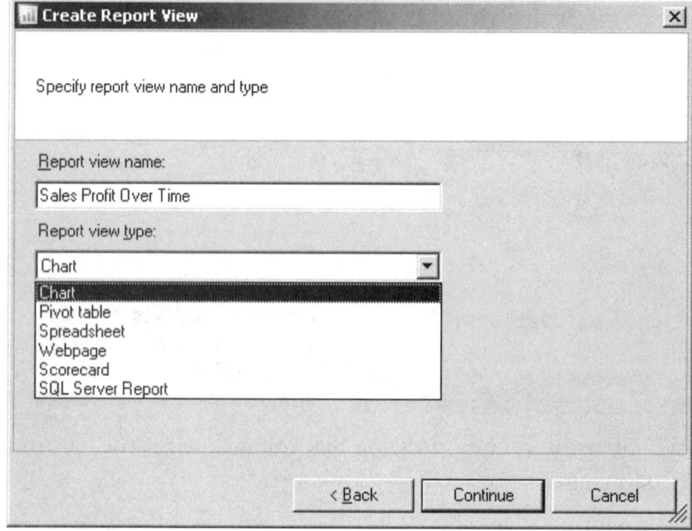

Figure 19.36 Use the Create Report View Wizard to create a report view and specify its type.

13. Click Continue to navigate to the Report View Editor (Figure 19.37) where you can configure the chart.

14. Behind the scenes, a chart report view uses the OWC PivotChart component which you are already familiar with. As a first step of configuring the chart, you need to connect to the data source. Click on the Chart Wizard (the right-most) button on the OWC toolbar to establish a connection to the SOS OLAP UDM.

15. Once connected, click on the Field List toolbar button and drag the *Data.Calendar Year* on the pages and filter the report to show data for year 2004 only.

16. Drag the *Sales Territory.Country* level on the chart categories axis and the Sales Profit measure on the chart series axis (see Figure 19.37). Click OK to create the report view.

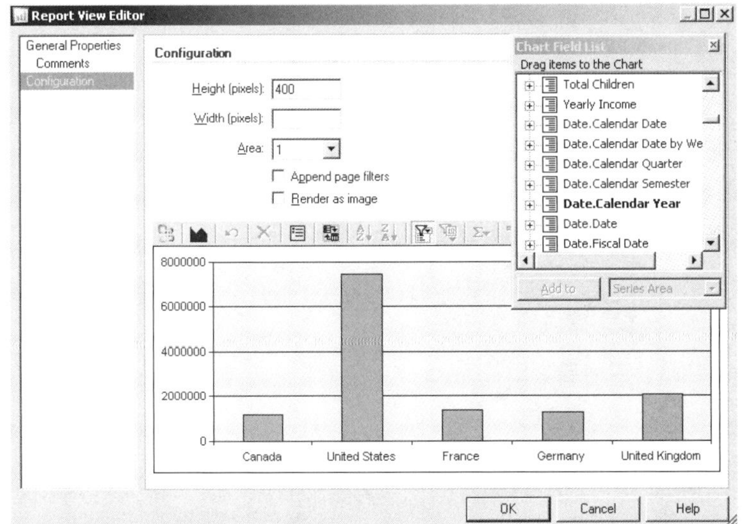

Figure 19.37 A Chart report view uses the OWC PivotChart component. You can render the report view as an image to avoid client-side dependencies to OWC.

Creating a Reporting Services report view

Besides a chart, you can associate a Reporting Services report to a scorecard. For example, suppose that your users would like to see a report that shows the details of Sales Profit KPI broken down by country. The Sales Profit report in the Ch18 solution fits exactly this purpose. Behind the scenes, it uses an MDX query to retrieve the Sales Profit KPI values from the SOS OLAP UDM (Figure 19.38). For end-user convenience, it also takes the report year as a parameter.

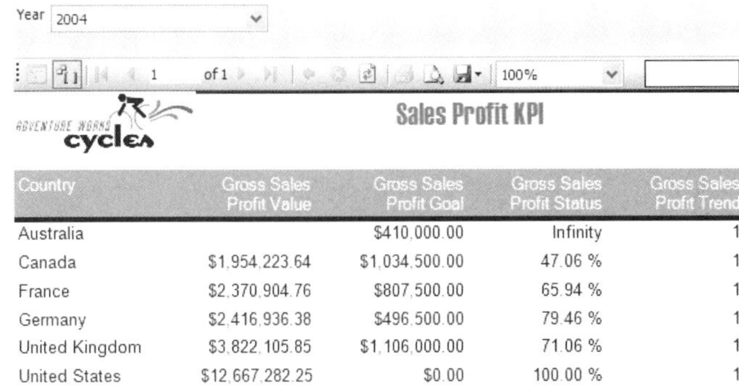

Sales Profit KPI

Country	Gross Sales Profit Value	Gross Sales Profit Goal	Gross Sales Profit Status	Gross Sales Profit Trend
Australia		$410,000.00	Infinity	1
Canada	$1,954,223.64	$1,034,500.00	47.06 %	1
France	$2,370,904.76	$807,500.00	65.94 %	1
Germany	$2,416,936.38	$496,500.00	79.46 %	1
United Kingdom	$3,822,105.85	$1,106,000.00	71.06 %	1
United States	$12,667,282.25	$0.00	100.00 %	1

Figure 19.38 The Sales Profit KPI report demonstrates how MDX functions can be used to retrieve the KPI values.

Hooking this report to a report view in the Scorecard Builder is trivial.

17. Create a new report view of a type *SQL Server Report* and name it **Sales Profit KPI by Country**.
18. In the Configuration tab, configure the report invocation details, as shown in Figure 19.39.
19. You can use the Area dropdown to specify in which zone of the SharePoint web page the view will be rendered. If two report views target the same area, SharePoint automatically generates a dropdown to allow the end-user to select the desired view. Expand the Area dropdown and select **2** to place the report in the second area.

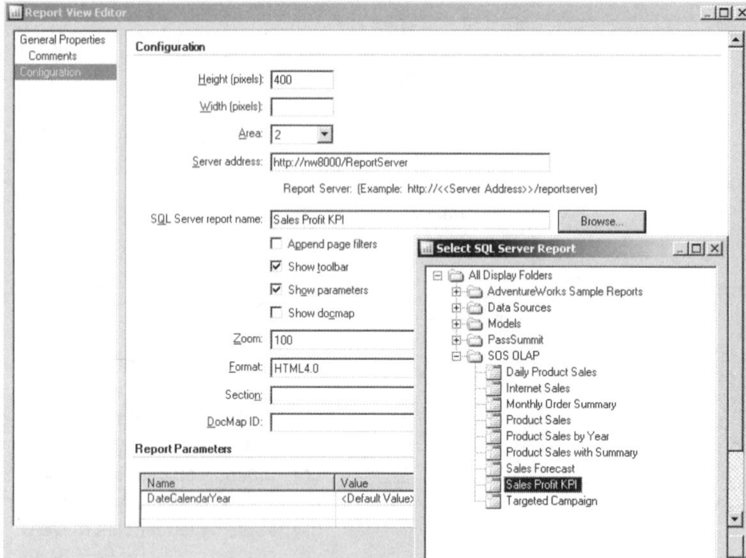

Figure 19.39 Use a SQL Server Report view to associate a standard report to a scorecard.

20. In the *Server address* textbox, enter the URL of the Report Server.

21. Click the Browse button to select the Sales Profit KPI report.

22. Use the Report Parameters grid to pass the report parameter values. In our case, we leave the Year parameter to its default value (2004), which is configured in the report itself.

19.3.3 Deploying Scorecards

Once the scorecard is ready, it can be published as a SharePoint web page or as a Reporting Services report. Follow these steps to publish the Sales Performance scorecard to the SharePoint portal.

Figure 19.40 Choose the SharePoint location where the scorecard will be deployed.

Generating the SharePoint page

1. Click Publish All toolbar button to publish the Sales Performance scorecard to the Scorecard Manager Database.

2. You can generate the initial SharePoint page from the Scorecard Builder. Once the SharePoint web page is generated, you can simply publish the modified scorecard elements and the web page will pick the changes automatically (no need to re-generate the page). Select *Tools* ⇨ *Deploy Scorecard* ⇨ *To SharePoint* to launch the *Deploy Scorecard in Sharepoint* Wizard.

Note To deploy the scorecard as a standard report, select *Tools ⇨ Deploy Scorecard ⇨ To SQL Server report*. Before doing so, make sure you run the Scorecard Manager Server setup program on the Report Server machine and install the Reporting component only. This option will install the Scorecard Custom Data Processing extension.

3. In the first wizard step, click the *Specify Scorecard on Server* button. In the Select Scorecard dialog that follows (Figure 19.40), expand the SOS OLAP folder and select *the Sales Performance* scorecard. Click OK to return back to the wizard and click Next to advance to the next step.

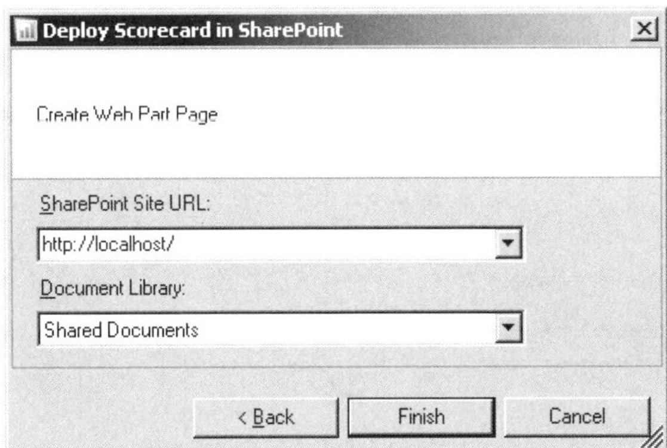

Figure 19.41 Specify the SharePoint web portal URL and document library.

4. In the *Specify the scorecard view* step, expand the Scorecard View Name dropdown and select *Sales Performance View* (the only item). If the scorecard has multiple views defined, this step sets the default scorecard view. You can subsequently overwrite the default view by modifying the SharePoint web page.

5. In the *Specify Name and Layout* step, enter **Sales Performance** as the web page name and accept the default page layout template.

6. Finally, in the *Crete Web Part Page* step, enter the SharePoint portal URL (e.g. http://localhost/) and the document library where the page will be generated. Click Finish to create the page.

Adjusting the page layout

Once the Scorecard Builder generates the page, it navigates to the page URL so you can see its rendered output. You can leverage the standard SharePoint page design features to make layout changes to the page. Notice that the chart report view is placed in area 1, while the SQL Server report view is in area 2, as we indicated during the scorecard configuration process.

7. Click the *Modify Shared Page* link to switch to the page design mode.

8. Drag the SSRS report web part below the scorecard view.

9. Expand the ▼ button of the Business Scorecard part (scorecard view) and choose the *Modify Shared Part* menu. The page reposts to itself and a Business Scorecard pane is shown on the right.

10. Change the width of the scorecard view to 800 pixels. Repeat the same with the SQL Server report view. Click the OK button to apply the settings and render the page (Figure 19.42). Experiment with the page design settings until you are satisfied with the layout.

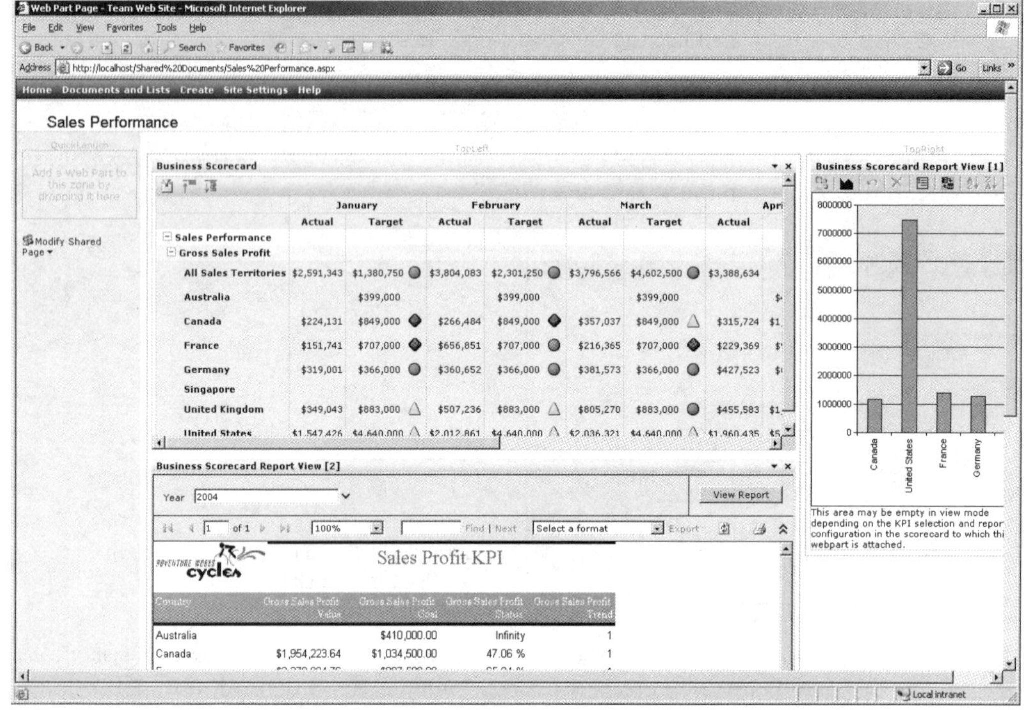

Figure 19.42 The finalized SharePoint page contains one scorecard view and two report views.

End users can request the page from the SharePoint portal. To try this scenario, navigate to the portal default page, e.g. *http://localhost/default.aspx*. In the *Shared Documents* folder, you will find a document link to the Sales Performance scorecard.

19.4 Summary

From end-user perspective, the best OLAP browser is the one that doesn't require MDX and OLAP knowledge. The analytics tools included in the Microsoft Office suite fulfill this requirement. Unfortunately, they all require a facelift to bring them on a par with the new UDM features. Many users rely on Microsoft Excel as a primary reporting and data crunching tool. Your users can leverage the built-in PivotTable Report component to generate structured reports. Alternatively, they can use the Excel Add-in for Analysis Services to author more feature-rich structured and free-form reports.

When you need to implement UDM browsing capabilities in custom applications, consider the PivotTable and PivotChart components, as I demonstrated with the Interactive Reporter demo. Finally, use the Scorecard Manager to build KPIs and scorecards that track the company performance. Well, we reached the last stop of the SSAS journey. I sincerely hope that this book has helped you perceive Analysis Services as a powerful platform for delivering rich and efficient OLAP and data mining solutions. If it has inspired you to use SSAS in your real-life projects, so much the better. Happy data analyzing with Microsoft Analysis Services and the Microsoft Business Intelligence Platform!

19.5 Resources

Microsoft Data Analyzer
(http://shrinkster.com/8nw) – Data Analyzer enables users to quickly view data, publish and share data.

Excel 2002/2003 Add-in for SQL Server Analysis Services
(http://shrinkster.com/7uc) – The Excel Add-in for Analysis Services enables users to access and analyze data from multiple Analysis Services Cubes, and to create rich, customized reports directly in Excel 2002/2003.

Office 2003 Add-in: Office Web Components
(http://shrinkster.com/8qs) – Microsoft Office Web Components are a collection of Component Object Model (COM) controls for publishing spreadsheets, charts, and databases to the Web.

PivotTable Service Download
(http://shrinkster.com/81v) – Download and install the PivotTable service version 9.0 to integrate Excel with UDM.

Business Intelligence Portal Sample Application for Microsoft Office 2003
(http://shrinkster.com/7ue) – Business intelligence portal sample application for Microsoft Office 2003 is an integrated, web-based OLAP solution that enables employees in an organization to create and share OLAP/Relational/XML based views, using SharePoint Portal Server, SQL Server Reporting Services, and Office Web components.

Microsoft Office Business Scorecard Manager 2005 Home Page
(http://shrinkster.com/7zc) – Use the Microsoft Office Business Scorecard Manager 2005 to visualize and manage scorecards and strategies across your organization.

Windows SharePoint Services with Service Pack 2
(http://shrinkster.com/8qt) – Microsoft Windows SharePoint Services is a Microsoft Windows Server 2003 component that helps organizations increase individual and team productivity by enabling them to create Web sites for information sharing and document collaboration.

Appendix A

Installing Analysis Services

The SQL Server setup program installs the SQL Server database engine and add-on services, including Analysis Services. If you are upgrading from SSAS 2000, before you run the SQL Server 2005 setup program, it may make sense to take the "think before you leap" approach and spend some time planning your deployment. Appendix B is meant to help you understand different upgrade scenarios and how to estimate the impact of the upgrade.

Start the SQL Server setup program by inserting the SQL Server 2005 Setup CD into your CD-ROM drive. If your computer has been set up with the CD Autoplay feature, the SQL Server Setup program starts automatically. Otherwise, run the *splash.hta* HTML application in the Server folder from the CD. If you just need to set up the client components, such as Management Studio and OLE DB Driver for Analysis Services 9.0, run the *splash.hta* HTML Application found in the Tools folder. The instructions that follow demonstrate the "happy" installation path that assumes that you are installing the server components on a clean machine.

A.1 Preparing to Set up Analysis Services

For the purposes of this book, I would recommend you install the SQL Server 2005 Developer Edition. It includes all the features of the Enterprise Edition but it is not licensed for production use. Moreover, this is the only edition that allows you to install Analysis Services on Windows XP.

Tip You can use Windows XP for development by installing SQL Server 2005 Development Edition. If you prefer to install SSAS 2005 on a Virtual PC instance with Windows XP firewall (SP2) installed, you need to open ports 2383 (SSAS 2005), 2382 (SQL Redirector) and ports 1433 and 5022 if you use SQL Server database as a data source that is hosted on the same VPC instance. In addition, depending on your domain infrastructure and security setup, you may need to open additional Active Directory ports if SSAS 2005 is configured to use Windows Integrated authentication to connect to the data source.

A.1.1 Reviewing Requirements

The Prepare section of the setup splash screen (Figure A.1) includes useful links that you may want to review before running the setup. For example, read the document *Review Hardware and Software Requirements* and install the dependent components, including Windows XP Service Pack 2 (if you are running Windows XP), IIS (required for Reporting Services and HTTP Connectivity to the Analysis Server), Internet Explorer 6.0 Service Pack1, etc. Don't worry that you may miss some of these components, since the Checking System Requirement step (see section 0) will verify them all.

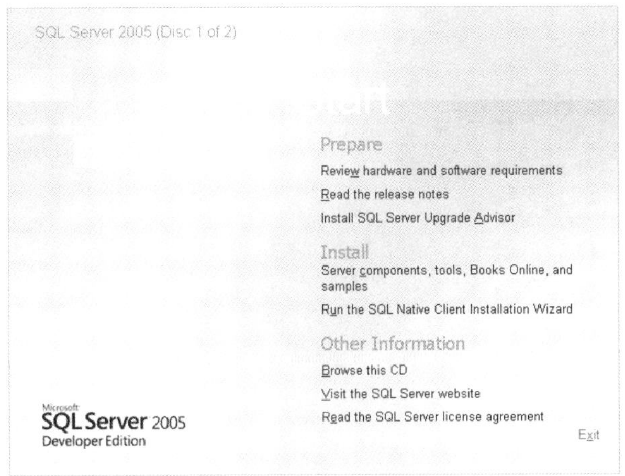

Figure A.1 Review the links in the Prepare section before you install SQL Server.

Another good resource to review beforehand is the topic *Installing SQL Server 2005* from the product documentation. The entire SQL Server 2005 product documentation is available online (see Resources). If you are upgrading, I highly recommend you install and run the *SQL Server Upgrade Advisor*, which is discussed in details in Appendix B. When you are done reviewing and installing the prerequisites, click on the Server components link (Install section) to start the SQL Server 2005 Installation Wizard.

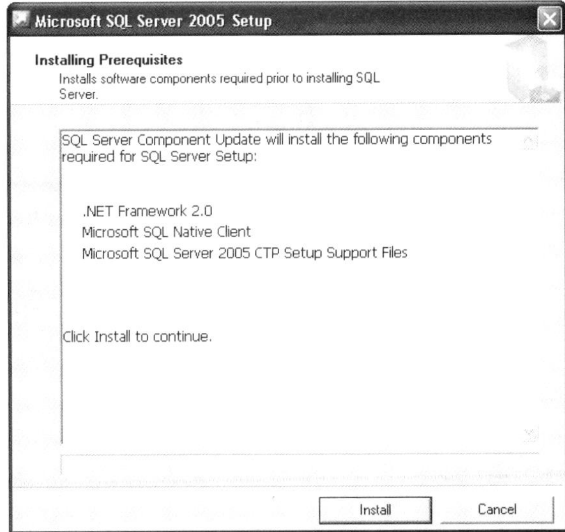

Figure A.2 Install the SQL Server prerequisites.

A.1.2 Installing Prerequisites

Once you confirm the End User License Agreement step, the Installation Wizard displays the Installing Prerequisites page (Figure A.2). SQL Server 2005 requires .NET Framework 2.0. The Microsoft SQL Native Client is a brand new data provider that is specifically designed for SQL

Server 2005. Click the Install button to install the required components to proceed to the System Configuration Check step.

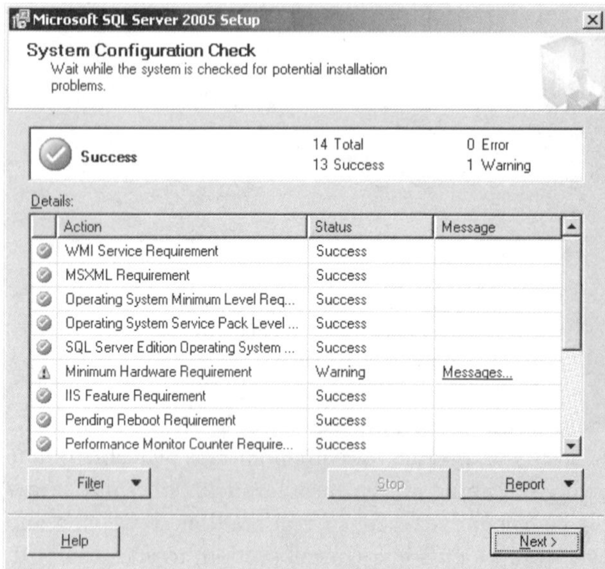

Figure A.3 Verify the system requirements.

A.1.3 Checking System Requirements

In the System Configuration Check (Figure A.3), the Installation Wizard verifies the system requirements. If a given requirement is not met, the Installation Wizard will flag it as a warning or error. You must address error conditions before continuing further. In comparison, warning conditions allow you to continue to the next step. For example, as Figure A.3 shows, the wizard has raised a warning that the installation machine doesn't meet the minimum hardware requirement. The issue in this case is that the computer memory is less than the recommended amount (1Gb for Developer Edition).

You also have an option to print a Configuration Check report, e.g. to send it to the system administrator who is responsible for fixing the issue. Next, the Installation Wizard scans the system to verify the state of the installed services and displays the Registration Information step where you fill in your name, company name, and product key.

A.2 Installing SQL Server Components

Once you pass successfully the setup prerequisites, you can select the SQL Server components to install. The add-on services are Analysis Services, Reporting Services, Notification Services, and Integration Services. You don't have to install the SQL Server Database Services if you need Analysis Services only. For example, if your data is located in a SQL Server database on another machine, you can select only the Analysis Services option.

Figure A.4 Select which components you need to install or upgrade.

A.2.1 Selecting Components

Use the Components to Install step (Figure A.4), to select the components you need to install or upgrade. If you choose not to install a component, and later change your mind after completing the setup process, you can add the component by re-running the setup from the Add/Remove Programs control panel (*Microsoft SQL Server 2005* program item). For the purposes of this book, you need *SQL Server Database Services* (the relational engine), *Analysis Services* (the topic of this book), *Reporting Services* (for report actions, standard and ad hoc reports, *Integration Services* (for the ETL demos and task automation), and *Workstation components, Books Online and development tools.*

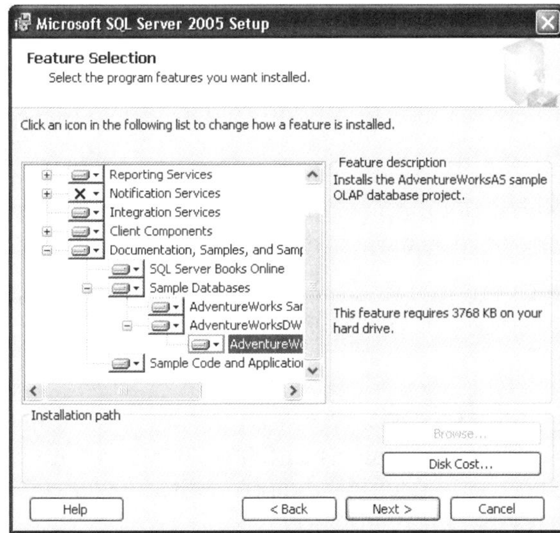

Figure A.5 Use the Feature Selection dialog to select the sample databases.

A.2.2 Choosing Features

You also need the sample databases (*AdventureWorks* and *AdventureWorksDW*) to run the code samples. They are not installed by default and can be selected in the Feature Selection step (Figure A.5) by clicking the Advanced button. Expand the Sample Databases folder and select the *AdventureWorks* and *AdventureWorksDW* databases. I recommend that you also install the *AdventureWorksAS OLAP database project* which the SSAS team has put together to demonstrate a sample UDM solution. Finally, I suggest you select the *Sample Code and Applications* option to install the SQL Server and Reporting Services samples.

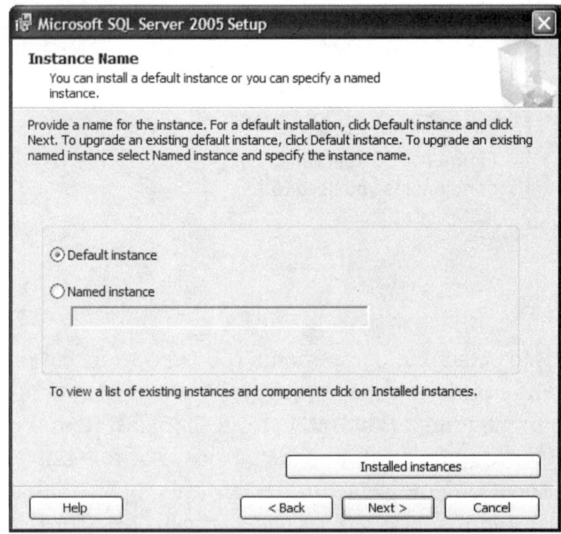

Figure A.6 When installing SQL Server side-by-side, use the Instance Name step to specify the instance.

A.2.3 Configuring Installation Instances

The SQL Server relational database and the add-on servers can be installed side-by-side. For example, you could have both the Express and Developer editions of the relational engine running on the same machine. Use the *Instance Name* step (Figure A.6) to configure side-by-side installation. If the Installation Wizard detects no other SQL Server instances, it enables only the Default instance option. Otherwise, you can select the *Named instance* option and specify the instance name. You can click on the *Installed instances* button to find what server instances are present on this machine. You can connect to a named instance using the *MachineName\InstanceName* naming convention.

Note Not all services are instance-aware. For example, Notification Services and Integration Services don't support multiple instances.

If the Installation Wizard determines that there is an SSAS 2000 instance running on the same machine, it will give you a choice to upgrade to SSAS 2005 or install SSAS 2005 as a named instance. In this case, you cannot install SSAS 2005 on the default instance because SSAS 2000 doesn't support named instances and it always takes the default instance.

A.2.4 Setting up Service Account

Use the Service Account step (Figure A.7) to specify the Windows account the services will run under. Choosing a correct account is important in a distributed environment. By default, the Installation Wizard suggests using a domain account instead of using the Local System account which can access local resources only.

Tip After the setup process is complete, use SQL Server Management Studio if you need to change the account under which a given service is running. Review the Setting Up Windows Service Accounts topic in the product documentation for more information about what rights are given to each service account.

For example, as we discussed in chapter 2, if your data source is installed on a separate machine than the Analysis Services server, the connection to the data source may fail under Local System if Windows Integrated security is used. That's because SSAS performs data operations (processing, writeback, etc.) under the account of the Analysis Services server.

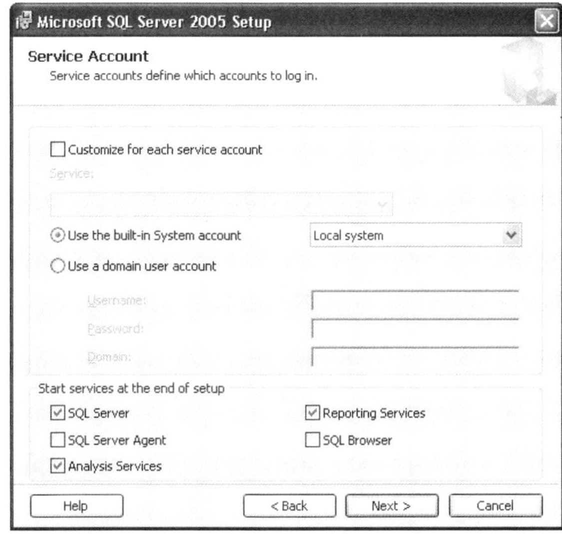

Figure A.7 Select a service account that the Windows services will run under.

For testing purposes or if your machine doesn't belong to a domain, running the services under the Local System account is fine. Just bear in mind that the Local System account is a highly privileged account and it may present security vulnerability.

The Service Account step allows you to select which services will be started automatically when the computer is rebooted. If you are planning to schedule SQL Server jobs, e.g. SSIS package execution, check the *SQL Server Agent* option. The SQL Browser service is only needed if you have multiple service instances installed. Its purpose is to redirect the incoming requests to the correct instance. The Installation Wizard grants the account the necessary privileges to perform the required actions, e.g. *Log on as a service* right is granted to the Analysis Server. You can use the same account for the SQL Server and add-on services or customize each service to use a different account.

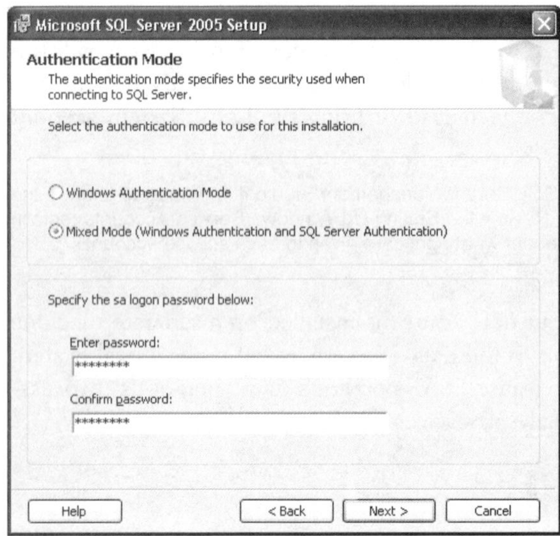

Figure A.8 Choose a Windows Authentication or mixed mode to connect to the SQL Server relational engine.

A.2.5 Choosing Authentication Mode

The Authentication Mode step (Figure A.8) is specific to the SQL Server relational engine. SQL Server supports Windows-based authentication or mixed authentication mode (Windows and standard authentication). Needless to say, although it may not always be feasible, the Windows-based authentication is the recommended option because you don't need to specify the password in the connection string.

If you need to support international users, change the default settings in the Collation Settings step to specify the sorting behavior of the SQL Server and Analysis Services. By default, Analysis Services uses the same collation and sort order settings as the SQL Server database engine. If you are installing both SSAS and the SQL Server relational engine under the same instance, you can choose to use the same settings or different settings for the two servers.

A.2.6 Configuring Reporting Services

The Report Server Installation Options step (Figure A.9) allows you to configure the Reporting Services settings. By default, the Installation Wizard will create a *ReportServer* virtual root in IIS for the Report Server and a *Reports* virtual root for the Report Manager. These settings can be overwritten by clicking on the Details button.

You may wonder why the Installation Wizard supports the option to install the Report Server files without configure the server. This could be useful if IIS is not installed and you don't want to interrupt the setup process. Use the Error and Usage Report Settings step to automatically send reports to Microsoft. Finally, review the setup tasks in the *Ready to Install* step and click Install to initiate the setup process.

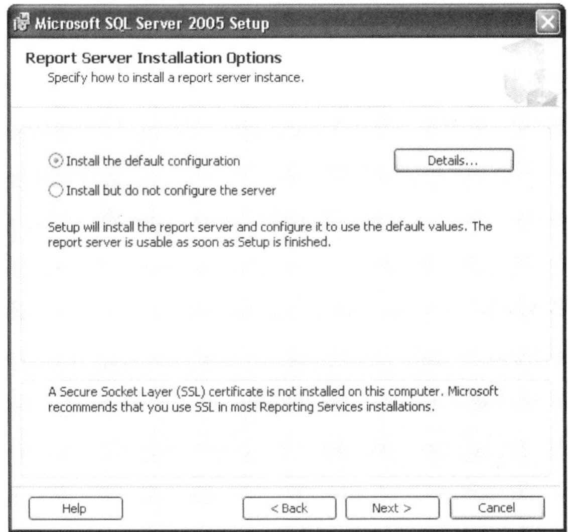

Figure A.9 Use the Report Server Installation Options step to configure Reporting Services.

A.3 Post-Installations Steps

If all is well, the setup program will complete successfully. The Completing Microsoft SQL Server 2005 Setup (Figure A.10) step allows you to review the Summary Log of the wizard activities. There are two post-installation tasks I suggest you consider right after you install the SQL Server 2005.

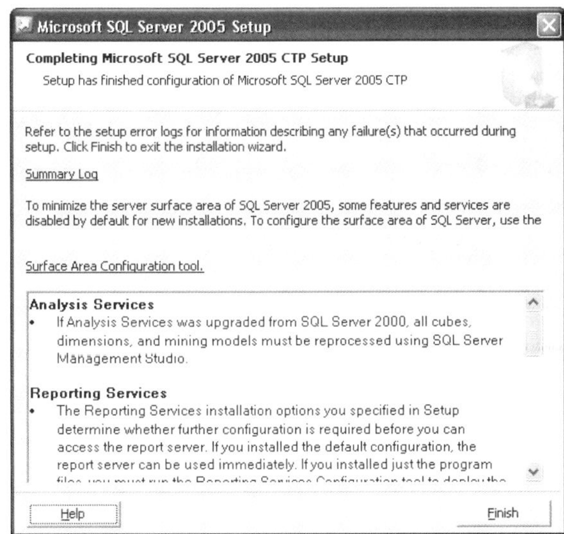

Figure A.10 Consider using the Surface Area Configuration tool to review the security and settings.

A.3.1 Configuring SQL Server 2005 Surface Area

By default, the Installation Wizard configures only the minimum features needed to run the SQL Server and add-on services. For example, ad hoc (*OpenRowset*) DMX queries and Analysis Services COM-based user-defined functions (UDF) are disabled by default. Similarly, only local connections to the SQL Server relational engine are allowed by default with Express and Developer editions. Click on the *Surface Area Configuration tool* (Figure A.10) link to open the SQL Server Surface Area Configuration tool (*Start ⇨ Microsoft SQL Server 2005 ⇨ Configuration Tools ⇨ SQL Server Surface Area Configuration*) to review the configured features and security settings.

A.3.2 Installing Analysis Services Samples

As noted, SSAS provides a few sample applications you may want to review and experiment with in addition to the SOS OLAP sample included in this book. Assuming that you've selected to install the Sample Code and Applications setup option, the programming samples are installed by default in C:\Program Files\Microsoft SQL Server\90\Tools\Samples\Analysis Services. The Adventure Works Analysis Services project is installed in a different location (C:\Program Files\Microsoft SQL Server\90\Tools\Samples\AdventureWorks Analysis Services Project). It comes with Standard and Enterprise versions. Use the appropriate version depending on the SQL Server edition you have.

The Enterprise edition of the Adventure Works project demonstrates all the features included in the Standard edition, plus features available only in the SSAS Developer and Enterprise editions, including partitions and account intelligence. For more information about how different SSAS editions compare, refer to the *SQL Server 2005 Features Comparison* document (see Resources).

A.3.3 Installing Visual Studio.NET

To support working with Business Intelligence projects (Analysis Services, Reporting Services, and Integration Services projects), SQL Server 2005 ships with Business Intelligence Studio -- a scale-down version of Visual Studio.NET. To open the sample Visual Basic.NET developer projects included with this book, you need the full-blown version of Visual Studio.NET. Always install Visual Studio.NET after you install SQL Server 2005. If you are budget-conscious, Visual Basic Standard Edition should be enough to run the code samples.

A.4 Resources

Installing SQL Server 2005
(http://shrinkster.com/81n) – The *Installing SQL Server 2005* topic from the SQL Server product documentation.

SQL Server 2005 Features Comparison
(http://shrinkster.com/81s) – Provides a feature comparison between the SQL Server editions -- Express, Workgroup, Standard, and Enterprise.

Appendix B

Upgrading Analysis Services

If you are using Analysis Services 2000, chances are that inspired by this book, you may be willing to move your existing Analysis Services 2000 databases to SSAS 2005 to take advantage of the new UDM features. Of course, one option is not to upgrade at all. Even if you are restricted to one server only, you could run both SSAS 2000 and 2005 side-by-side. As noted in Appendix A, this scenario requires that you keep the SSAS 2000 server under the default instance and install SSAS 2005 on a new named instance. In this way, you can keep the legacy SSAS 2000 cubes and use SSAS 2005 for new projects.

If you decided to upgrade, SSAS 2005 provides several options to do so. It is important to review the pros and cons of each option carefully and spend some time planning your upgrade path. Besides the tips outlined in this appendix, I recommend you review the *Upgrading or Migrating Analysis Services* topic in the product documentation. In addition, I highly recommend you read the excellent whitepaper *Analysis Services 2005 Migration*, which documents the real-life migration experience the Microsoft team has harvested in project REAL (see Resources).

B.1 Preparing For Upgrade

SSAS 2005 has been redesigned from the ground up and certain features have been deprecated, replaced, or simply don't exist in UDM anymore. Therefore, when planning your upgrade, you should have reasonable expectations about the outcome of the upgrade process. The SSAS team has done a great job maintaining backward compatibility wherever possible, but it may take some effort on your part to get the results you want. Let's start with a broad overview of how the SSAS 2000 functional areas map to UDM.

B.1.1 Analysis Services 2000 and UDM Equivalents

Readers who are planning to upgrade from SSAS 2000 to 2005 may be curious as to how both versions compare. Table B.1 is indented to give you a side-by-side correspondence map to help you with the transition. As you can see, UDM's feature set has been greatly enhanced. However, as radical as the new changes are, the core dimensional modeling concepts (cube, dimensions, levels, hierarchies, etc.) remain the same. Perhaps, the most important difference is that in UDM, a cube can have more than one fact table. In this respect, you could loosely relate a SSAS 2000 database to a SSAS 2005 cube, while the closest equivalent of a SSAS 2000 fact table is a SSAS 2005 measure group.

Table B.1 SSAS vs. SSAS 2005

Functionality Area	SSAS 2000	SSAS 2005
User interface and tools	Analysis Services Manager	Business Intelligence Development Studio
	Enterprise Manager, Query Analyzer	SQL Server Management Studio
	Connected (database) mode	Connected and project-based modes
Physical model	SSAS database	SSAS database
	Metadata in repository	No repository (XML-based metadata)
Dimensional model	No data source abstraction layer	Data Source Views
	One data source per cube	Many data sources per cube
	One fact table per cube	Many fact tables per cube
	Cube	Measure group
	Virtual cubes	Linked measure groups and dimensions
	Virtual dimensions	Multiple hierarchies in a single dimension
	Private dimensions	All dimensions are shared
	Changing/rigid dimensions	All dimensions are changing
	Limited to star /snowflake or parent/child dimensions	Flexible relationship types, e.g. many-to-many, referenced, role-playing, fact
	Hierarchical dimensions	Attributed-based dimensions
	Only one hierarchy in a single dimension	Many hierarchies in a single dimension
Programmability	Calculated members and cells	MDX scripts
	MDX Sample Application	SQL Server Management Studio MDX Editor
	Extensible by user-defined functions (need to deployed to the client)	Extensible by server-side .NET stored procedures
Data mining	Decision tree and clustering algorithms only	Five additional algorithms
	Mining Model Wizard and Data Mining Model Browser	Mining Model Wizard and Mining Model Editor
Architecture	OLE DB for OLAP connectivity through PTS	XML for Analysis (XML/A) native protocol
	Clent-side and server-side calculation cache	Server-side caching only
	Thick client (PivotTable Service)	Thin client
Management	No configuration management	Configuration management, e.g. production, development, etc
	Backup/restore (CAB) files	Deployment Wizard
	"Pull" cube processing model	Pull and push (real-time OLAP) models

Some SSAS 2000 features are discontinued in SSAS 2005, such as virtual cubes, virtual dimensions, and custom level formulas. Other features are deprecated (e.g. calculated cell, pass and solve order). Yet, other features have been re-architected, e.g. drillthrough. Finally, some features in SSAS 2005 don't have SSAS 2000 equivalents, including new dimensions types (fact, many-to-many, reference), semi-additive measures, KPIs, new action types (reporting, drillthrough), etc. For an extensive backward compatibly checklist, consult with the topic *Upgrading or Migrating Analysis Services* in the product documentation.

B.1.2 Understanding Upgrade Options

In general, you have four options for upgrading existing Analysis Services 2000 databases to UDM. These options are upgrade in-place when installing SQL Server 2005, migrate, migrate with enhancements, and redesign from scratch. Let's discuss each of these options in more details and outline their pros and cons.

Upgrading

This option is straightforward to execute because it takes place during setup. When the SQL Server 2005 Installation Wizard detects an existing SSAS 2000 installation on the same machine, it will prompt you to upgrade it to SSAS 2005 or install SSAS 2005 side-by-side. Once you select the upgrade path, the setup program will launch the Migration Wizard which will upgrade the SSAS 2000 databases on the server. Before upgrading or migrating to SSAS 2005, I highly recommend you run the Upgrade Advisor tool to analyze the SSAS 2000 metadata and estimate the upgrade effort. A step-by-step tutorial for using the Upgrade Advisor is provided in section B.2.1.

Note Both the upgrade and migrate options upgrade the metadata only. You need to reprocess the database once the upgrade process has completed.

What's upgraded?

The main goal of the upgrade process is duplicating the cubes you had in Analysis Services 2000. Therefore, the output of the upgrade process shouldn't be construed as UDM best practices. After you have completed the wizard, you need to determine the additional steps you need to best leverage the power of UDM. Table B.2 shows how some SSAS 2000 objects are upgraded and the recommended best practices.

Table B.2 SSAS 2000 objects and their equivalents.

SSAS 2000	SSAS 2005	Recommendation
Cube	Cube	Measure group
Virtual cube	Cube with linked measure groups	Single cube
Calculated members, calculated cells, named set	MDX script	Subcube expression for calculated cells
Mining model	Mining structure with one model	Host similar mining models in one structure
Database	Connected database	Project mode
Drillthrough	Not upgraded	Drillthrough action
Linked cubes	Not upgraded	Linked cubes

For example, the upgrade process will convert an SSAS 2000 virtual cube to a cube with linked measure groups. Although this will work, consider instead converting the linked measure groups into regular measure groups that reside in a single cube. Some SSAS 2000 features won't get migrated. For example, due to the radical architectural changes in UDM drillthrough, the SSAS 2000 drillthrough feature is not upgraded. If you want to keep them, you need to re-implement them manually.

Pros and cons

In comparison to the other options, the main advantages of the upgrade option are:

- *Automated process* – In the best case scenario, no manual intervention is required because the upgrade process is executed by the Installation Wizard.
- *Cost-effective* – You don't need two licenses (for SSAS 2000 and 2005) because the SSAS 2000 instance will no longer exist. No new hardware may be required either.
- *Backward compatibility* – In the ideal case, the Installation Wizard will preserve the cube structure and the upgraded cubes will be identical feature-wise to the original cubes.

The upgrade option has the following tradeoffs:

- *Not a best practice* – As noted, the Upgrade Wizard job is to provide backward compatibility, not best practices. As Table B.2 shows, consider revisiting UDM after upgrade to take advantage of the new UDM features.
- *Downtime* – Cubes are unavailable until the UDM cubes are re-processed.
- *Difficult validation* – Since the old cubes don't exist after upgrade, it may be difficult to validate the upgraded cubes.

Because of the above limitations, most upgrade scenarios will probably favor the migration option, which I will discuss next.

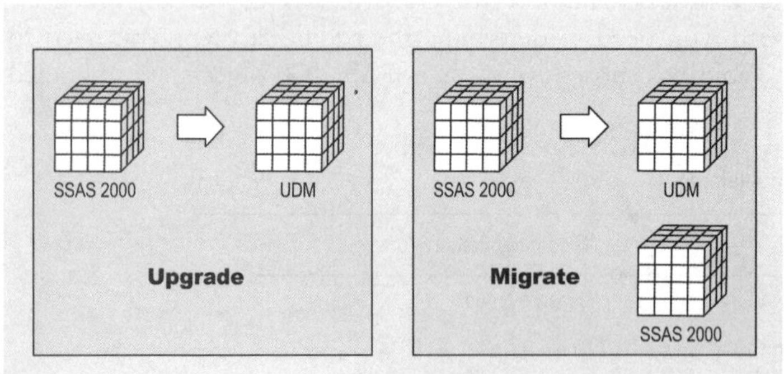

Figure B.1 With the migrate option, the SSAS 2000 database is not removed on install.

Migrating

You may wonder how migrating is different from upgrading. Figure B.1 is meant to clarify the migration process. When you upgrade, the SSAS 2000 server is uninstalled immediately after its databases are converted. As a result, you don't have SSAS 2000 and UDM databases co-existing on the same server at any point in time. In comparison, when you migrate, you install SSAS 2005 on a separate server or on a new instance in the same server (side-by-side installation) without upgrading the SSAS 2000 server. At some point in time, you could run the Analysis Services Migration Wizard to migrate an existing SSAS 2000 database to SSAS 2005. Once the Migration Wizard is done, it leaves the original SSAS 2000 database intact.

Note The Migration Wizard can be started from Management Studio (right-click on the SSAS server node and choose *Migrate Database*), or in a standalone mode (*C:\Program Files\Microsoft SQL Server\90\Tools\Binn\VSShell\Common7\IDE ⇨ MigrationWizard.exe*).

Both upgrade and migrate options use the same algorithm to convert the legacy databases to UDM. In other words, both options should produce the same results. The pros of the migration option include:

- *Side-by-side validation* – Since the original SSAS 2000 database is kept, you could verify the migrated data against the old data.
- *Backward compatibility* – As with the upgrade option, the Migration Wizard will make a best attempt to preserve the structure and model of the original cubes.
- *No downtime* – The legacy database is still functional while the migration and testing processes take place. Once UDM is validated, you can bring the legacy database offline.

The cons of the migration option are:

- *Not a best practice* – As with the upgrade option, you may need to revisit the migrated database and plan additional steps to optimize it.
- *Licensing cost* – You need to have two licenses until SSAS 2000 is no longer needed.

I believe that most organizations will embrace the migration option when moving to UDM. After the migration process is complete, I would recommend you evaluate the converted database and make appropriate design changes to incorporate best practices. This brings us to the third option.

Migrate and Enhance

With this option, you use the Migration Wizard to migrate the legacy database to UDM. Next, you would reverse-engineer the migrated SSAS 2005 database to a corresponding Analysis Services project. Then, you make design changes to incorporate UDM best practices, e.g. converting calculated cells into subcube expressions. Finally, if needed, you add new features not present in SSAS 2000 to enhance UDM, such as KPIs, perspectives, translations, etc.

A good practical scenario to use the Migrate and Enhance option is when you have many dimensions (e.g. 30-40) in the SSAS 2000 database and adding new features doesn't require complete redesign. The obvious disadvantage of the Migrate and Enhance option is that it takes more time. With complex cubes, identifying potential areas of improvement and implementing them may take longer than redesigning the cube from scratch.

Redesign

Finally, there is always an option to redesign the database from scratch and start anew. The advantage of this approach is that you follow best UDM design practices from the very start, such as multiple hierarchies per dimension, flexible dimension relationships (many-to-many, referenced), and so on. As an added bonus, this may be your opportunity to revisit the entire OLAP solution. For example, many of the data warehouse de-normalization techniques, e.g. database views, may not be needed anymore.

I would recommend the Redesign option with relatively simple databases (e.g. ten dimensions and a few cubes). Redesigning more complex databases could be time-consuming and may require a project of its own. To minimize the design effort, use the wizards available in BI

Studio, such as the DSV Wizard, Cube Wizard, Dimension Wizard, Mining Model Wizard, and Business Intelligence Wizard.

B.2 Migrating to UDM Example

Let's go through a hands-on lab that demonstrates upgrading an existing SSAS 2000 database to UDM. The legacy database that we will upgrade is the Foodmart 2000 sample database that ships with SSAS 2000. For the purposes of our demo, we will go for the third option – Migrate and Enhance. At a high-level, the migration process will take three steps. First, we will estimate the scope of the migration process using the Upgrade Advisor tool. Second, we will migrate the legacy database using the Migration Wizard. Finally, we will reverse-engineer the migrated database to an Analysis Services project, so we could optimize and enhance it.

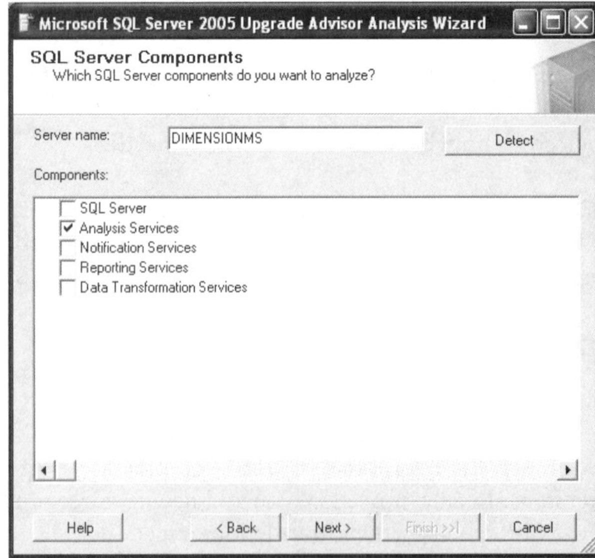

Figure B.2 The Upgrade Advisor can analyze the SQL Server relational engine and all add-on components.

B.2.1 Preparing for Upgrade with Upgrade Advisor

Upgrade Advisor is available as a separate download from the Microsoft website (see Resources). It is also available on the SQL Server setup CD in the Servers\Redist\Upgrade Advisor folder. Upgrade Advisor helps you to analyze SQL Server 7.0 and SQL Server 2000 database servers in preparation for upgrading to SQL Server 2005. Upgrade Advisor can be used to analyze all SQL Server components -- the SQL Server relational engine, Analysis Services, Notification Services, Reporting Services, and Data Transformation Services. For the purposes of our demo, we will focus on Analysis Services only.

1. Once you download and install Upgrade Advisor, run it and click the *Upgrade Advisor Analysis Wizard* link on the welcome screen to launch the Upgrade Advisor Analysis Wizard. Click Next to advance to the *SQL Server Components* step (Figure B.2).

2. In the *Server name* textbox, enter the server which has Analysis Services 2000 installed and select *Analysis Services* in the Components list. In my case, I've chosen to analyze a server called *DIMENSIONMS*. Click Next.

3. In the Confirm Upgrade Advisor Settings step, note the path where the report will be generated. Upgrade Advisor saves the results as an XML report. Each wizard run overwrites an existing report for the selected server. Click Next to advance to the Upgrade Advisor Progress step.

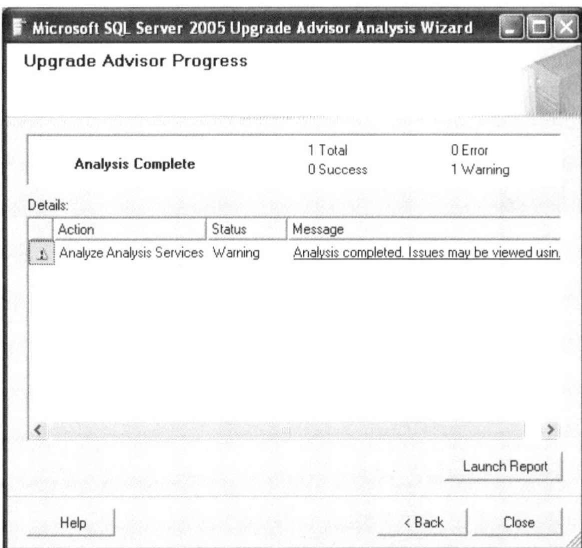

Figure B.3 In the Upgrade Advisor Progress step, the Upgrade Advisor analyzes the selected server and gives you an option to view the generated report.

4. Upgrade Advisor analyzes the SSAS 2000 metadata. If there are any issues detected, Upgrade Advisor displays a warning. Click the *Launch Report* button the view the generated report.

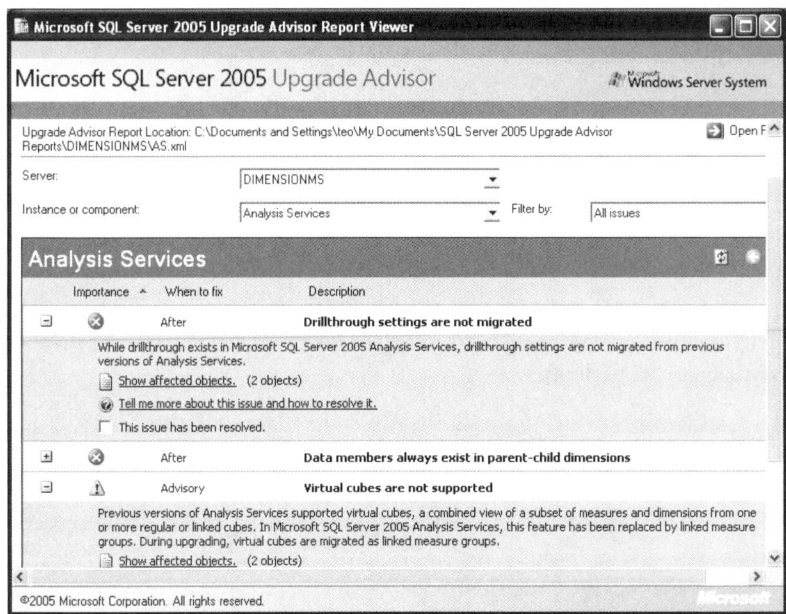

Figure B.4 The Upgrade Advisor report flags the issues as warnings and critical errors.

The Upgrade Advisor report identifies deprecated features and other issues that may impact the upgrade process. For example, the first critical error tells us the drillthrough settings will not be migrated.

5. Click on the *Show affected objects* link. Observe that the two objects are affected – the Sales and HR cubes.

6. Click the *Tell me more* link to obtain more information about this issue. Upgrade Advisor navigates to the corresponding help topic.

The *When to fix* column tells us when the issue needs to be addressed – before or after the upgrade process. In our case, the two critical issues need to be addressed after the cube is migrated, so we will proceed with the actual migration process.

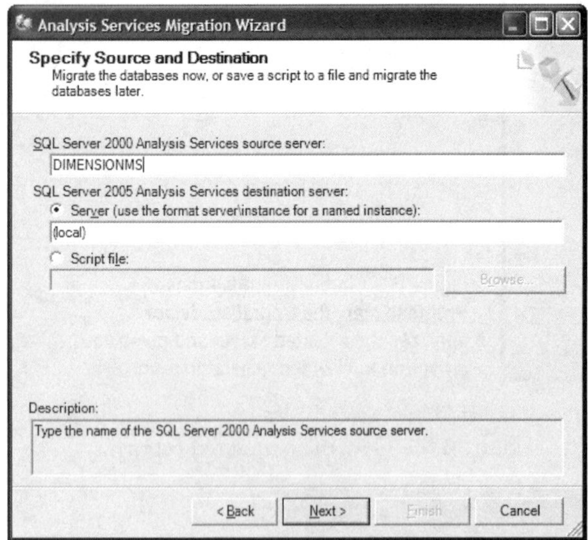

Figure B.5 The Migration Wizard allows you to migrate an existing SSAS 2005 database straight to UDM or generate an XMLA script for later execution.

B.2.2 Migrating Legacy Databases with Migration Wizard

Once you estimate the migration effort with Upgrade Advisor, the next step is to perform the actual migration using the Migration Wizard. Let's use the Migration Wizard to migrate the FoodMart 2000 database that we've just analyzed.

1. Open SQL Server Management Studio. Connect to the SSAS 2005 server that will host the migrated database. Right-click on the server node and select *Migrate Database* to launch the Migration Wizard. Click Next to skip the Welcome step.

2. In the Specify Sources and Destination step (Figure B.5), enter the name of the SSAS 2000 server as a source server. You can use the Migration Wizard to move an SSAS 2000 database straight to UDM or generate an XMLA script. You can run the script at a later time from Management Studio or schedule it to run in an unattended mode. Leave the default option (*Server*) selected and click Next.

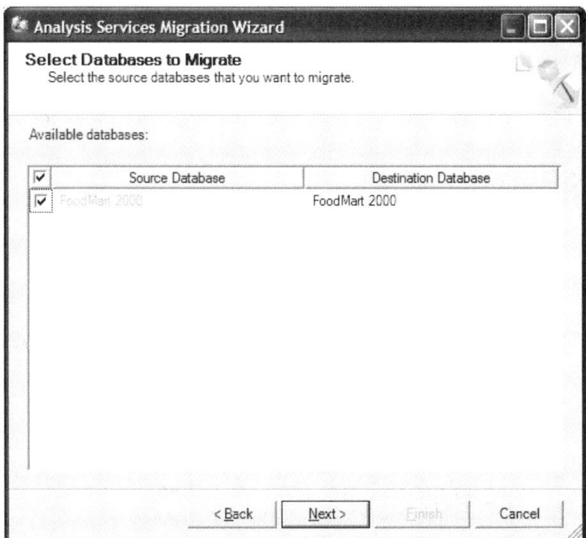

Figure B.6 Select the SSAS 2005 database(s) to migrate and specify the name(s) of the destination database.

3. In the Select Databases to Migrate step (Figure B.6), accept the default settings. By default, the Migration Wizard will migrate all legacy databases found on the SSAS 2000 server. If needed, you can change the names of the destination SSAS 2005 databases.

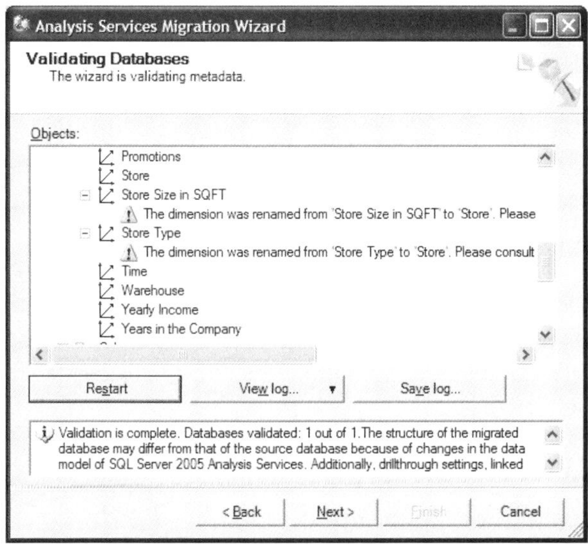

Figure B.7 Thc Migration Wizard validates the metadata of the source database and generates a validation log.

4. In the Validating Databases step, the Migration Wizard validates the SSAS 2000 metadata. It generates a validation log that contains errors and warnings that may impact the migration process. In our case, the Migration Wizard warns us that it will rename the *Store Size in SQFT* and *Store Type* dimensions. That's because it has correctly identified that these dimensions target the same dimension tables and has decided to convert them to attribute hierarchies.

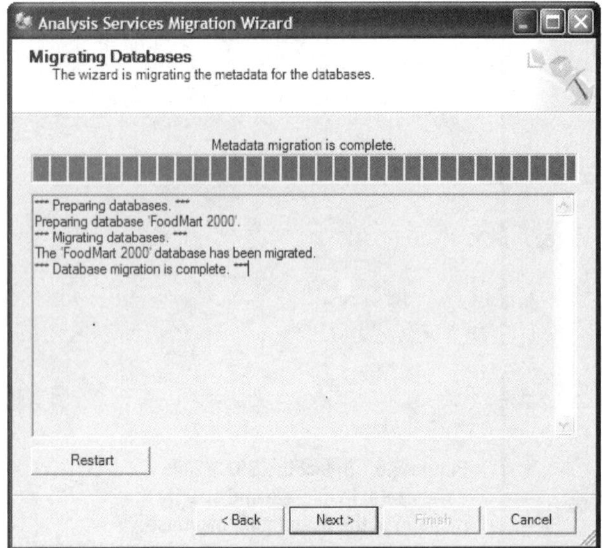

Figure B.8 The Migration Wizard converts the SSAS 2000 database to its UDM counterpart.

5. The Migration Database step (Figure B.8) is the workhorse of the migration process. Here, the wizard converts the SSAS 2000 metadata to its UDM equivalent. Once the migration process has completed, click Next to advance to the Completing the Wizard step. Review what the Migration Wizard has accomplished and click Finish to close the wizard.

As noted, the Migration Wizard migrates metadata only. You need to process the migrated database before you are able to browse the cubes.

B.2.3 Switching to Project Mode

The major objective of the Migration Wizard is to duplicate the cubes you had in SSAS 2000, not to optimize them and take advantage of the improved and new features in UDM. Therefore, once the migration process is completed, you need to plan the additional steps to optimize the migrated database. While you can make changes in online mode (a-la SSAS 2000), as a best practice, you should reverse-engineer the migrated database to generate an Analysis Services project. The project mode advantages are discussed in chapter 2. Follow these steps to create an Analysis Services project for the FoodMart 2000 database.

6. Start Business Intelligence Studio. Select *File* ⇨ *New* ⇨ *Project.*
7. In the New Project dialog, select *Import Analysis Services 9.0 Database.* Specify the location where the project files will be generated, and click OK.
8. BI Studio starts the *Import Analysis Services 9.0 Database Wizard.*
9. In the *Source database* step (Figure B.9), select the server that hosts the migrated database. Next, expand the Database dropdown and select *FoodMart 2000.* Click Next to initiate the project generation process

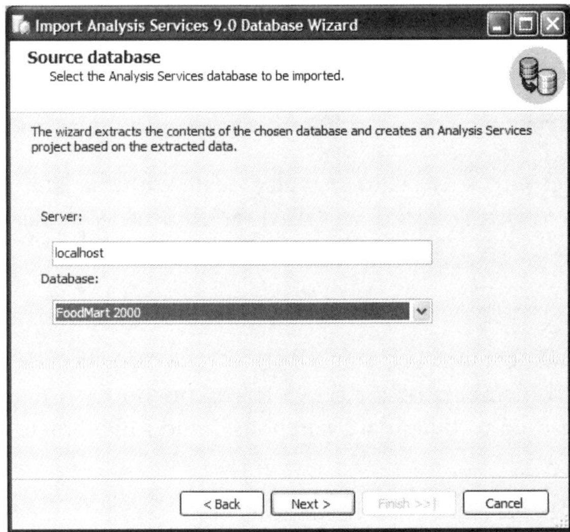

Figure B.9 Use the Import Analysis Services 9.0 Database Wizard to reverse-engineer the migrated database to its project equivalent.

Once the wizard has done reverse-engineering the Analysis Services database, it loads the generated project files in the Solution Explorer pane. From there, use the skills you learned in this book to optimize the UDM and add new features.

B.3 Resources

Microsoft SQL Server 2005 Upgrade Advisor
(http://shrinkster.com/81g) – This tool helps Database developers and administrators analyze SQL Server 7.0 and SQL Server 2000 database servers in preparation for upgrading to SQL Server 2005. It is also available on the SQL Server setup CD in the Servers\Redist\Upgrade Advisor folder.

Analysis Services 2005 Migration
(http://shrinkster.com/82k) – This paper guides you through the process of migrating to Analysis Services in SQL Server 2005. It includes many practical migration tips harvested from the Microsoft experience in Project REAL.

master resource list

Besides this book, you may find the following resources useful to stay up-to-date with the latest developments in the ever-changing and rapidly evolving world of OLAP and business intelligence.

Books

Professional SQL Server Analysis Services 2005 with MDX
(http://shrinkster.com/831) – Written by two members of the SSAS team, this book shows how Analysis Services 2005 and MDX can be used to build data warehouses and multidimensional databases.

MDX Solutions with Microsoft SQL Server Analysis Services 2005 and Hyperion Essbase
(http://shrinkster.com/833) – A sequel of the George Spofford's *MDX Solutions* book, this resource serves as both a tutorial and a reference guide to the MDX (Multidimensional Expressions) query language.

The Data Warehouse Toolkit: The Complete Guide to Dimensional Modeling, 2nd Edition
(http://shrinkster.com/616) – A great resource to get you up to speed with dimensional modeling and data warehouse design.

Data Mining with SQL Server 2005
(http://shrinkster.com/832) – Written by two member of the SSAS team, this book teaches you how to leverage the data mining features of UDM to to solve today's business problems.

Websites

Mosha Pasumansky's website
(http://www.mosha.com/msolap) – Tons of OLAP gems compiled by the development lead for the Microsoft Analysis Services engine.

SQL Server Analysis Services website
(http://www.sqlserveranalysisservices.com) – Maintained by Richard Tkatchuk, a Lead Program Manager with the Analysis Services team, this site includes white papers and code samples.

SQL Server Data Mining website
(http://www.sqlserverdatamining.com) – Personally, I am impressed by the commitment of the SSAS data mining team to assist the community. This is an excellent website designed by the SQL Server Data Mining team to provide the SQL Server community with access and information about the exciting data mining features.

Prologika website
(http://www.prologika.com) – Check my website for a discussion list, blog, and more...

Newsgroups

Analysis Services public newsgroup
(microsoft.public.sqlserver.olap) – The Microsoft public Analysis Services newsgroup.

Analysis Services OLAP private newsgroup
(microsoft.private.sqlserver2005.analysisservices.olap) – Requires subscription to the Microsoft Beta program (beta.microsoft.com).

Analysis Services Data Mining private newsgroup
(microsoft.private.sqlserver2005.analysisservices.datamining) – Requires subscription to the Microsoft Beta program (beta.microsoft.com).

Microsoft Analysis Services Developer Site
(http://groups.msn.com/olapservicesdevelopersforum) – Message board for implementation techniques, code samples, how-to and other OLAP application development issues are welcome on these pages.

Web logs

Mosha Pasumansky
http://sqljunkies.com/WebLog/mosha

Chris Webb
http://spaces.msn.com/members/cwebbbi/PersonalSpace.aspx

Marco Russo
http://sqljunkies.com/WebLog/sqlbi

Chris Harrington
http://www.activeinterface.com/thinolap.html

Read Jacobson
http://sqljunkies.com/WebLog/HitachiConsulting

Dejan Sarka
http://solidqualitylearning.com/Blogs/dejan/

Teo Lachev
http://www.prologika.com/blog

index

B

C

N

T

U

V

W

X

Y

Also by Teo Lachev

Use the ideas in this book and take Microsoft Reporting Services *to the next level*

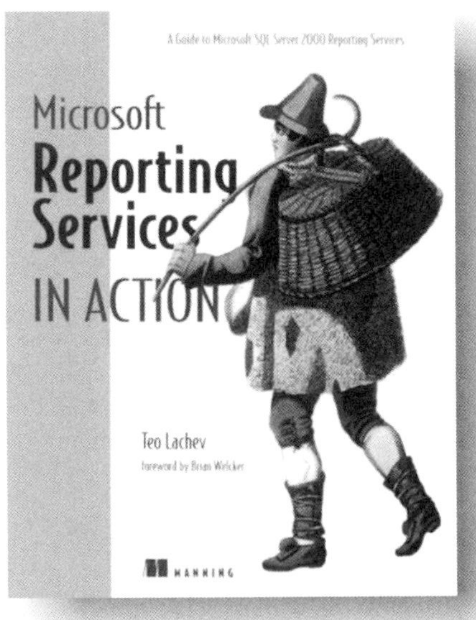

Serving as a guide to the functionality provided by Reporting Services, this book teaches developers to add reporting to any type of application, regardless of its targeted platform and development language. Following the report lifecycle's logical path, the book explains how to author, manage, and run RS reports.

Aimed at .NET developers who plan to fully utilize this product's features to add reporting capabilities to Windows Forms or web-based applications, this guide will also benefit developers who target other platforms but want to integrate their applications with RS because of its service-oriented architecture. The accompanying code samples are written in C# and Visual Studio .NET 2003 and many sample reports are included to demonstrate all aspects of report authoring.

ISBN 1-932394-22-2
Publisher website: www.manning.com/lachev
Amazon: http://shrinkster.com/8tw
B&N: http://shrinkster.com/8tx

The book is available in bookstores worldwide.
Prices and availability may be subject to change.

notes